Mastering™ Visual Basic® 6

Evangelos Petroutsos

SYBEX®

San Francisco • Paris • Düsseldorf • Soest

Associate Publisher: Gary Masters

Contracts and Licensing Manager: Kristine Plachy

Acquisitions & Developmental Editor: Peter Kuhns

Editors: Grace Wong, Pat Coleman

Project Editor: Dann McDorman

Technical Editor: Don Hergert

Book Designer: Kris Warrenburg

Electronic Publishing Specialist: Franz Baumhackl

Production Coordinator: Rebecca Rider

Indexer: Ted Laux

Companion CD: Ginger Warner

Cover Designer: Design Site

Cover Illustrator/Photographer: David Bishop

Library of Congress Card Number: 98-86251

ISBN: 0-7821-2272-8

Manufactured in the United States of America

10 9 8 7 6 5 4 3 2

To my family

ACKNOWLEDGEMENTS

Many people contributed to this book, and I would like to thank them all. I guess I should start with the programmers at Microsoft, for their commitment to Visual Basic. Visual Basic has evolved from a small, rather limited programming environment to an awesome development tool. This constant improvement and the gradual introduction of new and increasingly advanced topics is simply amazing. The choice of VBA as the programming language for Office applications and VBScript as the major scripting languages for Windows 98 itself indicates the commitment of Microsoft to Visual Basic. There will be plenty of new opportunities for those of us who have invested in Visual Basic.

Special thanks to the talented people at Sybex—to all of them and to each one individually. To Peter Kuhns, for his involvement in this book from conception to production. He worked on this project as developmental editor and advisor and offered his help generously when needed in every aspect of the book. To technical editor Don Hergert, for scrutinizing every paragraph and every line of code. To editors Grace Wong and Pat Coleman (who also edited the first edition of the book) for improving this book in numerous ways. To the project editor Dann McDorman, who has done more than I can guess to keep this project in order and on schedule. To production coordinator Rebecca Rider, electronic publishing specialist Franz Baumhackl, indexer Ted Laux, and everyone else who added their expertise and talent.

I want to thank Charles Brannon, long-time friend and occasional co-author, for lending his hardware expertise when needed. I wish him luck with his new life, and hope we'll meet soon in a future project.

Many thanks to the people who put together this book's CD. I haven't seen it yet, but I have seen their work in other titles, including one of mine.

Finally, this book would not have been possible (not on time, at least), without the Internet. I wrote much of it while in Greece. The technical editor was in Utah, the editors were in Texas and California, and, of course, the Sybex people were in Alameda. We all had to be in constant touch, and our cyberspace neighborhood trivialized large bodies of water and several time zones (which are pretty meaningless when a book is about to be published). And, so, finally, I would like to thank the people who maintain the servers, the routers, and the software, and who handle all the details of connecting users.

CONTENTS AT A GLANCE

TABLE OF CONTENTS

15 Building ActiveX Components   767

INTRODUCTION

Several years ago, when Visual Basic was a "small" language, a Mastering book would have covered every aspect of it. Since its first release, however, Visual Basic has evolved into a major development environment that covers every aspect of programming, from educational applications to databases, and from financial applications to Internet components. Writing a book that would even introduce all these topics was out of the question. Especially a Mastering book.

The topics covered in this book were chosen to provide a solid understanding of the principles and techniques involved in developing applications with Visual Basic. Programming isn't about new keywords and functions. I chose the topics I felt every programmer should learn in order to master the language. One of the largest chapters in the book discusses the graphics methods. There's nothing new in VB6 in this area, but graphics are such an important part of the language that the related techniques had to be explained in detail. Most chapters in this book are really version-independent. They will be just as useful to people who are still using version 4 or 5 of the language.

In choosing topics to include in the book I was also motivated by my desire to present useful, practical examples. Some of you may not find all topics equally interesting or important. My hope is that everyone will find something interesting and something of value to his or her daily work—whether it's an application such as DirMap, a clear explanation of a topic such as scanning the TreeView control, or the introduction to Internet programming techniques with Visual Basic.

Some chapters do deal with the new face of Visual Basic. Chapter 18, *The Active Data Objects*, is new in this version of the book. Yet, I have devoted more pages to Chapter 17, which covers Data Access Objects (DAO). It's an older database access technology, but most applications out there are still using the DAO component. It's simpler than ADO and more appropriate as an introduction to the topic of databases. As you will see, some keywords may change, but the underlying principles remain the same. After all, companies rely on databases for their daily operations, and they don't switch to a new technology just because it's newer, or fancier.

You will also notice that the last part of the book is about the Web. These chapters were added because of their broad appeal. The desktop and the Web are clearly merging, and VB programmers should be able to apply their knowledge to the Web. Actually, you'll also find out how to apply your VB programming knowledge to an entirely new field, Windows 98 scripting. In Chapter 20 you'll see how you can use VBScript (a subset of Visual Basic) and object-oriented techniques to script the desktop.

Although Visual Basic 6 comes with several tools for automating the development of Web pages (including plain HTML and Dynamic HTML) and the development of Web applications (or IIS applications), I do not discuss these tools. Because of the limited space, I decided that it was far more important to discuss the basic principles and show you what goes on behind the scenes. Once you understand the structure of Web pages, the basic HTML tags, Dynamic HTML, and how to activate the client and the server with VBScript, it will be much easier to use the automated tools.

Who Should Read This Book?

You don't need a solid knowledge of Visual Basic to read this book, but you do need a basic understanding of programming. You need to know the meaning of variables and functions and how an If…Then structure works. The first two chapters are introductory, but they are not meant for the absolute beginner. Instead, they were included to introduce Visual Basic to users with programming experience in a different environment. Occasional users of previous versions of Visual Basic will also find enough information in these chapters to catch up with the new environment.

Chapter 3, *Visual Basic: The Language*, is mostly reference information about data types and procedures. It's information that every programmer needs from time to time. While reading the rest of the book or exploring the code of an application, you might need to look up a topic you are not familiar with, such as how to use optional arguments with functions or how to implement a Collection. You'll find this kind of information in Chapter 3. Starting with Chapter 4, the book gets into real VB programming.

This book is addressed to the average programmer who wants to get the most out of Visual Basic. It covers the topics I felt are of use to most VB programmers, and it does so in depth. Visual Basic is an extremely rich programming environment, and I had to choose between a superficial coverage of many topics or an in-depth coverage of fewer topics. To make room for more topics, I have avoided including a lot of reference material and lengthy listings. For example, you won't find complete project listings or Form descriptions. I assume you can draw a few controls on a Form and set their properties, and you don't need long descriptions of the properties of the control. I'm also assuming that you don't want to read the trivial segments of each application. Instead, the listings concentrate on the "meaty" part of the code: the procedures that explain the topic at hand. If you want to see the complete listing, it's all on the CD.

Many books offer their readers long, numbered sequences of steps to accomplish something. Following instructions simplifies certain tasks, but programming isn't about following instructions. It's about being creative; it's about being able to apply the same techniques in several practical situations. And the way to creatively exploit the power of a language such as Visual Basic is to understand its principles and its programming model. You need to develop a sense of how to apply the language to daily programming situations.

In many cases, I provide a detailed, step-by-step procedure that will help you accomplish a task (such as designing a user interface). But this book goes beyond that. I explain why things must be done in a certain way, and I present alternatives and try to connect new topics to those explained earlier in the book. In several chapters, I expand on applications developed in earlier chapters. Associating new knowledge to something you have mastered already provides positive feedback and a deeper understanding of the language.

How About the Advanced Topics?

Some of the advanced topics in this book were missing in the book's first edition, *Mastering Visual Basic 5*. For example, I didn't discuss the TreeView and ListView controls because I felt they were too advanced for the book's audience. It turns out I was wrong. Many readers requested information on quite advanced topics, so I decided to discuss these topics as well. If you find them too advanced, you can skip them.

If you're looking forward to using the TreeView control in your user interfaces, you'll probably jump to Chapter 8 and read about it. Some of the examples will be difficult. I have tried to make the text and the examples easy to read and understand, but not unrealistically simple. You can do a lot with the TreeView control with very little programming, but in order to make the most out of this control, you must be ready for some advanced programming. Nothing terribly complicated, but some things just aren't trivial. Programming most of the operations of the TreeView control, for instance, is not complicated, but if your application calls for populating a TreeView control with an arbitrary number of branches (such as mapping a directory structure to a TreeView control), the code can get quite complex.

Some examples in this book are complicated, but I couldn't avoid them. The corresponding chapters would be incomplete without these examples. If you find some material to be over your head at first reading, you can skip it and come back to it after you have mastered other aspects of the language. But don't let a few advanced examples intimidate you. Most of the techniques are well within the reach of an average VB programmer. The few advanced topics were included for the readers who are willing to take that extra step and build elaborate interfaces using the latest tools and techniques.

The Structure of the Book

This book isn't meant to be read from cover to cover, and I know that most people don't read computer books this way. Each chapter is independent of the others, although all chapters contain references to other chapters. Each topic is covered in depth; however, I make no assumptions about the reader's knowledge on the topic. As a result, you may find the introductory sections of a chapter too simple. The topics become progressively more advanced, and even experienced programmers will find some new information in each chapter. Even if you are familiar with the topics in a chapter, take a look at the example. I have tried to simplify many of the advanced topics and demonstrate them with clear, practical examples.

This book tries to teach through examples. Isolated topics are demonstrated with short examples, and at the end of many chapters, you'll build a large, practical application (a real-world application) that "puts together" the topics and techniques discussed throughout the chapter. You may find some of the more advanced applications a bit more difficult to understand, but you shouldn't give up. Simpler applications would have made my job easier, but the book wouldn't deserve the Mastering title and your knowledge of Visual Basic wouldn't be as complete.

The Tutorials on the CD

In the course of writing this book, I developed a few interesting, yet lengthy applications. There wasn't room in this book for them, so I put them on the CD as tutorials. Some of them are quite basic. The tutorial on File Input/Output commands, for example, discusses Visual Basic's commands to write to and read from files.

The Annotate tutorial discusses an application that annotates bitmaps by placing simple shapes on top of them. This simple application illustrates some very interesting techniques that will come in handy if you're using Visual Basic to build graphics applications. The ImageBox tutorial also uses graphics methods, this time to build a scrolling ImageBox. This is a useful control, which you can use as is in your project. Having access to its source code will help you customize to meet specific requirements, too.

You should take a look at the tutorials on the CD and see if there's something of interest to you. I plan to post additional tutorials on the Sybex Web site (at http://www.sybex.com), so you should visit it from time to time for additional information on VB programming.

How To Reach The Author

Despite our best efforts, a book this size is bound to contain errors. Although a printed medium isn't as easy to update as a Web site, I will spare no effort to fix every problem you report (or I discover). The revised applications, along with any other material I think will be of use to the readers of this book, will be posted on the Sybex Web site. If you have any problems with the text or the applications in this book, you can contact me directly at:

76470.724@compuserve.com

Although I can't promise a response to every question, I will fix any problems in the examples and provide updated versions. I would also like to hear any comments you may have on the book, about the topics you liked or did not like and how useful the examples are. Your comments will be taken into consideration in future editions.

PART I

Visual Programming: The Fundamentals of Visual Basic

CHAPTER
ONE

Getting Started with Visual Basic

- Using the Integrated Development Environment (IDE)

- Developing your first VB project

- Designing the user interface

- Programming an application

- Developing event-driven programs in a visual environment

- Customizing your environment

This chapter introduces Visual Basic's Integrated Development Environment (IDE) and the basic principles of developing applications with visual tools and event programming. We will go through the steps of creating a few simple applications, and I'll explain the components of the visual development environment. In this chapter, I'll take you on a tour of the environment and discuss the basics of developing user interfaces. We'll then add a few lines of code. In the second chapter, we'll build more advanced, practical applications that demonstrate other features of the language.

NOTE   If you don't need the introductory material of this chapter, you can skip it entirely. You should, however, take a look at the new features of the Visual Basic IDE and its customization options. The corresponding sections are marked with a NEW icon.

One Language, Three Editions

I assume that you have installed Visual Basic 6. This means you have already decided which edition of Visual Basic you are going to use. Visual Basic comes in three flavors:

- The Visual Basic Learning edition

- The Visual Basic Professional edition

- The Visual Basic Enterprise edition

The *Visual Basic Learning edition* is the introductory edition that lets you easily create Windows applications. It comes with all the tools you need to build mainstream Windows applications; most of the examples and applications in this book will work with the Learning edition.

The *Visual Basic Professional edition* is for computer professionals and includes advanced features such as tools to develop ActiveX and Internet controls. The topics covered in Part VI, *Visual Basic and the Web,* require the Professional edition.

The *Visual Basic Enterprise edition* is the most advanced edition and is aimed at programmers who build distributed applications in a team environment. It includes all the features of the Professional edition, plus tools such as Visual SourceSafe (a version control system) and the Automation and Component Manager, which are not covered in this book.

Depending on which edition of Visual Basic you installed, you may see fewer or more options in the menus and toolbars of the Visual Basic IDE. The options discussed in most of this book are present in all three editions. If some of the menu options in the figures are not present on your system, you are probably using the Learning edition.

The Integrated Development Environment

Visual Basic is not just a language. It's an Integrated Development Environment in which you can develop, run, test, and debug your applications. Start Visual Basic, and you'll see the window shown in Figure 1.1. This is where you are prompted to select the type of project you want to create.

FIGURE 1.1:

The types of projects you can create with Visual Basic

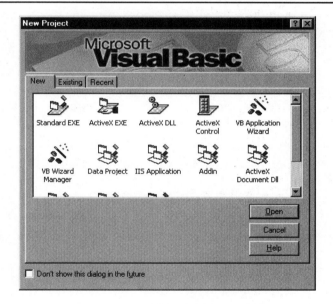

With Visual Basic, you can create the following types of applications.

Standard EXE   A Standard EXE project is a typical application. Most of the applications in this book are Standard EXE projects. These are the types of applications you developed with previous versions of Visual Basic.

ActiveX EXE, ActiveX DLL   These types of projects are available with the Professional edition. ActiveX components are OLE automation servers and are described in Chapters 14 and 15. ActiveX components are basic code-building components that don't have a visible interface and that can add special functionality to your applications. The two types of projects are identical in functionality, but are packaged differently (as executable files or Dynamic Link Libraries).

ActiveX Control   This type of project is also a feature of the Professional edition. Use it to develop your own ActiveX controls, which are described in Chapter 16. An ActiveX control such as a TextBox or Command button control, is a basic element of the user interface. If the ActiveX controls, that come with Visual Basic (the ones that appear in the Toolbox by default) don't provide the functionality you need, you can build your own custom controls.

ActiveX Document EXE, ActiveX Document DLL   ActiveX documents are in essence Visual Basic applications that can run in the environment of a container that supports hyperlinking (such as Internet Explorer). These types of documents are not discussed in this book.

VB Application Wizard, VB Wizard Manager   The Application Wizard takes you through the steps of setting up the skeleton of a new application. I believe that you shouldn't use this Wizard unless you can develop a project on your own. Modifying the skeleton code created by the Wizard is just as difficult as developing your own application from scratch, if not more. You should, however, experiment with this tool to see the types of applications it can prototype for you.

The Wizard Manager lets you build your own Wizard. A Wizard is a sequence of windows that collect information from the user. After the user fills out all the windows, the Wizard proceeds to build an application, install software, or carry out an automated operation for the end user.

NEW!> **Data Project**   This is a feature of the Enterprise edition, and it doesn't correspond to a new project type. It's identical to the Standard EXE project type, but it automatically adds the controls that are used in accessing databases to the Toolbox. It also adds the database ActiveX Designers to the Project Explorer window. The ActiveX Designers are visual tools for accessing and manipulating databases and generating reports. The DataEnvironment and DataReport ActiveX Designers are described in Chapter 18.

NEW!> **DHTML Application**   VB6 allows you to build Dynamic HTML pages that can be displayed in the browser's window on a client computer. I don't discuss this project type, but you'll find an introduction to HTML and Dynamic HTML in Part VI. Instead of showing you how to use Visual Basic's tools to automate the process of designing DHTML (and HTML) pages, I've included a section on the structure of DHTML documents. Even with Visual Basic's tools, you can't design DHTML pages without a basic understanding of Dynamic HTML.

NEW!> **IIS Application**   VB6 allows you to build applications that run on the Web server and interact with clients over the Internet with the Internet Information Server. I don't discuss this project type, but in Part VI you will find information on the basics of interacting with the server through a component called Active Server Pages (which is basically what IIS Applications do).

AddIn　You can create your own add-ins for the Visual Basic IDE. Add-ins are special commands you can add to Visual Basic's menus (they usually appear under the Add-Ins menu). To do so, select this type of project. This topic is rather advanced, and we won't look at it in this book.

VB Enterprise Edition Controls　This is not a new type of project. It simply creates a new Standard EXE project and loads all the tools of the Enterprise edition of Visual Basic. The window in Figure 1.1, earlier in this chapter, has three tabs: New, Existing, and Recent.

In the New tab, you can select the type of a new project, as explained already. Switch to the Existing tab to select an existing project and open it. To open a project you were working on recently, switch to the Recent tab, which contains the list of the most recently opened projects. In your daily projects, you'll be coming back to the project you were working on during the last few days, and this is where you can find them easily.

Select the Standard EXE icon in the New Project window, and then click OK to open the window shown in Figure 1.2.

FIGURE 1.2:

A new Visual Basic project

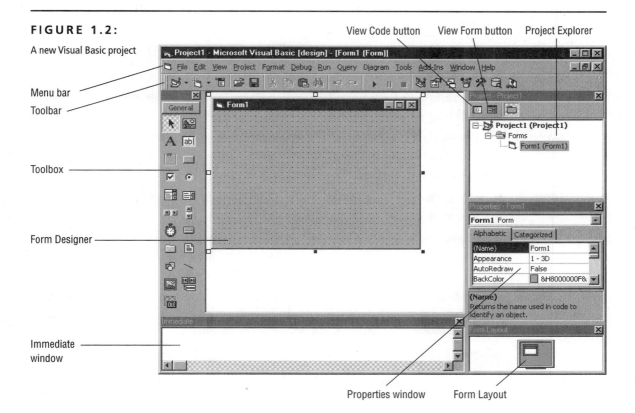

What you see on your screen now is the Visual Basic IDE, which is made up of a number of components. The main window, in the middle of the screen, contains a Form named Form1. The Form is the application's window, and in it you place the elements of your application's user interface (checkboxes, Command buttons, and so on). It is also the window that the user sees when running the application.

The Menu Bar

The menu bar contains the commands you need to work with Visual Basic. The basic menus are:

- **File** contains the commands for opening and saving projects and creating executable files and a list of recent projects.

- **Edit** contains editing commands (e.g., Undo, Copy, Paste) plus a number of commands for formatting and editing your code (e.g., Find, Replace).

- **View** contains commands for showing or hiding components of the IDE.

- **Project** contains commands that add components to the current project, references to Windows objects, and new tools to the Toolbox.

- **Format** contains commands for aligning the controls on the Form.

- **Debug** contains the usual debugging commands.

- **Run** contains the commands that start, break, and end execution of the current application.

- **Query** contains commands that simplify the design of Stuctured Query Language (SQL) queries. This menu is available when building database applications.

- **Diagram** contains commands for editing database diagrams. This menu is available when building database applications.

- **Tools** contains tools you need in building ActiveX components and ActiveX controls; contains the command to start the Menu Editor and the Options command, which lets you customize the environment.

- **Add-Ins** contains add-ins that you can add and remove as needed. By default, only the Visual Data Manager Add-In is installed in this menu. Use the Add-In Manager command to add and remove add-ins.

- **Window** is the standard Window menu of an application that contains commands to arrange windows on the screen.

- **Help** contains information to help you as you work.

The Toolbars

The toolbars give you quick access to commonly used menu commands. Besides the main toolbar, which is displayed by default below the menu bar, the Visual Basic IDE provides additional toolbars for specific purposes, such as editing, Form design, and debugging. To view the additional toolbars, choose View ➤ Toolbars.

- The Standard toolbar is just below the menu bar and is displayed by default.

- The Edit toolbar contains the commands of the Edit menu.

- The Debug toolbar contains the commands of the Debug menu.

- The Form Editor toolbar contains the commands of the Format menu.

To open and close toolbars, choose View ➤ Toolbars to display a submenu containing the names of the toolbars. These names are toggles and turn the corresponding toolbars on and off.

Choose the Customize command to customize the appearance and contents of menus. To customize default toolbars, choose View ➤ Toolbars ➤ Customize to open the Customize dialog box, as shown in Figure 1.3.

FIGURE 1.3:

The Customize dialog box lets you customize the default toolbars of the Visual Basic IDE.

The Customize dialog box has three tabs:

- **Toolbars** On this tab you can specify which toolbars will be visible, rename toolbars, delete them, and even create new ones. To create a new toolbar, click the New button and enter the new toolbar's name when prompted.

- **Commands** This tab contains a list of the main menu options and a list of the commands of the selected option. Use this tab to add commands to your custom toolbars (I'll describe the process in the following section).

- **Options** On this tab you can specify some general options for all toolbars. You can switch between small and large icons, specify whether ScreenTips display, and specify whether menus animate.

NOTE ScreenTips are small yellow boxes that contain a short description of each tool. Unless you specify not to display them, ScreenTips appear when the pointer hovers over a tool.

Creating a New Toolbar

To create a new toolbar, follow these steps:

1. Choose View ➤ Toolbars ➤ Customize to open the Customize dialog box.

2. Select the Toolbars tab, and click the New button.

3. Enter the name of the new toolbar (in Figure 1.3, it's **MyToolbar**). A small empty toolbar appears on your screen.

4. To add icons to your new toolbar, select the Commands tab, which contains all the commands of the IDE's menus organized according to the menu to which they belong.

5. Click the icon you want to add to your custom toolbar, and drag it from the Customize dialog box to your new toolbar.

6. Add as many command icons as necessary, and then close the Customize dialog box.

TIP If you can't see your custom toolbar on the screen, choose View ➤ Toolbars and click your custom toolbar's name.

The Project Explorer

The window titled Project is the Project Explorer, which displays the components of the project. Simple projects, such as the ones we develop in the early chapters of this book, are made up of a single Form. In later chapters, you'll see projects that have multiple Forms and other types of components, such as Class Modules and ActiveX controls.

The project components are organized in folders, and the Project window is called Project Explorer because it has the look of the Windows Explorer. As you will see in later chapters, Visual Basic 6 can manage projects and groups of projects.

The Toolbox

The Toolbox contains the icons of the controls you can place on a Form to create the application's user interface. By default, the Toolbox contains the pointer icon and the icons of 20 ActiveX controls (explained later in this chapter in the section "The Elements of the User Interface"). To place a control (such as a Command button) on a Form, you first select it with the mouse and then move the mouse over the Form. When the mouse is over the Form, the cursor turns into a cross, and you can draw the control on the Form, just as you would draw a rectangle using a drawing application. The size of the rectangle determines the size of the control.

In addition to the default Toolbox (called General), you can create custom layouts by right-clicking the Toolbox and selecting Add Tab from the shortcut menu. Instead of crowding the Toolbox with all the ActiveX controls you need for a project, you can create several tabs with icons on the Toolbox and organize the controls according to function.

To add a new tab to the Toolbox, follow these steps:

1. Right-click the Toolbox to open the shortcut menu.

2. Choose Add Tab, and enter the name of the new tab. Visual Basic displays a new button (such as the General button) in the Toolbox.

3. Click the new tab button to open the tab, and then right-click it to display a shortcut menu.

4. Select Components to display a list of all ActiveX controls installed on your system.

5. To add to the current tab, check the checkbox in front of the names of the controls, as shown in Figure 1.4.

FIGURE 1.4:

The Components dialog box contains all the ActiveX controls present on your system, and you can select the ones you want to use in your projects.

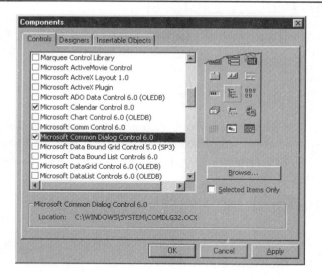

Where Do ActiveX Controls Come From?

Many places, indeed. Some ActiveX controls come with Windows, but are not installed by default. The Microsoft Common Dialog Control 6.0 (checked in Figure 1.4) comes with Windows, and if you place this control on your Forms, you can open the standard common dialog boxes, such as the Font and Color dialog boxes, from within your applications with just a few lines of code. Many ActiveX controls are manufactured by third-party companies, and you can use them in your projects. You can also find many ActiveX controls at Microsoft's Web site (http:// www.microsoft.com/activex).

The Properties Window

The Properties window contains the property settings for the selected control. *Properties* are attributes of an object, such as its size, caption, and color. You can adjust the appearance of the controls on the Form with point-and-click operations. For example, you can set the string that appears on a Command button by locating the Caption property in the Properties window and typing a new value, such as "Click me!". To change the color of a Form, locate the BackColor property in the Properties window, and click the arrow button next to the current value of the color. Visual Basic displays a color selection box, as shown in Figure 1.5. Select a color on this box to instantly fill the Form with the new color.

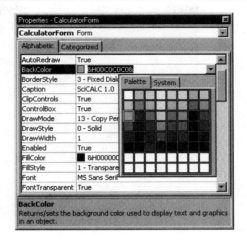

The Form Designer

The Form Designer is the main window in the middle of the screen, and in it you design and edit the application's user interface. The same window displays a text editor in which you can enter and edit the application's code. The Form Designer displays two windows for each Form:

- The Form itself (the elements of the visible user interface)
- A Code window (the code behind the elements of the Form)

To switch between the two views, click the little icons (View Code and View Form) at the top of the Project Explorer (see Figure 1.2, earlier in this chapter). Select the Form you want to view in the Project Explorer, and then click one of the two View buttons to see the Form or its code.

The Form Layout

You use the Form Layout window, which is in the lower-right corner of the Visual Basic IDE, to determine the initial positions of the Forms in your application. You can move Forms around and place them on top of each other. This window is useful in applications that use multiple Forms because you can specify how each Form is positioned with respect to the main Form. Figure 1.6 shows the placement of three Forms on the Desktop and their initial relative positions. The insert in the lower-right corner shows how the placement of the Forms was specified in the Form Layout window.

FIGURE 1.6:

Use the Form Layout window to specify the initial positions of your application's Forms.

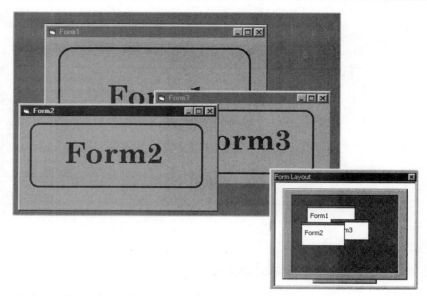

The Immediate Window

The Immediate window at the bottom of the IDE (if it's not visible, choose View ➤ Immediate Window) is a debugging aid. While an application is running, you can stop it and use the Immediate window to examine or change the values of the application's variables and to execute Visual Basic commands in Immediate mode. The Immediate window is one of the reasons for the popularity of Visual Basic and of the BASIC programming language in general. You can step into the application's code while it executes, change the values of the variables or even insert statements in the code, and then continue the execution of an application. You can use this window to execute immediate statements as if it was the window of an advanced calculator. If you enter the following statement in the Immediate window:

```
Print 1888/999
```

and press Enter, the following will be displayed:

```
1.88988988988989
```

You can also use variables in the Immediate window. If you enter the following lines:

```
A=1888
B=999
Print A/B
```

you'll see the same value as before. The Immediate window is a very versatile tool, and you'll learn more about it in the section "Using the Immediate Window," later in this chapter.

In the following sections, we will develop a few simple projects that demonstrate basic concepts of application development with visual tools and event-driven programming. It's introductory material, intended for people who are not familiar with visual development or who program with other languages. We'll look at how to set up an application, design its user interface, and add code. Toward the end of the chapter, I will summarize the principles of event-driven programming and show you how to customize the IDE. This topic is last so that those of you who are not familiar with Visual Basic will acquire some experience with the environment before you attempt to customize the environment.

Your First VB Project

When you select the Standard EXE type of project in the New Project window, Visual Basic creates a new project named Project1. Project1 is the top item in the Project Explorer window. The Forms folder under the project name contains the names of all Forms that make up the project. As you will see in the next chapter, a project can have more than one Form.

Renaming and Saving the Project

You should start your projects by renaming their components and saving them, preferably in a new folder. To do so, follow these steps:

1. In the Project Explorer window, click the project's name (Project1).

2. In the Properties window, select the value of the Name property (projects have a single property, the Name property) and enter the name **MVB6_1** (for Mastering Visual Basic 6).

3. In the Project Explorer window, select the name of the Form. The Properties window now displays the Form's properties.

4. Locate the Name property, select it, and change it to **Example1**.

Your Project Explorer window should now look like the one in Figure 1.7.

FIGURE 1.7:

The Project Explorer window after renaming the project's components

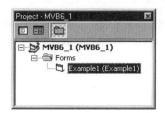

Now you are ready to save the project. To save a project, you must first save the Form(s) and then the project (more on this in Chapter 2, in which we'll look at the structure of a project and how it's saved on disk). When saving projects, try to use meaningful filenames so that you'll be able to locate them later. For the projects of this book, I had to use eight-character names, a limitation imposed by the CD production process.

Follow these steps to save the project:

1. Choose File (the File menu is shown in the left half of Figure 1.8) ➤ Save Example1 As. (Visual Basic suggests the default name for the Form, so you must select the Save As command, not the Save command.)

FIGURE 1.8:

The File menu and the Save File As window

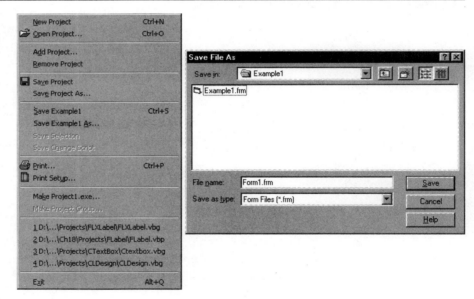

2. In the Save File As window (shown in the right half of Figure 1.8), click the New Folder button to create a new folder and save the project there. Each project and its files should be stored in a separate folder, but it is possible to store multiple projects in the same folder.

3. Name the new folder and click Save.

4. Choose File ➤ Save Project As. In the Save Project As window, enter a name for the project file and click Save.

NOTE The Form's name has nothing to do with the name of the file in which the Form is stored, and the Project's name has nothing to do with the name of the file in which the project is stored. It is customary, however, to use the same name for the Form or project and the file in which it is stored (or at least similar names). For more information on the structure of a project and how to move its files to a different folder, see Chapter 2.

The Elements of the User Interface

The user interface is what appears in the application's window when it runs. It consists of various elements with which the user can interact and control the application. The first element of the user interface is the Form. This is the window displayed at runtime, and it acts as a container for all the elements of the interface. The elements in the user interface are common to all Windows applications, and they are all shown as icons in the Toolbox.

The icons in the Toolbox of the Visual Basic IDE and their names are shown in Figure 1.9. Let's quickly run through the controls shown in the Toolbox.

FIGURE 1.9:

The icons on the Toolbox represent the elements you can use to build user interfaces.

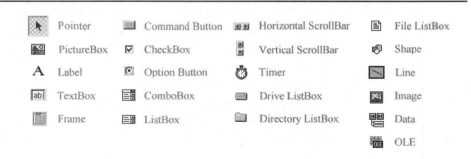

Pointer	Command Button	Horizontal ScrollBar	File ListBox
PictureBox	CheckBox	Vertical ScrollBar	Shape
Label	Option Button	Timer	Line
TextBox	ComboBox	Drive ListBox	Image
Frame	ListBox	Directory ListBox	Data
			OLE

 PictureBox   This control is used to display images, and the images are set with the Picture property. The PictureBox control supports a number of methods for generating drawings.

 Label   This control displays text on a Form that the user can't edit. Labels commonly identify other controls and can be transparent, so the text appears to be placed directly on the Form. You set the label's text with the Caption property.

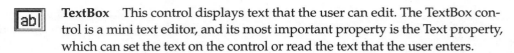 **TextBox**   This control displays text that the user can edit. The TextBox control is a mini text editor, and its most important property is the Text property, which can set the text on the control or read the text that the user enters.

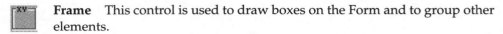 **Frame**   This control is used to draw boxes on the Form and to group other elements.

Command Button   This is the most common element of the Windows interface. A Command button represents an action that is carried out when the user clicks the button.

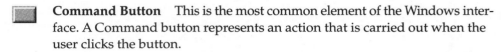 **CheckBox**   The CheckBox control presents one or more choices that the user can select. The CheckBox control's main property is Value, and it is 0 if the CheckBox is cleared, and 1 if the CheckBox is checked. The CheckBox is a toggle. Every time it's clicked, it changes status (from checked to cleared and back).

Option Button   Option buttons, or radio buttons, appear in groups, and the user can choose only one of them. The Option button's main property is Checked, and it is True if the control is checked, and False otherwise. The Option button is a toggle. Every time it's clicked, it changes status (from checked to cleared and back).

ComboBox   This control is similar to the ListBox control, but it contains a text Edit field. The user can either choose an item from the list or enter a new string in the Edit field. The item selected from the list (or entered in the Edit field) is given by the control's Text property.

ListBox   This control contains a list of options from which the user can choose one or more. Unlike a group of checkboxes or Option buttons, the ListBox control can contain many lines and the user can scroll the list to locate an item. The selected item in a ListBox control is given by the Text property. Another important property of the ListBox control is the Sorted property, which determines whether the items in the list will be sorted.

The Horizontal and Vertical ScrollBars   The horizontal and vertical scrollbars let the user specify a magnitude (the current location in a long piece of text, a numeric value, and so on) by scrolling the control's button between its minimum and maximum value.

Timer   You can use this control to perform tasks at regular intervals. The main property of the Timer control is Interval, which determines how often the Timer notifies your application. If the Interval property is set to 10000, the Timer control issues a Timer event every 10 seconds.

File System Controls   You use these controls to add file-handling capabilities to your application. They are normally used together to provide an interface for accessing and exploring drives, folders, and files. The File System controls are:

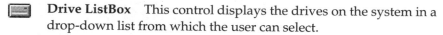 **Drive ListBox**   This control displays the drives on the system in a drop-down list from which the user can select.

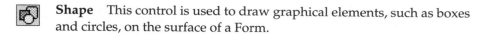 **Directory ListBox**   This control displays a list of all folders in the current drive and lets the user move up or down in the hierarchy of the folders.

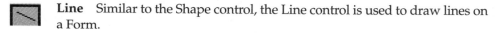 **File ListBox**   This control displays a list of all files in the current folder

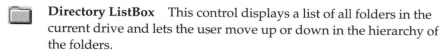 **Shape**   This control is used to draw graphical elements, such as boxes and circles, on the surface of a Form.

Line   Similar to the Shape control, the Line control is used to draw lines on a Form.

Image   This control is similar to the PictureBox control in that it can display images, but it supports only a few features of the PictureBox control (you can't draw on an Image control as you can on the PictureBox control) and requires fewer resources.

Data   This control provides point-and-click access to data stored in databases. It has many properties and methods, which are discussed in Chapter 17.

OLE   This control is a window you can place on your Form to host documents from other applications, such as Microsoft Word or Excel. Through this control, you can access the functionality of other applications, if they support OLE.

Designing the User Interface

Designing the application's user interface consists of drawing the elements on the Form. In our first application, the user can select one of the three major credit cards (the form of payment) and one or more of the three items listed on the right half of the Form shown in Figure 1.10.

FIGURE 1.10:

Designing a user interface
with Visual Basic controls

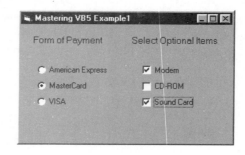

To design the Form shown in Figure 1.10, follow these steps:

1. In the Project Explorer, double-click the name of the Form to open it in design mode, and in the Properties window, find the Caption property. This is the value that appears in the Form's caption bar, and its default value is Form1. Change it to **Example1**. The new name appears on the Form's caption bar even as you type its value in the Properties window.

2. Place a Label control near the top left corner of the Form.

3. With the Label control selected, switch to the Properties window, and set the Label control's Caption property to **Form of Payment**. Notice that the Label control doesn't have a border by default.

4. Locate the Font property in the Properties window, and click the button with the ellipsis next to the current font to open the Font dialog box.

5. Select an easy-to-read font. The example in Figure 1.10 uses 10-point MS Sans Serif.

6. Place another Label control next to the first one, and set its Caption property to **Select Optional Items**.

7. Switch back to the Properties window, and set the Font property of the new Label control to the same setting as the first one.

8. Now you can place the Option button controls on the Form. Select the Option button icon in the Toolbox, and draw a control on the Form. Make it large enough to hold the **American Express** caption.

9. While the first Option button is still selected on the Form, move to the Properties window, and set its Caption property to **American Express**. Don't bother aligning the control or setting its Font or other properties yet.

10. Repeat steps 8 and 9 for the other two Option buttons. Their captions should be **Mastercard** and **VISA**.

11. Now add three CheckBox controls, and set their captions to **Modem**, **CD-ROM**, and **Sound Card**.

The elements of the interface are now on the Form, and you have two groups of controls that can be manipulated together. For example, you can change the setting of the Font property for a number of controls all at once by following these steps:

1. Select the three Option buttons with the mouse, and then locate the Font property in the Properties window.

2. Click the ellipsis button to open the Font dialog box.

3. Select a font to apply to all selected controls.

To select multiple controls on the Form, hold down the Shift (or Ctrl) key and click them. If the controls you want to select are clustered together, you can select them by drawing a box around them with the mouse. The selected controls are indicated with handles that appear along their perimeter.

Aligning the Controls

Now you must align the controls on the Form. This isn't a trivial step. Your application's user interface is its visible part, and what people think about your application depends a great deal on how the application looks. You are not expected to design the most spectacular user interface (not that it wouldn't help), but at the very least your controls must be perfectly aligned. If not, the Form will look crooked and out-of-whack. The Visual Basic IDE provides numerous commands for aligning controls, which are all on the Format menu, and they are explained next.

The Format Menu

The commands on the Format menu align and resize the selected controls on the Form.

Here's a quick rundown of the commands on the Format menu, arranged according to their corresponding submenu.

Align   The commands on this menu align the edges or middles of the selected controls:

> **Lefts, Centers, Rights** align the left, center, and right sides of the selected controls; these commands are meaningful only if controls are stacked in a column.

> **Tops, Middles, Bottoms** aligns the top, middle, and bottom sides of the controls; these commands are meaningful only if controls are placed next to each other.

> **To Grid** aligns the controls to the nearest grid point.

Make Same Size   The commands on this menu make all selected controls the same size.

> **Height, Width, Both** make the horizontal, vertical, or both dimensions of the controls equal.

Size to Grid   This command changes the size and/or position of the selected control(s) so that each corner aligns with the nearest grid point.

Horizontal Spacing   The commands on this menu control the horizontal spacing between selected controls.

> **Make Equal** makes all horizontal (vertical) distances between successive controls the same size.

> **Increase** increases the horizontal (vertical) distance between adjacent controls by one grid block.

> **Decrease** decreases the horizontal (vertical) distance between adjacent controls by one grid block.

> **Remove** removes any horizontal (vertical) space between adjacent controls.

Vertical Spacing   This menu controls the vertical spacing between selected controls and has the same commands as the Horizontal Spacing submenu, only these commands apply to the vertical arrangement of the controls.

Center in Form   This submenu contains two commands:

> **Horizontally** centers the selected control(s) in the width of the Form.

> **Vertically** centers the selected control(s) in the height of the Form.

Order   This submenu contains two commands that change the relative order of the selected control(s) by moving them in front or behind other controls.

Bring to Front brings the selected control in front of other overlapping controls.

Send to Back sends the selected control behind other overlapping controls.

They work just like the commands of the same name in a drawing application, and you use them to manipulate the depth of each control. The *depth* is equivalent to a layer on which one or more controls reside. Objects on layers closer to the viewer hide the objects on layers behind them and are hidden by objects on layers in front of them.

Lock Controls   This command allows you to select a number of controls on the Form and lock them. A locked control can't be moved on the Form and you don't risk misaligning it. You can still change its properties through the Properties window, but you can't move it by mistake or when you use it along with other controls in alignment operations.

Using the Format Menu

You can arrange your controls on the Form in many ways, and after you acquire some experience with the Visual Basic IDE, you'll be using these commands effectively.

To align the controls on the Example1 Form, follow these steps:

1. Select all three Option button controls with the mouse. (To select multiple controls, hold down Shift or Ctrl and click each one.) Alternatively, you can draw a rectangle on the Form that encloses the desired controls.

2. Choose Format ➤ Align ➤ Lefts to align the left edges of the three controls.

3. With the three controls selected, choose Format ➤ Vertical Spacing ➤ Make Equal to make the distance between successive controls equal.

4. While the three controls remain selected, move them around with the mouse to the desired position. Click any of the selected controls and drag it around. All the selected controls will move as a group.

Optionally, while the three controls remain selected, choose Format ➤ Lock Controls. This ensures that you won't ruin the alignment of the controls. Once a control is locked, you can't move it with the mouse or change its alignment. If your Form contains many carefully aligned controls, you should lock them; it doesn't take much to ruin the alignment. A simple action such as selecting a control to use as a reference to align other controls could move the control by a few pixels.

Running the Application

Now you can run and test the application. If you haven't had any experience with Visual Basic (or other visual development tools), you may be wondering, "What application?" We didn't type even a single line of code. Well, why do you think it's called Visual Basic and not Microsoft Basic or Windows Basic or anything else? Visual Basic uses visual tools to build a large section of the application. The user interface can be built almost entirely with point-and-click operations.

To run the application, choose Run ➤ Start or press F5. The application contains no code, but check out how much functionality is built into it. When you click an Option button, it is checked, and the previously checked Option button is cleared. The checkboxes behave differently. Each time you click a checkbox, it changes its state: if it is selected, it is cleared; if it is cleared, it becomes selected.

To stop the application, choose Run ➤ End. As you can see, the Visual Basic IDE is more than a program editor. It's an integrated environment in which you can design and run your applications.

Using the Immediate Window

Start the application again by pressing F5, and then interrupt it by pressing Ctrl+Break or by choosing Run ➤ Break. The application has been interrupted, but not terminated. At the bottom of the screen, you will see a window named Immediate, as shown in Figure 1.11. When you issue Visual Basic commands in this window, they execute immediately. Let's see how this works.

FIGURE 1.11:

Commands entered in the Immediate window execute immediately.

Immediate window ⎯⎯⎯

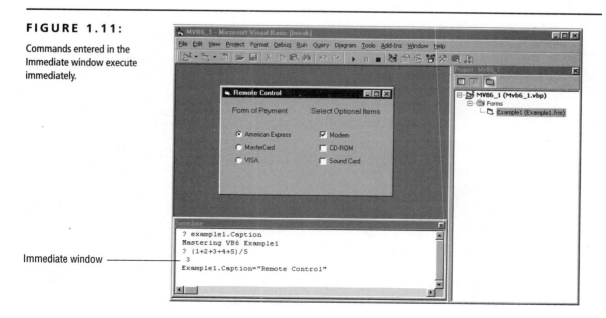

The States of Visual Basic

Visual Basic applications can be viewed in three distinct states: design, execution, and break.

In *design state*, you can edit the user interface or add code to the application. All the windows of the IDE and its commands are available to you.

In *execution state*, the application is running. Only a few menu commands are available, and none of the windows of the IDE are available. You can neither edit the user interface nor add code to an application while it's running.

In the *break state*, the application's execution has been interrupted temporarily and can resume when you press F5 or choose Run ➤ Continue. The Immediate window is activated, and you can edit the code and issue commands in it. However, you can't edit the user interface.

Let's explore the role of the Immediate window while the application is in break state. Place the pointer in the Immediate window and type the following:

```
Print Example1.Caption
```

As you recall, *Example1* is the name of the Form, and *Caption* is the name of the property that sets or reads the Form's caption. The previous statement displays the form's caption in the line below as soon as you press Enter.

TIP　To access the properties of the Form (such as the Caption property), the project must be in break state. Run the project by pressing F5, and then break it by pressing Ctrl+Break. If you attempt to read or set the value of the Caption property while the project is in design state, you'll get an error message. When a message box with an error appears, click OK to return to the editor.

The following statement displays the value 3:

```
Print (1+2+3+4+5)/ 5
```

This is a regular Visual Basic statement consisting of numeric values and arithmetic operators. It can appear anywhere in a Visual Basic application. You can issue all types of Visual Basic statements in the Immediate window, such as cos(3/100) or Rnd(), which returns a random number between 0 and 1.

The last statement shown in Figure 1.11:

```
Example1.Caption = "Remote Control"
```

does something quite interesting. It sets the value of the Form's Caption property. To display the application's window, press Alt+Tab. You will see that its caption has changed, as shown in Figure 1.11.

You use the Immediate window when you are designing and debugging applications to perform three common operations:

- Execute Visual Basic statements to perform simple tasks such as calculations
- Examine the values of the controls on the Form
- Set the values of the controls on the Form

These are extremely useful operations during an application's design and debugging phase. You don't have to write code to perform simple tasks. Merely type a statement in the Immediate window, and it executes as if it belongs to the current application.

You can issue even more complicated statements in the Immediate window, as long as you type them all on the same line. To display six random numbers in the range 1 to 49, for instance, you can either issue six separate Print statements or write a small For...Next loop that displays the numbers. In an application's code, you would use the following structure:

```
For lucky = 1 To 6
    Print 1 + Int(Rnd()*49)
Next lucky
```

To issue the same statements in the Immediate window, you must type them in a single line. To enter more than one statement in a line (whether in the Immediate window or in your code), use the colon as separator:

```
For lucky = 1 To 6: Print 1 + Int(Rnd()*49): Next lucky
```

Enter this line in the Immediate window and press Enter to display the next six lucky numbers, as shown in Figure 1.12.

FIGURE 1.12:

Executing multiple commands in the Immediate window

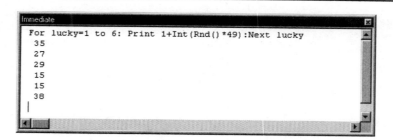

Programming an Application

Our next application is called MSVB_2, and you will find it in the Example2 folder in this chapter's folder on the CD. Start a new project, name the project **MSVB_2**, name its Form **Example2**, and then save it in its own folder. Figure 1.13 shows the application's main window.

Now, follow these steps:

1. When you are back in the Visual Basic IDE, select the Form and change its Caption property to **TextBox Demo**.

2. Place a textbox on the Form, as shown in Figure 1.13.

3. Select the textbox, and in the Properties window, set its MultiLine property to True.

FIGURE 1.13:

The Example2 Form demonstrates a few properties of the TextBox control.

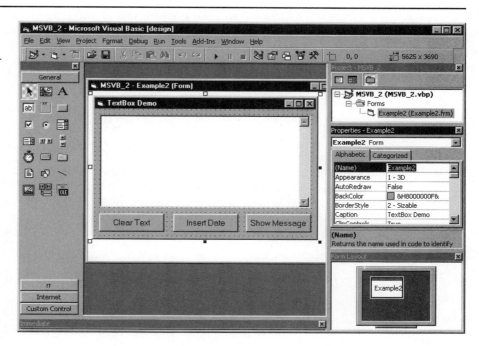

By default, the TextBox control accepts a single line of text, and the default setting of its MultiLine property is False. By setting it to True, you are specifying that the textbox can accept multiple lines of text.

Since the textbox can hold multiple lines of text, it is possible for the user to enter text that exceeds the height of the control. To make sure that every piece of the text in the control is visible, you must set its ScrollBars property to Vertical. When you do so, a vertical scroll bar appears on the right side of the control so that the user can scroll its contents up and down.

4. Locate the ScrollBars property in the Properties window, and expand the list of possible values by selecting the setting 2–Vertical. (The other possible values are 0–None, 1–Horizontal, and 3–Both.)

5. Add three Command buttons, and set their captions to **Clear Text**, **Insert Date**, and **Show Message**. We will program these buttons later to react when they are clicked.

6. From the Format menu, select the appropriate commands to make the size of all three Command buttons the same, align their tops, and align them with the textbox.

The application's interface is complete. Now run the application and check out the TextBox control. This control can add the basic functionality of a text editor to your applications. Notice how it wraps text as you type. Try out the editing keys. You can select text with the mouse and delete it, copy it to the Clipboard by pressing Ctrl+C, and paste it back by pressing Ctrl+V. You can even switch to another application, such as Notepad, copy some text with the other application's Copy command, and then paste it in the textbox by pressing Ctrl+V.

Programming the Command Buttons

Now we must add some code behind the Form's buttons to perform the actions indicated by their captions. Obviously, the Clear Text button must clear the control by deleting any text on it. The Insert Date button displays the date in the control, and the Show Message button displays a message on the control. Follow these steps:

1. If the application is running, stop it by choosing Run ➤ End.

2. When the Form appears on the screen, double-click the first Command button. Visual Basic opens the Code window, shown in Figure 1.14.

FIGURE 1.14:

The Code window for the Example2 application

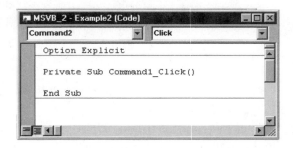

```
MSVB_2 - Example2 (Code)

Command2            Click

    Option Explicit

    Private Sub Command1_Click()

    End Sub
```

Command1 is the name of the control, and Click is the name of an event. This event is triggered every time the user clicks the first Command button. When this happens, Visual Basic looks for a subroutine named Command1_Click, and if it's found, it executes. In other words, if you want actions to execute every time the Command1 control is clicked, you must insert them in the Command1_Click subroutine.

Here is the command to clear the TextBox control:

```
Text1.Text = ""
```

Text1 is the name of the control (it's the default name Visual Basic assigned to it when it was created), and Text is the name of the property that sets (or reads) the text on the control. Setting the Text property to an empty string in effect clears the textbox. The Code window should now look like the one shown in Figure 1.15. Command1_Click() is an *event handler*, a procedure that specifies how the Command1 control must handle the Click event.

Preparing to Code

Before you start coding, choose Tools ➤ Options to open the Options dialog box:

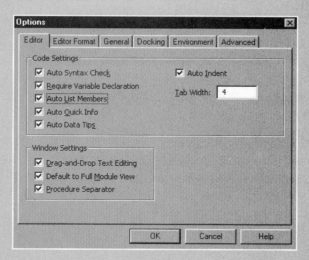

Select the Editor tab, and then clear the following checkboxes: Auto List Members, Auto Quick Info, and Auto Data Tips.

This action simplifies the process of entering code. I will explain later the meaning of these options and how they interfere with typing commands.

FIGURE 1.15:

The Code window of the
Example2 application with
the code of the Clear Text
button

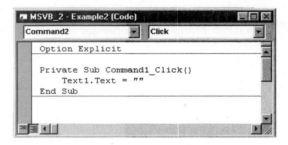

Visual Basic has inserted the following lines in the Code window and placed the pointer between them:

```
Private Sub Command1_Click()

End Sub
```

Now double-click the second Command button to display its subroutine for the Click event. To display the current date in the textbox, the subroutine must contain the following line:

```
Private Sub Command2_Click()
    Text1.Text = Date()
End Sub
```

The *Date()* function returns the current date. Assigning its value to the Text property replaces the current contents of the control with the date.

The Click event handler for the third button is:

```
Private Sub Command3_Click()
    Text1.Text = "Welcome to Visual Basic 6.0"
End Sub
```

This subroutine displays the string "Welcome to Visual Basic 6.0" in the textbox.

Run the application and test the operation of the Command buttons. They perform simple operations, but their code is even simpler. Each time you click the Insert Date or Show Message buttons, the current contents of the textbox are cleared. Ideally, we should be able to insert the date and message in the text, not replace it.

SelText   To insert a string in the textbox, you use the SelText property, which represents the selected text in the control. If you assign a value to the SelText property, the selected text (not the entire text) is replaced with the new value. Even if no text is selected, the new string is inserted at the location of the pointer in the text. The revised event handlers for the buttons Command1 and Command2 are shown next, along with the rest of the code. Implement these changes, and then run the application to see how the commands behave now. You have some practical and useful features in your editor, which is based on an ActiveX control.

Code 1.1:   The Example2 Application

```
Option Explicit

Private Sub Command1_Click()
    Text1.Text = ""
End Sub

Private Sub Command2_Click()
    Text1.SelText = Date()
End Sub

Private Sub Command3_Click()
    Text1.SelText = "Welcome to Visual Basic 6.0"
End Sub
```

Grouping Controls

Our next application is called MSVB6-3, and its interface is shown in Figure 1.16. This example is another typical design with a peculiar requirement and demonstrates how to group controls.

FIGURE 1.16:

The Example3 Form

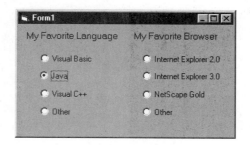

The design of this Form is straightforward. Place eight Option buttons grouped in two blocks on the Form, set their captions as shown in Figure 1.16, and left-align each group's controls by choosing Format ➤ Align ➤ Lefts. The titles are placed on Label controls.

Run the application, and check out how the Option buttons work. Each time you click a control, the other controls are cleared. But this isn't how this application should behave, is it? We want to be able to check one Option button in each column. By default, Visual Basic checks one Option button only, no matter how many you have placed on the Form. It can't group them without additional clues.

To create groups of controls, you place them on another control called a *container*. The most common choice for the container control is the Frame control. Option buttons placed on different frames form separate groups, and Visual Basic maintains one checked Option button in each group. Let's modify the application to create two groups of Option buttons, as shown in Figure 1.17. Follow these steps:

1. Select the Option buttons in the first group.

2. Choose Edit ➤ Cut. The Option buttons are removed from the Form and stored in the Clipboard. We will use the Paste command to place them back on the Form later.

3. Draw a frame large enough to hold the Option buttons you copied.

4. While the frame is selected, choose Edit ➤ Paste. The controls you removed from the Form earlier are pasted on the Frame control. They are not only grouped together, but they are a permanent fixture of the Frame control. You can't move them outside the frame.

5. Repeat steps 1 through 4 with the other four Option buttons. Select and copy them, place a second frame on the Form, and then paste the controls on it. Align the buttons as needed.

FIGURE 1.17:

The Option buttons of the Form shown in Figure 1.16, after they are grouped with the help of two frames

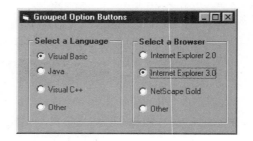

As you can see, the two labels are no longer needed because the two frames have their own captions. Let's delete the two labels and place the titles on the Frame controls. Follow these steps:

1. Select the first frame on the Form, and then locate its Caption property in the Properties window and set it to **Select a Language**.

2. Repeat step 1 for the second frame.

3. To turn on the bold attribute for both frames, select them, double-click their Font property in the Properties window, and in the Font dialog box, click Bold.

4. To delete the labels that are no longer needed, select each one and press Delete, or select them both with the mouse and press Delete. You can also select both labels and choose Edit ➤ Delete.

Run the application now, and check out how the Option buttons behave. Each group has its own checked button, and you can select both a language and a browser. You could have used the PictureBox control instead of the Frame control. I prefer the Frame, however, because it visually isolates the members of each group. You can also use a PictureBox control without a visible border so that the Option buttons appear as if they lie directly on the Form. They will behave as grouped buttons, just as they do when they are placed on a frame.

You now have an idea how Visual Basic works, and you have an understanding of the basic principles of application development with Visual Basic. The two main themes in developing applications with Visual Basic are:

- Visual design
- Event-driven programming

To design the user interface of the application, you don't need more than a basic understanding of the controls (and you know what each control does from your experience with other Windows applications) and basic drawing capabilities. If you have used drawing applications, you can design a user interface with Visual Basic.

Programming the application isn't as simple, but there's a methodology you can't escape. A Visual Basic application isn't a monolithic program such as applications you may have developed with other languages. When you program in Visual Basic, you must first decide how the application interacts with the user. In other words, you must decide how each control reacts to user actions, such as the click of a mouse, keystrokes, and so on, and you must program these reactions. This is called *event-driven programming*, because the application does not determine the flow; instead, the events caused by the user determine the flow of the application. You program the application to react to various external conditions (events), and the user's actions determine the application's flow.

Let's put together the knowledge acquired so far and summarize the basic principles of application development.

Visual Development and Event-Driven Programming

Forms and controls are the basic elements in the user interface of any Windows application. In Visual Basic, these elements are called *objects* because they are manipulated like objects. Objects have properties and methods, and they react to external events, as does any physical object. Your car, for example, is a physical object, and one of its properties is color. Normally, properties are set when an object is created. If you don't like the color of the car as you ordered it, you can still change it. Most control properties are set when the object is created (placed on the Form), but you can change a property later by assigning a new value to it. You can change a property at design time (through the Properties window) or at runtime (through your code).

Visual Basic assigns default properties to every new control you place on a Form. The default Name property, for example, is the name of the control, followed by a number (Command1, Command2, and so on). The background color of most controls is either gray or white. You can examine the property values of a newly created control in the Properties window.

> **TIP**
>
> Controls inherit some properties from the Form. For example, it's customary for all (or nearly all) controls on a Form to have the same Font property. If you place all the controls on the Form, you must change the Font property later. An alternative is to set the Form's Font property to the desired value so that all the controls placed on it will inherit the Form's font.

A few properties are available only at design time, and some others are available only at runtime. You can't specify an item in a ListBox control at design time because the control is empty. It is populated with Visual Basic statements when the program starts. (It is also possible to prepopulate the control at design time by assigning values to the List property, but the actual handling of the control's items takes place at runtime.) The Text property of the ListBox control, therefore, has no meaning at design time. At runtime, it is the control's most important property.

The MultiLine property of the TextBox control, on the other hand, determines whether the textbox holds multiple lines of text. You can set this property only at design time, and it can't be changed at runtime.

Some properties are only available at runtime and are read-only, for example, the number of items in a ListBox control. You can only find out the number of items in the control. To change their count, you must either add or remove items.

A Few Common Properties

The following properties apply to most objects.

- **Name**   This property sets the name of the control, through which you can access the control's properties and methods.

- **Appearance**   This property can be 0 for a flat look or 1 for a 3-D look. The examples in this book use the 3-D look for most controls.

- **BackColor**   This property sets the background color on which text is displayed or graphics are drawn.

- **ForeColor**   This property sets the foreground color (pen color or text color).

- **Font**   This property sets the face, attribute, and size of the font used for the text on the control (text in a TextBox control, the caption of a label or Command button, and so on).

- **Caption**   This property sets the text that is displayed on many controls that don't accept input, for example, the text on a Label control, the caption of a Command button control, and the strings displayed next to the CheckBox and Option button controls.

- **Text**   This property sets the text that is displayed on the controls that accept user input, for example, the TextBox control. Some other controls that can accept text, such as the RichTextBox control, don't appear by default in the Toolbox.

- **Width, Height**   These properties set the control's dimensions. Usually, the dimensions of a control are determined with the visual tools we have explored already. But you can read the control's dimensions or set them from within your code with these properties. The default units are twips, and there are 1,440 twips in an inch (see Chapter 6, for a discussion of the twips units).

- **Left, Top**   These properties set the coordinates of the control's upper-left corner, expressed in the units of the container (usually a Form). The placement of a control on the Form can be specified with the Form Layout window, but you can change it from within your code with these two properties. The default units are twips.

- **Enabled**   By default, this property's value is True, which means that the control can get the focus. Set it to False to disable the control. A disabled control appears gray and can't accept user input.

- **Visible**   Set this property to False to make a control invisible. Sometimes, you use invisible controls to store information that is used internally by the application and should not be seen or manipulated by the user.

A Few Common Methods

Objects have methods too, which are the actions they can carry out. You can think of methods as the actions of an object. For example, the methods of your VCR are the Play, Fast Forward, Rewind, Pause, and Record buttons. After you press one of these buttons, your VCR can perform without any further assistance from you. The Form object, for example, knows how to clear itself, and you can invoke the

Cls method to clear a Form. A Form also knows how to hide itself, an action that you can invoke from within your code with the Hide method.

WARNING   Don't confuse methods with a control's built-in functionality. The TextBox control, for example, knows how to handle keystrokes and convert them into lines of text and display them. You need not call a special method to perform these actions.

Clear   Some methods are simple verbs that tell the object the action to carry out. The Clear method tells the control to discard its contents. If the object is a ListBox, the Clear method removes all its item from the control. The Clear method can also be applied to the Clipboard object, to clear its contents.

Move   All controls that are visible at runtime (only the Timer control is invisible at runtime) provide a Move method that lets you move and resize them from within your application's code. The syntax of the Move method is:

```
Control.Move left, top, width, height
```

Control is a control's name (like Command1 or Text1).; *left* and *top* are the coordinates of the upper-left corner of the control's new position, and *width* and *height* are the control's new dimensions. Use the Move method to resize and reposition a control at once at runtime. For more information on coordinates see Chapter 6.

AddItem, RemoveItem   These methods are used to manipulate the items in a ListBox or ComboBox control. The application doesn't have to know how the items are stored in the control. It issues the AddItem method, and the control takes care of appending or inserting the new item in the list. And this is exactly why methods are used. They are the actions each control can perform without any assistance from the programmer. In effect, methods hide the implementation details of the controls' features, and the programmer can exploit these features by calling a method, which is similar to setting a property value.

For example, to add the item "Canada" in the ListBox control named Countries (which presumably maintains a list of countries), use the following statement:

```
Countries.AddItem "Canada"
```

The ListBox control appends the string "Canada" at the end of the list. If the list is sorted (its Sorted property was set to True at design time), the new item is inserted in the proper order in the list. The AddItem method does a good deal of work behind the scenes, but as a programmer, you needn't worry about the details. All you need to know is the name of the method.

As you can see, to apply a method to a control, you specify the name of the control followed by a period and then the name of the method. The syntax is nearly identical to the syntax of properties. The difference is that a method isn't assigned a value. Typically, a method accepts one or more parameters that tell it exactly how to perform an action.

Some methods, such as the Clear method, are quite simple. You merely specify the name of the control it applies to and the method's name. Some others require additional information. The AddItem method, for instance, which adds a new item to a ListBox control, must know the item to add. When you call this method, you must also supply the value of the item to be added to the list, as you saw in the previous example.

The PictureBox control provides a method for drawing lines. For the PictureBox control to draw a line, it must know the end coordinates of the line (line drawing and other drawing methods are explained in Chapter 6).

A Few Common Events

Events determine the control's reactions to external conditions. Controls recognize events, but your application handles them. A Command button will recognize that it was clicked, but it won't react to the event unless you provide some code. In other words, you must tell Visual Basic what to do when the user clicks the specific Command button, as we did in the second example in this chapter. Once you specify a subroutine for the control's Click event, this subroutine executes each time the control is clicked. The subroutine that determines how a control reacts to an event is called an event handler.

To write an event handler for a control, follow these steps:

1. Switch to the Code window, or double-click the control for which you want to write the event handler.

2. At the top of the Code window, which is shown in Figure 1.18, you will see two drop-down lists. The first contains the names of all the controls on the Form. Select the control for which you want to write an event handler. The second list contains all the events the selected control can recognize. Select the event for which you want to write an event handler.

The combination of the control's name and the event's name is unique and is the name of the event handler. Each time an event takes place, Visual Basic looks for the subroutine made up of the name of the control on which the event took place and the name of the event. If such a handler exists, it's executed. If not, your application won't react to the event. (Typically, applications react to a small number of events.)

The two most common groups of events are mouse (events caused with the mouse) and keyboard (events caused with the keyboard).

FIGURE 1.18:

To write an event handler, select the control's name from the list on the left and the event's name from the list on the right.

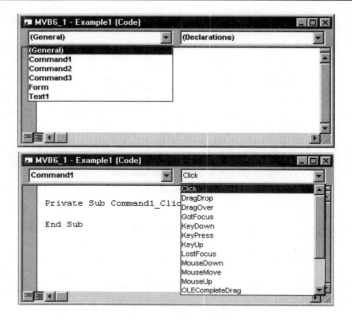

Mouse Events

The events triggered by mouse actions are the most common events in programming with Visual Basic. Most of the elements of the user interface can be manipulated with the mouse, and programming mouse events is your number one job as a VB programmer. However, many users prefer the keyboard, even for operations that are simpler to carry out with the mouse, so you must not favor mouse operations to the exclusion of their keyboard equivalents.

Click, DblClick   The Click event takes place when the user clicks the left mouse button; the DblClick event takes place when the user double-clicks the left mouse button.

MouseDown, MouseUp   The MouseDown event takes place when the mouse button is pressed, and the MouseUp event takes place as it is released.

MouseMove   This event takes place continuously as the mouse is moved over a control. The order in which mouse events take place is as follows:

1.   As the mouse is moved around, the MouseMove event is triggered continuously.

2.   When the user presses a mouse button, the MouseDown event is triggered.

3. If the user continues to move the mouse around while holding down the button, the program keeps receiving MouseMove events.

4. When the user releases the mouse button, the MouseUp event is triggered.

5. If the left mouse button was held down, the Click event is triggered immediately after the MouseUp event.

When the mouse button is double-clicked, the following events take place in the order listed: MouseDown, MouseUp, Click, Double-Click, and MouseUp.

It's a bit involved, but there will never be a reason to program all mouse events or the same control (unless you want to find out the order in which the events are received).

The mouse events you'll be using most often are the Click and DblClick events. If you want finer control of the mouse actions, you will have to program the MouseDown and MouseUp events. For example, if you want to know the coordinates of the point where the mouse was clicked, you will use the MouseDown and MouseUp events. The definitions of the Click and DblClick events are as follows:

```
Sub Click()

End Sub
```

and

```
Sub DblClick()

End Sub
```

Contrast these definitions with the definition of the MouseUp event:

```
Private Sub Text1_MouseUp(Button As Integer, Shift As Integer, _
                    X As Single, Y As Single)

End Sub
```

NOTE   The Visual Basic editor doesn't break the lines. Because we can't print long lines on the page, we break them by inserting an underscore character at the point where the line must break and continue on the following line. Broken lines are also indented. When you enter code, you can break long lines with the underscore character, or you can enlarge the Code window to view them. Notice that there must be a space in front of the underscore character.

The *Button* argument reports which mouse button caused the event. The *Shift* argument reports the status of the Shift, Ctrl, and Alt keys; and the *X* and *Y* arguments are the coordinates of the point where the mouse button was released. Table 1.1

shows the values of the *Button* argument, and Table 1.2 shows the values of the *Shift* argument.

TABLE 1.1: The Values of the *Button* Argument

CONSTANT	VALUE	DESCRIPTION
vbLeftButton	1	Left button is pressed
vbRightButton	2	Right button is pressed
vbMiddleButton	4	Middle button is pressed

TABLE 1.2: The Values of the *Shift* Argument

CONSTANT	VALUE	DESCRIPTION
vbShiftMask	1	Shift key is pressed
vbCtrlMask	2	Ctrl key is pressed
vbAltMask	4	Alt key is pressed

To find out which button caused the MouseDown or MouseUp event, use the following If structure:

```
If Button = vbLeftButton Then
    {process left button}
End If
```

You can write a mouse handler to simulate the double-click with the click of the middle mouse button (this will work with three-button mice only, but won't affect the operation of a two-button mouse). Insert the following lines in the MouseUp event handler:

```
Private Sub Form_MouseUp(Button As Integer, Shift As Integer, _
                        X As Single, Y As Single)
    If Button = vbMiddleButton Then Call Form_DblClick
End Sub
```

This event handler monitors the *MouseUp* event for the middle button, and when it detects the event, it invokes the *Form_DblClick* event handler. Notice that although you can't cause the DblClick event from within your code, you can call the event's handler.

Similarly, you can detect the state of the Shift key while the mouse button is pressed. Suppose you want to perform one action when the Command1 control is clicked and a different action when the same control is clicked with the Ctrl key pressed. To do so, test the *Shift* argument with an If structure like the following:

```
If Shift = vbCtrlMask Then
    {Mouse was pressed while Control key down}
End If
```

Keyboard Events

Keyboard events are generated by keystrokes. Usually, you must program the keyboard events for the controls that can accept text. In addition, you must provide code for the keyboard events of controls that can be manipulated with both the mouse and the keyboard, because many users prefer to work with the keyboard most of the time.

KeyDown, KeyUp   The KeyDown event is triggered when a key is pressed, and the KeyUp event is triggered when a key is released.

KeyPress   In practice, your code doesn't care about the KeyDown and KeyUp events. Most programs use the KeyPress event to find out which key was pressed. The KeyPress event is used frequently to write keyboard handlers for textboxes, because this event takes place before the character pressed is displayed in the textbox. The definition of the KeyPress event is:

```
Private Sub Text1_KeyPress(KeyAscii As Integer)

End Sub
```

The *KeyAscii* argument is the ASCII character of the key pressed. You can use this event to even reject the character typed. Setting the *KeyAscii* argument to 0 in effect chokes the keystroke, and the control never sees it. The character that corresponds to this ASCII code is:

```
Chr$(KeyAscii)
```

The ASCII codes of the numeric digits start at 48 (for the digit 0) and end at 57 (for the digit 9). The following event handler allows the user to enter only numeric digits in the Text1 textbox:

```
Private Sub Text1_KeyPress(KeyAscii As Integer)
    If KeyAscii < 48 Or KeyAscii > 57 Then KeyAscii = 0
End Sub
```

Change   The Change event is triggered by various controls when their contents change. The Change event is generated for the TextBox control each time a new character is typed or deleted. It is generated for the CheckBox control every time the user changes its status by clicking it.

Most Windows applications prompt you to save your data when it has been changed since the last Save operation. You can easily add this feature to your applications by setting a variable from within the Change event. When the user saves the contents of a textbox, reset this variable to indicate that the user can quit the application without saving the control's contents. If the user types even a single character after saving the file, the variable is set from within the Change event to indicate that the text has been changed and that the application should prompt the user before exiting.

Focus

A fundamental concept in developing user interfaces that comply with the Windows standards is the focus. *Focus* is the ability of a control to receive user input via the keyboard. When an object has the focus, it can receive input from a user. Suppose you have a Form with two TextBox controls on it. At any time, only one of them can accept input (in other words, can recognize the keys pressed). The control that can accept input is said to have the focus. To enter text in the other textbox, you must move the focus to it either with the mouse (by clicking the second TextBox control) or via the keyboard (by pressing the Tab key).

GotFocus and LostFocus

These are two related events. When the focus is moved from one control to the other, the first control (the one that had the focus) receives the LostFocus event, and after that the second control (the one to which the focus was moved) receives the GotFocus event.

You can use the GotFocus event to initialize a control for editing, and you can use the LostFocus event to validate the data entered by the user. For example, you can copy the contents of a textbox when it receives the focus so that you can restore its original contents later. After the user enters some data and moves to another control, you can examine the textbox's contents from within your code and either accept it or restore it by assigning the temporary variable to the control's Text property.

You can also move the focus to another control by using the *SetFocus* method in your code. Figure 1.19 shows a data-entry Form with three TextBox controls. Each textbox can store a single line of text (MultiLine property = False). The Enter key has no meaning on these controls because there is no second line to move to. You can detect this keystroke from within the KeyUp event and move the focus to the next control.

FIGURE 1.19:

The Focus application demonstrates how to move the focus from one control to the other from within your code.

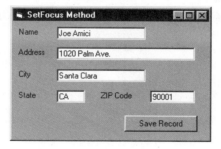

> **TIP**
>
> Why use the Enter key to move the focus to another control? Because most data-entry operators would much rather work with the keyboard than the mouse. If you are typing data, the last thing you want is to have to reach for the mouse to select the next field. The Tab key will do the same, but the Enter key is easier to reach and can speed up typing.

VB6 at Work: The Focus Project

The Focus application, which you will find in the Focus folder on the CD, has five single-line textboxes in which the user can enter data. Every time the user presses Enter, the focus moves to the next control. To capture the Enter key, you use the KeyUp event, which reports the code of the key pressed.

Code 1.2: **Capturing the Enter Key**

```
Private Sub Text1_KeyUp(KeyCode As Integer, Shift As Integer)

    If KeyCode = 13 Then Text2.SetFocus

End Sub
```

The other textboxes have similar event handlers for the KeyUp event. When the user presses Enter while the last textbox has the focus, the focus moves to the Save Record Command button, as follows:

```
Private Sub Text5_KeyUp(KeyCode As Integer, Shift As Integer)

    If KeyCode = 13 Then SaveBttn.SetFocus

End Sub
```

This button doesn't save the data anywhere. It simply displays a message, clears the textboxes, and then moves the focus to the first textbox.

Code 1.3:   **The Save Button**

```
Private Sub SaveBttn_Click()

    MsgBox "Record Saved. Click OK to enter another"
    Text1.Text = ""
    Text2.Text = ""
    Text3.Text = ""
    Text4.Text = ""
    Text5.Text = ""
    Text1.SetFocus

End Sub
```

Tab Order

All Windows applications allow the user to move the focus from one control to another with the Tab key. For this to happen, you must decide how the focus is moved from one control to the other. In other words, you must decide which control gets the focus each time the user presses Tab. This is known as Tab order. Each control has its own Tab order, which is by default the order in which the controls were created.

TIP   The Tab key doesn't produce spaces, even when used with a TextBox control. It always moves the focus to the next control in the Tab order.

Because controls are rarely placed on a Form in the same order they will be used, you need to be able to change the Tab order. You do so with the *TabIndex* property, which determines the control's position in the Tab order. The first control that is drawn has a TabIndex value of 0, the second has a TabIndex of 1, and so on. The focus is moved from each control to the one with the next TabIndex value. To change the order in which the focus moves from one control to another, you change the TabIndex property of the control. When the Tab order for a given control is changed, Visual Basic automatically renumbers the Tab order of the remaining controls on the Form to reflect insertions and deletions.

If you don't want the user to move to a specific control, you can remove it from the Tab order by setting its TabStop property to False. The *TabStop* property determines whether the control can get the focus, but does not determine its Tab order. Regardless of the setting of the TabStop property, you can always move the focus to any control with the mouse.

There is one control, the Option button, whose Tab order is handled specially. The members of an Option button group have a single Tab stop. Since only one Option button in the group can be checked at a time, it doesn't make sense to move the focus from one to the other. A user who wants to change the status of an Option button through the keyboard can use the arrow buttons to check an Option button—an action that clears the previously selected button.

Customizing the Environment

After familiarizing yourself with the IDE, you will probably want to customize it according to your taste and requirements. To access the customization tools, choose Tools ➤ Options to open the Options dialog box, as shown in Figure 1.20. Let's now look at the various ways you can customize the IDE by using the settings in this dialog box.

FIGURE 1.20:

The Editor tab of the Options dialog box

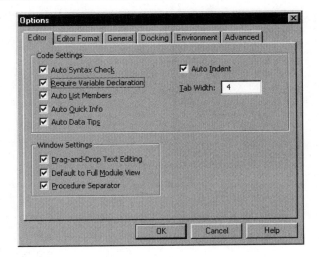

The Editor Tab

You use the settings in this tab to customize the behavior of the Code and Project windows. Visual Basic lets you customize these two windows according to your personal preferences and your experience.

Code Settings

The Code settings let you specify the behavior of the text editor of the Code window. Use the settings on this tab to specify how much help you want Visual Basic to provide as you enter your code. The Code Settings section of the Editor tab has the following options.

Auto Syntax Check   Check this checkbox if you want Visual Basic to verify the syntax of every line of code as you enter it. If you make a syntax error, Visual Basic issues a warning, and the line turns red when you press Enter.

Require Variable Declaration   Check this checkbox if you want to require explicit variable declarations. If you check this option, the statement Option Explicit is added automatically on each Form and Module.

Auto List Members   Check this checkbox to display a pop-up list with the members of a control. As soon as you type a control's name followed by a period (which means you are about to type a property or a method name), Visual Basic displays all the members (properties, methods, and events) of the control. Figure 1.21 shows the Auto List Members box with the members of the Text1 control (which is a TextBox control).

FIGURE 1.21:

Auto Listing the members of the TextBox control

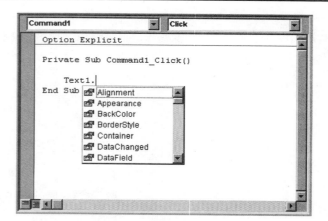

Auto Quick Info   Check this box to display information about functions and their parameters. For example, if you want to call the MsgBox() function in your code and the Auto Quick Info feature is enabled, Visual Basic displays the syntax of the function for you. As you enter the arguments of the function, the current argument is highlighted, as shown in Figure 1.22.

FIGURE 1.22:

Auto Quick Information for the MsgBox() function

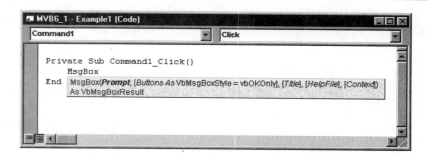

Auto Data Tips   Check this box to display the value of the variable over which your cursor is placed. Auto Data Tips are available in break state only. If you break the execution of an application and switch to the Code window, you can place the pointer over a variable to see its value. Figure 1.23 shows this feature in action for the MSVB6-2 application. The Stop statement was inserted to interrupt the execution of the application.

FIGURE 1.23:

The Auto Data Tips feature displays the values of the variables while the program is in break state.

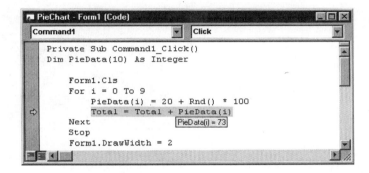

```
PieChart - Form1 (Code)

Command1                          Click

    Private Sub Command1_Click()
    Dim PieData(10) As Integer

        Form1.Cls
        For i = 0 To 9
            PieData(i) = 20 + Rnd() * 100
            Total = Total + PieData(i)
        Next            PieData(i) = 73
        Stop
        Form1.DrawWidth = 2
```

Auto Indent   Check this box if you want to be able to tab the first line of code; all subsequent lines start at that tab location.

Tab Width   Enter a number in this textbox to set the tab width; the default value is four spaces. Valid values are in the range 1 to 32.

Window Settings

Use the Window Settings to specify a few basic characteristics of the Code Editor.

Drag-and-Drop Text Editing   Check this box to allow drag-and-drop operations from the Code window to the Immediate or Watch windows.

Default to Full Module View   Check this box to view a scrollable list of procedures when you edit code in a Code window. If this box is not checked, you can view only one procedure at a time.

Procedure Separator   Check this box to display the separator bars that appear between procedures in the Code window.

The Editor Format Tab

You use this tab (see Figure 1.24) to set the attributes for the type of text selected in the Code Colors list. Select the type of text from this list, and then specify how you want it to appear in the Code window.

FIGURE 1.24:

The Editor Format tab of the Options dialog box

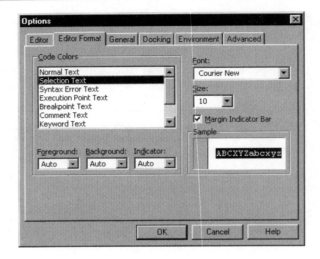

The General Tab

In this tab, you specify the settings of the grid, error-trapping, and compile options for the current project, as shown in Figure 1.25.

FIGURE 1.25:

The General tab of the Options dialog box

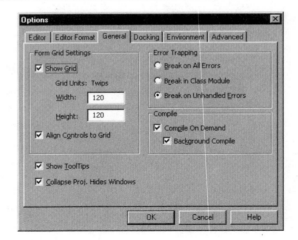

Form Grid Settings

The settings in this section let you specify the characteristics of the grid on which the controls are placed. These characteristics include the density of the grid points, whether the grid will be visible, and so on.

Show Grid   Check this box to specify that the grid on a Form is visible.

Grid Units   Displays the units used for measuring distances on the grid units, which are twips. This unit is explained in detail in Chapter 6.

Width, Height   In these textboxes, enter the numbers that determine the width and height of the grid cells.

Align Controls to Grid   Check this box if you want Visual Basic to automatically resize and reposition controls so that their outer edges are on grid lines.

Show ScreenTips   Check this box to display ScreenTips for the toolbar and Toolbox items.

Collapse Proj. Hides Windows   Check this box to hide the window when a project is collapsed in the Project Explorer.

Error Trapping

The options in this section of the General tab let you specify under what conditions an error in an application will generate a runtime error and be interrupted.

Break on All Errors   Check this box if you want Visual Basic to enter break state on any error, even if the error is handled by an error handler.

Break in Class Module   Check this box if you want any error in a Class Module without an error handler to cause the project to enter break state.

Break on Unhandled Errors   When you check this box, any error causes the project to enter break state if there is no active error handler.

Compile

The Compile options let you specify how and when Visual Basic will compile an application before it starts executing it.

Compile on Demand   Check this box if you want to compile code as needed, which allows the application to start sooner. If this checkbox is not cleared, Visual Basic compiles the entire project and then starts executing it. If you choose Run ➤ Start with Full Compile, Visual Basic ignores the Compile on Demand setting and performs a full compile.

Background Compile   When an application starts executing without a full compile, Visual Basic can use the idle time during runtime to finish the project's compilation in the background if this checkbox is checked.

The Docking Tab

In this tab (see Figure 1.26), you specify which windows will be dockable. A *dockable window* is attached (or "anchored") to other windows that are dockable or to the main window. When you move a dockable window, it "snaps" to the new location. You can move a nondockable window anywhere on the screen.

FIGURE 1.26:

The Docking tab of the Options menu

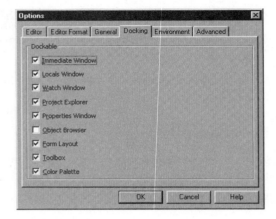

Check the box in front of the names of the windows that you want to behave as dockable, and clear the rest.

The Environment Tab

In this tab you specify various attributes of your Visual Basic development environment. Changes made in this tab (see Figure 1.27) are saved in the Registry and loaded every time you restart Visual Basic.

FIGURE 1.27:

The Environment tab of the Options menu

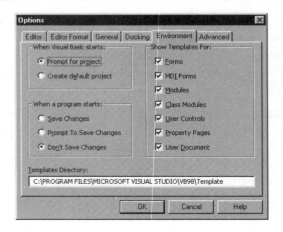

When Visual Basic Starts

The following options let you specify what happens when you start Visual Basic (whether it prompts you for a project name or starts a default executable program).

Prompt for Project Click this button if you want Visual Basic to display the New Project window when it starts.

Create Default Project Click this button if you want a default executable (EXE) project to open each time you start Visual Basic.

When a Program Starts

The following options let you specify what happens when you start an application (when you press F5 or choose Start ➤ Run).

Save Changes Click this option if you want to automatically save changes to a project (without prompting) every time you run it. If this option is selected, you won't lose changes when your application crashes Visual Basic. However, if you are making extensive changes to your application, you may want to go back to the previous version, and with this option selected, it will be too late.

Prompt to Save Changes Click this option if you want Visual Basic to always prompt you to save changes to your project when you run it.

Don't Save Changes Click this option if you want Visual Basic not to save the project automatically or to prompt you to save it when you run it.

Show Templates For

Check the boxes in this section to specify which templates are displayed in the Project menu when you add an item to a project.

Templates Directory

In this textbox, enter the full path name of the folder where template files are stored.

The Advanced Tab

In this tab (see Figure 1.28), you set the options that are described next.

Background Project Load Check this checkbox to specify that projects are loaded in the background. When projects are loaded in the background, control returns to the developer more quickly.

Notify When Changing Shared Project Items Check this checkbox if you want Visual Basic to notify you when you change a shared project item such as a Form or Module and try to save it.

The Advanced tab of the
Options dialog box

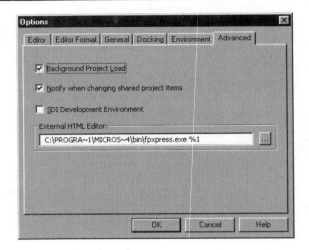

SDI Development Environment   Check this checkbox if you want to work
in an SDI (Single Document Interface) environment. In this book, we use the MDI
(Multiple Document Interface) environment.

External HTML Editor   If you are going to develop DHTML applications with
Visual Basic and you want to be able to invoke your favorite HTML editor (such
as FrontPage Express or Word) from within the Visual Basic IDE, enter the name
of the HTML editor in this textbox.

CHAPTER
TWO

Visual Basic Projects

- Developing a loan application

- Programming a math application

- Creating an application that uses multiple Forms

- Distributing executable files

2

The previous chapter introduced Visual Basic's development editor, basic controls, and the principles of event-driven programming. In this chapter, we expand on that introduction to the language by building some real-life applications. Among other topics, we'll look at how to write applications that have multiple windows, how to validate user input, and how to write error-trapping routines. We'll also look at several techniques you'll need as you work through the applications we develop in the rest of the book.

The bulk of the chapter demonstrates very basic programming techniques, such as building user interfaces, event programming, validating user input, and so on. The goal is to show you how to write simple applications using the most basic elements of the language. This chapter will explain the methodology for building applications. While the code of the applications will be rather simple, it will demonstrate user interface design and the basics of validating data and trapping errors.

If you're a beginner, you may be thinking, "All I want now is to write a simple application that works—I'll worry about data validation later." It's never too early to start thinking about validating your code's data and error trapping. As you'll see, making sure that your application doesn't crash requires more code than the actual operations it performs! If this isn't quite what you expected, welcome to the club. A well-behaved application must catch and handle every error gracefully, including user errors. This chapter only discusses the basic concepts of error handling you'll need to build a few simple applications.

Building a Loan Calculator

An easy-to-implement, practical application is one that calculates loan parameters. Visual Basic provides built-in functions for performing many types of financial calculations, and you only need a single line of code to calculate the monthly payment given the loan amount, its duration, and the interest rate. Designing the user interface, however, takes much more effort.

Regardless of the language you use, you must go through the following process to develop an application:

1. Decide what the application will do and how it will interact with the user.

2. Design the application's user interface.

3. Write the actual code.

Deciding How the Loan Application Works

Following the first step of the process outlined above, you decide that the user should be able to specify the amount of the loan, the interest rate, and the duration of the loan in months. You must, therefore, provide three textboxes where the user can enter these values.

Another parameter affecting the monthly payment is whether payments are made at the beginning or at the end of each month, so you must also provide a way for the user to specify whether the payments will be early (first day of the month) or late (last day of the month). The most appropriate type of control for entering Yes/No or True/False type of information is the CheckBox control. The CheckBox control is a toggle. If it's checked, you can clear it by clicking on it. If it's cleared, you can check it by clicking again. The user doesn't enter any data in this control and it's the simplest method for specifying values with two possible states. Figure 2.1 shows a user interface that matches our design specifications.

FIGURE 2.1:

The loan application is a simple financial calculator.

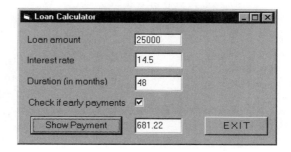

After the user enters all the information on the Form, they can click the Show Payment Command button to calculate the monthly payment and display it in a message box. All the action takes place in the Command button's Click subroutine. The function for calculating monthly payments is called Pmt(), and it must be called as follows:

```
MonthlyPayment = Pmt(InterestRate, Periods, Amount, FutureValue, Due)
```

The interest rate (variable *InterestRate*) is specified as a monthly rate. If the interest rate is 16.5%, this value should be 0.165/12. The duration of the loan *(Periods)* is specified in number of months, and *Amount* is the loan's amount. The *FutureValue* of a loan is zero (it would be a positive value for an investment), and the last parameter, *Due*, specifies when payments are due. If it's 0, payments are due at the beginning of the month; if it's 1, payments are due at the end of the month.

The present value of the loan is the amount of the loan with a negative sign. It's negative because you don't have the money now. You're borrowing it; it's money you owe to the bank. The future value of the loan is zero. The future value represents what the loan will be worth when it's paid off. This is what the bank owes you or what you owe the bank at the end of the specified period.

Pmt() is a built-in function that uses the five values in the parentheses to calculate the monthly payment. The values passed to the function are called *arguments*. Arguments are the values needed by a function (or subroutine) to carry out an action, such as a calculation. By passing different values to the function, the user can calculate the parameters of a different loan. The Pmt() function and other financial functions of Visual Basic are described in Appendix A, *Built-In Functions*, on the CD that accompanies this book.

You don't need to know how the Pmt() function calculates the monthly payment. The Pmt() function does the calculations and returns the result. To calculate the monthly payment on a loan of $25,000 with an interest rate of 14.5%, payable over 48 months, and due the last day of the payment period (which in our case is a month), you'd call the Pmt() function as follows:

```
Debug.Print Pmt(0.145 / 12, 48, -25000, 0, 0)
```

The value 689.448821287218 will be displayed in the Immediate window (you'll see later how you can limit the digits after the decimal point to two, since this is all the accuracy you need for dollar amounts). Notice the negative sign in front of the amount. If you specify a positive amount, the result will be a negative payment. The payment and the loan's amount have different signs because they represent different cash flows. The last two arguments of the Pmt() function are optional. If you omit them, Visual Basic assumes they are zero. You could also call the Pmt() function like this:

```
Debug.Print Pmt(0.145 / 12, 48, -25000)
```

NOTE   You'll see in Chapter 3, *Visual Basic: The Language*, that it's possible to write functions with optional arguments, but for now, we'll supply all values.

Calculating the amount of the monthly payment given the loan parameters is quite simple. What you need to know or understand are the parameters of a loan and how to pass them to the Pmt() function. You must also know how the interest rate is specified, to avoid invalid values. What you don't need to know is how the payment is calculated—Visual Basic does it for you. This is the essence of functions: they are "black boxes" that perform complicated calculations on their arguments and return the result. You don't have to know how they work, just how to supply the values required for the calculations.

Designing the User Interface

Now that you know how to calculate the monthly payment, you can design the user interface. To do so, start a new project, rename its Form to **LoanCalc**, rename the project to **LoanProject**, and save the project as **Loan**. The Form and the project files can be found in the Loan folder under this chapter's folder on the CD.

Your first task is to decide the font and size of the text you'll use for most controls on the Form. Although we aren't going to display anything on the Form directly, all the controls we place on it will have by default the same font as the Form (which is called the container of the controls). You can change the font later during the design, but it's a good idea to start with the right font. At any rate, don't try to align the controls if you're planning to change their fonts. This will, most likely, throw off your alignment efforts.

TIP Try not to mix fonts on a Form. A Form, or a printed page for that matter, that includes type in several fonts looks like it has been created haphazardly and is difficult to read.

The Loan application you'll find on the CD uses 10-point MS Sans Serif. To change it, select the Form with the mouse, double-click the name of the Font property in the Properties window to open the Font dialog box, and select the desired font and attributes.

To design the Form shown previously in Figure 2.1, follow these steps:

1. Place three labels on the Form and assign the following captions to them:

    Label1 Loan amount

    Label2 Interest rate

    Label3 Duration (in months)

    The labels should be large enough to fit their captions. You don't need to change the default names of the three Label controls on the Form because their captions are all we need. You aren't going to program them.

2. Place a TextBox control next to each label. Name the first textbox (the one next to the first label) **Amount** and set its Text property to 25,000, name the second textbox **IRate** and set its value to 14.5, and name the third textbox **Duration** and set its value to 48. These initial values correspond to a loan of $25,000 with an interest rate of 14.5% and a payoff period of 48 months.

3. Next, place a CheckBox control on the Form. By default, the control's caption is Check1, and it appears to the right of the checkbox. Because we want the titles to be to the left of the corresponding controls, we'll change this default appearance.

4. Select the checkbox with the mouse (if it's not already selected), and in the Properties window, locate the Alignment property. Its value is 0–Left Justify. If you expand the drop-down list by clicking the Arrow button, you'll see that this property has another setting, 1–Right Justify. Select the alternate value from the list.

5. With the checkbox selected, locate the Name property in the Properties window, and set it to PayEarly.

6. Change the caption by entering the string "Check if early payments" in its Caption property field.

7. Place a Command button control on the lower left corner of the Form. Name it **ShowPayment,** and set its caption to "Show Payment".

8. Finally, place a TextBox control next to the Command button and name it **txtPmt.** This is where the monthly payment will appear. Notice that the user isn't supposed to enter any data in this box, so you must set its Locked property to True. You'll be able to change its value from within your code, but users won't be able to type anything in it. (We could have used a Label control instead, but the uniform look of TextBoxes on a Form is usually preferred).

Aligning the Controls

Your next step is to align the controls on the Form. First, be sure that the captions on the labels are visible. Our labels contain lengthy captions, and if you don't make the labels long enough, the captions may wrap to a second line and become invisible like the one shown in Figure 2.2.

FIGURE 2.2:

The third label's caption is too long to be displayed in a single line.

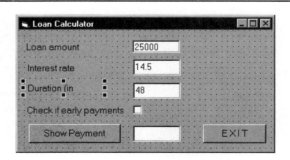

TIP

Be sure to make your labels long enough to hold their captions, especially if you're using a nonstandard font. A user's computer may substitute another font for a nonstandard font and the corresponding captions may increase in length.

To align the controls on the Form, Visual Basic provides a number of commands, all of which can be accessed through the Format menu. To align the controls that are already on the LoanCalc Form, follow these steps:

1. Select the three labels and the checkbox, and left-align them by choosing Format ➢ Align ➢ Left.

2. Select the four textboxes, and left-align them by choosing Format ➢ Align ➢ Left. Don't include the checkbox in this selection.

TIP

When you select multiple controls to align together, use the control with blue handles as a guide for aligning the other controls.

3. With all four textboxes still selected, use the mouse to align them above and below the box of the CheckBox control.

Your Form should now look like the one in Figure 2.1. Take a good look at it and check to see if any of your controls are misaligned. In the interface design process, you tend to overlook small problems such as a slightly misaligned control. The user of the application, however, instantly spots such mistakes. It doesn't make any difference how nicely the rest of the controls are arranged on the Form; if one of them is misaligned, it will attract the user's eye.

Programming the Loan Application

Now run the application and see how it behaves. Enter a few values in the textboxes, change the state of the checkbox, and test the functionality already built into the application. Clicking the Command button won't have any effect because we have not yet added any code. If you're happy with the user interface, stop the application, open the Form, and double-click the Command button. Visual Basic opens the Code window and displays the following three lines of the ShowPayment_Click event:

```
Option Explicit

Private Sub ShowPayment_Click()

End Sub
```

Place the pointer between the lines Private... and End Sub, and enter the following lines:

```
Dim Payment As Single

Payment = Pmt(0.01 * IRate.Text / 12, Duration.Text, _
          -Amount.Text, 0, PayEarly.Value)
txtPmt.Text = Format$(Payment, "#.00")
```

The Code window should now look like the one shown in Figure 2.3. Notice the underscore character at the end of the first part of the long line. The underscore lets you break long lines so that they will fit nicely in the Code window. I'm using this convention in this book a lot to fit long lines on the printed page. The same statement may appear in a single, long line in the project.

FIGURE 2.3:

The Show Payment button's Click event subroutine

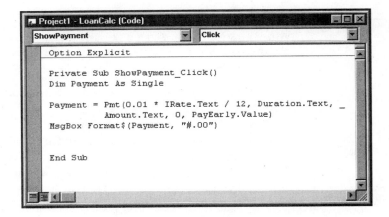

In Figure 2.3, the first line of code declares a variable. It lets the application know that *Payment* is a placeholder for storing a *floating-point number* (a number with a decimal part). The first really executable line in the subroutine calls the Pmt() function, passing the values of the controls as arguments:

- The first argument is the interest rate. The value entered by the user in the Irate textbox is multiplied by 0.01 so that the value 14.5 (which corresponds to 14.5%) is passed to the Pmt() function as 0.145. Although we humans prefer to specify interest rates as integers (8%) or floating-point numbers larger than 1 (8.24%), the Pmt() function expects to read a number less than 1. The value 1 corresponds to 100%. Therefore, the value 0.1 corresponds to 10%. This value is also divided by 12 to yield the monthly interest rate.

- The second argument is the duration of the loan in months (the value entered in the Duration textbox).

- The third argument is the loan's amount (the value entered in the Amount textbox). The fourth argument (the loan's future value) is 0 by definition.

- The last argument must be the value 0 or 1, which specifies when payments are due. If they are made early in the month, this value should be 0. If they are made at the end of the month, it should be 1. As you know, the CheckBox control's Value property can be either 0 (if cleared) or 1 (if checked). Therefore, you can pass the quantity PayEarly.Value directly to the Pmt() function.

The second line displays the result in the fourth TextBox control. The result is first formatted appropriately with the following statement:

```
txtPmt.Text = Format$(Payment, "#.00")
```

Because the Pmt() function returns a precise number, such as 372.2235687646345, you must round and format it nicely before displaying it. Since the bank can't charge you anything less than a penny, you don't need extreme accuracy. Two fractional digits are sufficient. That's what the Format$() function does. It accepts a number and a string and formats the number according to an argument you supply (it's called the *formatting string*).

To format a number with two fractional digits, you set the formatting string to "#.00". This tells Visual Basic to round the number to two fractional digits and throw away the rest. The integer part of the number isn't affected. Moreover, if the result is something like 349.4, Visual Basic will format it as 349.40.

TIP

You almost always use the Format$() function when you want to display the results of numeric calculations, because most of the time you don't need Visual Basic's extreme accuracy. A few fractional digits are all you need. In addition to numbers, the Format$() function can format dates and time (see Appendix A on the CD for more information on this function).

Run the application again, and when the Form opens, click the Show Payment button. The result for the loan described by the initial values of the controls on the Form is 689.45. This is the amount you'll be paying every month over the next four years to pay off a loan of $25,000 at 14.5%. Enter other values, and see how a loan's duration and interest rate affect the monthly payment.

The code of the Loan project on the CD is different than the one I have presented here and considerably longer. The statement discussed in the last paragraph is the bare minimum for calculating a loan payment. The user may enter any values on the Form and cause the program to crash. In the next section, we'll see how you can validate the data entered by the user, catch errors and handle them gracefully (that is, give the user a chance to correct the data and proceed).

Validating the Data

If you were to enter a non-numeric value in one of the fields, the program would crash and display an error message. For example, if you entered "twenty" in the Duration textbox, the program would display the error message shown in Figure 2.4. A simple typing error can crash the program. This isn't the way Windows applications should work. Your applications must be able to handle most user errors, provide helpful messages, and in general, guide the user in running the application efficiently. If a user error goes unnoticed, your application will either end abruptly, or produce incorrect results without an indication.

FIGURE 2.4:

The "Type mismatch" error message means that you supplied a string where a numeric value was expected.

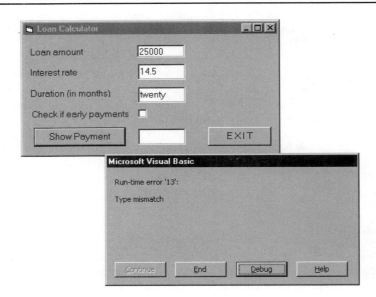

Click the End button, and Visual Basic will take you back to the application's Code window. Obviously, we must do something about user errors. Applications must be foolproof and not crash with every mistake the user makes. One way to take care of typing errors is to examine each control's contents, and if they don't contain valid numeric values, display your own descriptive message, and give the user another chance. Here's the revised ShowPayment_Click() subroutine that examines the value of each textbox before attempting to use it in the calculations.

Code 2.1:   **The Revised ShowPayment_Click() Subroutine**

```
Private Sub ShowPayment_Click()
Dim Payment As Single
Dim LoanIRate As Single
```

```
Dim LoanDuration As Integer
Dim LoanAmount As Integer

    If IsNumeric(Amount.Text) Then
       LoanAmount = Amount.Text
    Else
       MsgBox "Please enter a valid amount"
       Exit Sub
    End If
    If IsNumeric(IRate.Text) Then
       LoanIRate = 0.01 * IRate.Text / 12
    Else
       MsgBox "Invalid interest rate, please re-enter"
       Exit Sub
    End If
    If IsNumeric(Duration.Text) Then
       LoanDuration = Duration.Text
    Else
       MsgBox "Please specify the loan's duration _
             as a number of months"
       Exit Sub
    End If

    Payment = Pmt(LoanIRate, LoanDuration, -LoanAmount, 0, _
             PayEarly.Value)
    txtPmt.Text = Format$(Payment, "#.00")

End Sub
```

First, we declare three variables in which the loan's parameters will be stored: *LoanAmount, LoanIRate,* and *LoanDuration.* These values will be passed to the Pmt() function as arguments. Each textbox's value is examined with an If structure. If the corresponding textbox holds a valid number, its value is assigned to the numeric variable. If not, the program displays a warning and exits the subroutine without attempting to calculate the monthly payment. IsNumeric() is another built-in function that accepts a variable and returns True if the variable is numeric, False otherwise.

If the Amount textbox holds a numeric value, such as 21,000 or 21.50, the function IsNumeric(Amount.Text) returns True, and the statement following it is executed. The statement following it assigns the value entered in the Amount textbox to the *LoanAmount* variable. If not, the Else clause of the statement is executed, which displays a warning in a message box and then exits the subroutine. The Exit Sub statement tells Visual Basic to stop executing the subroutine immediately, as if the End Sub line was encountered.

You can run the revised application and test it by entering invalid values in the fields. Notice that you can't specify an invalid value for the last argument; the CheckBox control won't let you enter a value. You can only check or clear it and both options are valid. The LoanCalc application you'll find on the CD contains this last version with the error-trapping code.

The actual calculation of the monthly payment takes a single line of Visual Basic code. Displaying it requires another line of code. Adding the code to validate the data entered by the user, however, is an entire program. And that's the way things are.

Writing Well-Behaved Applications

A well-behaved application must contain data-validation code. This means that if the application crashes because of a typing mistake, nothing really bad will happen. The user will try again or give up your application and look for a more professional one. However, if the user has been entering data for hours, the situation is far more serious. It's your responsibility as a programmer to make sure that only valid data are used by the application and that the application keeps working, no matter how the user misuses or abuses it.

NOTE
The applications in this book don't contain much data-validation code because it would obscure the "useful" code that applies to the topic at hand. Instead, they demonstrate specific techniques. You can use parts of the examples in your own applications, but you should provide your own data-validation code (and error-handling code, as you'll see in the following section).

Now run the application one last time and enter an enormous loan amount. Try to find out what it would take to pay off our national debt with a reasonable interest rate in, say, 72 months. The program will crash again (as if you didn't know). This time the program will go down with a different error message. Visual Basic will complain about an "overflow."

TIP
An overflow is a numeric value too large for the program to handle. This error is usually produced when you divide a number by a very small value. Dividing by zero, for example, is sure to produce an overflow.

Actually, the Loan application will crash with a small loan value. Any value greater than 32,767 will cause an overflow condition. The largest value you can assign to an integer variable is 32,767 (quite small for storing financial figures). As you'll see in the next section, Visual Basic provides other types of variables, which can store enormous values (making the national debt look really small). In the meantime, if you want to use the loan calculator, change the declaration of the *LoanAmount* variable to:

```
Dim LoanAmount As Single
```

The Single data type can hold much larger values.

An overflow error can't be caught with data-validation code. There's always a chance your calculations will produce overflows or other types of math errors. Data validation isn't going to help here. We need something called error trapping. *Error trapping* tells Visual Basic to trap errors and, instead of stopping the program, inform your code that an error has occurred and give your code a chance to handle it. We'll see how to prevent these types of errors in the next example.

Building a Math Calculator

Our next application is more advanced, but not as advanced as it looks. It's a math calculator with a typical visual interface that demonstrates how Visual Basic can simplify programming. If you haven't tried it, you may think that writing an application such as this one is way too complicated, but it isn't. The Math application is shown in Figure 2.5, and you'll find it in this chapter's folder on the CD. The Math application emulates the operation of a hand-held calculator and implements the basic arithmetic operations. It has the structure of a working math calculator, and you can easily expand it by adding more features. Adding features like cosines and logarithms is actually simpler than performing the basic arithmetic operations.

FIGURE 2.5:

The Math application window

Designing the User Interface

The application's interface is straightforward, but it takes quite a bit of effort. You must align a number of buttons on the Form and make the calculator look like a hand-held calculator as much as possible. You don't have to redesign the interface or the operation of a calculator, so you can start building the application's Form. Start a new project, name its main Form **MathCalc,** and save the project as **Math** in a new folder (the project is stored in the Math folder on the CD). Now, follow these steps:

1. Select a font that you like for the Form. All the Command buttons you'll place on the Form will inherit this font. The MathCalc application on the CD uses 10-point Verdana font.

2. Add the Label control, which will become the calculator's display. Set its BorderStyle property to 1–Fixed Single so that it will have a 3-D look, as shown in Figure 2.5.

3. Draw a Command button on the Form, change its caption to "0", name it **Digits**, and set its Index to 0. We'll create an array of buttons.

4. Place the button in its final position on the Form.

Creating an array of controls may sound strange, but here's why you do it. We could create 11 buttons and give them different names, for example, Digit1, Digit2, and so on. But then we would have to provide a separate subroutine for their Click event, in other words, one subroutine per Command button. By creating an array of Command buttons, we can provide a single subroutine for the Click event of all buttons. You'll see later how this naming scheme simplifies our code.

5. Right-click the button and select Copy from the shortcut menu. The Command button is copied to the Clipboard, and now you can paste it on the Form (which is much faster than designing an identical button).

6. Right-click somewhere on the Form and from the shortcut menu select Paste to create a copy of the button you copied earlier. Visual Basic displays a dialog box with the following message:

    ```
    You already have a control named 'Digits'. Do you want to
    create a control array?
    ```

    You want to create an array of Command buttons, so click on Yes.

7. Repeat steps 5 and 6 eight more times, once for each numeric digit. Each time a new Command button is pasted on the Form, Visual Basic gives it the name Digits and sets its Index property to a value that's larger than the previous one by 1. Each button's Index property will be the same as its caption,

as long as you set the captions sequentially. If you place the Command buttons for the digits in any other order, the application won't work. As you have guessed, we'll be using the Index property to handle the buttons from within our code, and it's crucial that their captions are the same as their indices.

8. When the buttons of the numeric digits are all on the Form, place two more buttons, one for the C (Clear) operation and one for the Period button. Name them **ClearBttn** and **DotBttn**, and set their captions accordingly. Use a larger font size for the Period button to make its caption easier to read.

9. When all the Digit buttons of the first group are on the Form and in their approximate positions, align them with the commands on the Format menu.

    a. First, align the buttons in a row and make their horizontal spacing equal. Then do the same with the buttons in a column, and this time, make sure their vertical distances are equal.

    b. Now you can align the buttons in each row and each column separately. Use one of the buttons you aligned in the last step as the guide for the rest of them. The buttons can be aligned in many ways, so don't worry if somewhere in the process you ruin the alignment. You can always use the Undo command in the Edit menu.

10. Now, place the Command buttons for the operations. Table 2.1 lists their captions and names.

TABLE 2.1:   Captions and Names for MathCalc Application Command Buttons

Caption	Name
+	Plus
−	Minus
*	Times
/	Div
+/	PlusMinus
1/X	Over
=	Equals

11. Use the commands on the Format menu to align these buttons as shown in Figure 2.6. The control with the blue handles can be used as a reference for aligning the other controls into rows and columns.

FIGURE 2.6:

An alignment of Digit buttons created by using a single reference control (the one with the dark handles)

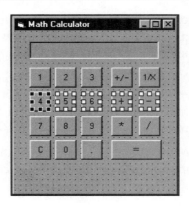

Programming the Math Application

Now you're ready to add some code to the application. Double-click one of the Digit buttons on the Form, and you'll see the following in the Code window:

```
Private Sub Digits_Click(Index As Integer)

End Sub
```

This is the Click event's handler for all Command buttons that represent digits. All buttons have the same name, and they are differentiated by their index. When the user clicks one of them, Visual Basic generates the Digits_Click event and uses the *Index* argument to report the index of the button that was clicked.

What happens on a hand-held calculator when you press a numeric button? The corresponding digit is appended to the display. To emulate this behavior, insert the following line in the Click event handler:

```
Display.Caption = Display.Caption + Digits(Index).Caption
```

This line appends the digit clicked to the calculator's display. The Caption property of the control that was clicked is the digit of the button. For example, if you have already entered the value 345, clicking the digit 0 displays the value 3450 on the Label control that acts as the calculator's display.

TIP

A single line of code in a single Click event takes care of all the numeric buttons. That's what an array of controls does for you. If you have multiple controls with identical behavior, create arrays of controls. All the members of the array have the same handler (subroutine) for each event, and you don't need to repeat the code over and over again.

The code behind the Digit buttons needs a few more lines. If you run the application now, you'll see what happens after an operation is performed and the result is displayed. If you click another digit, it's appended to the existing number. But this isn't the way a hand-held calculator works. The first time a Digit button is pressed after a result is displayed, the display must clear and then print the new digit. Revise the Digits_Click event handler as follows.

Code 2.2:	The Digits_Click Event

```
Private Sub Digits_Click(Index As Integer)
    If ClearDisplay Then
        Display.Caption = ""
        ClearDisplay = False
    End If
    Display.Caption = Display.Caption + Digits(Index).Caption
End Sub
```

The *ClearDisplay* variable is declared as Boolean, and it can take a True or False value. Suppose the user has performed an operation and the result is on the calculator's display. The user now starts typing another number. Without the If clause, the program would continue to append digits to the number already on the display. This is not how calculators work. When a new number is entered, the display must clear. And our program uses the *ClearDisplay* variable to know when to clear the display.

The Equals button sets the *ClearDisplay* variable to True to indicate that the display contains the result of an operation. The Digits_Click() subroutine examines its value each time a new Digit button is pressed. If it's True, it clears the display and then prints the new digit on it. It also sets it to False so that when the next digit is pressed, the program won't clear the display again.

What if the user makes a mistake and wants to undo an entry? The typical hand-held calculator has no backspace key. The Clear key erases the current number on the display. Let's implement this feature. Double-click the C button and enter the following code in its Click event:

```
Display.Caption = ""
```

And now we can look at the Period button. A calculator, no matter how simple, should be able to handle fractional numbers. The Period button works just like the Digit buttons, with one exception. A digit can appear any number of times in a numeric value, but the period can appear only once. A number like 99,991 is valid, but you must make sure that the user can't enter numbers such as 23.456.55. Once a period is entered, this button mustn't insert another one. The following code accounts for this.

Code 2.3:   **The Period Button**

```
Private Sub DotBttn_Click()
    If InStr(Display.Caption, ".") Then
        Exit Sub
    Else
        Display.Caption = Display.Caption + "."
    End If
End Sub
```

The `InStr(Display.Caption, ".")` function returns the location of the first instance of the period in the caption of the Label control. If this number is positive, the number entered contains a period already, and another can't be entered. In this case, the program exits the subroutine. If the InStr() function returns 0, the period is appended to the number entered so far, as is a regular digit.

The InStr() function accepts two string arguments and returns the location of the second string in the first one. The following function returns 12 because the string "Visual" appears in the 12th character position in the longer string:

```
InStr("Welcome to Visual Basic", "Visual")
```

However, the following function returns 0 because the string "Java" doesn't appear anywhere in the first string.

```
InStr("Welcome to Visual Basic", "Java")
```

The following expression returns a positive number if the value already on the display contains a period:

```
InStr(Display.Caption, ".")
```

If that's the case, the program exits the subroutine without taking any action. If the value returned by the InStr() function is a positive number, the value entered is an Integer, and the period is displayed.

Check out the operation of the application. We have already created a functional user interface that emulates a hand-held calculator with data entry capabilities. It doesn't perform any operations yet, but we have already created a functional user interface with only a small number of statements.

Math Operations

Now we can move to the interesting part of the application: considering how a calculator works. Let's start by defining three variables:

- *Operand1*   The first number in the operation
- *Operator*   The desired operation
- *Operand2*   The second number in the operation

When the user clicks a number, or *Operand1,* the value on the display is stored in a variable. If the user then clicks the Plus button, or *Operator,* the program must make a note to itself that the current operation is an addition, and then clear the display so that the user can enter another value. The user enters another value, or *Operand2,* and then clicks the Equals button to see the result. At this point, our program must do the following:

1. Read the *Operand2* value on the display.

2. Add that value to *Operand1.*

3. Display the result.

The Equals button must perform the following operation:

```
Operand1 Operator Operand2
```

Suppose the number on the display when the user clicks the Plus button is 3,342. The user then enters the value 23 and clicks the Equals button. The program must carry out the addition:

```
3342 + 23
```

If the user clicks the Division button, the operation is:

```
3342 / 23
```

In both cases, the result is displayed (and it may become the first operand for the next operation).

The variables in the previous examples are local in the subroutines where they are declared. Other subroutines have no access to them and can't read or set their values. Sometimes, however, variables must be accessed from many places in a program. If the *Operand1, Operand2,* and *Operator* variables in this application must be accessed from within more than one subroutine, they must be declared outside any subroutine. The same is true for the *ClearDisplay* variable. Their declarations, therefore, must appear outside any procedure, and they usually appear at the beginning of the code Module (the first lines in the Code window are usually declarations of variables that must be accessed from within any subroutine).

Let's see how the program uses the *Operator* variable. When the user clicks the Plus button, the program must store the value "+" in the *Operator* variable. This takes place from within the Plus button's Click event. But later on, the Equals button must have access to the value of the *Operator* variable in order to carry out the operation (in other words, it must know what type of operation the user specified). Because these variables must be manipulated from within more than a single subroutine, they must be declared outside any subroutine (see Figure 2.7).

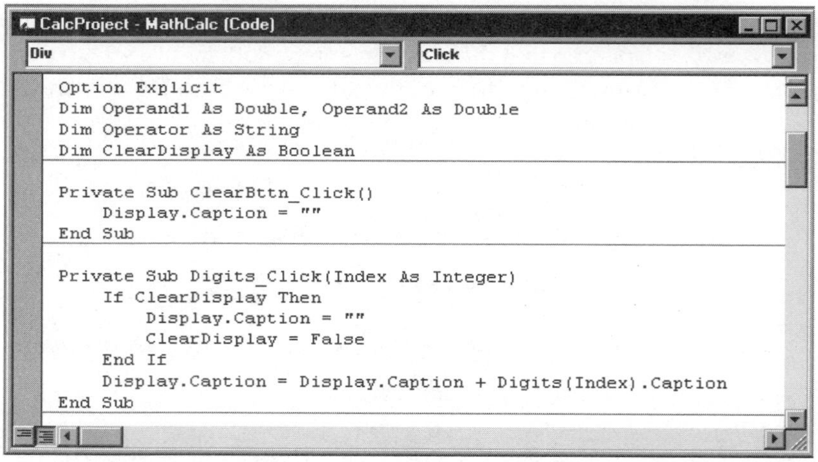

FIGURE 2.7:

The first few lines in the Math application's Code window. The variables declared outside any procedure are visible from any subroutine on this Form.

To declare the variables outside a subroutine, place the pointer at the top of the Code window, right after the Option Explicit statement, and enter the following declarations:

```
Dim Operand1 As Double, Operand2 As Double
Dim Operator As String
Dim ClearDisplay As Boolean
```

The keyword *Double* is new to you. It tells Visual Basic to create a numeric variable with the greatest possible precision for storing the values of the operators. (Numeric variables and their types are discussed in detail in the next chapter.) The Boolean type takes two values, True and False. You have already seen how the *ClearDisplay* variable is used.

The variables *Operand1*, *Operand2*, and *Operator* are called *Form-wide*, or simply *Form* variables, because they are visible from within any subroutine on the Form. If our application had another Form, these variables wouldn't be visible from within the other Form(s). In other words, any subroutine on a Form on which the variables are declared can read or set the values of the variables, but no subroutine outside that Form can do so.

With the variable declarations out of the way, we can now implement the Operator buttons. Double-click the Plus button and in the Click event's handler, enter the following lines:

```
Private Sub Plus_Click()
    Operand1 = Val(Display.Caption)
    Operator = "+"
    Display.Caption = ""
End Sub
```

The variable *Operand1* is assigned the value currently on the display. The Val() function returns the numeric value of its argument. As you may recall, a Label's Caption property is a string. For example, you can assign the value "My Label" to a Label's Caption property. The actual value stored in the Caption property is not a number. It's a String such as "428", which is different from the numeric value 428. That's why we use the Val() function to convert the value of the Label's caption to a numeric value.

WARNING   If you don't use the Val() function to convert the String to a Numeric value, adding two values like "355" and "8" will produce the String "3558" and not a numeric value. The + symbol tells Visual Basic to add two strings, as well as two numbers, depending on the type of operands. If you subtract the same two values, however, you'll get the correct result. Visual Basic can't subtract a string from another, so it assumes the two operands are numeric values and subtracts them numerically. Remove the Val() function from the code to see how it will perform the various operations. The other three Operator buttons do the same. The only difference is the symbol of the operator.

Code 2.4:   **The Click Event Handlers for the Operator Buttons**

```
Private Sub Minus_Click()
    Operand1 = Val(Display.Caption)
    Operator = "-"
    Display.Caption = ""
End Sub

Private Sub Times_Click()
    Operand1 = Val(Display.Caption)
    Operator = "*"
```

```
        Display.Caption = ""
    End

    Private Sub Div_Click()
        Operand1 = Val(Display.Caption)
        Operator = "/"
        Display.Caption = ""
    End Sub
```

So far, we have implemented the following functionality in our application: When an Operator button is clicked, the program stores the value on the display in the *Operand1* variable and the operator in the *Operator* variable. It then clears the display so that the user can enter the second operand. After the second operand is entered, the user can click the Equals button to calculate the result. When this happens, the following code is executed.

Code 2.5: **The Equals Button**

```
    Private Sub Equals_Click()
    Dim result As Double
        Operand2 = Val(Display.Caption)
        If Operator = "+" Then result = Operand1 + Operand2
        If Operator = "-" Then result = Operand1 - Operand2
        If Operator = "*" Then result = Operand1 * Operand2
        If Operator = "/" And Operand2 <> "0" Then _
            result = Operand1 / Operand2
        Display.Caption = result
    End Sub
```

The *result* variable is declared as Double so that the result of the operation will be stored with maximum precision. The code extracts the value displayed in the Label control and stores it in the variable *Operand2*. It then performs the operation with a string of If statements:

- If the Operator is "+", the result is the sum of the two operands.

- If the Operator is "-", the result is the difference of the first operand minus the second.

- If the Operator is "*", the result is the product of the two operands.

- If the Operator is "/", the result is the quotient of the first operand divided by the second operand, provided that the divisor is not zero.

NOTE

Division takes into consideration the value of the second operand because if it's zero, the division can't be carried out. The last If statement carries out the division only if the divisor is not zero. If *Operand2* happens to be zero, nothing happens.

Now run the application and check it out. It works just like a hand-held calculator, and you can't crash it by specifying invalid data. We didn't have to use any data-validation code in this example because the user doesn't get a chance to type invalid data. The data entry mechanism is foolproof. The user can enter only numeric values because there are only numeric digits on the calculator. The only possible error is to divide by zero, and that's handled in the Equals button.

Adding More Features

Now that we have implemented the basic functionality of a hand-held calculator, we can add more features to our application. Let's add two more useful buttons:

- The +/- button, which inverts the sign of the number on the display

- The 1/x button, which inverts the number on the display

Open the Code window for each of the Command buttons and enter the following code in the corresponding Click event handlers. For the +/- button, enter:

```
Private Sub PlusMinus_Click()
    Display.Caption = -Val(Display.Caption)
End Sub
```

For the 1/x button, enter:

```
Private Sub Over_Click()
    If Val(Display.Caption) <> 0 Then Display.Caption = _
        1 / Val(Display.Caption)
End Sub
```

As with the Division button, we don't attempt to invert a zero value. The operation 1/0 is undefined and causes a runtime error. Notice also that I use the value displayed on the Label control directly in the code. I could have stored the Display .Caption value to a variable and used the variable instead:

```
TempValue = Val(Display.Caption)
If TempValue <> 0 Then Display.Caption = 1 / TempValue
```

This is also better coding, but in short code segments, we all tend to minimize the number of statements.

You can easily expand the Math application by adding Function buttons to it. For example, you can add buttons to calculate common functions, such as Cos, Sin, and Log. The Cos button calculates the cosine of the number on the display. The code behind this button's Click event is a one-liner:

```
Display.Caption = Cos(Val(Display.Caption))
```

It doesn't require a second operand and it doesn't keep track of the operation. You can implement all math functions with a single line of code. Of course, you should add some error trapping, and in some cases, you can use data-validation techniques. For example, the Sqr() function, which calculates the square root of a number, expects a positive argument. If the number on the display is negative, you can issue a warning:

```
If Display.Caption < 0 Then
    MsgBox "Can't calculate the square root of a negative number"
Else
    Display.Caption = Sqr(Val(Display.Caption))
End If
```

The Log() function can calculate the logarithms of positive numbers only. Other functions, however, can easily cause overflows. For example, the Exp() function can easily produce very large numbers.

One more feature you could add to the calculator is a limit to the number of digits on the display. Most calculators can display a limited number of digits. To add this feature to the Math application (if you consider this a "feature"), use the Len() function to find out the number of digits on the display and ignore any digits entered after the number has reached the maximum number of allowed digits. But don't do anything about it yet. Let's see if we can crash this application.

Error Trapping

Crashing this application won't be as easy as crashing the Loan application, but it's not impossible either. Start multiplying very large numbers (start again with the national debt), and continue multiplying with large numbers. The result will eventually become larger than the largest number Visual Basic can represent and it will bring the program to a halt with an overflow error message.

The error's number is 6, and its description is "Overflow" (one of the worst, because it can't be remedied easily). Many errors are caused by conditions that can be remedied from within your code. If a file wasn't found, for instance, you can prompt the user for another filename. If a field's value is empty, you can ask the user to enter a different value or use a generic value. But the overflow is always the result of a series of math operations you can't undo.

How do you prevent this? Data validation isn't going to help. You just can't predict the result of an operation without actually performing the operation. And if the operation causes an overflow, you can't prevent it.

The solution is to *trap* the error. The overflow will occur no matter what, but you can trap it, and instead of letting the error message show up and embarrass you, you can handle it from within your code. To handle errors from within your code, you insert a so-called *error trap*, with the following statement:

```
On Error Goto ErrorLabel
```

The *ErrorLabel* entry is a label in your code. This statement asks Visual Basic to jump to the statement following the label ErrorLabel. (This has nothing to do with the Label control; it's a mark in the code that identifies a specific line and it can be any string.)

The structure of a subroutine with an error trap is as follows:

```
Sub MySubroutine()
On Error Goto ErrorHandler
    {statements}
    Exit Sub

ErrorHandler:
    MsgBox "Couldn't complete the operation. Aborting"
End Sub
```

The first statement isn't executable. It doesn't cause any action to be taken. It simply tells Visual Basic that if an error occurs, it must execute the lines following the label ErrorHandler. ErrorHandler is not a statement or keyword. It's a string that identifies the beginning of the error-handling code. Notice the colon at the end of the label. This is how Visual Basic knows that ErrorHandler is a label and not a procedure name.

If no error occurs during execution, the subroutine's statements are executed as if the error-trapping statements aren't there. After the subroutine's statements are executed and the Exit Sub statement is reached, the subroutine exits as usual. If an error occurs during the execution of the statements, however, the program jumps to the statement following the ErrorHandler label. The lines following the ErrorHandler label form an *error handler*, a subroutine that handles the error. The error handler shown in the example is generic; it displays a message and exits the subroutine.

Writing a Simple Error Handler

The error handler for the Math application must tell the user what kind of error occurred and then stop the operation. Let's examine its implementation. The overflow error will occur only when the Equals button is pressed, so this is the subroutine you must modify. Open the Code window, and in the button's Click event, add the underlined statements in Code 2.6.

Code 2.6: **The Revised Equals Button**

```
Private Sub Equals_Click()
Dim result As Double

On Error GoTo ErrorHandler
    Operand2 = Val(Display.Caption)
    If Operator = "+" Then result = Operand1 + Operand2
    If Operator = "-" Then result = Operand1 - Operand2
    If Operator = "*" Then result = Operand1 * Operand2
    If Operator = "/" And Operand2 <> "0" Then _
                result = Operand1 / Operand2
    Display.Caption = result
    ClearDisplay = True
    Exit Sub

ErrorHandler:
    MsgBox "The operation resulted in the following error" & _
            vbCrLf & Err.Description
    Display.Caption = "ERROR"
    ClearDisplay = True
End Sub
```

Most of the time, the error handler remains inactive and doesn't interfere with the operation of the program. If an error occurs, which most likely will be an overflow error, the program's control is transferred to the error handler. It doesn't make any difference which line in the code produces the error—all errors activate the same error handler. Of course, each procedure must have its own error handler.

The error handler displays a message box with the description of the error, prints the string "ERROR" on the calculator's display and sets the *ClearDisplay* variable to True so that when another Digit button is clicked, a new number will appear on the display. The vbCrLf constant inserts a line break between the literal string and the error's description.

NOTE   Err is the name of an object that represents the error. The two most important properties of the Err object are Number and Description. In the case of the overflow error, the error's number is 6, and its description is the string "Overflow". Notice that our error handler doesn't detect the type of error that occurred. It handles all errors in the same manner (by displaying the error message and the string "ERROR" on the calculator's display).

An Application with Multiple Forms

Few applications are built on a single Form. Most applications use two, three, or more Forms, which correspond to separate sections of the application. In this section, we are going to build an application that uses three Forms and lets the user switch among them at will. You'll see how to write an application that opens multiple windows on the Desktop. In Chapter 4, *Working with Forms*, we'll explore the topic of multiple Forms in depth.

VB6 at Work: The Calculators Project

The Calculators project combines the two Forms we have developed in this chapter into a single application. We'll create a new project, call it Calculators, and add the two Forms we have already designed (the project on the CD is called Calcs and you'll find it in the Calcs folder). We'll then design a third Form that will become our switching point. The new Form will let us load both calculators, as shown in Figure 2.8.

FIGURE 2.8:

The window of the Calculators application loads and displays the MathCalc and Loan calculators.

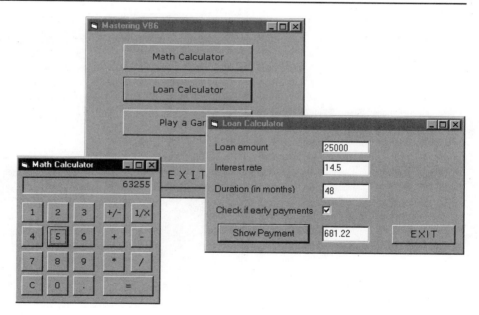

To implement the new, multi-window application, follow these steps:

1. Start a new Standard EXE project.

2. Choose Project ≻ Add Form to open the Add Form dialog box (see Figure 2.9). Click on the Existing tab, and locate the Form LoanCalc on your disk (or on the CD). The LoanCalc Form is added to the current project, and its name appears in the Forms folder under the project's name.

3. Choose Project ≻ Add Form, and locate the Form MathCalc in the Existing tab to add the Form to the project.

You now have a project with three Forms (the first one being an empty Form). If you run the application, you'll see the following error message:

```
Must have Startup Form or Sub Main()
```

To specify an application's start-up Form, do the following:

4. Open the Form1 Form in design mode, select it with the mouse, and in the Properties window, set its Name property to Calculators and its caption to Mastering VB6.

5. Now add four Command buttons to the Form, as previously shown in Figure 2.8. The names and captions of these buttons are listed in Table 2.2.

FIGURE 2.9:

When you ask Visual Basic to add a Form to a project, you have the option of creating a new Form or adding an existing one.

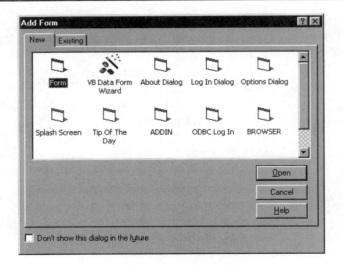

The code behind the first two buttons should show the MathCalc and Loan-Calc Forms. To show a Form from within another, you must use the Show method, which has the following syntax where *Form* is the name of the Form you want to show:

```
Form.Show
```

TABLE 2.2: Names and Captions of Command Buttons

CAPTION	NAME
NMath Calculator	bttnMath
Loan Calculator	bttnLoan
Play a Game	bttnGame
EXIT	bttnExit

6. Now, enter the following code in the Math Calculator button's Click event:

```
Private Sub ShowMath_Click()
    MathCalc.Show
End Sub
```

The code behind the Loan Calculator button is:

```
Private Sub ShowLoan_Click()
    LoanCalc.Show
End Sub
```

The Show method (as well as the Hide method, which hides an open window) is described in detail in Chapter 4, *Working with Forms*. Invoking a Form from within another is a simple task.

The code behind the Play a Game button should also call the Show method of another Form, but it doesn't. I regret not developing a game for your enjoyment, but I did implement a fun feature. When you click this button, it jumps to another place on the Form.

Code 2.7:   **The Play a Game Button**

```
Private Sub ShowGame_Click()
    ShowGame.Left = Rnd() * (Calculators.Width - _
                    ShowGame.Width)
    ShowGame.Top = Rnd() * (Calculators.Height - _
                    ShowGame.Height)
End Sub
```

This subroutine manipulates the Left and Top properties of the Command button to move the button to a different position.

The last button, Exit, ends the application with the End statement:

```
Private Sub ExitButton_Click()
    End
End Sub
```

This is all it takes to create a multi-window application based on some existing Forms. No changes in the existing Forms are required.

Now you can save the project. Choose File ➤ Save Project As, and in the Save dialog box, create a new folder and save the project in it.

On the CD, you'll find the Calculators project in the Calcs folder. You may notice that only the project file and the application's main Form are stored in this folder. The Math and Loan Forms are still in their original folders. The structure of a Visual Basic project and how its components are stored on disk are discussed shortly, in the section "A Project's Files."

The Startup Object

Now press F5 or choose Start ➤ Run to run the application described in the previous section. Instead of running the application, Visual Basic displays the following error message:

```
Must have a startup form or Sub Main()
```

Click OK to open the Project Properties dialog box shown in Figure 2.10. Visual Basic wants to know which Form to display when it starts. By default, Visual Basic displays the Form named Form1 or starts by executing a subroutine called Main. Our project has neither, so Visual Basic needs more information in order to start the application.

FIGURE 2.10:

Open the Project Properties dialog box to specify the Startup object.

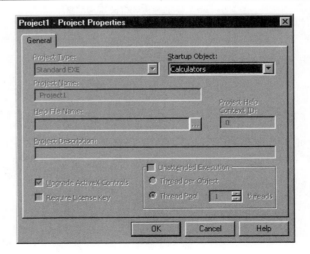

Obviously, the Startup object must call the Calculators Form, as shown in Figure 2.10. This is the only Form that can call the other two. Expand the Startup Object drop-down list and select Calculators. Click OK to start the application.

You can also open the Project Properties dialog box by choosing Project ➤ Project Properties. If you do so, the dialog box will have more tabs than those shown in Figure 2.10. I'll explain their contents later when we look at how to package an application as an EXE file.

Now, run the application and see how it works. Click the first two buttons in the main window to display the Loan and Math Forms. Switch from one window to the other, and click the main Form's buttons while the two windows are open. Visual Basic doesn't open the corresponding window again, but moves the *focus* to it (brings it on top of any other window on the Desktop).

To close a window, click the Close button (the little X button at the upper right corner of the window). You can close and open the Math and Loan windows as many times as you wish. If you close the application's Main window, though, you'll have to restart the application. This action is equivalent to clicking the Exit button of the main Form.

A Project's Files

Each Visual Basic project is made up of a number of files that are all listed in the Project Explorer window shown in Figure 2.11. This figure shows the components of the Calculators project. Notice that the files are grouped in folders, according to their types. As mentioned in Chapter 1, *Getting Started with Visual Basic*, there can be more types of files. Not only can you have more types of files in the same project, you can have multiple projects, or a project group (discussed in Chapter 15, *Building ActiveX Components*). In this section, we are going to look at the structure of the files that make up a typical project: the Form and project files.

The *project file* is a list of all the files and objects associated with the project, as well as information about the environment (if you have changed some of the default settings). The contents of the project file are updated every time the project is saved. It's a text file that you can open and view with a text editor.

Modifying the project file directly is not recommended, and you don't have good reason to do so.

FIGURE 2.11:

The components of the
Calculators project

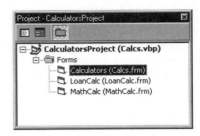

You can, however, create project files from within a special application, which
is usually called a code generator. A *code generator* is an application that creates
the code of an application based on user-supplied data. The various Wizards, for
instance, are code generators; they generate code for the programmer. This code
is usually the skeleton of an application that you must modify according to your
requirements.

The Project File

If you open the Calcs.vbp project file with a text editor, you'll find the following
references in it:

```
Form=Calcs.frm
Form=..\Math\MathCalc.frm
Form=..\Loan\LoanCalc.frm
Startup="Calculators"
```

It contains a list of the Forms that make up the project and the Start-up Form (which
is the Form displayed when the application starts). The project is stored in the
Calcs folder, and the Forms MathCalc and LoanCalc are stored in the Math and
Loan folder, respectively. The references to these files from within the Calcs project
file are relative. Thus, if you move the entire parent folder with its subfolder to a
new location on your disk, the project file will still be able to locate the project's
components.

The Form File

The Form files (FRM) are also text files and contain the descriptions of the controls
on the Form and the corresponding code. Here is the listing of the Calc.frm file:

```
VERSION 5.00
Begin VB.Form Calculators
   Caption        =   "Mastering VB6"
   ClientHeight   =   3675
```

```
ClientLeft       =    60
ClientTop        =    345
ClientWidth      =    4680
LinkTopic        =    "Form1"
ScaleHeight      =    3675
ScaleWidth       =    4680
StartUpPosition  =    3    'Windows Default
Begin VB.CommandButton bttnExit
   Caption          =    "E X I T"
   BeginProperty Font
      Name           =    "Verdana"
      Size           =    12
      Charset        =    0
      Weight         =    400
      Underline      =    0    'False
      Italic         =    0    'False
      Strikethrough  =    0    'False
   EndProperty
   Height         =    570
   Left           =    780
   TabIndex       =    3
   Top            =    2940
   Width          =    2820
End
Begin VB.CommandButton bttnGame
   Caption          =    "Play a Game"
   BeginProperty Font
      Name           =    "Verdana"
      Size           =    9.75
      Charset        =    0
      Weight         =    400
      Underline      =    0    'False
      Italic         =    0    'False
      Strikethrough  =    0    'False
   EndProperty
   Height         =    570
   Left           =    780
   TabIndex       =    2
   Top            =    1755
   Width          =    2820
End
Begin VB.CommandButton bttnLoan
   Caption          =    "Loan Calculator"
   BeginProperty Font
      Name           =    "Verdana"
```

```
            Size            =    9.75
            Charset         =    0
            Weight          =    400
            Underline       =    0     'False
            Italic          =    0     'False
            Strikethrough   =    0     'False
         EndProperty
         Height        =    570
         Left          =    780
         TabIndex      =    1
         Top           =    1005
         Width         =    2820
      End
      Begin VB.CommandButton bttnMath
         Caption        =    "Math Calculator"
         BeginProperty Font
            Name            =    "Verdana"
            Size            =    9.75
            Charset         =    0
            Weight          =    400
            Underline       =    0     'False
            Italic          =    0     'False
            Strikethrough   =    0     'False
         EndProperty
         Height        =    570
         Left          =    780
         TabIndex      =    0
         Top           =    270
         Width         =    2820
      End
   End
End
Attribute VB_Name = "Calculators"
Attribute VB_GlobalNameSpace = False
Attribute VB_Creatable = False
Attribute VB_PredeclaredId = True
Attribute VB_Exposed = False
Private Sub bttnExit_Click()
     End
End Sub

Private Sub bttnGame_Click()
bttnGame.Left = Rnd() * (Calculators.Width - bttnGame.Width)
bttnGame.Top = Rnd() * (Calculators.Height - bttnGame.Height)
End Sub
```

```
Private Sub bttnLoan_Click()
    LoanCalc.Show
End Sub

Private Sub bttnMath_Click()
    MathCalc.Show
End Sub
```

(No, I didn't create this listing with Visual Basic 5. The beta version I used to prepare this book inserts the line VERSION 5.0 at the beginning of the listing. The release version may use a different version number. It probably won't change because the project structure has not changed from version 5 to version 6.)

The first definition is that of the Form, which begins with the line:

```
Begin VB.Form Calculators
```

VB.Form is a Form object, and *Calculators* is its name. Following this line is a list of Form properties. The properties whose names begin with "Client" determine the position and size of the Form on the Desktop. The ScaleWidth and ScaleHeight properties determine the coordinate system of the Form. The positions of the controls on the Form are expressed in these units (coordinate systems are discussed in detail in Chapter 6, *Drawing with Visual Basic*).

After the properties of the Form and before the *End* keyword that closes the definition of the Form (the one that begins as Begin VB.Form), are the definitions of the controls. The following line:

```
Begin VB.CommandButton bttnExit
```

marks the beginning of the first Command button control on the Form, which is the Exit button. This definition ends with the *End* keyword. In between these two keywords are all the properties of the Exit Command button. Notice that the Font property has a number of members and that they are all enclosed in a pair of *BeginProperty/EndProperty* keywords.

Following the definition of the controls is the Form's code. Code 2.8 shows the structure of a FRM file. It contains the headers of the controls only. The lines that correspond to the properties of the controls and the actual statements in the subroutines are omitted to make the structure of the file easier to see. Ellipses denote the places where properties and code lines would otherwise appear.

Code 2.8:   The Object Headers of the Calculators Form

```
VERSION 5.00
Begin VB.Form Calculators
    ...
    Begin VB.CommandButton bttnExit
```

```
            BeginProperty Font

            ...
            EndProperty
        ...
        End
        Begin VB.CommandButton bttnGame
            BeginProperty Font

            ...
            EndProperty
        ...
        End
        Begin VB.CommandButton bttnLoan
            BeginProperty Font

            ...
            EndProperty
        ...
        End
        Begin VB.CommandButton bttnMath
            BeginProperty Font
            ...
            EndProperty
        ...
        End
    End
    Attribute VB_Name = "Calculators"
    Attribute VB_GlobalNameSpace = False
    Attribute VB_Creatable = False
    Attribute VB_PredeclaredId = True
    Attribute VB_Exposed = False

    Private Sub bttnExit_Click()

    End Sub

    Private Sub bttnGame_Click()

    End Sub

    Private Sub bttnLoan_Click()

    End Sub

    Private Sub bttnMath_Click()

    End Sub
```

As you can see, writing an application that automatically generates Visual Basic code is straightforward. You have to start with a similar project, see what information Visual Basic stores in the project and Form files, and use these files as guides.

Moving and Copying Projects

Sooner or later you'll have to move or copy a project to another folder. If you choose File ➤ Save Project As and save the project with the same (or a different) name in another folder, only the VBP file is stored in the new folder. The project's components remain in their original folders. This may not be what you expected, but that's how Visual Basic works. A project's components need not reside in the same folder, so Visual Basic doesn't copy all the files along with the project file.

TIP   Using components of existing projects is not only possible, it's desirable. You should never write code that duplicates existing code.

You shouldn't maintain multiple copies of the same file either. Suppose you create a custom Form for specifying colors. After this Form is tested and working, you can use it from within multiple projects. This Form shouldn't be replicated in each project's folder. If you decide to add a feature to it later (and believe me, you will), you'll have to update multiple files. If you save this Form in a special folder though, you can add it to any number of projects. If you update the Form in a single folder, all the projects that use it will see the new Form.

TIP   Another good way to save a Form is to place it in your vb\common\forms folder, for example, and add it to each project that needs its functionality.

This feature is why Visual Basic doesn't enforce the one-folder-per-project rule. Create a folder for each project, and store all the files that are unique to the project in it, but add existing components to a new project from their original folders.

To save a project in a different folder, you must first copy all the files of the project to a new folder and, only then, save the project file in the same folder. If you first save the project to a new folder or under a different filename, your project won't see the new files. Instead, it will refer to the original files.

As mentioned, the VBP file contains references to the project's components. Of course, if you change the name or path of even a single component in your project, Visual Basic will prompt you to save the project file before you close it. An awareness of this detail can save you a good deal of frustration.

There's nothing more frustrating than having identically named files in several folders and not knowing which ones are the latest versions. Even worse, you may end up updating one set of files and expect to see the changes in another set. This is an accident waiting to happen, and if you decide to move a project to another folder, always delete the files in the old folder.

You can also move projects to a different folder from within the Windows Explorer. Visual Basic uses relative path names in the VBP file, so if you move all the files to a new folder, the relative references are valid. However, you shouldn't count on this. It's possible that the VBP file will end up seeing files other than those you think it does, or it might not find the referenced files at all. It's best to use File menu commands when moving projects around. Select each component of the project in the Project Explorer window and save it under a different file name with the File ➤ Save As command. After you have saved all the components to the new folder, save the project in the same folder with the File ➤ Save Project As command.

Executable Files

So far, you have been executing applications within Visual Basic's environment. However, you can't expect the users of your application to have Visual Basic installed on their systems. If you develop an interesting application, you won't feel like giving away the code of the application (the *source code*, as it's called). Applications are distributed as executable files, along with their support files. The users of the application can't see your source code, and your application can't be modified or made to look like someone else's application (that doesn't mean it can't be copied, of course).

An *executable file* is a binary file that contains instructions only the machine can understand and execute. The commands stored in the executable file are known as *machine language*.

Applications designed for the Windows environment can't fit in a single file. It just wouldn't make sense. Along with the executable files, your application requires a number of so-called support files. If you're using any custom controls, the files in which they reside (they have the extension OCX) must be distributed with the application.

In general, Windows applications require a large number of support files, and these files may already exist on many of the machines on which your application will be installed. That's why it doesn't make sense to distribute huge files. Each user should install the main application and the support files that aren't already installed on their computer.

Using the Application Setup Wizard

Distributing applications would be a complicated process if it weren't for the Application Setup Wizard. The Application Setup Wizard takes care of packaging your application for distribution.

The Wizard creates a new application whose sole purpose is to install your application on the host computer. It also breaks the installation program into pieces so that you can distribute your application on diskettes. The Application Setup Wizard comes with Visual Basic, and it's straightforward to use.

TIP

There are also other tools you can use for creating setup applications. One of them is called InstallShield, and you'll find a demo version of this application on this book's CD.

Creating an Executable File

Before preparing the setup application, you must create an executable file for your application. This file will be represented as an icon on your Desktop, and you can run the application without starting Visual Basic and loading the project. Simply double-click the application's icon on the Desktop (or a folder) to start the application.

To make an executable file for your project, follow these steps:

1. Choose File ➢ Make *project*.exe (*project* is the name of the project).

2. Enter the name and the location of the file, and Visual Basic will create the executable file.

To set options for the executable files through the Project Properties dialog box, follow these steps:

1. Choose Project ➢ Project Properties to open the Project Properties dialog box, shown in Figure 2.12.

2. Select the Compile tab.

FIGURE 2.12:

In the Compile tab of the Project Properties dialog box, you specify compilation options.

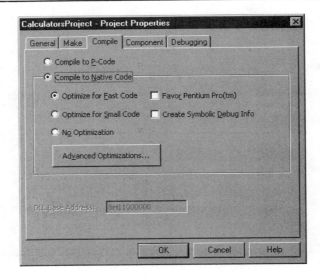

Now you're ready to specify options. Visual Basic can produce two types of executable files:

- P-code

- Native code

Compile to P-Code   When you select this option, Visual Basic compiles a project using *p-code*, which is pseudo-code that the CPU can't execute directly. BASIC has always been an interpreted language. Programs written in an interpreted language aren't translated into machine language before they are executed. Instead, each line of code is translated as needed and then executed.

Interpreted programs aren't as fast as compiled programs (which are translated into optimized machine language before execution). A p-code program is somewhere in between the two. It's highly efficient code, but it can't be executed as is. A translation step is required. P-code, however, is closer to machine language than it is to Visual Basic, and the process of translating p-code to executable code is efficient.

NOTE   The main benefit of p-code is that it's compact and not much slower than pure executable code. For more information on p-code and native code-compiled applications see Chapter 12, *Optimizing VB Applications*.

Compile to Native Code   When you select this option, Visual Basic compiles a project using *native code*, which is the machine language that the CPU understands and executes. The generated executable is faster than the equivalent p-code executable by as much as 20 times. This is a benchmark (a best-case scenario), and you shouldn't expect such dramatic improvements with your average applications. Use this option for applications that perform involved math operations.

When you compile to native code, you have the following options:

- **Optimize for Fast Code**   Maximizes the speed of the executable file by instructing the compiler to favor speed over size. To optimize the code, the compiler can reduce many constructs to functionally similar sequences of machine code.

- **Optimize for Small Code**   Minimizes the size of the executable file by instructing the compiler to favor size over speed

- **No Optimization**   Compiles without optimizations

- **Favor Pentium Pro™**   Optimizes code to favor the Pentium Pro processor. Use this option for programs meant only for the Pentium Pro. Code generated with this option runs on other Intel processors, but it doesn't perform as well as if compiled with other options.

- **Create Symbolic Debug Info**   Generates symbolic debug information in the executable. An executable file created using this option can be debugged with Visual C++ or with debuggers that use the CodeView style of debug information. Setting this option generates a PDB file with the symbol information for your executable. This option is most likely to be used by Visual C++ programmers who also use Visual Basic.

Selecting Advanced Optimization Options

When you select Advanced Optimizations, Visual Basic opens the Advanced Optimizations dialog box, shown in Figure 2.13. You use these options to turn off certain checks that normally take place and ensure that your application works properly. To increase the speed of the executable file, you can turn off some or all of these checks by selecting the appropriate checkbox.

WARNING   Enabling these optimizations may prevent the correct execution of your program. You must understand what each option does and be sure the application doesn't require any of the options you turn off.

FIGURE 2.13:

The Advanced Optimizations dialog box

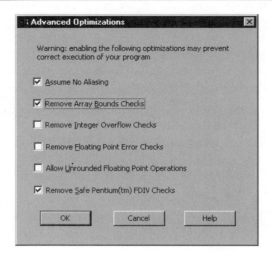

Assume No Aliasing   Select this checkbox to tell the compiler that your program doesn't use aliasing. *Aliasing* is a technique that lets your code refer to a variable (memory location) by more than one name. This technique is not used in this book, and you can safely select this option.

Remove Array Bounds Checks   By default, Visual Basic checks an array's bounds every time your code accesses the array to determine if the index is within the range of the array. If the index is not within array bounds, a runtime error is generated (which can be trapped from within the code). Select this option to turn off the array bounds checking and speed up applications that use arrays. However, the code that ensures that the array's bounds aren't exceeded may cost more in execution time. If an array bound is exceeded, the results will be unexpected.

Remove Integer Overflow Checks   By default, Visual Basic checks every calculation for integer-style data types—Byte, Integer, and Long—to ensure that the value is within the range of the data type. If the magnitude of the value being put into the data type is incorrect, a runtime error is generated. Select this option to turn off error checking and speed up integer calculations. If data type capacities are overflowed, you'll get incorrect results.

Remove Floating Point Error Checks   By default, Visual Basic checks every calculation of a floating-point data type—Single and Double—to be sure that the value is within range for that data type and that there are no divide-by-zero or invalid operations. If the magnitude of the value being put into the data type is incorrect, an error occurs. Select this option to turn off error checking and speed up floating-point calculations. If data type capacities are overflowed, no error occurs, and you'll get incorrect results.

Allow Unrounded Floating Point Operations   When this option is selected, the compiler uses floating-point registers more efficiently, avoids storing and loading large volumes of data to and from memory, and compares floating points more efficiently.

Remove Safe Pentium™ FDIV Checks   Selecting this option removes the safety checking so that the code for floating-point division is faster, but may produce slightly incorrect results on Pentium processors with the FDIV bug.

CHAPTER
THREE

Visual Basic: The Language

- Variables

- Constants

- Arrays

- Collections

- Procedures

- Subroutines

- Functions

- Arguments

- Statements

3

This chapter discusses the fundamentals of any programming language: variables and procedures. A *variable* stores data, and a *procedure* is code that manipulates variables. To do any serious programming with Visual Basic, you must be familiar with these concepts. To write efficient applications, you need a basic understanding of some fundamental topics, such as the types, scope, and lifetime of variables, and the procedures and argument-passing mechanisms.

As you have seen in the first two chapters, most of the code in a Visual Basic application deals with manipulating control properties. This chapter explores in greater depth how variables store data and how programs process variables. If you're familiar with Visual Basic, you might want to simply scan the following pages and make sure you're acquainted with the topics and the sample code discussed in this chapter.

If you're new to Visual Basic, you may find that some material in this chapter is over your head. This chapter covers basic concepts and definitions—in general, tedious, but necessary, material. You'll also learn how to use variants and how to write functions with optional arguments. Think of this chapter as a prerequisite for the more advanced techniques covered in the rest of the book.

Variables

In Visual Basic, as in any other programming language, variables store values during a program's execution. For example, you're writing a program that frequently prompts the user for data, and you decide to add a personal touch to the interface. Every time the program needs data, it will display the user's name. Instead of writing an application for Joe Doe, another for Mary Jones, and so on, you can declare a variable that will store the user's name. When the program starts, it asks the user to enter his or her name. It then stores this name in a variable and during the course of the program uses it to display the user's name.

Variables are placeholders in which you can leave values and recall them at will. A variable has a name and a value. The variable *UserName,* for example, can have the value "Joe," and the variable *Discount* can have the value 0.35. *UserName* and *Discount* are variable names, and "Joe" and 0.35 are their values. When a variable's value is text (or *string*, as it's called), it must be enclosed in double quotes. In your code, you can refer to the value of a variable by the variable's name. For example, the following statement calculates the discount for the amount of $24,500:

```
MsgBox "You will save " & 24500 * Discount
```

The message that this expression displays depends on the value of the *Discount* variable. If you decide to offer a better discount, all you have to do is change the value of the *Discount* variable. If you didn't use the *Discount* variable, you'd have to make many changes in your code. In other words, if you coded the previous line as follows:

```
MsgBox "You save " & 24500 * 0.35
```

you'd have to look for every line in your code that calculates discounts and change the discount from 0.35 to another value. By changing the value of the *Discount* variable in a single place in your code, the entire program is updated.

Declaring Variables

In most programming languages, variables must be declared in advance for the compiler. Historically, the reason for doing this has been to help the compiler. Every time a compiled application runs into a new variable, it has to create it. Doing so doesn't take a lot of statements, but it does produce a delay that could be avoided. If the compiler knows all the variables and their types that are going to be used in the application ahead of time, it can produce the most compact and efficient, or optimized, code. For example, when you tell the compiler that the variable *Discount* will hold a number, the compiler will set aside a number of bytes for the *Discount* variable to use.

One of the most popular, yet intensely criticized, features of BASIC was that it didn't force the programmer to declare all variables. As you will see, there are more compelling reasons than speed and efficiency for declaring variables. For example, if the compiler knows the types of the variables, it will catch many typing errors at design or compile time (errors that otherwise would surface at runtime). Later in the chapter, in the section "Forcing Variable Declarations," you'll see how variable declarations can simplify coding too.

Explicit Declarations

To declare a variable, use the *Dim* statement followed by the variable's name and type, as follows:

```
Dim meters As Integer
Dim greetings As String
```

We'll look at the various data types in detail in the next section. In the meantime, you should know that a variable declared *As Integer* can store only integer numbers.

The first variable, *meters*, will store integers, such as 3 or 1002, and the second variable, *greetings*, will store text, such as "Thank you for using Fabulous Software". You can declare multiple variables of the same type in the same line, as follows:

```
Dim meters As Integer, inches As Integer, centimeters As Integer
```

When Visual Basic finds a Dim statement, it creates one or more new variables, as specified in the statement. That is, it creates a placeholder by reserving some space in the memory and assigning a name to it. Each time this name is used in subsequent commands, Visual Basic accesses this area in the memory to read or set its value. For instance, when you use the following statement:

```
meters = 23
```

Visual Basic places the value 23 in the placeholder reserved for the *meters* variable. When the program asks for the value of this variable, Visual Basic reads it from the same area of memory. The following statement:

```
Print meters
```

causes Visual Basic to retrieve the value 23 from the area of memory named *meters*. It's also possible for a single statement to both read and set the value of a variable. The following statement increases the value of the *meters* variable:

```
meters = meters + 1
```

Visual Basic reads the value (say 23), adds 1 to it, and then stores the new value (24) in the same memory location.

Variable Naming Conventions

When declaring variables, you should be aware of a few naming conventions. A variable's name:

- Must begin with a letter
- Can't contain an embedded period or any of the type-declaration characters
- Mustn't exceed 255 characters
- Must be unique within its scope (we'll look at the variable's scope shortly)

One good reason for declaring variables is so that Visual Basic knows the type of information the variable must store and can validate the variable's value. Attempting to assign a value of the wrong type to a declared variable generates a "Type Mismatch" runtime error.

For example, if you attempt to assign the value "Welcome" to the *meters* variable, Visual Basic won't execute the statement because this assignment violates the variable's declaration. The *meters* variable was declared as Integer, and you're attempting to store a string in it. There are some interesting exceptions to this rule. For example, it's possible to assign the value "103" to the *meters* variable (it's a string, but it represents a numeric value) and to assign the value 103 to the *greetings* variable (it's converted to the string "103" and then assigned to the string variable). We'll look at more exceptions shortly.

You can also declare variables without specifying their type. Visual Basic creates a generic variable that can hold any type. The following statement creates three variables of the variant type:

```
Dim temp, var, generic
```

A *variant* can store all types of values and is an extremely flexible data type, but it requires more overhead than variables declared with a specific type. For a detailed discussion of variants and how they affect performance, see Chapter 12, *Optimizing VB Applications*.

Implicit Declarations

You can also choose not to declare variables. When Visual Basic meets an undeclared variable name, it creates a new variable on the spot and uses it. The new variable's type is variant, the generic data type that can accommodate all other data types. Using a new variable in your code is equivalent to declaring it without type. Visual Basic adjusts its type according to the value you assign to it. Declare two variables, *var1* and *var2*, with the following statement:

```
Dim var1, var2
```

and then assign a text value to one and a numeric value to the other:

```
var1 = "Thank you for using Fabulous Software"
var2 = 49.99
```

The *var1* variable is a string variable, and *var2* is a numeric one. You can verify this with the *TypeName()* function, which returns a variable's type. The following statements print the types shown below:

```
Debug.Print "Variable var1 is " & TypeName(var1)
Variable var1 is String
Debug.Print "Variable var2 is " & TypeName(var2)
Variable var2 is Double
```

NOTE   The TypeName() function is explained in Appendix A, *Built-In Functions*, on the CD.

Later in the same program you can reverse the assignments:

```
var1 = 49.99
var2 = "Thank you for using Fabulous Software"
```

If you execute the previous Print statements again, you'll see that the types of the variables have changed. The *var1* variable is now a double, and *var2* is a string.

Finally, you can omit declaration statements, yet create typed variables with the variable declaration characters. To create a variable without declaring it, but that is still of a specific data type, add a suffix that is one of the data declaration characters in Table 3.1.

TABLE 3.1: Data Type Definition Characters

SYMBOL	DATA TYPE	EXAMPLE
$	String	A$, messageText$
%	Integer	counter%, var%
&	Long	population&, colorValue&
!	Single	distance!
#	Double	ExactDistance#

You can also declare variables using the Def*xxx* statements. For example, you can declare that all variables beginning with *a* and *b* are integers, with the DefInt statement:

```
DefInt a-b
```

You can use the following statements to declare ranges of variables based on their first character:

DefBool	DefByte	DefInt
DefLng	DefCur	DefSng
DefDbl	DefDate	DefStr
DefOb	DefVar	

Variable types that are declared with variable declaration characters and the Def*xxx* statements are leftovers from older versions of BASIC and are, for the most part, obsolete.

Types of Variables

Visual Basic recognizes the following six types of variables:

- Numeric
- String
- Boolean
- Date
- Object
- Variant

The two major variable types are numeric and string. *Numeric variables* store numbers, and *string variables* store text. *Variant variables* can store any type of data. Why bother to specify the type if one type suits all? On the surface, using variants may seem like a good idea, but they have their disadvantages. *Date variables* are optimized for storing dates and *object variables* store objects (you'll see how to use object variables in your code later in the book). We'll use object variables a lot in Parts III and IV of the book.

We begin our discussion of variable types with numeric variables. Text is stored in string variables, but numbers can be stored in many formats, depending on the size of the number and its precision. That's why there are many types of numeric variables.

Numeric Variables

You'd expect that programming languages would use a single data type for numbers. After all, a number is a number. But this couldn't be farther from the truth. All programming languages provide a variety of numeric data types, including the following:

- Integers
- Single, or floating-point numbers with limited precision
- Double, or floating-point numbers with extreme precision

NOTE   Single and Double are the two basic data types for storing floating-point numbers. The Double type can represent these numbers more accurately than the Single type.

The names Single and Double come from single-precision and double-precision numbers. As you learned in Chapter 2, double-precision numbers are stored internally with greater accuracy than single-precision numbers. As you will see, there are many types of variables for storing numbers, and the reason is efficiency. For example, if you're manipulating the pixels of an image, you're calculating with integers. You don't need more precision than integer numbers can provide, and using integers speeds up the calculations considerably. In scientific calculations, you need all the precision you can get (and then some more); in that case, you should use the Double data type.

Different types of numbers are represented internally in different formats. All numeric values are truncated to a certain extent. The result of the operation ⅓ is 0.333333… (an infinite number of digits "3"). You could fill 16MB of RAM with the digit "3," and the result would still be truncated. Here's a simple, but illuminating, example:

In a new Form's Load event, declare two variables as follows:

```
Dim a As Single, b As Double
```

Then enter the following statements:

```
a = 1 / 3
Debug.Print a
```

Run the application and you should get the following result in the Immediate window:

```
0.3333333
```

There are seven digits to the right of the decimal point. Break the application by pressing Control+Break and execute the following statements in the Immediate window:

```
a = a * 100000
Debug.Print a
```

The following value will be printed in the Immediate window:

```
33333.34
```

The result is not as accurate as you might have expected initially—it isn't even rounded properly. If you divide *a* by 100000, the result will be:

```
0.3333334
```

which is different from the number we started with (0.3333333). This is an important point in numeric calculations, and it's called *error propagation.* In long sequences of numeric calculations, errors propagate. Even if you can tolerate the error introduced by the Single data type in a single operation, the cumulative errors may be significant.

Let's perform the same operations with double-precision numbers, this time using the variable *b*. Add these lines to the Form's Load event handler:

```
b = 1 / 3
Debug.Print b
b = b * 100000
Debug.Print b
```

This time, the following numbers are displayed in the Immediate window:

```
0.333333333333333
33333.3333333333
```

The results produced by the double-precision variables are more accurate.

NOTE   Smaller precision numbers are stored in fewer bytes and larger precision numbers are stored in more bytes. For example, integers are stored in two bytes, single-precision floating-point numbers in four bytes, and double-precision floating-point numbers in eight bytes. The actual format of the floating-point numeric types is complicated and won't be discussed in this book.

Numeric Data Types   The choice of data types for your variables can make a difference in the results of the calculations. The proper variable types are determined by the nature of the values they represent. The choice of data types is frequently a tradeoff between precision and speed of execution (less precise data types are manipulated faster). Visual Basic supports the numeric data types in Table 3.2.

TABLE 3.2:   Visual Basic Numeric Data Types

DATA TYPE	WHAT IT DOES
Integer	Stores integer values in the range -32,768 to 32,767.
Long	Stores long integers in the range −2,147,483,648 to 2,147,483,647.
Single	Stores single-precision floating-point numbers. It can represent negative numbers in the range -3.402823E38 to -1.401298E-45. The value 0 can't be represented precisely (it's a very, very small number, but not exactly 0).
Double	Stores double-precision floating-point numbers. It can represent negative numbers in the range −1.79769313486232E308 to −4.94065645841247E-324 and positive numbers in the range 4.94065645841247E-324 to 1.79769313486232E308.
Currency	Stores fixed-point numbers with four decimal digits. The Currency data type can represent numbers in the range -922,337,203,685,477.5808 to 922,337,203,685,477.5807.

Integers are stored internally in two bytes, and Visual Basic handles integers efficiently, but you can represent only so many numbers with two bytes. Integers that exceed the specified range must be stored as Long integers. Long integers are stored in four bytes, and they cover a much larger range of values. If you know that a specific variable (such as a loop counter, for instance) will hold a small integer, declare it as an Integer. If the value of the integer may exceed the range of values that can be represented with two bytes, use a Long integer. Integer operations are faster and consume less memory than other data types.

If your variable can contain a fractional part, declare it as a Single, Double, or Currency data type. The Single data type is stored in four bytes, and the Double data type is stored in eight bytes. The main difference between the two types is not the range of values, but the accuracy with which values are represented. If you divide 5 by 3 as a Single data type, the result is:

```
1.666667
```

If you divide 5 by 3 as a Double data type, the result is:

```
1.66666666666667
```

The Double data type provides more accuracy, which is needed in mathematical calculations. If you don't need more than a couple of fractional digits, use the Single data type. If you're concerned about accuracy, use the Double data type. Also use the Double data type if you're going to perform a series of math operations and the result of one operation will be used as an operand for the next. A little accuracy lost at every operation may substantially alter the final result.

The Currency data type can store fixed-point numbers and is suitable for financial calculations that don't need more accuracy than two fractional digits. This type supports four digits to the right of the decimal separator and 15 digits to the left. This accuracy is adequate for financial calculations, but not for scientific calculations.

The Byte Data Type   None of the numeric types is stored in a single byte. In some situations, however, data is stored as bytes, and you must be able to access individual bytes. The Byte type holds basically an integer in the range 0 to 255. Bytes are frequently used to access binary files, image and sound files, and so on. Some Windows Application Programming Interface (API) calls also use *Byte* arguments. API is a powerful set of functions that form the core of the operating system and they are discussed in Chapter 13. An *argument* is a value you pass to the procedure and on which the procedure usually acts. To declare a variable as a Byte, use the following statement:

```
Dim n As Byte
```

The variable *n* can be used in numeric calculations too, but you must be careful not to assign the result to another Byte variable if its value may exceed the range of the Byte type. If the variables *A* and *B* are initialized as follows:

```
Dim A As Byte, B As Byte
A = 233
B = 50
```

the following statement will display the correct result, even though it exceeds the value range of the Byte type:

```
MsgBox A + B
```

However, attempting to assign this value to a Byte variable with the following statement will generate an overflow runtime error:

```
B = A + B
```

The result (288) can't be stored in a single byte. Visual Basic generates the correct answer and stores it internally as an integer; that's why it can display the answer with the MsgBox function. But the assignment operation fails because the result can't fit in a single byte.

TIP
The operators that won't cause overflows are the Boolean operators AND, OR, NOT, and XOR, which are frequently used with Byte variables. These aren't logical operators that return True or False. They combine the matching bits in the two operands and return another byte. If you combine the numbers 199 and 200 with the AND operator, the result is 192. The two values in binary format are 11000111 and 11001000. If you perform a bitwise AND operation on these two values, the result is 11000000, which is the decimal value 192.

Accuracy of Numeric Types   The smaller the integer part of a floating-point number, the more fractional digits it can hold. For example, the result of the operation 5 divided by 3 expressed as a Double data type is:

```
1.66666666666667
```

The result of the operation 500000 divided by 3 expressed as a Double data type doesn't have as many fractional digits, however. Visual Basic reports the number as follows:

```
166666.666666667
```

The number had to be truncated at the ninth digit after the decimal point because Visual Basic has eight bytes in which to fit the number. Some bytes of the larger number are allocated to the integer part, so there are fewer bytes left to represent the fractional part.

Some Tricks for Improving Accuracy

If your calculations require the maximum precision possible, here are a few simple, but effective, tricks.

- *Bias the numbers.* If you're doing calculations in the range 100,010 to 100,100, subtract 100,000 from the initial numbers to reduce the values in the range to 10 to 100. When you're done, add the bias 100,000 to the result.

- *Manipulate your expressions.* Examine your expressions and try to remove any redundancy. An expression such as *(a * b) / a* need not be calculated. The result is *b*, no matter what. If the previous expression is evaluated, it can't yield a more accurate result, and it's likely that it will yield a less accurate result. This is a simple example, but long expressions may contain redundancy that's not as obvious.

- *Specify variables of the same type.* Don't expect that two floating-point numbers that are assigned the same value will be exactly the same! This is odd, but here's an example: Create a single-precision variable *a* and a double-precision variable *b*, and assign the same value to them:

```
a = 7.03007
b = 7.03007
```

Then print their difference:

```
Debug.Print a-b
```

The result won't be zero! It will be: -1.7196655299756E-07. Because different numeric types are stored differently in memory, they don't quite match. What this means to you is that all variables in a calculation should be of the same type. In addition, don't make comparisons like:

```
If a = b Then {do something}
```

Use a threshold instead. If the difference is smaller than a threshold, then the two values can be considered equal (depending on the nature of your calculations, of course):

```
If (a - b) < 0.000001 Then {do something}
```

Declaring Numeric Variables   To declare variables of any of the previous types, use the Dim statement, followed by the name of the variable, the *As* keyword, and the variable's type. The following are all valid declarations of numeric variables:

```
Dim count As Integer
Dim DaysInCentury As Long
Dim Length As Single
Dim Area As Double
```

You can also combine multiple declarations on the same line. If the variables are of the same type, separate them with commas:

```
Dim Area As Double, Volume As Double
```

You can also specify multiple variables with different types in the same statement:

```
Dim Area As Double, Count As Integer
```

In the following statement only the *C* variable will be declared as Integer; the other two, *A* and *B*, will be declared as variants:

```
Dim A, B, C As Integer
```

You can use other keywords in declaring variables, such as *Private, Public,* and *Static.* We'll look at these keywords in later sections of this chapter. In the meantime, bear in mind that all variables declared with the Dim statement exist in the Module in which they were declared. If the variable *Count* is declared in a function, it exists only in this function. You can't access it from outside the function. Actually, you can have a *Count* variable in multiple functions. Each variable is stored locally. Variables declared in different procedures have different values and don't interfere with one another.

String Variables

The String data type stores only text, and string variables are declared with the String type:

```
Dim someText As String
```

You can assign any text to the variable *someText.* You can store nearly 2GB of text in a string variable. The following assignments are all valid:

```
someText = "Now is the time for all good men to come to the _
            aid of their country"
someText = ""
someText = "There are approximately 15,000 words in this chapter"
someText = "15,000"
```

The second assignment creates an empty string, and the last one creates a string that just happens to contain numeric digits, which are also characters. The difference between the variables

```
someNumber = 15000
```

and

```
someText = "15,000"
```

is that they hold different values. The *someText* variable holds the digits "1", "5", ",", "0", "0", and "0", and *someNumber* holds a numeric value. You can, however, use the variable *someText* in numeric operations, and you can use the variable *someNumber* in string operations. Visual Basic performs the necessary conversions for you. After all, when you attempt to divide "15,000" by another number, your intentions are obvious, and your application need not crash with a runtime error (as it would with other versions of BASIC).

Declare and initialize two string variables, *A* and *B*, as follows:

```
Dim A As String, B As String
A = "123"
B = "10"
```

Dividing *A* by *B* is a valid operation, even though the two variables are defined as strings. The following statement prints 12.3 in the Immediate window:

```
Debug.Print A / B
```

This means that Visual Basic figured out that you wanted to use the two variables as numbers, converted them to integers, performed the division, and converted the result to the proper data type for you.

You can even use the two variables as both string and numeric values in the same expression. The following statement won't confuse Visual Basic:

```
Debug.Print A & " divided by " & B & " is " & A / B
```

It will actually display this message:

```
123 divided by 10 is 12.3
```

The & operator concatenates (joins) two variables as strings, even if their values are numeric. To make sure that the variables *A* and *B* will be concatenated and not added, use the & operator. The following statement will print the string 12310 and not the numeric value 133:

```
Debug.Print A & B
```

The same result would be printed even if the variables *A* and *B* were numeric.

Fixed-Length Strings   As you can see, string variables have variable lengths. They grow and shrink as needed to accommodate the values assigned to them. You can also specify fixed-length strings with a statement like:

```
Dim someText As String * 1000
```

This variable is long enough to hold 1,000 characters. If you assign a string with fewer than 1,000 characters to it, the variable is padded with spaces. If you assign a string that exceeds the maximum declared length, it will be truncated.

Fixed-length strings are used in several situations. For example, you can declare a fixed-length string variable to accept user input when its maximum length is known. If a string variable's size will change drastically during the course of an application, you might want to declare it as fixed-length to prevent Visual Basic from having to resize it constantly.

Boolean Variables

The Boolean data type stores True/False values. Although a single bit would be adequate, for efficiency reasons Visual Basic allocates two bytes to this data type. Boolean variables are, in essence, integers that take the value -1 (for True) and 0 (for False). Actually, any non-zero value is considered True.

Boolean variables are declared as:

```
Dim failure As Boolean
```

and they are initialized to False.

Boolean variables are used in testing conditions, such as the following:

```
If failure Then MsgBox "Couldn't complete the operation"
```

They are also combined with the logical operators AND, OR, NOT, and XOR. The NOT operator toggles the value of a Boolean variable. The following statement is a toggle:

```
running = Not running
```

If the variable *running* is True, it's reset to False, and vice versa. This statement is a shorter way of coding the following:

```
If running = True Then
    running = False
Else
    running = True
End If
```

Date Variables

Date and time values are stored internally in a special format, but you don't need to know the exact format. They are double-precision numbers: the integer part represents the date and the fractional part represents the time. A variable declared as Date can store both date and time values with a statement like the following:

```
Dim expiration As Date
```

The following are all valid assignments:

```
expiration = "01/01/1997"
expiration = "13:03:05 AM"
expiration = "02/23/1995 13:03:05 AM"
expiration = #02/23/1996 13:03:05 AM#
```

In the last statement, I didn't mistype pound signs instead of quotes. The pound sign tells Visual Basic to store a date and/or time value to the *expiration* variable, just as the quotes tell Visual Basic that the value is a string.

TIP

The date format is determined by the Regional Settings (open the Control Panel and double-click the icon Regional Settings). In the United States, it's mm/dd/yy (in other countries the format is dd/mm/yy). If you assign an invalid date to a date variable, like 23/04/99, Visual Basic will automatically swap the month and day values to produce a valid date. If you assign the previous value to a date (or variant) variable and then print the variable, you'll see that Visual Basic converts it to 04/23/99. If the date is invalid even after the swapping of the month and day values, then a runtime error will be generated.

The Date data type is extremely flexible; Visual Basic knows how to handle date and time values without performing complicated conversions. To manipulate dates and times, use the Date and Time functions, which are explained in Appendix A on the CD. You can, however, directly subtract two date variables to find out their difference in days. Let's initialize two date variables:

```
Dim day1 As Date, day2 As Date
day1 = Date()
day2 = "01/01/2000"
```

The *day1* variable will be the current date. The difference between the two dates is calculated by:

```
MsgBox day2 - day1
```

which is the number of days from the current date to the end of the millennium. On January 5, 1997, the difference was 1091 days. You can easily find the number of years, months, and days between the two dates with the help of the Year(), Month(), and Day() functions (also explained in Appendix A on the CD):

```
Years = Year(day2 - day1) - 1900
Months = Month(day2 - day1)
Days = Day(day2 - day1)
```

You can also add days to a date variable. Integer values correspond to days. To add an hour, add 1/24 of a day; to add a minute, add 1/(24*60) of a day; to add a second, add the value 1./(24.*60.*60.). If *day1* is:

```
day1 = #11/3/96 1:03:05 PM#
```

the following Print statements will display the results shown:

```
Print day1 + 1
11/4/96 1:03:05 PM
Print day1 + 1 / 24
11/3/96 2:03:05 PM
Print day1 + 1 / (24 * 60)
11/3/96 1:04:05 PM
```

When other numeric data types are converted to the Date data type, values to the left of the decimal represent date information, and values to the right of the decimal represent time. Midnight is 0 and midday is 0.5. Negative whole numbers represent dates before December 30, 1899. To arrive at the date and time six hours from now you would use:

```
now + 0.25
```

If the current time is less then six hours from midnight, the following statements will also change the date:

```
Debug.Print now
1/9/97 11:40:54 AM
Debug.Print now+0.5
1/9/97 11:40:54 PM
Debug.Print now+0.75
1/10/97 5:40:07 PM
```

TIP

As far as the infamous year 2000 problem goes, you shouldn't have to take any special actions in your Visual Basic applications. Visual Basic handles dates after the end of the millenium properly. The year value "00" corresponds to year 2000, the value "01" to year 2001 and so on. The expression:

```
DateDiff("d", "12/04/99", "12/04/00")
```

will evaluate to 366 days, and the expression:

```
DateDiff("d", "12/04/99", "12/04/09")
```

will evaluate to 3653 days (ten years and three days, due to leap years).

Object Variables

An object variable refers to one of Visual Basic's many objects, and you can use an object variable to access the actual object. You will see examples of object variables in Parts IV and V of the book.

Here is a simple example of an object variable. A Form has two Command buttons on it, Command1 and Command2. You can declare two object variables as:

```
Dim a As CommandButton, b As CommandButton
```

Each of these two object variables can be set to either one of the Command buttons with the following statements:

```
Set a = Command1
Set b = Command2
```

From now on, you can manipulate the two Command buttons' properties through the variables *a* and *b*. To change the Caption property of the first Command button, use a statement such as the following:

```
a.Caption = "Hi!"
```

To turn on the bold attribute of the second Command button (so that its caption appears in bold), use the following statement:

```
b.FontBold = True
```

You will find more examples of object variables in later chapters. You will also learn how to create your own objects that have their own properties and methods.

Variant Variables

This is the most flexible data type because it can accommodate all other types. A variable declared as variant (or a variable that hasn't been declared at all) is handled by Visual Basic according to the variable's current contents. If you assign an integer value to a variant, Visual Basic treats it as an integer. If you assign a string to a variant, Visual Basic treats it as a string. Variants can also hold different data types in the course of the same program. Visual Basic performs the necessary conversions for you.

To declare a variant, use the Dim statement without specifying a type, as follows:

```
Dim myVar
```

You can also specify the Variant type to make the code cleaner:

```
Dim myVar As Variant
```

however, it isn't necessary. Every time your code references a new variable, Visual Basic will create a variant for it. For example, if the variable *validKey* hasn't been declared, when Visual Basic runs into the following line:

```
validKey = "002-6abbgd"
```

it will create a new variant and assigns the value "002-6abbgd" to it.

You can use variants both in numeric and in string calculations. Suppose the variable *modemSpeed* has been declared as variant with the following statement:

```
Dim modemSpeed
```

and later in your code you assign the following value to it:

```
modemSpeed = "28.8"
```

The *modemSpeed* variable is a string variable that you can use in statements such as the following:

```
MsgBox "We suggest a " & modemSpeed & " modem"
```

This statement displays the following message:

```
"We suggest a 28.8 modem"
```

You can also treat the *modemSpeed* variable as a numeric value with the following statement:

```
MsgBox "A " & modemSpeed & " modem can transfer " & modemSpeed * _
       1000 / 8 & " bytes per second"
```

This statement displays the following message:

```
"A 28.8 modem can transfer 3600 bytes per second"
```

The first instance of the *modemSpeed* variable in the above statement is treated as a string, because this is the variant's type according to the assignment statement (we assigned a string to it). The second instance, however, is treated as a number (a single-precision number). Visual Basic converted it to a numeric value because it's used in a numeric calculation.

Another example of this behavior of variants can be seen in the following statements:

```
A = "10"
B = "11"
Debug.Print A + B
Debug.Print A & B
```

Both Print statements print the string "1011". You're asking Visual Basic to add two strings and this is how Visual Basic interprets your intentions. When applied to strings, the + and & operators are identical. If you change the definition of the second variable to the following:

```
B = 11
```

the first Print statement prints 21 (a numeric value), and the second Print statement prints the string "1011" as before.

Visual Basic knows how to handle variables in a way that "makes sense." The result may not be what you had in mind, but it certainly is dictated by common sense. If you really want to concatenate the strings "10" and "11", you should use the & operator, which would tell Visual Basic exactly what to do. Quite impressive, but for many programmers this is a strange behavior that can lead to subtle errors, and they avoid it. It's up to you to decide whether to use variants and how far you will go with them. Sure, you can perform tricks with variants, but you shouldn't overuse them to the point that others can't read your code.

WARNING   The plus operator is used in both numeric and string operations. In numeric operations, it adds two values. In string operations, it concatenates two values. This is the single operator that can introduce ambiguity when used with variants. Visual Basic attempts to add the two values by converting them into numbers. If the conversion is successful, the + operator adds the two values; if not, a Type Mismatch runtime error is generated. When adding or concatenating variants, use the operators + and & to help Visual Basic carry out the proper operation.

You can also store dates and times in the Variant type. To assign date or time values to variants, surround the values with the pound sign, as follows:

```
date1=#03/06/1999#
```

All operations that you can perform on date variables (discussed in the section "Date Variables") you can also perform with variants, which hold date and time values.

Converting Variable Types

In some situations you will need to convert variables from one type into another. Table 3.3 shows the Visual Basic functions that perform data type conversions.

TABLE 3.3:   Data Type Conversion Functions of Visual Basic

FUNCTION	Converts its argument to
CBool	Boolean
CByte	Byte
Ccur	Currency
Cdate	Date
CDbl	Double
Cint	Integer
CLng	Long
CSng	Single
CStr	String
Cvar	Variant
CVErr	Error

To convert the variable initialized as:

```
Dim A As Integer
```

to a Double, use the function:

```
B = CDbl(A)
```

Suppose you have declared two integers, as follows:

```
Dim A As Integer, B As Integer
A = 23
B = 7
```

The result of the operation A / B will be a single value. The following statement:

```
Debug.Print A / B
```

displays the value 3.285714. To get the same result with the greatest possible accuracy, use the CDbl() function:

```
Debug.Print CDbl(A / B)
```

which displays the value 3.28571438789368. It's the same value expressed as a Double, and therefore, more accurate.

User-Defined Data Types

In the previous sections, we assumed that applications create variables to store Single values. As a matter of fact, most programs store sets of data of different types. For example, a program for balancing your checkbook must store several pieces of information for each check: the check's number, its amount, the date, and so on. All these pieces of information are necessary to process the checks, and ideally, they should be stored together.

A structure for storing multiple values (of the same or different type) is called a *record*. For example, each check in a checkbook-balancing application is stored in a separate record, as shown in Figure 3.1. When you recall a given check, you need all the information stored in the record.

FIGURE 3.1:

Pictorial representation of a record

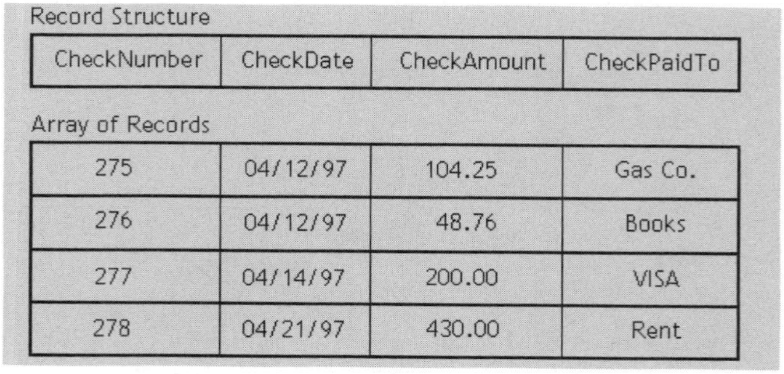

Record Structure			
CheckNumber	CheckDate	CheckAmount	CheckPaidTo

Array of Records			
275	04/12/97	104.25	Gas Co.
276	04/12/97	48.76	Books
277	04/14/97	200.00	VISA
278	04/21/97	430.00	Rent

To define a record in Visual Basic, use the *Type* statement, which has the following syntax:

```
Type varType
    variable1 As varType
    variable2 As varType
    ...
    variablen As varType
End Type
```

After this declaration, you have in essence created a new data type that you can use in your application. You can declare variables of this type and manipulate them as you manipulate all other variables (with a little extra typing). The declaration for the record structure shown in Figure 3.1 is:

```
Type CheckRecord
    CheckNumber As Integer
    CheckDate As Date
    CheckAmount As Single
    CheckPaidTo As String*50
End Type
```

The CheckRecord structure can be used in the same way as regular variables. To define variables of this type, use a statement such as this one:

```
Dim check1 As CheckRecord, check2 As CheckRecord
```

To assign value to these variables, you must separately assign a value to each one of its components (they are called *fields*), which can be accessed by combining the name of the variable and the name of a field separated by a period, as follows:

```
check1.CheckNumber = 275
```

You can think of the record as an object and its fields as properties. Here are the assignment statements for a check:

```
check2.CheckNumber = 275
check2.CheckDate = #02/12/97#
check2.CheckAmount = 104.25
check2.CheckPaidTo = "Gas Co."
```

You can also create *arrays of records* with a statement such as the following (arrays are discussed later in this chapter):

```
Dim Checks(100) As CheckRecord
```

Each element in this array is a CheckRecord record and holds all the fields of a given check. To access the fields of the third element of the array, use the following notation:

```
Checks(2).CheckNumber = 275
Checks(2).CheckDate = #04/12/1997#
Checks(2).CheckAmount = 104.25
Checks(2).CheckPaidTo = "Gas Co."
```

Records are used frequently to read from and write to random access files. For more informationon using files, see the *File Input/Output* tutorial on the CD.

Special Values

Variables have the values your program assigns to them. Before any value is assigned to them, numeric variables are zero, and string variables are zero length (""). There are, however, four special values: Empty, Null, Nothing, and Error.

The Empty Value

If a variant variable has been declared, but has not yet been assigned a value, its value is Empty. The Empty value is different from a zero-length string. To find out if a variable has been initialized with the *IsEmpty()* function, use:

```
If IsEmpty(var) Then MsgBox "Variable has not been initialized"
```

As soon as you assign a value to the variable, it's no longer Empty, and the IsEmpty() function returns False. You can also set a variable to Empty with the following statement:

```
var = Empty
```

The Empty value is used with numeric, string, and date variables. You can use the Empty value to reset variables before calling a procedure.

The Null Value

Null is commonly used in database applications to indicate that a field doesn't contain data or that an object variable hasn't been assigned a value. The Null value is different from the Empty value. A variable of the types we have examined so far is never Null, unless you assign the value Null to it with the following statement:

```
var = Null
```

Uninitialized variables that refer to database fields are Null, not Empty, as in the following:

```
If Not IsNull(varField) Then
    {process variable varField}
End If
```

If your code calls a function to create a new object, it must always check the value of the new object variable with the *IsNull()* statement to verify that the object has been created.

The Nothing Value

The Nothing value is used with objects and indicates that an object variable has not been initialized. If you want to disassociate an object variable from an object, set it to Nothing with the Set statement. The following statements create an object variable that references Excel and then releases it:

```
Set myVar = CreateObject("Excel.Application")
Debug.Print myVar.Name
If Not (myVar Is Nothing) Then
    Set myVar = Nothing
    Debug.Print myVar.Name
End If
```

The first Print statement will display the string "Microsoft Excel" on the Immediate window. The second Print statement will raise a runtime error, because the *myVar* variable does not point to any object (it is disassociated from Excel when it is set to Nothing). Visual Basic doesn't know where to look for the Name property and generates a runtime error. Of course, if Excel is not installed on your computer, the very first line will generate an error message.

The Error Value

This is a peculiar value that allows you to write functions that return Variant types or errors. If the function carries out its operations successfully, the result is returned as usual (it must be a Variant). If an error occurs, then the function can return an Error value. The calling program must examine the function's return value and act accordingly:

```
Result = myFunction(arguments)
If IsError(Result) Then
    {handle error}
Else
    {use result}
End If
```

For more information on using the Error type, see the section "Errors as Function Return Values" later in this chapter.

Examining Variable Types

Besides setting the types of variables and the functions for converting between types, Visual Basic provides two functions that let you examine the type of a variable. They are the *VarType()* and *TypeName()* functions. Both functions accept as argument the name of a variable, and they return a number (the VarType() function) or a string (the TypeName() function) indicating the type of the variable. The VarType() function returns one of the numbers shown in Table 3.4, depending on the type of its argument.

TABLE 3.4: Numbers Returned by VarType()

CONSTANT	VALUE	DESCRIPTION
vbEmpty	0	Empty (uninitialized)
vbNull	1	Null (no valid data)
vbInteger	2	Integer
vbLong	3	Long integer
vbSingle	4	Single-precision floating-point number

Continued on next page

TABLE 3.4 CONTINUED: Numbers Returned by VarType()

CONSTANT	VALUE	DESCRIPTION
vbDouble	5	Double-precision floating-point number
vbCurrency	6	Currency value
vbDate	7	Date value
vbString	8	String
vbObject	9	Object
vbError	10	Error value
vbBoolean	11	Boolean value
vbVariant	12	Variant (used only with arrays of variants)
vbDataObject	13	A data access object
vbDecimal	14	Decimal value
vbByte	17	Byte value
vbArray	8192	Array

Is It a Number or a String?

Another set of Visual Basic functions returns variables' data types, but not the exact type:

- **IsNumeric()**   Returns True if its argument is a number (Integer, Long, Currency, Single, or Double). Use this function to determine whether a variable holds a numeric value before passing it to a procedure that expects a numeric value or process it as a number.

- **IsDate()**   Returns True if its argument is a valid date (or time).

- **IsArray()**   Returns True if its argument is an array.

- **IsNull(), IsEmpty()**   Detects whether a variable has been initialized or is a Null/Empty value.

- **IsMissing()**   Returns True if a certain optional procedure argument is missing (you'll see how the IsMissing() function is used later in this chapter).

- **IsObject()**   Returns True if its argument is an object.

All these functions are described in Appendix A on the CD.

Forcing Variable Declarations

Visual Basic doesn't enforce variable declaration, which is a good thing for the average programmer. When you want to slap together a "quick-and-dirty" program, the last thing you need is someone telling you to decide which variables you're going to use and to declare them before using them.

But most programmers accustomed to the free format of Visual Basic also carry their habits of quick-and-dirty coding to large projects. When writing large applications, you will probably find that variable declaration is a good thing. It will help you write clean code and simplify debugging. Variable declaration eliminates the source of the most common and pesky bugs.

If you have gotten spoiled, you can ask Visual Basic to enforce variable declaration for you. To do so, place the following statement in the declarations section of a Form or Module:

```
Option Explicit
```

This statement tells the compiler to check each variable before using it and to issue an error message if you attempt to use a variable without declaring it. If you omit the Option Explicit statement, Visual Basic creates variables as needed.

The Option Explicit statement must be included in every Module in which you want to enforce variable declaration. If you decide to declare all variables in your projects, you can ask Visual Basic to insert the Option Explicit statement automatically in every Module by checking the Require Variable Declaration checkbox in the Options dialog box (choose Tools ➤ Options), as shown in Figure 3.2.

FIGURE 3.2:

The Options dialog box controls whether all variables in your projects must be declared explicitly.

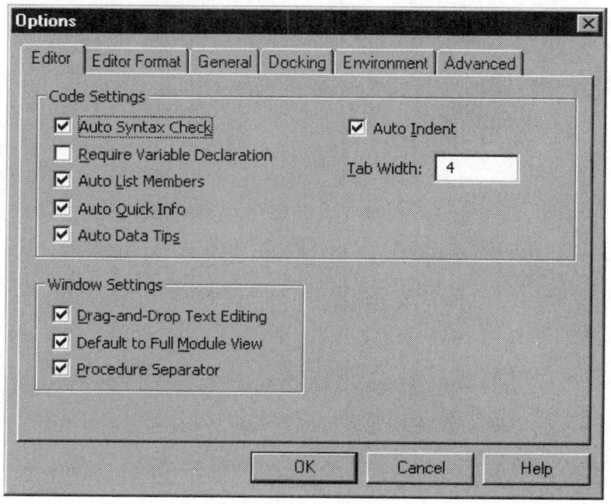

WARNING   If you check the Require Variable Declaration checkbox while you're working on a project, Visual Basic automatically inserts the Option Explicit statement in any new Modules but not in existing Modules. To enforce variable declaration in all Modules, you must add the Option Explicit statement to any existing Modules in your project manual.

Let's examine the side effects of implicit variable declaration in your application. You could use the following statements to convert German marks to U.S. dollars:

```
DM2USD = 1.562
USDollars = amount * DM2USD
```

The first time your code refers to the *DM2USD* variable name, Visual Basic creates a new variable and then uses it as if it was declared.

Suppose the variable *DM2USD* appears in many places in your application. If in one of these places you type *DM2UDS* instead of *DM2USD* and the program doesn't enforce variable declaration, the compiler will create a new variable, assign it the value zero, and then use it. Any amount converted with the *DM2UDS* variable will be zero! If the application enforces variable declaration, the compiler will complain (the *DM2UDS* variable hasn't been declared), and you will catch the error.

Many programmers, though, feel restricted by having to declare variables. Others live by it. Depending on your experiences with Visual Basic, you can decide for yourself. For a small application, you don't have to declare variables. It's too much typing. But for large applications that may take weeks or months to develop, you should consider variable declaration.

A Variable's Scope

In addition to its type, a variable also has a scope. The *scope* of a variable is the section of the application that can see and manipulate the variable. If a variable is declared within a procedure, only the code in the specific procedure has access to that variable. This variable doesn't exist for the rest of the application. When the variable's scope is limited to a procedure it's called *local*.

Suppose you're coding the Click event of a Command button to calculate the sum of all even numbers in the range 0 to 100. One possibility is the following:

```
Private Sub Command1_Click()
    Dim i As Integer
    Dim Sum As Integer
    For i = 0 to 100 Step 2
```

```
      Sum = Sum + i
   Next
   MsgBox "The sum is " & Sum
End Sub
```

The variables *i* and *Sum* are local to the Command1_Click() procedure. If you attempt to set the value of the *Sum* variable from within another procedure, Visual Basic will create another *Sum* variable and use it. But this won't affect the variable *Sum* in the Command1_Click() subroutine.

Sometimes, however, you'll need to use a variable with a broader scope, such as one whose value is available to all procedures within the same Form or Module. These variables are called *Form-wide* (or Module-wide) and can be accessed from within all procedures in a component. In principle, you could declare all variables in the Form's declaration section, but this would lead to problems. Every procedure in the Form would have access to the variable, and you would need to be careful not to change the value of a variable without good reason. Variables that are needed by a single procedure (such as loop counters, for example), should be declared in the procedure that uses them, not as Form variables.

Finally, in some situations the entire application must access a certain variable. In this case, the variable must be declared as *Public*. Public variables have a global scope (they are visible from any part of the application). To declare a public variable, use the Public statement in place of the Dim statement. Moreover, public variables may not appear inside procedures. They must be declared as Form variables or in a Module.

The Lifetime of a Variable

In addition to type and scope, variables have a *lifetime*, which is the period for which they retain their value. Variables declared as Public exist for the lifetime of the application. Local variables, declared within procedures with the Dim or Private statement, live as long as the procedure. When the procedure finishes, the local variables cease to exist and the allocated memory is returned to the system. Of course, the same procedure can be called again. In this case, the local variables are recreated and initialized again.

You also can force a local variable to preserve its value between procedure calls with the *Static* keyword. Suppose the user of your application can enter numeric values at any time. One of the tasks performed by the application is to track the average of the numeric values. Instead of adding all the values each time the user adds a new value and dividing by the count, you can keep a running total with the function *RunningAvg()*, which is shown next.

```
Function RunningAvg(newValue)
   CurrentTotal = CurrentTotal + newValue
   TotalItems = TotalItems + 1
   RunningAvg = CurrentTotal / TotalItems
End Function
```

You must declare the variables *CurrentTotal* and *TotalItems* outside the function so that their values are preserved between calls. Alternatively, you can declare them in the function with the *Static* keyword:

```
Function RunningAvg(newValue As Double) As Double
Static CurrentTotal As Double
Static TotalItems As Integer

   CurrentTotal = CurrentTotal + newValue
   TotalItems = TotalItems + 1
   RunningAvg = CurrentTotal / TotalItems

End Function
```

The advantage of using static variables is that they help you minimize the number of total variables in the application. All you need is the running average, which the RunningAvg() function provides without making its variables visible to the rest of the application. Therefore, you don't risk changing the variables' values from within other procedures.

TIP

You can declare all the variables in a procedure as static by prefixing the procedure definition with the keyword *Static*. The previous function could have been declared as

```
Static Function RunningAvg(newValue As Double) As Double
```

and the local variables could be declared with the Dim statement as usual. The keyword *Static* may appear in front of every subroutine or function, including event handlers.

Variables declared in a Form outside any procedure take effect when the Form is loaded and cease to exist when the Form is unloaded. If the Form is loaded again, its variables are initialized, as if it's being loaded for the first time.

Constants

Some variables don't change value during the execution of a program. These are *constants* that appear many times in your code. For instance, if your program does math calculations, the value of pi (3.14159…) may appear many times in your code. These values are best represented by constants. Instead of typing the value 3.14159 over and over again, you can define a constant, name it pi, and use the name of the constant in your code. The following statement:

```
Area = 2 * pi * Radius
```

is much easier to understand than the equivalent:

```
Area = 2 * 3.14159 * Radius
```

You could declare pi as a variable, but constants are preferred for two reasons:

- **Constants don't change value.** This is a safety feature. Once a constant has been declared, you can't change its value in subsequent statements, therefore, you can be sure that the value specified in the constant's declaration will take effect in the entire program.

- **Constants are processed faster than variables.** When the program is running, the values of constants don't have to be looked up. The compiler substitutes constant names with their values, and the program executes faster.

The manner in which you declare constants is similar to the manner in which you declare variables, except that in addition to supplying the constant's name you must also supply a value, as follows:

```
Const constantname [As type] = value
```

The *As type* part of the declaration is optional. If you omit it, the constant's type is determined by the value you assign to it. Constants also have a scope and can be Public or Private. The constant pi, for instance, is usually declared in a Module as Public so that every procedure can access it:

```
Public Const pi As Double = 3.14159265358979
```

The *constantname* variable is a valid constant name that follows the same rules as variable names. The constant's value is a literal value or a simple expression composed of numeric or string constants and operators. You can't use functions in declaring variables. One way to define the value of pi is as follows:

```
pi = 4 * Atn(1)
```

However, you can't use this assignment in the constant declaration. You must supply the actual value.

Constants can be strings too, such as:

```
Const ExpDate = #31/12/1997#
```

or:

```
Const ValidKey = "A567dfe"
```

Visual Basic uses constants extensively to define the various arguments of its methods and the settings of the various control properties. The value of a Check-Box control, for instance, can be 0 (unchecked), 1 (checked), or 2 (grayed). Instead of using statements like:

```
Check1.Value = 0
Check2.Value = 2
```

use the built-in constants *vbUnchecked* and *vbGrayed*:

```
Check1.Value = vbUnchecked
Check2.Value = vbGrayed
```

Visual Basic's constants are prefixed with vb, indicating that they are Visual Basic constants. The constants *vbUnchecked* and *vbGrayed* are built into the language, and you don't need to declare them. Their symbolic names make the code much easier to read and maintain. Avoid the *vb* prefix when declaring your own constants. Other components of the language use different prefixes. For example, the Database Access Objects use constants with the *db* prefix.

Constant declarations may include other constants. In math calculations, the value pi is as common as the value 2 * pi. You can declare these two values as constant:

```
Public Const pi As Double = 3.14159265358979
Public Const pi2 As Double = 2 * pi
```

You can also create circular constant definitions, such as the following:

```
Const constant1 = constant2 * 2
Const constant2 = constant1 / 2
```

This circular definition doesn't lead anywhere (none of the constants has a value) and should be avoided.

It's very unlikely that these two declarations will appear in the same Module, but you may forget how you defined *constant1* in one of the Modules and attempt to define *constant2* in terms of *constant1* in another Module. If this happens, Visual Basic generates a runtime error. If you declare all your constants in a single Module, they're easier to maintain and change.

TIP

When defining constants in terms of other constants, especially if they reside in different Modules, be sure to avoid circular definitions. Try to place all your constant declarations in the same Module. If you have Modules you use with several applications, try to include the Module's name in the constant names to avoid conflicts and duplicate definitions.

Arrays

A standard structure for storing data in any programming language is an array. Whereas individual variables can hold single entities, such as a number, date, or string, *arrays* can hold sets of related data. An array has a name, as does a variable, and the values stored in it can be accessed by an index.

For example, you could use the variable *Salary* to store a salary:

```
Salary = 34000
```

But what if you wanted to store the salaries of 16 employees? You could either declare 16 variables: *Salary1*, *Salary2*, up to *Salary16*, or you could declare an array with 16 elements.

Declaring Arrays

Unlike simple variables, arrays must be declared with the Dim statement followed by the name of the array and the maximum number of elements it can hold in parentheses, for example:

```
Dim Salary(15)
```

Using the salary example, *Salary* is the name of an array that holds 16 values (the salaries of the 16 employees). Salary(0) is the first person's salary, Salary(1) the second person's salary, and so on. All you have to do is remember who corresponds to each salary, but even this data can be handled by an array. To do this, you'd declare another array of 16 elements as follows:

```
Dim Names(15)
```

and then assign values to the elements of both arrays:

```
Names(0) = "Joe Doe"
Salary(0) = 34000
Names(1) = "Dave York"
Salary(1) = 62000
...
Names(15) = "Peter Smack"
Salary(15) = 10300
```

This structure is more compact and more convenient than having to hardcode the names of employees and their salaries in variables.

Optionally, you could specify the type of the array's elements with the *As* keyword:

```
Dim Names(15) As String
Dim Salary(15) As Long
```

All elements in an array have the same data type. Of course, when the data type is Variant, the individual elements can contain different kinds of data (objects, strings, numbers, and so on).

Specifying Limits

By default, the first element of an array has index 0. The number that appears in parentheses in the Dim statement is the array's upper limit (or upper bound) and is one less than the array's total capacity. In the previous example, the two arrays contained 16 elements each.

The array's first element doesn't need to be 0. You can specify the lower limit (or lower bound) explicitly in the Dim statement:

```
Dim Names(1 To 16) As String
Dim Salary(1 To 16) As Long
```

The lower bound can have any other value, provided it's smaller than the upper bound. The following declarations are valid although most arrays start at 0 or 1:

```
Dim Array1(10 To 20) As Double
Dim Array2(100 To 900) As Long
```

TIP

If you feel uncomfortable with zero-based arrays, you can declare your arrays with one more element than required. Declare an array with 20 elements as `Dim MyArray(20)` and ignore the first element. Even better, you can include the statement `Option Base 1` in your Form or Module to force array indexing to start at 1. The `Option Base 1` statement is similar to the `Option Explicit` statement and affects all the arrays in the current Form or Module.

Multidimensional Arrays

One-dimensional arrays, such as those presented so far, are good for storing long sequences of one-dimensional data (such as names, and temperatures). But how would you store a list of cities and their average temperatures in an array? Or names and scores, years and profits, or data with more than two dimensions, such as products, prices, and units in stock? In some situations you will want to store sequences of multidimensional data. You can use two one-dimensional arrays or one two-dimensional array. Figure 3.3 shows two one-dimensional arrays, one of them with city names, the other with temperatures. The name of the third city would be City(2) and its temperature would be Temperature(2).

FIGURE 3.3:

A two-dimensional array and the two equivalent one-dimensional arrays

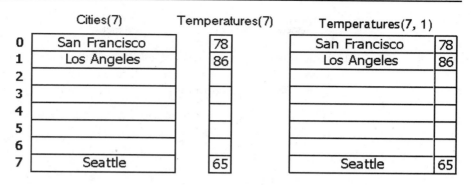

Two one-dimensional arrays   A two-dimensional array

You can store the same data more conveniently in a two-dimensional array. A two-dimensional array has two indices. The first identifies the row (the order of the city in the array), and the second identifies the column (city or temperature). To access the name and temperature of the third city in the two-dimensional array, use the following indices:

```
Temperatures(2, 0)     is the third city name
Temperatures(2, 1)     is the third city's average temperature
```

The benefit of using multidimensional arrays is that they're conceptually easier to manage. Suppose you're writing a game and you want to track the positions of certain pieces on a board. Each square on the board is identified by two numbers, its horizontal and vertical coordinates. The obvious structure for tracking the board's squares is a two-dimensional array, in which the first index corresponds to the row number and the second index corresponds to the column number. The array could be declared as follows:

```
Dim Board(10, 10) As Integer
```

When a piece is moved from the square on the first row and first column to the square on the third row and fifth column, you assign the value 0 to the element that corresponds to the initial position:

```
Board(1, 1) = 0
```

and you assign 1 to the square to which it was moved, to indicate the new state of the board:

```
Board(3, 5) = 1
```

To find out if a piece is on the upper-left square, you'd use the following statement:

```
If Board(1, 1) = 1 Then
    {piece found}
```

```
Else
    {empty square}
End If
```

Notice that this array is not zero-based. It just makes sense to waste the first element to code the application in a more familiar way. Board games don't have zero-numbered rows or columns.

This notation can be extended to more than two dimensions. The following statement creates an array with 1000 elements ($10 \times 10 \times 10$):

```
Dim Matrix(9, 9, 9)
```

You can think of a three-dimensional array as a cube made up of overlaid two-dimensional arrays, such as the one shown in Figure 3.4.

FIGURE 3.4:

Pictorial representations of one-, two-, and three-dimensional arrays

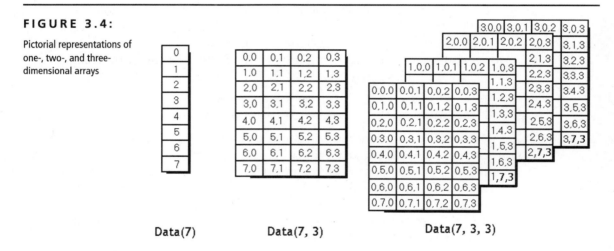

Data(7)   Data(7, 3)   Data(7, 3, 3)

Dynamic Arrays

Sometimes you may not know how large to make an array. Instead of making it large enough to hold the maximum number of data (which means that most of the array may be empty), you can declare a *dynamic array*. The size of a dynamic array can vary during the course of the program. Or, you might need an array until the user has entered a bunch of data and the application has processed it and displayed the results. Why keep all the data in memory when it is no longer needed? With a dynamic array, you can discard the data and return the resources it occupied to the system.

To create a dynamic array, declare it as usual with the Dim statement (or Public or Private), but don't specify its dimensions:

```
Dim DynArray()
```

Later in the program, when you know how many elements you want to store in the array, use the *ReDim* statement to redimension the array, this time with its actual size. In the following example, *UserCount* is a user-entered value:

```
ReDim DynArray(UserCount)
```

The ReDim statement can appear only in a procedure. Unlike the Dim statement, ReDim is executable—it forces the application to carry out an action at runtime. Dim statements aren't executable, and they can appear outside procedures.

A dynamic array also can be redimensioned to multiple dimensions. Declare it with the Dim statement outside any procedure as follows:

```
Dim Matrix() As Double
```

and then use the ReDim statement in a procedure to declare a three-dimensional array:

```
ReDim Matrix(9, 9, 9)
```

Note that the ReDim statement can't change the type of the array. Moreover, subsequent ReDim statements can change the bounds of the array *Matrix*, but not the number of its dimensions. For example, you can't use the statement ReDim Matrix(99, 99) later in your code. Once an array has been redimensioned the first time, its number of dimensions can't change. In the previous example, the *Matrix* array would remain three-dimensional.

NOTE

The ReDim statement can by issued only from within a procedure, and it can't appear in the declarations section of a Form or a Module. In addition, the array to be redimensioned must be visible from within the procedure that calls the ReDim statement.

The *Preserve* Keyword

Each time you execute the ReDim statement, all the values currently stored in the array are lost. Visual Basic resets the values of the elements as if they were just declared. (It resets Variants to Empty values, Numeric data types to zero, and Strings to empty strings.)

In most situations, when you resize an array, you no longer care about the data in it. You can, however, change the size of the array without losing its data. The ReDim statement recognizes the *Preserve* keyword, which forces it to resize the array without discarding the existing data. For example, you can enlarge an array by one element without losing the values of the existing elements by using the *UBound()* function as follows:

```
ReDim Preserve DynamicArray(UBound(DynArray) + 1)
```

Continued on next page

If the array *DynamicArray()* held 12 elements, this statement would add one element to the array *DynamicArray(12)*. The values of the elements with indices 0 through 11 wouldn't change. The *Ubound()* function returns the largest available index (the number of elements) in a one-dimensional array. Similarly, the *Lbound()* function returns the smallest index. If an array was declared with the statement:

```
Dim Grades(50)
```

then the functions LBound(Grades) and UBound(Grades) would return the values 0 (or 1, if the array was 1-based) and 49 (or 50), respectively. For more information on the functions LBound() and UBound(), see Appendix A on the CD.

Arrays of Arrays

One of the possibilities introduced to the Visual Basic language with the Variant data type is that of creating complex structures, such as arrays of arrays. If an array is declared as Variant, you can assign other types to its elements, including arrays. Suppose you have declared and populated two arrays, one with integers and another with strings. You can then declare a Variant array with two elements and populate it with the two arrays as follows:

```
Dim IntArray(10) As Integer
Dim StrArray(99) As String
Dim BigArray(2) As Variant

{populate array IntArray}
{Populate array StrArray}

BigArray(0) = IntArray()
BigArray(1) = StrArray()
```

Notice the empty parentheses after the array names. This notation signifies the entire array and is used in passing arrays to Dynamic Link Libraries (DLLs), which are discussed further in Chapter 13, *The Windows API*. The empty parentheses are equivalent to *IntArray(0)* and *StrArray(0)*. Had you supplied an index, part of the array would have been assigned to the corresponding element of *BigArray*. For example, the following statement assigns to the first element of *BigArray* the last nine elements (2 through 10) of the array *IntArray*:

```
BigArray(0) = IntArray(2)
```

BigArray was declared as a one-dimensional array, but because each of its elements is an array, you must use two indices to access it. To access the third element of *IntArray* in *BigArray*, use the indices 0 and 2. Likewise, the tenth element of the *StrArray* in *BigArray* is *BigArray(1) (9)*. The notation is quite unusual, but the indices of the *BigArray* must be entered in seperate parentheses.

Collections

Arrays are convenient for storing related data, but accessing individual elements can be a problem. To print the temperature in Atlanta, for instance, you would have to know the index that corresponds to Atlanta. If you didn't, you would have to scan each element in the array until you found Atlanta. Ideally, arrays should be accessed by their contents. For example, you should be able to look up the temperature in Atlanta with a statement such as:

```
Temperatures("Atlanta")
```

In the past, programmers had to resort to creative programming techniques to manipulate array data. Visual Basic provides an alternative: collections. Similar to an array, a *collection* stores related items, in this case, objects that have properties and methods. The advantage of a collection over an array is that the collection lets you access its items via a key. If a city name is the key in the Temperatures() array, you can recall the temperature in Atlanta instantly by providing the following key:

```
MsgBox "The temperature in Atlanta is " & Temperatures.Item("Atlanta")
```

The *Item* argument is a method of the collection object that returns a collection item based on its key or index. Or, if you know the index of Atlanta's entry in the collection, you can use a statement like:

```
MsgBox "The temperature in Atlanta is " & Temperatures.Item(6)
```

Of course, if you're going to access a collection's item with its index, there's no advantage to using collections over arrays.

To use a collection, you must first declare a collection variable, as follows:

```
Dim Temperatures As New Collection
```

The keyword *New* tells Visual Basic to create a new collection and name it *Temperatures*.

The collection object provides three methods and one property:

- **Add method**   Adds items to the collection
- **Remove method**   Deletes an item from the collection by index or key
- **Item method**   Returns an item by index or by key
- **Count property**   Returns the number of items in the collection

Let's look at each of these members in detail

Adding to a Collection

The *Add* method adds new items to the collection and it has the following syntax:

```
collection. Add value, key, before, after
```

To add a new element to a collection, assign its value to the *item* argument and its key to the *key* argument. To place the new item in a specific location in the array, specify one of the arguments *before* or *after* (but not both). To insert the new item before a specific element whose key (or index) you will specify, use the *before* argument. To place the new item after an item, specify this item's key or index with the *after* argument.

For example, to add the temperature for the city of San Francisco to the Temperatures collection, use the following statement:

```
Temperatures.Add 78, "San Francisco"
```

The number 78 is the value to be stored (temperature), and the string "San Francisco" is the new item's key. To insert this temperature immediately after the temperature of Santa Barbara, use the following statement:

```
Temperatures.Add 78, "San Francisco", , "Santa Barbara"
```

The extra comma denotes the lack of the *before* argument. The Add method supports named arguments, so the previous statement could also be written as:

```
Temperatures.Add 78, "San Francisco", after:= "Santa Barbara"
```

Collections aren't sorted, nor do they have a method to automatically sort their items. To maintain an ordered collection of objects, use the *before* and *after* arguments. In most practical situations, however, you won't care about sorting a collection's items. You sort arrays to simplify access to their elements; you don't have to do anything special to access the elements of collections.

Removing an Item from a Collection

The *Remove* method removes an item from a collection. The *index* argument can be either the position of the item you want to delete or the item's key. To remove the city of Atlanta from your collection of temperatures, use the following statement:

```
Temperatures.Remove "Atlanta"
```

Or, if you know the city's order in the collection, specify the index in place of the key:

```
Temperatures.Remove 6
```

Returning Items in a Collection

The *Item* method returns the value of an item in the collection. As with the Remove method, the index can be either the item's position in the collection or its key. To recall the temperature in Atlanta, use one of the following statements:

```
T1 = Temperatures.Item("Atlanta")
T1 = Temperatures.Item(3)
```

The Item method is the default method for a collection object, so you can omit it when you access an item in a collection. The previous example could also be written as:

```
T1 = Temperatures("Atlanta")
```

TIP   Collections maintain their indices automatically as elements are added and deleted. The index of a given element, therefore, changes during the course of a program and you shouldn't save an item's index value and expect to use it to retrieve the same element later in your program. Use keys for this purpose.

Counting a Collection

The *Count* property returns the number of items in the collection. To find out how many cities have been entered so far in the Temperatures collection, use the following statement:

```
Temperatures.Count
```

You can also use the Count property to scan all the elements of the collection, with a For...Next loop such as the following:

```
For city = 1 To Temperatures.Count
{process elements}
Next city
```

Actually, a better way to scan the elements of a collection is the ForEach...Next structure explained next.

Processing a Collection's Items

To scan all the items in a Collection, Visual Basic provides the For Each...Next structure. Its syntax is as follows:

```
For Each item in Collection
    {process item}
Next
```

The *item* variable is the loop counter, but you don't have to initialize it or declare its type. The For Each statement scans all the items in the collection automatically and at each iteration the *item* variable assumes the current item's value.

Using Collections

Let's implement a collection for storing city names and temperatures. Start a new project and add the following declaration in the Form:

```
Dim Temperatures As New Collection
```

This statement creates a new collection and names it Temperatures. Then enter the following code in the Form's Load event:

```
Private Sub Form_Load()
    Temperatures.Add 76, "Atlanta"
    Temperatures.Add 85, "Los Angeles"
    Temperatures.Add 97, "Las Vegas"
    Temperatures.Add 66, "Seattle"
End Sub
```

Of course, you can add as many lines as you wish, read the data from a disk file, or prompt the user to enter city names and temperatures at runtime. New items can be added to the collection at any time.

Next, create a Command button, set its Caption property to "Show City Temperature", and enter the following code in its Click subroutine:

```
Private Sub Command1_Click()
On Error GoTo NoItem
    city = InputBox("What City?")
    temp = Temperatures.Item(city)
    MsgBox temp
    Exit Sub
NoItem:
    MsgBox "This city was not found in our catalog"
End Sub
```

This subroutine prompts users to enter the name of the city whose temperature they want to find. The program then recalls the value of the collection's item, whose key is the city name supplied by the user. If the supplied key doesn't exist, a runtime error is generated, which is why we use the On Error statement. If the user enters a nonexistent city name, a runtime error is generated; Visual Basic intercepts it and executes the statements following the label NoItem. If the key exists in the array, then the temperature of the corresponding city is displayed in a message box.

Finally, add another Command button to the Form, set its caption to Show Average Temperature, and enter the following code behind its Click event.

```
Private Sub Command2_Click()
    For Each city In Temperatures
        total = total + city
        Debug.Print city
    Next
    avgTemperature = total / Temperatures.Count
    MsgBox avgTemperature
End Sub
```

The Print statement displays each element in the Immediate window. The name of the loop variable is *city*, which refers to the value of the current item, not the city name. In this case, it's the temperature in the current city. The counter of the For Each loop in the previous example could be named city, temp, or Boo.

> **NOTE**   The key values in a collection object aren't stored as array elements in the collection. They are only used for accessing the items of the collection, just as array indices are used for accessing an array's elements.

Procedures

The one thing you should have learned about programming in Visual Basic so far is that the *application* is made up of small, self-contained segments. Similarly, the code you write won't be a monolithic listing. It will be made up of small segments called *procedures* and you will work on one procedure at a time.

For example, when you write code for a control's Click event, you will concentrate on the event at hand, namely how the program should react to the Click event. What happens when the control is double-clicked is something you will worry about later, in the DoubleClick subroutine. This "divide and conquer" approach isn't unique to programming events. It permeates the Visual Basic language and even the longest applications are written by breaking them into small, well-defined tasks. Each task is performed by a separate procedure that is written and tested separately from the others.

Procedures are useful for implementing repeated tasks, such as frequently used calculations. Suppose you're writing an application that, at some point, must convert inches to centimeters or calculate the smaller of two numbers. You can always do the calculations inline and repeat them in your code wherever they are needed, or you can write a procedure that performs the calculations and call this procedure. The benefit of the second approach is that code is cleaner and easier to understand and maintain. If you discover a more efficient way to implement the task, you need change it in only one place. If the same code is repeated in several places throughout the application, you will have to change every instance.

The two types of procedures are subroutines and functions—the building blocks of your applications.

Subroutines

A *subroutine* is a block of statements that carries out a well-defined task. The block of statements is placed with a pair of *Sub/End Sub* statements and can be invoked by name. The following subroutine displays the current date in a Message Box and can be called by its name, ShowDate:

```
Sub ShowDate()
    MsgBox Date()
End Sub
```

A subroutine normally performs a more complicated task than this one, nevertheless, it's a block of code isolated from the rest of the application. All the event procedures in Visual Basic, for example, are coded as subroutines. The actions that must be performed each time a Command button is clicked are coded in the button's Click procedure. This subroutine is called each time the button is clicked.

The statements in a subroutine are executed, and when the End Sub statement is reached, control returns to the calling program. It's possible to exit a Subroutine prematurely with the Exit statement. For example, some condition may stop the subroutine from successfully completing its task.

Subroutines and Event Handlers

In the first couple of chapters, you learned to develop applications by placing code in event handlers. An *event handler* is a short segment of code that is executed each time an external (or internal to your application) condition triggers the event. When the user clicks a control, the control's Click event handler executes. This handler is nothing more than a subroutine, which performs all the actions you want to perform when the control is clicked. It is separate from the rest of the code and doesn't have to know what would happen if another control was clicked or if the same control was double-clicked. It's a self contained piece of code that's executed when needed.

Every application contains a number of event handlers, which contain code to react to user actions. Event handlers need not return any results and they're implemented as subroutines. For example, to react to the click of the mouse on the Command1 button, your application must provide the Command1_Click() subroutine. The code in this subroutine is executed independently of any other event handler and it doesn't return a result because there is no main program to accept it. The code of a Visual Basic application consists of event handlers, which may call other subroutines and functions, but they aren't called by a main program. They are automatically activated by Visual Basic in response to external events.

If you need a procedure to perform certain actions, such as change the background color of a control or display the fields of a record on the Form, you can implement it either as a function or subroutine. The choice of the procedure type isn't going to affect the code. The same statements can be used with either type of procedure. However, if your procedure doesn't return a value, then it should be implemented as a subroutine.

Functions

A *function* is similar to a subroutine, but a function returns a result. Subroutines perform a task and don't report anything to the calling program; functions commonly carry out calculations and report the result. The statements that make up a function are placed in a pair of *Function/End Function* statements. Moreover, because a function reports a result, it must have a type, for example:

```
Function NextDay() As Date
    NextDay = Date() + 1
End Function
```

The NextDay() function returns tomorrow's date by adding one day to the current date. Because it must report the result to the calling program, the NextDay() function has a type, as do variables, and the result is assigned to its name (something you can't do with subroutines).

The Abs() Function

This function returns the absolute value of its argument. If the argument is positive, it returns it as is; if it's negative, it inverts its sign. The Abs() function could be implemented as follows:

```
Function Abs(X As Double) As Double
    If X>=0 Then
        Abs = X
    Else
        Abs = -X
    End If
End Function
```

This is a trivial procedure, yet it's built into Visual Basic because it's used frequently in math and science calculations. Developers can call a single function rather than supplying their own Abs() functions. Visual Basic and all other programming languages provide a number of built-in functions for those needed most frequently by developers. But each developer has special needs and you can't expect to find all the procedures you may ever need in a programming language. Sooner or later, you will have to supply your own.

Calling Procedures

When you call a procedure, you must supply values for all the arguments specified in the procedure's definition and in the same order. To call a procedure, you use the *Call* statement and supply its name and arguments in parentheses as follows:

```
Call PrintLotto(Num1, Num2, Num3, Num4, Num5, Num6)
```

The values of the arguments must match their declared type. If a procedure expects an Integer value, you shouldn't supply a Double value.

Subroutines

You can omit the Call statement and call the subroutine by name. The arguments are supplied without the parentheses, as follows:

```
PrintLotto Num1, Num2, Num3, Num4, Num5, Num6
```

The number of arguments you supply to the subroutine and their types must match those in the procedure declaration. If the Subroutine expects six Integer values, but the variables you pass to it are long or floating-point numbers, a "Type Mismatch" runtime error will be generated. You'd expect Visual Basic to figure out what you intend to do and adjust the arguments accordingly, but it won't. Fortunately, you can instruct it to adjust the argument values so that they match with the arguments in the declaration of the subroutine, or function, by enclosing them in parentheses (see the sidebar "Automatic Argument Type Matching," later in this chapter).

Functions

Functions are called by name, and a list of arguments follows the name in parentheses as shown:

```
Degrees = Fahrenheit(Temperature)
```

In this example, the Fahrenheit() function converts the *Temperature* argument (which presumably is the temperature in degrees Celsius) to degrees Fahrenheit, and the result is assigned to the *Degrees* variable.

Functions can be called from within expressions as the following shows:

```
MsgBox "40 degrees Celsius are " & Fahrenheit(40) & _
" degrees Fahrenheit"
```

Suppose the function CountWords() counts the number of words and the function CountChars() counts the number of characters in a string. The average length of a word could be calculated as follows:

```
LongString = Text1.Text
AvgLen = CountChars(LongString) / CountWords(LongString)
```

The first statement gets the text of a TextBox control and assigns it to a variable, which is then used as an argument to the two functions. When the second statement executes, Visual Basic first calls the functions CountChars() and Count-Words() with the specified arguments and then divides the results they return.

You can call functions in the same way that you call subroutines, with the Call statement, but the result won't be stored anywhere. For example, the function Convert() may convert the text in a textbox to uppercase and return the number of characters it converts. Normally, you'd call this function as follows:

```
nChars = Convert()
```

If you don't care about the return value, you would call the Convert() function with the Call statement:

```
Call Convert()
```

Arguments

Subroutines and functions aren't entirely isolated from the rest of the application. Most procedures accept arguments from the calling program. Recall that an argument is a value you pass to the procedure and on which the procedure usually acts. This is how subroutines and functions communicate with the rest of the application.

In the previous examples, the subroutines that handled the various events either didn't provide arguments or had one or more. The Click subroutine, for instance, didn't have arguments because all that was needed was the name of the subroutine. It needed code to handle the user clicking a control, but it didn't need any additional information.

Unlike the argument-less Click event, the *KeyPress* subroutine provides an *integer* argument, which is the ASCII code of the character pressed. The definition of the KeyPress subroutine is as follows:

```
Private Sub Command1_KeyPress(KeyAscii As Integer)

End Sub
```

You specify arguments in the procedure declaration, but without the Dim statement. *KeyAscii* is an argument that conveys information about the key pressed. The code in the KeyPress subroutine will most likely process the keystroke, and it needs this information.

Functions also accept arguments, and in many cases, more than one. The function Min(), for instance, accepts two numbers and returns the smaller one:

```
Function Min(a As Variant, b As Variant) As Variant
   Min = IIf(a < b, a, b)
End Function
```

IIf() is a built-in function that evaluates the first argument, which is a logical expression. If the expression is True, the IIf() function returns the second argument. If the expression is False, the function returns the third argument. Because the arguments of the Min() function were declared As Variants, the function works with all types of data, not just Numeric data types. Test the Min() function with strings or date and time values to see how it behaves.

Argument-Passing Mechanisms

One of the most important procedural issues is the mechanism used to pass arguments. The examples so far have used the default mechanism: passing arguments by reference. The other mechanism is passing by value. Although most programmers use the default mechanism, it's important to know the difference between the two mechanisms and when to use each one.

Passing Arguments by Reference

Passing arguments by reference gives the procedure access to the actual variable. The calling procedure passes the address of the variable in memory so that the procedure can change its value permanently. In earlier versions of BASIC and Visual Basic, this was the only argument-passing mechanism.

Start a new Visual Basic project and enter the following function definition in the Form's Code window:

```
Function Add(num1 As Integer, num2 As Integer) As Integer
    Add = num1 + num2
    num1 = 0
    num2 = 0
End Function
```

This simple function adds two numbers and then sets them to zero.

Next, place a Command button on the Form and enter the following code in the button's Click event:

```
Dim A As Integer, B As Integer
A = 10
B = 2

Sum = Add(A, B)
Debug.Print A
Debug.Print B
Debug.Print Sum
```

This code displays the following results in the Immediate window:

```
0
0
12
```

The changes made to the function's arguments take effect even after the function has ended. The values of the variables *A* and *B* have changed permanently.

Now change the definition of the function by inserting the keyword *ByVal* before the names of the arguments as follows:

```
Function Add(ByVal num1 As Integer, ByVal num2 As Integer) As Integer
```

With this change, Visual Basic passes copies of the arguments to the function. The rest of the program remains the same. Run the application, click the Command button, and the following values display in the Immediate window:

```
10
2
12
```

The function has changed the values of the arguments, but these changes remain in effect only in the function. The variables *A* and *B* in the Command1_Click() subroutine haven't been affected.

When passing an argument by reference, the argument type must match the declared type. In other words, you can't pass an Integer value if the procedure expects a Double value, even if they have the same value. For example, if the function Degrees() converts temperature values from Celsius to Fahrenheit, the definition of the function is as follows:

```
Function Degrees(Celsius as Single) As Single
    Degrees = (9 / 5) * Celsius + 32
End Function
```

This function is usually called as:

```
CTemp = 37
MsgBox Degrees(CTemp)
```

If *CTemp* has been declared as an integer, Visual Basic generates a runtime error and displays the following message:

```
ByRef argument type mismatch
```

This error message tells you that the argument you're passing to the function doesn't match the function declaration. The function expects a Single value and is passed an Integer.

You can get around this problem in two ways. The first is to convert the Integer value to a Single value and then pass it to the function:

```
MsgBox Degrees(CSng(CTemp))
```

You can also change the variable's declaration to a single variable.

The second method is to let Visual Basic make the conversion by enclosing the argument in parentheses:

```
MsgBox Degrees((CTemp))
```

Visual Basic converts the value to the type that matches the function's declaration.

Automatic Argument Type Matching

This technique is more flexible than the example indicates. Suppose you're prompting the user for the Celsius degrees with the InputBox() function. The InputBox() function returns a String that you must convert to a numeric value before passing it to the Degrees() function. You can skip the conversion by enclosing the string argument in parentheses:

```
CTemp = InputBox("Enter temperature in degrees Celsius")
MsgBox Degrees((CTemp))
```

Visual Basic performs the necessary conversion, and the Degrees() function accepts a numeric argument. You can also combine the two statements into one:

```
MsgBox Degrees((InputBox("Enter temperature in degrees Celsius")))
```

In general, you pass arguments by reference only if the procedure has reason to change its value. If the values of the arguments are required later in the program, you run the risk of changing their values in the procedure. For example, if the Degrees() function changes the value of the *CTemp* argument, the variable won't have the same value before and after the call of the Degrees() function.

Passing Arguments by Value

When you pass an argument by value, the procedure sees only a copy of the argument. Even if the procedure changes it, the changes aren't permanent. The benefit of passing arguments by value is that the argument values are isolated from the procedure, and only the program in which they are declared can change their values.

Passing arguments by value requires a bit of extra typing, since this isn't the default argument-passing mechanism. For example, to declare that the Degrees()

function's arguments are passed by value, use the *ByVal* keyword in the argument's declaration as follows:

```
Function Degrees(ByVal Celsius as Single) As Single

    Degrees = (9 / 5) * Celsius + 32

End Function
```

To see what the *ByVal* keyword does, add a line that changes the value of the argument in the function:

```
Function Degrees(ByVal Celsius as Single) As Single

    Degrees = (9 / 5) * Celsius + 32
    Celsius = 0

End Function
```

Now call the function as follows:

```
CTemp = InputBox("Enter temperature in degrees Celsius")
MsgBox CTemp & " degrees Celsius are " & Degrees((CTemp)) & " degrees
Fahrenheit"
```

If the value entered in the InputBox is 32, the following message is displayed:

```
32 degrees Celsius are 89.6 degrees Fahrenheit
```

Remove the *ByVal* keyword from the function's definition and call the function as follows:

```
Celsius = 32.0
FTemp = Degrees(Celsius)
MsgBox Celsius & " degrees Celsius are " & FTemp & " degrees Fahren-
heit"
```

This time the program displays the following message:

```
0 degrees Celsius are 89.6 degrees Fahrenheit.
```

When the *Celsius* argument was passed to the Degrees() function, its value was 32. But the function changed its value, and upon return it was 0. Because the argument was passed by reference, any changes made by the procedure affected the variable permanently.

NOTE   When you pass arguments to a procedure by reference, you're actually passing the variable itself. Any changes made to the argument by the procedure will be permanent. When you pass arguments by value, the procedure gets a copy of the variable, which is discarded when the procedure ends. Any changes made to the argument by the procedure won't affect the variable of the calling program.

Using Optional Arguments

Normally, when you want to call a procedure that expects three arguments, you must pass three arguments to the procedure in the proper order. Suppose you write a function to evaluate math expressions, such as 3*cos(3.14159) + log(10). The function Evaluate() should expect a single argument, the expression to be evaluated, and return a Double value:

```
Function Evaluate(expression As String) As Double
```

The *expression* variable is the math formula to be evaluated.

What if you want to evaluate functions with an independent variable *X*, such as 3*cos(*X*) + log(10)? You'd have to specify not only the expression, but also the value of *X*. A function that evaluates all types of expressions should be able to accept one or two arguments.

The alternative of passing a dummy second argument when one is not needed will also work, but it will make your code more difficult to understand. Visual Basic lets you specify optional arguments with the *Optional* keyword preceding each optional argument. The definition of the *Evaluate()* function should be:

```
Function Evaluate(expression As String, Optional XValue As Double) As
Double
```

Once the first optional argument is specified, all following arguments in the definition must also be optional and declared with the *Optional* keyword. The Evaluate() function can now be called with one or two arguments:

```
Debug.Print Evaluate(397 / 3 - 102)
```

or

```
Debug.Print Evaluate(397 / sin(3) - 102)
```

Now, how does the procedure know which arguments it received and which it didn't? To find out whether an argument was supplied, use the *IsMissing()* function in the procedure. If an optional argument is not provided, the argument is actually assigned as a variant with the value of Empty. The example below shows how to test for missing optional arguments using the IsMissing() function. The function Evaluate() should contain a statement such as the following:

```
If IsMissing(XValue) Then
    {process expression without an x value}
Else
    {process expression for the specified x value}
End If
```

Here's an example of a generic function that supports optional arguments. It doesn't actually evaluate math expressions, but it demonstrates how to use the

IsMissing() function to check for missing arguments. First, declare the function as follows:

```
Function Evaluate(expression As String, Optional XValue As Double) As
Double
If IsMissing(XValue) Then
    MsgBox "Evaluating " & expression
Else
    MsgBox "Evaluating " & expression & " for x = " & XValue
End If
End Function
```

Next, call this function as follows:

```
Evaluate("3*x+5", 10)
```

and

```
Evaluate("3*10+5")
```

In each case, the Evaluate() function displays a different message. The first call to the function displays the following message:

```
Evaluating 3*x+5 for x = 10
```

The second call displays only this expression:

```
Evaluating 3*x+5
```

NOTE   A function that actually evaluates math expressions is really hard to implement. You will find more information on this topic in Chapter 20, *Scripting Objects*.

You can also specify a default value for an optional argument. If the Evaluate() function must have a value for the *XValue* argument, you can define the function as follows:

```
Function Evaluate(expression As String, Optional XValue=0) _
    As Double
```

If the function is called without a value for the *XValue* argument, the Evaluate() function uses the value 0 for the missing argument.

For example, Visual Basic's financial functions (described in Appendix A on the CD) accept optional arguments and specify default values for any missing arguments. The last argument of most Visual Basic financial functions is an integer that specifies whether loan payments are made at the beginning or at the end of the period. If you don't supply this value, these functions assume that payments are due at the end of the period.

The benefit of supplying default values for missing arguments is that your code doesn't have to check for missing arguments and then take a course of action depending on whether an argument's value was supplied. Using the default value, your program can proceed as if all arguments were supplied.

Passing an Unknown Number of Arguments

Generally, all the arguments that a procedure expects are listed in the procedure's definition, and the program that calls the procedure must supply values for all arguments. On occasions, however, you may not know how many arguments will be passed to the procedure. Procedures that calculate averages, or in general, process a number of values, can accept a few to several arguments whose count is not known at design time. In the past, programmers had to pass arrays with the data to similar procedures. Visual Basic 5 introduced the *ParamArray* keyword, which allowed you to pass a variable number of arguments to a procedure.

Let's look at an example. Suppose you want to populate a ListBox control with elements. The method for adding an item to the ListBox control is AddItem and is called as follows:

```
List1.AddItem "new item"
```

This statement adds the string "new item" to the List1 ListBox control.

If you frequently add multiple items to a ListBox control from within your code, you can write either repeated statements or a subroutine that performs this task. The following subroutine adds a number of arguments to the List1 control:

```
Sub AddNamesToList(ParamArray NamesArray())

    For Each x In NamesArray
       List1.AddItem x
    Next x
End Sub
```

This subroutine's argument is an array prefixed with the keyword *ParamArray*. This array holds all the parameters passed to the subroutine. To add a number of items to the list, call the AddNamesToList() subroutine as follows:

```
AddNamesToList "Robert", "Manny", "Richard", "Charles", "Madonna"
```

or

```
AddNamesToList "Mercury", "Earth", "Mars", "Jupiter"
```

If you want to know the number of arguments actually passed to the procedure, use the UBound() function on the parameter array. The number of arguments passed to the AddNamesToList() subroutine is determined as follows:

```
UBound(NamesArray())
```

Here is another method for scanning all the elements of the parameter array and posting them on a ListBox control:

```
For i = 0 to UBound(NamesArray())
    List1.AddItem NamesArray(i)
Next i
```

A procedure that accepts an unknown number of arguments relies on the order of the arguments. When calling this procedure, you can omit any number of arguments starting with the last one. To omit some of the arguments that appear first, you must use the corresponding comma. Let's say you want to call such a procedure and specify the first, third, and fourth arguments. The procedure must be called as:

```
ProcName arg1, , arg3, arg4
```

The arguments to similar procedures are usually of equal stature and their order doesn't make any difference. A function that calculates the mean or other basic statistics of a set of numbers, or a subroutine that populates a ListBox or ComboBox control, are prime candidates for implementing using this technique. If the procedure accepts a variable number of arguments that aren't equal in stature, then you should consider the technique described in the following section.

Named Arguments

You've learned how to write procedures with optional arguments and how to pass a variable number of arguments to the procedure. The main limitation of the argument-passing mechanism, though, is the order of the arguments. If the first argument is a string and the second argument is a date, you can't change their order. By default, Visual Basic matches the values passed to a procedure to the declared arguments by their order. That's why the arguments you've seen so far are called *positional arguments*.

This limitation is lifted by Visual Basic's capability to specify *named arguments*. With named arguments, you can supply arguments in any order, because they are recognized by name and not by their order in the list of the procedure's arguments. Suppose you've written a function that expects three arguments: a name, an address, and an e-mail address:

```
Function Contact(Name As String, Address As String, EMail As String)
```

When calling this function, you must supply three strings that correspond to the arguments *Name*, *Address*, and *EMail*, in that order. However, there's a safer way to call this function: supply the arguments in any order by their names. Instead of calling the Contact function as follows:

```
Contact("Peter Evans", "2020 Palm Ave. Santa Barbara,_
    CA 90000", "PeterEvans@SciNet.com")
```

you can call it this way:

```
Contact(Address:="2020 Palm Ave, Santa Barbara, CA 90000",_
    EMail:="PeterEvans@SciNet.com", Name:="Peter Evans")
```

The equals sign assigns values to the names of the arguments. Because the arguments are passed by name, you can supply them in any order.

To test this technique, enter the following function declaration in a Form's code:

```
Function Contact(Name As String, Address As String, EMail As String)

    Debug.Print Name
    Debug.Print Address
    Debug.Print EMail

    Contact = "OK"

End Function
```

Then, call the Contact() function from within a button's Click event with the following statement:

```
Debug.Print Contact(Address:="2020 Palm Ave, Santa Barbara, CA 90000",
    _
    Name:="Peter Evans", EMail:="PeterEvans@SciNet.com")
```

You'll see the following in the Immediate window:

```
Peter Evans
2020 Palm Ave, Santa Barbara, CA 90000
PeterEvans@SciNet.com
OK
```

The function knows which value corresponds to which argument and can process them the same way that it processes positional arguments. Notice that the function's definition doesn't change whether it's used with positional or named arguments. The difference is in how you call the function and how you declare it.

Named arguments make code safer and easier to read, but because they require a lot of typing, most programmers don't use them. Besides, programmers are so used to positional arguments that the notion of naming arguments is like having to declare variables when variants will do. Named arguments are good for situations in which you have optional arguments that require many consecutive commas, which may complicate the code. The methods of the various VBA objects (discussed in Chapter 14) require a large number of arguments and they accept named arguments.

Function Return Values

A new feature introduced with Visual Basic 6 is that function return values aren't limited to simple data types like Integers or Strings. Functions may now return custom data types and even arrays. This is a new feature of the language, so we'll explore it in depth and look at a few examples too. The ability of functions to return all types of data makes them very flexible and can simplify coding.

Functions Returning Custom Data Types

The custom data type returned by a function must be declared in a Module. Suppose you need a function that returns a customer's savings and checking balance. The custom data type must be defined as follows:

```
Type CustBalance
    BalSavings As Currency
    BalChecking As Currency
End Type
```

Then, you can define a function that returns a CustBalance data type as:

```
Function GetCustBalance(custID) As CustBalance
    {statements}
End Function
```

The GetCustBalance() function must be defined in the same Module as the declaration of the custom data type it returns. If you place the function's definition in a Form's code, then you'll get a syntax error during the compilation of the project.

When you call this function, you must assign its result to a variable of the same type. First declare the variable, then use it as shown here:

```
Private Balance As CustBalance
Balance = GetCustBalance(custID)
```

Here, *custID* is a customer's ID (a number or string, depending on the application). Of course, you must assign the proper values to the *CustBalance* variable's fields.

Here's the simplest example of a function that returns a custom data type. This example outlines the steps you must repeat every time you want to create functions that return custom data types:

1. Add a new Module to the project (or open the application Module, if it exists). Insert the declarations of the custom data type. For example:

    ```
    Type CustBalance
        BalSavings As Currency
    ```

```
        BalChecking As Currency
    End Type
```

2. Then implement the function. You must declare a variable of the type returned by the function and assign the proper values to its fields. The following function assigns random values to the fields *BalChecking* and *BalSavings*. Then, assign the variable to the function's name, as shown next:

```
Function GetCustBalance(ID As Long) As CustBalance
Dim tBalance As CustBalance
    tBalance.BalChecking = CCur(1000+ 4000 * rnd())
    tBalance.BalSavings = CCur(1000+15000 * rnd())
    GetCustBalance = tBalance
End Function
```

3. Switch to the Code window of the Form from which you want to call the function and declare a variable of the same type. Assign the function's return value to this variable and use it in your code. The example that follows prints the savings and checking balances on the Immediate window:

```
Private Sub Command1_Click()
Dim balance As CustBalance
    balance = GetCustBalance(1)
    Debug.Print balance.BalChecking
    Debug.Print balance.BalSavings
End Sub
```

For this example, I created a project with a Form and a Module. The Form contains a single Command button whose Click event handler is shown here. Create this project from scratch, perhaps using your own custom data type, to explore its structure and experiment with functions that return custom data types.

In the following section I'll describe a more complicated (and practical) example of a custom data type function.

VB6 at Work: The Types Project

The Types project, which you'll find in this chapter's folder on the CD, demonstrates a function that returns a custom data type. The Types project consists of a Form that displays record fields and is shown in Figure 3.5. Every time you click the Show Next button the fields of the next record are displayed. When all records are exhausted, the program wraps back to the first record.

FIGURE 3.5:

The Types project demonstrates functions that return custom data type.

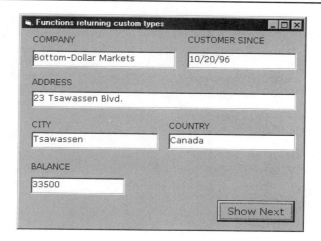

The project consists of a Form and a Module. The following custom data type appears in the Module:

```
Type Customer
    Company As String
    Manager As String
    Address As String
    City As String
    Country As String
    CustomerSince As Date
    Balance As Currency
End Type
Private Customers(1 To 10) As Customer
Private cust As Customer
```

The array *Customers* holds the data for 10 customers and the *cust* variable is used as a temporary variable for storing the current customer's data.

The Click event handler of the Show Next button keeps track of the current record and calls the GetCustomer() function with an index value (which is the order of the current customer) and displays its fields in the Label controls on the Form.

The GetCustomer() function returns a variable of Customer type (the variable *aCustomer*). The code behind the Show Next button follows.

```
Private Sub Command1_Click()
Dim aCustomer As Customer
Static currentIndex As Integer
    currentIndex = currentIndex + 1
    If currentIndex = CountCustomers() Then currentIndex = 1
```

```
      aCustomer = GetCustomer(currentIndex)
      lblCOMPANY.Caption = aCustomer.Company
      lblSINCE.Caption = aCustomer.CustomerSince
      lblADDRESS.Caption = aCustomer.Address
      lblCITY.Caption = aCustomer.City
      lblCOUNTRY = aCustomer.Country
      lblBALANCE.Caption = aCustomer.Balance
  End Sub
```

The CountCustomers() function returns the number of records stored in the *Customers()* array. The definitions of the CountCustomers() and GetCustomer() functions appear in the project's Module and they are:

```
Function CountCustomers() As Integer
    CountCustomers = 7
End Function


Function GetCustomer(idx As Integer) As Customer
    GetCustomer = Customers(idx)
End Function
```

The array *Customers* is populated when the program starts with a call to the InitData() subroutine (also in the project's Module). The program assigns data to the *Customers* array, one element at a time, with statements like the following:

```
      cust.Company = "Bottom-Dollar Markets"
      cust.Manager = "Elizabeth Lincoln"
      cust.Address = "23 Tsawassen Blvd."
      cust.City = "Tsawassen"
      cust.Country = "Canada"
      cust.CustomerSince = #10/20/1996#
      cust.Balance = 33500
      Customers(1) = cust
```

The code assigns values to the fields of the *cust* variable and then assigns the entire variable to an element of the *Customers* array. The data could originate in a file or even a database. This wouldn't affect the operation of the application, which expects the GetCustomer() function to return a record of Customer type. If you decide to store the records in a random access file, or a Collection, the Form's code need not change, only the implementation of the GetCustomer() function in the project's Module.

Functions Returning Arrays

In addition to returning custom data types, Visual Basic 6 functions can also return arrays. This is an interesting possibility that allows you to write functions that return more than a single value. With previous versions of Visual Basic, functions could return multiple values by setting the values of their arguments. Let's say you need a function that calculates the basic statistics of a data set. The basic statistics are the mean value (average), the standard deviation, and the minimum and maximum values in the data set. One way to declare a function that calculates all the statistics is the following:

```
Function ArrayStats(DataArray() As Double, Average As Double _
    StdDeviation As Double, MinValue As Double, MaxValue As Double)
```

The function's type doesn't really matter, since this function doesn't return a value. The *DataArray* array contains the data values. This argument is passed by the calling procedure and it's not modified by the function. The remaining arguments must be passed by reference, so that the ArrayStats() function can set their values. The calling procedure need not set their values. These arguments will be set by the function and will be read by the calling procedure upon the function's return.

With Visual Basic 6 you can declare a function that returns an array of values. The first element of the array could contain the average value, the second element could contain the standard deviation, and so on. The declaration of the new function should be:

```
Function ArrayStats(DataArray() As Double) As Double()
```

This function accepts an array with the data values and returns an array of doubles. This notation is more compact and helps you write easier-to-read code.

To implement a function that returns an array, you must do the following:

1. Specify a type for the function's return value and add a pair of parentheses after the type's name. Don't specify the dimensions of the array to be returned.

2. In the function's code, declare an array of the same type and specify its dimensions. If the function should return four values, use a declaration like the following one:

    ```
    Dim Results(3) As Double
    ```

    The *Results* array will be used to store the results and must be of the same type as the function. Its name can be anything.

3. Before exiting the function, assign the array to the function name:

    ```
    ArrayStats = Results()
    ```

4. In the calling procedure, you must declare an array of the same type without dimensions:

    ```
    Dim Stats() As Double
    ```

5. Finally, you must call the function and assign its return value to this array:

```
Stats() = ArrayStats(DataSet())
```

Here, *DataSet* is an array with the values whose basic statistics will be calculated by the ArrayStats() function. Your code can then retrieve each element of the array Stats() with an index value as usual.

VB6 at Work: The Stats Project

The next project demonstrates how to design and call functions that return arrays. It's the Stats project, which you can find in the Stats folder under this chapter's folder on the CD. When you run it, the Stats application creates a data set of random values and then calls the ArrayStats() function to calculate the data set's basic statistics. The results are returned in an array and the main program displays them in Label controls, as shown in Figure 3.6. Every time you click the button Show Statistics, a new data set is generated and its statistics are displayed.

FIGURE 3.6:

The Stats project calculates the basic statistics of a data set and returns them in an array.

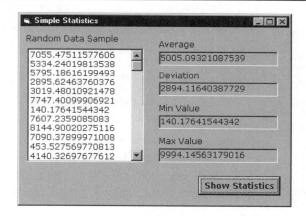

Let's start with the ArrayStats() function's code we find shown next:

```
Function ArrayStats(DataArray() As Double) As Double()
Dim Res(4) As Double
    Sum = 0
    SumSquares = 0
    DCount = 0
    DataMin = 999999
    DataMax = -999999
    For i = LBound(DataArray) To UBound(DataArray)
        Sum = Sum + DataArray(i)
        SumSquares = SumSquares + DataArray(i) ^ 2
        If DataArray(i) > DataMax Then DataMax = DataArray(i)
```

```
        If DataArray(i) < DataMin Then DataMin = DataArray(i)
        DCount = DCount + 1
    Next
    Avg = Sum / DCount
    StdDev = Sqr(SumSquares / DCount - Avg ^ 2)
    Res(1) = Avg
    Res(2) = StdDev
    Res(3) = DataMin
    Res(4) = DataMax
    ArrayStats = Res()
End Function
```

The function's return type is Double(), meaning the function will return an array of doubles. That's what the empty pair of parentheses signifies. This array is declared in the function's body with the statement:

```
Dim Res(4) As Double
```

This function returns four values, but we use 1-based arrays (that why its maximum index is 4 and not 3). The function performs its calculations and then assigns the values of the basic statistics to the elements of the array *Res*. The first element holds the average, the second element holds the standard deviation, and the other two elements hold the minimum and maximum data values. The *Res* array is finally returned to the calling procedure by the statement that assigns the array to the function name, just as you'd assign a variable to the name of the function that returns a single result.

The code behind the Show Statistics button, which calls the ArrayStats() function, is shown next:

```
Private Sub Command1_Click()
Dim SData(100) As Double
Dim Stats() As Double

    List1.Clear
    For i = 1 To 100
        SData(i) = Rnd() * 10000
        List1.AddItem SData(i)
    Next
    Stats() = ArrayStats(SData())
    For i = 1 To 4
        lblSTATS(i - 1).Caption = Stats(i)
    Next
End Sub
```

The code generates 100 random values and displays them on a ListBox control. Then, it calls the ArrayStats() function passing the data values to it through the

SData array. The function's return values are stored in the *Stats* array, which is declared as Double but without dimensions. Then, the code displays the basic statistics in the Label controls that form the *lblSTATS* array of controls with index values from 0 to 3.

Errors as Function Return Values

What happens when an error occurs during the course of the execution of a function? Many programmers will display an error message from within the function's code and exit. An alternative is to convert the return value of the function to an error object and exit the function normally. The calling program can examine the function's return value and determine whether an error occurred. If the function's return value is not an error, then it's the expected result.

Let's say you've implemented the function Calculate() to evaluate a math expression. In evaluating a math expression, all types of errors can occur. For example, the code may attempt to evaluate the square root of a negative number, or the exponential of a large number that results in an overflow. If the Calculate() function is called from many places in the application, it won't be easy to handle errors from within the function itself. Displaying a message describing a math error isn't going to help the user. However, if you let the main procedure handle the error, you may be able to display a more meaningful result like "The initial conditions you specified resulted in a math error" and give the user a chance to revise the data. This option isn't available from within the Calculate() function.

If everything goes well, the Calculate() function will return its result as usual. If an error occurs during the calculations, the function should return an error object. To convert a value to an error object, use the CVErr() function:

```
If Error Then
    Calculate = CVError()
End If
```

The procedure that calls the Calculate() function can examine the function's return value to determine whether an error occurred:

```
Result = Calculate(arguments)
If IsError(Result) Then
    {handle error}
Else
    {continue}
End If
```

The *Result* variable must be of variant type, so that it can store both the actual result (an Integer, Double, or other data type, including custom data types) and the error object returned by the function.

Control Flow Statements

What makes programming languages flexible and capable of handling every situation and programming challenge with a relatively small set of commands is the capability to examine external conditions and act accordingly. Programs aren't monolithic sets of commands that carry out the same calculations every time they are executed. Instead, they adjust their behavior depending on the data supplied; on external conditions, such as a mouse click or the existence of a peripheral; or even abnormal conditions generated by the program itself. For example, a program that calculates averages may work time and again until the user forgets to supply any data. In this case, the program attempts to divide by zero and your program must detect this condition and act accordingly.

An application needs a built-in capability to test conditions and take a different course of action depending on the outcome of the test. Visual Basic provides three control flow, or decision, structures:

- If…Then
- If…Then…Else
- Select Case

If…Then

The *If…Then* structure tests the condition specified, and if it's True, executes the statement(s) that follow. The If structure can have a single-line or a multiple-line syntax. To execute one statement conditionally, use the single-line syntax as follows:

```
If condition Then statement
```

Visual Basic evaluates the *condition*, and if it's True, executes the statement that follows. If the condition is False, it continues with the statement following the If structure.

You can also execute multiple statements by separating them with a colon:

```
If condition Then statement: statement: statement
```

Here's an example of a single-line If statement:

```
If Month(date) = 1 Then Year = Year + 1
```

You can break this statement into multiple lines, as shown here:

```
If Month(date) = 1 Then
    Year = Year + 1
End If
```

Some programmers prefer the multiple-line syntax of the If...Then statement, even if it contains a single statement, because the code is easier to read.

If...Then...Else

A variation of the If...Then statement is the *If... Then... Else* statement, which executes one block of statements if the condition is True and another if the condition is False. The syntax of the If...Then...Else statement is as follows:

```
If condition Then
    statementblock-1
Else
    statementblock-2
End If
```

Visual Basic evaluates the *condition*, and if it's True, it executes the first block of statements and then jumps to the statement following the End If statement. If the condition is False, Visual Basic ignores the first block of statements and executes the block following the *Else* keyword.

Another variation of the If...Then...Else statement uses several conditions, with the *ElseIf* keyword:

```
If condition1 Then
    statementblock-1
ElseIf condition2 Then
    statementblock-2
ElseIf condition3 Then
    statementblock-3
Else
    statementblock-4
End If
```

You can have any number of ElseIf clauses. The conditions are evaluated from the top, and if one of them is True, the corresponding block of statements is executed. The Else clause will be executed if none of the previous expressions are True. Here's an example of an If statement with ElseIf clauses:

```
score = InputBox("Enter score")
If score < 50 Then
    Result = "Failed"
ElseIf score < 75 Then
    Result = "Pass"
ElseIf score < 90 Then
    Result = "Very Good"
```

```
Else
    Result = "Excellent"
End If
MsgBox Result
```

Multiple If...Then Structures versus ElseIf

Notice that once a True condition is found, Visual Basic executes the associated statements and skips the remaining clauses. It continues executing the program with the statement immediately after End If. All following ElseIf clauses are skipped and the code runs a bit faster. That's why you should prefer the complicated structure with ElseIf statements to the equivalent series of simple If statements.

```
If score < 50 Then
    Result = "Failed"
End If
If score < 75 And score >= 50 Then
    Result = "Pass"
End If
If score < 90 And score > =75 Then
    Result = "Very Good"
End If
If score >= 90 Then
    Result = "Excellent"
End If
```

Visual Basic will evaluate all the conditions of the If statements, even if the score is less than 50.

You may have noticed that the order of the comparisons is vital in a nested *If...Then* structure that uses ElseIf statements. Had you written the previous code segment with the first two conditions switched, like this:

```
If score < 75 Then
    Result = "Pass"
ElseIf score < 50 Then
    Result = "Failed"
ElseIf score < 90 Then
    Result = "Very Good"
Else
    Result = "Excellent"
End If
```

the results would be quite unexpected. The code would compare the score variable (49) to the value 75. Since 49 is less than 75, it would assign the value "Pass" to the variable *Result* and then it would skip the remaining clauses. Thus, a student who made 49 would have passed the test! So, be extremely careful and test your code thoroughly if it uses multiple ElseIf clauses.

An alternative to the efficient, but difficult-to-read, code of the multiple ElseIf structure is the Select Case statement.

Select Case

The *Select Case* structure compares one expression to different values. The advantage of the Select Case statement over multiple If…Then…Else statements is that it makes the code easier to read and maintain.

The Select Case structure tests a single expression, which is evaluated once at the top of the structure. The result of the test is then compared with several values, and if it matches one of them, the corresponding block of statements is executed. Here's the syntax of the Select Case statement:

```
Select Case expression
Case value1
    statementblock-1
Case value2
    statementblock-2
    .
    .
    .
Case Else
    statementblock
End Select
```

A practical example based on the Select Case statement is:

```
Select Case WeekDay(Date)
Case 1
    DayName = "Monday"
    Message = "Have a nice week"
Case 6
    DayName = "Saturday"
    Message = "Have a nice weekend"
Case 7
    DayName = "Sunday"
    Message = "Did you have a nice weekend?"
Case Else
    Message = "Welcome back!"
End Select
```

The *expression* variable, which is evaluated at the beginning of the statement, is the number of the weekday, as reported by the WeekDay() function (a value in the range 1 to 7). The value of the expression is then compared with the values that follow each *Case* keyword. If they match, the block of statements up to the next *Case* keyword is executed, and the program skips to the statement following the End Select statement. The block of the Case Else statement is optional and is executed if none of the previous Case values match the expression.

Some Case statements can be followed by multiple values, which are separated by commas. Here's a revised version of the previous example:

```
Select Case WeekDay(Date)
Case 1
    Message = "Have a nice week"
    DayType = "Workday"
Case 2, 3, 4, 5
    Message = "Welcome back!"
    DayType = "Workday"
Case 6, 7
    Message = "Have a nice weekend"
    DayType = "Holiday"
End Select
```

The five workdays and the two weekend days are handled by two Case statements with multiple values. This structure doesn't contain a Case Else statement because all values are examined in the Case statements. The WeekDay() function can't return another value.

TIP   If more than one Case value matches the expression, only the statement block associated with the first matching Case executes.

For comparison, here are the equivalent If...Then...Else statements that would implement the previous example:

```
today = WeekDay(Date)
If today > 0 And today < 6 Then
    Message = "Welcome back!"
    DayType = "Workday"
Else
    Message = "Have a nice weekend"
    DayType = "Holiday"
End If
```

To say the least, this coding is verbose. If you attempt to implement a more elaborate Select Case statement with If...Then...Else statements, the code becomes even more difficult to read. Here is the first example, implemented with If…Then…Else statements:

```
today = WeekDay(date)
If today = 1 Then
    DayName = "Monday"
    Message = "Have a nice week"
ElseIf today = 6 Then
    DayName = "Saturday"
    Message = "Have a nice weekend"
ElseIf today = 7 Then
    DayName = "Sunday"
    Message = "Did you have a nice weekend?"
End If
```

Of course, the Select Case statement can't be substituted for any If…Then structures. The Select Case structure only evaluates the expression at the beginning. By contrast, the If…Then…Else structure can evaluate a different expression for each ElseIf statement.

Loop Statements

Loop statements allow you to execute one or more lines of code repetitively. Many tasks consist of trivial operations that must be repeated over and over again, and looping structures are an important part of any programming language. Visual Basic supports the following loop statements:

- Do…Loop
- For…Next
- While…Wend

Do…Loop

The Do…Loop executes a block of statements for as long as a condition is True. Visual Basic evaluates an expression, and if it's True, the statements are executed. If the expression is False, the program continues and the statement following the loop is executed.

There are two variations of the Do…Loop statement and both use the same basic model. A loop can be executed either while the condition is True or until the condition becomes True. These two variations use the keywords *While* and *Until* to specify how long the statements are executed. To execute a block of statements while a condition is True, use the following syntax:

```
Do While condition
    statement-block
Loop
```

To execute a block of statements until the condition becomes True, use the following syntax:

```
Do Until condition
    statement-block
Loop
```

When Visual Basic executes the previous loops, it first evaluates *condition*. If *condition* is False, the Do…While or Do…Until loop is skipped (the statements aren't even executed once). When the Loop statement is reached, Visual Basic evaluates the expression again and repeats the statement block of the Do…While loop if the expression is True, or repeats the statements of the Do…Until loop if the expression is False.

The Do…Loop can execute any number of times as long as *condition* is True (or nonzero if the condition evaluates to a number). Moreover, the number of iterations need not be known before the loops starts. If *condition* is initially False, the statements may never execute.

Here's a typical example of using a Do…Loop. Suppose the string *MyText* holds a piece of text (perhaps the Text property of a TextBox control), and you want to count the words in the text. (We'll assume that there are no multiple spaces in the text and that the space character separates successive words.) To locate an instance of a character in a string, use the InStr() function, which accepts three arguments:

- The starting location of the search
- The text to be searched
- The character being searched

The following loop repeats for as long as there are spaces in the text. Each time the InStr() function finds another space in the text, it returns the location (a positive number) of the space. When there are no more spaces in the text, the InStr() function returns zero, which signals the end of the loop, as shown.

```
position = 1
Do While position > 0
    position = InStr(position + 1, MyText, " ")
words = words + 1 Loop
Debug.Print words
```

The Do…Loop is executed while the InStr() function returns a positive number, which happens for as long as there are more words in the text. The variable *position* holds the location of each successive space character in the text. The search for the next space starts at the location of the current space plus 1 (so that the program won't keep finding the same space). For each space found, the program increments the value of the *words* variable, which holds the total number of words when the loop ends.

You may notice a problem with the previous code segment. It assumes that the text contains at least one word and starts by setting the *position* variable to 1. If the *MyText* variable contains an empty string, the program reports that it contains one word. To fix this problem, you must specify the condition as follows:

```
Do While InStr(position + 1, MyText, " ")
    position = InStr(position + 1, MyText, " ")
words = words + 1 Loop
Debug.Print words
```

The line words = words + 1 is necessary because the last word is not delimited by a space.

This code segment counts the number of words correctly, even if the *MyText* variable contains an empty string. If the *MyText* String variable doesn't contain any spaces, the function InStr(position + 1, MyText, " ") returns 0, which corresponds to False, and the Do loop isn't executed.

You can code the same routine with the *Until* keyword. In this case, you must continue to search for spaces until *position* becomes zero. Here's the same code with a different loop (the InStr() function returns 0 if the string it searches for doesn't exist in the longer string):

```
position = 1
Do Until position = 0
    position = InStr(position + 1, MyText, " ")
    words = words + 1
Loop
Debug.Print words
```

Another variation of the Do loop executes the statements first and evaluates the *condition* after each execution. This Do loop has the following syntax:

```
Do
statements
Loop While condition
```

or

```
Do
statements
Loop Until condition
```

The statements in this type of loop execute at least once, since the condition is examined at the end of the loop.

Could we have implemented the previous example with one of the last two types of loops? The fact that we had to do something special about zero-length strings suggests that this problem shouldn't be coded with a loop that tests the condition at the end. Since the loops' body will be executed once, the *words* variable is never going to be zero.

As you can see, you can code loops in a number of ways with the Do...Loop statement, and the way you use it will depends on the problem at hand and your programming style.

Of course, text is not made up of words seperated by single spaces. You may have multiple spaces between words, tabs, and multiple lines of text. The WCount application in this chapter's folder on the CD counts words with a more robust procedure. You can open the project and examine its code, which is thoroughly documented.

For...Next

The *For...Next* loop is one of the oldest loop structures in programming languages. Unlike the Do loop, the For...Next loop requires that you know how many times the statements in the loop will be executed. The For...Next loop uses a variable (it's called the loop's *counter*) that increases or decreases in value during each repetition of the loop. The For...Next loop has the following syntax:

```
For counter = start To end [Step increment]
statements
Next [counter]
```

The keywords in the square brackets are optional. The arguments *counter*, *start*, *end*, and *increment* are all numeric. The loop is executed as many times as required for the *counter* to reach (or exceed) the *end* value.

In executing a For...Next loop, Visual Basic completes the following steps:

1. Sets *counter* equal to *start*

2. Tests to see if *counter* is greater than *end*. If so, it exits the loop. If *increment* is negative, Visual Basic tests to see if *counter* is less than *end*. If it is, it exits the loop.

3. Executes the statements in the block

4. Increments *counter* by the amount specified with the *increment* argument. If the *increment* argument isn't specified, *counter* is incremented by 1.

5.   Repeats the statements

The following For...Next loop scans all the elements of the numeric array *data* and calculates their average:

```
For i = 0 To UBound(data)
   total = total + data(i)
Next i
Debug.Print total / UBound(a)
```

The single most important thing to keep in mind when working with For...Next loops is that the loop's *counter* is set at the beginning of the loop. Changing the value of the *end* variable in the loop's body won't have any effect. For example, the following loop will be executed 10 times, not 100 times:

```
endValue = 10
For i = 0 To endValue
   endValue = 100
   {more statements}
Next i
```

You can, however, adjust the value of the *counter* from within the loop. The following is an example of an endless (or infinite) loop:

```
For i = 0 To 10
   Debug.Print i
   i = i - 1
Next i
```

This loop never ends because the loop's *counter*, in effect, is never increased. (If you try this, press Control+Break to interrupt the endless loop.)

WARNING   Manipulating the *counter* of a For...Next loop is strongly discouraged. This practice will most likely lead to bugs such as infinite loops, overflows, and so on. If the number of repetitions of a loop isn't known in advance, use a Do...Loop or a While...Wend structure (discussed in the following section).

The *increment* argument can be either positive or negative. If *start* is greater than *end*, the value of increment must be negative. If not, the loop's body won't be executed, not even once.

Finally, the *counter* variable need not be listed after the Next statement, but it makes the code easier to read, especially when For...Next loops are nested within each other (nested loops are discussed in the section "Nested Control Structures" later in the chapter).

While...Wend

The While...Wend loop executes a block of statements while a condition is True. The While...Wend loop has the following syntax:

```
While condition
   statement-block
Wend
```

If *condition* is True, all statements are executed and when the Wend statement is reached, control is returned to the While statement which evaluates *condition* again. If *condition* is still True, the process is repeated. If *condition* is False, the program resumes with the statement following the Wend statement.

The following While...Wend loop prompts the user for numeric data. The user can type a negative value to indicate that all values are entered:

```
number = 0
While number => 0
   total = total + number
   number = InputBox("Please enter another value")
Wend
```

You assign the value 0 to the *number* variable before the loop starts because this value can't affect the total. Another technique is to precede the While statement with an InputBox function to get the first number from the user.

Nested Control Structures

You can place, or *nest*, control structures inside other control structures (such as an If...Then block within a For...Next loop). Control structures in Visual Basic can be nested in as many levels as you want. It's common practice to indent the bodies of nested decision and loop structures to make the program easier to read. Here is the structure of a nested For...Next loop that scans all the elements of a two-dimensional array:

```
For irow = 0 To Ubound(Array2(0))
   For icol = 0 To Ubound(Array2(1))
      { process element Array2(irow, icol)) }
   Next icol
Next irow
```

The outer loop (with the *irow* counter) scans each row of the array, and the inner loop scans each column. The outer loop scans each element in the first row of the array, the elements of the second row, and so on, until the entire array has been scanned. The loop's body can process the element *Array2(irow, icol)*.

TIP The presence of the *counter* names *icol* and *irow* aren't really required after the Next statement. Actually, if you supply them in the wrong order, Visual Basic generates an error message. In practice, few programmers specify *counter* values after a Next statement because Visual Basic matches each Next statement to the corresponding For statement. If the loop's body is lengthy, you can improve the program's readability by specifying the corresponding *counter* name after each Next statement.

You can also nest control flow structures. The following structure tests a user-supplied value to determine if it's positive and, if so, determines whether the value exceeds a certain limit:

```
Income = InputBox("Enter your income")
If Income > 0 Then
    If Income > 20000 Then
        MsgBox "You will pay taxes this year"
    Else
        MsgBox "You won't pay any taxes this year"
    End If
Else
    MsgBox "Bummer"
End If
```

The *Income* variable is first compared with zero. If it's negative, the Else clause of the If...Then statement is executed. If it's positive, it's compared with the value 20000, and depending on the outcome, a different message is displayed.

The Exit Statement

The Exit statement allows you to exit prematurely from a block of statements in a control structure, from a loop, or even from a procedure. Suppose you have a For...Next loop that calculates the square root of a series of numbers. Because the square root of negative numbers can't be calculated (the Sqr() function generates a runtime error), you might want to halt the operation if the array contains an invalid value. To exit the loop prematurely, use the Exit For statement as follows:

```
For i = 0 To UBound(nArray())
    If nArray(i) < 0 Then Exit For
    nArray(i) = Sqr(nArray(i))
Next
```

If a negative element is found in this loop, the program exits the loop and continues with the statement following the Next statement.

There are similar Exit statements for the Do loop (Exit Do), as well as for functions and subroutines (Exit Function and Exit Subroutine). If the previous loop was part of a function, you might want to assign an error code to the function and exit not only the loop, but the function itself:

```
For i = 0 To UBound(nArray())
    If nArray(i) < 0 Then
       MsgBox "Negative value found, terminating calculations"
        Exit Function
    End If
    nArray(i) = Sqr(nArray(i))
Next
```

If this code is part of a subroutine procedure, you use the Exit Subroutine statement. The Exit statements for loops are Exit For and Exit Do. There is no way (or compelling reason) to exit prematurely from an If or Case statement. There is also an Exit Property statement, which we'll look at in Chapter 16, *Building ActiveX Controls*.

CHAPTER

FOUR

4

Working with Forms

- Manipulating Forms

- Loading, showing, and hiding Forms

- Designing menus

- Developing shortcut and access keys

- Building dynamic Forms

- Using drag-and-drop operations

- Dragging list items

In Visual Basic, the *Form* is the container for all the controls that make up the user interface. When a Visual Basic application is executing, each window it displays on the Desktop is a Form. In previous chapters, we used Forms as containers on which we placed the elements of the user interface. Now, we'll look at Forms and at a few related topics, such as menus (Forms are the only objects that can have menus attached) and drag-and-drop operations. The Form is the top-level object in a Visual Basic application, and every application starts with the Form.

Forms have a built-in functionality that is always available without any programming effort on your part. You can move a Form around, resize it, and even cover it with other Forms. You do so with the mouse, with the keyboard, or through the Control menu. Forms have many trivial properties that won't be discussed here. Instead, let's jump directly to the properties that are unique to Forms and then look at how to manipulate Forms from within an application's code.

The Appearance of Forms

The main characteristic of a Form is the title bar on which the form's caption is displayed (see Figure 4.1). On the left end of the title bar is the Control Menu icon. Clicking this icon opens the Control menu. On the right side of the title bar are three buttons: Minimize, Maximize, and Close. Clicking these buttons performs the associated function. When a Form is maximized, the Maximize button is replaced by the Normal button. When clicked, the Normal button will restore the Form to its size and position before it was maximized.

FIGURE 4.1:

The elements of the Form

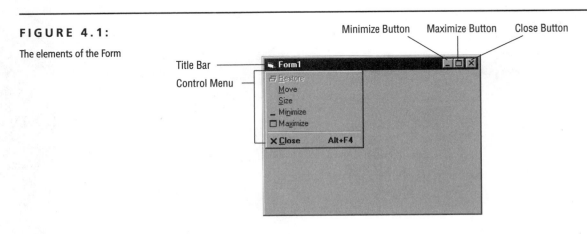

The Control menu contains the following commands:

- **Restore**   Restores a maximized Form to the size it was before it was maximized; available only if the Form has been maximized

- **Move**   Lets the user move the Form around with the mouse

- **Size**   Lets the user resize the control with the mouse

- **Minimize**   Minimizes the Form

- **Maximize**   Maximizes the Form

- **Close**   Closes the current Form

You can customize the appearance of the Form with the following Form properties:

- **MinButton, MaxButton**   These two properties are True by default. Set them to False to hide the corresponding buttons on the title bar.

- **ControlMenu**   This property is also True by default. Set it to False to hide the icon and disable the Control menu. Although the Control menu is rarely used, Windows applications don't disable it.

  When the ControlMenu property is False, the three buttons on the title bar are also disabled. If you set the Caption property to an empty string, the title bar disappears altogether.

- **BorderStyle**   The BorderStyle property determines the style of the Form's border and the appearance of the Form. The BorderStyle property can take one of the values shown in Table 4.1.

TABLE 4.1:   Values of the BorderStyle Property

VALUE	CONSTANT	DESCRIPTION
0–None	*vbBSNone*	Form has no border and can't be resized; this setting should be avoided
1–Fixed Single	*vbFixedSingle*	Form has a visible border, but can't be resized
2–Sizable	*vbSizable*	Border and a title bar and can be repositioned on the Desktop and resized
3–Fixed Dialog	*vbFixedDialog*	Fixed dialog box
4–Fixed ToolWindow	*vbFixedToolWindow*	Form has a Close button only and can't be resized; looks like a toolbar
5–Sizable ToolWindow	*vbSizableToolWindow*	Same as the Fixed ToolWindow, but can be resized

The Start-Up Form

A typical application has more than a single Form. When an application starts, the main Form is loaded. You can control which Form is initially loaded by setting the start-up object in the Project Properties window, shown in Figure 4.2. To open this dialog box, choose Project ➤ Project Properties.

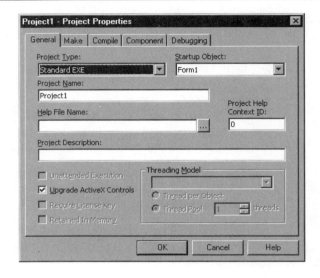

By default, Visual Basic suggests the name of the first Form it created when the project started, which is Form1. If you change the name of the Form, Visual Basic won't use the new name. Instead, when you try to start the application, Visual Basic will display an error message indicating that you must specify the start-up object, and then it will display the Project Properties window.

You can also start an application with a subroutine without loading a Form. This subroutine must be called Main and it must be inserted in a Module. If you specify the Main subroutine as the Start-up Object in the Project Properties window of Figure 4.2, you must load and display the application's Forms from within the Main subroutine with the statements described in the next section.

Loading, Showing, and Hiding Forms

Before we look at the methods and statements for displaying Forms, let's look at the three possible states of a Form:

- **Not loaded**   The Form lives on a disk file and doesn't take up any resources.

- **Loaded but not shown**   The Form is loaded into memory, takes up the required resources, and is ready to be displayed.

- **Loaded and shown**   The Form is shown, and the user can interact with it.

Loading and Unloading Forms

To load and unload Forms, use the *Load* and *Unload* statements. The Load statement has the following syntax:

```
Load formName
```

and the Unload statement has this syntax:

```
Unload formName
```

The *formName* variable is the name of the Form to be loaded or unloaded. Unlike the Show method, which takes care of both loading and displaying the Form, the Load statement doesn't show the Form. You have to call the Form's Show method to display it on the Desktop.

Once a Form is loaded, it takes over the required resources, so you should always unload a Form that's no longer needed. When a Form is unloaded, the resources it occupies are returned to the system and can be used by other Forms and/or applications. Because loading a Form isn't instantaneous, especially if the Form contains bitmaps or other resources that entail loading large files, don't unload a Form frequently in the course of an application. If your application contains many Forms, balance the benefit of having them all in memory versus loading certain Forms as needed. Opening a database and setting up the related structures (we'll look at them in Chapter 17, *Database Programming with Visual Basic*), for instance, doesn't take place instantly, and your application shouldn't load and unload Forms that access databases. It's best to keep the Form loaded in memory and display it when the user needs it.

Showing Forms

To show a Form, you use the *Show* method. If the Form is loaded but invisible, the Show method brings the specified Form on top of every other window on the Desktop. If the Form isn't loaded, the Show method loads it and then displays it. The Show method has the following syntax:

```
formName.Show mode
```

The *formName* variable is the Form's name, and the optional argument *mode* determines whether the Form will be modal or modeless. It can have one of the following values:

- 0–Modeless (default)

- 1–Modal

Modeless Forms are the norm. They interact with the user, and they allow the user to switch to any other Form of the application. If you don't specify the optional *mode* argument, the Show method displays the Form as modeless.

A modal Form takes total control of the application and won't let the applications proceed unless the Form is closed. A modal Form, therefore, must have a Close button or some means for the user to close it so that they can return to the Form from which the modal Form was loaded. The InputBox() function, for example, displays a Modal window. Unless the user clicks on the OK or Cancel button, the program can't continue. When an InputBox is displayed, you can't even switch back to the program's Main window.

WARNING   In effect, modal Forms disable all other parts of the application, but not any other applications that are running at the moment. When a modal Form is displayed, you can't switch to other Forms in the same application, but you can switch to other applications.

The Show method will also load the Form if necessary. You might wonder why you would load and then show a Form if the Show method takes care of both steps. There are two reasons for loading Forms separately:

1. Some Forms don't need to be displayed; they only need to be loaded. These Forms may contain procedures needed by other applications or have a special function, such as doing something in the background. For example, a Form with a Timer control that tracks time or other events doesn't need to have a visible user interface.

2. You can speed up the display of a Form by loading it ahead of time. Loading a Form takes time, especially if the Form contains large bitmaps or many controls. The delay associated with loading a Form can be avoided if the Form is loaded on start-up. The loading time won't be reduced by loading a Form at start-up, but after the application is loaded and running, there won't be any substantial delays. The Forms will be in memory, and the Show method can display them instantly.

Hiding Forms

If your application uses many Forms, you may want to hide some of them to make room on the Desktop for others. To hide a Form, use the Form's *Hide* method, whose syntax is:

```
Form.Hide
```

To hide a Form from within its own code, use the statement:

```
Me.Hide
```

Forms that are hidden are not unloaded; they remain in memory and can be displayed instantly with the Show method. Forms that may be opened frequently, such as a Search & Replace window, should be hidden when they are not needed. The next time the user opens the same window there will be no noticeable delay. Forms that aren't opened frequently in the course of an application, such as a Preferences or Options window, should be unloaded to reclaim the resources.

When a Form is hidden, you can still access its properties and code. For example, you can change the settings of its Control properties or call any Public functions in the Form, even its event handlers (as long as you make them public by changing the default "Private" declaration of the corresponding event handler to "Public"). The topic of manipulating a Form's controls from within another Form's code is discussed later in this chapter in the section "Controlling One Form from within Another." If you plan to manipulate the controls on a Form at runtime, you can do so while the Form is loaded but not visible (see also the section "Building Dynamic Forms at Runtime," later in this chapter). After you have manipulated the controls on the Form, you can display it with the Show method.

VB6 at Work: The FormLoad Project

By default, Visual Basic loads and displays the first Form of the project. If the loading process takes more than a second, the user simply has to wait. The Form-Load application demonstrates a technique for handling slow-loading Forms. You can't shorten the load time, but you can improve the *subjective delay*, which is the delay perceived by the user. The LoadForm application takes a while to load two Forms. The delay is artificial, but it simulates a real-world condition.

The FormLoad application has three Forms, as shown in Figure 4.3. The first one, shown on top of the others, is a simple, quick-loading Form with a couple of messages. You could place your company logo or other useful (or at least less boring) information on the first Form. Initially, the message on the main Form indicates that the application is loading and asks the user to wait. This Form loads the two slow-loading Forms in the background. As each Form is loaded, the main Form's caption changes to indicate which Form is currently loading. After both Forms are loaded, the two Command buttons at the bottom of the Form are enabled, and the messages on the Form change to those shown in Figure 4.3.

The absolutely essential code for loading the two Forms is as follows:

```
Load Form2
Load Form3
```

FIGURE 4.3:

The FormLoad application loads two Forms in the background, reducing the perceived delay.

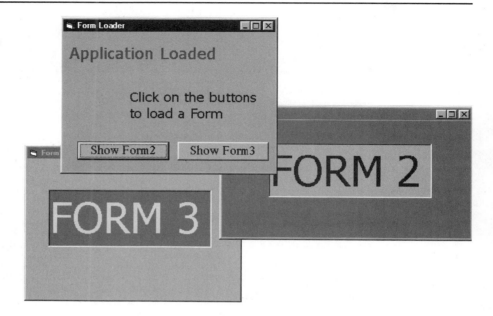

But if you just use these two lines to load the other Forms of the application, the first Form won't display properly before the loading process ends. This is because Windows loads the Form in memory and then waits for an opportunity to draw it on the screen. Windows gets this opportunity when other applications aren't running. The first Form is loaded, then the code on the Form starts executing. While the code is running, nothing happens on the display. To give Windows a chance to load the first Form, display it, and then load the other two Forms, insert the following code in the first Form's Load event.

Code 4.1:   **The Load Event Handler**

```
Private Sub Form_Load()

    Form1.Show
    Form1.Refresh
    Form1.Caption = "Loading Form2..."
    Load Form2
    Form1.Caption = "Loading Form3..."
    Load Form3

    Form1.Caption = "Form Loader"
    Command1.Visible = True
    Command2.Visible = True
```

```
    Label1.Caption = "Application Loaded"
    Label2.Caption = "Click the buttons to load a Form"

End Sub
```

If you omit the Form1.Show method, the main Form won't be displayed before the other two Forms are loaded. The Refresh method tells Visual Basic to update the display before executing the following commands. By default, Visual Basic refreshes the display only when it gets a chance, and this is when it's not executing any code. If you load a Form from within your code, you must call the Refresh method to redraw the screen instantly.

The program then sets the main Form's caption to a message indicating that Form2 is being loaded and loads Form2. After Form2 is loaded, it does the same for Form3. It displays a similar message in its caption and loads the Form. After both Forms are loaded, it resets its caption and makes the two buttons at the bottom visible so that the user can display Form2 and Form3. The code behind the Show Form2 button is:

```
Form2.Show
```

and the code behind the Show Form3 button is:

```
Form3.Show
```

Run the application and see how it works. To contrast this approach with the default behavior of Visual Basic, comment out the lines that load the two Forms by inserting a single quote in front of the line you want to comment out; to reinstate the line, remove the comment symbol. If you do so, the Forms will be loaded when the user clicks the corresponding button. They will be loaded just as slowly as before, but there's a big difference—this delay is perceived by the user. When users click a button, they want something to happen. But with a slow-loading Form, nothing happens for a few seconds. When an application is starting, though, the user will put up with some delay; in other words, the perceived delay. The Forms will take just as long to load in either case, but loading them when the user isn't actually working is less obtrusive, and therefore, more tolerable. A Form that takes more than a second to load at runtime makes your application look amateur-ish, not well designed, and certainly not as user-friendly as it should be.

You can simulate the delay by adding the following code to the Load events of Form2 and Form3:

```
Private Sub Form_Load()
    Dim LTime
    LTime = Timer()
    While Timer() - LTime < 5
```

```
    Wend
  End Sub
```

The Timer() function returns the number of seconds elapsed since midnight and is used to delay the loading for five seconds. The total delay is ten seconds, five for each Form. This code works well unless you start the application a few seconds before midnight. The Timer() function is reset at midnight.

The DoEvents Statement

As mentioned earlier, Windows doesn't deal with the display if it's busy executing code. In other words, the update of the display has a low priority in the Windows "to do" list. The code that implements the artificial delay in the loading of a Form is a tight loop. While it's executing, it takes over the application. You can switch to another application if you wish (Windows 95 is a multitasking environment), but the FormLoad application appears to be frozen. For example, you can't resize the application's main Form or move it around. Many users like to reposition Forms on the Desktop or resize them when the application starts. The FormLoad application is frozen because the code that's executing doesn't give Windows a chance to handle the display.

To give Windows a chance to do something about the display, you must call the DoEvents statement. The DoEvents statement tells your application to give Windows a chance to take care of its own chores. It doesn't relinquish control to the operating system; it simply gives it a little time to take care of any pending tasks, and the control is returned immediately to the application. To experiment with the DoEvents statement, modify the While loop as shown here:

```
  Private Sub Form_Load()
    Dim LTime
    LTime = Timer()
    While Timer() - LTime < 5
      DoEvents
    Wend
  End Sub
```

Now run the application and see how it reacts when you attempt to reposition or resize the main Form while the two Forms are being loaded. The application is no longer frozen. It reacts to external events as it should.

The DoEvents statement can introduce significant delays. If you have a loop that might execute a million times, you can't return control to the operating system with each iteration. Each time a new process takes control of the CPU, some overhead is required. It doesn't take long, but if you add up these delays, the DoEvents statement may harm your application rather than help it. Using the DoEvents statement effectively takes some experience and experimentation. We will come back to this topic in Chapter 6, *Drawing with Visual Basic*, where we'll look at techniques for balancing the requirements of quick code execution and proper application behavior.

Controlling One Form from within Another

You've learned how to load a Form from within another. In many situations, this is all the interaction you need between Forms. Each Form is designed to operate independently of the others, but they can communicate via global variables (see the discussion "Global versus Public Variables," later in the chapter). In other situations, however, you may need to control one Form from within another. Controlling the Form means accessing its controls and setting or reading its values from within another Form's code.

Look at the two Forms in Figure 4.4, for instance. These are Forms of the TextPad application, which we are going to develop in Chapter 5, *Basic ActiveX Controls*. TextPad is a text editor which consists of the main Form and an auxiliary Form for the Search & Replace operation. All other operations on the text are performed with the commands of the menu you see on the main Form. When the user wants to search for and/or replace a string, the program displays another Form on which the user specifies the text to find, the type of search, and so on. When the user clicks on one of the Search & Replace Form's buttons, the corresponding code must access the text on the main Form of the application and search for a word or replace a string with another. You'll see how this works in Chapter 5. In this chapter, we'll develop a simple example to demonstrate how you can access another Form's controls.

Accessing a Form's controls from within another is straightforward. Simply prefix the control's name with the name of the Form. For example, to access the Text property of the Text1 control on the Form, you could use the following expression:

```
Text1.Text
```

To access the same property from within another Form, you would use this expression:

```
Form1.Text1.Text
```

Form1 is the name of the Form to which the Text1 control belongs. You can actually have a Text1 control on two Forms. The expression Text1.Text is the Text property of the Text1 control on either control. If the following statement is executed from within Form1, it assigns the string "some text" to the Text1 control on Form1:

```
Text1.Text = "some text"
```

FIGURE 4.4:

The Search & Replace Form acts on the contents of a control on another Form.

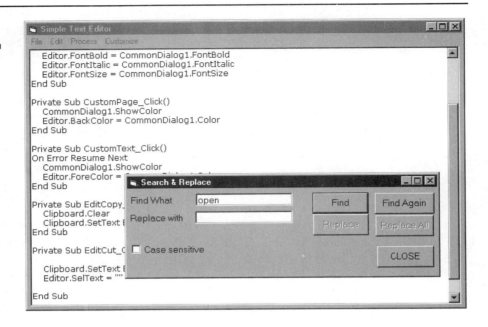

```
Simple Text Editor                                          _ □ ×
File  Edit  Process  Customize
    Editor.FontBold = CommonDialog1.FontBold             ▲
    Editor.FontItalic = CommonDialog1.FontItalic
    Editor.FontSize = CommonDialog1.FontSize
End Sub

Private Sub CustomPage_Click()
    CommonDialog1.ShowColor
    Editor.BackColor = CommonDialog1.Color
End Sub

Private Sub CustomText_Click()
On Error Resume Next
    CommonDialog1.ShowColor
    Editor.ForeColor =
End Sub

Private Sub EditCopy_
    Clipboard.Clear
    Clipboard.SetText
End Sub

Private Sub EditCut_(

    Clipboard.SetText
    Editor.SelText = ""

End Sub                                                  ▼
```

```
Search & Replace                          _ □ ×
Find What      open              [  Find  ]  [ Find Again ]
Replace with   [            ]    [ Replace ] [ Replace All ]
☐ Case sensitive                            [   CLOSE    ]
```

If the same statement is executed from within Form2, it assigns the same string to the Text1 control on Form2. To access the control on the other Form, you would prefix the expression with the name of the Form.

TIP

You can actually manipulate the properties of the controls on a Form that is not loaded. Visual Basic loads the Form and changes its property, but doesn't display the Form. When the Form is later displayed, you'll see that the property has changed value.

Accessing Forms from within Their Controls

You can also control the Form from within the various controls using the Parent property. The active control on a Form (the control that has the focus) is returned by the ActiveControl property. The expression `ActiveControl` returns a handle (a reference) to the active control. If the active control is the Command1 Command button, the expression `ActiveControl` is a synonym for `Command1`.

One of the properties of the ActiveControl object is the Parent property, which returns a handle to the object on which the active control is placed. Since most controls are placed

Continued on next page

on Forms, the expression `ActiveControl.Parent` is a reference to the current Form. To access the Form's Caption property, for instance, use a statement like:

```
ActiveControl.Parent.Caption = "I belong to this Form"
```

With similar expressions, you can access all the members of the Form (properties and methods) and even pass them as arguments to procedures.

Suppose you have a subroutine that can perform certain actions on Forms. In our example, the action is simple: it paints the Form red. Instead of writing a subroutine for each Form, you can pass to this subroutine a handle to the Form it must act upon. Here is the definition of the subroutine:

```
Sub DoSomethingWithForm(Frm As Object)
    MsgBox "I will paint the " & Frm.Name & " Form"
    Frm.BackColor = vbRed
End Sub
```

This subroutine accepts as an argument an object, which is presumably the Form whose background it must change. The subroutine can be called from within any control's code with a statement such as:

```
Private Sub Command1_Click()
    DoSomethingWithForm ActiveControl.Parent
End Sub
```

The expression `ActiveControl.Parent` is a reference to the object that contains the active control. If the command button is placed on another control, and not on the Form, this example may not work.

To use this technique in your applications, you must first examine the type of object passed to the DoSomethingWithForm() subroutine and make sure that it has a BackColor property. You can do so with the *TypeOf* keyword, which is explained in the section "Drag-and-Drop Operations," later in this chapter.

Global versus Public Variables

The simplest method for two Forms to communicate with each other is via global variables. These variables are declared in the application's Module with the *Global* or *Public* keyword. If the following declarations appear in a Module, then they can be accessed from any place in the application's (any Form or other Module) code:

```
Global NumPoints As Integer
Public DataValues(100) As Double
```

A Form's code, however, can't access variables declared in another Form directly. Two or more Forms can have a variable called *iCounter*, but each *iCounter* variable is separate and exists only in the context of the Form in which it has been declared.

It's also possible to access a variable declared in one Form from within another, as long as one of these Forms "exposes" the variable by declaring it as Public. To access public variables on one Form from within another Form's code, you must use an expression like the following one:

```
CustName = Form2.FName & ", " & Form2.LName
```

The variables *FName* and *LName* must be declared in Form2 with the following statement:

```
Public FName As String, LName As String
```

The PVars project on the CD demonstrates how to access the public variables of a Form from within another Form's code. The application consists of two Forms, Form1 and Form2, as shown in Figure 4.5.

FIGURE 4.5:

The customer's name is stored in public variables in Form2, which are read by the code in Form1.

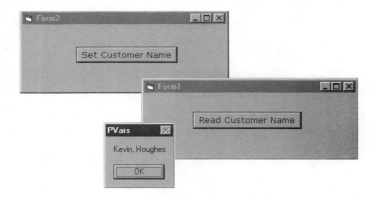

The code in Form2 consists of the declarations of two variables and the Command button's Click event that sets these two variables. Here's the entire code listing of Form2:

Code 4.2: The Code in Form2

```
Public FName As String, LName As String

Private Sub Command1_Click()
    LName = "Wong"
    FName = "Kevin"
End Sub
```

The variables *FName* and *LName* are declared as Public, so that they can be accessed from outside the Form's code. To assign some value to the variables, click the Command button on Form2. Then, you can retrieve their values from within Form1. The code behind the Read Customer Name button on Form1 is:

```
Private Sub Command1_Click()
    MsgBox Form2.FName & ", " & Form2.LName
End Sub

Private Sub Form_Load()
    Form2.Show
End Sub
```

The Form2.Show statement in the Form's Load event displays the second Form, where you can set the values of the public variables.

VB6 at Work: The Forms Project

The Forms application demonstrates the Load and Unload statements and the Show and Hide methods as well as how to access the properties and methods of one Form from within another. The application's main Form, shown in Figure 4.6, is called Form Handling. This Form contains two groups of identical controls under the headings Form2 and Form3. (Only Form2 is shown in Figure 4.6. Form3 is identical to Form2; it just contains a different graphic.) These two Forms are loaded, shown, and hidden from within the main Form. You can also specify whether the Forms will be shown as modal or modeless.

FIGURE 4.6:

The Forms application demonstrates how to manipulate Forms from within other Forms. Form2 is loaded from within the Form Handling Form.

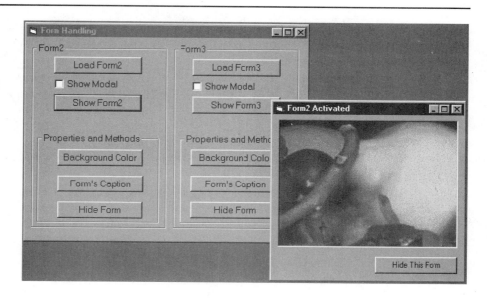

After Form2 and Form3 are loaded, you can use the buttons in the lower half of the main Form to set their BackColor and Caption properties and to call their Hide method. Let's look at the code behind the various buttons of the Forms application's main Form.

Code 4.3:   **The Load Form2 Button**

```
Private Sub LoadForm2_Click()
    If LoadForm2.Caption = "Load Form2" Then
        Load Form2
        LoadForm2.Caption = "Unload Form2"
    Else
        Unload Form2
        LoadForm2.Caption = "Load Form2"
    End If
End Sub
```

The Load Form2 button is a toggle. If the Form is already loaded, it unloads it and sets its own caption accordingly. The Show Form2 button calls the Show method to show Form2 (whether or not it's been loaded). The code behind the Show Form2 button takes into consideration the state of the Show Modal checkbox. If it's checked, it shows the Form as modal.

Code 4.4:   **The Show Form2 Button**

```
Private Sub ShowForm2_Click()
    Form2.Show Form2Modal.Value
End Sub
```

The checkbox's Value property is 0 or 1, which happens to be the same as the valid values of the Show method's *Mode* argument. That's why we can pass the checkbox's Value property as argument to the Show method.

The Background Color button sets the background color of Form2 to a random color.

Code 4.5:   **The Background Color Button**

```
Private Sub Form2Color_Click()
    Form2.BackColor = QBColor(Rnd() * 15)
End Sub
```

The Form's Caption button sets the caption of the Form with the following statement.

Code 4.6:   **The Caption Button**

```
Private Sub Form2Caption_Click()
    Form2.Caption = "Caption changed!"
End Sub
```

Finally, the Hide Form button hides the Form by calling its Hide method.

Code 4.7:   **The Hide Form Button**

```
Private Sub HideForm2_Click()
    Form2.Hide
End Sub
```

The code behind the buttons of the second group on the Forms application is quite similar, only it refers to Form3 instead of Form2.

The Activate and Deactivate Events

When more than one Form is displayed, the user can switch from one to the other with the mouse or by pressing Alt+Tab. Each time a Form is activated, the Activate event takes place. The Forms application uses the *Activate* event to set the Form's caption to a message indicating that this is the current Form:

```
Private Sub Form_Activate()
    Form2.Caption = "Form2 Activated"
End Sub
```

Likewise, when a Form is activated, the previously active Form receives the *Deactivate* event, which the application uses to change the Form's caption:

```
Private Sub Form_Deactivate()
    Form2.Caption = "Form2 Inactive"
End Sub
```

NOTE
It is possible to manipulate the properties and call the methods of the controls on a Form from within another Form, but the events are reported to the controls themselves. In other words, you can't capture the events of one Form's controls from within another Form.

Designing Menus

Menus are one of the most common and characteristic elements of the Windows user interface. Even in the old days of character-based displays, menus were used to display methodically organized choices and guide the user through an application. Despite the visually rich interfaces of Windows applications and the many alternatives, menus are still the most popular means of organizing a large number of options. Many applications duplicate some or all of their menus in the form of icons on a toolbar, but the menu is a standard fixture of a Form. You can turn the toolbars on and off, but not the menus.

The Menu Editor

Menus can be attached only to Forms, and you design them with the Menu Editor. To see how the Menu Editor works, start a new Standard EXE project, and when Form1 appears in the design window, choose Tools ➤ Menu Editor to open the Menu Editor, as shown in Figure 4.7. Alternatively, you can click the Menu Editor button on the toolbar.

FIGURE 4.7:

The Menu Editor's window displays a simple menu structure.

In the Menu Editor window you can specify the structure of your menu by adding one command at a time. Each menu command has two mandatory properties:

- **Caption**   This is the string that appears on the application's menu bar.

- **Name**   This is the name of the menu command. This property doesn't appear on the screen, but your code uses it to program the menu command.

The Caption and Name properties of a menu item are analogous to the properties that have the same name as the Command button or Label control. Caption is what the user sees on the Form, and Name is the means of accessing the control from within the code. As far as your code is concerned, each menu command is a separate object, just like a Command button or Label control.

To add commands to the Form's menu bar, enter a caption and a name for each command. As soon as you start typing the command's caption, it also appears in a new line in the list at the bottom of the Menu Editor window. Let's create the menu structure shown in Figure 4.7. This menu contains two commands, File and Edit. When the user clicks on either one, the submenus are displayed.

Table 4.2 shows the Caption and Name properties for each command.

TABLE 4.2:   Caption and Name Properties for File and Edit Commands

CAPTION	NAME
File	FileMenu
Open	FileOpen
Save	FileSave
Exit	FileExit
Edit	EditMenu
Copy	EditCopy
Cut	EditCut
Paste	EditPaste

The commands that belong to each menu form the corresponding submenu and are indented from the left. To design the menu, follow these steps:

1. Open a new Form in the Design pane, and choose Tools ➤ Menu Editor to open the Menu Editor window.

2. In the Caption box, type the caption of the first command (**File**).

3. In the Name box, enter the command's name (**FileMenu**).

4. Press Enter or click Next to enter the next command. Repeat steps 1 through 3 for all the commands listed.

If you run the application now, all the commands you've entered will be displayed along the Form's menu bar. If the window isn't wide enough to fit the entire menu, some of the menu's commands will be wrapped to a second line.

To create the menu hierarchy (make the commands appear under the File and Edit headings), you must indent them. Select the Open command in the list and click the button that has the right-pointing arrow. Do the same for the Save, Copy, Cut, and Paste commands. Your Menu Editor window should look like the one in Figure 4.7, shown earlier in this chapter.

If you run the application now, the menu has the proper appearance. Each subordinate command appears under the first-level menu command to which it belongs. To view the subordinate commands, click the corresponding top-level command. For example, to select the Paste command, first open the Edit menu.

You can nest menu commands to more than two levels by selecting a command and pressing the button with the right-pointing arrow more than once. When a menu command leads to a submenu, an arrow appears to its right, indicating that if selected, it will lead to a submenu.

NOTE   To create a separator bar in a menu, create a command as usual and set its caption to a hyphen (-). A horizontal line is displayed in the place of the command. Separator bars divide menu items into logical groups, and even though they have the structure of regular menu commands, they don't react to the mouse click.

The remaining fields on the Menu Editor window are optional and are described next.

The Index Field

Use the Index field to create an array of menu commands. All the commands of the array have the same name and a unique index that distinguishes them, just like arrays of controls. When appending a list of recently opened filenames in the File menu, it's customary to create an array of menu commands (one for each filename); all have the same name and a different index.

The Checked Field

Some menu commands act as toggles, and they are usually checked to indicate that they are on or unchecked to indicate that they are off. To display a checkmark next to a menu command initially, select the command from the list by clicking its name, and then check the Checked box in the Menu Editor window. You can also access this property from within your code to change the checked status of a menu command at runtime. For example, to toggle the status of a menu command called FrmtBold, use the statement:

```
FrmtBold.Checked = Not FrmtBold.Checked
```

The Enabled Field

Some menu commands aren't always available. The Paste command, for example, has no meaning if the Clipboard is empty. To indicate that a command can't be used at the time, you set its Enabled property to False. The command then appears grayed in the menu, and although it can be highlighted, it can't be activated. You can set the initial status of a command by checking or clearing the Enabled box in the Menu Editor window. You can also toggle the status of a menu command from within your code by manipulating its Enabled property, similar to the Checked command:

```
Paste CMP.Enabled = Not Paste CMP.Enabled
```

The Visible Field

To remove a command temporarily from the menu, set the command's Visible property to False. The Visible property isn't used frequently in menu design. In general, you should prefer to disable a command to indicate that it can't be used (some other action is required to enable it). Making a command invisible frustrates users, who may try to locate the command in another menu.

The Window Field

This option is used with MDI (Multiple Document Interface) applications to maintain a list of all open windows. The Window List option is explained in Chapter 10, *The Multiple Document Interface*.

TIP

The place to set menu control properties is the Menu Editor window. Each menu command is an object that belongs to the Form on which it appears (as are Command buttons). Therefore, it is possible to set a menu object's properties through the Properties window. You can't, however, select a command on the menu bar and then look up its properties in the Properties window. You must expand the list of objects at the top of the Properties window, select the menu object by name, and then view (or change) the menu object's properties. Likewise, you can program the Click event of each menu command by selecting the command's name in the Object list of the Code window.

Programming Menu Commands

Menu commands are similar to controls. They have certain properties that you can manipulate from within your code, and they recognize a single event, the Click event. If you select a menu command at design time, Visual Basic opens the code for the Click event in the Code window. The name of the event handler for the Click event is composed of the command's name followed by an underscore character and the event's name, as with all other controls.

You can also manipulate the menu command's properties from within your code. These properties are the ones you can set at design time, through the Menu Editor window. Menu commands don't have methods you can call.

Most menu object properties are toggles. To change the Checked property of the FontBold command, for instance, use the following statement:

```
FontBold.Checked = Not FontBold.Checked
```

If the command is checked, the checkmark will be removed. If the command is unchecked, the checkmark will be inserted in front of its name.

You can also change the command's caption at runtime, although this practice isn't common. The Caption property is manipulated only when you create dynamic menus by adding and removing commands at runtime, as you will see in the section "Adding Commands at Runtime."

Using Access and Shortcut Keys

Menus are a convenient way of displaying a large number of choices to the user. They allow you to organize commands in groups, according to their function, and they are available at all times. Opening menus and selecting commands with the mouse, however, can be an inconvenience. When using a word processor, for example, you don't want to have to take your hands off the keyboard and reach for the mouse. To simplify menu access, Visual Basic supports access keys and shortcut keys.

Access Keys

Access keys allow the user to open a menu by pressing the Alt key and a letter key. To open the Edit menu in all Windows applications, for example, you can press Alt+E. E is the Edit menu's access key. Once the menu is open, the user can select a command with the arrow keys or by pressing another key, which is the command's shortcut key. For example, with the Edit menu open, you can press P to invoke the Paste command or C to copy the selected text.

Access keys are designated by the designer of the application, and they are marked with an underline character. The underline under the character E in the Edit menu denotes that E is the menu's access key and that the keystroke Alt+E opens the Edit command. To assign an access key to a menu command, insert the ampersand symbol (&) in front of the character you want to use as an access key in the menu's caption.

NOTE

> If you don't designate access keys, Visual Basic will use the first character in each top-level menu as its access key. The user won't see the underline character under the first character, but will be able to open the menu by pressing the first character of its caption while holding down the Alt key. If two or more menu captions begin with the same letter, the first menu will open.

Because the & symbol has a special meaning in menu design, you can't use it as is. To actually display the & symbol in a caption, prefix it with another & symbol. For example, the caption "&Drag" produces a command with the caption Drag, (the first character is underlined because it's the access key). The caption "Drag && Drop" will create another command, whose caption will be Drag & Drop. Finally, the string "&Drag && Drop" will create another command with the caption Drag & Drop.

Shortcut Keys

Shortcut keys are similar to access keys, but instead of opening a menu, they run a command when pressed. Assign shortcut keys to frequently used menu commands, so that users can reach them with a single keystroke. Shortcut keys are combinations of the Control key and a function or character key.

To assign a shortcut key to a menu command, drop down the Shortcut list in the Menu Editor and select a keystroke. You don't have to insert any special characters in the command's caption, nor do you have to enter the keystroke next to the caption. It will be displayed next to the command automatically. Figure 4.8 shows some of the possible shortcut keys you can assign to your menus.

NOTE

> Unlike access keys, shortcut keys can't be assigned at all times. You must select them from the Shortcut list.

FIGURE 4.8:

The Shortcut list allows
users to assign shortcut
keys to a menu command.

TIP   When assigning access and shortcut keys, take into consideration some well-established Windows standards. Users expect Alt+F to open the File menu, therefore, don't use Alt+F for the Format menu. Likewise, when the Edit menu is open, pressing C selects the Copy command and pressing t selects the Cut command. Don't use the C key as a shortcut for the Cut command.

Manipulating Menus at Runtime

Dynamic menus change at runtime and display more or fewer commands, depending on the current status of the program. This section explores two techniques for implementing dynamic menus:

- Creating short and long versions of the same menu
- Adding and removing menu commands at runtime

Creating Short and Long Menus

A common technique in menu design is to create long and short versions of a menu. If a menu contains many commands, and most of the time only a few of them are needed, you can create one menu with all the commands and another with the most common ones. The first menu is the long one, and the second is the short one. The last command in the long menu should be Short Menu, and when selected, it should display the short menu. The last command in the short menu should be Long Menu, and when selected, it should display the long menu. Figure 4.9 shows a long and a short version of the same menu. The short version omits the infrequently used formatting commands and is easier to handle.

To implement the LongMenu command, start a new project and create a menu that has the structure shown in Table 4.3.

TABLE 4.3:   LongMenu Command Structure

Command Name	Caption
FontMenu	Font
mfontBold	Bold
mfontItalic	Italic
mfontRegular	Regular
mfontUline	Underline
mfontStrike	StrikeThru
mFontSmallCaps	SmallCaps
mFontAllCaps	All Caps
Separator	"-" (a hyphen without the quotes)
menuSize	Short Menu

Following is the code that shows/hides the long menu in the MenuSize command's Click event.

Code 4.8:	The MenuSize Menu Item's Click Event

```
Private Sub MenuSize_Click()
    If MenuSize.Caption = "Short Menu" Then
        MenuSize.Caption = "Long Menu"
    Else
        MenuSize.Caption = "Short Menu"
    End If
    mFontUline.Visible = Not mFontUline.Visible
    mFontStrike.Visible = Not mFontStrike.Visible
    mFontSmallCaps.Visible = Not mFontSmallCaps.Visible
    mFontAllCaps.Visible = Not mFontAllCaps.Visible
End Sub
```

This subroutine doesn't do much. It simply toggles the Visible property of certain menu commands and changes the command's caption to Short Menu or Long Menu, depending on the menu's current status.

Adding and Removing Commands at Runtime

We'll conclude our discussion of menu design with a technique for building dynamic menus, which grow and shrink at runtime. Many applications maintain a list of the most recently opened files in their File menu. When you first start the application, this list is empty, and as you open and close files, it starts to grow.

To create a dynamic menu, you first create a control array of menu commands. In the Menu Editor window, add a menu option and set its Index property to 0. You can then add commands with the same name and consecutive Index values. At design time, you don't have to add more than one option. One command with its Index property set to 0 is adequate to create the menu control array. You can use this array's name and an Index value to add new options at runtime.

Figure 4.10 shows the RTMenu application, which demonstrates how to add to and remove items from a menu at runtime.

FIGURE 4.10:

The RTMenu application

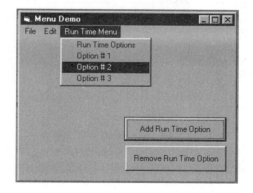

Initially, the form's menu contains the following items:

File

     Open

     Save

     Exit

Edit

     Copy

     Cut

     Paste

Run Time Menu

Commands grouped in submenus are indented from the left. The last command's name is RunTimeOptions and its index is 0. Once a command option is specified as a control array, you can easily add commands to the *RunTimeOptions* array with the Load method. After all, menu commands are very similar to controls.

The two buttons at the bottom of the Form add commands to and remove commands from the Run Time Menu. Each new command is appended at the end of the menu, and the commands are removed from the bottom of the menu (the most recently added commands). To change this order, and display the most recent command at the beginning of the menu, use a large initial index value (like 99) and increase it with every new command you add to the menu, as shown in Code 4.9.

Code 4.9:   **The RTMenu Application**

```
Option Explicit
Dim RTmenu

Private Sub AddCommand_Click()

    RTmenu = RTmenu + 1
    If RTmenu = 1 Then RunTimeOptions(0).Caption = "Run Time Options"
    Load RunTimeOptions(RTmenu)
    RunTimeOptions(RTmenu).Caption = "Option # " & RTmenu
End Sub

Private Sub RemoveCommand_Click()
    If RTmenu = 0 Then
        MsgBox "Menu is empty"
        Exit Sub
    End If
    Unload RunTimeOptions(RTmenu)
    RTmenu = RTmenu - 1
End Sub
```

New menu commands are appended to the existing menu with the Load method. The argument of the Load method is the name of a menu command with a new Index value. The variable *RTMenu* keeps track of the number of commands under the Run Time Menu object. Each time a new command is added to this menu, *RTMenu* increases by an increment of 1. The Remove Run Time Option button uses the Unload method to remove commands from the same menu. The argument to the Unload method is the index of the command to be removed. The sample application above removes commands from the bottom of the menu, but you could remove any command by specifying its order in the menu.

NOTE   The Load and Unload methods are not new to you. We used them in the first section of the chapter to load and unload Forms. In addition to these two methods, you can also call the Hide method to hide menu commands. Calling the Hide method is equivalent to setting the corresponding command's Visible property to False.

Creating Pop-Up Menus

Nearly every Windows application provides a context menu (or shortcut menu, as it's sometimes called) that the user can invoke by right-clicking a Form or a control. This *pop-up menu* (or floating menu) is a regular menu, but it's not anchored on the Form. It can be displayed anywhere on the Form.

Pop-up menus are invoked with the PopupMenu method. First, you create a menu as usual. Suppose you have designed the basic File and Edit menus for an application, and they are displayed on the Form as usual. To make the application a bit easier to use, you can also display the Edit menu as a pop-up menu. If the Edit menu's name is EditMenu, you can insert the following line in a control's MouseUp event:

```
Private Sub Form_MouseUp(Button As Integer, Shift As Integer, _
        X As Single, Y As Single)
   If Button = vbRightButton Then PopupMenu EditMenu
End Sub
```

(We use the MouseUp event because, unlike the Click event, it reports which button was pressed.)

If the right mouse button is pressed, the code calls the Form's PopupMenu method to display the Edit menu. The PopupMenu method is usually called from within TextBox and PictureBox controls, because these controls can carry out editing operations.

> **TIP**
>
> If you don't want the pop-up menu to appear in the application's menu bar, you must still create the menu as usual with the Menu Editor and then set its Visible property to False. Each time the menu is invoked with the PopupMenu method, Visual Basic ignores the setting of the Visible method.

The PopupMenu method has the following syntax:

```
PopupMenu menuname, flags, x, y, boldcommand
```

Only the first argument is required, and it's the menu's name, as shown in the Menu Editor window. The other arguments are optional. The *x* and *y* arguments are the coordinates of a point on the Form (or control) where the menu will be displayed. If you don't specify the *x* and *y* arguments, the pop-up menu will appear at the pointer's location. The *flags* argument defines the location and behavior of a pop-up menu and can have one of the values shown in Table 4.4.

The last argument, *BoldCommand*, specifies the name of a menu command that should appear in bold. Only one command in the menu can be bold, and bold is commonly used to denote the default (or suggested) option.

TABLE 4.4:   Values for the flags Argument

CONSTANTS	DESCRIPTION
Location	
vbPopupMenuLeftAlign	(default) The specified x location defines the left edge of the pop-up menu.
vbPopupMenuCenterAlign	The pop-up menu is centered around the specified *x* location.
vbPopupMenuRightAlign	The specified x location defines the right edge of the pop-up menu.
Behavior	
vbPopupMenuLeftButton	(default) The pop-up menu triggers the Click event when the user clicks a menu item with the left mouse button only.
vbPopupMenuRightButton	The pop-up menu triggers the Click event when the user clicks a menu item with either the right or the left mouse button.

To specify both a behavior and location constant, combine them with the Or operator. The following code displays a pop-up menu with its top border centered on the Form, which triggers Click events for menu items when either button is pressed.

```
x = ScaleWidth / 2
y = ScaleHeight / 2
Form1.PopupMenu EditMenu, vbPopupMenuCenterAlign Or _
        vbPopupMenuRightButton, X, Y
```

Building Dynamic Forms at Runtime

There are situations when you won't know in advance how many instances of a given control may be required on a Form. This isn't very common, but if you're writing a data entry application and you want to work with many tables of a database, you'll have to be especially creative. Since every table consists of different fields, it will be difficult to build a single Form to accommodate all the possible tables a user may throw at your application.

In these situations, it is possible to design dynamic Forms, which are populated at runtime. The simplest approach is to create more controls than you'll ever need and set their Visible property to False at design time. At runtime, you can display the controls by switching their Visible property to True. As you know already, quick-and-dirty methods are not the most efficient ones. The proper method to create dynamic Forms at runtime is described in this section.

Just as you can load (existing) Forms with the Load statement, you can also load new controls on a Form. The controls to be loaded don't need to exist on the Form; they can be members of an array of controls. At design time, you can create one control and make it the first member of an array. To do so, assign the value 0 to its Index property at design time. Figure 4.11 shows the CLoad project, which demonstrates this technique.

FIGURE 4.11:

The CLoad application creates this Form with code when it's loaded.

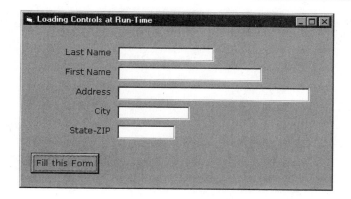

The Form of Figure 4.11 is a data entry Form and the fields are placed on the Form at runtime. The CLoad project, in this chapter's folder on the CD, builds the same Form every time it's executed, but in a practical situation, you would adjust the fields to reflect the structure of a table or a structure defined by the user on another Form.

To design the data entry Form of the CLoad application, you must place a Label and a TextBox control on the Form. Place them near the top of the Form, so that they can be used as guides for aligning the remaining controls. These two controls will remain invisible at all times. Then complete the following steps:

1. Name the Label control **Labels** and set its Index property to 0.

2. Set its Alignment property to 1 (Right Justify).

3. Name the TextBox control **TextBoxes** and set its Index to 0.

4. Then select both controls with the mouse and set their Visible property to False.

So far, you've created the structure necessary for loading new controls at runtime. These controls will be placed on the Form in pairs with the Load command and they'll be aligned with the two controls placed on the Form at design time. The code behind the Fill This Form button is shown in Code 4.10.

Code 4.10:   **Creating New Controls at Runtime**

```
Private Sub Command1_Click()
Dim Captions(10) As String
Dim Sizes(10) As Integer

Captions(1) = "Last Name"
Captions(2) = "First Name"
Captions(3) = "Address"
Captions(4) = "City"
Captions(5) = "State-ZIP"

Sizes(1) = 20
Sizes(2) = 30
Sizes(3) = 40
Sizes(4) = 15
Sizes(5) = 12
For i = 1 To 5
    Load Labels(i)
    Load TextBoxes(i)
    Labels(i).Top = Labels(i - 1).Top + 1.5 * Labels(0).Height
    Labels(i).Left = Labels(0).Left
    TextBoxes(i).Top = TextBoxes(i - 1).Top + 1.5 * TextBoxes(i).Height
    TextBoxes(i).Left = TextBoxes(0).Left
    TextBoxes(i).Width = Sizes(i) * TextWidth("A")
    Labels(i).Caption = Captions(i)
    Labels(i).Visible = True
    TextBoxes(i).Visible = True
Next
End Sub
```

The arrays *Captions* and *Sizes* hold the captions of the various fields and their lengths in number of characters. These two arrays don't change in the CLoad application. However, you can either extract these values from a table in a database or let the user design the structure of the desired record and then use it to construct the arrays. It's a simple method for creating data entry Forms that can be reused in many situations. By the way, this is how many Wizards work.

The code then places another pair of controls on the Form, aligns them with the previous ones, adjusts the size of the TextBox control according to the value of the corresponding element of the *Sizes* array, and sets the caption of the Label control to the value of the corresponding element of the *Caption* array. Finally, it displays them by setting their Visible property to True. Controls placed on a Form with the Load statement are invisible by default. Even if the first items in a control array were visible, the controls loaded with the Load statement would be invisible, so you must always turn on the Visible property from within your code.

This subroutine relies on the placement of the initial controls on the Form. There are more ways to position the controls on the Form, but this is probably the simplest method. Place a few controls on the Form at design time, and then use them as guides for aligning the new controls at runtime. You should open the CLoad project on the CD and see how it works. You can modify the project to accommodate other types of fields, such as True/False fields (which should be mapped to CheckBox controls), dates, and so on. To complete the CLoad application, you should also add a few Command buttons, including the code to handle the data entered by the user (validate them, save to random access file, and so on).

Drag-and-Drop Operations

A unique characteristic of the Windows user interface is the ability of the user to grab a control and drop it on another. This feature is called *drag-and-drop* and is used extensively in the Desktop. Nearly every item on the Desktop can be dragged and dropped on various other items, such as the Recycle Bin, the printers, folders, and so on.

The same techniques can be used in applications. For example, the Form in Figure 4.12 contains the three file controls that let the user select and view any folder on the disk. The two lists (Move to Temp and Move to Tape) are destinations for various files. You could provide buttons to move files from the FileListBox control to either list, but the most convenient way to move files to the two ListBox controls on the Form is to drag-and-drop them.

FIGURE 4.12:

The ListDrop application demonstrates the kind of functionality you can add to your user interface with drag-and-drop operations.

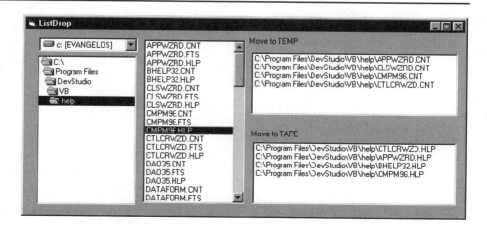

Open the ListDrop project to test-drive the application. To specify the files to be copied to the Temp folder or the tape drive (these features aren't implemented in the code, but you can easily add the code to actually move or copy the selected files), drag them from the FileListBox control (middle window) to the corresponding List. To undo an action, you can simply drag a file back. When a filename is moved from the file list to one of the two ListBox controls, the file isn't removed from the file control (you have to delete the file to remove it from the FileListBox control). However, when you move a selected filename from the Move to Temp or Move to Tape lists back to the FileListBox control, the name of the file is removed from the corresponding list, but it's not added again to the FileListBox control.

Load and run the ListDrop application and check out its ease of operation and functionality. Compare it with any other user interface design based on more traditional controls, such as Command buttons, and you will see that drag-and-drop features can significantly enhance your application's interface. User interfaces based on drag-and-drop operations aren't common, but when an application can benefit from this type of interface, you should implement it. As you will see, doing so is quite easy and based on a small number of properties, methods, and events.

The DragMode Property

Nearly all controls have a *DragMode* property, which determines whether a control can be dragged with the mouse. The DragMode property can have one of the following settings:

- **0–Manual**   Drag operations must be initiated from within the code.

- **1–Automatic**   The user can drag the control with the mouse.

When you set a control's DragMode property to Automatic, Visual Basic displays the control's outline as the user moves the control around and notifies the controls that happen to be underneath the control as it's dragged. Visual Basic doesn't perform any actions, such as copying one control's text onto another. This is the programmer's responsibility.

To implement drag-and-drop features in your applications, you must first decide which controls can be dragged and on which control they can be dropped. The control being dragged is the *source control*. All other controls on the Form are the *destinations* of the drag-and-drop operation. To initiate a drag-and-drop operation, you must either set a control's DragMode property to Automatic or call the control's Drag method. The DragMode=Automatic setting and the Drag method are identical, but the Drag method gives you more control over the operation. For example, you may not initiate a drag operation if the source control is empty.

The DragDrop and DragOver Methods

A drag operation ends with a drop operation; when the user releases the mouse button. By default, controls don't react to the drop operation. To make a control react when another control is dropped on it, you must supply some code in its *DragDrop* event, which is defined as follows:

```
Sub control_DragDrop(Source As Control, X As Single, Y As Single)
```

The *control* item can be any control on the Form. *Source* is an object that represents the control that was dropped. It's not a control's name or other property; it's an object variable. You can use it to access the various properties of the control that was dropped. *X* and *Y* are the coordinates of the mouse at the moment the source control was dropped on the destination control.

In addition to reacting to the dropping of a source control, the destination control can react to the movement of a control being dragged over it. This condition is detected with the *DragOver* event, which is generated as long as the source control is dragged over the destination control. The definition of the DragOver event is as follows:

```
Private Sub control_DragOver(Source As Control, X As Single, _
        Y As Single, State As Integer)
```

Source is the control being dragged, *X* and *Y* are the current coordinates of the mouse, and the *State* argument corresponds to the transition state of the control being dragged. It can have one of the following values:

- **0**   The source control enters the target's area.

- **1**   The source control leaves the target's area.

- **2**   The source control moves over the target's area.

Depending on whether the control under the pointer can accept the drop operation or not, use the DragOver event to prepare the destination control for the drop operation, or change the mouse pointer to a different icon.

VB6 at Work: The DrpEvnts Project

To see these drag-and-drop events in actions, let's design the application shown in Figure 4.13. The application is called DrpEvnts, and you will find it in this chapter's folder on the CD.

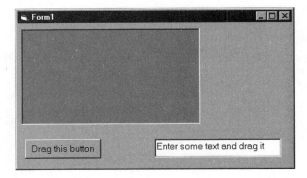

The application will monitor the dragging of the Command button and react as follows.

- When the button is first dragged over the picture box, the picture box is painted red.

- When the button leaves the picture box, the picture box is painted green.

- If the user drops the button while it's over the picture box, the picture box is painted blue.

To design the application, follow these steps:

1. Start a new project and place a picture box and a Command button on the Form.

2. Set the PictureBox control's Background property to a green color, and set the Command button's DragMode property to 1–Automatic.

3. Enter the following code in the PictureBox control's DragOver event handler:

```
Private Sub Picture1_DragOver(Source As Control, _
     X As Single, Y As Single, State As Integer)
   If State = 0 Then Picture1.BackColor = vbRed
   If State = 2 Then Form1.Caption = _
        "Source Control moves over the PictureBox"
   If State = 1 Then
       Picture1.BackColor = vbGreen
       Form1.Caption = "Drag & Drop Demo"
   End If
End Sub
```

4. Enter the following code in the control's DragDrop event:

```
Private Sub Picture1_DragDrop(Source As Control, _
        X As Single, Y As Single)
    Picture1.BackColor = vbBlue
End Sub
```

Run the application and see how it monitors the movement of the mouse. The *State* argument of the DragOver event takes the value 0 only when the button is dragged over the PictureBox control for the first time. After that, the DragOver event is triggered as the button is moved over the picture box, but the *State* argument is 2. Finally, as the button is moved outside the area of the PictureBox control, the DragOver event is triggered one last time, and this time, its *State* argument is 1.

Notice that the code of this application is concentrated in the two drag-related events of the Picture Box control and that you don't have to supply any code for the Command button's events. Simply setting its DragMode property to Automatic was enough to add the dragging capability to the control. Moreover, the code doesn't use the *Source* argument of the two events. The Picture Box control would react exactly the same no matter which control you dragged over or dropped on it.

The *TypeOf* Keyword

The DragDrop and DragOver events' *Source* argument represents an object so that the destination control can figure out which control was dropped on it. To access the name of the control that was dropped, use the following expression:

```
Source.Name
```

Suppose you want to read the Text property of TextBox controls and the Caption property of Label controls when they are dropped on the destination control. Normally, you would use the following expressions to retrieve these two properties:

```
Source.Text
Source.Caption
```

But you have to know whether the dropped control was a TextBox control or a Label control. If not, your code may attempt to access the Label's Text property or the TextBox's Caption property and crash with a runtime error.

To find out the type of object dropped, use the *TypeOf* statement, which has the following syntax:

```
TypeOf objectname Is objecttype
```

The *objectname* item is an object, and *objecttype* is an object type. To find out whether the source control is a TextBox control, use an If structure such as the following:

```
If TypeOf Source Is Textbox Then
    MsgBox Source.Text
End If
```

You can use the *TypeOf* keyword anywhere in a Visual Basic application, but it's commonly used in drag-and-drop operations. We'll use this keyword later in our applications to differentiate among the various types of controls being dropped.

Mouse Conflicts

Let's experiment a little with dragging operations. We'll add a line of code to the Command button's Click event to make the button react to the mouse click by displaying a message in the Immediate window with the following statement:

```
Debug.Print "I was clicked"
```

Run the application and click the Drag-and-Drop button with the mouse. No message will appear in the Immediate window. When Visual Basic starts a drag-and-drop operation, it doesn't generate the usual mouse events (Click or Mouse-Down). If you reset the button's DragMode property to 0 (Manual), Visual Basic will start responding to the mouse events on the button, but it won't drag it.

NOTE   When a control's DragMode property is set to True, it stops reacting to the usual mouse events. All you can do is drag the control around, but you can't count on its usual mouse events.

To make matters even worse, add a TextBox control on the Form, set its Drag-Mode property to Automatic, and then run the application again. You can enter text in the control, move the control around, but the editing operations of the mouse are gone. If you attempt to select some text with the mouse, a drag operation starts. The editing features of the mouse are taken over by the dragging operations.

Our experiments indicate that automatic dragging must be designed carefully. You can't simply set a control's DragMode to Automatic and expect it to work as before. If the control is a Label, you don't have to worry about editing it. Setting its DragMode property to Automatic isn't going to cause any serious problems, except that you won't be able to use the common mouse events. If you don't need the Click event handler of the Label control in your application, you can set the control's DragMode to Automatic and implement drag-and-drop features. If you set a Command button's DragMode to Automatic, you can no longer count on the control's Click event. The solution to these conflicts is to implement drag-and-drop features manually. You'll see how this is done, but first let's look at a couple of simpler applications that demonstrate typical uses of drag-and-drop operations.

VB6 at Work: The DragDrop Project

The DragDrop application, shown in Figure 4.14, consists of a single Form that contains a Label, TextBox, and PictureBox controls. The Label and TextBox controls' DragMode property is set to 1–Automatic, so you can drag them on any other control. Run the application, enter some text in the textbox (without using the mouse's editing features, just the keyboard), and then drop the TextBox control on the Label.

FIGURE 4.14:

The DragDrop application

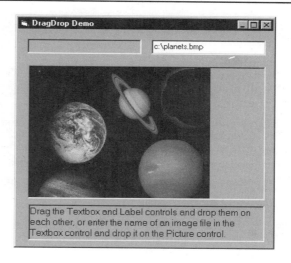

If you enter the full path name of an image file in the textbox and then drop the control on the Label control, the filename is copied to the Label control. If you drop it on the picture box, the image is displayed there. These are two common uses of drag-and-drop operations.

To make sure we make sure that the control being dropped is the Label control, and to assign the TextBox control's text to the Label control's caption, use the listing shown in Code 4.11 and 4.12.

Code 4.11: **The DragDrop Event Handler Code for the TextBox Control**

```
Private Sub Text1_DragDrop(Source As Control, X As Single, Y As Single)
    If TypeOf Source Is Label Then
        Text1.Text = Label1.Caption
```

```
        End If
End Sub
```

You may think that we don't have to test for the object being dropped since the Label is the only object that can be dropped on the TextBox control. That's not quite true. You can actually drop an object on itself.

The DragDrop event handler for the Label control is similar.

Code 4.12:   **The DragDrop Event Handler Code for the Label Control**

```
Private Sub Label1_DragDrop(Source As Control, _
        X As Single, Y As Single)
    If TypeOf Source Is TextBox Then
        Label1.Caption = Source.Text
    End If
End Sub
```

The Label control reacts to the drop of the TextBox control by copying the text to the Label's Caption property.

The PictureBox control reacts differently to the drop of either control. It assumes that the content of the label or the TextBox control is the filename of an image, which it attempts to display.

Code 4.13:   **The DragDrop Event Handler Code for the PictureBox Control**

```
Private Sub Picture1_DragDrop(Source As Control, _
        X As Single, Y As Single)
Dim imgName

    If TypeOf Source Is TextBox Then
        imgName = Source.Text
    Else
        imgName = Source.Caption
    End If
    On Error GoTo NOIMAGE
    Picture1.Picture = LoadPicture(imgName)
    Exit Sub

NOIMAGE:
```

```
        MsgBox "This is not a valid file name"
    End Sub
```

First, it extracts the label's caption or the textbox's text (depending on the source control), and then uses it as argument to the LoadPicture method to display the image on the PictureBox control. The error handler is there to prevent runtime errors, should the control contain an invalid filename.

NOTE   The drop event can trigger any action on the destination control. It's common to use drag-and-drop operations to allow the user to move information among textboxes or list boxes, but as this example demonstrates, you can process the data dropped on the destination control any way you see fit.

VB6 at Work: The DropForm Project

Our next application demonstrates drag-and-drop operations among multiple Forms. The DropForm application consists of three Forms. The main Form contains two columns of labels, with state and city names. The other two Forms each contain a ListBox control, and they are initially empty. The user can drag any of the labels on the main Form and drop them on one of the two lists, which reside on different Forms.

Design the Forms as shown in Figure 4.15. Place any type of data you want in the Label controls. The Label controls on the first column (which display state names) have their Tag property set to "STATE" and the Label controls on the second column have their Tag property set to "CITY." You'll see later how these tags are used in the code.

When the main Form is loaded, it must display the other two Forms. Enter the following code in its Load event handler:

```
Private Sub Form_Load()
    DropForm2.Show
    DropForm2.Move DropForm1.Left + DropForm1.Width + 500, _
        DropForm1.Top
    DropForm3.Show
    DropForm3.Move DropForm1.Left + DropForm1.Width + 500, _
        DropForm1.Top + DropForm2.Height
End Sub
```

The Move method is used to place the smaller Forms to the right of the main Form.

The DropForm application
lets you drag-and-drop
controls among different
Forms.

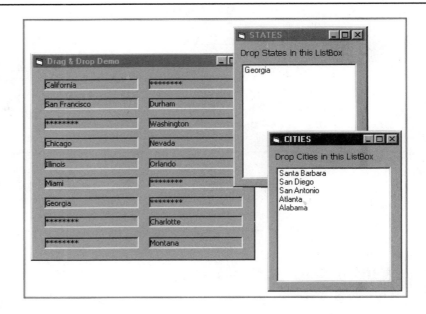

More interesting is the code is in the DragDrop event handlers of the two List-Box controls shown next.

Code 4.14: **The DragDrop Event Handler Code of the ListBox Control on the States Form**

```
Private Sub List1_DragDrop(Source As Control, X As Single, Y As Single)
    If Source.Caption = "********" Then
        Beep
        Exit Sub
    End If
    If Source.Tag = "STATE" Then
        List1.AddItem Source.Caption & "  (" & _
                Source.Parent.Name & ")"
        Source.Caption = "********"
    Else
        MsgBox "This list accepts states only!"
    End If
End Sub
```

When a label is dropped on this control, the code of the DragDrop event examines the source control's Tag property. If it's not STATE, then the control can't be dropped and the appropriate message is displayed. If the Tag property is STATE, it sets the caption of the source control to asterisks to indicate that it can't be dropped again. Since only Label controls can be dropped on the two ListBox controls, there is no need to test for the type of object being dropped. We use the `Source.Caption` expression directly to access the label's caption. The DragDrop event handler for the ListBox control on the Cities Form is identical. Only the name of the ListBox control changes (List2 instead of List1).

Notice that in addition to the caption of the control that is dropped on the list box, we add the name of the Form from which the label comes, in parentheses. The expression `Source.Parent` gives you access to the Form to which the source control belongs. Through this expression, you can access the properties of the Form from which the source control came. The expression `Source.Parent.Name` returns the name of the Form on which the labels with the city and state names are placed.

The drag operation's destination control doesn't care where the source control comes from. The argument *Source* has all the information it needs to access the source control's properties, regardless of whether it resides on the same or another Form.

Manual Drag

Now we'll see how to drag editable controls (such as TextBox controls) without sacrificing the control's editing features. To initiate a drag operation manually, call the *Drag* method. Calling the Drag method for a control is equivalent to setting its DragMode property to 1–Automatic for as long as the control is being dragged. After the control is dropped somewhere on the Form, the DragMode property is reset. The DragMode property doesn't change, but the control behaves temporarily as if it is set to 1–Automatic.

When do you call the Drag method of a control? First, you must decide how the application will differentiate between regular editing operations with the mouse and dragging operations. One safe approach is to use the Control or Alt key with the mouse to drag the control. All the functions of the mouse are available as usual. If the mouse button is pressed while the Control key is down, however, the code initiates a drag operation by calling the control's Drag method. Or, you can use the right mouse click to initiate a drag-and-drop operation.

VB6 at Work: The TextDrop Project

Let's see how manual dragging is done. Figure 4.16 shows a Form with two TextBox controls and a Label control. The project is called TextDrop and can be found in this chapter's folder on the CD.

The TextDrop application demonstrates the differences between automatic and manual dragging.

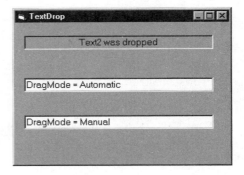

The two textboxes have their DragMode property set to Automatic and Manual, as indicated by their initial captions. Both TextBox controls can be dropped on the Label control. Let's start by looking at the code behind the Label control's DragDrop event.

Code 4.15: **The Label Control's DragDrop Event**

```
Private Sub Label1_DragDrop(Source As Control, _
        X As Single, Y As Single)
    Label1.Caption = Source.Name & " was dropped"
End Sub
```

This subroutine displays a message with the name of the control that is dropped on the label. There is no need to test for the type of the control, since all controls have a Name property.

The first control can be dropped automatically. This means that you can edit the contents of the first textbox using only the keyboard. To select a range of text on the control, you hold down the Shift key and press the arrow keys. If you drag the mouse on the first textbox, it will start moving. Drop it on the Label control and watch the label's caption change to reflect the name of the control that is dropped.

The second textbox can be edited as usual. To drag it, you must click the control while holding down the Control key and then start dragging it. The Drag method of the control is called from within the MouseDown event if the Control button is pressed, as shown in Code 4.16.

Code 4.16:   **The Second TextBox Control's MouseDown Event**

```
Private Sub Text2_MouseDown(Button As Integer, _
        Shift As Integer, X As Single, Y As Single)
    If Shift = 2 Then
        Text2.Drag
    End If
End Sub
```

Run the TextDrop application and see how it behaves. The Drag method is quite simple and will become your tool for adding drag-and-drop features to editable controls. You should also use the Drag method with noneditable controls, such as labels or Command buttons, which should also react to the common mouse events.

Dragging List Items

Another problem with drag-and-drop operations is that while you're dragging a large control, Visual Basic moves the control's outline around. If the source control is a ListBox control, there's no need to drag the entire control; drag only the selected element. The trick is to drag a smaller control, such as a Label control, whose dimensions are the same as the item's dimensions. In the last section, we're going to look at this technique with an example.

VB6 at Work: The ListDrop Project

The application shown in Figure 4.17 is called ListDrop, and you'll find it in the ListDrop folder on the CD. The operation of this application was explained in the section "Drag-and-Drop Operations," earlier in this chapter.

FIGURE 4.17:

The ListDrop application demonstrates how to simulate drag-and-drop operations with isolated List items.

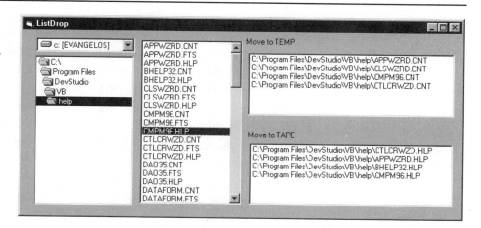

The Form contains all the controls you see on it plus an invisible Label control. When the user clicks the mouse over a ListBox control, the invisible Label control (called DragLabel) is resized to the width of the corresponding ListBox control and to the height of a line in the list. It is then repositioned over the selected item in the list. Its Drag method is called to initiate a drag operation, from within the ListBox control's MouseDown event, which is shown next.

Code 4.17:   **The FileListBox Control's MouseDown Event Handler**

```
Private Sub FileList_MouseDown(Button As Integer, _
        Shift As Integer, X As Single, Y As Single)
    Dim DY As Integer

    DY = TextHeight("A")    ' Height of an item
    DragLabel.Move FileList.Left, FileList.Top + Y - DY / 2, _
        FileList.Width, DY
    DragLabel.Drag          ' Drag label instead of item
End Sub
```

The DragLabel control can be dropped on any other control on the Form. When it's dropped on the TEMPList control, the following lines are executed:

```
Private Sub TEMPList_DragDrop(Source As Control, _
        X As Single, Y As Single)
    If ListDrop.ActiveControl.Name = "FileList" Then
        TEMPList.AddItem Dir1.Path & "\" & FileList.FileName
    End If
End Sub
```

The ListBox control can't use the *Source* argument to find out which control is dropped on it. It's always the label that's being dropped. The control in which the drag operation is initiated remains active to the end of the drag-and-drop operation, so the TEMPList control can access the ActiveControl property of the Form to figure out where the item is coming from. Since the TEMPList and TAPEList controls can only accept data from the FileList control, in their DragDrop event handler they must examine the ActiveControl's Name property. If it's FileList (the name of the FileListBox control), the selected item must be added to the corresponding list's contents. The code of the TAPEList_DragDrop event handler is identical.

When the user selects an item in the TEMPList and TAPEList controls to remove, the code in Code 4.18 is executed.

Code 4.18:   The TEMPList Control's DragDrop Event Handler

```
Private Sub TEMPList_MouseDown(Button As Integer, Shift As Integer,_
        X As Single, Y As Single)
Dim DY As Integer

    DY = TextHeight("A")     ' Height of item
    DragLabel.Move TEMPList.Left, _
            TEMPList.Top + Y - DY / 2, TEMPList.Width, DY
    DragLabel.Drag           ' Drag label instead of item
End Sub
```

Again, a drag operation is initiated.

The item is removed from the corresponding list if it's dropped on the FileList control. When the item is dropped on the FileList control, it signifies the user's intention to remove the file from the corresponding list. In the control's DragDrop event we must first examine the control from which the file name was dragged. Again, we can't use the *Source* argument of the DragDrop event; we must use the ActiveControl object. The FileList control's DragDrop event is shown next.

Code 4.19:   The FileList Control's DragDrop Event Handler

```
Private Sub FileList_DragDrop(Source As Control, _
    X As Single, Y As Single)
    If ListDrop.ActiveControl.Name = "TEMPList" Then
        TEMPList.RemoveItem TEMPList.ListIndex
    ElseIf ListDrop.ActiveControl.Name = "TAPEList" Then
        TAPEList.RemoveItem TAPEList.ListIndex
    End If
End Sub
```

There are a few more lines of code here because the program must figure out the control that initiated the drag-and-drop operation and remove the selected item from the corresponding list. Again, the code uses the form's ActiveControl property to figure out where the item came from.

You may notice that the DragLabel control doesn't become visible before the Drag method is called. Its outline is dragged as if it was visible. Normally, you wouldn't be able to drag an invisible control, but the Drag method doesn't seem to care about the control's Visible property.

If you open the ListDrop application on the CD, you will see that the controls that don't react to the dropping of the control have the following code in their DragOver event:

```
Private Sub Drive1_DragOver(Source As Control, X As Single, _
        Y As Single, State As Integer)
    If State = 0 Then Source.MousePointer = 12
    If State = 1 Then Source.MousePointer = 0
End Sub
```

The controls that can't be used as destinations for the drag-and-drop operation react to the DragOver event by setting the pointer to a stop icon, to indicate that they are not valid receptors for the current operation. It is customary to include these two lines of code in all the controls that won't react to the DragDrop event.

CHAPTER
FIVE

5

Basic ActiveX Controls

- The TextBox control

- The ListBox control

- The ComboBox control

- The ScrollBar control

- The Slider control

- The File controls

In the previous chapters, we explored the environment of Visual Basic and the principles of event-driven programming, which is the core of Visual Basic's programming model. In the process, we briefly examined a few basic controls through the examples. Visual Basic provides many more controls, and all of them have a multitude of properties. Most of the properties have obvious names, and you can set them either from the Properties window or from within your code.

This chapter explores several of the basic ActiveX controls in depth. These are the controls you'll be using most often in your applications because they are the basic building blocks of the Windows user interface.

Rather than look at controls' background and foreground color, font, and other trivial properties, we'll look at the properties unique to each control and how these properties are used in building a user interface.

NOTE   This chapter is not going to discuss every property and every method of every control. That would take another book, and its value would be questionable. Most properties are quite simple to use and easy to understand. This chapter focuses on the unique features of the basic controls you need to know in order to use them in your user interface.

The TextBox Control

The textbox is the primary mechanism for displaying and entering text and is one of the most common elements of the Windows user interface. The TextBox control is a small text editor that provides all the basic text-editing facilities: inserting and selecting text, scrolling the text if it doesn't fit in the control's area, and even exchanging text with other applications through the Clipboard.

The textbox is an extremely versatile data entry tool that can be used for entering a single line of text, such as a number or a password, or for entering simple text files. Figure 5.1 shows a few typical examples created with the TextBox control.

All the textboxes in Figure 5.1 contain text, some a single line, some several lines. The scroll bars you see in some textboxes are part of the control. These scroll bars are attached to the control automatically whenever the control's contents exceed the visible area of the control.

With the exception of graphics applications, the TextBox control is the bread and butter of any Windows application. By examining its properties and designing a text editor based on the TextBox control, you'll see that most of the application's functionality is already built into the control.

FIGURE 5.1

Typical uses of the
TextBox control

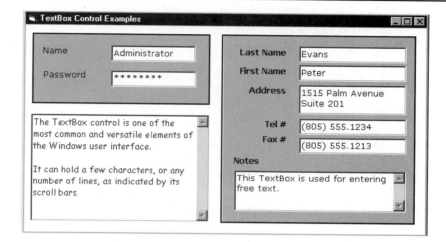

Basic Properties

Let's start with the properties that determine the appearance and, to some degree, the functionality of the TextBox control, which can be set through the Properties window. Then, let's look at the properties that allow you to manipulate the control's contents.

MultiLine

This property determines whether the TextBox control will hold a single line or multiple lines of text. By default, the control holds a single line of text. To change this behavior, set the MultiLine property to True.

ScrollBars

This property controls the attachment of scroll bars to the TextBox control if the text exceeds the control's dimensions. Single line textboxes can have a horizontal scroll bar so that the user can view any part of a long line of text. Multi-line textboxes can have a horizontal or a vertical scroll bar or both. Scroll bars will appear in multi-line textboxes even if they aren't needed or the text doesn't exceed the dimensions of the control.

If you attach a horizontal scroll bar to the TextBox control, the text won't wrap automatically as the user types. To start a new line, the user must press Enter. This arrangement is useful in implementing editors for programs in which lines must break explicitly. If the horizontal scroll bar is missing, the control inserts soft line breaks when the text reaches the end of a line, and the text is wrapped automatically.

MaxLength

This property determines the number of characters the TextBox control will accept. Its default value is zero, which means the text may be of any length, up to the control's capacity limit (discussed in a moment). To restrict the number of characters the user can type, set the value of this property accordingly.

NOTE   The MaxLength property of the TextBox control is often set to a specific value in data entry applications. This prevents users from entering more characters than can be stored in a database field.

A TextBox control with its MaxLength property set to 0, its MultiLine property set to True, and its ScrollBars property set to 2 (vertical) is, on its own, a functional text editor. Place a textbox with these settings on a Form, run the application, and check out the following:

- Enter text and manipulate it with the usual editing keys, such as Delete, Insert, Home, and End.

- Select multiple characters with the mouse or with the arrows while holding down the Shift key.

- Move segments of text around with Copy (Ctrl+C) and Paste (Ctrl+V) operations.

- Exchange data with other applications through the Clipboard.

You can do all this without a single line of code! Shortly you'll see what you can do with the TextBox control if you add some code to your application, but first, let's look at a few more properties of TextBox control.

The TextBox Maximum: 64Kb

The amount of text you can place in a TextBox control is limited to approximately 64Kb (a single line textbox can hold only 255 characters). This is adequate for moderately sized text files, but you may run into files that won't fit in a textbox. (In this case, you must resort to a RichTextBox control, which is covered in Chapter 9, *More Advanced ActiveX Controls*.)

Continued on next page

This is exactly what happens when you attempt to open a large file with Notepad, which is based on the TextBox control. Notepad will prompt you to open the file with WordPad, which is based on the RichTextBox control; it doesn't have a size limitation.

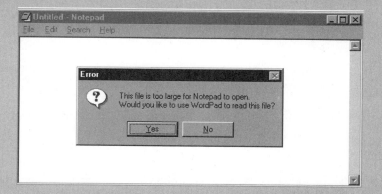

If you're using an application based on the TextBox control and enter the maximum number of characters, you won't be allowed to type any more characters. There will be no warnings; the control handles this situation silently by ignoring the characters typed. You can, however, perform certain editing operations, such as deleting characters to make room for additional text or sending data to the Clipboard, as long as the total number of characters in the textbox doesn't increase.

Another limitation of the TextBox control is that it can't mix multiple fonts or styles. It encapsulates the basic functionality of a text editor. If you want to implement a word processor, use the RichTextBox control, which is described in Chapter 9.

Manipulating the Control's Text

Most of the properties for manipulating text in a TextBox control are available at runtime only. Here's a breakdown of each property.

Text

The most important property of the TextBox control is the *Text* property, which holds the control's text. This property is also available at design time so that you can assign some initial text to the control. At runtime, use this property to extract the text entered by the user or to replace the existing text by assigning a new value to the Text property. The Text property is a string and can be used as an argument with the usual string manipulation functions of Visual Basic. The following function returns the number of characters in the textbox:

```
Len(Text1.Text)
```

The following Instr$ function returns the location of the first occurrence of the string "Visual" in the text:

```
Instr$(Text1.Text, "Visual")
```

To store the control's contents in a file, use a statement such as the following:

```
Write #fnum, Text.Text
```

Similarly, you can read the contents of a text file into a TextBox control with a statement such as the following:

```
Text1.Text=Input$(LOF(fnum), fnum)
```

The *fnum* entry is the file number, which is presumably opened for input with an Open statement. The functions and statements for reading from and writing to files are described in the *File Input/Output* tutorial on the CD.

WARNING   Before you use the Text property, you must make sure that the size of a file the user will open doesn't exceed the 64Kb limit of the control. If it does, you must reject the operation and prompt the user accordingly. Use the LOF() function, which returns the length of an open file, before attempting to assign the file's contents to the Text property of the control.

PasswordChar

Available at design time, the *PasswordChar* property turns the characters typed into any character you specify. If you don't want to display the actual characters typed by the user (when entering a password, for instance), use this property to define the character to appear in place of each character the user types.

The default value of this property is an empty string, which tells the control to display the characters as entered. If you set this value to an asterisk ("*"), for example, the user sees an asterisk in the place of every character typed. This property doesn't affect the control's Text property, which contains the actual characters. If a textbox's PasswordChar property is set to any character, the user can't even copy or cut the text. Any text that's pasted on the control will appear as a sequence of asterisks or as whatever character has been specified with the PasswordChar property.

Text Selection

The TextBox control provides three properties for manipulating the text selected by the user: SelText, SelStart, and SelLength. For example, the user can select a range of text with a click-and-drag operation and the selected text will appear in reverse color. You can access the selected text from within your code with the SelText property and its location in the control with the SelStart and SelLength properties.

SelText

The *SelText* property returns the selected text. If you want to manipulate the currently selected text from within your code, use the SelText property. For example, you can replace the current selection by assigning a new value to the SelText property. To convert the selected text to uppercase, use the UCase$() function, which does exactly that:

```
Text1.SelText =UCase$(Text1.SelText)
```

To delete the current selection, assign an empty string to the SelText property.

The other two properties, SelStart and SelLength, return (or set) the location and length of the selected text in the control.

SelStart and SelLength

The *SelStart* property returns or sets the position of the first character of the selected text, somewhat like placing the cursor at a specific location in the text and selecting text by dragging the mouse. The *SelLength* property returns or sets the length of the selected text. The most common use of these two properties is to extract the user's selection or to select a piece of text from within the application. One example is to extract the location of a string in the text.

The Form shown in Figure 5.2 contains a textbox and two labels. Each time the user selects some text with the mouse, the following lines are executed from within the control's MouseUp event, and they display the selected text's starting location and length in the two labels:

```
Label1.Caption = "SelStart = " & Text1.SelStart
Label2.Caption = "SelLength = " & Text1.SelLength
```

This example reads the values of the SelStart and SelLength properties. If you assign values to them, you can select text from within your application.

The SelStart and SelLength properties allow you to select text from within your application.

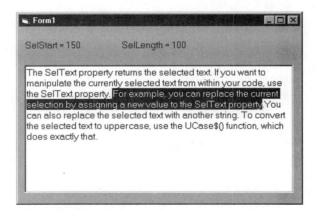

Suppose the user is seeking the word "Visual" in the control's text. The Instr$() function will locate the string, but it won't select it. The found string may even be outside the visible area of the control. You can add a few more lines of code to select the word in the text and highlight it so that the user will spot it instantly:

```
seekString = "Visual"
textStart = Instr$(Text1.Text, seekString)
If textStart > 0 Then
    Text1.SelStart = textStart
    Text1.SelLength = Len(seekString)
End If
```

These lines locate the string "Visual" (or any user-supplied string stored in the *seekString* variable) in the text and select it by setting the SelStart and SelLength properties. Moreover, if the string is outside the visible area of the control, the text can be scrolled with the appropriate scroll bar, so that the selected text becomes visible.

As far as the appearance of the selected text goes, it doesn't make any difference whether it was selected by the user or by the application; it appears in reverse color, as is common with all text editors.

The few lines of code shown above form the core of a text editor's Search command. Replacing the current selection with another string is as simple as assigning a new value to the SelText property and it provides you with an easy implementation of a Search & Replace operation. Designing a Form to include the control on which the Search & Replace strings will be entered and the Command buttons will take more effort than implementing the Search & Replace logic!

TIP

> The SelStart and SelLength properties always have a value even if no text has been selected. In this case, SelLength is 0, and SelStart is the current location of the pointer in the text. If you want to insert some text at the pointer's location, simply assign it to the SelText property.

The selected text will remain highlighted even when the user moves to another control or Form. If you want to change the appearance of the selected text, use the *HideSelection* property. Its default value is False, which is why the text remains highlighted even when the textbox loses the focus. If you set the HideSelection property to True, the selected text will be highlighted only as long as the TextBox control has the focus.

VB6 at Work: The TextPad Project

The TextPad application, shown in Figure 5.3, demonstrates most of the TextBox control's properties and methods described so far. TextPad is a basic text editor that you can incorporate in your programs and customize for special applications. The TextPad's Form is covered by a TextBox control. Every time the user changes the size of the Form the application adjusts the size of the TextBox control accordingly.

FIGURE 5.3:

The TextPad application is a text editor that demonstrates the most useful properties and methods of the TextBox control.

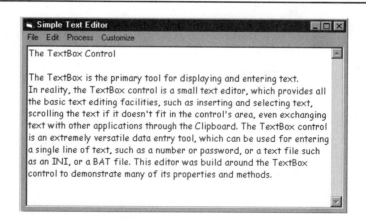

The menu bar of the Form contains all the commands you'd expect to find in text-editing applications:

> **File**
>
> > **New**   Clears the text
> >
> > **Open**   Loads a new text file from disk
> >
> > **Save**   Saves the text to its file on disk

Save As   Saves the text with a new filename on disk

Exit   Terminates the application

Edit

Copy   Copies selected text to the Clipboard

Cut   Cuts selected text

Paste   Pastes the Clipboard's contents to the text

Select All   Selects all the text in the control

Find   Displays a dialogbox with Find & Replace options

Process

Upper Case   Converts selected text to uppercase

Lower Case   Converts selected text to lowercase

Number Lines   Numbers the text lines

Customize

Font   Sets the text's font, size, and attributes

Page Color   Sets the control's background color

Text Color   Sets the color of the text

Design this menu using the techniques explained in Chapter 4, *Working with Forms*. The File menu options are implemented with the Common Dialogs control, which is discussed shortly. As you'll see, you don't have to design the File Open and File Save dialog boxes. All you have to do is place another control on the Form and set a few properties; Windows takes it from there. The application will display the standard File Open and File Save dialog boxes in which the user can select or specify a filename; the File Open common dialog control then reports this filename to the application.

The options on the Edit menu move selected text to and from the Clipboard. For the TextPad application, all you need to know about the Clipboard are the *SetText* method, which places a string on the Clipboard, and the *GetText* method, which retrieves text from the Clipboard and copies it to a string variable (see Figure 5.4).

The Copy command, for example, is implemented with a single line of code (*Editor* is the name of the TextBox control):

```
Private Sub EditCopy_Click()
    Clipboard.SetText Editor.SelText
End Sub
```

The Cut command does the same, but it also clears the selected text:

```
Private Sub EditCut_Click()
    Clipboard.SetText Editor.SelText
    Editor.SelText = ""
End Sub
```

FIGURE 5.4:

The Copy, Cut, and Paste operations can be used to exchange text with any other application.

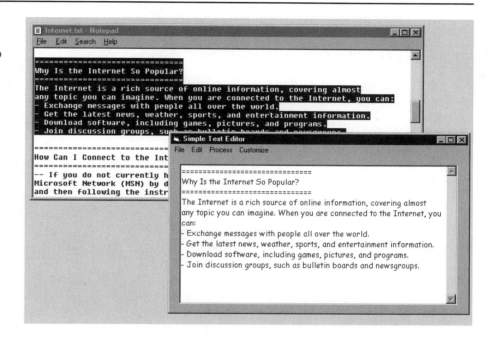

The Paste command assigns the contents of the Clipboard to the current selection:

```
Private Sub EditPaste_Click()
    Editor.SelText = Clipboard.GetText
End Sub
```

If no text is currently selected, the Clipboard's text is pasted at the pointer's current location. If the Clipboard contains a bitmap (placed there by another application), then the paste operation will fail. You can insert the statement:

```
On Error Resume Next
```

to prevent the application from crashing, should the Clipboard contain anything else than text.

The best method to handle the Paste operation is to use the *GetFormat* method of the Clipboard object, which lets you examine the contents of the Clipboard and act accordingly. The GetFormat method doesn't return the format of the data stored in the Clipboard. It lets you examine whether the Clipboard contains data of a specific format. To find out whether the Clipboard contains text, use the following If structure:

```
If Clipboard.GetFormat(vbCFText) Then
    Editor.SelText = Clipboard.GetText
Else
    MsgBox "Invalid Clipboard format."
End If
```

Search and Replace Operations

The last option in the Edit menu —and the most interesting—displays a Search & Replace dialog box (shown in Figure 5.5). This dialog box works like the Find and Replace dialog box of Word and many other Windows applications.

FIGURE 5.5:

The TextPad's Search & Replace dialog box

The buttons in the Search & Replace dialog box are relatively self-explanatory:

Find   Locates the first instance of the specified string in the text. In other words, Find starts searching from the beginning of the text, not from the current location of the pointer. If a match is found, the Find Again, Replace, and Replace All buttons are enabled.

Find Again   Locates the next instance of the string in the text

Replace   Replaces the current instance of the found string with the replacement string and then locates the next instance of the same string

Replace All   Replaces all instances of the string specified in the Find String box with the string in the Replace With box

Whether the search is case-sensitive depends on the status of the Case Sensitive CheckBox control. The Find command checks the status of this checkbox and sets the *compare* variable accordingly. This variable is then used with the InStr() function to specify the type of search.

The actual search is performed with the InStr() function, which searches the text in the TextBox control for the specified string. If the string is found, the program highlights it by selecting it and then stores its position in the *position* variable. The *position* variable is declared as a Form-wide variable so that it can be used later by the Find Again button to specify the starting location of the new search.

Code 5.1:   **The TextPad Application's Find Button**

```
Private Sub FindButton_Click()
Dim compare As Integer

    position = 0
    If Check1.Value = 1 Then
        compare = vbBinaryCompare
    Else
        compare = vbTextCompare
    End If
    position = InStr(Position + 1, Form1.Editor.Text, _
                Text1.Text, compare)
    If position > 0 Then
        ReplaceButton.Enabled = True
        ReplaceAllButton.Enabled = True
        Form1.Editor.SelStart = Position - 1
        Form1.SetFocus
    Else
        MsgBox "String not found"
        ReplaceButton.Enabled = False
        ReplaceAllButton.Enabled = False
    End If
End Sub
```

The Find button examines the value of the Check1 CheckBox control, which specifies whether the search will be case-sensitive and sets the value of the *compare* variable accordingly. The *compare* variable is passed to the InStr() function and the variable tells it how to search for the desired string. If the InStr() function locates the string, the program selects it by setting the textbox's SelStart and SelLength properties. If not, it displays a message and disables the Replace and Replace All buttons on the Form.

The code of the Find Again button is the same, but it doesn't reset the *position* variable to zero. This way, the InStr() function locates the next instance of the same string.

The Replace button replaces the current selection with the replacement string and then locates the next instance of the find string. The Replace All button, does the same thing as the Replace button, but it continues to replace the found string until no more instances can be located in the text.

The code behind the Find Again, Replace, and Replace All buttons is quite similar to the code of the Find button and really doesn't need repeating. If you open the TextPad sample application, you can see the differences.

When you have the application open, consider modifying the code so that the Find button starts searching for the string from the current pointer's location. To do this, pass the pointer's location as the first argument to the InStr() function:

```
position = InStr(Form1.Editor.SelStart, Form1.Editor.Text,_
           Text1.Text, compare)
```

You might also want to limit the search operation to the selected text only. To do so, pass the location of the first selected character to the InStr() function as before. In addition, you must make sure that the located string falls within the selected range, which is from `Form1.Editor.SelStart` to `Form1.Editor.SelStart + Form1.Editor.SelLength`:

```
If Position > Form1.Editor.SelStart + Form1.Editor.SelLength Then _
   MsgBox "String not found"
Else
   Form1.Editor.SelStart = Position - 1
   Form1.Editor.SelLength = Len(Text1.Text)
End If
```

Capturing Keystrokes

The TextBox control has no unique methods or events, but it's quite common in programming to use this control to capture and process the user's keystrokes. The *KeyPress* event occurs every time a key is pressed, and it reports the character that was pressed. You can use this event to capture certain keys and modify the program's behavior, depending on the character typed.

Suppose you want to use the TextPad application (discussed earlier) to prepare messages for transmission over a telex line. As you may know, a telex can't transmit lowercase characters or special symbols. The editor must convert the text to uppercase and replace the special symbols with their equivalent strings: DLR for $, AT for @, O/O for %, BPT for #, and AND for &. You can modify the default behavior of the TextBox control from within the KeyPress event so that it converts these characters as the user types.

The TLXPad application is identical to the TextPad application, but customized for preparing telex messages. (Not that the telex is growing in popularity, but there are situations in which some custom preprocessing of the data is required.) By capturing keystrokes, you can process the data as they are entered, in real time. For example, you could make sure that numeric values fall within a given range or that hexadecimal digits don't contain invalid characters, and so on. The only difference is the modified application's KeyPress event. The KeyPress event handler of the TLXPad application is shown next.

Code 5.2:   **TLXPad Application's KeyPress Event Handler**

```
Private Sub Editor_KeyPress(KeyAscii As Integer)
Dim TLXSymbols As String
Dim ch As String * 1

    TLXSymbols = "@#$%&"
    ch = Chr$(KeyAscii)
    If InStr(TLXSymbols, ch) Then
       KeyAscii = 0
    Else
       KeyAscii = Asc(UCase$(Chr$(KeyAscii)))
       Exit Sub
    End If
    Select Case ch
       Case "@": Editor.SelText = "AT"
       Case "#": Editor.SelText = "BPT"
       Case "$": Editor.SelText = "DLR"
       Case "%": Editor.SelText = "O/O"
       Case "&": Editor.SelText = "AND"
    End Select
End Sub
```

This event handler replaces the special symbols with a string, and it also converts alpha-numeric characters to uppercase. The line that converts the alphanumeric characters to uppercase needs some explanation. The *KeyAscii* argument of the KeyPress event reports the ASCII value of the key presses, not the actual character:

```
KeyAscii = Asc(UCase$(Chr$(KeyAscii)))
```

Before deploying the UCase$() function to convert the character to uppercase, you must convert the ASCII value to a character. This is what the function Chr$()

in the preceding long statement does. To understand it, read it from right to left: first it extracts the actual character typed from its ASCII value; then it converts the character to uppercase; and finally, it converts the character back to an ASCII value, which is returned to the application. The KeyPress event handler is executed before the keystroke is passed to the TextBox control, and that's why you can modify the keystrokes from within the control's KeyPress event.

Capturing Function Keys

Another common feature in text-editing applications is the assignment of special operations to the function keys. The Notepad application, for example, uses the F5 function key to insert the current date at the cursor's location. You can do the same with the TextPad application, but you can't use the KeyPress event—the *KeyAscii* argument doesn't report function keys. The events that can capture the function keys are the *KeyDown* event, which is generated when a key is pressed, and the *KeyUp* event, which is generated when a key is released. Also, unlike the KeyPress event, the KeyDown and KeyUp events don't report the ASCII value of the character, but instead, report its *keycode* (a special number that distinguishes each key on the keyboard, also known as the *scancode*).

The keycode is unique for each key, not each character. Lower- and uppercase characters have different ASCII values but the same keycode because they are on the same key. The number 4 and the $ symbol have the same keycode because the same key on the keyboard generates both characters. When the key's keycode is reported, the KeyDown and KeyUp events also report the state of the Shift, Control, and Alt keys.

To be able to use the KeyDown and KeyUp events, you must know the keycode of the key you want to capture. The keycode for the function key F1 is 112 (or the constant *vbKeyF12*), the keycode for F2 is 113 (or the constant *vbkeyF13*), and so on. To capture a special key, such as the F1 function key, and assign a special string to it, program the key's KeyUp event. The following event handler uses the F5 and F6 function keys to insert the current date and time in the document. It also uses the F7 and F8 keys to insert two predefined strings in the document.

Code 5.3:   **KeyUp Event Examples**

```
Const DateInputKey = vbkeyF5
Const TimeInputKey = vbkeyF6
Const SpecialInput1Key = vbkeyF7
Const SpecialInput2Key = vbkeyF8
{more code}
```

```
Select Case KeyCode
    Case DateInputKey:      Editor.SelText = Date
    Case TimeInputKey:      Editor.SelText = Time
    Case SpecialInput1Key: Editor.SelText = "MicroWeb Designs, Inc"
    Case SpecialInput2Key: Editor.SelText = "Another long,_
         common string you can insert with a single keystroke"
End Select
End Sub
```

Notice the definitions of the constants that make the code easier to read and simplify its maintenance.

With a little additional effort, you can provide users with a dialog box that lets them assign their own strings to function keys. You'll probably have to take into consideration the status of the *Shift* argument, which reports the status of the Shift, Control, and Alt keys (see Table 5.1). Windows already uses many of the function keys and you shouldn't reassign them. For example, the F1 key is the standard Windows context-sensitive Help key, and users will be confused if they press F1 and see the date appear in their documents.

TABLE 5.1:   Values of the Shift Argument of the KeyDown and KeyUp Events

Constant	Value	Description
vbShiftMask	1	Shift key is down
vbCtrlMask	2	Ctrl key is down
vbAltMask	4	Alt key is down

To find out whether another Shift key is down when a key is pressed, use the AND operator with the *Shift* argument. The following If structure detects the Shift key:

```
If Shift AND vbShiftMask Then
    {Shift key was down}
End If
```

To detect combinations of the Shift keys, use statements such as this one:

```
If (Shift AND vbShiftMask) AND (Shift AND vbAltMask) Then _
    {Shift and Alt keys were down}
End If
```

The ListBox and ComboBox Controls

The ListBox and ComboBox controls present lists of choices for the user to select. The ListBox control occupies a user-specified amount of space on the Form and is populated with a list of items; the user can select one or more with the mouse. The items must be inserted in the ListBox control through the code, or via the *List* property in the Properties window. Each new item in the List property must be entered on a separate line. To change lines, press Control+Enter. When you're done entering items, press Enter and the items will appear in the ListBox control on the Form. Users can't enter data in a list; they can only select items, which will be manipulated by the application when they click a button or take some other action.

The ComboBox control also contains multiple items but occupies less space on the screen. The ComboBox control is an expandable ListBox control: the user can expand it to make a selection and retract it after the selection is made. The real advantage to the ComboBox control, however, is that the user can enter new information in the ComboBox, rather than being forced to select only the items listed.

The ComboBox control may seem more useful, but its use isn't as common as ListBox controls. This section first examines the ListBox control's properties and methods. Later, you'll see how the same properties and methods can be used with the ComboBox control.

Basic Properties

The ListBox and ComboBox controls provide a few properties that can be set only at design time. Because they determine the basic functionality of the control and can't be changed at runtime, we'll start with these fundamental properties.

MultiSelect

This property determines how the user can select the list's items and must be set at design time (at runtime, you can only read this property's value). The *MultiSelect* property's values determine whether the user can select multiple items and which method will be used for multiple selection. The possible values of MultiSelect property are shown in Table 5.2.

TABLE 5.2: MultiSelect Property Values

Setting	Description
0	Multiple selection not allowed; the default.
1	Simple multiple selection. A mouse click (or pressing the spacebar) selects or deselects an item in the list. To move the focus to another item, use the arrow keys.
2	Extended multiple selection. Press Shift and click the mouse (or press one of the arrow keys) to span the selection. This will highlight all the items between the previously selected item and the current selection. Press Ctrl and click the mouse to select or deselect an item in the list.

Sorted

Items can be inserted by the application into a ListBox or ComboBox control, but inserting them in the proper place and maintaining some sort of organization can be quite a task for the programmer. If you want the items to be always sorted, set the control's *Sorted* property to True. This property must be set at design time and is read-only at runtime.

The ListBox control is basically a text control and won't sort numeric data properly. To use the ListBox control to sort numbers, you must first format them with leading zeros. For example, the number 10 will appear in front of the number 5, because the string "10" is smaller than the string "5". If the numbers are formatted as "010" and "005", they will be sorted correctly.

The items in a sorted ListBox control are in ascending and case-sensitive order. Moreover, there is no mechanism for changing this default setting. The items "aa", "aA", "AA", "Aa", "ba", and "BA" would be sorted as follows:

"AA"

"Aa"

"aA"

"aa"

"BA"

"ba"

Uppercase characters appear before the equivalent lowercase characters, but both upper- and lowercase characters appear together. All words beginning with B appear after the words beginning with A and before the words beginning with C. Within the group of words beginning with B, those beginning with B appear before those beginning with b.

Style

This property determines the appearance of the control. Its value can be 0 (Standard) or 1 (Checkbox). The two lists shown in Figure 5.6 illustrate the Standard and Checkbox appearance of the ListBox control. Notice that the list on the left is unsorted and the list on the right is sorted.

FIGURE 5.6:

The ListBox controls on this Form show the two distinct looks of the control.

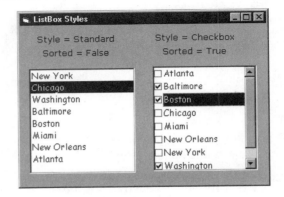

The ListBox Control's Methods

To manipulate a ListBox control from within your application, you should be able to:

- Add items to the list
- Remove items from the list
- Access individual items in the list

AddItem

To add items to the list, use the *AddItem* method. Its syntax is as follows:

```
List1.AddItem item, index
```

The *item* parameter is the string to be added to the list, and *index* is its order. The first item's order in the list is zero. The *index* argument is optional; if you omit it, the string is appended to the bottom of the list. If the control's Sorted property is set to True, the item is inserted in its proper place in the list, regardless of the value of the *index* argument.

RemoveItem

To remove an item from the list, you must first find its position *(index)* in the list, which you must then supply to the *RemoveItem* method. The syntax of the method is as follows:

```
List1.RemoveItem index
```

The *index* parameter is the order of the item to be removed, and this time, it's not optional. The following statement removes the item at the top of the list:

```
List1.RemoveItem 0
```

Clear

The *Clear* method removes all the items from the control. Its syntax is simple:

```
List1.Clear
```

To access individual items, you can use several properties that are unique to the ListBox (and ComboBox) control. Removing an item from a list requires that you know its order in the list, but the RemoveItem method's argument is rarely used. Usually, you rely on the user to select the items to be removed; otherwise, the items will be selected from within your code based on their values. The ListBox control provides several properties that let you read the items from within your code and they're described next.

ListCount

This is the number of items in the List. The items in the list can be accessed with an Index value, which goes from 0 to ListCount - 1.

List()

This is an array that holds the list's items. The element List(0) holds the first element of the list, List(1) holds the second item, and so on up to List(ListCount-1), which holds the last item. The *List()* array is used frequently in scanning all the

List items. The following loop, for instance, scans all the items of the List1 control, looking for blank strings to remove:

```
For itm = List1.ListCount - 1 to 0 Step -1
    If List1.List(itm) = "" Then
        List1.RemoveItem itm
    End If
Next
```

Notice that the loop scans the elements of the *List()* array backward. Can you see why? If the list was scanned forward, each time an item was removed, the list's length would decrease by 1: This would cause the loop to be executed more times than there are items in the List, resulting in a runtime error. Scanning the items backwards prevents this.

ListIndex

This is the index of the selected item in the List. If multiple items are selected, ListIndex is the index of the most recently selected item. Use this property to access specific elements in the list or delete specific items. The following statement removes the selected item from the List1 control, but only if an item is selected:

```
List1.RemoveItem List1.ListIndex
```

If no item is selected at the time the RemoveItem method is invoked, the ListIndex property has a negative value; any attempt to remove an item with a negative index results in a runtime error. To avoid this error, check the value of the ListIndex property first:

```
If List1.ListIndex >= 0 Then
    List1.RemoveItem List1.ListIndex
End If
```

After the removal of the item, the indices of the following items are adjusted accordingly.

Selected

This property is an array, similar to the List property, with elements that have a True or a False value, depending on the status of the corresponding list element (the value is True if the element is selected; otherwise, it's False). Because there is no property equivalent to the ListIndex property for multiple selected items, the only way to find out which elements have been selected is to examine all the elements of the *Selected* array (you'll see an example of this technique shortly).

SelCount

This property reports the number of selected items in a ListBox control with its MultiSelect property set to 1 (Simple) or 2 (Extended). It's commonly used in conjunction with the *Selected* array in processing the selected items in the control. If a ListBox control allows multiple elements to be selected, you might want to use the checkbox style for your list's items. Set the Style property to 1 so that the list's items will be displayed as checkboxes, like the ones shown in Figure 5.6, earlier in this chapter.

NewIndex

This property returns the index of the item most recently added to a ListBox control. This property is used commonly with the ItemData property, which will be discussed shortly in the section "Indexing with the List Control."

VB6 at Work: The ListDemo Project

The ListDemo application (shown in Figure 5.7) demonstrates the basic operations of the ListBox control. The two ListBox controls on the Form operate slightly different. The first one has the default configuration: only one item can be selected at a time, and new items are appended after the existing item. The second ListBox control has its Sorted property set to True and its MultiSelect property set to 2 (Extended). This means that the elements of this control are always sorted, and the user can select multiple cells with the mouse, while holding down either the Shift or the Control keys.

The code for the ListDemo application contains all the logic you'll need in your ListBox manipulation routines. It shows you how to:

- Add and remove items
- Transfer items between lists
- Handle multiple selected items
- Maintain sorted lists

Add New Element Button   The Add New Element buttons use the InputBox() function to prompt the user for input, and then they add the user-supplied string to the ListBox control. The code is identical for both buttons, and it's shown next.

Code 5.4: **Add New Element Buttons**

```
Private Sub Command5_Click()
Dim listItem As String

    listItem = InputBox("Enter item to add to the list")
    If Trim(listItem) <> "" Then
        List1.AddItem listItem
    End If
End Sub
```

FIGURE 5.7:

The ListDemo application demonstrates most of the operations you'll perform with ListBox controls.

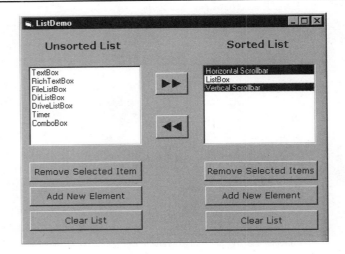

Notice that the subroutine examines the data entered by the user to avoid adding blank strings to the list. The code for the Clear List button is also straightforward; it simply calls the Clear method to remove all entries from the corresponding list.

Remove Selected Item(s) Button   The code for the Remove Selected Item button is different from that for the Remove Selected Items button. The reason is that the first ListBox can have only one selected item and the second can have multiple selected items. To delete an item, you must have at least one item selected (explained earlier).

Code 5.5: **Remove Selected Item Button**

```
Private Sub Command3_Click()
    If List1.ListIndex >= 0 Then
        List1.RemoveItem List1.ListIndex
```

```
        End If
    End Sub
```

The code for the Remove Selected Items button must scan all the items of the list and remove the selected one(s).

Code 5.6: **The Remove Selected Items Button**

```
Private Sub Command4_Click()
Dim i As Integer

    If List2.SelCount = 1 Then
        List2.RemoveItem List2.ListIndex
    ElseIf List2.ListCount > 1 Then
        For i = List2.ListCount - 1 To 0 Step -1
            If List2.Selected(i) Then
                List2.RemoveItem i
            End If
        Next i
    End If
End Sub
```

The code examines the control's SelCount property, which specifies the number of selected items. If SelCount equals one, it moves the item. If the number of selected items is more than one, the program scans the entire list and removes the items that have their Selected property set to True. Notice also that the list is scanned backward, as explained in the discussion of the RemoveItem method.

The Arrow Buttons   The two Command buttons between the two ListBox controls shown in Figure 5.7 transfer selected items from one list to another. The first arrow button can transfer a single element only, after it ensures that the list contains a selected item. First, it adds the item to the second list, and then it removes the item from the original list.

Code 5.7: **The Right Arrow Button**

```
Private Sub Command1_Click()
    If List1.ListIndex >= 0 Then
        List2.AddItem List1.Text
        List1.RemoveItem List1.ListIndex
    End If
End Sub
```

The second arrow button transfers items in the opposite direction. Its code is similar to that of the Remove Selected Items button. The arrow button examines the SelCount property, and if a single item is selected, it moves the item to the other list with the commands of previous list. If multiple items are selected, the arrow button scans the list backward, copying and deleting each selected item. Its code is as follows.

Code 5.8:   **The Left Arrow Button**

```
Private Sub Command2_Click()
Dim i As Integer

    If List2.SelCount = 1 Then
        List1.AddItem List2.Text
        List2.RemoveItem List2.ListIndex
    ElseIf List2.SelCount > 1 Then
        For i = List2.ListCount - 1 To 0 Step -1
            If List2.Selected(i) Then
                List1.AddItem List2.List(i)
                List2.RemoveItem i
            End If
        Next
    End If
End Sub
```

Before we leave the topic of the ListBox control, let's examine one more powerful technique: using the ListBox control to maintain a list of keys (the data items used in recalling the information) to an array or random access file with records of related information.

Indexing with the ListBox Control

A key property of the ListBox control is the *ItemData* property, which is an array similar to the *List* array, but instead of containing strings that appear in the control, it contains numbers. Each item displayed on a ListBox control has two entries: a string, given by the list's List(i) property; and a number, given by the ItemData(i) property (*i* is the index of the item in the list).

The ItemData property is a Long value that can store any type of numeric information associated with each item, as long as this information doesn't need to be displayed on the list. If you maintain a list of employee names, the *List()* array can hold names, and the *ItemData()* array can hold the salary of each employee. Each employee can be accessed by name, but his or her salary can appear in a TextBox control on the same Form.

The real value of the ItemData property, however, is not for storing additional pieces of information along with the item. If you want to store more information than is visible on the list, you probably would want to store more information than just a number. Suppose you need to maintain a list of names and addresses. Storing each entry in a ListBox control isn't practical. The control would have to be very wide to accommodate the entire string with each person's name, address, city, phone numbers, and so on.

A more practical approach is to store the names of the persons in the ListBox control and use the names as keys to access the elements of an array in which the rest of the information is stored. Each record is stored in an array element, which should match one of the items in the ListBox control. If the item's ItemData property is set to the index of the corresponding array element, you can access the array records instantly.

The same approach would also work with random access files, only this time, the value of the ItemData property would be the number of the matching record. The KeyList application demonstrates this technique.

VB6 at Work: The KeyList Project

KeyList, shown in Figure 5.8, maintains a list of books, indexed by ISBN. It could be a list of names and addresses, a price list, or any other collection of related items. The application is simple and doesn't justify the design of a database. To save space and time, the information is stored in an array and saved to a disk file between sessions.

FIGURE 5.8:

The KeyList application uses the ListBox control to maintain indexed information.

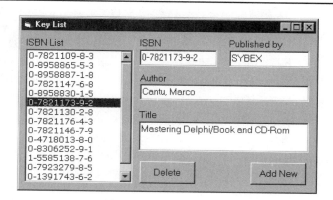

The array is a convenient storage mechanism for a few hundred entries, but it can't be sorted easily. Inserting each item in the proper array element requires massive copying. To insert a new item in the array's first element, you'd have to copy all the items to the next array position. In general, you should avoid sorting whenever possible, especially if it has to be repeated at runtime.

TIP
The ListBox control is frequently used as an array, especially to maintain sorted items. You can even hide the control by setting its Visible property to False and still use it in your application as an array. It provides the same functionality and can maintain its sorted items at all times.

The KeyList application uses a ListBox control to maintain a sorted list of items. We could have stored all the information in the ListBox control, but this is hardly practical. The list will be used for storing the keys which are the books' ISBN numbers. The remaining fields can be stored in an array.

Figure 5.9 shows how the keys are stored in the ListBox control and the matching data in the array. The *ItemData* array points to the appropriate element in the Data Array, which may contain a large number of fields.

All you need is a way to connect the ISBN numbers to the corresponding information in the array. This link is provided by the ListBox control, with its ItemData property. The ItemData property is an array of numbers, one per list item. Each item in the list has a value (what is displayed on the list) that can be accessed via the List property and a related value that isn't displayed on the List, but that can be accessed with the ItemData property.

The first element in the list is List1.List(0), and the related information is stored in the fourth array element, whose index is given by the property List1.ItemData(0). The List's Sorted property is set to True so that the user sees the keys sorted and can easily locate any item in the List. The fields that correspond to each key, though, are appended to the array. As a programmer, you don't have to worry about maintaining the elements of the array in any order. As long as you can instantly access the array element that corresponds to the selected key in the List control, it's as if the array is sorted too.

KeyList Code: Behind the Scenes   Now that we have looked briefly at the technique for maintaining sorted keys in the KeyList application, let's look at the code of the project. In the KeyList application (Figure 5.8), to add a new entry, the user must click the Add New button. The program will let the user enter data in the various fields. When done, the user clicks the OK button to commit the changes. (You don't see this button in Figure 5.8 because it appears only while the user is entering a new entry; its action is signaled to the program with the click of the Add New button.) The new record will be added to the array *DataArray()*, which is declared as follows:

```
Dim DataArray(999, 3) As String
```

FIGURE 5.9:

The *ItemData* array links the items of a ListBox control to the elements of an array or to the records in a random access file.

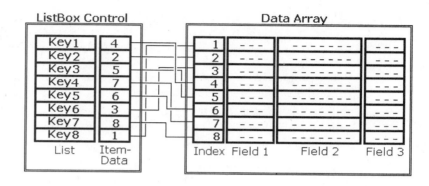

The element DataArray(i, 0) holds the ISBN of the book, the element DataArray(i, 1) holds the publisher, the element DataArray(i, 2) holds the author of the current title, and the element DataArray(i ,3) holds the book's title. The *i* parameter is the index stored in the List's ItemData property. Following is the code that's executed when the OK button is clicked.

Code 5.9:   **The OK Button**

```
Private Sub OKButton_Click()
   Key = Trim(Text1.Text)
   If Key = "" Then
      MsgBox "Key field must be non-empty"
      Exit Sub
   End If
   position = Search(Trim(Text1.Text))
   If position >= 0 Then
      reply = MsgBox("Key exists. Replace existing record?", vbYesNo)
      If reply = vbYes Then
      Else
         Text1.SetFocus
         Exit Sub
      End If
   End If
   ArrayIndex = ArrayIndex + 1
```

```
      List1.AddItem Key
      List1.ItemData(List1.NewIndex) = ArrayIndex
      DataArray(ArrayIndex, 1) = Text2.Text
      DataArray(ArrayIndex, 2) = Text3.Text
      DataArray(ArrayIndex, 3) = Text4.Text
      List1.ListIndex = List1.NewIndex
      ShowButtons
  End Sub
```

The program reads the data entered by the user in the various fields, searches the list with the *Search()* function (explained in the following section) to see if an entry with this key exists, and then inserts the key in the ListBox control and stores the other fields in the *DataArray()* array. Because the List's Sorted property is True, the item is automatically inserted in its proper position in the list.

The *ArrayIndex* variable is global and points to the last element of the array. Each time a new element is added, the *ArrayIndex* variable increases by an increment of 1. The value of the *ArrayIndex* property is stored in the *ItemData* array, in the position that corresponds to the newly added element. The following expression is the index of the newly added element in the list:

```
  List1.NewIndex
```

This expression is used to access the element of the *ItemData* array that corresponds to this item in the following statement:

```
  List1.ItemData(List1.NewIndex) = ArrayIndex
```

The List's *ItemData* array holds the keys to the array, and retrieving a book's title or author is a simple task once you have its ISBN. Each time the user clicks on an item in the list, the program extracts the item's ItemData property and uses it as an index to access the title's fields in the *DataArray()* array. The code that retrieves a record's fields each time a new item is selected on the list is shown next.

Code 5.10:   **Displaying a Record**

```
  Private Sub List1_MouseUp(Button As Integer, _
        Shift As Integer, X As Single, Y As Single)
     ShowRecord
  End Sub

  Sub ShowRecord()
     If List1.ListIndex < 0 Then
        txtISBN.Text = ""
```

```
            txtPublisher.Text = ""
            txtAuthor.Text = ""
            txtTitle.Text = ""
            Exit Sub
        End If
        ItemIndex = List1.ItemData(List1.ListIndex)
        txtISBN.Text = List1.List(List1.ListIndex)
        txtPublisher.Text = DataArray(ItemIndex, 1)
        txtAuthor.Text = DataArray(ItemIndex, 2)
        txtTitle.Text = DataArray(ItemIndex, 3)
    End Sub
```

If no item has been selected in the list, the program clears the contents of the various fields. If an element has been selected in the list, the program will display the matching record's fields on the corresponding textboxes, by calling the *ShowRecords()* subroutine. The *ShowButtons()* subroutine hides the OK and Cancel buttons and displays the Delete and Add New buttons. This action normally takes place after the user has added a new record and clicked the OK button. It's possible, however, to abandon the entry of a new record by clicking an element on the list.

TIP

Notice that I programmed the List's MouseUp event, but not the Click event. To understand why, try moving the code from the MouseUp to the Click event. You'll see that the ListBox control's Click event is called every time the control's ListIndex is set to select an item programmatically. This introduces side effects, which you can avoid by programming the MouseUp event. The MouseUp event is triggered every time the user clicks the control (that is, every time the user clicks a list item), but not when a new item is selected from within the code.

Locating an Item in the ListBox Control

The Search() function locates a specific item in the list. The ListBox control doesn't provide a specific method, but you can find out whether a specific item exists in the list and its index (if it exists) by setting the control's Text property to the desired value. The Text property of the ListBox control can also be set to a specific value at runtime. If you set it to the value of a specific list item from within your code, the item is automatically selected and the ListIndex property is set to the item's Index value.

The Search() function uses this trick to locate the item whose key has been entered in the TextBox control. The Search() function's code is shown next.

Code 5.11: **The Search() Function**

```
Function Search(KeyField) As Integer
    List1.Text = KeyField
    Search = List1.ListIndex
End Function
```

To locate an item in the ListBox control, you can provide a textbox where the user can enter a string. In the TextBox control's Change event, you must insert the following code to call the Search() function to locate the item whose key is entered in the TextBox control. To program the Change event handler of the ISBN textbox so that it can also locate items in the list, use the following code.

Code 5.12: **The ISBN TextBox's Change Event Handler**

```
Private Sub txtISBN_Change()
    position = Search(Trim$(txtISBN.Text))
    If position > -1 Then
        List1.ListIndex = position
         ShowRecord
    Else
        txtPublisher.Text = ""
        txtAuthor.Text = ""
        txtTitle.Text = ""
    End If
End Sub
```

This is how the KeyList application works. You can locate items in the list by using the mouse or entering their key in the ISBN box. However, this technique can't match partial keys. In other words, if the ISBN value doesn't match an entry in the list exactly, no item will be selected. For example, suppose the list contains the key *1984-2030-3*. The ISBN values 1984-2030 or 1984-20 won't cause a partial match as one would expect.

Ideally, the application should highlight the first item in the list that matches, even partially, the key value in the ISBN box. If its first five digits make it unique, then there's no reason to type the remaining digits. To perform partial matches on the list's items, you must use a more advanced searching technique, which is described next.

Searching a Sorted List

In this section we'll revise the KeyList application to incorporate the feature of partial matching. The revised application is called BSearch (for Binary Search), and you'll find it in the BSearch folder on the CD. As the user types characters in the ISBN field, the program selects the first item in the ListBox control that matches the partial entry of the ISBN field. This is a standard operation of the ListBox control. If the ListBox control has the focus and the user types characters, the matching item in the control is selected automatically. This operation is duplicated in the ISBN TextBox control for two reasons:

- **Convenience**   When users type characters in the TextBox control, they can see the string and edit it.

- **Practicality**   The algorithm that implements the search is practical, and it's likely that you'll use it in your applications.

Searching for a specific item in a sorted arrangement of data is a common operation, and it can be implemented efficiently with the *Binary Search algorithm*. The Binary Search algorithm starts by comparing the desired element with the middle element of the sorted list (or array). If it's alphabetically or numerically larger than the middle element of the list, the upper half of the list is rejected without further consideration. If the opposite is true, the lower half of the list is rejected. The same process continues with the selected half of the list. Another half is rejected again, and the algorithm continues until it finds a single element, which should be the desired one. If not, the element is not in the list. Figure 5.10 shows the steps in locating an item in a sorted list with eight items. The items rejected at each step are marked in gray.

FIGURE 5.10:

Locating the item "Bob" in a sorted list with eight elements takes three comparisons.

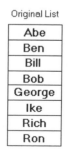  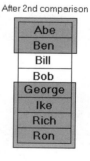 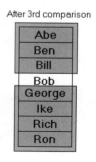

Suppose you have a list with 1,024 elements. After the first comparison, 512 elements will be rejected. Of the 512 remaining elements, 256 will be rejected with the second comparison. After the third comparison, only 128 of the initial 1,024 elements will be left. If this process continues, the size of the list will be reduced to 64 elements, then to 32, then to 16, and so on down to a single element. It will take only ten comparisons to reduce the 1,024 elements to a single element, which should be the desired one. The Binary Search algorithm exploits the sorted list and is extremely efficient.

The Implementation of the BSearch() Function

The burden of sorting the elements to be searched often lies with the programmer, but with a flexible tool such as a sorted ListBox control, maintaining a sorted list at all times is easy. Combining a sorted list of keys maintained by a ListBox control and the Binary Search algorithm is a powerful approach that can be used in situations in which you'd normally deploy database techniques. The database objects (discussed in Chapter 17, Database Programming with Visual Basic) require significant overhead, which isn't worthwhile for a small application such as KeyList or BSearch.

In the BSearch project, the ISBN field is editable (Locked property set to False), so that the user can enter an ISBN value. As the user edits the contents of the ISBN textbox, the Change event occurs with every character typed and the following code is executed.

Code 5.13:   **The ISBN TextBox's Change Event Handler**

```
Private Sub txtISBN_Change()
    position = BSearch(Trim$(txtISBN.Text))
    If position >= 0 Then
        List1.ListIndex = position
    Else
        List1.ListIndex = -1
        txtPublisher.Text = ""
        txtAuthor.Text = ""
        txtTitle.Text = ""
    End If
End Sub
```

The code calls the BSearch() function with the text entered in the *txtISBN* TextBox control. The BSearch() function searches the ListBox control for an item that partially matches its argument. If the item is found, the function returns its position in the list and highlights the key in the list. If the item is not found, it returns the value -1. If the item is found, the program also selects it in the list and calls the ListBox control's Click event to update the contents of the other TextBox controls in the data entry section of the Form. The listing of the BSearch() function follows.

Code 5.14:   **The BSearch() Function**

```
Function BSearch(KeyField) As Integer
Dim Lower As Integer, Upper As Integer, Middle As Integer
Dim MiddleItem As String

    Lower = 0
    Upper = List1.ListCount - 1

    While 1
       Middle = Fix((Lower + Upper) / 2)
       MiddleItem = List1.List(Middle)
       If Upper < Lower Then
          BSearch = -1
          Exit Function
       End If
       If StrComp(KeyField, Left(MiddleItem, Len(KeyField))) > 0 Then
          Lower = Middle + 1
       Else
          If StrComp(KeyField, Left(MiddleItem, Len(KeyField))) < 0 Then
             Upper = Middle - 1
          Else
             BSearch = Middle
             Exit Function
          End If
       End If
    Wend
End Function
```

The *Upper* and *Lower* variables delimit the section of the list that may contain the desired element. The items before *Lower* and after *Upper* have already been rejected. When the function starts, the *Lower* variable is set to the position of the first item, and the *Upper* variable is set to the position of the last item. The position of the middle element is then calculated (variable *Middle*), and the key field is compared with the middle element. If the key field is smaller than the middle item, the upper half of the list is rejected, by adjusting the value of the *Upper* variable. (The list is sorted in ascending order, that is, the "a" character shows up in the list before the "g.") If the key field is larger than the middle item, the lower half of the list is rejected by adjusting the value of the *Lower* variable.

NOTE   The BSearch() function calls the StrComp() function to compare strings. It compares only as many characters as there are in the key. If it compared the entire item to the key, it wouldn't report partial matches.

The BSearch project is identical to the KeyList project, only it uses the Binary Search algorithm to locate the first key in the ListBox control that partially or fully matches the string entered by the user in the ISBN box.

The ComboBox Control

The ComboBox control is similar to the ListBox control in the sense that it contains multiple items of which the user may select one, but it takes less space on-screen. The ComboBox is practically an expandable ListBox control, which can grow when the user wants to make a selection and retract after the selection is made. Normally, the ComboBox control displays one line with the selected item. The real difference, however, between ComboBox and ListBox controls is that the ComboBox control allows the user to specify items that don't exist in the list. Moreover, the Text property of the ComboBox control is read-only at runtime and you can locate an item by assigning a value to the control's Text property.

Three types of ComboBox controls are available in Visual Basic 6. The value of the control's *Style* property, whose values are shown in Table 5.3, determines which box is used.

TABLE 5.3:   Styles of the ComboBox Control

Value	Description
0	**(Default) DropDown Combo** The control is made up of a drop-down list and a textbox. The user can select an item from the list or type a new one in the textbox.
1	**Simple Combo** Includes a textbox and a list that doesn't drop down. The user can select from the list or type in the textbox.
2	**DropDown List** This style is a drop-down list, from which the user can select one of its items, but can't enter a new one.

The Combos project in this chapter's folder on the CD (see Figure 5.11) demonstrates the three styles of the ComboBox control. It's a common element of the Windows interface and its properties and methods are identical to those of the ListBox control. Load the Combos project in the Visual Basic IDE and experiment with the three styles of the ComboBox control.

The DropDown and Simple ComboBox controls allow the user to select an item from the list or enter a new one in the edit box of the control.

The DropDown List is similar to a List control in the sense that it restricts the user to selecting an item, but not entering a new one. However, it takes much less space on the Form. When the user wants to make a selection, the DropDown List expands to display more items. After the user has made a selection, the list contracts to a single line again.

FIGURE 5.11:

The Combos project demonstrates the various styles of the ComboBox control.

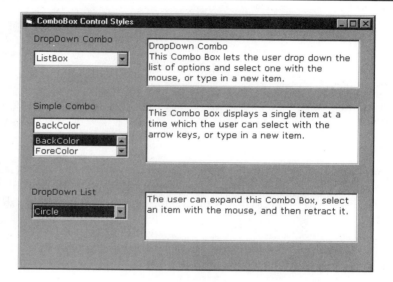

Most of the properties and methods of the ListBox control also apply to the ComboBox control. The AddItem method adds items to a ComboBox, and the RemoveItem method removes items from a ComboBox. To access the items of the control, you can use the *List* array, and the current selection in the control is given by its Text property.

You can also use the ItemData property to maintain sorted lists of keys, as you'll see in the KeyCombo example shortly. You can even set the control's MultiSelect property to 1 (Simple) or 2 (Extended) to allow the user to select multiple items in a ComboBox control. To find out whether an item has been selected, use the Selected property as before.

VB6 at Work: The KeyCombo Project

The KeyCombo application, shown in Figure 5.12, is similar to the KeyList application you saw earlier, but KeyCombo maintains three indexed lists, and the user can recall records based on any one key. Each record has four fields, three of them being potential keys. In a real application you could add any number of fields on the right-hand side of the Form.

FIGURE 5.12:

The KeyCombo application maintains a list of records, indexed by three keys (SSN, VISA #, and AMEX #).

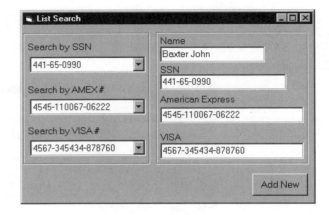

KeyCombo is a useful Form for incorporating into a larger payment tracking application. Customers can be recalled by their Social Security number, their American Express card number, or their VISA card number. All three keys are unique, and only one of the fields needs to be filled out for the application to run.

Adding a New Item to KeyCombo   The KeyCombo application uses each control's *ItemData* array to store the index of the array element (or record number, in the case of a random access file) in which the matching record is stored. When a user wants to add a new record, they click the Add New button (see Figure 5.12). When the new record is committed to the database, an OK button appears, and when it's clicked, the following code goes into action.

Code 5.15:   The OK Button

```
Private Sub OKButton_Click()
    Key = Trim(Text1.Text)
    If Key = "" Then
        MsgBox "Key field must be non-empty"
        Exit Sub
    End If
    ArrayIndex = ArrayIndex + 1
    Combo1.AddItem Text2.Text
    Combo1.ItemData(Combo1.NewIndex) = ArrayIndex
    If Text3.Text <> "" Then
        Combo2.AddItem Text3.Text
```

```
            Combo2.ItemData(Combo2.NewIndex) = ArrayIndex
        End If
        If Text4.Text <> "" Then
            Combo3.AddItem Text4.Text
            Combo3.ItemData(Combo3.NewIndex) = ArrayIndex
        End If
        DataArray(ArrayIndex, 0) = Text1.Text
        DataArray(ArrayIndex, 1) = Text2.Text
        DataArray(ArrayIndex, 2) = Text3.Text
        DataArray(ArrayIndex, 3) = Text4.Text
        Combo1.ListIndex = Combo1.NewIndex
        Combo2.ListIndex = Combo2.NewIndex
        Combo3.ListIndex = Combo3.NewIndex
        ShowButtons
        Text1.SetFocus
    End Sub
```

After ensuring that the name field is not empty, the program adds the corresponding fields to the three ComboBox controls. The SSN field is inserted in Combo1, the VISA # field is inserted in Combo2, and the AMEX # is inserted in Combo3. The *ArrayIndex* variable is the index of the element where the new record will be added in the array *DataArray()*; it's the index of the next available element in the array. This number is stored in each ComboBox control's *ItemData* array.

The NewIndex property returns the index of the newly added item in a ComboBox control; so the expression `ItemData(Combo3.NewIndex)` matches the location of the new record in the data array. The fields are stored in the data array. The last few lines cause the keys of the newly added record to appear in the edit box of the ComboBox controls, so that the selected entry matches the fields shown on the right side of the Form.

Selecting an Existing KeyCombo Item   When the user selects an item in one of the ComboBox controls, the program retrieves the matching record from the array and displays its fields in the data entry section of the Form. Following is the first ComboBox control's Click event handler, which displays the fields that correspond to the key selected in the ComboBox control.

Code 5.16:   **The Combo1 Control's Click Event**

```
    Private Sub Combo1_Click()
        If Combo1.ListIndex < 0 Then
            Text1.Text = ""
            Text2.Text = ""
```

```
        Text3.Text = ""
        Text4.Text = ""
        Exit Sub
    End If
    ItemIndex = Combo1.ItemData(Combo1.ListIndex)
    Text1.Text = DataArray(ItemIndex, 0)
    Text2.Text = DataArray(ItemIndex, 1)
    Text3.Text = DataArray(ItemIndex, 2)
    Text4.Text = DataArray(ItemIndex, 3)
End Sub
```

The event handlers for the other two ComboBox controls are identical.

The KeyCombo application is meant to be used for data retrieval only; it's not a data entry application. The Add New button was included to help you enter some data and test the program, which is why the application lacks a Delete button. The ComboBox controls with the alternative keys don't need to be visible at runtime. Depending on the user's needs, you might want to provide Command buttons that make one of the combo boxes visible. Another improvement would be to replace the TextBox controls with combo boxes so that the user can either select an existing item or type a new one.

The ScrollBar and Slider Controls

The ScrollBar and Slider controls let the user specify a magnitude by scrolling a selector between its minimum and maximum values. In some situations, the user doesn't know in advance the exact value of the quantity to specify (in which case, a textbox would suffice), so your application must provide a more flexible mechanism for specifying a value, along with some type of visual feedback.

The vertical scroll bar that lets a user move up and down a long document is a typical example of the use of a *ScrollBar* control. In the past, users had to supply line numbers to locate the section of the document they wanted to view. With a highly visual operating system, however, this is no longer even an option.

The scroll bar and visual feedback are the prime mechanisms for repositioning the view in a long document or in a large picture that won't fit entirely in its window. When scrolling through a document or an image to locate the area of interest, the user doesn't know or care about line numbers or pixel coordinates. Rather, the user uses the scroll bar to navigate through the document and the visible part of the document provides the required feedback. The example in Figure 5.13 was created with the ScrolPic application.

FIGURE 5.13:

The ScrollBar controls in this window bring the desired part of the image into view and also provide a clue as to the image's dimensions.

On the Mastering Visual Basic 6 CD-ROM: ScrolPic

The ScrolPic application shown in Figure 5.13 is in the Chapter 6 folder on the CD. The ScrolPic application displays a large picture in a small PictureBox control and lets the user scroll around the image until the desired part is located.

You have probably noticed that the PictureBox control doesn't have a ScrollBars property; if it did, scroll bars would automatically attach to the image if it exceeded the control's dimensions. To display an image larger than the control's dimensions, you must simulate this feature through your code, and the ScrolPic application shows you how it's done.

The ScrolPic application will be explained in the next chapter, as it makes extensive use of graphics methods. Nevertheless, you might want to open the application to see how it uses the two scroll bars as navigational aids.

The *Slider* control is similar to the ScrollBar control, but it doesn't cover a continuous range of values. The Slider control has a fixed number of tick marks, which the developer can label (e.g., Off, Slow, Speedy, as shown in Figure 5.14). The user can place the slider's indicator to the desired value. While the ScrollBar control relies on some visual feedback outside the control to help the user position the indicator to the desired value, the Slider control forces the user to select from a range of valid values.

FIGURE 5.14:

The Slider control lets the user select one of several discrete values.

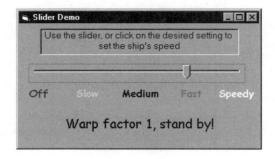

In short, the ScrollBar control should be used when the exact value isn't as important as the value's effect on another object or data element. The Slider control should be used when the user can type a numeric value and the value your application expects is a number in a specific range; for example, integers between 0 and 100, or a value between 0 and 5 inches in steps of 0.1 inches (0.0, 0.1, 0.2 inches, and so on, up to 5 inches). The Slider control is preferred to the TextBox control in similar situations because there's no need for data validation on your part. The user can only specify valid numeric values with the mouse.

The ScrollBar Control

The ScrollBar control is a long stripe with an indicator that lets the user select a value between the two ends of the control. The ScrollBar control comes in two versions: horizontal and vertical. Other than their orientation, there are no differences between the two versions. The left (or bottom) end of the control corresponds to its minimum value. The other end is the control's maximum value. The current value of the control is determined by the position of the indicator, which can be scrolled between the minimum and maximum values. The basic properties of the ScrollBar control, therefore, are properly named Min, Max, and Value (see Figure 5.15).

- **Min**   The control's minimum value

- **Max**   The control's maximum value

- **Value**   The control's current value, specified by the indicator's position

The Min and Max properties are positive Integer values, which means the valid range of values for a ScrollBar control is 0 to 32655. To cover a range of negative numbers or nonintegers, you must supply the code to map the actual values to Integer values. For example, to cover a range from 2.5 to 8.5, set the Min property to 25, set the Max property to 85, and divide the control's value by 10. If the range you need is from -2.5 to 8.5, set the Min property to 0 and the Max property to 110 (25 + 85). This time you'd not only divide the result by 10, you'd also have to subtract 2.5 from it to map the control's zero value to -2.5.

FIGURE 5.15:

The basic properties of the ScrollBar control

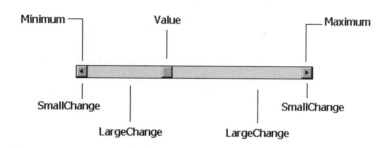

TIP

By default, scroll bars can be used to specify positive integers in the range 0 to 32655. To use them to specify negative or fractional numbers, you must use a little math in your code.

VB6 at Work: The Colors Project

Figure 5.16 shows another example that demonstrates how the ScrollBar control works. The Colors application lets the user specify a color by manipulating the value of its basic colors (red, green, and blue) through scroll bars. Each basic color is controlled by a scroll bar and they all have minimum values of 0 and maximum values of 255.

NOTE

If you aren't familiar with color definition in the Windows environment, see the section "Specifying Colors" in Chapter 7, *Manipulating Color and Pixels with Visual Basic*.

The Colors application demonstrates the use of the ScrollBar control.

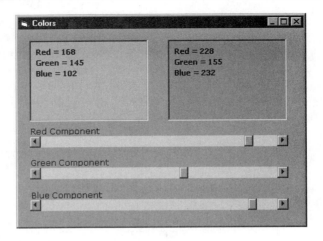

As the scroll bar is moved, the corresponding color is displayed, and the user can easily specify a color without knowing the exact values of its primary components. All the user needs to know is whether the desired color contains too much red or too little green. With the help of the scroll bars and the immediate feedback from the application, the user can easily pinpoint the exact value. Notice that this "exact value" is of no practical interest; only the final color counts.

Scroll bars and slider bars have minimum and maximum values that can be set with the Min and Max properties. The indicator's position in the control determines its value, which is set or read with the Value property. In the Colors application, the initial value of the control is set to 128 (the middle of the range). Before looking at the code for the Colors application, let's examine the control's events.

The ScrollBar Control's Events

The user can change the ScrollBar control's value in three ways:

- *By clicking the two arrows at its ends.* The value of the control changes by the amount specified with the *SmallChange* property.

- *By clicking the area between the indicator and the arrows.* The value of the control changes by the amount specified with the *LargeChange* property.

- *By scrolling the indicator with the mouse.*

You can monitor the changes on the ScrollBar's value from within your code with two events: Change and Scroll.

- **Change**   The Change event occurs every time the user changes the indicator's position and releases the mouse button. While the indicator is being moved, the Change event isn't triggered. For instance, if the user clicks on the indicator's button and holds down the mouse button while moving the mouse back and forth, no Change event is triggered. The Change event occurs only when the mouse button is released.

- **Scroll**   The Scroll event occurs continuously while the indicator is moving. This lets you update other controls on the Form from within your code as the user moves the indicator with the mouse. After the mouse button is released, the control stops triggering Scroll events and triggers a single Change event because the control's value has changed. In most situations, you should program both events to react to user actions.

Scroll and Change Events in the Colors Application

The Colors application demonstrates the difference between the two events. The two PictureBox controls, which display the color designed with the three scroll bars, react differently to the user's actions. The first PictureBox is updated from within the Scroll event, which occurs continuously as the user moves the indicator of a scroll bar. The second PictureBox is updated from within the Change event, which occurs after the indicator is moved to another position.

As the user moves the indicator with the mouse, the first PictureBox displays the current color and provides immediate feedback to the user. The other PictureBox doesn't follow the changes as they occur. When the mouse button is released, a Change event occurs, and the second PictureBox is updated. At this point, both PictureBoxes display the color specified by the three scroll bars.

If the user attempts to change the Color value by clicking the two arrows of the scroll bars or by clicking in the area to the left or to the right of the indicator, only the second PictureBox is updated. The user doesn't slide the scroll bar, and therefore, no Scroll event is generated. Open the Colors project and experiment by changing the values of the ScrollBar controls with the two techniques. The two PictureBoxes can have different colors if you set a Color value by clicking the arrows of the scroll bars.

The conclusion from this experiment is that you must program both the Scroll and the Change events to provide continuous feedback to the user. If this feedback requires too many calculations, which would slow down the reaction of the Scroll event, program only the Change event. This event may not take place continuously, but it will take place after the ScrollBar's value has changed, unlike the Scroll event, which occurs only during the sliding of the control.

The Slider Control

The Slider control is similar to the ScrollBar control, but it lacks the granularity of the ScrollBar control. Suppose you want the user of an application to supply a value in a specific range, such as the speed of a moving object. Moreover, you don't want to allow extreme precision; you need only a few settings, such as slow, fast, and very fast. A Slider control with three or four stops, such as the one shown earlier in Figure 5.14 will suffice. The user can set the control's value by sliding the indicator or by clicking either side of the indicator.

> **NOTE**
>
> *Granularity* is the degree of detail or accuracy desired for a given magnitude and is usually imposed by the quantity being measured. In measuring distances between buildings, a granularity on the order of a foot is adequate. In measuring (or specifying) the dimensions of a building, the granularity should be on the order of millimeters. The Slider control lets you set the type of granularity that's necessary for your application. You can do the same with a scroll bar, but not without some extra calculations.

The Slider control's icon doesn't appear on the Toolbox by default. To use the control in a project you must right-click the Toolbox or select Components in the Project menu. On the Components dialog box, check Microsoft Windows Common Controls 6.0. This will add a number of common controls to your Toolbox, including the Slider control.

As with the ScrollBar control, SmallChange and LargeChange properties are available. SmallChange is the smallest increment by which the Slider value can change. The user can only change the slider by the SmallChange value by sliding the indicator (unlike the ScrollBar control, there are no arrows at the two ends of the Slider control). To change the Slider's value by LargeChange, the user can click either side of the indicator.

The Slider on the Form in Figure 5.14 (also see the Slider project on the CD) has its Min property set to 1, its Max property set to 5 (that is, five stops), and its TickStyle set to sldNoTicks (3). The code behind the control's Change event, which sets the caption of the Label control at the bottom of the Form, is shown following.

Code 5.17:   **The Slider Control's Change Event**

```
Private Sub Slider1_Change()
    Select Case Slider1.Value
        Case 1: Label6.Caption = "Are we moving yet?"
        Case 2: Label6.Caption = "We're moving at 400 mph"
```

```
            Case 3: Label6.Caption = "We're cruising at 1000 mph"
            Case 4: Label6.Caption = "Warp factor 1, stand by!"
            Case 5: Label6.Caption = "Warp factor 9!"
        End Select
    End Sub
```

In the place of the tick marks under the Slider control are Label controls, which indicate the desired speed. In addition, each Label's Click event has also been programmed to change the position of the Slider control:

```
Private Sub Label2_Click()
    Slider1.Value = 2
End Sub
```

This simple subroutine enables you to make the Label a functional element of the program's interface.

VB6 at Work: The Inches Project

Figure 5.17 demonstrates another situation that calls for a Slider control. The Form in Figure 5.17 is an element of a program's user interface that lets the user specify a distance between 0 and 10 inches and in increments of 0.1 inches. As the user slides the indicator, the current value displays on a Label control, above the Slider. If you open the Inches application, you'll notice that there are more stops than there are tick marks on the control. This is made possible with the *TickFrequency* property, which determines the frequency of the visible tick marks.

FIGURE 5.17

This Slider control lets users specify a distance between 0 and 10 inches in increments of 0.1 inches. The tick marks correspond to whole inches.

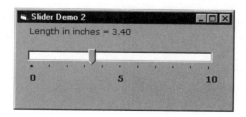

You may specify that the control has 50 stops (divisions) but that only 10 of them will be visible. The user can, however, position the indicator on any of the 40 invisible tick marks. You can think of the visible marks as the major tick marks and the invisible ones as the minor tick marks. If the TickFrequency property is 5, only every fifth mark will be visible. The slider's indicator, however, will stop at all tick marks.

TIP When using the Slider control on your interfaces, you should set the TickFrequency property to a value that helps the user select the desired setting. Too many tick marks are confusing and difficult to read. Without tick marks, the control doesn't look professional. You might also consider placing a few labels to indicate the value of selected tick marks, as I have done in the examples.

The slider in the Inches application was designed with the following settings:

```
Min = 0
Max = 50
SmallChange = 1
LargeChange = 10
TickFrequency = 5
```

The slider needs to cover a range of 10 inches in increments of 0.1 inches. To set the SmallChange property to 1, you have to set LargeChange to 10. Moreover, the TickFrequency is set to 5, so there will be a total of 10 divisions (corresponding to half and whole inches). The numbers below the tick marks were placed there with properly aligned Label controls.

The Label's contents need to be updated as the Slider's value changes. This is signaled with two events (which don't occur simultaneously): the Change event, which occurs every time the value of the control changes, and the Scroll event, which occurs as the user slides the control's indicator. While the Scroll event takes place, the Change event doesn't, so you must program both events if you want to update the Label at all times. The code is the same and quite simple:

```
Private Sub Slider1_Scroll()
    Label1.Caption = "Length in inches = " & _
        Format(Slider1.Value / 5,"#.00")
End Sub
```

This single line of Visual Basic code must be inserted into the control's Change event handler as well.

VB6 at Work: The TxtMargin Project

To see the Slider control in use, let's review a segment of another application, the RTFPad application, which is covered in Chapter 8, *Advanced ActiveX Controls*. The Form shown in Figure 5.18 contains a RichTextBox control and two sliders. The RichTextBox control will be explained in Chapter 9. All you need to know about the control to follow the code is that the RichTextBox control is similar to a TextBox control, but provides many more editing and formatting options. Two of the control's properties we'll use in this example are the SelIndent and SelHangingIndent properties and their functions are as follows:

- **SelIndent** Specifies the amount by which the currently selected paragraph(s) is indented from the left side of the control

- **SelHangingIndent** Specifies the amount of the hanging indentation (that is, the indentation of all paragraph lines after the first line)

The two sliders above the RichTextBox control let the user manipulate these two indentations. Because each paragraph in a RichTextBox control is a separate entity, it can be formatted differently. The upper slider controls the paragraph's indentation, and the lower slider controls the paragraph's hanging indentation.

You can open the TxtMargin application in this chapter's folder on the CD and check it out. Enter a few paragraphs of text and experiment with it to see how the sliders control the appearance of the paragraphs.

FIGURE 5.18:

The two Slider controls let the user format the paragraphs in a RichTextBox control.

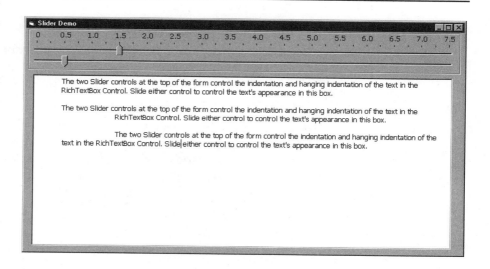

To create the Form shown in Figure 5.18, the left edge of the RichTextBox control must be perfectly aligned with the sliders' indicators at their leftmost position. When both sliders are at the far left, the SelIndent and SelHangingIndent properties are zero. As each slider's indicator is scrolled, these two properties change value, and the text is reformatted instantly. All the action takes place in the Slider controls' Scroll event. Here's the code of the Slider1 control, which controls the paragraph's indentation:

```
Private Sub Slider1_Scroll()
    RichTextBox1.SelIndent = RichTextBox1.RightMargin * _
        (Slider1.Value / Slider1.Max)
    Slider2_Scroll
End Sub
```

The paragraph's hanging indentation is not the distance of the text from the left edge of the control, but the distance of the paragraph from the leftmost character of the first line. That's why every time the paragraph's indentation changes, the program calls the Scroll event of the second slider to adjust the hanging indentation, even though the second slider hasn't been moved. The hanging indentation is expressed as a percentage, and we get the ratio of the difference between the two controls and their maximum value. This difference can become negative too, in which case the hanging indentation is to the left of the normal indentation. Remove the following line from the Slider1 control's Scroll event and see what happens:

```
Slider2_Scroll
```

Since the slider's tick marks don't correspond to physical units, we set the text's indentation to a percentage of its total width, which is given by the RightMargin property of the RichTextBox control. The *RightMargin* property is the distance of the text's right edge from the left side of the control.

This percentage is the same as the percentage of the slider's value divided by its maximum value. As soon as the SelIndent property is set, the entire paragraph is indented accordingly. The program then calls the second slider's Scroll event, which adjusts the hanging indentation. The code for this event is shown here:

```
Private Sub Slider2_Scroll()
    RichTextBox1.SelHangingIndent = RichTextBox1.RightMargin * _
            ((Slider2.Value - Slider1.Value) / Slider2.Max)
End Sub
```

The numbers (which don't correspond to any real units, but you could easily map them to inches, centimeters, or any other unit) are Label controls, carefully placed on the Form. The length of the two Slider controls is 7.5 inches (on a monitor with 92 dpi) and the Labels above the tick marks are arranged from within the Form's Load event. The length of both Slider controls is 11,360 twips, which is slightly larger than 7.5 inches. On a 92 dpi monitor, 7.5 inches correspond to 10,800 twips. This value is returned by the function:

```
ScaleX 7.5, vbInches, vbTwips
```

This value is increased by 28 pixels to account for the fact that the control's Width property is larger than the width of the slider (the carved line that runs across the control). Ideally, the Slider control should provide a property to return the width of the actual slider, excluding the left and right margins. Since you don't know the size of the margins, sizing a Slider control precisely is not a simple task. After setting the Slider control's Width property, you must also reposition and resize the RichTextBox on the Form, so that its two margins coincide with the minimum and maximum values of the Slider control, respectively. By default, the dimensions of the various controls on a Form are returned by the *Width* and *Height* properties in twips. To convert twips to pixels, you must first find out how many twips correspond to a pixel on the specific monitor resolution with the Screen.TwipsPerPixelX and Screen.TwipsPerPixelY properties and then use them in your code.

The Labels above the control's tick marks are placed there from within the Form's Load event with the following code. The Labels are members of the Margin control array (Margin(0) being the Label that displays 0, Margin(1) the Label that displays 0.5, and so on). The first Label, Margin(0), must be placed over the first tick manually.

```
Private Sub Form_Load()
    Me.Show
' The Sliders' settings will work for monitors with 92 dpi ONLY!
    RichTextBox1.RightMargin = _
            RichTextBox1.Width - Screen.TwipsPerPixelX * 30
    Disp = (Slider1.Width - 28 * Screen.TwipsPerPixelX) / 15
    For i = 1 To 15
        Margin(i).Left = Margin(i - 1).Left + Disp
    Next
End Sub
```

The File Controls

Three of the controls on the Toolbox let you access the computer's file system. They are the DriveListBox, DirListBox, and FileListBox controls (see Figure 5.19), which are the basic blocks for building dialog boxes that display the host computer's file system. Using these controls, the user can traverse the host computer's file system, locate any folders or files on any hard disk, even on network drives. The file controls are independent of one another, and each can exist on its own, but they are rarely used separately. The file controls are described next.

FIGURE 5.19:

Three File controls are used in the design of Forms that let users explore the entire structure of their hard disks.

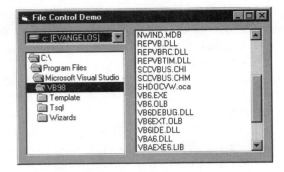

- **DriveListBox**   Displays the names of the drives within and connected to the PC. The basic property of this control is the *Drive* property, which sets the drive to be initially selected in the control or returns the user's selection.

- **DirListBox**   Displays the folders of the current drive. The basic property of this control is the *Path* property, which is the name of the folder whose sub-folders are displayed in the control.

- **FileListBox**   Displays the files of the current folder. The basic property of this control is also called Path, and it's the path name of the folder whose files are displayed.

The three File controls aren't tied to one another. If you place all three of them on a Form, you'll see the names of all the drives in the DriveListBox. If you select one of them, you'll see the names of all the folders under the current folder, and so on. Each time you select a folder in the DirListBox by double-clicking its name, its subfolders are displayed. Similarly, the FileListBox control will display the names of all files in the current folder. Selecting a drive in the DriveListBox control, however, doesn't affect the contents of the DirListBox.

To connect the File controls, you must assign the appropriate values to their basic properties. To force the DirListBox to display the folders of the selected drive in the DriveListBox, you must make sure that each time the user selects another drive, the Path property of the DirListBox control matches the Drive property of the Drive-ListBox. The following is the minimum code you must place in the DriveListBox control's Change event:

```
Private Sub Drive1_Change()
    Dir1.Path = Drive1.Drive
End Sub
```

Similarly, every time the current selection in the DirListBox control changes, you must set the FileListBox control's Path property to point to the new path of the DirListBox control:

```
Private Sub Dir1_Change()
    File1.Path = Dir1.Path
End Sub
```

This is all it takes to connect the three File controls and create a Form that lets users traverse all the disks on their computers. Although the DriveListBox control displays all the drives and the DirListBox control displays all the subfolders, in most cases you'll want to limit the files displayed in the FileListBox. To do this, use the control's *Pattern* property, which lets you specify which files will be displayed with a file-matching string such as "*.TXT" or "1997*.XLS".

It's also customary to display a list of available file-matching specifications in a ComboBox control, where the user can select one of them. The ComboBox control, shown in Figure 5.20, is populated when the Form is loaded and its selection is changed. The new file pattern is assigned to the Pattern property of the File control.

Changes in the ComboBox control are reported to the application with two distinct events: Change (the user enters a new file pattern) and Click (the user selects a new pattern from the list with the mouse). Both events contain the following line of code:

```
File1.Pattern = Combo1.Text
```

FIGURE 5.20:

The ComboBox control below the ListBox control lets you specify a pattern, which will be used to populate the FileList control with file names that match the pattern.

But why bother with the File controls when you can use the FileOpen and File-Save controls? The answer is that sometimes you want to build your own custom applications that manipulate disk files. In Chapter 11, *Recursive Programming*, you'll be introduced to the FileScan application, which scans a folder and its subfolder to locate specific files and then processes them. This application can't be implemented with the standard common dialog controls.

A program that scans the hard disk relies on the contents of these controls, and when it switches to a specific folder, it expects to find the names of the files in this folder in a FileListBox control. The ScanFolder application examined in Chapter 11 is a good example of the use of these controls, not only as elements of the user interface, but as functional elements of an application.

To access the contents of the three File controls, use their List property, which is similar to the List property of the ListBox control. The DriveListBox and FileListBox controls are linear; they display a list of drives and files, respectively, all of them being equal. To access the contents of these two controls use the List property with an Index value, which is 0 for the first item and ListCount - 1 for the last item. The following two loops scan the drives and the files of the current folder and print their names to the Immediate window:

```
' Scan the contents of the DriveListBox control
For i = 0 To Drive1.ListCount - 1
    Debug.Print Drive1.List(i)
Next

' Scan the contents of the FileListBox control
For i = 0 To File1.ListCount - 1
    Debug.Print File1.List(i)
Next
```

Scanning the folders of the DirListBox control is a bit more involved because this control's contents are structured. The folder names above the current folder are parent folders, and the folders under the current folder are subfolders. To access the subfolders of the current folder, use a loop similar to the previous ones:

```
' Scan the contents of the DirListBox control
For i = 0 To Dir1.ListCount - 1
    Debug.Print Dir1.List(i)
Next
```

The current folder is Dir1.List(-1) and the folders above (the parent folders) can be accessed with increasingly negative indices. The expression Dir1.List(-2) is the current folder's parent folder, Dir1.List(-3) its parent's parent folder, and so on. There is no property that returns the number of parent folders, so you can't set up a For...Next loop to scan the parent elements. One method is to create a While...Wend loop like the following one:

```
pDepth = -1
While Dir1.List(pDepth) <> ""
```

```
        Debug.Print Dir1.List(pDepth)
        pDepth = pDepth - 1
Wend
Debug.Print "The current folder is nested" _
        & -pDepth +  & "folders deep"
```

When you attempt to access a non-existent parent folder (with the expression Dir1.List(-99), for instance), Visual Basic won't generate a runtime error, as one might expect. It will return an empty string, which you can examine from within your code to find out whether there are more parent folders or not.

The project FileDemo on the CD demonstrates the techniques for accessing the contents of the file controls. You can open the project in the Visual Basic IDE to experiment with it and see how it uses the List and ListCount properties of the various controls to retrieve their contents and print them on a ListBox control, as shown in Figure 5.21.

FIGURE 5.21:

The FileDemo application demonstrates the techniques for enumerating the contents of the three file controls.

PART II

Advanced Visual Basic

CHAPTER
SIX

6

Drawing with Visual Basic

- The PictureBox control

- The ImageBox control

- Coordinate systems

- Drawing lines and circles

- Drawing rubber shapes

- Drawing transparent shapes

- Optimization issues

One of the most interesting and fun parts of a programming language, is its graphics elements. In general, graphics fall into two major categories: vector and bitmap. *Vector graphics* are images generated by graphics commands such as the Line and Circle commands. *Bitmap graphics* are images that can be displayed on various controls and processed on a pixel-by-pixel basis. The difference between vector and bitmap graphics is that vector graphics aren't tied to a specific monitor resolution; that is, they can be displayed at various resolutions. Figure 6.1 shows an interesting curve that was designed with the Spiral application, which we'll explore later in the chapter. The vector image on the left was generated with drawing commands, and the image on the right is the equivalent bitmap.

FIGURE 6.1:

Although these two images appear to be identical, the image on the left was created with drawing commands and the image on the right is its bitmap.

Figure 6.2 shows a detail of the same curve. The curve designed with drawing commands (the vector image) looks just as good when enlarged, whereas the bitmap reveals its blocklike structure. The vector drawing can be easily generated at the new resolution, but the bitmap can only be enlarged. And as you know, you can't blow-up an image without some loss in quality. On the printed page, Figures 6.1 and 6.2 may not reveal the detail of the vector and bitmap drawing.

Despite their inherent limitations, bitmap graphics are quite useful and much more common than vector graphics. For example, you can't create the image of a landscape with graphics commands. On the other hand, it doesn't make sense to display the bitmap of a circle when a simple Circle command can produce the same image faster and cleaner. Both types of graphics have their place, and you can mix them to produce the desired result.

This chapter explores both types of graphics and the many Visual Basic tools for manipulating them.

FIGURE 6.2:

When enlarged, the vector drawing retains its detail, but the bitmap reveals its structure.

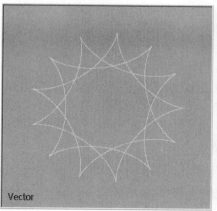
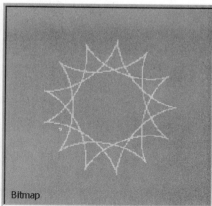

Vector

Bitmap

Graphics Controls

You can place graphics on three controls:

- Form
- PictureBox
- ImageBox

The main difference in these three controls is that the ImageBox control is designed specifically for displaying images and not for creating new images or manipulating them. The other two controls provide drawing methods that let you design graphics at runtime.

The methods for loading graphics on the various controls are simpler than creating graphics from scratch. You can place graphics on controls at design time and runtime. To load a graphic (bitmap or icon) on a control at design time, you assign its filename to the *Picture* property of the control in the Properties window. This same procedure can't change the image displayed at runtime; instead, you must use the LoadPicture() function, which is described shortly.

If the graphic is assigned to a control at design time, it's stored along with the application. One of the files that the Visual Basic editor generates for each Form in a project has the extension FRX. This is where the image (the actual bitmap) is stored. As a consequence, the size of the application will increase if its Forms contain bitmaps that must be loaded at runtime. The alternative is to load the graphic at runtime with the LoadPicture() function. This reduces the size of the FRX file, but your application must make sure the file is available at runtime.

Vector drawings aren't loaded, they are generated on the fly (we'll explore the drawing commands in the second part of the chapter).

Sizing Images

When an image is loaded on a Form or a PictureBox, you must make sure it will fill the available space, unless you let the user select the graphic at runtime. Graphics are usually placed on ImageBox or PictureBox controls. The *ImageBox* is good for displaying graphics and uses fewer resources than PictureBox controls. The *Picture-Box* control provides methods for drawing at runtime and is much more flexible than the ImageBox control. As a consequence, the PictureBox control uses more resources. Each control provides a different property for controlling the appearance of the picture displayed.

The ImageBox Control

If the *Stretch* property is True, the image is resized to fill the area of the ImageBox control. Unless the control's dimensions have the same aspect ratio as the image's dimensions, the image is distorted as it's resized. If the Stretch property is False, the ImageBox control behaves like a PictureBox with its AutoSize property set to True. Figure 6.3 shows two ImageBox controls, both containing the same image. Notice how the image is resized in the ImageBox control whose Stretch property is True.

The PictureBox Control

If the *AutoSize* property is True, the control is resized to the dimensions of the image it contains. If the AutoSize property is False, only the part of the image that can fit on the control is displayed.

Loading and Saving Images

To load a graphic on a control at runtime, use the LoadPicture method as follows:

```
Form1.Picture = LoadPicture(fileName)
```

FIGURE 6.3:

The Stretch property of the ImageBox control allows images to be resized.

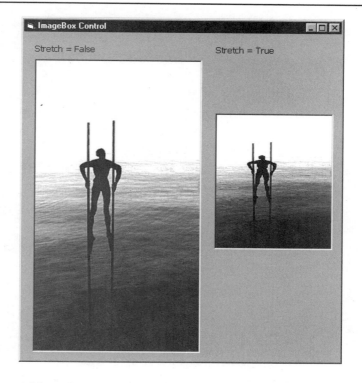

The *fileName* variable is the name of the file containing the graphic. This file can have one of the following extensions:

- **BMP**   Bitmap
- **GIF**   Graphics Interchange Format
- **JPG**   Joint Photographic Experts Group
- **DIB**   Device Independent Bitmap
- **WMF**   Windows MetaFile
- **EMF**   Enhanced MetaFile
- **ICO**   Icons

At present, Visual Basic doesn't support other types of graphic files.

If you use the LoadPicture method without an argument, the current picture is unloaded (along with any drawing or printing painted onto the control or Form with the Circle, Line, PSet, or Print commands). Calling the LoadPicture without an argument clears the control. To remove a graphic from a PictureBox (or any control that can display graphics), issue the following command:

```
Picture1.Picture = LoadPicture()
```

This technique is similar to the Cls method, which clears any drawing or printing from a Form or a control.

If your application processes the displayed image during the course of its execution and you want to save the image, you can use the *SavePicture* statement. Its syntax is as follows:

```
SavePicture picture, filename
```

The *picture* argument is the Picture property of the PictureBox or ImageBox control whose contents you want to save, and *filename* is the name of the file that will store the image.

To save the contents of the Picture1 control to a file, you must use a statement like the following:

```
SavePicture Picture1.Picture, "c:\tmpImage.bmp"
```

WARNING   If you use the SavePicture statement to save the contents of a PictureBox control, you will end up with an empty BMP file if the AutoRedraw property of the control is False. If you plan to save the contents of a PictureBox control to a file, be sure that its AutoRedraw property is set to True before loading any image or otherwise creating graphics. The AutoRedraw property is an important property of controls that can display images, and we'll look at it in detail at the end of the chapter.

The SavePicture statement supports only BMP files, even if the original image loaded on the control comes from a GIF or a JPG file. When prompting the user with the FileOpen common dialog box to select an image file to open, you can use the extensions BMP, GIF, or JPG. In the corresponding FileSave common dialog box though, you can specify only the BMP (or DIB) extension.

Setting Picture and Image Properties

Another related property is the *Image* property, which is a pointer to a structure in memory where the bits of the image are stored. Unlike the Picture property, the Image property is read-only and used to pass bitmaps to API functions, as you'll see in Chapter 13, *The Windows API*. Another difference between the Image and Picture properties is that the bitmap returned by the Picture property is the one saved along with the other Form elements in the FRX file and doesn't include any shapes drawn on top of the bitmap at runtime. The PicImg application, shown in Figure 6.4, demonstrates the basic difference between the two properties.

The PicImg application demonstrates the difference between the Picture and Image properties.

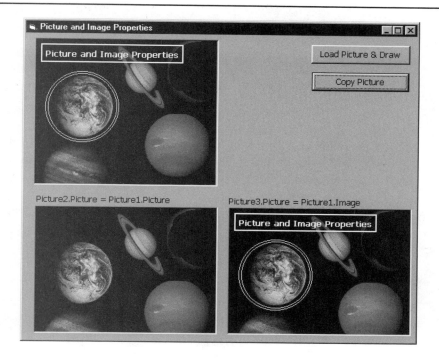

Click the Load Picture & Draw button to load the Planets.bmp image on the PictureBox control in the upper-left control and draw a couple of shapes over the bitmap with Visual Basic's drawing commands. Click the Copy Picture button to copy the contents of the top PictureBox control onto the other two PictureBox controls. The bitmap is copied onto the left PictureBox control with the following command:

```
Picture2.Picture = Picture1.Picture
```

The same bitmap is copied onto the other PictureBox with this command:

```
Picture3.Picture = Picture1.Image
```

Using the Picture property, you can copy only the bitmap loaded with the Load-Picture method. On the other hand, the Image property copies everything on the control, including the shapes. The Image property points to the persistent bitmap, which consists of the shapes drawn while the AutoRedraw property is True. Any shapes drawn while the AutoRedraw property is False won't be copied with either method. Another use of the Image property is to copy the image of a control to the Clipboard, as you'll see in the next section.

Exchanging Images through the Clipboard

Whether you use bitmap images or create graphics from scratch with the Visual Basic drawing methods, sooner or later you'll want to exchange them with other Windows applications. To do so, you use the Clipboard and its SetData, Get-Data(), and GetFormat methods, which are described next.

The ImgCopy application, shown in Figure 6.5, demonstrates how to use the Clipboard to exchange data with other applications. Click the Load Image button to load the Planets.bmp image on the top PictureBox control, and click the Draw on Image button to draw a couple of shapes on top of the control's bitmap. If the AutoRedraw checkbox is checked, the AutoRedraw property of the top Picture-Box is set to True before drawing. If not, the drawing takes place on a PictureBox with its AutoRedraw property set to False, and the drawing isn't copied to the Clipboard along with the bitmap. The other two buttons copy the first PictureBox control's image to the Clipboard and paste the contents of the Clipboard on the second PictureBox control. The code behind the first two Command buttons is straightforward. We used similar code in the PicImg application.

FIGURE 6.5:

The ImgCopy application uses the Clipboard to exchange images with any Windows application that can handle them.

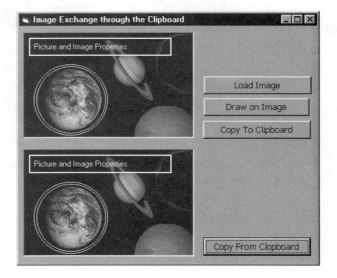

Using SetData

To copy the contents of a control to the Clipboard, you use the *SetData* method:

```
Clipboard.SetData Picture1.Image, vbCFBitmap
```

The *vbCFBitmap* argument is a built-in constant that corresponds to the bitmap format (one of the formats the Clipboard object can handle). The first argument of the SetData method specifies the bitmap to be copied and it can be either the Picture or the Image property of the control. If you use the Picture property, any shapes drawn on the control at runtime won't be copied.

Before copying a bitmap to the Clipboard, you must clear its contents with the Clear method. If you attempt to copy a bitmap to the Clipboard without clearing its current contents, nothing will be copied. The Clipboard's contents can't be overwritten.

The Copy to Clipboard button clears the Clipboard and then uses the SetData method to add data to the Clipboard.

Code 6.1:   **The Copy to Clipboard Button Code**

```
Private Sub Command1_Click()
    Clipboard.Clear
    Clipboard.SetData Picture1.Image, vbCFBitmap
End Sub
```

Whatever is copied to the Clipboard with the SetData method is available to any application in the Windows environment. For instance, if you start an image processing application after copying the contents of the first PictureBox to the Clipboard, the application's Paste command will be enabled, indicating that the Clipboard's contents can be pasted on the current document. Notice that any shapes drawn on top of the bitmap while AutoRedraw is set to False aren't copied to the Clipboard. For more information in the AutoRedraw property and its role in graphics, see the section "Optimization Issues" toward the end of this chapter.

Using GetData()

The Paste from Clipboard button uses the *GetData()* method to retrieve data from the Clipboard. The code behind this button examines the contents of the Clipboard, and if the Clipboard contains an image, it's copied onto the second PictureBox control.

Code 6. 2:   **The Paste from Clipboard Button**

```
Private Sub Command2_Click()
    If Clipboard.GetFormat(vbCFBitmap) Then
        Picture2.Picture = Clipboard.GetData()
```

```
    Else
        MsgBox "The clipboard doesn't contain image data"
    End If
End Sub
```

The Paste from Clipboard button pastes the Clipboard's contents on the PictureBox control regardless of which application placed it there.

Using GetFormat

The *GetFormat* method of the Clipboard object returns a True/False value, indicating whether the Clipboard's current contents match the format specified as the parameter. In other words, the GetFormat method asks the Clipboard whether it contains a specific format, rather than what is the format of the data it contains. Other common values for the *GetFormat* argument are the constants *vbCFMetafile* (Windows Metafile), *vbCFPalette* (Windows Palette), *vbCFText* (plain text), and *vbCFRTF* (Rich Text Format). Notice how the Paste from Clipboard command uses the GetFormat method to make sure the Clipboard contains a bitmap before attempting to move it to the PictureBox.

Coordinate Systems

Visual Basic provides two basic methods for drawing shapes on controls and a method for displaying text:

- **Line**   Draws lines and boxes
- **Circle**   Draws circles and ellipses
- **Print**   Displays text strings

(A fourth method, Point, turns individual pixels on and off, and we'll explore this method in the following chapter.)

Before you draw anything, you must know the dimensions of the control you're about to draw on and the units it uses. To do this, you must understand coordinates and coordinate systems and how they are used in drawing.

Coordinates describe the position of the individual pixels on the screen or of the points on a piece of paper in the printer. The coordinate system is similar to a city map. Each square on the map has its own unique address: a combination of a column and a row number. The column number is the vertical coordinate, or Y coordinate. The row number is the horizontal coordinate, or X coordinate. Any point on the Form can be identified by its X and Y coordinates, and we refer to it as the point at coordinates (X, Y) or simply the point (X, Y). An example is shown in Figure 6.6. The values along the x-axis in the coordinate system of the figure go from 0 to 100, and the values along the y-axis go from -50 to 50. Any pair of numbers in the ranges 0 to 100 and -50 to 50 specifies a point on the Form.

FIGURE 6.6:

Any point on a Form can be identified by its X and Y coordinates.

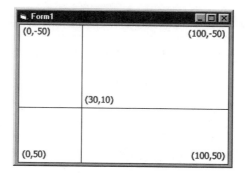

The point with the smallest coordinates is the *origin of the coordinate system*. In Visual Basic, the origin of the coordinate system is the upper-left corner of the control or Form. The X coordinates increase to the right and the Y coordinates increase downward. Each coordinate is a number and it may or may not correspond to a meaningful unit. For example, the letter and number coordinates on a city map don't correspond to meaningful units; they are arbitrary. The coordinates on a topological map, though, correspond to physical distances (e.g., kilometers, miles). It all depends on the intended application.

For example, if you want to draw a plan for your new house, you need to use a coordinate system in inches or centimeters so that there will be some relation between units and the objects you draw. If you're going to draw some nice geometrical shapes, any coordinate system will do. Finally, if you're going to display and process images, you'd want a coordinate system that uses pixels as units.

Visual Basic supports several coordinate systems, including a user-defined coordinate system that lets users set up their own units. If you're familiar with computer graphics in older languages or operating systems, you'd probably expect that the most common coordinate system to be based on pixels. Actually, pixels aren't the best units for all applications. If you use pixels to address a control's contents, you're tied to a particular resolution. If the monitor's resolution is increased, your designs are going to look different. Even the aspect ratio may not be the same, and the circles will become ellipses.

Visual Basic's default coordinate system uses a unit called *twip*, which equals 1/20 of a point. A point is a typographical measure of unit; there are 72 points in an inch and 1,440 twips in an inch. The twip is a precise unit of measurement, probably more precise than we need today. It does, however, allow us to draw shapes that will look good even when printed on a 1,200 dpi laser printer. But because twips aren't convenient in all situations, Visual Basic provides the eight coordinate systems listed in Table 6.1.

TABLE 6.1: Visual Basic Coordinate Systems

CONSTANT NAME	VALUE	DESCRIPTION	COMMENTS
vbUser	0	User-defined coordinate system	
vbTwips	1	Twips	1,440 twips per inch
vbPoints	2	Points	72 points per inch
vbPixels	3	Pixels	
vbCharacters	4	Characters	120 twips wide, 240 twips high
vbInches	5	Inches	
vbMillimeters	6	Millimeters	
vbCentimeters	7	Centimeters	

To change the default coordinate system, assign the appropriate value to the Scale-Mode property. If you set ScaleMode to Inches, distances on the control must be specified in inches. In this case, two points that are one unit apart are one inch from each other. You can also specify decimal distances such as 0.1, which corresponds to 1/10 of an inch. Changing the ScaleMode property doesn't resize or otherwise affect the control. It simply changes the density of the grid you use to address the points on the control.

If none of the pre-defined coordinate systems suit your needs, you can create your own. Suppose you want to implement a game board with 12 squares along the x-axis and eight squares along the y-axis. The pieces of the game can only rest on a square of the grid, so you don't need the precision of units such as twips or pixels. You can set up a coordinate system that extends from 0 to 11 in the horizontal direction and from 0 to 7 in the vertical direction. If the game board is 32 × 32 squares, you set up a coordinate system that extends 32 units in both directions. The size of the PictureBox control doesn't change. There is, however, enough space for 32 × 32 squares, and each square is addressed with integer coordinates. To set up a user-defined coordinate system, you can use the Scale method or the Scale-related properties, which are explained next.

Scale Properties and Methods

Now we can look at the properties and methods that relate to the control's position and the coordinate system. There are two groups of properties: those that control the size and position of the control and those that affect (and are affected by) the choice of coordinate system.

Width and Height Properties

These two properties determine the actual dimensions of the control and are always expressed in the units of the container of the control. Suppose you're placing a PictureBox control on a Form whose coordinate system is the default, twips. The Width and Height properties of the PictureBox control are expressed in twips. If you change the control's coordinate system, the values of these two properties won't change. If you resize the control on the Form by dragging its handles with the mouse, the Width and Height properties will change value to reflect the new size of the control. These properties will also change value if you change the container's coordinate system to reflect the control's dimensions in the new coordinate system.

Left and Top Properties

The *Left* and *Top* properties are the coordinates of the control's upper-left corner, and they are expressed in the container's coordinate system. If you change their values, the control is repositioned. They also change value if you change the container's coordinate system to reflect the control's position in the new coordinate system.

ScaleMode Property

The *ScaleMode* property sets (or returns) the control's current coordinate system. Set this property to one of the values shown in Table 6.1 to establish a new coordinate system. If you set this property to 0 (User), you must also set the ScaleWidth and ScaleHeight properties. Conversely, if you set the ScaleWidth and/or ScaleHeight properties, the ScaleMode property is reset to 0.

ScaleWidth and ScaleHeight Properties

These two properties are the control's inner dimensions in units of the current coordinate system. Changing the coordinate system doesn't change the size of the control, but it does change the number of units that can fit along the two axes of the control. For example, a PictureBox control placed on a Form that's 2,880 twips wide and 2,880 twips tall is approximately two inches wide and two inches tall.

Its Width and Height properties are 2,880. If you change the Form's coordinate system to inches, the control won't be resized, but its ScaleWidth and ScaleHeight properties will become two (inches). Where the X coordinate of the control's middle point in the previous coordinate system was 1,440, it's now one. You can also assign values to these properties, in which case you're automatically switching to a user-defined coordinate system (the ScaleMode property is reset to zero).

ScaleLeft and ScaleTop Properties

ScaleLeft and *ScaleTop* are the coordinates of the upper-left corner of the control in a user-defined system of coordinates. Coordinate systems need not start at zero. ScaleLeft is the minimum value an X coordinate can assume. The maximum X coordinate is ScaleLeft+ScaleWidth. Suppose you want to draw an object with dimensions 12 × 10, but you want the X coordinate to start at 100 and the Y coordinate to start at 300. This coordinate system must be defined as follows:

```
Form1.ScaleWidth = 12
Form1.ScaleHeight = 10
Form1.ScaleLeft = 100
Form1.ScaleTop = 300
```

The X coordinates in this system extend from 100 to 112, and the Y coordinates extend from 300 to 310.

Scale Method

Using the *Scale* method is the most convenient way to set up a user-defined coordinate system. It has the following syntax:

```
Form1.Scale (X1, Y1) - (X2, Y2)
```

The coordinates of the upper-left corner of the control are *(X1, 1)*, and *(X2, Y2)* are the coordinates of the lower-right corner. The Scale method tells Visual Basic that the horizontal dimension of the control is *(X2 - X1)* units and that the vertical dimension is *(Y2 - Y1)* units. This is the address space of the control and it doesn't affect its external dimensions.

To set up the game board mentioned earlier, you can call the Scale method as follows:

```
Form1.Scale (0, 0) - (11, 7)
```

The statement is equivalent to the following assignments:

```
Form1.ScaleTop = 0
Form1.ScaleLeft = 0
```

```
Form1.ScaleWidth = 11
Form1.ScaleHeight = 7
```

(Of course, setting any of the Scale properties resets the ScaleMode to 0, so you don't have to explicitly set the ScaleMode.)

Setting any of the ScaleWidth, ScaleHeight, ScaleTop, and ScaleLeft properties or calling the Scale method resets the ScaleMode property to 0 (user-defined).

All properties that begin with the prefix Scale use the user-defined coordinate system. Setting any of these properties switches you to a user-defined coordinate system and resets the ScaleMode property to 0 but doesn't reposition or rescale the control or the Form. Similarly, every time you issue a Scale command such as `Picture1.Scale (0, 0) - (11, 7)`, these four properties change value according to the Scale command's arguments.

ScaleX, ScaleY Methods

On occasion, you'll want to express the control's new size in a given coordinate system without changing the container's coordinate system. Let's say the Form's coordinate system is 1 (twips) and you want to place a PictureBox on it with the exact dimensions of 1.20 x 2.00 inches. First, calculate how many twips correspond to 1.20 and 2.00 inches, and then assign these values to the control's Width and Height properties. Given that there are 1,440 twips in an inch, mapping inches to twips is straightforward. Visual Basic, however, provides the *ScaleX* and *ScaleY* methods to convert units between any two coordinate systems. Both methods have the identical syntax, which is:

```
Form1.ScaleX (width, fromscale, toscale)
```

The *width* argument is the number of units you want to convert, *fromscale* is the coordinate system from which the units will be converted, and *toscale* is the coordinate system into which the units will be converted. The arguments *fromscale* and *toscale* can have one of the values shown earlier in Table 6.1.

HiMetric is another scale that can be used only with the Image object (a property that represents the image on a control). The Picture property of a PictureBox or Form is an object which exposes the Width and Height properties. These two properties return the dimensions of the picture regardless of the size of the control. Even if the picture doesn't fit on the control, the properties Picture1.Picture.Width and Picture1.Picture.Height return the original dimensions of the picture in HiMetric units. To convert HiMetric units to pixels, use the ScaleX and ScaleY methods with the constant *vbHiMetric* as its second argument.

Suppose you want to make the Picture1 control 200 pixels wide by 140 pixels tall. The Form on which the PictureBox lies has the default coordinate system, twips. The Width and Height properties of the Picture1 control, therefore, must be expressed in twips. To convert 200 pixels to twips, use the following statement:

```
WidthTwips = Form1.ScaleX(200, vbPixels, vbTwips)
```

Similarly, to convert the height of 140 pixels to twips, use the following statement:

```
HeightTwips = Form1.ScaleY(140, vbPixels, vbTwips)
```

And then use the results to set the control's size in twips:

```
Picture1.Width = WidthTwips
Picture1.Height = HeightTwips
```

Since the Form's coordinate system is twips, you can omit the last argument of the ScaleX and ScaleY methods. You can resize the Picture1 control with the following statements:

```
Picture1.Width = Form1.ScaleX(200, vbPixels)
Picture1.Height = Form1.ScaleY(140, vbPixels)
```

TwipsPerPixelX, TwipsPerPixelY Properties

These two properties apply to the Screen object, and they return the number of twips per pixel for an object measured horizontally (*TwipsPerPixelX*) or vertically (*TwipsPerPixelY*).

CurrentX, CurrentY Properties

A basic concept in drawing with Visual Basic methods is the *current point*. Visual Basic allows you to draw shapes, a line for instance, without specifying a starting point. If the starting point isn't specified, the current point becomes the line's starting point. After the line is drawn, its endpoint becomes the current point. The properties *CurrentX* and *CurrentY* set or read the coordinates of the current point in the units of the current coordinate system. To display a string at specific coordinates on a Form, set the CurrentX and CurrentY properties to the desired coordinates and then issue the Print method to display the string (the Print method is described later in this chapter).

VB6 at Work: The Coords Project

To help you visualize the various coordinate systems and the related properties, I've included the Coords project on the CD, which is shown in Figure 6.7. The

Option buttons on the left side of the Form set the ScaleMode of the PictureBox control on the right side. The PictureBox control has fixed dimensions, but you can easily change its internal coordinate system by clicking one of the Option buttons. Each time you set a new coordinate system, the coordinates of the PictureBox control's opposite corners are updated. Set a coordinate system, place the pointer over the PictureBox, and then move it around while holding down the left mouse button. As the pointer slides over the control, its coordinates are displayed.

FIGURE 6.7:

The Coords application

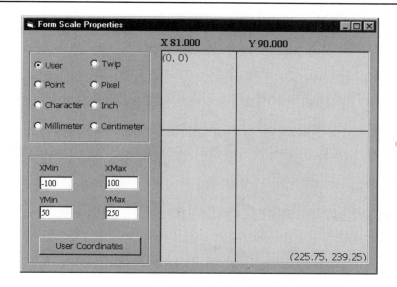

You can also set your own coordinate system by supplying the proper values in the four TextBox controls in the lower-left segment of the window. You can use both positive and negative coordinates and then slide the pointer over the PictureBox to see its coordinates.

The most interesting part of the Coords application's code is in the PictureBox control's MouseMove event. You can open the Coords application with the Visual Basic editor to find out how it works. You can also interrupt the application and move or resize the PictureBox control by setting its Top, Left, Height, and Width properties. The code for the application manipulates the control's Scale properties only, and you can't change the control's position with these properties. Let's start by looking at the code of the Option buttons.

Code 6. 3:	The Twip Option Button

```
Private Sub Option2_Click()
    Label1.Caption = "X " & Format$(Picture1.ScaleX(currX,_
            Picture1.ScaleMode, 1), "#.000")
    Label2.Caption = "Y " & Format$(Picture1.ScaleY(currY,_
            Picture1.ScaleMode, 1), "#.000")
    Picture1.ScaleMode = 1
    ShowSize
End Sub
```

First, it displays the current coordinates in their new units, then it changes the coordinate system, and finally it calls the ShowSize subroutine, which displays the minimum and maximum coordinate values on the PictureBox control. Many of the methods used in this example are explained later in the chapter, so you might want to come back to this example later and examine its code again.

Graphics Methods

Now we can look at the drawing methods of Visual Basic, which are the following:

- **Print**   Displays a string

- **Line**   Draws lines and boxes

- **Circle**   Draws circles and arcs

- **Point**   Retrieves the Color value of a point

- **PSet**   Sets the color of a point

The Print method has nothing to do with your printer; it draws text on a Form or a control. The Line and Circle methods accept many arguments that extend Visual Basic's drawing capabilities. For example, you can draw elaborate geometric shapes such as ellipses, filled shapes, and pie charts. The Point and PSet methods manipulate pixels and are used frequently in image processing applications and for drawing curves, which must be plotted point by point. The last two methods are discussed in detail in the following chapter, *Manipulating Color and Pixels with Visual Basic.*

Drawing Text

The simplest drawing method is the *Print* method, which draws text on a Form or a PictureBox control starting at the current point. The text is drawn in the control's current font and size, and after it's drawn, the current point is moved to the end of the text. The following statement will display a string at the top of the PictureBox:

```
Picture1.Print "Drawing with Visual Basic"
```

It will also move the current point below the string, as if you were printing on a multi-line TextBox control. The next string you'll print on the same control will appear below the first one.

> **TIP**
>
> Keep in mind that long lines of text don't wrap automatically when the control's right edge is reached. Your code must take care of breaking long lines of text into smaller ones before drawing them.

TextWidth, TextHeight Methods

Two methods commonly used to align text on a Form or a PictureBox control are *TextWidth* and *TextHeight*. These methods accept a string as argument and they return their arguments' width and height, respectively. The TextWidth and TextHeight properties apply to the objects that accept graphics methods, which are the Form object, Printer object, and the PictureBox control, and they report the length and width required to print a string on the printer at the current font.

VB6 at Work: The TxtPrint Project

The TxtPrint project (see Figure 6.8) demonstrates how to use the Print method along with the TextWidth and TextHeight properties to draw aligned text on a Form. To place a string in the middle of the Form, you must first calculate the Form's middle point:

```
Form1.ScaleWidth/2, Form1.ScaleHeight/2
```

You must then subtract one-half of the text's width from the X coordinate and one-half of the text's height from the Y coordinate. Setting the current point to these coordinates and then issuing the Print command centers the text on the Form:

```
Form1.CurrentX = (Form1.ScaleWidth - TextWidth("Centered Text")) / 2
Form1.CurrentY = (Form1.ScaleHeight - TextHeight("Centered Text")) / 2
Form1.Print "Centered Text"
```

TIP   Notice that the code shown here uses the ScaleWidth and ScaleHeight properties. These two properties return the width and height of the "useful" area of the Form; the Form's frame and title bar are excluded. The Width and Height properties report the external dimensions of the Form, including the frame and the title bar. Also, for the purposes of centering a string on a Form, the actual scale mode won't make any difference. The middle point will be the same with any scale; only the absolute values will differ.

You can open the TxtPrint application in Visual Basic's editor to examine the rest of the code.

FIGURE 6.8:

The TxtPrint application demonstrates how to use the TextWidth and Text-Height properties to align text on a Form with the Print method.

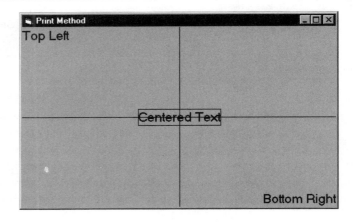

Drawing Lines and Shapes

The method for drawing lines is called *Line*, and it has the following syntax:

```
Line[Step] (X1, Y1) - [Step] (X2, Y2) ,[color], [B][F]
```

The arguments that appear in square brackets are optional. The coordinates of the line's starting point are *X1, Y1*, and *X2, Y2* are the coordinates of the ending point. The following statement demonstrates the simplest form of the method:

```
Line (X1, Y1) - (X2, Y2)
```

The coordinates of the line's endpoints are expressed in the units of the control's coordinate system. The thickness of the line is determined by the *DrawWidth* property, and its style, by the *DrawStyle* property, whose settings are shown in Table 6.2. If the width of the line is greater than one pixel, the settings 1 through 4 are identical to setting 0—that is, you can't draw dashed or dotted lines that are thicker than one pixel.

TABLE 6.2: Values of the DrawStyle Property

CONSTANT NAME	VALUE	DESCRIPTION
vbSolid	0	(Default) Solid
vbDash	1	Dash
vbDot	2	Dot
vbDashDot	3	Dash-dot
vbDashDotDot	4	Dash-dot-dot
vbInvisible	5	Transparent
vbInsideSolid	6	Inside solid

The meaning of each property is obvious, except for the last value, InsideSolid. When drawing with a line width larger than one pixel, Visual Basic splits the width of the line on both sides of the specified coordinates. If you set the DrawStyle property to 6 (Inside Solid), the shape (line, box, or circle) will be drawn entirely within the specified coordinates.

The following short program draws lines of different styles on the Picture1 control:

```
Private Sub Picture1_Click( )
Hstep = Picture1.ScaleHeight / 6
For i% = 1 to 6
Picture1.DrawStyle = i% - 1
Picture1.Line (.1 * Picture1.ScaleWidth, Hstep * i%) - _
        (.9 * Picture1.ScaleWidth, Hstep * i%)
Next
End Sub
```

Specifying Color

The *ForeColor* property of the Picture Box or Form determines the color of the shapes you draw. However, you can draw lines in different colors by specifying the optional argument *color*, available with the Line and Circle methods (the Circle method will be discussed shortly). The following statements show how the *color* argument is used.

```
Line (10, 10) - (100, 100), RGB(255, 0, 0)
Line (10, 10) - (100, 100), &H0000FF
Line (10, 10) - (100, 100), QBColor(3)
RedColor# = RGB(255, 0, 0)
Line (10, 10) - (100, 100), RedColor#
```

All three examples draw a red line from (10, 10) to (100, 100), regardless of the current setting of the ForeColor property. The method's *color* argument can be any valid color expression. Normally, the line's color is determined by the control's ForeColor property, but the *color* argument of the Line method overwrites the ForeColor property for the current line. If you draw another line, without specifying a *color* argument, it will be drawn in the control's Foreground color.

Using Relative Coordinates (The Step Option)

With the *Step option* of the Line method, you can define the second endpoint of the line relative to the first endpoint. In other words, the Step option defines a point not in terms of its coordinates, but in terms of its distance from the line's first endpoint. The coordinates we have used so far are absolute because they specify a unique point on the screen as measured from the control's upper-left corner. The coordinates following the Step option are relative. The difference between the two types of coordinates is their origin. Absolute coordinates are always measured from the origin (ScaleLeft, ScaleTop), and relative coordinates are measured from the current position, wherever this might be. The following statement draws a line that starts at point (100, 100) and extends 100 units down and 200 units to the right from its starting point:

```
Line (100, 100) - (300, 200)
```

The following command draws a line from the same starting point, but this one extends 200 units down and 300 units to the right:

```
Line (100, 100) - Step (300, 200)
```

The two numbers following the Step option aren't the coordinates of the second endpoint, but its distance from the current point. You can also use the *Step* keyword in front of the Line method's first argument, in which case the line's starting point is defined relative to the current point (CurrentX, CurrentY).

Relative coordinates are used frequently in drawing closed shapes, because it's easier to define an endpoint by its distance from the previous one. Suppose you want to draw a box with dimensions 100 × 300, with its upper-left corner at the point (100, 400). You can draw this box in absolute coordinates, with the following commands:

```
Line (100,400) - (200,400)    ' Line to the right along the X-axis
Line (200,400) - (200,700)    ' Line down along the Y-axis
```

```
Line (200,700) - (100,700)    ' Line to the left along the X-axis
Line (100,700) - (100,400)    ' Line to the starting point
```

For each of the previous commands, you calculate the absolute coordinates of each corner of the frame by adding the appropriate dimensions to the previous endpoint. It is much easier, however, to draw the same box with relative coordinates. Here's how:

```
Line (100, 300) - Step (100, 0)
Line - Step(0,300)
Line - Step(-100,0)
Line - Step(0,-300)
```

You must define the starting point in absolute coordinates, but for the remaining points, it makes sense to use relative coordinates. Notice that you don't even need to define the first endpoint of each side because it coincides with the second endpoint of the previous side. The numbers following the Step option represent the distance of the next corner of the box from the previous one.

Drawing Boxes

Visual Basic offers a convenient way to draw boxes: the B *option* (Box) of the Line method. If you include this option, you can draw a box whose upper-left corner is defined by the first coordinate pair and whose lower-right corner is defined by the second coordinate pair. The last four commands in the Step option example could be replaced with the following line:

```
Line (100,400) - (200,700), , B
```

You must type the two consecutive commas if you omit the *color* argument; if you don't, Visual Basic assumes that B is a variable name specifying the color of the box.

As you may have guessed, there is an even easier way to draw a box on the screen using relative coordinates. If all we wanted was a rectangle with known dimensions and its upper-left corner fixed at point (100, 400), the following command would create just that:

```
Line (100, 400) - Step (100, 300), , B
```

You need to specify the coordinates of the upper-left corner and the dimensions of the box. The advantage of the last command is that you don't have to perform any calculations—you simply type the dimensions of the box, which is what you usually know.

The Line method accepts one more option that can be used only with the B option. If you want to fill a box, use the *F option* (Fill) immediately after the B option without a comma in between. It might be easier to think of the two options as the B (for box) and BF (for filled box) options, since you cannot use the F option alone. The FillColor property determines the color used for filling the box. The BF option overwrites the current setting of the FillColor property for a single box, just as the *color* argument overwrites the ForeColor property of the control or Form for the current statement.

Filling Shapes

Closed shapes can also be filled with various patterns, depending on the setting of the FillStyle property. By default, closed shapes are transparent. To draw solid or hatched shapes, you must set the FillStyle property, which can take any of the values shown in Table 6.3.

TABLE 6.3: Values of the FillStyle Property

CONSTANT	VALUE	DESCRIPTION
vbFSSolid	0	Solid
vbFSTransparent	1	(Default) Transparent
vbHorizontalLine	2	Horizontal line
vbVerticalLine	3	Vertical line
vbUpwardDiagonal	4	Upward diagonal
vbDownwardDiagonal	5	Downward diagonal
vbCross	6	Cross
vbDiagonalCross	7	Diagonal cross

NOTE If the FillStyle property is set to any value other than 1 (transparent), any closed shape is automatically filled with the specified pattern. The FillColor property determines the color used for drawing the pattern.

The effect of the FillStyle property in drawing filled shapes is shown in Figure 6.9. Each circle is filled with a different pattern and a different color. If the FillStyle property of a PictureBox control or Form is set to any value other than 1 (Transparent), all the boxes and circles you draw on the control will be filled with the corresponding pattern. Moreover, the color used for drawing the pattern is given by the FillColor property. The FillColor property is the color with which the shape will be filled if the FillStyle is 0 (Solid) or the color of the lines in the pattern.

If the FillStyle property is 1 and you still want to draw boxes filled with a solid color, use the BF option of the Line method. This option overwrites the FillStyle temporarily and subsequent boxes are filled according to this property's setting. The Circle method (discussed next) doesn't have an equivalent option for drawing filled circles.

FIGURE 6.9:

The various values of the FillStyle property applied to boxes and circles

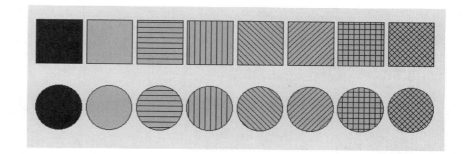

Using the Circle Method

The *Circle* method draws circles, arcs, and ellipses. The method's complete syntax is:

```
Circle [Step] (X, Y), radius, [color], [start] ,[end] ,[aspect]
```

The coordinates of the circle's center are X and Y, and R is its radius. These are the only mandatory arguments, and they are expressed in units of the current coordinate system.

Drawing Circles

The simplest form of the Circle method is Circle (X,Y), R. The following statement uses it to draw a circle at the center of the Form1 Form:

```
Circle (Form1.ScaleWidth / 2, Form1.ScaleHeight / 2), _
      Form1.ScaleHeight / 3
```

The circle's radius equals one-third of the Form's height. If the Form is taller than it is wide, part of the circle may be invisible.

As with the Line command, the Step option makes the coordinates of the center relative to the current point. Unlike the Line method, the Circle method doesn't allow you to use the current point as the center of the circle and omit its coordinates. To draw a circle centered at the current point, use the following command:

```
Circle Step (0, 0), R
```

You must specify the relative coordinates, even if they are zero.

You should specify the radius of the circle in the units of the horizontal axis. With most coordinate systems, you could use the units of the horizontal or the vertical axis; however, in a user-defined coordinate system, the units of the horizontal and vertical axes might be different. The circle won't be distorted in any way, but you must be aware of this detail when defining the length of the radius, because it will affect the size of the circle.

Some Tips about Circles

If you set a coordinate system such as the following:

```
Form1.Scale (0, 0) - (100, 1000)
```

and then draw a circle with a radius of 50 units, the circle fills the Form. If the coordinate system is defined as:

```
Form1.Scale (0, 0) - (1000, 100)
```

a circle with the same radius will be only 1/10 of the Form's width (its radius being 1/20 of the Form's width). The circle won't be distorted, but the choice of radius will affect its size.

Drawing Ellipses

You can also use the Circle method to draw ellipses if you include the *aspect* argument. *Aspect* is the ratio of the vertical to the horizontal radius of the ellipse and it can be an integer, floating-point number, or even less than 1, but it cannot be a negative number. If the aspect is smaller than 1, the ellipse extends horizontally and is squeezed in the vertical direction. If the aspect is larger than 1, the ellipse extends vertically. Figure 6.10 shows how the aspect ratio is defined. The two ellipses of Figure 6.10 and their bounding boxes were drawn with the following statements:

```
SideX = 1
SideY = 0.75
Side = 2000
```

```
Form1.DrawWidth = 2
Form1.Line (100, 100)-Step(Side * SideX, Side * SideY), , B
XC = 100 + Side * SideX / 2
YC = 100 + Side * SideY / 2
Form1.DrawWidth = 1
Form1.Circle (XC, YC), Side / 2, , , , SideY / SideX

SideX = 0.75
SideY = 1
Form1.DrawWidth = 2
Form1.Line (3000, 100)-Step(Side * SideX, Side * SideY), , B
XC = 3000 + Side * SideX / 2
YC = 100 + Side * SideY / 2
Form1.DrawWidth = 1
Form1.Circle (XC, YC), Side / 2, , , , SideY / SideX
```

FIGURE 6.10:

The aspect ratio determines how a circle is distorted to produce an ellipse.

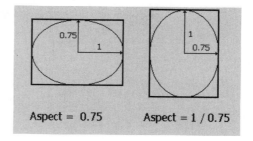

Aspect = 0.75   Aspect = 1 / 0.75

Drawing Arcs

You also can use the Circle method to draw arcs. The arguments *start* and *end* specify the arc's starting and ending angles in radians.

TIP

Remember that a full circle contains 360 degrees, which corresponds to 2*pi radians (pi = 3.14159625...). To convert an angle of D degrees to radians, use the formula 2*pi*D/360 or pi*D/180.

The arc's starting and ending angles are measured counterclockwise. Negative angles don't reverse the direction of the arc. They simply tell Visual Basic to draw the arc as if they were positive numbers and then connect the endpoint that corresponds to the negative angle with the center of the circle. As you may have guessed, this technique is used for drawing pie charts.

Because circles (and connected arcs) are closed shapes, they are automatically filled with the pattern specified with the FillStyle property and take on the color specified by the FillColor property. For a discussion of these two properties, see the section "Filling Shapes," earlier in this chapter.

VB6 at Work: The PieChart Project

The PieChart application uses the Circle method to draw pie charts with connected arcs, as shown in Figure 6.11. Because a connected arc is a closed shape, it can also be filled with a pattern or a solid color, as specified by the FillStyle and FillColor properties. The PieChart application lets you select whether the pie's slices will be filled with a pattern or a solid color or remain hollow. The PieChart application also serves as an example of how to use the FillStyle and FillColor properties to fill closed shapes.

FIGURE 6.11:

The PieChart application uses connected arcs to draw the pie's wedges.

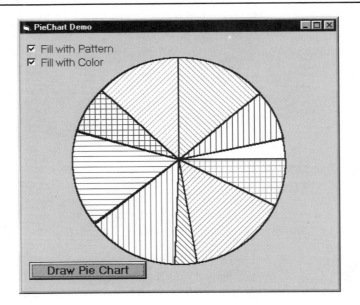

The program generates 10 random numbers in the range 20 to 100, stores them in the *PieData()* array, and then calculates the arc that corresponds to each number. Because the total must be a full circle (2*pi), each element of the *PieChart()* array corresponds to an arc of 2*pi*PieData(i)/Total. Each slice's starting angle is the ending angle of the previous slice, and its ending angle is the starting angle plus the angle corresponding to its element in the *PieData()* array. The following code implements the technique just described for drawing pie charts.

Code 6 . 4:   The PieChart Application

```
Private Sub Command1_Click()
Dim PieData(10) As Integer

    Form1.Cls
    For i = 0 To 9
        PieData(i) = 20 + Rnd() * 100
        Total = Total + PieData(i)
    Next

    Form1.DrawWidth = 2
    For i = 0 To 9
        arc1 = arc2
        arc2 = arc1 + 6.28 * PieData(i) / Total
        If Check1.Value Then
            Form1.FillStyle = 2 + (i Mod 5)
        Else
            Form1.FillStyle = 0
        End If
        If Check2.Value Then
            Form1.FillColor = QBColor(8 + (i Mod 6))
        Else
            Form1.FillColor = QBColor(9)
        End If
        Form1.Circle (Form1.ScaleWidth / 2, Form1.ScaleHeight / 2),_
                Form1.ScaleHeight / 2.5, , -arc1, -arc2
    Next
End Sub
```

Using the Drawing Modes

When you draw shapes with Visual Basic's graphics methods, the pixels that make up the shape replace any existing pixels on the control by default. Visual Basic can, however, combine the new pixels with the existing ones in various ways, depending on the settings of the control's DrawMode property. The settings of this property are shown in Table 6.4. Most of them correspond to logical operators such as AND, OR, and NOT. The default DrawMode setting is 13 (Copy Pen), which transfers the new pixels onto the control, replacing the underlying pixels. Setting 4 (Not Copy Pen) works the same way, except that it reverses the color of the pixels being drawn. Setting 9 combines the new pixels with the existing ones with the logical operator AND. As you can see, there are many ways to combine the color of the new pixels with the existing ones.

TABLE 6.4: Values of the DrawMode Property

Constant	Value	MEANING
vbBlackness	1	Draws in black color
vbNotMergePen	2	Inverse of Setting 15 (Merge Pen)
vbMaskNotPen	3	Combination of the colors common to the background color and the inverse of the drawing color
vbNotCopyPen	4	Inverse of Setting 13 (Copy Pen)
vbMaskPenNot	5	Combination of the colors common to both the drawing color and the inverse of the background color
vbInvert	6	Inverse of the drawing color
vbXorPen	7	Combination of the colors in the background color and drawing color, but not in both
vbNotMaskPen	8	Inverse of Setting 9 (Mask Pen)
vbMaskPen	9	Combination of the colors common to the drawing color and the display
vbNotXorPen	10	Inverse of Setting 7 (Xor Pen)
vbNop	11	Output remains unchanged
vbMergeNotPen	12	Combination of the control's background color and the inverse of the drawing color
vbCopyPen	13	Color specified by the ForeColor property
vbMergePenNot	14	Combination of the drawing color and the inverse of the background color
vbMergePen	15	Combination of the drawing color and the background color
vbWhiteness	16	Draws in white color

The default setting of the DrawMode property is *vbCopyPen*, which replaces the underlying pixels with the new ones. We'll return to the topic of the drawing mode in the section "Using the PaintPicture Method," in the following chapter, where you'll find an application that allows you to experiment with the various settings. First, however, let's explore an especially interesting and useful drawing mode: XOR.

Using the XOR Operator

One of the most practical settings of the DrawMode property is 7 *(vbXorPen)*. With this setting, the values of the new pixels are combined with the existing ones by means of the XOR operator. The bits are combined as shown in Table 6.5.

TABLE 6.5: Combining Bits with the XOR Operator

BIT 1	BIT 2	RESULT
0	0	0
0	1	1
1	0	1
1	1	0

The result of the operation is 1 only if the bits are different. If they are the same (both 0 or both 1), the result is 0. Let's see how the XOR operator works. In the Immediate window (if it's not visible, choose View ➢ Immediate Window), enter the following statements (press Enter after each Print statement to see the result):

```
print 184 XOR 45
       149
print 149 XOR 45
       184
print 149 XOR 184
       45
```

As you can see, the number 184 is XORed with the value 45, and the result is a new number (149). When the result is again XORed with one of the two original numbers it yields one of the other numbers. This is a unique property of the XOR operator, which makes it useful in many situations, including cryptography. Indeed, at the heart of every encryption algorithm you'll find the XOR operator. Let's run a small experiment with characters. As you know, characters are represented by numbers, which you can find with the Asc() function. Here are a few experiments with characters and the XOR operator:

```
print asc("d") XOR 88
60
print chr$(60)
<
print chr$(60 XOR 88)
d
```

When the character "d" is XORed with the number 88, it becomes the character "<". If the new character is XORed with 88, it becomes the original character. Repeating this process for every character in a text file encrypts the text. To recover the original text, you must XOR each character of the encrypted text with the key. The number 88 in the previous example is the key (something like an encryption password). Without the key, you'll find it difficult to recover the original text. More secure encryption algorithms use long encryption keys or other variations on this technique, but they are all based on this unique property of the XOR operator.

Now how does this relate to Visual Basic graphics? If the XOR operator can mask and then reveal a number, why not use it to do the same with a line? If you draw a line in XOR mode, you'll see a line superimposed over the existing pixels. If you draw another line on top of the first one, the line will disappear, revealing the underlying pixels. The XOR drawing mode has an interesting property: The first time you draw a shape on the screen, it's displayed on top of everything else and the colors change, but not the shape. If you draw the same shape again, the net result is to remove the shape without affecting the background.

The two PictureBox controls on the Form shown in Figures 6.12 and 6.13 have the same dimensions and display the same image. They differ only in the setting of their DrawMode property, which is 13 (Default) for the first one and 7 *(vbXorPen)* for the second one. Figure 6.12 shows the result of drawing a solid rectangle on both of them. Figure 6.13 shows the result of drawing the same rectangle again. Nothing is changed in the first PictureBox, but the rectangle is removed from the second control.

FIGURE 6.12:

When you draw a solid rectangle over an image in XOR mode, its pixels change color, but you can still make out the original shape.

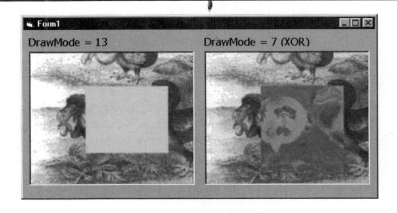

FIGURE 6.13:

When you draw another solid rectangle on top of the previous one in XOR mode, the underlying pixels are revealed.

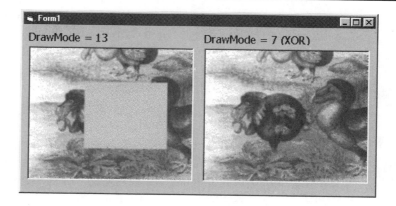

Drawing Rubber Lines

The most common example of the XOR drawing mode is in drawing rubber lines. A *rubber line* is a line with one of its endpoints fixed on the screen and the other endpoint moving around, following the movement of the pointer. Using rubber lines, the user can verify the final position of a line (and practically every other shape) before committing it to the screen. You have seen this tool in action in just about any drawing application you've used, and now you'll learn how to incorporate this technique in your applications.

To implement a rubber line feature in an application, you must make use of the three mouse events: MouseDown, MouseMove, and MouseUp.

The *MouseDown* event signals the starting point of the rubber line. The coordinates of this point must be stored in two Form-wide variables, which we'll call *XStart* and *YStart.* Set the DrawMode to 7 (XOR) so that you can continuously erase the previous line.

As long as the pointer is moving, Visual Basic generates *MouseMove* events. With each MouseMove event, you must erase the previous line and draw a new one from the starting point to the current point. To be able to erase the old line, you must store the coordinates of the old ending point in two more Form-wide variables, *XOld* and *YOld.* The MouseMove handler must draw two lines, one between the points *(XStart, YStart)* to *(XOld, YOld)* and another from the same starting point to the current point. The first line erases the previous rubber line, and the second becomes the current rubber line, which is erased with the next MouseMove event.

When the mouse button is released, you must draw the last line in the standard (COPY_PEN) mode. However, you must first erase the previous line, from *(XStart,*

YStart) to *(XOld, YOld),* by drawing another line on top of it in XOR mode. There-fore, the event handler must erase the last rubber line, change the drawing mode momentarily to COPY_PEN, and draw a line between the original point *(XStart, YStart)* and the point where the button is released (X, Y).

VB6 at Work: The Rubber Project

The Rubber application implements the technique just described and lets you draw rubber lines on a Form. Run it and press the left mouse button at the start-ing point of the line. When you move the mouse around without releasing the button, the second endpoint of the line follows the movement of the mouse. Every time you move the mouse, a new line is drawn between the starting point and the current position of the pointer. This line is called a rubber line because it can swing, shrink, and stretch, as needed, to follow the mouse. It's as if you had a rubber band attached to the starting point on one end and to the mouse pointer on the other end.

Once you decide on the exact placement of the line, release the mouse button, and the last rubber line is committed on the Form.

Code 6. 5:   **The Rubber Application**

```
Dim XStart, YStart As Single
Dim XOld, YOld As Single

Private Sub Form_MouseDown(Button As Integer, Shift As Integer, _
        X As Single, Y As Single)
    If Button <> 1 Then Exit Sub
    XStart = X
    YStart = Y
    XOld = XStart
    YOld = YStart
    Form1.DrawMode = 7
End Sub

Private Sub Form_MouseMove(Button As Integer, Shift As Integer, _
        X As Single, Y As Single)
    If Button <> 1 Then Exit Sub
    Form1.Line (XStart, YStart)-(XOld, YOld)
    Form1.Line (XStart, YStart)-(X, Y)
    XOld = X
    YOld = Y
End Sub
```

```
Private Sub Form_MouseUp(Button As Integer, Shift As Integer, _
        X As Single, Y As Single)
    If Button <> 1 Then Exit Sub
    Form1.DrawMode = 13
    Form1.Line (XStart, YStart)-(XOld, YOld)
    Form1.Line (XStart, YStart)-(X, Y)
End Sub
```

It's easy to modify this application so that it draws rubber rectangles or even rubber circles. You'll see how this technique is used in the context of a drawing application in the next section.

VB6 at Work: The Draw Project

The Draw project (see Figure 6.14) demonstrates just about every method and technique presented in this chapter. It's a simple application that lets the user draw various shapes, such as lines, boxes, and circles, and even display text. All the shapes are drawn in rubber mode. The menus of the application let the user set the drawing parameters, such as the drawing or filling color, the width of the shapes, the style of the lines, and so on. The File menu contains commands for storing the drawings in BMP files and loading images from disk files (images that were saved earlier with the Draw application or images in BMP format).

FIGURE 6.14:

The Draw application can become your starting point for a custom drawing application.

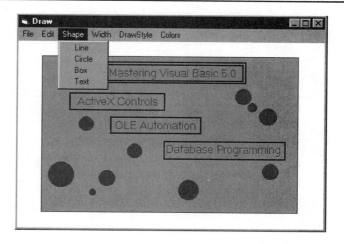

The Edit menu contains the usual Copy, Cut, and Paste commands that manipulate rectangular sections of the drawing. The parts of the drawing being copied aren't transferred to the Clipboard, though. They are saved temporarily on an invisible PictureBox control from which they can be pasted back in the same document (you'll see shortly why we aren't using the Clipboard for the Copy and Paste operations). The Width, DrawStyle, and Colors menus contain commands to change the width of the pen, the drawing style and the pen, and fill and background colors. These commands should be icons on a toolbar, but I wanted to focus on the drawing features of the project rather than its interface.

Drawing Rubber Shapes The Draw application's listing is too long to print in its entirety, so we'll focus on its most important aspects. Let's start with the code for drawing rubber shapes. When the user selects the shape to be drawn from the Shape menu, the program sets the *Shape* global variable to LINE, CIRCLE, BOX, or TEXT. This variable is used in the MouseDown, MouseUp, and MouseMove event handlers as explained earlier. In the MouseDown event, the program stores the starting coordinates of the rubber shape in the variables *Xstart* and *YStart*. These are the coordinates of a line's first endpoint, a box's upper-left corner, or a circle's center.

Code 6. 6:   **The MouseDown Event**

```
If Button = 1 Then
        XStart = X
        YStart = Y
        XPrevious = XStart
        YPrevious = YStart
        Form1.DrawMode = 7
End If
```

In the MouseMove event, the program draws the rubber shape by erasing the shape at the old coordinates and then drawing another one at the new coordinates. The MouseMove event handler is a Case switch, which erases the previous rubber lines and draws the new one (more on the Case switch later).

Code 6. 7:   **The MouseMove Events**

```
Select Case Shape
    Case "LINE":
        Form1.Line (XStart, YStart)-(XPrevious, YPrevious)
        Form1.Line (XStart, YStart)-(X, Y)
    Case "CIRCLE":
        Form1.Circle (XStart, YStart), Sqr((XPrevious - _
            XStart) ^ 2 + (YPrevious - YStart) ^ 2)
        Form1.Circle (XStart, YStart), Sqr((X - _
```

```
                    XStart) ^ 2 + (Y - YStart) ^ 2)
        Case "BOX":
            Form1.Line (XStart, YStart)-(XPrevious, YPrevious), , B
            Form1.Line (XStart, YStart)-(X, Y), , B
    End Select
    XPrevious = X
    YPrevious = Y
```

In the MouseUp event, the program draws the final shape in COPY_PEN mode.

```
    Form1.DrawMode = 13
    Select Case Shape
        Case "LINE":
            Form1.Line (XStart, YStart)-(X, Y)
        Case "CIRCLE":
            Form1.Circle (XStart, YStart), Sqr((X - XStart) ^ 2 _
                + (Y - YStart) ^ 2)
        Case "BOX":
            Form1.Line (XStart, YStart)-(X, Y), , B
    End Select
```

Drawing Text Unlike drawing standard shapes, printing the text requires a few extra steps. When the user selects Text from the Draw project's Shape menu, the program prompts for the string to be printed on the Form. It then waits for the user to click the mouse on the Form and move it around. As the pointer moves, the text follows the movement of the pointer and is printed on the Form when the user releases the mouse button.

WARNING   Visual Basic's drawing commands combine the pixels of the new shapes with the existing ones, except for the Print method, which overwrites the underlying pixels, regardless of the setting of the DrawMode property.

The Print method isn't affected by the drawing mode, so you can't count on the XOR drawing mode to erase the text. The Draw application does the trick by placing the text on a transparent, borderless Label control. As the user moves the pointer around on the Form, the program moves the Label by changing its Left and Top properties. When the mouse is released, the program calls the Print method to print the text on the Form.

The process just described is implemented in the Text command and in the MouseDown and MouseUp events. The Text command of the Shape menu executes the code in Code 6.8.

Code 6. 8:   **The Text Command**

```
Private Sub DrawText_Click()
Dim DrawString As String

    DrawString = InputBox("Enter string")
    Label1.Caption = DrawString
    PrintText = True

End Sub
```

The *PrintText* variable is global, and we'll use it in the Form's mouse events.

The Form's MouseDown event executes the code in Code 6.9.

Code 6. 9:   **The MouseDown Event**

```
If PrintText Then
        Label1.ForeColor = Form1.ForeColor
        Label1.Visible = True
        Label1.Left = X
        Label1.Top = Y
        Exit Sub
End If
```

Notice that the Label control used for moving the text around is invisible, except when needed (which is while the Label is dragged around).

Finally, in the MouseUp event, the program calls the Print method to place the string at the current location on the Form and hide the Label control again, as shown in Code 6.10.

Code 6.10:   **The MouseUp Event**

```
If PrintText Then
    Form1.AutoRedraw = True
    Form1.CurrentX = X
    Form1.CurrentY = Y
    Form1.Print Label1.Caption
    Label1.Visible = False
```

```
            PrintText = False
            Exit Sub
    End If
```

The text is drawn in the current drawing color and the Draw application doesn't have a menu option for changing the font, its size, and style. You can easily add this feature to the program, as long as you change the font of both the Label control and the Form. The Label's text is displayed while the user moves the string around to its final position, where it's printed in the Form's font with the Print method.

Using the Copy Command   When choosing the Copy or the Cut command, the user can select a rectangular area of the drawing with the mouse. A rubber rectangle is drawn around the selection as the user presses the button and moves the mouse. As soon as the user releases the button, the program copies the selected area of the bitmap to a hidden PictureBox control with the PaintPicture method. You can't use the Clipboard's SetData method because it doesn't provide any arguments to let you specify which part of the image will be copied. This method transfers the entire bitmap to the Clipboard. Thus, to copy part of the image, you must first move it to a "local Clipboard," which is PictureBox control. It's the project's internal clipboard in which bitmaps are stored between Copy and Paste operations. The Copy operation is implemented from within the Form's Mouse events, as follows:

1. In the MouseDown event, the program sets the rectangle's starting coordinates. It also temporarily resets the DrawWidth property to 1 (pixel).

2. In the MouseMove event, the program draws a rubber rectangle, which encloses the area to be copied.

3. Finally, in the MouseUp event, the rectangular area is transferred to the PictureBox control, with the following statements:

```
If X > XStart Then X1 = XStart Else X1 = X
If Y > YStart Then Y1 = YStart Else Y1 = Y
Picture1.PaintPicture Form1.Image, 0, 0, Abs(X - XStart), _
    Abs(Y - YStart), X1, Y1, Abs(X - XStart), _
    Abs(Y - YStart), &HCC0020
CopyBMP = False
CopyWidth = Abs(X - XStart)
CopyHeight = Abs(Y - YStart)
```

The two If statements ensure that the proper segment of the bitmap is copied, even if the user starts the selection from its lower-left corner. The *CopyWidth* and *CopyHeight* global variables hold the dimensions of the rectangle being copied so that later on, the program will paste only this area of the hidden PictureBox control.

Picture1 is the name of a hidden container where copied images (or parts of images) are stored with the Copy command and retrieved with the Paste command.

TIP　　　　Visual Basic doesn't provide a means for copying part of an image to the Clipboard. To exchange pictorial data with other Windows applications, you must copy the segment of the image you want to a PictureBox control, resize the control to the dimensions of the copied bitmap, and only then, use the SetData method of the Clipboard object to copy the bitmap to the Clipboard.

Using the Paste Command　　The Paste operation is simpler. When the user selects the Paste command, the program waits until the mouse button is pressed and then moves the bitmap to be pasted around, following the movement of the pointer. The pasted bitmap is drawn in XOR mode until the user releases the mouse button, and then the program copies the bitmap in COPY_PEN mode. This process is also implemented from within the Form's mouse events.

Moving an image segment around by redrawing it continuously in XOR mode is a slow process. This section of the application will be revised later in the chapter, in "Better Rubber Shapes," where I will first discuss the AutoRedraw property in detail, and then use it to implement a better method of refreshing the Form.

Further Improvements　　The Draw application is a functional application that you can use as a starting point for many custom applications. Because it can draw on top of bitmaps, you can use it to annotate drawings and graphics such as fax images.

You can also specify the font for printing text and add an Undo feature. To implement an Undo command, temporarily store the drawing in another hidden PictureBox control after each drawing operation. When the user selects the Undo command, copy this PictureBox control's contents back on the Form.

You can even implement a hierarchical Undo by tracking the drawing commands. To do this, you must set up a structure in which each command will be stored. This structure could be a list, such as the following:

```
Form1.DrawWidth = 3
Load "c:\drawings\cards.bmp"
Form1.Line (143, 193) - (302, 221), , B
Form1.FillColor = 134745&
Form1.Copy (0, 0) - (150, 100)
```

You must encode all the operations and save their descriptions in a list. If the user wants to undo an operation, you can present this list, let the user delete certain entries or change their order, and then clear the Form and execute all the commands in the list. This requires quite a lot of coding, but in principle, it's a straightforward process.

A problem with this application is that the rubber shapes can assume strange colors, depending on the values of the underlying pixels. This is a side effect of the XOR drawing mode, which isn't a problem when you draw shapes over a solid background, but it becomes a problem when you draw on top of bitmaps. We'll fix this problem later in the chapter, after we look at the AutoRedraw property and the Refresh method. We'll also look at the QDraw application, which is practically identical to the Draw application, except it uses a more robust method for drawing rubber shapes.

Drawing Curves

The Line and Circle methods are sufficient for drawing bar graphs or pie charts, but what if you want to draw interesting, mathematically defined curves like the ones shown in Figures 6.15 and 6.16? To graph curves, you must provide the code that plots every single point of the curve. As you can guess, drawing curves isn't going to be nearly as quick as drawing lines, but Visual Basic isn't too slow.

FIGURE 6.15:

The graph of the function exp(2/t)*sin(2*t)

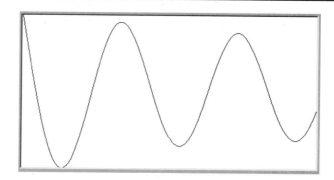

FIGURE 6.16:

The graph of the function cos(3*t)*sin(5*t)

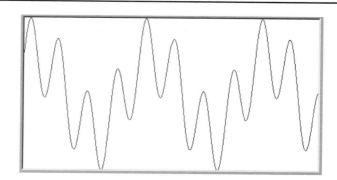

Suppose you want to plot a function, such as exp(2/t)*sin(2*t), for the values of t from 1 to 10. The t variable is time and it will be mapped to the x-axis. Clearly, you must set up a user-defined scale mode that extends from 1 to 10 along the x-axis. But what about the vertical axis? You must either guess or calculate the minimum and maximum values of the function in the range 1 to 10 and then set up the scale.

To plot the function, you calculate the function at consecutive X values and turn on the point that corresponds to this value. So, at how many points along the x-axis must you calculate the function? The function must be evaluated at each pixel along the x-axis. If you evaluate the function at more points, some will map to the same pixel. If you evaluate the function at fewer points, gaps will appear between successive points on the graph.

TIP   To draw a curve, you must calculate and display each and every point along the curve. To speed up applications that draw mathematically defined curves, compile them to native code.

Since you're going to calculate the function at every pixel along the x-axis, you must map the pixels to the corresponding values of the t variable. Let's assume that the t variable goes from *XMin* to *XMax* and that the number of pixels along the x-axis is *XPixels*. The following loop scans all the pixels along the x-axis and calculates the value of the time variable at each pixel:

```
For i = 0 To XPixels
    t = XMin + (XMax - XMin) * i / XPixels
Next
```

The variable t starts at *XMin*. When i reaches *XPixels*, its maximum value, the variable t becomes *XMax*. This loop goes through all the pixels along the x-axis and calculates the value of the t variable that corresponds to each pixel. All you have to do now is calculate the function for each value of the time variable.

Let's write a function that calculates the function for any given value of the independent variable:

```
Function FunctionEval1(ByVal X As Double) As Double
    FunctionEval1 = Exp(2 / X) * Cos(2 * X)
End Function
```

The function *FunctionEval1()* accepts as argument the value of the independent variable, calculates the function at the point, and returns the value of the function.

Let's now modify the main loop so that it plots the function.

```
For i = 0 To XPixels
    t = XMin + (XMax - XMin) * i / XPixels
    Picture1.PSet (t, FunctionEval1(t))
Next
```

In essence, the loop breaks the plot in as many points as there are pixels along the x-axis, calculates the value of the function at each point, and then turns the corresponding pixel on. Now that you have a technique for mapping the values of the variable *t* to pixel values, creating the actual plot is straightforward.

The last issue to be resolved is the value of the variable *XPixels*. You can switch the PictureBox control's ScaleMode property to 3 (Pixels) temporarily, use the ScaleWidth property to find out the control's horizontal resolution, and then set up a user-defined coordinate system that's appropriate for the plot, as follows:

```
Picture1.ScaleMode = 3
XPixels = Picture1.ScaleWidth - 1
```

The last step is to figure out the dimensions of the user-defined coordinate system for each function you want to plot. Use a loop similar to the one that produces the plot, only this time, instead of plotting the function, track its minimum and maximum values:

```
For i = 1 To XPixels
    t = XMin + (XMax - XMin) * i / XPixels
    functionVal = FunctionEval1(t)
    If functionVal > YMax Then YMax = functionVal
    If functionVal < YMin Then YMin = functionVal
Next
```

After the completion of the loop, the variables *YMin* and *YMax* hold the minimum and maximum values of the function in the range *XMin* to *XMax*. To set up the coordinate system for the specific function, you can call the Scale method with the following arguments:

```
Picture1.Scale (XMin, YMin) - (XMax, YMax)
```

You've seen all the important pieces of the code for plotting functions. Let's put it all together to build the application shown in Figure 6.17. The application is called Graph and you'll find it on this chapter's folder on the CD.

The Draw First Function and Draw Second Function buttons plot the two functions shown in Figures 6.15 and 6.16, and the Draw Both Functions button draws them both on the same PictureBox.

FIGURE 6.17:

The Graph application draws mathematically defined curves.

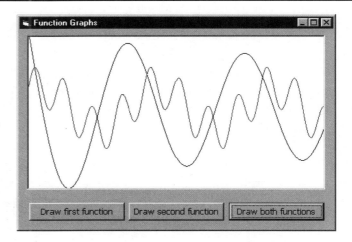

The Draw First Function Button

```
Private Sub Command1_Click()
Dim t As Double
Dim XMin As Double, XMax As Double, YMin As Double, YMax As Double
Dim XPixels As Integer

' Draw functions in for X=2 to X=10
YMin = 1E+101
YMax = -1E+101
XMin = 2
XMax = 10
Picture1.Cls
Picture1.ScaleMode = 3
XPixels = Picture1.ScaleWidth - 1

' Calculate Min and Max for Y axis
For i = 1 To XPixels
    t = XMin + (XMax - XMin) * i / XPixels
    functionVal = FunctionEval1(t)
    If functionVal > YMax Then YMax = functionVal
    If functionVal < YMin Then YMin = functionVal
Next

' Set up a user defined scale mode
Picture1.Scale (XMin, YMin)-(XMax, YMax)
Picture1.ForeColor = RGB(0, 0, 255)
```

```
' Move to the first point
Picture1.PSet (XMin, FunctionEval1(XMin))
' Plot the function
For i = 0 To XPixels
    t = XMin + (XMax - XMin) * i / XPixels
    Picture1.Line -(t, FunctionEval1(t))
Next

End Sub
```

The Draw Second Function button's code is identical, only instead of calling the FunctionEval1() function, it calls the FunctionEval2() function, which calculates a different function:

```
Function FunctionEval2(ByVal X As Double) As Double
    FunctionEval2 = Cos(3 * X) * Sin(5 * X)
End Function
```

The actual graph of the function is shown in Figure 6.18. The problem with the code so far is that there are gaps between successive points of the function. To "close" these gaps, you can replace the *PSet* method (which turns on a single pixel) with the Line method to draw a line segment from the last point to the new one. In other words, drawing the line segments between successive points on the control will close the gaps you see in the plot of Figure 6.18.

FIGURE 6.18:

The function of Figure 6.16 drawn by turning on isolated points

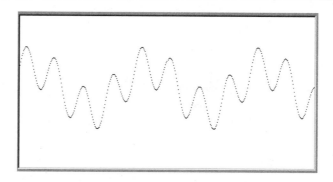

If you replace the line that turns on the pixels with the following one:

```
Picture1.Line -(t, FunctionEval1(t))
```

the plot of the same function will look like Figure 6.15. The solid line is much more suitable for plotting functions. Notice that the coordinates of the Line method are relative to the current point, which is the second endpoint of the previous line segment drawn. The previous Line method draws a line segment that joins two adjacent points on the plot. In the application's code, the lines that use the PSet method to turn on isolated pixels are commented out.

The Graph application is the core of a data plotting application. You can supply your own functions and add features such as axis numbering, major and minor ticks along the axes, legends, and so on. You can also add color, graph multiple functions at once, and in general, use the Graph application as a starting point for a custom data plotting application. The code behind the Draw Both Functions button, for instance, plots both functions, each in a different color. The user-defined coordinate system is based on the values of the first function only. The drawback of the Graph application is that the functions to be plotted must be hard-coded, which makes the application less flexible. In Chapter 21, you'll learn how to evaluate any math function supplied by the user at runtime, with the Script control (a new control introduced with Visual Basic 6).

VB6 at Work: The Spiral Project

The Spiral application demonstrates how to draw complicated, mathematically defined curves with Visual Basic's methods. It is a computer rendition of an old toy that literally made drawing curves a child's game. The actual toy consists of two plastic circles dented along their circumference. The large circle remains fixed on a piece of paper while the smaller one slides around the larger one with the help of a pen. The pen is inserted in a small hole somewhere off the center of the smaller circle. The dents around the circumference of the two circles help the user keep them in contact as the outer circle slides around the inner one. As the outer circle moves around the inner one, the pen leaves intricate patterns on the paper.

If you find this description complicated, open the Spiral application and draw a few curves. The curves shown in Figures 6.19 and 6.20 are the traces left by a point fixed on a small circle that rotates around a bigger circle. The operation of the program is really easy to understand if you spend a moment with it and watch the curves being drawn.

The curves drawn with this toy can be described mathematically. The following equations describe the curve where the diameters of the two circles are *R1* and *R2*, and the pen is fixed at a point that's *r* units from the smaller circle's center (see Figure 6.21):

```
X = (R1 + R2) * Cos(t) - (R2 + r) * Cos(((R1 + R2) / R2) * t)
Y = (R1 + R2) * Sin(t) - (R2 + r) * Sin(((R1 + R2) / R2) * t)
```

FIGURE 6.19:

The Spiral application draws interesting, mathematically defined curves.

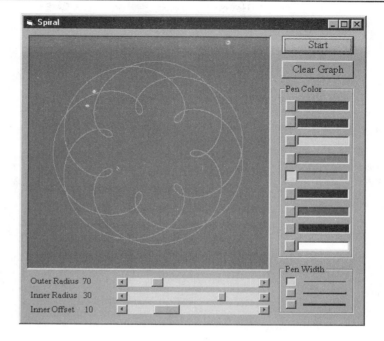

FIGURE 6.20:

Another pattern made up of two spiral curves

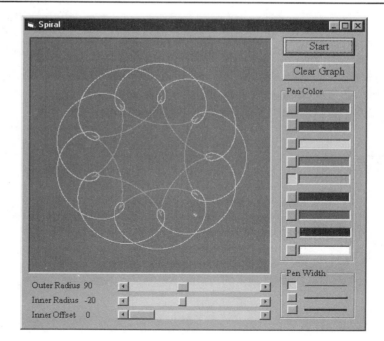

The *t* variable is the angle of rotation and it increases with time. Each complete rotation of the small circle around the large one takes 360 degrees (or 2*pi radians). One complete rotation of the outer circle, however, doesn't complete the curve. The smaller circle must rotate many times around the inner circle to produce the entire curve. The exact number of rotations depends on the ratio of the radii of the two circles.

FIGURE 6.21:

(Left) The spiral curve is generated by the trace of a point on the smaller circle, which slides around the larger one. (Right) The thick line in the figure is the trace left by the pen.

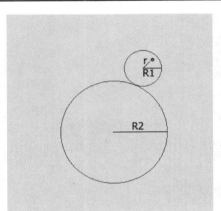
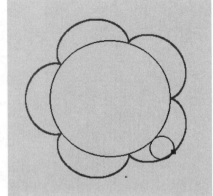

The Spiral application uses a quick-and-dirty algorithm to figure out how many rotations are required to complete a curve. If the ratio of the two radii is an integer, the algorithm works. If the ratio is not an integer, the algorithm may not recognize the end of the curve in time and will continue drawing over the existing curve. In this case, you can always click the Stop button to stop the drawing.

To plot the actual curve, you can turn on the pixel at (X, Y), or you can draw a line segment from the previous point to the new one. The complete code for drawing the spiral curves of Figures 6.19 and 6.20 is shown next.

Code 6.12:   **The DrawRoulette() Subroutine**

```
Sub DrawRoullette()
Dim R1, R2, r, pi

R1 = Form1.HScroll1.Value
R2 = Form1.HScroll2.Value - 80
If R2 = 0 Then R2 = 10
r = Form1.HScroll4.Value
pi = 4 * Atn(1)
```

```
Dim loop1, loop2
Dim t, X, Y As Double
Dim Rotations As Integer

If Int(R1 / R2) = R1 / R2 Then
    Rotations = 1
Else
    Rotations = Abs(R2 / 10)
    If Int(R2 / 10) <> R2 / 10 Then Rotations = 10 * Rotations
End If

For loop1 = 1 To Rotations
    If BreakNow Then
        Form1.Command1.Caption = "Start"
        BreakNow = False
        Exit Sub
    End If

    For loop2 = 0 To 2 * pi Step pi / (4 * 360)
        t = loop1 * 2 * pi + loop2
        X = (R1 + R2) * Cos(t) - (R2 + r) * Cos(((R1 + R2) / R2) * t)
        Y = (R1 + R2) * Sin(t) - (R2 + r) * Sin(((R1 + R2) / R2) * t)
        Form1.Picture1.PSet (Form1.Picture1.ScaleWidth / 2 + X,_
            Form1.Picture1.ScaleHeight / 2 + Y), PenColor
    Next
    DoEvents
Next
Form1.Command1.Caption = "Start"
BreakNow = False

End Sub
```

The program consists of two nested loops. The inner loop draws the trace of a complete rotation of the small circle around the large one. The outer loop determines how many times the small circle must rotate around the large one to produce a closed curve.

Experiment with the Spiral application. Try various combinations of the inner and outer radii by adjusting their values with the corresponding scroll bar. You will notice that the inner radius can assume negative values too. The negative values correspond to a small circle that slides inside the larger one. The last scroll bar controls the position of the pen in the small circle. It's the distance of the pen from the center of the smaller circle. For points on the circumference of the smaller circle, set the last scroll bar to 0.

Optimization Issues

If you experiment with Spiral application, you'll see that it has a major flaw: if you switch to another application and then return to the Spiral window, the curve is erased. This isn't really a problem with the application per se, rather, it's a thorny issue in drawing with Visual Basic. You can overcome it in several ways, but first you must understand how Visual Basic handles graphics.

One of the most important properties affecting Visual Basic graphics is *AutoRedraw*, which has two possible settings, True and False. When you draw on a control with its AutoRedraw property set to False, every shape appears instantly on the screen. This is how the Spiral application works. However, this setting has two problems. First, the drawing disappears when the window is covered by another one because any shapes placed on a control aren't stored permanently; that's why Windows can't refresh the control. Which leads us to the second problem: since Windows doesn't maintain a permanent copy of the control's contents, it can't save the contents with the SavePicture method.

Let's see if the other setting eliminates these problems. Open the Spiral application in design mode and set the PictureBox control's property to True. Previously, with AutoRedraw=False, you could watch the curve slowly being drawn, but now you must wait until Visual Basic completes the drawing to see the curve on the control. The program now is half as fun to watch, not to mention that if you didn't know better, you'd think that it didn't work. So, what's the problem with this setting of the AutoRedraw property?

When you draw with the AutoRedraw property set to True, Visual Basic draws in a special area of memory called a device context. A *device context* is a copy of the actual picture on the Picture Box or Form, and Visual Basic uses it to update the image of the actual object from time to time. The contents of the device context are transferred to the control under two circumstances:

- Whenever Visual Basic gets a chance

- When you instruct Visual Basic to do so with the Refresh method

The *Refresh* method refreshes the contents of the control to which it's applied, including any graphics. If you apply the Refresh method to the Form object, the entire window is refreshed. To refresh the contents of a PictureBox control, apply the Refresh method to the control like this:

```
Picture1.Refresh
```

As mentioned, Visual Basic also updates the controls when it gets a chance, and this happens whenever the application isn't busy executing code. When the

DrawRoulette() subroutine is executing, Visual Basic doesn't get a chance to do anything else. When the subroutine ends and Visual Basic is waiting for an external event, it gets a chance to redraw the controls. That's why you don't see anything on the screen until the entire curve has been calculated.

When to Refresh

As you can see, the setting of the AutoRedraw property can seriously affect your application. If you set it to False, users are able to watch the progress of the drawing, as they should. But you won't have a permanent copy of the drawing, which means you can't save it in a file. Also, if the user switches to another application, the control will be cleared, and you'll have to repeat the drawing. It looks as if we have a no-win situation here, but as always, there are ways to overcome the problem.

One solution is to draw with AutoRedraw set to True and to refresh the control frequently. How about refreshing the control after each point is plotted? You can try this by inserting the following statement right after the Line method in the DrawRoulette() subroutine:

```
Picture1.Refresh
```

This statement causes the program to refresh the PictureBox control so often that it behaves as if its AutoRedraw property is set to False. Run the program now and you'll see that this approach is out of the question. The program is too slow. This is the penalty of refreshing controls frequently.

How about refreshing the control after each rotation of the outer circle around the inner one? Simply remove the Refresh statement you just inserted in the code, insert it between the two loops, and run the program again. The DoEvents statement between the two loops has the same effect. It interrupts the program and gives Windows the chance to refresh the screen. (This statement was placed there to give the program a chance to process external events, such as the click of a Command button.) The curve is drawn in pieces, a rather unnatural progression. This approach is quite useful in other situations but it's not as helpful here. For instance, when you process an image, you can refresh the image one row at a time. This is what we'll do in the image processing application we'll develop in the following chapter, but the Spiral application requires a more complicated approach.

You could refresh the PictureBox control more frequently, or you might try another interesting approach: draw on two identical PictureBox controls. This is requires the following:

- A visible control that has its AutoRedraw property set to False, so that all points appear as they are plotted

- An invisible control that has its AutoRedraw property set to True, so the bitmap of the curve is always available to your code

If you want to save the curve as a bitmap to a disk file, you can use the Picture property of the invisible PictureBox.

The other problem you must cope with is updating the visible control when its contents are cleared because the user has switched to another window. This condition is signaled to your application by the Paint event. Therefore, every time the application receives a Paint event, the program must copy the contents of the invisible PictureBox control onto the visible one. This approach has all the benefits of the True setting of the AutoRedraw property and the curve is always visible, even while it's being drawn.

Spirals Revised

The Spirals1 application implements the technique just described. The Picture2 control is invisible and has its AutoRedraw property set to True. It also has the exact position and dimensions as the visible Picture1 control. The revised Draw-Roulette() routine, which draws on both controls, is shown next.

Code 6.13:   **The Revised DrawRoulette() Subroutine**

```
Form1.Picture1.PSet (Form1.Picture1.ScaleWidth / 2 + X, _
    Form1.Picture1.ScaleHeight / 2 + Y), PenColor
Form1.Picture2.PSet (Form1.Picture2.ScaleWidth / 2 + X, _
    Form1.Picture2.ScaleHeight / 2 + Y), PenColor
```

When the program receives the Paint event, the contents of the Picture2 control are copied onto the Picture1 control.

Code 6.14:   **The Paint Event**

```
Private Sub Form_Paint()
    Picture1.Refresh
    Picture1.PaintPicture Picture2.Image, 0, 0, Picture2.Width,_
        Picture2.Height, 0, 0, _
        Picture2.Width, Picture2.Height, _
        &HCC0020
End Sub
```

The Refresh method seems unnecessary, but the program won't work without it. Run the Spirals1 application, watch its behavior, and compare it with the Spirals application. You gain all the convenience of the immediate refreshing of the Picture control, and at the same time, the contents of the control are persistent.

Of course, the Spirals1 application requires a few more additional lines of code. For example, when the user changes the pen's width, you must change the Draw-Width property for both PictureBox controls. Likewise, when the Clear Graph button is clicked, the program must clear both PictureBox controls. Other than that, the code of the two applications is identical.

Transparent Drawing

The AutoRedraw property isn't only a source of problems. For instance, since everything you draw while the AutoRedraw Property is set to False appears on the control but doesn't update the internal copy, you can manipulate the AutoRedraw property at runtime to draw on layers that can be instantly removed from the control. Figure 6.22 shows the TRGrid application, which turns on and off a grid over the contents of a PictureBox control. The grid is drawn while the AutoRedraw property is False and can be easily removed with a single call to the Refresh method. The Refresh method copies the contents of the device context to the control. Because the grid is not saved in the device context, it disappears when the control is refreshed. Click the two buttons at the bottom of the Form to superimpose a linear or polar grid on top of the image.

FIGURE 6.22:

The grid on top of this PictureBox can be removed with a call to the control's Refresh method because it's drawn with Auto-Redraw set to False.

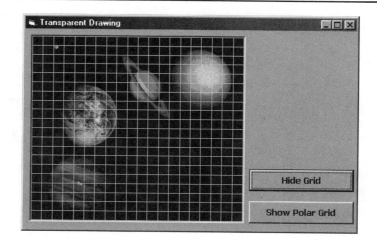

The following code draws the linear grid on top of the image already loaded onto the Picture1 control.

Code 6.15:   **The Show Linear Grid**

```
Sub DrawLinearGrid()
    GridLines = 20
    Picture1.AutoRedraw = False
    GridSpaceX = Int(Picture1.ScaleWidth / GridLines)
    GridSpaceY = Int(Picture1.ScaleHeight / GridLines)
    For i = 0 To GridLines + 1
        Picture1.Line (GridSpaceX * i, 0)-(GridSpaceX * i, _
            Picture1.Height - 1)
        Picture1.Line (0, GridSpaceY * i)-(Picture1.Width - 1, _
            GridSpaceY * i)
    Next
End Sub
```

To remove the grid, you must either reload the graphic to overwrite the contents of the Picture Box or refresh the contents of the control with the Refresh method. The RemoveGrid subroutine that removes the grid from the Picture Box couldn't be simpler:

```
Picture1.Refresh
```

The trick is in the second line of the ShowGrid() subroutine:

```
Picture1.AutoRedraw = False
```

Everything drawn after this command (in other words, everything drawn while the AutoRedraw property is False) is ignored when Visual Basic updates the contents of the control, because it's not part of the device context. This simple technique allows you to display all kinds of graphics on top of an image and then remove them with a Refresh command, as if they were drawn on a transparency over the actual image. You can even assign different colors to different users and let them annotate the same drawing (e.g., the image of a received fax or a technical drawing).

Better Rubber Shapes

In the Draw application, with the help of the XOR drawing mode, you learned how to draw rubber shapes and how to temporarily place elements on a background without disturbing it. The XOR drawing mode has the unique property of being reversible, but it also has a serious side effect: the rubber shapes assume strange colors. A better approach is to draw the rubber shape in copy mode (Draw-Mode=13), but switch to AutoRedraw=False mode. Then, instead of erasing the previous rubber shape as we did before, you can refresh the control. With each refresh, the rubber shape is erased, revealing the background, which is drawn with Auto-Redraw set to True.

The QDraw application works just like the Draw application presented earlier, but it uses the technique just described to draw rubber shapes (see Figure 6.23). The rubber shapes don't change color, so they are much more convincing. The QDraw application is identical to the Draw application, but instead of switching to the XOR mode to draw rubber shapes and erasing the previous rubber shape from within the MouseMove event, it turns off the AutoRedraw property and then uses the Refresh method to erase the previous shape. If you open the QDraw application and examine its code, you'll see that only a few lines are changed.

FIGURE 6.23:

The QDraw application can draw shapes over a bitmap without resorting to the XOR mode, which means that the underlying pixels don't affect the color of the shape.

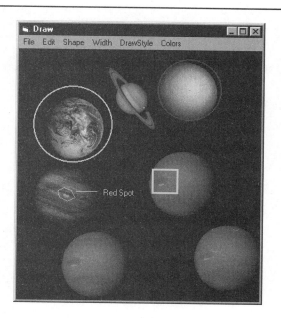

The Case switch that draws rubber shapes in the MouseMove event in the revised application is where most of the changes can be found.

Code 6.16:   **The Case Switch**

```
Select Case Shape
    Case "LINE":
        'Form1.Line (XStart, YStart)-(XPrevious, YPrevious)
```

```
        Form1.Refresh
        Form1.Line (XStart, YStart)-(X, Y)
    Case "CIRCLE":
        'Form1.Circle (XStart, YStart), _
            Sqr((XPrevious - XStart)^ 2 + (YPrevious - YStart) ^ 2)
        Form1.Refresh
        Form1.Circle (XStart, YStart), _
            Sqr((X - XStart) ^ 2 + (Y - YStart) ^ 2)
    Case "BOX":
        'Form1.Line (XStart, YStart)-(XPrevious, YPrevious), , B
        Form1.Refresh
        Form1.Line (XStart, YStart)-(X, Y), , B
End Select
```

Notice that the line that used to erase the previous line in XOR mode is commented out. Its function is now accomplished with a call to the Form's Refresh method.

This example concludes our discussion of Visual Basic's drawing commands. However, we're not done with the graphics methods. In the following chapter, we are going to discuss the methods for manipulating pixels and we'll demonstrate them with an image processing application.

Manipulating Color and Pixels with Visual Basic

- Specifying and using Color values

- The PaintPicture method

- The PSet and Point methods

- Processing images

- Using palettes

In the last chapter, we explored the methods and techniques for drawing shapes. There are only three shape-drawing methods, but when coupled with the various properties of the PictureBox control or the Form object, they're quite powerful and flexible. The examples you've seen illustrate how far you can go with Visual Basic's drawing methods.

This chapter explores Visual Basic's two methods for manipulating pixels: PSet and Point. *PSet* turns on pixels, and *Point* reads their values. Similar to their drawing counterparts, the methods for manipulating pixels are quite flexible, and you can do a lot with them, but they are slow.

In the latter part of this chapter, you'll see how image processing applications work, and you'll learn how to implement your own image processing techniques in Visual Basic. The Image application isn't nearly as fast or as elaborate as professional image processing applications, but you can use it to experiment. In Chapter 12, *Optimizing VBApplications*, we'll optimize the speed of the Image application using API functions. The optimized application is also called Image and can be found in Chapter 12's Image2 folder. Use Chapter 12's Image project if you like this chapter's Image application and want to process your images or incorporate it in your own applications. In this chapter we'll look at the basic image processing techniques and the core of an image processing application, without worrying too much about efficiency. Finally, we'll take a quick look at how to use palettes.

Let's begin by examining how computers manipulate color, and then look at Visual Basic's function for specifying Color values.

Specifying Colors

Many of you probably have already used the Color common dialog box, which lets you specify colors by manipulating their basic components. If you attempt to specify a Color value through the common dialog box, you'll see three boxes—Red, Green, and Blue (RGB)—whose values change as you move the cross-shaped pointer over the color spectrum. (The Color common dialog box will be discussed in detail in Chapter 8, *Advanced ActiveX Controls*.) These are the values of the three basic colors that computers use to specify colors. Any color that can be represented on a computer monitor is specified by means of the RGB colors. By mixing percentages of these basic colors, you can design almost any color.

The model of designing colors based on the intensities of their RGB components is called the *RGB model*, and it's a fundamental concept in computer graphics. If you aren't familiar with this model, this section might be well worth reading. Every color you can imagine can be constructed by mixing the appropriate percentages of the three basic colors. Each color, therefore, is represented by a triplet (Red, Green, Blue), in which red, green, and blue are three bytes that represent the basic color components. The smallest value, 0, indicates the absence of color. The largest value, 255, indicates full intensity, or saturation. The triplet (0, 0, 0) is black, because all colors are missing, and the triplet (255, 255, 255) is white. Other colors have various combinations: (255, 0, 0) is a pure red, (0, 255, 255) is a pure cyan (what you get when you mix green and blue), and (0, 128, 128) is a mid-cyan (a mix of mid-green and mid-blue tones). The possible combinations of the three basic color components are $256 \times 256 \times 256$, or 16,777,216 colors.

> **NOTE** Each color you can display on a computer monitor can be defined in terms of three basic components: red, green, and blue.

Notice that we use the term *basic colors* and not *primary colors*, which are the three colors used in designing colors with paint. The concept is the same; you mix the primary colors until you get the desired result. The primary colors used in painting, however, are different. They are the colors red, yellow, and blue. Painters can get any shade imaginable by mixing the appropriate percentages of red, yellow, and blue paint. On a computer monitor, you can design any color by mixing the appropriate percentages of red, green, and blue.

The process of generating colors with three basic components is based on the RGB Color Cube, shown in Figure 7.1. The three dimensions of the color cube correspond to the three basic colors. The cube's corners are assigned each of the three primary colors, their complements, and the colors black and white. Complementary colors are easily calculated by subtracting the Color values from 255. For example, the color (0, 0, 255) is a pure blue tone. Its complementary color is (255-0, 255-0, 255-255), or (255, 255, 0), which is a pure yellow tone. Blue and yellow are complementary colors, and they are mapped to opposite corners of the cube. The same is true for red and cyan, green and magenta, and black and white. If you add a color to its complement, you get white.

Notice that the components of the colors at the corners of the cube have either zero or full intensity. As you move from one corner to another along the same edge of the cube, only one of its components changes value. For example, as you move from the green to the yellow corner, the red component changes from 0 to 255. The other two components remain the same. As you move between these two corners, you get all the available tones from green to yellow (256 in all). Similarly, as you move from the yellow to the red corner, the only component that changes is the green, and you get all the available shades from yellow to red. This range of similar colors is called *gradient*.

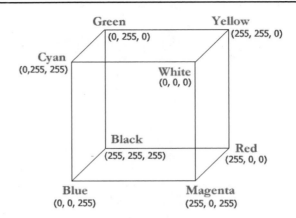

Although you can specify more than 16 million colors, you can't have more than 256 shades of gray. The reason is that a gray tone, including the two extremes (black and white), is made up of equal values of all three primary colors. You can see this on the RGB cube. Gray shades lie on the cube's diagonal that goes from black to white. As you move along this path, all three basic components change value, but they are always equal. The value (128, 128, 128) is a mid-gray tone, but the values (127, 128, 128) and (129, 128, 128) aren't gray tones, although they are too close for the human eye to distinguish. That's why it's wasteful to store grayscale pictures using 16-million-color True Color file formats (see the True Color and Palette Systems sidebar for more information). A 256-color file format stores a grayscale just as accurately and more compactly. Once you know an image is grayscale, you needn't store all three bytes per pixel. One value is adequate (the other two components have the same value).

Defining Colors with the RGB() Function

For defining colors, Visual Basic provides the *RGB() function*, which accepts three arguments:

```
RGB(Red, Green, Blue)
```

With the RGB() function, you can define any color imaginable. I mentioned earlier that the triplet (255, 255, 0) is a pure yellow tone. To specify this Color value with the RGB() function, you can use a statement such as the following:

```
newColor = RGB(255, 255, 0)
```

The *newColor* variable is a Long integer (a Long integer is made up of four bytes) and it can be assigned to any color property. To change the Form's background color to yellow, you can assign the *newColor* variable to the BackColor property, like this:

```
Form1.BackColor = newColor
```

or you can combine both statements into one like this:

```
Form1.BackColor = RGB(255, 255, 0)
```

Recall in Chapter 5, *Basic ActiveX Controls,* the Colors application used the RGB() function to design colors. You can open this application again to see how it translates the values of the three scroll bars to RGB values. It simply plugs the values of the scroll bars into the RGB() function and assigns the result to the PictureBox control's BackColor property.

True Color and Palette Systems

To display an image with the best possible color quality, the computer must store the three bytes for each pixel (one for each basic color). This image quality is called *True Color* and systems that can display these images are said to support True Color. For a computer to display True Color images at a resolution of 1024 × 768, a total of 1024 × 768 × 3, or approximately 2.1 MB of Video RAM (VRAM) is required. The most common notebook computers, for instance, can display True Color at a resolution no greater than 800 × 600, because they have 2MB of VRAM or less.

Many computers don't have as much VRAM, and they use 16 bits for storing each pixel's Color value. They assign six bits to the red color and five bits each to the green and blue colors. This is called *HiColor* and it's the most common color resolution for notebook computers that have a resolution of 800 × 600.

Finally, there are computers with even less VRAM that use only 256 colors to display color images. To display 256 color images, only one byte per pixel is needed. In other words, you can display 256 color images on a monitor with resolution of 1024 × 768 with less than 1 MB of VRAM. This color quality is called *Palette Color.* To display an image, the computer must select 256 colors that best describe the image. Each image is stored along with its palette, so that it can be displayed properly on every system.

For most computer images, 256 colors are plenty (the images you see on Web pages rarely contain more), but the smaller number doesn't mean they're easy to handle. When two images with different palettes must be displayed on a monitor, the computer must decide how to handle the conflicts between the two palettes. Visual Basic, for example, lets you determine how images with conflicting images will be displayed with the Palette and Palette-Mode properties of the Form object. These properties are discussed in the section "Image Quality" in Appendix C on the CD, *Using Multimedia Elements to Enhance Applications.*

continued on next page

Some of the applications for this chapter, such as the Image or the ClrGrads application that generates color gradients, will work properly on True Color or HiColor systems only. If your computer supports 256 colors only, you can decrease the resolution and increase the color depth to 16 bits or more. On palette systems, these applications won't show their "true colors." To learn more about what to do with palettes, see the section at the end of the chapter on "Using Palettes."

Specifying Gradients with the RGB() Function

Another interesting application of the RGB() function is to generate gradients. When you move from one corner to another on the same side of the RGB cube (as from red to black or from green to blue), one or more components change value. The colors along the path that connects any two points in the RGB cube form a gradient.

To specify a gradient, you must call the RGB() function many times, each time with a slightly different argument. Suppose you want to fill a rectangle with a gradient. Because there's no function to produce the gradient, you must draw vertical or horizontal lines with slightly different colors and cover the area of the rectangle. Figure 7.2 shows the ClrGrads application, which lets you specify the starting and ending colors of the gradient (with the two narrow PictureBox controls on either side of the Form), and then it generates linear and circular gradients. When you click the two narrow PictureBox controls at the two ends of the Form, the Color common dialog box is displayed, where you can select the gradient's starting and ending colors.

FIGURE 7.2:

The ClrGrads application generates a linear and a circular gradient between any two user-specified colors.

The starting color is the triplet (startRed, startGreen, startBlue), and the ending color is the triplet (endRed, endGreen, endBlue). If the rectangle's width in pixels is *PWidth*, you must write a loop that increases the red component by *redInc*, which is `(EndRed - StartRed)/PWidth`; the green component by *greenInc*, or `(EndGreen - StartGreen)/Pwidth`, and the blue component by *blueInc*, or `(EndBlue - StartBlue)/PWidth`. Following is the complete code for painting the rectangle with a gradient.

Code 7.1:   **The ClrGrads Application**

```
PWidth = Picture1.ScaleWidth
redInc = (EndRed - StartRed) / PWidth
greenInc = (EndGreen - StartGreen) / PWidth
blueInc = (EndBlue - StartBlue) / PWidth

For ipixel = 0 To PWidth - 1
   newColor = RGB(StartRed + redInc * ipixel, StartGreen + _
         greenInc * ipixel, StartBlue + blueInc * ipixel)
   Picture1.Line (ipixel, 0)-(ipixel, Picture1.Height - 1), _
         newColor
Next
```

This code draws as many vertical lines as there are pixels along the PictureBox. (The control Scale Mode should be 3–Pixel.) Each new line's color will be quite similar to the color of the previous line, with its three components adjusted by the amount *redInc*, *greenInc*, and *blueInc*. The values of the increments are chosen so that the first line has the gradient's starting color and the last line has the gradient's ending color. With variations on this technique, you can design vertical, diagonal, and even circular gradients. For a circular gradient, draw circles, starting with the outer one, and then decrease the radius at each step. You'll see this technique in the Gradients application, later in the chapter.

The code in the ClrGrad applications for generating gradients is straightforward, but it requires that you supply the color components of the starting and ending colors. Although this may be feasible in some applications, it's best to let the user select two colors and then have the program generate the gradient between them. The tricky part for you will be extracting the three basic color components from a Color value, a topic covered in the following section.

Color Components

The RGB() function combines the three color components to produce a Color value, which is a Long number, but Visual Basic lacks a function to return the three color components from a Color value. Suppose the user selects a Color value from the Color common dialog box, and your application needs to know its color components. In an image processing application, such as the one we'll develop later in this chapter, you want to read pixel values, isolate their RGB color components, and then process them separately. The Gradient application must calculate the three basic components of the starting and ending colors selected by the user with the help of the Color common dialog box. It's necessary, therefore, to write a function that extracts the RGB color components from any Color value.

To do so, you must first look at how the three color components are stored in a Long integer. A Long integer is made up of four bytes, three of which store the values of the RGB components and one that stores zero. The most significant byte is zero, followed by the blue, green, and red components, respectively.

The Long integer that corresponds to the triplet (64, 32, 192) is 12591168. This number bears no similarity to the original numbers. If you represent the color components with their hexadecimal values, the RGB triplet is (40, 20, C0). If you place these numbers next to one another, the result is the hexadecimal format of the Long number. If you get the hexadecimal representation of the number 12591168 (with the Hex() function), the value is C02040. The last two digits correspond to the red component, the next two digits correspond to the green component, and the two most significant hexadecimal digits correspond to the Blue value.

When you place the decimal values of the color components next to each another, the result bears no resemblance to the Long Integer value they represent. If you place the hexadecimal values of the color components next to each other, you get the hexadecimal representation of the Long integer that corresponds to the Color value. And this explains why hexadecimal numbers are used so frequently in specifying Color values. The following three statements extract the values of the three color components from a Color value stored in the *pixel&* variable:

```
pixel& = Form1.Picture1.Point(j, i)
red = pixel& Mod 256
green = ((pixel& And &HFF00FF00) / 256&)
blue = (pixel& And &HFF0000) / 65536
```

The *i* and the *j* variables are the coordinates of the point whose value we're examining. Since the Red value is stored in the least significant byte of the number, it's the remainder of dividing the number by 256.

To extract the next most significant byte, you must set the byte in front of it and after it to zero. This is done by combining the number with the hex number 00FF00 using the AND operator. If you type this number, though, Visual Basic truncates it to FF00 automatically, because the leading zeros make no difference. But when Visual Basic ANDs the two numbers, it takes into consideration the last two bytes (the length of the number FF00) and doesn't AND the *high order bytes* (the first two bytes). To force Visual Basic to AND all the digits, you must use the number FF00FF00. The high order byte of the Color value is zero anyway, so it doesn't make any difference what value it's ANDed with. The Green value is stored in the results' second least significant byte. To reduce it to a Byte value, divide it by 256. Finally, you do something similar with the third byte from the right. You AND the Color value with FF0000 to zero the other bytes and then divide the result by 65536 (which is 256 * 256).

If you aren't familiar with hexadecimal number operations, print the intermediate results to see why this technique works. Let's start with the Color value 12591168. If you AND it with FF00FF00, the result is 12591104. The hexadecimal format of this number is 002000. The byte 20 is there already, but it must be shifted down to the least significant byte position, which is what happens when it's divided by 256. The result is the value of the green color component. To extract the Blue value, the Color value is ANDed with FF0000. The result of the operation 12591168 AND FF0000 is 12582912 in decimal format, and C00000 in hexadecimal. The Blue component's value is there, but this time it must be shifted to the right by two bytes, which is accomplished by dividing it with 65536. The process is depicted graphically in Figure 7.3.

FIGURE 7.3:

The process of extracting the values of the basic colors from a Long Color value

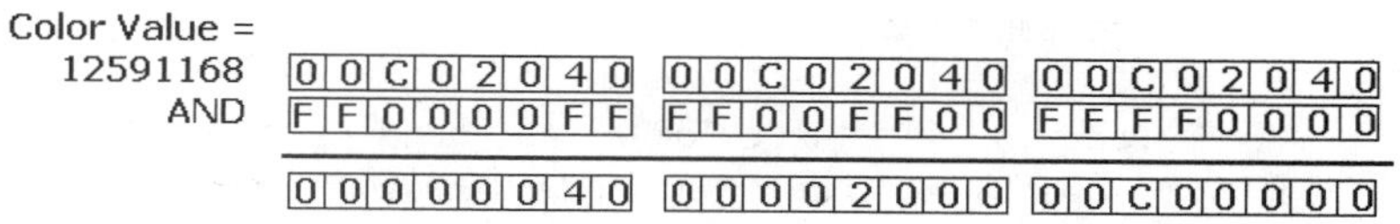

In Figure 7.3, the number at the top is the hexadecimal representation of a Long Color value and the number below is the mask, which must be ANDed with the Color value to extract the RGB components of the color. The left-most value is the Red component (always in hexadecimal notation). The next value must be shifted to the right by two digits to yield the Green component, and the last value must be shifted to the right by four digits to yield the Blue component. To shift a hexadecimal value to the right by a digit, you must divide it by 16 (to shift it by two digits divide by 16*16, or 256, and so on).

There's also another technique to extract the color components from a Color value, which is conceptually simpler, but a bit slower. If you use the hexadecimal representation of the original Color value, the values of all three color components already exist. All you have to do is extract them with string manipulation functions. The hexadecimal format of the number 12591168 is the string "C02040".

The Red color component is the value of the hexadecimal number formatted with the two right-most digits of the number. The Green component is the value of the hexadecimal number formatted with the next two digits, and the Red component is the value of the hexadecimal number formatted with the two left-most digits of the number. Here's the equivalent code:

```
n$ = Hex(Form1.Picture1.Point(j, i))
red = Val("&H" & Right(n$, 2))
green = Val("&H" & Mid$(n$, 3, 2))
blue = Val("&H" & Mid$(n$, 5, 2))
```

Now you can write three functions, GetRed(), GetGreen(), and GetBlue(), which accept as an argument a Color value and return the value's RGB components. The code for the three functions that extract a color's basic components follows.

Code 7.2:   **Extracting the Color Components from a Color Value**

```
Function GetRed(colorVal As Long) As Integer
    GetRed = colorVal Mod 256
End Function

Function GetGreen(colorVal As Long) As Integer
    GetGreen = ((colorVal And &HFF00FF00) / 256&)
End Function

Function GetBlue(colorVal As Long) As Integer
    GetBlue = (colorVal And &HFF0000) / (256& * 256&)
End Function
```

(You should replace the term 256& * 256& with 65536 to speed up the calculations a little. I've used the product to make the code easier to read and understand.) With the help of these functions, you can extract the color components of the gradient's starting and ending colors, calculate the increment, and use it to generate and display the desired gradient.

Following is the complete code behind the Linear Gradient button.

Code 7.3:   **Linear Gradient Button**

```
Private Sub Command1_Click()
Dim newColor As Long
Dim ipixel, PWidth As Integer
Dim redInc, greenInc, blueInc As Single
Dim color1 As Long, color2 As Long
```

```
color1 = StartColor.BackColor
color2 = EndColor.BackColor

StartRed = GetRed(color1)
EndRed = GetRed(color2)
StartGreen = GetGreen(color1)
EndGreen = GetGreen(color2)
Blue = GetBlue(color1)
EndBlue = GetBlue(color2)

PWidth = Picture1.ScaleWidth

redInc = (EndRed - StartRed) / PWidth
greenInc = (EndGreen - StartGreen) / PWidth
blueInc = (EndBlue - StartBlue) / PWidth

For ipixel = 0 To PWidth - 1
    newColor = RGB(StartRed + redInc * ipixel, StartGreen _
        + greenInc * ipixel, StartBlue + blueInc * ipixel)
    Picture1.Line (ipixel, 0)-(ipixel, Picture1.Height - 1),_
        newColor
Next
End Sub
```

The code behind the Circular Gradient button is quite similar, but instead of drawing lines, it draws circles of varying colors. First, it draws the largest circle, then it draws all the successive circles, each having a radius smaller than that of the previous circle by one pixel. You can try other types of gradients on your own, such as diagonal gradients or off-center circular gradients. You can also use this technique to fill your Forms or certain controls with gradients when a Form is loaded. Grayscale gradients make quite interesting backgrounds. They have a subtle effect and add a nice three-dimensional look to your application's user interface.

The FrmGrad application (which you'll find in the chapter's folder on the CD), shown in Figure 7.4, uses the code of the ClrGrads application to design a gradient as a background. (The buttons on the Form don't do anything; the figure simply shows how to use the gradient as a backdrop on a Form.) The gradient is generated as the program loads. The code is nearly identical to that presented earlier in the ClrGrads application and is executed from within the Form's Resize event so that the gradient is adjusted each time the user changes the Form's size. The FrmGrad Form won't look as nice on systems with 256 colors because the current palette doesn't contain all the colors required by the gradient.

FIGURE 7.4:

This Form's background gradient is generated on the fly in the Resize event handler.

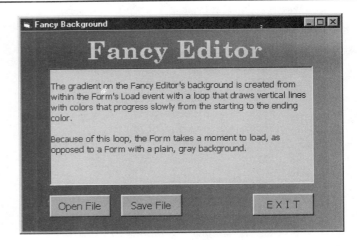

Using the PaintPicture Method

So far, we've explored the Visual Basic methods for manipulating individual pixels. Manipulating an entire image pixel by pixel is a slow process. In some situations, you may need a quick way to copy an image or part of an image from one container to another. Windows provides a powerful mechanism for moving pixels around, known as BitBlt (pronounced "BIT BLIT"). *BitBlt* stands for Bit Block Transfers and is nothing but highly optimized code for moving bits around in memory. Visual Basic programmers can access the services of the BitBlt routines, which are built into the operating system, via the *PaintPicture* method. The Paint-Picture method allows you to copy a rectangular area of pixels from one object (a PictureBox or Form) onto another. Moreover, the source pixels need not replace the pixels at the destination control. They can be combined with them in various ways to yield interesting effects.

The syntax of the PaintPicture method is as follows:

```
Picture1.PaintPicture picture, DestX, DestY, DestWidth, DestHeight, _
     SourceX, SourceY, SourceWidth, SourceHeight, RasterOp
```

This method accepts a number of arguments, but their use is straightforward:

- The *picture* argument is the source of the transfer. It's the Picture property of a PictureBox, an ImageBox, or a Form, whose contents will be transferred to the Picture1 control.

- *DestX* and *DestY* are the coordinates of the transfer's destination. The rectangle can be transferred anywhere on the destination control.

- *DestWidth* and *DestHeight* are the dimensions of the destination area, in pixels.

- *SourceX* and *SourceY* are the coordinates of the upper-left corner of the rectangular area to be transferred.

- *SourceWidth* and *SourceHeight* are the dimensions of the rectangle to be copied, in pixels.

- *RasterOp* specifies how the pixels being transferred will be combined with the existing pixels at the destination.

NOTE If the *SourceWidth* and *SourceHeight* arguments don't match the *DestWidth* and *DestHeight* arguments, the area being copied will be stretched accordingly to fill its destination.

The most common operation is to replace existing pixels with the pixels being transferred. But the PaintPicture method lets you combine the source with the destination pixels using the logical operators AND, OR, XOR, and NOT. For example, you can OR the source pixels with the inverse (NOT) of the destination pixels. Or you can replace the destination pixels with the inverse of the source pixels. In all, there are 256 ways to combine source and destination pixels, but you'll never need most of them. Table 7.1 shows a few of the *RasterOp* argument's values, which you may find useful in your applications. The names of the constants shown in Table 7.1 are different from the ones listed in Table 6.4, but they have the same effect.

TABLE 7.1: The Most Common Values for the `RasterOp` Argument

CONSTANT	VALUE	DESCRIPTION
vbDstInvert	&H00550009	Inverts the destination bitmap
vbMergePaint	&H00BB0226	Combines the inverse of the source bitmap with the destination bitmap using the OR operator
vbNotSrcCopy	&H00330008	Copies the inverse of the source bitmap to the destination
vbNotSrcErase	&H001100A6	Combines the source and destination bitmaps using the OR operator and then inverts the result
vbSrcAnd	&H008800C6	Combines the source and destination bitmaps using the AND operator

Continued on next page

TABLE 7.1 CONTINUED: The Most Common Values for the RasterOp Argument

CONSTANT	VALUE	DESCRIPTION
vbSrcCopy	&H00CC0020	Copies the source bitmap to the destination bitmap
vbSrcErase	&H00440328	Combines the inverse of the destination bitmap with the source bitmap using the AND operator
vbSrcInvert	&H00660046	Combines the source and destination bitmaps using the XOR operator
vbSrcPaint	&H00EE0086	Combines the source and destination bitmaps using the OR operator

The values of the constants are given in hexadecimal because this is how they appear in Microsoft's documentation. In your code, you should use the constants listed in the first column of the table. The constant *vbSrcCopy* overwrites the existing pixels at the destination and is the one you'll be using most often.

To copy the contents of the Picture1 PictureBox to the Picture2 control, use the following statement:

```
Picture2.PaintPicture _
Picture1.Picture _                              ' source image
0, 0, _                                         ' destination origin
Picture2.ScaleWidth, Picture2.ScaleWidth, _     ' destination dimen-
sions
0, 0, _                                         ' source origin
Picture1.ScaleWidth, Picture1.ScaleWidth, _     ' source dimensions
VbSrcCopy                                       ' copy mode
```

This rather lengthy statement copies the pixels of the Picture1 control onto the Picture2 control. If the two controls don't have the same dimensions, the image will be distorted to cover the entire destination control. If you don't want the image to be distorted during the transfer, replace the arguments *Picture2.ScaleWidth* and *Picture2.ScaleHeight* with *Picture1.ScaleWidth* and *Picture1.ScaleHeight*. If the destination PictureBox is smaller than the source PictureBox, only part of the image will be displayed. If it's larger, the image won't fill it entirely. But in either case, the image won't be distorted during the process because the width and height arguments are the same on both the source and the destination.

To better understand how to use the various settings of the *RasterOp* argument and what effect they have on the destination bitmap, experiment with the various settings and images. In this chapter's folder on the CD you'll find the PaintPic project, which lets you combine two bitmaps with the various raster operators, as well as with the remaining arguments of the PaintPicture method.

VB6 at Work: The PaintPic Project

The PaintPic application, shown in Figure 7.5, lets you combine the pixels of the source (left) and destination (right) PictureBox controls with the various values of the *RasterOp* argument of the PaintPicture method. The eight sliders let you set the origin of the rectangle to be copied and its dimensions, the destination coordinates of the transfer, and the transfer's dimensions on the destination PictureBox control.

You can copy the entire source image, or part of it, and place it anywhere on the destination control. You can also specify different dimensions on the two controls to see how the PaintPicture method distorts the image's dimensions during the transfer. Also, try the various settings for the raster operator with different images.

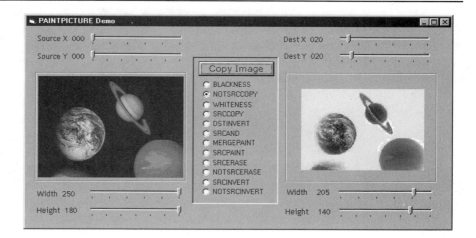

Notice that since most raster operations combine the source with the destination pixels, the result of the transfer depends on the destination control's current contents. The *vbSrcInvert* operation, for instance, merges the pixels of the source image with the destination pixels using the XOR operator. If you copy the source image again with the same setting, you'll get the original contents of the destination image. That's because the XOR operator works like a toggle that merges the two images and then restores the original. The first time, it's actually encrypting the original image; the second time, it reveals it.

You can also experiment with successive transfers of the same image with different settings for the raster operation. Some settings will yield interesting effects, especially if you change each successive image's destination by one or two pixels. Finally, you can set the destination PictureBox control's background color to black or white by checking the Blackness or Whiteness checkbox. You can also reset the destination PictureBox control's background color by right-clicking it.

Flipping an Image with PaintPicture

Another interesting application of the PaintPicture method is to flip an image as it copies it. If the image's width is negative, the image flips horizontally; if the image's height is negative, the image flips vertically. If both width and height are negative, the image flips in both directions. The negative sign in the width of the destination, for example, tells the PaintPicture method to copy the pixels to the left of the origin (the same is true for the height of the destination). Thus, the pixels are copied to the left of the destination control's left edge. The entire image is copied outside the destination control. To compensate, set the origin to the other corner of the destination. Figure 7.6 shows the PicFlip application, which uses the PaintPicture method to flip an image as it copies it.

FIGURE 7.6:

The PicFlip application flips an image using the Paint-Picture method.

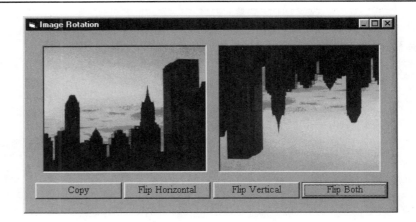

The Copy button transfers the source image to the destination. Let's look at the code of the Copy button in the PicFlip application next.

Code 7.4:	The Copy Button

```
Private Sub Command3_Click()
     Picture2.PaintPicture Picture1.Picture, 0, 0, _
     Picture1.ScaleWidth, Picture1.ScaleHeight, 0, 0, _
     Picture1.ScaleWidth, Picture1.ScaleHeight, &HCC0020
End Sub
```

Compare the Copy button code with the code of the Flip Horizontal button shown next.

Code 7.5:   **The Flip Horizontal Button**

```
Private Sub Command1_Click()
    Picture2.PaintPicture Picture1.Picture, 0, 0, _
        Picture1.ScaleWidth, Picture1.ScaleHeight, _
        Picture1.ScaleWidth, 0, _
        -Picture1.ScaleWidth, Picture1.ScaleHeight, &HCC0020
End Sub
```

Notice that in order to flip the image horizontally, the destination's X origin is not 0, but the actual image width. The destination's width is the negative of the actual width. The code behind the Flip Vertical button is similar, but instead of the X coordinate and the width of the image, it inverts the Y coordinate and the height of the image. The Flip Both button inverts both the X and Y coordinates and the width and height of the destination.

NOTE   For a more interesting example of the PaintPicture method, see the Wipes application in Appendix C on the CD, *Using Multimedia Elements to Enhance Applications*. The Wipes application displays images on top of one another with various transition effects.

Processing Images

Images are arrays of pixels, much like a PictureBox control. The values of the image's pixels are stored in disk files and when an image is displayed on a PictureBox or Form control, each one of its pixels is mapped to a pixel on the PictureBox or Form. As you'll see, image processing is nothing more than simple arithmetic operations on the values of the image's pixels. The Image application we'll build to demonstrate the various image processing techniques is slow compared with professional applications, but it demonstrates the principles of image processing techniques that can be used as a starting point for custom applications.

We'll build a simple image processing application that can read BMP, GIF, and JPEG image files, process them, and then display the processed images. There are simpler ways to demonstrate Visual Basic pixel-handling methods, but image processing is an intriguing topic, and I hope many readers will experiment with its techniques in the Image application. In Chapter 12, we'll optimize the Image application and make it considerably faster.

An image is a two-dimensional array of pixels in which each pixel is represented by one or more bits. In a black-and-white image, each pixel is represented by a single bit. In the most common types of images, or those with 256 colors, each pixel is represented by a byte. The best quality images, however, use three bytes per pixel, one for each RGB color component. For a discussion of the various methods of storing and displaying colors, see the sidebar "True Color and Palette Systems," earlier in this chapter.

Images composed of 256 colors are based on a palette; that's why they're sometimes called palette images. The program that creates the image selects the 256 colors that best describe the image and stores them in a palette, along with the image. Each byte in the image is a pointer to the pixel's color in the palette. If the original image happens to contain more than 256 colors, some of them must be approximated with the existing colors. The best approach for processing this image would be to create a new palette that best describes the new image, but this topic is beyond the scope of this book. Palette manipulation is a complicated topic and requires extensive use of API functions.

A total of 256 colors is sufficient for describing a typical image. Even if some of the colors must be approximated, the quality of the image is relatively good. Most pages on the World Wide Web contain no more than 256 colors and they look fine. The problem with palettes isn't with the image, but with the computers that display them. If your computer can display True Color, it can display any number of images, even when opened at the same time. But systems that can display only 256 colors at a time will have a problem. The palette system won't be able to correctly display the new colors introduced by the processing algorithm (see the sidebar "True Color and Palette Systems," earlier in this chapter).

For example, if the original image contains 256 colors, the processing algorithm will most likely introduce additional colors that aren't present in the palette. Because the computer can't display more than 256 colors, some of them must be approximated. The Image application works best on True Color systems. It will also work on systems capable of displaying palette images, but some of the colors may not look quite right.

Because images are two-dimensional arrays of integers, their processing is nothing more than simple arithmetic operations on these integers. Let's look at a simple technique, the inversion of an image's colors. To invert an image, you must change all pixels to their complementary colors—black to white, green to magenta, and so on (the complementary colors are on opposite corners of the RGB cube, shown in Figure 7.1, earlier in this chapter).

To calculate complementary colors, you subtract each of the three color components from 255. For example, a pure green pixel whose value is (0, 255, 0) will be converted to (255-0, 255-255, 255-0) or (255, 0, 255), which is magenta. Similarly, a mid-yellow tone (0, 128, 128) will be converted to (255-0, 255-128, 255-128) or (255, 127, 127), which is a mid-brown tone. To invert an image's colors, you set up two loops that scan the image's pixels and invert the colors of the pixels. The result is the negative of the original image (what you'd see if you looked at the negative from which the picture was obtained).

Other image processing techniques aren't as simple, but the important thing to understand is that, in general, image processing is as straightforward as a few arithmetic operations on the image's pixels. After we go through the Image application, you'll probably come up with your own techniques and be able to implement them.

VB6 at Work: The Image Project

The application we'll develop in this section is called Image and it's shown in Figure 7.7. It's not a professional tool, but it can be easily implemented in Visual Basic, and it will give you the opportunity to explore various image processing techniques on your own. To process an image with the Image application, choose File ➤ Open to load it to the PictureBox control and then select the type of processing from the Process menu. Using the Image application, you can apply the following effects to an image:

- **Smooth**   Reduces the amount of detail

- **Sharpen**   Brings out the detail

- **Emboss**   Adds a raised (embossed) look

- **Diffuse**   Gives a painterly look

- **Solarize**   Creates a special effect based on selective pixel inversion

- **Custom Filter** Allows the user to specify the effect to be applied to the image

FIGURE 7.7:

The Image application demonstrates several image processing techniques that can be implemented with Visual Basic.

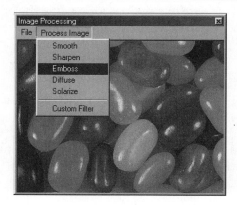

Next, let's look at how each algorithm works and how it's implemented in Visual Basic.

How the Image Application Works

Let's start with a general discussion of the application's operation before we get down to the actual code. Once the image is loaded on a PictureBox control, you can access the values of its pixels with the Point method, which returns a Long integer representing each pixel's color. The basic color components must be extracted from this Long Integer value and used to implement the algorithms. This is a time-consuming step, and for most algorithms, it must be performed more than once for each pixel. To speed up the processing, you can choose to read the values of all the pixels when the image is loaded and store them in an array. In effect, it introduces a delay while the image is loaded, to speed up the rest of the application.

The array that stores the values of the pixels is called *ImagePixels* and is declared as follows:

```
Global ImagePixels(2, 800, 800) As Integer
```

The largest image you can process with the Image application can't exceed these dimensions. Of course, you can either change the dimensions of the array or abandon the array altogether and read the pixel values from the PictureBox, as needed. The application will run slower overall, but it will be able to handle any size image you throw at it.

> **NOTE**
>
> Since the valid range for Color values is the same as the value range of the Byte data type, why don't we declare the *ImagePixels* array as an array of bytes? Because Visual Basic handles integers more efficiently than bytes, so we give up some memory for speed. You can modify the declaration of the *ImagePixels* array to save memory.

There are two options for reading the image's pixels into the *ImagePixels* array:

- Use the Point method
- Read the pixels directly from the file

The Point method, which is simpler and used in the Image application, reads the pixel values directly off the PictureBox. Most image processing applications use the other option, reading the pixels directly from the file. This technique is faster, but you have to supply different routines for each image type. Visual Basic currently supports three image types: BMP, GIF, and JPEG. Instead of learning the file structure for all three types of images and implementing a different routine for each one, we'll let Visual Basic read the image into a PictureBox control and then read the control's pixels with the Point method.

Reading Pixel Values

Next, let's look at the code behind the Open command of the File menu. The program calls the File Open common dialog box, which lets the user select an image and then loads the image on the PictureBox. The PictureBox's ScaleMode property is set to 3 (pixels), and its AutoSize property is set to True, so we can find out the image's dimensions from the PictureBox's dimensions. If either of the image's dimensions exceeds 800, the process ends with the appropriate message and the image isn't loaded. If the image's dimensions are smaller, the program proceeds by reading the pixel values into the *ImagePixels* array. The value returned by the Point method is a Long Integer, which contains all three color components, but can't be used in any operation as is. You must first extract the three color components with the GetRed(), GetGreen(), and GetBlue() functions, which were presented in the section "Color Components," earlier in this chapter.

Once extracted, the color components are stored in the appropriate elements of the *ImagePixels* array. The first index in the array corresponds to a color component (0 for red, 1 for green, 2 for blue), the second index corresponds to the pixel's column, and the third index corresponds to the pixel's row. While the image's pixels are read, the program updates a ProgressBar control that acts as a progress indicator. The ProgressBar control is updated after reading an entire row of pixels from the PictureBox control.

Code 7.6:   **The Open Command**

```
Private Sub FileOpen_Click()
Dim i As Integer, j As Integer
Dim red As Integer, green As Integer, blue As Integer
Dim pixel As Long
Dim PictureName As String

CommonDialog1.InitDir = App.Path
CommonDialog1.Filter = "Images|*.BMP;*.GIF;*.JPG;*.DIB|All Files|*.*"
CommonDialog1.Action = 1
PictureName = CommonDialog1.FileName
If PictureName = "" Then Exit Sub
Picture1.Picture = LoadPicture(PictureName)
Form1.Refresh
```

```
X = Picture1.ScaleWidth
Y = Picture1.ScaleHeight
If X > 500 Or Y > 500 Then
   MsgBox "Image too large to process. _
           Please try loading a smaller image."
   X = 0
   Y = 0
   Exit Sub
End If

Form1.Width = Form1.ScaleX(Picture1.Width + 6, vbPixels, vbTwips)
Form1.Height = Form1.ScaleY(Picture1.Height + 30, vbPixels, vbTwips)
Form1.Refresh

Form3.Show
Form3.Refresh

   For i = 0 To Y - 1
      For j = 0 To X - 1
         pixel = Form1.Picture1.Point(j, i)
         red = pixel& Mod 256
         green = ((pixel And &HFF00) / 256&) Mod 256&
         blue = (pixel And &HFF0000) / 65536
         ImagePixels(0, i, j) = red
         ImagePixels(1, i, j) = green
         ImagePixels(2, i, j) = blue
      Next
      Form3.ProgressBar1.Value = i * 100 / (Y - 1)
   Next
   Form3.Hide
End Sub
```

Smoothing Images

Now we're ready to look at the image processing techniques. One of the simplest and most common operations in all image processing programs is the smoothing (or blurring) operation. The smoothing operation is equivalent to low-pass filtering: just as you can cut off a stereo's high frequency sounds with the help of an equalizer, you can cut off the high frequencies of an image. If you're wondering what the high frequencies of an image are, think of them as the areas with abrupt changes in the image's intensity. These are the areas that are mainly affected by the blurring filter.

The smoothed image contains less abrupt changes than the original image and looks a lot like the original image seen through a semitransparent glass. Figure 7.8 shows an image and its smoothed version, obtained with the Image application.

Original Image   Smoothed Image

To smooth an image, you must reduce the large differences between adjacent pixels. Let's take a block of nine pixels, centered around the pixel we want to blur. This block contains the pixel to be blurred and its eight immediate neighbors. Let's assume that all the pixels in this block are green, except for the middle one, which is red. This pixel is drastically different from its neighbors, and for it to be blurred, it must be pulled toward the average value of the other pixels. Taking the average of a block of pixels is, therefore, a good choice for a blurring operation. If the current pixel's value is similar to the values of its neighbors, the average won't affect it significantly. If its value is different, the remaining pixels will pull the current pixel's value toward them. In other words, if the middle pixel was green, the average wouldn't affect it. Being the only red pixel in the block though, it's going to come closer to the average value of the remaining pixels. It's going to assume a green tone.

Here's an example with numbers: if the value of the current pixel is 10 and the values of its eight immediate neighbors are 8, 11, 9, 10, 12, 10, 11, and 9, the average value of all pixels will be (8+11+9+10+12+10+11+9+10)/9=10. The pixel under consideration happens to be right on the average of its neighboring pixels. The results would be quite different if the value of the center pixel was drastically different. If the center pixel's value was 20, the new average would be 11. Because the neighboring pixels have values close to 10, they would pull the "outlier" toward them. This is how blurring works. By taking the average of a number of pixels, you force the pixels with values drastically different from their neighbors to get closer to them.

Another factor affecting the amount of blurring is the size of the block over which the average is calculated. We used a 3×3 block in our example, which yields an average blur. To blur the image even more, use a 5×5 block. Even larger blocks will blur the image to the point that useful information will be lost. The actual code of the Smooth operation scans all the pixels of the image (excluding the edge pixels that don't have neighbors all around them) and takes the average of their RGB components. It then combines the three values with the RGB() function to produce the new value of the pixel.

Code 7.7:   **The Smooth Operation**

```
Private Sub ProcessSmooth_Click()
Dim i As Integer, j As Integer
Dim red As Integer, green As Integer, blue As Integer

    For i = 1 To Y - 2
        For j = 1 To X - 2
            red = ImagePixels(0, i - 1, j - 1) __
            + ImagePixels(0, i - 1, j) + ImagePixels(0, i - 1, j + 1)_
            + ImagePixels(0, i, j - 1) + ImagePixels(0, i, j) _
            + ImagePixels(0, i, j + 1) + ImagePixels(0, i + 1, j - 1)_
            + ImagePixels(0, i + 1, j) + ImagePixels(0, i + 1, j + 1)
            green = ImagePixels(1, i - 1, j - 1) _
            + ImagePixels(1, i - 1, j) + ImagePixels(1, i - 1, j + 1)_
            + ImagePixels(1, i, j - 1) + ImagePixels(1, i, j) _
            + ImagePixels(1, i, j + 1) + ImagePixels(1, i + 1, j - 1)_
            + ImagePixels(1, i + 1, j) + ImagePixels(1, i + 1, j + 1)
            blue = ImagePixels(2, i - 1, j - 1) _
            + ImagePixels(2, i - 1, j) + ImagePixels(2, i - 1, j + 1)_
            + ImagePixels(2, i, j - 1) + ImagePixels(2, i, j) _
            + ImagePixels(2, i, j + 1) + ImagePixels(2, i + 1, j - 1)_
            + ImagePixels(2, i + 1, j) + ImagePixels(2, i + 1, j + 1)
            Picture1.PSet (j, i), RGB(red / 9, green / 9, blue / 9)
        Next
        Picture1.Refresh
    Next
End Sub
```

In the code, I used a 3×3 block, but you can change a few numbers in the code to blur the image with an even larger block. The pixels involved in the calculations are the neighboring pixels on the same, previous, and next rows, and the pixel being processed is always at the center of the block.

You may have noticed that the code is quite verbose. I could have avoided the very long line that adds the color components with a couple of For...Next loops, but I chose this verbose coding over the more compact version to speed up the computations. Setting up loop counters introduces some small additional delays, which we can do without. The program is slow as is, and every trick counts. Visual Basic is not the most efficient language for this type of operation, but it surely is the most convenient.

Sharpening Images

Since the basic operation for smoothing an image is addition, the opposite operation will result in sharpening the image. The sharpening effect is more subtle than smoothing, but more common and more useful. Nearly every image published, especially in monochrome publications, must be sharpened to some extent. For an example of a sharpened image, see Figure 7.9. Sharpening an image consists of highlighting the edges of the objects in it, which are the very same pixels blurred by the previous algorithm. Edges are areas of an image with sharp changes in intensity between adjacent pixels. The smoothing algorithm smoothed out these areas; now we want to pronounce them.

In a smooth area of an image, the difference between two adjacent pixels will be zero or a very small number. If the pixels are on an edge, the difference between two adjacent pixels will be a large value (perhaps negative). This is an area of the image with some degree of detail that can be sharpened. If the difference is zero, the two pixels are nearly identical, which means that there's nothing to sharpen there. This is called a "flat" area of the image. (Think of an image with a constant background. There's no detail to bring out on the background.)

FIGURE 7.9:

The sharpening operation brings out detail that isn't evident in the original image.

Original Image   Sharpened Image

The difference between adjacent pixels isolates the areas with detail and completely flattens out the smooth areas. The question now is how to bring out the detail without leveling the rest of the image. How about adding the difference to the original pixel? Where the image is flat, the difference is negligible, and the processed pixel practically will be the same as the original one. If the difference is significant, the processed pixel will be the original plus a value that's proportional to the magnitude of the detail. The sharpening algorithm can be expressed as follows:

```
new_value = original_value + 0.5 * difference
```

If you simply add the difference to the original pixel, the algorithm brings out too much detail. You usually add a fraction of the difference; a 50 % factor is common.

Code 7.8:   The Sharpening Algorithm

```
Private Sub ProcessSharpen_Click()
Dim i As Integer, j As Integer
Const Dx As Integer = 1
Const Dy As Integer = 1
Dim red As Integer, green As Integer, blue As Integer

    For i = 1 To Y - 2
        For j = 1 To X - 2
            red = ImagePixels(0, i, j) + 0.5 * (ImagePixels(0, i, j)_
                - ImagePixels(0, i - Dx, j - Dy))
            green = ImagePixels(1, i, j) + 0.5 * (ImagePixels(1, i, j)_
                - ImagePixels(1, i - Dx, j - Dy))
            blue = ImagePixels(2, i, j) + 0.5 * (ImagePixels(2, i, j)_
                - ImagePixels(2, i - Dx, j - Dy))
            If red > 255 Then red = 255
            If red < 0 Then red = 0
            If green > 255 Then green = 255
            If green < 0 Then green = 0
            If blue > 255 Then blue = 255
            If blue < 0 Then blue = 0
            Picture1.PSet (j, i), RGB(red, green, blue)
        Next
        Picture1.Refresh
    Next

End Sub
```

The variables Dx and Dy express the distances between the two pixels being subtracted. You can subtract adjacent pixels on the same row, adjacent pixels in the same column, or diagonally adjacent pixels, which is what I did in this subroutine. Besides adding the difference to the original pixel value, this subroutine must check the result for validity. The result of the calculations may exceed the valid value range for a Color value, which is 0 to 255. That's why you must clip the value if it falls outside the valid range.

Embossing Images

To sharpen an image, we add the difference between adjacent pixels to the pixel value. What do you think would happen to a processed image if you took the difference between adjacent pixels only? The flat areas of the image would be totally leveled, and only the edges would remain visible. The result would be an image like the image on the right in Figure 7.10. This effect clearly sharpens the edges and flattens the smooth areas of the image. By doing so, it gives the image depth. The processed image looks as if it's raised and illuminated from the right side. This effect is known as *emboss* or bas relief.

FIGURE 7.10:

The Emboss special effect

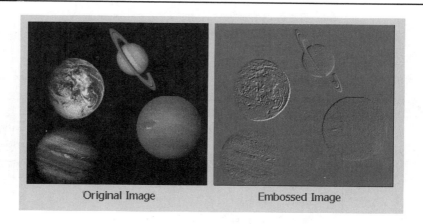

Original Image   Embossed Image

The actual algorithm is based on the difference between adjacent pixels. For most of the image, however, the difference between adjacent pixels is a small number, and the image will turn black. The Emboss algorithm adds a constant to the difference to bring some brightness to areas of the image that would otherwise be dark. The algorithm can be expressed as follows:

```
new_value = difference + 128
```

As usual, you can take the difference between adjacent pixels in the same row, adjacent pixels in the same column, or diagonally adjacent pixels. The code that implements the Emboss filter in the Image application uses differences in the X and Y directions (set the values of the variables Dx or Dy to 0 to take the difference in one direction only). The Emboss filter's code is shown next.

Code 7.9:   **The Emboss Algorithm**

```
Private Sub ProcessEmboss_Click()
Dim i As Integer, j As Integer
Const Dx As Integer = 1
Const Dy As Integer = 1
Dim red As Integer, green As Integer, blue As Integer

    For i = 1 To Y - 2
      For j = 1 To X - 2
         red = Abs(ImagePixels(0, i, j)_
                - ImagePixels(0, i + Dx, j + Dy) + 128)
         green = Abs(ImagePixels(1, i, j)_
                - ImagePixels(1, i + Dx, j + Dy) + 128)
         blue = Abs(ImagePixels(2, i, j) _
                - ImagePixels(2, i + Dx, j + Dy) + 128)
         Picture1.PSet (j, i), RGB(red, green, blue)
      Next
      Picture1.Refresh
    Next

    End Sub
```

The variables Dx and Dy determine the location of the pixel being subtracted from the one being processed. Notice that the pixel being subtracted is behind and above the current pixel. If you set the Dx and Dy variables to -1, the result is similar, but the processed image looks engraved rather than embossed.

Diffusing Images

The *Diffuse* special effect is different from the previous ones, in the sense that it's not based on the sums or the differences of pixel values. The Diffuse special effect uses the *Rnd()* function to introduce some randomness to the image and give it a painterly look, as demonstrated in Figure 7.11.

This time we won't manipulate the values of the pixels. Instead, the current pixel will assume the value of another one, selected randomly in its 5×5 neighborhood with the help of the Rnd() function.

FIGURE 7.11:

The Diffuse special effect gives the image a painterly look.

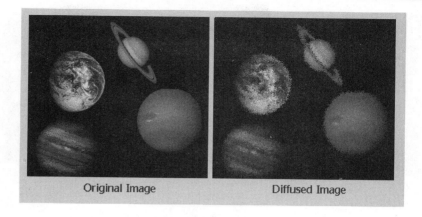

Original Image   Diffused Image

Code 7.10:   **The Diffuse Algorithm**

```
Private Sub ProcessDiffuse_Click()
Dim i As Integer, j As Integer
Dim Rx As Integer, Ry As Integer
Dim red As Integer, green As Integer, blue As Integer

    For i = 2 To Y - 3
        For j = 2 To X - 3
            Rx = Rnd() * 4 - 2
            Ry = Rnd() * 4 - 2
            red = ImagePixels(0, i + Rx, j + Ry)
            green = ImagePixels(1, i + Rx, j + Ry)
            blue = ImagePixels(2, i + Rx, j + Ry)
            Picture1.PSet (j, i), RGB(red, green, blue)
        Next
        DoEvents
    Next

    End Sub
```

Solarizing Images

The last special effect in the Image application is based on a photographic technique, and it's called *solarization*. Figure 7.12 shows an example of a solarized image. Part of the image is unprocessed and part of it is inverted. You can use many rules to decide which pixels to invert, and you should experiment with this algorithm to get the best possible results for a given image.

FIGURE 7.12:

The Solarize special effect

The algorithm as implemented in the Image application inverts the basic color components whose values are less than 128. If a pixel value is (58, 199, 130), then only its Red component will be inverted, while a pixel with a value (32, 99, 110) will be inverted completely. The code behind the Solarize menu command follows.

Code 7.11:   **The Solarize Algorithm**

```
Private Sub ProcessSolarize_Click()
Dim i As Integer, j As Integer
Dim red As Integer, green As Integer, blue As Integer

    For i = 1 To Y - 2
        For j = 1 To X - 2
            red = ImagePixels(0, i, j)
            green = ImagePixels(1, i, j)
            blue = ImagePixels(2, i, j)
            If ((red < 128) Or (red > 255)) Then _
                red = 255 - red
            If ((green < 128) Or (green > 255)) Then _
                green = 255 - green
            If ((blue < 128) Or (blue > 255)) Then _
```

```
            blue = 255 - blue
        Picture1.PSet (j, i), RGB(red, green, blue)
    Next
    DoEvents
Next
Picture1.Refresh
End Sub
```

Notice the If statements that invert the Color values. The second comparison operator is not really needed because a Color value can't exceed 255. However, you can set it to another smaller value to experiment with the algorithm (in other words, invert a Color value in a specific range).

Implementing Custom Filters

The last operation on the Process menu is a versatile technique for implementing many filters. The Custom Filter command leads you to another Form, shown in Figure 7.13. You can use this Form to specify a 3×3 or 5×5 block over which the calculations will be performed. Imagine that this block is centered over the current pixel. The coefficients in each cell of this block are multiplied by the underlying pixel values, and all the products are added together. Let's call this sum SP (sum of products). The sum of the products is then divided by the Divide factor, and finally the Bias is added to the result. The code that processes an image with a custom filter, as specified in the Custom Filter window is shown next.

FIGURE 7.13:

The Custom Filter specification Form of the Image application

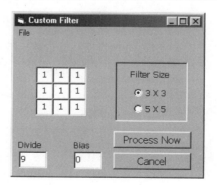

Code 7.12:   **The Custom Filter Command**

```
Private Sub ProcessCustom_Click()
    Dim RedSum As Integer, GreenSum As Integer, BlueSum As Integer
    Dim red As Integer, green As Integer, blue As Integer
```

```
      Dim fi As Integer, fj As Integer
      Dim i As Integer, j As Integer
      Dim Offset As Integer

      Form2.Show 1    Î wait for user to define filter
      If FilterCancel = True Then Exit Sub

      If FilterNorm = 0 Then FilterNorm = 1

      If Form2.Option1.Value Then
         Offset = 1
      Else
         Offset = 2
      End If
      For i = Offset To Y - Offset - 1
         For j = Offset To X - Offset - 1
            RedSum = 0: GreenSum = 0: BlueSum = 0
             For fi = -Offset To Offset
                 For fj = -Offset To Offset
                     RedSum = RedSum + ImagePixels(0, i + fi, j + fj) _
                        * CustomFilter(fi + 2, fj + 2)
                     GreenSum = GreenSum + ImagePixels(1, i + fi, j + fj)_
                        * CustomFilter(fi + 2, fj + 2)
                     BlueSum = BlueSum + ImagePixels(2, i + fi, j + fj)_
                        * CustomFilter(fi + 2, fj + 2)
                 Next
             Next
             red = Abs(RedSum / FilterNorm + FilterBias)
             green = Abs(GreenSum / FilterNorm + FilterBias)
             blue = Abs(BlueSum / FilterNorm + FilterBias)
             Picture1.PSet (j, i), RGB(red, green, blue)
         Next
         DoEvents
      Next
   End Sub
```

The subroutine reads the values of the various controls on Form2 (the filter's Form) and uses them to process the image as described. The custom filter is the slowest one, but it's quite flexible.

To understand how this filter works, let's implement the smoothing algorithm as a custom filter. The smoothing algorithm adds the values of the current pixel and its eight neighbors and divides the result by 9. If you set all the coefficients in the filter to 1, the sum of the products will be the sum of all pixel values under the filter's block. Multiplying each pixel by 1 won't change their values, and so the sum of the products will be the same as the sum of the pixel values. To calculate the average, you must divide by 9, so set the Divide field on the Custom Filter Form to 9. The Bias field should be 0. If you apply this custom filter to the image, it will have the same effect on the image as the smoothing algorithm. The values of all nine pixels under the block are added, their sum is divided by 9, and the result, which is the average of the pixels under consideration, is assigned to the center pixel of the block. The same process is repeated for the next pixel on the same row, and so on, until the filter is applied to every pixel of the image.

Let's look at one more example of the Custom Filter command, this time one that uses the Bias field. The Emboss algorithm replaces each pixel with its difference from the one on the previous row and column and then adds the bias 128 so that the embossed image won't be too dark. To implement the Emboss algorithm as a Custom Filter, set the coefficients as shown in Figure 7.14.

FIGURE 7.14:

The coefficients of the Custom Filter Form for the Emboss filter

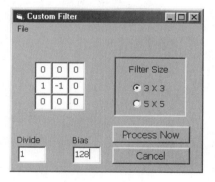

The pixel to the right of the current pixel is subtracted from the current pixel, and the bias 128 is added to the result, which is exactly what the actual algorithm does.

Using Edge Detection Filters

You can use another type of custom filter to extract the edges of an image. Because an image contains both horizontal and vertical edges, the two types of edge detection filters detect the corresponding types of edges.

The horizontal edge detection filter detects and extracts horizontal edges by subtracting a row of pixels above the center pixel from the corresponding pixels below the center pixel. The vertical edge detection filter subtracts columns of pixels instead of rows, and its definition is shown in Figure 7.15. Figure 7.16 shows the result.

FIGURE 7.15:

A vertical edge detection filter

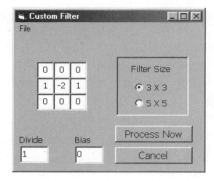

FIGURE 7.16:

The result of applying the filter in Figure 7.15 to an image

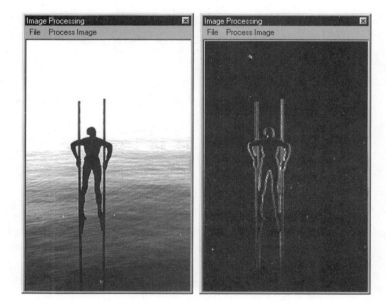

In the Cfilters folder in this chapter's folder on the CD, you'll find a few additional figures that show pairs of filters and processed images. These figures show some special effects implemented with custom filters: two "neon" effects, an "outline" effect, and a "shake" effect. Open the images in the Cfilters folder to see some interesting effects you can create with the custom filter option of the Image application.

Using Palettes

In concluding this chapter, let's briefly review a technique for accessing palette colors. Although specifying colors with the RGB() function is straightforward, you can't be sure that the color displayed is the same as the one you specified with the RGB() function's arguments. For example, you may draw a yellow circle on top of an image and see a "greenish" circle. This is because computers that can't display more than 256 colors must approximate Color values with existing colors. Therefore, if the bitmap displayed doesn't already contain a yellow tone, then the computer may try to approximate the yellow color with a tone that's not even close.

Most of the time, your computer will approximate colors quite nicely. Sometimes, however, you must be able to access the colors in the current palette so that the color you specify in your code is the color being displayed. Visual Basic provides a mechanism for accessing the entries of the current palette by index. (There are many Windows API functions for manipulating palettes, but this is a complicated topic that won't be covered in the book.) To retrieve the palette entry *PIndex*, use the expression:

```
clr = &H1000000 + PIndex
```

clr is a Long Color value, which can be used in your code in the place of the RGB() function. For example, to paint a point with the 120th entry in the current palette, call the PSet method with the following arguments (the first entry in the palette has zero index):

```
Form1.Pset (X, Y), &H1000000 + 119
```

Forms and PictureBoxes don't have a default palette. You must first load a palette by assigning it to the Palette property of the control. To load a palette to a Form, assign the name of the file with the palette to the Form1.Palette property and set the PaletteMode property to 2 (Custom Palette). For more information on these two properties, see the section "True Color and Palettes" of Appendix C.

A *palette file* is a BMP or DIB file with a single pixel and a 256-color palette. Most image processing applications let you edit an image's palette. To create a palette file, open an image that contains many of the colors you like with an application like Paint Shop Pro and look at its palette. Edit it if you like, or create an entirely new palette. Then resize the image to a single pixel (1 × 1) and save it as BMP or DIB file. This single pixel image contains its own palette and you can use it to load the palette onto a Form. Every PictureBox and ImageBox control on the form will use this palette.

In the PalColor folder in this chapter's folder on the CD, you'll find the sample projects of this section and a number of palette files (stored in the DIB folder). They are the Bluewhit.dib, Earth.dib, ManyClrs.dib, Mono.dib, MoonLite.dib, Neon.dib, SeaSky.dib, and Smooth.dib files, and they are all single pixel images with the desired palette. You can open these files with an image processing application and see their palettes.

VB6 at Work: The PaletteColor Project

The PaletteColor project, shown in Figure 7.17, demonstrates how to load a palette on a Form and access its colors (you'll find the project in the PalColor folder under this chapter's folder on the CD). The PaletteColor application loads a user-specified palette on a PictureBox control and then creates a grid of 256 small boxes, arranged in 16 rows of 16 columns. Each box on the grid is colored with a different palette color. It paints the upper left box with the first entry in the palette, the one below with the next entry in the palette, and so on. When the first column is exhausted, the program continues with the second column, and so on.

FIGURE 7.17:

The PaletteColor application demonstrates how to read palette colors and display them on a PictureBox control.

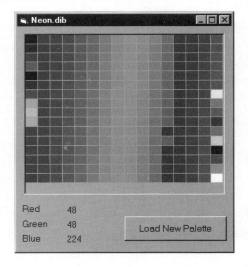

Every time the user selects a new palette with the Load Palette button, the following lines are executed, which create the grid and paint every box with a different color.

Code 7.13:	**Creating the Color Grid**

```
BSpace = 2
BWidth = Int((Picture1.ScaleWidth - 32) / 16)
BHeight = Int((Picture1.ScaleHeight - 32) / 16)

For ih = 0 To 15
    For iv = 0 To 15
        CIndex = ih * 16 + iv
        bxStart = ih * (BWidth + BSpace)
        byStart = iv * (BHeight + BSpace)
        clr = &H1000000 + CIndex
        Picture1.Line (bxStart, byStart)- _
                Step(BWidth, BHeight), clr, BF
    Next
Next
```

When the user selects a color by clicking in a box, the following lines read the color's value and display its RGB components in the Label controls at the bottom of the Form.

Code 7.14:	**Displaying a Color's Components**

```
Private Sub Picture1_MouseUp(Button As Integer, _
                Shift As Integer, X As Single, Y As Single)
Dim pixel As Long
Dim Red As Integer, Green As Integer, Blue As Integer

    pixel = Picture1.Point(X, Y)
    Red = pixel Mod 256
    Green = ((pixel And &HFF00FF00) / 256&)
    Blue = (pixel And &HFF0000) / 65536
    Label2.Caption = Red
    Label3.Caption = Green
    Label4.Caption = Blue
End Sub
```

VB6 at Work: The PaletteGradient Project

If you attempt to display a gradient on a palette system you may see three or four different colors only. Obviously, this isn't much of a palette. To see how the gradient will be drawn, set your monitor's color depth to 256 colors (right-click on the Desktop, and from the shortcut menu select Properties ➤ Settings) and run the ClrGrads application. To create smooth gradients on palette systems, you must create a custom palette, load it on the PictureBox control or Form, and then access the palette's colors. The PaletteGradient project, shown in Figure 7.18, does exactly that. (The PaletteGradient project is called PalGrad and can be found in the PalColor folder on the CD. The project uses the palette files in the DIB folder.)

FIGURE 7.18:

The PaletteGradient application draws gradients using a palette's colors.

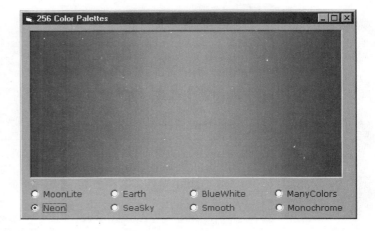

The PictureBox control on which the gradients are drawn has a width of 472 pixels. The gradient is drawn with 236 vertical lines, each one having a width of two pixels. The program makes use of 236 of the palette's 256 colors. The first 10 and last 10 colors in the palette are reserved by Windows for displaying the standard colors (the colors used for the title bars, scrollbars, and other elements of the user interface are always the same and they aren't affected by the palette). If you open the palettes in the DIB folder, you'll also see the standard Windows colors at the beginning and end of the palette. Since you don't have control over the basic colors in the palette, you shouldn't use them.

The gradient is drawn by the DrawGradient() subroutine each time you select a new palette by clicking on another Option button at the bottom of the Form. The DrawGradient() subroutine is shown in Code 7.15.

Code 7.15:	**The DrawGradient() Subroutine**

```
Sub DrawGradient()
DoEvents
For i = 0 To 235
    Picture1.Line (i * 2, 0)-(i * 2, Picture1.ScaleHeight), _
        &H1000000 + 10 + i
Next
End Sub
```

If you want to add a gradient (or any other pattern with many custom colors), create the appropriate palette and load it on the Form. Then, you can access the palette's entries and make sure that the gradient will appear with its proper colors on the palette system. You'll find more examples, as well as a discussion of the Form's palette-related properties in Appendix C on the CD, *Using Multimedia Elements to Enhance Applications*.

CHAPTER

EIGHT

Advanced ActiveX Controls

■ The Common Dialogs control

■ The ImageList control

■ The TreeView control

■ The ListView control

In the first part of the book you learned how to use the basic ActiveX controls to build user interfaces. These controls appear on the Toolbox of the Visual Basic editor every time you start a new project, and they are the basic elements of the Windows interface. Windows applications also use other controls which aren't displayed on the Toolbox by default, such as the File Open and Color dialog boxes. Other interesting and relatively common ActiveX controls are the TreeView control, which displays hierarchical lists of items, such as those in the left pane of the Windows Explorer, and the RichTextBox control, an advanced word processor. We'll explore more advanced ActiveX controls in the next chapter.

To use any of the controls presented in this chapter, you must first add them to the Toolbox and make them a part of the project. To add a new control to the Toolbox, right-click the Toolbox and from the shortcut menu, select Components. You can also open the Project menu and select the Components command. Either way, you'll see the Components dialog box, shown in Figure 8.1.

FIGURE 8.1:

Use the Components dialog box to add new ActiveX controls to the Toolbox.

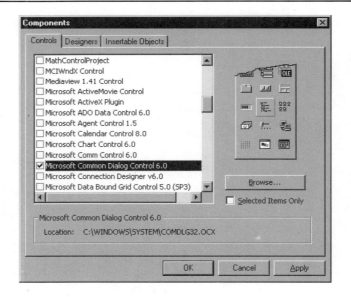

Select the component(s) you want to add by checking the box in front of their name and clicking the OK button. To add the ImageList, TreeView, and ListView controls, which we're going to discuss in the second half of this chapter, check the box Microsoft Common Dialog Control 6.0. To add the Common Dialogs control, which displays familiar common dialog boxes such as File Open, Color, and Font, check the Windows Common Dialogs Control box. To remove certain ActiveX controls from a project, simply uncheck them, and then click the OK button. You should always remove ActiveX controls that aren't going to be used in a project, since they only add to the size of the distribution files.

The Common Dialogs Control

A rather tedious, but quite common, task in nearly every application is to prompt the user for filenames, font names and sizes, or colors to be used by the application. Designing your own dialog boxes for these purposes would be a hassle, not to mention that your applications wouldn't have the same look and feel of all Windows applications. In fact, all Windows applications use some standard dialog boxes for common operations, such as selecting a font or opening a file. Figure 8.2 shows a couple of examples. These dialog boxes are built into the operating system and any application can use them.

FIGURE 8.2:

The Font and File Open common dialog boxes

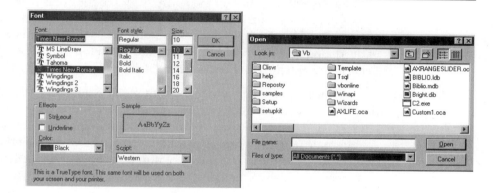

If you ever want to display a File Open or Font dialog box, don't design it—it already exists. To use it, just place the Common Dialogs control on your Form and call the appropriate method. For instance, the ShowOpen method invokes the File Open dialog box; the ShowColor method invokes the Color dialog box.

Using the Common Dialogs Control

The Common Dialogs control is a peculiar one. It provides its services to the application, but it doesn't need to be displayed on the Form at runtime (similar to the Timer control). The Common Dialogs control provides the following built-in Windows dialog boxes:

- **Open** The File Open common dialog box lets users select a file to open.

- **Save As** The File Save common dialog box lets users select or specify a filename in which the current document will be saved.

- **Color** The Color dialog box lets users select colors or specify custom colors.

- **Font**   The Font common dialog box lets users select a typeface and style to be applied to the current text selection.

- **Print**   The Print common dialog box lets users select and set up a printer.

- **Help**   The Help common dialog box displays Help topics.

You'll see many examples of the Common Dialogs control in the following chapters. This section explores the basic properties and methods of the control, especially the Flags property, which modifies the default behavior of each common dialog box.

To call upon the services of the Common Dialogs control, you must first place an instance of the control on the Form. After the control is placed on the Form, you can't adjust its size because the Common Dialogs control remains hidden at runtime. You can, however, set several properties to adjust the appearance of any of the dialog boxes it displays, such as the initial font in the Font dialog box or a default filename in the Open or Save As dialog boxes.

To display a common dialog box from within your code, you must assign the proper value to the control's *Action* property. The Action property acts as a method: after you assign a value to it, the corresponding common dialog box is displayed. An alternate (and preferred) way of invoking the same dialog boxes is to use the more descriptive methods instead of numeric values. The methods of the control and their equivalent Action property values are listed in Table 8.1.

T A B L E 8 . 1 :   Methods and Values of the Common Dialogs Control's Action Property

Method	Value	Action
ShowOpen	1	Displays the Open dialog box
ShowSave	2	Displays the Save As dialog box
ShowColor	3	Displays the Color dialog box
ShowFont	4	Displays the Font dialog box
ShowPrinter	5	Displays the Printer dialog box
ShowHelp	6	Invokes the Windows Help engine

After you assign a value to the Action property or call the equivalent method, the corresponding dialog box appears on-screen and execution of the program is suspended until the dialog box is closed. Using the Open and the Save dialog boxes, for example, the user can traverse the entire structure of his or her hard disk and locate the desired filename. When the user clicks the Open or Save button, the program control is returned to the application, which can read the name of the file selected by the user (*FileName* property) and use it to open the file or to store the current document there.

Here is the sequence of statements used to invoke the File Open dialog box and retrieve the selected filename:

```
CommonDialog1.ShowOpen
fileName = CommonDialog1.FileName
```

The variable *fileName* is the full path name of the file selected by the user. You can also set the FileName property to a filename that's displayed when the common dialog box is first opened. This allows the user to click the Open button to open the preselected file or choose another file.

```
CommonDialog1.FileName = "C:\Documents\Doc1.doc"
CommonDialog1.ShowOpen
fileName = CommonDialog1.FileName
```

Similarly, you can invoke the Color dialog box and read the value of the selected color with the following statements:

```
CommonDialog1.ShowColor
Color=CommonDialog1.Color
```

The dialog box sets the FileName and Color properties, and your application simply reads them.

The Common Properties

Each common dialog box has a number of properties that you can adjust in appearance and/or function. Most of the properties are optional, and they should be set before you open the dialog box. Some of the properties common to nearly all the common dialog boxes are discussed next. Afterwards, we'll look at the properties that are unique to each common dialog box.

CancelError

Each dialog box has a Cancel button, which should signal to your application the user's intention to cancel the current operation. The Cancel action can be reported to your application by means of an error. To specify whether an error is generated when the user clicks the Cancel button, set the *CancelError* property to True. If you don't want to handle this situation through an error handler, set the CancelError property to False and examine the value returned by the Common Dialogs control (such as the FileName or Color property). If the user has canceled the operation, this value will be an empty string.

If you set the CancelError property to True, you must also provide an error handler that will detect this condition and act accordingly. All common dialog boxes return the same error, which is error number 32755 (constant *cdlCancel*). Your error handler must examine the error number, and if it's 32755, cancel the operation. You can open the Open common dialog box and detect whether the user has canceled the operation with the following code.

Code 8.1:   **Checking for the Cancel Operation**

```
On Error Goto NoFile
CommonDialog1.CancelError=True
CommonDialog1.ShowOpen
Fname=CommonDialog1.Filename
{more commands}
Exit Sub

NoFile:
If Err.Number=32755 Then
    Exit Sub    ' operation cancel, do nothing
Else
    MsgBox "Unknown error in opening file " & Fname
End If
```

DialogTitle

The second common property is the *DialogTitle* property, which returns or sets the string displayed in the title bar of the dialog box. The default title on the dialog box's title bar is the name of the dialog box (e.g., Open, Save, Color).

Flags

A third property of all the common dialog boxes is *Flags,* which you use to adjust the function of each common dialog box. The values of this property will vary depending on the specific common dialog box being opened. These values are discussed in the following sections devoted to each type of dialog box.

Min and Max

These properties apply to the Print and Font common dialog boxes. In the Print dialog box, they determine the minimum and maximum allowable values for the print range that the user can specify (see the fields *From* and *To* of the Print common dialog box in Figure 8.11, later in this chapter). In the Font common dialog box, the properties determine the minimum and maximum size displayed in the Size list (the range of font sizes from which the user will be allowed to select).

VB6 at Work: The CDBox Project

The Flags property of the Common Dialogs control may take on a large number of values, and remembering them is out of the question. When programming the Common Dialogs control, you should have a reference at hand.

In this chapter's folder on the CD, you'll find the CDBox application. You can use it to experiment with the various settings of the common dialog boxes; see what each property does and determine which flag combinations you might need for a specific application. Or you can create an executable, run it (outside the Visual Basic IDE) to get the settings of a control right, and then use the constants in your code.

The CDBox application is based on a Tab control with one tab per common dialog box. The tab for the Color common dialog box, shown in Figure 8.3, contains a list of all the flags you can set in the Color common dialog box as well as the value of the Color property. Each tab will be explained as we examine each common dialog box in the following sections.

The Color Common Dialog Box

The Color common dialog box, shown in Figure 8.3, is one of the simplest dialog boxes. It has a single property, *Color*, which returns the color selected by the user or sets the initially selected color when the user opens the dialog box.

Before opening the *Color* dialog box with the ShowColor method, you can set a number of flags through its Flags property, whose values are shown in Table 8.2. To combine multiple flags, add their values or use the OR operator.

T A B L E　8 . 2 :　Flag Constants for the Color Common Dialog Box

Constant	Value	Description
cdCClFullOpen	&H2	Displays the full dialog box, including the Define Custom Colors section
cdlCCHelpButton	&H8	Displays a Help button in the dialog box
cdlCCPreventFullOpen	&H4	Hides the Define Custom Colors section (prevents the user from defining custom colors)
cdlCCRGBInit	&H1	Sets the value of the color initially selected when the dialog box is opened

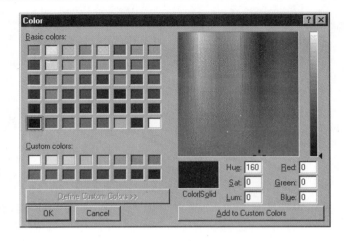

The Color tab of the CDBox application lets you set (or reset) the various flags and the value of the color that's initially selected in the Color dialog box. You can specify this value in decimal or hexadecimal format (the latter is more common). The Show Dialog Box button displays the Color common dialog box. When you select a color and then exit the Color dialog box, the PictureBox control at the bottom is filled with the selected color (see Figure 8.4). In addition, the color's value is displayed in decimal and hexadecimal format in the two TextBox controls under the Color Value heading.

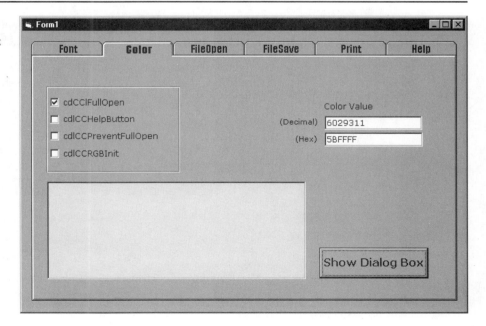

The Font Common Dialog Box

The Font common dialog box, shown in Figure 8.5, lets the user review and select a font and its size and style. To open the Font dialog box, set the Action property to 4 or invoke the ShowFont method of the Common Dialogs control.

FIGURE 8.5:

The Font common dialog box

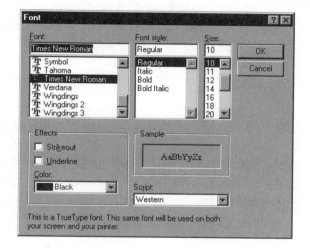

After the user selects a font, its size and style, and possibly some special effects (color or the underline attribute), and clicks the OK button, the Common Dialogs control returns the attributes of the selected font through the following properties:

- **Color**   Returns the font's selected color; to allow the user to set this property, you must first set the Flags property to *cdlCFEffects* (see Table 8.3 for a description)

- **FontBold**   It's True if the bold attribute is set

- **FontItalic**   It's True if the italic attribute is set

- **FontStrikethru**   It's True if the strikethrough attribute is set; to allow the user to set this property, you must first set the Flags property to *cdlCFEffects*

- **FontUnderline**   It's True if the underline attribute is set; to allow the user to set this property, you must first set the Flags property to *cdlCFEffects*

- **FontName**   Returns the selected font's name

- **FontSize**   Returns the selected font's size

When the Font common dialog box is closed, the values of the corresponding checkboxes on the tab are updated to match the settings specified by the user in the dialog box. You can also set the value of any of the previous properties to specify the initial settings of the Font dialog box before clicking the Show Dialog Box button.

You may have noticed that some properties require the *cdlCFEffects* flag to be set. This flag displays a few additional settings that are considered special effects, such as strikethrough, underline, and the color of the font.

WARNING   If you attempt to call the Font dialog box by invoking only the ShowFont method, you'll get an error message stating that no fonts are installed. To open the Font dialog box, you must first set the Flags property to *cdlCFScreenFonts*, *cdlCFPrinter-Fonts*, or *cdlCFBoth*, which determine which fonts will be displayed (screen fonts only, printer fonts only, or both; see Table 8.3 for more details).

Using the Flags Property with the Font Dialog Box

The CDBox Form shown in Figure 8.6 provides checkboxes for every type of flag you can set with the Font common dialog box. The Flags property of the Font common dialog box can take on any of the values shown in Table 8.3.

FIGURE 8.6:

Switch to the Font tab of the CDBox application to experiment with the various settings of the Font common dialog box.

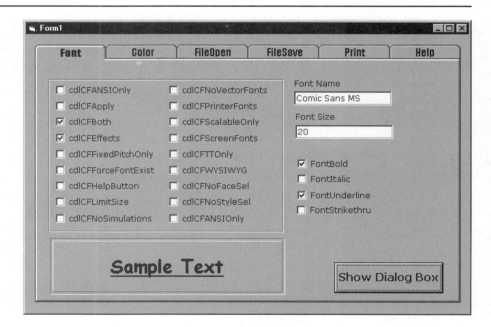

TABLE 8.3: Flag Constants for the Font Common Dialog Box

Constant	Value	Description
cdlCFANSIOnly	&H400	Specifies that the dialog box display only the fonts that use the Windows character set. If this flag is set, the user won't be able to select a font that contains only symbols, such as Wingdings.
cdlCFApply	&H200	Enables the Apply button in the dialog box
cdlCFBoth	&H3	Displays both printer and screen fonts in the dialog box. (You must also set the hDC property to specify the current printer.)
cdlCFEffects	&H100	Specifies that the dialog box let the user set the strikethrough, underline, and color effects
cdlCFFixedPitchOnly	&H4000	Specifies that the dialog box display only monospaced (fixed-pitch) fonts. These fonts are commonly used for program lists.
cdlCFForceFontExist	&H10000	Specifies that an error message box appear if the user attempts to select a font or style that doesn't exist
cdlCFHelpButton	&H4	Displays a Help button in the dialog box
cdlCFLimitSize	&H2000	Specifies that the dialog box display only font sizes within the range specified by the Min and Max properties
cdlCFNoSimulations	&H1000	Specifies that the dialog box doesn't display simulated fonts
cdlCFNoVectorFonts	&H800	Specifies that the dialog box doesn't display vector-font selections
cdlCFPrinterFonts	&H2	Causes the dialog box to list only the fonts supported by the printer specified by the hDC property
cdlCFScalableOnly	&H20000	Specifies that the dialog box display only fonts that can be scaled
cdlCFScreenFonts	&H1	Causes the dialog box to display only the screen fonts supported by the system
cdlCFTTOnly	&H40000	Specifies that the dialog box display only TrueType fonts
cdlCFWYSIWYG	&H8000	Specifies that the dialog box display the fonts supported by the printer and on-screen. If this flag is set, the cdlCFBoth and cdlCFScalableOnly flags should also be set.
cdlCFNoFaceSel	&H80000	No font name selected
cdlCFNoSizeSel	&H200000	No font size selected
cdlCFNoStyleSel	&H100000	No style selected

When the Font common dialog box is first opened, the font name, size, and attributes of the font selected the last time the same dialog box was opened are displayed.

If you want these fields to be empty when the user opens this dialog box, set the Flags property to the following value:

```
CommonDialog1.Flags = cdlCFNoFaceSel OR cdlCFNosizeSel OR _
    cdlCFNoStyleSel
```

This line displays the Font dialog box without an initial font, size, or style selection.

The FileOpen and FileSave Common Dialog Boxes

FileOpen and FileSave (see Figure 8.7) are the two most widely used common dialog boxes. Nearly every application prompts the user for a filename. Windows 95 provides two highly customizable common dialog boxes for this purpose. The two dialog boxes are nearly identical and most of their properties are common, so let's look at the properties of both.

FIGURE 8.7:

The FileSave common dialog box

When a File common dialog box is opened, it rarely displays all the files in any given folder. Usually the number of files displayed is limited to the ones that the application recognizes so that users can easily spot the file they want. The Filter property determines which files appear in the File Open or File Save dialog box.

It's also standard for the Windows 95 interface not to display the extensions of files (although Windows distinguishes files using invisible extensions, which is why I've turned on the option to display file extensions for Figure 8.7). The Save As Type ComboBox contains the various file types recognized by the application. The various file types can be described in plain English with long descriptive names and without their extensions.

The extension of the default file type for the application is described by the DefaultExt property, and the list of the file types displayed in the Save As Type box is described by the Filter property. Both the DefaultExt and the Filter properties are available in the control's Properties window at design time. At runtime, you must set them manually from within your code.

- **DefaultExt**   Sets the default extension of the dialog box. Use this property to specify a default filename extension, such as TXT or DOC, so that when a file with no extension is saved, the extension specified by this property is automatically appended to the filename.

- **Filter**   The Filter property is used to specify the type(s) of files displayed in the dialog box's file list box. To display text files only, set the Filter property to "Text file | *.txt". The pipe symbol separates the description of the files (what the user sees) from the actual extension (how the operating system distinguishes the various file types).

> **TIP**
>
> If you want to display multiple extensions, such as BMP, GIF, and JPG, use a semicolon to separate extensions with the Filter property. The string "Imagesl*.BMP;* .GIF;*.JPG" displays all the files of these three types when the user selects Images in the Save As Type box.

Don't include spaces before or after the pipe symbol because these spaces will be displayed with the description and Filter values. In the FileOpen dialog box of an image processing application, you'll probably provide options for each image file type, as well as an option for all images:

```
CommonDialog1.Filter = "Bitmaps|*.BMP|GIF Images|*.GIF|JPEG _
            Images|*.JPG|All Images|*.BMP;*.GIF;*.JPG"
```

The FileOpen dialog box has four options which determine what appears in the Save As Type box (see Figure 8.8).

- **FilterIndex**   When you specify more than one filter for a dialog box, the filter specified first in the Filter property becomes the default. If you want to use a Filter value other than the first one, use the FilterIndex property to determine which filter will be displayed as the default when the Open or Save dialog box is opened. The index of the first filter is 1 and there's no reason to ever set this property to 1. If you want to use the Filter property value of the previous example and set the FilterIndex property to 2, the Open dialog box will display GIF files by default.

- **FileTitle**   This property returns the name of the file to be opened or saved. The FileTitle property doesn't include the path name. If you set this property before opening the dialog box, the specified filename will appear in the File Name field.

- **InitDir** This property sets the initial directory (folder) in which files are displayed the first time the Open and Save dialog boxes are opened. Use this property to display the files of the application's folder or to specify a folder in which the application will store its files by default. If you don't specify an initial folder, it will default to the last folder where the dialog box opened or saved a file. It's also customary to set the initial folder to the application's path, with the following statement:

```
CommonDialog1.InitDir = App.Path
```

- **MaxFileSize** This property returns or sets the maximum size of the filename opened using the Common Dialogs control. Its default value is 256, which is plenty for any reasonable filename. Normally you won't use this property unless you allow the user to select multiple files; in that case, you must allocate enough memory to store the names of the selected files. See the descriptions of the flags of this common dialog box in Table 8.4 to find out how you can allow multiple file selection in the Open and Save common dialog boxes. The section "Multiple File Selection," later in this chapter, contains an example.

FIGURE 8.8:

Switch to the FileOpen tab of the CDBox application to experiment with the various settings of the File common dialog box.

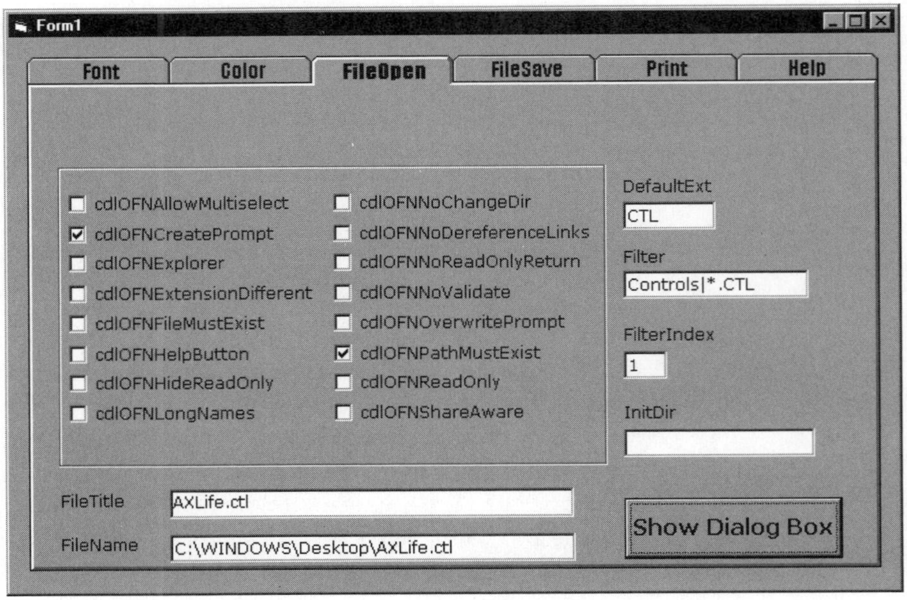

TABLE 8.4: Flag Constants for the FileOpen and FileSave Common Dialog Boxes

Constant	Value	Description
cdlOFNAllowMultiselect	&H200	Permits multiple file selection. The user can select more than one file at runtime by pressing the Shift key and using the Up and Down arrow keys to select the desired files. On return, the File-Name property returns a string containing the names of all selected files, delimited by spaces.
cdlOFNCreatePrompt	&H2000	Prompts the user to create a file that doesn't currently exist. This flag automatically sets the *cdlOFNPathMustExist* and *cdlOFNFile MustExist* flags.
cdlOFNExplorer	&H80000	Uses the Explorer-like Open a File dialog box template
cdlOFNExtensionDifferent	&H400	Indicates that the extension of the returned filename is different from the extension specified by the DefaultExt property. This flag isn't set if the DefaultExt property is Null, if the extensions match, or if the file has no extension. This Flag value is set by the Common Dialogs control, and the application must examine it when the dialog box is closed.
cdlOFNFileMustExist	&H1000	Specifies that the user can enter only names of existing files in the File Name textbox. If this flag is set and the user enters an invalid filename, a warning is displayed. This flag automatically sets the *cdlOFNPathMustExist* flag.
cdlOFNHelpButton	&H10	Displays the Help button in the dialog box
cdlOFNHideReadOnly	&H4	Hides the read-only *cdlOFNReadOnly* checkbox
cdlOFNLongNames	&H200000	Allows long filenames
cdlOFNNoChangeDir	&H8	Forces the dialog box to set the current directory to what it was when the dialog box was opened. Use this flag to force the user of the application to use a predetermined folder for storing the files.
cdlOFNNoDereferenceLinks	&H100000	Prevents the shell from dereferencing shortcuts. By default, choosing a shortcut causes it to be dereferenced by the shell.
cdlOFNNoReadOnlyReturn	&H8000	Disables the selection of files that have the read-only attribute set and won't be in a write-protected directory. This attribute won't allow the user to save to a file on a CD-ROM drive.
cdlOFNNoValidate	&H100	Normally, the File Open dialog box validates filenames. To skip this validation step, set this Flag value.
cdlOFNOverwritePrompt	&H2	Causes the Save As dialog box to generate a message box if the selected file already exists. The user must confirm the intention to overwrite a file before the file is overwritten.

Continued on next page

TABLE 8.4 CONTINUED: Flag Constants for the FileOpen and FileSave Common Dialog Boxes

Constant	Value	Description
cdlOFNPathMustExist	&H800	Specifies that the user can enter only valid paths. If this flag is set and the user enters an invalid path, a warning message is displayed.
cdlOFNReadOnly	&H1	Checks the read-only checkbox the first time the dialog box is opened. This flag also indicates the state of the read-only checkbox on exit. Test this flag to find out whether the user wants to open a file as read-only.
cdlOFNShareAware	&H4000	Specifies that sharing violation errors will be ignored

To specify that the user must select an existing file only (in other words, the user won't be allowed to type a nonexistent filename in the File Name field), set the Flags to *cdlOFNFileMustExist*, with the following statement:

```
CommonDialog1.Flags = cdlOFNFileMustExist
```

To set multiple flags, combine their values with the OR operator:

```
CommonDialog1.Flags = cdlOFNFileMustExist OR cdlOFNLongNames _
    OR cdlOFNExplorer
```

Each value sets certain bits in the Flags property; when multiple flags are combined with the OR operator, all corresponding bits are set. To test for a Flag value, you must use AND with the flag's corresponding value or constant. To find out the status of the read-only checkbox, use a structure such as the following:

```
If CommonDialog1.Flags AND cdlOFNReadOnly Then
{open file for input}
Else
{open file for random access}
End If
```

TIP   By default, the File Open common dialog box will dereference shortcuts. In other words, it will report the complete path name of the file referenced by the shortcut. If you don't want to dereference shortcuts, set the *cdlOFNNoDereferenceLinks* flag.

Multiple File Selection

The first *Flag* constant in Table 8.4 allows for the selection of multiple files on the dialog box. This option isn't very common, but it can come in handy in situations when you want to process a number of files en masse. You can let the user select many files and then process them one at a time. Or, you may wish to prompt the user to select multiple files to be moved or copied.

To allow the user to select multiple files on the File Open common dialog control, specify the *cdlOFNAllowMultiselect* flag as follows:

```
CommonDialog1.Flags = CommonDialog1.Flags Or cdlOFNAllowMultiselect
```

This flag allows the user to select multiple files with the mouse by holding down the Shift or Ctrl key.

The names of the selected files are reported by the property FileName, but unlike single file selections, you can't use this property to open the files directly. The File-Name property contains the path names of all selected files and in order to use them, you must first extract each one. Extracting the filenames from the FileName property is straightforward string manipulation code, but there's a small glitch you have to deal with.

With the simple (Windows 3.11) File Open common dialog box, the filenames are separated by a space. All you have to do is to scan the property value for spaces and extract the names of the selected files. If you specify the *cdlOFNExplorer* flag, which opens a Windows 98/NT Explorer-style dialog box, the filenames are delimited by the null character (Chr(0)) because long paths and filenames may contain spaces too (this excludes the use of the space as a delimiter, of course). So, the code for extracting the names of the selected files from the FileName property is different, depending on the type of File Open common dialog box.

> **NOTE**   Normally, the FileTitle property returns the name of the selected file, without path information. If multiple files are selected, the FileTitle property is an empty string. All the information you need is stored in the FileName property. In processing a File Open common dialog box, however, you can test the FileTitle property and act accordingly. If it's empty, then multiple files have been selected; if not, a single file has been selected and its name is given by the FileTitle property (see the MFiles and MFiles95 sample projects of the following section).

VB6 at Work: The MFiles Project

In this chapter's folder on the CD, you'll find the MFiles project, which demonstrates the use of the *cdlOFNAllowMultiselect* flag of the Open common dialog box. The application's Form is shown in Figure 8.9. Besides the controls you see on the Form at runtime, there is also an instance of the Common Dialogs control that's invisible at runtime. The Command button at the bottom of the Form opens a File Open dialog box, where you can select multiple files. After closing the dialog box by clicking the OK or Open button (depending on the version of the dialog box you open), the application displays the names of the selected files in the ListBox control. Notice that only the names of the files are displayed. The path, which is common for all files, is displayed on a Label control near the top of the Form.

FIGURE 8.9:

The MFiles project lets the user select multiple files on a File Open dialog box and it displays the names on a ListBox control.

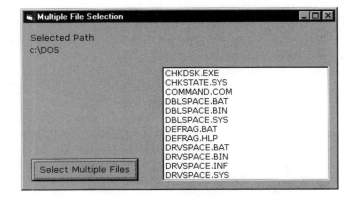

The code behind the Select Multiple Files button is shown next.

Code 8.2: **Processing Multiple Selected Files**

```
Private Sub Command1_Click()
    CommonDialog1.Flags = cdlOFNAllowMultiselect
    Label1.Caption = ""
    List1.Clear
    CommonDialog1.Filter = "All Files|*.*"
    CommonDialog1.ShowOpen
    filenames = CommonDialog1.FileName
    If Len(filenames) = 0 Then
        MsgBox "No files selected"
        Exit Sub
    End If
' Extract path name:
' IF FILETITLE IS NOT EMPTY, THEN A SINGLE FILE
' HAS BEEN SELECTED. DISPLAY IT AND EXIT
    If CommonDialog1.FileTitle <> "" Then
        List1.AddItem CommonDialog1.FileTitle
        Exit Sub
    End If
' FILETITLE IS NOT EMPTY, THEN MANY FILES WERE SELECTED
' AND WE MUST EXTRACT THEM FROM THE FILENAME PROPERTY
    spPosition = InStr(filenames, " ")
    pathName = Left(filenames, spPosition - 1)
```

```
        Label1.Caption = pathName
        filenames = Mid(filenames, spPosition + 1)
' then extract each space delimited file name
        If Len(filenames) = 0 Then
            List1.AddItem "No files selected"
            Exit Sub
        Else
            spPosition = InStr(filenames, " ")
            While spPosition > 0
                List1.AddItem Left(filenames, spPosition - 1)
                filenames = Mid(filenames, spPosition + 1)
                spPosition = InStr(filenames, " ")
            Wend
' Add the last file's name to the list
' (the last file name isn't followed by a space)
            List1.AddItem filenames
        End If
End Sub
```

The code isn't complicated, but it's quite lengthy compared to the code that retrieves and uses a single filename. Before opening the dialog box, the code sets the control's MaxFileSize property to a large value to make sure the FileName property will hold all the selected files (you may want to increase this value, depending on the nature of the application). After the user selects the files and closes the dialog box, the code extracts the name of the path; it's the first segment of the FileName property up to the first instance of the space delimiter. The path is displayed on a Label control and applies to all selected files. The *cdlOFNAllow-Multiselect* flag allows the selection of multiple files in the same folder, but you can't select multiple files in more than one folder. Each time you switch to another folder, the current selection is cleared.

Then, the program scans the FileName property searching for spaces. Each time a space is found, it extracts another filename by isolating the characters to the left of the delimiter and removes it from the FileName string. The last filename isn't delimited by the space character. After all other filenames have been extracted, the FileNames string contains the name of the last selected file.

Notice how the code uses the FileTitle property: if the FileTitle property isn't empty, then the user has selected a single file, whose name is displayed on the ListBox control, and the program exits.

```
If CommonDialog1.FileTitle <> "" Then
    List1.AddItem CommonDialog1.FileTitle
    Exit Sub
End If
```

TIP

The MaxFileSize property determines the memory allocated for storing the actual names of the selected file(s). When using the *cdlOFNAllowMultiselect* flag, you should increase its value (it's 256 characters by default) to allow enough memory for the selected filenames. You can also include an error handler to trap a possible runtime error, as follows:

```
On Error Goto SelectionError
    {your code for processing file names} SelectionError:
    If Err.Number = 20476 Then
        CommonDialog1.MaxFileSize = CommonDialog1.MaxFileSize + 1024
        Resume
    Else
        MsgBox "Unknown Error"
        Exit Sub
    End If
```

VB6 at Work: The MFiles95 Project

The MFiles95 project, shown in Figure 8.10, opens an Explorer-style dialog box that displays long filenames, some of which may contain spaces. The code of the Select Multiple Files button is identical to the listing in Code 8.2, but uses the delimiter Chr(0) instead of the space character. You can open the project in the Visual Basic editor and examine its code.

FIGURE 8.10:

An Explorer-style File Open dialog box displays long filenames. Multiple selected files are delimited in the FileName property of the Common Dialogs control with the Chr(0) character.

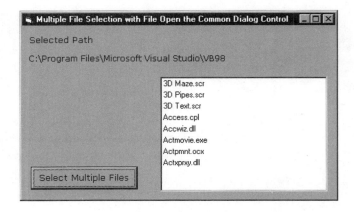

The Print Common Dialog Box

The Print common dialog box enables users to select a printer, set certain properties of the printout (number of copies, pages to be printed, and so on), and set up a specific printer (see Figure 8.11).

FIGURE 8.11:

The Print common dialog box

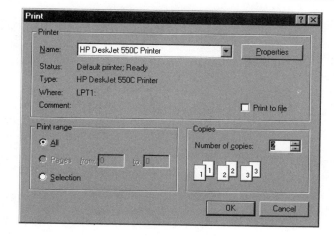

To open the Print dialog box, set the Action property of the Common Dialogs control to 5 or invoke the *ShowPrinter* method of the Common Dialogs control. After the user selects a printer and clicks OK, the Common Dialogs control returns the printer's device context and the attributes of the desired printout to the calling program through the following properties:

- **Copies** Specifies the number of copies to print

- **FromPage** Specifies the page on which to start printing

- **ToPage** Specifies the page on which to stop printing

- **hDC** Specifies the device context for the selected printer. The RichTextBox control's Print method, for example, requires an *hDC* argument to tell it where to send its printout (see the description of the RichTextBox control in the next chapter).

When the Print common dialog box is closed, the application reads the values of these properties to determine the settings specified by the user.

You can also set the value of any of the previous properties before calling the ShowPrinter method so that initial settings will appear when the dialog box is first opened. The Flags property of the Print common dialog box enables you to specify these initial settings. These values are shown in Table 8.5.

TABLE 8.5: Flag Constants for the Print Common Dialog Box

Constant	Value	Description
cdlPDAllPages	&H0	Returns or sets the state of the All Pages Option button
cdlPDCollate	&H10	Returns or sets the state of the Collate checkbox
cdlPDDisablePrintToFile	&H80000	Disables the Print to File checkbox
cdlPDHidePrintToFile	&H100000	Hides the Print to File checkbox
cdlPDNoPageNums	&H8	Disables the Pages Option button and the associated edit control
cdlPDNoSelection	&H4	Disables the Selection Option button
cdlPDNoWarning	&H80	Prevents a warning message from being displayed when there is no default printer
cdlPDPageNums	&H2	Returns or sets the state of the Pages Option button
cdlPDPrintSetup	&H40	Causes the system to display the Print Setup dialog box rather than the Print dialog box.
cdlPDPrintToFile	&H20	Returns or sets the state of the Print to File checkbox
cdlPDReturnDC	&H100	Returns a device context for the printer selection made in the Printer dialog box. If this flag is set, the device context is returned in the dialog box's hDC property.
cdlPDReturnDefault	&H400	Returns the name of the default printer
cdlPDReturnIC	&H200	Returns an information context for the printer selected in the dialog box. An information context provides a fast way to get information about the device without creating a device context. The information context is returned in the dialog box's hDC property.
cdlPDSelection	&H1	Activates the Pages option on the Print dialog box, so that the user can specify a range of pages to be printed
cdlPDUseDevModeCopies	&H40000	If a printer driver doesn't support multiple copies, setting this flag disables the Number of Copies control in the Print dialog box. If a driver does support multiple copies, setting this flag indicates that the requested number of copies is stored in the Copies property.

To experiment with the various settings of the Print common dialog box, you can use the Print tab of the CDBox application, shown in Figure 8.12.

TIP	The constant *cdlPDSelection* will have no effect on the appearance of the dialog box, unless the Min and Max properties have already been set. The user can set page numbers in the range of Min to Max only.

FIGURE 8.12:

Switch to the Print tab of the CDBox application to experiment with the various settings of the Print common dialog box.

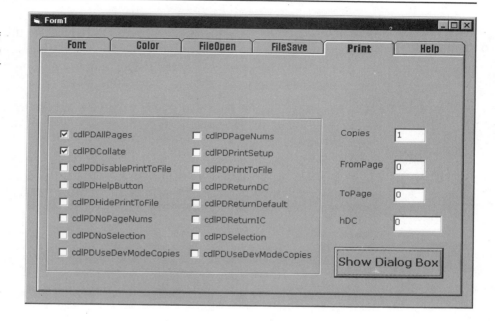

The Help Common Dialog Box

The Help common dialog box is as simple to use as the other ones, but you must first prepare your Help files. I won't discuss how to build Help files in this book; you can purchase many specialized tools for this task. If you don't have your own Help files, you can use ones that come with an application like Visual Basic. Visual Basic's Help file is called VB6. You don't have to specify an extension or a path; WinHelp knows where the Help files are located.

The basic properties of the Help common dialog box are the following:

- **HelpFile**   Specifies the filename of a Windows Help file that will be used to display online Help. This file must be supplied by your application, but for the purposes of learning the Help common dialog box, you can use any Help files already on your hard drive.

- **HelpCommand**   Sets or returns the type of Help requested. The values of this property are listed in Table 8.6. The constants listed in the table look like flags, but they are actually parameters for the HelpCommand property. You can combine multiple commands by using the OR operator or by adding them together.

- **HelpContextID**   Sets or returns a context number for an object. This ID is a number that tells WinHelp where in the Help file it will find the pages describing the specific topic. If you've created a Windows Help file for your application, Visual Basic searches the Help file for the topic identified by the current context ID when a user opens the Help common dialog box (by pressing the F1 key, for instance).

- **HelpKey**   Sets or returns the keyword that identifies the requested Help topic. To use this property, you must also set the HelpCommand property to *cdlHelpKey*.

TABLE 8.6:   Values of the Common Dialogs Control's HelpCommand Property

Constant	Value	Description
cdlHelpCommand	&H102&	Executes a Help macro
cdlHelpContents	&H3&	Displays the Help contents topic as defined by the Contents option in the [OPTION] section of the HPJ file
cdlHelpContext	&H1&	Displays Help for a particular context. When using this setting, you must also specify a context for using the HelpContext property.
cdlHelpContextPopup	&H8&	Displays a particular Help topic in a pop-up window identified by a context number defined in the [MAP] section of the HPJ file
cdlHelpForceFile	&H9&	Ensures that WinHelp displays the correct Help file. If the correct Help file is currently displayed, no action occurs. If the incorrect Help file is displayed, WinHelp opens the correct file.
cdlHelpHelpOnHelp	&H4&	Displays Help for using the Help application itself
cdlHelpIndex	&H3&	Displays the index of the specified Help file. An application should use this value only for a Help file with a single index.
cdlHelpKey	&H101&	Displays Help for a particular keyword. When using this setting, you must also specify a keyword for using the HelpKey property.
cdlHelpPartialKey	&H105&	Displays the topic found in the keyword list that matches the keyword passed in the dwData parameter if there is one exact match. If more than one match exists, the Search dialog box is displayed with the topics listed in the Go To list box. If no match exists, the Search dialog box is displayed. To display the Search dialog box without passing a keyword, use a long pointer to an empty string.

Continued on next page

TABLE 8.6 CONTINUED: Values of the Common Dialogs Control's HelpCommand Property

Constant	Value	Description
cdlHelpQuit	&H2&	Notifies the Help application that the specified Help file is no longer in use
cdlHelpSetContents	&H5&	Determines which content's topic will be displayed when a user presses the F1 key
cdlHelpSetIndex	&H5&	Sets the context specified by the HelpContext property as the current index for the Help file. Used with Help files with more than one index.

You can use the CDBox application to experiment with some of the Windows Help files (see Figure 8.13). They are all located in the Help folder under the Windows folder, and you need to specify only their name in the Help File box. If you set the *cdlHelpIndex* flag, the Index tab of the Help file is opened automatically. Or you can check the *cdlHelpKey* flag and supply a key such as "text" in the Help Key box. The Help dialog box opens the specified Help file, locates the topic, and takes you there.

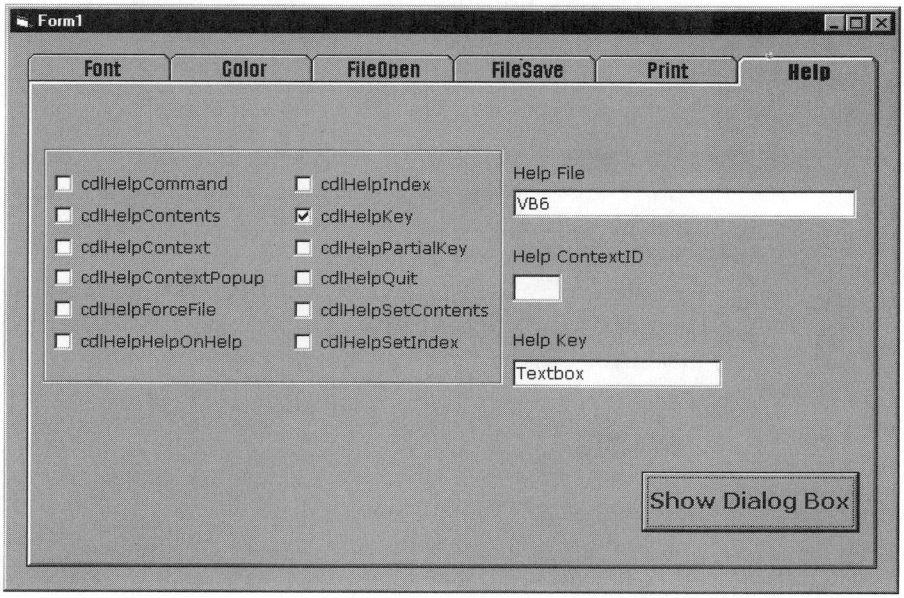

FIGURE 8.13:

Switch to the Help tab of the CDBox application to experiment with the various settings of the Help common dialog box.

The TreeView and ListView Controls

The last two ActiveX controls we're going to explore in this chapter are among the more advanced ones, and they are certainly more difficult to program than the previous ones. If you're new to Visual Basic or programming, you may find this material over your head. You can safely skip the rest of this chapter and come back to it after you've learned more about Visual Basic and familiarized yourself with the topic of object programming. The two controls discussed in this section, however, are the basic makings of unique applications, as you'll see in the examples.

The TreeView and ListView controls implement two of the more advanced data structures (a topic that's not terribly popular even among computer science students). These controls were designed to hide much of the complexity of the data structures they implement, and they do this very well. However, they are more difficult to use than the other controls.

I will start with a general discussion of the two controls to help you understand what they do and when to use them. A basic understanding of the data structures they implement is also required to use them efficiently in your applications. Then, I'll discuss their members and demonstrate how to use the controls. If you find the examples too difficult to understand, you can always postpone the use of these controls in your applications. Some of the code I will present in this chapter can be used as is in many situations, so you should take a look at the examples and see if you can incorporate them in your applications.

In Chapter 5, you learned that the ListBox control is a simple control for storing string items. The items of a ListBox control can be sorted, but they don't have any particular structure. I'm sure most of you wish the ListBox control had more "features," such as the means to store structured items or additional information along with each item and display them at will. For instance, a list with city and state names should be structured so that each city appears under the corresponding state name. In a ListBox control, you can indent some of the entries, but the control itself can't impose or maintain any structure on its data. The answer to the shortcomings of the ListBox control can be found in the TreeView and ListView controls.

Figure 8.14 shows the TreeView and ListView controls used in tandem. What you see in Figure 8.14 is the Windows Explorer, a utility for examining and navigating your hard disk's structure. The left pane, where the folders are displayed, is a *TreeView*. The folder names are displayed in a manner that reflects their structure on the hard disk. You can expand and contract certain branches and view only the segment(s) of the tree structure you're interested in.

FIGURE 8.14:

The Windows Explorer is made up of a TreeView control (left pane) and a List-View control (right pane).

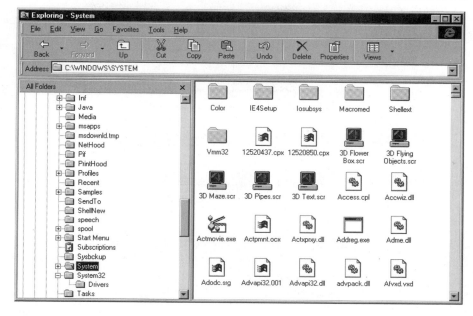

The right pane is a *ListView* control. The items on the ListView control can be displayed in four different ways (Icons, Small Icons, List, or Report). Although most people prefer to look at the contents of the folders as icons, the most useful view is the Report view, which displays not only filenames, but their attributes as well. In the Report view, the list can be sorted according to any of its columns, making it very easy for the user to locate any item based on various criteria (file-type, size, creation date, and so on).

How Tree Structures Work

The TreeView control implements a data structure known as a *tree.* A tree is the most appropriate structure for storing hierarchical information. The organizational chart of most companies is a tree structure. Every person reports to another person above them, all the way to the president or CEO. Figure 8.15 depicts a possible organization of continents, countries, and cities as a tree. Every city belongs to a country and every country to a continent. In the same way, every computer file belongs to a folder that may belong to an even bigger folder. You can't draw large tree structures on paper, but it's possible to create a similar structure in the computer's memory without size limitations.

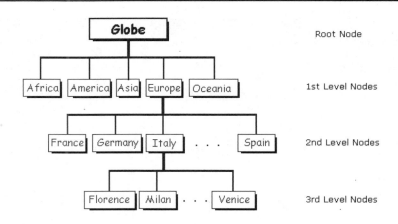

Each item in the tree of Figure 8.15 is called a *node*, and nodes can be nested to any level. Oddly, the top node is the *root* of the tree and the subordinate nodes are called *child nodes*. If you try to visualize this structure as a real tree, think of it as an upside-down tree with the branches emerging from the root.

To locate a city, you must start at the root node and select the continent to which the city belongs. Then, you must find the country in the selected continent to which the city belongs. Finally, you must find the city you're looking for. If it's not under the appropriate country node, then it doesn't exist. You also can traverse a tree in the opposite direction. You can start with a city and find its country. The country node is the city node's *parent node*. Notice that there is only one route from child nodes to their parent nodes, which means you can instantly locate the country or continent of a city. The same data shown in Figure 8.15 are shown in Figure 8.16 on a TreeView control. Only the nodes we're interested in are expanded. The plus sign indicates that the corresponding node contains child nodes. To view them, click a plus sign to expand the node.

The tree structure is ideal for data with parent-child relationships (items that can be described as "belongs to" or "owns"). The continents-countries-cities data is a typical example. The folder structure on a hard disk is another typical example. Any given folder is the child of another folder, or the root folder. If you need a method to traverse the folder structure of your hard disk quickly and conveniently, you must store the folders in a TreeView control. This is exactly what happens when you use the Windows Explorer to navigate your hard disk. Of course, there are other ways to navigate your hard disk (you can do the same with a File Open dialog box), but the TreeView control helps you visualize the structure of the entire disk. With the File Open dialog box, you can only view one segment of the disk, namely, the path to the current folder.

FIGURE 8.16:

The tree of Figure 8.15 implemented with a Tree-View control

FIGURE 8.16:

The tree of Figure 8.15 implemented with a Tree-View control

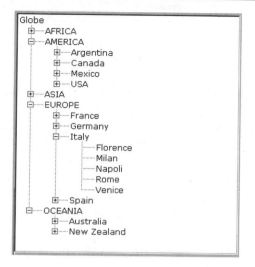

Many programs are actually based on tree structures. Computerized board games use a tree structure to store all possible positions. Every time the computer has to make a move, it locates the board's status on the tree and selects the "best" next move. For instance, in tic-tac-toe, the tree structure that represents the moves in the game has nine nodes on the first level, which correspond to all the possible positions for the first token on the board (the X or O mark). Under each possible initial position, there are eight nodes, which correspond to all the possible positions of the second token on the board (one of the nine positions is already taken). On the second level, there are 9*8, or 72 nodes. On the third level, there are seven nodes under each node that correspond to all the possible positions of the third token, a total of 72*7, or 504 nodes on this level, and so on. In each node, you can store a value that indicates whether the corresponding move is good or bad. When the computer has to make a move, it traverses the tree to locate the current status of the board, and then it makes a good move.

Of course, tic-tac-toe is a very simple game. In principle, you could design a chess-playing game using a tree. This tree, however, would grow so large so quickly that it couldn't be stored in any reasonable amount of memory. Moreover, scanning the nodes of this enormous tree would be a slow process. If you also consider that chess moves aren't good or bad (there are better and not so good moves), and you must look ahead many moves to decide which move is the best for the current status of the board, you'll realize that this ad-hoc approach is totally impractical. Practically speaking, such a program requires either infinite resources or infinite time. That's why the chess-playing algorithms use *heuristic approaches* which store every recorded chess game and consult this database to pick the best next move.

Maintaining a tree structure is a fundamental operation in software design; computer science students spend a good deal of their studies implementing tree structures. Even the efficient implementation of a tree structure is a research subject. Fortunately, with Visual Basic you don't have to implement tree structures on your own. The TreeView control is a mechanism for storing hierarchically structured data packaged as an ActiveX control. The TreeView control hides (or *encapsulates* in object-oriented terminology) the details of the implementation and allows you to set up tree structures with a few lines of code. In short, all the gain without the pain. You may find this too good to be true, but if you've ever had to implement tree structures, you'll appreciate the simplicity of the TreeView control.

Programming the TreeView control is not as simple as programming other controls, but keep in mind that the TreeView control implements a complicated data structure. It's far simpler to program the TreeView control than to implement tree structures from scratch. There's not much you can do about efficiency, and unless you're developing highly specialized applications that rely on tree structures, the TreeView control is your best bet.

The ListView control implements a simpler structure, known as a *list*. A list's items aren't structured in a hierarchy. They are all on the same level and can be traversed serially, one after the other. You can also think of the list as an array, but the list offers more features. A list item can have subitems and can be sorted in many ways. For example, you can set up a list of customer names (the list's items) and assign a number of subitems to each name, like an address, a phone number, and so on. Or, you can set up a list of files with their attributes as subitems. Figure 8.17 shows a Windows folder mapped on a ListView control. Each file is an item and its attributes are the subitems. As you already know, you can sort this list by filename, size, file type, and so on. All you have to do is click the header of the corresponding column. You can also display the list of files in different views: as icons, as a list of filenames only, or as a report (the view shown in Figure 8.17). All this functionality is built into the ListView control, and all you have to do is populate the control and set various properties to change the sort order or the view.

The ListView control is a glorified ListBox control. If all you need is a control to store sorted strings, use a ListBox control. If you want more features, like storing multiple items per row, sorting them in different ways, or locating them based on any subitem's value, then you must consider the ListView control. It's simpler to program than the TreeView control, but still more involved than the simple ListBox control.

FIGURE 8.17:

A folder's files displayed in a TreeView control (Report view)

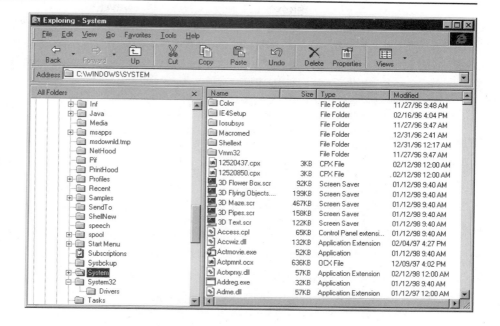

To program the TreeView and ListView controls, you must understand the concept of collections. You can't simply add items to these controls with the AddItem method as you'd do with the ListBox control. Each level of nodes in the TreeView control is a *collection*. Each item in this collection represents a node, which may have child nodes. Each node's child nodes form another collection. Each item in this collection is a *Node object*, which in turn may have its own child Form, which is represented by another collection, and so on. We'll discuss these techniques in detail, but there's something else I would like to mention briefly and get out of the way as early as possible.

The TreeView and ListView controls are commonly used along with the Image-List control. The ImageList control is a very simple control for storing images, so they can be retrieved quickly and used at runtime. Before we get into the details of the TreeView and ListView controls, a quick overview of the ImageList control is in order.

The ImageList Control

The ImageList control is a really simple control that stores a number of images used by other controls at runtime. For example, a TreeView control may use a number of icons to identify its nodes. The simplest and quickest method of setting up the Tree-View is to create an ImageList with icons to use. The ImageList control maintains a series of bitmaps in its memory that the TreeView control can access very quickly at runtime. Keep in mind that the ImageList control can't be used on its own and remains invisible at runtime.

The images stored in the ImageList control can be used for any purpose by your application, but in this book, we'll use them in conjunction with the TreeView and ListView controls, which use them to identify their nodes and list items, respectively. So, before we start the discussion of the TreeView and ListView controls, let's look at how to store images in an ImageList control and how to use this control in your code.

To use the ImageList control in a project, add the Windows Common Controls–2 component. To load images to an ImageList control, right-click it and select Properties. On the first tab of the control's property pages, specify the size of the images, which can have one of the following values: 16 × 16, 32 × 32, 48 × 48, or Custom. If you check the Custom checkbox you must supply the desired dimensions, which will be the same for all images.

On the second tab, shown in Figure 8.18, you can add as many images as you need to the control. To add a new image, click the Insert Picture button and you'll be asked to select an image with a standard File Open dialog box. You can add all types of images recognized by Visual Basic (BMP, GIF, JPEG files), as well as icons (ICO files) and cursors (CUR files).

FIGURE 8.18:

Use the Images tab of the control's property pages to add images to the Image-List control.

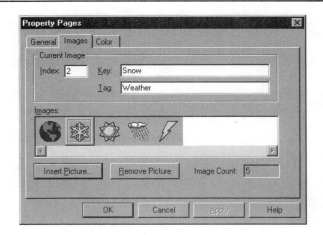

Each image stored in the ImageList control can be identified by an Index value or a key. The Index value is determined by the position of the image in the control and the Key value must be supplied on the Images tab. You can also set a tag for each image.

The other method of adding images to an ImageList control is to call the Add method of the *ListImages* collection, which contains all the images stored in the control. To add an image at runtime, you must make sure that the image file exists on the target computer and then call the Add method as follows:

```
ImageList1.ListImages.Add index, key, picture
```

The arguments of the Add method are the same properties you can set on the control's property pages at design time. To specify additional properties such as the Tag property, use the following alternate syntax of the Add method:

```
Set thisImage = ImageList1.ListImages.Add(index, key, picture)
```

The variable *thisImage* is a ListImage object and it's declared as:

```
Dim thisImage As ListImage
```

The Add method returns a ListImage object representing the newly added image. To set the image's Tag property, use the statement:

```
ThisImage.Tag = "Weather Element"
```

ListImages is a collection of Picture objects, not the file where the pictures are stored. Therefore, the last argument of the Add method must the Picture property of another control (a PictureBox control, for example). To add an image from a file, you must use the LoadPicture function (the same function you'd use to load an image on a PictureBox control). To load the image stored in the "Sun.bmp" file in the application's folder, use this statement:

```
ImageList1.ListImages.Add 0, "SUN", LoadPicture(App.Path & "\Sun.bmp"
```

To use one of the pictures stored in the ImageList control, extract the corresponding item's Picture property and assign it to the Picture property of another control:

```
Picture1.Picture = ImageList1.ListImages(0).Picture
```

You can also access the properties of the Picture object, such as its dimensions, with the following statements:

```
ImageList1.ListImages(0).Picture.Width
ImageList1.ListImages(0).Picture.Height
```

As you'll see in the following sections, the simplest method of accessing the pictures of the ImageList control is to assign the control to the ImageList property of a control. Not all controls have an ImageList property, but the two controls we'll explore in the following section do.

Using the TreeView Control

Let's start our discussion with a few simple properties that you can set at design time through the control's property pages. To experiment with the settings of the property pages, open the TView1 project in this chapter's folder on the CD. The project's main Form is shown in Figure 8.19. After setting some properties (they are discussed next), run the project, and click the Populate Sorted button to see the effects these property settings have on the control. We'll discuss the other buttons on the Form in the following sections.

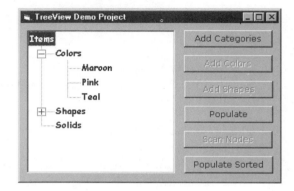

With the TView1 project open in the Visual Basic IDE, right-click the control and from the shortcut menu select Properties. The TreeView control's property pages contain three tabs: the Font and Picture tabs (which are trivial) and the General tab (see Figure 8.20).

On the General tab, you can set the style of the list, as well a few general attributes. The *Style* property of the TreeView control can have one of the values shown in Table 8.7. This property determines the appearance of the data on the control and the navigation model too. Set the TreeView control's style on the first property page, run the project, and then open the nodes Shapes and Colors to see how they are displayed. Stop the project, change the Style property, and run the project to test all the settings.

TABLE 8.7: Settings of the TreeView Control's Style Property

Constant	Value	Description
tvwTextOnly	0	Text only
tvwPictureText	1	Picture and text
tvwPlusMinusText	2	Plus/minus and text
tvwPlusPictureText	3	Plus/minus, picture, and text
tvwTreelinesText	4	Treelines and text
tvwTreelinesPictureText	5	Treelines, picture, and text
tvwTreelinesPlusMinusText	6	Treelines, plus/minus, and text
tvwTreelinesPlusMinusPictureText	7	Treelines, plus/minus, picture, and text

The checkboxes on the right let you specify the general attributes of the control:

- **HideSelection**   This property determines whether the selected item will remain highlighted when the focus is moved to another control.

- **Sorted**   This property determines whether the items in the control will be automatically sorted or not.

NOTE   Unlike the Sorted property of the ListBox control, the Sorted property of the Tree-View control must be set either at design time or at runtime. When you set the Sorted property to True, the existing items will be sorted, and any new ones will be inserted automatically in the proper positions in the control. If you set it back to False, the already sorted elements won't be rearranged. Only the new elements will be appended to the end of the tree as they are entered.

- **FullRowSelect**   This True/False value determines whether the entire row of the selected item will be highlighted and whether an item will be selected even if the user clicks outside the item's text.

- **CheckBoxes**   If this option is enabled, a checkbox appears in front of each item. If the control will allow the user to select multiple items, you should consider placing checkboxes in front of each item.

- **SingleSel**   Check this property to enable multiple item selection (to select multiple items click their name while holding down the Shift or Ctrl key).

- **Scroll**   This True/False value determines whether the appropriate scrollbars will be attached automatically to the control should the control's contents exceed its dimensions.

- **HotTracking**   This True/False value determines whether items are highlighted as the pointer hovers over them. When this property is True, the ListView control behaves like a Web document with the items acting as hyperlinks.

Adding New Items

The items or nodes on a TreeView control are members of the Nodes collection. To access the Nodes collection use the following expression where *Treeview1* is the control's name:

```
TreeView1.Nodes
```

As a collection, Nodes exposes the following members (for more information on collections see Chapter 4):

- **Add method**   Adds a new node to the Nodes collection

- **Count property**   Returns the number of nodes in the Nodes collection

- **Clear method**   Removes all the nodes from the collection

- **Item property**   Retrieves a node specified by an Index value or a key

- **Remove method**   Removes a node from the Nodes collection

The Nodes collection's methods have straightforward syntax, except for the Add method. To add a new node with the Add method, you must specify its position in the hierarchy, the node's text (which will appear on the control), its key, an image that will be displayed in front of the node, and an image that will be displayed when the node is selected. Here's the complete syntax of the Add method:

```
Nodes.Add Relative, Relationship, Key, Text, Image, SelectedImage
```

Since most of the arguments are optional (only the *Text* argument is required), let's start with the simpler forms of the Add method. To add the first-level items to a TreeView control, use this syntax:

```
TreeView1.Nodes.Add,  , "node's key", "node's text"
```

You may omit any of the optional arguments, but you must still insert the appropriate commas to indicate the absence of the corresponding argument(s).

In this and the following sections, we're going to examine the code of the TView1 project. The Add Categories button adds the three top-level nodes to the TreeView control with the following statements.

Code 8.3:   **The Add Categories Button's Code**

```
Private Sub Command1_Click()
    TreeView1.Nodes.Add , , "SHAPE", "Shapes"
    TreeView1.Nodes.Add , , "SOLID", "Solids"
    TreeView1.Nodes.Add , , "COLOR", "Colors"
End Sub
```

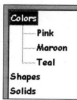

When these statements are executed, three nodes will be added to the list. The strings "COLOR", "SHAPE", and "SOLID" are keys of the corresponding nodes. They are required if you want to place items under the Colors, Shapes, and Solids nodes. After clicking the Add Categories button, your TreeView control looks like the one shown at the left.

To add a few nodes under the node Colors, use the following statements:

Code 8.4:   **The Add Colors Button's Code**

```
Private Sub Command2_Click()
    TreeView1.Nodes.Add "COLOR", tvwChild, , "Pink"
    TreeView1.Nodes.Add "COLOR", tvwChild, , "Maroon"
    TreeView1.Nodes.Add "COLOR", tvwChild, , "Teal"
End Sub
```

When these statements are executed, three nodes will be added under the Colors node, but the Colors node won't be expanded; therefore, its child nodes won't be visible. To see its child nodes, you must double-click the Colors node to expand it. The same TreeView control with its Colors node expanded is shown to the left.

The lines of Code 8.4 are the Add Colors Command button's Click event handler. Run the project, click the first button (Add Categories) and then the second button (Add Colors). If you click the Add Colors button first, you'll get an error message, indicating that there's no node with the "COLOR" key. Child nodes can't be inserted unless their parent nodes exist already. (The TView1 project's code on the CD contains a few additional statements that disable the buttons that generate similar run-time errors.)

The syntax of the three statements for both buttons is identical. The first argument is the key of the node, under which you want to place the new one. The second argument indicates the relationship between the node specified in the first argument and the new node. Since we want the color names to appear under the Colors node, their relationship is *tvwChild* (the new nodes are children of the existing node). Because we aren't going to place any nodes under the color names, there's no reason for the color names to have a key, so the third argument is omitted. The fourth argument is the text of the node, and the remaining arguments are also omitted (the last two arguments, which are images, will be discussed later in this chapter).

To add child nodes under the Shapes node, use the following statements. This is the Shapes button's Click event handler.

Code 8.5: **The Add Shapes Button's Code**

```
Private Sub Command3_Click()
    TreeView1.Nodes.Add "SHAPE", tvwChild, , "Square"
    TreeView1.Nodes.Add "SHAPE", tvwChild, , "Triangle"
    TreeView1.Nodes.Add "SHAPE", tvwChild, , "Circle"
End Sub
```

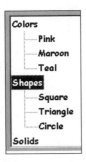

Add a third Command button on the Form, name it Add Shapes, and insert these lines in its Click event handler. If you run the project and click the three buttons in the order in which they appear on the Form, the TreeView control will be populated with Colors and Shapes. If you double-click the items Colors and Shapes, the TreeView control's contents will be expanded and the control will look like the one shown to the left.

You'll notice that the child nodes have treelines in front of them, but their parents don't have the plus sign, which indicates that a node has child nodes and can be expanded. It's always a good idea to display a plus symbol in front of the nodes that have child nodes. Let's revise the code we've written so far, to display all the nodes under a header called Items.

First, we must add the header, a node that will contain all other nodes as children:

```
TreeView1.Nodes.Add , , "ITEM", "Items"
```

As you probably expected, there is no parent node or relationship for this node, just a key and the node's text.

Then, we must revise the statements that add the first-level items. They now belong to the Items node, so their first argument *(Relative)* must be the key of the parent node and their second argument *(Relationship)* must be *tvwChild*. Revise the Add Categories button's Click event handler as follows:

```
TreeView1.Nodes.Add "ITEM", tvwChild, "COLOR", "Colors"
TreeView1.Nodes.Add "ITEM", tvwChild, "SHAPE", "Shapes"
TreeView1.Nodes.Add "ITEM", tvwChild, "SOLID", "Solids"
```

The remaining statements need to be modified. They add child nodes to existing nodes. By making the Colors node a child of the Items node, all the child nodes for Colors will also follow. The same is true for the Shapes node.

Since the TreeView control's nodes aren't expanded by default, you can expand the Item node from within your code with the following statement:

```
TreeView1.Nodes.Item("ITEM").Expanded = True
```

As I mentioned already, the items of the Nodes collection can be accessed by an Index value or their key. The last statement expands the top node in the collection, but none of its child nodes. To expand all the nodes that have child nodes, you must scan the items of the Nodes collection and set their Expanded property to True. You'll learn how to scan the nodes of a TreeView control later in this chapter..

Place a new Command button on the Form, name it **Populate**, and insert the following statements in its Click event handler:

Code 8.6:   **The Populate Button's Code**

```
Private Sub Command4_Click()
    TreeView1.Nodes.Add , , "ITEM", "Items"
    TreeView1.Nodes.Add "ITEM", tvwChild, "SHAPE", "Shapes"
    TreeView1.Nodes.Add "ITEM", tvwChild, "SOLID", "Solids"
    TreeView1.Nodes.Add "ITEM", tvwChild, "COLOR", "Colors"

    TreeView1.Nodes.Add "COLOR", tvwChild, , "Pink"
    TreeView1.Nodes.Add "COLOR", tvwChild, , "Maroon"
    TreeView1.Nodes.Add "COLOR", tvwChild, , "Teal"

    TreeView1.Nodes.Add "SHAPE", tvwChild, , "Square"
    TreeView1.Nodes.Add "SHAPE", tvwChild, , "Triangle"
    TreeView1.Nodes.Add "SHAPE", tvwChild, , "Circle"
    TreeView1.Nodes.Item("ITEM").Expanded = True
End Sub
```

When the Populate button is clicked, it will produce the output shown on the left. If you open the TView1 project and examine its code, you'll see that it contains additional statements that enable various Command buttons. Most of the buttons on the Form are initially disabled to prevent user errors. For example, the Add Colors and Add Shapes buttons are initially disabled because you can't add child nodes before their parent nodes exist. You'll also see the statement `TreeView1.Nodes.Clear` in several buttons' handlers. This statement clears the contents of the TreeView control, so that the program won't keep adding the same items every time its buttons are clicked.

In the examples of the next section, we'll use only the *tvwChild* value for the *Relationship* argument of the Add method. The possible values of the *Relationship* argument are shown in Table 8.8.

TABLE 8.8: Settings of the *Relationship* Argument

Constant	Value	Description
tvwFirst	0	Places the new node before all other nodes at the same level of the node specified by the *Relative* argument
tvwLast	1	Places the new node after all other nodes at the same level of the node specified by the *Relative* argument
tvwNext	2	(Default) Places the new node after the node specified by the *Relative* argument
tvwPrevious	3	Places the new node before the node specified by the *Relative* argument
tvwChild	4	Instructs the new node to become a child of the node specified by the *Relative* argument

NOTE   Notice that the *Relationship* argument specifies the relationship of the new node to an existing one, which is specified by the *Relative* argument. The value *tvwChild* specifies that the new node is a child of the node specified by the *Relative* argument, and the value *tvwNext* specifies that the new node must be inserted after the node specified by the *Relative* argument.

Assigning Images to Nodes

The last two arguments of the Add method, *Image* and *SelectedImage*, are the two pictures that will appear in front of the node. The Image picture will appear by default in front of the node and the SelectedImage picture will replace the default picture when the node is selected. These two arguments are Picture objects; they can be the Picture property of a PictureBox control or they can be loaded from a file at runtime with the LoadPicture function. For example, to assign the bitmap stored in the C:\CONTROLS\IMAGES\SHAPES1.BMP file to a new node, use a statement like the following one:

```
TreeView1.Nodes.Add "SHAPE", tvwChild, , "Square", _
        LoadPicture("c:\controls\images\shapes1.bmp")
```

The simplest method, however, is to set up an ImageList control, populate it with the images that you'll later assign to the nodes of the TreeView control, and use those images. To do this, add an ImageList control to the Form, add to it all the images (usually icons) you want to use with the TreeView control, and then assign the ImageList control to the ImageList property of the TreeView control.

The following statements set up an ImageList control with three small images for the Globe project (discussed in the next section) and assign it to the TreeView1 control's ImageList property. The code assumes that the three images are stored in the same folder as the project that uses them:

```
ImageList1.ListImages.Add , , LoadPicture(App.Path & "\shape.bmp")
ImageList1.ListImages.Add , , LoadPicture(App.Path & "\color.bmp")
ImageList1.ListImages.Add , , LoadPicture(App.Path & "\solid.bmp")
TreeView1.ImageList = ImageList1
```

To add three new nodes and assign the three bitmaps to them, use the following statements:

```
TreeView1.Nodes.Add , , "SHAPE", "Shapes", 1
TreeView1.Nodes.Add , , "SOLID", "Solids", 2
TreeView1.Nodes.Add , , "COLOR", "Colors", 3
```

The numbers correspond to the indices of the bitmaps in the ImageList control. You can also use the keys of the various images if you assign keys when you add the images to the ImageList control.

Sorting Items

The last property demonstrated by the TView1 project is the Sorted property, which sorts the child nodes of the node to which it's applied. When you set the Sorted property of a node to True, every child node you attach to it will be inserted automatically in alphabetical order. The Sorted property, however, won't affect the other nodes on the same level or a child node's children. In other words, a child node doesn't inherit its parent's Sorted property setting. So each time you add a node that you anticipate will have its own child nodes, set its Sorted property to True.

The Populate Sorted button's code is shown in Code 8.7. This handler populates the control with the same data as the Populate button, but it also sets to True the Sorted property of all nodes that have child nodes. Notice that the Sorted property of the node Solids doesn't need to be set because this node doesn't have any children. The same is true for the end nodes.

Code 8.7: **The Populate Sorted Button's Code**

```
Private Sub Command6_Click()
Dim thisNode As node

    Set thisNode = TreeView1.Nodes.Add(, , "ITEM", "Items")
    thisNode.Sorted = True
    Set thisNode = TreeView1.Nodes.Add("ITEM", tvwChild, "SHAPE", "Shapes")
    thisNode.Sorted = True
    Set thisNode = TreeView1.Nodes.Add("ITEM", tvwChild, "SOLID", "Solids")
    thisNode.Sorted = True
    Set thisNode = TreeView1.Nodes.Add("ITEM", tvwChild, "COLOR", "Colors")
    thisNode.Sorted = True

    TreeView1.Nodes.Add "COLOR", tvwChild, , "Pink"
    TreeView1.Nodes.Add "COLOR", tvwChild, , "Maroon"
    TreeView1.Nodes.Add "COLOR", tvwChild, , "Teal"

    TreeView1.Nodes.Add "SHAPE", tvwChild, , "Square"
    TreeView1.Nodes.Add "SHAPE", tvwChild, , "Triangle"
    TreeView1.Nodes.Add "SHAPE", tvwChild, , "Circle"
    TreeView1.Nodes.Item("ITEM").Expanded = True
End Sub
```

NOTE If you reset the Sorted property to False and add another node, it will be appended to the end of the existing (and sorted) nodes. This is how new child nodes are added to a parent node when its Sorted property is False.

Enumerating Nodes

Storing items in a TreeView control is one of the basic operations you can perform with the control. But how do you retrieve the nodes of the tree? The simplest method is to scan the Nodes collection, which contains all the nodes of the tree. The most appropriate loop for scanning a collection is the For Each...Next loop, which is shown next:

```
Dim node As Node
For Each node In TreeView1.Nodes
    {process node}
Next
```

The *node* variable represents a different node at each iteration. To process the current node, use the *node* variable's members. The following statement will print the node's text on the Immediate window:

```
Debug.Print node.Text
```

The Scan Nodes button prints all the nodes in the order they were entered. Its Click event handler is shown next:

```
Dim node As Node
For Each node In TreeView1.Nodes
    Debug.Print node.Text
Next
```

This loop enumerates the Nodes collection of the control, and the variable *node* returns the next node at each iteration. The following strings will appear in the Immediate window:

```
Items
Colors
Shapes
Solids
Pink
Maroon
Teal
Square
Triangle
Circle
```

The node names will appear in the order they were entered without any indication of their structure. A better technique for scanning a tree and enumerating its items will be discussed later on in the section "Scanning the TreeView Control." In the next section, we're going to put together all the information presented so far to build a "real" application based on the TreeView control.

VB6 at Work: The Globe Project

The Globe project, which you can find in this chapter's folder on the CD, demonstrates many of the techniques we've discussed so far. It's not the simplest example of a TreeView control, and its code is lengthy, but it will help you understand how to manipulate nodes at runtime. As you know by now, TreeView is not a simple control, so I would like to end this section with an advanced example that you can use as a starting point for your own custom applications. You'll also see how to save the nodes of a TreeView control to a disk file and retrieve them later, a basic operation that can't be performed with a method call (as one might expect).

The Globe project contains a single Form, which is shown in Figure 8.21. The TreeView control at the left contains a tree structure with continents, countries, and cities, with a rather obvious structure. Each city belongs to a country and each country belongs to a continent. The control is populated at runtime from within the Form's Load event. When a node is selected in the TreeView control, its text is displayed on the TextBox controls at the bottom of the Form. When a continent name is selected, the continent's name appears in the first TextBox and the other two TextBoxes are empty. When a country is selected, its name appears in the second TextBox and its continent appears in the first TextBox. Finally, when a city is selected, it appears in the third TextBox, along with its country and continent in the other two TextBoxes.

You can also use the TextBox controls to add new nodes. To add a new continent, just supply the name of the continent in the first TextBox. To add a new country, supply its name in the second TextBox and the name of the continent it belongs to in the first one. Finally, to add a city, supply a continent, country, and city name in the three TextBoxes.

NOTE   You should be aware of a limitation in the Globe application: you can't add identically named cities in different countries. In other words, you can't have nodes like Europe-Greece-Athens and America-United States-Athens. You'll soon learn about the design considerations that impose this limitation. In the next section, you'll see how this limitation can be overcome.

Run the Globe application and expand the continents and countries to see the tree structure of the data stored in the control. Add new nodes to the control, and enumerate its nodes by clicking the appropriate button on the right-hand side of the Form. These buttons list the nodes at a given level (continents, countries and cities). When you add new nodes, the code places them in their proper place in the list. If you specify a new city and a new country, then a new country node will be created under the specified continent and a new city node will be inserted under the specified country. Or, you can add a new country node and then a city node. Just remember that country names and city names must be unique throughout the tree structure, not only in the continent or country to which they belong.

Coding the Globe Project   Let's take a look at how the Globe project is coded. We'll start by looking at the code that populates the TreeView control. First, the root node (Globe) is added. This is the top-level node and all other nodes are children of this node:

```
Set Nd = TreeView1.Nodes.Add(, , "GLOBE", "Globe", 1)
Nd.Tag = "GLOBE"
Nd.Sorted = True
```

FIGURE 8.21:

The Globe project demonstrates how to populate and search a TreeView control, as well as how to add new nodes at runtime.

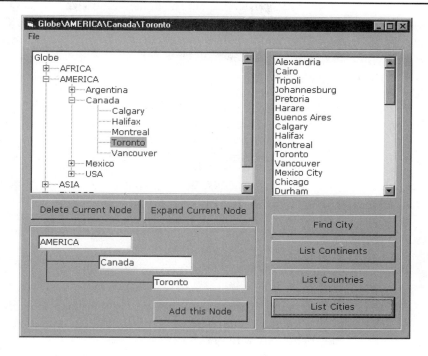

Notice that the reference to the newly created node returned by the Add method is stored to the *Nd* variable. This node's tag is set to "GLOBE" and its Sorted property is set to True. This means that the continent names placed directly under the Globe node will be automatically sorted.

Then, the code adds the continents directly under the Globe node. The continents are child nodes of the node whose key is "GLOBE". This is done using the following statements (I'm only showing the statements for adding the first two continents; the remaining continents are added with similar statements):

```
Set Nd = TreeView1.Nodes.Add("GLOBE", tvwChild, "EUROPE", "EUROPE", 2)
Nd.Tag = "Continents"
Nd.Sorted = True    ' this statement sorts all countries under EUROPE
Set Nd = TreeView1.Nodes.Add("GLOBE", tvwChild, "ASIA", "ASIA", 2)
Nd.Tag = "Continents"
Nd.Sorted = True    ' this statement sorts all countries under ASIA
```

After the continents are in place, the code adds the countries to each continent, and cities to each country. Here are the statements that add the "Germany" node:

```
Set Nd = TreeView1.Nodes.Add("EUROPE", tvwChild, "GERMANY", "Germany", 3)
Nd.Tag = "Countries"
Nd.Sorted = True    ' this statement sorts all German cities
```

Germany is placed under the node with the key "EUROPE", its Tag property is set to "Countries", and its Sorted property is set to True. This means that all German cities will be sorted automatically. Finally, the following statements insert city nodes under Germany:

```
Set Nd = TreeView1.Nodes.Add("GERMANY", tvwChild, "BERLIN", "Berlin")
Nd.Tag = "Cities"
Set Nd = TreeView1.Nodes.Add("GERMANY", tvwChild, "MUNICH", "Munich")
Nd.Tag = "Cities"
```

Notice that you don't have to set the Sorted property of the city nodes, because they don't have child nodes. The cities will appear sorted because the Sorted property of the country node they belong to has its Sorted property set to True. As you can see, populating the TreeView control from within the application's code is straightforward. As long as you assign meaningful keys to the items and add them in their natural order, you can create very elaborate tree structures. You can create long trees with many branches, which you couldn't possibly draw on paper. Yet, with the navigational tools built into the control, it's still easy to traverse them and locate the information you need.

The keys of the nodes are the same as their text (keys are in uppercase to simplify searching). That's why you can't have two cities with the same name, even if they belong to different countries.

The following code segment adds Africa and all its child nodes to the Globe node.

Code 8.8: **Adding the Nodes of Africa**

```
Set Nd = TreeView1.Nodes.Add("GLOBE", tvwChild, "AFRICA", "AFRICA", 2)
Nd.Tag = "Continents"
Nd.Sorted = True    ' this statement sorts all countries under AFRICA
Set Nd = TreeView1.Nodes.Add("AFRICA", tvwChild, "EGYPT", "Egypt", 3)
Nd.Tag = "Countries"
Nd.Sorted = True    ë this statement sorts all cities under EGYPT
Set Nd = TreeView1.Nodes.Add("EGYPT", tvwChild, "CAIRO", "Cairo")
Nd.Tag = "Cities"
Set Nd = TreeView1.Nodes.Add("EGYPT", tvwChild, "ALEXANDRIA", "Alexandria")
Nd.Tag = "Cities"
Set Nd = TreeView1.Nodes.Add("AFRICA", tvwChild, "LIBYA", "Libya", 3)
Nd.Tag = "Countries"
Nd.Sorted = True
Set Nd = TreeView1.Nodes.Add("LIBYA", tvwChild, "TRIPOLI", "Tripoli")
Nd.Tag = "Cities"
Set Nd = TreeView1.Nodes.Add("AFRICA", tvwChild, "SOUTH AFRICA", "South Africa", 3)
Nd.Tag = "Countries"
```

```
Nd.Sorted = True
Set Nd = TreeView1.Nodes.Add("SOUTH AFRICA", tvwChild, "JOHANNESBURG", "Johannesburg")
Nd.Tag = "Cities"
Set Nd = TreeView1.Nodes.Add("SOUTH AFRICA", tvwChild, "PRETORIA", "Pretoria")
Nd.Tag = "Cities"
Set Nd = TreeView1.Nodes.Add("AFRICA", tvwChild, "ZIMBABWE", "Zimbabwe", 3)
Nd.Tag = "Countries"
Nd.Sorted = True
Set Nd = TreeView1.Nodes.Add("ZIMBABWE", tvwChild, "HARARE", "Harare")
Nd.Tag = "Cities"
```

Figure 8.22 shows a segment of a TreeView control and the commands for adding a few of the nodes. The text above the statements shows how to read the arguments of the Add method (that's the trick to understanding where each node belongs). The third argument, *Key,* has a relationship to the first argument, *Relative,* which is specified by the second argument, *Relationship.* The top statement reads "America is a child of Globe"; the next statement reads "Canada is a child of America," and so on.

FIGURE 8.22:

Adding nodes to a TreeView control with the Add method

Adding Nodes to a TreeView control

Retrieving the Selected Node

When the user clicks a node in the *TreeView* control, the *NodeClick* event is triggered. This event reports the node clicked as a Node object, and you can use the object it returns from within the NodeClick event's handler to manipulate the selected node. The event handler shown in Code 8.9 displays the path of the selected node in the three textboxes at the lower-left section of the Form. The continent is displayed in the first textbox, the country in the second textbox, and the city in the third textbox.

The program examines the node's Tag property. If it's "Cities", it displays the Text property on the Text3 control and then extracts its parent with the statement:

```
Set Nd = Nd.Parent
```

The expression Nd.Parent returns the *Nd* node's parent node (which is the continent). This node's Text property is assigned to the Text2 control. Finally, with the same statement, it extracts the country's parent node and displays its Text property in the Text1 control. If the selected node's Tag property is "Countries", the code leaves the last textbox blank and displays only the country and continent names in the other two textboxes, using similar statements.

Code 8.9:   **Processing the Selected Node**

```
Private Sub TreeView1_NodeClick(ByVal Node As ComctlLib.Node)
Dim Nd As Node, childNd As Node
Dim i As Integer

    Text1.Text = ""
    Text2.Text = ""
    Text3.Text = ""
    Set Nd = Node
    Me.Caption = Nd.FullPath
    Nd.Expanded = Not Nd.Expanded
    Set Nd = Node
     If Nd.Tag = "GLOBE" Then Exit Sub
     If Nd.Tag = "Cities" Then
        Text3.Text = Nd.Text
        Set Nd = Nd.Parent
        Text2.Text = Nd.Text
        Set Nd = Nd.Parent
        Text1.Text = Nd.Text
    ElseIf Nd.Tag = "Countries" Then
        Text3.Text = ""
        Text2.Text = Nd.Text
        Set Nd = Nd.Parent
        Text1.Text = Nd.Text
    Else
        Text1.Text = Nd.Text
        Text2.Text = ""
        Text3.Text = ""
    End If
End Sub
```

The code behind Delete Current Node and Expand Current Node is simple. To delete a node, call the node's *Remove* method, passing the node's index as argument. The index of the selected node is given by the property `TreeView1.SelectedItem.Index`. In addition, the event handler must also clear the three TextBox controls. Here's the Delete button's code:

```
Private Sub DeleteNodeBttn_Click()
    TreeView1.Nodes.Remove (TreeView1.SelectedItem.Index)
```

```
        Text1.Text = ""
        Text2.Text = ""
        Text3.Text = ""
    End Sub
```

The other button expands the current node by setting its Expanded property to True:

```
Private Sub ExpandNodeBttn_Click()
    TreeView1.SelectedItem.Expanded = True
End Sub
```

Adding Nodes at Runtime

The Add Node button lets the user add new nodes to the tree at runtime. The number and type of the node(s) added depends on the contents of the TextBox controls:

- If only the Text1 control contains text, then a new continent will be added.

- If the first two TextBox controls contain text, then:
    - If a continent exists, a new country node is added under the specified continent.

    - If a continent doesn't exist, a new continent node is added, then a new country node is added under the continent's node.

- If all three TextBox controls contain text, the program adds a continent node (if needed), then a country node under the continent node (if needed), and finally, a city node under the country node.

Obviously, you can omit a city, or a city and country, but you can't omit a continent name. Likewise, you can't specify a city without a country or a country without a continent. The code will prompt you accordingly when it detects a condition that prevents it from adding the new node for any reason. If the node exists already, then the program selects the existing node and doesn't issue any warnings. The Add Node button's code is shown next.

Code 8.10:   **Adding Nodes at Runtime**

```
Private Sub AddEntry_Click()
Dim newNode As Node
Dim NodeContinent As Node, NodeCountry As Node, NodeCity As Node

On Error Resume Next
    Text1.Text = Trim(Text1.Text)
    Text2.Text = Trim(Text2.Text)
```

```
        Text3.Text = Trim(Text3.Text)
        If Trim(Text1.Text) = "" Then
            MsgBox "You didn't supply a continent name"
            Exit Sub
        End If
        Set newNode = TreeView1.Nodes.Item(UCase$(Text1.Text))
        If Error Then
            Set newNode = TreeView1.Nodes.Add("GLOBE", _
                    tvwChild, UCase$(Text1.Text), Text1.Text, 2)
            newNode.Tag = "Continents"
        End If
        If Trim(Text2.Text) = "" Then Exit Sub
        Set newNode = TreeView1.Nodes.Item(UCase$(Text2.Text))
        If Error Then
            Set newNode = TreeView1.Nodes.Add(UCase$(Text1.Text), _
                    tvwChild, UCase$(Text2.Text), Text2.Text, 3)
            newNode.Tag = "Countries"
        End If
        If Trim(Text3.Text) = "" Then Exit Sub
        Set newNode = TreeView1.Nodes.Item(UCase$(Text3.Text))
        If Error Then
            Set newNode = TreeView1.Nodes.Add(UCase$(Text2.Text), _
                    tvwChild, UCase$(Text3.Text), Text3.Text)
            newNode.Tag = "Cities"
        End If
        TreeView1.SelectedItem = newNode
    End Sub
```

The On Error Resume Next statement tells Visual Basic to continue the execution of
the code with the following statement, should it detect an error:

```
Set newNode = TreeView1.Nodes.Item(UCase$(Text1.Text))
```

The entire subroutine is based on this statement. The code will attempt to access a
node to find out if it exists. The statement retrieves the node that corresponds to
the continent specified in the first TextBox control and assigns the node retrieved
to the *newNode* variable. However, if such a node doesn't exist, a runtime error will
be generated. Without the On Error statement, the application would end here with
an error message.

NOTE   The *Item* method of the Nodes collection retrieves a node based on its key. The
Globe project's code uses the name of the city/country/continent as key (it first
converts to uppercase), which makes searching for a specific node really easy.

Because of the `On Error` statement, the code continues with the following statement that examines the built-in *Error* variable:

```
If Error Then
    Set newNode = TreeView1.Nodes.Add("GLOBE", tvwChild,_
        UCase$(Text1.Text), Text1.Text, 2)
    newNode.Tag = "Continents"
End If
```

If Error is True, the program knows it must add a continent node because it doesn't exist. The same process is repeated for the country and city nodes. The program attempts to retrieve the nodes that correspond to the keys entered by the user in the TextBox controls. If they don't exist, they are added automatically.

As you can see, adding new nodes at runtime isn't really complicated, but you must make sure the node you're about to add doesn't already exist. The Globe application uses the node's Key value to determine whether a node exists or not. Each node's key must be unique, and this raises some problems. For example, how can you add two identically named cities in different countries? The following section describes how to handle this situation.

VB6 at Work: The Revised Globe Project

To add identically named cities under different countries, you must modify the key so that it still identifies the node uniquely. The obvious choice is to prefix the keys of the cities with the names of the countries and continents to which they belong, for example, "Europe-Italy-Venice" and "America-United States-Venice". You'd then be able to add a Venice node under both countries.

This technique comes with a price—it prevents you from locating a city by name instantly. For example, you'd no longer be able to search for "Venice". You would need to know which Venice you were looking for and supply the entire key: "Europe-Italy-Venice" or "America-United States-Venice".

TIP

If the tree isn't very long or the application doesn't search it frequently, there's an even simpler approach to adding two nodes with identical names: don't assign keys to the tree's nodes, and scan the tree with a For. . .Next loop to locate the desired item. It's not a very efficient approach, but it will work on trees of moderate size.

In the MEntries folder under the Globe folder on the CD, you'll find a different version of the Globe project, which uses long keys made up of the continent, country, and city name. The revised Globe project's code is very similar to the original code, except for the following:

1. The statements that populate the control prefix the old key with the keys of the parent nodes. The statements that add the nodes for Germany and German cities are:

```
Set Nd = TreeView1.Nodes.Add("EUROPE", tvwChild, _
        "EUROPE-GERMANY", "Germany", 3)
Nd.Tag = "Countries"
Nd.Sorted = True     ' this statement sorts all German cities
Set Nd = TreeView1.Nodes.Add("EUROPE-GERMANY", tvwChild, _
        "EUROPE-GERMANY-BERLIN", "Berlin")
Nd.Tag = "Cities"
Set Nd = TreeView1.Nodes.Add("EUROPE-GERMANY", tvwChild, _
        "EUROPE-GERMANY-MUNICH", "Munich")
Nd.Tag = "Cities"
Set Nd = TreeView1.Nodes.Add("EUROPE-GERMANY", tvwChild, _
        "EUROPE-GERMANY-BAYREUTH", "Bayreuth")
Nd.Tag = "Cities"
Set Nd = TreeView1.Nodes.Add("EUROPE-GERMANY", tvwChild, _
        "EUROPE-GERMANY-FRANKFURT", "Frankfurt")
Nd.Tag = "Cities"
```

Germany's key is no longer "GERMANY", but "EUROPE-GERMANY", and Berlin's key is no longer "BERLIN", but "EUROPE-GERMANY-BERLIN".

2. The code that adds new nodes at runtime is also modified to use long keys. The following statements add a new country node:

```
Set newNode = TreeView1.Nodes.Item _
            (UCase$(Text1.Text & "-" & Text2.Text))
    If Error Then
        Set newNode = TreeView1.Nodes.Add _
          (UCase$(Text1.Text), tvwChild, _
          UCase$(Text1.Text & "-" & Text2.Text), Text2.Text, 3)
        newNode.Tag = "Countries"
    End If
```

Notice that it prefixes the country's key by the continent's key. Likewise, the following statements add a city node:

```
Set newNode = TreeView1.Nodes.Item _
            (UCase$(Text1.Text & "-" & _
            Text2.Text & "-" & Text3.Text))
    If Error Then
        Set newNode = TreeView1.Nodes.Add_
          (UCase$(Text1.Text & "-" & Text2.Text), _
```

```
            tvwChild, UCase$(Text1.Text & "-" & _
            Text2.Text & "-" & Text3.Text), Text3.Text)
        newNode.Tag = "Cities"
    End If
```

3. Finally, the Find button's code expects that a full key will be supplied. In other words, it won't locate items like "China" or "Kyoto". Instead, you must provide the full key such as "Asia-China" or "Asia-Japan-Kyoto". Open the project in the Visual Basic IDE and examine the differences in the code that searches the TreeView control for a key.

Listing Selected Nodes

The three buttons List Continents, List Countries, and List Cities, populate the List-Box control with the names of the continents, countries, and cities, respectively. The code is straightforward and it's based on the *Next* method of the Node object, which returns the next node on the same level. The List Continents button, for example, retrieves the first child of the "GLOBE" node, which is the first continent name, with the statement:

```
Set Nd = TreeView1.Nodes.Item("GLOBE")
Set childNd = Nd.Child
```

The variable *childNd* represents the first continent node. To retrieve the remaining ones, you must call the *childNd* object variable's Next method as many times as there are continents in the tree. Each time, the Next method will return the next node on the same level. Here's the complete listing of the List Continents button.

Code 8.11: **Retrieving the Continent Names**

```
Private Sub ListContinents_Click()
Dim Nd As Node, childNd As Node
Dim continent As Integer, continents As Integer

    List1.Clear
    Set Nd = TreeView1.Nodes.Item("GLOBE")
    continents = Nd.Children
    Set childNd = Nd.Child
    For continent = 1 To continents
        List1.AddItem childNd.Text
        Set childNd = childNd.Next
    Next
End Sub
```

The code behind the List Countries names is equally straightforward, although longer. It must scan each continent, and within each continent, it must scan in a similar fashion the continent's child nodes. To do this, you must set up two nested loops, the outer one to scan the continents and the inner one to scan the countries. The complete listing of the List Countries button is shown next.

Code 8.12:   **Retrieving the Country Names**

```
Private Sub ListCountries_Click()
Dim Nd As Node, countryNd As Node, continentNd As Node
Dim continent As Integer, continents As Integer
Dim country As Integer, countries As Integer

    List1.Clear
    Set Nd = TreeView1.Nodes.Item("GLOBE")
    continents = Nd.Children
    Set continentNd = Nd.Child
    For continent = 1 To continents
        countries = continentNd.Children
        Set countryNd = continentNd.Child
        For country = 1 To countries
            List1.AddItem countryNd.Text
            Set countryNd = countryNd.Next
        Next
        Set continentNd = continentNd.Next
    Next
End Sub
```

When the `continentNd.Next` method is called, it returns the next node in the Continents level. Then the `continentNd.children` method is called and it returns the first node in the Countries level. As you can guess, the code of the List Cities button uses the same two nested lists as the previous listing and an added inner loop, which scans the cities of each country.

The code behind these Command buttons requires some knowledge of the information stored in the tree. It will work with trees that have two or three levels of nodes like the Globe tree, but what if the tree's depth is allowed to grow to a dozen levels? A tree that represents the structure of a folder on your hard disk, for example, may easily contain half a dozen nested folders. Obviously, to scan the nodes of this tree you can't put together unlimited nested loops. The next section describes a technique for scanning any tree, regardless of how many levels it contains. The code in the following section uses recursion, and if you're not familiar with recursive programming you should first read Chapter 11.

Scanning the TreeView Control

The items of a TreeView control can all be accessed through the Nodes collection. You have seen how to scan the entire tree of the TreeView control with a For...Next loop. This technique, however, doesn't reflect the structure of the tree; it simply lists all the nodes. The proper method to scan a tree is to exhaust each node, including its child nodes, before moving to the next node on the same level, as if you were scanning a folder. Displaying all the files in a folder along with the files in its subfolders isn't very practical. We try to organize files under their folder and folders under their parent folders. We'll do the same with the TreeView control.

VB6 at Work: The TreeViewScan Project

To demonstrate the process of scanning a TreeView control, I have included the TreeViewScan project on the CD (you'll find it in the TVWScan folder). The application's Form is shown in Figure 8.23. The Form contains a TreeView control on the left, which is populated with the same data as the Globe's TreeView control, and a ListBox control on the right, where the tree's nodes are listed. Child nodes on the ListBox control are indented according to the level of the tree to which they belong.

FIGURE 8.23:

The TVWScan application demonstrates how to scan the nodes of a TreeView control recursively.

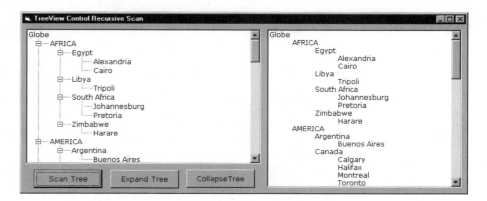

Scanning the child nodes in a tree calls for a *recursive procedure*, or a procedure that calls itself. Think of a tree structure that contains all the files and folders on your C: drive. If this structure contained no subfolders, you'd need to set up a loop to scan each folder, one after the other. Since most folders contain subfolders, the process must be interrupted at each folder to scan the subfolders of the current folder. The process of scanning a drive recursively is described in detail in Chapter 11, *Recursive Programming*. Here, I will present the code to scan a tree and explain it a little. If you can't follow the example of this section, you should read the discussion of the DirMap project of Chapter 11, and then you'll be able to understand how a tree structure is scanned recursively.

Recursive Scanning   To start the scanning of the TreeView1 control, start at the top node of the control with the statement:

```
ScanNode TreeView1.Nodes(1)
```

The ScanNode() subroutine scans the nodes under the node that is passed as argument. By passing the root node to the ScanNode() subroutine, we're in effect asking it to scan the entire tree. Let's look now at the ScanNode() subroutine.

Code 8.13:   **Scanning a Tree Recursively**

```
The ScanNode() Subroutine
Sub ScanNode(aNode As Node)
Dim thisNode As Node
Dim i As Long

    List1.AddItem aNode.Text
    If aNode.Children > 0 Then
        Set thisNode = aNode.Child
        For i = 1 To aNode.Children
            ScanNode thisNode
            Set thisNode = thisNode.Next
        Next
    End If
End Sub
```

This subroutine is deceptively simple. First, it adds the name of the current node to the List1 ListBox control. If this node (represented by the *aNode* variable) contains child nodes, the code must scan them all. The aNode.Child method returns the first child node of *aNode*. After this method is called, the aNode.Next method returns the next child of the *aNode* node. Each time the aNode.Next is called, it returns a reference to the next node in the tree.

So, after we retrieve the first child node, we need to set up a loop, which must scan the child nodes of the current node, one at a time. To do this, the ScanNode() subroutine must call itself by passing a different argument. After the child nodes have been scanned, the code moves to the next node under *aNode*. If you're familiar with recursive procedures, you'll find the code quite simple. If not, this coding probably will raise many questions. You can use the ScanNode() subroutine as is to scan any TreeView control. All you need is a reference to the root node (or the node you want to scan recursively), which you must pass to the ScanNode() subroutine as argument. The subroutine will scan the entire tree and display its nodes on a ListBox control. The nodes will be printed one after the other. To make the list easier to read, indent the names of the nodes by an amount that's proportional to the levels of nesting. Nodes of the first level aren't indented at all. Nodes on the first level can be indented by 10 spaces, nodes on the second level can be indented by 20 spaces, and so on. The variable *RDepth* keeps track of the level of nesting and is used to specify the indentation of the corresponding node. The revised ScanNode() subroutine follows.

Code 8.14:   **The ScanNode Subroutine**

```
Sub ScanNode(aNode As Node)
Dim thisNode As Node
Dim i As Long
Static RDepth As Integer

    List1.AddItem Space(RDepth * 10) & aNode.Text
    If aNode.Children > 0 Then
        RDepth = RDepth + 1
        Set thisNode = aNode.Child
        For i = 1 To aNode.Children
            ScanNode thisNode
            Set thisNode = thisNode.Next
        Next
        RDepth = RDepth - 1
    End If
End Sub
```

The *RDepth* variable is declared as Static because it must maintain its value between calls. When we run into a node that has child nodes, we increase the *RDepth* variable by one level. After we have scanned all the child nodes, we decrease it by one level.

Run the TVWScan project and click the Expand Tree button to see all the nodes of the tree. Then click the Scan Tree button to populate the list on the right with the names of the continents/countries/cities. Obviously, the ListBox control is not a substitute for the TreeView control. The data have no particular structure; even when they're indented there are no treelines on front of its nodes, and users can't expand and collapse the control's contents. So why bother to map the contents of the Tree-View control to a ListBox control? The goal was to demonstrate how to scan a tree structure and extract all the nodes along with their structure. You can use the Scan-Code() subroutine to store the nodes of a TreeView control to a disk file or transfer them to a database or another control. The ScanNode() subroutine is the core of the subroutine you need and can be adjusted to accommodate all the operations just mentioned.

The Globe project has a small menu, which contains the Save and Load commands. Although these commands could have been implemented with a code similar to the

ScanCode(), I used a non-recursive procedure. The Save command uses three nested loops, which scan each continent, each country within each continent, and each city within each country. Each level's nodes are prefixed by a space, so that the code that reads the data can easily figure out whether a specific node is a child of another node. The actual code is based on the code discussed in the section "Enumerating Nodes." Here's the code behind the Save command of the File menu.

Code 8.15:   **The Save Command's Code**

```
Private Sub FileSave_Click()
Dim Nd As Node, countryNd As Node, continentNd As Node, cityNd As Node
Dim continent As Integer, continents As Integer
Dim country As Integer, countries As Integer
Dim city As Integer, cities As Integer
Dim FNum As Integer

    FNum = FreeFile()
    Open App.Path & "\Globe.txt" For Output As #FNum
    Set Nd = TreeView1.Nodes.Item("GLOBE")
Debug.Print Nd.Text
    Write #FNum, Nd.Text
    continents = Nd.Children
    Set continentNd = Nd.Child
    For continent = 1 To continents
Debug.Print continentNd.Text
        Write #FNum, " " & continentNd.Text
        countries = continentNd.Children
        Set countryNd = continentNd.Child
        For country = 1 To countries
Debug.Print "   " & countryNd.Text
            Write #FNum, "   " & countryNd.Text
            cities = countryNd.Children
            Set cityNd = countryNd.Child
            For city = 1 To cities
Debug.Print "      " & cityNd.Text
                Write #FNum, "      " & cityNd.Text
                Set cityNd = cityNd.Next
            Next
            Set countryNd = countryNd.Next
        Next
        Set continentNd = continentNd.Next
    Next
    Close #FNum
End Sub
```

The Print statements are inserted to help you visualize the structure of the tree as it's saved in a disk file. Part of the output produced by the Print statements is shown next:

```
EUROPE
    France
        Lyon
        Nice
        Paris
    Germany
        Bayreuth
        Berlin
        Frankfurt
        Munich
    Italy
        Florence
        Milan
        Napoli
        Rome
        Venice
```

You can also open the text file created by the Save command with a text editor. The Load command's code reads one item at a time and inserts it in the TreeView control in the proper order. The program examines the number of spaces in front of the node's text. If there's a single space, the current node is a country and it's added under the continent that was added last to the tree. If there are two spaces, the current node is a city and it's added under the most recently added country node. The Load command's code follows.

Code 8.16:   **The Load Command's Code**

```
Private Sub FileLoad_Click()
Dim FNum As Integer
Dim Nd As Node
Dim level1 As String, level2 As String
Dim key As String
Dim nodeText As String

TreeView1.Nodes.Clear
' set up the ListImage object
Dim Images As ListImage

    Set Images = ImageList1.ListImages.Add( , , _
                LoadPicture(App.Path & "\cont.bmp"))
    Set Images = ImageList1.ListImages.Add( , , _
                LoadPicture(App.Path & "\country.bmp"))
```

```
        Set Images = ImageList1.ListImages.Add(, , _
                     LoadPicture(App.Path & "\city.bmp"))
        TreeView1.ImageList = ImageList1
' THERE'S NO NEED TO DO ANYTHING ABOUT SORTING KEYS, BECAUSE
' THE ITEMS WERE SORTED WHEN THE TREEVIEW CONTROL WAS SAVED
        FNum = FreeFile()
        Set Nd = TreeView1.Nodes.Add(, , "GLOBE", "Globe", 1)
        Nd.Tag = "GLOBE"
        Nd.Sorted = True

        Open App.Path & "\Globe.txt" For Input As #FNum
        While Not EOF(FNum)
            Input #FNum, nodeText
            key = UCase(Trim(nodeText))
            If Left(nodeText, 3) = "    " Then
                Set Nd = TreeView1.Nodes.Add(level2, tvwChild, key, _
                         Trim(nodeText), 3)
                Nd.Tag = "Cities"
            ElseIf Left(nodeText, 2) = "  " Then
                level2 = key
                Set Nd = TreeView1.Nodes.Add(level1, tvwChild, key, _
                         Trim(nodeText), 2)
                Nd.Tag = "Countries"
            ElseIf Left(nodeText, 1) = " " Then
                level1 = key
                Set Nd = TreeView1.Nodes.Add("GLOBE", tvwChild, key, _
                         Trim(nodeText), 1)
                Nd.Tag = "Continents"
            End If
        Wend
        Close #FNum
End Sub
```

The code of the Save and Load commands is lengthy but straightforward. A recursive procedure would have been shorter, but not as easy to follow for readers who aren't familiar with recursive programming techniques. After reading Chapter 11, *Recursive Programming*, you should try to implement these two subroutines recursively as an exercise.

Using the ListView Control

The ListView control is similar to the ListBox control only it can display its items in many forms along with any number of subitems for each item. To do the same with the ListBox control in Chapter 5, we had to make use of its ItemData property to store a pointer to the remaining items. With the ListView control, you can store all the subitems along with the key item.

The basic properties of the ListView control can be set through the control's property pages. Place an instance of the ListView control on a Form, right-click the control, and select Properties. The property pages shown in Figure 8.24 will appear on your screen.

FIGURE 8.24:

The ListView control's property pages

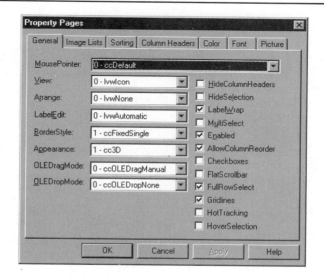

You can set up most of the control's properties using the property pages, but you can't populate the control. Soon you'll see how to populate the ListView control through code, but let's start with the basic properties:

- **General Tab**   This tab contains the basic properties that determine the control's appearance and its operation.

  - In the MousePointer box you can specify the shape of the pointer, while it's hovering over the ListView control.

  - The *View* property determines how the items will be displayed on the control, and it can have one of the values shown in Table 8.9.

  - The *Arrange* property determines how the items are arranged on the control, and it can have one of the values in Table 8.10.

TABLE 8.9:   Settings of the ListView Control's View Property

Constant	Value	Description
lvwIcon	0	(Default) Each item is represented by an icon and a text label below the icon
lvwSmallIcon	1	Small icon; each item is represented by a small icon and a text label that appears to the right of the icon
lvwList	2	List; each item is represented by a small icon and a text label that appears to the right of the icon
lvwReport	3	Report; each item is displayed in a column with its subitems in adjacent columns

TABLE 8.10:   Settings of the ListView Control's Arrange Property

Constant	Value	Description
lvwNone	0	(Default) None
lvwAutoLeft	1	Left; ListItem objects are aligned along the left side of the control
lvwAutoTop	2	Top; ListItem objects are aligned along the top of the control

- The *LabelEdit* property lets you specify whether the user will be allowed to edit the text of the items. Its default value is *lvwAutomatic* and you should set it to *lvwManual* if you want to control from within your code when the user can edit the labels.

- The checkboxes on the right-hand side of the General tab let you specify options that affect both the appearance and operation of the control. The names of the properties you can set here are self-explanatory. Open the LVDemo project in the Visual Basic IDE, change the settings of these properties, and then run the project to see how they affect the ListView control.

- **Image Lists Tab**   Use this tab to specify the ImageList controls with the icons that will be (optionally) displayed along with the text of the items. In the Normal box you specify the icons that appear in the Large Icons view. In the Small box you specify the small icons, which are displayed in the Small Icons view, and in the last box you select the icons to appear next to the headers.

- **Sorting Tab**   Use this tab to specify whether the items of the ListView will be sorted or not. *SortKey* is the index of the column with the sort field. If the Index value is larger than zero, then the items will be sorted according to a subitem. You can also specify the order of the sort (ascending or descending).

- **Column Headers Tab** If you plan to display the items in Report view, use this tab to set the headers of the columns. Use the Insert Column and Delete Column buttons to insert new columns or delete existing ones, respectively. Each column has a title (Text field) and its own width (Width field). In addition to the text of the column header, you can specify a key, tag, and icon for each column. To edit an existing column header, specify its index in the Index box.

- **Color Tab** Use this tab to specify the control's background and foreground (text) colors.

- **Font Tab** Use this tab to specify the font for the item labels.

- **Picture Tab** Use this tab to specify a custom pointer and the image to appear on the control's background.

Adding New Items

The items of the ListView control can be accessed through the *ListItems* property, which is a collection. As such, it exposes the standard members of a collection, which are:

- **Add method** Adds a new item to the ListItems collection

- **Count property** Returns the number of items in the collection

- **Clear method** Removes all the items from the collection

- **Item property** Retrieves an item specified by an Index value or key

- **Remove method** Removes an item from the ListItems collection

The ListItems collection's methods have straightforward syntax, except for the Add method. To add a new item with the Add method, you must specify its index (the first item's index is 1), a key, its text, and two icons: a large one and a small one. Depending on the setting of the View property, one of these icons is displayed with each item. The syntax of the Add method is:

```
ListView1.Add Index, Key, Text, Icon, SmallIcon
```

The Add method returns a ListItem object, which represents the newly added item and has the following alternate syntax:

```
LItem = ListView1.Add(Index, Key, Text, Icon, SmallIcon)
```

You can use the *LItem* variable in your code to manipulate the properties of the new item. Notice that none of the Add method's arguments are mandatory. Of course, you can't omit all the arguments. You can add an item specifying only its icon and no text or a Key value. Or, you can add an item with text only and omit its key or icon, if the application doesn't allow the user to view the items as icons. Actually, the following statement will insert a new item in the list:

```
LItem = ListView1.ListItems.Add
```

but you must use the *LItem* variable to set some of its properties, as in the following statements:

```
LItem.Text = "New Item"
LItem.Key = "New_Key"
```

The *Index* argument specifies the order of the new item in the control and it's usually omitted. If you want to sort the items, use the Sorted property instead. The *Key* is a string that uniquely identifies an item. No two items in the ListView control can share the same Key value. If you attempt to insert an item with a key that exists already, a trappable runtime error will be generated.

The last three arguments, *Text*, *Icon*, and *SmallIcon*, determine how the item will be displayed on the control. Which of the three values is used depends on the setting of the View property. If View = lvwIcon, then the *Icon* argument will specify that the large icon be displayed above the item's label. If the control's View property is *lvwList* or *lvwReport*, you must provide a value for the *Text* argument.

Using SubItems

Each item in the ListView control may also have subitems. You can think of the item as the key of a record and the *subitems* as the other fields of the record. The subitems are displayed only in the Report mode, but they are available to your code in any view. For example, you can display all items as icons, and when the user clicks on an icon, show the values of the selected item's subitems on other controls, or simply access them from within your code.

To access the subitems of a given item, use its *SubItems* collection. The first subitem is SubItem(1), the second one is SubItems(2), and so on. The following statements add an item and three subitems to the ListView1 control:

```
Set LItem = ListView1.ListItems.Add(, , "Alfreds Futterkiste")
LItem.SubItems(1) = "Maria Anders"
LItem.SubItems(2) = "030-0074321"
LItem.SubItems(3) = "030-0076545"
```

To access the SubItems collection, you must have a reference to the item to which the subitems belong. The Add method returns a reference to the newly added item, the *LItem* variable, which is then used to access the item's subitems. SubItems is a property of the ListItem object, which is not a collection. It's an array of strings that holds the values of the subitems.

Displaying the subitems on the control requires some overhead. Subitems are displayed only in the Report view mode. However, setting the View property to *lvwReport* is not enough. You must first create the headers of the Report view, as shown in Figure 8.25. The ListView control will display only as many subitems as there are headers in the control. The first column, with the header Company, displays the items of the list. The following columns display the subitems. Moreover, you can't specify which subitem will be displayed under each header. The first subitem ("Maria Anders" in the above example) will be displayed under the second header, the second subitem ("030-0074321" in the same example) will be displayed under the third header, and so on. At runtime, the user can rearrange the columns by dragging them with the mouse. To disable the rearrangement of the columns at runtime, set the control's *AllowColumnReorder* property to False (its default value is True).

The simplest way to define the headers is through the Column Headers tab of the control's property pages. To add a column, click Insert Column and then specify the header's properties in the text fields: the header's text, its alignment, width, key, and tag. There's no reason to index the columns, except that it's easier to refer to them by a name (their key), than by their index, which is a numeric value.

You can also insert columns and headers from within your code. The headers of a ListView control can be accessed through another collection, the *ColumnHeaders* collection. The ColumnHeaders collection exposes the standard members of a collection. Here's the syntax of its Add method:

```
ColumnHeaders.Add Index, Key, Text, Width, Alignment, Icon
```

FIGURE 8.25:

Displaying subitems on a ListView control in the Report mode.

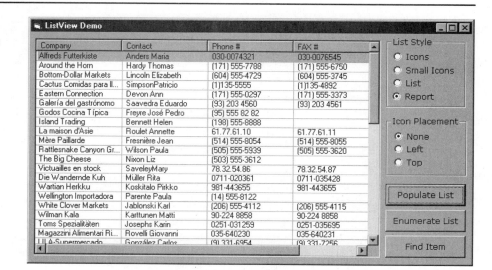

The alternate form of its syntax is:

```
CHeader1 = ColumnHeaders.Add(Index, Key, Text, Width, Alignment, Icon)
```

The arguments of the Add method are the same ones you can specify through the Column Headers property page. As with the ListItems collection's Add method, all arguments are optional. Usually the text, an icon, and the column's width are specified.

Unless you set up each column's width, all columns will have the same width. The width of individual columns is usually specified as a percentage of the total width of the control. The following code sets up a ListView control with four headers, all having the same width:

```
Private Sub Form_Load()
Dim LHeader As ColumnHeader

    LWidth = ListView1.Width - 5 * Screen.TwipsPerPixelX
    ListView1.ColumnHeaders.Add(1, , "Company", LWidth / 4)
    ListView1.ColumnHeaders.Add(2, , "Contact", LWidth / 4)
    ListView1.ColumnHeaders.Add(3, , "Phone", LWidth / 4)
    ListView1.ColumnHeaders.Add(4, , "FAX", LWidth / 4)
    ListView1.View = lvwReport
End Sub
```

This subroutine sets up four headers and then sets the control's View property to *lvwReport*. The first header corresponds to the item (not a subitem). The number of headers you set up must be equal to the number of subitems you want to display on the control plus one.

VB6 at Work: The ListViewDemo Project

Let's put together the members of the ListView control to create a sample application that populates a ListView control and enumerates its items. The application is called ListViewDemo and you'll find it in the LVWDemo folder under this chapter's folder on the CD. The application's Form, shown in Figure 8.26, contains a ListView control whose items can be displayed in all possible views, depending on the status of the OptionButton controls in the List Style section on the right side of the Form.

When the application starts, it sets up the headers (columns) of the ListView control. The headers are displayed only in the Report view, but they are required for the list's subitems. Unless you create the appropriate headers, you won't be able to add subitems. You can comment out the lines that insert the headers in the Form's Load event and then run the project to see what happens when Visual Basic runs into a statement that attempts to add subitems.

The LVWDemo application demonstrates the basic members of the ListView control.

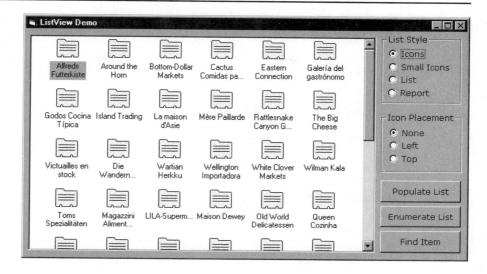

Let's start by looking at the code of the Form's Load event. In this event, we set up the control's headers. All columns have the same width, but you can adjust their widths according to the data to be displayed. The ListView control's headers can also be resized by the user at runtime.

Code 8.17:   Setting up the Headers of the ListView Control

```
Private Sub Form_Load()
Dim LHeader As ColumnHeader

    LWidth = ListView1.Width - 5 * Screen.TwipsPerPixelX
    Set LHeader = ListView1.ColumnHeaders.Add(1, , "Company", LWidth / 4)
    Set LHeader = ListView1.ColumnHeaders.Add(2, , "Contact", LWidth / 4)
    Set LHeader = ListView1.ColumnHeaders.Add(3, , "Phone #", LWidth / 4)
    Set LHeader = ListView1.ColumnHeaders.Add(4, , "FAX #", LWidth / 4)
    ListView1.View = lvwReport
End Sub
```

To populate the ListView control click the Populate List button, whose code is shown next. To add an item, the code calls the control's Add method, which returns a *ListItem* variable. This variable is used to append the item's subitems with the SubItems property. Notice that SubItems doesn't provide an Add method. It's an array with as many elements as there are columns in the control, and you can assign values to its elements.

Code 8.18 shows the statements that insert the first two items in the list. The remaining items are added with similar statements, which need not be repeated here. The sample data I used in the ListViewDemo application came from the NWind sample database, which comes with Visual Basic and is installed in the Visual Basic 6 folder.

Code 8.18:   **Populating a ListView Control**

```
Private Sub Command1_Click()
Dim LItem As ListItem

Set LItem = ListView1.ListItems.Add(, , "Alfreds Futterkiste")
    LItem.SubItems(1) = "Maria Anders"
    LItem.SubItems(2) = "030-0074321"
    LItem.SubItems(3) = "030-0076545"

Set LItem = ListView1.ListItems.Add(, , "Around the Horn")
    LItem.SubItems(1) = "Thomas Hardy"
    LItem.SubItems(2) = "(171) 555-7788"
    LItem.SubItems(3) = "(171) 555-6750"
{more statements}
End Sub
```

Enumerating the List

The Enumerate List button scans all the items in the list and displays them along with their subitems on the Immediate window. To scan the list, you must set up a loop that enumerates all the items in the ListItems collection. For each item in the list, set up a nested loop that scans all the subitems of the current item. The complete listing of the Enumerate List button is shown next.

Code 8.19:   **Enumerating Items and SubItems**

```
Private Sub Command3_Click()
Dim i As Integer, j As Integer

    For i = 1 To ListView1.ListItems.Count
        Debug.Print ListView1.ListItems(i).Text
        For j = 1 To ListView1.ColumnHeaders.Count - 1
            Debug.Print Space(5) & ListView1.ColumnHeaders(j + 1).Text _
                & "     " & ListView1.ListItems(i).SubItems(j)
        Next
    Next
End Sub
```

The output of this code on the Immediate window is shown in Figure 8.27. The subitems appear under the corresponding item and they are indented by five spaces.

FIGURE 8.27:

The output of the Enumerate List button on the Immediate window

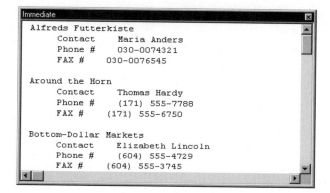

Code 8.19 uses the ListView control's SubItems property to access the current item's subitems. An alternate method for accessing the same subitem is to assign the current item to an item variable, *LItem,* and then use this object's ListSubItems property, which is a collection that contains the current item's subitems. The following subroutine does the exact same thing as Code 8.19, only it uses the List-SubItems collection.

Code 8.20:   An Alternate Method for Accessing Subitems

```
Private Sub Command3_Click()
Dim i As Integer, j As Integer
Dim LItem As ListItem

    For i = 1 To ListView1.ListItems.Count
        Set LItem = ListView1.ListItems(i)
        Debug.Print LItem.Text
        For j = 1 To LItem.ListSubItems.Count
            Debug.Print Space(5) & ListView1.ColumnHeaders(j + 1).Text _
                    & "    " & LItem.ListSubItems(j)
        Next
    Next
End Sub
```

Sorting and Searching

The ListView control provides the mechanisms for sorting its ListItems and searching for specific items. To sort the ListItems in the control, you must assign the value True to the Sorted property. This is a Boolean value that determines whether the ListItems in the collection will be sorted. Two related properties are the SortOrder and SortKey properties. The *SortOrder* property determines whether the ListItems are sorted in ascending or descending order, and the *SortKey* property determines the sorting key. If SortKey is 0, the list is sorted according to the item's Text property. If you want to sort the list according to a subitem, assign the subitem's Index value to the SortKey property.

The SortOrder property's values are listed in Table 8.11.

TABLE 8.11: Settings of the SortOrder Property

Constant	Value	Description
IvwAscending	0	(Default) Ascending order; sorts from the beginning of the alphabet (A-Z) or the earliest date. Numbers are sorted as strings (e.g., the number 22 will appear before the value 3).
IvwDescending	1	Descending order; sorts from the end of the alphabet (Z-A) or the latest date. Numbers are sorted as strings (e.g., the number 22 will appear after the value 333).

It's common to sort a list when the column header is clicked. For this reason, the SortKey property is commonly set from within the *ColumnClick* event to sort the list using the clicked column, as determined by the sort key and demonstrated in the following example:

```
Private Sub ListView1_ColumnClick (ByVal ColumnHeader as ColumnHeader)
    ListView1.SortKey=ColumnHeader.Index-1
End Sub
```

The *FindItem* method finds and returns a reference to a ListItem object. You can use this reference in your code to manipulate the properties of the found item. The syntax of the FindItem method is:

```
FindItem string, value, index, match
```

The *string* argument is the search argument (the value being searched). The FindItem method can search for a string in the ListItem objects' Text and Tag properties, or in the SubItems collection. *Value* is an optional argument, which specifies where the search will take place, and its possible values are shown in Table 8.12.

TABLE 8.12: Settings of the *Value* Argument of the FindItem Method

Constant	Value	Description
lvwText	0	(Default) Searches for a match in the ListItem objects' Text property
lvwSubItem	1	Searches for a match in the ListItem objects' ListSubItems collection
lvwTag	2	Searches for a match in the ListItem objects' Tag property

Index is another optional argument, which specifies where the search will begin. To search for an ListItem after the 10th item in the list, set the index argument of the FindItem method to 11. Its default value is 1 (the first item in the control).

The last argument, *match*, is another optional argument that specifies how the specified search argument will be matched. It can have one of the values in Table 8.13.

TABLE 8.13: Settings of the *Match* Argument of the FindItem Method

Constant	Value	Description
lvwWholeWord	0	(Default) The match successful if the item's Text property matches the whole word being searched. This setting doesn't apply to numeric search arguments.
lvwPartial	1	The match is successful if the item's Text property begins with the string being searched. This setting doesn't apply to numeric search arguments.

The last button of the ListViewDemo application searches the list for specific items using the control's FindItem method. When you click the Find Item button, you'll be prompted to enter a string to search for. The code will search among the ListItems' Text properties to locate the desired string. The following statement locates the FindItem string among the items' Text properties:

```
Set LItem = ListView1.FindItem(FindItem, lvwText, , lvwPartial)
```

If the string isn't found in any ListItem object's Text property, the *LItem* variable is Nothing. In this case, the program will attempt to locate the same string in the subitems with the statement:

```
If LItem Is Nothing Then
    Set LItem = ListView1.FindItem(FindItem, lvwSubItem)
```

Notice that you can't specify a partial match when searching the subitems. The last two arguments of the FindItem method are ignored when the value argument is *lvwSubItem*. If the string isn't found in the subitems either, then a message is displayed. If the search string is located (either in a Text property or subitem), the matching item is highlighted and it's brought into view. The code behind the Find Item button is shown next.

Code 8.21:   Finding a ListItem

```
Private Sub Command2_Click()
Dim LItem As ListItem

    FindItem = InputBox("Find what?")
    Set LItem = ListView1.FindItem(FindItem, lvwText, , lvwPartial)
    If LItem Is Nothing Then
        Set LItem = ListView1.FindItem(FindItem, lvwSubItem)
        If LItem Is Nothing Then
            NotFound = True
        End If
    End If
    If NotFound Then
        MsgBox "Item not found"
        Exit Sub
    Else
        LItem.EnsureVisible
        LItem.Selected = True
    End If
End Sub
```

The *EnsureVisible* method scrolls the control's content so that the selected item comes into the control's visible area. The *Selected* property is set to True to highlight the item just located.

Selecting Items

If you experiment a little with the ListViewDemo application you'll see that the ListView control reacts when items are clicked and/or double-clicked. A common task in programming the ListView control is have it detect the item that's clicked or double-clicked upon. The mouse-click on an item is reported to the application with the *ItemClick* event, whose declaration is as follows:

```
Private Sub ListView1_ItemClick(ByVal Item As ComctlLib.ListItem)
```

The *Item* argument represents the list item that's clicked, and you can use it from within your code to access the members of the item. However, there is no equivalent ItemDoubleClick event. Yet, many applications must react when the user double-clicks an item in the ListView control.

It is possible to detect the item that has been double-clicked, but the process is a bit involved. The ListView control provides the *HitTest* method, which returns the item displayed at a specific pair of coordinates. The HitTest method's declaration is:

```
Set LItem = ListView1.HitTest(X, Y)
```

The HitTest method returns an object variable, which represents the item at coordinates (X, Y). These coordinates must be expressed in pixels. You can use the HitTest method to detect the item under a drop operation (the DragDrop event reports the coordinates of the point where the control is dropped). You can also use the HitTest method to detect the item that has been double-clicked, as long as you can find out the coordinates of the point where the mouse was double clicked. This can't be done with straight Visual Basic statements; you'll need the GetCursorPos() API function. API (Application Programming Interface) functions are built into the operating system and you can use them from within your Visual Basic code. The process is described in Chapter 13, *The Windows API*. In the section "Using the HitTest Method" of Chapter 13 you'll see the code that enables the ListViewDemo application to react to the double-click event.

VB6 at Work: The Explorer Project

The last example in this section combines the TreeView and ListView controls. It's a fairly advanced example, but I've included it here for the most ambitious readers. It can also be used as the starting point for many custom applications, so give it a try. You can always come back to this project after you've mastered other aspects of the language.

The Explorer project, shown in Figure 8.28, is the core of a custom Explorer window, which displays a structured list of folders on the left pane and the list of files in the selected folder on the right pane. The left pane is populated when the application starts, but it takes a while. On my Pentium system, it takes nearly five seconds to populate the TreeView control with the structure of the C:\WINDOWS folder. You can expand any folder on this pane and view its subfolders. To view the files in a folder, click its name and the right pane will be populated with the names of the files, along with vital data, such as the file size, date of creation, and date of last modification. Later in the book you'll read about the FileSystemObject object, how to access other file data, and how to enhance the Explorer application.

This section's project is not limited to displaying folders and files; you can populate the two controls with data from several sources. For example, you can display customers in the left pane (and organize them by city or state) and their related data on the right pane (e.g., invoices, payments). Or you can populate the left pane with product names and the right pane with the respective sales. In general, it can be used as an interface for many types of applications.

FIGURE 8.28:

The Explorer project demonstrates how to combine a TreeView and a ListView control on the same Form.

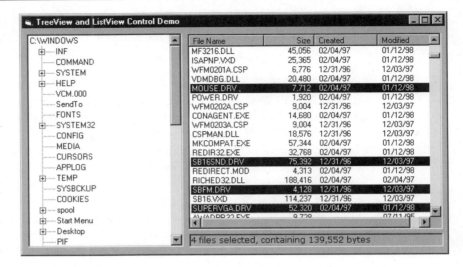

The left pane is populated from within the Form's Load event. The code makes use of the FileSystemObject object, which is discussed later in the book. In this section, I will go quickly through the code and explain only the members of the FileSystemObject used in this project. Following is the code that populates the TreeView control with the subfolders of the C:\WINDOWS folder.

Code 8.22: **The Explorer Project's Load Event**

```
Private Sub Form_Load()
    LWidth = ListView1.Width - 5 * Screen.TwipsPerPixelX
    ListView1.ColumnHeaders.Add 1, , "File Name", 0.3 * LWidth
    ListView1.ColumnHeaders.Add 2, , "Size", _
                0.2 * LWidth, lvwColumnRight
    ListView1.ColumnHeaders.Add 3, , "Created", _
                0.25 * LWidth
    ListView1.ColumnHeaders.Add 4, , "Modified", _
                0.25 * LWidth
    Set FSys = CreateObject("Scripting.FileSystemObject")
' Specify the folder you wish to map in the following line
    InitPath = "C:\WINDOWS"
    TreeView1.Nodes.Add , tvwFirst, UCase(InitPath), InitPath
    Me.Show
    Screen.MousePointer = vbHourglass
    DoEvents
    ScanFolder (InitPath)
    Screen.MousePointer = vbDefault
End Sub
```

The program sets up the ListView control with four columns and then it creates the *FSys* variable, which represents the computer's file system. Through this variable, which is declared on the Form level, other subroutines will be able to access the file system. From within the Load event, only the top-level node, C:\WINDOWS, is added to the TreeView control. Its child nodes are added by the ScanFolder() subroutine.

The ScanFolder() subroutine is a short, recursive procedure that scans all the folders under C:\WINDOWS and their subfolders. The subroutine's listing is shown next.

Code 8.23:   **The ScanFolder() Subroutine**

```
Sub ScanFolder(folderSpec)
Dim thisFolder As Folder
Dim allFolders As Folders

    Set thisFolder = FSys.GetFolder(folderSpec)
    Set allFolders = thisFolder.SubFolders
    For Each thisFolder In allFolders
        TreeView1.Nodes.Add UCase(thisFolder.ParentFolder.Path), _
            tvwChild, UCase(thisFolder.Path), thisFolder.Name
        ScanFolder (thisFolder.Path)
    Next
End Sub
```

The variable *thisFolder* represents the current folder (the one passed to the Scan-Folder() subroutine as argument). Using this variable, the program creates the *all-Folders* collection, which contains all the subfolders of the current folder. Then, it scans every folder in this collection and adds its name to the TreeView control. The newly added node's key is the folder's path name, so each key will be unique. After adding a folder to the TreeView control, the procedure must scan the subfolders of the current folder. It does so by calling itself and passing another folder's name as argument. If you find the recursive implementation of the subroutine difficult to understand, go through the material of Chapter 11, *Recursive Programming*. You can use the ScanFolder() subroutine as is in your projects; just pass to it a reference to the folder you want to scan. The argument to the ScanFolder() subroutine is a Folder object, not just the name of the folder. The ScanFolder() subroutine must be used along with the FileSystemObject, which is discussed in detail in Chapter 20, *Scripting Objects*.

Viewing a Folder's Files

To view the files of a folder, click the folder's name in the TreeView control. Every time the user clicks an item in the TreeView control, the NodeClick event is triggered.

This event passes a single argument, which is a reference to the selected node. We use this argument to process the selected node. The processing consists of displaying the selected folder's files on the ListView control. The listing for TreeView control's NodeClick handler follows.

Code 8.24:   **Programming the NodeClick Event**

```
Private Sub TreeView1_NodeClick(ByVal Node As ComctlLib.Node)
Dim thisFolder As Folder
Dim thisFile As File
Dim allFiles As Files
Dim thisItem As ListItem

    Screen.MousePointer = vbHourglass
    ListView1.ListItems.Clear
    Set thisFolder = FSys.GetFolder(Node.Key)
    Set allFiles = thisFolder.Files
    If allFiles.Count > 0 Then
    On Error Resume Next
        For Each thisFile In allFiles
            Set thisItem = ListView1.ListItems.Add(, , thisFile.Name)
            thisItem.SubItems(1) = Format(thisFile.Size, "###,###,###")
            thisItem.SubItems(2) = Left(thisFile.DateCreated, 8)
            thisItem.SubItems(3) = Left(thisFile.DateLastModified, 8)
            If thisFile.Attributes And System Then thisItem.Ghosted = True
        Next
    End If
    Screen.MousePointer = vbDefault
End Sub
```

After reading the discussion of the FileSystemObject object (in Chapter 20), you'll find this code really easy to understand. The expression `FSys.GetFolder(Node.Key)` returns a reference to the selected folder, which is stored in the variable *thisFolder*. This variable is then used to retrieve the folder's files. The statement `thisFolder.Files` returns a collection of all the files in the selected folder. This collection can be accessed through the *allFiles* variable. The following loop scans all the files in the *allFiles* collection:

```
For Each thisFile In allFiles
    . . .
Next
```

At each iteration of the loop, the variable *thisFile* references a different file and it's used to access the file's properties:

- **thisFile.Name**   The file's name

- **thisFile.Size**   The file's size

- **thisFile.DateCreated**   The file's creation date and time

- **thisFile.DateModified**   The date and time the file was last modified

These properties are used to populate the subitems of the current item in the List-View control.

Processing the Selected Files

At the bottom of the ListView control, there is a Label where the number of selected files and their total size is printed. Keeping the label updated at all times is tricky. Try setting the ListView control's MultiSelect property to True and inserting the following code in the control's ItemClick event.

Code 8.23:   **Processing the Selected Files**

```
Dim totFiles As Integer, totSize As Long
    totFiles = 0
    totSize = 0
    On Error Resume Next
    For i = 1 To ListView1.ListItems.Count
        If ListView1.ListItems(i).Selected Then
            totFiles = totFiles + 1
            totSize = totSize + ListView1.ListItems(i).SubItems(1)
        End If
    Next
    Label1.Caption = Format(totFiles, "###,##0") & _
            " files selected, containing " & _
            Format(totSize, "###,###,###,##0") & " bytes"
```

Here's how the code works: Because the user may select or deselect a file by clicking its name, we can't simply add the size of the file that was clicked to the total size. Every time the ItemClick event is triggered, the computer must scan all the ListItems and examine their Selected property. If they're True, then it increases the number of selected files by one and adds the file's size to the total size.

This code works in principle, but it has two drawbacks. For one thing, it's slow—quite slow when the ListView control is filled with many filenames. For some reason, the code in the ItemClick event must be as short as possible.

The second, and more annoying, drawback is that it works only when the user selects files with mouse-clicks (while holding down the Shift and Ctrl keys, of course). If you select multiple files on the ListView control with a mouse drag operation (just press the mouse button, draw a rectangle that encloses a number of files, and then release the mouse button) the label below the ListView control won't be updated because the ItemClick event won't be triggered. So, the ItemClick event isn't where the code belongs.

To figure out where the code should be placed, I tried and discarded the Mouse-Move event (it doesn't trigger when the user selects multiple files) and the Selection-Changed event (the ListView control doesn't provide a similar event), before using a Timer control to handle all possible selection mechanisms. You can change the Interval property of the Timer control to repeat the operations more or less often, but I set the control to repeat the operations every 100 milliseconds. By placing the statements of Code 8.23 in the Timer control's Timer event, this managed to keep the statistics displayed on the Label control updated at all times, regardless of how the files were selected (with point-and-click or click-and-drag operations).

Even when I select multiple files with the mouse button and the Shift key, the processing of the files from within the Timer event is much faster than processing them from within the ItemClick event. Instead of removing the identical code from within the ItemClick event, I've commented it out so you can experiment with it. Uncomment the lines in the ItemClick event and run the program to see for yourself how slow the ItemClick event can be, especially with folders that contain many files. Notice that it doesn't make any difference how many files you select, because the code scans all the files to locate the selected ones.

CHAPTER

NINE

9

More Advanced
ActiveX Controls

- ◼ The RichTextBox control

- ◼ The MSFlexGrid control

This chapter explores a few of the more advanced ActiveX controls that you'll find useful in building elaborate applications such as word processors and spreadsheets, and they are:

- **The RichTextBox control,** the core of a word processor, wrapped as an ActiveX control

- **The MSFlexGrid control,** the core of a spreadsheet application, also wrapped as an ActiveX control

The RichTextBox control provides all the functionality you'll need to build a word processor, and the MSFlexGrid control provides the necessary functionality for a spreadsheet application. To add data plotting features to your applications, especially applications based on the MSFlexGrid control, you can use the MSChart control, which is presented in Appendix B on the CD.

NOTE You may be wondering why you shouldn't just use the Microsoft Office application and VBA (Visual Basic for Applications) for these functions and control them from within a Visual Basic application. The answer is that many of your users may not have Microsoft Office installed on their systems. Also, why put up with the monstrous functionality of the Office applications when a sleek, quick-loading, fast-executing Visual Basic application will do the trick?

The RichTextBox Control

The RichTextBox control is the core of a full-blown word processor. It provides all the functionality of a TextBox control; it gives you the capability to mix different fonts, sizes, and attributes; and it gives you precise control over the margins of the text (see Figure 9.1). You can even place images in your text on a RichTextBox control (although you won't have the kind of control over the embedded images that you have with Word 97).

The fundamental property of the Rich TextBox control is its *TextRTF* property. Similar to the Text property of the TextBox control, this property is the text currently displayed by the control. Unlike the Text property, which returns (or sets) the text of the control but doesn't contain formatting information, the TextRTF property returns the text along with any formatting information. Therefore, you can use the RichTextBox control to specify the text's formatting including paragraph indentation, font, and font size or style, among other things.

FIGURE 9.1:

The RTFPad application uses the functionality of the Rich-TextBox control to implement a word processor.

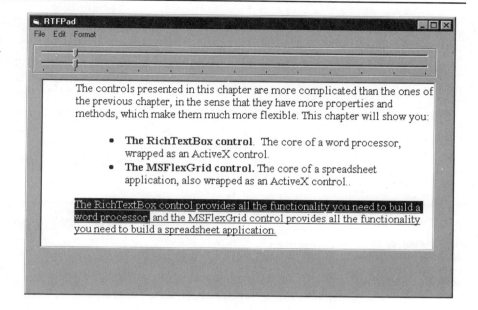

RTF stands for *Rich Text Format,* which is a standard for storing formatting information along with the text. The beauty of the RichTextBox control for programmers is that they don't need to supply the formatting codes. The control provides simple properties that turn the selected text into bold, change the alignment of the current paragraph, and so on. The RTF code is generated internally by the control and used to save and load formatted files. It's possible to create elaborately formatted documents without knowing the RTF language.

The RTF Language

A basic knowledge of the RTF format, its commands, and how it works, will certainly help you understand how the RichTextBox control works. RTF is a document formatting language that uses simple commands to specify the formatting of a document. These commands, or *tags*, are ASCII strings, such as \par (the tag that marks the beginning of a new paragraph) and \b (the tag that turns on the bold style). And this is where the value of the RTF format lies. RTF documents don't contain special characters and can be easily exchanged among different operating systems and computers, as long as there is an RTF-capable application to read the document. Let's look at the RTF document in action.

Open the WordPad application (choose Start ➤ Programs ➤ Accessories ➤ WordPad) and enter a few lines of text (see Figure 9.2). Select a few words or sentences and format them in different ways with any of WordPad's formatting commands. Then save the document in RTF format. Choose File ➤ Save As, select Rich Text Format, and then save the file as Document.rtf. If you open this file with a text editor such as NotePad, you'll see the actual RTF code that produced the document. You can find the RTF file for the document shown in Figure 9.2 in this chapter's folder on the CD.

FIGURE 9.2:

The formatting applied to the text using WordPad's commands is stored along with the text in RTF format.

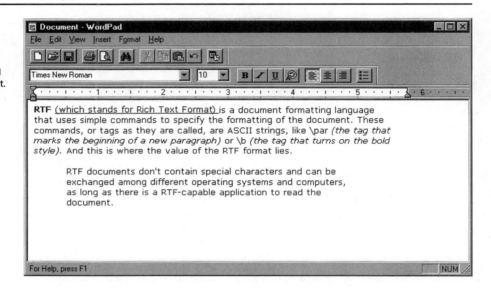

Code 9.1:   **The RTF Code for the Document in Figure 9.2**

```
{\rtf1\ansi\deff0\deftab720{\fonttbl{\f0\fswiss MS Sans Serif;}
{\f1\froman\fcharset2
Symbol;}{\f2\fswiss\fprq2 Verdana;}{\f3\froman Times New Roman;}}
{\colortbl\red0\green0\blue0;}
\deflang1033\pard\plain\f2\fs20\b RTF\plain\f2\fs20  \plain\f2\
fs20\ul (which stands for
Rich Text Format) \plain\f2\fs20 is a document formatting language that
uses simple
commands to specify the formatting of the document. These commands, or
tags as they are
```

```
called, are ASCII strings, like \\par \plain\f2\fs20\i (the tag that
marks the beginning of
a new paragraph) \plain\f2\fs20 or \\b \plain\f2\fs20\i (the tag that
turns on the bold style). \plain\f2\fs20 And this is where the value of
the RTF format lies.
\par
\par \pard\li720\ri1109\plain\f2\fs20 RTF documents don't contain spe-
cial characters and can be exchanged among
different operating systems and computers, as long as there is an RTF-
capable application to read the document.
\par \pard\plain\f3\fs20
\par }
```

As you can see, all formatting tags are prefixed with the backslash (\) symbol. To display the \ symbol itself, insert an additional slash. Paragraphs are marked with the \par tag, and the entire document is enclosed in a pair of curly brackets. The \li and \ri tags followed by a numeric value specify the amount of the left and right indentation. If you assign this string to the TextRTF property of a RichTextBox control, the result will be the document shown in Figure 9.2, formatted exactly as it appears in WordPad.

RTF is similar to HTML (Hypertext Markup Language), and if you're familiar with HTML, a few comparisons between the two standards will provide helpful hints and insight into the RTF language. Like HTML, RTF was designed to create formatted documents that could be displayed on different systems. The RTF language uses tags to describe the document's format. For example, the tag for italics is \i, and its scope is delimited with a pair of curly brackets. The following RTF segment displays a sentence with a few words in italics:

```
{{\b RTF} (which stands for Rich Text Format) is a {\i document
formatting language} that uses simple commands to specify the
formatting of the document.}
```

The following is the equivalent HTML code:

```
<B>RTF</B> (which stands for Rich Text Format) is a <I>document format-
ting language</I> that uses simple commands to specify
the formatting of the document.
```

The <B> and <I> tags of HTML are equivalent to the \b and \i tags of RTF. RTF, however, is much more complicated than HTML. It's not nearly as easy to understand an RTF document as it is to understand an HTML document because RTF was meant to be used internally by applications. As you can see in the RTF segment presented earlier, RTF contains information about the font being used, its size, and so on. Just as you need a browser to view HTML documents, you need an RTF-capable application to view RTF documents. WordPad, for instance, supports RTF and can both save a document in RTF format and read RTF files.

You're not expected to supply your own RTF code to produce a document. You simply select the segment of the document you want to format and apply the corresponding formatting command from within your word processor. Fortunately, the RichTextBox control isn't any different. It doesn't require you or the users of your application to understand RTF code. The RichTextBox control does all the work for you while hiding the low-level details.

VB6 at Work: The RTFDemo Application

The RTFDemo application, shown in Figure 9.3, demonstrates the principles of programming the RichTextBox control. The RichTextBox control is the large box in the upper section of the Form where you can type text as you would with a regular TextBox control.

FIGURE 9.3:

The RTFDemo application demonstrates how the RichTextBox control handles RTF code.

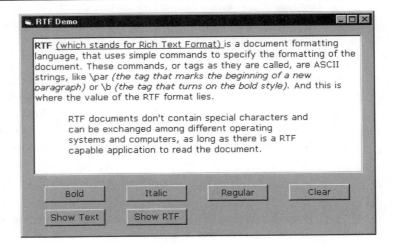

Use the buttons on the top row to set styles for the selected text. The Bold and Italic buttons are self-explanatory; the Regular button restores the regular style of the text. All three buttons set (or reset) the value of the properties *SelBold* (for the bold attribute) and *SelItalic* (for the italic attribute). By setting one of these properties to True, the corresponding attribute is turned on for the selected text; if set to False, it will be turned off. Here's the code behind the Bold button:

```
RichTextBox1.SelBold = True
```

The code for the Italic button is:

```
RichTextBox1.SelItalic = True
```

The Regular button's code contains the following two lines:

```
RichTextBox1.SelBold = False
RichTextBox1.SelItalic = False
```

The Clear button clears the contents of the control by setting its Text property to an empty string:

```
RichTextBox1.Text = ""
```

The two buttons on the second row demonstrate the nature of the RichTextBox control. Select a few words on the control, turn on their bold and/or italic attribute, and then click the Show Text button. You'll see a message box that contains the control's text. No matter how the text is formatted the control's Text property will be the same. This is the text you would copy from the control and paste into a text editing application that doesn't support formatting commands (for example, Notepad).

The RTF Code

If you click the Show RTF button, you'll see the actual RTF code that produced the formatted document in Figure 9.3. The message box with the RTF code is shown in Figure 9.4. This is all the information the RichTextBox control requires to render the document. As complicated as it may look, it isn't difficult to produce. In programming the RichTextBox control, you'll rarely have to worry about inserting actual RTF tags in the code. The control is responsible for generating the RTF code and for rendering the document. You simply manipulate a few properties (the recurring theme in Visual Basic programming) and the control does the rest.

FIGURE 9.4:

The RTF code for the formatted document shown in Figure 9.3

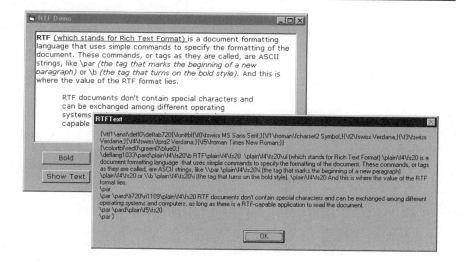

On rather rare occasions, you may have to supply RTF tags. You'll see an example of this in Chapter 11, *Recursive Programming*, with the DirMap application, which produces RTF code on the fly. You don't have to know much about RTF tags, though. Simply format a few words with the desired attributes using the RTFDemo application (or experiment with the Immediate window), copy the tags that produce the desired result, and use them in your application. If you are curious about RTF, experiment with the RTFDemo application.

One of the most interesting applications on the book's CD-ROM is the RTFPad application, a word processing application that's discussed in detail later in this chapter. This application duplicates much of the functionality of Windows Word-Pad, but it's included in this book to show you how the RichTextBox control is used. The RTFPad application can become your starting point for writing custom word processing applications (a programmer's text editor with color-coded keywords, for example).

Text Manipulation Properties

The RichTextBox control's properties for manipulating selected text start with the prefix Sel. The most commonly used properties related to the selected text are shown in Table 9.1.

TABLE 9.1: RichTextBox Control's Properties for Manipulating Selected Text

Property	What it manipulates
SelText	The selected text
SelStart	The position of the selected text's first character
SelLength	The length of the selected text
SelBold, SelItalic, SelUnderline, SelStrikethru, SelColor, SelFontName, SelFontSize	Various font attributes of the selected text
SelIndent, SelRightIndent, SelHangingIndent	The indentation of the selected text
SelRightMargin	The right margin of the selected text
SelRTF	The RTF code of the selected text

SelText, for example, represents the selected text. To assign the selected text to a variable, use the following statement:

```
SText=RichTextbox1.SelText
```

RichTextbox1 is the name of the control. You can also modify the selected text by assigning a new value to the SelText property. The following statement converts the selected text to uppercase:

```
RichTextbox1.SelText=UCase(RichTextbox1.SelText)
```

If you assign a string to the SelText property, the selected text in the control is replaced with the string. The following statement replaces the current selection on the RichTextbox1 control with the string "Revised string":

```
RichTextbox1.SelText="Revised string"
```

If no text is selected, the statement inserts the string at the location of the pointer. It is possible, therefore, to insert text automatically by assigning a string to the SelText property.

To simplify the manipulation and formatting of the text on the control, two additional properties, *SelStart* and *SelLength*, report the position of the first selected character in the text and the length of the selection, respectively. You can also set the values of these properties to select a piece of text from within your code. One obvious use of these properties is to select (and highlight) the entire text (or a segment of the text):

```
RichTextBox1.SelStart=0
RichTextBox1.SelLength=Len(RichTextBox1.Text)
```

NOTE   The SelText property is similar to the Text property. The difference is that SelText applies to the current selection instead of the entire text of the control.

SelIndent, *SelRightIndent*, and *SelHangingIndent* allow you to manipulate the indentation of the text. These properties apply to the selected text only. The text is aligned with the left side of the control. However, if you set the SelIndent property while the control is still empty, every time the user presses Enter, new paragraphs inherit the same left margin setting.

The RichTextBox Control's Methods

The first two methods of the RichTextBox control you will learn about are SaveFile and LoadFile:

- **SaveFile** saves the contents of the control to a disk file.

- **LoadFile** loads the control from a disk file.

The syntax of the SaveFile method is as follows:

```
RichTextBox1.SaveFile(filename, filetype)
```

The *filename* argument is the full path name of the disk file where the contents of the control will be saved, and *filetype* determines how the control's contents will be saved. The *filetype* argument, which is optional, can have one of the two values shown in Table 9.2.

TABLE 9.2: Two File Types Recognized by the RichTextBox Control

Constant	Value	Type	Description
rtfRTF	0	(Default) RTF	The RichTextBox control saves its contents as an RTF file; this is equivalent to saving the value of the TextRTF property to a disk file.
rtfText	1	Text	The RichTextBox control saves its contents as a text file; this is equivalent to saving the value of the control's Text property.

Similarly, the LoadFile method loads a text file or an RTF file to the control. Its syntax is identical to the syntax of the SaveFile method:

```
RichTextBox1.LoadFile(filename, filetype)
```

The *filetype* argument is optional. Saving and loading files to and from disk files are as simple as presenting a File Save or File Open common dialog control to the user and then calling one of the SaveFile or LoadFile methods with the filename returned by the common dialog box.

NOTE　You can also use the RichTextBox control to display nicely formatted instructions to the user. To specify the RTF file to be loaded on the control at design time, you can assign its path name to the control's FileName property. In addition, you can set the control's Locked property to True to prevent the user from changing the control's contents.

Advanced Editing Features

The RichTextBox control provides all the text editing features you'd expect to find in a text editing application. You can use the arrow keys to move through the text and press Ctrl+C to copy text or Ctrl+V to paste text. To facilitate the design of advanced text editing features, the RichTextBox control provides the Span and UpTo methods. Both of these interesting methods operate similarly, and their syntax is nearly identical.

- **Span** selects text in a RichTextBox control based on a set of specified characters.

- **UpTo** moves the pointer up to, but not including, the first character that's a member of the specified character set.

Many text editors provide special keystrokes that either let the user select an entire word or sentence or move the pointer to the end of a word or a sentence. By using the Span and UpTo methods, you can add the exact same capabilities to your application. Use the Span method to specify the characters that signal the end of the selection; use the UpTo method to specify the characters that identify where the pointer will move.

When you call the Span method, the RichTextBox control starts searching from the current position for one of the characters in the specified character set. The first character found causes the search to stop, and the text from the pointer's location to the position of the character found is selected. When you call the UpTo method, the pointer moves to the position of the first character found instead of selecting a range of text.

The Span method has the following syntax:

```
RichTextBox1.Span characterset, forward, negate
```

UpTo has a similar syntax:

```
RichTextBox1.UpTo characterset, forward, negate
```

The *characterset* argument is a string variable or constant that contains all the characters that mark the end of the selection or the new position of the pointer. The *forward* argument is a Boolean variable that determines the direction of the search:

- **True** causes a forward search from the current position of the pointer to the end of the text.

- **False** causes a backward search.

The *negate* variable is usually False and means that the search should locate one of the characters specified in the *characterset* variable. If you want to search for all characters except for a few, you can specify the characters you want to exclude from the search and set the *negate* argument to True. To implement a "select whole word" or "select sentence" feature in your text editing application, capture the KeyUp event and check for the key pressed, as explained in the following section.

Selecting Words and Sentences

Suppose you want the program to select the current word when Ctrl+W is pressed and the current sentence when Ctrl+S is pressed. First, the program must check the status of the Ctrl key, and if it's pressed, check the status of the W and S keys. If the W key is pressed, it should call the Span method to select everything from the pointer's location to the end of the word. If the S key is pressed, it should call the

Span method to select everything from the pointer's location to the end of the sentence. You must also supply the characters that commonly mark the end of a word or a sentence. See Figure 9.5 for an example of how this works.

FIGURE 9.5:

These two paragraphs show how Ctrl+W selects the word (top) and how Ctrl+S selects the sentence (bottom).

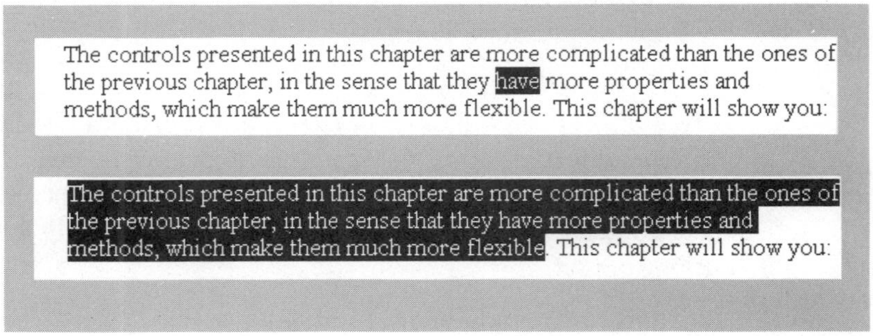

If the pointer is in the middle of a word, this technique selects only the characters from the pointer's location to the end of the word. However, selecting part of a word or a sentence is usually not what users want—they want to select the whole word with a single keystroke. Since you can't expect the user to position the pointer at the beginning of a word or sentence, you have to call the Span method twice, once to select the characters that belong to the word to the left of the pointer and again to select the characters to the right. In the first call of the function, you must set the *forward* argument to False (to search backward), and in the second call, you must set the *forward* argument to True (to search forward). This is what the first segment of Code 9.2 does.

Code 9.2:   **The Ctrl+W and Ctrl+S Key Combinations**

```
Private Sub RichTextBox1_KeyUp(KeyCode As Integer, Shift As Integer)
' Select word, or sentence
    If Shift = vbCtrlMask Then
        Select Case KeyCode
            ' If Ctrl+S:
            Case vbKeyS
                RichTextBox1.Span ".?!", False, True
                SelectionStart = RichTextBox1.SelStart
                ' Select to the end of the sentence.
                RichTextBox1.Span ".?!", True, True
                ' Extend selection to include punctuation.
                SelectionEnd = RichTextBox1.SelStart + _
                        RichTextBox1.SelLength
                RichTextBox1.SelStart = SelectionStart
                RichTextBox1.SelLength = SelectionEnd - SelectionStart
```

```
              ' If Ctrl+W:
              Case vbKeyW
                  ' Select to the end of the word.
                  RichTextBox1.Span " ,;:.?!", False, True
                  SelectionStart = RichTextBox1.SelStart
                  ' Select to the end of the word
                  RichTextBox1.Span " ,;:.?!", True, True

                  SelectionEnd = RichTextBox1.SelStart + _
                          RichTextBox1.SelLength
                  RichTextBox1.SelStart = SelectionStart
                  RichTextBox1.SelLength = SelectionEnd - SelectionStart
              End Select
          End If
' Move pointer by word or sentence
      If Shift = (vbCtrlMask Or vbShiftMask) Then
          Select Case KeyCode
          Case vbKeyS
              ' Move pointer to end of sentence.
              RichTextBox1.UpTo ".?!", True, False
          Case vbKeyW
              ' Move pointer to end of word.
              RichTextBox1.UpTo " ,;:.?!", True, False
          End Select
      End If
End Sub
```

This subroutine is used in the RTFPad application to implement the select word and select sentence features. The Ctrl+W keystroke selects the current word, and the Ctrl+S keystroke selects the current sentence; Ctrl+Shift+W moves the pointer to the end of the current word, and Ctrl+Shift+S moves the pointer to the end of the current sentence. Notice the similarities between the Span and UpTo methods. You can open the RTFPad application in this chapter's folder on the CD, enter some text in the control, and see how these keystrokes behave.

TIP

The same technique can be used to select keywords in a programmer's editor. In HTML programming, for example, all tags are enclosed in a pair of angle brackets (< and >). You can use the Span method to select an entire tag (everything from the opening < symbol to the closing > symbol) or to highlight the arguments of a function which are enclosed in parentheses. The Span method is a great tool for implementing advanced editing features for programmers' editors.

Searching in a RichTextBox Control

The *Find* method locates a string in the control's text and is similar to the InStr() function. You can use InStr() with the control's Text property to locate a string in the text, but the Find method is optimized for the RichTextBox control and supports a couple of options that the InStr() function doesn't. The syntax of the Find method is as follows:

```
RichTextBox1.Find(string, start, end, options)
```

The *string* argument is the string you want to locate in the RichTextBox control, *start* and *end* are the starting and ending locations of the search (use them to search for a string within a specified range only), and *options* is the sum of one or more of the constants listed in Table 9.3.

TABLE 9.3:   Search Options of the RichTextBox Control's Find Method

Constant	Value	Description
rtfWholeWord	2	Determines whether whole words (if True) or a fragment of a word (if False) will be matched
rtfMatchCase	4	Determines whether the match will be case sensitive (if True) or not (if False)
rtfNoHighlight	8	Determines whether the matched string will be highlighted in the control

To combine multiple options, you can add their values or you can combine them with the OR operator. All the arguments of the Find method are optional except for the string to be matched. If you omit them, they take on their default values. As a result, the search isn't case-sensitive, the entire text is searched, and the matching text is highlighted. If you specify only the *start* argument, the search is performed on the text from the specified position to the end of the text. Likewise, if you specify only the *end* argument, the search is performed on the text from the first character up to the specified character position.

The RTFPad application's Find command demonstrates how to use the Find method and its arguments to build a Find & Replace dialog box that performs all the types of text searching operations you might need in a text editing application. The code is identical to the code of the Search & Replace dialog box of the Notepad application presented in Chapter 5 in "Search and Replace Operations."

Text Formatting Properties

The RichTextBox control provides a number of properties for setting the appearance of the text in the control. Through the formatting properties, you can format the text in any of the ways possible through a word processing application such as WordPad. This section discusses all the text formatting properties of the Rich-TextBox control and how they are used.

Font Properties and Attributes

The following properties apply user-specified font, size, and attributes to the selected text. They can also be used to read the settings from within your code.

SelFontName, SelFontSize Properties   To change the font and size of the selected text, use these properties. The following statements render the selected text in 24-point Verdana font:

```
RichTextBox1.SelFontName = "Verdana"
RichTextBox1.SelFontSize = 24
```

You must supply the name of a font that exists on the user's computer; if you don't, a similar font will be substituted. Use the Font common dialog box (discussed in Chapter 8, *Advanced ActiveX Controls*) to let the user select one of the available fonts, as well as the desired attributes.

SelBold, SelItalic, SelUnderline Properties   You can read the value of these properties to check the formatting of the selected text from within your code, or you can set them to change the formatting accordingly. The following statements turn on the bold and italic attributes of the selected text:

```
RichTextbox1.SelBold=True
RichTextbox1.SelItalic=True
```

If no text is selected, the attributes are set for the character at the current location of the pointer. By setting the character-formatting properties accordingly (usually with the click of a button or a menu command), the user is, in effect, changing the style of the selected text.

The character-formatting properties are frequently used as toggles. Every time the user clicks a Bold button (or selects Bold from the application's menu), the following code is executed:

```
RichTextbox1.SelBold=NOT RichTextbox1.SelBold
```

If the selected text is in bold, it's turned back to normal; if it's normal, it's turned to bold. There is no property to reset the text style to normal. To do so, you must manually set all three properties to False:

```
RichTextbox1.SelBold=False
RichTextbox1.SelItalic=False
RichTextbox1.SelUnderline=False
```

SelCharOffset Property   This property determines whether the selected characters appear on, above, or below the text baseline. Normally, text appears on the baseline. You can raise characters above their baseline to create superscripts (you must also reduce the text's font size by a point or two) or place it below the baseline to create subscripts. To lower the selected text, assign a negative number to the SelCharOffset property. This value must be expressed in twips.

NOTE   Twips are a peculiar unit of length, used extensively in the Windows environment. A *twip* is 1/20 of a point, and there are 72 points in an inch. To raise selected characters one point above the baseline, use the statement `RichTextBox1`
`.SelCharOffset = 20`. To lower the selected text by 1/20 of an inch, use the statement `RichTextBox1.SelOffset = -72`.

Text Alignment Properties

The next group of properties control (or return) the alignment and indentation of the selected text in the RichTextBox control.

SelAlignment Property   Use this property to read or change the alignment of one or more paragraphs. It can have one of the values shown in Table 9.4.

TABLE 9.4: Alignment Values of the RichTextBox Control

Value	Description
0	(Default) Left-aligns selected paragraph(s)
1	Right-aligns selected paragraph(s)
2	Centers selected paragraph(s)

NOTE   The user doesn't have to actually select the entire paragraph to align it. Placing the pointer anywhere in the paragraph or selecting a few characters in the paragraph will do, because there is no way to align only a part of a paragraph.

SelIndent, SelRightIndent, SelHangingIndent Properties   When designing applications with the RichTextBox control, the most meaningful values for the container's ScaleMode property are points, inches, and millimeters (more on this property can be found in Chapter 6, *Drawing with Visual Basic*). Setting the values of the indentation properties is rather trivial, but designing a user interface that enables the user to intuitively and conveniently set these properties isn't. You can set the indentation of the selected text with the following properties:

- **SelIndent** sets (or returns) the amount of the text's indentation from the left edge of the control.

- **SelRightIndent** sets the indentation of the right side of the text from the right margin.

- **SelHangingIndent** specifies the distance between the left edge of the first line of the selected paragraph(s) (including any indentation specified by the SelIndent property) and the left edge of subsequent lines in the paragraph(s).

The hanging indentation can also be negative, in which case, the first line of text extends to the left farther than the rest of the paragraph. Figure 9.6 shows three possible combinations of the left and hanging indentation, all made possible with the two slider controls above the text.

FIGURE 9.6:

Various combinations of the SelIndent and Sel-HangingIndent properties produce interesting paragraph formatting.

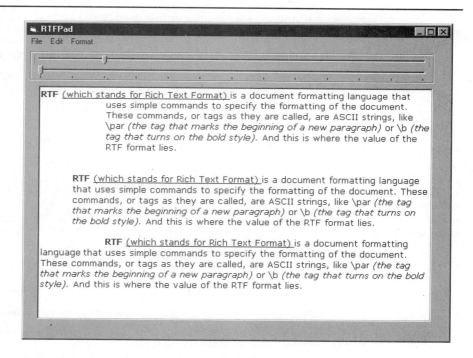

SelBullet Property   You use this property to create a list of bulleted items. If you set the SelBullet property to True, the selected paragraphs are formatted with a bullet style, similar to the <UL> tag in HTML. To create a list of bulleted items, select them with the pointer and then assign the value True to the SelBullet property. To change a list of bulleted items back to normal text, select the items and then assign the value False to the SelBullet property.

The paragraphs formatted with the SelBullet property set to True are also indented from the left by a small amount. To change the value of the indentation, use the *BulletIndent* property, whose syntax is as follows:

```
RichTextBox1.BulletIndent = value
```

You can also read the BulletIndent property from within your code to find out the bulleted items' indentation. Or you can use this property, along with the SelBullet property, to simulate nested bulleted items. If the current selection's SelBullet property is True and the user wants to apply the bullet format, you can increase the indentation of the current selection.

VB6 at Work: The RTFPad Project

Creating a functional, even fancy, word processor based on the RichTextBox control is quite simple. The challenge is to provide a convenient interface that lets the user select text, apply attributes and styles to it, and then set the control's properties accordingly. This chapter's application does just that. It's called RTFPad, and you can find it in this chapter's folder on the CD.

The RTFPad application (see Figure 9.7) is based on the TextPad application developed in Chapter 5, *Basic ActiveX Controls*. It contains the same text editing commands and some additional text formatting commands that can only be implemented with the RichTextBox control; for example, it allows you to mix font styles in the text. This section examines the code and discusses a few topics unique to this application's implementation with the RichTextBox control.

FIGURE 9.7:

The RTFPad application is a word processor based on the RichTextBox control.

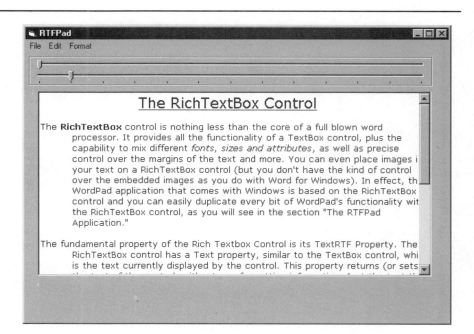

The two slider controls above the RichTextBox control manipulate the indentation of the text. We've already explored this arrangement in the discussion of the Slider control in Chapter 5, but let's review the operation of the two slider controls again. Every time they are scrolled, the following code is executed.

Code 9.3:   **Setting the Slider Controls**

```
Private Sub Slider1_Scroll()
    RichTextBox1.SelIndent = RichTextBox1.RightMargin _
        * (Slider1.Value / Slider1.Max)
    Slider2_Scroll
End Sub

Private Sub Slider2_Scroll()
    RichTextBox1.SelHangingIndent = RichTextBox1.RightMargin _
        * ((Slider2.Value - Slider1.Value) / Slider2.Max)
End Sub
```

The Slider1 control sets the text's left indentation as a percentage of the control's width (same percentage as the control's value compared with the maximum value). Next, the code of the other control's Scroll event is executed to set the hanging indentation. If the user changes the hanging indentation, the Slider1_Scroll subroutine isn't called from within the Slider2 control's code because there's no reason to adjust the overall indentation.

Enter some text in the control, select one or more paragraphs, and check out the operation of the two sliders. Unfortunately, there's no Slider control that has indicators for setting both left and right values, thereby controlling both margins.

The Scroll events of the two slider controls adjust the text's indentation. The opposite action must take place when the user rests the pointer on another paragraph: the Sliders' positions must be adjusted to reflect the new indentation of the text. The selection of a new paragraph is signaled to the application by the SelChange event. Among the statements that are executed from within the SelChange event (they are discussed in the next sections), the following one adjusts the two slider controls to reflect the indentation of the text.

Code 9.4:   **Setting the Slider Controls**

```
' Change the sliders' positions according to the selection's indentation
    If IsNull(RichTextBox1.SelIndent) Then
        Slider1.Enabled = False
        Slider2.Enabled = False
        Exit Sub
```

```
        Else
            Slider1.Enabled = True
            Slider2.Enabled = True
    On Error Resume Next
            Slider1.Value = RichTextBox1.SelIndent _
                * Slider1.Max / RichTextBox1.RightMargin
            Slider2.Value = (RichTextBox1.SelHangingIndent / _
                RichTextBox1.RightMargin) * Slider2.Max + Slider1.Value
        End If
```

If the user selects multiple paragraphs with different indentations, the SelIndent property returns Null. The code examines the value of the SelIndent property and if it's Null, it disables the two slider controls (since it can't set their position). If it's not Null, it sets the positions of the controls according to the values of the SelIndent and SelHangingIndent properties.

NOTE   Disabling the slider controls if the user selects multiple paragraphs with different indentations is not the best approach. The user might wish to apply a uniform indentation to multiple paragraphs, but this can't be done while the sliders are disabled. You should experiment with different approaches, such as changing the background color of the frame, but keeping the sliders enabled. Or, you can set the sliders according to the indentation of the first or last paragraph in the selection. Unfortunately, you can't gray the sliders and keep them enabled.

The File Menu

The RTFPad application's File menu contains the usual Open and Save commands, which are implemented with the LoadFile and SaveFile methods, and the Print command. Here is the implementation of the Open command in the File menu.

Code 9.5:   **The Open Command**

```
Private Sub FileOpen_Click()
Dim txt As String
Dim FNum As Integer

On Error GoTo FileError:
    CommonDialog1.CancelError = True
    CommonDialog1.Flags = cdlOFNFileMustExist
    CommonDialog1.DefaultExt = "RTF"
    CommonDialog1.Filter = "RTF Files|*.RTF|Text Files|*.TXT|All _
        Files|*.*"
    CommonDialog1.ShowOpen
```

```
        RichTextBox1.LoadFile CommonDialog1.filename, rtfRTF
        OpenFile = CommonDialog1.filename
        Exit Sub
FileError:
    If Err.Number = cdlCancel Then Exit Sub
    MsgBox "Unknown error while opening file " & _
            CommonDialog1.filename
    OpenFile = ""
End Sub
```

The *OpenFile* variable is global and holds the name of the currently open file. It's set every time a new file is successfully opened and used by the Save command to automatically save the open file, without prompting the user for a filename.

The Save menu's code is similar, only it calls the SaveFile method to save the RTF code to a disk file.

Printing the RTF Document

The Print command is implemented with a few lines of code that select all the text on the control and then call the *SelPrint* method to print the selected text. The EditSelect_Click subroutine is the event handler of the Select All command of the Edit menu. The SelPrint method's argument is the hDC property of the printer where the text is printed. The code uses the default printer, but you can display the Print common dialog box, where the user can select any of the available printers. If you do so, don't give your users the option to select a range of pages, because the SelPrint method doesn't provide a mechanism for this. It's a very simple method that prints the selected text and offers no options. Hopefully, a future version of the RichTextBox control will provide a more flexible Print method. I should warn you that implementing your own printing procedure is quite a task. Here's the listing for the Print command's event handler:

Code 9.6:　　　　**The Print Command of the RTFPad Project**

```
Private Sub FilePrint_Click()
Dim lastPosition As Long, lastSelection As Long

    EditSelect_Click
    RichTextBox1.SelPrint Printer.hDC
    RichTextBox1.SelStart = lastPosition
    RichTextBox1.SelLength = lastSelection
End Sub
```

The Edit Menu

The RTFPad application's Edit menu commands are quite simple. Instead of the SelText property, they use the control's *SelRTF* property to move information to the Clipboard and back so that the copied text carries its formatting information with it. If you aren't familiar with the Clipboard's methods, all you need to know to follow this example are the SetText method, which copies a string to the Clipboard, and the GetText method, which copies the Clipboard's contents to a string variable. The Copy and Cut commands are shown next.

Code 9.7:   The Copy and Cut Commands

```
Private Sub EditCopy_Click()
    Clipboard.SetText RichTextBox1.SelRTF
End Sub

Private Sub EditCut_Click()
    Clipboard.SetText RichTextBox1.SelRTF
    RichTextBox1.SelRTF = ""
End Sub
```

The Paste command examines the type of the contents stored in the Clipboard, with the *GetFormat()* method and pastes them at the current location in the control either in text or RTF format. The Paste command's code follows.

Code 9.8:   The Paste Command

```
Private Sub EditPaste_Click()
    If Clipboard.GetFormat(vbCFRTF) Then
        RichTextBox1.SelRTF = Clipboard.GetData(vbCFRTF)
    ElseIf Clipboard.GetFormat(vbCFText) Then
        RichTextBox1.SelText = Clipboard.GetText
    End If
End Sub
```

You can also insert bitmaps, or other objects in the RTFPad's window. To do so, open an image with Paint (or another image processing application), copy it to the Clipboard, and then paste it in the RTFPad application by pressing Shift+Insert. The Paste command won't paste bitmaps. You'll see how to paste other types of objects in the RichTextBox control, as well as how to access these objects in Chapter 14, *OLE Automation and VBA*.

The Search & Replace Dialog Box

The Find command in the RTFPad Edit menu opens the dialog box shown in Figure 9.8, which the user can use to perform various search and replace operations (whole word or case-sensitive match, or both). The code behind the Command buttons on this Form is quite similar to the code for the Find & Replace dialog box of the TextPad application, with one basic difference: it uses the control's Find method and the options of this method that aren't available with the InStr() function.

FIGURE 9.8:

The Search & Replace dialog box of the RTFPad application

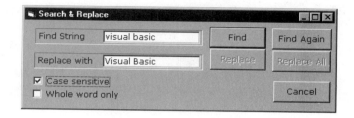

Code 9.9:   **The Find Button**

```
Private Sub FindButton_Click()
Dim FindFlags As Integer

    Position = 0
    FindFlags = Check1.Value * 4 + Check2.Value * 2
    Position = Form1.RichTextBox1.Find(Text1.Text, Position + 1, ,_
            FindFlags)
    If Position >= 0 Then
        ReplaceButton.Enabled = True
        ReplaceAllButton.Enabled = True
        Form1.SetFocus
    Else
        MsgBox "String not found"
        ReplaceButton.Enabled = False
        ReplaceAllButton.Enabled = False
    End If
End Sub
```

The *FindFlags* variable takes its value from the CheckBox controls that determine the type of match. When a checkbox is checked, its Value property is 1. The code multiplies the first CheckBox control's value by 4 and the second CheckBox control's value by 2 to set the *rtfWholeWord* and *rtfMatchCase* options. This value is passed as the last argument of the Find method.

The search starts with the first character of the text and moves forward. To implement a "backward search" option, add another CheckBox control on the Find Form, and adjust the *start* and *end* arguments of the Find method accordingly.

NOTE
The Find command of the Edit menu calls an API function to display the Search & Replace dialog box using SetWindowPos(). You can invoke the same Form with the following simple statement:

```
SearchForm.Show
```

(This statement is commented out in the project's code). The API function I use in the code causes the Search & Replace dialog box to remain on top of the main Form, even when it's not active. This is the standard behavior of the Seach & Replace dialog box of every word processor. The SetWindowPos() API function is explained in detail in Chapter 13.

The Format Menu

The Format menu lets the user set the font, size, and attributes of the selected text. The first command of the Format menu is Font, and it opens the Font common dialog box, in which the user can select the font, size, and attributes of the currently selected text. Although the font doesn't change frequently in a document, the attributes do, and the application shouldn't force the user to open the Font common dialog box just to turn a word into bold or italics. That's why the font attributes are also implemented as commands on the Format menu.

NOTE
If you'd like to enable all the options in the Font common dialog box when the user opens it, you need to set a number of flags. Chapter 8, *Advanced ActiveX Controls*, lists all the flags related to the Font common dialog box and shows you how to set these flags in your code.

The Bold, Italic, Underline, and Regular commands on the Format menu turn on and off the corresponding attribute. A checkmark next to one of these commands indicates the attribute of the current selection. If only part of the selection is bold, the SelBold property returns Null to indicate that the selection isn't uniform. You must always check the values of the SelItalic, SelBold, and SelUnderline properties for Null values. You will see an example of how these properties are used to read the attributes of the selected text in the next section, "The SelChange Event."

The first function of the Bold, Italic, and Underline commands is quite simple: to turn on the corresponding attribute of the selected text. If the selected text isn't bold, selecting the Bold command turns on the attribute. If the selected text is bold already, this command turns off the attribute. The second function of these commands is to reflect the attributes of the selected text; that is, you must set or rest the checkmark in front of their names depending on the attributes of the selected text. The RTFPad application must track the user's actions through the SelChange event, which is triggered every time the current selection changes. From within this event, we must examine the values of the SelBold, SelItalic, and SelUnderline properties and set (or reset) the checkmark in front of the corresponding menu command. The three font attribute commands are implemented with code from within two events: the menu command's Click event and the RichTextBox control's SelChange event. The Click event handler for the Bold command is shown next.

Code 9.10:   The Bold Command

```
Private Sub FormatBold_Click()
    FormatBold.Checked = Not FormatBold.Checked
    RichTextBox1.SelBold = FormatBold.Checked
End Sub
```

First, the program switches the current state of the menu command (if it's checked, it unchecks it, and vice versa). It then turns on or off the bold attribute of the selected text according to the recently updated state of the Bold command.

The SelChange Event   To be able to set the status of the various commands of the Format menu, your code must be able to detect when the user changes the current selection. This action is reported to your application by the control's SelChange event. In the RichTextBox control's SelChange event, the program does the opposite. It examines the attribute of the selected text and sets the command state accordingly. Following are the statements that manipulate the state of the formatting commands from within the SelChange event.

Code 9.11:   The SelChange Event

```
Private Sub RichTextBox1_SelChange()
    If Not IsNull(RichTextBox1.SelBold) Then _
        FormatBold.Checked = RichTextBox1.SelBold
    If Not IsNull(RichTextBox1.SelItalic) Then _
        FormatItalic.Checked = RichTextBox1.SelItalic
    If Not IsNull(RichTextBox1.SelUnderline) Then _
        FormatUnderline.Checked = RichTextBox1.SelUnderline
End Sub
```

Notice the use of the IsNull() function. If part of the selected text has an attribute turned on and part of it has the same attribute turned off, the SelBold property is neither True nor False. Instead, it's undefined, and the program must check for this condition. If the SelBold property is defined, the Bold command is checked or unchecked, depending on the value of the property.

If the SelBold attribute is undefined, the menu command doesn't change. (You could replace the Bold title with another string, such as "mixed", indicating that the corresponding attribute is not uniform for the current selection.) Earlier in the chapter, you learned that the SelChange event handler also contains statements that adjust the positions of the slider controls to reflect the indentation of the selected text.

The font attributes menu commands are best implemented with Tri-state buttons. For example, when the selected text is bold and the user presses the Bold button, the text is reset to regular. If the current selection's bold attribute is undefined, the corresponding button should assume a third (grayed) appearance.

When the user clicks the Bold button, RTFPad should turn the bold attribute on and off. This feature is relatively easy to implement, except perhaps for designing the pictures for the three states (on, off, mixed) of the Command buttons. Visual programming requires some artistic talent; your programming abilities won't help you much here.

You've learned basically everything there is to know about the RichTextBox control. It provides the basic functionality of a word processing application, and adding more features to an editor is as simple as setting the values of its various properties.

The Objects Collection   If you experiment a little with the RTFPad application, you'll find out that it can accept more than text. You can copy a bitmap in an image processing application and paste it into the RichTextBox control by pressing Shift+Insert. The Paste command of the Edit menu doesn't recognize anything more than text (plain or RTF format), but the control itself is capable of accepting other data types, including objects. For example, you can insert a sound file or video file (AVI or MPEG file) at the current location in the text. The various objects that can exist on the RichTextBox control along with the text can be accessed through the *Objects* collection. This is a rather advanced topic, and I will postpone its discussion until Chapter 14, *OLE Automation and VBA*. In this chapter, you'll learn how to manipulate the objects embedded in the RichTextBox control and even how to recognize when an object is about to be pasted and how to react to this action.

The MSFlexGrid Control

One of the most impressive controls of Visual Basic is the MSFlexGrid control. As you can guess by its name, the MSFlexGrid control is a descendant of the old Grid control. The MSFlexGrid control provides all the functionality for building spreadsheet applications, just as the RichTextBox control provides all the functionality for building word processing applications. Once you master its basic properties, writing spreadsheet-like applications for displaying data will just be a question of setting its properties.

The MSFlexGrid control is an extremely useful tool for displaying information in a tabular form. You can place it on your Forms to present nicely organized data to the user. Figure 9.9 shows a MSFlexGrid control displaying financial data. At first glance, it looks a lot like a spreadsheet: the first row and column are fixed and they contain titles, and the rest of the cells contain text (including numbers) or graphics arranged in rows and columns, which can vary in width and height. The scroll bars give the user easy access to any part of the control (although all the cells can scroll, the fixed cells always remain visible).

NOTE   The grid shown in Figure 9.9 was created with the Grid1 application, which you can find in this chapter's folder on the CD. The Grid1 application demonstrates the basic properties of the MSFlexGrid control.

FIGURE 9.9:

The MSFlexGrid control looks very much like an Excel spreadsheet. The title is placed on a Label control, but everything else (including the scroll bars) belongs to the control.

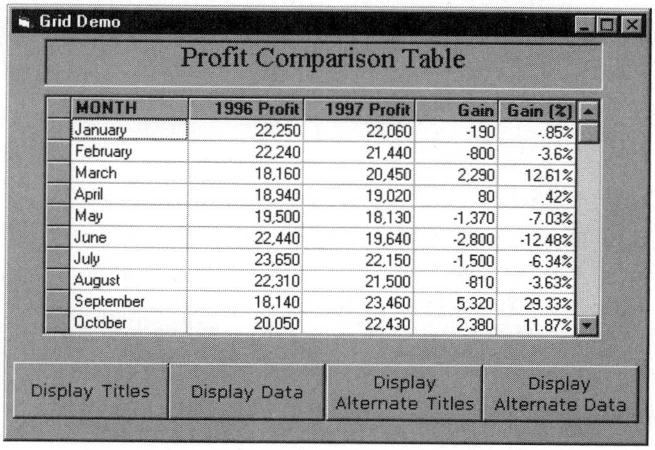

MONTH	1996 Profit	1997 Profit	Gain	Gain (%)
January	22,250	22,060	-190	-.85%
February	22,240	21,440	-800	-3.6%
March	18,160	20,450	2,290	12.61%
April	18,940	19,020	80	.42%
May	19,500	18,130	-1,370	-7.03%
June	22,440	19,640	-2,800	-12.48%
July	23,650	22,150	-1,500	-6.34%
August	22,310	21,500	-810	-3.63%
September	18,140	23,460	5,320	29.33%
October	20,050	22,430	2,380	11.87%

Profit Comparison Table — Grid Demo

Display Titles | Display Data | Display Alternate Titles | Display Alternate Data

Despite external similarities, the MSFlexGrid control is not a complete spreadsheet in the same sense that the TextBox control is not a complete word processor. Although it can be the basis of a spreadsheet, this is not the purpose for which the MSFlexGrid control was designed. It is meant to display information in tabular form, but not for data entry.

Most of the properties of this control pertain to the placement of the data and their appearance; there are no properties or events for the immediate editing of the cells' contents. However, it's not too difficult to take control of the KeyPress event to capture keystrokes and add data entry capabilities to the control, as you'll see later on in the section "The FlexGrid Application."

Basic Properties

Let's review the basic properties of the control by examining its operation. Recall that the grid's cells can contain text, numbers, or images. You can assign a value to a cell in several ways, but all methods require that you first select the cell by means of its address on the grid and assign the desired value to its Text property.

The address of a cell is given by its *Row* and *Col* properties, whose values start at 0. Row 0 is the fixed title row, and column 0 is the fixed title column. To address the first non-fixed cell in the grid of Figure 9.9, you would use the following statements:

```
Grid.Row = 1
Grid.Col = 1
```

After you specify the cell's address, you can examine its contents with a statement like:

```
CellValue = Grid.Text
```

or set its contents with a statement like:

```
Grid.Text = "January"
```

This method of reading or setting cell values requires too many statements for such a simple task, and it's probably available to be compatible with the old Grid control. The simplest way to address a cell on the grid is by means of the *TextMatrix* property, which has the following syntax :

```
Grid.TextMatrix(row, col)
```

The *row* and *col* arguments are the cell's coordinates in the grid. To extract the value of the first editable cell, use a statement like:

```
CellValue = Grid.TextMatrix(1, 1)
```

The names of the months and the corresponding profit figures of the grid shown in Figure 9.9 are assigned with the following loop, which is executed from within the Display Data button's event handler.

Code 9.12:   **Using the FormatString Property**

```
Dim irow As Integer
For irow = 1 To 12
    Grid.TextMatrix(irow, 1) = MonthNames(irow)
    Grid.TextMatrix(irow, 2) = Format$(Profit97(irow), "#,###")
    Grid.TextMatrix(irow, 3) = Format$(Profit96(irow), "#,###")
    Grid.TextMatrix(irow, 4) = Format$(Grid.TextMatrix(irow, 3) _
            - Grid.TextMatrix(irow, 2), "#,###")
    Grid.TextMatrix(irow, 5) = Format$(100 * _
            - (Grid.TextMatrix(irow, 3) _
            - Grid.TextMatrix(irow, 2)) / Grid.TextMatrix(irow, 2), _
            - "#.##") & "%"
Next
```

The array *MonthNames* holds the names of the months and the arrays *Profit96* and *Profit97* contain the numeric values. Notice that the contents of the last two columns (Gain and Gain [%]) are calculated.

A third way to access the cells of the grid is by means of the *TextArray* property, which is similar to the TextMatrix property, but it uses a single index to address a cell. It has the following syntax:

```
Grid.TextArray(cellindex)
```

To calculate the *cellindex* argument, which determines the location of the desired cell, multiply the desired row by the Cols property and add the desired column. The following statement calculates the value of the *cellindex* argument, given its row (*row*) and column (*col*) number:

```
cellindex = row * Cols + col
```

The TextArray property is less convenient than the TextMatrix property because you have to convert the actual address of the desired cell to a single number. Use the TextArray property to assign values to the grid's cells if the values are already stored in a one-dimensional array.

Displaying Rows and Columns

In Figure 9.9, the cells of the first row and column have a gray background because they are meant to be used as titles for the corresponding columns and rows. The unique feature of these cells is that they don't scroll along with the rest of the cells, so the titles always remain visible. You can change the number of the title rows and columns with the FixedCols and FixedRows properties, use the Format String property to set up the control's headers, and adjust column width and row height with the AllowUserResizing property.

FixedCols, FixedRows Properties   The most common value for these two properties is 1, which translates into one fixed row and one fixed column. The fixed row and column contain titles that can be assigned with any of the methods mentioned earlier or with the help of the FormatString property (discussed in next section). Other than their different background color and the fact that they don't scroll, the fixed cells are the same as the other cells of the grid.

Another characteristic of the title row and column is that clicking one of their cells selects the entire row or column (see Figure 9.10). Clicking the very first fixed cell of the grid, in the upper left corner, selects the entire grid. This behavior can be changed by setting the *AllowBigSelection* property to False instead of True (its default value).

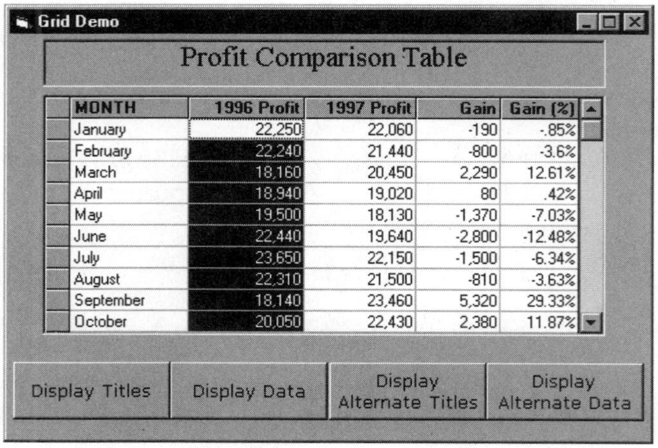

FIGURE 9.10:

Clicking a column header such as "Profit 1996" will automatically select the entire column.

Grid Demo

Profit Comparison Table

MONTH	1996 Profit	1997 Profit	Gain	Gain (%)
January	22,250	22,060	-190	-.85%
February	22,240	21,440	-800	-3.6%
March	18,160	20,450	2,290	12.61%
April	18,940	19,020	80	.42%
May	19,500	18,130	-1,370	-7.03%
June	22,440	19,640	-2,800	-12.48%
July	23,650	22,150	-1,500	-6.34%
August	22,310	21,500	-810	-3.63%
September	18,140	23,460	5,320	29.33%
October	20,050	22,430	2,380	11.87%

Display Titles   Display Data   Display Alternate Titles   Display Alternate Data

FormatString Property   This property can be assigned a string variable that sets up the control's column width, alignments, and fixed row and column text. The FormatString property is made up of segments separated by pipe characters (|). The text between two pipes defines a new column or row, and it can contain text and the alignment characters shown in Table 9.5.

TABLE 9.5: The Alignment Characters

Character	What It Does
<	Left-aligns the column
^	Centers the column
>	Right-aligns the column

The text becomes the column's header, and its width defines the width of the column. The semicolon denotes that the text following it applies to the next row. The text also becomes the row's header, and the longest string defines the width of the fixed column. Similar to column titles, successive row titles are separated with the pipe symbol.

Figures 9.11, 9.12, and 9.13 demonstrate the use of the FormatString property to set up a grid with a fixed row, column, or both. These figures were created with the FString application, which you will find in this chapter's folder on the CD.

FIGURE 9.11:

The titles on the fixed row of this grid are placed there with a format string.

The header row of Figure 9.11 is created with the following format string:

```
s$ = "<Country|^Athletes|^Gold|^Silver|^Bronze"
MSFlexGrid1.FormatString = s$
```

Successive column headers are separated by the pipe character. Some spaces are inserted before and after the titles to create some space between the headers and the cell dividers.

The header column of Figure 9.12 is created with a similar format string:

```
s$ = ";|Country|Athletes|Gold|Silver|Bronze"
MSFlexGrid1.FormatString = s$
```

FIGURE 9.12:

The titles on the fixed column of this grid are placed there with a format string.

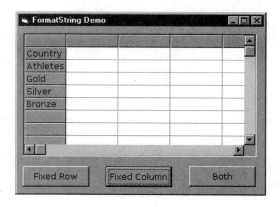

This string starts with the semicolon, which indicates that the following entries are row headers. After the semicolon, the pipe symbol is used to delimit each row's header.

In the grids in Figures 9.11 and 9.12, the user is expected to enter the country names along with the other information.

The grid in Figure 9.13 displays the headers of the previous examples, as well as the country names; the user needs to supply only the numeric data.

FIGURE 9.13:

The titles on the fixed row and column of this grid are placed there with a format string.

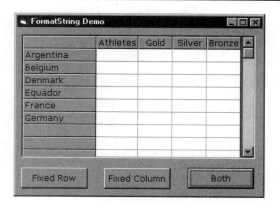

This grid's headers are set up with a format string that is a combination of the two previous format strings:

```
s$ = "<Country|^Athletes|^Gold|^Silver|^Bronze;| Argentina "
s$ = s$ & " |Belgium | Denmark | Ecuador | France | Germany"
MSFlexGrid1.FormatString = s$
```

Notice again that there's only one semicolon in the string, which denotes that all the entries that follow are row headers. The country names are separated by the pipe symbol, and the longest country name determines the width of the fixed column.

Each column in the grid may have its own width, which is controlled by the *ColWidth* property. To set the width of the first column (the title column), use the following statement:

```
Grid1.ColWidth(0)=500
```

The Width's value is expressed in twips, and as mentioned earlier, there are 20 twips in a point. The previous statement sets the width of the first column to approximately 25 points. Likewise, each row can have a different height, which is controlled by the RowHeight property, whose syntax is quite similar. It's quite common to use the TextWidth property to set up the width of the column. The MSFlex-Grid control doesn't have a TextWidth property, so you must set the Form's Font property to the same value as the grid's Font property and use the Form's Text-Width property. Open the FString project in the Visual Basic IDE and examine its code; it uses the ColWidth property to set the width of the grid's columns.

AllowUserResizing Property   The user can change the width of columns and height of rows at runtime by dragging the column and row separators with the mouse. If you place the mouse over a dividing line between two columns (or rows) in the title section of the grid, it assumes the shape of a double arrow indicating that it can be dragged to resize a row or column of cells. To disable row and/or column resizing, set the AllowUserResizing property to one of the values shown in Table 9.6.

TABLE 9.6:   Values of the AllowUserResizing Property

Constant	Value	Description
flexResizeNone	0	(Default) User can't resize the cells
flexResizeColumns	1	User can resize columns only
flexResizeRows	2	User can resize rows only
flexResizeBoth	3	User can resize columns and rows

Working with Multiple Cells

One of the most useful aspects of a spreadsheet is the ability to select multiple cells and perform certain operations on them, such as copying, pasting, and formatting. Unfortunately, you can't insert formulas for calculated fields in an MSFlexGrid control, but you can perform simpler, useful operations such as sorting the grid's rows, as you will see later in the section "Sorting the Grid."

Properties for Selecting a Range of Cells   The user can select a range of cells with a click-and-drag operation over multiple cells. By clicking a fixed column (or row) cell, the user can select the entire column (or row). The selected range is always a rectangle, and the coordinates of the first selected cell (where the mouse button is pressed) are given by the properties Row and Col. The coordinates of the last selected cell (where the mouse button is released) are given by the properties RowSel and ColSel. If you set these properties, you can select a range from within your code. The following statements select the month names on the grid previously seen in Figure 9.9:

```
Grid.Row = 1
Grid.Col = 0
Grid.RowSel = 12
Grid. ColSel = 0
```

The selected range is highlighted and all its cells appear in reverse background color except for the first one. This cell is distinguished from the rest because it also happens to be the active cell, or the cell that was clicked at the start of the click-and-drag operation. You can also restrict the way cells are selected with the *SelectionMode* property; its settings are shown in Table 9.7.

TABLE 9.7:   Values of the SelectionMode Property

Constant	Value	Description
flexSelectionFree	0	Allows selections to be made normally, spreadsheet-style
flexSelectionByRow	1	Forces selections to be made by rows
flexSelectionByColumn	2	Forces selections to be made by columns

FillStyle Property   The simplest operation you can perform on a range of cells is to assign an initial value to them. Normally, the value assigned to the control's Text property applies to the active cell. However, the property FillStyle determines whether a value is assigned to the active cell or to the entire range of selected cells. The FillStyle property is a property of the control, and its values are shown in Table 9.8.

The same property can be used to specify whether other cell properties, such as alignment or background color, will be applied to the active cell or to an entire range of cells.

TABLE 9.8: Values of the FillStyle Property

Constant	Value	Description
flexFillSingle	0	(Default) Changes only affect the active cell.
flexFillRepeat	1	Changes affect all selected cells.

Clip Property   This property holds the contents of the selected cells on the grid. Values of adjacent cells on the same row are delimited by a tab character (Chr$(9)), and successive rows are delimited by a new line or carriage return character (Chr$(13)). The most common operation of the Clip property is to transfer data to and from the Clipboard. The following statement transfers the values of the selected cells to the Clipboard, where they are stored as text:

```
Clipboard.SetText Grid.Clip
```

To paste these cell values to another area of the control, first select the destination of the paste operation, and then use the following statement:

```
Grid.Clip = Clipboard.GetText
```

Observe that the contents of the Clipboard are pasted only on the selected cells, that is, on the cells that are part of the current Clip property. If the number of selected cells is larger than the number of cells in the Clip property, some cells won't be affected. On the other hand, if there are fewer selected cells than the Clipboard's entries, some of the Clipboard's data will not end up in the grid.

NOTE   The Clip property is all you need to implement the Copy, Cut, and Paste operations in an application that uses the MSFlexGrid control. However, you must make sure that enough cells have been selected to accommodate all the data on the Clipboard before you actually paste them.

The MSFlexGrid control doesn't provide a method for storing its contents to a disk file that's similar to the SaveFile and LoadFile methods of the RichTextBox control. The simplest way to store the contents of an entire grid to a disk file is to use the Clip property. First, select the entire grid, then write the Clip property (which by now holds the contents of the entire grid) to a file. The following statements store the current grid to the Grid.GRD file (the extension is arbitrary; no known file type uses it):

```
Open "Grid.GRD" For Output As #1
Write #1, Grid.Clip
Close #1
```

This method is used in the FlexGrid application to implement the Save and Save As commands.

You can also prepare data to append to a spreadsheet from within another application. First, create a long string with data, using the Tab character to delimit successive values on the same row and the carriage return character to delimit successive columns. Then, assign this string to the MSFlexGrid control's Clip property.

Cell Appearance and Alignment

Another group of properties relate to the font, style, and color of the cells. With the MSFlexGrid control, you have the flexibility to control the appearance of individual cells with the following properties:

- **CellFontBold** and **CellFontItalic** set (or return) the style of the text in the selected cells. To change the style of multiple cells, you first select the cells and then set the FillStyle property to *flexFillRepeat*.

- **CellFontName** sets (or returns) the font to be used in rendering the text in the selected cells.

- **CellFontSize** sets (or returns) the font's size in points.

- **CellFontWidth** sets (or returns) the width of the selected cell(s) in points.

When you change the font's width, its height remains the same, as specified by the CellFontSize property (or whatever font size you specified at design time in the control's Properties window).

CellFontSize, CellFontWidth Properties   To find out how these properties affect the appearance of the text on an MSFlexGrid control, experiment with the Font-Size application in the Grid folder on the CD (shown in Figure 9.14). The two Combo-Boxes at the bottom of the form let you set the size of both properties in points.

FIGURE 9.14:

The FontSize application demonstrates the difference between the Cell-FontSize and CellFont-Width properties.

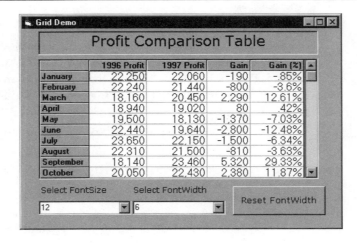

	1996 Profit	1997 Profit	Gain	Gain (%)
January	22,250	22,060	-190	-.85%
February	22,240	21,440	-800	-3.6%
March	18,160	20,450	2,290	12.61%
April	18,940	19,020	80	.42%
May	19,500	18,130	-1,370	-7.03%
June	22,440	19,640	-2,800	-12.48%
July	23,650	22,150	-1,500	-6.34%
August	22,310	21,500	-810	-3.63%
September	18,140	23,460	5,320	29.33%
October	20,050	22,430	2,380	11.87%

As you change the CellFontSize property, both the width and height of the characters change. Change the CellFontWidth property, and only the width of the characters changes. In general, when you set the width of the text, you should consider its height. If you have a large amount of data to display, you can set both the Cell-FontSize and CellFontWidth properties to squeeze more data in the available area by making the numbers narrow, yet easy-to-read.

CellForeColor, CellBackColor Properties   To change the color of the text or the background color in the selected cell(s), use the following properties. The value of these properties can be an RGB Color value or a QB Color value.

- **BackColorBgk** returns or sets the background color of various elements of the control (the area outside the grid).

- **ForeColorFixed** returns or sets the foreground color of the fixed rows and columns.

- **BackColorFixed** returns or sets the background color of the fixed rows and columns.

- **ForeColorSel** returns or sets the foreground color of the selected cells.

- **BackColorSel** returns or sets the background color of the selected cells.

You will see how these properties are used in the FlexGrid application later in the chapter. The FlexGrid application allows the user to select a range of cells and set their foreground and background colors independently of the rest of the grid.

CellAlignment Property   You can give each cell in the grid a different alignment by using this property. You can use it to set the alignment of the active cell or the range of selected cells (as long as the FillStyle property is set to True, of course), and it can take on one of the values listed in Table 9.9.

TABLE 9.9: Values of the CellAlignment Property

Value	Alignment	Value	Alignment
0	Left top	5	Center bottom
1	Left center	6	Right top
2	Left bottom	7	Right center
3	Center top	8	Right bottom
4	Center center	9	Left center for strings, right center for numbers

As you can see, the cell's contents can be aligned both vertically and horizontally. To align a range of cells from within your code, follow these steps:

1. Select the range by setting the Row, Col, SelRow, and SelCol properties to the appropriate values.

2. Make sure that the FillStyle property is set to True.

3. Assign one of the values in Table 9.9 to the CellAlignment property.

ColAlignment Property   If you want to align an entire column, you can use this property instead of CellAlignment. It's an array with one element per column. Its syntax is as follows:

```
MSFlexGrid1.ColAlignment(column) = value
```

The *column* argument is the number of the column whose alignment you want to set. The ColAlignment property may take on any of the values previously shown in Table 9.9. The following statement centers the text in the first (most likely fixed) column, regardless of the current selection:

```
MSFlexGrid1.ColAlignment(0)= 4
```

Notice that there is no RowAlignment property to set the alignment of the cells of an entire row.

Sorting the Grid

Nearly every application you will develop with the MSFlexGrid control will require a sorting feature. The control's Sort property does just that. Sort is not a method, as you might expect, but a property. Each time the Sort property is set to a value, the selected rows of the grid are sorted according to selected criteria. If no rows are selected, the entire grid is sorted.

Sort Property   Before setting this property, you must select one or more columns, which are the *keys* used in the sorting. The keys are the values according to which the rows of the grid are sorted, and they must be the elements of one or more rows. If you select a single column, the (selected) rows are sorted according to the entries of this column. If you select multiple columns, their entries are combined to create the sort key. If you set the Col property to 1 and the ColSel property to 3, the entries in the first column are the primary sorting keys. If two or more rows have the same primary key, they are sorted according to their values in the second column. If these keys are identical, the same cells in the third column are used as keys.

TIP

The columns used in the sorting process must be adjacent. In other words, the columns used as sorting keys can be selected only with the Col and ColSel properties. Moreover, the order of the selection doesn't matter, because the key columns are used from left to right. Whether you specify Col = 1 and ColSel = 3, or Col = 3 and ColSel = 1, the rows are sorted according to the contents of column 1, then column 2, and then column 3.

The syntax of the Sort property is as follows:

```
MSFlexGrid1.Sort = value
```

The variable *value* can be one of the values shown in Table 9.10.

TABLE 9.10:   Values of the Sort Property

Value	Description
0	None
1	Generic Ascending (the control guesses whether text is string or number)
2	Generic Descending
3	Numeric Ascending (strings are converted to numbers)
4	Numeric Descending
5	String Ascending, case-insensitive
6	String Descending, case-insensitive
7	String Ascending, case-sensitive
8	String Descending, case-sensitive
9	Custom; uses the Compare event to compare rows

If the Sort property is set to 4, for example, the rows are sorted according the numeric value of the selected column(s). The Sort menu of the FlexGrid application (discussed later in this chapter) contains commands for all types of sorting operations, as shown in Figure 9.15. When an option from this menu is selected, the code assigns the appropriate value to the Sort property and the selected rows are sorted instantly.

FIGURE 9.15:

This menu structure contains commands for sorting a grid's rows in all available ways.

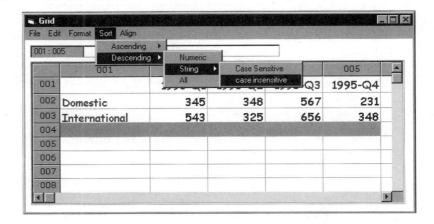

Sort's Custom Setting (9) and Compare Event   All but the last value of the Sort property are self-explanatory. When Sort is set to Custom, the program must specify the order of the columns through a series of Compare events. The Compare event is peculiar in that it's triggered a number of times. It's triggered as many times as there are rows in the grid, and it prompts your program to specify which of two columns will appear first.

The first Compare event determines the order of the first and second rows. When the first two columns are in place, the Compare event is triggered for the second and third rows, then for the third and fourth rows, and so on. As you can imagine, the custom value of the Sort property is slow compared with the other values, but it's the most flexible value. The Custom setting of the Sort property allows you to sort rows according to any criteria and to use nonadjacent columns as sorting keys.

The syntax of the Compare event is as follows:

```
Sub MSFlexGrid1.Compare(row1, row2, cmp)
```

In this event's handler, your code must decide how the rows *row1* and *row2* will be sorted and set the *cmp* argument according to one of the values in Table 9.11.

TABLE 9.11: Custom Values of the Sort Property

Value	Description
-1	Row1 appears before row2
0	Both rows are equal, or either row can appear before the other
1	Row1 appears after row2

The Compare event arranges two rows at a time, so if the Sort property is set to 9, it's triggered many times. The first time it's triggered, the *row1* argument is 1 and the *row2* argument is 2 (assuming that the first row is fixed). The second time it's triggered, the two arguments are 2 and 3; the third time, they are 3 and 4; and so on up to the rows Rows-1 and Rows. Depending on the type of sorting you want to achieve, you may have to set the Sort property to 9 several times, however, your code will become really slow.

TIP

A trick to avoid the Compare event for unusual sorting is to create a sorting key in the form of an invisible column that contains all the sorting keys. Set this column's width to 1 pixel (or twip) and it will be practically invisible. This invisible column is usually the last one in the grid.

Merging Cells

Another useful operation you may want to perform on a grid's data is to merge cells with identical data. Figure 9.16A shows a grid with duplicate data, and Figure 9.16B shows the same grid after certain cells were merged. The MSFlexGrid control provides a mechanism for merging adjacent cells automatically if their contents happen to be identical. To control the merging of the cells with identical values, use the properties discussed in this section.

MergeCells Property   This property determines whether adjacent cells will be merged; it can take one of the values shown in Table 9.12.

TABLE 9.12:   Values of the MergeCells Property

Value	Description	Purpose
0	Never (default value)	Prohibits the merging of cells
1	Free	Merges cells in both rows and columns
2	Restrict rows	Merges cells across rows
3	Restrict columns	Merges cells across columns
4	Restrict both	Similar to free merging; merges cells only if selected cells are next to other cells that have been merged already

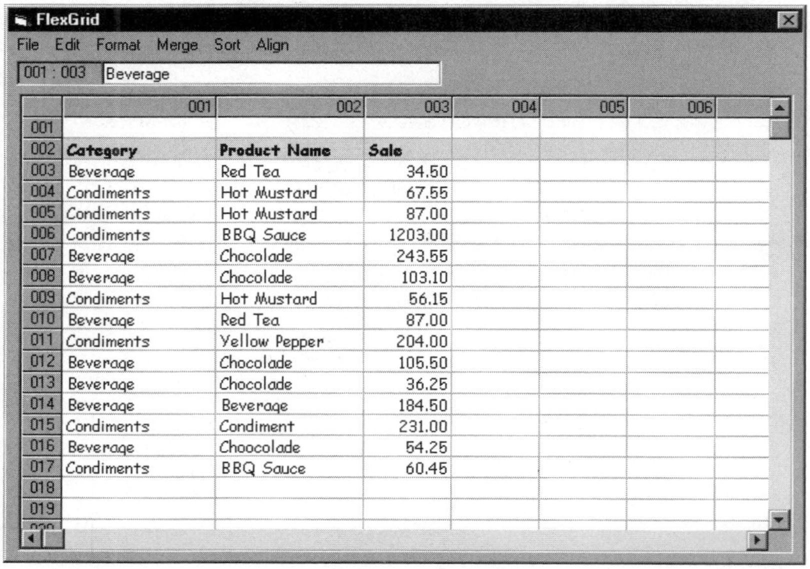

FIGURE 9.16A:

This grid's appearance could be greatly improved if certain cells were merged.

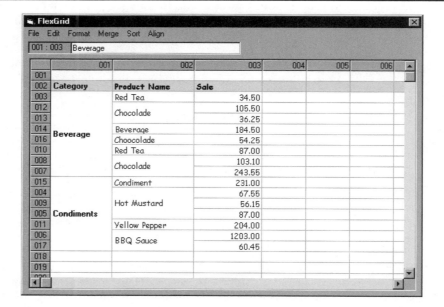

FIGURE 9.16B:

The cell-merging mechanism of the MSFlexGrid control enables you to present tabular data in appealing formats.

MergeRow(), MergeCol() Properties   Setting the MergeCells property to True doesn't necessarily merge the cells. For a cell to be merged, it must belong to a row or to a column and its MergeRow() or MergeCol() property must be set to True. The *MergeRow()* and *MergeCol()* properties are arrays that determine whether the cells of any given row or column can be merged. In other words, you can specify the rows and columns whose cells will be merged and through the MergeRow() and MergeCol() properties, have absolute control over the appearance of your grid. To merge consecutive cells on the first column of the grid, use the following settings:

```
Grid1.MergeCol(1) = True
Grid1.MergeCells = 3
```

Likewise, if you want to merge consecutive cells that have identical contents on the grid's first three rows, use the following settings:

```
Grid1.MergeRow(1) = True
Grid1.MergeRow(2) = True
Grid1.MergeRow(3) = True
Grid1.MergeCells = 2
```

NOTE
The Merge menu of the FlexGrid application in this chapter's folder on the CD enables you to experiment with the various settings of the MergeCells, MergeRow(), and MergeCol() properties. Ideally, these properties should be set by the application for specific data on the grid and should not rely on the user to select the rows and/or columns to merge.

WARNING
A side effect of the merging operation is that multiple selected cells aren't highlighted. To be able to select multiple cells and highlight them, you must select the Do Not Merge command from the Merge menu.

Data Entry

The MSFlexGrid control is an extremely useful tool for displaying data, but it lacks a basic capability: the user cannot edit a single cell. This limitation can be easily overcome with the help of an edit control, namely, the TextBox control. The grid itself provides a few properties and events that make the task of combining the MSFlexGrid control with the TextBox control easy.

There are two approaches to editing a grid's cells. The first is to place a TextBox control on the Form. Each time the user clicks on a cell, the program copies the contents of the active cell to the TextBox control and lets the user edit it. This simple approach is used in the FlexGrid application later in this chapter. The second approach is a bit more elegant, but it involves more complex coding: if you place a TextBox control with the exact same dimensions of the cell being edited right on top of the cell, the user gets the impression of editing a cell directly on the grid.

To integrate the TextBox control with the MSFlexGrid control, use the *CellWidth*, *CellHeight*, *CellTop*, and *CellLeft* properties of the grid, which determine the current cell's dimensions and placement on the grid. If you assign the location and size properties of the current cell to the TextBox control, the TextBox control will be overlaid on top of the current cell. At design time, you can place the TextBox anywhere on the Form. It only becomes visible when it's placed on top of a cell at runtime (see Figures 9.17 and 9.18).

After the text control is placed exactly on top of the cell, the contents of the current cell are copied to the TextBox. When the user moves to another cell by clicking it, the TextBox's contents are copied to that cell, and then the TextBox control is placed over it.

VB6 at Work: The GridEdit Project

The GridEdit application, shown in Figure 9.17, implements the second technique described previously for editing the MSFlexGrid control. The Form of the application contains an MSFlexGrid control and a TextBox control.

FIGURE 9.17:

The GridEdit application simulates data entry operations on a grid by combining the MSFlexGrid control with a TextBox control.

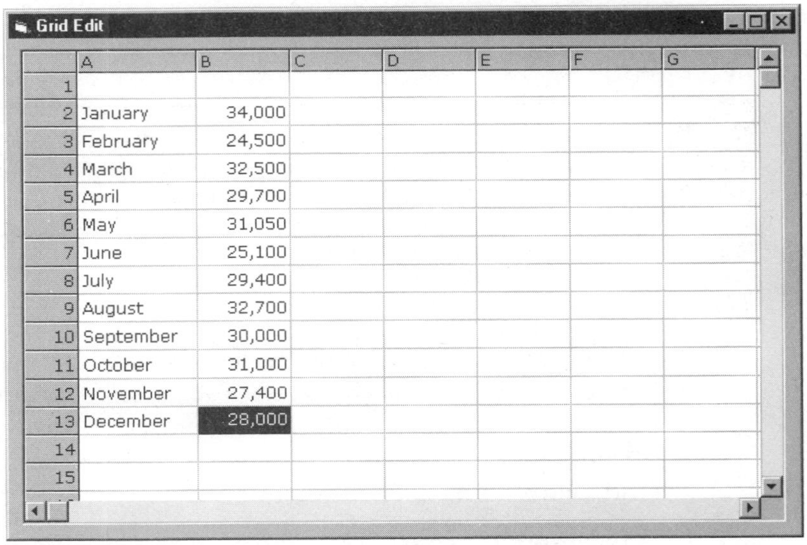

Figure 9.18 shows the GridEdit application at design time. The TextBox control will remain practically invisible at runtime. Because it will be moved from cell to cell, users won't be able to distinguish it from the underlying cell.

FIGURE 9.18:

The GridEdit application at
design time. The TextBox
control, partially overlapping the Grid control, is
seamlessly integrated with
the active cell at runtime.

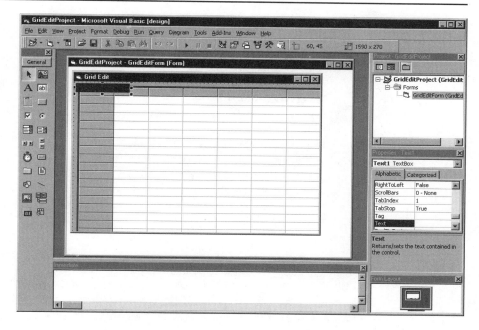

FIGURE 9.18:

The GridEdit application at
design time. The TextBox
control, partially overlapping the Grid control, is
seamlessly integrated with
the active cell at runtime.

In order to program the application, you must first select the events to code. The
two events that signal the change of the active cell are the *EnterCell* and *LeaveCell*
events. No matter how the focus is moved from one cell to another, these events will
take place. It's a good idea, therefore, to place your code behind them.

The EnterCell Event   This event takes place every time a new cell is activated.
In its handler you must:

1. Clear the contents of the TextBox control.

2. Place the TextBox control over the active cell and resize it to fit the cell.

3. Assign the contents of the active cell to the TextBox control's Text property.

4. Move the focus to the TextBox control.

These instructions are translated directly to code with the following lines.

Code 9.13:   **Positioning and Sizing the TextBox Control**

```
Private Sub Grid1_EnterCell()
' Make sure the user doesn't attempt to edit the fixed cells
    If Grid1.MouseRow = 0 Or Grid1.MouseCol = 0 Then
        Text1.Visible = False
```

```
          Exit Sub
      End If
' clear contents of current cell
      Text1.Text = ""
' place Textbox over current cell
      Text1.Visible = False
      Text1.Top = Grid1.Top + Grid1.CellTop
      Text1.Left = Grid1.Left + Grid1.CellLeft
      Text1.Width = Grid1.CellWidth
      Text1.Height = Grid1.CellHeight
' assign cell's contents to Textbox
      Text1.Text = Grid1.Text
' move focus to Textbox
      Text1.Visible = True
      Text1.SetFocus
End Sub
```

Notice the lines that check the MouseCol and MouseRow properties to see if the user has clicked on a fixed cell (these two properties return the current mouse position in row and column coordinates). If the user clicks on a fixed cell, the subroutine terminates. Also, the entire column is selected, yet the fixed cell can't be edited. To disable multiple cell selections, set the AllowBigSelection property to False.

The LeaveCell Event When the user is done editing the current cell and moves to another one, the application must copy the text from the TextBox control to the cell just edited. This is done by a single line of code from within the MSFlexGrid's LeaveCell event:

```
Private Sub Grid1_LeaveCell()
    Grid1.Text = Text1.Text
End Sub
```

If you run the application as is, two more problems will surface. First, the EnterCell event isn't fired when the Form is first loaded, so we must invoke it from within the Form's Load event. To force the code of the EnterCell event to be executed, insert the following lines in the Form's Load event.

Code 9.14:	The Form's Load Event

```
Private Sub Form_Load()
    Grid1.Row = 1
    Grid1.Col = 1
End Sub
```

Notice that we don't have to explicitly call the control's EnterCell subroutine. Setting a cell's address from within the code causes the EnterCell event to be executed.

The code presented so far is the absolute minimum required for a functional data entry application based on the MSFlexGrid control. A serious limitation is that the user can't change the active cell with the help of the keyboard. When the user presses the Enter key, for example, the focus should move to the next cell on the same column or row. No such luck. Not even the arrow keys work.

Although it's relatively easy to adjust the code to add more features that will facilitate data entry operations, I've omitted them from the example. The GridEdit application's code demonstrates the basic principles of adding data entry capabilities to the MSFlexGrid control. The properties and methods discussed so far will allow you to add advanced editing features to your application.

VB6 at Work: The FlexGrid Project

The FlexGrid application demonstrates most of the methods and properties of the MSFlexGrid control. FlexGrid is a functional spreadsheet application with data entry capabilities, which you can customize for your specific needs. The application's Form is shown in Figure 9.19.

FIGURE 9.19:

The FlexGrid application is a functional spreadsheet application based on the MSFlexGrid control.

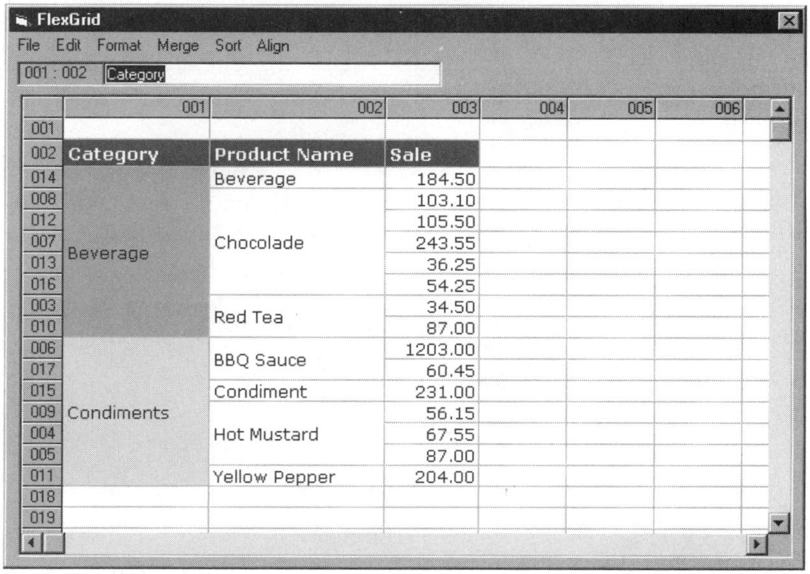

The top-level menus of the FlexGrid application are as follows:

- **File** contains the usual Open and Save commands.

- **Edit** contains commands for exchanging information with the Clipbo

- **Format** contains commands for setting the appearance of individual ce. (font, text color, and background color) and formatting for numeric valu￯.

- **Merge** contains commands for merging cells in all possible ways.

- **Sort** contains commands to sort selected rows in all possible ways.

- **Align** contains the commands for left-aligning, right-aligning, and centering the contents of selected cells.

Data Entry in FlexGrid   The code for data entry in FlexGrid uses a technique different from the one described earlier in GridEdit. GridEdit adds data entry capabilities to the MSFlexGrid control using a TextBox control that is placed over the cell being edited. In the FlexGrid application, the data entry mechanism relies on a TextBox control above the grid.

Each time the user selects a cell to edit, the program copies the contents of this cell to the TextBox control, where the editing takes place. The coordinates of the selected cell are displayed on a Label control in front of the TextBox control. When the user is done editing, the contents of the TextBox control are copied to the original cell, the contents of the next cell are copied to the TextBox control , and the process is repeated. The data entry mechanism is implemented in the MSFlexGrid control's EnterCell and LeaveCell events.

Code 9.15:   **The EnterCell and LeaveCell Events**

```
Private Sub Grid_EnterCell()
    Label1.Caption = Grid.TextMatrix(Grid.Col, 0) & " : " & _
        Grid.TextMatrix(0, Grid.Row)
    Text1.Text = Grid.Text
    Text1.SetFocus
    Text1.SelStart = 0
    Text1.SelLength = Len(Text1.Text)
End Sub

Private Sub Grid_LeaveCell()
    Grid.Text = Text1.Text
End Sub
```

On entering a new cell, the program updates the Label control with the coordinates of the newly selected cell and then copies its contents to the TextBox control. It also selects the text in the control. On leaving the cell, the program copies the TextBox control's text to the original cell. This code works nicely, but it requires the user to select the next cell with the mouse.

To simplify the data entry process, a few lines of code have been added in the TextBox's KeyPress event. When the user presses Enter, the TextBox control's contents are copied to the corresponding cell, and the focus moves to the next cell on the same column. If this cell is the last one in the current column, the focus moves to the first cell of the next column. Or, you can move the focus to the next cell on the same row, and when the end of the row is reached, move to the next row. In other words, Enter signals the user's intent to commit the changes in the current cell and edit the next one.

You can add more lines in the same event handler to let the user move to other cells with different keystrokes. You can use the Tab key, for instance, to move to the next cell on the same row, or you can use the up and down arrow keys to move to the previous or next cell in the same column. The other two arrow keys are reserved for editing the text and can't be used for navigation purposes. Following is the TextBox control's KeyPress event handler as implemented in the FlexGrid application.

Code 9.16:   **The KeyPress Event Handler**

```
Private Sub Text1_KeyPress(KeyAscii As Integer)
Dim SRow, SCol As Integer

    If KeyAscii = 13 Then 'Enter Key = 13
        Grid.Text = Text1.Text
        SRow = Grid.Row + 1
        SCol = Grid.ColSel
        If SRow = Grid.Rows Then
            SRow = Grid.FixedCols
            If SCol < Grid.Cols - Grid.FixedCols Then SCol = SCol + 1
        End If
        Grid.Row = SRow
        Grid.Col = SCol
        Grid.RowSel = SRow
        Grid.ColSel = SCol
        Text1.Text = Grid.Text
        Text1.SetFocus
        KeyAscii = 0
    End If
End Sub
```

Saving and Loading Data   The MSFlexGrid control doesn't provide any methods for storing or loading its contents to and from a disk file. To implement the Open, Save, and Save As commands in the File menu, you can select the entire spreadsheet, copy it to a string variable, and then save it with the *Write* statement. To load an existing file to the grid, use the *Input* statement.

After the entire grid has been selected, the Clip property holds the values of all cells in the grid, and the problem of saving them to a disk file is reduced to writing a string variable to the file. The grid's data are stored in files with the extension GDT (for Grid DaTa) so that the FileOpen and FileSave dialog boxes can use a default extension unique to this application.

Code 9.17:   **The Save As Command**

```
Private Sub FileSaveAs_Click()
Dim allCells As String
Dim FNum As Integer
Dim curRow, curCol As Integer

    curRow = Grid.Row
    curCol = Grid.Col
On Error GoTo FileError
    CommonDialog1.DefaultExt = "GDT"
    CommonDialog1.ShowSave
    EditSelect_Click
    allCells = Grid.Clip
    FNum = FreeFile
    Open CommonDialog1.filename For Output As #FNum
    Write #FNum, allCells
    Close #FNum
    OpenFile = CommonDialog1.filename
    Grid.Row = curRow
    Grid.Col = curCol
    Grid.RowSel = Grid.Row
    Grid.ColSel = Grid.Col
    Exit Sub
FileError:
    If Err.Number = cdlCancel Then Exit Sub
    MsgBox "Unknown error while opening file " & _
         CommonDialog1.filename
    OpenFile = ""
End Sub
```

As you can see, most of the lines set up the FileSave common dialog box. The code that actually extracts the data and writes them to the file consists of a few lines that select the entire grid (by calling the Select All command of the Edit menu), assign the Clip property to the *allCells* variable, and then write to a disk file. The Save command uses the *openFile* global variable to save the grid's contents without prompting the user for a filename. (The FreeFile() function returns the next available file handle and is described in the *File Input/Output* tutorial on the CD.) The Open command is quite similar: it reads the string variable from the disk file, selects the entire grid, and then assigns the *allCells* variable to the control's Clip property.

NOTE   Although the FlexGrid application contains commands for formatting individual cells, the formatting of the cells isn't saved by the Save command. The MSFlexGrid control lacks a Save method to save the complete status of the cells, including their formatting. Until the release of a better version of the control, you can save the formatting of the cells along with the data. If your application calls for storing and retrieving spreadsheets along with their formatting or editing the cells, you should consider a third party component. The MSFlexGrid control was meant for displaying, rather than editing, data.

The Edit Menu   The FlexGrid application's Edit menu contains the usual Cut, Copy, and Paste commands, which manipulate the control's Clip property. The Copy command extracts the selected cells from the grid via its Clip property and assigns them to the Clipboard with the SetText method as follows:

```
Private Sub EditCopy_Click()
Dim tmpText As String
    tmpText = Grid.Clip
    Clipboard.Clear
    Clipboard.SetText tmpText
End Sub
```

The Paste command does the opposite. It extracts the data from the Clipboard with the GetText method and then assigns them to the grid as follows:

```
Private Sub EditPaste_Click()
Dim tmpText As String

    tmpText = Clipboard.GetText
    Grid.Clip = tmpText
End Sub
```

As implemented in the preceding code, the Paste command has a rather serious drawback: the copied cells are pasted in the selected range only. In other words, the user must select a range (its dimensions should match the dimensions of the range of cells currently in the Clipboard) and then issue the Paste command.

To improve the Paste command, your program must first examine the string that holds the Clipboard's contents. Successive cell values are separated by a Tab character (Chr$(9)), and successive columns are separated by a new line character (chr$(13)). Your program must first select a range with as many columns as there are cells in a row and as many rows as there are rows in the Clipboard's string and then assign the variable to the Clip property.

The Format Menu   The FlexGrid's Format menu contains the following commands:

- **Font** lets the user specify the font attributes of the selected cell(s) through a Font common dialog box.

- **Text Color** lets the user specify the text color for the selected cell(s).

- **Cell Color** lets the user specify the background color for the selected cell(s).

Also included is a group of commands for formatting Numeric data. To apply the desired format to the selected cells, select one of these commands:

- **###**   Formats 1802.5 as 1802

- **###.00**   Formats 1802 as 1802.00

- **#,###.00**   Formats 1802.5 as 1,802.50

- **$#,###.00**   Formats 1802.5 as $1,802.50

These commands call the *FormatCells()* subroutine with the proper argument. The subroutine scans the entire range of selected cells and formats each cell with the *Format$()* function.

Code 9.18:   **Formatting the Selected Cells**

```
Sub FormatCells(formatString)
Dim irow, icol As Integer

    For irow = Grid.Row To Grid.RowSel
        For icol = Grid.Col To Grid.ColSel
            Grid.TextMatrix(irow, icol) = _
                Format$(Grid.TextMatrix(irow, icol), formatString)
        Next
    Next

End Sub
```

The Sort and Align Menus   The Sort menu contains a number of nested commands that let the user specify all types of possible sorting methods with the MSFlexGrid control, except for the Custom sort. Through the Sort menu's commands, you can sort the rows of the grid as strings or numbers and in ascending or descending rows. Moreover, the sorting process can be case-sensitive or case-insensitive.

Implementing the Sort menu is simple. Each command in this menu assigns the appropriate value to the MSFlexGrid control's Sort property (see Table 9.10 earlier in this chapter for a list of these values and how they affect the sorting process). The Sort command relies on the user to select the columns to be used as keys with the mouse. To sort all the rows in the grid, the user would select all the key columns by clicking on their fixed cells. To sort a range of rows only, the user would select the cells in the column(s) with the sorting keys and the rows to be sorted.

The code behind the command Sort | Descending | Numeric consists of a single line:

```
Private Sub DescNumeric_Click()
    Grid.Sort = 4
End Sub
```

The grid's rows will be sorted according to the values of the cells in the selected column(s). If part of a column has been selected, only the selected rows will be sorted (see Figure 9.20). Notice that the MSFlexGrid control switches the rows around, including the cells of the fixed column. If the titles of the fixed column are not part of the data (in other words, if they are sequence numbers, as in the FlexGrid application), you should renumber them after each sort operation.

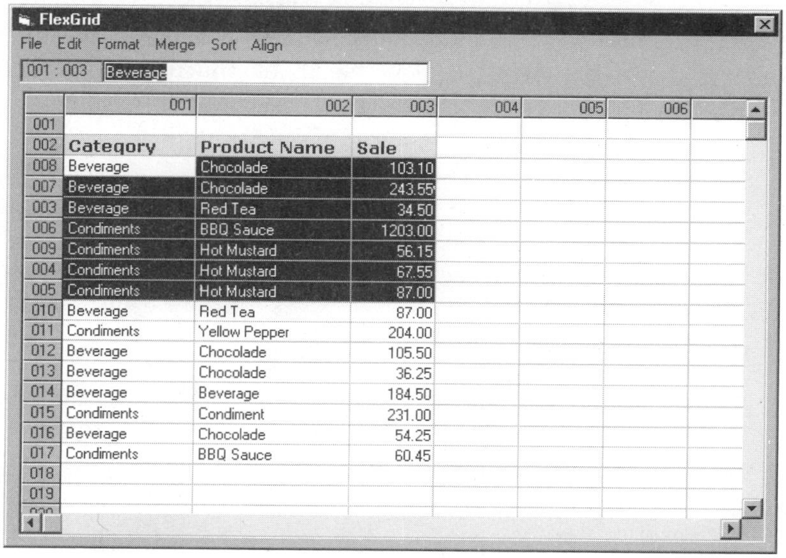

FIGURE 9.20:

The highlighted rows on this spreadsheet are sorted. To partially sort the grid, select only the rows you want to sort in the key column.

The Align menu contains the commands that let the user left-align, right-align, and center selected cells. After the alignment property for a cell is set, it remains in effect even if the cell's contents are edited. The same is true for the font attributes of the cell, but not for the number formatting commands.

Enhancing the FlexGrid Project   FlexGrid has most of the functionality you'll need to write complicated spreadsheet applications. For instance, you can easily add data processing capabilities to the application. Inserting formulas won't be easy, but you can calculate the average of a range of cells or normalize them. The code for formatting a range of numeric values, which scans the range of the selected cells, is the structure you need. Instead of formatting the cells' contents, add their values and divide the sum by the number of selected cells. Or you can fill a column with a function of the values of the cells to its left.

A few commands that automatically fill a range of cells are also quite common. You can implement a command that reads the value of a cell and fills the following cells in the same column with the initial value incremented by a user-supplied step. These values can also be dates. The user can supply the initial day and an increment in days, and your program can fill the following cells with the appropriate dates.

Thus, you can easily add functionality to the FlexGrid control for many practical situations that require a gridlike structure for displaying or entering data, as long as you don't need something like Excel. If you need the data processing capabilities of Excel, especially data processing with formulas, or if you need a built-in programming language, you should look into more specialized spreadsheet controls. In Chapter 15, you'll see how to program and control Excel from within a Visual Basic application.

This example concludes the rather extensive discussion of ActiveX controls in this book. The controls in Chapter 8 and this chapter are rather advanced, but they are the makings of elaborate, highly functional user interfaces. Using these controls in your applications will not be easy, but the examples in this book should serve as starting points for many applications.

PART III

Special Topics

CHAPTER

TEN

10

The Multiple Document Interface

- Built-in MDI capabilities

- Parent and child menus

- The Window menu

- The Arrange property

- Child Forms

- The QueryUnload event

- Scrolling Forms

The *Multiple Document Interface (MDI)* was designed to simplify the exchange of information among documents, all under the same roof. With an MDI application, you can maintain multiple open windows, but not multiple copies of the application. Data exchange is easier when you can view and compare many documents simultaneously.

You almost certainly use Windows applications that can open multiple documents at the same time and allow the user to switch among them with a mouse-click. Microsoft Word is a typical example, although most people use it in single document mode. Each document is displayed in its own window, and all document windows have the same behavior. The main form, or MDI Form, is not duplicated, but it acts as a container for all other windows, and it's called the *parent window*. The windows in which the individual documents are displayed are called *child windows* (or document windows). When you reposition the parent window on the Desktop, its child windows follow. Child windows, however, exist independently of the parent window. You can open and close child windows as you want, and child windows can even have different functions. For example, you can open a few text windows and a few graphics windows next to one another, although this is rare.

Figure 10.1 shows Word in MDI mode. The application's main window contains five documents, three of them in custom-size windows and two of them minimized. The menus and the toolbars of the parent window apply to all the child windows. In reality, the menu bar of the MDI Form contains the menu of the active child Form.

Paint Shop Pro is a popular MDI application (see Figure 10.2), and most mail applications display each message in a separate window and allow the user to open multiple messages. Most of the popular text editors (NotePad excluded) are MDI applications too.

MDI applications aren't very common; not too many applications lend themselves to MDI implementation. Most of them are easier to implement with multiple Forms, but some applications should be implemented with an MDI interface. These are the applications that can open multiple documents of the same type and use a common menu structure that applies to all open documents. In the following sections we are going to discuss the basic behavior of MDI applications, their differences from regular *Single Document Interface (SDI)* applications, and how to build MDI applications.

FIGURE 10.1:

Using Word in MDI mode

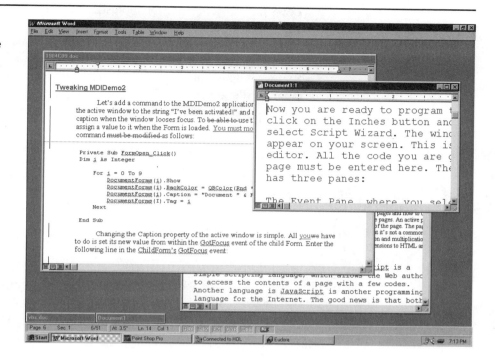

FIGURE 10.2:

Paint Shop Pro, one of the most popular shareware applications, uses the MDI user interface.

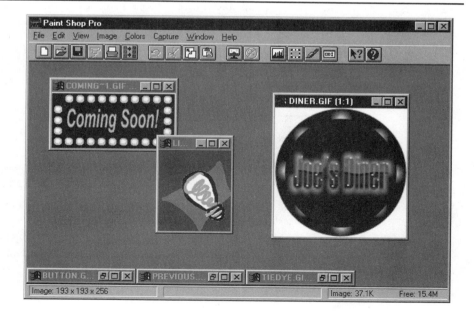

Even if you don't plan to develop MDI applications, you should take a look at the last section of this chapter, "Implementing Scrolling Forms," to see how the MDI techniques can be used to build regular SDI Forms with scrolling capabilities. By default, Visual Basic's Forms can't be scrolled. If you want to build a really long or wide Form, you must either provide your own mechanism for scrolling it or break it into two or more smaller Forms. The techniques discussed in this chapter will enable you to build scrolling Forms that can fit in small windows and low resolution monitors.

MDI Applications: The Basics

An MDI application must have at least two Forms, the parent Form and one or more child Forms. Each of these Forms has certain properties. There can be many child Forms contained within the parent Form, but there can be only one parent Form.

The parent Form may not contain any controls. While the parent Form is open in design mode, the icons on the Toolbox aren't disabled, but you can't place any controls on the Form. The parent Form can, and usually does, have its own menu.

To create an MDI application, follow these steps:

1. Start a new project and then choose Project ➤ Add MDI Form to add the parent Form.

NOTE   After you add an MDI Form to your application, the Add MDI Form command in the Project menu is disabled. The reason: you can't have a second MDI Form in the same application.

2. Set the Form's caption to MDI Window.

3. Choose Project ➤ Add Form to add a regular Form.

4. Make this Form the child Form by setting its *MDIChild* property to True. To denote that this is a child Form, set its Caption property to MDI Child Form.

Visual Basic automatically associates this new Form with the parent Form. This child Form can't exist outside the parent Form; in other words, it can only be opened within the parent Form.

Built-In Capabilities of MDI

You've just created an MDI application. It doesn't do much, but if you run the project now, you'll see two Forms, one inside the other, as shown in Figure 10.3. Simply make Form1 the application's start-up Form. To do this, open the project's Properties window and set Form1 as the start-up object. If the start-up object is the MDI Form the child window won't be displayed by default; you must load it from within the application code. Notice that the child Form is contained entirely within the parent Form and exists only in that context. If you close or minimize the parent Form, the child Form also will be closed or minimized.

Use the mouse to move the child Form around and change its size. If you click the child Form's Maximize button, the two Forms are combined into one, as shown in Figure 10.4.

FIGURE 10.3:

The framework of an MDI application with a single child Form

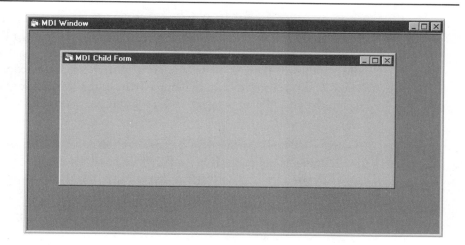

FIGURE 10.4:

The MDI application from Figure 10.3 after the child window has been maximized

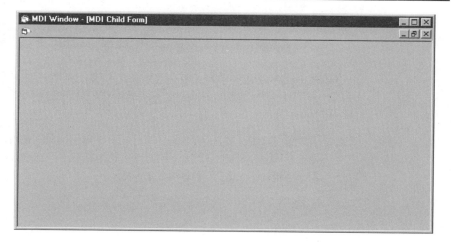

Notice that the window's caption is now the parent Form's caption, followed by the caption of the child Form. You can also move the child Form outside the parent Form, in which case, the appropriate scroll bars will be attached to the parent Form. In addition, both the child window and the MDI Form have a Control menu (which you can open by clicking the icon in the upper-left corner) and their own Minimize, Normal, and Close buttons (in the upper-right corner).

NOTE

Later in this chapter, when you start to create MDI applications, you'll see that how you name parent and child windows is important to maintaining the Windows Graphic User Interface (GUI) guidelines. The most important rule for parent and child windows is that the parent Form's caption should be the name of the application and the captions of the child Forms should be the names of the documents in each one of them.

Clicking the child Form's Minimize button reduces the child Form to an icon, but always within the parent Form. You'll never see a child Form's icon on the Desktop's status bar, even if its *ShowInTaskbar* property is set to True. To restore the minimized Form to its original size, double-click the icon. A child window is usually minimized instead of being closed to make room for other documents. In short, the child Form behaves like a regular Form on the Desktop, only its "desktop" is the parent window.

I have just demonstrated the basic operations of an MDI application without writing a single line of code. These capabilities are built into the language and are available to your applications through the settings of certain properties.

To see how useful and powerful MDI applications can be, let's add a second child Form to the application and throw in a few commands. Follow these steps:

1. Add one more Form to the project, and make it an MDI child Form by setting its MDIChild property to True.

2. Set the Form's Caption property to MDI Child 2.

If you run the application now, you won't see the second child Form. This makes perfect sense because you must be able to open and close child Forms under program control.

3. To display the second Form, you need to add the following line behind a menu command or in the MDI Form's Load event so that both Forms display when the MDI Form is loaded:

```
Form2.Show
```

In a later example, you'll see how to design menus for MDI applications with commands for opening and closing child Forms.

If you run this small MDI program now, its main window will look much more like an MDI application, thanks to its two child Forms. You can add more child Forms and open them when the MDI Form is loaded with the Show method.

By default, the first child Form is displayed when the MDI Form is loaded. You can also start an MDI application without showing any child Forms, by setting the MDI Form's *AutoShowChildren* property to False. In this case, you must either provide a menu command that enables the user to open new documents in child Forms or load one or more child Forms from within your code.

WARNING   It's possible for a child Form to be displayed on the MDI Form even if the MDI-Form's AutoShowChildren property is False. This will happen if the child Form is the project's start-up object. Since child Forms can't exist outside the context of an MDI Form, the start-up object is loaded on the application's MDI Form when the application starts.

Parent and Child Menus

MDI Forms can't contain objects other than child Forms, but MDI Forms do have their own menus. However, because most of the operations of the application have meaning only if there is at least one child Form open, there's a peculiarity about the MDI menus. The MDI Form usually has a menu with a couple of commands for loading a new child Form and quitting the application. The child Form can have any number of commands in its menu, depending on the application. When the child Form is loaded, the child Form's menu replaces the original menu on the MDI Form.

VB6 at Work: The MDIDemo1 Form

To see how child Form menus replace the MDI Form's menu, let's design an MDI Form with a simple menu. Start a new project, add an MDI Form, and design a menu that has the following structure:

MDIMenu Menu caption

    MDIOpen Opens a new child Form

    MDIExit Terminates the application

Then design the following menu for the child Form:

ChildMenu Menu caption

> **Child Open** Opens a new child Form
>
> **Child Save** Saves the document in the active child Form
>
> **Child Close** Closes the active child Form

You don't need to add any code to the previous menus at this point. If you run this application now (it's the MDIDemo1 application in this chapter's folder on the CD), you'll see the child Form's menu on the MDI Form's menu bar (see Figure 10.5). If you close the child Form, the original menu of the MDI Form will replace the child Form's menu. The reason for this behavior should be obvious. The operations available through the MDI Form are quite different from the operations of the child window. Moreover, each child Form shouldn't have its own menu.

FIGURE 10.5:

The MDI Form's menu (MDI Menu) is displayed only while no child Forms are opened. When a child Form (Child Menu) is loaded, its menu becomes the application's menu.

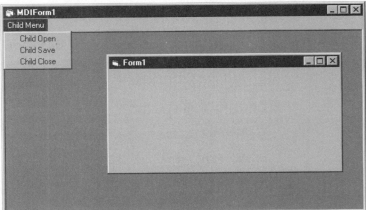

A different menu on the container (the MDI Form) and a different menu on the individual child Forms would confuse the user. You should be aware of this idiosyncrasy when designing menus for MDI applications. The common practice is to attach a limited menu to the MDI Form, which is repeated in the child Form's menu. You'll see an example of MDI menu design in the section "Adding Child Forms to the MDIEditor," later in this chapter.

The Window Menu

A few more features are built into MDI Forms. These features aren't available through properties, but with a minimum of coding you can include them in your programs. All MDI applications in the Windows environment have a submenu called *Window* that contains two groups of commands. The first group of commands positions the child windows on the MDI Form, and the second group consists of the captions of the open child windows (see Figure 10.6). With the commands on this menu, you can change the arrangement of the open windows (or the icons of the minimized windows) and activate any child window.

FIGURE 10.6:

Visual Basic automatically maintains the list of windows in the Window submenu.

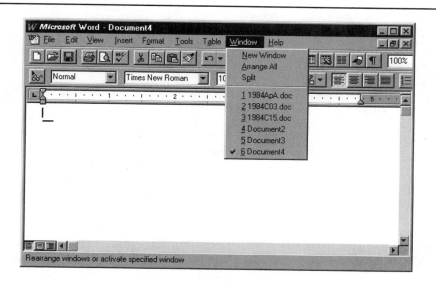

Let's design an MDI Form that maintains its Window menu:

1. Select a child Form in the Project window and design a menu for this window.

2. Add a single command named **Window**.

3. Check the WindowList checkbox in the Menu Editor, as shown in Figure 10.7.

FIGURE 10.7:

The Window menu shown in Figure 10.6 is implemented with the WindowList command in the Menu Editor.

You have just told the MDI application to maintain a list of all child windows that appear on the Form and display their names in the Window menu. The active child window is denoted with a checkmark next to its entry in the menu. Even the separator line between the two groups of commands is placed there automatically.

WARNING   You can add the Window menu to the MDI Form, but only if the child windows don't have their own menus. If a child window has a menu, this menu takes over the MDI Form's menu when the child Form is loaded.

The Arrange Property

Windows offers three ways of arranging the windows on an MDI Form. You can cascade them, tile them vertically, or tile them horizontally. Of course, the user can resize and move the windows around, but the automatic placement comes in handy when the MDI Form becomes messy and the user can no longer easily locate the desired window. The placement of the child windows on the Form is controlled with the *Arrange* property, which can take one of the values shown in Table 10.1.

TABLE10.1: Values of the MDI Form's Arrange Property

Constant	Value	Description
vbCascade	0	Cascades all child Forms
vbTileHorizontal	1	Tiles all child Forms horizontally
vbTileVertical	2	Tiles all child Forms vertically
vbArrangeIcons	3	Arranges the icons for minimized child Forms at the bottom of the MDI Form

The Arrange property isn't available at design time, and it's usually set by the commands in the Window menu. The first three values in Table 10.1 concern the arrangement of the windows when they are in normal state; the last value concerns the arrangement of the icons of minimized windows. As the user minimizes and maximizes the windows, it's possible for the icons to end up in the four corners of the MDI Form, some of them even outside the Form's visible area.

When the Arrange property is set to 3, the icons are placed next to one another in the lower-left corner of the MDI Form. This property acts as a method in the sense that it causes an action when it's set. To see how the Arrange property works, design a menu with the following structure (the menu belongs to the child Form of the application, not the MDI Form):

Menu Command	Name	Remarks
Window	WindowMenu	Check the WindowList checkbox
Tile Horizontally	WindowTileH	
Tile Vertically	WindowTileV	
Cascade	WindowCascade	
Arrange Icons	WindowArrangeIcons	

Don't do anything about the list of child windows; just check the WindowList checkbox in the Menu Edit window for the Window menu command. If you run the application now, you'll see the name of the child Form attached to the Window menu. This is taken care of by Visual Basic, which maintains the list of current child windows and displays their names at the bottom of the Window menu. The name of the active child window is checked in this list, and you can select another window by clicking its name in the Window list. To implement the commands that rearrange the windows on the MDI Form, you must provide a few lines of code. The code is really trivial and it sets the MDI Form's Arrange property. For example, the code for the Cascade command is shown next.

Code 10.1:   **The Cascade Command**

```
Private Sub WindowCascade_Click()
    MDIForm1.Arrange vbCascade
End Sub
```

The subroutines for the Tile Vertically, Tile Horizontally, and Arrange Icons commands are similar. Run the application and check out all the features that are already built into the MDI Form (or open the MDIDemo2 application in this chapter's folder on the CD). Move the child windows around, minimize and maximize them, arrange them and their icons on the MDI Form, and switch from one to the other with the help of the Window menu's commands.

With just a few lines of code, you can create a good deal of functionality. By the way, although the name of this menu doesn't need to be Window (any menu name will do), this is the name used by all Windows applications, so you should probably stick with it.

Despite its simplicity, you may have noticed a problem with the approach just described. You may be wondering if you have to design a separate child Form for each document you need to display on the MDI Form. And, even worse, do you have to refer to each child window with a different name? It would be so much easier if you could declare an array of child Forms and access them with an index. Actually, this is the way child Forms are handled, and this is the next topic we'll explore.

Accessing Child Forms

Visual Basic is an object-oriented language and most of the applications developed with it work by manipulating the values of objects or invoking the methods of the various objects to perform certain tasks. Recall that an *object* is the instance of a control or Form. Not surprisingly, a fundamental concept in the design of MDI applications is that of objects and their instances. All the controls you use in building an application's user interface are control objects. Forms are objects too, and they are called Form objects. It's actually possible to create new objects and delete existing ones at runtime from within your code.

To help you handle objects from within your code, Visual Basic allows the declaration of variables that represent objects. These object variables allow you to manipulate objects (create new instances or delete existing instances) just as you'd manipulate any other type of variable. For example, you can design a single Form object and create multiple instances of this Form from within your code. You can even declare an array of object variables and manipulate them through the application's code.

The Form you design is the prototype. An instance of a Form is a copy that inherits all the properties of the original but exists in your application independently of the original. On an MDI Form, all child Forms are usually instances of one basic Form. The Forms all have the same behavior, but the operation of each one doesn't affect the others. When a child Form is loaded, for example, it will have the same background color as its prototype, but you can change this from within your code by setting the Form's BackColor property.

An MDI Form can contain a number of child Forms, therefore, you might start the design process by designing each one of them. You could call the first one DocumentForm1, the second one DocumentForm2, and so on. Unfortunately, this setup would require a lot of programming effort to handle individual Forms. The most common approach to designing MDI applications is to design a single child Form and use it as the prototype for as many child Forms as you want to place on the MDI Form. To do this, use an array of Forms, like *DocumentForms()*. As with control arrays (discussed in Chapter 2, *Visual Basic Projects*), you only need to design the first element of the array. With this index structure, each child Form can be accessed by an index, and the maintenance of the child Forms is simplified. The application in Figure 10.8 shows an MDI Form with three child Forms, all members of the *DocumentForms()* array.

FIGURE 10.8:

The child windows of this application were designed as an array of Forms, not as separate elements.

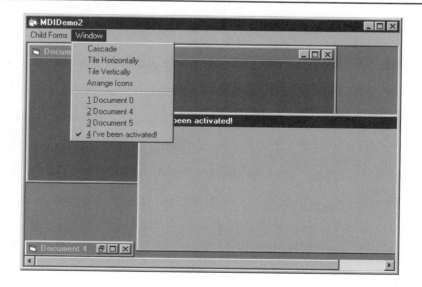

To create a Form that can be used as a prototype, follow these steps:

1. Start a new project, add an MDI Form, and set its caption to MDIDemo2.

2. Add a new Form to the project, name it **ChildForm**, and set its MDIChild property to True.

3. Set other properties of the child Form (such as its background color) and add a few controls if you want.

When you're done, you can use this Form as a prototype and declare an array of child Forms with a statement such as the following:

```
Dim DocumentForms(9) As New ChildForm
```

ChildForm is the name of the child Form. This declaration must appear in a Module or be a Form-wide declaration. Each element of the *DocumentForms()* array is an instance of the ChildForm Form you just designed.

To change the Caption property of the third child Form, use the following statement:

```
DocumentForms(2).Caption = "Document #3"
```

The name of the *DocumentForms()* array followed by an Index value is equivalent to the name of the child Form.

The keyword *New* tells Visual Basic to create 10 new instances of the Form Child-Form. The one you designed doesn't exist until it's loaded. The ChildForm Form you see in the Project window is just the prototype. The next example illustrates the difference between the ChildForm Form and the array of child Forms.

Loading and Unloading Child Forms

Let's design a menu that will load and unload the child Forms. This menu, shown earlier in Figure 10.8, has two commands on the first level, Child Forms and Window. The Window menu is identical to that in Figure 10.8. The Child Forms command leads to a submenu with two commands:

Open Forms Opens all child Forms

Close Forms Closes all open child Forms

This section's application is called MDIDemo2, and you'll find it in this chapter's folder on the CD.

VB6 at Work: The MDIDemo2 Project

The MDIDemo2 project demonstrates how to load and unload child Forms on an MDI window from within your code. The project's complete code is shown next.

Code 10.2:   **The Open Forms and Close Forms Commands**

```
Option Explicit
Dim DocumentForms(10) As New ChildForm

Private Sub FormsClose_Click()
Dim i As Integer

  For i = 0 To 9
    Unload DocumentForms(i)
  Next
End Sub

Private Sub FormOpen_Click()
Dim i As Integer

  For i = 0 To 9
    DocumentForms(i).Show
    DocumentForms(i).BackColor = QBColor(Rnd * 14 + 1)
    DocumentForms(i).Caption = "Document " & Format(i)
  Next
End Sub
```

The Open Forms command loads all 10 child Forms and assigns a different background color and caption to each one as it's loaded. The Close command closes the Forms. If you run the application now, you'll see 11 child Forms—the original ChildForm (the one with caption Form1), which is loaded automatically, and the 10 child Forms of the *DocumentForms()* array. To prevent the automatic loading of the first instance of the Form1 child Form, set the AutoShowChildren property of the MDI Form to False.

You can rearrange the child Forms on the MDI window, minimize and maximize them as usual, and close them by clicking on their Close buttons. You can also choose Forms ➤ Close Forms to close them all. If you do so, the original child Form will remain on the MDI window. This is because the window isn't part of the array. It's the first child window that Visual Basic loads automatically each time the MDI Form is loaded. You can modify this default behavior by changing the

Start-up Form in the project's Properties window. To do so, right-click the project's name, select Project Properties, and change the value of the Start-up Object box.

By default, the start-up object is the first child Form, but because a child Form can't exist on its own, the MDI Form is loaded first and the child Form is displayed in it. Select the MDI Form in the Start-up Object ComboBox control and run the application again. This time, the MDI Form appears without any child Forms. To display a child Form, you must load it explicitly from within your code.

<table>
<tr><td>NOTE</td><td>Notice that the MDI Form's menu didn't change when the child Form was loaded because a child Form doesn't have its own menu. If it did, its menu would replace the MDI Form's menu. Thus, menus that you want always to remain visible, such as the Window menu, must be designed on the child Form.</td></tr>
</table>

Tracking the Active Window   Since MDI applications manipulate multiple windows at once, you need to be able to keep track of the active window from within your code. A useful keyword in working with MDI and child Forms is the *Me* keyword, which refers to the active child Form. If you consider that the MDI Form is the Desktop environment for its child Forms, the *Me* keyword is equivalent to the Screen object's ActiveForm property (which is the active Form). *Me* is the active child Form in an MDI Form, and you can address any of its properties through the Me object. Me.BackColor is the background color of the current child Form, Me.Caption is its caption, and so on.

In most situations, however, you'll want to know the index of the active child Form in your code. Say you can't find out whether a specific child Form is open with the *Me* keyword. Visual Basic doesn't report the index of the active window, so you must implement a method for keeping track of the active child Form. The solution is to use the Form's Tag property. Every time a new child Form is loaded, you can store its index in the Form's Tag property, as follows:

```
DocumentForms(i).Tag = i
```

When the Form is unloaded, Visual Basic resets its tag (you needn't worry about resetting it). After the Form is loaded, you can use the Form's Tag property in your code to find the index of the active child Form and access its properties and methods.

Tweaking MDIDemo2   Let's add a command to the MDIDemo2 application that changes the caption of the active window to the string "I've been activated!" and resets it to the original caption when the window loses focus. To use the Tag property to keep track of the active window, as described in the previous section, you must assign a value to it when the Form is loaded. You modify the Open Forms command as follows:

```
Private Sub FormOpen_Click()
Dim i As Integer

  For i = 0 To 9
    DocumentForms(i).Show
    DocumentForms(i).BackColor = QBColor(Rnd * 14 + 1)
    DocumentForms(i).Caption = "Document " & Format(i)
    DocumentForms(i).Tag = i
  Next
End Sub
```

Changing the Caption property of the active window is simple. All you have to do is set its new value from within the *GotFocus* event of the child Form. Enter the following line in the child Form's GotFocus event:

```
Private Sub Form_GotFocus()
  Me.Caption = "I've been activated!"
End Sub
```

The *Me* keyword is equivalent to *DocumentForms(i)*, in which *i* is the index of the active window. Instead of tracking the active window's index, use the *Me* keyword.

Similarly, the caption must be reset each time the window loses the focus. But this time you have to know the index of the active window in the *DocumentForms()* array, which is given by its *Me.Tag* property. The *LostFocus* event handler is again only a single line:

```
Private Sub Form_LostFocus()
  Me.Caption = "Document " & Format(Me.Tag)
End Sub
```

This example concludes our introduction to the structure and mechanics of MDI applications. In the following section we'll put this information to use by designing a couple of practical MDI applications. We'll start by converting the TextPad application of Chapter 5, *Basic ActiveX Controls*, to an MDI editor that will open multiple documents at once.

VB6 at Work: The MDIPad Project

In Chapter 5, we reviewed the development of the TextPad application. Now you're going to convert it to an MDI application. An MDI application lets you open and edit multiple documents simultaneously. You can also copy information from one window and paste it into another, and you can arrange multiple documents on-screen so that you can view any other document while editing the active one. All this is possible without invoking multiple instances of the application. Figure 10.9 shows the TextPad application, and Figure 10.10 shows the MDIPad application.

FIGURE 10.9:

The TextPad application

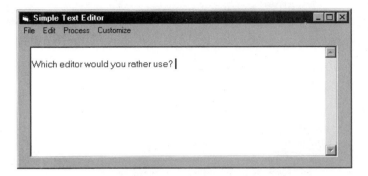

FIGURE 10.10:

The MDIPad application

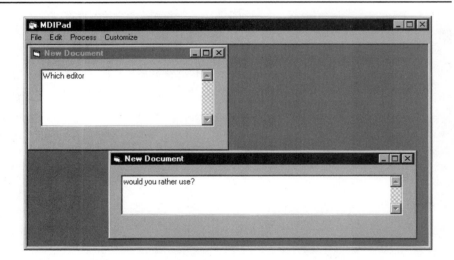

To convert TextPad to an MDI application, follow these steps:

1. Open the TextPad project and save it in a different folder.

2. Select the Editor Form and make sure its name is **Editor**.

3. Set its MDIChild property to True. It will become the child Form in which the documents will be opened and processed.

4. Choose Project ➤ Add MDI Form to add the MDI Form, and set its Caption property to MDIPad.

5. Run the application now to see how it works.

The child Form's menu appears in the MDI Form's menu bar and all its commands work as before. The code refers to the Editor TextBox control of the Form1 Form and it still works. You can open and save the active window's document with the Open, Save, and Save As commands on the File menu, resize the child Form, and do everything you could do with the TextPad application.

Adding Child Forms to MDIEditor

The modified TextPad application isn't an MDI application yet. For one thing, you can't open a new child Form. The Open command loads another document in the child Form, and if you close the child Form by clicking on its Close button, you won't be able to open it again. Some programming is needed to convert a regular application to an MDI application.

Let's start by adding multiple child Forms. Add a Module to the application, and in its declaration section add these lines:

```
Global DocumentForms(10) As New Form1
Global OpenFile(10) As String
Global currentDocument As Integer
```

The *DocumentForms()* array tracks the active document. The *OpenFile()* array has the same role as the *OpenFile* variable of the TextPad application: it holds the names of the documents open in each child Form. *OpenFile()* is used by the Save command of the File menu to save the active window's contents to the text files from which they were read.

When a new file is opened, its name is stored in the *OpenFile()* array. When a new document is created, the corresponding entry in the *OpenFile()* array is blank. The *currentDocument* variable is the index of the active window in the *DocumentForms()* array. Each time the focus is moved to a new child window, the *currentDocument* variable is updated with the following code:

```
Private Sub Form_GotFocus()
    currentDocument = Me.Tag
End Sub
```

To continue updating the TextPad application, you must now create a new File menu for the MDI Form. This menu will contain the following commands:

New Opens a new child window

Open Opens an existing document in a new child window

Exit Terminates the application

NOTE

Notice the lack of a Save command? The MDI Form's menu is visible only if no documents are open. Therefore, the Save and Save As commands won't be of any use in the MDI Form's File menu. Moreover, there's no need to attach the Edit, Format, and Customize menus to the MDI Form.

Programming the New Command

Start the Menu Designer for the MDI Form and create the File menu with the commands New, Open, and Exit. Then, include the following code for the New menu command.

Code 10.3: **The New Command**

```
Private Sub MDINew_Click()
Dim windex As Integer

  windex = FindFree()
  If windex = -1 Then
    MsgBox "You must close one of the documents before _
            another one can be opened"
    Exit Sub
  End If
Load DocumentForms(windex)
  DocumentForms(windex).Caption = "New Document"
  DocumentForms(windex).Tag = windex
  DocumentForms(windex).Show
End Sub
```

The New command doesn't clear the contents of the active child window, as was the case with the TextPad application. Instead, it opens a new, blank child window. As you can see in this code, before the New command can create a new child window, it must first find out if a child Form is available. This is done with the *FindFree()* function, which returns the index of the first available child Form. The FindFree() function scans all the elements of the *DocumentForms()* array looking for the first available one (an instance of the child Form with an empty tag). If all 10 child Forms are open, the program will prompt the user to close one of the open windows and try again. If a free child window is found, the program does the following:

1. Loads the corresponding element of the *DocumentForms()* array

2. Sets its caption to New Document

3. Sets its tag to its index in the *DocumentForms()* array

4. Displays the window

Later in the program, the window's caption will be set to this file's name if the user saves its document to a disk file. Here's the code of the FindFree() function:

```
Function FindFree() As Integer
Dim i As Integer
    For i = 0 To 9
        If DocumentForms(i).Tag = "" Then
            FindFree = i
            Exit Function
        End If
    Next
End Function
```

Programming the Open Command

The Open command's code is longer, but not drastically different from the Open command of the TextPad application. Like the New command, it doesn't display the file in the active child window. Instead, it loads a new child Form and displays the file in it.

Code 10.4: **The Open Command**

```
Private Sub MDIOpen_Click()
Dim FNum As Integer
Dim txt As String
Dim windex As Integer

  windex = FindFree()
  If windex = -1 Then
    MsgBox "You must close one of the" & _
" documents before another one can be opened"
Exit Sub
  End If

  Load DocumentForms(windex)
  DocumentForms(windex).Show
  currentDocument = windex
On Error GoTo FileError
  CommonDialog1.CancelError = True
  CommonDialog1.Flags = cdlOFNFileMustExist
  CommonDialog1.DefaultExt = "TXT"
  CommonDialog1.Filter = "Text files|*.TXT|All files|*.*"
```

```
CommonDialog1.ShowOpen
FNum = FreeFile
Open CommonDialog1.filename For Input As #1
txt = Input(LOF(FNum), #FNum)
Close #FNum
DocumentForms(currentDocument).Editor.Text = txt
OpenFiles(currentDocument) = CommonDialog1.filename
DocumentForms(currentDocument).Tag = OpenFile(currentDocument)
DocumentForms(currentDocument).Caption = OpenFiles(currentDocument)
Exit Sub

FileError:
  If Err.Number = cdlCancel Then Exit Sub
  MsgBox "Unknown error while opening file " & CommonDialog1.filename
  OpenFiles(currentDocument) = ""
End Sub
```

The Open command first opens a new child window (as does the New command) and then prompts the user with the FileOpen common dialog box to select a file to open. The child window's caption is set to the file's name, which is also stored in the corresponding element of the *OpenFile()* array. Every instance of the *OpenFile* variable in the program must be replaced with *OpenFiles(currentDocument)*. This is the name of the file in which the document of the current child window must be saved. The Save and Save As commands are implemented similarly, so I won't list the corresponding code here.

Programming the Exit Command

The Exit command of an MDI application is a bit more complicated than a simple End statement. See the code behind this command in the section "Ending an MDI Application," later in this chapter.

Differences between TextPad and MDIPad

Some commands of the MDI Form's menu have a different function than the commands with the same name on the child Form's File menu. In the TextPad application, the New command clears the contents of the editor. In the MDI version of the application, the New command opens a new, empty child window. Likewise, the Open command in the TextPad application reads a file into the editor. In the MDI version of the application, the Open command reads a file into a new child window. The differences in the operation of most MDI applications need to be kept in mind as you convert applications from the SDI to the MDI model. You can't simply duplicate the code of the New and Open commands of the equivalent SDI application to its MDI version.

The problems arising out of the different behaviors of the New and Open commands in the two types of applications can be overcome easily by duplicating the code of the MDI Form's File menu. Simply copy the code behind the New and Open commands of the MDI Form's menu to the equivalent subroutines of the child Form. Even better, you can call the corresponding event handler of the MDI Form from within the subroutines of the child Form's File commands. The File ➤ New and File ➤ Open commands of the child Form in the MDIPad project are implemented as follows:

```
Private Sub FileNew_Click()
    MDIForm1.MDINew_Click
End Sub

Private Sub FileOpen_Click()
    MDIForm1.MDIOpen_Click
End Sub
```

In spite of the differences between the two applications, you can get the File commands, which represent the most important differences between single and multiple window applications, to work in the MDI application. The next task is to ensure that the rest of the program references the Editor TextBox of the current child Form.

In the TextPad application, the program references the textbox control as `Form1`.`Editor`. The name of the child Form is no longer Form1; it's *DocumentForms-(currentDocument)*, in which *currentDocument* is the index of the active window in the *DocumentForms()* array. Replace all instances of *Form1* in the code with *DocumentForms(currentDocument)*—this is all it takes. Even the Find & Replace Form's code will reference the correct window in the MDI Form. The *Form1* variable is also referenced in the child Form's Resize event.

Ending an MDI Application

In most cases ending an application with the End statement isn't necessarily the most user-friendly approach. Before you end an application, you must always offer your users a chance to save their work. Ideally, you should maintain a *True/False* variable whose value is set every time the user edits the open document (the Change event of many controls is a good place to set this variable to True) and reset every time the user saves the document (with the Save or Save As commands).

This simple setup doesn't require too much code, but it's one of the finishing touches I have skipped in many of the examples in this book. The error-catching code required is usually unrelated to the point I'm trying to make, and it would make the examples too lengthy (the objective is to demonstrate the core of various applications, not provide truly professional applications). In a real-world application, however, these "details" can make all the difference for your application's future.

Handling unsaved data in normal applications is fairly simple, as there's only one document to deal with. But in an MDI application, you have to cope with several possible scenarios:

- The user closes a child window by clicking its Close button. You should detect this condition and provide the same code you'd use with a single Form application.

- The user quits a single document only. This situation is easy to handle—it's just like a normal application.

- The user closes the MDI Form. If the MDI Form is closed, all the open documents will close with it! If losing the edits in a single document is bad, imagine losing the edits in multiple documents.

Therefore, terminating an MDI application with the End statement is unacceptable. One approach would be to go through all child Forms, examine whether they are open, and prompt the user for each open document. This is possible, but it would take a lot of programming, and as you may have guessed, there's a simpler way, which we'll explore next.

Using QueryUnload to Protect Data

The MDI mechanism provides a better solution for terminating an MDI application, via the *QueryUnload* event. This event is triggered when a child window is unloaded. If the entire MDI Form is unloaded, the QueryUnload event is triggered for each open child Form and it gives your code a chance to cancel the action. The QueryUnload event's syntax is as follows:

```
QueryUnload(cancel As Integer, unloadmode As Integer)
```

The application can set the *cancel* argument to halt the termination process. If you set the *cancel* argument to True in your code, the child Form won't be unloaded, which in turn, prevents the unloading of the MDI Form.

The *unloadmode* argument tells you which event caused the QueryUnload event according to the values in Table 10.2.

TABLE 10.2: Values of the QueryUnload's *unloadmode* Argument

Constant	Value	Description
vbFormControlMenu	0	The user clicked the Form's Close button or selected Control ➤ Close
vbFormCode	1	The Unload statement was invoked from within the code
vbAppWindows	2	Windows itself is shutting down
vbAppTaskManager	3	The application was shut down through the Task Manager
vbFormMDIForm	4	The MDI Form is closing

As you can see, the QueryUnload event is triggered even if Windows itself is shutting down. If you program the QueryUnload event of the child Forms, you can rest assured that the users of your application won't lose any data unless their computer crashes or they reset it. You can examine the value of this argument from within your code to find out why the Form is being unloaded and act accordingly. On certain occasions, you may want to handle the situation differently, depending on the external event that caused the Form to unload, but the process is practically the same. Offer your users a chance to save the data, discard the data, or cancel the program's termination altogether (see Figure 10.11).

FIGURE 10.11:

If you shut down the MDI-Pad application, you'll be prompted to save each and every open document.

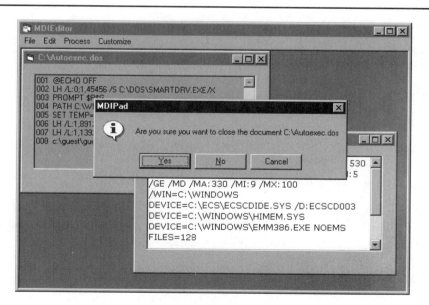

To use the QueryUnload event, you must unload the child Form from within its Exit menu command. The code behind the End command of the MDIEditor's File menu is shown in Code 10.5.

Code 10.5:	**The End Command**

```
Private Sub FileExit_Click()
  Unload MDIForm1
  End
End Sub
```

Notice that this is the Exit command of the child Form's File menu. The MDI Form's File menu is visible only if no child windows are open, in which case there's nothing to save and a single End statement will suffice. To terminate the MDI application, first unload the MDI Form and then End the application.

Unloading the MDI Form triggers a QueryUnload event for all its child Forms. In each child Form's Unload event, you can prompt the users accordingly and give them a chance to save their data, discard the data, or cancel the operation. Here's how you can handle this event in the MDIEdit application.

Code 10.6:	**The QueryUnload Event**

```
Private Sub Form_QueryUnload(Cancel As Integer, UnloadMode As Integer)
Dim reply As Integer

    reply = MsgBox("Are you sure you want to close the document " & _
            Me.Tag,vbYesNoCancel + vbInformation)
    If reply = vbCancel Then
      Cancel = True
    ElseIf reply = vbYes Then Exit Sub
    Else
      FileSaveAs_Click
    End If
End Sub
```

These few lines of code enable the user of the application to discard unsaved data, cancel the operation, or save any unsaved data with a call to the child Form's FileSave_Click subroutine.

Handling the unloading of multiple Forms in a single point in your code is a great convenience because you can make the process of terminating the application as simple or as complicated as you wish for all child Forms. For instance, you can create temporary files with unsaved information in case the user decides that the discarded information is valuable after all.

Implementing Scrolling Forms

One of the shortcomings of regular Visual Basic Forms is that they can't be scrolled. If you resize a fairly long Form to make room on your Desktop, you'll see only part of the Form (its upper-left corner is always shown). Ideally, a pair of scroll bars should be attached to the Form automatically to help the user scroll it and bring the desired area of the Form in view. The problem is even worse when a large Form, which can fit on a 1024×768 (or larger) monitor, is displayed on a monitor with lower resolution. The user may have to move the Form with the mouse beyond the right or left edge of the screen to see the other end of it.

To overcome this limitation, you can create MDI Forms that look and feel like regular Forms. Scroll bars are attached automatically to an MDI Form when the child Forms no longer fit in the designated area. To display a long Form, design it as usual, set its MDIChild property to True, and place it within an MDI Form. When the user resizes the main window of the application to a smaller size, the corresponding scroll bar(s) will be attached automatically, allowing any portion of the Form to come into view.

Scrolling Forms can be built in two ways, and we'll demonstrate them both with examples. The simplest scrolling Form is an MDI Form with a large child Form. The MDI Form can be set to any size initially, and the user can resize it at will. Whenever the MDI is smaller than its child Form, the user can bring any part of the child Form into view with the help of the two scroll bars. The MDI window can be made as large as the monitor's resolution allows. If you don't want this to happen, insert the appropriate code in the Form's Resize event to restrict the size of the window.

Figure 10.12 shows a section of a large Form displayed as a child Form within an MDI Form. The MDI Form is smaller than the child Form, and the scroll bars are attached automatically. The Form shown in the figure is the main Form of the LongForm project, which is discussed later in this chapter.

The second method is to design several smaller child Forms and place them next to each other (from within the MDI Form's Load event). The tiled windows should have no title bars, so that the user can't change their placement on the container Form. This method is very useful when the child Forms are identical and you don't know in advance how many of them may be needed at runtime. Figure 10.13 shows an MDI Form with several sections. Normally, each section would be a smaller Form, displayed as needed. With the MDI approach, you can place them next to each other on a child Form and create a long Form. The user can adjust the length of this Form and bring the desired section into view with the help of the MDI Form's scroll bars.

FIGURE 10.12:

To create a scrolling Form, design it as a child Form and place it on an MDI Form.

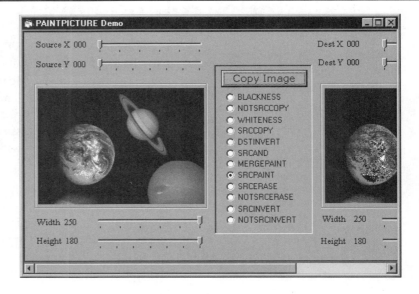

FIGURE 10.13:

This scrolling Form is an MDI Form with several borderless child Forms displayed next to each other.

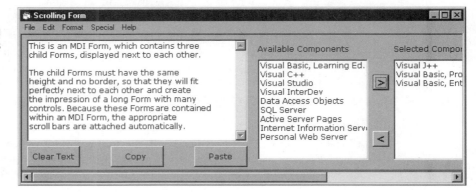

VB6 at Work: The ScrollImage Project

The first scrolling Form I'll demonstrate is a Form with a large image that can be scrolled in all four directions. Visual Basic's ImageBox and PictureBox controls don't provide any scroll bars when the image exceeds the dimensions of the controls, and in many cases, this is a serious problem in designing Forms with images. The best approach to this problem is to design a custom ActiveX control that does exactly what the PictureBox control does and also provides a pair of scroll bars that are activated whenever the image's dimensions exceed those of the control. The MDI approach works well enough and many applications don't really call for a custom control.

Figure 10.14 shows a Form with an image and the appropriate scroll bars attached to it. From a user's point of view, it looks just like a Form with scroll bars. In fact, this is an MDI Form with a child Form. The child Form is as large as the image it contains and it has neither a title bar nor a control box. The child Form is aligned to the top left corner of the MDI Form and it can't be moved by the user because it doesn't have a title bar.

FIGURE 10.14:

Using an MDI Form to simulate a scrolling PictureBox control.

The Form shown in Figure 10.14 belongs to the ScrlImg project, which you'll find in this chapter's folder on the CD. To implement the scrolling Form, follow these steps:

1. Start a new project.

2. Rename the Form to **ImageForm** and set its MDIChild property to True.

3. Set the child Form's Caption property to a blank string and its ControlBox property to False. Also set its BorderStyle property to 1 (Fixed Single).

4. Add an MDI Form to the project with the Project ➢ Add MDI Form command. Set the MDI Form's Name property to ScrollImageForm.

5. To display an image on the child Form, assign the image file's name to the Picture property of the ImageForm Form. You must also set the same Form's PaletteMode property to 1 (UseZOrder), so that the image's colors will be properly displayed even on palette systems (systems that can display 256 colors only).

6. The last step is to add the code for resizing the child Form to fit the size of the image it contains. This code must be inserted in the child Form's Load event:

```
Private Sub Form_Load()
    PictWidth = Me.ScaleX(Me.Picture.Width, vbHimetric, vbTwips)
    PictHeight = Me.ScaleY(Me.Picture.Height, vbHimetric, vbTwips)
    Me.Move 0, 0, PictWidth, PictHeight
End Sub
```

Notice that the dimensions of the image are returned by the Width and Height properties of the Picture object in HiMetric units, and they must be converted to twips. This conversion is carried out by the ScaleX and ScaleY methods of the Form. If you have set the child Form's ScaleMode property to another value (pixels, for instance), you must change the second argument of the method accordingly.

This is all the code needed by the application. If you load another image on the child Form, you must call the child Form's Load event handler to resize the Form accordingly. The project's MDI Form has a single menu command, the Load Image command, which does exactly that. The menu is added to the child Form so that it's attached to the MDI Form when a child Form is loaded. The Load Image command is implemented with the following code:

```
Private Sub LoadImage_Click()
    CommonDialog1.Filter = "Images|*.bmp;*.gif;*.jpg"
    CommonDialog1.DialogTitle = "Select Image"
    CommonDialog1.InitDir = App.Path
    CommonDialog1.FileName = ""
    CommonDialog1.ShowOpen
    If CommonDialog1.FileName = "" Then Exit Sub
    Me.Picture = LoadPicture(CommonDialog1.FileName)
    Call Form_Load
End Sub
```

The first seven lines set up the Windows Common Dialogs control and the last two lines load the image on the child Form and call the Form's Load event handler, which resizes the child Form according to the new image's dimensions.

VB6 at Work: The LongForm Project

The same approach will work with a really long or wide Form. Design it as a child Form in the Visual Basic IDE, then display it on an MDI Form. Designing an exceptionally large Form in the IDE is not difficult because scroll bars are attached automatically to the Form design window at design time. Give it a try now to see how easy it is to implement large scrolling Forms with the MDI approach. Remember to remove the child Form's title bar so users can't move it, and set its border to a fixed style so users can't resize it.

Earlier, Figure 10.12 showed a long Form we used in Chapter 5. It's the main Form of the PaintPic application, implemented as a child Form on an MDI Form. The revised project can be run on a monitor of any resolution. To make the Paint-Pic Form scroll, follow these steps:

1. Start a new project and remove its Form1 component. Right-click the Form1 entry in the Project Window and from the shortcut menu, select Remove Form1.

2. Add the PaintPic Form. Open the Project menu, select Add Form and in the Add Form dialog box, locate the PaintPic Form (you'll find it in the LongForm folder in this chapter's folder on the CD).

3. Change the PaintPic Form's BorderStyle property to 1 (Fixed Single), the Caption property to an empty string and the ControlBox property to False.

Now run the application to see how the PaintPic Form can fit in a smaller window. If you want to save the project, use the Save PaintPic.frm As command in the File menu to save the revised Form to another folder. If you simply save the project's components, you'll break the PaintPic project.

VB6 at Work: The ScrollForm Project

The next example demonstrates how to build a scrolling Form with different zones, which would normally correspond to different regular Forms. Figure 10.15 shows a Form with several sections placed next to each other. At nearly 1,000 pixels wide, it's too big for the window. It also shows the separate child Forms that make up the long Form at design time.

FIGURE 10.15:

The MDI Form of the Scroll-Form project looks like a wide scrolling Form.

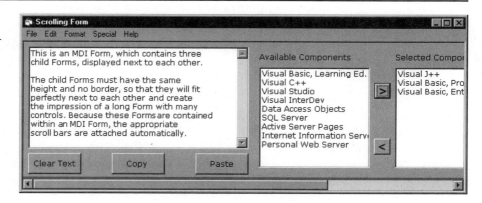

FIGURE 10.16:

The three child Forms of the ScrollForm project at design time

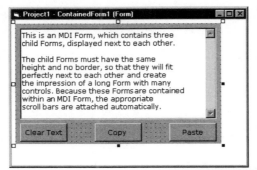
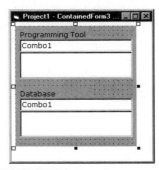
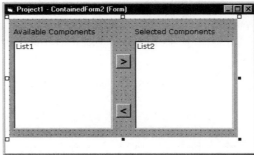

To design this Form, you must create three child Forms that correspond to the three sections of the MDI Form (shown in Figure 10.16 above). In doing so, make sure that they:

- Are all child Forms (property MDIChild is set to True)

- Don't have a TitleBar (property Caption is set to "" and property Control-Box is set to False)

- All have the same height, so that they can be displayed next to each other and give the impression of a continuous long Form

- Have their BorderStyle property set to 0 (None). If you want to display the borders between the sections of the Form, set the BorderStyle property of the child Forms to 1 (Fixed Single).

The placement of the child Forms on the MDI Form is critical to this approach. The child Forms can't be arranged on the MDI Form at design time. To display the three child Forms next to each other, insert the following code in the MDI Form's *Initialize* event:

```
Private Sub MDIForm_Initialize()
    MDIScrollForm.Show
    MDIScrollForm.Enabled = False
```

```
ContainedForm1.Show
ContainedForm2.Top = ContainedForm1.Top
ContainedForm2.Left = ContainedForm1.Left + ContainedForm1.Width
ContainedForm2.Show
ContainedForm3.Top = ContainedForm2.Top
ContainedForm3.Left = ContainedForm2.Left + ContainedForm2.Width
ContainedForm3.Show

    MDIScrollForm.Height = ContainedForm1.Height + 70 * Screen.Twips-
PerPixelY
    MDIScrollForm.Enabled = True
End Sub
```

TIP

If you place this code segment in the Form's Load event, the child Forms won't be placed next to each other properly. The reason is that the child Forms are displayed after the MDI Form is loaded, therefore, you can't specify their positions from within the Load event. The Initialize event takes place after the Load event and this is the event that must be used to arrange the child windows on the MDI Form.

MDIScrollForm is the name of the MDI Form and the three child Forms are called ContainedForm1, ContainedForm2 and ContainedForm3. The first one is placed flush against the top left corner of the MDI Form, the second child Form is placed flush against the right edge of the first child Form, and so on. The MDIScrollForm's Height property is set to the height of the child Forms plus the height of the Form's title bar and horizontal scroll bar. If you want to prevent the user from changing the Form's height, insert a line that sets its height in the Resize event.

The ListBox controls are populated from within the corresponding Form's Load event, which is fired for child Forms as well. There's no code behind the menu commands of the MDI Form. I designed the menu structure for the MDI Form to demonstrate how you can make an MDI application mimic a regular Form, with the added benefit of allowing its contents to be scrolled.

As I mentioned at the beginning of this chapter, MDI Forms aren't very common in user interface design, but they are unique. With some creative programming, you can put this technique to good use. Applications that open multiple documents are prime candidates for implementing with MDI. The technique of implementing scrolling Forms with MDI Forms masquerading as regular Forms is a useful and practical trick for designing Forms that can be viewed on monitors with lower resolutions.

CHAPTER

ELEVEN

11

Recursive Programming

- Understanding recursion

- Performing a binary search with recursion

- Building a custom File Manager with recursion

- Building a custom Explorer with recursion

- Exploring the stack and recursive programming

- Determining when to use recursive programming

This chapter is slightly different from the previous ones because it doesn't describe specific Visual Basic techniques or controls. Instead, it introduces a powerful technique for implementing efficient, compact programs. Recursion is a special topic in computer programming that's one of the least understood among beginners and even among some advanced programmers. It's surrounded by an aura of mystery and most BASIC programmers ignore it. The truth is, recursive programming is no more complicated than any other programming approach, once you understand how it works and when to use it.

Some readers may think that the material in this chapter is of little use to the average programmer. They are probably right, but there is some valuable information in this chapter. Toward the end of it, you'll learn how to write applications that scan an entire folder and its subfolders. The DirMap application is a customized Windows Explorer that you can incorporate in your applications even if you don't quite understand how it works.

Basic Concepts

Recursive programming is used for implementing algorithms, or mathematical definitions, that are described recursively, that is, in terms of themselves. A recursive definition is implemented by a procedure that calls itself; thus, it is called a *recursive procedure*.

Code that calls functions and subroutines to accomplish a task, such as the following segment, is quite normal:

```
Function MyPayments()
{other statements}
CarPayment = CalculatePayment(CarCost, Interest, Duration)
MonthlyCost = MonthlyCost + CarPayment
HomePayment = CalculatePayment(Mortgage, Interest, Duration)
MonthlyCost = MonthlyCost + HomePayment
{more statements}
End Function
```

In the preceding code, the MyPayments() function calls the CalculatePayment() function twice to calculate the monthly payments for a car and home loan. There's nothing puzzling about this piece of code because it's linear. Here's what it does:

1. The MyPayments() function suspends execution each time it calls the CalculatePayment() function.

2. It waits for the CalculatePayment() function to complete its task and return a value.

3. It then resumes execution.

But what if a function calls itself? Examine the following code:

```
Function DoSomething(n As Integer) As Integer
{other statements}
value = value - 1
If value = 0 Then Exit Function
newValue = DoSomething(value)
{more statements}
End Function
```

If you didn't know better, you'd think that this program would never end. Every time the DoSomething() function is called it gets into a loop by calling itself again and again and it never exits. In fact, this is a clear danger with recursion. It's not only possible, but quite easy, for a recursive function to get into an endless loop. A recursive function must exit explicitly. In other words, you must tell a recursive function when to stop calling itself and exit. The condition that causes the DoSomething() function to end is met when *value* becomes zero.

Apart from this technicality, you can draw a few useful conclusions from this example. A function performs a well-defined task. When a function calls itself, it has to interrupt the current task to complete another, quite similar task. The DoSomething() function can't complete its task (whatever this is) unless it performs an identical calculation, which it does by calling itself.

Recursion in Real Life

Do you ever run into recursive processes in your daily tasks? Suppose you're viewing a World Wide Web page that describes a hot new topic. The page contains a term you don't understand and the term is a hyperlink. When you click the hyperlink, another page that defines the term is displayed. This definition contains another term you don't understand. The new term is also a hyperlink, so you click it and a page containing its definition is displayed. Once you understand this definition, you click the Back button to go back to the previous page where you re-read the term knowing its definition. You then go back to the original page.

The task at hand involves understanding a topic, a description, and a definition. Every time you run into an unfamiliar term, you interrupt the current task to accomplish another identical task such as learning another term.

The process of looking up a definition in a dictionary is similar and it epitomizes recursion. For example, if the definition of *Active page* is "Web pages that contain ActiveX controls," you'd probably have to look up the definition of *ActiveX controls*. Let's say *ActiveX controls* are defined as "elements used to build Active Web pages." This is a sticky situation, indeed. At this point, you'd either have to interrupt your search and find out what *Active Web pages* are or look up its definition elsewhere. Going back and forth between these two definitions won't take you anywhere. This is the endless loop mentioned earlier.

Because endless loops can arise easily in recursive programming, you must be sure that your code contains conditions that will cause the recursive procedure to stop calling itself. In the example of the DoSomething() function, this condition is as follows:

```
If value = 0 Then Exit Function
```

The code reduces the value of the variable *value* by increments of 1 until it eventually reaches 0, at which point, the sequence of recursive calls ends. Without such a condition, the recursive function would call itself indefinitely. Once the DoSomething() function ends, the suspended instances of the same function resume their execution and terminate.

Now, let's look at a few practical examples and see these concepts in action.

A Simple Example

I'll demonstrate the principles of recursive programming with a simple example: the calculation of the factorial of a number. The factorial of a number, denoted with an exclamation mark, is described recursively as follows:

```
n! = n * (n-1)!
```

The factorial of n (read as n factorial) is the number n multiplied by the factorial of (n-1), which in turn is (n-1) multiplied by the factorial of (n-2) and so on, until we reach 0!, which is 1 by definition.

Here's the process of calculating the factorial of 4:

```
4! = 4 * 3!
   = 4 * 3 * 2!
   = 4 * 3 * 2 * 1!
   = 4 * 3 * 2 * 1 * 0!
   = 4 * 3 * 2 * 1 * 1
   = 24
```

For the mathematically inclined, the factorial of the number *n* is defined as follows:

```
n! = n * (n-1)!      if n is greater than zero
n! = 1               if n is zero
```

The factorial is described in terms of itself and it's a prime candidate for recursive implementation. The Factorial application, shown in Figure 11.1, lets you specify the number whose factorial you want to calculate in the box on the left and displays the result in the box on the right. To start the calculations, click the Factorial button.

FIGURE 11.1:

The Factorial application

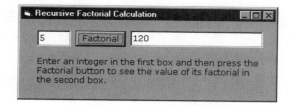

Here's the factorial() function that implements the previous definition:

```
Function factorial(n As Integer) As Double

    If n = 0 Then
        factorial = 1
    Else
        factorial = factorial(n - 1) * n
    End If

End Function
```

The recursive definition of the factorial of an integer is implemented in a single line:

```
factorial = n * factorial(n-1)
```

As long as the argument of the function isn't zero, the function returns the product of its argument times the factorial of its argument minus 1. With each successive call of the factorial() function, the initial number decreases by an increment of 1 and eventually, *n* becomes 0 and the sequence of recursive calls ends. Each time the factorial() function calls itself, the calling function is suspended temporarily. When the called function terminates, the most recently suspended function resumes execution. To calculate the factorial of 10, you'd call the factorial() function with the argument 10, as follows:

```
MsgBox "The factorial of 10 " & factorial(10)
```

The execution of the factorial(10) function is interrupted when it calls factorial(9). This function is also interrupted when factorial(9) calls factorial(8), and so on. By the time factorial(0) is called, ten instances of the function have been suspended and made to wait for the function they called to finish. When that happens, they resume execution.

Let's see how this happens by adding a couple of lines to the factorial() function. Open the Factorial application and add a few statements that print the function's status in the Immediate window:

```
Function factorial(n As Integer) As Double

Debug.Print "Starting the calculation of " & n & " factorial"
    If n = 0 Then
        factorial = 1
    Else
Debug.Print "Calling factorial(n) with n=" & n - 1
        factorial = factorial(n - 1) * n
    End If
Debug.Print "Done calculating " & n & " factorial"

End Function
```

Watching the Algorithm

The Print statements are commented out in the Factorial application. You can remove the apostrophes from in front of them and then run the application to watch the sequence of function calls while the factorial of a number is being calculated.

The first Print statement tells us that a new instance of the function has been activated and gives the number whose factorial it's about to calculate. The second Print statement tells us that the active function is about to call another instance of itself and shows which argument it will supply to the function it's calling. The last Print statement informs us that the factorial function is done. Here's what you'll see in the Immediate window if you call the factorial() function with the argument 4:

```
Starting the calculation of 4 factorial
Calling factorial(n) with n=3
```

```
Starting the calculation of 3 factorial
Calling factorial(n) with n=2
Starting the calculation of 2 factorial
Calling factorial(n) with n=1
Starting the calculation of 1 factorial
Calling factorial(n) with n=0
Starting the calculation of 0 factorial
Done calculating 0 factorial
Done calculating 1 factorial
Done calculating 2 factorial
Done calculating 3 factorial
Done calculating 4 factorial
```

This list of messages is lengthy, but it's worth examining for the sequence of events. The first time the function is called, it attempts to calculate the factorial of 4. It can't complete its operation and calls factorial(3) to calculate the factorial of 3, which is needed to calculate the factorial of 4. The first instance of the factorial() function is suspended until factorial(3) returns its result.

Similarly, factorial(3) doesn't complete its calculations because it must call factorial(2). So far, there are two suspended instances of the factorial() function. In turn, factorial(2) calls factorial(1), and factorial(1) calls factorial(0). Now, there are four suspended instances of the factorial() function, all waiting for an intermediate result before they can continue with their calculations. Figure 11.2 shows this process.

When factorial(0) completes its execution, it prints the following message and returns a result:

```
Done calculating 0 factorial
```

This result is passed to the most recently interrupted function, which is factorial(1). This function can now resume operation, complete the calculation of 1! (1×1) and then print another message indicating that it finished its calculations.

As each suspended function resumes operation, it passes a result to the function from which it was called, until the very first instance of the factorial() function finishes the calculation of the factorial of 4. Figure 11.3 shows this process. (In the figure, factorial is abbreviated as *fact*.)

FIGURE 11.2:

You can watch the progress of the calculation of a factorial in the Immediate window.

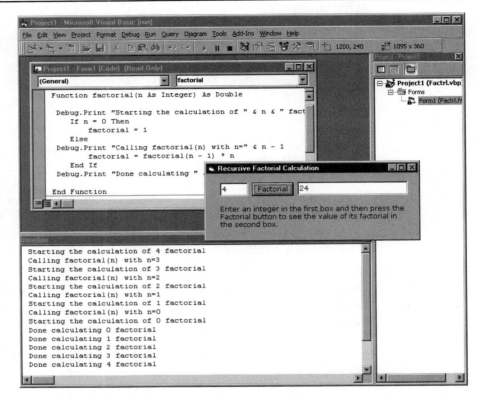

FIGURE 11.3:

The process of the recursive calculation of the factorial of 4. The arrows pointing to the right show the direction of recursive calls, and the ones pointing to the left show the propagation of the result.

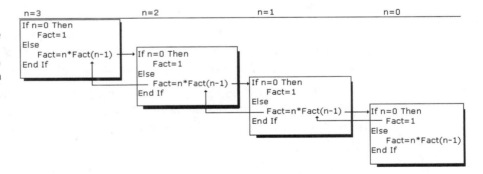

What Happens When a Function Calls Itself

If you're completely unfamiliar with recursive programming, you're probably uncomfortable with the idea of a function calling itself. Let's take a closer look at what happens when a function calls itself. As far as the computer is concerned, it doesn't make any difference whether a function calls itself or another function. When a function calls another function, the calling function suspends execution and waits for the called function to complete its task. The calling function then resumes (usually by taking into account any result returned by the function it called). A recursive function simply calls itself instead of another one.

Let's look at what happens when the factorial in the previous function is implemented with the following line in which factorial1() is identical to factorial():

```
factorial = n * factorial1(n-1)
```

When the factorial() function calls factorial1(), its execution is suspended until factorial1() returns its result. A new function is loaded into the memory and executed. If the factorial() function is called with 3, the factorial1() function calculates the factorial of 2.

Similarly, the code of the factorial1() function is:

```
factorial1 = n * factorial2(n-1)
```

This time, the function factorial2() is called to calculate the factorial of 1. The function factorial2() in turn calls factorial3(), which calculates the factorial of zero. The factorial3() function completes its calculations and returns the result 1. This is in turn multiplied by 1 to produce the factorial of 1. This result is returned to the function factorial1(), which completes the calculation of the factorial of 2 (which is 2*1). The value is returned to the factorial() function, which now completes the calculation of 3 (3*2, or 6).

Recursive Calls and the Operating System

You can think of a recursive function calling itself as the operating system supplying another identical function with a different name; it's more or less what happens. Each time your program calls a function, the operating system does the following:

1. Saves the status of the active function
2. Loads the new function in memory
3. Starts executing the new function

If the function is recursive—in other words, if the new function is the same as the one currently being executed—nothing changes. The operating system saves the status of the active function somewhere and starts executing it as if it was another function. Of course, there's no reason to load it in memory again because the function is already there.

When the newly called function finishes, the operating system reloads the function it interrupted in memory and continues its execution. I mentioned that the operating system stores the status of a function every time it must interrupt it to load another function in memory. The *status information* includes the values of its variables and the location where execution was interrupted. In effect, after the operating system loads the status of the interrupted function, the function continues execution as if it was never interrupted. We'll return to the topic of storing status information later on in the section "The Stack Mechanism."

Recursion by Mistake

Recursion isn't as complicated as you may think. Here's an example of a recursive situation you may have experienced without knowing it. Figure 11.4 shows a simple application that fills the background of a picture box with a solid color. Instead of setting the control's BackColor property though, it draws vertical lines from one end of the control to the other. Every time the New Color button is clicked, the Picture-Box control is filled slowly with vertical lines. The color of the lines is chosen randomly. This application is quite similar to the ClrGrads application of Chapter 7, *Manipulating Color and Pixels with Visual Basic,* which fills the background of the control with a gradient. I used a solid color in this example to simplify the code.

FIGURE 11.4:

Click the New Color button before the program has a chance to fill the control to watch a recursive behavior.

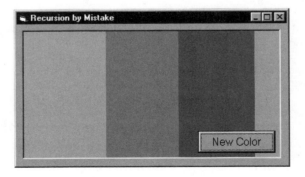

VB6 at Work: The Recurse Project

You'll find the Recurse application in this chapter's folder on the CD. Load it and run it. Click the New Color button and the program starts filling the picture box with a random color from left to right. Because the control's ScaleMode is twips, the progress of the drawing is slow, even on a fast Pentium. The code behind the New Color Command button follows.

Code 11.1:   **The New Color Button Code**

```
Private Sub Command1_Click()
RGBColor = Rnd * 16000000
For i = 0 To Picture1.Width
    Picture1.Line (i, 0)-(i, Picture1.Height), RGBColor
    DoEvents
Next
End Sub
```

Suppose the program starts filling the picture box with red lines. Before the program has a chance to complete its operation, click the New Color button again. The subroutine Command1_Click() is interrupted, and the program starts filling the control with a new color, perhaps fuchsia. Interrupt the process again. This time, yellow kicks in and starts filling the control from left to right. Let this operation complete.

As soon as the picture box is filled with yellow, the interrupted process continues. The program completes the drawing of the fuchsia lines, but it doesn't start drawing from the left edge of the control. It picks up from where it was interrupted. When the fuchsia color reaches the right edge of the control, red kicks in! Can you see what's going on here? Each time you click the New Color button, the Command1_Click() subroutine is interrupted, and a new copy of the same subroutine starts executing. The interrupted (or suspended) instance of the subroutine doesn't die. It waits for a chance to complete, which it gets when the newer instance of the subroutine completes its task.

This recursion is made possible by the DoEvents() statement placed in the loop's body. Without it, you wouldn't be able to interrupt the subroutine and invoke another instance of it. Normally, you wouldn't use the DoEvents() statement to avoid the very behavior you witnessed in this example. Most of the procedures you've written so far don't use the DoEvents() statement; these procedures won't allow another procedure to start executing before they have finished.

I need to mention one important aspect of recursion here. The *RGBColor* variable is local and it maintains its value while the subroutine is interrupted. Visual Basic stores the values of the local variables of the interrupted procedures and recalls them when the procedure gets a chance to complete. This is possible because each new copy of the procedure that starts executing has its own set of local variables. Local variables are part of the procedure's status.

Binary Search: A Recursive Implementation

If you're mathematically inclined, the examples that were used to introduce the concepts of recursive programming are quite interesting. But most people aren't, so let's look at a couple of practical examples. We'll return to the Binary Search algorithm we explored in Chapter 5, *Basic ActiveX Controls*, and implement it with a recursive function.

The Binary Search algorithm searches a list of ordered (sorted) entries to locate any given item. This algorithm starts by comparing the desired item with the middle entry of the list. Because the entries are sorted, depending on the outcome of the comparison, half the list will be rejected. If the desired element is above the middle element of the list, the lower half of the list will be rejected. The search continues in the upper half, and the process is repeated. The desired element is located somewhere in the upper half of the list, and the algorithm now compares the desired element with the middle element of the upper half of the list. Depending on the outcome of this comparison, one half of the already reduced list is rejected again, and the process is repeated until we are left with a single element, which is the desired element. If it isn't, you know that the element you're looking for doesn't belong to the list.

The idea behind the Binary Search algorithm is to halve the list at each iteration and reach the location of the desired element quickly. If you start with a list of 1,024 items, after the first comparison you'll be left with 512 elements, after the second comparison you'll be left with 256 elements, after the third comparison you'll be left with 128 elements, and so on. It will take only 10 comparisons to narrow the list down to the item you want. The definition of the Binary Search algorithm is recursive in nature and it can be implemented easily and efficiently with a recursive function.

The BSearch() Function

Following is a description of the BSearch() function, which implements the Binary Search algorithm:

1. First, BSearch() retrieves the list's middle element.

2. It then compares the desired element with the list's middle element.

3. If the desired element is found, the task is finished.

4. If the desired element is larger than the list's middle element:

    • The lower half of the list is rejected.

    Or else

    • The upper half of the list is rejected.

5. If the list has one or no element(s), it quits. The element isn't in the list.

6. BSearch() then searches the rest of the list.

The last test is essential; without it, the search would never end. If the list's size is reduced to a single element, you know that this element is the desired one or that the desired element doesn't exist. The implementation of the BSearch() function in Visual Basic follows.

Code 11.2:   **The BSearch() Function**

```
Function BSearch(lower As Integer, upper As Integer, KeyField As
String) As Integer
Dim middle As Integer

    middle = Fix(lower + upper) / 2
    If DataArray(middle) = KeyField Then
      BSearch = middle
      Exit Function
    End If

    If lower >= upper Then
      BSearch = -1
      Exit Function
    End If

    If KeyField < DataArray(middle) Then
      upper = middle - 1
    Else
      lower = middle + 1
    End If
    BSearch = BSearch(lower, upper, KeyField)

End Function
```

The BSearch() function is a straightforward coding of the verbal explanation of the algorithm. Here's what it does:

1. First, it calculates the index of the list's middle element and compares the list's middle element with the desired element (*KeyField*).

2. If both elements are the same, the desired element has been located and the search need not continue. The function returns the index of the desired element in the list.

3. If both elements aren't the same, the values of the two limits of the array are compared.

4. If the upper limit is equal to or less than the lower limit (that is, if the list has been reduced to a single element), the desired element is not in the list, and instead of an index, the function returns the value -1.

5. If the end of the list has not been reached, the function compares the desired element with the array's middle element and shortens the array accordingly by changing the values of the upper and lower variables, which are the indices delimiting the section of the array in which the desired element resides.

Figure 11.5 shows the BSearch application of Chapter 5, *Basic ActiveX Controls*, only this time, the BSearch() function is implemented recursively. The new BSearch application (in this chapter's folder on the CD) demonstrates how to use the BSearch() function presented earlier in this section to search for an item in a sorted list.

FIGURE 11.5:

The revised BSearch application uses a recursive implementation of the Binary Search algorithm.

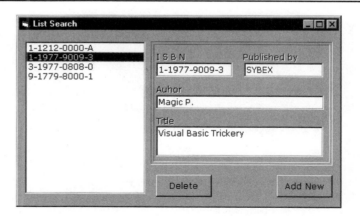

Recursive functions are also used in some very efficient searching and sorting algorithms which I won't go into in this book. They are rather advanced topics, and with all the programming tools that Visual Basic provides, it's doubtful that you'll ever need them. Instead, let's look at a more practical example and application, which you might find quite useful.

Scanning Folders Recursively

The examples of recursive functions we have looked at so far probably haven't entirely convinced you of the usefulness of recursion. The factorial of a number can be easily calculated with a For...Next loop, and the Binary Search algorithm was implemented nonrecursively earlier in this book. So, what good is recursion?

The answer is the FileScan application, which can't be implemented non-recursively. I hope that the previous examples helped you understand the principles of recursive programming and that you're ready for some real recursion. We'll design an application similar to the Windows Explorer, which scans an entire folder, including its subfolders. As the application scans the files and sub-folders of a folder or an entire volume, it can locate files by name, size, and date. It can also move files around, and in general, perform all the operations of the Windows Explorer, plus any other custom operation you might require. Much of the functionality of this application is provided by Windows Explorer, but as you'll see shortly, this application is highly customizable. It can serve as your starting point for many file operations that Windows Explorer doesn't provide. For example, your custom Explorer could expand all the subfolders each time you open a folder or display the full path name of each folder. Later in the chapter, you'll see an application that generates a list of all the files in a folder, including its subfolders, organized by folder.

A file scanning application is ideal for implementing with a recursive function because its operation is defined recursively. Suppose you want to scan all the entries of a folder and locate the files whose size exceeds 1MB or count the files. If an entry is another folder, the same process must be repeated for that subfolder. If the sub-folder contains a folder, the process must be repeated. This application calls for a recursive function, because every time it runs into a subfolder, it must interrupt the scanning of the current folder and start scanning the subfolder by calling itself. If you spend some time thinking about the implementation of this algorithm, you'll conclude that there's no simple way to do it without recursion. Actually, once you've established the recursive nature of a process, you'll know you must code it as a recursive procedure.

Describing a Recursive Procedure

When you're about to write a recursive procedure, it's helpful to start with a general written description of the procedure. For the FileScan application, we need a subroutine (since it's not going to return a result) that scans the contents of a folder: let's call it ScanFolders(). The ScanFolders() subroutine must scan all the entries of the initial folder and process the files in it. If the current entry is a file, it must act upon the file, depending on its name, size, or any of its attributes. If the current entry is a folder, it must scan the contents of this folder. In other words, it must interrupt the scanning of the current folder and start scanning the subfolder. And the most efficient way to scan a subfolder is to have it to call itself. Here's the ScanFolders() function in pseudocode:

```
Sub FileScan()
Process files in current folder
If current folder contains subfolders
For each subfolder
    Switch to subfolder
    FileScan()
Next
Move to parent directory
End If
```

Translating the Description to Code

Now, let's translate this description to actual code. Because we need access to each folder's files and subfolders, we'll use a DriveListBox control, a DirListBox control, and a FileListBox control, as shown in Figure 11.6. Using these controls, we can enumerate the subfolders of any given folder with the DirListBox control and its files with the FileListBox control.

FIGURE 11.6:

The FileScan application scans the files and subfolders of any folder on your disk, performing a custom operation on each file along the way.

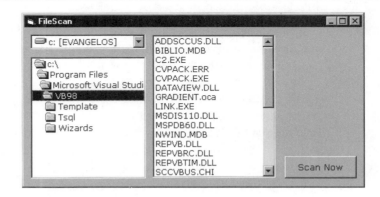

Using the File Controls

The three file controls (DriveListBox, DirListBox, and FileListBox) are connected with the following subroutines.

Code 11.3:   The DriveListBox

```
Private Sub Drive1_Change()
    ChDrive Dir1.Path
    Dir1.Path = Drive1.Drive
    Dir1.Refresh
End Sub
```

When the user selects a different drive from the DriveListBox control, the program switches to the new drive and updates the contents of the DirListBox control. Likewise, when the user selects a folder in the DirListBox control, the program switches to the selected folder and updates the contents of the FileListBox.

Code 11.4:   The DirListBox

```
Private Sub Dir1_Change()
    ChDir Dir1.Path
    File1.Path = Dir1.Path
End Sub
```

Since we are only scanning folders, we don't need to display the FileListBox control on the Form, but I decided to include it so that you can watch the progress of the scanning process.

The subfolders of a given folder are displayed in a DirListBox control (Dir1) and are accessed with the help of the *Dir1.List* array. The first subfolder is Dir1.List(0), the second subfolder is Dir1.List(1), and so on. Similarly, you can access the files of the current folder through the *File1.List()* array. After the user selects the folder to be scanned in the DirListBox control and clicks the Scan Now button, the program starts scanning.

Code 11.5:   The Scan Now Button

```
Private Sub Command1_Click()
    ChDrive Drive1.Drive
    ChDir Dir1.Path
    InitialFolder = CurDir
    ScanFolders
    MsgBox "There are " & totalFiles & _
          " under the " & InitialFolder & " folder"
End Sub
```

The global variable *InitialFolder* is used later in the code to determine whether we have exhausted all the subfolders of the current folder and must end the process.

The ScanFolders() Subroutine

Now, let's look at the actual code of the ScanFolders() subroutine. The number of subfolders in the current folder is given by the number of entries in the DirListBox control, which is `Dir1.ListCount`. If this number is positive, the program scans each subfolder with a For…Next loop. With each iteration, it switches to the next subfolder, updates the contents of the DirListBox and FileListBox controls, and calls itself to scan the new folder.

This process is repeated as long as there are subfolders to be scanned. When a folder without subfolders is reached, the If statement is skipped, and the ScanFolders() subroutine moves to the parent folder and returns. The ScanFolders() subroutine doesn't do any real processing. It simply counts the total number of files in the folders visited with the following statement:

```
totalFiles = totalFiles + File1.ListCount
```

First, ScanFolders() updates the File control. Then it scans the subfolders under the current folder and adds the number of files in the current folder to the *totalFiles* global variable. Finally, it moves up to the parent directory and exits. When an instance of the ScanFolders() subroutine terminates, the most recently suspended instance of the subroutine resumes and scans the remaining entries of the current folder.

Code 11.6:   **The ScanFolders() Subroutine**

```
Sub ScanFolders()
Dim subFolders As Integer

    totalFiles = totalFiles + File1.ListCount
    subFolders = Dir1.ListCount
    If subFolders > 0 Then
        For i = 0 To subFolders - 1
            ChDir Dir1.List(i)
            Dir1.Path = Dir1.List(i)
            File1.Path = Dir1.List(i)
            Form1.Refresh
            ScanFolders
        Next
    End If
    File1.Path = Dir1.Path
    MoveUp
End Sub
```

At first, the program processes the files in the current folder. The processing in this example consists of counting the files, but as you'll see shortly, you can insert many types of custom file processing here.

The variable *subFolders* holds the number of subfolders in the current folder. If that number is positive (that is, if the current folder contains subfolders), the ScanFolders() function scans each one of them by calling itself. If some of these folders happen to contain subfolders of their own, they are scanned by another call to the same subroutine.

The For…Next loop scans all the subfolders of the current folder by switching to each subfolder (with the *ChDir* command). Once in a subfolder, the program changes the contents of the Directory and FileListBox controls. The `Form1.Refresh` statement updates the contents of all controls on the Form so that they reflect the contents (subfolders and files) of the current folder. Then the ScanFolders() subroutine is called recursively to scan the entire folder.

The MoveUp() Subroutine

The MoveUp() subroutine is called every time the program finishes scanning the files and subfolders of the current folder and backs up to the parent folder. The current folder's parent folder is Dir1.List(-2). Likewise, Dir1.List(-1) is the name of the current folder. The MoveUp() subroutine first makes sure that the program is not at the folder where it started. If so, it doesn't move to the parent folder. If the program is at a subfolder, it moves to the parent folder.

Code 11.7:   **The MoveUp() Subroutine**

```
Sub MoveUp()
    If Dir1.List(-1) <> InitialFolder Then
      ChDir Dir1.List(-2)
      Dir1.Path = Dir1.List(-2)
    End If
End Sub
```

If you run the FileScan application, you can watch the folder names in the Dir-ListBox control and the current folder's files in the FileListBox control. In a real application, you won't want to display the name of the folder visited and its files, so these controls should be invisible. But if you're trying to learn how the program operates, it might be helpful to watch the folder-scanning process through the changing contents of these two controls on the Form.

Building a Custom Explorer

FileScan is an interesting example of recursive programming, but why duplicate functionality that's already available for free? All the features of the FileScan application are built into Windows Explorer. One reason is that the FileScan application is highly customizable. In the previous section, you learned how to count all the files of a given folder, including those in its subfolders. You can add many more useful features to the FileScan application that aren't available through Windows Explorer.

For example, you can implement a version of the Find utility that locates files and/or folders based on criteria that aren't available through the Find utility. A limitation of the Find utility is that you can't specify exclusion criteria. For instance, you can't ask it to find all the files whose size exceeds 1MB that aren't system files (e.g., EXE, DLL) or images (e.g., BMP, TIF, JPG). But with FileScan, you can modify the application to handle all types of file selection or rejection criteria by designing the proper user interface.

VB6 at Work: The DirMap Project

Here's another customization idea for the FileScan application: Have you ever had to prepare a hard copy of your hard disk's structure? (If you ever have to submit the contents and structure of an entire CD to a publisher, this utility will save you a good deal of work.) As far as I know, there is no simple way to do it. However, you can easily modify the FileScan application so that it prints the contents of a folder, including its subfolders, to a textbox. Figure 11.7 shows the DirMap application, which does exactly that. The structure of a user-specified folder is printed on a RichTextBox control so that folder names can be displayed in bold and stand out. The contents of the textbox can be copied and pasted in any other document or used in a mail message.

The code of the DirMap application is quite similar to the code of the FileScan application, with the exception of a few additional lines that create the output shown in the lower half of the Form.

Code 11.8: **The Map This Folder Button**

```
Private Sub Command1_Click()
'T1 = Timer
    totalFiles = 0
    totalFolders = 0
    currentDepth = 1
    InitialFolder = CurDir
```

```
        DirStructure = "{"
        DirStructure = DirStructure & "{\b " & _
                DoubleSlashes(Dir2.List(-1)) & "}" + newLine
        Screen.MousePointer = vbHourglass
        ScanFolders
        DirStructure = DirStructure & "}"
        RichTextBox1.TextRTF = DirStructure
        Label1.Caption = "Scanned " & totalFolders & _
                " folders containing " & totalFiles & " files"
        Screen.MousePointer = vbDefault
    'MsgBox Timer - T1
    End Sub
```

FIGURE 11.7:

The DirMap application generates a text file with the structure of any given folder.

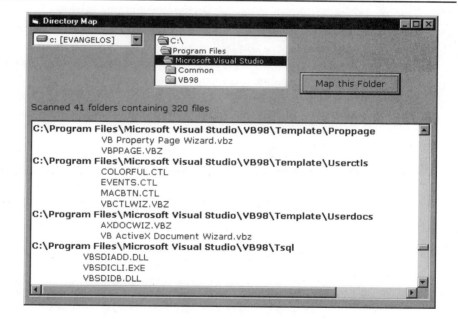

Let's examine the code of the DirMap application. The *DirStructure* variable is a long string variable that holds the RTF description of the contents of the RichTextBox control. This string is slowly built as the program scans each folder along the way. Folder names are displayed in bold and filenames are displayed in regular font and indented from the right according to their level within the parent folder.

The \b tag in RTF causes everything that appears within a pair of curly braces to appear in bold. Folder names are printed as {\b c:\windows\desktop}, and when rendered in the RichTextBox control, they appear in bold. Files in the first directory level are indented by five spaces, files in the second directory level are indented by 10 spaces, and so on. Everything placed in the *DirStructure* string must be enclosed in a pair of curly brackets so that when they're assigned to the TextRTF property of the RichTextBox control they will be interpreted as RTF code and not simply displayed as is.

The pointer's icon then switches to an hourglass, indicating that the process will take a while. Depending on the total number of files under the folder you're mapping, the program may run quite slowly. The *DirStructure* variable can grow large because it holds the entire contents of the RichTextBox control. Although Visual Basic 6 doesn't impose any practical limitations on the variable's length (a string variable can hold as many as two million characters), appending more characters at the end of a long string introduces delays. Visual Basic continuously reallocates space for the growing *DirStructure* variable and this causes the delay.

An alternative is to append the filenames to disk file rather than a memory variable, then open the file and read its contents into the RichTextBox control. Or, if you don't care about displaying folder names in bold, you could abandon the RichTextBox control and use a plain TextBox control. Instead of updating the *DirStructure* variable you would append each new filename directly to the TextBox control. If the folder being mapped is of moderate size, the following approach works well. I think the benefit of richly formatting the folder structure offsets the less than optimal execution speed.

The ScanFolders() subroutine is the same as before, but lines have been added that will append the file and folder names to the *DirStructure* variable.

Code 11.9:   **The Revised ScanFolders() Subroutine**

```
Sub ScanFolders()
Dim subFolders As Integer
Dim txtLine As String
Dim i As Integer, j As Integer

    txtLine = ""
    For j = 0 To File1.ListCount - 1
        txtLine = txtLine & Space(currentDepth * 5) + File1.List(j) &
newLine
    Next
    totalFiles = totalFiles + File1.ListCount
    DirStructure = DirStructure & txtLine

    subFolders = Dir2.ListCount
    If subFolders > 0 Then
        currentDepth = currentDepth + 1
        For i = 0 To subFolders - 1
```

```
'msgbox "moving from " & CurDir & " to " & Dir2.List(i)
            DirStructure = DirStructure & "{\b " & _
                        DoubleSlashes(Dir2.List(i)) & "}" & newLine
            File1.Path = Dir2.List(i)
            ChDir CurDir
            Dir2.Path = Dir2.List(i)
            ScanFolders
        Next
        totalFolders = totalFolders + subFolders
        Label1.Caption = "Processed " & totalFolders & " folders"
        currentDepth = currentDepth - 1
        DoEvents
    End If
    MoveUp
    File1.Path = Dir2.Path
End Sub
```

Every time this subroutine visits a new folder, it prints the names of all the files in it with the first For...Next loop. Likewise, every time it switches to another folder, it prints its name in bold with the following line:

```
DirStructure = DirStructure & "{\b " & DoubleSlashes(Dir2.List(i)) _
    & "}" & newLine
```

The *newLine* constant is defined as follows:

```
Const newLine = "{\par }"
```

Notice that the Chr$(10)+Chr$(13) combination won't cause a line break in a Rich-TextBox control. The DoubleSlashes() function replaces the slashes in the path name with two slashes. The slash is a special character in RTF; to cause the RichTextBox control to print a slash instead of interpreting a slash, you must prefix the slash with another slash.

Hidden Controls in the DirMap Application

Figure 11.8 shows the window of the DirMap application at design time. Notice that the Form contains a second DirListBox control and a FileListBox control, both of which remain invisible at runtime. The FileListBox control is where the program looks for the current folder's files. Since there's no reason for the user to watch its contents change a few dozen times a second as new folders are mapped, you can choose to hide it from the user. The other DirListBox control is where the current folder's subfolders are displayed. Again, once the user selects the folder to be mapped, there's no reason for them to watch the names of the various sub-folders as the program scans a folder. Therefore, this control isn't updated while the application scans the selected folder.

FIGURE 11.8:

The DirMap application's
main Form at design time

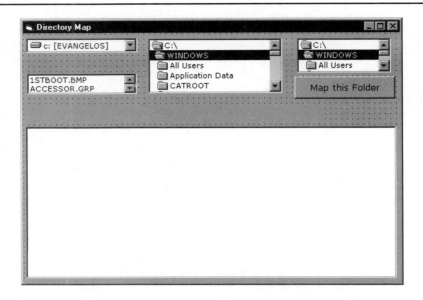

The user selects the folder to be mapped on the visible DirListBox control. The program uses the hidden DirListBox control for its own purposes and lets the visible DirListBox control display the selected folder. The two DirListBox controls are kept in sync from within the Change events of the visible controls. As a new drive or folder is selected, both DirListBox controls are updated.

Code 11.10: **The File Controls**

```
Private Sub Dir1_Change()

    ChDir Dir1.Path
    Dir2.Path = Dir1.Path
    File1.Path = Dir2.Path

End Sub

Private Sub Drive1_Change()

    ChDrive Drive1.Drive
    Dir1.Path = Drive1.Drive
    Dir2.Path = Drive1.Drive

End Sub
```

The DirMap application is rather slow. If you attempt to map a folder like Windows or an entire disk, it will probably take more than a minute to display the list of files and folder on the RichTextBox control. We'll return to this project in Chapter 12, *Optimizing VB Applications,* to optimize the application and make it considerably faster.

Further Customization

Another customization idea is to process selected files with a specific application. Suppose your DownLoad folder is full of ZIP files you have downloaded from various sources. Unzipping these files in the DownLoad folder would be a disaster. Ideally, you should create a separate folder for each ZIP file, copy a single ZIP file there, and then unzip it. You can do this manually or you can let a variation of the FileScan application to do it for you. All you need is a small program that creates the folder, moves the ZIP file there, and then unzips it with PKUNZIP (of course, any zipping/unzipping utility will work in a similar manner.) You could even write a DOS batch file to process the ZIP files with the following statements:

```
md c:\Shareware\%2
copy %1 c:\Shareware\%2\
del %1
pkunzip c:\Shareware\%1
```

TIP

A *batch file* is a program that can be started with the Shell function. To start the PKUNZIP application from within Visual Basic, use a statement like `Shell("pkunzip c:\zipfiles\*.ZIP")`.

If this batch file is named MVFiles.bat, you can call it with two arguments:

```
MVFILES CuteUtility.zip CuteUtility
```

The first argument is the name of the ZIP file to be moved and unzipped, and the second argument is the name of the folder where the ZIP file will be moved and unzipped. You can modify the FileScan application so that every time it runs into a ZIP file, it calls the MVFiles.bat program with the appropriate arguments and lets it process the ZIP file.

The Stack Mechanism

Now that you have seen examples of recursive programming and have a better understanding of this powerful technique, let's look at the mechanism that makes recursion possible. I mentioned earlier that each time a procedure (function or subroutine) calls another, its status must be stored in memory so that it can later resume execution. The status of an interrupted procedure includes the location of the line where it was interrupted and the values of the local variables the moment it was interrupted. This information is enough for a procedure to resume operation and never be aware that it was interrupted.

Stack Defined

The area of memory in which the procedure's status is stored is called the *stack*. The stack is a protected area of the system's memory that's handled exclusively by the operating system. The stack memory is regular memory, but the operating system handles it differently from the way it handles the rest of memory. For one thing, programs can't grab any byte from the stack. The items in this memory are stacked on top of one another and only the topmost item can be extracted.

Each time a program places a value on the stack, the new item is placed at the top of the stack. When a program reads a value from the stack, it can only read the item on top, which is the item that was placed on the stack last. This type of memory organization is called *Last-In-First-Out*, or *LIFO*. The item that is placed on the stack last is the first one to be read from. This is exactly the mechanism used to pass arguments between procedures.

Recursive Programming and the Stack

If you aren't familiar with the role of stack in the computer's operation, the following discussion will probably help you understand the mechanics of recursion a little better. The stack is one of the oldest models used in programming, and it's still as useful and as popular as ever. In fact, it's an important part of the operating system, and microprocessors provide special commands for manipulating the stack. Fortunately, you don't have to worry about the stack, since it's handled exclusively by the operating system and your favorite programming language. The description of the stack you'll find in this section is a bit simplified. The goal is to explain how recursive procedures work without getting too technical.

Suppose the recursive procedure is a subroutine and it accepts no arguments, similar to the ScanFolders() subroutine. When the ScanFolders() subroutine calls itself, it must first store its status on the stack so that it can later resume. One component of the subroutine's status is the line that's executing when the program is interrupted. The ScanFolders() subroutine calls itself from within a loop. When it resumes, it should be able to continue with the remaining loops, not start all over again. The loop's counter, i, is part of the subroutine's status, and it must also be stored on the stack along with all the information that makes up the function's status.

The ScanFolders() subroutine's status is stored on top of the stack, and the same subroutine starts executing again with a fresh set of local variables (a new loop counter, for example). When this copy of the ScanFolders() subroutine calls itself again, its status is stored on the stack on top of the status of the previously interrupted subroutine. As more instances of the same subroutine are called, the status of each is stored on top of the previously interrupted subroutine's status. Eventually, the active ScanFolders() subroutine terminates, and the most recently interrupted one takes over. Its status is on the top of the stack. The operating system removes the values of its local variables from the stack so that the subroutine can resume execution.

What's left on the top of the stack now is the status of the subroutine that must resume execution when the active subroutine terminates. When these values are removed from the stack, the status of another interrupted function surfaces on the stack. This simple mechanism allows procedures to interrupt each other and keep track of each other's status without any complicated operations. Each procedure finds its status on the stack, as if no other information was ever placed on top of it.

Passing Arguments through the Stack

The same mechanism is used to pass arguments from one procedure to another. Suppose your program calls the function Payment(Amount, Interest), which expects to read two arguments (the loan amount and an interest rate) and return the monthly payment. As you know so well by now, you must supply the arguments in this order: first the amount, then the interest. The calling program leaves its status and the two arguments on the stack in the same order: first its status (the values of its local variables), then the value of the *Amount* argument, and finally, the value of the *Interest* argument. When the Payment() function takes over, it retrieves the two arguments from the top of the stack: first the value of the last argument, then the value of the first argument. After the removal of these two values from the stack, the status of the calling procedure is at the top of the stack. When the Payment() function finishes, it leaves its result on the top of the stack and relinquishes control to the calling procedure.

The calling procedure removes the value from the top of the stack (the result of the Payment() function) and uses it for its own purposes. It then removes the values of the local variables (its status) so that it can resume execution. As you can see, the LIFO structure is ideal for exchanging data between procedures.

Suppose the Payment() function calls another function. Again, the arguments of the new function are placed on the stack where the new function will find them. When the other function returns, it leaves its result on the top of the stack where the Payment() function will find it and remove it from the stack. It also finds its status information on the stack. No matter how many functions are called in such a nested manner, the information required is always at the top of the stack.

The only requirement when passing arguments through the stack is that they are placed there in the order they are needed. The procedure being called has no other means to decipher which value corresponds to which argument. That's why these arguments are also known as *positional arguments.*

Many Visual Basic functions now also support named arguments, and you can pass to them arguments in any order, as long as you provide both the name and the value of the argument. Even these procedures use the stack mechanism to pass the named arguments, but the mechanics are a bit more complicated. The basic idea is the same: the information is always placed on top of the stack, and when it's read, it's removed from the stack. In this way, each procedure is guaranteed to find the information it leaves on the stack the moment it needs it.

A Real–Life Example

Imagine that you are so disciplined and organized that you can place every document you use in your office on top of a document stack. Every time you're interrupted by a visitor or a phone call, you leave the document you were working on on top of this paper stack and remove another document from your filing cabinet to work on. When you're done, you take the document in front of you and place it back in the filing cabinet (or if you're interrupted again you place this document on the stack and retrieve another one from the filing cabinet).

What you now have in front of you is the document you were working on when you were interrupted. When you're done with this document, you put it back where it belongs and another document surfaces on the stack—the document you were working on before you were interrupted. After you work with this document, revise it, and put it away, you have another document before you from an even earlier interruption. If you can maintain this type of organization, you'll never need to waste time looking for documents (and your productivity will be at an all-time high!). Everything will be in its filing space, and most of the time, the document you need will be right in front of you. Thankfully, we're not as simplistic as our computers nor do we need to be so rigid. But you'll probably agree that this type of memory organization makes perfect sense for keeping track of interrupted tasks on your computer.

Some Special Issues in Recursive Programming

Recursion is not a technique that most programmers regularly use. Only a few situations call for recursive programming, and unfortunately, these programs can't be implemented otherwise. The following sections discuss the dangers of recursion and give you a few hints to help you recognize a procedure that calls for recursive programming.

It's Easy to Write a Never-Ending Program

If you forget to specify an exit condition with a few statements that stop the procedure from calling itself, you'll end up with a never-ending program, or an endless loop. If this happens, your computer will run out of memory for storing the intermediate results and the program will end with the "Out of stack space" error message (see Figure 11.9). The memory available for storing intermediate results between procedure calls is limited and it's easy to exhaust.

FIGURE 11.9:

The "Out of stack space" error message

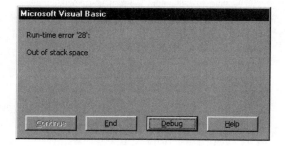

The stack isn't used only for recursive procedures. Each time a function is called, the status of the one that's interrupted, along with the arguments of the function being called, are stored on the stack. It's practically impossible to run out of stack space with regular procedures; to do so, you'd have to call several hundred procedures, one from within the other. You can run out of stack space with recursive procedures, though, because you don't have to write several hundred routines—only one that calls itself and doesn't provide an exit mechanism.

Knowing When to Use Recursive Programming

In addition to knowing how to implement recursive programming, you need to know *when* to use it. The recursive nature of many problems isn't obvious, so it may take a while to get the hang of it. (We humans aren't trained to think recursively, but once you've established the recursive nature of a problem, the recursive algorithm will follow quite naturally.) An algorithm that, in the middle of carrying out a task, has to start and complete an identical task is a prime candidate for recursive implementation. Consider the Binary Search algorithm, which rejects half the original list and then has to do the same with the other half. Or consider a procedure for scanning the contents of a folder. First, it counts the files. If the folder has subfolders, the same process must be repeated for each subfolder.

If you find yourself nesting loops in many levels or if you're trying to set up conditions to exit these loops prematurely, your code would probably benefit from a recursive implementation. Recursion bears some resemblance to iteration, and in many situations, you can implement a recursive algorithm with a loop. The factorial algorithm, for instance, can be easily implemented with a For…Next loop. But there are situations in which iterations won't help.

Try It!

If you're interested in recursion and would like to experiment a little, here's a problem that can be solved both recursively and nonrecursively: write a program that accepts a phone number and produces all possible seven-letter combinations that match the phone number (vanity numbers, as they are called). (This is not a trivial task, no matter how you look at it.)

Elsewhere in this book you'll find more examples of recursive procedures. In Chapter 8, there is a recursive procedure for scanning a TreeView control. In Chapter 16, you'll see how to use recursion to scan all the messages under the Inbox folder of Outlook, including subfolders. Now that you have a better understanding of how recursion works, you may wish to take a closer look to these applications.

CHAPTER
TWELVE

12

Optimizing VB Applications

- The Visual Basic compiler

- Optimizing for speed

- String and math optimization tricks

- Optimizing the Image application

- Optimizing the DirMap application

In this chapter, I will present the basics of code optimization and a few tricks for writing faster running code. To demonstrate the importance of code optimization, I will also present a few examples based on applications developed earlier in the book. Visual Basic is the simplest, most popular language for rapid application development, and in most respects, as powerful as any other language for Windows application development, such as Visual C++ or Delphi. But Visual Basic has limitations. For one, you shouldn't expect that an environment with the simplicity of Visual Basic will be the most efficient or speedy. Yet, it's very efficient, and after the release of version 5 (the first version of the language with native code compatibility), it's closing the gap in execution speed when compared to languages like Visual C++.

Visual Basic 6 comes with a *native code compiler,* which can generate optimized code similar to the code produced by the VC++ compiler. In this chapter, we're going to discuss the Visual Basic compiler, look at what the native code compiler can do for your applications, and give you a few tips on how to optimize your code for maximum execution speed. Of course, the speed of an application isn't determined exclusively by the compiler. If the source code is sloppy, the executable's speed won't be optimal.

An application can be optimized in many ways. Some programmers will spend most of their time tweaking the user interface. Sometimes, a funky interface can make an application really fun to use. Most programmers will tweak the code to optimize speed. They may also consider tweaking the size of the application (the total size of the installation files, since you can no longer distribute stand-alone EXE files). As far as the appearance goes, it's a question of artistic talent more than anything else. And since CD-ROMs are the most common distribution medium, there's not much point in optimizing the size of the application. Therefore, this chapter will deal exclusively with execution speed.

When you optimize an application, you should also try to optimize your own time. Decide which parts of the application will benefit from optimization and focus on them. Try to optimize areas where a little work will make a lot of difference. For example, if you're developing an image processing application, you should focus on the code that processes the image. Subroutines that aren't going to be called often, such as a procedure that rotates the image, aren't going to disturb the user as much. But if the basic procedures of the application (the ones that are called again and again in the course of the application) are slow, users will most likely consider an equivalent, but faster, application.

You should also know when to stop. Optimization is a challenging process and you may find yourself in a situation where you're competing with yourself or trying to prove something to yourself by seeking further improvements in speed. This is great motivation while learning, but when you develop as a professional, you should know when to stop. It doesn't make much sense to delay an entire project in order to speed up by 5% some feature of the application that most users will never need.

The optimization process practically never ends. You can always find places in your code that can be rewritten to make the program run 2% faster. For experienced programmers, almost all applications of considerable size can be further optimized. But what's the point in wasting a few hours of the development cycle to make a calculation run faster if the entire calculation doesn't take more than half a second? Or, what's the point in calculating a section of an application that very few users will invoke (for example, the code that converts a file to a newer format)? Similar "special" sections of an application don't need to be optimized. I'm not suggesting that you make them terribly slow, but they probably won't be worth your time or effort to optimize.

Develop or Buy?

At some point in your program development, you're likely to face a decision: develop or buy? Sometimes, it doesn't pay to develop every piece of your application on your own. If you can purchase components that will simplify or speed up the development process, do it. Before spending a week to develop a special ActiveX control, see if you can purchase it for a few hundred dollars. A week of your time is worth far more than the price of the component, not to mention the fact that off-the-shelf components have other benefits, such as timely upgrades with newer versions of Visual Basic and thorough testing (components used by hundreds of developers are bound to have fewer problems and more features than the ones you develop). In short, try to optimize your own time and budget too. Modern programming is a team effort, and this maxim also applies to programmers who don't work in corporate environments.

Of course, buying components also has a downside. For one thing, your application will be dependent on this component being available with the next version of your programming language. Most importantly, if the custom component doesn't provide all the features you need, you can't adjust its source code. But as mentioned already, third party components are feature-rich, and in most cases, they provide more, not fewer, features.

The most important aspect of optimizing applications written with Visual Basic is speed, so we'll concentrate on it. You'll rarely have to optimize the size of your executable. Besides, the size of the support files you may have to distribute with your application will probably diminish any size optimization effort on your part (which will only affect your own EXE file and not the support files). The size of the application may become an issue for utilities that must be loaded really quickly. You should create both a native code and a p-code executable and see how long they each take to load.

The Visual Basic Compiler

Visual Basic applications can be executed in two modes: as *p-code* (from within the Visual Basic IDE) and as *native code* (when compiled to EXE files). Prior to version 5, Visual Basic could only produce p-code. Where native code is understood directly by the processor and executed as is, p-code is a special form of executable that must first be translated into native code and then executed. Even with Visual Basic 6, when you run a project in the IDE, you're actually running p-code. Any project will run faster (marginally or significantly faster, depending on the nature of the calculations it performs) when it's compiled to native code and executed outside the Visual Basic IDE. To understand why native code performs better than p-code, you must first understand the nature of p-code and how Visual Basic uses it.

When you design and test an application, you'll be executing it from within the IDE. When you're done and ready to distribute the application or use it on a daily basis yourself, you should compile it to native code. Depending on the nature of the application, the compilation may speed it up considerably or not at all. If the compiled application doesn't run faster and its size is considerably larger than the size of the equivalent p-code executable, this may lead to longer loading times. In these instances, you may decide to use the p-code executable.

> **NOTE**
>
> In short, p-code is what makes the environment of Visual Basic so unique and so popular. Without p-code, you wouldn't be able to stop your applications, edit the code, and resume execution. Even if you plan to compile every application to native code, you must still understand what p-code is and how it works.

What Is P-Code?

P-code is close to machine language, but it's not quite machine language. In other words, it can't be executed as is; it must be translated into commands for a specific processor. Whether you develop on a Pentium or a PowerPC, the p-code is the same. But before it can be executed on either processor, it must be translated into the target processor's *command set*. Moreover, this translation must take place while the application is running, which means that p-code will never be as fast as native code.

The text you enter in the Visual Basic editor is translated into p-code as you enter it. Each time you press Enter to move to the next line, the IDE translates the line you're leaving into p-code. All the syntax checking and color coding of the statements takes place after the line is translated into p-code, which explains why the current line isn't colored as you type.

To run p-code, Visual Basic uses a so-called *execution engine*: a DLL (Dynamic Link Library) that translates p-code into machine-executable code, or native code. This is how projects are executed in the Visual Basic IDE. To distribute the application, you can create an executable file that contains the p-code plus the execution engine. The EXE files produced by previous versions of Visual Basic were nothing more than p-code and the runtime DLL. That's why running an executable file outside the IDE wasn't any faster than running the application in it.

NOTE   Interpreted Visual Basic applications always have been slower than applications compiled with other languages. All benchmarks showed that languages such as Visual C++ and Delphi were consistently faster than Visual Basic. The reason is that every line of p-code must be translated into machine-specific instructions before it can be executed. This is the price we have to pay in exchange for an unmatched development environment in which we can edit, run, and resume execution of the application.

The Visual Basic 6 native code compiler is similar to a traditional compiler, such as the one used by Visual C++. It produces processor-specific instructions that can be executed directly without any additional translation. Thus, it's easy to understand why native code executes faster than p-code. In reality, Visual Basic's p-code is so highly optimized that you might not get a great improvement in speed in native code over p-code. (It seems that Microsoft couldn't improve p-code any further, and the introduction of a native code compiler was inevitable.)

Another reason native code outperforms p-code is that it can do global optimizations. P-code is generated on the fly and executed one line at a time. By contrast, the native code compiler can see the big picture (many lines of source code at once) and produce optimal executable code that takes into consideration the peculiarities of and dependencies among multiple lines of code.

Compiler Options

So, now that we have a native code compiler, which produces faster-running executables, you might think that we could just forget all about p-code. But the native code compiler comes with a price. It produces longer files that take longer to load, and if you're distributing your software on the Internet, it will also take longer to download. If these restrictions don't apply to you, you can compile your applications to native code, see what difference the compiler makes, and then decide how to distribute them.

Applications compiled to native code don't always run faster. Real-world business applications spend most of their time doing disk I/O (input/output), screen updates, and other tasks that you can't speed up from within your Visual Basic code. For example, when you call an API function, you're no longer in control. While the API function is executed, there's nothing you can do to improve its speed no matter how much you've optimized the rest of the code. In a way, this is a barrier you can't break regardless of whether you compile to p-code or native code. In the section "Optimizing the DirMap Application," at the end of this chapter, you'll see that the code that manipulates the properties of ActiveX controls can't be made to go any faster.

With these issues in mind, let's go through the process of compiling applications and look at the various options of the native code compiler. To create the executable file, start Visual Basic (if necessary) and choose File ➤ Make file.exe (file.exe is the application's name). Before you create the EXE file, however, you must specify the compiler's options. Open the Project menu and select the last command, Project Properties, to see the Project Properties dialog box.

The type of executable that will be created depends on the settings you choose in the Compile tab of the Project Properties dialog box shown in Figure 12.1.

- **Compile to P-Code** compiles a project using p-code. The main benefit of p-code is that it's compact and (in many practical cases) not much slower than purely executable code.

- **Compile to Native Code** compiles a project using native code, which is the machine language the CPU can understand and execute.

FIGURE 12.1:

The Compile tab of the Project Properties dialog box

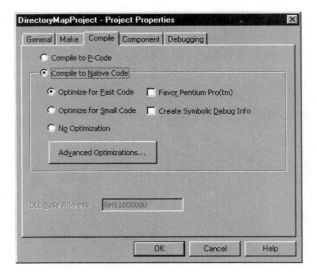

Options for Optimizing Native Code   The native code compiler must balance a number of requirements, some of which conflict. For example, it can't produce the most compact and fastest possible code. The Compile to Native Code section of the Project Properties dialog box contains processor-specific optimizations and a number of advanced options that may or may not apply to your project. You should specify the options that will produce the type of executable that best matches your application and the target systems.

- **Optimize for Fast Code** maximizes the speed of the executable file by instructing the compiler to favor speed over size. To optimize the code, the compiler reduces many constructs to functionally similar sequences of machine code. This will inevitably increase the size of the executable file.

- **Optimize for Small Code** minimizes the size of the executable file by instructing the compiler to favor size over speed.

- **No Optimization** compiles without specific optimizations. It balances speed and size.

- **Favor Pentium Pro™** optimizes the code to favor the Pentium Pro processor. Use this option for programs meant only for the Pentium Pro. Code generated with this option will run on other Intel processors, but it may not perform as well.

- **Create Symbolic Debug Info** generates symbolic debug information in the executable. An executable file created using this option can be debugged using Visual C++ or debuggers that use the CodeView style of debug information. Setting this option generates a PDB file with the symbol information for your executable. This option is most often used by Visual C++ programmers who also use Visual Basic.

- **Advanced Optimizations** displays the Advanced Optimizations dialog box, which is shown in Figure 12.2. Use the options in this dialog box to turn off certain checks that normally take place to ensure that your application works properly. To increase the speed of the executable file, you can turn off some or all these options by checking the appropriate checkbox.

WARNING   Enabling the options in the Advanced Optimizations dialog box may prevent the correct execution of your program. You must understand what each option does and be sure that your application doesn't require any of the options you turn off.

FIGURE 12.2:

The Advanced Optimizations dialog box

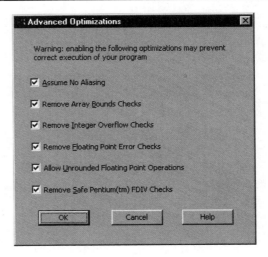

- **Assume No Aliasing** tells the compiler that your program doesn't use aliasing. Aliasing is a technique that lets your code refer to the same variable (memory location) by more than one name. We don't use this technique (of dubious value, anyway) in this book, so you can safely turn off this option.

- **Remove Array Bound Checks** tells the program not to check for array bounds. By default, Visual Basic checks an array's bounds every time your code accesses the array to determine if the index is within the range of the array. If the index is not within the array's bounds, a runtime error is generated (the "Out-of-bounds" error), which can be trapped from within the code. However, the code that ensures that the array's bounds aren't exceeded is costly in terms of execution time. If an array bound is exceeded, the results will be unexpected. You can turn on this option if the application doesn't use arrays or if you know that your code will not attempt to access non-existent array elements. For example, a loop that uses the LBound() and UBound() functions to scan the elements of an array won't cross the array's boundaries.

- **Remove Integer Overflow Checks** speeds up integer calculations when checked. By default, Visual Basic checks every calculation for integer-style data types—Byte, Integer, and Long—to ensure that the result is within the range of the data type. If the magnitude of the value being put into the data type is incorrect, a runtime error is generated. If this option is checked and data type capacities overflow, you'll get incorrect results, but no errors. It's really difficult to make sure that calculations with integers do not result in overflows, and it's even trickier to find out where the overflow occurred.

- **Remove Floating Point Error Checks** speeds up floating-point calculations when checked. By default, Visual Basic checks every calculation of a floating-point data type—Single and Double—to make sure that the result is within range for that data type and that there are no divide by zero or invalid operations. If the magnitude of the value being put into the data type is incorrect, an error occurs. Select this option to turn off the error checking and speed up floating-point calculations. If this option is checked and data type capacities are overflowed, no error will occur, and you may get incorrect results.

- **Allow Unrounded Floating Point Operations** uses floating-point registers more efficiently, avoids storing and loading large volumes of data to and from memory, and performs floating point comparisons more efficiently (floating-point numbers are slightly truncated when moved from registers to memory).

- **Remove Safe Pentium™ FDIV Checks** removes safety checking so that the code for floating-point division is faster. Selecting this option may produce slightly incorrect results on Pentium processors with the FDIV bug. (The new Pentiums that are 120MHz or faster are exempt from the floating-point division flaw.)

Use the native code compiler with these advanced options to automatically speed up your application. Of course, how much faster the application will become depends in the nature of the application, but the compiler will do its best to produce the fastest code possible. Unless the EXE is really large (and you plan to distribute it by means other than a CD-ROM), you should generate EXE files optimized for speed. However, a few bad coding techniques can easily offset any benefit introduced by the native code compiler. For example, if your application calculates squares in a loop that's executed many times and you code it as x^2, no advanced optimization option is going to help your application. As you'll see shortly, by coding this operation as x*x, it will make a p-code executable run faster than a native code executable that uses the expression x^2. The trick to writing fast-running applications is to start by optimizing the code itself. In the following sections, we're going to present a few useful optimization techniques. They are quite simple, but very efficient. Even if you're an experienced Visual Basic programmer, you should take a look at the following pages. You may discover some new optimization tricks.

Optimizing VB Code

Code optimization depends on the type of application you're writing. In most cases, you'll be optimizing small, tight sections of code that are executed frequently (such as loops or frequently called procedures). Code optimization requires a combination of experience, an eye for detail, and a basic understanding of the architecture of the language and how processors work. Seasoned programmers who have done some assembly language programming in their days have an advantage, but you can pick up a lot along the way.

You should never consider your code to have been optimized completely, and never underestimate your capabilities. Some expert programmers start optimizing with the code produced by the compiler, so don't count on the machine too much. Learn its limitations and work around them. Although there are no hard and fast rules for optimizing code, there are some tricks you can use and some guidelines you can follow. We'll discuss them in the following sections, where we'll see how these tricks affect the native code and p-code compiler.

Use Proper Data Types

The simplest optimization trick is to use the proper data types for your calculations. If your application manipulates integers, don't use doubles, or even worse, variants. They will slow down the calculations without increasing numerical accuracy. In general, the shorter the data type, the more efficiently it's handled. Many programmers use floating-point numbers even when they are manipulating integers. Some extra accuracy can't hurt, so why spare it? The extra accuracy comes at a price, and when it's not really called for, it should be avoided.

If you're not accustomed to declaring variables, you may end up using variants for mundane tasks such as loop counters. Even if you don't use the Explicit option, which forces you to declare every variable before using it, at a minimum, you should declare integer variables.

Let's say you must set up a nested loop like the following one:

```
For iCounter = 1 To 5000
    For jCounter = 1 To 5000
        {your statements}
    Next
Next
```

If you're going to use the loop counters (variables *iCounter* and *jCounter*) in the loop's body, you may be tempted to declare them as Doubles to match the accuracy of the remaining variables in the loop. If the loop counters are declared as Doubles, the nested loop will take more than twice as long to complete than if the same variables were declared as Integers. Sometimes the loop's counter may exceed the capacity of the Integer data type. A loop that must repeat 50,000 times can't be set up with an integer counter. In this case, you should declare the loop counter as Long.

When working with Integer data types, you should take into consideration both the nature of the data and the results. For example, consider the difference between two date values that are within the same month:

```
Date1 = #4/14/99#
Date2 = #4/22/99#
DDiff = Date2 - Date1
```

The *DDiff* variable holds a Double value, as we discussed in Chapter 3. However, the integer part of the difference is the number of days between the two dates. To express this difference in seconds, you must multiply it by 24*60*60. The following statement will fail:

```
MsgBox "The difference in seconds is: " & DDiff / (24 * 60 * 60)
```

The reason is that Visual Basic will see three integers and assume that the result of the operation 24*60*60 is also an integer. Even if the variable *DDiff* is declared as Double (as it should be), Visual Basic will fail to calculate the expression 24*60*60 because the result doesn't fit into an integer. To work around this problem, convert the integers to floating-point numbers as follows:

```
MsgBox "The difference in seconds is: " & DDiff / (24.0 * 60.0 * 60.0)
```

This little trick will force Visual Basic to generate a floating-point number (whose decimal part will be zero) and the calculations will complete.

TIP   Variables declared without a type, with a statement like:

```
Dim iCounter, jCounter
```

are variants. Also notice that you can't declare multiple variables on the same statement without repeating the type for each variable. The following statement will not create two integer variables. It will create a variant *(iCounter)* and an integer *(jCounter)*.

```
Dim iCounter, jCounter As Integer
```

Avoid Variants

Variants are convenient when you're putting together a short program to display the ASCII character set or the ASCII values of the function keys, but otherwise, you should avoid variants in your code. They take up much more memory than other data types and can't be processed immediately. When the compiler encounters them, it must find out their proper type, convert them to their type, and then use them in a calculation. For example, if a variant holds the value 45, the compiler must convert it to a numeric value before using it in a numeric calculation or to a string before using it in a string operation.

Some developers defend variants, pointing out that they free the programmer from having to declare variables and use them consistently. They may give you some neat examples—mostly one-liners that normally could be implemented with two or three lines of code. If you're trying to squeeze every drop of performance from your application, avoid variants. Or, if you're the type that likes to learn the hard way, use them and see for yourself.

Let's write some code that performs math calculations with variants and doubles. Place a Command button on a Form, and then insert the following code in the button's Click event handler.

Code 12.1:   Timing Math Operations with Variants and Doubles

```
Private Sub Command1_Click()
Dim v1, v2
Dim d1 As Double, d2 As Double
Dim vCounter
Dim dCounter As Long

    T1 = Timer
    Screen.MousePointer = vbHourglass
    For vCounter = 1 To 1000000
        v1 = Rnd() * 100
        v2 = v1 ^ 2
        v2 = Sin(v1) * Cos(v2) * Log(vCounter)
    Next
    vtime = Timer - T1
    MsgBox "Done with variants in " & Format(vtime, "##.000")
    Screen.MousePointer = vbDefault

    T1 = Timer
    Screen.MousePointer = vbHourglass
    For dCounter = 1 To 1000000
        d1 = Rnd() * 100
        d2 = d1 ^ 2
        d2 = Sin(d1) * Cos(d2) * Log(dCounter)
    Next
    dtime = Timer - T1
    MsgBox "Done with doubles in " & Format(dtime, "##.000")
    Screen.MousePointer = vbDefault
End Sub
```

This subroutine declares the variables *v1, v2,* and *vCounter* as Variants and the variables *d1, d2,* and *dCounter* as Double and Long, respectively. Then, it performs the same calculations a million times. The calculations are really trivial:

```
For vCounter = 1 To 1000000
    v1 = Rnd() * 100
    v2 = v1 ^ 2
    v2 = Sin(v1) * Cos(v2) * Log(vCounter)
Next
```

The first time, the calculations are executed with the variant variables by using them as the loop counter. The same calculations are then repeated with double variables, using a long variable as the loop counter. The time required for the completion of each loop is then displayed on a message box. On a 166MHz Pentium, the loop with variants takes 24.500 seconds and the loop with the declared variables takes only 13.125 seconds. The declared variables loop is nearly twice as fast! This difference may become even greater for more complicated calculations.

You may ask, "How many applications perform the same calculations a million times?" It's not as rare as you may think. Consider an image processing application or an application that generates fractals: the same calculations must be performed for each pixel in the image or in the PictureBox control where the fractal will be displayed.

If you compile this application to native code, the results will favor the loop with the declared variables even more. To compile the application, follow these steps:

1. In the Project Properties dialog box, check the Compile to Native Code and the Optimize for Fast Code options.

2. Click the Advanced Optimizations button to open the Advanced Optimizations dialog box.

3. Check all the options to enable all optimizations.

4. Now choose File ➤ Make PROJECT1.EXE to generate the executable file (or use whatever name you've assigned to your project).

5. Minimize the Visual Basic window, locate the PROJECT1.EXE file, and run it.

The times for the compiled application on the same computer are 17.578 seconds (for the loop with variants) and 6.977 seconds (for the loop with doubles)—two-and-a-half times faster! Clearly, you must always declare your variables with their proper types. You will experience similar gains with strings versus variants.

Now let's experiment with the optimization options to see what effect they have on speed. Go back to the Advanced Optimizations dialog box and clear the Allow

Unrounded Floating-Point Operations option. This will tell the compiler to round the results of each operation in-between calculations, as if they were moved to memory. This will add a few cycles and cause some loss in accuracy too (one wonders why this is even an option). If you run the program again, the calculations with the declared variables will take 6.703 seconds and those with variants will take 27.898 seconds. In short, rounding intermediate results will have a profound effect on execution time. Any additional operation introduced by the compiler will affect your code's speed adversely, especially if it's applied to variants. The rounding of the values requires intermediate results to be moved from registers to memory and back, resulting in additional execution time. Registers can store numbers with greater accuracy than memory and you should enable this option in applications that perform lots of math operations.

WARNING　　It's possible to use variants by calling the wrong form of certain functions. String functions such as Mid() and Left() are different than the functions Mid$() and Left$(). The functions without the dollar sign in their names are more flexible (they work on both strings and numbers), but they return variants. If you work exclusively with strings, use Left$() instead of Left() and Right$() instead of Right().

Simplify the Math

Now we're going to optimize the code in the loop. There isn't much you can do other than to replace the ^ operator, which raises a number (integer and non-integer) to a power. Raising a number to a non-integer power is accomplished with a rather complicated algorithm, but you can also do this by squaring or cubing a number, which is a far simpler operation. You can square a number by simply multiplying it by itself. Many programmers will use the proper operator (x^2) to calculate the square of x because they don't know better, or in most cases, because they are translating a math formula into Visual Basic statements.

Start a new project, place a Command button on the Form, and insert the following code in its Click event handler.

Code 12.2:   **Coding Squares**

```
Private Sub Command1_Click()
Dim d1 As Double, d2 As Double
Dim iCounter As Long

    T1 = Timer
    Screen.MousePointer = vbHourglass
```

```
    For iCounter = 1 To 1000000
        d1 = 1342.344345456
        d2 = d1 ^ 2
        d1 = 8856452#
        d2 = d1 ^ 2
    Next
    vtime = Timer - T1
    MsgBox "Done with variants in " & Format(vtime, "##.000")
    Screen.MousePointer = vbDefault

    T1 = Timer
    Screen.MousePointer = vbHourglass
    For iCounter = 1 To 1000000
        d1 = 1342.344345456
        d2 = d1 * d1
        d1 = 8856452#
        d2 = d1 * d1
    Next
    dtime = Timer - T1
    MsgBox "Done with doubles in " & Format(dtime, "##.000")
    Screen.MousePointer = vbDefault

End Sub
```

This subroutine consists of two loops which calculate squares with two different methods. The first loop uses the ^ operator, while the second loop multiplies the two numbers. Both loops use double variables (I couldn't ignore the conclusions of the previous section, could I?) and the loop's counter is a long variable. If you run this application now in the IDE, the results will probably surprise you. The ^ operator will take 11.430 seconds, while the multiplication will take 1.867 seconds. This difference suggests that you should avoid the ^ operator whenever possible. Likewise, don't use the ^ operator to calculate the square root, as in the following statement:

```
X2 = X ^ 0.5
```

Use the *Sqr()* function instead, which is much faster:

```
X2 = Sqr(X)
```

Now that you've learned these basic math tricks, you can combine them in more complicated expressions. For instance, the expression X^2.5 is equivalent to the expression X*X*Sqr(X), but the second expression is evaluated more than twice as fast. Change the body of the first loop in the previous example to the following code segment:

```
d1 = 1342.344345456
d2 = d1 ^ 2.5
d1 = 8856452#
d2 = d1 ^ 2.5
```

Change the second loop to the following:

```
d1 = 1342.344345456
d2 = d1 * d1 * Sqr(d1)
d1 = 8856452#
d2 = d1 * d1 * Sqr(d1)
```

Even in the Visual Basic IDE, the second (optimized) loop will complete its execution in 4.1 seconds and the first loop will finish in 9.5 seconds. This trick suggests that you should scrutinize the math expressions you're coding. Don't just translate the math into Visual Basic statements. Rearrange terms, and whenever possible, try to simplify them to help the compiler.

Another way to optimize code that implements math operations is to save intermediate results. For example, the following statements:

```
Xnew = X * X + X0: Ynew = Y * Y + Y0
{other calculations}
If X * X + Y * Y > 0 Then ...
```

will execute faster if you save the results of the operation X*X to a temporary variable, as shown next:

```
XSquare = X * X : YSquare = Y * Y
Xnew = Xsquare + X0: Ynew = Ysquare + Y0
{other calculations}
If Xsquare + Ysquare > 0 Then ...
```

The improvement will be more impressive if you store more complicated operations, such as $X^{2.8}$ or $Y^{-0.3}$, to temporary variables and reuse them.

Avoid Large Strings

The single most important trick in speeding up string operations is to remember that *Mid()* is not only a function, it's also a statement. In the following line, the Mid() function returns the third through the tenth characters of a string:

```
subString = Mid$(originalStrig,3,10)
```

But in the following line, Mid$() is used as a statement to change part of the string:

```
Mid$(originalString,3,10) = "1234567890"
```

Let's say you want to reverse a long string. Many Visual Basic programmers would start by building a new string and appending to it the characters of the string to be reversed. They would start with the last character and work up to the first with a loop like this:

```
For i = 1 To Len(AString)
    BString = BString & Mid$(AString, Len(AString) - i + 1, 1)
Next
```

In this listing, *AString* is the string to be reversed, and *BString* is the new string. If you run this code with a 30KB string, you'll spend almost a minute looking at the hourglass. You won't wait as long with a shorter string, say 5KB, but as the length of the string increases, so does the amount of time Visual Basic needs to handle it. Reversing a 30KB string isn't six times slower than reversing a 5KB string six times. It's not even close, as you'll see in the following paragraphs.

TIP

To reverse a string in a Visual Basic 6 application, you must use the *StrReverse()* function, which accepts a string as argument and returns the reversed string. This is a new function introduced with VB6, along with a number of new string functions, which are discussed in Appendix A on the CD.

Let's build a string using random characters. Start by setting up a long string, which is a more fundamental problem. In a practical application, the long strings can be read from a file or an incoming stream from a Web server. The basic problem is that as strings grow longer, Visual Basic takes longer to process them. The following code appends random characters to the end of the string variable *AString*:

```
AString = ""
For i = 1 To 30000
    AString = AString & Chr(Rnd() * 26 + 48)
Next
```

The ASCII value of the character *A* is 48. The expression Chr(Rnd() * 26 + 48) returns an uppercase character. The code is simple, but very slow. On a Pentium 166MHz system, it takes more than a minute to complete execution. But if the string was only 3,000 characters, filling it with random characters would take less than a second. Is there something wrong here? The length of the string and the time it takes to process it aren't proportional. As the string grows longer, Visual Basic needs disproportionately more time to manipulate it. This is a consequence of the way Visual Basic stores strings in memory, but it isn't something you can change.

To speed up the code, you can set up two nested loops, like the following:

```
AString = ""
For j = 1 To 10
    BString = ""
```

```
        For i = 1 To 3000
            BString = BString & Chr(Rnd() * 26 + 48)
        Next
        AString = AString & BString
    Next
```

The inner loop creates 3,000-character strings (variable *BString*) at a time and appends it to the *AString* variable. It must build ten such strings to fill the long string. Yet, this structure takes only 6.7 seconds on the 166 MHz Pentium. By limiting the size of the string variable used to append individual characters, you can bring the total execution time from more than 60 seconds down to less than seven seconds. Notice that the *AString* variable is updated only 10 times, not with every new character. That's where the gain in execution time comes from.

TIP   The conclusion is that you shouldn't manipulate very long strings with Visual Basic. Break long strings into shorter ones, manipulate them individually, and when you're done, concatenate the processed strings. Execution times will be reduced tremendously.

Access Object Properties Indirectly

Another simple, effective optimization technique is to avoid referencing the same property many times. Let's say you have an incoming stream of data that you want to display on a TextBox control. You already know what to do: create small string variables and append them to the control's Text property.

Another common mistake is to reference a property like Text1.Text in a loop. Let's say you want to reverse the characters of the text displayed on a TextBox control. Even if you use the Mid() statement in a loop such as the following, the process is going to be very slow:

```
Dim Astring As String
Astring = " "
With Text1
    For i = 1 To Len(.Text)
        tmpChar = Mid(.Text, Len(.Text) - i + 1, 1)
        Mid(AString, i, 1) = tmpChar
        Astring = Astring + " "
    Next
    .Text = Astring
End With
```

Because a lot of overhead is involved every time you access a control's property, avoid too many references to the same property. Copy the Text property's value to an intermediate variable and process this variable. Then, assign the processed variable to the Text property. Reversing 3,000 characters on a TextBox control takes 8.6 seconds using the Text property, while the same operation using a temporary string variable takes less than half a second on the same computer. Clearly, you should avoid referencing control properties directly in your code, especially within loops that are executed many times.

The same is true for all properties, but they don't usually appear in loops. The Text property can appear in a loop, especially if you append to it characters read from a file or when you save its value to a file. You should always use intermediate string variables and assign to them the value of the Text property.

Optimizing for Worst-Case Scenarios

Many times we write less than optimal code because we don't test our applications with real world data or under worst-case scenarios. We write code that works well with short text files and we assume it will behave similarly with any text file. After all, if an operation takes 90 milliseconds, why optimize it? Because, as we have demonstrated, it may deteriorate by a factor of 100 when the string's length is increased by a factor of 20. So don't trust anyone's code—not that of the compiler, a code generator, your colleagues or boss, your professors, or book authors. No code (except for truly trivial segments) can be proven optimal; so if you're not happy with its speed, optimize it.

Maximize Subjective Speed

No amount of optimization is going to do you much good unless the users of your application think it's fast. Conversely, the sloppiest application need not be optimized if users think it's fast. The most important measure of the speed of an application is its so-called *subjective speed* (also called perceived speed or apparent speed). Subjective speed can't be measured in time units (or any units, for that matter). Subjective speed describes how fast the application appears to the user. If your Forms load slowly, no amount of optimization in the code that follows the loading of the Form is going to help. An application that loads, responds, and repaints the screen quickly, may actually be preferred to an application that does its math faster, but takes too long to load, or one that doesn't respond quickly to user actions.

Subjective speed can be improved in many ways, but there are a few goals you should always try to attain, they are:

- Try to load the Forms quickly.

- Make sure the application starts quickly.

- Display flash screens, animation, or at least a progress indicator if the program is busy for more than a few seconds.

- Wisely use the AutoRedraw property to speed up graphics.

Your best bet is to load Forms at start-up and keep them in memory. The Load command loads a Form, but doesn't display it. Once the Form is in memory, you can display it instantly with the Show method. The application may take longer to start, but once it's started, Forms can be displayed and hidden instantly (unless they contain large bitmaps).

But how about the initial delay, when the user has to wait for your application's Forms to load? This initial delay is just about the worse thing you can do for the application's subjective speed, but it helps the subjective speed of the rest of the application. Design a simple initial Form that can be loaded very quickly. Once this Form is shown, load other larger Forms while the initial Form is displayed. This technique is demonstrated in Chapter 4, in the section "VB6 at Work: The Form-Load Project."

You should also avoid lengthy (or slow) code segments in a Form's Load event. If the Load event takes a few seconds to execute, the Form won't be drawn until the Load event handler has completed its execution. If you must place a significant amount of code in the Form's Load event, call the Form's Show method at the beginning. The following statements will force Visual Basic to draw the Form on the screen before it starts executing the code:

```
Me.Show
DoEvents
```

The DoEvents statement will give Windows a chance to redraw the screen. If you omit this statement, you'll see only the outline of the Form. Even if the code that follows loads another Form, you must call the Show method and the DoEvents statement.

When a time-consuming operation takes place, you can use the hourglass to indicate that the user should wait. We've all watched more than our fair share of hourglasses. Sometimes users go as far as shake them to see if the sand will move. An hourglass won't improve the application's subjective speed, so we need something more amusing, something fresher. An animated cursor or an AVI file with a few small frames isn't going to make the application run faster, but it's not going to slow it down noticeably either. A typical example is the animation that takes place when documents are sent to the Recycle Bin. Another example is the information displayed on the screen while applications are being installed. The flash screens keep the user from getting utterly bored, and they are more fun to watch than an hourglass.

Some operations are inherently slow and no amount of optimization will make them fast. If an operation takes more than a few seconds to complete, you should provide an indicator to let the user know the progress of the calculations. An hourglass tells the user that the application is busy doing something, but it gives no cues as to how long it will take to complete. The ProgressBar control is the ideal control for this purpose. The progress indicator lets the user know how the calculations are proceeding and how much longer they will take to complete. You should also provide a Cancel button, just in case the user decides to cancel an operation that takes too long.

Finally, if your application makes extensive use of graphics methods, estimate the effect of the setting of the AutoRedraw property of the Form or PictureBox where the drawing takes place. The graphics methods are slower when AutoRedraw is True, but the Form will be repainted instantly when the user switches to it if it has been temporarily hidden by another window. If AutoRedraw is False, then the Form won't be repainted automatically and you'll have to redraw the Form from within the Paint event. The effects of the AutoRedraw setting were discussed in detail in the section "Optimization Issues" of Chapter 6.

Case Studies

To help you better understand how to apply the rules that have been mentioned so far and optimize your applications, let's explore a few practical situations and follow the optimization process. In the rest of the chapter we'll optimize two of the applications developed earlier in the book: the DirMap application we developed in Chapter 11 and the Image application of Chapter 7.

Before you can optimize your application's execution speed, you must find out which sections of the code call for optimization. Optimizing the statements that display the results isn't going to help an application if it spends several minutes performing the calculations. Most of the code in an application is rarely executed, and in many cases, not at all. Some statements are executed thousands or millions of times. This is the code that must be optimized. You must locate the sections of the code that are responsible for most of the execution time and focus your efforts there.

Sometimes, it's not easy to locate the statements responsible for an application's execution speed, especially in large projects developed by programming teams. When you reach that point, you should consider some professional tools (called *code profilers*), which analyze your code and pinpoint the sections of the code where you should focus your efforts.

Timing Your Applications

In the course of application optimization, you'll be comparing the optimized applications to the original, non-optimized versions of the same applications. Since the same application will be executed on all types of different systems (some of them on 100MHz systems, others on 300MHz systems), the absolute numbers are meaningless. You should always look at the improvement ratio or how much faster the optimized application runs. These numbers shouldn't change on different processors. The code in this chapter is tested on a Pentium 166MHz computer.

Another issue you should keep in mind is how much memory is installed on the target computer. Even if your computer has plenty of memory for a specific application, you should also test the application on a system with less memory and include a warning for the users, should the program slow down considerably if executed on a computer with the minimum amount of memory. This isn't going to affect the execution speed per se (in other words, you can't make your application run faster by adding memory), but too little memory can cause other side effects.

If there's not enough memory on your computer and the operating system can't keep all open Forms in the memory, it will have to use the swap file on the computer's hard disk. The *swap file* is a large area on the disk that the operating system uses as memory when it runs out of physical RAM. The swap file practically eliminates the "out of memory" problems, but the hard disk isn't nearly as fast as the RAM. This will introduce unacceptable delays that aren't caused by your code. Therefore, when you test an application, you should keep an eye on the usage of the hard disk. If the disk is spinning when the code isn't accessing files, chances are you don't have enough memory installed and the same application will execute much faster on a system with more RAM. The system I used for testing the code in this chapter is equipped with 64MB of RAM.

WARNING You may not know it, but the books you buy when a new version of a language is released are prepared with a beta version of the software. The information is quite accurate, but beta versions contain code that simplifies its debugging. The extra code, which is removed from the release version, will affect the timing. The comparison of optimized versus non-optimized applications may be more favorable on your system. If this happens, it's due to the differences between the beta and the final production release of Visual Basic.

To time an operation, you must use the *Timer()* function, which returns the number of seconds (and fractions thereof) that have elapsed since midnight. However, it has a resolution of 55 milliseconds, so to time operations that take less than half a second or so, you should use the API time functions (discussed in Chapter 13). For the purposes of this chapter, the Timer() function is more than adequate. Save the function's value to a local variable before the first executable statement of the section you want to time. At the end of this section, call the Timer() function again and subtract the two values. Here's a typical code timing section:

```
{other statements}
T1 = Timer()
{code you want to time}
TDiff = Timer() - T1
Debug.Print TDiff
```

You can also place the operations you want to time in a loop that's repeated many times, but you should be very careful. If the time it takes Visual Basic to set up the loop and update the loop's counter isn't negligible compared to the time it takes to complete the calculations, you'll be timing the loop as well.

Optimizing the Image Application

The Image application presented in Chapter 7 processes images by manipulating each and every pixel of the image individually. This application easily performs a few million operations for a small image, so it's no surprise that it's slow. For instance, it takes over 20 seconds to sharpen a 400 × 400 image. This time is clearly unacceptable for a commercial or shareware-grade application. My goal in Chapter 7 was to demonstrate the basics of image processing and how the Image project can become your vehicle for experimenting with other image processing techniques. The code presented in Chapter 7 is straightforward Visual Basic code.

If you really like image processing and you're ready to build your own image processing application, then you probably want to make it as fast as typical image processing applications like PaintShop or PhotoStyler. That's not easy. Even after optimization, our Image application won't be as fast, but we'll make it as fast as it can get. Professional image processing applications are written in C++ with parts of the code written in machine language for maximum speed. Our application won't process the same image in a second or so, but we can drop the processing time from 30 seconds down to two or three seconds, which will make a world of difference. This is as fast as you can make it with Visual Basic (but that shouldn't stop you from trying to prove me wrong).

This section is rather lengthy but it will pay to read it. If you like, you can jump to end of the section and read the optimized code, but I'm going to optimize the code one step at a time. It's a process you'll find useful in optimizing your applications later on. I'll start by locating the code that's responsible for most of the delay (the code that contributes the most to the execution of the application) and then I'll try to improve this code.

Optimization Targets

Let's start by timing the Image application. Open an image file (like the NYSTRT .GIF file, which you'll find on the CD) and select an effect from the Process menu. On a 166MHz Pentium with 64MB of RAM, it takes 30 seconds to sharpen the image and slightly more to smooth it. The code that implements the sharpening operation is shown next:

```
For i = 1 To y - 2
    For j = 1 To x - 2
      red = ImagePixels(0, i, j) + 0.5 * (ImagePixels(0, i, j) - _
            ImagePixels(0, i - Dx, j - Dy))
      green = ImagePixels(1, i, j) + 0.5 * (ImagePixels(1, i, j) - _
            ImagePixels(1, i - Dx, j - Dy))
      blue = ImagePixels(2, i, j) + 0.5 * (ImagePixels(2, i, j) - _
            ImagePixels(2, i - Dx, j - Dy))
      If red > 255 Then red = 255
      If red < 0 Then red = 0
      If green > 255 Then green = 255
      If green < 0 Then green = 0
      If blue > 255 Then blue = 255
      If blue < 0 Then blue = 0
      Picture1.PSet (j, i), RGB(red, green, blue)
    Next
  Picture1.Refresh
Next
```

This is the double loop that scans the rows of the image and the pixels within each row and processes them. There's not much room for optimizing the calculations (at least, not to the point that it would make the application run significantly faster); after all, they are operations with integers. The If statements introduce some delay, but as you'll see, they aren't responsible for much of the execution time. As you may have guessed, the PSet method is a slow one. Break the application and comment out the line that sets the current pixel's value by inserting the comment character in front of it:

```
    Picture1.PSet ('i,j), RGB(red, green, blue)
```

Run the application again and time it. This time it takes 9.34 seconds to complete the processing. The processed image isn't displayed, but the required calculations do take place. It may come as a surprise, but the PSet method is responsible for two-thirds of the execution time. Visual Basic can handle the math quite efficiently, but painting is a real hog. (The times mentioned were measured in the Visual Basic IDE and they will be better if the application is compiled to native code).

Since drawing operations are so time consuming, let's also remove the line that refreshes the Form by commenting out the line:

```
Picture1.Refresh
```

This time, the smoothing operation is completed in 2.42 seconds, which is an impressive speed. Let's see how close to this time we can get. Paint Shop is even faster, but unless you're willing to code parts of the application in Visual C++ or assembly language, you can't do any better.

So far, we have figured out what part of the code we can improve. At this point, it doesn't make sense to even consider optimizing the math. Even if you could get rid of the math calculations, you'd bring the execution time from 30 seconds down to slightly less than 28. This is not nearly as time-saving as speeding the display operations.

The SetPixelV() API Function

In Chapter 13, *The Windows API,* you'll learn about the SetPixelV() function, which does the same thing as the PSet method, but faster. Let's replace the call to the PSet method in the code with a call to the SetPixelV() function. Just replace all the instances of the line:

```
Picture1.PSet (j, i), RGB(red, green, blue)
```

with the line

```
SetPixelV Picture1.hdc, j, i, RGB(red, green, blue)
```

This is an API function, and in order to use it, you must first declare it in a Module. The SetPixelV() function's declaration is:

```
Declare Function SetPixelV Lib "gdi32" (ByVal hdc As Long, _
    ByVal x As Long, ByVal y As Long, ByVal crColor As Long) As Long
```

Since we replaced the PSet method with the equivalent API function for setting a pixel, we might as well replace the method Point, which reads a pixel's value, with the GetPixelV() API function, whose declaration must also appear in the application's Module:

```
Declare Function GetPixel Lib "gdi32" (ByVal hdc As Long, _
    ByVal x As Long, ByVal y As Long) As Long
```

The line that reads the current pixel's Color value in the Open command should be:

```
pixel = GetPixel(Form1.Picture1.hdc, j, i)
```

To revise the Image application you must first add a Module (with the Project ≻ Add Module command) and insert the two declarations in it. Then replace the instances of the Pset method with the SetPixelV() function. Now run the application and time it again. The total processing time on the same system is 16.25 seconds. By replacing a Visual Basic method with a call to an API function, we improved the speed of the application by more than 40%.

The revised application can be found in the folder IMAGE1 on the CD. It's also called Image and it's identical to the Image application, except for the statement that reads pixel values (in the Open command) and the statement that paints the processed pixel in the processing commands.

Comment out the statement that refreshes the Form and repeat the sharpen operation. It will take 9.9 seconds. This statement is executed as many times are there are rows in the image. If you omit it altogether, you'll gain another five seconds or so, but this comes with a price: the image won't be updated on the screen as it's processed.

You could add a progress bar, as many image processing applications do, but displaying the processing progress for nearly 10 seconds isn't the best you can do. Ten seconds is a long time for a user to wait without receiving clues about the result of the processing. It would be a reasonable choice if the total time was a second or two, but 10 seconds is probably too much.

So, what do you do next? If you're happy with the application's speed, you can stop here. Compile the application to native code to gain another second or two and you'll have a reasonably fast application you can use for your own custom image processing algorithms. To save a few more seconds, you can avoid refreshing the screen and display a progress bar that indicates the progress of the operation. This way, users won't think that the application has stopped responding. But from your experience with image processing applications, you know that this application can be made faster. There's room for improvement, and you probably know what the next step is. The painting of the pixels is still responsible for most of the application's execution time, so this is where we should focus our efforts next. Let's redesign the part of the program that paints the Form.

Drawing on Device Contexts

To speed up the drawing operations, we are going to draw directly on the bitmap that corresponds to the rectangle of the control on the screen. Visual Basic doesn't draw directly on the PictureBox control. Instead, it updates a special area in the memory where a copy of the image is stored. Whenever Windows gets a chance, it transfers the contents of this memory area to the screen. This happens when no code is executed or when the DoEvents or Picture1.Refresh statements are executed. This indirect method of drawing on controls places a significant burden on Visual Basic.

It's possible to access the memory where the copy of the bitmap is stored and update the pixel values there. After the entire bitmap has been modified, we can transfer it to the PictureBox control. The drawback of this method is that while drawing on the bitmap, the image on the PictureBox control won't be updated. But if the image is processed in a few seconds, that's something we can live with. As you'll see shortly, updating the bitmap in memory is quite fast.

Before we start coding though, let's review the process. In Chapter 13 you'll find more information on the API functions used here. In this section we are going to outline the process and briefly discuss what each API function does. In order to access the bitmap that stores the image of the PictureBox control, you must create a bitmap structure. This is done with the CreateCompatibleBitmap() API function, which creates a bitmap of specific dimensions and makes it compatible with the bitmap displayed on the control. The variable *hBMP* created with the following statement points to a bitmap that's compatible with the bitmap displayed on the Picture1 control and has the same dimensions as the control.

```
hBMP = CreateCompatibleBitmap(Picture1.hdc, _
            Picture1.ScaleWidth, Picture1.ScaleHeight)
```

The *hBMP* structure can't be accessed directly by Visual Basic either. The drawing API functions, in particular, the SetPixelV() function, can only write to a *device context*. To use the SetPixelV() function, you must also create a device context with the CreateCompatibleDC() API function:

```
hDestDC = CreateCompatibleDC(Picture1.hdc)
```

The device context is compatible with the PictureBox control and you can use any of the drawing functions to draw on it. However, your drawing won't end up on the PictureBox control unless you connect the *hDestDC* device context and the compatible bitmap *hBMP*. This is taken care of by the SelectObject() API function, which connects the two objects (or mounts the bitmap on the device context):

```
SelectObject hDestDC, hBMP
```

The *hDestDC* device context is the device context of the PictureBox control. In other words, it's equivalent to the hDC property of the PictureBox control. Before, you were drawing on the PictureBox control with the statement:

```
SetPixelV Picture1.hdc, j, i, RGB(red, green, blue)
```

and now you can draw with the statement:

```
SetPixelV hDestDC, j, i, RGB(red, green, blue)
```

After the entire device context has been updated, you must transfer it to the PictureBox control with the BitBlt()function. In other words, the new bitmap exists in the control's device context and you must transfer it to the PictureBox control with the BitBlt() function:

```
BitBlt Picture1.hdc, 1, 1, Picture1.ScaleWidth - 2, _
     Picture1.ScaleHeight - 2, hDestDC, 1, 1, &HCC0020
```

The copied portion of the device context is slightly smaller than the original image, because the edge pixels aren't processed. The corresponding pixels in the device context have random values. By omitting them, we keep the original values of the edge pixels on the PictureBox control instead of displaying random values.

Sharpening an Image on the Device Context

You have seen all the statements that are new to the revised Image application. The new application is called Image and can be found in the IMAGE2 folder on the CD. It's nearly identical to the initial Image application, with the exception of the statements that change the pixel values. Here's the code that implements the Sharpen command:

```
Private Sub ProcessSharpen_Click()
Dim i As Long, j As Long
Dim Dx As Integer, Dy As Integer
Dim red As Integer, green As Integer, blue As Integer

    Dx = 1: Dy = 1
    T1 = Timer
    Form3.Show
    Form3.Caption = "Sharpening image ..."
    Form3.Refresh

    hBMP = CreateCompatibleBitmap(Picture1.hdc, _
          Picture1.ScaleWidth, Picture1.ScaleHeight)
    hDestDC = CreateCompatibleDC(Picture1.hdc)
    SelectObject hDestDC, hBMP

    For i = 1 To y - 2
        For j = 1 To x - 2
            red = ImagePixels(0, i, j) + _
        0.5 * (ImagePixels(0, i, j) - ImagePixels(0, i - Dx, j - Dy))
            green = ImagePixels(1, i, j) + _
        0.5 * (ImagePixels(1, i, j) - ImagePixels(1, i - Dx, j - Dy))
            blue = ImagePixels(2, i, j) + _
        0.5 * (ImagePixels(2, i, j) - ImagePixels(2, i - Dx, j - Dy))
            If red > 255 Then red = 255
            If red < 0 Then red = 0
            If green > 255 Then green = 255
            If green < 0 Then green = 0
```

```
        If blue > 255 Then blue = 255
        If blue < 0 Then blue = 0
        SetPixelV hDestDC, j, i, RGB(red, green, blue)
    Next
    Form3.ProgressBar1.Value = i * 100 / (y - 1)
    DoEvents
Next
Form3.Hide
BitBlt Picture1.hdc, 1, 1, Picture1.ScaleWidth - 2, _
    Picture1.ScaleHeight - 2, hDestDC, 1, 1, &HCC0020
Picture1.Refresh
Call DeleteDC(hDestDC)
Call DeleteObject(hBMP)

MsgBox "Processing completed in " & Format(Timer - T1, "##.000")
End Sub
```

If you run the revised Image application, you'll see that it's quite fast. Most of the processing algorithms finish in less than five seconds in the Visual Basic IDE. If you compile it and turn on all the optimization switches (it's safe to do so), the same image will be processed in less than three seconds. This is a very good speed for a Visual Basic application. It's still slower than professional image processing applications, but its speed is acceptable. Of course, my goal was to demonstrate how to optimize a Visual Basic application. Image can't be considered a typical VB application, but it's the type of application that benefits immensely from the optimization process. It shows what some additional programming effort can do. With the exception of the lines that read and write the pixels, the rest of the application is fairly simple, and you can modify it to use with your own custom image processing techniques.

Providing Feedback with a Progress Bar

Notice that the revised Image application uses an additional Form with a Progress-Bar control, which shows the progress of the algorithm. The ProgressBar control's value is set after each completion of the inner loop, which processes one line of pixels. Since the image on the PictureBox control isn't updated in real time, the progress bar provides some feedback to the user, so that they know how the processing is going. At each step, the ProgressBar control's value is updated with the statement:

```
Form3.ProgressBar1.Value = i * 100 / (y - 1)
```

The outer loop's counter is i and it goes from 1 to $y - 1$ (y is the vertical resolution of the image). The ProgressBar control's Min property is 0 and its Max property is 100, and it's the same control that's used to indicate the progress of an image when it loads. Figure 12.3 shows the Image application as it processes an image.

FIGURE 12.3:

The optimized Image application doesn't update the image during processing. It uses a ProgressBar to indicate the progress of the operation instead.

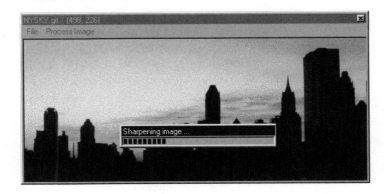

To appreciate the full effect of the optimization effort, you should load the Image applications from the CD, check all the advanced optimization switches in the Advanced Optimizations dialog box, and compile the images to native code. Then, run the executables and time the three versions of the application to see the effect of the various optimization techniques. Feel free to further customize the application and see if you can make it any faster. Most likely, further optimization isn't going to show such apparent improvements.

Optimizing the DirMap Application

Another useful application in this book that could use some optimization is the Dir-Map application of Chapter 11. This application iterates recursively through the files of a given folder (or drive) and creates a list like the one shown in Figure 12.4. The DirMap application, which uses a recursive function to scan a specific folder and its subfolders, is described in detail in Chapter 11.

The DirMap application can scan a small folder (one with a small number of sub-folders), but if you attempt to scan an entire drive, it will deteriorate rapidly. The DirMap application can scan the Program Files folder on my system in 25 seconds. This specific folder contains 2,673 files in 186 subfolders. By contrast, my main hard disk contains 12,363 files in 1,054 folders, and it takes the original DirMap application 374 seconds to scan it. This is an awful lot of time for a rather simple operation. As you can see, the program gets disproportionately slower as the number of folders/files increases. You will also notice that the number of processed files, which is displayed on the Form and updated every time the program visits a new subfolder, increases quickly initially and not so quickly as more and more files are processed.

FIGURE 12.4:

The DirMap application scans the contents of a folder recursively to display its contents on a Rich-TextBox control.

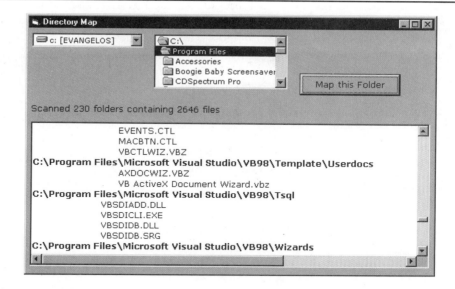

As you can guess, the source of the delay is the line that appends new data to the *DirStructure* string variable. As we mentioned earlier in this chapter, manipulating long strings with Visual Basic is very costly in execution time. To verify that the source of the delay is the manipulation of the *DirStructure* variable, comment out the lines that append a folder/file name to the variable *DirStructure*. These lines are shown next:

```
DirStructure = DirStructure & txtLine
DirStructure = DirStructure & "{\b " & DoubleSlashes(Dir2.List(i)) _
               & "}" & newLine
```

The revised application scans the same hard disk in approximately 75 seconds (versus 374 seconds). These two lines are really slowing down the application, especially when it scans large drives or folders.

One of the simple optimization tricks we mentioned earlier in this chapter is to avoid manipulating long strings. The DirMap application builds the list of folders and files as an *RTF* string, which is then assigned to the RTFText property of the RichTextBox control. This string can become quite long, and each time we add a new folder and file name, this string grows. The longer the string, the more time it takes to append characters to it. For a fair-sized folder, like the Program Files folder on my system, the contents of the RichTextBox control exceed 140KB. Considering the string variable experiments we carried out earlier in the chapter, you can easily see that the manipulation of this variable is responsible for most of the application's execution time.

Clearly, we must limit the size of the string that holds the contents of the Rich-TextBox control. To avoid a very large string, we can build it piece-by-piece: append a number of file and folder names to an intermediate string variable, and every time this variable's length exceeds a threshold, append it to the long string variables, reset the intermediate variable to an empty string, and continue.

The core of the DirMap application's code is the ScanFolders() subroutine, which is shown here:

```
Sub ScanFolders()
Dim subFolders As Integer
Dim txtLine As String
Dim i As Integer, j As Integer

txtLine = ""
For j = 0 To File1.ListCount - 1
    txtLine = txtLine & Space(currentDepth * 5) + _
                File1.List(j) & newLine
Next
totalFiles = totalFiles + File1.ListCount
DirStructure = DirStructure & txtLine
subFolders = Dir2.ListCount
If subFolders > 0 Then
    currentDepth = currentDepth + 1
    For i = 0 To subFolders - 1
        DirStructure = DirStructure & "{\b " & _
                    DoubleSlashes(Dir2.List(i)) & "}" & newLine
        File1.Path = Dir2.List(i)
  ChDir CurDir
  Dir2.Path = Dir2.List(i)
  ScanFolders
    Next
    totalFolders = totalFolders + subFolders
    Label1.Caption = "Processed " & totalFolders & " folders"
    currentDepth = currentDepth - 1
    DoEvents
End If
MoveUp
File1.Path = Dir2.Path
End Sub
```

The variable that holds the RTF string to be displayed on the RichTextBox control is the *DirStructure* variable and it can become extremely long. We must use another variable, the *tmpDirStructure* variable, whose length we're going to keep under control. Every time the *tmpDirStructure* variable's length exceeds a threshold (5,000 characters or so), we'll append it to the *DirStructure* variable and reset the *tmpDirStructure* variable. The process will continue for as long as the program is running.

To do this, we must first replace the line:

```
DirStructure = DirStructure & "{\b " & _
              DoubleSlashes(Dir2.List(i)) & "}" & newLine
```

with the following one:

```
tmpDirStructure = tmpDirStructure & "{\b " & _
              DoubleSlashes(Dir2.List(i)) & "}" & newLine
```

Then, we must examine the length of the new string variable, and if it has exceeded a predefined maximum length, append it to the *DirStructure* variable:

```
If Len(tmpDirStructure) > 8000 Then
    DirStructure = DirStructure & tmpDirStructure
    tmpDirStructure = ""
End If
```

A threshold value of 8,000 characters is a reasonable compromise. You can experiment with this setting and see for yourself that very small or very large values are actually bad choices. A very small value means that the body of the previous If...Then structure is executed very frequently, and in effect, diminishes any gain from not allowing the *DirStructure* variable to grow too long. A very large threshold gets us back to the situation we wanted to avoid in the first place.

When the ScanFolder() subroutine is called for the last time, we must move the contents of the temporary variable to the actual variable. This takes place from within the Click event's handler of the Command button on the Form, after the ScanFolder() subroutine is called. The revised handler is shown next (the new lines are underlined):

```
Private Sub Command1_Click()
T1 = Timer
    totalFiles = 0
    totalFolders = 0
    currentDepth = 1
    InitialFolder = CurDir
    tmpDirStructure = ""
    DirStructure = "{"
    DirStructure = DirStructure & _
              "{\b " & DoubleSlashes(Dir2.List(-1)) & "}" + newLine
    Screen.MousePointer = vbHourglass
    DoEvents
```

```
        ScanFolders
        If tmpDirStructure <> "" Then
            DirStructure = DirStructure & tmpDirStructure
        End If
        DirStructure = DirStructure & "}"
        RichTextBox1.TextRTF = DirStructure
        Label1.Caption = "Scanned " & totalFolders _
                        & " folders containing " & totalFiles & " files"
        Screen.MousePointer = vbDefault
        MsgBox Timer - T1
    End Sub
```

The optimized DirMap application is stored in the OPTIMZD folder on the CD, and it's identical to the original DirMap application, except for the changes explained in the previous paragraphs. If you run the optimized DirMap application (it doesn't make much difference whether you compile it to native code or execute it from within the Visual Basic IDE) and time it, you'll see that it's consistently more than three times faster than the original application. Overall, it's still a slow application when you use it to map a folder like Windows or Program Files, but this application is useful in mapping smaller folders.

If you compile the DirMap application to native code and execute it, you won't see a considerable improvement in execution time. This is because p-code is quite efficient at manipulating strings. The rest of the code can't be optimized. Most of the code manipulates the DirListBox and FileListBox controls and these operations can't be made any faster. When an ActiveX control takes over, there's nothing you can do from within the code to speed it up. This is the "speed barrier" I talked about earlier in the chapter

There are certainly more applications in this book whose execution speeds aren't optimal, and you can use them to experiment with the optimization techniques we have looked at in this chapter. For example, you can use the technique of drawing on a device context to speed up the Spiral application of Chapter 6, *Drawing with Visual Basic*. This can be an interesting exercise, as you'll have to be creative with the AutoRedraw property to increase the subjective speed of the application.

PART IV

Extending Visual Basic

CHAPTER

THIRTEEN

13

The Windows API

- Accessing the Win32 API from Visual Basic

- Passing arguments by value and reference

- Determining free disk space

- Creating menus with bitmaps

- Detecting mouse movements

- Accessing the system

- Manipulating graphics

So far you've been programming within the limits of Visual Basic. You've designed with point-and-click operations and used Visual Basic statements to program the controls on the Forms. You've seen how far you can go with Visual Basic, and there's a lot you can do with straight Visual Basic code. Sometimes, however, you must get into the core of the operating system and access of its many functions. To do advanced programming, such as detecting mouse movements outside a Form, you need some additional functions. These functions are provided by the *Win32 Application Programming Interface (API).*

The Win32 API is a set of functions developed primarily for C programmers, but there's no reason why you can't use it from within your Visual Basic applications. Many Visual Basic programmers resort to the Win32 API functions to accomplish what is simply impossible (or too complicated) from within Visual Basic. As you'll see in Chapter 12, *Optimizing VB Applications,* API calls can also significantly speed up certain operations that are inherently slow with Visual Basic (especially graphics operations).

The API functions aren't complicated and they're not as exotic as Visual Basic programmers might think. The problem is that the API is documented for C programmers, so you may find it difficult to map the function and data type declarations from C jargon to Visual Basic.

All Win32 API functions are available from within the Visual Basic environment. In fact, the graphics methods of Visual Basic are masqueraded API functions. In Chapter 7, *Manipulating Color and Pixels with Visual Basic,* we looked at the PaintPicture method, which copies bitmaps from one control to another. The PaintPicture method was introduced with Visual Basic 4. Before that, Visual Basic programmers had to use an API function to achieve similar functionality. The Bit-Blt() function can copy pixels to and from Visual Basic controls from anywhere on the Desktop. To copy part of the Desktop to a PictureBox control (for instance, to implement a custom screen capture utility) you have to use the BitBlt() function, not the PaintPicture method.

Many Windows applications use the API to some extent. Fortunately, Visual Basic hides a lot of the complexities of Windows programming from you while providing access to the API. This chapter will not even attempt to explain all API functions (there are more than 1,000 of them), but only a few that I think you'll find useful.

The goal of this chapter is to introduce the basics of calling the API functions and to explain how to use the API viewer to add API function declarations to your code. Instead of quickly presenting many API functions, I will present a few useful ones and build small applications that use them. These applications will demonstrate not only how to call the corresponding functions, but how to use them in the context of a Visual Basic application as well. The functions I've chosen to discuss and demonstrate with examples are not among the simpler ones. Many of the API functions are quite easy to understand and use, and although they would make for simple examples, these functions have Visual Basic counterparts, so there's no need to learn them.

Basic Concepts

Before we dive into the examples of using specific API functions, let's go over the fundamental concepts. The Win32 API consists of functions, structures, and messages that can be accessed to build Windows 95/98 and Windows NT applications.

The four functional categories of the Windows API are:

- Windows Management (User)
- Graphics Device Interface (GDI)
- System Services (Kernel)
- Multimedia (MMSystem)

The functions in these categories are implemented as *DLLs (Dynamic Link Libraries)* and can be called from any language. A DLL is loaded at runtime and it doesn't need to be linked to your application. Actually, that's where the name comes from: the contents of a DLL are linked to your application dynamically at runtime, not at design time. Because the API functions are required for the proper operation of Windows itself, the DLLs are always available to your application.

Windows Management provides the essential functions to build and manage your applications. All the basic input and output of the system goes through this layer of the Win32 API, including mouse and keyboard input and all processing of messages sent to your application. The Windows Management functions give your application better control over the mouse movement than Visual Basic's mouse events.

The *Graphics Device Interface* provides the functions you use to manage all supported graphical devices on your system, including the monitor and printer. In addition, you can define fonts, pens, and brushes. The GDI provides support for the line and circle drawing operations and for bit-blit operations with the BitBlt() function. (For details on bit-blit, see the discussion of the PaintPicture method in Chapter 7, *Manipulating Color and Pixels with Visual Basic*.)

System Services provides functions to access the resources of the computer and the operating system. You'll see how to call some of these functions to figure out the free resources on the system running your application.

The *Multimedia* functions allow you to play waveform audio, MIDI music, and digital video. You can achieve this with the MCI command string and MCI command message interface, which are discussed in detail in Appendix B on the CD, *Using Multimedia Elements to Enhance Applications*.

Accessing Win32 API from Visual Basic

The only difference between Visual Basic functions and the Win32 API functions is that API functions must be declared before they can be used. In essence, you must tell Visual Basic the name and location of the DLL in which an API function resides and the arguments it requires. You can then use it as you would use any other Visual Basic function.

Declaring API Functions

You declare the Win32 API functions with the Declare statement. One way is to enter the function along with the arguments, as in the following:

```
Declare Function mciSendString Lib "winmm.dll" _
    Alias "mciSendStringA" (ByVal 1pstrCommand As String, _
    ByVal 1pstrReturnString As String, ByVal uReturnLenght As Long, _
    ByVal hwndCallback As Long) As Long
```

> **NOTE** Long declarations are usually broken into multiple lines with an underscore character at the end of each line. You can also enter them in a single long line.

The Win32 API function *mciSendString()* is part of the Winmm multimedia library (which is in the Winmm.dll file in the Windows/System folder). The A suffix is a leftover from older versions of the API, where 16- and 32-bit functions coexisted. Under Windows 95/98, you must use 32-bit functions and ignore the alias of the function.

Nearly all API functions have their arguments passed by value. Only arguments that must be modified by the function are passed by reference. By default, Visual Basic passes arguments by reference, so you must always precede the argument names with the *ByVal* keyword.

Using the API Viewer Application

You aren't expected to remember the arguments of every API function or even the function names. It's assumed you'll look them up in a reference. This reference is available from within Visual Basic's IDE, and it's the API Viewer shown in Figure 13.1.

FIGURE 13.1:

The API Viewer application

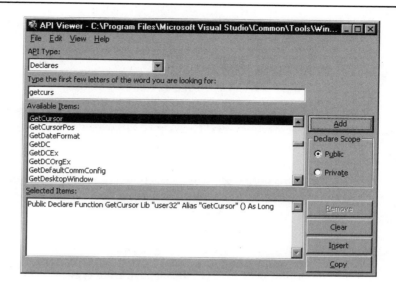

You can easily copy and paste any function into your Visual Basic programs. To do so, follow these steps:

1. Choose Add-Ins ➤ API Viewer. If the API Viewer command doesn't appear in the Add-Ins menu, select Add-Ins Manager, and in the Add-Ins Manager dialog box double-click the entry Visual Basic 6 API Viewer to add it to the Add-Ins menu.

2. In the API Viewer window, choose File ➤ Load Text File or File ➤ Load Database File. The Load Database File loads faster (except for the first time, when the test file is converted to a database).

3. In the Available Items list box, select the function you want, and click the Add button. API Viewer displays the selected function(s) in the Selected Items list box.

4. Select the functions you need for your application and then click the Copy button to copy the function's declaration to the Clipboard.

5. Open your application's Code window and paste in the function declarations.

TIP

The Win32 Software Development Kit provides full documentation for each function, including all structures and messages. The Microsoft Developer Network (MSDN) contains everything you need to develop Windows applications. For more information on the MSDN, visit the site at http://www.microsoft.com/msdn.

Most of the API functions require a large number of arguments and some of the arguments can be complicated data types. The argument types of the API functions are described the next.

API Function Arguments

When using the Win32 API functions, you must supply the functions' declarations and their arguments. The Win32 API was written for programmers writing in the C or C++ language, so the documentation uses the C data structures, which you must map to their Visual Basic equivalents. Table 13.1 summarizes the C declarations and the corresponding Visual Basic data types. The third column shows how the arguments are passed to the API function. All types are passed by value, except Internet and Long Integer pointers.

TABLE 13.1: Visual Basic and C Data Types

C Declaration	Visual Basic Data Type	Argument Type
Integer	Integer	ByVal
Integer Pointer (LPINT)	Integer	ByRef
Long	Long	ByVal
Long Integer Pointer	Long	ByRef
String Pointer (LPSTR)	String	ByVal
Handle	Long	ByVal
Char	String	ByVal
Void Pointer	Any	ByRef

Passing Arguments by Value

To use API functions in your code, you must understand two argument-passing mechanisms, *ByVal* and *ByRef*. They are explained in detail in Chapter 3, *Visual Basic: The Language*, but I'm including an overview of Visual Basic's argument-passing mechanisms in this section.

When you pass arguments by value, you pass a copy of the argument to the called procedure. The procedure can change the value, but the change affects only the copy, not the argument itself. Visual Basic uses the *ByVal* keyword to indicate that the argument is passed by value. Code 13.1 shows the AnySub() procedure with the argument *anyNumber* passed by value. Within the AnySub() procedure, the argument *anyNumber* is set to the value 10. When the program exits this procedure, however, *anyNumber* reverts to its assigned value.

Code 13.1:   **Passing Arguments by Value**

```
Sub AnySub( ByVal anyNumber as Integer)
     anyNumber = 10
     Debug.Print anyNumber
End Sub
```

If you call the AnySub() function with the following lines:

```
x=1
Call AnySub(x)
Debug.Print
```

you'll see the following messages on the Immediate window:

```
AnyNumber = 10
AnyNumber = 1
```

The Print statement in the AnySub() procedure displays the value assigned to the *anyNumber* variable from within its code. The main program displays the value 1 on the Immediate window. The value 10 of the procedure's argument takes effect only while AnySub() executes; it's invalid outside of the procedure.

Passing Arguments by Reference

When you pass arguments by reference, you give the procedure access to the actual contents of the argument. The procedure to which the argument is passed has the actual memory address where the argument resides and can permanently change the value of the argument. In Visual Basic, this is the default argument-passing mechanism. The AnySub() procedure in the following example changes the value of its argument permanently.

Coded 13.2:   **Passing Arguments by Reference**

```
Sub AnySub( myInt As Integer )
     myInt = 20              'myInt is now 20
End Sub
```

If you call this subroutine with the following lines:

```
Dim x As Integer
{other statements}
x = 4
Debug.Print "Before calling AnySub x= " & x
Call AnySub(x)
Debug.Print "After calling AnySub x = " & x
```

the Print statements will display the following lines in the Debug window:

```
Before calling AnySub x= 4
After calling AnySub x = 20
```

The changes made to the *x* variable in the AnySub() subroutine have a global effect because the argument is passed by reference. If the called procedure has no reason to change the value of an argument, the argument must be passed by value. Some API functions store results in their arguments. These functions expect that their arguments will be passed by reference. In C, these arguments are called *pointers* (they point to the memory location where the variable is stored).

Declaring 32-Bit Functions and Structures

Some API functions use structures for their arguments. The MousePos application (you'll find it in the MousePos folder on the CD) demonstrates how to declare and use a simple structure. It uses the GetCursorPos() function to get the current mouse position when the mouse is clicked. This function must report back to the application two values: the X and Y coordinates of the mouse. These values are stored in a structure called POINTAPI, which has two members, X and Y. You can access these values from within your code with the expressions `PointAPI.X` and `PointAPI.Y`.

To design the MousePos project follow these steps:

1. Open the API Viewer (choose Add-Ins ➤ API Viewer).

2. In the API Viewer window, choose File ➤ Load Text File.

3. Select the file Win32api.txt, and in the Available Items list double-click the GetCursorPos entry.

4. The following declaration will appear in the Selected Items list:

```
Declare Function GetCursorPos Lib "user32" Alias "GetCursorPos" _
        (lpPoint As POINTAPI) As Long
```

The argument required for the function is a data structure named POINTAPI, which holds the coordinates of a point on the screen. To find the definition of the POINTAPI data structure with the API Viewer, complete the next steps.

5. Select Types in the API Type drop-down list. The Available Items list is populated with all the data structures used by the API functions.

6. Locate the POINTAPI data structure and double-click its name. Its definition will appear in the Selected Items list as follows:

```
Type POINTAPI
    x As Long
    y As Long
End Type
```

7. Click the Copy button to copy this definition (along with the declaration of the GetCursorPos() function) into your application's Code window.

TIP Function declarations may appear anywhere, but it's customary to place them in a Module so that they will be available from within any procedure.

8. Add a new Module to the project and paste the selected declaration there. You'll paste the following declarations from the API Viewer via the Clipboard:

```
Type POINTAPI
    x As Long
    y As Long
End Type
Declare Function GetCursorPos Lib "user32" Alias "GetCursorPos" _
            (lpPoint As POINTAPI) As Long
```

TIP If you want to paste these declarations on a Form because they won't be used outside a single Form, prefix the declarations with the *Private* keyword.

Now you can use the GetCursorPos() function in your code. Suppose you want to know the location of the pointer in the Click event. Visual Basic's Click event doesn't report the coordinates of the point where the mouse is clicked, but you can request them with the GetCursorPos() function. With the previous declarations in the application's Module, enter the following code in the Form's Click event:

```
Private Sub Form_Click()
Dim MouseLoc As POINTAPI
Dim retValue As Boolean
```

```
        retValue = GetCursorPos(MouseLoc)
        Debug.Print "X Pos = " & MouseLoc.x
        Debug.Print "Y Pos = " & MouseLoc.y
End Sub
```

The GetCursorPos() function returns the pointer's coordinates in pixels. The values you see in the Immediate window correspond to screen pixels. The origin is (0, 0) and it corresponds to the pixel at the upper-left corner of the screen. If the display is set to a resolution of 800 × 600, the pixel at the lower-right corner of the screen will be (799, 599). To actually click that coordinate, you must move the Form to the lower-right corner of the screen and then click a pixel. The GetCursorPos() function reports the mouse coordinates in absolute screen units, but the Form_Click event is triggered only when the mouse is clicked somewhere on the Form. That's why you must move the Form to another location on the screen, then click. You'll see later how you can track the pointer, even outside the Form.

Determining Free Disk Space

This section describes the functions you use to determine a drive's medium type and its free disk space and the functions you use to find the Windows directory and the current directory; they are:

- GetDriveType()

- GetDiskFreeSpace()

- GetWindowsDirectory()

- GetCurrentDirectory()

These functions add capabilities that are normally not available with Visual Basic. For example, you can use them to determine the amount of free space on a disk drive or if a certain drive is a CD-ROM drive.

GetDriveType()

This function determines the drive type and is declared as follows:

```
Private Declare Function GetDriveType Lib "kernel32" Alias _
        "GetDriveTypeA" (ByVal nDrive As String) As Long
```

You pass the drive that you want to check with the *nDrive* argument and the function returns a Long value, which describes the type of the drive. Table 13.2 lists and describes the values.

TABLE 13.2: Values for Drive Types

VALUE	DESCRIPTION
0	Drive type cannot be determined
1	There is no root directory
DRIVE_REMOVABLE	Drive can be removed, for example, a ZIP drive
DRIVE_FIXED	Drive cannot be removed, for example, drive C
DRIVE_REMOTE	Drive is remote, for example, a network drive
DRIVE_CDROM	Drive is CD-ROM drive
DRIVE_RAMDISK	Drive is a RAM drive

VB6 at Work: The Drives Project

The Drives application (see Figure 13.2) displays information about the selected drive on the DriveListBox, as well as the current folder and the Windows folder on the system. Every time you select a different drive, the information on the application's Form is updated. The Drives application uses three API functions: GetDiskFreeSpace(), GetCurrent Directory(), and GetWindowsDirectory().

FIGURE 13.2:

The Drives application

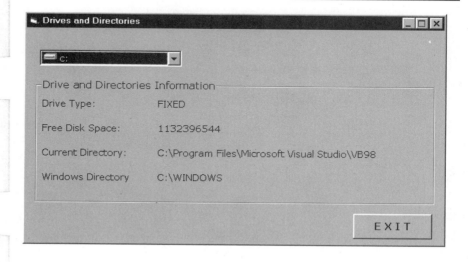

GetDiskFreeSpace()

This function gets specific information about a disk, including the amount of free space. It also returns the number of sectors per cluster, the number of bytes per sector, the total number of free clusters on the disk, and the total number of clusters. The free disk space isn't reported directly by the GetDiskFreeSpace() function; instead, it must be calculated by taking the product of the bytes per sector, sectors per cluster, and the number of free clusters. Here's how you declare the function:

```
Private Declare Function GetDiskFreeSpace Lib "kernel32" Alias _
        "GetDiskFreeSpaceA" (ByVal lpRootPathName As String, _
        lpSectorsPerCluster As Long, lpBytesPerSector As Long, _
        lpNumberOfFreeClusters As Long, _
        lpTtoalNumberOfClusters As Long) As Long
```

The arguments of this function have intuitive names, and you'll see how they are used in the FileInfo application, later in this chapter.

To find out the free space on drive C, use the following statements:

```
retValue = GetDiskFreeSpace("c:\", Sectors, Bytes, _
        freeClusters, totalClusters)
FreeSpace = Sectors * Bytes * freeClusters
```

The total free space is calculated as the product of free clusters, sectors per cluster, and bytes per sector.

GetCurrent Directory()

Use this function to retrieve the current directory where your program is running; it's similar to the App.Path property of Visual Basic. This function expects two arguments: the buffer length and the buffer in which the pathname will be stored. The function is declared as follows:

```
Private Declare Function GetCurrentDirectory Lib "kernel32" _
        Alias "GetCurrentDirectoryA" (ByVal nBufferLength As Long, _
        ByVal lpBuffer As String) As Long
```

When the function returns, you can read the value of the *lpBuffer* argument to find out the current path.

GetWindowsDirectory()

Use this function to find where Windows is installed on the hard drive. You may need this information to install any initialization files or help files in the Windows directory. Its arguments are identical to the arguments of the GetCurrentDirectory() function, and it's declared as follows:

```
Private Declare Function GetWindowsDirectory Lib "kernel32" _
        Alias "GetWindowsDirectoryA" (ByVal lpBuffer As String, _
        ByVal nSize As Long) As Long
```

The complete listing of the Drives project is shown next.

Code 13.3:   The Drives Project

```
Option Explicit

Private Declare Function GetDriveType Lib "kernel32" _
        Alias "GetDriveTypeA" (ByVal nDrive As String) As Long
Private Declare Function GetDiskFreeSpace Lib "kernel32" _
        Alias "GetDiskFreeSpaceA" (ByVal lpRootPathName As String, _
        lpSectorsPerCluster As Long, lpBytesPerSector As Long, _
        lpNumberOfFreeClusters As Long, _
        lpTtoalNumberOfClusters As Long) As Long
Private Declare Function GetCurrentDirectory Lib "kernel32" _
        Alias "GetCurrentDirectoryA" (ByVal nBufferLength As Long, _
        ByVal lpBuffer As String) As Long
Private Declare Function GetWindowsDirectory Lib "kernel32" _
        Alias "GetWindowsDirectoryA" (ByVal lpBuffer As String, _
        ByVal nSize As Long) As Long
Const DRIVE_CDROM = 5
Const DRIVE_FIXED = 3
Const DRIVE_RAMDISK = 6
Const DRIVE_REMOTE = 4
Const DRIVE_REMOVABLE = 2

Private Sub Command1_Click()
    End
End Sub

Private Sub Drive1_Change()
Dim driveType As Long
Dim freeSpace As Long, Sectors As Long
Dim Bytes As Long
Dim freeClusters As Long, totalClusters As Long
Dim retValue As Long
Dim buffer As String * 255
Dim DName As String

    Screen.MousePointer = vbHourglass
    DoEvents
    DName = Left(Drive1.Drive, 2) & "\"
    driveType = GetDriveType(DName)
    Select Case driveType
        Case 0
            Label5.Caption = "UNDETERMINED"
        Case DRIVE_REMOVABLE
            Label5.Caption = "REMOVABLE"
        Case DRIVE_FIXED
            Label5.Caption = "FIXED"
```

```
            Case DRIVE_REMOTE
                Label5.Caption = "REMOTE"
            Case DRIVE_CDROM
                Label5.Caption = "CDROM"
            Case DRIVE_RAMDISK
                Label5.Caption = "RAMDISK"
        End Select
        'Get free space
        retValue = GetDiskFreeSpace(DName, Sectors, Bytes, _
                freeClusters, totalClusters)
        Label6.Caption = Sectors * Bytes * freeClusters
        'Get current directory
        retValue = GetCurrentDirectory(255, buffer)
        Label7.Caption = buffer
        'Get windows directory
        retValue = GetWindowsDirectory(buffer, 255)
        Label8.Caption = buffer
        Screen.MousePointer = vbDefault
        DoEvents
        Debug.Print App.Path
    End Sub

    Private Sub Form_Load()
        Drive1_Change
    End Sub
```

Other File Functions

Sometimes you want information about a file such as its path, attributes, or size. The FileInfo application on the CD (see Figure 13.3) demonstrates how to retrieve information about a file using API functions.

FIGURE 13.3:

The FileInfo application

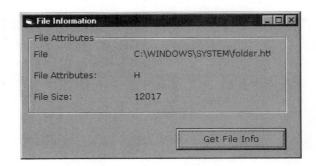

VB6 at Work: The FileInfo Project

This FileInfo application uses the following functions:

- GetFullPathName()
- GetFileAttributes()
- GetFileSize()

GetFullPathName()   This function obtains the full path name of a file, and its declaration is as follows:

```
Private Declare Function GetFullPathName Lib "kernel32" _
        Alias "GetFullPathNameA" (ByVal lpFileName As String, _
        ByVal nBufferLength As Long, ByVal lpBuffer As String, _
        ByVal lpFilePart As String) As Long
```

In the FileInfo application, the GetFullPathName()function returns the path for the file selected by the user in a standard File Open dialog box. It accepts as an argument the name of the file whose full path you want and returns the path of the filename in the *filePath* variable.

GetFileAttributes()   This function returns a flag that indicates the status of the file: read-only, hidden, normal, and so on. It's similar to the Visual Basic Get-FileAttributes() function, and its declaration is as follows:

```
Private Declare Function GetFileAttributes Lib "kernel32" Alias _
        "GetFileAttributesA" (ByVal lpFileName As String) As Long
```

Table 13.3 lists the attributes that a file can have. The FileInfo application demonstrates the use of this function.

TABLE 13.3: File Attributes

VALUE	DESCRIPTION
FILE_ATTRIBUTE_ARCHIVE	File is archived; e.g., it's marked for backup or removal
FILE_ATTRIBUTE_COMPRESSED	File is compressed
FILE_ATTRIBUTE_DIRECTORY	Name is a directory
FILE_ATTRIBUTE_HIDDEN	The file or directory is hidden; that is, you can't see it in a normal listing
FILE_ATTRIBUTE_NORMAL	File has no other attributes
FILE_ATTRIBUTE_READONLY	File is read-only
FILE_ATTRIBUTE_SYSTEM	File is part of the operating system

GetFileSize() To determine the file size, first open the file using the Create-File() function (described previously in the section "Managing Large Data Files") with the OPEN_EXISTING flag to make sure the file already exists. You can now use the GetFileSize() function to return the file size in bytes. Of course, you must close the file with the CloseHandle() function when you're done.

The complete listing of the FileInfo project is shown next.

Code 13.4:   **The FileInfo Project**

```
Option Explicit

Private Declare Function GetFileAttributes Lib "kernel32" _
        Alias "GetFileAttributesA" (ByVal lpFileName As String) As Long
Private Declare Function GetFullPathName Lib "kernel32" _
        Alias "GetFullPathNameA" ByVal lpFileName As String, _
        ByVal nBufferLength As Long, ByVal lpBuffer As String, _
        ByVal lpFilePart As String) As Long
Private Declare Function CreateFile Lib "kernel32" Alias _
        "CreateFileA" (ByVal lpFileName As String, _
        ByVal dwDesiredAccess As Long, ByVal dwShareMode As Long, _
        ByVal lpSecurityAttributes As Any, _
        ByVal dwCreationDisposition As Long, _
        ByVal dwFlagsAndAttributes As Long, _
        ByVal hTemplateFile As Long) As Long
Private Declare Function GetFileSize Lib "kernel32" _
        (ByVal hFile As Long, lpFileSizeHigh As Long) As Long
Private Declare Function CloseHandle Lib "kernel32" _
        (ByVal hObject As Long) As Long

Const FILE_ATTRIBUTE_ARCHIVE = &H20
Const FILE_ATTRIBUTE_COMPRESSED = &H800
Const FILE_ATTRIBUTE_DIRECTORY = &H10
Const FILE_ATTRIBUTE_HIDDEN = &H2
Const FILE_ATTRIBUTE_NORMAL = &H80
Const FILE_ATTRIBUTE_READONLY = &H1
Const FILE_ATTRIBUTE_SYSTEM = &H4
Const GENERIC_READ = &H80000000
Const OPEN_EXISTING = 3
Const GENERIC_WRITE = &H40000000

Private Sub Command1_Click()
Dim retValue As Long
Dim filePath As String * 255
Dim attrFlag As Long, attrStr As String
```

```
Dim fileName As String, filePointer As Long
Dim fileSize As Long

    CommonDialog1.ShowOpen
    If CommonDialog1.fileName <> "" Then fileName = CommonDialog1.fileName
    'Get full path for file name
    retValue = GetFullPathName(fileName, 255, filePath, 0)
    Label5.Caption = filePath

    'Get file attributes
    attrFlag = GetFileAttributes(fileName)

    If (attrFlag And FILE_ATTRIBUTE_ARCHIVE) Then _
            attrStr = "Archive "
    If (attrFlag And FILE_ATTRIBUTE_COMPRESSED) Then _
            attrStr = attrStr & "Compressed"
    If (attrFlag And FILE_ATTRIBUTE_DIRECTORY) Then _
            attrStr = attrStr & "Directory"
    If (attrFlag And FILE_ATTRIBUTE_HIDDEN) Then _
            attrStr = attrStr & "Hidden"
    If (attrFlag And FILE_ATTRIBUTE_NORMAL) Then _
            attrStr = attrStr & "Normal"
    If (attrFlag And FILE_ATTRIBUTE_READONLY) Then _
            attrStr = attrStr & "Read-Only"
    If (attrFlag And FILE_ATTRIBUTE_SYSTEM) Then _
            attrStr = attrStr & "System"
    Label6.Caption = attrStr

    'Get file size
    filePointer = CreateFile(fileName, GENERIC_READ Or _
                    GENERIC_WRITE, 0&, 0&, OPEN_EXISTING, _
                    FILE_ATTRIBUTE_NORMAL, 0&)
    fileSize = GetFileSize(filePointer, 0&)
    Label7.Caption = fileSize
    CloseHandle (filePointer)
End Sub
```

Forms and Windows

This section describes Win32 API functions that you can use to extend the usual Visual Basic functions to enhance your Forms, windows, and menus. Using these functions, you can create menus that incorporate bitmaps and dynamically change menu items. You'll also learn how to track the mouse and manipulate windows of other active applications on the Desktop.

Creating Menus with Bitmaps

The menus you create with Visual Basic's Menu Editor can contain text only. Some applications, however, can display images in their menus. It's possible to add bitmaps to your menus by calling several Win32 API functions. The process is time-consuming, but well worth it. The MenuBMP application (see Figure 13.4) creates a menu with bitmaps at runtime.

FIGURE 13.4:

The MenuBMP application

VB6 at Work: The MenuBMP Project

This application uses the following functions:

- GetMenu()
- GetSubMenu()
- ModifyMenu()
- CreateCompatibleDC()
- CreateCompatibleBitmap()
- SelectObject()

To manipulate menus with API functions, you must obtain the menu's handle. Menus are objects, and as such, they have a handle that identifies them to the operating system (just as Forms and bitmaps do). In effect, you can manipulate the menus of other applications that are running at the time by obtaining the handle of their menu.

To obtain a menu's handle, use the *GetMenu()* function, which is declared as follows:

```
Private Declare Function GetMenu Lib "user32" (ByVal hWnd As Long)
    As Long
```

The *hWnd* argument is the handle of the Form whose menu you want to manipulate. To obtain the handle of the current Form's menu, use the following expression:

```
MenuHandle = GetMenu(Me.hWnd)
```

First-level menus contain submenus that are identified by their order in the main menu. Submenus also have handles, which can be obtained with the *GetSubMenu()* function:

```
Private Declare Function GetSubMenu Lib "user32" _
    (ByVal hMenu As Long, ByVal nPos As Long) As Long
```

The *hMenu* argument is the menu handle returned by the GetMenu() function, and *nPos* is the position of the submenu. If *nPos* is 0, the GetSubMenu() function returns the handle of the first submenu, which quite often, is the File menu.

After you retrieve the handle of a submenu, you can modify it with the *ModifyMenu()* function, which is declared as follows:

```
Private Declare Function ModifyMenu Lib "user32" Alias _
            "ModifyMenuA" (ByVal hMenu As Long, ByVal nPosition As Long, _
            ByVal wFlags As Long, ByVal wIDNewItem As Long, _
            ByVal lpString As Any) As Long
```

This function can change a menu entry, and it requires some explanation. The *hMenu* argument is the handle of the submenu retrieved by the GetSubMenu() function. The *nPosition* argument identifies the menu item to be changed. If the MF_BYCOMMAND flag in the *wFlags* argument is set, this argument refers to the ID of the command to be changed. If the MF_BYPOSITION flag is set, this argument specifies the position of the item in the submenu. The *wFlags* argument is a combination of flags, described in Table 13.4.

TABLE 13.4: Menu Flags

VALUE	DESCRIPTION
MF_BITMAP	Specifies that a menu item is a bitmap; the bitmap should remain in memory while it's used in the menu
MF_BYCOMMAND	Specifies the menu entry by the command ID of the menu
MF_BYPOSITION	Specifies the menu entry by its position in the submenu; the position of the first item is zero
MF_CHECKED	Displays a checkmark next to the specified menu item
MF_DISABLED	Disables the specified menu item

Continued on next page

TABLE 13.4 CONTINUED: Menu Flags

VALUE	DESCRIPTION
MF_ENABLED	Enables the specified menu item
MF_GRAYED	Disables the specified menu item and draws it in gray (instead of making it invisible)
MF_MENUBARBREAK	Places the specified item on a new column with a vertical bar, which separates the columns
MF_MENUBREAK	Places the specified item on a new column
MF_POPUP	Places a pop-up menu at the specified item location
MF_SEPARATOR	Places a separator line at the specified item's location
MF_STRING	Places a string at the specified item location
MF_UNCHECKED	Clears the checkmark in front of the specified item (if it is checked)

To assign a bitmap to a menu item, you set the MF_BITMAP flag in the *wFlags* argument of the ModifyMenu() function. Modifying the menu is relatively simple, but specifying the bitmap to be assigned in the place of the item's caption isn't. First, you must create a device context (a memory area where a bitmap can be stored) with the *CreateCompatibleDC()* function. The bitmap comes from an image (a BMP file) that is first loaded onto a hidden PictureBox control. The bitmap on the hidden PictureBox control is copied to the device context with the *CreateCompatibleBitmap()* function. When the bitmap is selected into the device context, you can assign it to a menu item, as if it was a string. Code 13.5 shows how the bitmaps are added to the menu of the MenuBMP application.

Notice that the bitmap's dimensions must be passed as arguments to the Create-CompatibleBitmap() function. When you design the bitmap with an image processing application, you must size the bitmap so that it will fit nicely in the menu. Don't make the bitmaps too long or too narrow. The bitmaps used in this section's examples were designed with the Paint Shop Pro application. You can use any image processing application to design bitmaps for your menus, including ImageEdit, which can be found in the Tools folder on the Visual Basic CD.

The Bitmaps menu of the MenuBMP application contains three commands, which correspond to three different fonts, as you can see in Figure 13.4. The three bitmaps are stored in the Verdana.bmp, Serif.bmp, and Comic.bmp files, in the same folder as the application. After the bitmaps have been designed, you can start coding the application. The MenuBMP application's complete listing is shown next.

Code 13.5:   **The MenuBMP Application**

```vb
Option Explicit

Private Declare Function GetMenu Lib "user32" _
        (ByVal hwnd As Long) As Long
Private Declare Function GetSubMenu Lib "user32" _
        (ByVal hMenu As Long, ByVal nPos As Long) As Long
Private Declare Function GetMenuItemID Lib "user32" _
        (ByVal hMenu As Long, ByVal nPos As Long) As Long
Private Declare Function ModifyMenu Lib "user32" _
        Alias "ModifyMenuA" (ByVal hMenu As Long, _
        ByVal nPosition As Long, ByVal wFlags As Long, _
        ByVal wIDNewItem As Long, ByVal lpString As Any) As Long
Private Declare Function CreateCompatibleDC Lib "gdi32" _
        (ByVal hdc As Long) As Long
Private Declare Function CreateCompatibleBitmap Lib "gdi32" _
        (ByVal hdc As Long, ByVal nWidth As Long, _
        ByVal nHeight As Long) As Long
Private Declare Function SelectObject Lib "gdi32" _
        (ByVal hdc As Long, ByVal hObject As Long) As Long
Private Declare Function BitBlt Lib "gdi32" _
        (ByVal hDestDC As Long, ByVal x As Long, ByVal y As Long, _
        ByVal nWidth As Long, ByVal nHeight As Long, _
        ByVal hSrcDC As Long, ByVal xSrc As Long, _
        ByVal ySrc As Long, ByVal dwRop As Long) As Long
Private Declare Function DeleteDC Lib "gdi32" _
        (ByVal hdc As Long) As Long

Const SRCCOPY = &HCC0020
Const MF_BYPOSITION = &H400&
Const MF_BITMAP = &H4&

Private Sub Form_Load()
Dim Width As Integer, Height As Integer
Dim hTmpDC As Long, hMenuID As Long
Dim hBitmap As Long, retValue As Long
Dim tmpID As Long
Dim fileName As String
Dim menuPos As Integer, menuID As Long

    'Set menu position and file name
    menuPos = 0
    fileName = App.Path & "\verdana.bmp"
```

```
Picture1.Picture = LoadPicture(fileName)
Width = 64
Height = 16
'Get handle to menu
hMenuID = GetSubMenu(GetMenu(Me.hwnd), menuPos)
'Create device context to store bitmap
hTmpDC = CreateCompatibleDC(Picture1.hdc)
'Create the bitmap for the picture
hBitmap = CreateCompatibleBitmap(Picture1.hdc, Width, Height)
'Select bitmap into temporary dc
tmpID = SelectObject(hTmpDC, hBitmap)
'Copy contents from picture control to DC
retValue = BitBlt(hTmpDC, 0, 0, Width, Height, _
        Picture1.hdc, 0, 0, SRCCOPY)
'Deselect bitmap
tmpID = SelectObject(hTmpDC, tmpID)
'Modify the menu
menuID = GetMenuItemID(hMenuID, menuPos)
retValue = ModifyMenu(hMenuID, menuPos, _
        MF_BYPOSITION Or MF_BITMAP, menuID, hBitmap)
'Second menu item
menuPos = 1
fileName = App.Path & "\serif.bmp"
Picture1.Picture = LoadPicture(fileName)
'Create the bitmap for the picture
hBitmap = CreateCompatibleBitmap(Picture1.hdc, Width, Height)
'Select bitmap into temporary dc
tmpID = SelectObject(hTmpDC, hBitmap)
retValue = BitBlt(hTmpDC, 0, 0, Width, Height, _
        Picture1.hdc, 0, 0, SRCCOPY)
tmpID = SelectObject(hTmpDC, tmpID)
menuID = GetMenuItemID(hMenuID, menuPos)
retValue = ModifyMenu(hMenuID, menuPos, _
        MF_BYPOSITION Or MF_BITMAP, menuID, hBitmap)
'Third menu item
menuPos = 2
fileName = App.Path & "\comic.bmp"
Picture1.Picture = LoadPicture(fileName)
'Create the bitmap for the picture
hBitmap = CreateCompatibleBitmap(Picture1.hdc, Width, Height)
'Select bitmap into temporary dc
tmpID = SelectObject(hTmpDC, hBitmap)
retValue = BitBlt(hTmpDC, 0, 0, Width, Height, _
        Picture1.hdc, 0, 0, SRCCOPY)
```

```
        tmpID = SelectObject(hTmpDC, tmpID)
        menuID = GetMenuItemID(hMenuID, menuPos)
        retValue = ModifyMenu(hMenuID, menuPos, _
                   MF_BYPOSITION Or MF_BITMAP, menuID, hBitmap)
        'Clean up
        retValue = DeleteDC(hTmpDC)
End Sub

Private Sub MyMenu_Click(Index As Integer)
Dim fName(3) As String
fName(0) = "Verdana"
fName(1) = "Serif"
fName(2) = "Comic Sans MS"
    Me.Cls
    Me.CurrentX = (Me.ScaleWidth - TextWidth(fName(Index))) / 2
    Me.CurrentY = (Me.ScaleHeight - TextHeight(fName(Index))) / 2
    Me.Font.Name = fName(Index)
    Me.Print fName(Index)
End Sub
```

Changing Menus at Runtime

At times, you'll want to change the menus dynamically. The MenuMod application, which is based on the MenuBMP application, shows how this can be done.

VB6 at Work: The MenuMod Project

The MenuMod application lets you switch the menu items from bitmaps to text and back. The application has the same menu as the MenuBMP application, plus a third item, whose caption is Display Graphics (when the menu displays text) or Display Text (when the menu displays graphics). The Click event handler for this menu item calls the *DisplayTextMenu()* or *DisplayBitmapMenu()* function to switch the menu between text and graphics. In the ModifyMenu() procedure, you use the MF_STRING flag to change the menu item to text, and you use the MF_BITMAP flag to change the menu item to graphics.

Code 13.6:   **The MenuMod Application**

```
Option Explicit
Private Declare Function GetMenu Lib "user32" _
       (ByVal hwnd As Long) As Long
Private Declare Function GetSubMenu Lib "user32" _
```

```
                    (ByVal hMenu As Long, ByVal nPos As Long) As Long
        Private Declare Function GetMenuItemID Lib "user32" _
            (ByVal hMenu As Long, ByVal nPos As Long) As Long
        Private Declare Function ModifyMenu Lib "user32" _
            Alias "ModifyMenuA" (ByVal hMenu As Long, _
            ByVal nPosition As Long, ByVal wFlags As Long, _
            ByVal wIDNewItem As Long, ByVal lpString As Any) As Long
        Private Declare Function CreateCompatibleDC Lib "gdi32" _
            (ByVal hdc As Long) As Long
        Private Declare Function CreateCompatibleBitmap Lib "gdi32" _
            (ByVal hdc As Long, ByVal nWidth As Long, _
            ByVal nHeight As Long) As Long
        Private Declare Function SelectObject Lib "gdi32" _
            (ByVal hdc As Long, ByVal hObject As Long) As Long
        Private Declare Function BitBlt Lib "gdi32" _
            (ByVal hDestDC As Long, ByVal x As Long, ByVal y As Long, _
            ByVal nWidth As Long, ByVal nHeight As Long, _
            ByVal hSrcDC As Long, ByVal xSrc As Long, _
            ByVal ySrc As Long, ByVal dwRop As Long) As Long
        Private Declare Function DeleteDC Lib "gdi32" (ByVal hdc As Long) As Long

        Const MF_STRING = &H0&
        Const SRCCOPY = &HCC0020
        Const MF_BYPOSITION = &H400&
        Const MF_BITMAP = &H4&

        Private Sub Exit_Click()
            Unload Me
        End Sub

        Private Sub Form_Load()
            Call DisplayBitmapMenu
        End Sub

        Private Sub Graphics_Click()
            'Display text
            If Graphics.Checked Then
                Graphics.Checked = False
                Call DisplayTextMenu
            Else
                Graphics.Checked = True
                Call DisplayBitmapMenu
            End If
        End Sub
```

```vb
Private Sub MyMenu_Click(Index As Integer)
    Me.Cls
    Me.Font.Name = MyMenu(Index).Caption
    Me.CurrentX = (Me.ScaleWidth - _
                Me.TextWidth(MyMenu(Index).Caption)) / 2
    Me.CurrentY = (Me.ScaleHeight - _
                Me.TextHeight(MyMenu(Index).Caption)) / 2
    Me.Print MyMenu(Index).Caption
End Sub


Private Sub DisplayTextMenu()
Dim hMenuID As Long, menuID As Long
Dim menuPos As Integer
Dim retValue As Long

    'Get handle to menu
    hMenuID = GetSubMenu(GetMenu(Me.hwnd), 0)
    menuPos = 0
    menuID = GetMenuItemID(hMenuID, menuPos)
    retValue = ModifyMenu(hMenuID, menuPos, _
                MF_BYPOSITION Or MF_STRING, menuID, "Verdana")
    menuPos = 1
    menuID = GetMenuItemID(hMenuID, menuPos)
    retValue = ModifyMenu(hMenuID, menuPos, _
                MF_BYPOSITION Or MF_STRING, menuID, "Serif")

    menuPos = 2
    menuID = GetMenuItemID(hMenuID, menuPos)
    retValue = ModifyMenu(hMenuID, menuPos, _
                MF_BYPOSITION Or MF_STRING, menuID, "Comic Sans")
End Sub


Private Sub DisplayBitmapMenu()
Dim Width As Integer, Height As Integer
Dim hTmpDC As Long, hMenuID As Long
Dim hBitmap As Long
Dim retValue As Long
Dim tmpID As Long
Dim fileName As String
Dim menuPos As Integer, menuID As Long

    'Set menu position and file name
    menuPos = 0
    fileName = App.Path & "\verdana.bmp"
```

```
Picture1.Picture = LoadPicture(fileName)
Width = 64
Height = 16
'Get handle to menu
hMenuID = GetSubMenu(GetMenu(Me.hwnd), menuPos)
'Create device context to store bitmap
hTmpDC = CreateCompatibleDC(Picture1.hdc)
'Create the bitmap for the picture
hBitmap = CreateCompatibleBitmap(Picture1.hdc, Width, Height)
'Select bitmap into temporary dc
tmpID = SelectObject(hTmpDC, hBitmap)
'Copy contents from picture control to DC
retValue = BitBlt(hTmpDC, 0, 0, Width, Height, _
            Picture1.hdc, 0, 0, SRCCOPY)
  'Deselect bitmap
tmpID = SelectObject(hTmpDC, tmpID)
  'Modify the menu
menuID = GetMenuItemID(hMenuID, menuPos)
retValue = ModifyMenu(hMenuID, menuPos, _
            MF_BYPOSITION Or MF_BITMAP, menuID, hBitmap)
' Second menu item
menuPos = 1
fileName = App.Path & "\serif.bmp"
Picture1.Picture = LoadPicture(fileName)
' Create the bitmap for the picture
hBitmap = CreateCompatibleBitmap(Picture1.hdc, Width, Height)
'Select bitmap into temporary dc
tmpID = SelectObject(hTmpDC, hBitmap)
retValue = BitBlt(hTmpDC, 0, 0, Width, Height, _
            Picture1.hdc, 0, 0, SRCCOPY)
tmpID = SelectObject(hTmpDC, tmpID)
menuID = GetMenuItemID(hMenuID, menuPos)
retValue = ModifyMenu(hMenuID, menuPos, _
            MF_BYPOSITION Or MF_BITMAP, menuID, hBitmap)
' Third menu item
menuPos = 2
fileName = App.Path & "\comic.bmp"
Picture1.Picture = LoadPicture(fileName)
'Create the bitmap for the picture
hBitmap = CreateCompatibleBitmap(Picture1.hdc, Width, Height)
'Select bitmap into temporary dc
tmpID = SelectObject(hTmpDC, hBitmap)
retValue = BitBlt(hTmpDC, 0, 0, Width, Height, _
            Picture1.hdc, 0, 0, SRCCOPY)
```

```
        tmpID = SelectObject(hTmpDC, tmpID)
        menuID = GetMenuItemID(hMenuID, menuPos)
        retValue = ModifyMenu(hMenuID, menuPos, _
                    MF_BYPOSITION Or MF_BITMAP, menuID, hBitmap)

        'Clean up
        retValue = DeleteDC(hTmpDC)
    End Sub
```

Detecting Mouse Movements

A common event in programming with Visual Basic is the MouseMove event, which lets you monitor the movement of the mouse. The MouseMove event reports the coordinates of the mouse as it moves on a Form. In some situations, we want to monitor the coordinates of the point from within the Click or DblClick events (which don't report where the mouse was clicked) or even monitor the movement of the mouse outside a Form. To find out the location of the mouse at any time, use the GetCursorPos() function, which has the following syntax:

```
Private Declare Function GetCursorPos Lib "user32" _
        (lpPoint As POINTAPI) As Long
```

> **NOTE**
>
> The arguments of the GetCursorPos() function were discussed in the section "Declaring 32-Bit Functions and Structures," earlier in this chapter.

VB6 at Work: The MouseMov Project

The MouseMov application (shown in Figure 13.5) uses an endless loop to track the mouse, but also releases control to Windows with the DoEvents statement. This allows Windows to process other events such as ending the program when the user clicks the Stop button. Without the DoEvents statement, we would not be able to stop the program.

The GetCursorPos() function returns a POINTAPI variable, which you can pass to the *WindowFromPoint()* function to get the handle of the window under the pointer. Once you've obtained the window handle, you can find out the class name of the window with the *GetClassName()* function, which returns the name of the window's class. If the name is SysListView32, the mouse is over the Windows Desktop. Otherwise, the mouse is over some other window.

FIGURE 13.5:

The MouseMov application tracks the mouse location, even outside the application's Form.

The main portion of the code is the tracking loop. The code gets the current mouse position and uses this information to get the window handle and the class name. The class name is then displayed and updated each time the mouse moves over a new window.

Code 13.7: **The MouseMov Application**

```
Option Explicit

Private Declare Function GetCursorPos Lib "user32" _
        (lpPoint As POINTAPI) As Long
Private Declare Function WindowFromPoint Lib "user32" _
        (ByVal xPoint As Long, ByVal yPoint As Long) As Long
Private Declare Function GetClassName Lib "user32" Alias _
        "GetClassNameA" (ByVal hwnd As Long, _
        ByVal lpClassName As String, ByVal nMaxCount As Long) As Long
Private Type POINTAPI
    X As Long
    Y As Long
End Type
Private gStop As Boolean

Private Sub Command1_Click()
Dim mousePT As POINTAPI
Dim prevWindow As Long, curWindow As Long
Dim X As Long, Y As Long
Dim className As String
Dim retValue As Long

    'Track mouse here
    If Command1.Caption = "Start" Then
      Command1.Caption = "Stop"
      gStop = False
      prevWindow = 0
```

```
            'Track until user stops
            Do
              'Stop tracking
              If gStop = True Then Exit Do
              Call GetCursorPos(mousePT)
              X = mousePT.X
              Y = mousePT.Y
              'Get window under mouse
              curWindow = WindowFromPoint(X, Y)
              If curWindow <> prevWindow Then
                className = String$(256, " ")
                prevWindow = curWindow
                retValue = GetClassName(curWindow, className, 255)
                className = Left$(className, InStr(className, vbNullChar) - 1)
                If className = "SysListView32" Then
                  Label1.Caption = "The mouse is over the desktop."
                Else
                  Label1.Caption = "The mouse is over " & className
                End If
              End If
              DoEvents
            Loop
          'Stop tracking the mouse
          Else
            Command1.Caption = "Start"
            gStop = True
          End If
      End Sub

      Private Sub Form_QueryUnload(Cancel As Integer, _
                 UnloadMode As Integer)
        gStop = True
      End Sub
```

A related project is the previously discussed MousePos project, which you'll find in this chapter's folder on the CD.

Using the HitTest Method

Many controls have a *HitTest* method whose function is to retrieve an object at a specific pair of coordinates. We used this method in the LVWDemo project in Chapter 8, but now it's time to look at this method and see how it's used with the GetCursorPos() function.

The HitTest method applies only to a few controls that can act as containers for multiple objects. The ListView control, for example, can host many ListItem objects. When the user double-clicks the ListView control, the *DblClick* event is triggered, but this event doesn't report where the mouse was clicked. To find out which item was double-clicked, use the GetCursorPos()function to retrieve the pointer's coordinates and pass them to the control's HitTest method, which will return a reference to the object at this location.

Let's return to the LVWDemo project and look at the ListView control's Dbl-Click event handler. The ListView control is populated with company names and related data. When these items are displayed as icons, as shown in Figure 13.6, we should be able to detect the item that was clicked or double-clicked. The single click is reported by the *ItemClick* event, which reports the clicked item. The declaration of the ItemClick event handler is:

```
Private Sub ListView1_ItemClick(ByVal Item As ComctlLib.ListItem)
```

However, there's no ItemDblClick event and the declaration of the DblClick event is simply:

```
Private Sub ListView1_DblClick()
```

FIGURE 13.6:

The LVWDemo demonstrates how to use the GetCursor-Pos() function to retrieve the item that has been clicked or double-clicked in a ListView control.

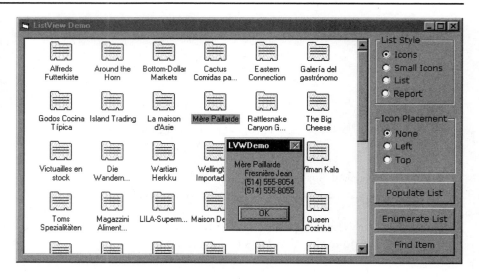

Even though the DblClick event doesn't report the double-clicked item, it's quite common in programming the ListView control to provide code that reacts to the double-clicking of an item. Applications can indirectly detect the double-clicked item with the help of the GetCursorPos()function and the HitTest method. To detect the coordinates of the point where the mouse was double-clicked, follow the steps presented next.

First, declare the GetCursorPos() function and the POINTAPI data structure in a Module as:

```
Type POINTAPI
    x As Long
    y As Long
End Type
Declare Function GetCursorPos Lib "user32" Alias "GetCursorPos" _
            (lpPoint As POINTAPI) As Long
```

In the DblClick event handler, call the GetCursorPos() function to find out the coordinates of the pointer where the button was double-clicked:

```
GetCursorPos dPoint
```

The members of the *dPoint* variable are the X and Y coordinates of the mouse pointer in pixels. They are screen coordinates. In other words, if you call the Get-CursorPos() event from within the ListView control's DblClick event, it will report a pair of coordinates. If you move the Form to another location on screen and then double-click the same icon, the coordinates will be drastically different. Therefore, we must map the screen coordinates to the control coordinates. To do so, we must subtract the Left and Top properties of the control and the Form from the values of the coordinates returned by the GetCursorPos() function. We need two statements like the following ones:

```
X = dPoint.X - Me.Left - ListView1.Left
Y = dPoint.Y - Me.Top - ListView1.Top
```

These statements are not quite right because the coordinates *dPoint.X* and *dPoint.Y* are expressed in pixels and the other coordinates are expressed in twips. Before subtracting them, we must convert them to pixels with the ScaleX and ScaleY methods. Here are the statements that map the screen coordinates to the internal coordinates of the ListView control:

```
X = dPoint.X - ScaleX(Me.Left + ListView1.Left, vbTwips, vbPixels)
Y = dPoint.Y - ScaleY(Me.Top + ListView1.Top, vbTwips, vbPixels)
```

X and *Y* are the coordinates of the pointer in pixels the moment it was double-clicked. The coordinates (0, 0) correspond to the control's upper-left corner. The variables *X* and *Y* must be passed to the HitTest method, which will return a reference to the double-clicked item. However, the HitTest method requires that the coordinates be specified in twips. The HitTest method is called as follows:

```
Set LItem = ListView1.HitTest(ScaleX(X, vbPixels, vbTwips), _
            ScaleY(Y, vbPixels, vbTwips))
```

The variables *X* and *Y* are first converted to twips, then passed to the HitTest method. The method returns a reference to the double-clicked item, which is stored in the *LItem* variable. The *LItem* variable must be declared as ListItem:

```
Dim LItem As ListItem
```

Using the *LItem* variable, you can access the properties of the double-clicked item. For example, you can highlight it from within your code with the following statement:

```
LItem.Selected = True
```

or read its subitems through the collection:

```
LItem.ListSubItems
```

If the mouse double-clicked an empty area of the ListView control rather than an item, the *LItem* variable will be Nothing. If you attempt to access its properties, a runtime error will be generated. To avoid the runtime error, use the *On Error Resume Next* statement and examine the value of the *LItem* variable.

```
On Error Resume Next
Set LItem = ListView1.HitTest(ScaleX(X, vbPixels, vbTwips), _
            ScaleY(Y, vbPixels, vbTwips))
If LItem Is Nothing Then Exit Sub
{statements to access the LItem's properties}
```

Here's the complete listing of the ListView control's DblClick event handler. If you open the LVWDemo project, you'll see that it's adequately documented. You can reuse this code as is (without the statements that process the *LItem* variable's members, of course) in your code to react to the double-click event on a ListView control.

Code 13.8:   **The ListView Control's DblClick Event Handler**

```
Private Sub ListView1_DblClick()
Dim dPoint As POINTAPI
Dim LItem As ListItem

    GetCursorPos dPoint
    X = dPoint.X - ScaleX(Me.Left + ListView1.Left, vbTwips, vbPixels)
    Y = dPoint.Y - ScaleY(Me.Top + ListView1.Top, vbTwips, vbPixels)
On Error Resume Next
    Set LItem = ListView1.HitTest(ScaleX(X, vbPixels, vbTwips), _
                ScaleY(Y, vbPixels, vbTwips))
    If LItem Is Nothing Then Exit Sub
```

```
        If ListView1.View = lvwIcon Or ListView1.View = lvwSmallIcon Then
            LItem.Selected = True
            msg = LItem.Text & vbCrLf
            For i = 1 To LItem.ListSubItems.Count
                msg = msg & "        " & LItem.ListSubItems(i).Text & vbCrLf
            Next
            MsgBox msg
        End If
    End Sub
```

This is not the only use of the HitTest method or even the most common one. However, it's not a trivial one and that's why I presented it in detail. The HitTest method was designed to be used primarily with the DragDrop event. The DragDrop event reports the coordinates of the point where an object is dropped. If the destination of the drag-and-drop operation is a ListView or TreeView control, we usually want to know the item on which the source object was dropped. The declaration of the DragDrop event is:

```
Private Sub TreeView1_DragDrop(Source As Control, x As Single, y As Single)
```

Since the coordinates of the point where the object was dropped are known, you can pass them to the HitTest method to find out on which item the source object was dropped. Notice that you need not convert or adjust the coordinates, since the DragDrop event reports them in the control's internal coordinate system in twips.

Keeping a Window on Top

You've often seen applications that keep a window on top regardless of whether the window is active. Microsoft Word does this with its Find window. This is done with a single call to the *SetWindowPos()* API function, which is declared as follows:

```
Private Declare Function SetWindowPos Lib "user32" _
        (ByVal hwnd As Long, ByVal hWndInsertAfter As Long, _
        ByVal x As Long, ByVal y As Long, _
        ByVal cx As Long, ByVal cy As Long, _
        ByVal wFlags As Long) As Long
```

The *hWnd* argument is the handle of the window, *x* and *y* are the coordinates of the window's upper-left corner, and *cx* and *cy* are the window's width and height. The *hWndInsertAfter* argument is the handle of a window, after which the hWnd window is in the window list. It can also be one of the values shown in Table 13.5.

TABLE 13.5: Values of the *hWnd* Argument

VALUE	WHERE WINDOW IS PLACED
HWND_BOTTOM	At the bottom of the window list
HWND_TOP	At the top of the z order
HWND_TOPMOST	At the top of the window list
HWND_NOTOPMOST	At the top of the window list, behind any topmost window

The *wFlags* argument is an integer that contains one or more of the flags shown in Table 13.6.

TABLE 13.6: Flags of the *wFlags* Argument

FLAG	WHAT IT DOES
SWP_DRAWFRAME	Draws a frame around the window
SWP_HIDEWINDOW	Hides the window
SWP_NOACTIVATE	Does not activate the window
SWP_NOMOVE	Retains the window's current position (the *x* and *y* arguments are ignored)
SWP_NOREDRAW	Does not automatically redraw the window
SWP_NOSIZE	Retains the window's current size
SWP_NOZORDER	Retains window's current position in the window list
SWP_SHOWWINDOW	Displays the window

TIP

You can copy the values of the constants from the API Viewer's window into your application. You should avoid hardcoding constant values in your code.

The sample application that demonstrates the SetWindowPos() function is called WinTop, and its listing is shown next.

Code 13.9:   The WinTop Application

```
Option Explicit

Private Declare Function SetWindowPos Lib "user32" _
        (ByVal hwnd As Long, ByVal hWndInsertAfter As Long, _
        ByVal x As Long, ByVal y As Long, _
        ByVal cx As Long, ByVal cy As Long, _
        ByVal wFlags As Long) As Long

Const HWND_TOPMOST = -1
Const SWP_SHOWWINDOW = &H40

Private Sub Form_Load()
Dim retValue As Long

    retValue = SetWindowPos(Me.hwnd, HWND_TOPMOST, _
            Me.CurrentX, Me.CurrentY, 300, 300, SWP_SHOWWINDOW)
End Sub
```

You can use this technique to create the Search & Replace window of the RTFPad project (see Chapter 9, *More Advanced ActiveX Controls*). This window remains on top and visible even when the user switches to the editor's Form (see Figure 13.7). All you've to do in order to always keep the Search & Replace window on top is to insert the declaration of the SetWindowPos() function and a couple of constants in a Module:

```
Public Declare Function SetWindowPos Lib "user32" _
    (ByVal HWND As Long, ByVal hWndInsertAfter As Long, _
    ByVal x As Long, ByVal y As Long, ByVal cx As Long, _
    ByVal cy As Long, ByVal wFlags As Long) As Long
Public Const HWND_TOPMOST = -1
Public Const SWP_SHOWWINDOW = &H40
```

Also, change the code of the Find menu command's event handler. The line:

```
SearchForm.Show
```

must be replaced by the following statement:

```
SetWindowPos SearchForm.hwnd, HWND_TOPMOST, _
        Me.CurrentX, Me.CurrentY, 470, 155, SWP_SHOWWINDOW
```

The values 470 and 155, which are hardcoded into the listing, are the dimensions of the Search & Replace window in pixels. The BorderStyle property of the Search-Form must also be set to Fixed, so that users can't resize it.

FIGURE 13.7:

The Search & Replace dialog box remains visible, even when another Form is active (as indicated by its title bar color).

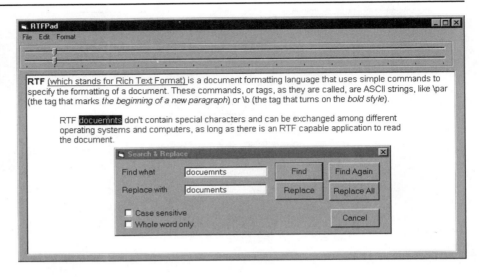

Accessing the System

The API functions described in this section let you look at other running applications from within your Visual Basic application and obtain information about an application and even its parent window.

Querying Other Applications

To query an application, you must be able to tell your program which application to query. One way to do this is to place the mouse pointer over the other application's window. This is how the Query application (see Figure 13.8) works. This application demonstrates how to spy on other active applications and it uses the GetCursorPos() and SetWindowPos() functions, as well as a number of new functions which are discussed in the following section.

VB6 at Work: The Query Project

The window of the Query application displays information about the current active window and retrieves information about its parent window.

FIGURE 13.8:

The Query application

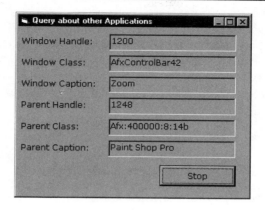

This program uses the following functions to retrieve information about any other window that happens to be open:

- SetWindowPos()
- GetCursorPos()
- WindowFromPoint()
- GetClassName()
- GetWindowText()
- GetParent()

SetWindowPos()   The program keeps the window on top of other applications with the SetWindowPos() function call. The key element is the HWND_TOPMOST flag, which tells Windows to keep a particular window on top of the Z order. You track the mouse to see which window the mouse is over and obtain information about the window. This is accomplished with the GetCursorPos() and the WindowFromPoint() functions.

GetCursorPos(), WindowFromPoint()   The GetCursorPos() function returns the screen coordinates of the mouse pointer. These coordinates are then used by the WindowFromPoint() function to retrieve the name of the window that is visible at the pointer's coordinates. The declaration of the WindowFromPoint() function is:

```
Declare Function WindowFromPoint Lib "user32" (ByVal xPoint As _
        Long, ByVal yPoint As Long) As Long
```

The arguments *xPoint* and *yPoint* are a pair of coordinates. The function returns a Long Integer, which is the handle of the window at the specified location (the window that would be brought on top of the Z order if the user clicked the specific point).

GetClassName(), GetWindowText To spy on other applications, you can use the GetClassName() and GetWindowText() functions. The GetClassName() function obtains a window's class name, and the GetWindowText() function retrieves the window's title bar if there is one. If the window is a control, the text of the control is returned.

GetParent() This function gets the window's parent window.

The complete listing of the Query application follows.

Code 13.10: **The Query Application**

```
Option Explicit

Private Declare Function SetWindowPos Lib "user32"
        (ByVal hwnd As Long, ByVal hWndInsertAfter As Long, _
         ByVal X As Long, ByVal Y As Long, ByVal cx As Long, _
         ByVal cy As Long, ByVal wFlags As Long) As Long
Private Declare Function GetCursorPos Lib "user32" _
        (lpPoint As POINTAPI) As Long
Private Declare Function WindowFromPoint Lib "user32" _
        (ByVal xPoint As Long, ByVal yPoint As Long) As Long
Private Declare Function GetParent Lib "user32" _
        (ByVal hwnd As Long) As Long
Private Declare Function GetClassName Lib "user32" _
        Alias "GetClassNameA" (ByVal hwnd As Long, _
        ByVal lpClassName As String, ByVal nMaxCount As Long) As Long
Private Declare Function GetWindowText Lib "user32" _
        Alias "GetWindowTextA" (ByVal hwnd As Long, _
        ByVal lpString As String, ByVal cch As Long) As Long

Const HWND_TOPMOST = -1
Const SWP_SHOWWINDOW = &H40

Private Type POINTAPI
    X As Long
    Y As Long
End Type

Private gStop As Boolean
```

```vb
Private Sub Command1_Click()
Dim mousePT As POINTAPI
Dim prevWindow As Long, curWindow As Long
Dim X As Long, Y As Long
Dim tmpStr As String
Dim parentWnd As Long, retValue As Long

  ' Start tracking the mouse here
  If Command1.Caption = "Start" Then
    Command1.Caption = "Stop"
    gStop = False
    prevWindow = 0
    'Track until user stops
    Do
      'Stop tracking
      If gStop = True Then Exit Do
      Call GetCursorPos(mousePT)
      X = mousePT.X
      Y = mousePT.Y
      'Get window under mouse
      curWindow = WindowFromPoint(X, Y)
      If curWindow <> prevWindow Then
        tmpStr = String$(256, " ")
        prevWindow = curWindow
        retValue = GetClassName(curWindow, tmpStr, 255)
        tmpStr = Left$(tmpStr, InStr(tmpStr, vbNullChar) - 1)
        Text1(0).Text = curWindow
        Text1(1).Text = tmpStr
        retValue = GetWindowText(curWindow, tmpStr, 255)
        Text1(2).Text = tmpStr
        'Get parent window
        parentWnd = GetParent(curWindow)
        retValue = GetClassName(parentWnd, tmpStr, 255)
        tmpStr = Left$(tmpStr, InStr(tmpStr, vbNullChar) - 1)
        Text1(3).Text = parentWnd
        Text1(4).Text = tmpStr
        retValue = GetWindowText(parentWnd, tmpStr, 255)
        Text1(5).Text = tmpStr
      End If
      DoEvents
    Loop
  'Stop tracking the mouse
  Else
    Command1.Caption = "Start"
```

```
        gStop = True
    End If
End Sub

Private Sub Form_QueryUnload(Cancel As Integer, _
        UnloadMode As Integer)
    gStop = True
End Sub

Private Sub Form_Load()
Dim retValue As Long

    If Command1.Caption = "Start" Then
        gStop = False
        'Command1.Caption = "Stop"
        retValue = SetWindowPos(Me.hwnd, HWND_TOPMOST, _
                Me.CurrentX, Me.CurrentY, _
                Me.Width, Me.Height, SWP_SHOWWINDOW)
    Else
        gStop = True
        Command1.Caption = "Start"
    End If
End Sub
```

Registry Functions

The Windows 95/98 Registry is a hierarchical database of settings used by Windows that includes information on users, system hardware configuration, and application programs. The Registry system replaces the old INI files, where applications used to store information between sessions, used in previous versions of Windows.

You access the Registry using a program called Regedit. To run Regedit, follow these steps:

1. Choose Start ➢ Run.

2. In the Run window, type **regedit** and press Enter to open the Registry Editor window shown in Figure 13.9.

FIGURE 13.9:

The main Registry Editor
window

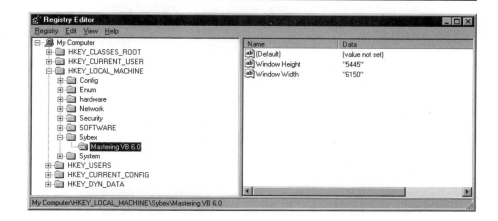

As you can see, if you double-click one of the items in the main Registry Editor
window, the Registry stores data in a TreeView structure. The first item is usually
referred to as the *Registry key*, and subsequent items are referred to as *subkeys*. The
Registry keys are predefined to organize the data as follows:

- **HKEY_CLASSES_ROOT** holds OLE information about applications that
  have been installed or documents with particular filename extensions, such
  as TXT or DOC. In addition, it maintains the list of programs that can handle
  each file type.

- **HKEY_CURRENT_USER** describes settings and configuration information
  about the user currently logged on to the computer.

- **HKEY_LOCAL_MACHINE** contains the settings for the hardware installed
  on the computer. The following are its subkeys:

  - **HKEY_USERS** contains profiles for all users who can log on to the
    machine. If only one person uses the machine, this key contains only
    the .Default subkey.

  - **HKEY_CURRENT_CONFIG** contains font and printer information.

  - **HKEY_DYN_DATA** contains dynamic information that should be read
    into the system's RAM, because it has to be readily available to the
    operating system.

WARNING
If you're not familiar with the Registry, you should not fool around with it. Ruining a few items in the Registry is a sure way to crash your machine. You can even disable the operating system. Before you manipulate any keys from within your Visual Basic applications, be sure to back up the files SYSTEM.DAT and USER.DAT. This is where the Registry information is stored, and should anything go wrong with your code, you can always restore the original contents of the Registry. If you're not familiar with the Registry, you should consult the Windows documentation on Registry back-up and restore procedures. Even better, you should start with the Visual Basic's Registry functions, which are quite safe to use, and they are described in Appendix A on this book's CD. Once you've familiarized yourself with the Registry, you can use the API functions of this chapter.

You can browse the Registry Editor to find out the type of information stored by other applications. It's relatively safe to use the Registry to store information about your application. For example, you can store initialization information about an application in the Registry so that the next time it's run, it looks up the settings of the previous execution. The list of most recently opened files, which you'll find in nearly every Windows application, is stored in the Registry. As you manipulate the Registry, be sure you don't touch other applications' entries. Manipulate only your own application's entries.

The topic of manipulating the Registry can get quite messy. In this section, I'll show you how to create a new branch in the Registry and store the information from within your application (which will presumably read this information back the next time it's executed). It's a simple example, but this is what most developers will use the Registry for.

VB6 at Work: The Registry Project

The Registry application (see Figure 13.10) demonstrates how to create keys, store values, and get Registry data. It creates three subkeys under the HKEY_LOCAL_ MACHINE key, where it stores the dimensions of the Form from the last time it was executed:

- \Sybex\Mastering VB 6.0
- Window Width
- Window Height

The program uses the Window Width and Window Height subkeys to store and retrieve the window width and height (the data values stored in the Registry by the Registry application are shown in Figure 13.9).

FIGURE 13.10:

The Registry program remembers the Form's dimensions from the last time it was executed.

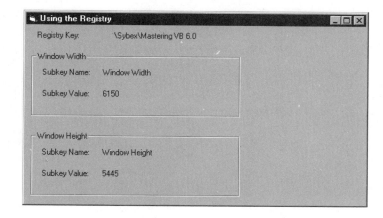

When the program starts, it attempts to retrieve the values of the subkeys Window Width and Window Height with the *RegQueryValueEx()* function. If these subkeys contain values, the program simply retrieves them and sets the window width and height. If these subkeys don't contain values, there are no entries in the Registry. The program then gets the current window width and height and stores that information in the Registry with the *RegSetValueEx()* function. The *RegCreateKey()* function creates the specified key; if the key already exists, this function opens the key.

If you resize the window, the program saves the new window width and height to the Registry with the QueryUnload method. The next time you run the program, the application window will open at this new size. Thus, you can store you program initialization settings using the Registry and retrieve them when your application starts up. To test the Registry project, you must close the Form by clicking the Close button. If you end the application with the Run ➤ End command in the Visual Basic IDE, the QueryUnload event will not be triggered.

The Registry program's listing follows.

Code 13.11:   Using the Registry Program

```
Option Explicit

Private Declare Function RegCreateKey Lib "advapi32.dll" _
        Alias "RegCreateKeyA" (ByVal hKey As Long, _
        ByVal lpSubKey As String, phkResult _
        As Long) As Long
Private Declare Function RegDeleteKey Lib "advapi32.dll" _
        Alias "RegDeleteKeyA" (ByVal hKey As Long, _
        ByVal lpSubKey As String) As Long
```

```vb
Private Declare Function RegDeleteValue Lib "advapi32.dll" _
        Alias "RegDeleteValueA" (ByVal hKey As Long, _
        ByVal lpValueName As String) As Long
Private Declare Function RegQueryValueEx Lib "advapi32.dll" _
        Alias "RegQueryValueExA" (ByVal hKey As Long, _
        ByVal lpValueName As String, ByVal lpReserved As Long, _
        lpType As Long, lpData As Any, lpcbData As Long) As Long
Private Declare Function RegSetValueEx Lib "advapi32.dll" _
        Alias "RegSetValueExA" (ByVal hKey As Long, _
        ByVal lpValueName As String, ByVal Reserved As Long, _
        ByVal dwType As Long, lpData As Any, _
        ByVal cbData As Long) As Long

Const ERROR_SUCCESS = 0&
Const ERROR_BADDB = 1009&
Const ERROR_BADKEY = 1010&
Const ERROR_CANTOPEN = 1011&
Const ERROR_CANTREAD = 1012&
Const ERROR_CANTWRITE = 1013&
Const ERROR_REGISTRY_RECOVERED = 1014&
Const ERROR_REGISTRY_CORRUPT = 1015&
Const ERROR_REGISTRY_IO_FAILED = 1016&
Const HKEY_CLASSES_ROOT = &H80000000
Const HKEY_CURRENT_USER = &H80000001
Const HKEY_LOCAL_MACHINE = &H80000002
Const REG_SZ = 1

'Dim regKey As String
Const regKey = "\Sybex\Mastering VB 6.0"

Private Sub Form_Load()
Dim retValue As Long, result As Long
Dim keyID As Long, keyValue As String
Dim subKey As String
Dim bufSize As Long

    Label6.Caption = regKey
    ' Create key
    retValue = RegCreateKey(HKEY_LOCAL_MACHINE, regKey, keyID)
    If retValue = 0 Then
    ' Save width
    subKey = "Window Width"
    retValue = RegQueryValueEx(keyID, subKey, 0&, _
            REG_SZ, 0&, bufSize)
    ' No value, set it
```

```
            If bufSize < 2 Then
            keyValue = Me.Width
            retValue = RegSetValueEx(keyID, subKey, 0&, _
                    REG_SZ, ByVal keyValue, Len(keyValue) + 1)
        Else
            keyValue = String(bufSize + 1, " ")
            retValue = RegQueryValueEx(keyID, subKey, _
                    0&, REG_SZ, ByVal keyValue, bufSize)
            keyValue = Left$(keyValue, bufSize - 1)
            Me.Width = keyValue
        End If

        ' Set values on form
        Label4.Caption = subKey
        Label5.Caption = Me.Width
          ' Save height
         subKey = "Window Height"
         retValue = RegQueryValueEx(keyID, subKey, 0&, _
                    REG_SZ, 0&, bufSize)
        If bufSize < 2 Then
          keyValue = Me.Height
          retValue = RegSetValueEx(keyID, subKey, 0&, _
                    REG_SZ, ByVal keyValue, Len(keyValue) + 1)
        Else
          keyValue = String(bufSize + 1, " ")
          retValue = RegQueryValueEx(keyID, subKey, 0&, REG_SZ, _
                    ByVal keyValue, bufSize)
          keyValue = Left$(keyValue, bufSize - 1)
          Me.Height = keyValue
        End If
        ' Set values on form
        Label8.Caption = subKey
        Label7.Caption = Me.Height
    End If
End Sub

Private Sub Form_QueryUnload(Cancel As Integer, _
            UnloadMode As Integer)
Dim keyValue As String
Dim retValue As Long, keyID As Long

    retValue = RegCreateKey(HKEY_LOCAL_MACHINE, regKey, keyID)
    keyValue = Me.Width
    retValue = RegSetValueEx(keyID, "Window Width", 0&, _
            REG_SZ, ByVal keyValue, Len(keyValue) + 1)
```

```
      keyValue = Me.Height
      retValue = RegSetValueEx(keyID, "Window Height", 0&, _
                  REG_SZ, ByVal keyValue, Len(keyValue) + 1)
  End Sub
```

The Registry application works on Windows 95/98 only, not on Windows NT 4.

Manipulating Graphics

Graphics attract users and are an important part of any application. A graphic can be a simple icon or a complex bitmap. This section describes some techniques for manipulating the display of bitmaps using the Win32 APIs. In this section, we'll look at the API graphics functions, BitBlt()and StretchBlt(), which are more or less equivalent to the PaintPicture method of the graphics controls of Visual Basic. The main difference is that the PaintPicture method applies to a given control (Picture-Box or Form), but the BitBlt() and StretchBlt() functions can copy pixels from anywhere on the Desktop. As a result, you can use them for applications, such as screen capture programs, for which the PaintPicture method is inadequate.

The BitBlt() Function

The *BitBlt()* function is used to blit, or copy, an image from a source to a destination object. The function transfers a rectangle of pixels from the specified source device context into a destination device context. Earlier in this chapter, the MenuBMP application demonstrated the use of BitBlt(). Now, let's look at it in detail and compare it with the PaintPicture method provided with Visual Basic.

Declare the BitBlt() function as follows:

```
Declare Function BitBlt Lib "gdi32" Alias "BitBlt" (ByVal _
    hDestDC As Long, ByVal x As Long, ByVal y As Long, ByVal _
    nWidth As Long, ByVal nHeight As Long, ByVal hSrcDC As Long, _
    ByVal xSrc As Long, ByVal ySrc As Long, ByVal dwRop As Long) _
    As Long
```

Unlike the PaintPicture method, the BitBlt() function requires you to supply all the arguments. You must supply the starting X and Y coordinates, the height and width, and the starting coordinates of the source.

Before you can use the BitBlt() function, you must create a device context for the source and destination objects with the CreateCompatibleDC() and Create-CompatibleBitmap() functions. If you plan to use the BitBlt() function to copy from a PictureBox control, the control's device context is its hWnd property. However, the BitBlt function can be used with any device context, even with the device context of a bitmap loaded into memory.

With the exceptions of *hDestDC* and *hSrcDC*, the remaining arguments of the BitBlt() function are the same as those of the PaintPicture method. They specify the origin of the rectangle to be copied (the source arguments) and the origin and dimensions of the rectangle to which the pixels will be copied to (the destination arguments). The dimensions of the source and destination rectangles must be the same. Table 13.7 lists the raster operation codes for the *dwRop* argument. These codes define how the pixels of the source rectangle are combined with the pixels of the destination rectangle.

The StretchBlt() Function

Another way to draw bitmaps is to use the *StretchBlt()* function. With this function, you can copy a bitmap from a source rectangle into a destination rectangle, stretching or compressing the bitmap to fit the destination rectangle. Here's the declaration for StretchBlt():

```
Declare Function StretchBlt Lib "gdi32" Alias "StretchBlt" _
    (ByVal hdc As Long, ByVal x As Long, ByVal y As Long, ByVal _
    nWidth As Long, ByVal nHeight As Long, ByVal hSrcDC As Long, _
    ByVal xSrc As Long, ByVal ySrc As Long, ByVal nSrcWidth As _
    Long, ByVal nSrcHeight As Long, ByVal dwRop As Long) As Long
```

As you can see, StretchBlt() has all the arguments of the BitBlt() function plus two more arguments that specify the size of the source rectangle. StretchBlt() can compress a picture, stretch it backward, or turn it inside out by using different signs for the arguments. The raster operation codes in Table 13.7 define how Windows combines the colors of the source and destination rectangle to achieve the final color.

TABLE 13.7: Raster Operation Codes for BitBlt() and StretchBlt()

VALUE	DESCRIPTION
BLACKNESS	Fills in the destination rectangle with black
DSTINVERT	Inverts the destination rectangle
MERGECOPY	Merges the source rectangle with a pattern using the AND operator
MERGEPAINT	Merges the inverted source rectangle with the destination rectangle using the OR operator

Continued on next page

TABLE 13.7 CONTINUED: Raster Operation Codes for BitBlt() and StretchBlt()

VALUE	DESCRIPTION
NOTSRCCOPY	Copies the inverted source rectangle to the destination
NOTSRCERASE	Combines the source and destination rectangle with the OR operator and inverts the final color
PATCOPY	Copies a pattern to the destination rectangle
PATINVERT	Combines a pattern with the destination rectangle using the XOR operator
PATPAINT	Combines the colors of the pattern with the inverted source rectangle using the OR operator. The result is combined with the destination rectangle using the OR operator.
SRCAND	Combines the source and destination rectangles using the AND operator
SRCCOPY	Copies the source rectangle into the destination rectangle
SRCERASE	Combines inverted colors of the destination rectangle with the source rectangle using the AND operator
SRCINVERT	Combines the source and destination rectangles using the XOR operator
SRCPAINT	Combines the source and destination rectangle using the OR operator
WHITENESS	Fills the destination rectangle with the color white

These settings are also explained in Chapter 7, *Manipulating Color and Pixels with Visual Basic*. You can also open the PaintPic application discussed in Chapter 7 to experiment with various settings of the raster operation codes. The PaintPic application uses the PaintPicture method, but the raster operations are the same.

Drawing Functions

Visual Basic provides a few methods for drawing on Forms and PictureBoxes, which are discussed at length in Chapter 6. There are only a few drawing methods, but they accept a variety of arguments and they are quite flexible. However, they are not as fast as their API counterparts (the functions a C++ program would call). Windows is a visually rich environment and it provides a number of API functions for drawing and painting. In this section, I will discuss a few of the API drawing functions that will help you speed up your Visual Basic application (a discussion of all related API functions is beyond the scope of this book). In the last section of the chapter, I will present a few basic concepts of the Windows API drawing functions, device contexts, and bitmap structures. These techniques will help you write very fast code for drawing and pixel manipulation.

NOTE   You'll notice that a good part of this chapter is devoted to graphics functions and drawing techniques. Drawing is the slowest operation in the Windows operating system and Visual Basic can use all the help you can offer. The examples of this section will show you how to speed up your drawing code.

Drawing Lines and Circles

The two basic API drawing functions are the *LineTo()* and *Ellipse()* functions which draw lines and ellipses/circles, respectively. The LineTo() function's syntax is:

```
Public Declare Function LineTo Lib "gdi32" Alias "LineTo" _
      (ByVal hdc As Long, ByVal x As Long, ByVal y As Long) As Long
```

The LineTo() function draws a line from the current point to the coordinates X, Y on the specified device context. To set the current point, use the *MoveToEx()* function, whose declaration is:

```
Private Declare Function MoveToEx Lib "gdi32" Alias "MoveToEx" _
      (ByVal hdc As Long, ByVal x As Long, ByVal y As Long, _
      lpPoint As POINTAPI) As Long
```

The arguments x and y of the MoveToEx() function are the coordinates of the new current point. The last argument is a POINTAPI structure, and it holds the coordinates of the current point before it was changed by the function (in other words, the coordinates of the current point before the function changed it). The POINTAPI structure was explained previously in the section "Declaring 32-Bit Functions and Structures."

The coordinates for both functions (and all the API drawing functions) must be expressed in pixels. If you're going to mix Visual Basic drawing methods and API drawing functions, you should set the coordinate system of the respective control(s) to 3 (Pixels). To draw a line from the point (10, 10) to the point (85, 130) on Form1, use the following statements:

```
Dim point As POINTAPI
MoveToEx Form1.hDC, 10, 10, point
LineTo Form1.hDC, 85, 130
```

To draw circles and ellipses, use the Ellipse() function, whose syntax is:

```
Public Declare Function Ellipse Lib "gdi32" Alias "Ellipse" _
      (ByVal hdc As Long, ByVal X1 As Long, ByVal Y1 As Long, _
      ByVal X2 As Long, ByVal Y2 As Long) As Long
```

The Ellipse() function draws an ellipse on the *hdc* device context. The ellipse is enclosed by the rectangle defined by the coordinates *(X1, Y1)* and *(X2, Y2)*. To draw a square, make the sides of the rectangle equal.

If you use these commands to draw on a Form or PictureBox control, the shapes will be drawn in the control's drawing color (property ForeColor) and with the control's drawing width (property DrawWidth). You can change these settings using the properties of the Form or control or you can use the *CreatePen()* API function as follows:

```
Public Declare Function CreatePen Lib "gdi32" Alias "CreatePen" _
        (ByVal nPenStyle As Long, ByVal nWidth As Long, _
        ByVal crColor As Long) As Long
```

The *nPenStyle* argument is an integer, which can take any of the values shown in Table 13.8. These values correspond to the settings of the DrawMode property.

TABLE 13.8: Settings of the *nPenStyle* Argument of the CreatePen() Function

CONSTANT	VALUE
PS_SOLID	0
PS_DASH	1
PS_DOT	2
PS_DASHDOT	3
PS_NULL	5
PS_DASHDOTDOT	4
PS_INSIDEFRAME	6

To create a solid red pen, two pixels wide, call the following function:

```
myPen = CreatePen(0, 2, RGB(255, 0, 0))
```

Creating a Pen object doesn't mean that it will be automatically used by subsequent drawing operations. To use the new pen, you must register the Pen object with the device context to which it applies. To do so, you must call the *Select-Object()* function, whose syntax is:

```
Public Declare Function SelectObject Lib "gdi32" Alias "SelectObject" _
        (ByVal hdc As Long, ByVal hObject As Long) As Long
```

The first argument is the handle of the device context where the drawing will take place, and the second argument is the handle of the Pen object. To specify that the myPen object be used in subsequent operations, you must call the following function:

```
SelectObject Form1.hDC, myPen
```

After this statement is executed, the Line() and Ellipse() functions will use the myPen pen to draw on the device context. Analogous to the Pen object is the Brush object, which is used for filling areas (you'll see how it is done later). The simplest function for creating a Brush object is the *CreateSolidBrush()* function, whose syntax is:

```
Public Declare Function CreateSolidBrush Lib "gdi32" Alias _
        "CreateSolidBrush" (ByVal crColor As Long) As Long
```

crColor is a Long Color value. You can use the RGB() function to specify the brush's color or use the Color common dialog box's Color property. To use the Brush object with subsequent operations, you must select it into the device context with the SelectObject() function.

VB6 At Work: The APIDraw Project

The APIDraw project demonstrates the API drawing functions discussed in the previous section. It's a simple application that draws a circle and an ellipse and their bounding rectangles, as shown in Figure 13.11. In the next section, you'll see how to fill the various closed sections of the drawing.

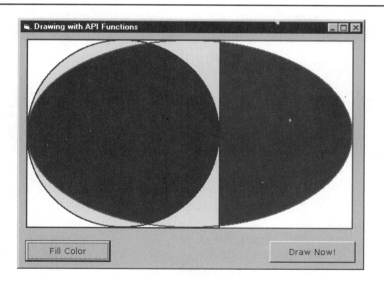

The following API function declarations appear at the beginning of the code:

```
Private Declare Function LineTo Lib "gdi32" (ByVal hdc As Long, _
        ByVal x As Long, ByVal y As Long) As Long
Private Declare Function Ellipse Lib "gdi32" (ByVal hdc As Long, _
        ByVal X1 As Long, ByVal Y1 As Long, ByVal X2 As Long, _
        ByVal Y2 As Long) As Long
```

```
Private Declare Function MoveToEx Lib "gdi32" (ByVal hdc As Long, _
        ByVal x As Long, ByVal y As Long, lpPoint As POINTAPI) As Long
Private Declare Function CreateSolidBrush Lib "gdi32" _
        (ByVal crColor As Long) As Long
Private Declare Function ExtFloodFill Lib "gdi32" (ByVal hdc As Long, _
        ByVal x As Long, ByVal y As Long, ByVal crColor As Long, _
        ByVal wFillType As Long) As Long
Private Declare Function SelectObject Lib "gdi32" _
        (ByVal hdc As Long, ByVal hObject As Long) As Long
Private Declare Function DeleteObject Lib "gdi32" _
        (ByVal hObject As Long) As Long
```

The code behind the Draw Now button uses the *MoveToEx()* and *LineTo()* functions to draw the bounding rectangles and the Ellipse() function to draw the ellipses. The first ellipse is bound by a rectangle that extends from (10, 10) to (500, 300), and the second one is bound by a rectangle that extends from (10, 10) to (300, 300). Because the second rectangle is a square, the ellipse is actually a circle. The code behind the Draw Now Command button follows.

Code 13.12:   **Drawing Ellipses**

```
Private Sub Command1_Click()
Dim point As POINTAPI
    Form1.Cls
    Form1.ForeColor = RGB(255, 0, 0)
    MoveToEx Form1.hdc, 10, 10, point
    LineTo Form1.hdc, 500, 10
    LineTo Form1.hdc, 500, 300
    LineTo Form1.hdc, 10, 300
    LineTo Form1.hdc, 10, 10
    Ellipse Form1.hdc, 10, 10, 500, 300

    Form1.ForeColor = RGB(0, 0, 255)
    MoveToEx Form1.hdc, 10, 10, point
    LineTo Form1.hdc, 300, 10
    LineTo Form1.hdc, 300, 300
    LineTo Form1.hdc, 10, 300
    LineTo Form1.hdc, 10, 10
    Ellipse Form1.hdc, 10, 10, 300, 300
End Sub
```

Filling Closed Shapes

A very useful drawing feature missing from Visual Basic is a method that fills a closed area. You can draw filled circles and rectangles, but what about shapes that are defined as intersections of other basic shapes, like the filled areas of the drawing shown in Figure 13.11? To fill irregular shapes, you must use the *ExtFloodFill()* function, whose declaration is:

```
Public Declare Function ExtFloodFill Lib "gdi32" _
        Alias "ExtFloodFill"(ByVal hdc As Long, ByVal x As Long, _
        ByVal y As Long, ByVal crColor As Long, _
        ByVal wFillType As Long) As Long
```

This function fills a solid area starting with the point at coordinates (x, y) with the color specified by the argument *crColor*. The last argument, *wFillType*, specifies the type of filling and it can have one the following values:

- **FLOODFILLBORDER (0)**   The function fills the area colored with *crColor*. The point (x, y) must lie in the area to be filled.

- **FLOODFILLSURFACE (1)**   The *clColor* argument specifies the bounding color.

The area is filled with a brush, so you must first create a Brush object, select it into the device context, and then call the ExtFloodFill() function. The drawing produced by the Draw Now button of the Ellipse application contains interesting areas to fill with the ExtFloodFill() function, so we'll add some code to this application to fill closed areas with a color selected by the user on a Color common dialog box. To fill an area, click the Fill Color button (which will display the Color common dialog box, where you can select the fill color) and then click a point in the area you want to fill. The filling takes place from within the MouseUp event with the following statements.

Code 13.13   **Filling a Closed Area**

```
Private Sub Form_MouseUp(Button As Integer, Shift As Integer, _
        x As Single, y As Single)
    brush = CreateSolidBrush(CommonDialog1.Color)
    SelectObject Me.hdc, brush
    ExtFloodFill Me.hdc, x, y, Me.point(x, y), FLOODFILLSURFACE
    DeleteObject brush
End Sub
```

The code extracts the selected color from the *CommonDialog1* control and uses it to create a solid brush. The brush object is selected into the Form's device context and used by the ExtFloodFill() function to fill the area.

Pixel Painting Functions

I can't think of many applications that spend more than a few milliseconds drawing lines, except for a few really elaborate math curves, so it's probably not worth the effort to use the API functions to draw shapes. But as you may recall from Chapter 7, the Image application had to read and set the values of nearly one million pixels during image processing. In this instance, every millisecond you can squeeze out of the processing cycle of a single pixel really adds up. In Chapter 12, *Optimizing VB Applications*, you learned about the GetPixelV() and SetPixelV() functions, which are significantly faster than their Visual Basic counterparts (Point and PSet methods) in reading and setting a pixel value, respectively.

The GetPixelV() function returns the value of the pixel at coordinates (x, y) on the device context specified by the argument *hdc* as follows.

```
Public Declare Function GetPixel Lib "gdi32" Alias "GetPixel" _
        (ByVal hdc As Long, ByVal x As Long, ByVal y As Long) As Long
```

The pixel's value is returned as a Long value, just like the value that the Point method would return. The first argument of the GetPixel() function is the hDC property of a Form, PictureBox, or any other control that you can draw on.

The SetPixel() function's syntax is analogous:

```
Public Declare Function SetPixel Lib "gdi32" Alias "SetPixel" _
        (ByVal hdc As Long, ByVal x As Long, ByVal y As Long, _
        ByVal crColor As Long) As Long
```

The handle of the control's device context is *hdc*, *x* and *y* are the pixel's coordinates, and *crColor* is the color to be assigned to the specified pixel.

Figure 13.12 shows the CopyPix application, which copies the pixels of the top PictureBox to the bottom one using either straight Visual Basic code (the Copy VB button), or the GetPixelV() and SetPixelV() API functions (the Copy API button). Run the project to see how much faster the API functions are compared with the equivalent Visual Basic methods. You don't even have to time the two operations; you can "see" the difference in execution speed. Notice that the AutoRedraw property of the second PictureBox is set to False, so that you can watch the progress of the pixel copying operation.

The CopyPix project should be executed on system that can display more than 256 colors. If your system supports 256 colors only, make sure that the color you select to fill an area is solid. If it's a dithered color, the area will be filled with a pattern of different colored dots. If you attempt to fill this area again, the code will most likely fill a single pixel. The ExtFloodFill() function fills an area of solid color only and will fail with dithered colors.

FIGURE 13.12:

The CopyPix project demonstrates the difference in execution speed between the VB pixel manipulation methods and the equivalent API functions.

The application's code is straightforward, so I will only list the code of the Copy API button. The program scans every pixel in the source image with a double loop, reads its value, and then assigns it to the pixel at the same coordinates in the lower PictureBox. The actual code is shown next.

Code 13.14:   **Copying Pixels with API Functions**

```
Private Sub Command2_Click()
Dim i As Integer, j As Integer
Dim clrValue As Long

    For i = 0 To Picture1.ScaleWidth - 1
        For j = 0 To Picture1.ScaleHeight - 1
            SetPixel Picture2.hdc, i, j, GetPixel(Picture1.hdc, i, j)
        Next
    'DoEvents
    Next
End Sub
```

To copy images between controls you must use the PaintPicture method or the BitBlt() API function; they are both nearly instantaneous. If you have to process pixels, however, the two API functions discussed in this section will speed up the application considerably. In Chapter 12, we used the pixel manipulation functions to optimize the Image application, which spends most of its time reading and setting pixel values.

Speeding Up Drawing Operations

Manipulating pixels with the SetPixelV() and GetPixelV() functions is significantly faster than using their Visual Basic counterparts, but it is still slow. There's a better method, but it requires even more API functions.

When you draw with Visual Basic methods on a Form, the drawing takes place in an area of the memory that is mapped on the Form's window. Visual Basic has a handle to this memory, and there are several layers between your Visual Basic code and the actual window. The API functions discussed in the previous section do the same, but they are faster than Visual Basic code. (After all, Visual Basic has to call the same function internally; it hides some of the complexity of drawing operations, but it's slower.)

Windows doesn't allow an application to draw directly on the screen. Remember, under Windows, you can run multiple applications, switch between them, and rely on Windows to take care of chores such as updating the windows on the screen and manipulating palettes. Windows simply wouldn't be able to handle all these details if applications had direct access to the windows' bitmaps on the screen. That's why drawing operations under Windows are inherently slow.

No matter how Windows handles drawing and painting operations, eventually, the bitmap must be stored somewhere in memory. There are API functions that allow applications to access this area of the memory and draw by setting bits and bytes in memory. Drawing in memory is faster than drawing on device contexts, but more complicated. Moreover, when you're drawing in memory, nothing appears on the screen. You must also provide the code to transfer the bitmap from the memory to a window on the monitor. Even with this additional step, drawing in memory is considerably faster than drawing on device contexts.

To draw in memory, you must create a bitmap structure in memory. This structure must also be compatible with the device context on which it will be displayed. In other words, a different bitmap structure is required for the monitor and a different one for a printer. To create a bitmap structure in memory, use the CreateCompatible-Bitmap() function, whose syntax is:

```
Public Declare Function CreateCompatibleBitmap Lib "gdi32" _
        Alias "CreateCompatibleBitmap" (ByVal hdc As Long, _
        ByVal nWidth As Long, ByVal nHeight As Long) As Long
```

The first argument of the function is the device context with which the bitmap must be compatible. This is also the device context where the bitmap's contents must be transferred in order to be displayed on the monitor. The other two arguments are the dimensions of the bitmap in pixels.

Since you'll be drawing off-screen, you must also create a device context with CreateCompatibleDC() function and then select the bitmap structure into the device context with the SelectObject() function. The syntax of the CreateCompatibleDC() function is:

```
Public Declare Function CreateCompatibleDC Lib "gdi32" _
    ,    Alias "CreateCompatibleDC" (ByVal hdc As Long) As Long
```

Its argument is the device context of the control (or the Form) where the drawing will be displayed. If you want to prepare a bitmap in memory and then display it on the PictureBox1 control, use the following statements:

```
hBMPSource = CreateCompatibleBitmap(Picture1.hdc, _
            Picture1.ScaleWidth, Picture1.ScaleHeight)
hSourceDC = CreateCompatibleDC(Picture1.hdc)
SelectObject hSourceDC, hBMPSource
```

After these statements are executed, you can draw on the *hSourceDC* device context using the drawing functions we have discussed already. Notice that the *hSourceDC* device context isn't directly mapped to the monitor. It lives in the memory and can be updated really quickly. To display it, you must transfer its contents to the PictureBox2 control with the BitBlt() function.

The third Command button on the CopyPix project's Form, Copy Fast, uses this technique to read the pixels of the top PictureBox control and set the pixels on the bottom PictureBox. The code behind the Copy Fast button is shown next.

Code 13.15: **The Copy Fast Command Button's Code**

```
Private Sub Command3_Click()
    Picture2.Cls
' set up source bitmap
    hBMPSource = CreateCompatibleBitmap(Picture1.hdc, _
            Picture1.ScaleWidth, Picture1.ScaleHeight)
    hSourceDC = CreateCompatibleDC(Picture1.hdc)
    SelectObject hSourceDC, hBMPSource
' set up destination bitmap
    hBMPDest = CreateCompatibleBitmap(Picture2.hdc, _
            Picture2.ScaleWidth, Picture2.ScaleHeight)
    hDestDC = CreateCompatibleDC(Picture2.hdc)
    SelectObject hDestDC, hBMPDest
' Copy picture bitmap to source bitmap
    BitBlt hSourceDC, 0, 0, Picture1.ScaleWidth - 1, _
            Picture1.ScaleHeight - 1, Picture1.hdc, 0, 0, &HCC0020
```

```
' Copy pixels between bitmaps
    For i = 0 To Picture1.ScaleWidth - 1
        For j = 0 To Picture1.ScaleHeight - 1
            clr = GetPixel(hSourceDC, i, j)
            SetPixel hDestDC, i, j, clr
        Next
    Next
' transfer the copied pixels to the second PictureBox
    BitBlt Picture2.hdc, 0, 0, Picture1.ScaleWidth - 1, _
        Picture1.ScaleHeight - 1, hDestDC, 0, 0, &HCC0020
    'Picture2.Refresh
' finally, clean up memory
    Call DeleteDC(hSourceDC)
    Call DeleteObject(hBMPSource)
    Call DeleteDC(hDestDC)
    Call DeleteObject(hBMPDest)
End Sub
```

The code starts by creating two device contexts in memory, the *hSourceDC* (which represents the bitmap of the top PictureBox control) and the *hDestDC* (which represents the bitmap of the bottom PictureBox control). Then it copies the pixels of the PictureBox1 control into the corresponding device context (when a device context is first created in memory it contains random data). The double loop that follows copies the pixels from the *hSourceDC* context to the *hDestDC* context with the GetPixelV() and SetPixelV() API functions. As you can see, the same methods that draw on actual device contexts can also draw on memory device contexts.

While the pixels are being copied, the screen isn't updated. You're drawing something in memory and Windows doesn't know what you intend to do with it, so it doesn't display it anywhere. After all the pixels have been copied, we must move the bitmap from the memory (the *hDestDC* context) into the destination control (PictureBox2 control). This is done with the BitBlt() function. Finally, the program releases all the resources it created during its operation by calling the *DeleteDC()* and *DeleteObject()* functions.

Run the CopyPix project, and click the Copy Fast button to see how much faster it is than the other two methods. The drawback of this method is that you can't watch the progress of the pixel copying operation. You'll see the second image only after all pixels have been copied. If you're manipulating large images, you may wish to call the BitBlt() function more often (after copying each column of pixels, for example). This will introduce some delay, but the method described in this section is still faster than the other two. You may want to use a progress indicator to let the user know that the program is running and to estimate how much time is left before the operation is finished.

This example concludes the discussion of API functions. Next, you'll see how to extend Visual Basic by contacting external applications, such as Excel and Word, and manipulating their objects through VBA. Office applications provide so many features you can use from within your Visual Basic applications that it doesn't make much sense implement them from scratch on your own.

CHAPTER

FOURTEEN

14

OLE Automation and VBA

- Extending Visual Basic with OLE

- Understanding OLE terminology

- Linking and embedding

- Using OLE Container control properties and methods

- OLE Automation and VBA

- Programming Word's objects

- Programming Excel's objects

- Programming Outlook's objects

Visual Basic is a highly successful object-oriented language because it manages to hide many of the details of using and manipulating objects. The elements you use to build a user interface are objects, and you manipulate them via their properties and methods. By now, you should be quite familiar with Visual Basic's object nature.

This chapter explores two more major aspects of Visual Basic's object nature: OLE and OLE Automation. *OLE* (pronounced "OH-LAY") lets Visual Basic applications access the functionality of other applications in the Windows environment. The controls you've used so far are built into Visual Basic. They appear in the editor's Toolbox and you can place them on Forms with point-and-click operations. Some objects in the Windows environment, however, aren't unique to Visual Basic and don't come with the language. They are supplied by other applications, but you can use them within your own applications.

A Word document is such an object, and you can incorporate DOC files in your applications. You don't have to know much about Word files or how documents are stored on disk to use them. After you incorporate them in your applications and the need arises to edit them, you can momentarily borrow Word's menus and toolbars and display them in your own application. Your users can then edit the document as if they were using Word—all from within your application's window.

In addition, you can program applications like Word by manipulating the objects they expose through *VBA (Visual Basic for Applications).* VBA is an increasingly popular and significant language that allows programmers to customize popular applications (like Word and Excel) rather than develop new applications to meet the specific requirements of the workflow in small businesses and corporations. You can easily apply your Visual Basic knowledge to VBA, and you should familiarize yourself with the structure and basic principles of VBA.

In the first part of the chapter, you'll learn how to extend Visual Basic by using OLE to incorporate objects exposed by other applications into your applications. The second half of the chapter is an introduction to VBA. It shows you how to exploit the rich features of Word, Excel, and Outlook from within your Visual Basic applications by OLE automating them with VBA.

What Is OLE?

In the past, software development tools were uniform throughout, allowing little, if any, variation and component exchange with other tools. Programming environments were thought of as islands, somewhat isolated from other applications.

Programmers used structured programming techniques to analyze programming problems in terms of procedures and then implement those procedures.

However, with the introduction of OLE, software development has been significantly transformed from procedural to object-oriented programming. You no longer have to work with prepackaged tools. You can create self-contained Modules, or *objects*, that greatly simplify programming, especially when it comes to building large applications. In the previous chapters, you learned how to use Visual Basic objects to build applications. With OLE, you can use both Visual Basic objects and objects exposed by other applications to do the same. As a result, your applications no longer will be islands of functionality. They will be an integral part of the operating system and its applications.

Component Software

The essence of OLE is *component software*. A component is an item (a control or an application) that someone else has developed. You don't have to reinvent it to use it in your applications. If the component supports OLE, you can "borrow" its functionality for your own purposes. Microsoft Word, for example, comes with a powerful spell-checker. Why buy another spell-checker or write your own when you can borrow this functionality from Word?

A developer of component software views a program as a combination of components working together to provide a common interface standard for OLE applications. For example, the functionality of a spreadsheet can be available in a word processing document and vice versa. Or, a Visual Basic application can borrow functionality from both a word processor and a spreadsheet.

Compound Documents

A document that contains more than a single type of object is called a *compound document*. For example, a Microsoft Word document that contains an Excel worksheet or an image is a compound document. There have been attempts to develop all-in-one applications to handle text, numbers, images, communications, and every other aspect of computing upon which the average user relies, but they have all failed—until the advent of OLE technology.

The folks at Microsoft recognized the need of the average user to integrate favorite applications. They also understood that the all-in-one approach was not feasible, so they came up with OLE, which is a way for applications to exchange both data and functions. Because OLE applications can communicate with each other, end users can put together the pieces they need to create their own all-in-one software. The beauty of OLE is that the application that calls upon the services of another application doesn't need to know much about it, short of how to accomplish the task. In the same way, you, the Visual Basic programmer, don't need to know much about the operation of the RichTextBox or MSFlexGrid control, short of the properties and methods that let you manipulate them.

A Data-Centered Approach

OLE allows the user to take a data-centered approach to a program instead of a product approach. The user needs to consider *what* needs to be done, not *how* it should be done or *which application* should be used for the task at hand. For example, in a component software environment, the user doesn't have to work exclusively with an Excel spreadsheet to manipulate numbers or with WordPerfect to manage text. An OLE application provides the user access to the functionality of a spreadsheet, a word processor, or a graphics application, within one environment called a *container application*. As you'll soon see, Visual Basic lets you build components that can share functionality with other applications, as well as applications that can host compound documents.

> **NOTE** Whereas traditionally structured applications focus on the *how* of processing data, OLE applications focus on the *what* of processing data. As you're learning OLE techniques, keep this simple principle in mind. It's the essence of OLE. It's what makes OLE useful for the end user, which must always be your goal. OLE programming may get complicated, but the end product must be a simple and easy-to-use application.

OLE Terminology

At this point, we would normally look at a few examples that demonstrate the items discussed so far, but before doing so, we must look at some OLE terms that we'll be using in this chapter. OLE has its own terminology. You may not quite understand all the terms presented next, but they will be used later with examples.

OLE Object

An *OLE object* is an item that is *exposed*, or made available, by an OLE server application. *OLE server applications* expose different types (or *Classes*) of objects. OLE objects are used in *container applications* (see the next section). As Figure 14.1 illustrates, Excel (the OLE server) can expose a worksheet (the OLE object) that can be inserted as is in a Word document (the container application).

FIGURE 14.1:

An Excel worksheet is
embedded in a Word
document.

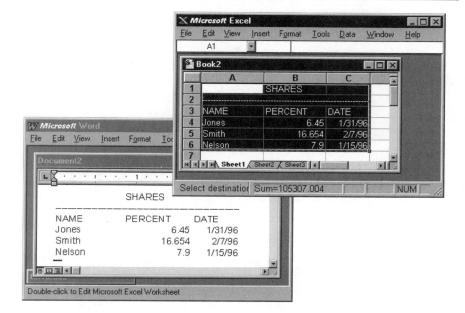

Server Application

This is the application that exposes the objects your Visual Basic application contacts. When your application must edit a document created by a server application, it contacts the server application that will be used to edit the document.

Container Application

This is an application that contains the OLE objects. Objects can be linked or embedded (more on this next). A container itself is also an object. A good example of this in
Visual Basic is the Form (FRM) object, which contains controls. The container is also
referred to as a *client* because it uses the services of OLE servers to obtain the objects.
In the example of Figure 14.1, Excel is the server application and Word is the container
application.

Object Embedding

With this technique, you can insert an object from one application (the server application) into another application (the container application). The inserted object is a
copy of the original and can be manipulated and stored separately and apart from
the original object. For example, you can embed a range of cells from an Excel worksheet in a Word document. To edit the cells, you switch to Excel by double-clicking
the embedded Excel object. If the container application supports in-place editing,

you'll see the menus of the server application right in the container application (see the section "In-Place Editing").

Object Linking

This technique is similar to embedding, except that the embedded data are also *linked* to the document from which they come. Changes to the object in the server application are reflected automatically in the container application. Linking doesn't store the object, it makes a reference to the object exposed by the server application. Each time you open the document that contains the linked object, the container application contacts the server application, which actually opens the most up-to-date version of the linked object. Linked objects are not copies. They *are* the originals, viewed from within different containers.

In-Place Editing

In-place editing is also known as in-place activation. The functionality of the server application is incorporated into the container application, thus enabling you to edit the object using the menus and tools of the server application. For example, if a Word document contains a range of cells from an Excel spreadsheet, double-clicking the Excel object replaces the Word menus with the Excel menus. You can now edit the cells without switching to another application.

In-place editing is the most obvious manifestation of what was previously called "borrowing another application's functionality." For it to happen, both server and container applications must support OLE Automation (discussed next).

OLE Automation

This method allows you to programmatically manipulate objects exposed by another application from within your Visual Basic applications. It's also a standard that defines how code is shared between applications and how applications can be controlled from within other applications. For example, when you copy a range of cells from an Excel spreadsheet onto a Word document, you embed the range of cells. With OLE Automation, your application can request that Excel perform some calculations and return the result to Word. For example, you can pass a table to Excel and request that Excel manipulate the numeric data in ways that are not possible with Word's tools and then return the processed data to Word. You'll see examples of Visual Basic applications that control (or OLE automate, as it's called) Excel and Word, later in this chapter.

OLE Drag-and-Drop

This method allows you to pick up objects that have been exposed in a server application and place or drop them into your container application. For example, you can create an embedded object in a Word document by dragging-and-dropping a range of cells from an Excel worksheet. In Chapter 4, you learned how to code drag-and-drop operations. Later in this chapter, you'll learn how to a drag a document, or part of it, and drop it on a control that can recognize both the data being dropped and the control.

An Example of Embedding and Linking

Let's look at an example of embedding and linking objects from a user's point of view. To create a compound document with WordPad, follow these steps:

1. Choose Start ➤ Programs ➤ Accessories ➤ WordPad.

2. Choose Insert ➤ Object to display the Insert Object dialog box, as shown in Figure 14.2.

3. Check the Create from File option, and then click the Browse button.

4. In the Browse dialog box (which is identical to a File Open dialog box), select a bitmap image, and click OK. The selected bitmap will be embedded in the WordPad document.

When you save the document, the bitmap is saved with it. WordPad is the container application that contains the bitmap object, which is saved along with the document. If you edit the original bitmap, the contents of the WordPad document won't be affected.

FIGURE 14.2:

The Insert Object dialog box lets the user select an existing object (or create a new one) and embed it in or link it to the current document.

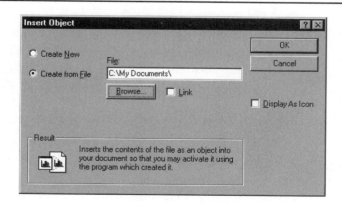

If you check the Create New option on the Insert Object dialog box, you'll see a list of objects known to the system. Every application that can act as a server application registers the objects it exposes with the system, so that every container application can use them. When you insert a new object, the application that knows how to handle it starts automatically with a new document. Go back to the Insert Object dialog box, check the option Create New, and from the Object Types list select Bitmap Image. By default, bitmap images are handled by Paint. If you haven't changed the application associated with bitmap images, WordPad will contact Paint and "borrow" its user interface. WordPad's menu will be replaced by Paint's menu and Paint's toolbox will appear on the screen (see Figure 14.3). You can create a new bitmap with Paint's tools as usual, only the process will take place from within WordPad. You won't have to start another application, copy the bitmap, and then paste it to the other application.

Regardless of whether you inserted a new bitmap or an existing one, to edit it, simply double-click the image. The operating system searches the Registry to find an application associated with bitmaps. The default application is Paint, which comes with Windows. If you haven't changed this setting, the Paint application starts, and its menus and toolbars appear in place of WordPad's menus (as shown in Figure 14.3). (If you did change it, that image processing application starts.) You can edit the bitmap and then return to the main document by clicking somewhere outside the image. Paint is the server application that knows how to manipulate bitmaps.

The bitmap in the WordPad document and the bitmap in the disk file are two separate objects. You can change the disk file, even remove it from the disk, and the WordPad document won't be affected. What you have in the WordPad document is a copy of the bitmap.

Furthermore, you can edit the embedded object in the same window that contains it. You don't need to understand which program created which object, nor do you have to work with that object in a separate window. You can remain in the window of the container application and edit the object without switching applications or windows. One benefit of this approach is that it makes it easy to resize the object with respect to the surrounding text.

If you click the Link checkbox in the Insert Object dialog box, the object in the WordPad document will be linked to the original object. When linking an object, there will be only one object (bitmap file) in the system. WordPad will contain a reference to it, not a copy of the object. The same object can be linked to another document, perhaps with a different application. No matter how many documents make references to this object, there will be a single object in the system. If this object is updated, all documents that reference this object will see its updated version (see Figure 14.4).

NOTE If the object inserted in the container application is linked to the source object (the source file), you won't be able to edit it from within the container application. You'll have to do so from within the server application. The essence of linking is that the user shouldn't be able to edit the object from within various applications. Only one copy of the object is on the computer, and it can be revised only from within the application that created it. As soon as the object is edited, any applications that contain links to this object are updated.

FIGURE 14.3:

The menus and toolbars of the container application (WordPad) are replaced by those of the server application (Paint).

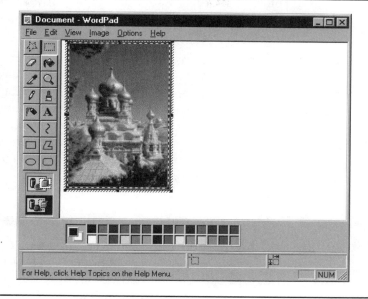

FIGURE 14.4:

When you edit a linked object from within the server application, its linked image in the container application is updated as you edit the original object.

The OLE Container Control

Now, we'll look at how you can exploit the OLE technology from within your Visual Basic applications. To incorporate OLE functionality into your VB applications, you need the OLE Container control, which allows you to insert objects from other applications into your program. You can place only one object in the Container control at a time, but you can have multiple OLE Container controls on the same Form, each one with its own object.

The OLE Container control is your door to the various objects available within the operating system that Visual Basic can't handle on its own, including Word documents, sounds, bitmaps, and Excel spreadsheets. The OLE Container control can host any of the objects listed in the Insert Object dialog box, and in essence, make your Visual Basic application act like a container application. The good news is that the OLE Container control hides nearly all the complexity of OLE and you can easily build OLE-capable applications. You can embed objects in an OLE Container control at design time or at runtime.

Object Linking and Embedding at Design Time

In this section, we are going to create a simple OLE Container control to demonstrate object embedding at design time. Embed objects at design time if you know in advance the object to be embedded and you want to limit the users of the application to a specific object or type of object (a Word document, for example). It's also possible to link objects with the following techniques, but at design time, you usually embed, rather than link, documents. You can embed objects in two ways at design time:

- By pasting an existing object (or dragging-and-dropping the object on the control)

- By selecting the object through the Insert Object dialog box

Embedding with Drag-and-Drop

To embed with drag-and-drop, follow these steps:

1. Start a new Visual Basic project and double-click the OLE Container control's icon in the Toolbox to place an instance of the control on the Form. Visual Basic will display the Insert Object dialog box, where you can specify the object to be embedded in the OLE Container control.

2. In the Insert Object dialog box (previously shown in Figure 14.2), click the Cancel button. (You want an empty OLE Container control of Form1 so that you can later drop an OLE object on it.)

3. In the OLE Container control's Properties window, change the SizeMode property to 1–Stretch (if it's a drawing that can be resized) or to 2–AutoSize

(if it's text or a bitmap that will look bad when resized) to adjust the size of the object or the container.

The settings of the SizeMode property are explained in Table 14.1.

TABLE 14.1: Values for the SizeMode Property

VALUE	DESCRIPTION
Clip	The object is displayed at actual size. If it's larger than the OLE Container control, its image is clipped.
Stretch	The object's image is sized to fill the OLE Container control. The image may be distorted if you allow the object to be resized.
AutoSize	The control is resized to display the entire object.
Zoom	The object is resized to fill the as much of OLE Container control as possible while still maintaining its original proportions.

4. Next, start an application that supports OLE and open a file. In this example, we will embed a Word document in our OLE Container control by dragging-and-dropping the document from the source application (Word) onto the OLE Container control.

5. With both Visual Basic and Word visible on your screen, drag the document (or part of it) onto the empty OLE Container control.

TIP

To drag part of a Word document and drop in onto an OLE Container control, select it with the mouse, click somewhere on the selected paragraphs, and start dragging. If the Visual Basic window isn't visible, press Alt+Tab to switch to it, *without releasing the mouse button*. When the Visual Basic Form is visible on the Desktop, drop the selection on the OLE Container. The selected text will be removed from the original object (the Word document). To embed a copy of the selected text, hold down the Ctrl key as you drag the selection. Plain drag-and-drop operations move the source, even when you move a file on the Desktop. To make a copy, use the Ctrl key while you drag-and-drop.

6. As you drag the object, an oblong shape appears under the pointer arrow. Drop this onto the empty OLE Container control. After a few seconds, the Word document will appear in your OLE Container control (see Figure 14.5).

FIGURE 14.5:

The object dragged from a Word document appears in the OLE Container control where it's dropped.

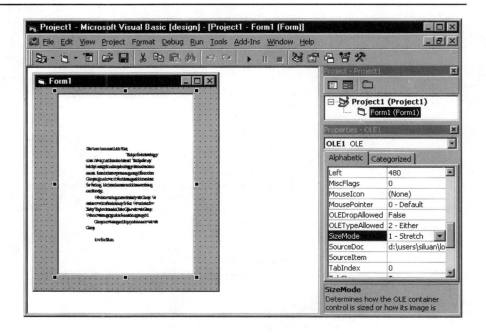

Your Form now contains a Word document. When you run the application, the Word document will be displayed in the OLE Container control. You can edit it with Word's menus and toolbars.

Class, SourceDoc, and SourceItem Properties   Let's look at a few more basic properties of the OLE Container control. When you create an object on your Form, the Properties window contains the following information:

- The name of the application that produced the object (property *Class*)

- The data or a reference to the data (property *SourceDoc*)

- The image of the data (property *SourceItem*). This applies to linked objects only. It specifies the data within the source file that are linked to the OLE control.

OLETypeAllowed Property   Whether the source document is embedded in or linked to the OLE Container control depends on the setting of the control's *OLEType-Allowed* property. Select the OLE Container control on the Form and locate the OLETypeAllowed property in the Properties window. Table 14.2 shows the valid values for this property. The default is 2–Either.

TABLE 14.2: Values for the OLETypeAllowed Property

CONSTANT	VALUE	DESCRIPTION
vbOLELinked	0	Linked; the OLE Container control can contain only a linked object
vbOLEEmbedded	1	Embedded; the OLE Container control can contain only an embedded object
vbOLEEither	2	(Default) Either; the OLE Container control can contain either a linked or an embedded object

Let's make a linked object by setting OLETypeAllowed property to 0 (Linked). The default setting of this property doesn't determine what kind of OLE type you're going to use, but rather what type *can* be used. The actual OLE type is indicated in the Insert Object dialog box. For example, if OLETypeAllowed is 2, the Create New and Create from File buttons and the Link CheckBox control are enabled in the Insert Object dialog box. If the OLETypeAllowed property is 0 (Linked), the Create New button is disabled (you can't link a nonexistent object). If you select 1 (Embedded), the Link checkbox is disabled.

Linking with the Insert Object Dialog Box

Dragging-and-dropping is not the only way to embed or link objects in an OLE Container control. You can also do so through the Insert Object dialog box by following these steps:

1. Delete the OLE Container control in Form1 and create a new OLE Container control as you did earlier.

2. In the Insert Object dialog box, check the Create from File option and the Link checkbox, as shown in Figure 14.6. As mentioned, the Link checkbox is sometimes disabled. This occurs when you've set OLETypeAllowed to 1–Embedded. To make the Link checkbox available, set the OLETypeAllowed to 2–Either.

3. Click the Browse button to locate the file you want.

4. The selected file will appear on the OLE Container control. You'll see part of the linked file. To fit the entire object in the container, resize the control.

Depending on the setting of the *SizeMode* property, the image of the linked file may be distorted. The OLE Container control now contains a reference to the object, not a copy of the object that embedded objects use. Whenever the server application changes the linked object, the object in your container will be updated.

FIGURE 14.6:

To link an object, check the Link checkbox in the Insert Object dialog box.

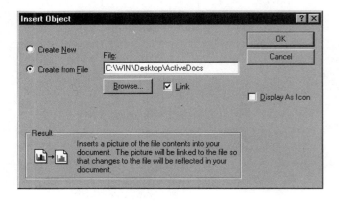

> **NOTE**
>
> When the inserted object is linked to the original, the container application doesn't hold any data. What you see in the container application is an image of the object you inserted, not a copy of the object's data, as happens with an embedded object.

If the linked object is a Word document it will appear in your OLE Container control as shown in Figure 14.5. You'll notice that the SourceDoc property is now the path\filename of the linked object.

5. Keep the Visual Basic window open while you open the document in Word. Make some changes to the document and watch the linked document in the Visual Basic window get updated in real time. You don't have to run the application for this to happen. Even in design mode, the linked document is updated in real time as the original is edited.

Saving and Retrieving Embedded Objects

Embedded objects are created by server applications, but are stored in your container application. Once an object is embedded, there is no connection between the contents of the OLE Container control and the original object. To edit the embedded object, you access the resources of the application that supplied the object, but the data is supplied by the container application. Moreover, data in an embedded object is not automatically saved. To save the embedded object and any changes made by the server application, you use the *SaveToFile* method. It has the following syntax:

```
OLE1.SaveToFile filenumber
```

The *filenumber* variable is a numeric expression specifying an open file's number. The number must correspond to a file opened in binary mode. The following code demonstrates how to prompt the user for a filename and save the embedded document in it with the SaveToFile method.

Code 14.1:   Saving OLE Data

```
Private Sub mnuFileSaveas_Click()
Dim fnum As Integer
    On Error GoTo Cancel
    fnum = FreeFile
    CommonDialog1.ShowSave         ' show Save As dialog
    Open CommonDialog1.FileName For Binary As #fnum
    OLE1.SaveToFile (fnum)
    Close #fnum
    Exit Sub
Cancel:
    MsgBox "Could not save file"
    Close #fnum
End Sub
```

To load an object that has been saved to a data file, use the *ReadFromFile* method. Its syntax is similar to that of SaveToFile. The following code demonstrates how to read the contents of an OLE container from a file (where it was stored earlier with the SaveToFile method).

Code 14.2:   Reading OLE Data

```
Private Sub mnuFileOpen_Click()
Dim fnum As Integer
    On Error GoTo Cancel
    CommonDialog1.ShowOpen          ' show Open dialog
    Fnum = FreeFile
    Open CommonDialog1.FileName For Binary As #fnum
    OLE1.ReadFromFile (fnum)
    Close #fnum
    Exit Sub
Cancel:
    MsgBox "Could not load file"
    Close #fnum
End Sub
```

NOTE   If the property OLEType is 0 *(vbOLELinked),* only the link information and an image of the data are saved to the specified file. If the property OLEType is 1 *(vbOLEEmbedded),* the object's data are saved by the SaveToFile method.

When you save an embedded file, the following information is saved:

- The name of the application that created the object
- The object's data
- A metafile image of the object

When you save a linked file, the following information is saved:

- The name of the application that created the object
- The filename of the object
- A metafile image of the object

The data saved by the SaveToFile method is only accessible by the container application and only through the *ReadFromFile* method. These are Visual Basic methods that you can invoke from within your applications without knowing anything about the object's native format.

Using In-Place Editing

If you run the application now, you'll see the embedded or linked object right on your Visual Basic Form. The user of the application can actually edit the object by double-clicking it. You can open the embedded object for editing in several ways, which are discussed in the sections "Common OLE Container Control Properties" and "Common OLE Container Control Methods," later in this chapter. The simplest way to open the application that provides the embedded object and edit the object using its menus and toolbars is to double-click the object.

In-place editing, or in-place activation, is an enhancement to embedded objects in Visual Basic. With this feature, you can edit the embedded object within the OLE container. The functionality of the server application is incorporated into the container. In-place editing is available only if the server application supports OLE Automation. When you select the embedded object, the menus and toolbars of the server application replace the menus and toolbars of the Visual Basic application (see Figure 14.7). In-place editing allows your container application to borrow the functionality of the embedded object's server application.

FIGURE 14.7:

In-place editing of a Word document on an OLE Container control in a Visual Basic application

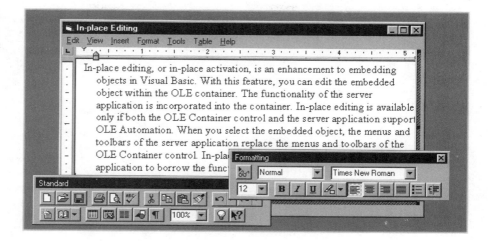

WARNING   Some OLE-capable applications may not be able to display their toolbars for in-place editing of an object. This problem is specific to the applications and can't be fixed from within your Visual Basic application.

The OLE Control's Shortcut Menu

Another way to embed objects in an OLE Container control is through the control's shortcut menu. Right-click an OLE Container control at design time to display the shortcut menu shown in Figure 14.8. Use this menu to insert a new object or to edit the embedded document if the control already contains an object. To embed (or link) another object in an OLE Container control, first delete the existing object.

The commands on the shortcut menu depend on the state of the selected object. The shortcut menu in Figure 14.8 contains the Edit and Open commands since the selected object is a Word document. If the embedded object is a sound file, the shortcut menu will contain the Edit and Play commands. If the control doesn't contain an object (because you clicked the Cancel button in the Insert Object dialog box), the Edit and Open commands, which depend on the control's contents, will be missing from the shortcut menu.

FIGURE 14.8:

To display the OLE Container control's shortcut menu, right-click the control at design time.

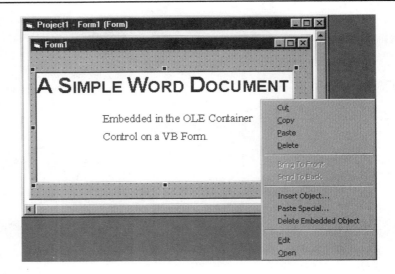

The shortcut menu of the OLE Container may contain some or all of the following commands:

- **Cut**   Copies the object in the container to the Clipboard and clears the container

- **Copy**   Copies the object in the container to the Clipboard

- **Paste**   Pastes an object from the Clipboard to the control

- **Delete**   Removes the OLE object from the OLE control

- **Insert Object**   Deletes the existing object and opens the Insert Object dialog box so that the user can insert a new or an existing object in the OLE Container control

- **Paste Special**
  Opens the Paste Special dialog box, which allows you to paste an object copied to the Clipboard from another OLE application. Whereas the Paste command embeds the object in the control, the Paste

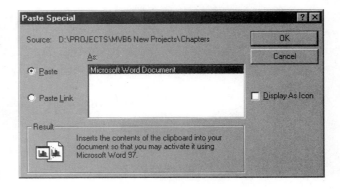

Special command creates a link to the object on the Clipboard. The Paste Special dialog box is similar to the Insert Object dialog box, except that its options apply to the object currently stored on the Clipboard.

- **Create Link**   Appears only if the SourceDoc property of the OLE Container control is set; creates a linked object

- **Delete Link**   Breaks a link and turns a linked object into an embedded object

- **Create Embedded Object**   Appears if either the SourceDoc or the Class properties are set; creates an embedded object

NOTE   To share your program with other users, they must have a copy of the application that created the file. If the OLE control contains a Word document, users of your application won't be able to view and edit the document unless they have Word installed on their system. Also, they must have a valid link (path name) to the linked file. Otherwise, when users run your program, only an image of the original data will be displayed.

Object Linking and Embedding at Runtime

In this section, we are going to create linked and embedded objects at runtime. This section's example is called OLERTime, and you'll find it in this chapter's folder on the CD. The OLERTime application demonstrates how to:

- Insert an object

- Choose between linking and embedding

- Set the size of the container control or the size of the object

- Display information about the object

The OLERTime application demonstrates how you can embed objects in and link them to an OLE Container control by opening the Insert Object dialog box from within your code. It programmatically does what you've been doing manually in the previous examples. Operations are performed from within the framework of a Visual Basic application, which lets the user select the object and set some of its basic properties. The application's main Form is shown in Figure 14.9.

FIGURE 14.9:

The OLERTime application's
main window

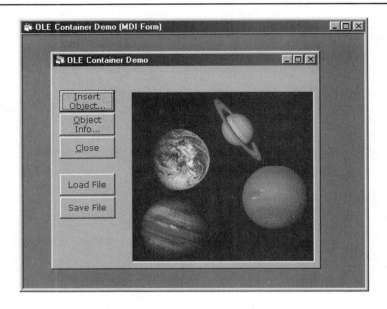

When you click the Insert Object button, the application displays the Object Type dialog box (see Figure 14.10) in which you set the container's Stretch mode and OLE type (link or embed). If you click OK, you'll display the Insert Object dialog box, in which you can specify a new object or select an existing one.

FIGURE 14.10:

The OLERTime application's
Object Type dialog box

To test the application, check the Stretch Container Control and Embedded options in the Object Type dialog box, and click OK. In the Insert Dialog box that appears, select the Excel Chart object. A chart with random data will appear on the control. You can edit the chart from within the OLERTime application, resize the graph (because the Stretch Container Control option is checked), and even save the revised chart to a local file. You can stop the program, run it again, and load the chart saved in the local file.

VB6 at Work: The OLERTime Application

To design the application, follow these steps:

1. Start a new Visual Basic project, and change the Form's name to **frmOLE**. This Form contains an OLE Container control, five Command buttons (as shown in Figure 14.9), and the Windows Common Dialogs control.

2. When you place the OLE Container control on the Form, the Insert Object dialog box will appear. Click Cancel to place an empty container on the Form. Resize the OLE Container control, and place on it the Command buttons shown in Figure 14.10.

3. Add a new Form to the project and place the controls you see in Figure 14.10 on it.

4. Save all the Forms and the project in a new folder.

Now, you'll add the code that will do the following:

- Display the second window (frmType) and activate the Insert Object dialog box
- Display information about the object

Open the Insert Object button's Click handler and enter the following:

```
Private Sub cmdInsObj_Click()
    frmType.Show
End Sub
```

The Object Info button displays information about the object that has been inserted in the container (you'll see shortly how the object is selected and inserted). The following code is executed when you click the Object Info button (*oleDisplay* is the name of the OLE control).

Code 14.3:   **The Object Info Button**

```
Private Sub cmdObjInfo_Click()
    Dim SourceText As String
    Dim TypeText As String
    Dim MsgText As String
    SourceText = "The object's source file is " + oleDisplay.SourceDoc
    TypeText = "The type of object is " + oleDisplay.Class
    MsgText = SourceText + Chr(13) + TypeText
    MsgBox MsgText, vbInformation, "Object Information"
End Sub
```

The carriage return character *(vbCrLF)* breaks the message into multiple short lines. If the embedded (or linked) object is a Word document, the following information is displayed:

```
The object's source file is C:\My Documents\FileName
The type of object is Word.Document
```

(*FileName* will be replaced by the name of the file you actually embed in the OLE control.) Figure 14.11 shows what the Object Info button displays if an Excel Chart object is embedded to the OLE Container control. The SourceItem is blank for a new Excel Chart object.

FIGURE 14.11:

The information reported by OLERTime for a linked bitmap

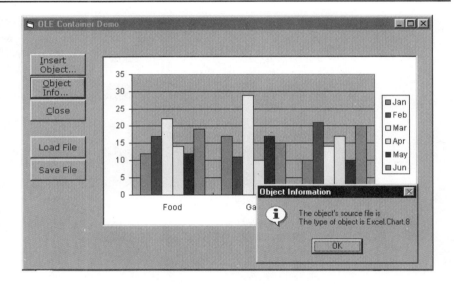

SourceDoc and Class Properties   The Object Info button displays the values of the SourceDoc and Class properties. The SourceDoc property is the name of the linked or embedded file. The Class property sets or returns the class name of an embedded object, which is its type. Other object types you'll find on your computer are Excel spreadsheets (Excel.Sheet), Paint pictures, and the objects you'll create in the remaining sections of this chapter. If you create a new object using Excel, Word, or another compatible OLE application, there will be no SourceDoc property because the embedded object is not yet a document that resides on the disk.

The SourceItem Property   The SourceItem property indicates the part of the document that is embedded or linked. In many cases, this property is undefined because the entire object is linked. You can, however, select part of some objects for embedding. You can't select part of a Word document or a bitmap, but you can select part of an Excel spreadsheet. If you select a range of cells, the SourceItem property might be something like "R1C1:R1C10." Although the OLERTime application allows you to select the file to be embedded, it doesn't support drag-and-drop, so the SourceItem property is empty.

When you click the Insert Object button, the application displays a window that offers you a choice of data types. You can select Linked or Embedded. You can also determine the size of the object to be displayed by setting the size mode in the OLE Container control's Properties window. The choices are:

- Stretch the OLE Container control to fit the object (2–AutoSize)

- Stretch the object to fit the container (1–Stretch)

When you click OK, the Insert Object dialog box opens, and you can select the data to insert.

Draw the Command buttons, Option buttons, and frames as shown previously in Figure 14.10. Then add the following code for Cancel button.

Code 14.4:   **The frmType**

```
Option Explicit
Private Sub cmdCancel_Click()
  Unload frmType
End Sub
```

This Sub procedure closes the application by unloading *frmType*.

Setting the Size of the OLE Container Control   Let's digress for a moment and set the size for the OLE Container control. When embedding objects in an OLE Container control at runtime, you must take into consideration the size of the control because the user can't change it with the mouse. Let's declare the variables *OLE-Height* and *OLEWidth* so that the size of the control will be the size you select at design time. Instead of hardcoding the height and width of the container control, we'll use *OLEHeight* and *OLEWidth*, which are more flexible. In the frmOLE Form's declaration section enter the following:

```
Public OLEHeight As Integer
Public OLEWidth As Integer
```

In the Form's Load event add the following lines:

```
OLEHeight = oleDisplay.Height
OLEWidth = oleDisplay.Width
```

Now return to frmType and add the code to call the Insert Object dialog box after the user sets the desired options.

Code 14.5:   **Invoking the Insert Object Dialog Box**

```
Private Sub cmdOK_Click()
    With frmOLE.oleDisplay
        .Height = frmOLE.OLEHeight
        .Width = frmOLE.OLEWidth
    End With
    If optStretchObject.Value = True Then
        frmOLE.oleDisplay.SizeMode = 1      ' Stretch
    Else
        frmOLE.oleDisplay.SizeMode = 2      ' AutoSize
    End If
```

Add the following line to hide the Form:

```
frmType.Hide
```

Finally, the following lines open the Insert Object dialog box and insert the object:

```
frmOLE.oleDisplay.InsertObjDlg
If frmOLE.oleDisplay.Class <> "" Then
    frmOLE.cmdObjInfo.Enabled = True
End If
Unload frmType
```

The Object Info button becomes enabled only if an object is inserted.

InsertObjDlg is a method of the OLE Container control that displays the Insert Object dialog box so that the user can create a linked or an embedded object by choosing its type and the application that provides the object. The user's choices are automatically assigned to the appropriate properties of the OLE control.

To size the container, follow these steps:

1. Run the application and click the Insert Object button to display the Object Type dialog box.

2. Click one of the Size Mode buttons, and then click one of the Object Type buttons. The Insert Object dialog box appears as shown in Figure 14.12.

Here's the complete listing of the frmOLE Form. Notice the Resize event handler of the OLE Container control. If the control is allowed to be resized at runtime, the Resize event is triggered every time the user resizes it. This event reports the new dimensions of the control with the *HeightNew* and *WidthNew* arguments. These values are used by the event handler to resize the Form accordingly.

FIGURE 14.12:

The Insert Object dialog box shows the Create from File Option button selected and displays the path to the data file.

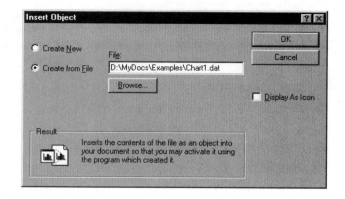

Code 14.6:   **The frmOLE Form**

```
Option Explicit

Private Sub cmdClose_Click()
    Dim Quit As String
    Quit = MsgBox("Are you sure you want to quit?", vbYesNo + vbQuestion)
    If Quit = vbYes Then
        End
    End If
End Sub

Private Sub cmdInsObj_Click()
    frmType.Show
End Sub

Private Sub cmdObjInfo_Click()
    Dim SourceText As String
    Dim TypeText As String
    Dim MsgText As String
    SourceText = "The object's source file is " + oleDisplay.SourceDoc
    TypeText = "The type of object is " + oleDisplay.Class
    MsgText = SourceText + Chr(13) + TypeText
    MsgBox MsgText, vbInformation, "Object Information"
End Sub

Private Sub bttnLoad_Click()
Dim fnum As Integer
    On Error GoTo LoadCancel
```

```
        fnum = FreeFile
        CommonDialog1.ShowOpen          ' show Open dialog
        Open CommonDialog1.FileName For Binary As #1      ' Open file
        oleDisplay.ReadFromFile (fnum)  ' Read file No. 1
        Close #fnum
        Exit Sub
LoadCancel:
        MsgBox "Could not load file"
        Close #fnum
End Sub

Private Sub bttnSave_Click()
Dim fnum As Integer
        On Error GoTo SaveCancel
        CommonDialog1.ShowSave          ' show Save As dialog
        fnum = FreeFile
        Open CommonDialog1.FileName For Binary As #1      ' Open file
        oleDisplay.SaveToFile (fnum)    ' Write to file No. 1
        Close #fnum                     ' Close file
        Exit Sub
SaveCancel:
        MsgBox "Could not save file"
        Close #fnum
End Sub

Private Sub oleDisplay_Resize(HeightNew As Single, WidthNew As Single)
        frmOLE.Width = oleDisplay.Left + WidthNew _
                + 20 * Screen.TwipsPerPixelX
        frmOLE.Height = oleDisplay.Top + HeightNew _
                + 80 * Screen.TwipsPerPixelY
End Sub
```

Code 14.7:   The frmType Form

```
Option Explicit
Private Sub cmdCancel_Click()
        Unload frmType
End Sub

Private Sub cmdOK_Click()
        With frmOLE.oleDisplay
            .Height = frmOLE.OLEHeight
            .Width = frmOLE.OLEWidth
```

```
        End With
        If optStretchObject.Value = True Then
            .SizeMode = 1
        Else
            .SizeMode = 2
        End If

        If optTypeEmbedded.Value = True Then
            frmOLE.oleDisplay.OLETypeAllowed = 1      ' Linked
        Else
            frmOLE.oleDisplay.OLETypeAllowed = 0      ' Embedded
        End If

    'Hide frmType
      frmType.Hide
    'Insert Object
      frmOLE.oleDisplay.InsertObjDlg
      If frmOLE.oleDisplay.Class <> "" Then
          frmOLE.cmdObjInfo.Enabled = True
      End If
      Unload frmType
End Sub
```

Try embedding various objects in the OLE control of the OLERTime Form and double-click the control to edit them. You'll see that the OLE Container control is still somewhat rough around the edges. It takes a while to embed or link a document, and sometimes when you switch to edit mode, the server application's toolbars may not be visible. Embedding objects in the OLE Container control is not used commonly in Visual Basic programming. Later in this chapter, you'll learn how to OLE automate server applications and how to instruct the server application to carry out some tasks and return the results to the Visual Basic application.

Common OLE Container Control Properties

This section summarizes the properties and methods used in creating embedded and linked documents at runtime. The same properties are set by Visual Basic when the object is inserted at design time with any of the methods already described.

Class

This property identifies the type of object held by the OLE Container control. To see this, run the OLERTime application, select various types of objects registered on your system, and then click the Object Info button to view their Class property.

DisplayType

This property specifies whether the object displays with the content (0) of the object or as an icon (1) of the OLE server. The related constants are:

- *vbOLEDisplayContent* (0) This setting displays the object's contents.
- *vbOLEDisplayIcon* (1) This setting displays the object as an icon.

OLETypeAllowed

This property determines the type of object you can create:

- 0–Linked
- 1–Embedded
- 2–Either

The type of object is specified in the Insert Object dialog box. The related constants are:

- *vbOLELinked* (0) The object will be linked.
- *vbOLEEmbedded* (1) The object will be embedded.
- *vbOLEEither* (2) The object can be linked or embedded.

OLEDropAllowed

If this property is set to True, a user can drag-and-drop an object onto the OLE Container control at runtime. This has the same effect as copying an object onto the Clipboard and the application calling the Paste Special method on the OLE Container control.

SizeMode

This property determines how an object's icon or data image is displayed in the OLE Container control, and its settings are as follows:

- *vbOLESizeClip* (0) This is the default. The object is displayed at its actual size. If the object is larger than the OLE Container control, its image is clipped by the control's borders.
- *vbOLESizeStretch* (1) The object's image is sized to fill the OLE Container control. The image may not maintain the original proportions of the object.

- *vbOLESizeAutosize* (2)   The OLE Container control is resized to display the entire object.

- *vbOLESizeZoom* (3)   The object is resized to fill as much of the OLE Container control as possible while maintaining its original proportions.

SourceDoc

When you create a linked object, this property determines which source file to link. When you create an embedded object, this property determines which file to use as a template.

SourceItem

This property is for linked objects only. It specifies the data to link within a file. For example, if you're linking a range of Excel worksheet cells, the SourceItem property specifies the range of cells that are linked.

OLEType

This property is read-only and returns the status of an object at runtime. Its value is 0 for linked objects, 1 for embedded objects, and 2 if no object is inserted. The related constants are:

- *vbOLELinked* (0)   The object is linked in the OLE control.

- *vbOLEEmbedded* (1)   The object is embedded in the OLE control.

- *vbOLENone* (2)   The OLE Container control is empty.

AutoActivate

This property determines whether the contents of the OLE Container will be activated by a double-click or each time the focus moves to the control. The AutoActivate property can take the following values:

- *vbOLEActivateManual* (0)   The object isn't activated automatically. You use the DoVerb method to activate it.

- *vbOLEActivateGetFocus* (1)   The object is activated for editing each time the OLE Container control gets the focus.

- *vbOLEActivateDoubleclick*(2)   This is the default value. The object in the OLE Container control is activated when the user double-clicks the control.

- *vbOLEActivateAuto* (3)   The object is activated normally, either when the control receives the focus or when the user double-clicks the control.

Common OLE Container Control Methods

To manipulate embedded or linked objects, the OLE Container control provides the following methods, in addition to the properties already mentioned.

CreateEmbed

This method creates an embedded object. It has the following syntax:

```
CreateEmbed sourcedoc, class
```

The *sourcedoc* argument is the filename of a document used as a template for the embedded object. To create a new embedded document, supply a zero-length string ("") for the *sourcedoc* argument.

The *class* argument is an optional argument that specifies the name of the class of the embedded object. This argument is required only if the *sourcedoc* argument is omitted. To find out the registered classes, select the OLE Container control's Class property in the Properties window and click the button with the ellipsis.

CreateLink

This method creates a linked object from the contents of a file. It has the following syntax:

```
CreateLink sourcedoc, sourceitem
```

The *sourcedoc* argument is the file from which the object will be created, and *sourceitem* is the data within the file to be linked in the linked object. For example, to link the contents of the OLE Container control to a range of Excel cells, specify the file with the *sourcedoc* argument and the range of cells to be linked with the *sourceitem* argument. The *sourceitem* argument can be a single cell, such as R10C12, or a range of cells, such as R1C1:R10C20. You can also specify a named range.

After the linked document is created, the SourceItem property is reset to a zero-length string, and its original value is appended to the SourceDoc property, which becomes something like the following:

```
"c:\data\revenus\rev1997.xls|R1C1:R20C25"
```

An easy way to determine the syntax of the two commands is to select the object you want to link (or a similar one) and then paste it with the Paste Special command on the OLE Container control at design time. After the object is linked, look up the value of the SourceDoc property and use it in your code.

DoVerb *verb*

The DoVerb method executes a command (which is a verb like Edit, Play and so on). The object knows how to carry out the command The optional *verb* argument can have one of the values in Table 14.3.

TABLE 14.3: Values of the *verb* Argument

CONSTANT	VALUE	DESCRIPTION
vbOLEPrimary	0	Default action for the object
vbOLEShow	-1	Opens the object for editing. This activates the application that created the document in the OLE Container.
vbOLEOpen	-2	Opens the object for editing. This activates the application that created the document in a separate window.
vbOLEHide	-3	For embedded objects, this hides the application that created the object
vbOLEUIActivate	-4	Activates the object for in-place editing and shows any user interface tools. If the object doesn't support in-place editing, an error occurs.
vbOLEInPlaceActivate	-5	When the user moves the focus to the OLE Container control, this action creates a window for the object and prepares the object to be edited
vbOLEDiscardUndoState	-6	When the object is activated for editing, this method can discard all the changes that the object's application can undo

InsertObjDlg

This method displays the Insert Object dialog box. The user's selections are reported to the application via the properties of the OLE Container control.

PasteSpecialDlg

This method displays the Paste Special dialog box. The user's selections are reported to the application via the OLE Container control's properties.

To find out the intrinsic constants you can use with the various methods and properties of the OLE Container control, use the Object Browser.

1. Choose View ➤ Object Browser.

2. Select the Visual Basic object library, and then choose the Constants object to display the names of the constants under Methods/Properties.

If you experiment a little with OLE techniques and the OLE Container control, you'll realize that OLE is still rough around the edges. You don't have complete control over the appearance of the embedded or linked object, and sometimes the server application's toolbars are not visible. In general, OLE is not quite mature, even though it's been around for a few years.

In reality, not many Visual Basic applications embed and link documents provided by server applications. However, there's another aspect of OLE, OLE Automation, which has matured and is one of the most powerful features of major Windows applications such as the Office application. We'll discuss OLE Automation in the second half of the chapter, but first let's look briefly at OLE drag-and-drop operations.

OLE Drag-and-Drop Operations

In Chapter 4, you learned how to program drag-and-drop operations. Drag-and-drop operations allow the user to drag a control on a Form and drop it on another control (which may reside on the same or another Form). The destination control knows when another control is dropped and can be programmed to react to this action. However, you must supply some code in the destination control's Drag-Drop event or nothing will happen.

Many applications allow you to drag-and-drop not only controls, but also documents, or parts of documents. For example, you can select a range of cells in an Excel worksheet and drop them on a Word document. If you use the right mouse button for this operation, you can link the source data into the destination document. This operation is called OLE drag-and-drop, because it relies on OLE (you can drag-and-drop parts of documents only among applications that support OLE).

To add OLE drag-and-drop capabilities to certain controls on a Form, you must set the following properties of the controls:

- **OLEDragMode** Determines whether a control can initiate a drag-and-drop operation, similar to the DragMode. This property can be set to 0–Manual (the control can be dragged under program control) or 1–Automatic (the control can be dragged automatically).

- **OLEDropMode** This property is equivalent to the DropMode property and determines whether a control can act as the destination of an OLE drag-and-drop operation. This property can be set to 0–None (the control can't be used as a destination), 1–Manual (the control must be programmed to react to OLE drag-and-drop operations), or 2–Automatic (the control automatically becomes the destination).

The simplest method to incorporate OLE drag-and-drop functionality in your applications is to set the OLEDragMode property of the source control to 1 (Automatic) and the OLEDropMode of the destination control to 2 (Automatic).

Figure 14.13 shows the OLEDDAUTO project (you'll find it in the Oledd folder on the CD), whose main Form contains a RichTextBox control, a TextBox control, and a PictureBox control. Click the Load Image button to load an image to the PictureBox control and enter some text in the TextBox and RichTextBox controls. You can also open a text file in the TextBox control by clicking the Load Text File button.

FIGURE 14.13:

The OLEDDAUTO project demonstrates automatic OLE drag-and-drop operations.

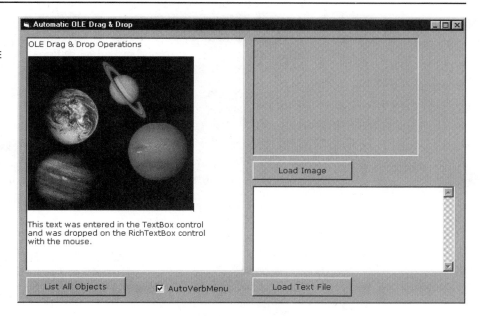

If you drag the image and drop it on the RichTextBox control, it will be inserted in the text at the pointer's location. You can also select part of the text in the Text-Box control and drop it to the RichTextBox control. It will be inserted at the current location. As you can see, by using the Automatic setting for the OLEDragMode and OLEDropMode properties, you can bring OLE drag-and-drop operations into your application with no coding at all.

Obviously, the destination of an OLE drag-and-drop operation must be able to recognize and display multiple types of information, and in this sense, the Rich-TextBox control is an ideal candidate. This application also demonstrates a very important property of the RichTextBox control: OLEObjects. The RichTextBox control's *OLEObjects* property is a collection that contains all the objects in the control except for text. Drop an image or two on the RichTextBox control of the OLEDDAUTO application. Then drop a few files from the Desktop or any other folder. Just make sure that the application and the folder's window with the desired file are visible, then drag a file's icon and drop it on the RichTextBox control. To drop the text of the TextBox control, you must first select it with the mouse, then drag it across to the RichTextBox control.

After you've placed a few objects on the RichTextBox control, click the List All Object files button and you'll see a description of each object in the control. The code behind the Command button scans the OLEObjects collection and prints out the Class property of each item in the collection in the Immediate window. The Class of a bitmap is StaticDIB.

The items of the OLEObjects collection have other properties too, such as the *DisplayType* property (which determines whether an object appears on the control as contents or as an icon) and the *ObjectVerbs* collection (contains all the verbs, or commands, recognized by the object). To find out which actions an embedded object can carry out, you must first call the *FetchVerbs* method as follows:

```
Set AllVerbs = RichTextBox1.OLEObjects(1).FetchVerbs
For i = 1 to AllVerbs.Count
    {enumerate the commands}
    {at each iteration the current verb is AllVerbs(i)}
Next
```

To invoke a specific verb (like the Play verb for a multimedia file) on one of the objects, use the following statement:

```
RichTextBox1.OLEObjects(1).DoVerb("Play")
```

Programming OLE Drag-and-Drop Operations

Manual OLE drag-and-drop operations are more flexible than automatic operations because your program is in control. The OLEDDMAN project (also in the OLEDD folder on the CD) has the same interface as the OLEDDAUTO project, but it uses the manual setting of the OLEDropMode property. The TextBox's OLEDragMode property is set to Automatic, so no code is needed to initiate the operation. The same is true for the PictureBox and RichTextBox controls.

Each control detects when an object is dropped on it and they react to the action differently. Let's start with the simpler control, the TextBox control. When an object is dropped, the OLEDragDrop event takes place, which is equivalent to the Drag-Drop event. The OLEDragDrop event's definition is:

```
Private Sub Text1_OLEDragDrop(Data As DataObject, _
    Effect As Long, Button As Integer, Shift As Integer, _
    x As Single, y As Single)
```

Data is an object variable that represents the object that was dropped. The *Data* variable provides several properties for accessing the object (they are discussed shortly). *Effect* is a constant that determines the type of the drop (whether it's a Move or Copy operation). The *Button* argument reports the button that triggered the drop operation; the *Shift* argument contains information about the status of the Shift, Alt, and Ctrl keys; and the last two arguments are the coordinates of the point where the drop operation took place.

The methods of the Data object are similar to the methods of the Clipboard object. The GetFormat method lets you find out the format of the data. The GetFormat method doesn't return a data type; instead, it must be called with a data type, and it returns True if the data is of the specified type, False otherwise. To find out whether the Data object contains text, use an If structure like the following one:

```
If Data.GetFormat(vbCFText) Then
    {process text}
End If
```

(The constants that describe the various data types are the same ones used with the Clipboard.)

To actually retrieve the data, use the *GetData* method. The GetData method returns an object, which must be assigned to the proper variable. If the data format is text, you can assign the value returned by the GetData method to the Text property of a TextBox control. If the data is a bitmap, you can assign it to the Picture property of a control that can display images.

The syntax of the GetData method is:

```
Data.GetData(format)
```

where *format* is a constant that determines the desired data format. Many times, the same object can have different formats. When you select a paragraph from a Word document, you can drop it on a TextBox control as text or you can drop it on a Rich-TextBox control as formatted text. The data itself can be retrieved in multiple formats, depending on the capabilities of the destination control. The EditCopy method of the Graph control (discussed in Appendix B, *The MSChart Control*) has a similar behavior. The EditCopy method copies the current graph from a Graph control. The same data can be pasted as a bitmap on an image processing application or as text on a text editor.

If the user has dropped one or more files on the control (the expression Get-Format *(vbCFFiles)* is True), you can use the *Files* collection of the Data object to retrieve their names:

```
If Data.GetFormat(vbCFFiles) Then
    For i = 1 To Data.Files.Count
        {process file Data.Files(i) }
    Next
End If
```

Here's how the TextBox control handles OLE drag-and-drop operations:

```
Private Sub Text1_OLEDragDrop(Data As DataObject, _
     Effect As Long, Button As Integer, Shift As Integer, _
     x As Single, y As Single)
Dim pic As Picture
    If Data.GetFormat(vbCFFiles) Then
        Text1.Text = "You dropped the following files:" & vbCrLf
        For i = 1 To Data.Files.Count
            Text1.Text = Text1.Text & Data.Files(i) & vbCrLf
        Next
    End If
    If Data.GetFormat(vbCFRTF) Then
        Text1.Text = Data.GetData(vbCFText)
    End If
If Data.GetFormat(vbCFBitmap) Then
        imgWidth = Round(ScaleX(Data.GetData _
            (vbCFBitmap).Width, vbHimetric, vbPixels))
        imgHeight = Round(ScaleY(Data.GetData _
            (vbCFBitmap).Height, vbHimetric, vbPixels))
        Text1.Text = "You dropped an image with the _
            following specifications:" & vbCrLf
        Text1.Text = Text1.Text & "WIDTH  " & _
                imgWidth & vbCrLf
        Text1.Text = Text1.Text & "HEIGHT " & imgHeight
    End If
```

If you drop one or more files on the TextBox control, their names will be listed. If you drop the RichTextBox control's text, then the same text (without formatting) will appear on the TextBox control. Finally, if you drop the image of the PictureBox control, then the image's characteristics will be displayed. Notice how the program retrieves the dimensions of the image. The object returned by the GetData method is a Picture object; therefore, we can call its Width and Height properties to read its dimensions.

The code in the RichTextBox control's OLEDragDrop event handler is similar. The RichTextBox control understands more types of data and it must handle each one differently. You can open the project in Visual Basic's IDE and examine the code. If you attempt to drop the image on the RichTextBox control, you'll get an error message. The following statements should insert the bitmap in the RichTextBox control, but they fail. Instead of moving the image, they produce a runtime error.

```
If Data.GetFormat(vbCFBitmap) Or Data.GetFormat(vbCFDIB) Then
        RichTextBox1.OLEObjects.Add , , Data.GetData(vbCFDIB)
        GoTo PasteDone
    End If
```

The only workaround I'm able to suggest is to momentarily switch the Rich-TextBox control's OLEDropMode property to Automatic, then reset it to manual. The first action must take place from within the PictureBox control's OLEStart-Drag event:

```
Private Sub Picture1_OLEStartDrag(Data As DataObject, _
        AllowedEffects As Long)
    RichTextBox1.OLEDropMode = rtfOLEDropAutomatic
End Sub
```

After the drop operation completes, you can reset the RichTextBox control's OLEDropMode property back to manual. This action must take place in the Text-Box control's OLECompleteDrag event, which signals the end of the OLE drag-and-drop operation:

```
Private Sub Picture1_OLECompleteDrag(Effect As Long)
    RichTextBox1.OLEDropMode = rtfOLEDropManual
End Sub
```

OLE drag-and-drop operations are similar to plain drag-and-drop operations, but they can get quite a bit more complicated because of the variety of objects that can be dropped. The destination control must be able to decipher the type of object that is dropped and handle it accordingly. The ability to detect the drop of files on a Visual Basic Form means that you can write applications that can interact with the Desktop (receive the files dropped by the user, process them, move them to a different folder, and so on). OLE drag-and-drop is a very interesting capability which you may wish to further explore on your own. See the Visual Basic Help files for more information on related properties and events.

OLE Automation

OLE Automation goes one step beyond linking. When you link, you borrow the functionality of another application. When you use OLE Automation, you control the source document from within your application. Applications that support OLE Automation expose their objects to other applications. For example, an object that Word exposes could be a sentence, a paragraph, or an entire document. An object that Excel exposes could be a macro, a range of cells, or an entire worksheet.

You can control exposed objects from your Visual Basic application via the properties and methods exposed by the source application. An important feature of Visual Basic is that you can both access the objects of an OLE server application and use the functionality of the server application. The benefit of OLE Automation is that you can work in a single environment and use any OLE tools that are available from other applications.

When Microsoft developed OLE Automation, their basic idea was really simple: create a common language and programming environment for a number of applications so that people could customize applications and add capabilities to suit their own environments. The result was the language Visual Basic for Applications.

You can't use VBA to develop any type of application you may need or think of. VBA provides only basic control structures, math and string functions, and variable manipulation capabilities. The real power of VBA comes from the objects of the applications that support it.

With the introduction of VBA 5, Microsoft started licensing the language to manufacturers who wanted to add programmable features to their products, for example, Autodesk's AutoCAD. AutoCAD had been a programmable environment for many years, but its programming language was unique to AutoCAD and couldn't be shared with other applications. Many other manufacturers included scripting languages or other means of automating their software, but the need for a global language that could act as the glue in putting together pieces of many applications was clear. Finally, Microsoft came up with a version of VBA (version 5) that met the needs of other manufacturers. VBA is now on its way to becoming a universal language for automating applications under Windows.

Most businesses today buy off-the-shelf software and need to customize it. More than half the corporations in the United States use Microsoft Office products. Many of them use VBA to customize these applications to suit their specific business needs. This trend will continue and become stronger in the future. There is already a need not only to customize applications, but to tie them together so that they can communicate. VBA serves both functions, and as a result, the need for VBA programmers will increase in the next few years.

Today's applications are so powerful and feature-rich that it no longer makes sense to develop custom applications. Even the Office 97 applications are adequate for addressing most of the day-to-day computer operations of a typical corporation. With a host of third-party applications supporting VBA, you can easily guess its importance in corporate environments. Let's start our exploration of OLE Automation by looking at a few examples.

Contacting an OLE Server

To access the services of an OLE server application, you must first create a variable that references Excel. This variable is called an *object variable*, because it represents an object rather than an integer or other simple data types. The characteristic of object variables is that they expose the members of the application or Class that they represent. Excel, for instance, exposes the Evaluate method, which lets you evaluate any math expression. This method can't be accessed directly; it must be accessed through an object variable that represents the Excel application. In other words, you can't use a statement like:

```
Excel.Evaluate "Log(499/0.785)"    ' WRONG!
```

You must first create an object variable, for instance, *ExcelObj,* and then call the *ExcelObj* variable's Evaluate method:

```
ExcelObj.Evaluate "Log(499/0.785)"
```

There are two functions that create object variables. The *CreateObject()* function, which creates a new instance of the application you want to reference, and the *GetObject()* function, which contacts an instance of the application that's already running on the computer. These functions are explained next.

NOTE   To be able to access OLE Automation servers from within your Visual Basic application, you must add the appropriate reference to the project through the References dialog box (Project ➤ References). To reference Excel, add the entry "Microsoft Excel 8.0 Object Library," to reference Word, add the entry "Microsoft Word 8.0 Object Library," and to reference Outlook 98 add the entry "Microsoft Outlook 98 Object Model" to your project.

Creating a New Instance

The first method of contacting an OLE server application is to start a new instance of the application with the CreateObject() function, whose syntax is:

```
Set AppObject = CreateObject(Class, ServerName)
```

Class is the server application's Class name as it's registered in the Registry. The Class name of Word is the string "Word.Application" and the Class name of Excel is "Excel.Application". This is the *Class* argument of the CreateObject() function.

The second argument is optional and it's the name of the network server on which the object will be created. If the server application resides in another machine, you must also specify the name of the machine on which the Class will be created. If the server application has been installed on the machine "Toolkit," then use the following statement to create a new instance of Excel:

```
Set EXLApp = CreateObject("Excel.Application", "Toolkit")
```

Contacting an Existing Instance

If the application you want to contact is running already, there's usually no reason to start a new instance. You can contact the running instance of the application and open a new document. To contact a running instance of a server application use the GetObject() function, whose syntax is:

```
Set AppObject = GetObject(pathname, class)
```

Both arguments of the GetObject() are optional, but one of them must be specified. The full path and file name of the document to be opened with the server application is *pathname*. The second argument, *class,* is the name of the application's Class as it's registered with the system Registry.

If you specify a document to be opened by the application, you don't have to supply the application's Class name. For example, you don't have to specify that a worksheet be opened with Excel. The system knows that files with extension XLS are handled by Excel, for example:

```
Set EXLApp = GetObject("C:\sample files\Sales98.xls")
```

The previous statement will also start Excel and load the specified file if no instance of Excel is running at the time. Finally, to contact the running instance of Excel use the statement:

```
Set EXLApp = GetObject(, "Excel.Application")
```

In many situations, it doesn't make any difference whether you start a new instance of the server application or contact an existing one. To call the Evaluate method of Excel, for instance, you don't need a new instance of Excel. If one is running already, you can contact it to evaluate the math expression. After this action completes, the running instance of Excel is in the exact same state as before. Therefore, it's more efficient to attempt to contact an existing instance of the server application. Only if there are no currently active instances should you start a new instance. The following code segment does exactly this. It attempts to contact a running instance of Word. If Word isn't running at the time, a runtime error is generated. The `On Error Resume Next` statement causes Visual Basic to suppress the error message and continue with the statement that follows, which examines the Err object. If an error occurs, then it knows that the GetObject() function failed and it uses the CreateObject() function to start a new instance of Word.

Code 14.8:   **Contacting or Starting Word**

```
On Error Resume Next
Set AppWord = GetObject("Word.Application")
If AppWord Is Nothing Then
    Set AppWord = CreateObject("Word.Application")
    If AppWord Is Nothing Then
        MsgBox "Could not start Word. Application will quit"
        End
    End If
End If
```

Declaring Object Variables

The object variable that represents an OLE server application can be declared either as Object or as a specific type (like Excel.Application or Word.Application). If you declare the *EXLApp* variable as Object, then every time you call its properties or methods, Visual Basic must first make sure these members exist before contacting them. Because Object is a generic variable type that can accommodate all types of objects, Visual Basic doesn't know which object an object variable represents at design time and it can't detect syntax errors when you enter the code. For example, if you mistype a member name, Visual Basic won't catch it at design time. Excel, for example, supports the Evaluate method, which evaluates math expressions. If you declare *EXLApp* as Object and then attempt to access its Calculate method, Visual Basic won't spot the error.

If you've declared the variable *EXLApp* as Excel.Application, then Visual Basic won't only catch any references to nonexistent members, it will also display the list of members in a list as soon as you type the period following the *EXLApp* variable's name. In other words, by declaring variables with their proper type, syntax errors are caught as you enter code. The application is not going to crash because you've misspelled one of its member's name. Even if the option Member AutoList is turned off, these errors will be caught during compilation.

Another far more serious implication of proper object type declaration is performance. When Visual Basic sees an expression like EXLApp.Property, it must first make sure that the specified property exists, then contact the server application represented by the *EXLApp* object and invoke its Property member. The compiler will produce additional statements that contact the application represented by an object variable to make sure that it exposes the requested member. Even worse, these statements will be executed every time your application requests a member of the *EXLApp* object. To avoid this unnecessary delay, simply declare the *EXLApp* object variable with its proper type.

Object variables declared with specific types are called *early-bound*, because Visual Basic can bind them to the objects they represent at design time. Object variables declared generically (as Object) are called *late-bound*. Visual Basic can't bind them to specific objects at design time and any errors will surface at runtime.

To take advantage of the early binding of object variables, declare them with the proper types. Late binding of variables is not always a bad practice. Sometimes, we don't know the type of object we'll store in a variable and our only option is to declare it as Object. For example, you may have to switch between the Form and Printer objects from within your code. An elegant method of printing on either object is to declare an *OutputObject* variable and then set it to the desired device with one of the following two statements:

```
Set OutputObject = Printer
Set OutputObject = Screen
```

When you issue the Print method of the *OutputObject*, it applies to the object that was most recently assigned to the *OutputObject* object variable. In situations like this one, the *OutputObject* variable can't be early-bound.

Accessing Excel through an Object Variable

The *EXLObject* variable is an object variable that exposes the objects of Excel. To access the current workbook, for instance, use the expression:

```
EXLObject.ActiveWorkbook
```

To access the currently active sheet in the active workbook, use the expression:

```
EXLObject.ActiveWorkbook.ActiveSheet
```

The objects we usually want to access on a worksheet are the cells, which are represented by the Cells collection. To access the first cell of the second row and assign the value 99 to it, use the following expression:

```
EXLObject.ActiveWorkbook.ActiveSheet.Cells(2, 1).Value = 99
```

The properties and methods for accessing Excel that give you access to the cells and allow you to manipulate them are discussed later in the chapter. What you should keep in mind is that they are accessed through the variable returned by the CreateObject() function. The CreateObject() function, as well as the GetObject() function, return a reference to an OLE server. This variable is your gateway to the *object model* exposed by the server application. The object model is a hierarchy of objects that correspond to the objects of the server application (e.g., Excel's cells and macros, Word's sentences and dictionaries).

In the remaining sections of this chapter, I will describe the most basic objects of the Word 97, Excel 97, and Outlook 98 (the beta version that was made available before the release of Visual Basic 6). By the time you read this book, Windows 98 versions of Word and Excel may be available. The following examples should work without adjustments. If you experience any problems, you'll find the newer version at Sybex's Web site, on the page for this book.

Discussing all the objects exposed by these applications would probably require three different books. I've limited the discussion to the basic objects exposed by the applications and provide examples that you can experiment with. Using your understanding of the basic objects of these applications and the help of the Object Browser, which lists the objects exposed by each application, you should be able to develop interesting applications that rely on the services of OLE server applications.

Automating Word

Microsoft Word provides numerous objects which you can use to program any action that can be carried out with menu commands. For example, you can open a document, count words and characters, replace certain words in it, and save it back on disk without user intervention. You can actually do all this in background without even displaying Word's window on the Desktop.

The top-level Word object is the *Application* object, which represents the current instance of the application. You can use the Application object to access some general properties of the Word's window including its Visible property (to make the application visible or not) and the active document (to switch to one of the open documents).

Under the Application object is the *Documents* collection, which contains a *Document* object for each open document. Using an object variable of Document type, you can access any open document (or open and create new documents). The most important object that each document exposes is the *Range* object, which represents a contiguous section of text. This section can be words, part of a word, characters, or even the entire document. Using the Range object's methods, you can insert new text, format existing text (or delete it), and so on.

To address specific units of text, use the following collections:

- The *Paragraphs* collection, which is made up of *Paragraph* objects that represent text paragraphs

- The *Words* collection, which is made up of *Word* objects that represent words

- The *Characters* collection, which is made up of *Character* objects that represent individual characters

For example, you retrieve all the paragraphs of a document through the Paragraphs collection of the Document object. If you apply the same method to the current selection (represented by the Selection object), you retrieve all the paragraphs in the selected text. In the following section, we are going to explore the members of the basic objects exposed by Word and show you how to use them from within your Visual Basic code.

The Documents Collection and the Document Object

The first object under the Word Application object hierarchy is the Document object, which is any document that can be opened with Word or any document that can be displayed in Word's window. All open documents belong to a Documents collection that is made up of Document objects. Like all other collections, it supports the Count property (the number of open documents); the Add method, which adds a new document; and the Remove method, which closes an existing one. To access an open document, you can use the Item method of the Documents collection, specifying the document's index as follows:

```
Application.Documents.Item(1)
```

Or, you can specify the document's name:

```
Application.Documents.Item("MasteringVB.doc")
```

Since Item is the collection default property, you can omit its name altogether:

```
Application.Documents(1)
```

To open an existing document, use the Documents collection's Open method, whose syntax is:

```
Documents.Open(fileName)
```

The *fileName* argument is the document file's path name.

To create a new document, use the Documents collection's Add method, which accepts two optional arguments:

```
Documents.Add (template, newTemplate)
```

The argument *template* specifies the name of a template file to be used as the basis for the new document. The *newTemplate* argument is a Boolean value. If it's set to True, Word creates a new template file.

Most of the operations you'll perform apply to the active document (the document in the active Word window), which is represented by the *ActiveDocument* object, a property of the Application object. To access the selected text in the active document, use the following expression:

```
Application.ActiveDocument.Selection
```

You can also make any document active by calling the *Activate* method of the Document object. To make the document *MyNotes.doc* active, use the following statement:

```
Documents("MyNotes.doc").Activate
```

After the execution of this statement, the MyNotes.doc document becomes the active one, and your code can refer to it through the object *Application.ActiveDocument*.

Printing and Saving Documents

To print a document, call its Printout method, which has the following syntax:

```
Printout Background, append, range, outputfilename, _
         from, to, item, copies, pages, PrintToFile, _
         Collate, ActivePrinterMacGX, ManualDuplexPrint
```

All the arguments are optional and they correspond to the properties you can set on Word's Print dialog box. The *Background* argument is an optional value that specifies whether the printout will take place in the background, and this argument is usually set to True when we're automating applications.

TIP

When calling methods with a large number of arguments (most of which are omitted anyway), you should use named arguments to specify only a few arguments. For example, to print the first three pages of the active document, use the following syntax:

```
AppWord.ActiveDocument.Printout from:=1, to:=3
```

When you use VBA to instruct Word to print a document, the process of spooling the document to the printer queue is not instantaneous. If you attempt to quit the application immediately after calling the Printout method, Word will inform you that quitting at this point will cancel the printout. To make sure that the document has been spooled (which means you can safely quit Word), you must set up a loop that examines the value of the BackgroundPrintingStatus property. As long as this property is not 0, the application is busy spooling the document. After all the information has been queued, you can quit Word. We'll use this technique in the section "VB6 at Work: The WordVBA Project," later in this chapter.

To save a document, use the *SaveAs* method of the Document object, which has the following syntax:

```
SaveAs FileName, FileFormat, LockComments, Password, _
       AddToRecentFiles, WritePassword, ReadOnlyRecommended, _
       EmbedTrueTypeFonts, SaveNativePictureFormat, _
       SaveFormsData, SaveAsOCELetter
```

As with the Print method, the arguments of the SaveAs method's arguments correspond to the settings of the application's Save As dialog box. If the file has been saved already, use the Save method, which accepts no arguments at all. It saves the document to its file on disk using the options you specified in the SaveAs method when the document was saved for the first time. To save the active document under a different file name, use the following statement:

```
AppWord.ActiveDocument.SaveAs "c:\Documents\Report99.doc"
```

A related property of the Document object is the *Saved* property, which returns a True/False value indicating whether a document has been changed since the last time it was saved. Use the Saved property in your code to find out whether you must call the Save method before you quit the application.

The following code segment opens an existing document, prints it, and then quits. Notice that I use the CreateObject() function to create a new instance of Word. I did this to simplify the code. You've already seen how to contact the existing instance of Word if it exists.

Code 14.9:   **Opening and Printing a DOC File**

```
Dim WordApp As Word.Application
Dim thisDoc As Document
Dim prnTime As Date
Dim breakLoop As Boolean

    Set WordApp = CreateObject("Word.Application")
    WordApp.Visible = False
    WordApp.Documents.Open ("c:\sample.doc")
    thisDoc.PrintOut True, True
    prnTime = Time
    breakLoop = False
    While WordApp.BackgroundPrintingStatus <> 0 And Not breakLoop
        If Minute(Time - prnTime) > 1 Then
            Reply = MsgBox("Word is taking too long to print." _
                    & vbCrLf & "Do you want to quit?", vbYesNo)
            If Reply = vbYes Then
                breakLoop = True
            Else
                prnTime = Time
            End If
        End If
    Wend
    WordApp.Quit
    MsgBox "Document saved and printed!"
```

The BackgroundPrintingStatus property returns a non-zero value while Word is spooling the document. While the loop is executing, the application won't quit.

Because of hardware errors, this process may never end, and we don't want our application to lock up. Every minute, the program asks the user whether they want to wait or not. If the user decides to terminate the printout, the *breakLoop* Boolean variable is set to True from within the loop's code and the While loop breaks. This approach is rather simplistic and takes up too much computer time. It would be far more efficient to place a Timer control on the Form and monitor the printout's progress from within the Timer event.

Objects That Represent Text

The basic object for accessing text in a Word document is the Range object, which represents a contiguous segment of text. To extract some text from a document, you can use the Document object's *Range* method, which accepts as arguments the positions of the starting and ending characters in the text. The syntax of the Range method is:

```
Document.Range(start, end)
```

The *start* and *end* arguments are two numeric values. Oddly enough, the first character's position in the document is 0. The following statement extracts the first 100 characters of the document represented by the *Document* object variable:

```
Range1 = Document.Range (0, 99)
```

These characters are assigned to the *Range1* object variable. The *Range1* variable can be a variant, but it can also be declared as Range type:

```
Dim Range1 As Range
```

In the previous expressions, the *Document* variable must first be set to reference an existing object with a statement like the following one:

```
Set Document1 = Documents(1)
```

The *Document1* variable can be a variant, or it must be declared as Document type:

```
Dim Document1 As Document
```

You can also replace the variable *Document1* with the built-in object *Active-Document,* which represents the active document. The selected text in the active document can be accessed by the following expression:

```
Application.ActiveDocument.Selection
```

Words, sentences, and paragraphs are more meaningful units of text than characters. The Word, Sentence, and Paragraph objects are better suited for text manipulation, and you commonly use these objects to access documents. These objects, however, don't support all the properties of the Range object. All units of text can be converted to a Range object with the Range property. For example, the following statement returns the third paragraph in the specified document as a Range object:

```
Document1.Paragraphs(3).Range
```

You can then access the Range object's properties to manipulate the third paragraph.

The Paragraph object doesn't have a Font property or a Select method. To change the appearance of the third paragraph in the document, you must first convert the paragraph to a Range object with a statement like the following one:

```
Set Range1 = Document1.Paragraphs(3).Range
Range1.Font.Bold = True
```

Document1 is a properly declared Document variable, and *Range1* is a properly declared Range variable. You can also combine both statements into one and avoid the creation of the *Range1* object variable as follows:

```
Document1.Paragraphs(3).Range.Font.Bold = True
```

The following statement selects (highlights) the same paragraph:

```
Document.Paragraphs(3).Range.Select
```

Once a paragraph (or any other piece of text) is selected, you can apply all types of processing to it (e.g., edit it, move it to another location, format it).

The two methods of the Range object that you'll use most often are *InsertAfter,* which inserts a string of text after the specified Range, and *InsertBefore,* which inserts a string of text in front of the specified Range. The following statements insert a title at the beginning of the document and a closing paragraph at the end:

```
AppWord.ActiveDocument.Select
AppWord.ActiveDocument.Range.InsertBefore _
          "This is the document's title"
AppWord.ActiveDocument.Range.InsertAfter _
          "This is the closing paragraph"
```

The *Select* method of the ActiveDocument object selects the entire text. The selected text is then converted to a Range object, so that the Range object's methods can be applied to it. The InsertBefore and InsertAfter methods place some text before and after the Range object.

VB6 at Work: The WordVBA Project

With the objects and methods described so far, you have enough information to create a new document, place some text into it, format it, and then save it to a disk file. The first step is to start an instance of Word and connect to it. The WordVBA project demonstrates how to:

- Create a new document.

- Insert some text and format it.

- Count the paragraphs, words, and characters in the new document and display them in a message box (see Figure 14.14).

These actions take place from within the Visual Basic application while Word is running in the background. The user doesn't see Word's window, not even as an icon on the taskbar. The new document is saved as C:\SAMPLE.DOC and you can open it later with Word and edit it.

FIGURE 14.14:

The Word VBA project demonstrates how to create and manipulate a DOC file from within a Visual Basic application.

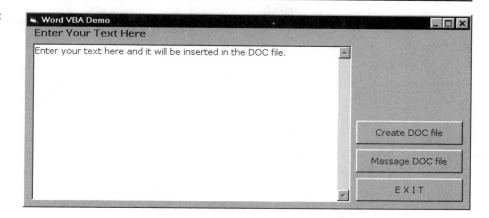

The code behind the Create DOC File button is straightforward. It uses the Paragraph property of the Document object to manipulate the text (insert new paragraphs and manipulate them). Notice how it changes the alignment of the first text paragraph with the Alignment property of the Paragraph object.

Code 14.10:   The Create DOC File Button

```
Private Sub Command1_Click()
Dim thisDoc As Document
Dim thisRange As Range
Dim prnTime As Date
Dim breakLoop As Boolean

    Me.Caption = "Creating document..."
    Set thisDoc = WordApp.Documents.Add
    thisDoc.Range.InsertBefore "Document Title" & vbCrLf & vbCrLf
    Set thisRange = thisDoc.Paragraphs(1).Range
    thisRange.Font.Bold = True
    thisRange.Font.Size = 14
    thisRange.ParagraphFormat.Alignment = wdAlignParagraphCenter
    thisRange.InsertAfter "This sample  document was created _
        automatically with a Visual Basic application." & vbCrLf
    thisRange.InsertAfter "You can   enter additional text _
        here  " & vbCrLf
    thisRange.InsertAfter vbCrLf & vbCrLf
    thisRange.InsertAfter "This  project was   created for _
        Mastering VB6 "
    thisRange.InsertAfter "(Sybex,  1999) and was tested _
```

```
                with Word 97."
        thisRange.InsertAfter vbCrLf
        thisRange.InsertAfter "Your text follows"
        thisRange.InsertAfter Text1.Text
        Me.Caption = "Saving document..."
        thisDoc.SaveAs "c:\sample.doc"
        Me.Caption = "Printing document..."
        thisDoc.PrintOut True, True
        prnTime = Time
        breakLoop = False
        While WordApp.BackgroundPrintingStatus <> 0 And Not breakLoop
            If Minute(Time - prnTime) > 1 Then
                Reply = MsgBox("Word is taking too long to print." _
                        & vbCrLf & "Do you want to quit?", vbYesNo)
                If Reply = vbYes Then
                    breakLoop = True
                Else
                    prnTime = Time
                End If
            End If
        Wend
        WordApp.Quit
        MsgBox "Document saved and printed!"
        Command2.Enabled = True
        Command3.Enabled = True
        Me.Caption = "Word VBA Demo"
End Sub
```

The Massage DOC File button shows you how to manipulate the text in a Word document through OLE Automation. The initial text contains multiple spaces between words that shouldn't be there. To reduce multiple spaces to single space characters (a common task in editing), you can use the Find & Replace dialog box. The WordVBA application does the same by calling the Find method.

The Find method accepts a large number of arguments, most them optional. For the WordVBA application we must specify the string to search for and the replacement string. The program searches for two consecutive spaces, and if found, replaces them with a single space. The process can't end here, because the document may contain three consecutive spaces that need to be reduced to two. So the Find & Replace operations must continue. As long as the code finds two consecutive spaces, it repeats the replace operation and reduces them to one space.

Code 14.11:   **Massaging a Word Document**

```
Private Sub Command2_Click()
Dim thisDoc As Document
Dim thisRange As Range

    WordApp.Documents.Open ("c:\sample.doc")
    WordApp.Visible = False
    Set thisDoc = WordApp.ActiveDocument
    thisDoc.Content.Find.Execute FindText:="VB5", _
            ReplaceWith:="VB6", Replace:=wdReplaceAll
    While thisDoc.Content.Find.Execute(FindText:="  ", _
            Wrap:=wdFindContinue)
        thisDoc.Content.Find.Execute FindText:="  ", _
            ReplaceWith:=" ", Replace:=wdReplaceAll, _
            Wrap:=wdFindContinue
    Wend
End Sub
```

Spell-Checking Documents

One of the most useful features of Word (and of every Office application) is its ability to spell-check a document. This functionality is also exposed by Word's VBA objects, and you can borrow it for use within your Visual Basic applications. This is not only possible, it's actually quite simple. To call upon Word's spell-checking routines, you need to know about two objects: the *ProofReadingErrors* collection and the *SpellingSuggestions* collection.

The ProofReadingErrors collection is a property of the Range object and it contains the misspelled words in the Range. To ask Word to spell-check a range of text and populate the ProofReadingErrors collection, call the Range object's *SpellingErrors* method. This method returns a result that must be stored in an object variable of type *ProofreadingErrors*:

```
Dim SpellCollection As ProofreadingErrors
Set SpellCollection = DRange.SpellingErrors
```

DRange is Range object (a paragraph or an entire document). The second line populates the *SpellCollection* variable with the misspelled words. You can then set up a For Each…Next loop to read the words from the collection.

Besides locating spelling errors, Word can also suggest a list of alternate spellings or words that sound like the misspelled one. To retrieve the list of alternate words, you call the *GetSpellingSuggestions* method of the Application object, passing the misspelled word as an argument. Notice that this is a method of the Application object, not of the Range object you're spell-checking. The results returned by the GetSpellingSuggestions method must be stored in a similar object variable, whose declared type is *SpellingSuggestions*:

```
Dim CorrectionsCollection As SpellingSuggestions
Set CorrectionsCollection = _
        AppWord.GetSpellingSuggestions("antroid")
```

The second line retrieves the suggested alternatives for the word *antroid*. To scan the list of suggested words, you set up a loop that retrieves all the elements of the CorrectionsCollection collection. The example in the next section demonstrates the use of both methods from within a Visual Basic application.

VB6 at Work: The SpellDoc Project

SpellDoc is an application that uses Word's methods to spell-check a document. You'll find the SpellDoc application in this chapter's folder on the CD. The application's main Form, shown in Figure 14.15, consists of a multimine TextBox control on which the user can enter some text (or paste text from another application) and spell-check it by clicking the SpellCheck Document button.

FIGURE 14.15:

The SpellDoc application's main Form

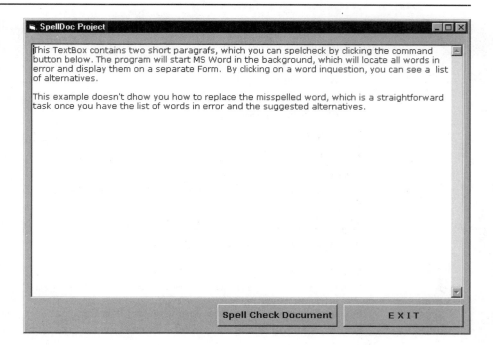

The application will contact Word and request the list of misspelled words. The list of misspelled words will be displayed on a different Form, shown in Figure 14.16. The ListBox control on the left shows all the misspelled words returned by Word. Word can not only locate misspelled words, but suggest alternatives as well. To view the alternate spellings for a specific word, select the word in the left list with the mouse.

To replace all instances of the selected misspelled word with the selected alternative, click the replace button. You can design your own interface to allow the user to select which and how many instances of the misspelled word in the original document will be replaced.

FIGURE 14.16:

This Form of the SpellDoc application displays the misspelled words and possible alternatives.

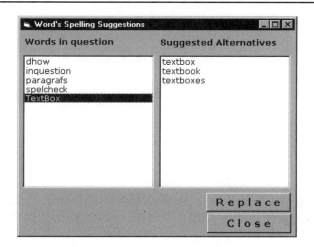

The program uses three public variables, which are declared as follows:

```
Public AppWord As Application
Public CorrectionsCollection As SpellingSuggestions
Public SpellCollection As ProofreadingErrors
```

The *SpellCollection* variable is a collection that contains all the misspelled words, and the *CorrectionsCollection* variable is another collection that contains the suggested spellings for a specific word. The *CorrectionsCollection* variable's contents are assigned every time the user selects another misspelled word in Word's Spelling Suggestions window.

When the SpellCheck Document button is clicked, the program contacts the Word application. First, it attempts to connect to an existing instance of Word with the GetObject() function. If no instance of Word is currently running, it starts a new instance of Word. This is done with the following lines in Code 14.12.

Code 14.12:   **Contacting Word**

```
Set AppWord = GetObject("Word.Application")
    If AppWord Is Nothing Then
        Set AppWord = CreateObject("Word.Application")
        If AppWord Is Nothing Then
            MsgBox "Could not start Word. Application will end"
            End
        End If
    End If
```

After contact with Word is established, the program creates a new document and copies the TextBox control's contents to the new document using the Insert-After method of the Range object, as follows:

```
AppWord.Documents.Add
DRange.InsertAfter Text1.Text
```

Now comes the interesting part. The Visual Basic code calls the Range object's SpellingErrors method, which returns a collection of Word objects. The result of the SpellingErrors method is assigned to the object variable *SpellCollection*:

```
Set SpellCollection = DRange.SpellingErrors
```

The following lines add the words contained in the *SpellCollection* variable to the left list of the second Form and then they display the Form.

Code 14.13:   **The Check Document Button**

```
Private Sub Command1_Click()
Dim DRange As Range
    Me.Caption = "starting word ..."
On Error Resume Next
    Set AppWord = GetObject("Word.Application")
    If AppWord Is Nothing Then
        Set AppWord = CreateObject("Word.Application")
        If AppWord Is Nothing Then
            MsgBox "Could not start Word. Application will end"
            End
        End If
    End If
On Error GoTo ErrorHandler
    AppWord.Documents.Add
    Me.Caption = "checking words..."
```

```
        Set DRange = AppWord.ActiveDocument.Range
        DRange.InsertAfter Text1.Text
        Set SpellCollection = DRange.SpellingErrors
        If SpellCollection.Count > 0 Then
            SuggestionsForm.List1.Clear
            SuggestionsForm.List2.Clear
            For iWord = 1 To SpellCollection.Count
                SuggestionsForm!List1.AddItem _
                            SpellCollection.Item(iWord)
            Next
        End If
        Me.Caption = "Word VBA Example"
        SuggestionsForm.Show
        Exit Sub
ErrorHandler:
        MsgBox "The following error occurred during the _
                document's spelling" & vbCrLf & Err.Description
    End Sub
```

On the second Form of the application, all the code is concentrated in the Words in Question list's Click event. Every time an entry in this ListBox is clicked, the code calls the AppWord object's *GetSpellingSuggestions* method, passing the selected word as an argument. Notice that we add 1 to the List's ListIndex property to offset the fact that the indexing of the elements of a collection starts at 1, while the indexing of the elements of a ListBox control starts at 0. The GetSpellingSuggestions method returns another collection with the suggested words, which are placed in the second ListBox control on the Form with the following statements.

Code 14.14:   **The List's Click Event**

```
    Private Sub List1_Click()
        Screen.MousePointer = vbHourglass
        Set Correctionscollection = _
            AppWord.GetSpellingSuggestions(SpellCollection.Item _
                    (List1.ListIndex + 1))
        List2.Clear
        For iSuggWord = 1 To Correctionscollection.Count
            List2.AddItem Correctionscollection.Item(iSuggWord)
        Next
        Screen.MousePointer = vbDefault
    End Sub
```

The SpellDoc application can become the starting point for many custom Visual Basic applications that require spell-checking, but don't need powerful editing features. In some cases, you might want to customize spelling, although it's not a very common situation. In a mail-aware application, for example, you can spell-check the text and exclude URLs and e-mail addresses. You would first scan the words returned by the SpellingErrors method to check which ones contained special characters and omit them.

As you can see, tapping into the power of the Office applications isn't really complicated. Once you familiarize yourself with the objects of these applications, you can access the Office applications by manipulating a few properties and calling the methods of these objects.

Automating Excel

The objects that Excel exposes have different names, but they form an equally sensible and structured hierarchy for accessing data stored in a tabular arrangement. Just as Word's basic unit of information is the text segment (not characters or words), Excel's basic unit of information is also called Range. A Range object can contain a single cell or an entire worksheet (and everything in between).

The Application object represents an instance of Excel, and it supports most of the basic properties and methods of Word's Application object. In addition, it supports a few more methods that are unique to Excel. Two important methods of Excel's Application object are the *Calculate* method, which recalculates all open worksheets, and the *Evaluate* method, which evaluates math expressions and returns the result. The following statement returns a numeric value that is the result of the math expression passed to the Evaluate method as argument:

```
Application.Evaluate "cos(3/1.091)*log(3.499)"
```

You can also use variables in your expressions as long as you store their values in specific cells and use the addresses of these cells in the expression. The following statement returns the logarithm of the numeric value stored in cell A1:

```
Application.Evaluate "log(" & Application.Range("A1") & ")"
```

The Range object represents one or more cells, depending on the address you supply. In this example, we addressed a single cell (A1). You'll see how you can address and access specific cells in an Excel worksheet in the following two sections.

The Worksheets Collection and the Worksheet Object

Each workbook in Excel contains one or more worksheets. The *Worksheets* collection, which is similar to Word's Documents collection, contains a *Worksheet* object for each worksheet in the current workbook. To add a new worksheet, use the Add method, whose syntax is as follows:

```
Application.Worksheets.Add(before, after, count, type)
```

The *before* and *after* arguments let you specify the order of the new worksheet in the workbook. You can specify one of the two arguments; if you omit both, the new worksheet is inserted before the active worksheet (and also becomes active). The *type* argument specifies the new worksheet's type and it can have one of the following values:

- **xlWorksheet**   The default value

- **xlExcel4MacroSheet**   A worksheet with Excel 4 macros

- **xlExcel4IntlMacroSheet**   A worksheet with Excel 4 international macros

To access a worksheet, use the Worksheet collection's Item method, passing the index or the worksheet's name as an argument. If the second worksheet is named *SalesData.xls*, the following expressions are equivalent:

```
Application.WorkSheets.Item(2)
```

and

```
Application.Worksheets.Item("SalesData.xls")
```

Since Item is the collection default property, you can omit its name altogether:

```
Application.Worksheets(2)
```

Objects That Represent Cells

Excel is an application for manipulating units of information stored in cells, but the basic object for accessing the contents of a worksheet is the Range object, which is a property of the Worksheet object. There are several ways to identify a Range, but here's the basic syntax of the Range method:

```
Worksheet.Range(cell1:cell2)
```

Here, *cell1* and *cell2* are the addresses of the two cells that delimit a rectangular area on the worksheet. They are the addresses of the upper-left and lower-right corners of the selection. In this section, we are going to use the standard Excel notation, which is a number for the row and a letter for the column, for example, C3 or A103. To select the 10×10 upper-right section of the active Worksheet, use the expression:

```
Worksheet.Range("A1:J10")
```

You can also retrieve a single cell as a Range object with the *Cells* method, whose syntax is:

```
Worksheet.Cells(row, col)
```

The *row* and *col* arguments are the coordinates of the cell as numbers. Finally, the Rows and Columns methods return an entire row or column by number. The following expressions return the third row and the fourth column as Range objects:

```
Worksheet.Rows(3)
```

and

```
Worksheet.Columns("D")
```

The Range object is not a collection, but you can access individual cells in a Range object with the Cells method. The Cells method accepts a single argument, which is the index of the cells in the range. The index 1 corresponds to the upper-left cell in the range, the index 2 corresponds to the second cell of the first row, and so on, up to the last cell in the first row. The next index corresponds to the first cell of the second row, and so on, up to the last row. The Text property returns the cell's contents as a string, and the Value property returns the cell's contents as a string (if it's text) or as a numeric value (if it's numeric).

Another way to work with cells is to make a selection and access the properties and methods of the Selection object. To create a *Selection* object (which represents the cells that are highlighted with the mouse), use the Range object's Select method:

```
Range("A2:D2").Select
```

This statement creates a new Selection object which you can access by name. Because a worksheet has only one selection, you don't have to specify any arguments. To change the appearance of the selection, for instance, use the Font property:

```
Selection.Font.Bold = True
Selection.Font.Size = 13
```

Notice that the selection is always rectangular; you can't select non-adjoining cells on a worksheet. However, you can specify a multiple-range area consisting of multiple selections. The following statements combine two different ranges with the *Union* method and assigns them to a new Range object:

```
Set Titles = WorkSheet.Range ("A1:A10")
Set Totals = WorkSheet.Range ("A100:A110")
Set CommonFontRange = Union(Titles, Totals)
```

The Union method returns a Range object, which you can use to manipulate all the cells in the *Titles* and *Totals* ranges together. For example, you can apply common formatting to all the cells in the Range.

In the following section, we are going to create a new spreadsheet from within a Visual Basic application, insert formulas, and print the document.

VB6 at Work: The ExcelVBA Project

The ExcelVBA application's Make New Sheet button demonstrates how to access a worksheet, populate it with data, and then format the data (see Figure 14.17). The program starts by setting the *AppExcel* object variable, which references the Excel application.

FIGURE 14.17:

The ExcelVBA project demonstrates how to contact Excel with VBA from within a Visual Basic application.

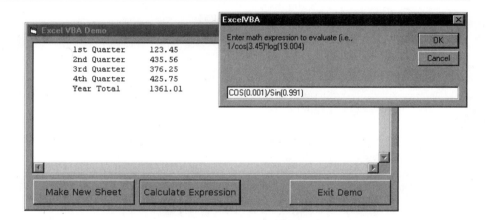

The new spreadsheet is populated and formatted with the MakeSheet() subroutine, whose code is shown next. The code uses the Cells collection to access individual cells and assign their values. To format a group of cells, it creates a Range object that contains all the cells to be formatted alike, selects the range, and then manipulates the cells through the Selection object.

Code 14.15:   **Preparing a New Spreadsheet**

```
Sub MakeSheet()
Dim wSheet As Worksheet
Dim wBook As Workbook

    Set wBook = AppExcel.Workbooks.Add
    Set wSheet = AppExcel.Sheets(1)
```

```
        wSheet.Cells(2, 1).Value = "1st Quarter"
        wSheet.Cells(2, 2).Value = "2nd Quarter"
        wSheet.Cells(2, 3).Value = "3rd Quarter"
        wSheet.Cells(2, 4).Value = "4th Quarter"
        wSheet.Cells(2, 5).Value = "Year Total"

        wSheet.Cells(3, 1).Value = 123.45
        wSheet.Cells(3, 2).Value = 435.56
        wSheet.Cells(3, 3).Value = 376.25
        wSheet.Cells(3, 4).Value = 425.75

' Format column Headings
    Range("A2:E2").Select
    With Selection.Font
        .Name = "Verdana"
        .FontStyle = "Bold"
        .Size = 12
    End With
    Range("A2:E2").Select
    Selection.Columns.AutoFit
    Selection.ColumnWidth = Selection.ColumnWidth * 1.25
    Range("A2:E2").Select
    With Selection
        .HorizontalAlignment = xlCenter
    End With
' Format numbers
    Range("A3:E3").Select
    With Selection.Font
        .Name = "Verdana"
        .FontStyle = "Regular"
        .Size = 11
    End With
    wSheet.Cells(3, 5).Value = "=Sum(A3:D3)"
    MsgBox "The year total is " & wSheet.Cells(3, 5).Value

End Sub
```

While the worksheet is being populated and formatted, Excel is running in the background. Users can't see Excel, although they will notice activity (the disk is spinning, and the pointer assumes an hourglass shape for several seconds). See Figure 14.18.

FIGURE 14.18:

This spreadsheet was created by the ExcelVBA application with OLE Automation.

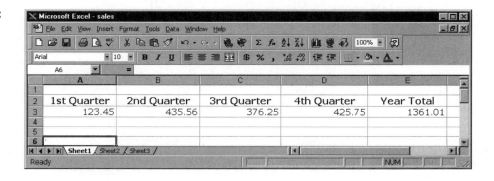

After the grid is populated, the code reads the values from the spreadsheet and displays them in two columns on the TextBox control of the ExcelVBA Demo Form. To read the data, you can use different technique. The following code creates a selection on the spreadsheet and then brings it into the Visual Basic application in a single move. The selected cells are read into the *CData* array by assigning the Selection object to the name of the array:

```
AppExcel.Range("A2:E3").Select
Set CData = AppExcel.Selection
```

These two statements read a range of cell values into the array. The array is created the moment it's used and you don't need to declare it separately. Then, you can use straight Visual Basic code to iterate through the array's elements and create the two columns of text, shown previously in Figure 14.17. The lines that read Excel's cell values are shown next.

Code 14.16:   Importing Data from Excel

```
AppExcel.Range("A2:E3").Select
Set CData = AppExcel.Selection
For icol = 1 To 5
    For irow = 1 To 2
        Text1.Text = Text1.Text & Chr(9) & CData(irow, icol)
    Next
    Text1.Text = Text1.Text & vbCrLf
Next
```

Using Excel as a Math Parser

In the earlier section "Spell-Checking Documents," you learned how to borrow the spell-checking capabilities of Word. Now, we'll do something similar with Excel. Excel is a great tool for doing math. At the same time, Visual Basic doesn't provide a function or method for calculating math expressions. If Excel is installed on the host computer, you can contact it from within your Visual Basic application and use it to evaluate complicated math expressions.

The simplest method to calculate a math expression is to call the Evaluate method of the Excel.Application object. Assuming you've initialized the *ExcelApp* object variable, you can calculate a math expression like the following one:

```
1/cos(0.335)*cos(12.45)
```

by calling the *ExcelApp* object's Evaluate method and passing the expression as a string argument:

```
y = ExcelApp.Evaluate "1/cos(0.335)*cos(12.45)"
```

The Calculate Expression button on the ExcelVBA Form does exactly that. Its listing is shown next.

Code 14.17:   The Calculate Expression Button

```
Private Sub bttnCalculate_Click()
Dim wSheet As Worksheet
Dim wBook As Workbook
Dim expression

    StartExcel
    expression = InputBox("Enter math expression to evaluate _
                (i.e., 1/cos(3.45)*log(19.004)")
On Error GoTo CalcError
    If Trim(expression) <> "" Then
        MsgBox AppExcel.Evaluate(expression)
    End If
    GoTo Terminate
    Exit Sub

CalcError:
    MsgBox "Excel returned the following error: " & vbCrLf & _
                Err.Description
Terminate:
    AppExcel.Quit
    Set AppExcel = Nothing
End Sub
```

The code prompts the user to enter any math expression at runtime. Calculating arbitrary math expressions supplied at runtime with straight Visual Basic code is quite difficult. In Chapter 20, you'll see how to use the Script control (a new control introduced with Visual Basic 6) to do the same.

Another method to calculate math expressions with Excel is to prefix the expression with the equals sign ("=") and assign the entire expression to a cell. Excel will assign the result of the calculation to the cell, and if you read back the value of the same cell, it will be a number and not the actual expression you supplied.

```
wSheet.Cells(1, 1).Value = "=" & expression
wSheet.Calculate
result = wSheet.Cells(1, 1).Value
MsgBox "The value of the expression " & expression & _
       vbCrLf & " is " & result
```

NOTE   Using Excel to evaluate simple expressions may seem like overkill, but if you consider that Visual Basic doesn't provide the tools for evaluating expressions at runtime, automating Excel is not such a bad idea. This is especially true if you want to evaluate complicated expressions and process statistically large data sets. In Chapter 20, *Scripting Objects,* you'll see how to use the Script control to evaluate math expressions. However, the Script control doesn't provide the rich set of math functions of Excel.

Automating Outlook 98

Incorporating e-mail capabilities into Desktop applications is becoming increasingly popular in today's software. To make your applications e-mail-aware, you can use the MAPI control or program Outlook's objects. We are going to discuss how to mail-enable your Visual Basic applications through the Outlook VBA because Outlook is simple, manages more types of information than just messages, and it's a very practical tool for carrying out day-to-day operations. Many corporations use Outlook to automate common tasks like appointment scheduling and routing e-mail. Because of the variety of tasks that can be performed from within Outlook's environment, you should learn the basics of programming its objects. Whereas Excel and Office can be programmed with VBA, Outlook can only be programmed with Visual BasicScript. However, you can use VBA to automate Outlook.

To contact Outlook and program the objects it exposes, you must first create an object variable, such as the *OLApp* variable:

```
Dim OLApp As Outlook.Application
Set OLApp = CreateObject("Outlook.Application")
```

Unlike Word and Excel, Outlook 98 doesn't expose a single object like a Document or Worksheet that gives you access to the information it can handle. Outlook 98 contains several objects including mail messages, contacts, and tasks. The most likely candidate to use as the basic unit of information in Outlook is a folder. Depending on the operation you want to perform with Outlook, you must first select the appropriate folder in the Shortcuts bar. For example, to view the incoming e-mail messages, you must select the InBox folder; to add a contact, you must first select the Contacts folder. You can't expect the find information about your contacts in the InBox folder or the pending messages in the Calendar folder. Since every operation in Outlook is initiated with the selection of the proper folder, the various folders of the application are the top-level objects.

To access the folder objects, you must create a MAPI message store. A *MAPI message store* is a data source that provides all types of information that can be stored by Outlook. If you've used Outlook before, you know that it's essentially a front end for a database that can store many different types of information. To access this information, you must create a *mNameSpace* object variable with the following statement:

```
Set mNameSpace = OLApp.GetNamespace("MAPI")
```

The necessary code for accessing the information stored by Outlook is shown next:

```
Dim OLApp As Outlook.Application
Dim mNameSpace As NameSpace
    Set OLApp = CreateObject("Outlook.Application")
    Set mNameSpace = OLApp.GetNamespace("MAPI")
```

Through the *mNameSpace* variable you can access the various folders of Outlook. The method for accessing a folder is the *GetDefaultFolder* method, which accepts the name of the folder as argument and returns an object variable. The object variable returned by GetDefaultFolder method provides properties and methods that give your application access to the items stored in the folder.

The various folders maintained by Outlook can be accessed with the following constants (their names are self-explanatory):

olFolderContacts	*olFolderDeletedItems*	*olFolderDrafts*
olFolderInBox	*olFolderJournal*	*olFolderNotes*
olFolderOutBox	*olFolderSentMail*	*olFolderTask*

To retrieve all the items in the Contacts folder, use the following statement:

```
Set AllContacts = _
        mNameSpace.GetDefaultFolder(olFolderContacts).Items
```

The Items property returns a collection that contains all the items in the specified folder.

Each folder contains different types of information. The Contacts folder is made up of *ContactItem* objects, the InBox and OutBox folders contain *MailItem* objects, and the Calendar folder contains a collection of *AppointmentItem* objects. Each one of these objects provides numerous properties, which are the attributes of the item it represents. For example, a ContactItem object provides properties for setting just about any attribute of a contact.

To see the properties of the ContactItem object, open the Object Browser, select Outlook in the Class box, and in the Classes list click the ContactItem entry, as shown in Figure 14.19. The members of the selected Class will appear in the right pane. The properties you'll use most often in your applications are LastName, First-Name, Email1Address, Title, and the properties that begin with HomeAddress and BusinessAddress. These are the fields you can set in the Contact dialog box when you add or edit Contact with Outlook. If you need additional fields, you can create your own custom properties. The custom properties are also accessed by name, but I'm not going to discuss them here. You should see Outlook's Help files for more information on adding custom properties.

FIGURE 14.19:

The properties of the ContactItem object

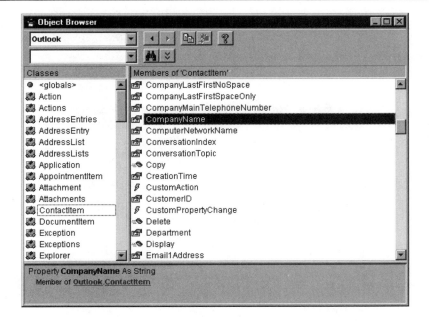

A property that's common to all items is the *EntryID* property, which is a Long value that uniquely identifies each item. EntryID values are similar to IDs you assign to the various records in a database (they identify the record, but they have no other apparent meaning). Of course, you can't have the user select a contact or message based on its EntryID (it makes much more sense to present a list of names or companies to select from) but you can use them to bookmark items. If you populate the nodes of a TreeView control with the messages or contacts stored in Outlook, you can use the EntryID fields as keys for their nodes. This way, the user can select items based on more meaningful information, such as name, company, or message subject. Then, you can instantly locate the desired item in the corresponding folder by its ID. You'll see how the EntryID property is used in the examples of the following sections.

Retrieving Information

Outlook stores different types of information in different files. Contact information is stored in the Contacts file, incoming messages are stored in the InBox folder, and so on. Most users, however, customize Outlook's folder structure by adding subfolders to the default folders. To organize your contacts, for instance, you can create Business and Personal subfolders under the Contacts folders. Likewise, you can create Business, Personal, and Junk folders under the InBox folder.

One of the most common programming tasks in automating Outlook is the extraction of the desired information. In the following examples, you'll see how to access the contacts and incoming messages in the Contacts and InBox folders, respectively.

VB6 at Work: The Contacts Project

The first example of how to OLE automate Outlook is the Contacts application, whose Form is shown in Figure 14.20. The Contacts application assumes that all contact items are stored in the Contacts folder. If you've organized your contacts differently, perhaps in subfolders under the Contacts folder, copy a few contacts temporarily to the Contacts folder so that you can test the application. Later, in the section "Recursive Scanning of the Contacts Folder," you'll see how you can scan the entire Contacts folder recursively, including its subfolders.

The Contact project's main Form contains two lists. The first list is populated with company names, which are read from the contact items. This list doesn't contain any duplicate entries, even though a typical Contacts folder contains multiple contacts from the same company. To view the contacts in a company, click the company's name and the corresponding contacts will appear in the Contacts list. Then, each time you click a contact name, more information about the selected contact will be displayed in the lower half of the Form.

FIGURE 14.20:

The Contacts project demonstrates how to retrieve contact items from Outlook's Contacts folder.

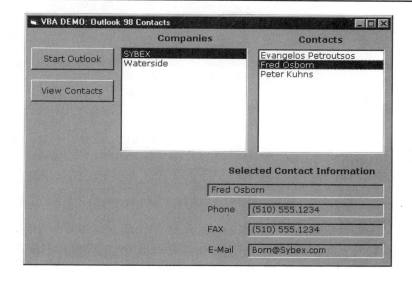

The program starts by contacting Outlook when the Start Outlook button is clicked. The button's code is shown next.

Code 14.18:   Contacting Outlook

```
Private Sub Command1_Click()
On Error GoTo OutlookNotStarted
    Set OLApp = CreateObject("Outlook.Application")
On Error GoTo NoMAPINameSpace
    Set mNameSpace = OLApp.GetNamespace("MAPI")
    List1.Clear
    List2.Clear
    Command2.Enabled = True
    Exit Sub

OutlookNotStarted:
    MsgBox "Could not start Outlook"
    Exit Sub
NoMAPINameSpace:
    MsgBox "Could not get MAPI NameSpace"
    Exit Sub
End Sub
```

If Outlook is contacted successfully, the View Contacts button is enabled. When this button is clicked, the program creates a collection with all the items in the

Contacts folder and sorts the *allContacts* collection according to the company name. Duplicate company names are removed from the list with the If statement at the end of the subroutine. The code of the View Contacts button follows.

Code 14.19: **Populating the Contacts List**

```
Private Sub Command2_Click()
    Set allContacts = _
            mNameSpace.GetDefaultFolder(olFolderContacts).Items
    allContacts.Sort "CompanyName"
On Error Resume Next
    For Each mContact In allContacts
        If Trim(mContact.CompanyName) <> "" Then _
            List1.AddItem mContact.CompanyName
        If List1.List(List1.NewIndex) = _
            List1.List(List1.NewIndex - 1) Then _
                List1.RemoveItem List1.NewIndex
    Next
End Sub
```

The code that retrieves the contacts in the selected folder on the left list must be placed in the ListBox control's Click event; it's shown next.

Code 14.20: **Selecting Contacts from a Company**

```
Private Sub List1_Click()
Dim CompanyName As String
Dim filterString As String

    If List1.ListIndex = -1 Then Exit Sub
    CompanyName = List1.Text
    filterString = "[CompanyName] = """ & CompanyName & """"

    Set thiscontact = allContacts.Find(filterString)
    If IsNull(thiscontact) Then
        MsgBox "Fatal error in locating a contact. _
                Program will exit"
        End
    End If
    List2.Clear
```

```
        While Not thiscontact Is Nothing
            If Trim(thiscontact.FullName) <> "" Then _
                    List2.AddItem thiscontact.FullName
            Set thiscontact = allContacts.FindNext
        Wend
    End Sub
```

To display additional information about a contact, the following code needs to be executed from within the List control's Click event.

Code 14.21:   **Displaying Contact Information**

```
        Private Sub List2_Click()
        Dim ContactName As String
        Dim filterString As String
            If List2.ListIndex = -1 Then Exit Sub
            ContactName = List2.Text
            filterString = "[FullName] = """ & ContactName & """"
            Set thiscontact = allContacts.Find(filterString)
            If IsNull(thiscontact) Then
                MsgBox "Fatal error in locating a contact's name. _
                        Program will exit"
            End
        End If
        lblName.Caption = " " & thiscontact.FullName
        lblPhone.Caption = " " & thiscontact.BusinessTelephoneNumber
        lblFAX.Caption = " " & thiscontact.BusinessFaxNumber
        lblEMail.Caption = " " & thiscontact.Email1Address
    End Sub
```

VB6 at Work: The Messages Project

The Messages project demonstrates some techniques for retrieving mail items. Messages are stored in the InBox and OutBox folders, as well as any custom folders created under these two folders by the user. The Messages example retrieves the messages from the InBox folder only. If you don't have any messages in this folder, temporarily move some incoming messages from your custom folders to the InBox folder to test the application. Later in the chapter, you'll see how to retrieve all the messages under InBox, including its subfolders nested to any depth. If you've read the previous chapters, you probably know you're facing another recursive procedure.

The Messages application (shown in Figure 14.21) lets you select messages based on their sender or the date they were sent. The user can specify the criteria with the controls on the upper-right section of the Form and then click the Show Selected Messages button to display the messages that meet the criteria in the Selected Messages ListBox. The program displays only each message's sender and subject. Then, each time the user selects a message on this list by clicking a message item, more information about the selected message is displayed in the controls in the lower half of the Form (including the message's body). If the message contains attachments, the names of the attached files are displayed in a message box. Run the project and experiment with it. There are two issues you should be aware of. First, the Messages application can see only the messages in the InBox folder. If you've organized your messages into subfolders under the InBox folder, you must move a few messages to the InBox folder temporarily. The second issue is that the sender names are read from the Contacts folder. If the names in the Contacts folder don't match the names that appear in the messages, then you won't see the messages sent by the selected contact.

FIGURE 14.21:

The Messages project demonstrates how to read Outlook's incoming messages from within your Visual Basic applications.

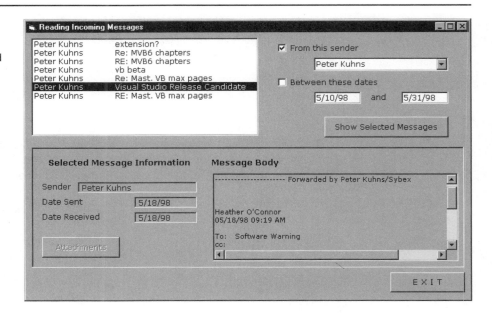

The Application's Code

In the Form's Load event we create two object variables, the *OLApp* variable, which references the Outlook application, and the *mNameSpace* variable, which references

Outlook's folders. These variables are declared in the Form's declaration section with the following statements:

```
Dim OLApp As Application
Dim mNameSpace As NameSpace
```

Then, the code sets up the *AllContacts* variable, which references the items of the Contacts folder. This variable is also declared in the Form's declaration section, with the following statement:

```
Dim AllContacts As Items
```

The code scans all the items in the *AllContacts* collection and adds the names of the contacts (property FullName) to the Combo1 box. The Sorted property of the ComboBox control is set to True and the code removes any duplicate entries (which will appear in consecutive positions in the list). Following is the code that contacts Outlook and sets up the *AllContacts* object variable.

Code 14.22:   Initializing the Messages Project

```
Private Sub Form_Load()
On Error GoTo OutlookNotStarted
    Set OLApp = CreateObject("Outlook.Application")
On Error GoTo NoMAPINameSpace
    Set mNameSpace = OLApp.GetNamespace("MAPI")
    Set AllMessages = _
            mNameSpace.GetDefaultFolder(olFolderInbox).Items
    Set AllContacts = _
            mNameSpace.GetDefaultFolder(olFolderContacts).Items
    Combo1.Clear
    For Each mcontact In AllContacts
        Combo1.AddItem mcontact.FullName
        If Combo1.List(Combo1.NewIndex) = _
                Combo1.List(Combo1.NewIndex + 1) Then _
                Combo1.RemoveItem Combo1.NewIndex
    Next
    Combo1.ListIndex = 0
    Exit Sub

OutlookNotStarted:
    MsgBox "Could not start Outlook"
    Exit Sub
```

```
NoMAPINameSpace:
    MsgBox "Could not get MAPI NameSpace"
    Exit Sub

End Sub
```

Filtering Messages

The user can select a name and/or a date range to limit the selected messages. If the checkboxes "From this sender" and "Between these dates" are cleared, then clicking the Show Selected Messages button will display all the messages in the InBox folder on the ListBox control. If you check either or both checkboxes, then the program will display only the messages that meet the specified criteria.

To filter the messages, use the *Find* and *FindNext* methods of the *AllMessages* object variable. The *AllMessages* variable is declared as Items, and the Items object supports these two methods for retrieving selected messages. The syntax of the Find method is:

```
Items.Find(filterstring)
```

filterstring is an expression that specifies the desired criteria. The Find method returns an object, whose type depends on the type of the Items collection. If you apply the Find method to the InBox folder, it will return a MailItem object; if you apply it to the Contacts folder, it will return a ContactItem object. After you've retrieved the first item that meets the criteria, you can retrieve the remaining ones by calling the FindNext method without specifying any arguments.

The *filterstring* argument is a string expression that combines field names, logical operators, and values. To retrieve the messages sent by Site Builder Network, use the following string:

```
"[SenderName] = "Site Builder Network"
```

To retrieve all messages sent in October 1997, use the following string:

```
"[SentOn] => ""10/01/97"" And [SentOn] <= ""10/31/97""
```

(The consecutive double quotes indicate embedded double quotes, which are inserted in the string with the expression Chr(34).)

You can combine as many fields as needed with the usual comparison and logical operators. The field names for each item type can be found in the Object Browser. Select the desired item (e.g., MailItem, ContactItem) and look up its properties in the Members pane.

In the Messages project you use the values of various controls on the Form to build the filter string as follows. First, you validate the dates, then you build the filter string with the following statements:

```
If chkCompany.Value And Combo1.ListIndex >= 0 Then
     ContactName = Combo1.Text
     filterString = "[SenderName] = """ & ContactName & """"
End If
If chkDate.Value Then
     If filterString = "" Then
         filterString = "[SentOn] > """ & _
         DateFrom.Text & """ And [SentOn] < """ & _
         DateTo.Text & """"
     Else
         filterString = filterString & " and _
             [SentOn] > """ & DateFrom.Text & """ _
             And [SentOn] < """ & DateTo.Text & """"
     End If
End If
If filterString = "" Then
     filterString = "[SentOn] > ""01/01/1980"""
End If
```

Notice the multiple quotes in the expressions. Two double quote characters are needed to insert a double quote character in a string. If the value of the *Contact-Name* variable is "Sybex" then the statement:

```
"[SenderName] = """ & ContactName & """"
```

will produce the following string:

```
[SenderName] = "Sybex"
```

The *filterstring* variable is built slowly, according to the values entered by the user on the Form. If the user specifies a name, the *SenderName* property is set to the appropriate value. If the user specifies dates, the *SentOn* property is set accordingly.

The *filterstring* variable is then passed to the Find method of the AllMessages object. Then, the program loops through the selected messages by calling the FindNext method. At each iteration, another message's sender and subject are displayed on the ListBox control. At the same time, the selected messages are also appended to the *SelectedMessages* collection:

```
Set thismessage = AllMessages.Find(filterString)
    If thismessage Is Nothing Then
        MsgBox "No messages sent in the specified interval."
```

```
Else
    List1.Clear
    While Not thismessage Is Nothing
        List1.AddItem thismessage.SenderName & _
                Chr(9) & thismessage.Subject
        SelectedMessages.Add thismessage
        Set thismessage = AllMessages.FindNext
    Wend

End If
```

The rest of the code is straightforward. When an item on the ListBox control is clicked, the program recalls the selected item in the SelectedMessages collection and displays its basic entries in the corresponding Label control at the bottom of the screen and its body in the TextBox control (whose Locked property must be set to True to prevent editing of the message). Following is the listing of the List-Box control's Click event handler.

Code 14.23: **Viewing a Message Item**

```
Private Sub List1_Click()
Dim thismessage As Object
Dim MessageAttachments As Attachments

    selectedEntry = List1.ListIndex + 1
    If selectedEntry < 1 Then Exit Sub
    Set thismessage = SelectedMessages.Item(selectedEntry)
    lblSender.Caption = " " & thismessage.SenderName
    lblSent.Caption = " " & thismessage.SentOn
    lblRecvd.Caption = " " & thismessage.ReceivedTime
    txtBody.Text = " " & thismessage.Body

    Set MessageAttachments = thismessage.Attachments
    If MessageAttachments.Count = 0 Then
        Command4.Enabled = False
    Else
        Command4.Enabled = False
    End If

End Sub
```

Open the Messages project in the Visual Basic IDE to examine its code and see how it combines the items of the Contacts folder and uses them to retrieve mail items from the InBox folder. You can modify the code to add more selection criteria or work with different folders (for example, the OutBox folder or a subfolder under the InBox folder).

WARNING   The Messages project uses the *FullName* property of the contacts to display the names of possible message senders. If the names you've used in the Contacts folder are not the same as the sender names in the incoming messages, then the program won't select all the messages as you'd expect. There are many methods for matching contacts and messages, but they require additional effort. For example, you can use each contact's e-mail address, which is the same in both the Contacts and InBox folders. However, contacts may have multiple e-mail addresses, so you must make sure you search the mail items for all e-mail addresses (aliases) of the selected contact.

VB6 at Work: The AutoMssg Project

The AutoMssg application demonstrates how to create e-mail messages from within your Visual Basic applications and use Outlook to deliver them. It also shows another technique for retrieving and organizing contacts. Initially, the application retrieves the names of the companies only and displays them in the Companies list. The user can select a company and see the contacts in this company in the Contacts list. To add new names to the list of recipients, the user must double-click their names in the Contacts. The list of recipients is sorted, but it doesn't prevent duplicate entries. The reason for this is that you'll find "Smiths" in every other company, so eliminating duplicate entries based on names is not a good idea. Displaying more information to make the entries in the recipients list unique would clutter the display. So, for this project, I've decided to use a sorted ListBox control so that duplicate names appear together and allow the user to decide which ones to select.

The AutoMssg project's code is straightforward and I will not include its listing here. You can open the project in the Visual Basic IDE and see how it prepares the messages.

Recursive Scanning of the Contacts Folder

The Contacts project of the previous section assumes that all contacts are stored in the Contacts folder (likewise, the other projects assume that all messages reside in a single folder). This may be the case for users with a small number of contacts (or totally unorganized users), but it's not common. Most users organize their contacts in subfolders to simplify searching. Scanning a Contacts folder with subfolders is not as simple. This operation calls for recursive programming. If you thought that Chapter 11, *Recursive Programming,* was uncalled for in an introductory book, this is another attestation to the usefulness of recursive programming. It's not an obsession of mine, but some tasks just can't be carried out without recursion. Nor could I have skipped these tasks either. You may find the related programming techniques difficult, but without them you wouldn't be able to recursively scan the Contacts folder if it contained subfolders (just as you wouldn't be able to scan a TreeView node with child nodes nested to multiple levels).

VB6 at Work: The AllContacts Project

The application that demonstrates how to recursively scan the Contacts folder is called AllContacts and can be found in the ALLCONTS folder in this chapter's folder on the CD. When the application's Form is loaded, click the Populate Tree button to populate the TreeView control with the names of all subfolders under the Contacts folder (as shown in Figure 14.22). Expand the various folders on the TreeView control, and click a folder's name to see its contact items in the ListBox control on the right.

FIGURE 14.22:

The AllContacts project populates the TreeView control on the left with the names of the subfolders under Outlook's Contracts folder.

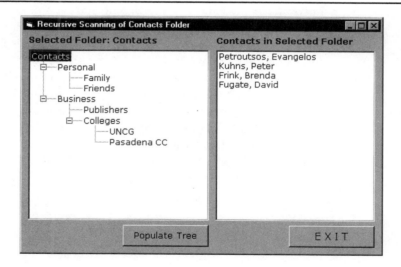

The Project's Code

Let's start with the trivial code. First, declare the following object variables, which are used by most procedures:

```
Public OutlookApp As outlook.Application
Public OlObjects As outlook.NameSpace
Public OlContacts As outlook.MAPIFolder
```

Then, in the Form's Load event, enter the following statements to create a new instance of Outlook and the object variables needed to access the folders of Outlook.

Code 14.24:   **Creating an Outlook Object Variable**

```
Private Sub Form_Load()
    Set OutlookApp = CreateObject("Outlook.Application.8")
    If Err Then
        MsgBox "Could not create Outlook Application object!"
        End
    End If
    Set OlObjects = OutlookApp.GetNamespace("MAPI")
    Set OlContacts = OlObjects.GetDefaultFolder(olFolderContacts)
    If Err Then
        MsgBox "Could not create MAPI Namespace!", vbCritical
    End If
End Sub
```

The *OutlookApp* variable represents the application. The *OlObjects* variable represents all the folders exposed by Outlook and *OlContacts* represents the Contacts folder. The declarations of these variables are:

```
Public OlObjects As outlook.NameSpace
Public OlContacts As outlook.MAPIFolder
```

The core of the application is the Populate button's Click event handler, which populates the TreeView control recursively.

Code 14.25:   **Populating the TreeView control**

```
Private Sub Command1_Click()
Dim allFolders As outlook.Folders
Dim Folder As outlook.MAPIFolder
Dim Folders As outlook.Folders
Dim thisFolder As outlook.MAPIFolder
Dim newNode As Node

' Add root node
Set newNode = TreeView1.Nodes.Add(, , OlContacts.EntryID, _
              "Contacts")
newNode.Expanded = True
' Get all Folders under Contacts
Set allFolders = OlContacts.Folders
' Process each Folder under Contacts
```

```
For Each Folder In allFolders
    Set newNode = TreeView1.Nodes.Add(OlContacts.EntryID, _
                tvwChild, Folder.Name, Folder.Name)
    Set Folders = Folder.Folders
    For Each thisFolder In Folders
        Set newNode = TreeView1.Nodes.Add(Folder.Name, _
                    tvwChild, thisFolder.EntryID, _
                    thisFolder.Name)
        newNode.Expanded = True
        ' now scan the current folder's subfolders
        ScanSubFolders thisFolder
    Next
Next
End Sub
```

To populate the TreeView control, we first add the root node, which is the Contacts folder. This node has no parent node and its key is the Contacts folders EntryID property value:

```
Set newNode = TreeView1.Nodes.Add( , , OlContacts.EntryID, _
            "Contacts")
newNode.Expanded = True
```

As soon as the node is added, it's expanded so that the user will see the names of the subfolders under it and the plus sign in front of their names. Then we must create the *allFolders* collection, which contains all the subfolders of the Contacts folder:

```
Set allFolders = OlContacts.Folders
```

The loop of Code 14.26 scans each item in this collection and adds the name of the current folder to the TreeView control. The new node becomes a child node of the Contacts node, and its key is the EntryID property of its parent node.

Then, we must create another collection, the *Folders* collection, with the current folder's subfolders. This collection's items are added to the TreeView control and then we call the ScanSubFolders() subroutine to scan the subfolders of each item. The code of the ScanSubFolders() subroutine is shown next.

Code 14.26:   **The ScanSubFolders() Subroutine**

```
Sub ScanSubFolders(thisFolder As Object)
Dim subFolders As outlook.Folders
Dim subFolder As outlook.MAPIFolder
```

```
        Set subFolders = thisFolder.Folders
        If subFolders.Count <> 0 Then
            strFolderKey = thisFolder.EntryID
            For Each subFolder In subFolders
                TreeView1.Nodes.Add thisFolder.EntryID, _
                    tvwChild, subFolder.EntryID, subFolder.Name
                ScanSubFolders subFolder
            Next
        End If
    End Sub
```

This subroutine's code is quite simple (for a recursive procedure, that is). It creates a collection of the current folder's subfolders, the *subFolders* collection. Then, it scans each item in the collection, adds its name to the TreeView control, and scans it recursively, which means it calls itself passing the name of the current folder as argument.

Viewing a Folder's Contacts

After populating the TreeView control with the structure of the subfolders under the Contacts folder, you can select a folder in the TreeView control with the mouse to display its contacts on the ListBox control in the right-hand side of the Form. When an item in the TreeView control is clicked, the *NodeClick* event is triggered. This event reports the node clicked, and you can use the event's argument to retrieve the node's key, which is the ID of the selected folder. Once you know the ID of the selected folder, you can create a reference to this folder (variable *thisFolder*) and use it to scan the contact items in the actual folder. The code of the TreeView control's NodeClick event is shown next.

Code 14.27:   Listing the Items of the Selected Folder

```
Private Sub TreeView1_NodeClick(ByVal Node As ComctlLib.Node)
Dim thisFolder As outlook.MAPIFolder
Dim contacts As outlook.Items
Dim Contact As outlook.ContactItem

On Error Resume Next
    List1.Clear
    Label1.Caption = "Selected Folder: " & Node.Text
    Set thisFolder = OlObjects.GetFolderFromID(Node.Key)
    If Err Then
        Exit Sub
```

```
        Else
            Set contacts = thisFolder.Items
            For Each Contact In contacts
                List1.AddItem Contact.LastName & ", " & _
                                Contact.FirstName
            Next
        End If
End Sub
```

The code displays only the contact's LastName and FirstName properties. You can modify the code to display any fields. For example, you can retrieve the contact's e-mail address and send automated messages as we did in the previous example. If you think these examples are interesting and you have good reason to automate Outlook, you should try to incorporate the code of the AllContacFs project into the Contacts project.

The introduction to the topic of OLE Automation ends with this example. If you add references to the various Office applications in your projects and then open the Object Browser, you'll realize that the Office applications expose many objects, which in turn, provide numerous properties and methods. Automating Office applications with VBA is well within the reach of the average Visual Basic programmer, as long as you familiarize yourself with the objects exposed by the Office applications (or any other application that supports VBA). After reading and studying this chapter, you should know the basics of VBA programming and understand that it's not fundamentally different from Visual Basic programming.

Building ActiveX Components

- Modules and Class Modules

- Builing Class Modules

- Implementing properties and methods

- Raising Events from within Classes

- Creating and using object variables

- Registering ActiveX components

- Handling Class errors

In the last chapter, you learned how to contact server applications and program (or OLE automate) them through the objects they expose. In this chapter, you'll learn how to build your own OLE server applications, or ActiveX components. An *ActiveX component* is a general term that encompasses three types of projects (perhaps more in the future): ActiveX DLLs, ActiveX EXEs, and ActiveX controls. In this chapter, you'll learn how to build *code components* (ActiveX DLLs and ActiveX EXEs), which are server applications that expose their functionality through an interface consisting of properties, methods, and events.

In the following chapter, you'll learn how to create your own custom ActiveX controls, which can be added to any project's Toolbox and used by developers in building user interfaces. In Chapter 20, you'll see how custom ActiveX controls can be used on Web pages.

The main differences between ActiveX controls and code components lie in their interface and integration into the Visual Basic IDE. ActiveX controls are integrated into the Visual Basic IDE and they have a visible interface. While code components provide a functionality similar to that of ActiveX controls, they aren't as integrated with the development environment (e.g., you can't drop a code component on a Form like you can with a control), and they don't have a visible interface. Instead, code components are Classes, which must be accessed through a properly declared object variable.

Another category of ActiveX components is the ActiveX document. *ActiveX documents* are applications that can be hosted in containers such as Internet Explorer and the Office Binder. At this time, there aren't many ActiveX documents on the Internet (personally, I haven't seen any), and it seems it will be a while before they catch up. The practicality of developing applications for Office Binder is even more questionable. This book doesn't cover ActiveX documents, which are really simple compared to ActiveX code components and ActiveX controls.

Modules and Class Modules

Code components are implemented in Visual Basic as Class Modules. Modules have existed in Visual Basic since its first version. They store variable declarations and code (functions and subroutines), which are available to all the other components of an application. Many of the examples developed in previous chapters have their own Modules. If the function ConvertTemperature(degrees As Double) is going to be called from several places in your code and from within multiple Forms, then you should implement it in a Module. Procedures stored in a Module can be called from any part of an application; the same is true for variables that must be accessed by multiple procedures. This is one method by which Forms and procedures in different Forms can exchange information.

You can think of the procedures as methods of the Module, only you don't have to prefix them with the name of the Module when you call them. The public variables you store in a Module can also be thought of as properties of the Module. Therefore, a Module is similar to a Class, and Classes are implemented as special types of Modules called Class Modules.

A question some readers might raise at this point is, "Why bother with Classes when a Module can provide the functionality I need in my application?" If you only need a few procedures and global variables for a single project, you're probably better off dumping them in a Module. If you plan to use the same procedures in multiple projects, however, then you should build a Class Module. Let's say you've implemented several functions in a Module, tested them with Project A, and you're satisfied with them. Later on, you build another project, Project B, which uses the same Module. You realize that the functions in the Module need some tweaking, so you introduce a few additional public variables, and then the Module works well with Project B—but you've inadvertently broken Project A. And even if you're disciplined enough not to touch the Module, what if you belong to a group working on a common project? Allowing many programmers to access the same Module from within their projects is an accident waiting to happen. One of them will inevitably tweak the code and break some of the existing projects.

Another potential danger is conflicting names. If you add a Module with many public variables to a project, some of the Module's variables may have the same names as other variables you've used in your other project. In that case, the scope rules will determine which variable is referenced (which may not be the one *you* think is being used). The properties in a Class Module can't be accessed by their name only. The must be accessed with an expression like `ClassName.VariableName`, which makes the property unique not only in the project, but in the operating system itself.

In-Process and Out-of-Process Servers

A Class Module is a server, or an application that provides its services to client applications. When you create an object variable to access the properties and methods of a Class, you're actually invoking an executable file (DLL or EXE), which runs in the background and waits to be contacted. Every time you set or read a property value or call a method, this executable activates, performs some actions, and optionally, returns some results to your application.

Servers can be implemented as ActiveX EXE or ActiveX DLL components. The difference between the two lies in how the server is executed. An ActiveX DLL component is an *in-process server*. The DLL is loaded in the same address space as the executable that calls the server and runs on the same thread as the client. At any given moment, however, either the client application or the DLL is running. The benefit of DLLs is that they are faster because, in effect, they become part of the application that uses them.

An ActiveX EXE component is an *out-of-process server* that runs as a separate process. When a client application creates an object provided by an EXE server for the first time, the server starts running as a separate process. If another client application creates the same object, the new object is provided by the running EXE server. In other words, a single EXE server can service multiple clients. Out-of-process servers seem to be more efficient in resource allocation, but exchanging information between servers is a slow process, so execution speed in in-process servers is faster. The communication between two processes is a complicated process known as *marshaling*.

An example of an out-of-process server is Excel. You can run two or more applications that request Excel's services (as explained in the last chapter), and they will all be serviced by a single instance of Excel. For an application the size of Excel, it wouldn't make much sense to invoke a new instance of it every time a Visual Basic application needs to evaluate an expression with the Evaluate method. If the VB applications must access different worksheets, they can all be opened by the same instance of Excel.

VB Modules: A Quick Review

It's usually easier to understand new concepts if you associate them with others you've already mastered. Let's start by reviewing Visual Basic Modules and then see how the same concepts are applied to Class Modules. We'll implement a short application that will count time (it can become part of another application that needs to time its operations). In the application, we want to be able to start and stop the timer at will. When the application executes auxiliary code, we should be able to pause the timer, then continue timing. After the operation to be timed completes, we must be able to read the elapsed time. Let's implement the timing logic in a Module. By implementing the timing logic in a Module, we can reuse the component with other projects. (In general, you shouldn't include the logic of timing or other auxiliary operations in your code. It's best to isolate this logic and make it available to your application with a few procedure calls). The application we'll develop in this section is called TimerMod, and you'll find it in this chapter's folder on the CD.

Start a new project, add a Module to the project, and then insert the following lines in the Module.

Code 15.1:   **The TimerMod Module's Code**

```
Public TotalInterval As Double
Dim T1 As Double, t2 As Double

Sub StartCounting()
    T1 = Time
End Sub

Sub StopCounting()
    TotalInterval = TotalInterval + Time - T1
End Sub

Sub ResetTimer()
    TotalInterval = 0
End Sub
```

The subroutine *StartCounting()* starts the timer and the subroutine *StopCounting()* pauses the timer. Each time the timer is stopped, the *TotalInterval* variable is updated. To find out the elapsed time, the application must read the value of this variable. Finally, the *ResetTimer()* subroutine resets the timer. The timing logic doesn't allow you to read the elapsed time while the timer is running; you must first call the Stop-Counting method to update the variable *TotalInterval*, then read the variable's value.

Now switch to the application's Form and place two buttons on the Form. Set their captions to Start Timing and Show Interval, as shown in Figure 15.1. Then insert the following lines in the Form's Code window.

Code 15.2:   **The TimerMod Test Form's Code**

```
Private Sub Command1_Click()
    If Command1.Caption = "Start" Then
        StartCounting
        Command1.Caption = "Stop"
    Else
        StopCounting
        Command1.Caption = "Start"
    End If
End Sub
```

```
Private Sub Command2_Click()
    MsgBox "I've been counting for " & vbCrLf & _
        Hour(TotalInterval) & " hours" & vbCrLf & _
        Minute(TotalInterval) & " minutes and " & vbCrLf & _
        Second(TotalInterval) & " seconds" & vbCrLf
End Sub
```

FIGURE 15.1:

The TimerMod
project's Form

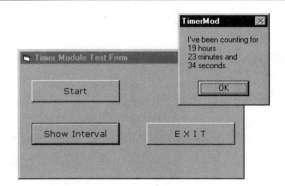

Run the application, start the timer, and stop and restart it a few times. Then click the Show Interval button to see the elapsed time in hours, minutes, and seconds.

The code works, but there are a couple of problems. If another developer gets his hands on this Module, he may attempt to set the *TotalInterval* variable with a statement like:

```
TotalInterval=0.00453567
```

This is possible and the value shown is a valid time value, but what if he attempts to set the variable to an invalid value like:

```
TotalInterval = 99
```

The program will most likely work, but it will no longer report the correct elapsed time. Another programmer may ignore the ResetTimer() subroutine and attempt to reset the *TotalInterval* variable from within the StartCounting subroutine. Perhaps, he doesn't really care about pausing and resuming the timing process and it suits him to reset the *TotalInterval* variable every time the StartCounting subroutine is called. His project will work (with fewer calls too), but yours will no longer work. And this is the most important benefit of implementing auxiliary procedures as Class Modules: to create a component that's consistent across multiple applications. In addition, by implementing the timing logic separately and apart from the application, you hide the details of its implementation from the developers who use it. In the same way, you don't have to know how Excel evaluates a complicated math expression in order to call its Evaluate method.

Using a Class Module

Let's implement the same project, but this time with a Class Module. The Class Module will completely hide the implementation details. It will expose its functionality and the developer will never see or edit its source code.

WARNING   If you're going to open the sample projects from the CD (or the folder of your hard disk they have been copied to), you'll get an error message indicating that the project references a component that's not available. Each of the projects in this chapter creates a new Class, which is not known to the system. Ignore the message, open the project, select the test project, and add to it a reference to the Class. The process is explained shortly, but I've inserted this warning here so that you won't be alarmed by the error message.

Save the existing project and then start a new project (it's the CTIMER project in this chapter's folder on the CD). Follow these steps to create a new Class:

1. In the New Project dialog box select ActiveX DLL. Visual Basic will add a Class Modules folder in the Project Explorer window and a Class Module under it. The Class Module is named Class1 by default. The ActiveX DLL project doesn't have Forms.

2. Change the Class Module's Name property to **CTimer.**

    The Class Module doesn't have a visible interface, so the Code window for the new component will be displayed.

3. Enter the lines in Code 15.3 in the Class Module's Code window.

Code 15.3:   **The CTimer Class' Code**

```
Dim totalInterval As Double
Dim T1 As Double
```

```
Public Sub StartCounting()
    T1 = Time
End Sub

Public Sub StopCounting()
    totalInterval = totalInterval + Time - T1
End Sub

Property Get ElapsedTime() As Double
    ElapsedTime = totalInterval
End Property

Public Sub ResetTimer()
    totalInterval = 0
End Sub
```

The code of the Class Module is quite similar to the Module's code, but it doesn't have a public variable. The *totalInterval* variable can't be accessed directly from any procedure outside the Class Module. It can only be read through the ElapsedTime() procedure. Notice that this is a special type procedure called *Property Get*. Every time an application attempts to read the value of the *totalInterval* variable, the Elapsed-Time() procedure is invoked. Its code reads the value of the *totalInterval* local variable and assigns it to the ElapsedTime() procedure. This value is then passed to the calling application.

When an application attempts to set a property value, a similar procedure is invoked, only it's a *Property Let* procedure. This Class doesn't have any properties that can be set, so there are no Property Let procedures in it. We'll discuss both Property procedures after looking at this simple example. The Property Let and Property Get procedures act like buffers between the Class and the application that uses it. For one thing, the application can't set the variable directly.

NOTE   The CTimer Class project doesn't provide a Property Let procedure for the totalInterval property. As a result, this property is read-only.

The methods of the Class Module are identical to the methods of the Module. Adding a method to a Class is as simple as declaring a Public function or subroutine. Any procedure that can appear in your code can become a method of a Class if it's entered in a Class Module and declared as Public.

NOTE   Some members can be implemented both as methods and properties, and it isn't always easy to say which way to go. Fortunately, this isn't extremely important. You should try to follow the paradigm of the built-in, or third party, controls. For example, if Class is an ActiveX control, a member you would like to see in the Properties window should be implemented as a property (the opposite isn't necessarily true). Methods should correspond to actions, while properties are attributes. The naming scheme is also important. A name like GetElapsedTime suggests a method, while a name like ElapsedTime is closer to a property.

Private and Friend Members

Class Modules may contain private procedures too. These procedures can be called from within the Class' code, but other applications that use the Class can't call them. If you want to keep track of how many times a method has been called during the course of an application, you can include a function like the following one:

```
Private Function CallCounter() As Integer
Static Popularity As Integer
    Popularity = Popularity + 1
    CallCount = Popularity
End Function
```

This function can be called from within the Class' code, but applications that use this Class can't see the CallCounter() function. Because CallCounter() is private, it's not a method of the Class, it's a regular function in the Class' code. You can add this function to the CTimer project and see that you can't access it from within another application.

In addition to private and public members, Classes have a third type of scope modifier, which is called *Friend*. A Friend member is public for the entire project and can be accessed by all the Classes in the project. Public variables in a Standard EXE project can be accessed by all other Modules and Forms. In a standard EXE application, this is the broadest scope a variable can have. With ActiveX components whose public members also can be accessed from other applications, there has to be another type that makes members accessible from anywhere in the project, but not from outside. Keep in mind that only methods (functions or subroutines) and Property properties can be declared as Friend. Variables are either private or public. This means that the Class Modules of an ActiveX DLL project can communicate with each other by calling Friend methods and properties.

Testing the CTimer Class

The CTimer ActiveX DLL can't be tested as is. A Class Module exposes its objects to other applications, but it can't be executed on its own. Normally, you'd compile the Class Module and then start a new project that would reference the newly created Class. To simplify the process of testing ActiveX components, Visual Basic allows you to build project groups. In other words, you can have the ActiveX component and its test project in the same project group. To add a test project to the CTimer project, follow these steps:

1. Add a new project with the File ≻ Add Project command. Visual Basic will add a new folder to the Explorer window, the Project1 folder, and it will place a Form under it. Project1 is a regular Visual Basic project.

2. Change the name of the new project to **TestProject** and the name of its Form to **TestForm.**

3. Place the controls you see in Figure 15.1 on the TestForm.

4. In order to use the CTimer Class in the test project, we must first add a reference to the Class. Open the Project menu and select References. In the References dialog box select the entry TimerProject by checking it, as shown in Figure 15.2. The References dialog box displays the name of the project, not the name of the Class.

FIGURE 15.2:

Add the CTimer Class to a project through the References dialog box.

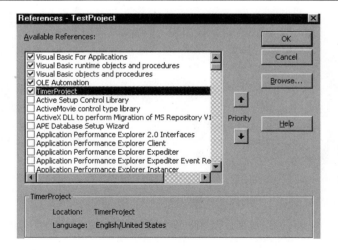

TIP

> If you haven't saved the project yet, you will most likely see the entry Project1 (which is the default name of the project). Do not add this reference to your project yet. Rename the project's components, save them to a new folder, then add the reference. It's not that you can't add a reference to Project1, rather, the next time you open the References dialog box, you won't remember what the Project1 Class does.

5. Then, open the test Form's Code window and enter the lines in Code 15.4.

Code 15.4: **The CTimer Test Form's Code**

```
Dim TMR As New CTimer

Private Sub Command1_Click()
    If Command1.Caption = "Start Timing" Then
        TMR.StartCounting
        Command1.Caption = "Stop Timing"
    Else
        TMR.StopCounting
        Command1.Caption = "Start Timing"
    End If
End Sub

Private Sub Command2_Click()
    ETime = TMR.ElapsedTime
    MsgBox "I've been counting for " & vbCrLf & _
        Hour(TMR.ETime) & " hours" & vbCrLf & _
        Minute(TMR.ETime) & " minutes and " & vbCrLf & _
        Second(TMR.ETime) & " seconds" & vbCrLf
End Sub

Private Sub Command3_Click()
    End
End Sub
```

6. Right-click the name of the TestProject in the Project Explorer window and select the command Set as StartUp. When you press F5, the TestForm will appear.

Run the project and exercise the CTimer Class. Click the Start Timer button to start the timer. Its caption will change to "Stop Timer" and when you click it again it will pause the timing. Stop the timer and restart it again. You can read the elapsed time at any point, but the reading will be correct only if the timer isn't running. If you examine the Class' code you'll see that the *totalInterval* variable is updated every time you stop the timer.

The Test Project's Code

Let's look at the test project's code. The first line is a declaration of an object variable:

```
Dim TMR As New CTimer
```

TMR is an object variable of CTimer type. *CTimer* is the new Class you've just implemented. Just like you need an object variable to access Word's methods and properties, you need an object variable to access the methods of the CTimer Class. The *New* keyword tells Visual Basic to create a new instance of the CTimer object (you could have used the CreateObject() function instead, and we'll discuss this shortly). Your code will access the properties and methods exposed by the CTimer Class through the *TMR* object variable. As soon as you enter the name of the object variable and a period in the code, a list of its members will appear in the Code window, provided that the AutoList Members feature of the editor is on. I suggest that you turn on this feature when working with Classes. The new Class is registered and Visual Basic treats it like any other Class.

The code behind the buttons of the application is trivial. The Start/Stop button calls the StartCounting and StopCounting methods of the Class to start and stop the timing. The Show Interval button reads the value of the ElapsedTime property and formats it as hours, minutes, and seconds, and displays it on a message box.

Class Module Properties

Although a Class' properties can be implemented as public variables, Visual Basic provides the Property Let and Property Get procedures for accessing them. The proper method of implementing a property in your Class is to add the following procedures:

```
Private m_IntProperty
Public Property Let IntProperty(newValue As Integer)
    m_IntProperty = newValue
End Property

Public Property Get IntProperty() As Integer
    IntProperty = m_IntProperty
End Property
```

The private variable *m_IntProperty* is local copy of the property's value. Every time an application sets this property's value, the Property Let procedure is automatically invoked and the new value specified is passed as argument. In other words, the line:

```
IntProperty = 100
```

invokes the following procedure in your Class:

```
Property Let IntProperty(100)
```

Assignments to property values invoke a Property Let procedure (one with the same name as the property) to be executed. The procedure's code can validate the new value and either accept it (and assign it to a local variable) or reject it. Likewise, when the host application requests the value of the IntProperty property, the value of the local variable *m_IntProperty* is passed to it.

In the Property Let procedure, you can insert all the validation code you see fit. For example, here's how you would implement an Age property:

```
Private m_Age
Public Property Let Age(newValue As Integer)
    Select Case newValue
        Case < 0: m_Age = 0
        Case > 100 : m_Age = 100
        Else m_Age=newValue
    End Select
End Property

Public Property Get Age() As Integer
    IntProperty = m_Age
End Property
```

If the application specifies an invalid age value, the Class takes some action that will prevent some serious errors later in the code. The amount of validation code depends on the nature of the property, and you can insert as little or as much as you like.

You can also raise errors from within your Property Let procedure, which can be trapped by the application's code. For example, you could implement the Age property as follows:

```
Public Property Let Age(newValue As Integer)
    If newValue < 0 or newValue > 100 Then
            Err.Raise 1999, _
                "Invalid Age. It must be greater than _
                zero and less than 100"
    Else
            m_Age = newValue
End Property
```

The error is passed back to the application, and it will either generate a runtime error or it will be trapped by the application's code. You will find more information on raising errors from within a Class in the section "Raising Errors in a Class."

You may think of displaying a message with the MsgBox() function from within the procedure's code. This isn't such a good idea for two reasons:

1. The message box may not be displayed on the user's monitor. If the Class resides on a server and is used remotely by an application on a network (or the Internet), the message box will be displayed on the server, not on the client computer. Since the user of the application never sees the message box, he will never get a chance to click the OK button, and as a result, the application will freeze.

2. Since the error isn't produced by the application's code, you can't really offer the user descriptive information, just a generic message like "Please enter a valid value." This action must take place in the application's code, and the best method of reacting to errors in Classes is to raise errors to the calling application and let the application handle it.

However, it's possible to display message boxes from within a Class or even bring up an entire Form or dialog box and request user input, as long as you keep in mind that the Class' visible user interface may become invisible if the Class is executed remotely.

Some Classes provide read-only properties. The simplest method of implementing a read-only property is to omit the Property Let procedure, as we have done with the CTimer Class. You can also raise a trappable runtime error, which the host application can intercept, and then act accordingly. You will see how to raise errors from within your Class later in this chapter.

Creating Object Variables

In the last chapter, you learned how to access objects through object variables. You also learned two methods for declaring object variables:

1. Declare an object variable with the *New* keyword:

    ```
    Private objectVar As New objectType
    ```

2. Declare an object variable, and then set it to the object you want to access:

    ```
    Private objectVar As objectType
    Set objectVar = New objectType
    ```

Both methods require that Visual Basic knows the object's type.

You also would expect Visual Basic to know about Forms, controls, and other types of built-in objects, but what about your custom objects? Visual Basic doesn't know anything about the objects you create, so you must tell it that a specific project must access an object by adding a reference to this object to your project. For example, if you want to add the CTimer Class to a project, open the Project menu and select References. In the References dialog box that appears, locate the object you want to reference from within your code, and click OK.

If you open the Object Browser window after adding a new reference to your project, you will see the Type Library of the recently added object. Select it in the Type Library box to see the Classes it exposes in the Classes pane. The CTimer project exposes a single Class, the CTimer Class. Click the name of the Class to see its members.

So, unless you add a reference to a specific object to your project, you won't be able to declare variables of this type. There's also a third method of declaring object variables, the CreateObject() function, which requires you to supply the application and Class name. First, declare an object variable, and then assign an object instance to it:

```
Private TMR As Object
Set TMR = CreateObject("TimerProject.CTimer")
```

The Set statement is usually placed in the Form_Load event or in the procedure that needs to access the object. You can change the declaration of the object variable *TMR* in the test application with the CreateObject method shown. The rest of the code remains the same.

Raising Events from within Classes

This topic is rather advanced and you can safely skip it. Raising events from within Classes is not a very common practice. Since Classes don't have a visible user interface, there are no external events to react to and from which to raise events. In the following chapter, you'll learn how to raise events from within ActiveX controls. ActiveX controls have a visible interface and they must react to many external events, such as mouse and keyboard events. As you will see, it's actually quite common to raise events from within ActiveX controls and quite simple too.

The situation is quite different with ActiveX DLLs. Classes raise events based on internal events such as timeouts. We will revise the CTimer Class so that it raises a Minute and an Hour event every time a minute or an hour has passed. The revised CTimer project, along with its test project, can be found in the EVNTimer folder in this chapter's folder on the CD.

Since the CTimer Class doesn't keep track of time constantly, we must help it with a Timer control. But the Class Module doesn't have a Form, so how can we use a Timer control? We'll add a Form to the project, but we'll never show it. It will be a hidden Form with a Timer control. The Class Module will be able to access the Timer control on the Form and intercept its Timer event. Here's how you can access an ActiveX control from within a Class Module.

1. In the Project Explorer select the CTimer component and rename it to Event-Timer, as shown in Figure 15.3. Then open the Project menu, select Add Form, and add a new Form to the Class Module project.

NOTE Make sure the new Form appears under the EventTimer component and not under the TestProject component. If the Form is added to the test project, remove it and repeat the process.

2. Open the Form1 Form in design mode and place an instance of the Timer control on it. Set its Enabled property to True and its Interval property to 10000. This value corresponds to 10 seconds. We don't want our TimerClass to spend too much computer time processing Timer events, so we set a large timeout interval.

Figure 15.3 shows the EventTimer project in the Visual Basic IDE. Notice the project components in the Project window, the Form1 in the Design window, and the Class' Code window. The new Class is called EventTimerClass and the Project is called EventTimer. When you open this sample project, remember to select the test project and add a reference to the EventTimer to it.

FIGURE 15.3:

The EventTimer project is the same as the CTimer project, but uses an internal Timer to keep track of time.

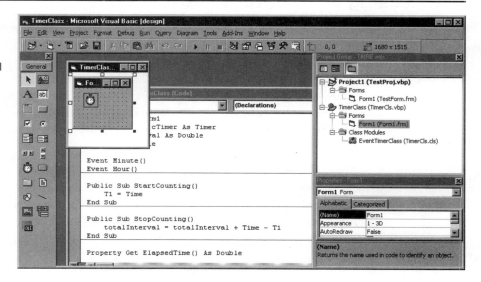

Our goal is to intercept the Timer control's Timer event from within the Class Module and use it to raise the Minute and Hour events. The Minute event takes place for the first time 60 seconds after the timer is started and then every 60 seconds thereafter. Likewise the Hour event takes place for the first time 60 seconds after the Class is started and every 60 minutes after that.

3. In order to access a control on another Form, you must create a Form variable in the Class itself. Insert the following declarations in the Class' code:

```
Dim cFrm As Form1
Dim WithEvents eTimer As Timer
```

The keyword *WithEvents* tells Visual Basic that the *eTimer* control must carry with it its properties, methods, *and* events (which is why I named it eTimer). These variables will come to life when you set them to the appropriate objects. This action must take place from within the Class' Initialize event.

4. Insert the following lines in the Class_Initialize event:

```
Private Sub Class_Initialize()
    Set cFrm = New Form1
    Load cFrm
    Set eTimer = cFrm.Timer1
End Sub
```

The first statement assigns a new instance of the Form1 object to the *cFrm* variable. Then, the new Form is loaded. At this point we can access the controls on the Form. The last line makes the *eTimer* variable equivalent to the Timer1 control on the Form1 Form. The Class can now access the Timer1 control on the Form1 Form as *eTimer*, just as the Form1 can access it as Timer1. The two expressions are equivalent, but you can't access the Timer control as Form1.Timer1 from within the Class Module.

If you expand the Objects drop-down list in the Class Module's Code window, you will see the object *eTimer*. Because the *eTimer* object variable is declared with the *WithEvents* keyword, we should be able to program its events. That's why its name appears in the Objects list. Select the *eTimer* object on the Objects list and then open the Events list in the Code window. You will see the name of the Timer event. Select it and you're ready to program the eTimer_Timer() event, which is equivalent to programming the Timer1_Timer event.

5. Insert the lines of Code 15.5 in the eTimer_Timer event handler.

Code 15.5:   **Raising Events from within a Class**

```
Private Sub eTimer_Timer()
Static seconds As Long
Static minutes As Long
Static hours As Long
Dim RaiseMinutes As Boolean, RaiseHours As Boolean

    If Not Counting Then Exit Sub
    RaiseMinutes = False
    RaiseHours = False
    seconds = seconds + eTimer.Interval / 1000
    If seconds = 60 Then
        minutes = minutes + 1
        seconds = 0
        RaiseMinutes = True
        If minutes = 60 Then
            hours = hours + 1
            minutes = 0
            RaiseHours = True
        End If
    End If
    If RaiseHours Then
        RaiseEvent Hour
    ElseIf RaiseMinutes Then
        RaiseEvent Minute
    End If
End Sub
```

The *Counting* Boolean variable is declared in the Form's declaration section and indicates whether the timer is counting. If the timer is paused, we shouldn't process the Timer event. This variable is set to True from within the StartCounting method and reset to False from within the StopCounting method.

This subroutine is invoked every 10 seconds and increases the number of seconds elapsed by increments of 10. Every 60 seconds, it increases the number of minutes by increments of 1, and every 60 minutes it increases the number of hours by increments of 1. If the *minutes* variable is 0 (that is, if it has reached 60 and is reset back to 0), the Hour event must be raised. If not, we examine the value of the *seconds* variable. If it's 0, then the Minute event must be raised. This coding raises 59 consecutive Minute events, then an Hour event, and the process is repeated. Since we can't issue to events at once, we skip the Minute event when the Hour event is due. Obviously, the Hour event implies that a Minute event should take place.

6.	In order for a Class to raise an event, you must also declare the names of the events. Insert the following lines in the Class Module's code window (outside any procedure):

```
Event Minute()
Event Hour()
```

The complete listing of the EventTimerClass is shown next. Notice its similarities to and differences from the plain CTimer Class. The Property Get procedures and the Class' method don't change. Only the code for accessing a Timer control on an invisible Form is added, and the Timer control's Timer event is programmed to raise the appropriate events.

**Code 15.6:	The EventTimerClass Listing**

```
Dim cFrm As Form1
Dim WithEvents eTimer As Timer
Dim totalInterval As Double
Dim T1 As Double
Dim Counting As Boolean

Event Minute()
Event Hour()

Public Sub StartCounting()
    T1 = Time
    Counting = True
End Sub

Public Sub StopCounting()
    totalInterval = totalInterval + Time - T1
    Counting = False
End Sub

Property Get ElapsedTime() As Double
    ElapsedTime = totalInterval
End Property

Public Sub ResetTimer()
    totalInterval = 0
End Sub

Private Sub Class_Initialize()
    Set cFrm = New Form1
    Load cFrm
    Set eTimer = cFrm.Timer1
End Sub

Private Sub eTimer_Timer()
```

```
Static seconds As Long
Static minutes As Long
Static hours As Long
Dim RaiseMinutes As Boolean, RaiseHours As Boolean

    If Not Counting Then Exit Sub
    RaiseMinutes = False
    RaiseHours = False
    seconds = seconds + eTimer.Interval / 1000
    If seconds = 60 Then
        minutes = minutes + 1
        seconds = 0
        RaiseMinutes = True
        If minutes = 60 Then
            hours = hours + 1
            minutes = 0
            RaiseHours = True
        End If
    End If
    If RaiseHours Then
        RaiseEvent Hour
    ElseIf RaiseMinutes Then
        RaiseEvent Minute
    End If
End Sub
```

Testing the EventTimer Class

To test the EventTimer Class, add a new project to the existing one with the File ➢ Add Project command. On the test project's Form, add a Command button and four Labels. Arrange the Labels in pairs and align them as shown in Figure 15.4. The controls Label3 and Label4 are where the number of elapsed minutes and hours are displayed.

FIGURE 15.4:

The EventTimer Class
Test Form

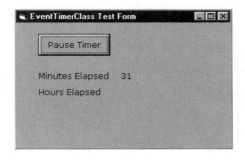

The Command button lets you start and pause the timer. When you click it for the first time, its caption changes to Pause Timer. To pause the timer, click the button again. To resume timing, click the button and its caption will change back to Start Timer.

When the Form is first loaded, an *eventTimerClass* object variable is created from within the Form's Load event with the following statement:

```
Private Sub Form_Load()
    Set TMR = New eventTimerClass
End Sub
```

The *TMR* variable is declared as:

```
Dim WithEvents TMR As eventTimerClass
```

As soon as you've entered the above declaration in the Form's declarations section, the TMR object will be added to the Code window's Objects drop-down list and its events to the Events list. Select the TMR object in the Objects list and examine its events in the Events list. Then select the Minute and Hour events and enter the following code in their handlers:

```
Private Sub TMR_Hour()
    Label4.Caption = Val(Label4.Caption) + 1
End Sub


Private Sub TMR_Minute()
    Label3.Caption = Val(Label3.Caption) + 1
End Sub
```

Finally, add the following code to the Command button's Click event handler to start and pause the timing:

```
Private Sub Command1_Click()
    If Command1.Caption = "Start Timer" Then
        Command1.Caption = "Pause Timer"
        TMR.StartCounting
    Else
        Command1.Caption = "Start Timer"
        TMR.StopCounting
    End If
End Sub
```

The hours and minutes reported on the Form's Labels correspond to the time elapsed while the timer is counting. When the timer is paused, the EventTimer Class doesn't count seconds or fire any events.

Setting Project Properties

At this point, we'll take a break to discuss the Project Properties dialog box. Most of the entries in this dialog box are obvious, but some aren't. Also, some seemingly obvious options may have ramifications you must be aware of. You can skip this section if you want and come back to it when you need additional information. The Project Properties dialog box, shown in Figure 15.5, lets you select a project type and set various options for the project. The tabs of the dialog box are explained next.

FIGURE 15.5:

The General tab of the Project Properties window

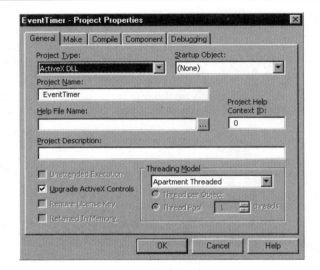

General Tab

- **Project Type** This list contains the types of projects as they appear in the File Open dialog box. The project types available in this list are Standard EXE, ActiveX DLL, ActiveX EXE, and ActiveX control. Changing the project type when you want to isn't always feasible, or simple, but many times it is. Switching between ActiveX DLL and Standard EXE projects is possible and fairly easy. Let's say you want to build an ActiveX DLL. To simplify the testing and debugging process, you can start a Standard EXE project and add a Class Module to the project. When the Class is working in the context of the current project, you can remove the project's Forms and change the type of the project from Standard EXE to ActiveX DLL. After the DLL has been created and registered (as explained in the section "Registering a Component," later in this chapter), you can use the Class from within any project.

- **Startup Object**   This entry lets you specify what will happen when the project runs. ActiveX DLL and EXE projects can't be executed; the ActiveX component must be called from within a Standard EXE project's code. For Standard EXE projects, the start-up object can be a Form or the subroutine Main. The Main subroutine must reside in a standard Module of the project, and it must bring up the first visible Form of the application. Code components can't start by displaying Forms. The start-up object of an ActiveX EXE or DLL component must be None or the subroutine Main. If you change the type of a project during its implementation, you must also change the start-up object.

  For project groups, you can set a different start-up object for each project in the group. To specify the start-up project, right-click the project's name in the Project window and select Set as Start-up.

- **Project Name**   This property is the component's name in the Object Browser. In other words, this is how developers will locate your component in the Object Browser and look up its members. It's important to set a proper project name in this field or else you'll have to differentiate among various Project1 components on your disk. If the component's name is MyComponent and it exposes a Class called MyClass, then you must create an object variable to reference the Class from within another application with a statement like the following one:

  ```
  Set Object1 = CreateObject("MyObject.MyClass")
  ```

  As you've probably realized, changing the project's name (or the Class' name, for that matter) after the fact, requires that the code be revised too. Use descriptive project names and avoid generic names like Test, Example, or Server. ActiveX components are registered to the system, they aren't just files that live in a folder.

- **Help File Name, Project Help Context ID**   These two fields let you specify the Help file for the project and the ID in this file. Although we won't discuss Help files in this book, any component you plan to release (especially ActiveX controls) must have a Help file.

- **Project Description**   This is the project's description and it appears in the Object Browser when a user selects your component.

- **Upgrade ActiveX Controls**   Check this option to have Visual Basic automatically upgrade ActiveX controls to newer versions should the user upgrade one or more of the controls used in the project.

- **Require License Key**   This field enables you to protect your components with a license key. The ActiveX components you will create with the process outlined here will work on any system on which they are installed. Let's say you've developed a custom ActiveX DLL, which you will use from within your applications. The control must also be installed on the host systems that will run your application. The end users should be able to use your component at runtime only. This is possible with license keys. Once you reach this level of component development, you must consult the documentation to learn how to create license keys for your components.

- **Unattended Execution**   The options in this section apply to multithreaded EXE servers and won't be discussed in this book. This option tells Visual Basic to skip any message boxes or other forms of input/output so that the component can be executed without user attention. If you call an ActiveX EXE component that runs on a server machine, you don't want the component to display an input box (which you probably inserted as a debugging aid) on the server and wait for user input forever.

Component Tab

- **Start Mode**   In this section, you can specify whether an ActiveX EXE server will start as a stand-alone application or an ActiveX server. This option applies to ActiveX EXE components only and the default option is ActiveX component.

- **Remote Server**   When checked, Visual Basic creates a file with a .vbr file name extension and the same filename as the .dll file. This .vbr file contains information needed by the Windows Registry to run an ActiveX server on a remote computer.

- **Version Compatibility**   The options in this section allow you to set the level of version compatibility, they are:

  - **No Compatibility**   If this option is checked, compatibility is not enforced.

  - **Project Compatibility**   If checked, the Location box is activated which allows you to search for the file compatible with this project. If cleared, the Location box is not available. If you design an ActiveX control or code component to be used with a specific project, click this option and select the name of the project in the last field on the tab. By default, this option is checked for all ActiveX projects so that every time you change the control or component's code, the project is also updated.

  - **Binary Compatibility**   Check this option to maintain compatibility among projects that have been compiled using your component.

The Class Instancing Property

As you've noticed, Classes have a few properties. In this chapter, we discuss only two of them: the Name property and the Instancing property. The *Instancing* property determines whether and how applications can use the Class. Its six possible settings are discussed next.

Private

Private objects can only be accessed by components in the same application. If you're developing a Class that can't be used in other projects, or you don't want to make it available to other developers, set its Instancing property to Private.

SingleUse

This setting applies to ActiveX EXE code components only. An ActiveX EXE server is an executable file (an application) that can service one or more clients. If the server's Instancing property is SingleUse, for every client that calls the Class' objects, a new instance of the server is started. This setting is an inefficient method of creating and using objects, and it's usually avoided. If you need a new instance of the server for each client, you might as well implement the server as an ActiveX DLL.

MultiUse

This setting is the opposite of Private and can be used with code components only. It allows a single instance of the server to provide as many objects as are required by the client applications. Every new ActiveX EXE or ActiveX DLL project you start has its Instancing property set to MultiUse by default.

GlobalSingleUse

This setting creates a global object with SingleUse characteristics. If you're going to implement a global object, make it SingleUse so that all clients that call it can be serviced by a single instance of the server. It's also available with ActiveX EXE and ActiveX DLL components.

GlobalMultiUse

This setting is available with ActiveX EXE and ActiveX DLL projects and should be used rarely. The objects exposed by GlobalMultiUse component are available to the entire system and can be accessed by any application, as if they were system components. Visual Basic provides system-wide objects called global objects. For example, the Screen and Printer objects are global objects because you don't need to add a reference to them in the applications that use them. If you think you have an object that's important for the rest of the system to know about (and not just the application that needs it), then set its Instancing property to GlobalMultiUse.

PublicNotCreatable

The objects of a Class with this setting can be accessed by other applications, but can't be created. Now what good is this? The objects of a PublicNotCreatable Class must be first created by another component in the same object and then accessed through this component's objects. For example, if you have a Class that implements database operations, one of the objects exposed by the Class represents the database. Another Class in the project represents a Table of the database. If you allow the developer to access the second object directly, there's a chance he may attempt to open the Table without first opening the database. Instead, if you make the Class that exposes the Database object MultiUse and the Class that exposes the Table object PrivateNotCreatable, and then you create a reference to the object that represents the table as soon as the database is opened, the developer can access the Table object directly, but only after it has been created.

The remaining properties of the Class object are briefly described but will not be used in this book:

- **DataBindingBehavior** Determines whether the Class will act as a data consumer (a Class that connects to databases and provides records and/or fields to the host application)

- **DataSourceBehavior** Determines whether the Class can be used as a data source (whether other Classes of controls can be bound to this Class)

- **MTSTransactionMode** Allows you specify whether the Class will support the Microsoft Transaction Server. This setting will be used for Classes meant to be executed on a server and carry out multiple transactions at once. If one of the transactions fails, then all transactions are aborted.

Registering an ActiveX Component

Classes are registered automatically on the system on which they are designed. When you create the DLL or EXE file that implements the Class, Visual Basic also registers it. But what if you want to make the Class available to other developers working on different systems? If the component is an EXE server, you can distribute the EXE file. Once it's run on the target computer, the Class will be registered automatically. No messages or Forms will be displayed. All you have to do is simply execute the server and it will register itself.

The situation is different for DLL components because they can't be executed on their own. They must be loaded in the address space of another application (that's why ActiveX DLLs are called in-process servers—they service only the process that hosts them). ActiveX DLLs must be registered with the REGSVR32 utility, which comes with Visual Basic (it's in the Tools/RegUtils folder on the Visual Basic CD). REGSVR32 is a program that allows you to register and unregister in-process servers. Being able to unregister out-of-process servers is just as important. For example, removing the DLL files that implement the code components isn't enough. You must also unregister the components themselves from the Registry, which can be done with the REGSVR32 utility.

To register an ActiveX DLL, create the DLL file with the Make ClassName.dll command of the File menu (ClassName being the name of your Class, of course). Then copy this file to your Windows System folder or any other folder. To register the DLL, open a Command Prompt window (a DOS window), switch to the folder where the DLL resides, and issue the following command:

```
C:\WINDOWS\SYSTEM\REGSVR32 ClassName.dll
```

ClassName.dll is the file that implements the server. There are several options you can use with the REGSVR32 utility. The /u option will uninstall a previously registered DLL. To uninstall the file ClassName.dll, use the command:

```
REGSVR32 /u ClassName.dll
```

When a new DLL is registered, the REGSVR utility reports the results of the operation in a message box. To suppress this message box, use the /s (silent) option. REGSVR32 is the simplest mechanism for distributing DLL servers. All you have to do is write a small application that copies the DLL file to a folder and then run the REGSVR32 utility on the target computer to register it. If your decide to create distribution files for your component with the Package & Deployment Wizard, any component that must be installed with the application will be installed by the distribution application.

Referencing the EventTimer Class in Other Projects

To use a Class in another project, you must first add a reference to the Class. This means that you must make the component available to the system by registering it as explained in the previous section. Once the DLL (or EXE) file of the component has been created and registered with the host system, any project or other application on the system can use it. To add the EventTimer Class to another project, follow these steps:

1. Start a new project, open the Project menu, and select References to see the References dialog box. This dialog box contains all the objects you can reference in your projects.

2. Select the entry EventTimer (objects are listed by their project name, not the Class name) and click OK. After the Class has been added to the project, you can examine its interface with the Object Browser.

3. From the View menu, select Object Browser to see the window of Figure 15.6. In the top drop-down list select the newly added reference.

FIGURE 15.6:

The EventTimer Class' members viewed with the Object Browser

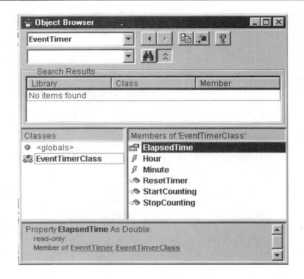

4. The EventTimer project exposes a single Class, the EventTimerClass, whose name appears in the Classes pane. In the Members pane you see the properties, methods, and events of the Class.

If you select ElapsedTime property in the Members pane with the mouse, you'll see its description in the lower pane of the Object Browser. It's a property of the EventTimer.EventTimerClass object and it's read-only because the Class contains a Property Get procedure for this property. The other members are methods and events of the Class. A developer could probably figure out what this Class does by just looking at the members it exposes.

Implementing Collection Properties

Some ActiveX components provide array or Collection properties. For example, the ListBox control exposes the List property, which is an array. The items of the ListBox control are stored in the *List* array, which is a property of the control, and they can be accessed by an index that goes from 0 to ListCount(-1). Implementing array properties from within your component isn't complicated, but you must declare an array and the methods for adding, retrieving, and removing elements from the array. Arrays aren't the best structures for storing multiple items because you can't quickly remove an element of the array. To delete an element, you must move all the elements that follow up by one position. A structure that's better suited for this type of task is the Collection object.

Implementing a Collection

To implement a public collection in your custom component, you must expose the following properties and methods of the Collection object:

- **Add Method**   Adds a new item to the collection
- **Remove Method**   Removes an item from the list
- **Clear Method**   Removes all items from the list
- **Count Property**   Returns the number of items in the list
- **Item Property**   Returns a specific item

To do so, insert the following collection declaration at the beginning of the Class Module's Code window:

```
Dim DataCollection As New Collection
```

DataCollection is a new variable that can hold multiple items. Then, insert the following property and method definitions so the developer can manipulate the collection (add/remove items to and from the collection, enumerate it, and retrieve selected items by their key). The Class' Count property returns the value of the collection's Count property.

Code 15.7:   **The Count Property of DataCollection**

```
Public Property Get Count() As Long
    Count = DataCollection.Count
End Property
```

The Add method is a public function that returns True if its arguments are successfully added to the collection. If an error occurs, then the method returns False.

Code 15.8:   **The Add Method of DataCollection**

```
Public Function Add(dValue As Double) As Boolean
On Error GoTo AddError
```

```
        DataCollection.Add dValue
        Add = True
        Exit Function
AddError:
        Add = False
End Function
```

The Remove method is also a Boolean function that returns True if the specified element is successfully removed from the list. In addition, it generates a trappable runtime error, which the host application can handle with the On Error statement. Notice that the `Err.Raise` statement in Code 15.9 triggers a trappable error with a number and a description (you must add the *vbObjectError* constant to avoid conflicts with the standard Visual Basic error message). As far as the application that uses the Class is concerned, it's as if it has received a Visual Basic error. Notice that Visual Basic may trigger its own error 1. Our error 1 is for our custom Class, which is why we added the *vbObjectError* constant.

Code 15.9: **The Remove Method of DataCollection**

```
Public Function Remove(index As Long) As Boolean
    If index < 0 Or index > DataCollection.Count Then
        DataCollection.Remove index
        Remove = True
    Else
        Err.Raise vbObjectError + 2, "ClassName", _
                "Couldn't remove item"
        Remove = False
    End If
End Function
```

The syntax of the Raise method of the Err object is:

```
Err.Raise number, source, description
```

source is the name of the component where the error occurred (it's possible that multiple components will raise the same error). The host application must read both the error's number and source and then take some action (e.g., correct the condition that triggered the error, repeat the operation).

The Item method retrieves a specific item from the collection based on the index that's passed to the method as argument. If the index is beyond the collection's bounds, the trappable runtime error 2 is triggered.

Code 15.10:   **The Item Method of DataCollection**

```
Public Function Item(index As Long) As Double
    If index < 0 Or index > DataCollection.Count Then
        Err.Raise vbObjectError + 1, "ClassName", _
                "Index out of bounds"
    Else
        Item = DataCollection(index)
    End If
End Function
```

The last method is the Clear method, which removes all the items in the collection. Because the collection doesn't have a Clear method, we must remove every item in the collection with its Remove method. Notice also that the loop scans the collection's items backward. A forward loop would cause a runtime error because after the removal of the first item, the DataCollection.Count property will be less by one; however, this change won't affect the number of iterations.

Code 15.11:   **The Clear Method of DataCollection**

```
Public Function Clear() As Boolean
On Error GoTo ClearError
    For i = DataCollection.Count To 1 Step -1
        DataCollection.Remove i
    Next
    Clear = True
    Exit Function

ClearError:
    Clear = False
End Function
```

VB6 at Work: The AXStat Class

The AXStat Class project demonstrates the process of designing Classes that expose collections. The AXStat Class exposes the members of a standard collection and the following custom members:

- **Average property**   Returns the average of the data set currently stored in the control

- **Min property**   Returns the minimum value in the data set
- **Max property**   Returns the maximum value in the data set

The custom properties are quite trivial and their implementation is shown next.

Code 15.12:   **The AXStat Class' Custom Members**

```
Public Property Get Average() As Double
Dim dSum As Double
Dim itm As Long

    For itm = 1 To DataCollection.Count
        dSum = dSum + DataCollection(itm)
    Next
    Average = dSum / DataCollection.Count
End Property

Public Property Get Min() As Double
Dim itm As Long
    Min = 1E+202
    For itm = 1 To DataCollection.Count
        If DataCollection(itm) < Min Then _
            Min = DataCollection(itm)
    Next
End Property

Public Property Get Max() As Double
Dim itm As Long
    Max = -1E+202
    For itm = 1 To DataCollection.Count
        If DataCollection(itm) > Max Then _
            Max = DataCollection(itm)
    Next
End Property
```

The code reads the data values stored in the DataCollection collection and calculates their basic statistics. You can implement Property Get procedures to calculate more advanced statistics than the ones shown here. Notice that the properties are read-only (it doesn't make sense to set their values) and there's no equivalent Property Let procedure.

The code that implements the standard collection methods is identical to the code presented earlier in the section "Implementing a Collection." Just change the name of the Class in the lines that raise runtime errors.

Testing the AXStat Class   The test project for the AXStat Class is shown in Figure 15.7. The Create Data Set button adds 100 random values to the Class' collection. The Display Data button retrieves the data values from the Class and displays them on the ListBox control. Finally, the Show Statistics button calls the Class' methods to calculate the basic statistics of the data set and display them. The buttons on the right demonstrate how to handle errors raised by the Class (we'll get to them later).

FIGURE 15.7:

The AXStat Class' test Form

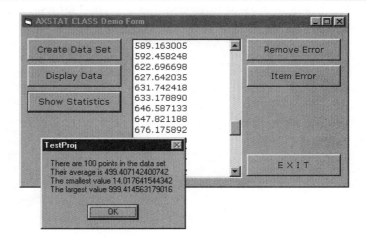

To use the AXStat Class in a project, you must first add a reference to the Class to the project and then create an object variable that references the Class. The following declaration appears at the top of test Form's Code window:

```
Dim STATS As New Statistics
```

The *New* keyword tells Visual Basic to create a new instance of the Statistics Class Module. The first Command button uses the *STATS* variable's Add method to create a data set of 100 random values.

Code 15.13:   Populating the STATS Object with Random Data

```
Private Sub Command1_Click()
    List1.Clear
    STATS.Clear
    For i = 1 To 100
        STATS.Add Rnd() * 1000
    Next
    Command2.Enabled = True
```

```
        Command3.Enabled = True
    End Sub
```

The Display Data button retrieves these values from the *STATS* variable with its Item method. The data values are retrieved with a loop that goes from 1 to STATS.Count.

Code 15.14:   **Reading the Data Values from the STATS Object**

```
    Private Sub Command2_Click()
    Dim i As Long
        List1.Clear
        For i = 1 To STATS.Count
            List1.AddItem Format(STATS.Item(i), "000.000000")
        Next
    End Sub
```

The Show Statistics button calls the variable's Average, Min, and Max methods to calculate the basic statistics of the data set. The code behind the Show Statistics button is shown next.

Code 15.15:   **Using the AXStat Class to Calculate Statistics**

```
    Private Sub Command3_Click()
        StatsMsg = "There are " & STATS.Count & _
                    " points in the data set" & vbCrLf
        StatsMsg = StatsMsg & "Their average is " & _
                    STATS.Average & vbCrLf
        StatsMsg = StatsMsg & "The smallest value " & _
                    STATS.Min & vbCrLf
        StatsMsg = StatsMsg & "The largest value " & STATS.Max
        MsgBox StatsMsg
    End Sub
```

Handling Class Errors

The AXStat Class contains code that raises errors from within the Class. As far as the application is concerned, these errors are identical to the ones generated by Visual Basic and they can be trapped. If the user attempts to access a non-existent item (an item whose index is larger than the Count property), the Class will raise an error. The Class could handle the error by displaying an error message, but this isn't the way we handle errors that occur in Classes. We simply raise a custom error and let the host application handle it.

To generate a trappable runtime error from within a Class (or ActiveX control, as you will see in the following chapter) you must use the *Raise* method of the Err object. The error number can be any Integer value, but you should make sure it doesn't coincide with a Visual Basic error number. The range 0 to 512 is reserved for Visual Basic and you should never use error numbers in this range. You can use any other error number, but it's recommended that you use small integers and add the *vbErrorObject* constant to them. For example, if your Class can detect 8 types of errors, you can assign to them the values 1 through 8 and add the constant *vbErrorObject*. Should another control use the same error numbers, you can find out which control generated the error by examining the Err object's Source property. To find out the original error number, the application can subtract the same constant from the Err.Number value.

TIP

Another interesting property of the *vbErrorObject* constant is that its value is a very large negative number (-2147221504). Thus, all error numbers returned by custom Classes will be negative and you can easily distinguish them from regular Visual Basic errors in your code.

The two buttons on the right side of the test Form generate runtime errors by invoking the members of the AXStat Class with invalid arguments. The next listing shows how they call the Item and Remove methods and the corresponding error-trapping code.

Code 15.16:   **Handling Errors Raised by the AXStat Class**

```
Private Sub Command5_Click()
On Error Resume Next
    STATS.Remove 9999
    If Err.Number <> 0 Then
        MsgBox "ERROR # " & Err.Number - vbObjectError & vbCrLf & Err
.Description & vbCrLf & "In " & Err.Source
    End If
End Sub

Private Sub Command6_Click()
On Error Resume Next
    STATS.Item 9999
```

```
    If Err.Number <> 0 Then
        MsgBox "ERROR # " & Err.Number - vbObjectError & vbCrLf & Err
.Description & vbCrLf & "In " & Err.Source
    End If
End Sub
```

The error number and the error's source are set from within the Class' code with Raise method of the Err object as previously discussed. To find the actual error number raised by the Class, subtract the constant *vbErrorObject* from the Err.Number value. Even better, you can declare a few constants in your code that correspond to the error values. Here's an enumerated type with the errors raised by the AXStats Class:

```
Public Enum AXStatErrors
    AddError = 1
    RemoveError = 2
End Enum
```

The constants for the error values will appear in the Object Browser under the Class AXStatsErrors and you can use them from within your application's code with the expressions AXStatErrors.AddError and AXStatErrors.RemoveError.

Start the application and click one of the two buttons on the right side of the Form. Both buttons cause a runtime error by attempting to access the item with the index 9999. The application will stop with an error message. Why didn't the test project catch the runtime error with its own error-handling routines?

The answer is that, by default, Visual Basic breaks at the location of the error while in design mode. This way you can see the line that is causing the error and debug the appropriate procedure in the Class Module. If you create an executable file and run it outside the Visual Basic IDE, the runtime error will be trapped by the host application. You can also change the default behavior of Visual Basic's error-trapping mechanism at design time. Open the Tools menu and select Options. In the Options dialog box that will appear on the screen, select the General tab, as shown in Figure 15.8.

In the Error Trapping section of the General tab, the option Break in Class Module is selected by default. That's why Visual Basic breaks as soon as the error occurs and the test project doesn't get a chance to handle it with its own error handler. Select the Break on Unhandled Errors option (as shown in Figure 15.8), close the Options dialog box, and run the test project again. Click the Remove Error or Item Error button and this time the project will not end with a runtime error. Instead, a dialog box with an error message like the one shown in Figure 15.9 will be displayed.

FIGURE 15.8:

Changing the default
behavior of the Error
Trapping mechanism
at design time

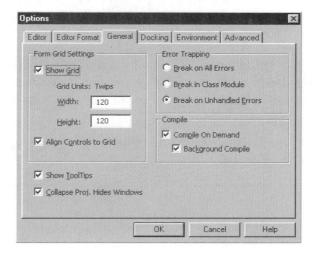

FIGURE 15.9:

Trapping runtime errors
generated by the AXStats
Class

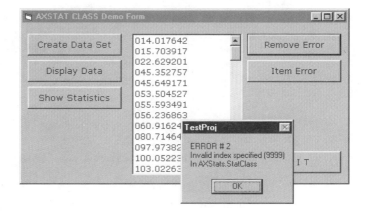

The String Class

The last example in this section is a very simple Class that implements a few useful string operations. The String Class provides three methods, which are implemented as Public functions, and they are:

- **Integer2Binary(number As Long)**   Converts its numeric argument to a binary number and returns the binary value as a string

- **Number2String(number As Integer)**   Converts its numeric argument to a string and returns it. If the number 395 is passed to this method as argument, the return value will be the string "three hundred ninety-five."

- **LowerCaps(str As String)**   Converts its argument to lower caps and returns the new string. If the value "three hundred ninety-nine" is passed to this method as argument, the return value will be "Three Hundred Ninety-Nine."

The members of the String Class are quite simple, but they can serve as your starting point for creating a custom Class with all the string and number manipulation functions you frequently use in your projects that are not readily available in Visual Basic.

The three methods of the String Class are implemented as Public functions, and they are listed next.

Code 15.17:   **The Methods of the String Class**

```
Public Function Number2String(Number)
Dim tenth As Integer
Dim leftover As Integer
Dim hundred As Integer
Dim thousand As Integer

    If Number < 20 Then          'Reads unique numbers
        NumString = ReadSingle(Number)
    ElseIf Number < 100 Then     'Reads numbers less than 100
        tenth = Fix(Number / 10)
        NumString = ReadTenths(tenth * 10)
        leftover = Number - (tenth * 10)
        If leftover > 0 Then
            NumString = NumString & " " & ReadSingle(leftover)
        End If
    ElseIf Number < 1000 Then    ' values between 100 and 999
        hundred = Fix(Number / 100)
        NumString = ReadSingle(hundred) & " hundred"
        leftover = Number - (hundred * 100)
        If leftover > 0 Then
            tenth = Fix(leftover / 10)
            If tenth > 0 Then NumString = _
                NumString & " " & ReadTenths(tenth * 10)
            leftover = Number - (hundred * 100) - (tenth * 10)
            If leftover > 0 Then
                NumString = NumString & " " & _
                    ReadSingle(leftover)
            End If
        End If
    Else              'Reads number between 1000 and 9999
        thousand = Fix(Number / 1000)
```

```
            NumString = ReadSingle(thousand) & " thousand"
            leftover = Number - (thousand * 1000)
            If leftover > 0 Then
                hundred = Fix(leftover / 100)
                If hundred > 0 Then
                    NumString = NumString & " " & _
                        ReadSingle(hundred) & " hundred"
                End If
                leftover = Number - (thousand * 1000) - _
                    (hundred * 100)
                If leftover > 0 Then
                    tenth = Fix(leftover / 10)
                    If tenth > 0 Then
                        NumString = NumString & " " & _
                            ReadTenths(tenth * 10)
                    End If
                    leftover = Number - (thousand * 1000) - _
                        (hundred * 100) - (tenth * 10)
                    If leftover > 0 Then
                        NumString = NumString & " " & _
                            ReadSingle(leftover)
                    End If
                End If
            End If
        End If
    End If
    Number2String = NumString
End Function

Public Function LowerCaps(str As String) As String
Dim newWord As String, newStr As String
Dim tempStr As String
Dim WDelimiter As Integer

    tempStr = Trim(str)
    WDelimiter = InStr(tempStr, " ")
    While WDelimiter > 0
        newWord = Left(tempStr, WDelimiter)
        tempStr = Right(tempStr, Len(tempStr) - WDelimiter)
        newStr = newStr & UCase(Left(newWord, 1)) & _
                Mid(newWord, 2, Len(newWord) - 1)
        WDelimiter = InStr(tempStr, " ")
    Wend
    newWord = tempStr
    newStr = newStr & UCase(Left(newWord, 1)) & _
            Mid(newWord, 2, Len(newWord) - 1)
    LowerCaps = newStr
```

```
End Function

Public Function Integer2Binary(ByVal Number As Long) As String
    HexNum = Hex(Number)
    For i = 1 To Len(HexNum)
        BinNum = BinNum & BinaryDigits("&H" & Mid(HexNum, i, 1))
    Next
    Integer2Binary = BinNum
End Function
```

The Number2String() function is the most complicated one. It's similar to a function used by the READNUM project in Appendix C (on the CD) to read out numeric values. The Number2String() function can convert Integer values in the range from 0 to 9999, but you can easily add the code to make it work with larger values and non-integer values. The Number2String() function calls the functions ReadTenths() and ReadSingle(), which are private to the Class, meaning they can be called from within the Class, but outside programs can't contact them. If you view the members of the StringClass Class with the Object Browser, you will see the private members of the Class. However, they will be listed as Private, which lets you know that you can't access them from within your application.

The test Form of the StringClass is shown in Figure 15.10. The user can enter a numeric value in the textbox at the top of the Form and click the Convert to String or Convert to Binary buttons to convert the value to a string or binary value, respectively. Although the textbox under the Convert to String button contains a string (the string that corresponds to the numeric value or a user-supplied value), the user can click the Convert to LCaps button to convert the string to lower caps.

FIGURE 15.10:

The test Form of the String Class

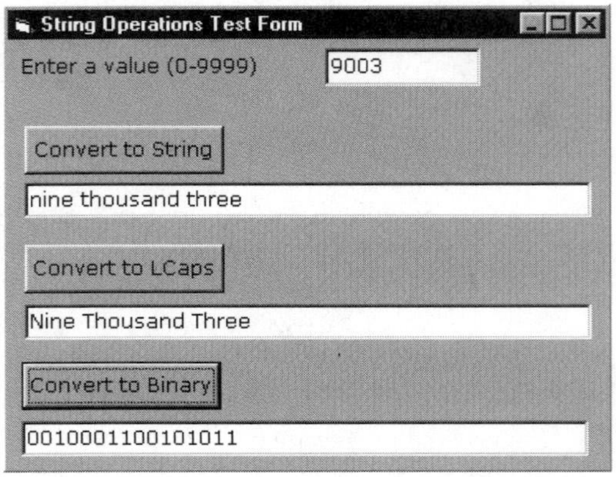

The code of the test Form is quite simple. First, an object variable that will be used to access the String Class is declared:

```
Dim NS As New NumStrings.StringClass
```

NumStrings is the name of the project and *StringClass* the name of the Class Module. The code behind the three Command buttons is shown next:

```
Private Sub Command1_Click()
    Text2.Text = NS.Number2String(Text1.Text)
End Sub

Private Sub Command2_Click()
Dim NStr As String
    NStr = NS.Number2String(Text1.Text)
    Text3.Text = NS.LowerCaps(NStr)
End Sub

Private Sub Command3_Click()
    Text4.Text = NS.Integer2Binary(Text1.Text)
End Sub
```

Each button calls a different method of the *NS* variable. The code behind the Command2 button calls two methods, one after the other. First, it converts the numeric value in the Text1 control to a string, then it calls the LowerCaps method to convert the string to lower caps. The two calls can be combined in a single statement, as shown next:

```
Text3.TextNStr = NS.LowerCaps(NS.Number2String(Text1.Text))
```

In this chapter's folder on the CD, you'll find the NumStr project. Open it with Visual Basic and examine its code or add new members to it. Now is a good time to register this Class with your system so you can use it in the examples of Chapter 22, where we'll build an Active Server Page that contacts this component to create HTML pages.

In the following chapter, we are going to look at the second category of ActiveX components, the ActiveX controls. ActiveX controls are far more common than ActiveX DLLs and quite a bit more interesting because they have a visible user interface. The programmatic interface of ActiveX controls is identical to that of ActiveX code components. The process of implementing properties and methods for ActiveX controls is also identical to the one described in this chapter. In addition, you must design the visible interface of the control, which is quite similar to designing Forms.

CHAPTER

SIXTEEN

16

Building ActiveX Controls

- Designing ActiveX controls

- Building the FLEXLabel control

- Interacting with the Container object

- Designing Property Pages

- Building a generic control

- Enhancing existing controls

If there's one feature of Visual Basic that attracts all kinds of developers, this is it. There is now a simple, easy-to-learn, and fun-to-use language for building ActiveX controls. An ActiveX control is what was formerly called an OLE control. You can think of ActiveX controls as extensions to the Visual Basic language. They are the objects that are represented on Visual Basic's toolbox with a small icon, and you can include them on any Form to add functionality to the applications that use them.

The first question is, Why are they now called ActiveX controls? More than anything else, it's a question of marketing. OLE controls were synonymous with difficult, tricky C programming. A name such as ActiveX will certainly help the average VB programmer feel less intimidated. And, indeed, this feature of Visual Basic has been so well implemented that developing ActiveX controls is within the reach of the average VB programmer. It's not only that Visual Basic 6 can produce ActiveX controls, it's how easily it can do so. In addition, you can use ActiveX controls on Web pages, one of the fastest-growing arenas for Visual Basic program development.

Now, who should be developing ActiveX controls? If I have managed without ActiveX controls, why bother now? Indeed, many of you may not develop custom ActiveX controls for a while. But sooner or later, you will. If you come up with an interesting utility that can be used from within several applications, why not package it as an ActiveX control? Besides, why not indulge in the latest, truly hot stuff? ActiveX controls are cool and will help you leverage your capabilities as a Visual Basic programmer. Being able to design components that can be used both on the Desktop and on the Internet is a great prospect for anyone who makes a living with Visual Basic.

On Designing ActiveX Controls

In this section, I'm going to discuss briefly the similarities and differences among ActiveX controls, ActiveX components, and standard projects. Before I get to the details of how to build ActiveX controls, I want to show you how they relate to other types of projects. This information will help you get the big picture and put together the pieces of the following sections.

A standard application consists of a main Form and several (optional) auxiliary Forms. The auxiliary Forms usually support the main Form, as they usually accept user data that are processed by the code in the main Form. You can think of an ActiveX control as a Form and think of its Properties window and Property Pages as the auxiliary Forms.

An application interacts with the user through its interface. The designer of the application decides how the Forms interact with the user, and the user has to follow these rules. Something similar happens with ActiveX controls. The ActiveX control provides a well-defined interface, which consists of properties and methods. This is the only way to manipulate the control. Just as users of your applications don't have access to the source code and can't modify the application, developers can't see the control's source code and must access an ActiveX control through the interface exposed by the control.

In the last chapter, you learned how to implement interfaces consisting of properties and methods and how to raise events from within an ActiveX component. This is how you build the interface of an ActiveX control. You implement properties as Property procedures, and you implement methods as Public procedures. Whereas an ActiveX component may provide a few properties and methods, an ActiveX control must provide a large number of properties. When a developer places your custom control on a Form, he or she expects to see the properties that are common to all the controls that are visible at runtime (properties to set the control's dimensions, its color, the text font, the Index and Tag properties, and so on). The developer also expects to be able to program all the common events, such as the mouse and keyboard events, as well as some events that are unique to the custom control.

The design of an ActiveX control is similar to the design of a Form. You place controls on a Form-like object, called UserControl, which is the control's Form. It provides nearly all the methods of a standard Form, such as the Print method, the Line method, and so on. In other words, you can use familiar programming techniques to draw an ActiveX control, or you can use existing controls to build a custom ActiveX control.

The Forms of an application are the windows you see on the Desktop when the application is executed. When you design the application, you can rearrange the controls on a Form and program how they react to user actions. At runtime, these Forms will appear on the Desktop. ActiveX controls are also windows, only they can't exist on their own and they can't be placed on the Desktop. They must be placed on Forms.

The major difference between applications and custom controls is that custom controls can exist in two runtime modes. When the developer places a control on a Form, the control is actually running. When you set a control's property through the Properties window, something happens to the control; its appearance changes, or the control rejects the changes. This means that the code of the custom control is executing, even though the project on which the control is used is in design mode. When the developer starts the application, the custom control is already running. However, the control must be able to distinguish when the project is in design or execution mode and behave accordingly.

Consider a simple TextBox control at design time. Its Text property is Text1. If you set its MultiLine property to True, and the Scrollbar property to Vertical, a vertical scroll bar will be attached to the control automatically. Obviously, some statements are executed while the project is in design mode. Then you start the application, enter some text in the TextBox control, and end it. When the project is back in design mode, the control's Text property is reset to Text1. The control has stored its settings before the project switched from design time to runtime mode and restored them when the project returned to design mode again.

This dual runtime mode of an ActiveX control is something new to VB programmers, and you'll have to get used to it. When you design custom ActiveX controls, you must also switch between the roles of the ActiveX developer (the programmer who designs the control) and the role of the application developer (the programmer who uses the control).

In summary, a custom ActiveX control is an application with a visible user interface, as well as an invisible programming interface. The visible interface is what the developer sees when placing an instance of the control on the Form, which is also what the user sees on the Form when the project is placed in runtime mode. The developer can manipulate the control through the properties exposed by the control (at design time) and through its methods (at runtime). The properties and methods constitute the control's invisible interface (or the *developer interface*, as opposed to the *user interface*). You, the ActiveX control developer, will develop the visible user interface on a UserControl object, which is almost identical to the Form object. It's like designing a standard application. As far as the control's invisible interface goes, it's like designing a Class Module.

The FLEXLabel Custom Control

We'll start our exploration of custom ActiveX controls with a simple example. The first control we'll develop in this chapter is the FLEXLabel control, which is an enhanced Label control and is shown in Figure 16.1. It provides all the members of the Label control, plus a few highly desirable new features, such as the ability to align the text in all possible ways on the control, as well as in three-dimensional type.

To implement the FLEXLabel control, here's what we must do:

1. Include all the members of the standard Label control.

2. Add the custom members and provide the code to implement the custom members.

3. Test the control on a standard Form.

FIGURE 16.1:

The FLEXLabel control is an enhanced Label control that can display 3-D text and align it vertically and horizontally on the control.

At this point, you're probably thinking about the code that aligns the text and renders it as carved or raised. A good idea is to start with a standard project, which displays a string on a Form and aligns it in all possible ways. A control is an application packaged in a way that allows it to be displayed on a Form, instead of on the Desktop. As far as the functionality is concerned, in most cases it can be implemented on a regular Form. Figure 16.2 shows the FLabel project's Form, which does exactly what the FLEXLabel control will do. You'll find the project in this chapter's folder on the CD, and you can open it to see how the code works.

FIGURE 16.2:

The FLabel project displays a string in 3-D type and aligns it vertically and horizontally, like the FLEXLabel control.

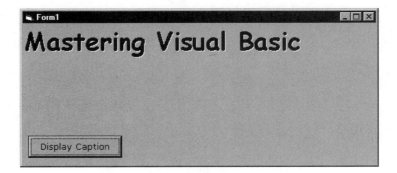

I'm not suggesting you start your custom controls as Standard EXE applications, but for your first few projects, this approach will probably help you. Once you get the code that handles the control's visible interface out of the way, you can concentrate on the procedures that are specific to the development of ActiveX controls. There's another good reason I've chosen this approach, namely to juxtapose the similarities and differences in designing standard applications and custom ActiveX controls.

Start a new Standard EXE project, and add the code that aligns a string vertically and horizontally and renders a string with 3-D type on a Form. The code is lengthy, but straightforward. To align the string, you must calculate the width and height of the string in the current font, set the current point on the Form accordingly, and then display the string with the Print method. To align a string vertically, you must find out the difference between the Form's height and the string's height and then split this difference above and below the string.

To achieve the 3-D effect, you must display the same string twice, first in white and then in black on top of the white. The two strings must be displaced slightly, and the direction of the displacement determines the effect (whether the text will appear as raised or carved). The amount of displacement determines the depth of the effect. Use a displacement of 1 pixel for a light effect, a displacement of 2 pixels for a moderate effect, and a displacement of 3 pixels for a heavy effect. The following code displays the string on the Form, taking into consideration the values of the Form variables *m_Caption* (the string), *m_TextAlignment* (the alignment of the text on the Form), and *m_Effect* (the special effect that will be applied on the text). The meanings of the possible settings of these variables are listed in the code as comments. Here's the code that duplicates the functionality of the FLEXLabel control on a Form.

Code 16.1:   Implementing a More Flexible Label Control

```
Sub DrawCaption()
Dim CaptionWidth As Long, CaptionHeight As Long
Dim CurrX As Long, CurrY As Long
Dim oldForeColor As OLE_COLOR

    CaptionHeight = Me.TextHeight(m_Caption)
    CaptionWidth = Me.TextWidth(m_Caption)
    Select Case m_TextAlignment
        Case 0: ' Top-left
            CurrX = 30
            CurrY = 0
        Case 1: ' Top-center
            CurrX = (Me.ScaleWidth - CaptionWidth) / 2
            CurrY = 0
        Case 2: ' Top-right
            CurrX = Me.ScaleWidth - CaptionWidth - 30
            CurrY = 0
        Case 3: ' Middle-left
            CurrX = 30
            CurrY = (Me.ScaleHeight - CaptionHeight) / 2
        Case 4: ' Middle-center
            CurrX = (Me.ScaleWidth - CaptionWidth) / 2
            CurrY = (Me.ScaleHeight - CaptionHeight) / 2
        Case 5: ' Middle-left
            CurrX = Me.ScaleWidth - CaptionWidth - 30
```

```
            CurrY = (Me.ScaleHeight - CaptionHeight) / 2
        Case 6: ' Bottm-right
            CurrX = 30
            CurrY = Me.ScaleHeight - CaptionHeight - 45
        Case 7: ' bottom-center
            CurrX = (Me.ScaleWidth - CaptionWidth) / 2
            CurrY = Me.ScaleHeight - CaptionHeight - 45
        Case 8: ' Bottom-right
            CurrX = Me.ScaleWidth - CaptionWidth - 30
            CurrY = Me.ScaleHeight - CaptionHeight - 45
End Select

oldForeColor = Me.ForeColor
Select Case m_Effect
    Case 0: ' Plain text
        Me.Cls
        Me.CurrentX = CurrX
        Me.CurrentY = CurrY
        Me.Print m_Caption
    Case 1: ' carved light
        Me.Cls
        ' displace by 15 twips (1 pixel)
        Me.CurrentX = CurrX + 15
        Me.CurrentY = CurrY + 15
        Me.ForeColor = RGB(255, 255, 255)
        ' and print caption in white
        Me.Print m_Caption
        ' restore original coordinates for current point
        Me.CurrentX = CurrX
        Me.CurrentY = CurrY
        Me.ForeColor = oldForeColor
        ' and print caption in black
        Me.Print m_Caption
    Case 2: ' Carved medium
        Me.Cls
        Me.CurrentX = CurrX + 30
        Me.CurrentY = CurrY + 30
        Me.ForeColor = RGB(255, 255, 255)
        Me.Print m_Caption
        Me.CurrentX = CurrX
        Me.CurrentY = CurrY
        Me.ForeColor = oldForeColor
        Me.Print m_Caption
    Case 3: ' Carved heavy
        Me.Cls
```

```
            Me.CurrentX = CurrX + 45
            Me.CurrentY = CurrY + 45
            Me.ForeColor = RGB(255, 255, 255)
            Me.Print m_Caption

            Me.CurrentX = CurrX + 30
            Me.CurrentY = CurrY + 30
            Me.ForeColor = RGB(255, 255, 255)
            Me.Print m_Caption

            Me.CurrentX = CurrX + 15
            Me.CurrentY = CurrY + 15
            Me.ForeColor = RGB(255, 255, 255)
            Me.Print m_Caption

            Me.CurrentX = CurrX
            Me.CurrentY = CurrY
            Me.ForeColor = oldForeColor
            Me.Print m_Caption
    Case 4: ' Raised light
            Me.Cls
            Me.CurrentX = CurrX - 15
            Me.CurrentY = CurrY - 15
            Me.ForeColor = RGB(255, 255, 255)
            Me.Print m_Caption
            Me.CurrentX = CurrX
            Me.CurrentY = CurrY
            Me.ForeColor = oldForeColor
            Me.Print m_Caption
    Case 5: ' Raised medium
            Me.Cls
            Me.CurrentX = CurrX - 30
            Me.CurrentY = CurrY - 30
            Me.ForeColor = RGB(255, 255, 255)
            Me.Print m_Caption
            Me.CurrentX = CurrX
            Me.CurrentY = CurrY
            Me.ForeColor = oldForeColor
            Me.Print m_Caption
    Case 6: ' Raised heavy
            Me.Cls
            Me.CurrentX = CurrX - 45
            Me.CurrentY = CurrY - 45
            Me.ForeColor = RGB(255, 255, 255)
            Me.Print m_Caption
```

```
        Me.CurrentX = CurrX - 30
        Me.CurrentY = CurrY - 30
        Me.ForeColor = RGB(255, 255, 255)
        Me.Print m_Caption

        Me.CurrentX = CurrX - 15
        Me.CurrentY = CurrY - 15
        Me.ForeColor = RGB(255, 255, 255)
        Me.Print m_Caption
        Me.CurrentX = CurrX
        Me.CurrentY = CurrY
        Me.ForeColor = oldForeColor
        Me.Print m_Caption

    End Select

End Sub
```

The DrawCaption() subroutine draws the string, taking into consideration the values of the variables that determine the alignment and special effect. The Draw-Caption() subroutine is called from within the Display Caption button's code:

```
Private Sub Command1_Click()
    m_Caption = "Mastering Visual Basic"
    m_TextAlignment = 0
    m_Effect = 1
    DrawCaption
End Sub
```

This code sets the values of the Form variables *m_Caption*, *m_TextAlignment*, and *m_Effect* and then calls the DrawCaption() subroutine to display the caption on the Form. The DrawCaption() subroutine is the core of the FLEXLabel control, and as you will soon see, we'll use it as is in the control's code. You might want to open the FLabel project now and familiarize yourself with the code, before proceeding to build the control.

Building the FLEXLabel Control

We'll get to the implementation of the control shortly, but first I want to discuss the benefits of building an ActiveX control. Some of you may be wondering, Why bother with an ActiveX control? I have the code to display 3-D text on my Forms and align it any way I like. If I want to, I can modify the code to work with a Picture-Box control, which I can place anywhere on my Forms.

Indeed, a custom control such as the FLEXLabel control is nothing more than an application wrapped in a different package. There are benefits in packaging some applications as ActiveX controls, and here are the most convincing ones:

- The control's code won't interfere with the application code. Your application will not even be aware of the control's code.

- You can change the text alignment and the special effect in the Properties window. No need to edit the code that displays the text. In addition, you can edit the control visually and see the effects of the changes without executing the project.

- The control can cover only part of the Form. Moreover, you can place multiple controls with different captions on the same Form.

- Finally, you can distribute the control easily, and other developers can use it without touching its code.

The first step in designing a custom control is to design the control's interface: what it will look like when placed on a Form (its visible interface) and how developers can access this functionality through its members (the programmable interface). Sure, you've heard the same advice over and over, and many of you still start coding an application without spending much time designing it. In the real world, especially if you are not a member of programming team, people design as they code (or the other way around).

The situation is quite different with ActiveX controls. Your custom control must provide a number of properties, which will be displayed automatically in the Properties window. The developer should be able to adjust every aspect of the control's appearance by manipulating the settings of these properties. In addition, developers expect to see the standard properties shared by most standard controls (such as the background color, the text's font, and so on). You must carefully design the methods so that they expose all the functionality of the control that should be accessed from within the application's code, and the methods shouldn't overlap. Finally, you must provide the events necessary for the control to react to external events. You can start coding other types of applications without much design, but ActiveX controls (and database applications) require thoughtful preparation. Don't start coding a custom control unless you have formulated a very clear idea of what the control will do and how it will be used by developers at design time.

The FLEXLabel Control's Specifications

The FLEXLabel control displays a caption like the standard Label control, so it must provide the Caption and Font properties, which let the developer determine the text and its appearance. In addition, the FLEXLabel control can align its caption both vertically and horizontally. This functionality will be exposed by the Text-Alignment property, whose settings are shown in Table 16.1.

TABLE 16.1: The Settings of the FLEXLabel Control's TextAlignment Property

Value	Description
0	Top Left
1	Top Middle
2	Top Right
3	Center Left
4	Center Middle
5	Center Right
6	Bottom Left
7	Bottom Middle
8	Bottom Right

The names that appear under the Description heading are the strings that will appear in the drop-down list of the TextAlignment property. As you have noticed, properties with a limited number of settings display a drop-down list in the Properties window. This list contains descriptive names (instead of numeric values), and the developer can select only a valid setting.

Similarly, the text effect is manipulated through the Effect property, whose settings are shown in Table 16.2.

TABLE 16.2: The Settings of the FLEXLabel Control's Effect Property

Value	Description
0	None
1	Carved Light
2	Carved
3	Carved Heavy
4	Raised Light
5	Raised
6	Raised Heavy

Like the TextAlignment property, the Effect property has a small number of valid settings, which will be identified in the Properties window with descriptive names.

In addition to the custom properties, the FLEXLabel control should also expose the standard properties of a Label control, such as Font, Tag, BackColor, and so on. Developers expect to see standard properties in the Properties window, and you should implement them. The FLEXLabel control doesn't have any custom methods, but it should provide the standard methods of the Label control, such as the Move method. Similarly, although the control doesn't raise any special events, it must support the standard events of the Label control, such as the mouse and keyboard events.

Except for a few custom properties, this control must expose the standard functionality of the Label control. Most of the custom control's functionality exists already, and there should be a simple technique to borrow this functionality from other controls, rather than implementing it from scratch. And this is indeed the case. Visual Basic provides a Wizard, which will generate the code for implementing standard members. The ActiveX Control Interface Wizard will generate the code that implements the standard members, and you only have to provide the code for the custom properties.

Designing a Custom Control

To start a new ActiveX control project, follow these steps:

1. Choose File ➤ New Project.

2. In the New Project window, select the ActiveX Control icon. Visual Basic creates a new project named Project1, which contains a UserControl named UserControl1.

The initial setup for an ActiveX control project is shown in Figure 16.3 (the names in the project window are different, and I'll show you immediately how to change them).

Let's rename the project and the control. These two names will be used to register your control in your system, so they should be meaningful. Follow these steps:

1. Select Project1 in the Project window, and when its properties appear, change the Name property to FLEXLabel.

2. Select UserControl1 in the Project window, and when its properties appear, change the Name property to Label3D.

FIGURE 16.3:

An ActiveX control project contains a User control instead of a Form.

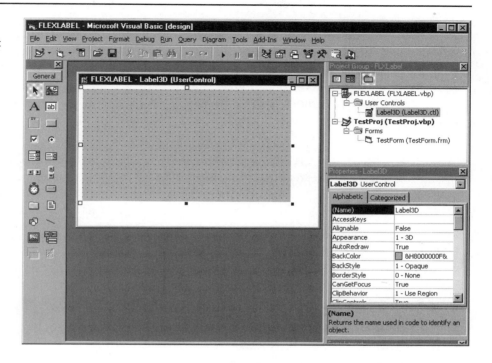

TIP

Every time you place an ActiveX control on a Form, it's named according to the UserControl object's name and a sequence digit. The first instance of the custom control you place on a Form will be named Label3D1, the next one will be named Label3D2, and so on. Obviously, it's important to choose a meaningful name for your UserControl object.

A new object was just introduced: the *UserControl* object. As you will soon see, the UserControl is the "Form" on which the custom control will be designed. It looks, feels, and behaves like a regular VB Form, but it's called a UserControl. User-Control objects have additional unique properties that don't apply to a regular Form, but in order to start designing new controls, think of them as regular Forms. Whereas the FLabel application aligns and displays the caption on a Form, the Label3D custom control uses the same code to draw the caption on the UserControl object (we'll simply change all instances of "Me" to "UserControl").

You've set the scene for a new ActiveX control. Before we insert even a single line of code, we'll let a Wizard generate as much of the custom control as it can for us. Among other things, it will design the control's structure.

The ActiveX Control Interface Wizard

Now, choose Add-Ins ➤ ActiveX Control Interface Wizard to open the Wizard. This Wizard will guide you through the steps of creating a new ActiveX control. It will create the control's interface (its properties, methods, and events) and prepare the basic code for it. You will have to provide only the code that draws the caption and a few more features that can't be automated. The Wizard will take care of the bulk of the work for you. The ActiveX Control Interface Wizard has six windows, which are explained next.

If the ActiveX Control Interface Wizard doesn't appear in the Add-Ins menu, select Add-In Manager, and in the Add-In Manager dialog box, double-click the entry VB6 ActiveX Control Interface Wizard. The indication *Loaded* will appear in the Load Behavior column next to the Wizard's name, as shown in Figure 16.4. If you want the Wizard to load every time you start Visual Basic, check the Load on Startup checkbox. Now, click the OK button, and the add-in's name will appear in the Add-In menu.

FIGURE 16.4:

The Add-in Manager
dialog box

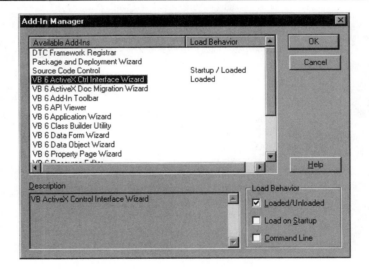

The ActiveX Control Interface Wizard will guide you through the steps of designing the skeleton of a custom ActiveX control. The Wizard will not add the code to align or even display the caption, but it will create a functional control with most of the standard members of a typical ActiveX control.

Introduction

The first screen of the Wizard is a welcome, and you can disable it in the future by checking the Skip This Screen in the Future checkbox. Click the Next button to start the design of your control's user interface.

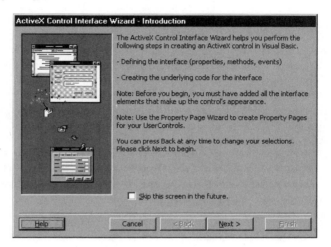

Selecting Interface Members

The next window of the Wizard prompts you to select the standard members of the control. On the left is a list of standard properties, methods, and events that you can include in your custom control. On the right is a list of common members of the user interface, already selected for you. Visual Basic suggests that your control should support these members.

To add a new member, select it from the left list, and click the button that has a single right-pointing arrow. Add the following members to the custom control:

Appearance	Font	MouseMove	OLEGiveFeedback
BackColor	ForeColor	MousePointer	OLESetData
BackStyle	HDC	MouseUp	OLEStart Drag
BorderStyle	HWnd	OLEDrag	Picture
Click	KeyDown	OLEDragDrop	Resize
DblClick	KeyPress	OLEDragOver	
Enabled	KeyUp	OLEDropMode	

As you can see, I've included all the standard properties, events, and methods you'd expect to find in any control that's visible at runtime. I've omitted the data-bound properties, but the FLEXLabel control won't be connected to a database field. Click the Next button.

Creating Custom Interface Members

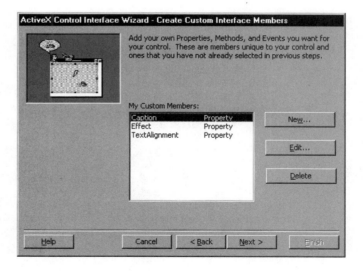

In this window, you add the properties, events, and methods that are unique to your custom control. Follow these steps:

1. Click the New button to display the Add Custom Member dialog box.

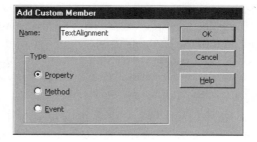

2. In the Name box, enter **Caption** (which is the name of a property), and select the Property radio button.

3. Click OK. The name of the first custom property is now displayed in the My Custom Members box of the Create Custom Interface Members window.

4. Repeat steps 1 through 3 to add the TextAlignment and Effect properties.

If you have misspelled any of the property names or if you want to delete one and re-enter it, use the Edit and Delete buttons. When you are done, click the Next button.

Setting Member Mapping

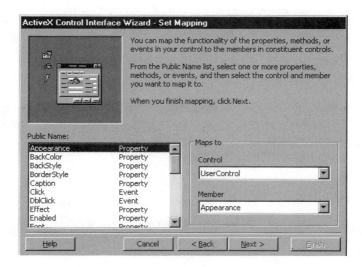

You use this window to map certain properties of your custom control to properties of the so-called constituent controls. A *constituent control* is a regular VB control that your custom control uses. Suppose your custom control contains a Label control, and you want the label's background color to become your control's background color (or foreground color, for that matter). In this window, you map the properties of the controls used by your custom control to the properties of any of the controls it uses. When calling one of the mapped members, the user thinks he or she is setting a control's properties, but in reality is setting a constituent control's member.

You must map all the members (properties, methods, and events) to the User-Control object (except for the custom members, of course). When the user clicks the control, for instance, the Click event is passed to the host application, as if it were generated by the custom control. Any properties, methods, or events that you don't want to handle with your own code must be mapped to the UserControl object. The Click event is a typical example. There's no action you want to take from within your control's code when it's clicked with the mouse. The event must be reported to the host application to handle it accordingly.

To map properties, follow these steps:

1. From the Public Name list, select a property or an event.

2. Click the Control drop-down list's down arrow, and select UserControl. The Wizard immediately selects the UserControl member with the same name.

3. Map all members of the new control (except for custom members) to the equivalent members of the UserControl object.

4. Click the Next button.

Setting Attributes

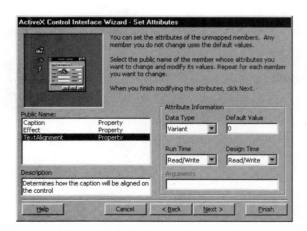

In this window, you set the attributes of the new members (or change the attributes of some default members, if you want, but this isn't recommended). Members that have already been mapped will not appear in this list. The Wizard has declared all new properties as variants, because it can't decipher their types from their names. Our TextAlignment and Effect properties, however, are integers, and the Caption property is a string.

To set attributes, follow these steps:

1. In the Public Name box, select TextAlignment.

2. Click the Data Type drop-down arrow, and select Integer.

Notice that you can set an initial value too. Set the TextAlignment property's initial value to 4 (which displays the caption in the center of the control).

3. In the Default Value box, enter the value **4.** This is the value that is displayed by default in the Properties window for the FLEXLabel control. You will see later in the chapter how to assign custom data types to your properties.

4. Repeat steps 1 through 3 for the Effect property. Set its data type to Integer and its initial value to 2 (carved).

TIP

Don't forget to supply a short description of each property in the Description box. These descriptions are displayed below the Properties window when the user selects a property. The standard members have a description already, but you must supply descriptions for your custom properties.

In the Arguments box, you supply the arguments of the events. This project doesn't have any custom events, but you'll see examples of custom events later in the chapter.

Notice that the properties can have different design-time and runtime properties, which is the first really unique characteristic of a user control. If you think that the developer has no reason to change the alignment or the effect at runtime, make these properties Read-Only at runtime.

Finishing

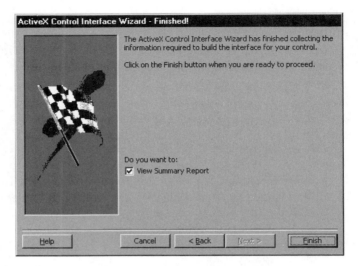

In this window, you are prompted to click Finish to generate the control. Leave View Summary Report checked.

Your hard disk will spin for a few seconds, and you will see the summary report. Read the summary report (which basically tells you how to proceed), and close or save the editor window.

You have created the FLEXLabel control. Not that it does much (you haven't entered the code for displaying the caption yet), but you are ready to test its behavior as a control. At this point, your control has its own Properties page, and you can place it on your Forms.

There's nothing on the screen except a Form. This is the UserControl object, which for all intents and purposes is a Form. There's also a new icon in the toolbox. This is your new control's icon. The icon of a matrix with a pen on top is the default icon for all ActiveX controls. To change the icon, design a new bitmap and assign it to the UserControl object's ToolboxBitmap property. Let's first make sure the control works, and then we'll customize it. The ActiveX control's icon is disabled because you are still designing the control. The control won't be activated while it's being designed.

Testing Your New ActiveX Control

To test your new control, you would normally have to create an OCX file, start a new project, and then place the new custom control on a Form. To simplify development, Visual Basic lets you add a new project to the existing project. In this way, you can test and modify the control without loading a new project each time. The next steps are standard, and you will follow them every time you design an ActiveX control:

1. Choose File ➤ Add Project, to open the New Project window.

2. Select Standard EXE. A new project is added in the New Project window, with its default Form named Form1. Change the name of the Form to TestForm, and change the name of the new project to TestProject.

3. Close the UserControl Design window by clicking its Close button. Close the control's Code window, if it's open.

When the TestForm is selected, the custom control's icon in the toolbox is enabled. From this point on, you can use the FLEXLabel control just as you use any other VB control.

To place an instance of the FlxLabel control on the test Form, follow these steps:

1. Select the icon of the custom ActiveX control in the toolbox and draw the control as usual. The control is automatically named Label3D1, following the Visual Basic convention for naming controls.

2. With the control selected on the Form, locate the Effect property in the Properties window, and set it to another value (it must be an integer and in the valid range of 0 to 6).

You can, however, set both the TextAlignment and Effect property to any value. As long as you specify an integer value, Visual Basic accepts it. You'll see what can be done about that shortly.

As you may have noticed already, ActiveX controls have an Appearance property that by default is 3-D, which gives the controls a 3-D type edge. But the Appearance property doesn't take effect unless the BorderStyle property is also set to 1 - Fixed Single. The default value of the BorderStyle property is 0 - Flat (a rather peculiar choice, considering the effect it has on the Appearance property). Open the Border-Style property and set it to 1 - Fixed Single.

Now double-click the FLEXLabel control on the Form to see its events. Your new control has its own events, and you can program them just as you would program the events of any other VB control. Enter the following code in the control's Click event:

```
Private Sub Label3D1_Click()
    MsgBox "My properties are " & vbCrLf & _
      "Caption = " & Label3D1.Caption & Chr$(13) & _
      "TextAlignment = " & Label3D1.TextAlignment & Chr$(13) & _
      "Effect = " & Label3D1.Effect
End Sub
```

To run the control, press F5 and then click the control. You will see the control's properties displayed in a message box, as shown in Figure 16.5. (At this point no caption is displayed on the control, because we have not yet implemented the Caption custom property.)

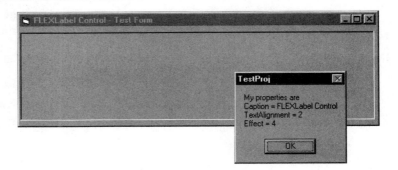

You can program other events too. There's nothing peculiar about programming the custom control. For the developer, it's a regular control. VB has done quite a lot for us. It generated a working ActiveX control. Of course, we must still add the code that makes the control tick. Creating something that looks and feels like a control with point-and-click operations was quite a feat, but our final goal is to design something practical and useful.

The Skeleton of the ActiveX Control

Before adding the custom code, you must understand what the Wizard did for you. Switch to the Project Explorer window, and double-click the name of the control to open it in design mode. Then, double-click the UserControl to open the code pane and see the lines inserted by the Wizard.

Code 16.2: **The ActiveX Control**

```
Private m_Caption As String
Private m_Effect As Integer
Private m_TextAlignment As Integer

'Default Property Values:
Const m_def_Caption = "3D Label"
Const m_def_Effect = 2
Const m_def_TextAlignment = 4
'Property Variables:
'Event Declarations:
Event DblClick()
Event Click()
```

```
Event KeyUp(KeyCode As Integer, Shift As Integer)
Event KeyPress(KeyAscii As Integer)
Event KeyDown(KeyCode As Integer, Shift As Integer)
Event MouseUp(Button As Integer, Shift As Integer, _
      X As Single, Y As Single)
Event MouseMove(Button As Integer, Shift As Integer, _
      X As Single, Y As Single)
Event OLEStartDrag(Data As DataObject, AllowedEffects As Long)
Event OLESetData(Data As DataObject, DataFormat As Integer)
Event OLEGiveFeedback(Effect As Long, DefaultCursors As Boolean)
Event OLEDragOver(Data As DataObject, Effect As Long, _
      Button As Integer, Shift As Integer, X As Single, Y As Single, _
      State As Integer)
Event OLEDragDrop(Data As DataObject, Effect As Long, _
      Button As Integer, Shift As Integer, X As Single, Y As Single)
Event Resize()

Public Property Get Font() As Font
    Set Font = UserControl.Font
End Property

Public Property Set Font(ByVal New_Font As Font)
    Set UserControl.Font = New_Font
    PropertyChanged "Font"
End Property

Public Property Get BorderStyle() As Integer
    BorderStyle = UserControl.BorderStyle
End Property

Public Property Let BorderStyle(ByVal New_BorderStyle As Integer)
    UserControl.BorderStyle() = New_BorderStyle
    PropertyChanged "BorderStyle"
End Property

Public Property Get BackStyle() As BackgroundStyle
    BackStyle = UserControl.BackStyle
End Property

Public Property Let BackStyle(ByVal New_BackStyle As BackgroundStyle)
    UserControl.BackStyle() = New_BackStyle
    PropertyChanged "BackStyle"
End Property

Public Property Get Appearance() As Integer
    Appearance = UserControl.Appearance
End Property
```

```vb
Private Sub UserControl_DblClick()
    RaiseEvent DblClick
End Sub

Private Sub UserControl_Click()
    RaiseEvent Click
End Sub

Public Property Get Enabled() As Boolean
    Enabled = UserControl.Enabled
End Property

Public Property Let Enabled(ByVal New_Enabled As Boolean)
    UserControl.Enabled() = New_Enabled
    PropertyChanged "Enabled"
End Property

Public Property Get ForeColor() As OLE_COLOR
    ForeColor = UserControl.ForeColor
End Property

Public Property Let ForeColor(ByVal New_ForeColor As OLE_COLOR)
    UserControl.ForeColor() = New_ForeColor
    PropertyChanged "ForeColor"
End Property

Public Property Get hDC() As Long
    hDC = UserControl.hDC
End Property

Public Property Get hWnd() As Long
    hWnd = UserControl.hWnd
End Property

Private Sub UserControl_KeyUp(KeyCode As Integer, Shift As Integer)
    RaiseEvent KeyUp(KeyCode, Shift)
End Sub

Private Sub UserControl_KeyPress(KeyAscii As Integer)
    RaiseEvent KeyPress(KeyAscii)
End Sub

Private Sub UserControl_KeyDown(KeyCode As Integer, Shift As Integer)
    RaiseEvent KeyDown(KeyCode, Shift)
End Sub
```

```
Private Sub UserControl_MouseUp(Button As Integer, _
        Shift As Integer, X As Single, Y As Single)
    RaiseEvent MouseUp(Button, Shift, X, Y)
End Sub

Public Property Get MousePointer() As Integer
    MousePointer = UserControl.MousePointer
End Property

Public Property Let MousePointer(ByVal New_MousePointer As Integer)
    UserControl.MousePointer() = New_MousePointer
    PropertyChanged "MousePointer"
End Property

Private Sub UserControl_MouseMove(Button As Integer, _
        Shift As Integer, X As Single, Y As Single)
    RaiseEvent MouseMove(Button, Shift, X, Y)
End Sub

Private Sub UserControl_OLEStartDrag(Data As DataObject, _
        AllowedEffects As Long)
    RaiseEvent OLEStartDrag(Data, AllowedEffects)
End Sub

Private Sub UserControl_OLESetData(Data As DataObject, _
        DataFormat As Integer)
    RaiseEvent OLESetData(Data, DataFormat)
End Sub

Private Sub UserControl_OLEGiveFeedback(Effect As Long, _
        DefaultCursors As Boolean)
    RaiseEvent OLEGiveFeedback(Effect, DefaultCursors)
End Sub

Public Property Get OLEDropMode() As Integer
    OLEDropMode = UserControl.OLEDropMode
End Property

Public Property Let OLEDropMode(ByVal New_OLEDropMode As Integer)
    UserControl.OLEDropMode() = New_OLEDropMode
    PropertyChanged "OLEDropMode"
End Property

Private Sub UserControl_OLEDragOver(Data As DataObject, _
        Effect As Long, Button As Integer, Shift As Integer, _
        X As Single, Y As Single, State As Integer)
```

```
                RaiseEvent OLEDragOver(Data, Effect, Button, Shift, X, Y, State)
        End Sub

        Private Sub UserControl_OLEDragDrop(Data As DataObject, Effect As Long, _
                    Button As Integer, Shift As Integer, X As Single, Y As Single)
            RaiseEvent OLEDragDrop(Data, Effect, Button, Shift, X, Y)
        End Sub

        Public Sub OLEDrag()
            UserControl.OLEDrag
        End Sub

        Public Property Get Picture() As Picture
            Set Picture = UserControl.Picture
        End Property

        Public Property Set Picture(ByVal New_Picture As Picture)
            Set UserControl.Picture = New_Picture
            PropertyChanged "Picture"
        End Property

        Private Sub UserControl_Resize()
            RaiseEvent Resize
        End Sub

        Public Property Get Caption() As String
            Caption = m_Caption
        End Property

        Public Property Let Caption(ByVal New_Caption As String)
            m_Caption = New_Caption
            PropertyChanged "Caption"
        End Property

        Public Property Get Effect() As Integer
            Effect = m_Effect
        End Property

        Public Property Let Effect(ByVal New_Effect As Integer)
            m_Effect = New_Effect
            PropertyChanged "Effect"
        End Property

        Public Property Get TextAlignment() As Integer
            TextAlignment = m_TextAlignment
        End Property
```

```vb
Public Property Let TextAlignment(ByVal New_TextAlignment As Integer)
    m_TextAlignment = New_TextAlignment
    PropertyChanged "TextAlignment"
End Property

'Initialize Properties for User Control
Private Sub UserControl_InitProperties()
    Set Font = Ambient.Font
    m_Caption = m_def_Caption
    m_Effect = m_def_Effect
    m_TextAlignment = m_def_TextAlignment
    UserControl.BorderStyle = 1
    UserControl.BackStyle = 1
End Sub

'Load property values from storage
Private Sub UserControl_ReadProperties(PropBag As PropertyBag)

    Set Font = PropBag.ReadProperty("Font", Ambient.Font)
    UserControl.BorderStyle = PropBag.ReadProperty("BorderStyle", 0)
    UserControl.BackStyle = PropBag.ReadProperty("BackStyle", 1)
    UserControl.Enabled = PropBag.ReadProperty("Enabled", True)
    UserControl.ForeColor = PropBag.ReadProperty("ForeColor", _
                    &H80000012)
    UserControl.MousePointer = PropBag.ReadProperty("MousePointer", 0)
    UserControl.OLEDropMode = PropBag.ReadProperty("OLEDropMode", 0)
    Set Picture = PropBag.ReadProperty("Picture", Nothing)
    m_Caption = PropBag.ReadProperty("Caption", m_def_Caption)
    m_Effect = PropBag.ReadProperty("Effect", m_def_Effect)
    m_TextAlignment = PropBag.ReadProperty("TextAlignment", _
                    m_def_TextAlignment)
    UserControl.BackColor = PropBag.ReadProperty("BackColor", _
                    &H8000000F)
End Sub

'Write property values to storage
Private Sub UserControl_WriteProperties(PropBag As PropertyBag)

    Call PropBag.WriteProperty("Font", Font, Ambient.Font)
    Call PropBag.WriteProperty("BorderStyle", UserControl.BorderStyle, 0)
    Call PropBag.WriteProperty("BackStyle", UserControl.BackStyle, 1)
    Call PropBag.WriteProperty("Enabled", UserControl.Enabled, True)
    Call PropBag.WriteProperty("ForeColor", UserControl.ForeColor, _
        &H80000012)
    Call PropBag.WriteProperty("MousePointer", _
        UserControl.MousePointer, 0)
```

```
      Call PropBag.WriteProperty("OLEDropMode", _
           UserControl.OLEDropMode, 0)
      Call PropBag.WriteProperty("Picture", Picture, Nothing)
      Call PropBag.WriteProperty("Caption", m_Caption, _
           m_def_Caption)
      Call PropBag.WriteProperty("Effect", m_Effect, _
           m_def_Effect)
      Call PropBag.WriteProperty("TextAlignment", _
           m_TextAlignment, m_def_TextAlignment)
      Call PropBag.WriteProperty("BackColor", _
           UserControl.BackColor, &H8000000F)
  End Sub

  'WARNING! DO NOT REMOVE OR MODIFY THE FOLLOWING COMMENTED LINES!
  'MappingInfo=UserControl,UserControl,-1,BackColor
  Public Property Get BackColor() As OLE_COLOR
      BackColor = UserControl.BackColor
  End Property

  Public Property Let BackColor(ByVal New_BackColor As OLE_COLOR)
      UserControl.BackColor() = New_BackColor
      PropertyChanged "BackColor"
  End Property
```

It's quite lengthy, but not as complicated as it appears. Let's look at each section of the code in detail, starting with the declaration section:

```
Option Explicit
'Default Property Values:
Private m_Caption As String
Private m_Effect As Integer
Private m_TextAlignment As Integer
```

These variables will hold the values of the control's custom properties. The control's properties are mapped to private variables in the control's code, because that's what they are. As is the case with an ActiveX component, what the applications perceive and access as properties from the outside are actually plain variables in the control. Later, you'll see how the control gets the values entered by the user in the Properties window (or the code at runtime) and assigns them to these private variables. (Do you remember how you were manipulating the properties of your own OLE server in the previous chapter with the Property Let and Property Get procedures? The same approach works with ActiveX controls. But more on this later.)

Following are the definitions of a few constants that correspond to the values we specified in the Set Attributes window of the Wizard. These constants will be used later in the code as initial values for various properties. Notice that you don't have to run the Wizard to change these values. You can easily edit the control's code. Notice also that the names of the constants are based on the actual property names and that you can easily edit the code.

```
'Default Property Values:
Const m_def_Caption = "3D Label"
Const m_def_Effect = 2
Const m_def_TextAlignment = 4
```

The event declarations follow. These are the events we specified in the first two windows of the Wizard, and we mapped them to the UserControl object. Clicking on the custom control generates a Click event, which is reported to the application as if it were generated by the ActiveX control. There are more event definitions in the listing, but I need not repeat them here.

```
'Event Declarations:
Event DblClick()
Event Click()
Event KeyUp(KeyCode As Integer, Shift As Integer)
Event KeyPress(KeyAscii As Integer)
Event KeyDown(KeyCode As Integer, Shift As Integer)
Event MouseUp(Button As Integer, Shift As Integer, _
        X As Single, Y As Single)
Event MouseMove(Button As Integer, Shift As Integer, _
        X As Single, Y As Single)
```

NOTE   If the Click event weren't mapped to the UserControl object, only the UserControl would see the Click event. If you want to perform a special action when the control is clicked, you program the Click event in the custom control's Code window. The user won't be able to program the Click event unless you raise the Click event in the control's code.

In our custom control, we don't have any exclusive use for the Click event (and the other common mouse and keyboard events), so we are exposing them to the application that uses the ActiveX control.

Setting and Reading Property Values

Next, you see a number of subroutines, two for each property.

Code 16.3:   **The Caption Property Procedures**

```
Public Property Get Caption() As String
    Caption = m_Caption
End Property
```

```
Public Property Let Caption(ByVal New_Caption As String)
    m_Caption = New_Caption
    PropertyChanged "Caption"
End Property
```

Each property is defined by two Public procedures:

- Property Let
- Property Get

The Property Let procedure is invoked every time the property is changed, either via the Properties window (at design time) or via code (at runtime). The code that's executed when a property changes value consists of two lines. The first line gets the value supplied by the procedure's argument (which is the new value of the property) and assigns it to the private variable that represents the property in the control. The rest of the code sees only the *m_Caption* local property, not the actual property. The second line notifies Visual Basic that the property has changed value. The PropertyChanged method is important and must be included in the Property Let procedure, because this is how Visual Basic saves any changes made to the property at design time so that it will take effect at runtime.

The Property Get procedure is invoked every time the program recalls the value of the property. This procedure reads the value of the *m_Caption* private variable and assigns it to the Caption property. There must be a Property Let and a Property Get procedure for each property, and they must include the lines shown here. They represent the minimum functionality of the mechanism for setting and reading property values.

Of course, you can add validation code here too. The TextAlignment property's value must be in the range 0 through 9. As is, the custom control allows the user to enter any value in the Properties window for this property. Let's add some validation code in the Property Let procedure of the TextAlignment property. The validation code is simple: It rejects any values that are smaller than 0 or larger than 8.

Code 16. 4:   **Validation Code for the Property Let Procedure**

```
Public Property Let TextAlignment(ByVal New_TextAlignment As Integer)
    If m_TextAlignment >=0 And m_TextAlignment<=8 Then
        m_TextAlignment = New_TextAlignment
        PropertyChanged "TextAlignment"
    Else
        MsgBox "Invalid value for this property"
    End If
End Property
```

The If statement tests the validity of the supplied value, and if the new value is outside the valid range, the attempt to set the property is rejected. Modify the Property Let procedure according to the previous listing, and then switch to the test Form of the test project. Select the FLEXLabel control on the Form, open the Properties window, and set the TextAlignment property to an invalid value (13 or 1000, for example). As soon as you attempt to change the property's value to an invalid setting, the control displays the warning and rejects the changes. You may be wondering now, How can I make this property display its valid settings only in a drop-down ListBox control, like other Visual Basic controls? It is possible, of course, but it takes a bit of code, and you'll see how shortly.

After the Property Let and Property Get procedures for all properties of the control comes some initialization code.

Code 16.5:   **The Initialization Code**

```
'Initialize Properties for User Control
Private Sub UserControl_InitProperties()
    Set Font = Ambient.Font
    m_Caption = m_def_Caption
    m_Effect = m_def_Effect
    m_TextAlignment = m_def_TextAlignment
    UserControl.BorderStyle = 1
    UserControl.BackStyle = 1
End Sub
```

The statements of the InitProperties() subroutine assign initial values to the private variables that represent the control properties. The constants *m_def_Caption*, *m_def_TextAlignment*, and *m_def_Effect* were defined earlier in the program. When this control is placed on a Form, Visual Basic looks up the values of the *m_Caption*, *m_TextAlignment*, and *m_Effect* variables and uses them to assign the proper values to the corresponding entries of the Properties window.

Saving and Retrieving Property Values

Now come two interesting subroutines:

- ReadProperties
- WriteProperties

When you set some properties through the Properties window, the new values must be saved somewhere. The reason? So that the control won't forget them. An application may (and usually does) change the values of certain properties at runtime. But when the application stops and you're back in design mode, the properties changed at runtime must be reset to their values before the application is started—*not to their default values, but to whatever values you assigned to them at design time.*

Visual Basic provides a special object for storing all property values: the PropertyBag. The PropertyBag object exposes two methods, one for saving a property's value and one for reading a property's value. You, the control developer, need not know anything about how the values are stored. Visual Basic stores them, and when you request their values, it furnishes them. The two methods are properly named WriteProperty and ReadProperty.

The WriteProperty Method   This method has the following syntax:

```
WriteProperty propertyName, value, defaultValue
```

The *propertyName* variable is the name of the property (Effect, for instance), *value* can be a literal (such as 1 or "some sizzling effect") but is nearly always the name of the private variable that holds the property value, and *defaultValue* is the property's default value.

NOTE   Why specify both a value and a default value in the WriteProperty method? Visual Basic compares the value with the default setting, and if that value and the default value are the same, Visual Basic doesn't save it (to speed up the process of saving and restoring property values). When you later request the property's value with the ReadProperty method, Visual Basic provides the same default value.

The ReadProperty Method   This method has the following syntax:

```
ReadProperty propertyName, defaultValue
```

The *propertyName* variable is the name of the property, and *defaultValue* is the value stored earlier in the Property Bag object for this property. In the UserControl's WriteProperties event's code, you must call the WriteProperty method once for each property. Likewise, in the control's ReadProperties subroutine, you must call the ReadProperty method once for each property. Here are the listings for the WriteProperties and ReadProperties events of the FLEXLabel control as generated by the Wizard.

Code 16.6:   **The Control's ReadProperties Procedure**

```
'Load property values from storage
Private Sub UserControl_ReadProperties(PropBag As PropertyBag)

    Set Font = PropBag.ReadProperty("Font", Ambient.Font)
    UserControl.BorderStyle = PropBag.ReadProperty("BorderStyle", 0)
    UserControl.BackStyle = PropBag.ReadProperty("BackStyle", 1)
```

```
UserControl.Enabled = PropBag.ReadProperty("Enabled", True)
UserControl.ForeColor = PropBag.ReadProperty("ForeColor", _
                        &H80000012)
UserControl.MousePointer = PropBag.ReadProperty("MousePointer", 0)
UserControl.OLEDropMode = PropBag.ReadProperty("OLEDropMode", 0)
Set Picture = PropBag.ReadProperty("Picture", Nothing)
m_Caption = PropBag.ReadProperty("Caption", m_def_Caption)
m_Effect = PropBag.ReadProperty("Effect", m_def_Effect)
m_TextAlignment = PropBag.ReadProperty("TextAlignment", _
                  m_def_TextAlignment)
UserControl.BackColor = PropBag.ReadProperty("BackColor", _
                        &H8000000F)
End Sub
```

Code 16.7:   The Control's WriteProperties Procedure

```
'Write property values to storage
Private Sub UserControl_WriteProperties(PropBag As PropertyBag)

    Call PropBag.WriteProperty("Font", Font, Ambient.Font)
    Call PropBag.WriteProperty("BorderStyle", UserControl.BorderStyle, 0)
    Call PropBag.WriteProperty("BackStyle", UserControl.BackStyle, 1)
    Call PropBag.WriteProperty("Enabled", UserControl.Enabled, True)
    Call PropBag.WriteProperty("ForeColor", UserControl.ForeColor, _
        &H80000012)
    Call PropBag.WriteProperty("MousePointer", _
        UserControl.MousePointer, 0)
    Call PropBag.WriteProperty("OLEDropMode", _
        UserControl.OLEDropMode, 0)
    Call PropBag.WriteProperty("Picture", Picture, Nothing)
    Call PropBag.WriteProperty("Caption", m_Caption, _
        m_def_Caption)
    Call PropBag.WriteProperty("Effect", m_Effect, _
        m_def_Effect)
    Call PropBag.WriteProperty("TextAlignment", _
        m_TextAlignment, m_def_TextAlignment)
    Call PropBag.WriteProperty("BackColor", _
        UserControl.BackColor, &H8000000F)
End Sub
```

Reporting Events

The last section of the code maps the various controls' events to the equivalent
events of the UserControl object. When the user clicks on the ActiveX control,

Windows reports the Click event to the UserControl object. As a control developer, you can process the event from within the control (in which case, the application that uses the control doesn't see the Click event), you can pass it to the host application (in which case, the application receives Click events for the control and the application programmer can program them), or you can do both (do something within your code and then pass them to the host application).

You pass an event to the application via the RaiseEvent method. The UserControl object's Click event is coded as follows:

```
Private Sub UserControl_Click()
    RaiseEvent Click
End Sub
```

The code for the remaining events is nearly identical. These events call the Raise-Event statement to pass the event to the host application. If the event reports any arguments, such as the KeyPress event, these arguments are listed in parentheses next to the event's name.

The Wizard hasn't done anything terribly special; it simply inserted some straight-forward code. With the exception of the ReadProperty and WriteProperty methods, everything else should be more or less familiar to most VB programmers. The ActiveX control, therefore, is slightly more complicated than a standard project. Now it's time to enter a few lines of code. After all, we must tell our control how to align the caption and render it with a 3-D effect.

Drawing on the UserControl

We now have a functional control, and it wasn't difficult to develop. Visual Basic created the skeleton of a working control. It hooked it into the environment, its icon appears in the toolbox, and we can use it in our projects just as we use any other control; it even manages its own Properties window. Now, it's time to make this control "tick." We must add the code that's unique to this control: the code that draws the caption.

The code for drawing the custom control's visible interface is usually placed in the Paint event. Visual Basic raises this event every time a control must be redrawn, and you must supply the code to redraw it. What we are going to do now is copy the DrawCaption() subroutine we developed earlier in the chapter and paste it into the custom control. Open the UserControl object's Code window, and paste the DrawCaption() subroutine. In the UserControl's Paint event handler, insert the following line, which calls the DrawCaption() subroutine:

```
DrawSubroutine
```

This statement in the Paint event ensures that every time the developer resizes the control on the Form or the Form needs to be refreshed at runtime, the entire UserControl object will be redrawn.

The DrawCaption() subroutine draws on a Form object. The UserControl object is practically identical to the Form object, and it supports the same drawing methods. Open the UserControl's Code window, locate the DrawCaption() subroutine's code, and replace all instances of "Me" with "UserControl" so that it will draw the caption on the UserControl object.

The DrawCaption() subroutine must also be called every time a custom property is changed, to redraw the caption. The properties that affect the appearance of the caption on the UserControl object are the custom properties Caption, Text-Alignment, and Effect, as well as the standard properties Picture and BackColor. Locate the Property Let procedures for these properties, and insert a line to invoke the UserControl_Paint event. The revised Property Let procedure for the Effect property is shown next (with the new statement underlined):

```
Public Property Let Effect(ByVal New_Effect As Effects)
    m_Effect = New_Effect
    PropertyChanged "Effect"
    UserControl_Paint
End Property
```

Drawing on the UserControl object is identical to drawing on the Form object. Custom controls that draw their visible interface and don't rely on the standard controls, such as the FLEXLabel control, are called *user-drawn*. Later in the chapter, you'll see how to build custom controls based on constituent controls.

You should also try to set a color property in the FLEXLabel control's Properties window. You will see the familiar color box, where you select and specify new colors. You didn't do anything special about this property. If you look at the control's code, you'll see that the Wizard declared the BackColor and ForeColor properties as OLE_COLOR type. When Visual Basic sees the OLE_COLOR type, it knows how to handle the corresponding property in the Properties window.

NOTE   OLE_COLOR is not a general data type you can use in normal variable declarations in Visual Basic, and it has special meaning here. It places a Color Selection dialog box that pops up every time the user tries to set a new value for a color-related property. If you set the BackColor or ForeColor property's data type to Long, the user of the control would have to type a long value (for example, &H00FF00 for green) in the Properties window.

Enumerated Properties

If you switch to the test Form and exercise the new control, you'll see that it doesn't quite behave like the standard controls. The custom properties on the Properties window can be set to any value. We need to add some code that will display only valid values for the TextAlignment and Effect properties and limit the user's choices to valid settings. Figure 16.6 shows the Properties window for the control when the TextAlignment property is selected.

FIGURE 16.6:

Some custom properties may have limited values, which should be displayed in a drop-down list such as this one.

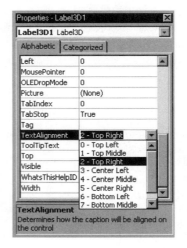

A data type that can hold a small number of values is called Enumerated type. The Integer, Double, and other numeric data types are generic and can represent numeric values. If your application uses a variable that can take on only a limited number of integer values, you can use the Enumerated data type. The TextAlignment property is such a variable. It can take only one of two integer values. The days of the week and the months of the year are also examples of Enumerated data types. To create an Enumerated data type, you must first declare the Enumerated type's values so that Visual Basic knows which ones are valid. Insert the following Enumerated type declaration at the beginning of the code, right after the Option Explicit statement:

```
Enum Align
     [Top Left]
     [Top Middle]
     [Top Right]
     [Center Left]
     [Center Middle]
     [Center Right]
     [Bottom Left]
```

```
        [Bottom Middle]
        [Bottom Right]
    End Enum
```

This declaration tells Visual Basic that any variable defined as *Align* can have the values 0 through 8 (Enumerated types correspond to numeric values, starting with 0). The strings that appear in the declaration are synonyms of the corresponding numeric values, which will be displayed in the Properties window. The square brackets are necessary only if the corresponding strings have embedded spaces (or, in general, are invalid variable names).

For this to happen, we must change the type of the TextAlignment property from Integer to Align (the Enumerated type we just declared). The TextAlignment property shouldn't be an integer, but an Enumerated type. Open the FLXLabel project group and implement the following changes:

1. Select the UserControl, open its Code window, and at the beginning of the code insert the following type definition:

    ```
    Enum Align
        [Top Left]
        [Top Middle]
        [Top Right]
        [Center Left]
        [Center Middle]
        [Center Right]
        [Bottom Left]
        [Bottom Middle]
        [Bottom Right]
    End Enum
    ```

2. Now, change the definitions of the TextAlignment property's Let and Get procedures so that their type is Align and not Integer. Make the following changes to these two procedures:

    ```
    Public Property Get TextAlignment() As Align
        TextAlignment = m_TextAlignment
    End Property

    Public Property Let TextAlignment(ByVal New_TextAlignment As
    Align)
        m_TextAlignment = New_TextAlignment
        PropertyChanged "TextAlignment"
    End Property
    ```

Notice that the validation code in the Property Let procedure is no longer needed because the user can't select an invalid value for this property in the Properties window. If you attempt to assign an invalid value to this property from within your code, the command will be ignored without any warnings or error messages. The property will simply not change value. If you attempt to set an enumerated property to an invalid value from within your code, a trappable runtime error will be generated.

Using the Custom Control in Other Projects

By adding the test project to the custom control project, we were able to design and test the control in the same environment. A great help indeed, but the custom control can't be used in other projects. If you start another instance of Visual Basic and attempt to add your custom control to the toolbox, you won't see the FLEXLabel entry in the Components dialog box. Other projects see only components that were registered with the system.

To register your custom control, you must create the corresponding OCX file. Choose File ➢ Make FlxLabel.ocx. The OCX file is all your need to include the control in your projects. OCX files can be placed anywhere on your disk, but they are usually stored in the Windows\System folder. You can create the OCX file in the same folder as the project. While Visual Basic creates the OCX file, it also registers it in the system Registry, so you shouldn't move the OCX file to another location later. To use a custom control with a new project, follow these steps:

1. Start a new Standard EXE project, and add the new control to the toolbox.

2. Right-click the toolbox, and from the shortcut menu, select Components to display the Components dialog box:

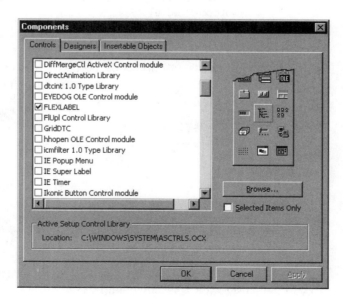

3. Check the FLEXLABEL checkbox, and click OK. The custom control's icon will appear on the project's toolbox. Notice that the name of the control is the same as the project's name.

If you use this icon to place a FLEXLabel control on a Form, Visual Basic automatically names it Label3D1 (if it's the first control on the Form; the second will be named Label3D2, and so on).

The custom control has been registered with the system Registry on your computer, but how about other computers? When you distribute an application that uses the custom control, the new control must be installed on the host computer before your application can use it. To install a custom control to another system, use the Regsvr32 utility, passing the name of the OCX file as an argument. Assuming you have copied the FLXLABEL.OCX file to the Windows\System folder, use the following command from the DOS prompt to install it on the host system:

```
REGSVR32 FLXLABEL.OCX
```

If the OCX file resides in another folder, switch to its folder and issue this command:

```
C:\WINDOWS\SYSTEM\REGSVR32 FLXLABEL.OCX
```

To uninstall a custom control, use the REGSVR32 program with the /U option. The following command will uninstall the FLXLABEL control:

```
C:\WINDOWS\SYSTEM\REGSVR32 FLXLABEL.OCX /U
```

Interacting with the Container

ActiveX controls are meant to be used as building blocks in application development. As such, they are sited on Forms or other controls that can act as containers. As an ActiveX control designer, you should be able to access the properties of a control's container and adjust the control's appearance according to the properties of the container. You will find two objects useful in designing custom controls: Extender and Ambient.

The Extender Object

The Extender object provides some of your control's basic properties, such as its Name, Width, and Height. These are the properties that are maintained by Windows itself, and they don't trigger a Property Let procedure when they are set. As you know, the control's Name property can be changed at any time while the control is used in design mode, but there are no Property procedures for this property. To find out the name assigned to the control by the user, you must call the Extender object's Name property. The Extender object is also your gateway to certain properties of the *parent control*, the control on which the custom control is sited.

The Name Property   You can find out the Name of the container control and its dimensions. To access the Extender object, use the following expression:

```
UserControl.Extender.extProperty
```

The *extProperty* entry is an Extender property name. The name of the custom control is returned by the following expression:

```
UserControl.Extender.Name
```

> **NOTE**   But do I really have to invoke the Extender object to find out the custom control's name from within the custom control? Isn't this overkill? If you think about it, the control doesn't know its own name! The user can set the control's Name property at any time during the control's design, and to read this name from within the control's code, you must indeed call upon the services of the Extender object. There are no Property Let and Property Get procedures for the Name property.

The Width and Height Properties   These properties return the control's dimensions, as specified by the user. To find out the control's dimensions, use the expressions:

```
UserControl.Extender.Width
```

and

```
UserControl.Extender.Height
```

The Tag and Index Properties   These are two more properties that Visual Basic maintains for you. Tag and Index aren't properties of the Extender object (although the syntax indicates that they are). They are properties of your custom control that can't be accessed directly. I didn't include any code for maintaining these properties, but they appear in the control's Properties window anyway. Because their values are maintained by Visual Basic, you can't access them directly; you must go through the Extender object.

The Parent Property   This property returns the object on which your control is sited. The UserControl.Extender.Parent object is one way of accessing the container control's properties. To find out the container control's dimensions, you can use the following statements:

```
PWidth = UserControl.Extender.Parent.Width
PHeight = UserControl.Extender.Parent.Height
```

You can use similar statements to read the container control's name (UserControl .Extender.Parent.Name), it's background (UserControl.Extender.Parent.BackColor), and so on.

TIP

Notice this important difference: UserControl.Extender.Name is the custom control's name (for example, Label3D1); UserControl.Extender.Parent.Name is the container's name (for example, Form1).

To experiment with a few of the Extender object's dimensions, insert the following lines in the FlxLabel UserControl's Click event, run the test Form, and click the FLEXLabel control.

Code 16.8:   Accessing the Extender Object

```
Private Sub UserControl_Click()
Dim ExtProp As String
    ExtProp = "I'm a custom control. My name is " _
            & UserControl.Extender.Name
    ExtProp = ExtProp & "I'm located at (" & UserControl.Extender.Left _
            & ", " & UserControl.Extender.Left & ")"
    ExtProp = ExtProp & vbCrLf & " My dimensions are " _
            & UserControl.Extender.Width & " by " _
            & UserControl.Extender.Height
    ExtProp = ExtProp & vbCrLf & "I'm tagged as " _
            & UserControl.Extender.Tag
    ExtProp = ExtProp & vbCrLf & "I'm sited on a control named " _
            & UserControl.Extender.Parent.Name
    ExtProp = ExtProp & vbCrLf & "whose dimensions are " _
            & UserControl.Extender.Parent.Width _
            & " by " & UserControl.Extender.Parent.Height
    MsgBox ExtProp
    RaiseEvent Click
End Sub
```

You will see the message box shown in Figure 16.7 (you must assign a value to the Tag property, which is by default empty).

NOTE

This message is displayed from within the custom control's Click event, not from the test application. Only after the message is displayed does the test application receive the Click event. If you have programmed the control's Click event in the test application as discussed earlier in the chapter, you will see two message boxes. The first one is displayed from the UserControl's code; the second is displayed from the application's code.

Use the Extender object to access certain properties of the custom control and its container.

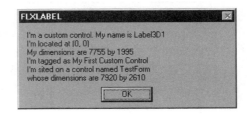

The Default and Cancel Properties   These two properties determine whether the custom control can be used as the Default (Extender.Default is True) or the Cancel (Extender.Cancel is True) control on the Form. These are two more properties you can't set from within your code. You can read them only while the control is used in the design of another application.

> **NOTE**   The DefaultCancel property of the UserControl object determines whether one of the Default and Cancel properties of the control can be set, and not whether the control will be the Default or Cancel control on the Form. If DefaultCancel is True, properties Default or Cancel will appear in the control's Properties window, and you can find out the values of these properties through the Extender object.

The Ambient Object

The Ambient object is similar to the Extender object, in that it provides information about the custom control's environment, and the two actually overlap in some ways. The Ambient object gives your control's code hints about the control's environment, such as the container's background color, its font, and so on. The single most important property of the Ambient object is UserMode, which indicates whether the control is operating in design or runtime mode.

As you know from working with regular controls, all VB controls operate in design and runtime modes. Because our control behaves identically in both modes, there's no need to distinguish between the two. In designing custom ActiveX controls, however, you frequently need to differentiate between the two modes from within your code and react to certain events differently, depending on whether the control is being used in design-time or runtime mode.

The UserMode Property   This property is True when the control is operating in runtime mode and False when the control is operating in design mode. To see how this property works, let's display the text "Design Mode" while the control is in design mode. Open the Paint event's subroutine, and insert the following lines at the end of the Paint event's handler.

Code 16.9:   **Using the UserMode Property**

```
Private Sub UserControl_Paint()
    DrawCaption
    OldFontSize = UserControl.Font.Size
    UserControl.Font.Size = 10
    If Not Ambient.UserMode Then
        UserControl.CurrentX = 0
        UserControl.CurrentY = 0
        UserControl.Print "Design Mode"
    End If
    UserControl.Font.Size = OldFontSize
End Sub
```

These statements determine whether the control is being used in design or run-time mode. In design mode, the string "Design Mode" is displayed in its upper left corner, as shown in Figure 16.8. The statements that save and restore the font size are needed, because without them either the "Design Mode" string will be displayed in a large font (same as the caption), or the caption will be printed in the same (small) size as the string. The code sets the font size to a small value, displays the "Design Mode" string at the upper left corner of the control, and then restores the original font size.

FIGURE 16.8:

The "Design Mode" string is displayed in the control's upper left corner when it's open in design mode.

The ForeColor, BackColor Properties   These two properties report the foreground and background colors of the container. Use them to initialize the equivalent properties of your custom control.

The Font Property   This property reports the font used by the control's container. All controls inherit the font settings of the container on which they are sited, the moment they are created. If the Form's font is changed after your custom control has been sited on it, the control's Font setting won't be affected.

The ShowGrabHandles Property   This property lets you hide the grab handles that are used to resize the control at design time.

The ShowHatching Property   If, under certain circumstances, you want to disable the control, set this property to True to draw a hatch pattern over the control, which will indicate that some other action must take place before the control can be manipulated.

The AmbientChanged Event   Besides its properties, the Extender object provides the AmbientChanged() event, which informs your code about changes in the Ambient object. This event is recognized by the UserControl object and its declaration is:

```
Private Sub UserControl_AmbientChanged(PropertyName As String)
```

The AmbientChanged() event has a single argument, which is the name of the property that changed. Use this event to stay on top of changes in the control's container and to adjust the control's appearance or behavior accordingly.

To test this event, insert the following line in the AmbientChanged() event of a custom control (use the FLEXLabel control, if you haven't designed any other yet):

```
Private Sub UserControl_AmbientChanged(PropertyName As String)
    Debug.Print "The property " & PropertyName & " changed"
End Sub
```

Then switch to the test Form and change a few of the container's properties. Every time an Ambient property changes value, a message will be displayed in the Immediate window. Notice that only a few of the container's properties trigger the AmbientChanged() event. They are the ones that can affect the appearance of the control on the Form. If you change the Form's Name or Caption property, no AmbientChanged() event is raised in the UserControl object.

Designing Property Pages

ActiveX controls can also have Property Pages. Property Pages are similar to the Properties window, in that they allow the developer (the programmer who is using your control in a VB project) to set the control's properties. Unlike the Properties window, however, the Property Pages offer a better and more flexible user interface, including instant visual feedback, for setting up a control.

Property Pages are basically design elements. Figure 16.9 shows the Property Pages for the TabStrip control. Through this interface, you can set up the TabStrip control in ways that are simply impossible through the Properties window. The properties you can set through the Properties window apply to the entire control, and you can't set the titles and appearance of the individual tabs, their number, and so on. The Property Pages for this control contain several pages (General, Tabs, Font, and Picture) on which related properties are grouped.

FIGURE 16.9:

The Property Pages for the TabStrip control

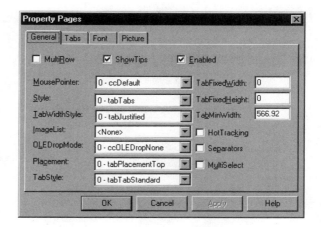

The design of Property Pages is greatly simplified by (what else?) the Property Page Wizard. Let's add some Property Pages to the FLEXLabel control. The control has three custom properties—two enumerated properties and a string property—which we'll place on the same page. In addition, the control has several standard properties, which will be placed on different property pages. The Font property, for example, must appear on its own Property Page, which is similar to the Font common dialog box. Similarly, the Color property must appear on its own property page, which resembles the Color common dialog box.

Using the Property Page Wizard

To use the Property Page Wizard, follow these steps:

1. Open the FlxLabel project if it's not already the active project.

2. Choose Add-Ins ➢ Property Page Wizard to open the Add Property Page dialog box.

3. Select VB Property Page Wizard.

The Property Page Wizard will take you through the steps of setting up the control's property pages.

Introduction

This is an introductory window, which you can skip in the future by checking the Skip This Screen in the Future checkbox.

Selecting the Property Pages

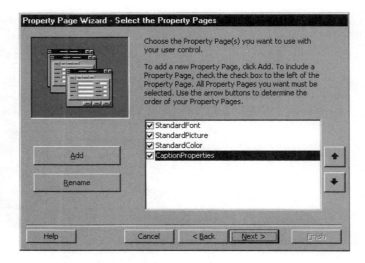

In this window, you select the Property Pages for your control. This window contains some (or all) of the standard Property Pages:

- **StandardFont**, which allows you to set the font

- **StandardPicture**, which allows you to set Picture properties

- **StandardColor**, which allows you to set color

For our control's Property Pages, we need the StandardColor page, plus a custom one, which we can add by clicking on the Add button. The Wizard prompts you to enter the name of the custom page. Enter **TextProperties**, and then click the Next button.

Can you see why the Wizard selected the StandardColor page for us? Our custom control provides the BackColor and ForeColor properties, which are set through the StandardColor property page. If you don't want a Property Page for the color-related properties, clear the checkbox that precedes the property name. But we do need the page for specifying color, so leave this page checked. You can also rename the pages with the Rename button.

Assigning Properties to the Property Pages

In this window, you specify the properties to be displayed in each Property Page. The Wizard has already assigned the color-related properties to the StandardColor page, the Font property to the StandardFont page, and the Picture property to the StandardPicture page. The custom properties, however, have not been assigned to any page, because the Wizard doesn't know where they belong. To add the Caption property to the Text Properties page, follow these steps:

1. Select the Text Properties tab.

2. Select the Caption property from the list on the left, and then click the single right-arrow button to add it to the Text Properties page.

3. Click Next to display the last page of the Property Page Wizard, and then click Finish.

If you examine this window of the Wizard carefully, you'll probably notice something strange. Not all of the custom properties appear in the Available Properties list. Instead, some other property names appear in the list. The Wizard can't handle properties of custom type. The TextAlignment and Effect properties are custom data types (the Align and Effects enumerated types we declared in the code), so they are omitted. If you want a Property Page on which the developer can specify the appearance of the control, you must add the TextAlignment and Effect properties to the Text Properties page. Unfortunately, you can't add these properties through the Wizard; you'll have to do it manually.

But first, let's see what the Wizard has done for us. Follow these steps:

1. Switch to the test Form, and right-click on the FLEXLabel control

2. From the shortcut menu, choose Properties to display the two Property Pages shown in Figures 16.10 and 16.11.

FIGURE 16.10:

The Color Property Page of the FLEXLabel control

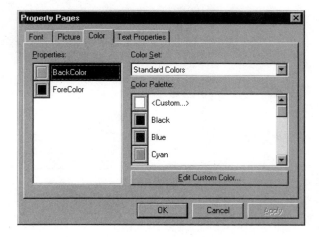

FIGURE 16.11:

The Text Properties Property Page of the FLEXLabel control

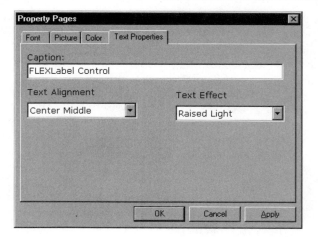

The Color page looks fine, but the Text Properties page needs drastic improvement. The Wizard just dumped a Label and a TextBox control on it, and you should not only fix their appearance, but provide the actual code as well.

The Color tab has a Properties list that contains the names of the color-related properties. Had you created more color properties for the custom control, they would appear on the same page. To assign a new value to a color-related property, do one of the following:

- Select it and then chose a standard color from the Windows palette.

- Specify a custom color by clicking the Edit Custom Color button.

The new color appears in front of the property's name in the Properties list. If you click the Apply button, the gradient on the control is redrawn according to the new selection. The Text Properties page lets you specify the Caption property's value by entering a value in a TextBox control. Click Apply for the property to take effect on the control. You should experiment with the other tabs of the Property Pages to see how they behave.

If you look at the Project window, you will see that the Wizard has added another folder, the Property Pages folder. This new folder contains the Caption Properties file. Double-click it to open the page's Form in design mode. Notice that the OK, Cancel, and Apply buttons are not part of the Form. They belong to a TabStrip control, which displays the Property Pages at runtime (this control isn't available to you and can't even be customized). Moreover, there is no Form for the Color, Font, and Picture Property Pages. These are standard Property Pages, and they are manipulated entirely by Visual Basic. You can't modify the Font Property Page built by the Wizard, but you can create a new custom page for specifying colors if you really don't like the standard one.

Let's examine the code created by the Wizard for the CaptionProperties Property Page.

Code 16.10:   The CaptionProperties Property Page

```
Private Sub txtCaption_Change()
    Changed = True
End Sub

Private Sub PropertyPage_ApplyChanges()
    SelectedControls(0).Caption = txtCaption.Text
End Sub

Private Sub PropertyPage_SelectionChanged()
    txtCaption.Text = SelectedControls(0).Caption
End Sub
```

The subroutine txtCaption_Change() takes place every time the user changes the direction by typing something in the txtCaption TextBox. By setting the *Changed* variable to True, the code enables the Apply button (which is disabled as long as the Caption property doesn't change value). Visual Basic uses the Changed property to determine when the Apply button must be enabled.

The new setting of a property isn't applied to the control automatically, of course. The code that actually applies the changes must be entered in the PropertyPages_ ApplyChanges event, which is triggered every time the Apply button is clicked. From within this event, you must update the control's property. Because the Property Page is a separate Form and can't know the name of the selected control (there could be multiple instances of the same control on the Form), the code uses the Selected-Controls(0) object to access the selected control and set its properties. SelectedControls() is a collection that represents all the selected controls on the Form. The item of the collection with index 0 is the first selected control.

Finally, the PropertyPage_SelectionChanged() event occurs whenever the user selects another tab on the Property Pages dialog box. This is a good place to insert initialization code. The PropertyPage_SelectionChanged() subroutine's code assigns the current setting of the Caption property of the selected control to the TextBox control, in which the user is supposed to enter the property's value.

Editing a Property Page

Run the test project and check out the operation of the Property Pages generated by the Wizard. This is a good point to add a few more controls on the Text Properties tab, which will allow developers to set the other custom properties. The finished Property Page should look like the one shown in Figure 16.12.

FIGURE 16.12:

The Property Page with the FLEXLabel control's custom properties

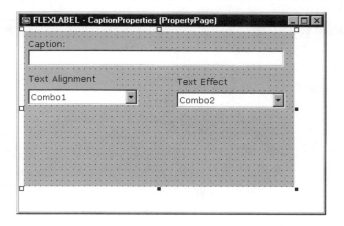

Open the Property Page in design mode and add two ComboBox controls and the matching Label controls on top of them. Adjust their size, and specify a nice font and size for all the controls.

Now you are ready to adjust the code. The two ComboBox controls must be populated with the valid setting for the two properties. The best place to insert the initialization code is in the page's Initialize event.

Code 16.11:   Initializing the CaptionProperties Page

```
Private Sub PropertyPage_Initialize()
    Combo1.AddItem "Top Left"
    Combo1.AddItem "Top Middle"
    Combo1.AddItem "Top Right"
    Combo1.AddItem "Center Left"
    Combo1.AddItem "Center Middle"
    Combo1.AddItem "Center Right"
    Combo1.AddItem "Bottom Left"
    Combo1.AddItem "Bottom Middle"
    Combo1.AddItem "Bottom Right"

    Combo2.AddItem "None"
    Combo2.AddItem "Carved Light"
    Combo2.AddItem "Carved"
    Combo2.AddItem "Carved Heavy"
    Combo2.AddItem "Raised Light"
    Combo2.AddItem "Raised"
    Combo2.AddItem "Raised Heavy"

End Sub
```

Now, we must revise the SelectionChanged event's code. We must add the statements to initialize the two ComboBox controls that correspond to the two new properties. Enter the following code in the Property Page's SelectionChanged event handler.

Code 16.12:   Initializing the ComboBox Controls

```
Private Sub PropertyPage_SelectionChanged()
    txtCaption.Text = SelectedControls(0).Caption
    Combo1.ListIndex = SelectedControls(0).TextAlignment
    Combo2.ListIndex = SelectedControls(0).Effect
End Sub
```

Next, you must update the *Changed* variable from within the events that signify a new selection in the two ComboBox controls. Since the ComboBox controls don't allow the entry of new values, the selection can only change with the Click event; so add the following subroutines in the Property Page's code window:

```
Private Sub Combo1_Click()
    Changed = True
End Sub

Private Sub Combo2_Click()
    Changed = True
End Sub
```

The last step is to revise the ApplyChanges event so that it applies the current settings of the ComboBox controls to the custom control. Here is the code that implements the Apply button.

Code 16.13:   **Applying the Changes**

```
Private Sub PropertyPage_ApplyChanges()
    SelectedControls(0).Caption = txtCaption.Text
    SelectedControls(0).TextAlignment = Combo1.ListIndex
    SelectedControls(0).Effect = Combo2.ListIndex
End Sub
```

You can now switch to the test Form and check out the operation of the Property Pages. As you can see, Property Pages aren't new objects; they are regular VB Forms, on which you can place all kinds of controls and do all kinds of neat tricks, as long as you observe a few rules inserted in the code by the Wizard:

1. Set the Changed property to True each time a property changes value and you want the Apply button enabled.

2. Update the control's property by using the expression SelectedControls(0) .propertyName, in which the *propertyName* variable is an actual property name.

3. Initialize the properties each time the user switches to a new Property Page from within the PropertyPage_SelectionChanged event.

If you look up the Properties window for the UserControl object, you will see that its PropertyPages property is set to 4 to indicate that four Property Pages were added. Click the ellipsis button to display the Connect Property Pages dialog box shown in Figure 16.13. To exclude a page from the control, clear the box in front of its name.

Visual Basic's standard Property Pages are displayed in this dialog box, along with the custom page we designed for the FLEXLabel control.

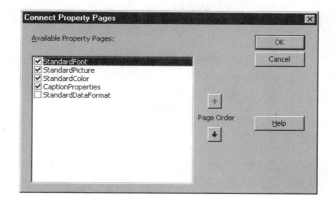

Building a custom ActiveX control isn't a big deal after all. The ActiveX Control Interface Wizard takes care of many details for you. It sets up a skeleton for the control's code, and you supply the code that actually does something (presumably something that other controls can't do). The code you supply is the type of code you would write for any VB application. There are, however, a few differences between developing regular applications and developing controls. The more you familiarize yourself with these differences, the better equipped you will be to develop ActiveX controls. The following section focuses on these differences.

Building a Generic Control

In the first section of this chapter, you learned how to build ActiveX controls with the ActiveX User Interface Wizard. Even though the Wizard took care of many details for you and constructed a functional control, you had to know a few things about a control's modes of operation in order to attach the desired type of functionality. The Wizard creates the skeleton of the control, but you have to flesh it out.

There are a few important topics I didn't cover earlier, and we will look at them in this section, including how to initialize and terminate controls and how to use unique properties, methods, and events. To simplify the discussion, we are not going to build another control. Instead, we'll use a generic control. This time we will not use the Wizard but will implement all the properties and methods manually so that you'll get some experience in editing controls.

Creating a Generic Control

Let's start by creating a generic control. Follow these steps:

1. Choose File ➤ New Project to open the New Project window.

2. Click the ActiveX Control icon. Visual Basic creates a new project that contains a UserControl, named UserControl1. This is the control's Form on which the visible interface will be built.

3. Choose File ➤ Add Project to add a Standard EXE project. Visual Basic creates a new project with a single Form, named Form1. You'll use Form1 to test the control. (Form1 is frequently called the "test Form," and the project it belongs to is called the "test project.") What you have on your screen now is a generic control.

4. This is a good point at which to rename and save your project's files. For this generic project, use the default names.

5. Close the control's design window to enable the control's icon in the toolbox.

6. Place an instance of the new control on the Form. The newly created Form doesn't have a background color or a border that will distinguish it from the Form on which it lies.

7. With the control selected, open the Properties window.

By default, a UserControl object has the following properties:

DragIcon	TabStop
DragMode	Tag
Height	ToolTipText
HelpContextID	Top Left
Index	Visible
Left	WhatIsThisHelpID
TabIndex	Width

These properties are actually provided by the container. The Left property is determined by the container and has meaning only in the context of a container. Likewise, the TabIndex and TabStop properties aren't managed by the control itself, because the control doesn't know what other controls exist on the Form. Only the Form does, and therefore the Form must maintain these properties for its controls.

Test a few of these properties. Assign the value "My generic control" to the ToolTipText property. Run the application, and then rest the pointer for a second over the control. The string you entered is displayed in a ToolTip box. In a similar manner, you can test the Tag property by assigning a string to it, or you can test the Index property by creating multiple instances of the same control on the Form with the same name and a different Index value. There's not a single line of code you should add to the control to implement these properties.

Adding a Property

Let's add a property to our generic control. We'll call it Title, and we'll store its value internally to the m_Title private property. Select UserControl1 in the Project window, and in the Code window, insert the following declaration:

```
Private m_Title As String
```

and then the procedures:

```
Public Property Get Title() As String
    Title = m_Title
End Property

Public Property Let Title(ByVal vNewValue As String)
    m_Title = vNewValue
End Property
```

Close the UserControl design window and the Code window, switch to the test Form, select the new control, and look up its new property in the Properties window. The mere presence of the Let and Get procedures is all that Visual Basic needs to add a property to the control. Enter a new value in the Title property's box (for example, Control Title). As expected, the title won't appear on the control.

We must also write a few lines of code to display the title. Switch back to the UserControl window, double-click it to open the Code window, and in the Paint event, enter the following:

```
Private Sub UserControl_Paint()
    UserControl.CurrentX = 0
    UserControl.CurrentY = 0
    UserControl.Print m_Title
End Sub
```

TIP   The first two statements aren't really needed to display something at the control's upper left corner, but you must set them accordingly if you want to display something elsewhere on the control.

Switch back to the test Form. If you have followed any of the previous suggestions and experimented with the custom control on the Form, delete all controls on the test Form.

Add an instance of the custom control (it will automatically be named User-Control1 unless you have changed the name of the UserControl object), and then assign a value to the Title property. Set the title to **My Generic Control**, for instance. The title won't appear the moment you enter it because the Paint event isn't triggered when a property changes values. You must resize the control to force a Paint event and display the title. If you don't like the font, change the UserControl's Font property (our control doesn't have a Font property yet).

Every time a new property is set, the Property Let procedure is invoked. You must, therefore, call the Paint method from within the Property Let procedure so that the title is displayed as soon as it's entered. Switch back to the UserControl, and add the following line to the Property Let Title procedure:

```
UserControl_Paint
```

Your VB window should like the one shown in Figure 16.14. Now assign a value to the Title property and watch the string appear on the control.

FIGURE 16.14:

The VB window during the first steps of the design of the generic control

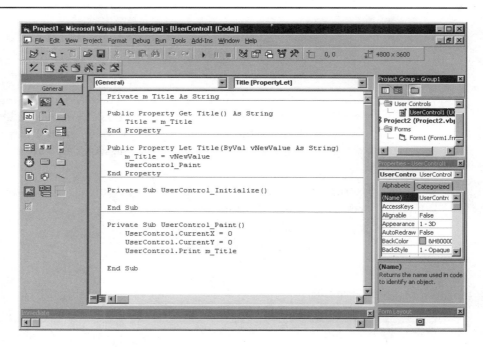

Now, press F5 to run the application. The title won't appear on the control. It was there at design time, but it disappeared at runtime. You probably want to stop the application and look up the value of the Title property to make sure it still contains its value. But you're in for a surprise. The Title property's value is a blank string. It wasn't your fault, so don't repeat the process. Any properties set at design time lose their value at runtime. It's a strange behavior, but this is how controls work.

Your experience with Visual Basic tells you that any properties set at design time keep their values at runtime. To make this happen, you must first save the property values to the Property Bag. What's not so easy to guess is when an action must take place. Let's explore the control's life cycle.

The Life of a Control

Let's experiment a little with the control's key events. Follow these steps:

1. Switch to the UserControl window and double-click it to open the Code window.

2. Locate the Initialize, InitProperties, and Terminate events in the drop-down list on the right. In each, enter the Debug.Print statement, followed by the event's name, as shown here:

```
Private Sub UserControl_Initialize()
     Debug.Print "initializing control"
End Sub

Private Sub UserControl_InitProperties()
     Debug.Print "initializing properties"
End Sub

Private Sub UserControl_Terminate()
     Debug.Print "terminating control"
End Sub
```

3. Close the UserControl window and return to the test Form. Place an instance of the new control on the Form, and watch the Immediate Execution window. The following messages are displayed:

```
initializing control
initializing properties
```

When you place a control on a Form, it is initialized, and then its properties are initialized.

NOTE The Print statements executed when you switched from the UserControl to the test Form. Even though you are not running the application, the code is running! To understand this behavior, you must put on your ActiveX designer's hat. When you place a regular ActiveX control, such as a TextBox control, on a Form, some code is executed. This is what you just witnessed. ActiveX controls are always in run mode, regardless of whether the Form they belong to is running. How else would the control's appearance change every time you set a different font or a background color?

---

4. Now set the Title property and run the test application. Two new messages appear in the Immediate Execution window (clear the current contents of the Immediate Execution window first):

```
terminating control
initializing control
```

The control that was on the Form at design time was terminated, and a new one was initialized. All its properties were initialized to their default values, and the default value for the Title property was a blank string. That's why it disappeared.

If you stop the application now, the following message appears once again in the Debug window:

```
initializing control
```

This time, the runtime instance of the control is terminated, and another design-time instance of the control is initialized. Each time you switch from design-time mode to runtime mode, the instance(s) of the control is(are) terminated, and a new one is created.

During this transition, the properties must be saved somehow. To do so, follow these steps:

1. Switch back to the UserControl Code window and enter a Print statement in the ReadProperties and WriteProperties events.

2. Switch back to the test project, set the Title property, run the application again, and you will see the following sequence of events:

   ```
   writing properties
   terminating control
   initializing control
   reading properties
   ```

Visual Basic saves the values of the properties in the Properties window and terminates the design-time instance of the control. It then initializes the runtime instance of the control and reads the same properties. This is the life cycle of an ActiveX control.

> **NOTE**   But if Visual Basic knows which values to save, why can't it remember them until the new instance of the control is created? Why does Visual Basic save the property values and then read them again? It seems so simple, but notice the Terminate event between the writing and reading of the property values. In between these two instances, the control ceases to exist! Even if this behavior doesn't make sense right now, this is how controls behave.

Let's summarize the events that mark the life of a control. To execute some code at each of these events, place it in the corresponding event handler.

Key Events in a Control's Lifetime

When you place an instance of a control on the Form, the following events take place:

Initialize initializes the design-time instance of the control.

InitProperties assigns initial values to the properties.

When you switch from design time to runtime, the following events take place:

WriteProperties saves the properties listed in the Properties window.

Terminate terminates the design-time instance of the control.

Initialize initializes a new, runtime instance of the control.

ReadProperties reads the saved properties.

When you switch from runtime to design time, the following events take place:

Initialize initializes the design-time instance of the control.

ReadProperties reads the values from the Properties window and assigns them to the corresponding properties.

TIP   When you switch from runtime to design-time mode, no WriteProperties event takes place. As expected, Visual Basic doesn't save the properties that changed at runtime and resets the ActiveX control to the properties set in the Properties window at design time. In other words, changes made to the control's properties at design time are valid at runtime too. The opposite isn't true; changes made at runtime are reset when you switch back to design mode.

To maintain the values of the properties when the control switches from design to runtime, you must add a few lines of code in the ReadProperties and Write-Properties events. We have looked at how property values are written to and read from the Property Bag object, so here's the code for the Title property:

```
Private Sub UserControl_WriteProperties(PropBag As PropertyBag)
    Debug.Print "writing properties"
    PropBag.WriteProperty "Title", m_Title, "Control Title"
End Sub

Private Sub UserControl_ReadProperties(PropBag As PropertyBag)
    Debug.Print "reading properties"
    Title = PropBag.ReadProperty("Title", "Control Title")
End Sub
```

Initializing the Control and Its Properties

You can use two events to maintain the control—Initialize and InitProperties. The InitProperties event is the place to assign initial values to the various properties.

The ActiveX User Interface Wizard does it so well for us. The Initialize event can be used to enter initialization code that doesn't involve properties. If you attempt to set a property value or do something on the control (for instance, printing the Title on the control with the statement UserControl.Print "Control"), you'll get the following error message:

```
Object Required
```

The UserControl object is being initialized. It doesn't exist yet. That's why the following statement:

```
UserControl.Print "Control"
```

works when executed from within other events, but not from within the Initialize event.

So, what can you do from within this event? Very little. You can assign initial values to the private variables of the control, but you can't access the control's properties, not even the Ambient object.

The event of interest is the InitProperties event, which takes place after the control is created. This behavior may strike you as strange: The Initialize event takes place every time you switch between design and runtime mode, but the InitProperties event doesn't follow.

TIP

The InitProperties event takes place the first time a control is created and placed on a container. After that, the role of the InitProperties event in the control's life cycle is taken over by the ReadProperties event. If you changed the values of certain properties on the control, it wouldn't make much sense for Visual Basic to reset them to their initial values. Instead, it reads them from the Property Bag, when the ReadProperties event is triggered.

In the InitProperties event, you can insert initialization code that controls the appearance of a "newborn" control. For instance, you can determine what happens if the user places the control on a Form by double-clicking on its icon instead of actually drawing the control on the Form. Visual Basic places an instance of the control on the Form, and it will have a certain size (which is the same for all controls). If your control contains a long default title, a shape, or any element you want to be entirely visible, you can adjust the initial size of the control with a couple of statements such as the following:

```
UserControl.Width = 2400
UserControl.Height = 1200
```

When your control is placed on a Form with a double-click of its icon, its initial size is 2400 by 1200 twips.

The Extender and Ambient objects are also available from within the InitProperties control, because the control has been sited. You can display a title on the control in the same font as the container's font, as follows:

```
Set Font = Ambient.Font
UserControl.Print "FabControl"
```

These two lines display the string "FabControl" in the control's upper left corner, in the font of the container. In addition, your control's font will also be initially set to the Form's font.

NOTE   The title "FabControl" appears on the new instance of the control only if its Auto-Redraw property is set to True. The control is created behind the scenes and is actually displayed after all the initialization code has been executed. If the control's AutoRedraw property is False, the string will be printed on the control initially, but when the control is displayed, the string is not part of the persistent bitmap (discussed in Chapter 6) and will not be refreshed.

A Control's Key Properties

As you have learned, the UserControl object is basically a Form on which you can place other controls, draw shapes, display text, and detect events. It even has properties such as AutoRedraw and ScaleMode, which make it suitable for drawing at runtime. But it's not called Form; it's called UserControl. In addition, it has a few properties that are unique to ActiveX controls, and we are going to look at them in this section.

CanGetFocus   Set this property to True if the control can receive the focus, either with the mouse or with the Tab key. A user control can get the focus if the UserControl object gets the focus or if one of its constituent controls can get the focus. If the control can get the focus, the EnterFocus and ExitFocus events are triggered every time the focus is moved in or out of the control.

Set the CanGetFocus property of the generic control to True and then enter the following lines in the control's EnterFocus and ExitFocus events:

```
Private Sub UserControl_EnterFocus()
    UserControl.BackColor = vbRed
End Sub

Private Sub UserControl_ExitFocus()
    UserControl.BackColor = vbGreen
End Sub
```

Then switch to the test Form, and place two instances of the new control on it (or one instance of the control and a couple of regular controls). Run the application, and move the focus from one control to the other. The generic control that has the focus is filled with red, and the other control is filled with green.

Custom controls with a visible user interface should be able to receive and handle the focus. If the control contains multiple constituent controls, you should also decide which one takes the focus. By default, the constituent control that was placed first on the user control takes the focus. To set the focus to another constituent control, use the SetFocus method and follow these steps:

1. Go back to the generic control, and place two Command Buttons on the User-Control. Don't change their names.

2. Add the following lines to move the focus to the Command2 button in the EnterFocus event:

```
Private Sub UserControl_EnterFocus()
    UserControl.BackColor = vbRed
    Command2.SetFocus
End Sub
```

3. Switch to the test Form, delete all controls on the Form, and place an instance of the new control (large enough to display both buttons) and another Command Button on the Form.

4. Run the project, and check out how the focus is moved from one control to the other. Notice that when the user control takes the focus, it passes it to the Command2 button. You can't move the focus to the Command1 button with the Tab key. The user control is a single entity, and it gets the focus once.

ControlContainer   If this property is set to True, the user control can become a container for other controls. Normally, the controls placed on a container are grouped with the container, and they all move together. When you reposition the container control on the Form, all the controls contained in it are moved along.

By default, a user control is not a container. In other words, it is possible to draw a Command Button that lies half on the user control and half outside. To change this behavior, set the ControlContainer property to True.

Alignable   If the Alignable property is set to True, the user control has an Align property at design time. The Align property determines whether and how the control is aligned on the Form. The Align property's settings are shown in Table 16.3.

TIP   The Align property is not available at design time if the user control's Alignable property is False. Set the Alignable property to True for toolbarlike controls, which must always be aligned with the edges of the container, even when the container is resized.

TABLE 16.3: The Values of the Align Property

VALUE	DESCRIPTION
VbAlignNone	The control is aligned manually (the default).
VbAlignTop	The control is always aligned with the top of the Form.
VbAlignLeft	The control is always aligned with the left edge of the Form.
VbAlignRight	The control is always aligned with the right edge of the Form.
VbAlignBottom	The control is always aligned with the bottom of the Form.

InvisibleAtRuntime   Some controls, the Timer being the most typical example, are invisible at runtime. If your user control does not have a user interface and need not appear on the Form, set its InvisibleAtRuntime property to True.

ToolboxBitmap   Use this property to display a BMP file in the toolbox in place of the ActiveX Control generic icon. The ToolboxBitmap property's value is a BMP file's path name, but the bitmap is stored in the control and distributed with it.

AccessKeys   You use the AccessKeys property to specify which keys will act as hot keys for the control. If you want the user to move the focus instantly to your control by pressing a hot-key combination (Alt+Key), assign the key value to the AccessKeys property. Follow these steps:

1. Assign the value "A" to the user control's AccessKeys property (without the quotes).

2. Switch to the test Form and run it. Notice that you can switch the focus to the user control by pressing Alt+A.

3. Now stop the application, return to the user control, and open the Access-KeyPress event. This event is invoked every time the access key is pressed. Enter the following lines to display the key's ASCII value:

```
Private Sub UserControl_AccessKeyPress(KeyAscii As Integer)
Debug.Print "Access key pressed " & KeyAscii
End Sub
```

To move the focus to a specific constituent control or to perform some action when the focus is moved to the user control, enter the appropriate code in the AccessKeyPress event. Let's add access keys to the two Command buttons of the last example. Follow these steps:

1. Switch to the UserControl object, and add two Command buttons, Command1 and Command2, as shown in Figure 16.15. (If you have followed the steps of

the examples in the section "CanGetFocus," the two Command buttons are already on the Form.)

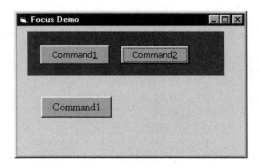

2. Switch to the test Form, and place an instance of the new control, another button, or another VB control on the Form.

3. Run the test project and move the focus back and forth. Notice the following:

    • When you move the focus to the custom control with the mouse, the first Command button takes the focus.

    • When you move the focus to the custom control with the Tab key, the ASCII value of the shortcut key is displayed in the Immediate Execution window.

4. Now switch back to the UserControl object, and assign shortcut keys to the two Command buttons. Change their caption properties to Command&1 and Command&2 so that the keys 1 and 2 will become their access keys.

5. Run the test project, and experiment with moving the focus among the various controls on the Form.

You can use a hot-key combination to access not only the user control, but also the individual constituent components on it. To activate a specific constituent control every time the focus is moved to a custom control, insert the SetFocus method in the UserControl_AccessKeyPress() subroutine. If the custom control contains a text box as a constituent control, you can set the focus to this control each time the user control receives the focus with the following subroutine:

```
Private Sub UserControl_AccessKeyPress(KeyAscii As Integer)
    Text1.SetFocus
End Sub
```

VB6 at Work: The Alarm ActiveX Control

The next example demonstrates an ActiveX control that contains all three types of members—properties, methods, and events. It's a simple alarm that can be set to go off at a certain time, and when it times out, it triggers a TimeOut event. Moreover, while the timer is ticking, the control updates a display, showing the time elapsed since the timer started (the property CountDown must be False) or the time left before the alarm goes off (the property CountDown must be True). Figure 16.16 shows the test Form for the Alarm control. The first instance of the Alarm control (Process A) counts the time since the Timer started, and the second instance (Process B) counts down the time left before the alarm goes off.

FIGURE 16.16:

The test Form for the Alarm custom control

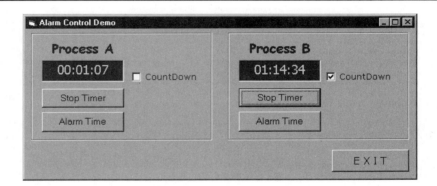

| TIP | When you load the Alarm project for the first time, Visual Basic will issue a warning to the effect that it couldn't load the Alarm control. This simply means that the Alarm control hasn't been installed on your system yet, and the test Form that uses it can't be loaded. Continue loading the project and then open the test Form. The two instances of the Alarm control will be replaced by two PictureBox controls. Delete these two controls, and place two instances of the Alarm control on the test Form, as shown in Figure 16.16. |

The Alarm Control's Interface

The Alarm control has two custom properties:

- AlarmTime
- CountDown

AlarmTime is the time when the alarm goes off, expressed in AM/PM format. CountDown is a True/False property that determines what's displayed on the control. If CountDown is True, the alarm displays the time remaining. If you set the alarm to go off at 8:00 PM and you start the timer at 7:46 PM, the control displays 0:14.00, then 0:13.59, and so on until the alarm goes off 14 minutes later. If CountDown is False, the control starts counting at 00:00.00 and counts until the AlarmTime is reached. If the AlarmTime property is ahead of the current time, the Alarm control assumes that you want the alarm to go off at the specified time on the next day. For example, if the time is 8:00.00 PM on April 1, and the AlarmTime is 6:30.00 PM, the alarm will go off at 6:30.00 PM on April 2 (which is 22 hours and 30 minutes later).

The Alarm control has two methods for starting and stopping the alarm:

StartTimer starts the alarm.

StopTimer stops the alarm.

Finally, the Alarm control has a TimeOut event which notifies the application that the alarm has gone off (which happens when the time has reached AlarmTime). The application can use this event to trigger another action or simply to notify the user.

Testing the Alarm Control

The Alarm control's test Form is shown in Figure 16.16, earlier in this chapter. It contains two instances of the control, and you can change their CountDown property at runtime. The AlarmTime property of the controls is set from within the test Form's Load event to a random value with the following statements:

```
Private Sub Form_Load()
    Randomize Time
    AlarmCtl1.AlarmTime = Rnd()
    AlarmCtl2.AlarmTime = Rnd()
End Sub
```

If you run the Alarm test project, comment out the lines in the Form's Load event, and set the alarm time a few minutes ahead of the current time so that you won't have to wait long before the alarm goes off.

When the two CheckBox controls are clicked, the CountDown property is changed with the following code:

```
Private Sub Check1_Click()
    If Check1.Value Then
        AlarmCtl1.CountDown = True
    Else
        AlarmCtl1.CountDown = False
    End If
End Sub
```

The code for the Check2 control's Click event is identical, only it applies to the AlarmCtl2 control. Finally, when an Alarm control times out, the following code is executed:

```
Private Sub AlarmCtl1_TimeOut()
    MsgBox "The Alarm " & AlarmCtl1.Tag & " has Timed out"
End Sub
```

You must set the control's Tag property to a meaningful name, since the program uses this property to differentiate between the two controls. The test project uses the tags ProcessA and ProcessB.

The Start Timer button under each Alarm control starts the timer of the corresponding control. At the same time, it changes its Caption to Stop Timer so that the user can stop the countdown at any time. The code behind the first Start Timer button is shown next.

Code 16.14:   Starting and Stopping the Alarm

```
Private Sub StartButton1_Click()
    If StartButton1.Caption = "Start Timer" Then
        AlarmCtl1.StartTimer
        StartButton1.Caption = "Stop Timer"
    Else
        StartButton1.Caption = "Start Timer"
        AlarmCtl1.StopTimer
    End If
End Sub
```

Finally, the Alarm Time buttons display the time when the corresponding alarm will go off, with the following code:

```
Private Sub AlarmButton1_Click()
    MsgBox "The alarm will go off at " & AlarmCtl1.AlarmTime
End Sub
```

Load the Alarm project (continue loading even after the warning that will appear), and replace the two PictureBox controls that will appear in place of the Alarm controls with two instances of the Alarm control. Experiment with the interface of the control and examine the code of the test project.

Open the test project, comment out the statements in the Form's Load event (which set the AlarmTime properties to random values), and set the AlarmTime property a minute or so ahead of your system's time (the current time displayed in the lower right corner of the task bar). Run the project, and then click the CountDown box. The

Alarm will start counting downward the difference between the current time and the alarm time. When this difference reaches zero, a message box informs you that time's up. If the CountDown box is cleared, you'll see how much time has passed since you started the timer. To see when the alarm will go off, click the Alarm Time button.

Designing the Alarm Control

Your first step is to design the control's interface. Unlike the Timer control of Visual Basic, the Alarm control has a visible interface. Its operation is based on two constituent controls:

> **Timer,** which updates its display every second
>
> **Label,** which displays the time

Designing the User Interface

To design the control's interface, follow these steps:

1. Place a Label control on the UserControl Form, and set its Font property to a font and size that looks nice for our purposes.

2. Align the Label with the upper left corner of the control, and resize the control so that it just fits the label. (Make a note of the values of the control's Width and Height properties. You'll need them later when you write the code to prevent this control from being resized.)

3. Place a Timer control on the UserControl object. It doesn't make any difference where the Timer control is placed; it will be invisible at runtime. You can place the timer outside the visible area of the user control or even on top of the label.

4. To complete the design of the control and prevent it from being resized, add the following code to the control's Resize event:

```
Private Sub UserControl_Resize()
    UserControl.Size 1800, 500
End Sub
```

The Size method forces the control to remain at a fixed size. You must change the values 1800 (width) and 500 (height) to the size of the control, according to the size of the Label control.

Now you can test the behavior of your new control. Place it on a Form and try to resize it. Even though you can drag the handles of the control, you won't be able to resize it.

Implementing the Control's Members

Now we are ready to implement the control's properties, its methods, and its event. Let's start with the properties. You have seen how to add properties to a control with the ActiveX Control Interface Wizard and how to do it manually. Now let's look at one more tool. We will do something similar with the Wizard, but this time one property or method at a time.

Let's start with the variable declarations. Insert the following lines in the User-Control object's Code window:

```
Private startTime As Date
Private Running As Boolean
Private m_CountDown As Boolean
Private m_AlarmTime As Date
```

As you have guessed, *m_CountDown* and *m_AlarmTime* are the two private variables that will hold the values of the CountDown and AlarmTime properties. The *Running* variable is True while the alarm is running and is declared outside any procedure so that all procedures can access its value. The *startTime* variable is set to the time the alarm starts counting and is used when the control is not counting down (you'll see how it's used shortly).

To add the skeletons for the control's properties with the Add Procedure command, follow these steps:

1. Switch to the UserControl window, and double-click its Form to open the Code window.

2. Choose Tools ➢ Add Procedure to open the Add Procedure dialog box:

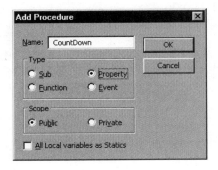

3. Add the name of the CountDown property, and check the Property radio button. The following lines are inserted in the code window:

```
Public Property Get CountDown() As Variant
End Property
```

```
Public Property Let CountDown(ByVal vNewValue As Variant)
End Property
```

4. Change the property's type to match its declaration, and then supply the code for the two Property procedures:

```
Public Property Get CountDown() As Boolean
    CountDown = m_CountDown
End Property

Public Property Let CountDown(ByVal vNewValue As Boolean)
    m_CountDown = vNewValue
End Property
```

> **NOTE**
>
> The code should be quite trivial by now. All Property procedures map the property name to a private variable, and they have the same structure. You must not forget to change their types from Variant to whatever type best describes the variables.

5. Do the same for the *AlarmTime* variable. The procedures for this property are as follows:

```
Public Property Get AlarmTime() As Date
    AlarmTime = m_AlarmTime
End Property

Public Property Let AlarmTime(ByVal vNewValue As Date)
    If IsDate(vNewValue) Then m_AlarmTime = vNewValue
End Property
```

This Property procedure validates the property value to make sure you enter a valid time. If you specify a date, the program assumes that the time is 00:00:00 (midnight).

6. Now you're ready to add the two methods. In the Code window choose Tools ➤ Add Procedure. Enter the name of the method, StartTimer, but this time check the Sub radio button. The following lines will be inserted in the code:

```
Public Sub StartTimer()
End Sub
```

7. In the StartTimer() subroutine, insert the code to start the alarm:

```
Public Sub StartTimer()
    If Not Running Then
        Timer1.Enabled = True
        Running = True
        startTime = Time
```

```
        If Time - m_AlarmTime > 0 Then NextDay = True
        Label1.Caption = "00:00:00"
    End If
End Sub
```

This subroutine doesn't do anything if the alarm is already running. If it isn't, it enables the Timer control and sets the variable *startTimer* to the current time and the display to "00:00:00". The *Running* variable is also set to True to prevent this subroutine from being executed again while the alarm is running. The variable *NextDay* is set to True if the alarm time is behind the current time. This means that the control should go off at the specified time on the next day.

8. Now choose Tools ➤ Add Procedure again to create another public subroutine, the StopTimer() method. Here is the code for this subroutine:

```
Public Sub StopTimer()
    If Running Then
        Timer1.Enabled = False
        Running = False
    End If
End Sub
```

As with the StartTimer method, the alarm stops only if it's running. If that's the case, the code disables the Timer control and sets the *Running* variable to False.

9. Now, add the control's event. Chose Tools ➤ Add Procedure to open the Add Procedure dialog box.

10. Specify the name TimeOut, and check the Event radio button. This time, a single line is added to the code, right after the declarations:

```
Event TimeOut()
```

How do you cause this event to take place? With the RaiseEvent statement from any place in your code. Whenever the alarm goes off, you can raise the TimeOut event with the following statement:

```
RaiseEvent TimeOut
```

The TimeOut event is raised from within the Timer's code, which is the core of the control (we'll see this code shortly).

You just completed the skeleton of the Alarm control, the kind of thing we did earlier with the ActiveX Control Interface Wizard. This time, you've added all the members of the control's interface manually, with the help of the Tools menu. It's easier to let the Wizard build the control for you, but knowing how it can be done manually will help you add a property or two to an existing control, without having to go through all the steps of the ActiveX Control Interface Wizard.

TIP

> If you run the ActiveX Control Interface Wizard to update an existing control, you will find that the Wizard comments out some of your code. Always check your code after processing it with the Wizard.

The Add Procedure command will not insert the appropriate lines in the Read-Properties and WriteProperties events. You must insert the following code manually.

Code 16.15:   **Saving and Reading the Alarm Control's Properties**

```
Private Sub UserControl_ReadProperties(PropBag As PropertyBag)
    CountDown = PropBag.ReadProperty("countdown", CountDown)
    m_AlarmTime = PropBag.ReadProperty("AlarmTime", AlarmTime)
End Sub

Private Sub UserControl_WriteProperties(PropBag As PropertyBag)
    PropBag.WriteProperty "CountDown", m_CountDown, False
    PropBag.WriteProperty "AlarmTime", m_AlarmTime, 0
End Sub
```

Finally, you must insert the following code, also manually, to initialize the values of the properties:

```
Private Sub UserControl_InitProperties()
    m_CountDown = True
    Running = False
End Sub
```

Updating the Display

Now we can write the code that updates the display and raises the TimeOut event. The code we develop in this section has nothing to do with ActiveX control development. It's the type of code you write to implement an alarm as a standalone application.

TIP

> If you're not quite accustomed to the ActiveX development environment yet, you can develop a regular application that does the job (that is, counts down time, displays elapsed or remaining time on a Label control, and detects when the alarm timed out). Then copy the essential procedures and paste them in the ActiveX project window.

You must supply the code for the Timer control's Timer event, which takes place every second. So, set the Timer control's Interval property to 1000. From within the Timer control's Timer event, you must update the display and test whether the alarm should go off.

Code 16.16: **The Alarm Control's Timer Event**

```
Private Sub Timer1_Timer()
Dim TimeDiff As Date
Dim StopNow As Boolean

    If Time - m_AlarmTime > 0 Then
        If NextDay = False Then
            StopNow = True
        Else
            TimeDiff = 24 - Time + m_AlarmTime
        End If
    Else
        If NextDay = True Then
            StopNow = True
        Else
            TimeDiff = m_AlarmTime - Time
        End If
    End If
    If m_CountDown Then
        Label1.Caption = Format$(Hour(TimeDiff) & ":" & _
            Minute(TimeDiff) & ":" & Second(TimeDiff), "hh:mm:ss")
    Else
        Label1.Caption = Format(Hour(Time - startTime) & ":" & _
            Minute(Time - startTime) & ":" & _
            Second(Time - startTime), "hh:mm:ss")
    End If

    If StopNow Then
        Timer1.Enabled = False
        RaiseEvent TimeOut
    End If
End Sub
```

The logic for stopping the timer and invoking the TimeOut event depends on whether the control is set to count down. When counting down, it displays the time remaining; when counting up, it displays the time elapsed since the timer started (the *startTime* variable set by the StartTimer method) and stops when the AlarmTime is reached. This condition is detected with the last If structure in the code. The variable *NextDay* is set in the StartTimer method. When it's time for the alarm to go off, the *NextDay* variable will change value, an event that signals that the alarm must go off.

You may think of detecting the TimeOut event by comparing the AlarmTime with the current time, with a statement such as the following:

```
If Time = AlarmTime Then
    Timer1.Enabled = False
    RaiseEvent TimeOut
End If
```

This code will not always work. If the computer is too busy when it's time for the alarm to go off (starting another application or scanning the hard disk, for example), the Timer event for the last second may not be triggered. If this event is skipped, you'll have to wait for another 24 hours before you get the next time out (and then you may not get it again!). The implementation I've chosen for the example will set off the alarm, even if this happens a second or two later.

See how simple it is to generate your own events? Simply call the RaiseEvent method from within your code, and Visual Basic sees that the event is reported to the host application. Any condition in your application can trigger an event at any time. In addition, you must insert the declaration of the event, along with the variable declarations, at the beginning of the code:

```
Event TimeOut()
```

Open the Alarm project and examine the code of the UserControl object, as well as the code of the test project. The code is straightforward, and that's why I've chosen to implement this control manually. It's usually easier to implement custom controls with the help of the ActiveX Control Interface Wizard, but it's important that you understand what goes on and what the Wizard does for you.

Enhancing Existing Controls

You can also develop custom ActiveX controls that enhance existing controls. There's not a single user who wouldn't like to add "new" features to existing controls. Many programmers add new features to standard ActiveX controls with the appropriate code from within their applications. A shortcoming of the ComboList control, for instance, is that any new entries added to its Edit box are not appended to the list of options. In other words, the ComboBox control lets you specify a new entry, but this entry isn't automatically added to the control's list of options. Many programmers capture the Enter keystroke in the ComboBox control and append new entries to the control's list manually.

I'm sure each of you would like to add your own little feature to the standard VB controls. In this section, you'll learn how to enhance existing ActiveX controls and package them as custom controls. Obviously, you can't change the basic functions of an existing control, as you don't have access to their code. But there's a lot you can do by adding some code and packaging the existing control along with your code as a new control.

In this section, I'm going to enhance the TextBox control. The CTextBox custom control is a regular TextBox control that changes its default behavior depending on whether it accepts an optional or a required field.

In this chapter's folder on the CD, you will also find the CLDesign project, which demonstrates how to add runtime characteristics to a control at design time. Did you ever try to set the value of a Scrollbar control at design time by scrolling its button? Most of us have tried this at one time or another, and the result was to move the entire control on the Form. The ScrollBar control's value can't be set visually at design time. An interesting enhancement to the ScrollBar control would be to provide a mechanism that would allow the developer to specify whether the control should be moved or operate as it would at runtime, even though it's in design mode. The CLDesign project is straightforward, and I will not discuss it in this chapter. All the information you need to make a control exhibit runtime behavior at design time is the *EditAtDesignTime* property of the UserControl object. If you set this property to True, the Edit command will be appended to its shortcut menu. Right-click the control on the test Form and select Edit; the control will behave as if it were in runtime mode. If it contains a Scrollbar control, for example, you can adjust the control's value with the mouse. The CLDesign control, shown on a Form in Figure 16.17, lets the developer select the initial color at design time by sliding the three scrollbars.

FIGURE 16.17:

The CLDesign project exhibits runtime behavior at design time.

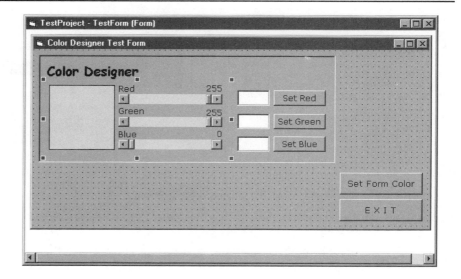

An Enhanced TextBox Control

The CTextBox control is a custom ActiveX control that enhances the operation of the standard TextBox control. It's a simple control (it inherits all of the TextBox control's functionality), but I found it very useful in designing data-entry applications. As you will see, the enhancements are quite simple and really trivial to implement.

Most of you have developed data-entry screens in which some fields are required, and you may have designed Forms with TextBoxes colored differently, depending on whether the corresponding field is required. Or you may have used the required field's LostFocus event to keep the focus in the required field until the user enters a value.

How about an enhanced TextBox control that changes color after a value is entered? Figure 16.18 shows a data-entry Form using the enhanced TextBox control. The fields First Name, Last Name, and E-Mail are required, and the corresponding TextBox controls are initially colored red. If the user moves the focus without entering a value in these fields, they remain red. If a value is entered, their color changes to white. Another feature of the enhanced TextBox control is that it changes color when it receives the focus so that the user can quickly spot the active control on the Form. As you can probably guess, I got the idea from data-entry Forms on Web pages, which use an asterisk to indicate the required fields.

FIGURE 16.18:

The CTextBox control enhances the standard TextBox control by adding a few custom properties.

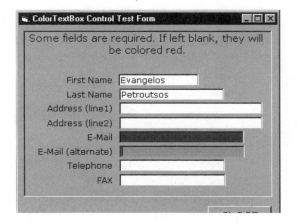

VB6 at Work: The CTextBox Project

Open the CTextBox project on the CD and run it. When you open the project for the first time, you'll see an error message, indicating that the CTextBox control can't be loaded. Continue loading the project, and then open the project's test

Form. All instances of the CTextBox control are replaced by PictureBoxes. Delete the PictureBox controls on the Form, and create an array of seven CTextBox controls. Place them on the Form as shown in Figure 16.18, aligning them with their corresponding captions and with one another. Then run the project by pressing F5, and check out the functionality of the new control.

The CTextBox Control's Specifications

The design of the CTextBox control is fairly simple. It's identical to the standard TextBox control, and it provides a few additional properties.

EnterFocusColor   When the control receives the focus, its background color is set to this value. If you don't want the currently active control to change color, set its EnterFocusColor to white.

LeaveFocusColor   When the control loses the focus, its background color is set to this value (this property is usually white for optional fields and has the same value as the MandatoryColor for required fields).

Mandatory   This property indicates whether the control corresponds to a required field, if Mandatory = 1 (Required), or an optional field, if Mandatory = 0 (Optional).

MandatoryColor   This is the background color of the control if its Mandatory property is 1 (Required). The MandatoryColor overwrites the LeaveFocusColor setting. In other words, if the user skips a mandatory field, the corresponding control is painted with the MandatoryColor and not with the LeaveFocusColor. Notice that required fields (those with Mandatory=1) behave like optional fields after they have been assigned a value.

To understand how these properties are used in the design of a data-entry Form, open the CTextBox project and experiment with the settings of its custom properties to see how they affect its operation. Because the CTextBox control is not a standard element of the Windows interface, your users may not understand what the changing colors mean, but it won't take long for anyone to get the hang of it and use this feature efficiently.

Designing the CTextBox Control

The design of the CTextBox control is straightforward. We'll use the ActiveX Control Interface Wizard to design a custom control that has all the members of the standard TextBox control (except for the properties that relate to data binding). The Wizard will create the source code for us, and we'll add a few statements that change the control's background color according to the settings of its properties and its contents.

Start a new ActiveX control project and add a test project as usual. Then name the project's components as follows:

1. Select the project and change its name to ColorTextBox.

2. Select the UserControl object and change its name to CTextBox.

3. Select the test project and change its name to TestProject.

4. Select the test Form and change its name to TestForm.

Since the custom control is nothing less than a TextBox control, place an instance of the TextBox control on it. The TextBox control must cover the entire UserControl object, so you must enter the following code in the UserControl object's Resize event handler:

```
Private Sub UserControl_Resize()
    Text1.Move 0, 0, UserControl.Width, UserControl.Height
End Sub
```

The remaining custom code must use the Mandatory property, so we can't add it now. At this point, you can start the ActiveX Control Interface Wizard to generate most of the code. Our goal is to incorporate all the functionality of the TextBox control into our custom control.

In the Select Interface Members window, move the following members from the Available Names list to the Selected Names list:

Appearance	KeyDown	MouseUp	OLEGiveFeedback
BackColor	KeyPress	MultiLine	OLESetData
Click	KeyUp	OLECompleteDrag	OLEStartDrag
Change	MaxLength	OLEDrag	PasswordChar
DblClick	MouseDown	OLEDragDrop	Refresh
Enabled	MouseIcon	OLEDragMode	Text
Font	MouseMove	OLEDragOver	ToolTip
ForeColor	MousePointer	OLEDropMode	

These are the basic members of the TextBox control, with the exception of the data-binding properties (DataSource, DataMember, and so on). When you duplicate the functionality of an existing control with your custom control, you must make sure that all the members a developer expects to find in the custom control are there. I have skipped the data-binding properties because I don't plan to use this control with databases. (The topic of creating data-bound controls is fairly advanced and is not covered in this book.)

Click the Next button to display the next window, Create Custom Interface Members. Here you must add the following custom members:

EnterFocusColor The control's background color when it receives the focus.

LeaveFocusColor The control's background color when it loses the focus.

Mandatory If this property is True, the control's background is set to the MandatoryColor property's value, to indicate that the control is used for a required field.

MandatoryColor The control's background color when its Mandatory property is True.

In the next window of the Wizard, map all members except the custom member to the corresponding properties of the TextBox1 control. No members of the CTextBox control are mapped to the UserControl object, simply because the TextBox takes over the entire UserControl object.

In the next window, Set Attributes, you define the properties of the custom properties. Enter the attributes shown in Table 16.4 in the appropriate fields in the Set Attributes window of the Wizard.

TABLE 16.4: Properties of the Custom Properties

Property Name	Data Type	Default Value	Runtime	Design Time
EnterFocusColor	OLE_COLOR	&H00FFFF	Read/Write	Read/Write
LeaveFocusColor	OLE_COLOR	&HFFFFFF	Read/Write	Read/Write
Mandatory	Boolean	False	Read/Write	Read/Write
MandatoryColor	OLE_COLOR	&HFF0000	Read/Write	Read/Write

In the same window, you also enter a description for each property, which will appear in the Properties window when the corresponding property is selected. Click the Next button, and then click Finish to generate the control's code.

You can now open the UserControl object's Code window and see the code generated by the Wizard. The following variables and initial values appear at the top of the Code window:

```
'Default Property Values:
Const m_def_Mandatory = False
Const m_def_EnterFocusColor = &HFF00FF
Const m_def_MandatoryColor = &HFF
Const m_def_LeaveFocusColor = &HFFFFFF
```

```
'Property Variables:
Dim m_Mandatory As Boolean
Dim m_EnterFocusColor As Variant
Dim m_MandatoryColor As OLE_COLOR
Dim m_LeaveFocusColor As OLE_COLOR
```

These variable and constant definitions correspond to the properties we specified in the windows of the Wizard. All standard members have already been implemented for you, and you need not change them, except for the Property procedures of the Appearance property. The Wizard will implement this property as an Integer, but an Enumerated type works better for properties with a limited number of settings. So, insert the following Type declaration:

```
Enum Flat3D
    Flat
    [3D]
End Enum
```

and then change the Property procedures as follows.

Code 16.17:   The Revised Appearance Property Procedures

```
Public Property Get Appearance() As Flat3D
    Appearance = Text1.Appearance
End Property

Public Property Let Appearance(ByVal New_Appearance As Flat3D)
    Text1.Appearance() = New_Appearance
    PropertyChanged "Appearance"
End Property
```

You must also modify the code of the Property Let procedure for the MandatoryColor property. This property can be set only if the control's Mandatory property is True. If it's False, the user must first change it and then set the MandatoryColor property.

Code 16.18:   The Revised MandatoryColor Property Procedures

```
Public Property Let MandatoryColor(ByVal New_MandatoryColor As
OLE_COLOR)
    m_MandatoryColor = New_MandatoryColor
    If m_Mandatory Then Text1.BackColor = New_MandatoryColor
    PropertyChanged "MandatoryColor"
End Property
```

The Mandatory property is an integer, and you can enter any integer values in its field, in the Properties window. Define the following Enumerated type:

```
Enum ReqOpt
    [Optional]
    Required
End Enum
```

Notice that the Optional value must be enclosed in square brackets, because it's a Visual Basic keyword. Modify the definitions of the Property procedures of the Mandatory property as follows.

Code 16.19:   **The Modified Mandatory Property Procedures**

```
Public Property Get Mandatory() As ReqOpt
    Mandatory = m_Mandatory
End Property

Public Property Let Mandatory(ByVal New_Mandatory As ReqOpt)
    m_Mandatory = New_Mandatory
    If m_Mandatory = Required Then
        Text1.BackColor = m_MandatoryColor
    Else
        Text1.BackColor = m_def_LeaveFocusColor
    End If
    PropertyChanged "Mandatory"
End Property
```

When the Mandatory property is set to True, the control automatically sets its background color property to the color value of the MandatoryValue property.

This takes care of the trivial code necessary for the control's proper operation. You're now ready to add the custom code to enhance the operation of the TextBox control. The code that enhances the operation of the TextBox control is located in the UserControl object's LostFocus event. When the user moves the focus away from a CTextBox control, the code examines the control's contents and its Mandatory property. If the control is empty and its Mandatory property is True, the TextBox control's background is set to the value of the MandatoryColor property.

Code 16.20:   **The UserControl's LostFocus Event Handler**

```
Private Sub Text1_LostFocus()
    If Len(Trim(Text1.Text)) = 0 And m_Mandatory = Required Then
        Text1.BackColor = m_MandatoryColor
    Else
```

```
            Text1.BackColor = LeaveFocusColor
        End If
    End Sub
```

Notice that the code isn't raising the LostFocus event. Although the control's
behavior when it loses the focus is determined by its code, you may still want to
be able to program the LostFocus event. You *can* use the LostFocus event,
because this event can't be triggered by the control itself. It's triggered by the control's container (the Form), and you can't raise it from within the control's code.
So, even though the statement RaiseEvent LostFocus() doesn't appear anywhere in
the control's code, the Lostfocus event can still be programmed. The same is true
for the GotFocus event, which is also raised by the container, not by the control.

The CTextBox control has another feature: when it's active, it changes its background color to the value of the EnterFocusColor property:

```
Private Sub Text1_GotFocus()
    Text1.BackColor = EnterFocusColor
End Sub
```

If you don't like this behavior, simply set the EnterFocusColor to the same value
as the control's Background color.

To summarize, ActiveX controls combine design elements from both standard
VB applications and ActiveX component design. Their properties, methods, and
events are handled just as their counterparts in ActiveX components:

- Properties are private variables, which can be read or set through Property
  procedures.

- Methods are public subroutines.

- Events can be raised from anywhere in an ActiveX control with the Raise-
  Event method.

The control's visible interface is drawn on a UserControl object, which is quite
similar to a Form. It supports nearly all of a Form's properties and methods, including the Drawing methods. There are no means for loading and unloading User-
Controls as there are for Forms, but you can make a control visible or invisible at
runtime from within your code.

The code of the control resides in key events of the control, such as the Paint
and Resize events, and is no different from the code you use to develop a stand-
alone application with similar functionality.

The integration of an ActiveX control in the development environment is the responsibility of Visual Basic. The properties you attach to the control are automatically displayed in the Properties window, and the syntax of its methods is displayed as you type code (they are incorporated into the AutoList Members feature of the Visual Basic IDE). In short, developing an ActiveX control is strikingly similar to developing a standard VB application. The result is a new animal that can live in various environments, including Web pages, as you'll see in the last part of this book.

PART V

Database Programming with Visual Basic

CHAPTER

SEVENTEEN

17

Database Programming
with Visual Basic

- Working with databases and database management systems

- Understanding relational concepts

- Using the Visual Data Manager

- Exploring the structure of the BIBLIO database

- Validating data

- Entering data

- Accessing fields in RecordSets

- Introducing SQL

- Using advanced data-bound controls

- Mapping databases

If there is one topic that's too big to fit in a single chapter, it's database programming. This chapter, therefore, is an introduction to the basic concepts of database programming with Visual Basic. It's primarily for those who want to set up small databases and for those familiar with other database management systems, such as dBase. If you are familiar with database programming in other environments, the information in this chapter will help you get up to speed quickly in database programming with Visual Basic.

NOTE   The applications in this chapter use the sample databases BIBLIO and NWIND, which come with the Professional Edition of Visual Basic. The names of the databases are hardcoded in many of the examples. In particular, the databases are expected to reside in the default folder that is created during installation. If you didn't install Visual Basic to its default folder, you must change the name of the database to match its location on your system. You must change the Database-Name property of the Data control (if the application uses the Data control) or the path of the database in the OpenDatabase() method in the code (if the application opens the database directly). Because you can't change these settings on the CD, you must first copy the sample applications to a folder on your hard disk and then run or modify them.

Understanding Databases and Database Management Systems

Nearly all business applications need to store large volumes of data, organized in a format that simplifies retrieval. This is accomplished with a *database management system (DBMS)*, a mechanism for manipulating tabular data with high-level commands. The database management system hides low-level details, such as how data are stored in a database, and frees the programmer to concentrate on managing information, rather than on the specifics of manipulating files or maintaining links among them.

.Visual Basic provides a wealth of tools for creating and accessing databases on both individual machines and networks. The two major tools are:

- The Data control
- The Data Access object

The *Data control* gives you access to databases without any programming. You can set a few properties of the control and use regular controls such as textboxes to display the values of the fields in the database. This is the no-code approach to database programming, which is implemented quite nicely in Visual Basic. But as you can guess, this approach can't take you far. Sooner or later, you will have to write code.

The *Data Access object* is a structure of objects for accessing databases through your code. All the functionality of the Data control is also available to your code, through the Data Access object (DAO).

Just what is a database? In its basic sense, a database is simply a grouping of related information organized for easy processing and retrieval. Figure 17.1 shows how this works. The actual data in a database is stored in *tables*, which are similar to random access files. Data in a table is made up of *columns* and *rows*. The rows contain identically structured pieces of information, which are equivalent to the records of random access files. A *record* is a collection of values (called *fields*).

FIGURE 17.1:

A pictorial representation of a database and the structure of tables

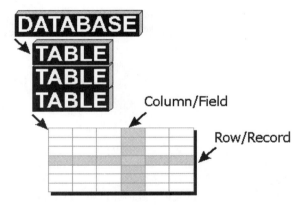

RecordSets

RecordSets are objects that represent collections of records from one or more tables. In database programming, RecordSets are the equivalent of variables in regular programming. You can't access the tables of a database directly. The only way to view or manipulate records is via RecordSet objects. A RecordSet is constructed of columns and rows and is similar to a table, but it can contain data from multiple tables. The contents of the grid shown in Figure 17.2 come from a single table, and they form a RecordSet. Such records are the result of queries, such as all the customers and the total of their invoices in a given month.

FIGURE 17.2:

The Products table of the NWIND database. The selected row is a record of the Products table.

ID	ProductName	SupplierID	egoryID	QuantityPerUnit	UnitPrice
1	Chai	1	1	10 boxes x 20 bags	18
2	Chang	1	1	24 - 12 oz bottles	19
3	Aniseed Syrup	1	2	12 - 550 ml bottles	10
4	Chef Anton's Cajun Seasoning	2	2	48 - 6 oz jars	22
5	Chef Anton's Gumbo Mix	2	2	36 boxes	21.35
6	Grandma's Boysenberry Spread	3	2	12 - 8 oz jars	25
7	Uncle Bob's Organic Dried Pears	3	7	12 - 1 lb pkgs.	30
8	Northwoods Cranberry Sauce	3	2	12 - 12 oz jars	40
9	Mishi Kobe Niku	4	6	18 - 500 g pkgs.	97
10	Ikura	4	8	12 - 200 ml jars	31

NOTE

One way to think of RecordSets is as object variables. They store the results of queries or an entire table of the database, just as numeric variables store numbers. The contents of a RecordSet, however, have a more complicated structure (they are made of rows and columns), and each cell on this grid can be of a different type. To access the contents of the RecordSet, you use its properties and methods.

A RecordSet, therefore, is a view of some of the data in the database, selected from the database according to user-specified criteria. The three types of Record-Sets are:

- **DynaSets,** which are updatable views of data

- **SnapShots,** which are static (read-only) views of data

- **Tables,** which are direct views of tables

DynaSets and SnapShots are usually created with SQL (Structured Query Language) statements. We will look at SQL statements later in this chapter, but all you need to know about SQL statements for now is that they are commands that you use to specify criteria for recalling data from a database. (You can also use SQL commands to update a database and even to create a new database, but I'm not going to discuss these commands in this book.) DynaSets are updated every time users change the database, and changes they make to the corresponding RecordSet are reflected in the underlying tables. SnapShots are static views of the same data. A SnapShot contains the records requested the moment the SnapShot was generated (changes made to the underlying tables are not reflected in SnapShots), and you can't update SnapShots.

The DynaSet is the most flexible and powerful type of RecordSet, although a few operations (such as searches) may be faster with the Table RecordSets. The Table type, however, requires a lot of overhead. The least flexible RecordSet type, the SnapShot, is the most efficient in terms of overhead. If you don't need to update the database and simply want to view records, choose the SnapShot type.

There's also a variation of the SnapShot type, the *forward-only SnapShot*, which is even more limited than the SnapShot type, but faster. Forward-only SnapShots let you move forward only. You can use them in programming situations in which you want to scan a number of records and process them sequentially (use their values in a calculation, copy selected records to another table, and so on). By not providing any methods to go back in the records, this RecordSet type requires the least overhead of all.

The Table RecordSet is a reference to a table in the database. The Table is faster than the other types of RecordSets, always in sync with the table's data, and can be used to update the database. But the Table type is limited to a single table. In addition, when accessing a table through a Table RecordSet, you can take advantage of the Table's indices to perform very fast searches.

The Data Control

RecordSets are the foundation of database programming. Let's look at an example that will help you visualize RecordSets and explore the Data control. The Data1 application, shown in Figure 17.3, is nothing less than a front end for an existing table in a database.

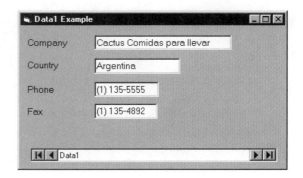

VB6 at Work: The Data1 Project

To build this application, follow these steps:

1. Start a new Standard EXE project and design a Form like the one shown in Figure 17.3. Start by drawing a Data control at the bottom of the Form. The Data control is your gateway to the database.

2. With the Data control selected, open the Properties window, locate its DatabaseName property, and then click on the ellipsis button to open the Open dialog box.

3. Select the NWIND database that comes with Visual Basic.

4. Locate the RecordSource property in the Properties window, and drop down the list of available entries. You'll see a list of all the tables in the NWIND database. Select the Customers table.

5. Place four textboxes on the Form, as shown in Figure 17.3.

6. Select the first textbox, and in the Properties window locate its DataSource property. Set it to **Data1**.

7. Set the DataField property of the textbox to **CompanyName**. The DataField property is a drop-down list with the names of all fields in the Customers table.

8. Set the DataSource property of the other three textboxes to **Data1**, and set the DataField property to **Country**, **Phone**, and **Fax**.

Now run the application. The textboxes will display the values of the corresponding fields of the Customers table in the NWIND database. Using the Data control's buttons, you can move through the records (rows) of the table. Clicking the leftmost button displays the first record of the table, and clicking the button next to it displays the previous record. Clicking the rightmost button displays the last record of the table, and clicking the button next to it displays the next record.

Not only can you navigate through the table's records with the Data control, you can also edit its fields. Change the value of a field, move to the next record, and then come back to the previous record. The changes you made to the record are saved to the database, and now you see the updated value of the record.

You should also attempt to enter invalid data in the table's fields. The program won't allow you to enter invalid values and will let you know why. If you attempt to enter a very long phone number, for example, the application displays a message indicating that the entry is too long for the field and gives you a chance to correct the value. The field was obviously declared with a limited length in the definition of the database. It is actually the database management system that issues the warning, not Visual Basic, and certainly not the application. You have yet to enter a single line of code.

Figure 17.4 shows the relationship among the TextBox controls on the Form, the Data control, and the database. The controls on the Form can't see the database directly. Instead, they see the database through the Data control. The Data control, in turn, sees a RecordSet, which happens to be a table of the database. You'll learn later how to specify other types of RecordSets for the Data control.

The Data control sees one row of the RecordSet and updates the data-bound controls on the Form with the values of the specific fields of the current record.

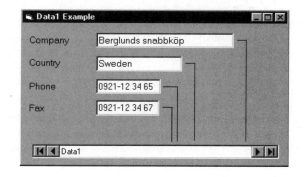

CompanyName	Country	Phone	Fax
454545			
Alfreds Futterkiste	Germany	030-0074321	030-0076545
Ana Trujillo Emparedados y helados	Mexico	(5) 555-4729	(5) 555-3745
Antonio Moreno Taquería	Mexico	(5) 555-3932	
Around the Horn	UK	(171) 555-7788	(171) 555-6750
Berglunds snabbköp	Sweden	0921-12 34 65	0921-12 34 67
Blauer See Delikatessen	Germany	0621-08460	0621-08924
Blondel père et fils	France	88.60.15.31	88.60.15.32
Bólido Comidas preparadas	Spain	(91) 555 22 82	(91) 555 91 99
Bon app'	France	91.24.45.40	91.24.45.41

The Data Control's Properties

The most important properties of the Data control are:

- **DatabaseName,** which specifies the database to be used

- **RecordSource,** which specifies the part of the database seen by the control

At any given time, the Data control is positioned at a single row (record) of its RecordSet. The user can move to any other record with the help of the navigation buttons on the Data control.

The textboxes see a field in the current row. Each time the Data control is repositioned in its RecordSet, the textboxes are updated. If the data in a textbox change, the new value is written to the database when the Data control is repositioned. The TextBox controls are connected to a field of the RecordSet through the Data control, and they are called *data-bound* (they have been bound to a field in the RecordSet).

The most important properties of a data-bound control are:

- **DataSource,** which is the name of a Data control through which the controls (e.g., TextBox, CheckBox) are bound to a Data control; in other words, it's the name of a Data control through which the data bound control "sees" the database.

- **DataField,** which is the name of a field in the RecordSet that the control displays and updates.

When TextBox controls are bound to a specific field, and they are called data-bound. There are other controls that you can bind to the Data control's RecordSet. If you want to prevent users of the application from editing the contents of the table, you can use Label controls. If the table contains Boolean fields (that have the values True/False only), you can bind them to CheckBox controls. Some common controls aren't data-bound. The ListBox control, for example, isn't data-bound. Microsoft provides an enhanced version of the ListBox control, the data-bound List-Box control, which can be automatically populated with the values of a column in the RecordSet. You'll see later how to use this control in your applications.

You can set the following properties of the Data control from the Properties window, or you can use them from within your code to manipulate the control.

EOF   The EOF (End of File) property returns a True/False value that indicates whether the current record position is after the last record in a RecordSet object.

BOF   The BOF (Beginning of File) property returns a True/False value that indicates whether the current record position is before the first record in a RecordSet object.

BOFAction   This property sets or returns a value indicating what action the Data control should take when the BOF property is True, which can be one of the actions in Table 17.1.

TABLE 17.1: The Values Returned by the BOFAction Property

CONSTANT	VALUE	ACTION
vbBOFActionMoveFirst	0	(Default) Repositions the control on the first record.
vbBOFActionBOF	1	Moves past the beginning of a RecordSet and lands on an invalid record. At the same time, it triggers the Data control's Validate event for the first record. You'll see later how to handle this situation.

EOFAction   This property sets or returns a value indicating what action the Data control takes when the EOF property is True, which can be one of the actions in Table 17.2.

TABLE 17.2: The Values Returned by the EOFAction Property

CONSTANT	VALUE	ACTION
vbEOFActionMoveLast	0	(Default) Repositions the control on the last record.
vbEOFActionEOF	1	Moves past the end of a RecordSet and lands on an invalid record. At the same time, it triggers the Data control's Validate event for the last record. You'll see later how to handle this situation.
vbEOFActionAddNew	2	Adds a new blank record to the RecordSet, which the user can edit. The new record is written to the database when the user repositions the Data control.

ReadOnly   This property returns or sets a value that determines whether the control's RecordSet is opened for read-only access.

RecordsetType   This property returns or sets a value indicating the type of RecordSet object you want the Data control to create. It can have one of the values shown in Table 17.3.

TABLE 17.3: The Values of the RecordsetType Property

CONSTANT	VALUE	DESCRIPTION
vbRSTypeTable	0	A Table type of RecordSet
vbRSTypeDynaset	1	(Default) A DynaSet type of RecordSet
vbRSTypeSnapshot	2	A SnapShot type of RecordSet

Options   This property sets one or more characteristics of the RecordSet object and can have one of the values shown in Table 17.4.

TABLE 17.4: The Values of the Options Property

CONSTANT	VALUE	DESCRIPTION
dbDenyWrite	1	In a multiuser environment, other users can't make changes to records in the RecordSet.
dbDenyRead	2	In a multiuser environment, other users can't read records (Table type of RecordSet only).
dbReadOnly	4	The user of the application can read but can't make changes to records in the RecordSet.

Continued on next page

TABLE 17.4 CONTINUED: The Values of the Options Property

CONSTANT	VALUE	DESCRIPTION
dbAppendOnly	8	The user of the application can add new records to the RecordSet but can't read existing records.
dbInconsistent	16	Updates can apply to all fields of the RecordSet, even if they violate the join condition (applies to RecordSets based on SQL queries).
dbConsistent	32	(Default) Updates apply only to those fields that don't violate the join condition (applies to RecordSets based on SQL queries).
dbSQLPassThrough	64	When using Data controls with an SQL statement in the Record-Source property, sends the SQL statement to an ODBC database, such as a SQL Server or an Oracle database, for processing.
dbForwardOnly	256	The RecordSet object supports forward-only scrolling. The only Move method allowed is MoveNext. This option cannot be used on RecordSet objects manipulated with the Data control.
dbSeeChanges	512	Generates a trappable error if another user is changing data you are editing.

Bookmark   This property is a Variant that identifies a row in the RecordSet. Each row has its own, unique bookmark that isn't related to the record's order in the RecordSet. Save the Bookmark property to a variable so that you can return to this record later by assigning the variable to the Bookmark property.

The Data Control's Methods

The built-in functionality of the Data control, which is impressive indeed, can be accessed through an application's code with the Data control's methods. The simplest methods are the navigation methods, which correspond to the actions of the four buttons on the control, and they are as follows:

- **MoveFirst** repositions the control to the first record.

- **MoveLast** repositions the control to the last record.

- **MovePrevious** repositions the control to the previous record.

- **MoveNext** repositions the control to the next record.

You can use these methods to implement navigation buttons. However, you must take care of three special cases: (1) what happens when the Data control is positioned at the first or last record; (2) what happens when the Previous button is clicked while the Data control is on the first record; and (3) what happens when the Next button is clicked while the Data control is on the last record.

VB6 at Work: The Data2 Project

The Data2 application is similar to the Data1 application, but this time we'll use a different database. The BIBLIO database, which also comes with Visual Basic, is a database of book titles, publishers, and authors. We will look at the structure of this database later in the chapter, but in this application we are going to build a front end for navigating through the Titles table, which contains Title, ISBN, Description, Subject, and Comments fields, among others. The Form of the Data2 application is shown in Figure 17.5.

FIGURE 17.5:

The Data2 application uses the methods of the Data control to implement the four navigation buttons.

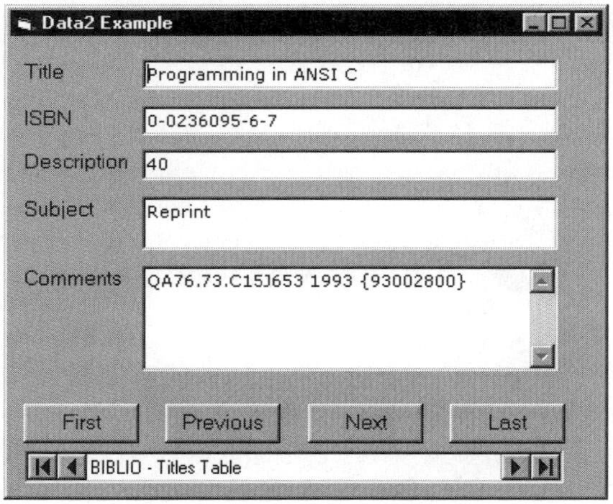

Designing the Form is straightforward. Follow these steps:

1. Place a Data control and connect it to the BIBLIO database by setting its DatabaseName property to the path of the database on your system and setting its RecordSource property to the Titles table.

2. Place the data-bound controls on the Form and bind them to the Data control by setting their DataSource property to **Data1** and their Datafield properties to the fields they display.

The code behind the First and Last buttons is simple. It calls the corresponding navigation method of the control.

Code 17.1:	The First and Last Buttons

```
Private Sub firstBttn_Click()
    Data1.Recordset.MoveFirst
End Sub

Private Sub LastBttn_Click()
    Data1.Recordset.MoveLast
End Sub
```

The code behind the other two buttons is a bit more complicated, as it takes into consideration the EOF property of the control.

Code 17.2:	The Next Button's Click Event

```
Private Sub NextBttn_Click()
    Data1.Recordset.MoveNext
    If Data1.Recordset.EOF Then
        MsgBox "You are on the last record"
        Data1.Recordset.MoveLast
    End If
End Sub
```

The program moves to the next record, and then it examines the EOF property. If EOF is True, we have landed on a record after the last one. The program displays a message to let the user know that the last record has been reached and then moves to the last record.

NOTE   Landing on a record beyond the last one isn't catastrophic. It's a blank record, which you can let the user edit and then append to the table. A problem will arise, however, if the Next button is clicked again. Attempting to move even further beyond this record will cause a runtime error. That's why we must handle this situation as soon as we hit the EOF=True condition. You will also notice that the fields are blank while the message is displayed. Normally, you should display the message after moving to the last valid record. I used this order here to demonstrate that after the last record in the RecordSet there's indeed a blank record.

The code behind the Previous button is quite similar. It calls the MovePrevious method, and instead of the EOF property, it examines the BOF property of the Data control.

Code 17.3:   **The Previous Button**

```
Private Sub PreviousBttn_Click()
    Data1.Recordset.MovePrevious
    If Data1.Recordset.BOF Then
        MsgBox "You are on the first record"
        Data1.Recordset.MoveFirst
    End If
End Sub
```

The Find Methods

In addition to the navigation methods, the Data control provides four methods for finding records in the RecordSet. One of the basic operations you perform on databases is locating specific records. The following methods locate records:

- **FindFirst** finds the first record that meets the specified criteria.

- **FindLast** finds the last record that meets the specified criteria.

- **FindNext** finds the next record that meets the specified criteria.

- **FindPrevious** finds the previous record that meets the specified criteria.

These methods can locate any record in the RecordSet, based on user-specified criteria. The syntax of all these methods is the same and is as follows:

```
RecordSet.FindFirst criteria
```

The *criteria* argument is a string expression specifying a relation between field values and constants. The following statement:

```
Data1.RecordSet.FindFirst "State='NY'"
```

locates the first record in the RecordSet in which the state is NY. Notice that literals within the *criteria* string are delimited with single quotes. The user-specified criteria can be more complicated and can combine values of multiple fields with logical and relational operators. For example, the following statement:

```
Data1.RecordSet.FindFirst "InvoiceDate > '12/31/1996' AND Invoice >= 1000"
```

locates the first invoice issued in 1997 with a total of $1,000 or more.

In addition to the usual relational operators, you can use the LIKE operator, which allows you to locate records that match a pattern. For example, to locate any book in the BIBLIO database with SQL in its title, use the following Find method:

```
RecordSet.FindFirst "Title LIKE '*SQL*'"
```

The string *SQL* is a pattern that allows any number of characters to appear before and after SQL. In other words, it matches titles such as *SQL: An Introduction*, *Mastering SQL*, or *The SQL Handbook*.

How the Find Methods Search

The search performed by the Find methods is case-insensitive. Thus, the argument *SQL* matches SQL, sql, and SqL. To change the default search mode, use the following statement to make comparisons case-insensitive:

```
Option Compare Text
```

Use the following statement to make comparisons case-sensitive:

```
Option Compare Binary
```

The Option Compare statement must appear in the Form's declarations or in a Module.

When a Find method is called, Visual Basic locates a record that matches the criteria and repositions the Data control to this record. In your code, however, you must first examine the value of the *NoMatch* property, which is set to False if a record is found, and True otherwise. The following code segment shows how the Find methods are used:

```
Data1.Recordset.FindFirst "City='Berlin'"
If Data1.Recordset.NoMatch Then
    MsgBox "No such record found"
Else
    MsgBox Data1.Recordset.Fields("Country")
End If
```

This code segment searches for the first record whose City field has the value Berlin. If no such record is found, the program displays a message. If it's found, the program displays the value of the field Country.

VB6 at Work: The FindDemo Project

The FindDemo application demonstrates how to use the Find methods on a RecordSet. You can actually include this little utility in a larger application to implement a general Find feature. The application is shown in Figure 17.6. The first ComboBox control lets you select a table, and the second ComboBox control lets you select a field. You can then type a search argument for the operation in the Search Value textbox and click the buttons to locate the records that meet the specified criteria. (The code that extracts the table names from the NWIND database and the field names of the selected table is discussed in the section "Mapping Databases," later in this chapter.)

FIGURE 17.6:

The FindDemo application demonstrates the Find methods.

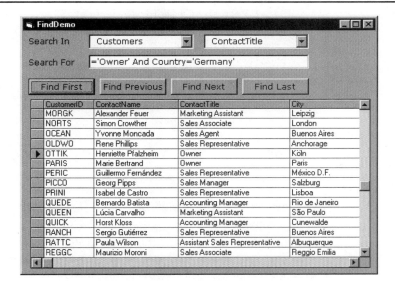

As you can see in Figure 17.6, it is possible to specify additional fields in the search argument beyond the one selected in the ComboBox. Any strings in the Search Value field must be enclosed in single quotes. Alternatively, you can write a small procedure that replaces any double quotes found in the string with single quotes.

If you run the FindDemo application, you'll see columns that are different from the ones shown in Figure 17.6. If you place the pointer on the dividing line between two columns in the data-bound Grid control, it turns into a double arrow, indicating that you can resize the column. To prepare Figure 17.6, I eliminated some columns with meaningless data by setting their width to 0 and resized other columns to display the data of interest (contact names and cities).

The Form of the FindDemo application contains a data-bound Grid control and a hidden Data control. The data-bound Grid control is discussed later in this chapter. For purposes of this example, all you need to know is that this control can be bound to a Data control and can display the Data control's RecordSet in a tabular arrangement. The code that populates the two ComboBox controls accesses the values of the fields through code, and this will be explained in the section "Accessing Fields in RecordSets" later in this chapter.

Code 17.4:   **The Find First Button**

```
Private Sub firstBttn_Click()
On Error GoTo SQLError
    Data1.Recordset.FindFirst GenerateSQL()
    If Data1.Recordset.NoMatch Then
        MsgBox "No such record found"
    End If
    Exit Sub

SQLError:
    MsgBox Err.Description

End Sub
```

The GenerateSQL() Function   The GenerateSQL() function generates the search argument for all Find operations. The value returned by the GenerateSQL() function is used with the Find methods. After calling the FindFirst method, the program examines the NoMatch property. If it's True, the program displays a message. If a record matching the criteria is found, the Data control is automatically repositioned at this record.

The code of the GenerateSQL() function extracts the text from the txtsearchValue textbox, appends it to the selected field, and returns a string that is used as an argument with the Find methods. Most of the application's code handles potential errors. All the work is done by the GenerateSQL() function, which prepares the search criteria, and it's shown next.

Code 17.5:   **The GenerateSQL() Function**

```
Private Function GenerateSQL() As String
    GenerateSQL = cmbFields.Text & " " & txtsearchValue
End Function
```

Understanding Relational Concepts

The databases described and used so far are *relational* because they are based on relations among the tables. The foundation of a relational database system is to break the data into multiple tables that are related by common information (keys).

Suppose you are designing a database for storing invoices. This database should have a table with customer names, product names, and prices and, of course, a table for the invoices. Each invoice that is issued to a customer contains a number of products. Instead of storing product names and customer names in the invoice, you store numbers that uniquely identify the customers and the products. These numbers are the *keys* that connect rows in one table to rows in another table. The keys establish relationships among the tables and make it possible to break the information into separate tables and avoid duplicating information.

> **NOTE** The relational database model was created in 1970 by Dr. E. F. Codd of IBM, who also created the query language that became SQL.

Let's look at a few basic concepts of the relational model, and then we'll develop some applications to demonstrate these principles.

The Primary Key

In a relational database system, each record has a unique identifier that is used to indicate the record and to relate it to other records in other tables. Often, a close inspection of your data will reveal an existing characteristic that makes each record unique; frequently, this can become the primary key. This type of primary key is called *composite*. For example, in an employees database, an employee's Social Security number is a composite primary key.

When there is not an apparent field or set of fields that can be used to form a composite primary key, Visual Basic's database management system (the JET engine, as it's known) can automatically generate a unique numeric key for each record. This type of key is made by adding a field to your table and setting it to the AutoNumber field type. An *AutoNumber* field automatically increases by increments of one whenever a new record is added. This ensures that the key is unique, although the key may not necessarily mean anything. As long as all tables refer to the same record with the same key, the key need not be meaningful. Sometimes an auto-numbered primary key can be made to fit a business purpose, for example, using an auto-numbered field for an invoice number.

Regardless of the type of primary key, it is wise to *always* make the primary key of a table a field of the type Long (a standard Visual Basic data type, as explained in Chapter 3). By doing so, you greatly simplify design of other tables.

Foreign Key

A field (column) in a table that stores a value and relates the value to another table is called a *foreign key*. For example, a field in an Invoices table that stores the customer number is a foreign key. The same value in the Customers table is the primary key. A foreign key should be of the same type as the primary key of the table to which it is relating.

Indices

Indices are structures that determine the order of the records in a table. Normally, data aren't maintained in any special order in the table. In most practical situations, though, you want to access them in a specific order. When you print a list of customers's names, you want them in alphabetic order. If you print mailing labels, you probably want the labels in ZIP code order. In general, the type of processing you want to perform determines the order in which a table's rows should be furnished, and it is common for a table to be furnished in different orders for different operations.

Rearranging the rows of a table each time the application needs them in a different order is out of the question. This would take too much time. The solution is to maintain small tables, called *indices*, that dictate the order in which records will be read from the table. The index file doesn't contain any of the information that appears in the table itself. It contains only the numbers that determine the order of the records.

Suppose that the fifth record in a table should appear first when the table's rows are requested in alphabetic order. The first element of the index file contains the value 5, so when the database supplies the rows of the specific table, it retrieves the fifth element first.

NOTE In Chapter 5, we looked at an application that used the List's ItemData property to maintain sorted data with the help of a ListBox control. The index files are similar to the elements of the ItemData property.

A table can have more than a single index. The indices of all tables in a database are maintained by the JET engine, and you need not do anything more than specify the fields on which the index will be based.

When Shouldn't I Index?

When a record is updated, the indices must be updated as well. This obviously increases the amount of time needed to update a record. Indices also increase the amount of storage space and consequently increase both the time and media needed for routine backups.

So, even though maintaining multiple indices for each table, just in case, sounds like a good idea, there's a performance penalty for the index files, and you should specify additional indices only as needed for the proper operation of the database. Too many indices, especially with very large tables that must be updated frequently, will decrease performance.

Using the Visual Data Manager

The Visual Data Manager is a Visual Basic tool for designing databases. Although it's rather crude, you can use the Visual Data Manager to create and modify tables, to implement security, and to experiment with SQL. When you open an existing database, the Visual Data Manager displays a database window listing the tables and properties of that database. Figure 17.7 shows the Visual Data Manager window with the BIBLIO database open in design mode. We'll look at the structure of the BIBLIO database shortly, but first let's explore the basic operations of the Visual Data Manager application.

FIGURE 17.7:

Examining and modifying a database's structure with the Visual Data Manager

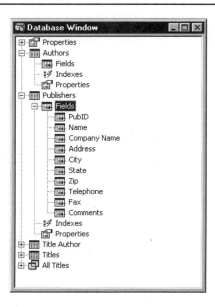

BIBLIO
C:\Program Files\Microsoft
VISUAL STUDIO\VB98

To create new tables, right-click in the database window to open the shortcut menu and select New Table. In the Table Structure dialog box that appears, create your fields.

Each time you add a new field to the table by clicking the Add Field button, the Add Field dialog box opens, as shown in Figure 17.8.

FIGURE 17.8:

Adding tables to a database and fields to tables with the Visual Data Manager

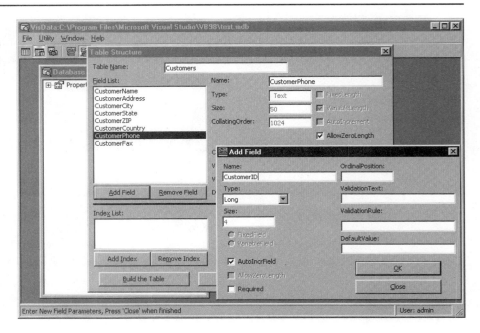

The Add Field dialog box has the options shown in Table 17.5. Some of the options are disabled in the figure and may not be readable. Follow the steps outlined to open the Add Field dialog box and see all the options on it.

TABLE 17.5: The Options in the Add Field Dialog Box

Option	What It Is
Name	The name of the field
OrdinalPosition	The position of the field within the field roster
Type	The field type. A field can have the usual types of any variable, plus two additional types: Binary and Memo. Binary fields store binary data, such as sounds and images. Memo fields store long segments of text. The size of Memo fields is not specified during the design of the database. (Text fields have a predetermined length for efficiency.)

Continued on next page

TABLE 17.5 CONTINUED: The Options in the Add Field Dialog Box

Option	What It Is
ValidationText	The text to be displayed if an attempt is made to place invalid data into the field
Size	The field's size in bytes
FixedField	The field must have a fixed length.
VariableField	The field can have variable length.
ValidationRule	Simple rules used to validate the values entered for the field
DefaultValue	The initial value for the field whenever a record is created
AutoIncrField	If a field is going to be used as a key, you can set its type to Long and check this box. Each time a new record is added to the table, this field is assigned a value, which is plus one the value of the same field in the last record.
AllowZeroLength	Check this box if a blank string is a valid value for the field.
Required	Check this box if the field can't be omitted. In a table with invoices, for example, the customer ID is a required field and so is the date.

Specifying Indices with the Visual Data Manager

You can also use the Visual Data Manager to manage indices within a database. At the bottom of the database window is a list of the indices currently in the database. Click the Add Index button to open the Add Index To dialog box, shown in Figure 17.9. The Add Index To dialog box has the options listed in Table 17.6.

FIGURE 17.9:

The Add Index To dialog box

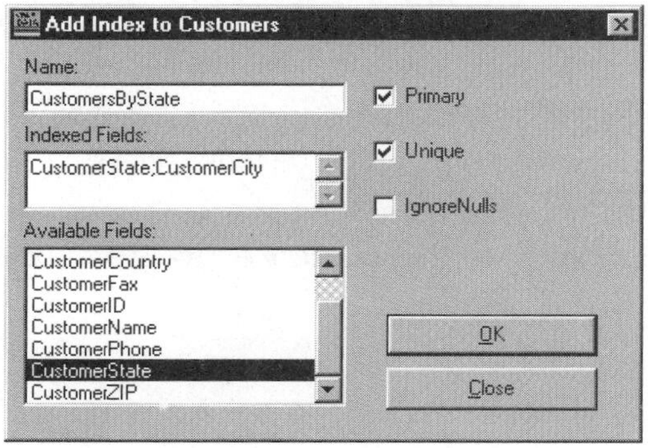

TABLE 17.6:   The Options in the Add Index To Dialog Box

OPTION	WHAT IT DOES
Name	The name of the index. As a programmer, you will only use the name of the index when you are programming a Table type of RecordSet. In query situations, the Rush-More technology automatically uses index information to optimize queries.
Indexed Fields	A list of the fields on which the table is indexed, separated by semicolons
Available Fields	A list box of the available fields; clicking one will add it to the list of index fields
Primary	Check this box to indicate whether the index's field should be considered the primary key for the table.
Unique	Check this box if you want to force unique values for the field. If you are indexing the Customers table on the customer's name field, this index need not be unique. There can be two customers with the same name. The index based on the customer's ID, though, must be unique. Two customers can't have the same key, even if they have the same name.
IgnoreNulls	This property indicates whether any of the fields used in the index can contain a Null value. If it's set to False and the Required property is True, a runtime error is generated if the corresponding field is Null.

NOTE   Null is a special value; it's described in Chapter 3. A field is Null if it hasn't been initialized (in other words, if it contains nothing). It's common to test field values against the Null value before using them in operations.

Entering Data with the Visual Data Manager

In addition, you can use the Visual Data Manager for data entry. Double-clicking the name of a table in the Database window opens the table in data entry mode, as shown in Figure 17.10, and you can edit, add, and delete records.

You will learn how to implement these operations from within your code in the following sections, but first we must look at the basic concepts of database design by exploring the structure of the BIBLIO database.

FIGURE 17.10:

You can also use the Visual Data Manager for data entry.

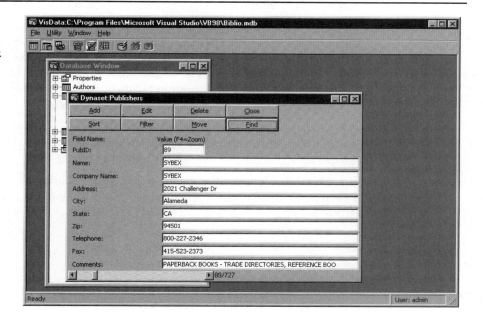

The Structure of the BIBLIO Database

One of the two sample databases that comes with Visual Basic is called BIBLIO. The BIBLIO database has a simple structure, almost trivial, but it demonstrates many of the topics we have covered so far. You can open the BIBLIO database with the Visual Data Manager and explore its structure.

The BIBLIO database contains book titles, authors, and publishers, and it's made up of four tables, as shown in Figure 17.11. Instead of showing the names of the fields of each table, this figure shows some of the data they contain, and it shows only the fields needed to demonstrate the relationships among the tables. The field names are displayed as column headings.

FIGURE 17.11:

The structure of the BIBLIO database

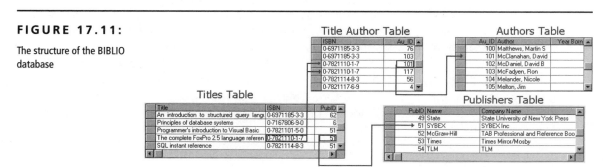

The first rule in database design is to avoid data duplication. Storing author names along with the titles would violate this rule because an author may have written more than one book. In this case, you would have to repeat the same author name in more than one row of the Titles table. Author names are stored in a separate table, the Authors table. The same is true for publishers. Since each publisher appears in many books, you shouldn't store information about publishers in the Titles table. Why repeat the publisher's address with each title?

So far, we have established the reasons for the presence of three tables in the database. But the BIBLIO database has a fourth table. Each book can have more than one author, and an author's name may appear with more than a single title. Think about this for a moment. Storing multiple author names, even author IDs, for each title would require a field for each author. This field would be analogous to the PubID field, but because a book might have multiple authors, you would have to provide a number of fields for storing Author IDs (AuthorID1, AuthorID2, and so on). It is clear that authors can't be handled like publishers.

The Title Author table sits between the Titles and Authors tables and connects them with a pair of fields, which are the Title's ISBN and the Author's ID. When you want to see a specific title's author, you will do the following:

1. Locate the desired title in the Titles table.

2. Read the Title's ISBN and use it as a key to locate the matching row(s) in the Title Author table.

3. For each of the matching rows in the Title Author table, read the author's ID and use it as a key to locate the author's name in the Authors table.

If you are not familiar with database programming, this procedure may sound complicated, but it isn't (perhaps you should just get used to it). Later in this chapter, you'll see two ways to search for specific records with keys. The technique just described won't work efficiently unless there's a quick way to locate a record based on the value of a specific field. And this can be accomplished with the proper indexing of the tables.

As you can see, the indices are an essential part of database design. The Title Author table, for example, must be indexed on the ISBN field. If you want to be able to search in the opposite direction (given an author's name, locate the books on which this name appears), you should also index the Title Author table on the AuID field. Obviously, the Authors table must be indexed on the AuID field, since the information in the Title Author table is the author's ID, not their name. The Publishers table must be indexed on the PubID field so that you can go quickly from a title to its publisher.

Validating Data

You have seen in the first example of this chapter that the Data control can also be used for editing records. Database applications, however, should have the means to validate user input before attempting to save data to the database. The Data control provides a few events and methods that let you validate the input before committing it to the database.

The Validate Event

The validation of input takes place in the Data control's *Validate* event, whose declaration is as follows:

```
Private Sub object_Validate (action As Integer, save As Integer)
```

The *action* entry is an integer indicating the operation that caused this event to occur, and it can have one of the values shown in Table 17.7.

TABLE 17.7:   The Values of the *Action* Argument of the Validate Event

CONSTANT	VALUE	DESCRIPTION
vbDataActionCancel	0	Cancel the operation when the Sub exits
vbDataActionMoveFirst	1	MoveFirst method
vbDataActionMovePrevious	2	MovePrevious method
vbDataActionMoveNext	3	MoveNext method
vbDataActionMoveLast	4	MoveLast method
vbDataActionAddNew	5	AddNew method
vbDataActionUpdate	6	Update operation (not UpdateRecord)
vbDataActionDelete	7	Delete method
vbDataActionFind	8	Find method
vbDataActionBookmark	9	The Bookmark property has been set
vbDataActionClose	10	The Close method
vbDataActionUnload	11	The Form is being unloaded

The value *vbDataActionCancel* can be set from within code to cancel the operation that triggered the Validate event. For example, if the user changes the data on a data-bound control and then clicks the Move Next button of the control, you can reject the changes from within your code and cancel the Move Next operation.

The *save* argument is a Boolean expression specifying whether bound data has changed. You can set this argument to False to reject the changes.

The Error Event

Another useful event in data validation operations is the Error event. When you update records in a database, the JET engine ensures that the data entered don't invalidate the rules incorporated in the design of the database. For example, if an index requires that a specific field be unique, it won't update the record if the value entered has already been used. If a field exceeds its maximum length, the changes will also be rejected. In other words, the JET engine performs some data validation on its own. It also performs any validation steps you specified in the Validation Rule field, in each table's design.

If the data violates rules specified in the design of the database, a runtime error is generated. Before the error message is displayed, the Error event is generated. You can find the condition that generated the error and handle it from within your code.

The declaration of the Error event is as follows:

```
Sub Error (dataerr As Integer, response As Integer)
```

The *dataerr* entry is the error number, and *response* is an integer that you can set from within the event to specify how the error will be handled. The *response* argument can take one of the values shown in Table 17.8. You must handle the error from within the Error event and then set the *response* argument to 0 to prevent the runtime error.

TABLE 17.8: The Values of the Response Argument of the Error Event

CONSTANT	VALUE	DESCRIPTION
vbDataErrContinue	0	Continue
vbDataErrDisplay	1	(Default) Display the error message

Entering Data

The Data control is a great tool for browsing tables and editing their contents, but how about entering new information or deleting existing records? These actions require a few lines of code. Nothing extreme, but you can't rely on the no-code approach of the Data control for data entry. To write data entry applications, you use the following methods:

- **AddNew** appends a record to the table.
- **Delete** deletes the current record.
- **Update** writes the current record to the database.
- **Refresh** reloads the data from the database (refreshes the RecordSet).

> **NOTE** It is also possible to use the Data control for data entry. To do so, set the EOF action of the Data control to 2–Add New. Every time the user is at the last record and clicks the Next button, the Data control displays a new empty record, which can be filled and written to the database. The method is not intuitive (to say the least), and it doesn't reflect the way in which professional data entry applications are written.

AddNew   To add a new record to a table, you call the AddNew method of the control's RecordSet (it must be a Table type of RecordSet). A new blank record is appended at the end of the RecordSet, and the Data control is positioned at this record. The user can now enter data in the data-bound controls.

Update, Refresh   When the user signals an intention to commit the new record to the database (by clicking OK or moving to a new record), you call the Update method of the control's RecordSet. To reject the data, call the Refresh method, which refreshes the RecordSet by reading it from the database. Since the newly appended record hasn't been committed to the database, it is lost when the RecordSet is refreshed.

Delete   To delete a record, call the Delete method of the control's RecordSet. The current record is removed from the RecordSet, but only after the JET engine checks any relations that might be affected. If the database enforces certain references, you won't be able to remove a record that's referenced by another one. I'm not going to discuss referential integrity at length in this book, but let's see how the JET engine maintains the integrity of the references in a database.

Referential Integrity

The NWIND database, which also comes with Visual Basic, enforces the integrity of certain relations. To see how this works, follow these steps:

1. Using the Visual Data Manager, open the NWIND database, and double-click the Orders table, which contains all the invoices.

2. Select an invoice and make a note of the customer ID to which the invoice was issued.

3. Close this table, and double-click the name of the Customers table to open it in data entry mode.

4. Select the customer whose ID appeared in the invoice, and click Delete. The JET engine displays the error message shown in Figure 17.12.

FIGURE 17.12:

Some relations can be enforced by the JET engine itself.

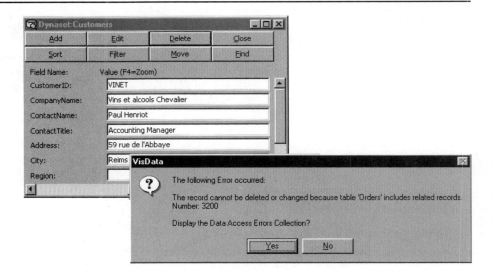

This error message tells you that the customer you are trying to delete is referenced in another table and can't be removed.

If a relation is important for the integrity of the database, you can ask the JET engine to enforce it. Enforcing referential integrity is one of the most important features of a database management system. Without it, your program would have to ensure that important relations are enforced (not a simple task).

Although you can enforce certain references from within your code, the best way to implement this feature is by incorporating referential integrity in the database itself. You can't use the Visual Data Manager for this purpose, but if you use a more advanced tool for designing databases, such as Microsoft Access, you can specify which relations must be enforced by the system, and this information is stored in the database itself.

VB6 at Work: The Data Entry Project

Now we are ready to build a real data entry application with add and delete features, as shown in Figure 17.13. When the user clicks the Add Record button, the application calls the AddNew method and hides the two buttons on the Form. In their place, it displays the usual OK and Cancel buttons. The user can commit the new record to the database by clicking OK or reject it by clicking Cancel. In either case, the OK and Cancel buttons are hidden, and the Add Record and Delete Record buttons are displayed again.

FIGURE 17.13:

The Data Entry application demonstrates the basic data entry methods of the Data control.

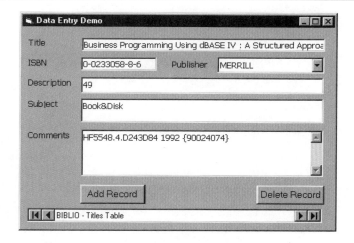

The Form of the Data Entry application contains a Data control, whose RecordSet is the Titles table of the BIBLIO database. The textboxes are all bound to the Data control, and they display the Title, ISBN, Description, Subject, and Comments fields of the table.

As you recall from the discussion of the structure of the BIBLIO database, each record in the Titles table has a key that links the title to a publisher. Instead of providing a textbox in which the user can type the ID of the title's publisher, we provide a CombobBox control with the names of all publishers; the user can select one of the publishers by name. This control isn't the usual Visual Basic CombobBox control. It's a data-bound CombobBox control, and we will look at it in the section "Advanced Data-Bound Controls," later in the chapter.

To build this application, follow these steps:

1. Add a Data control to the Form and set its DatabaseName property to the path of the BIBLIO database and its RecordSource property to the Titles table.

2. Place the five textboxes you see on the Form in Figure 17.13 and bind them to the Data1 Data control. Set each text box's DataField property to the appropriate field of the table.

3. Now, create four Command buttons and set their Name and Caption properties as shown in Table 17.9.

TABLE 17.9: The Name and Caption Properties for the Command Buttons

CAPTION	NAME
Add Record	AddBttn
Delete Record	DelBttn
OK	OKBttn
Cancel	CancelBttn

4. Position the buttons on the Form so that the OK and Add Record buttons coincide and so that the Cancel and Delete buttons coincide.

Now you are ready to program the application.

Code 17.6:   **The Add Button's Click Event**

```
Private Sub AddBttn_Click()
    HideButtons
    Data1.Recordset.AddNew
End Sub
```

The HideButtons subroutine hides the Add Record and Delete Record buttons and displays the other two buttons. The AddNew button appends a new blank record at the end of the RecordSet and repositions the Data control at this record. The user can enter new data in the TextBox controls and then click OK to write the changes to the database.

Code 17.7: **The OK Button's Click Event**

```
Private Sub OKBttn_Click()
On Error GoTo CancelUpdate
    Data1.Recordset.Update
    ShowButtons
    Exit Sub

CancelUpdate:
    MsgBox Err.Description
    Data1.Recordset.CancelUpdate
    ShowButtons
End Sub
```

The Update method commits the temporary record to the database. The Show-Buttons subroutine then hides the OK and Cancel buttons and displays the other two buttons.

WARNING If an error occurs while the database is being updated (an error triggered most likely by the JET engine), the operation must be canceled. Because the Update method has been called already, it's too late to call the Refresh method. Instead, you must call the *CancelUpdate* method.

The Cancel button deletes the temporary record (the one displayed) by calling the Refresh method and then hides the OK and Cancel buttons.

Code 17.8: **The Cancel Button's Click Event**

```
Private Sub CancelBttn_Click()
    Data1.Refresh
    Data1.Recordset.FindFirst "Isbn='" & prevISBN & "'"
    ShowButtons
End Sub
```

If you cancel an add operation, you'll be brought back to the first record in the table (that's what happens when you refresh a RecordSet). To return to the last record displayed, the code stores the record's ISBN field in the variable *prevISBN*. This action takes place when the Add button is clicked. If the user cancels the operation, the program searches for the record with the same ISBN and displays it again.

Code 17.9: **The Delete Button's Click Event**

```
Private Sub DelBttn_Click()
On Error Resume Next

    Data1.Recordset.Delete
    If Not Data1.Recordset.EOF Then
        Data1.Recordset.MoveNext
    ElseIf Not Data1.Recordset.BOF Then
        Data1.Recordset.MovePrevious
    Else
        MsgBox "This was the last record in the table"
    End If
End Sub
```

The Delete method deletes the current record. After a delete operation, the RecordSet isn't moved to another record automatically. Instead, it remains on the deleted record until a Move button is pressed. The code moves to the next record, unless the record deleted was the last one, in which case it moves to the previous record. If the deleted record was the only record in the table, the program displays a message and remains on the current record.

The ShowButtons and HideButtons subroutines manipulate the Visible properties of the buttons. In addition, they hide and display the Data control so that the user can end a data entry operation with only the OK or Cancel button.

Code 17.10: **The ShowButtons Subroutine**

```
Sub ShowButtons()

    AddBttn.Visible = True
    DelBttn.Visible = True
    OKBttn.Visible = False
    CancelBttn.Visible = False
    Data1.Visible = True

End Sub
```

If you open the Data Entry application with Visual Basic, you will find a few more interesting subroutines. In the Data control's Error event, for example, the program displays the error message and cancels the update operation. This may happen if the user edits the current record and enters invalid information in one of the fields.

Code 17.11:	The Data Control's Error Event

```
Private Sub Data1_Error(DataErr As Integer, Response As Integer)
    MsgBox Err.Description
    Response = 0
    Data1.Recordset.CancelUpdate
End Sub
```

In the Data control's Validate event, the program finds out whether any data-bound control has been changed, and if so, it prompts the user as to whether it should save the changes to the table.

Code 17.12:	The Validate Event

```
Private Sub Data1_Validate(Action As Integer, Save As Integer)
Dim reply

    If txtTitle.DataChanged Or txtISBN.DataChanged Or _
       txtDescription.DataChanged Or txtSubject.DataChanged _
       Or txtComments.DataChanged Then
        reply = MsgBox("Record has been changed. Save?", vbYesNo)
        If reply = vbNo Then
            Save = False
        End If
    End If
End Sub
```

Typically, the code behind the Validate event takes into consideration the value of the *Action* argument and reacts according to the action that caused the error.

Accessing Fields in RecordSets

The data-bound controls can display the fields of the current record in the Record-Set of a Data control, but you must also be able to access the fields' values from within the application. The field values can be accessed via the Fields object of the RecordSet. The following expression:

```
recordset.Fields
```

represents the fields (columns) of the RecordSet. The *recordset* variable represents a RecordSet (it could be a Data control's RecordSet property, Data1.RecordSet, or a *RecordSet* variable).

You access individual fields through the field's name or through the field's ordinal position in the table. If the Data1 Data control is connected to the Titles table of the BIBLIO database, you can access the Title field of the current record with either of the following statements:

```
bookTitle = Data1.Recordset.Fields(0)
bookTitle = Data1.Recordset.Fields("Title")
```

Two more properties of interest are the *RecordCount* property of the RecordSet object (which returns the number of records in the RecordSet) and the *Count* property of the Fields object (which returns the number of fields in the RecordSet's row). These two properties are actually the dimensions of the RecordSet. The number of rows in the RecordSet of the Data1 Data control is:

```
Data1.RecordSet.RecordCount
```

and the number of columns in the same RecordSet is:

```
Data1.RecordSet.Fields.Count
```

VB6 at Work: Scanning a RecordSet

Let's develop a short application to demonstrate how you can scan the records in a RecordSet and process their fields. The processing is quite trivial: We will place the rows of a RecordSet on a ListBox control. However, the code demonstrates how to scan a RecordSet and extract specific fields.

To build this application, follow these steps:

1. Start a new project and place a ListBox control and a Data control on it, as shown in Figure 17.14.

FIGURE 17.14:

This application loads the fields of a RecordSet to a ListBox control.

2. Set the Data control's Visible property to False. You can't use the Data control to navigate through the RecordSet, since all the records will be in the ListBox control.

3. Set the DatabaseName and RecordSource properties of the Data control to any table of the BIBLIO or NWIND database.

4. Now, enter the following code in the Form's Load event:

```
Private Sub Form_Load()
Dim i As Integer

    Data1.Refresh
    Data1.Recordset.MoveLast
    Data1.Recordset.MoveFirst
    For i = 1 To Data1.Recordset.RecordCount
        List1.AddItem Data1.Recordset.Fields(1)
        Data1.Recordset.MoveNext
    Next
End Sub
```

TIP

If you run this application, the ListBox control will be populated with the entries of the second field in the table. This code segment is meant to be used in a larger application and not on its own, of course. In the section "Advanced Data-Bound Controls," later in this chapter, you will learn about the data-bound ListBox control, which can be populated automatically. The Refresh method causes the Data control to read the RecordSet from the database, and you should call it before using the Data control's properties. When a RecordSet is first created or refreshed, it doesn't know how many records it has. Actually, it thinks it has one record (the first one). If the user clicks the Next button, the RecordSet thinks it has two records, because it hasn't seen the other ones yet. To find out the number of records, you must visit the last record with the MoveLast method. After calling this method, you can use the RecordCount property to find out the number of rows in the RecordSet.

Seek   The Seek method of the RecordSet object can instantly locate a record in a table based on the value of an index field. The Seek method is extremely fast because it uses the index of a table, and in effect, locates an item in a sorted list. The Seek method has the following syntax:

```
Seek operator, key
```

The *operator* argument is one of the following relational operators:

- = (equal)

- > (greater than)

- < (less than)

- >= (greater or equal)

- <= (less or equal)

The *key* argument is the value to be compared with the key field of the index. If the index is made up of a single field, *key* is a single value. If the index is made up of multiple fields, the *key* argument may contain multiple values, separated by commas.

For example, if the Customers table is indexed according to its State field, you can seek the first customer in California with the following statement:

```
Data1.Recordset.Seek "=", "CA"
```

The Seek method is much faster than the Find method, but it's not as flexible. If you frequently need to locate records based on a specific field's value, create an index on this field and use the Seek method. You can use the Find method to perform all types of searches involving multiple fields and the LIKE operator, but it's not nearly as fast as the Seek method.

VB6 at Work: The ManyTblsProject

The ManyTbls application (see Figure 17.15) demonstrates the use of the Seek method to quickly locate records based on their primary keys. This application combines all the tables in the BIBLIO database to display the titles, along with their authors, publishers, and related data (comments and descriptions).

FIGURE 17.15:

The ManyTbls application displays all the titles in the BIBLIO database, along with their authors and publishers, which are stored in different tables.

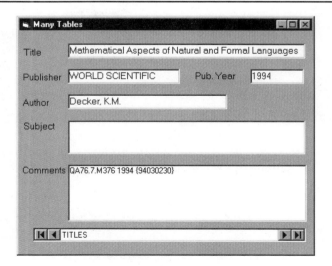

NOTE

If you are familiar with SQL, you have already realized that this application can be implemented without resorting to the Seek method. In essence, you don't need to write a single line of code, just an SQL statement. This example was meant to demonstrate the use of the Seek method. We will revise the ManyTbls application later in the chapter, and you will see how to implement it with a single SQL statement.

As the user navigates through the titles with the navigation buttons of the TITLES Data control, the program displays the next or previous title in the first textbox and the book's Comments and Description fields in their corresponding textboxes. These textboxes are bound directly to the Data control on the Form.

To display the publisher of the title, the application uses the PubID field of the Titles table as a key to the Publishers table, where it locates (using the Seek method) the record with the same PubID.

To display the author of the title, the application uses the ISBN field to locate the matching record in the Title Author table. When the record that corresponds to the current title is found, the program uses the Au_ID field as a key to the Authors table to locate the primary author's name.

These actions must take place within the Data control's *Reposition* event, which is triggered every time the user clicks one of the navigation buttons to move to another record in the Titles table. The application uses all four tables in the database, and you must therefore use four RecordSets, one for each table. The Form of the application at design time contains four Data controls, as shown in Figure 17.16, but only one of them is visible at runtime.

FIGURE 17.16:

The ManyTbls application at design time

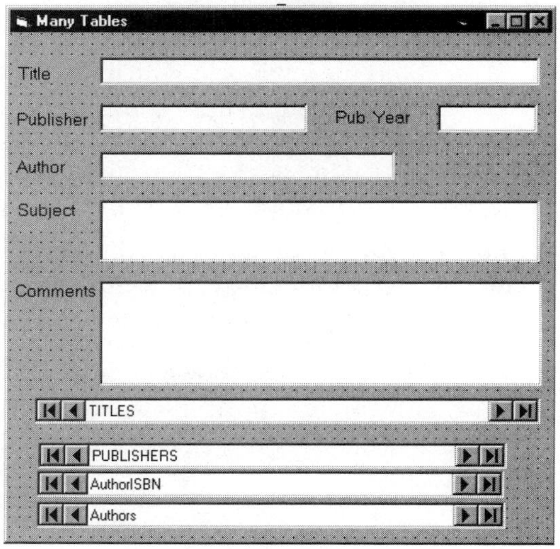

To design the ManyTbls application, follow these steps:

1. Start a new project and place the Label and TextBox controls you see in Figure 17.16.

2. Place four Data controls on the Form: TITLES, PUBLISHERS, AUTHORISBN, and AUTHORS. Set their DatabaseName property to the path of the BIBLIO database.

3. Each Data control sees a different table of the database, so you must set the RecordSource property of each control according to Table 17.10.

TABLE 17.10: The RecordSource Settings for the Data Control on the ManyTbls Form

DATA CONTROL NAME	RECORDSOURCE SETTING
TITLES	Titles
PUBLISHERS	Publishers
AUTHORISBN	Title Author
AUTHORS	Authors

4. Now bind the textboxes to the corresponding fields of the Data controls on the Form.

   - Bind the textbox in which the title is displayed to the Title field of the TITLES Data control.

   - Bind the textbox in which the publisher is displayed to the Publisher field of the PUBLISHERS Data control.

   - Bind the textbox in which the author is displayed to the Author field of the AUTHORS Data control.

Bind the remaining textboxes to the corresponding fields of the proper Data control. You can open the ManyTbls application in Visual Basic's IDE and examine how the various data-bound controls are bound to the Data controls. At this point, you can combine any title with any author and any publisher because the three Data controls are not connected and can be positioned at will in the corresponding tables.

We are going to use the Seek method of the Data control to connect the controls, so we must use the primary indices of the tables. This must take place when the Form is loaded.

5.   Enter the following code in the Form's Load event:

```
Private Sub Form_Load()

    PUBLISHERS.Refresh
    AUTHORISBN.Refresh
    AUTHORS.Refresh

    PUBLISHERS.Recordset.Index = "PrimaryKey"
    AUTHORISBN.Recordset.Index = "ISBN"
    AUTHORS.Recordset.Index = "PrimaryKey"

End Sub
```

To open an index file for a Table RecordSet, you must assign the name of the index to the Index property of the RecordSet. Once the Index property has been set, all Seek operations on the RecordSet will use this index.

6.   Enter the following code in the TITLES Data control's Reposition event:

```
Private Sub TITLES_Reposition()

    PUBLISHERS.Recordset.Seek "=", _
            TITLES.Recordset.Fields("PubID")
    If PUBLISHERS.Recordset.NoMatch Then _
            lblPublisher.Caption = "***"
    AUTHORISBN.Recordset.Seek "=", _
            TITLES.Recordset.Fields("ISBN")
    If AUTHORISBN.Recordset.NoMatch Then
        lblAuthor.Caption = "***"
        Exit Sub
    End If
    AUTHORS.Recordset.Seek "=", _
        AUTHORISBN.Recordset.Fields("Au_ID")

End Sub
```

All the action takes place in the Reposition event. Each time the user repositions the Data control in the RecordSet, the program does the following:

1.   It uses the Seek method on the PUBLISHERS RecordSet to locate the record whose PubID field matches the PubID field of the title displayed.

2.   If no such record exists, it prints asterisks in the textbox where the publisher's name would normally appear. If a matching record is found, the program doesn't do anything. The Seek method repositions the PUBLISHERS Data

control to the row of the Publishers table with the title's publisher, and the corresponding data-bound textbox is updated automatically.

3. The program then locates the record of the Title Author table whose ISBN field is the same as the current book's ISBN. If no such record exists, it prints asterisks and exits the subroutine. If a matching record is found, its Au_ID field becomes the key for the last seek operation, which locates the record in the AUTHORS table, whose Au_ID field matches the Au_ID field located in the Title Author table.

The Seek method is fast; the fields on the Form are updated instantly. Even with large files, this approach works well and doesn't introduce any significant delays. Notice that you can seek records in a RecordSet based on more than one index. Each Seek operation must be performed with a specific index, but you can change the current index by setting the Index property of the RecordSet to another value.

Displaying Multiple Authors

You may have noticed that this program displays only the primary author of each title. In an application such as this, you would probably have to display all the authors for each title.

You could, for example, add the author names in a ComboBox or ListBox control. You can easily adjust the program to display all author names if you consider that the second, third, and other authors of any title will appear right after the first matching record in the Title Author table. You can issue the MoveNext method on the AUTHORISBN RecordSet, and if its ISBN is the same as the current book's ISBN, then the book has another author and you can display it. If the ISBN field is different, the book has no more authors.

The Move methods of a RecordSet take into consideration the index of the RecordSet. For example, issuing the MoveNext method on a RecordSet with an index takes you to the next record in the index.

An Introduction to SQL

SQL, or *Structured Query Language*, is a nearly universal language used for database management. SQL is a *declarative language*, as opposed to a procedural language such as Visual Basic. In a declarative language, you specify *what* you want, not *how* to do it. You do not need to tell SQL *how* to access a database; you only need to tell it what you *want* from the database. In a procedural language, you must tell the language to some degree *how* to accomplish a given task.

Procedural versus Declarative is the primary dividing line between a third-generation language, such as Visual Basic, and a fourth-generation language, such as SQL. Whether SQL is a fourth-generation language is a tricky question. It was designed in the 1970s by Dr. E. F. Codd at IBM. At that time, languages were not even classified by generations.

We'll start by examining the structure of SQL statements and the keywords used in them, and then we'll look at numerous examples of SQL statements and develop a tool for retrieving data from databases with SQL statements.

You can use the SQLExec application, discussed later in this chapter, to experiment with SQL statements. The SQLExec application lets you select a database, execute SQL statements, and view the results (which is a RecordSet) on a grid.

The Format of SQL Statements

There are SQL statements for all types of operations you can perform on a database. You can use SQL statements to create a new database and to create and add tables and indices to it. You can use other SQL statements to update a database. SQL is a complete database manipulation language, but the most common use of SQL is to retrieve data from databases. Retrieving data from a database is called *querying* the database, and the SQL statements for querying databases are called *Select* statements, because they begin with the SELECT verb.

The general format of a Select SQL statement is:

```
SELECT (field list) FROM (table list) WHERE (expression)
```

> **NOTE**
>
> The SQL keywords in this book appear in uppercase, but SQL is not case-sensitive. Using uppercase is a matter of style. It helps readers who are not familiar with SQL to spot the keywords and understand the components of a complicated SQL statement.

(field list)

This part of the statement is a list of fields to be included in the query, separated by commas. If the name of an element (field or table) contains a space, you must enclose the name in square brackets ([]). For example, to include the Customer Name field in a query, you would enter **[Customer Name]**.

Prefix the full name of each field with the name of the table to which it belongs. This notation ensures that field names are unique, even if multiple tables have fields with the same name. For example, the full name of the Total field in the Customer Orders table is [Customer Orders].Total. If the field name Total doesn't appear in any other table, you can omit the table's name and refer to it as Total.

The output of a Select query contains the rows that match the criteria, plus a row of headers. The headers are the names of the fields by default. When you display the results of a query on a data-bound Grid control, the names of the fields are displayed as headers. To change the headers, use the AS keyword after the field name. This addition can be handy when a field name that is appropriate in the context of a table would be unclear from the context of a query consisting of several tables or would clash with the field name in another table involved in the query. For example, if you have a Total field in the Customer Orders table, you can display the header Order Total for this field with the following syntax:

```
[Customer Orders].[Total] AS [Order Total]
```

To select all the fields in a table, you can use the asterisk (*) instead of entering all the field names. For example, the following statement selects all the fields in the Orders table: SELECT * FROM Orders.

(table list)

This part of the statement is a list of all the tables on which the query is based. To retrieve fields from multiple tables, separate the field names with a comma. If your SQL statement is based on more than one table, it's a good idea to prefix the field names with the name of the table to which they belong.

When you select fields from multiple tables, you must tell the SQL engine how to combine the tables. If you specify only the names of the tables, the result of the query will contain all possible combinations of the fields in each table. To combine fields from multiple tables, you must create a so-called *join*, which is a fundamental concept in SQL Select statements that we will look at shortly.

(expression)

This part of the statement is a logical expression that is used to filter the data and report back a subset of the RecordSet. You can use most Visual Basic built-in functions and operators to form this expression as well as the following SQL-specific operators.

field_name BETWEEN value1 AND value2   Only rows in which the *field_name* is between *value1* and *value2* are returned. See the entry #date# for an example.

field_name IN(value1, value2, ...)   Only rows in which *field_name* is one of the values listed in parentheses are returned. You can specify any number of list elements inside the parentheses. The following statement retrieves customer records from certain cities:

```
SELECT Customers.CompanyName, Customers.ContactTitle, Customers.City,
Customers.Country  FROM Customers WHERE
```

```
UCase(customers.city) IN("BERLIN", "LONDON", "BERN", "PARIS")
ORDER BY Customers.Country
```

#date#   This operator specifies dates within an expression. Dates are always specified using the U.S. system of month/day/year. The following SQL statement retrieves all the orders placed in 1994 from the NWIND database:

```
SELECT Orders.ShipName, Orders.OrderDate , Orders.CustomerID
FROM Orders WHERE OrderDate BETWEEN #1/1/94# AND #12/31/94#
```

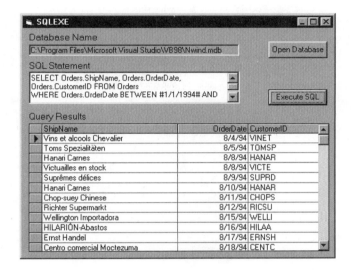

LIKE   This operator is one of the more powerful and complex of the SQL operators, and you can use it to select rows with a pattern string. To build the expression, use the special characters in Table 17.11.

TABLE 17.11: Special Characters for Use with the LIKE Operator

SYMBOL	USAGE	EXAMPLE
*	Any group of characters	Joh* locates John, Johnson, and John's.
?	Any single character	?t locates at and it.
#	Any single numeric digit	1234#67 locates 1234167, 1234267, 1234367, 1234467, and so on.
[ ]	Individual character in the brackets	[ai]t locates at and it, but not bt.
[!]	Any character *not* in the brackets	[!a]t locates it but not at.
[-]	Any character within a range	[i-k]t locates it, jt, and kt, but not at or st.

ORDER BY (field list) This operator orders the rows of the RecordSet according to the values of the specified fields. The following SQL statement creates a RecordSet of the names of all the customers in the Customers table of the NWIND database, sorted by country. Customers in the same country appear in the order of their city:

```
SELECT Customers.CompanyName, Customers.ContactName, Customers.Country,
    Customers.City FROM Customers ORDER BY Customers.Country, Customers.City
```

(The table name need not appear in front of the field names in this statement.) The results of this statement are shown below:

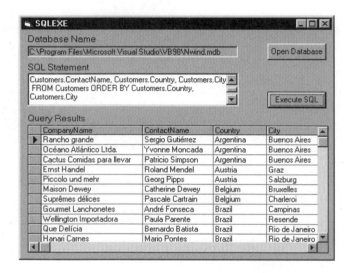

SQL Joins

Joins specify how you connect multiple tables in a query, and there are three types of joins:

- Left Outer
- Right Outer
- Inner

A *join* operation combines all the rows of one table with the rows of another table. Joins are usually followed by a condition, which determines which records in either side of the join will appear in the RecordSet.

Left Outer   This join displays all the records in the left table and only those records of the table on the right that match certain user-supplied criteria. This join has the following syntax:

```
FROM (primary table) LEFT JOIN (secondary table) ON (primary
table).(field) (comparison) (secondary table).(field)
```

In a Left Outer join, all records in the primary table are matched according to specified criteria with records from a secondary table. Records from the left table (the one whose name appears to the left of the *Left Join* keyword) are included even if they do not match any records in the secondary table.

Right Outer   This join is similar to the Left Outer join, except that all the records in the table on the right are displayed and only the matching records from the left table are displayed. This join has the following syntax:

```
FROM (secondary table) RIGHT JOIN (primary table) ON (secondary
table).(field) (comparison) (primary table).(field)
```

In a Right Outer join, all records in the primary table are matched according to specified criteria with records from a secondary table. Records from the primary table are included even if they do not match any records in the first table.

Outer joins return enormous RecordSets, and you should avoid using them. Inner joins, on the other hand, are common, and most SQL statements are built with them.

Inner   This join returns the rows of both tables involved in the operation that match according to specified criteria. The Inner join has the following syntax:

```
FROM (primary table) INNER JOIN (secondary table) ON (primary
table).(field) (comparison) (secondary table).(field)
```

Because Inner joins are so useful, we'll look at a couple of examples in detail. In their simplest format, Inner joins are similar to WHERE clauses. The following SQL statement combines records from the Titles and Publishers tables of the BIB-LIO database if their PubID fields match. It returns a RecordSet with all the titles and their publishers:

```
SELECT Titles.Title, Publishers.Name FROM Titles, Publishers
WHERE Titles.PubID = Publishers.PubID
```

You can retrieve the same RecordSet using an Inner join, as follows:

```
SELECT Titles.Title, Publishers.Name FROM Titles, Publishers, INNER
JOIN Titles ON Titles.PubID = Publishers.PubID
```

The results of this statement are shown below:

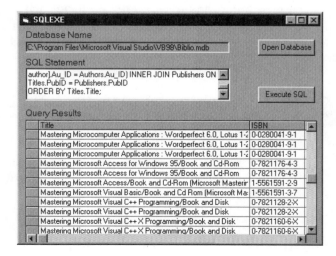

Let's look at a more complicated join operation. This time we are going to retrieve all titles along with their authors and publishers from the BIBLIO database. The following statement is quite complicated and represents a real-world situation:

```
SELECT Titles.Title, Titles.ISBN, Authors.Author, Titles.[Year.Pub-
lished], Publishers.[Company Name] FROM ((([title author] INNER JOIN
Titles ON [title author].ISBN = Titles.ISBN) INNER JOIN Authors ON
[title author].Au_ID = Authors.Au_ID) INNER JOIN Publishers ON Titles
.PubID = Publishers.PubID ORDER BY Titles.Title
```

The results of this statement are shown below:

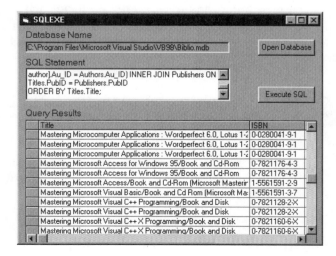

In the previous statement, brackets indicate the field names that contain spaces. Also, all field names are prefixed with the corresponding table's name, even though most field names are unique, to make the statement easier to read and understand.

The field list specifies the following fields:

- **Titles.Title**   The book's title
- **Titles.ISBN**   The book's ISBN
- **Authors.Author**   The book's author
- **Titles.[Year Published]**   The book's publication year
- **Publishers.[Company Name]**   The book's publisher

As you may recall from our discussion of the BIBLIO database, four tables are involved, and our query requires data from all tables. Actually, no data from the Title Author table are displayed in the query's results, but this table links titles and authors (via the book's ISBN), and we must use it in the SQL statement.

The fields won't come directly from any single table. Instead, they come from a series of Inner joins. The first Inner join is as follows:

```
[title author] INNER JOIN Titles ON [title author].ISBN = _
        Titles.ISBN
```

This expression extracts (and matches) each title with its author's ID if the ISBNs on both tables match. In essence, you get an author ID for each title. Let's call this expression, which represents a RecordSet, `Title-AuthorIDs`. This RecordSet is placed in parentheses and joined with another RecordSet:

```
(Title-AuthorIDs INNER JOIN Authors ON [title author].Au_ID =
Authors.Au_ID)
```

This RecordSet joins the Author IDs of the previous RecordSet with actual author names. So far, we have created a RecordSet with author names and titles. Let's call it `Titles-Author`. The last join operation joins the RecordSet that has author names and titles with the Publishers table as follows:

```
(Title-Author) INNER JOIN Publishers ON Titles.PubID = Publishers.PubID
```

This time, the publishers' IDs must match. The final RecordSet contains titles, authors, and publishers, and our data will come from it. The last keyword in this SQL statement, *ORDER BY*, determines the order in which the orders will be displayed.

Using SQL Statements

You now know the basic SQL statements, and you can extract data from a database with SQL statements using the SQLExec application (described in the section "VB6 at Work: The SQLExec Project," later in this chapter). But how can you use SQL statements in your application?

SQL statements are basically RecordSet definitions. The RecordSet property of the Data control need not be a table's name. You can be more specific by identifying certain rows of the table or combining data from more than one table. The RecordSet that the SQL statement selects from the database is assigned to the Data control, and the bound fields see the fields of this RecordSet. Let's look at a simple example.

The Data1 application, presented earlier in this chapter, displays a few fields from the Customers table in the NWIND database. The Data control's RecordSource property was set to the name of the Customers table, which you selected from a drop-down list. The list next to the name of the RecordSource property in the Properties window is a combo box, and you can also enter data in it.

Suppose you want the Data1 application to display customers from Germany only. To select part of a table, you supply the SQL statement that will create the corresponding RecordSet in the RecordSource property's field. Follow these steps:

1. Open the Data1 application and select the Data control.

2. In the Properties window, locate the RecordSource property and enter the following SQL statement (as shown in Figure 17.17):

   ```
   SELECT * FROM Customers WHERE Country = "Germany"
   ```

3. Now run the application and use the Data control's buttons to navigate through the customers of the NWIND database whose country is Germany.

FIGURE 17.17:

Set the RecordSource property to a SQL statement to retrieve a RecordSet that is part of a table or that combines multiple tables.

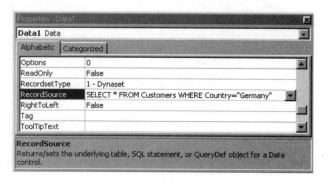

Because SQL statements are so common in databases, you can incorporate them in the design of the database itself. If you expand the list of the RecordSource property for a Data control connected to the NWIND database, you will see that the list contains more than table names. It contains the names of SQL queries that are stored in the database itself. The Category Sales for 1995 item, for example, is not a table name. It's the name of a query that returns sales for 1995, grouped according to product category. If you set the RecordSource property to this item, the resulting RecordSet's fields will appear in the list next to the DataField property of the data-bound controls. For the Categories Sales for 1995 query, the field names that can be displayed in data-bound controls are CategoryName and CategorySales.

Attaching Queries to a Database

Before I end this section of the chapter, we must look at the process of specifying queries with SQL statements and attaching them to the database. To get started, follow these steps:

1. Start the Visual Data Manager and open the BIBLIO database.

2. In the Database window, right-click the All Titles query, and from the shortcut menu, select Design. Visual Data Manager displays another window containing the definition of the query, as shown in Figure 17.18.

FIGURE 17.18:

In addition to tables, a database can contain queries, which are SQL statements that are incorporated into the design of the database.

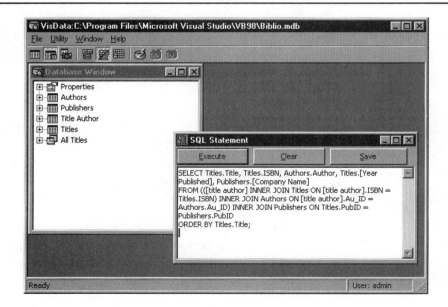

The Query icon is different from the Table icon, as you can see when you open the Database window.

The name of the query appears in the RecordSource property of a Data control connected to the BIBLIO database. We will use this query later to revise the Many-Tbls application, but first let's look at the tools of the Visual Data Manager for building SQL queries.

Building SQL Queries

If you have found SQL difficult to learn, you'll be pleasantly surprised to find out that the Visual Data Manager can generate simple SQL statements with point-and-click operations. Right-click in the Database window of the Visual Data Manager, and from the shortcut menu, select New Query to open the Query Builder window, as shown in Figure 17.19.

FIGURE 17.19:

The Query Builder of the Visual Data Manager lets you build SQL statements with point-and-click operations.

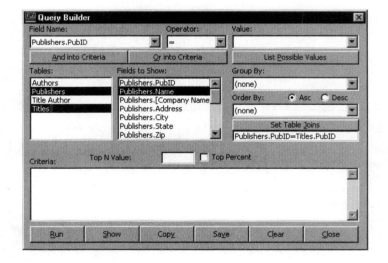

Let's use the Visual Data Manager to build a simple SQL statement. Follow these steps to create a query that retrieves all titles and their publishers:

1. Select the names of the Publishers and Titles tables by clicking their names in the Tables list. The fields of the selected tables will appear in the Fields to Show list.

2. Now click the names of the fields you want to include in the query (the RecordSet that this query will return). Click the following field names: Titles .Title, Titles.[Year Published], and Publishers.Name.

Now we'll get the difficult part of the SQL statement out of the way. Click the Set Table Joins button to define the joins (in other words, to specify how the tables will be combined). The Visual Data Manager doesn't use the JOIN operator. It implements joins with the *WHERE* keyword, which means you can't rely on this tool to implement advanced queries.

3. In the Select Table Pair list, click the names of the tables Titles and Publishers. The fields of the two tables will appear in the lists under the heading Select Fields to Join On, as shown in Figure 17.20.

FIGURE 17.20:

The Join Tables dialog box of the Query Builder lets you easily specify inner Joins with point-and-click operations.

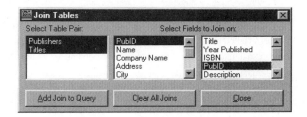

4. Now click the PubID field in both lists. The Titles and Publishers tables are joined on the value of the PubID field. Records with matching PubID fields are joined.

5. Click the Add Join to Query button to add the join to the query.

6. Click the Close button to return to the Query Builder window. The query is defined.

7. Click the Show button to display the SQL statement that implements the query, or click the Run button to execute it. When prompted as to whether this is a SQLPassThrough Query, click No. You will see a new Form with a Data control that lets you navigate through the retrieved records.

8. Click the Save button to attach the query to the database. Visual Data Manager prompts you for the name of the query and attaches it to the database. The next time you connect a Data control to the database, you will see the query's name in the list of available RecordSource items.

You can use the Query Builder to specify selection criteria, which are also implemented with the *WHERE* keyword, to group and order the results of the query and to limit the size of the RecordSet to a number of records if it's too long.

To add selection criteria, for example, select a field name in the Field Name list, select the operator, and then specify a value in the Value box. If you don't remember the values of a specific field, click the List Possible Values button, and the

Visual Data Manager retrieves all the values of the specified list and displays them in the list, from which you can select one.

The SQL statements generated by the Query Builder are relatively simple and are adequate for simple queries (in case you were wondering why I chose such a simple example). For example, the Query Builder can't create multiple joins. However, you can always edit the SQL statement (by opening the query in design mode) and add more keywords to it. If you must create SQL statements, yet you don't feel comfortable with the language, you can use a more elaborate tool, such as Microsoft Access.

VB6 at Work: SQLTbls, ManyTbls Revised

The ManyTbls application combined all the tables of the BIBLIO database to display the titles, along with their authors and publishers. It used the Seek method to combine the tables, not because this was the most efficient implementation but to demonstrate the use of indices and the Seek method. Now, we are going to implement a similar application, but we'll use SQL statements to define the RecordSet with the fields we need. Follow these steps:

1. Open the ManyTbls application and save it as **SQLTbls** (change the name of the Form to **SQLTbls** too) and store it in a new folder.

2. Delete all the Data controls on the Form and place a new one on it. Name it **TITLES**, and set its Caption property to **Titles-Authors-Publishers**.

3. Connect this control to the BIBLIO database by setting the DatabaseName property to the path name of the database on your hard disk.

4. Now, expand the RecordSource property list and select All Titles. This is the name of a SQL query stored in the database, and it returns the desired Record-Set (the titles with their authors and publishers).

5. Because this RecordSet is created with a SQL statement, it's a DynaSet-type RecordSet, so you must set the Data control's RecordSetType property to **1–DynaSet**.

6. Now, adjust the DataSource and DataFields properties of the data-bound controls on the Form so that they see the corresponding fields of the RecordSet via the Data1 Data control. You must set their DataSource property to **Data1** and their DataField properties to **Title**, **Company Name**, **Year Published**, and **Author**.

7. The last two fields on the application's main Form (Description and Comments) are not part of the All Titles query, so delete them from the Form. You can also change the query or create a new one that contains these fields, based on the All Titles query.

8.   Now, delete all the code in the application, because you don't need it any longer.

The SQL statement, in effect, takes the role of the application's code. It does the same thing, only it's as compact and as efficient as it can be.

Advanced Data-Bound Controls

In this section, we are going to look at three data-bound controls that are quite different from those we've used so far:

- The data-bound List control
- The data-bound ComboBox control
- The data-bound Grid control

Unlike the other data-bound controls, these controls can display fields from multiple rows. The data-bound List control is similar to the regular ListBox control and can be populated with an entire column of a RecordSet. The data-bound List control has all the functionality of the regular ListBox control, and in addition, allows the use to enter new values (records). The data-bound Grid control is similar to the Grid control and can display an entire RecordSet. Each row of the grid holds a row (record) of the RecordSet, and the RecordSet's columns correspond to the columns (fields) of the RecordSet.

These two data-bound controls aren't installed by default. To use them in your projects, you must first add them to the Toolbox. To do so, follow these steps:

1.   Right-click the Toolbox and select Components to open the Components dialog box.

2.   Check the Microsoft Data Bound Grid Control and the Microsoft Data Bound List Control boxes.

3.   Click the Close button to close the Components dialog box.

Using the Data-Bound List Control

The data-bound List control can be bound to a specific column of the RecordSet and is commonly used as a lookup table. Figure 17.21 shows how the data-bound List control can be used as a lookup table to simplify navigation in a RecordSet.

This list contains the names of all products in the Products list of the NWIND database, which are loaded when the program starts. Each time you click a new item, the program updates the data-bound controls on the Form to display the fields of the selected record.

FIGURE 17.21:

The DBList application shows how to use the List control as a navigation tool in browsing applications.

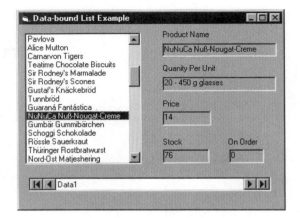

The data-bound List control is different from the data-bound controls we have looked at thus far: it can connect to two data controls. It has the standard Data-Source/DataField properties, which are used just like any other data-bound control, and it has RowSource/ListField properties that determine how the control is populated:

- **RowSource** specifies the source (RecordSet or Data control) for populating the list.

- **ListField** specifies the field that will be used to fill the list.

VB6 at Work: The DBList Project

The DBList application demonstrates the use of the data-bound List control as a navigation tool. The Form you see in Figure 17.21 contains a number of fields from the Products table in the NWIND database. Design the Form shown in Figure 17.21 by binding the various textboxes to their corresponding fields through a Data control, as if you were going to navigate through the list of products with the buttons on the Data control.

The problem with the Data control is that you can't really use it to navigate through a RecordSet, even if it's indexed, because you only see one record at a time. If you could place the key values in a ListBox control and use it as a navigation tool, you would have a much more convenient user interface.

Place a data-bound List control on the Form, and set its RowSource property to the name of the Data1 Data control and its ListField property to the name of the field you want to display in the list. For the DBList application, this is the Product-Name field. The DataSource and DataField properties of the data-bound List control are empty.

If you run the application now, nothing will happen, because you haven't specified how the List control should react to the Click event. Basically, you want to reposition the Data control to the row of the RecordSet that has the matching ProductName field. To do this, insert the following code in the List control's Click event:

```
Private Sub DBList1_Click()
    Data1.Recordset.Bookmark = DBList1.SelectedItem
End Sub
```

The *Bookmark* property identifies a row in the RecordSet. By setting this property to a value, you are in effect forcing the Data control to be repositioned to the specified row. The control's SelectedItem property is not the text displayed in the edit box of the control, but the bookmark of the record to which the selected field belongs. This code repositions the Data control in the RecordSet and updates the data-bound labels on the Form. For a single line, the DBList application sure does a lot.

Using the Data-Bound ComboBox Control

The ComboBox control is commonly used as a lookup table, as demonstrated in the Data Entry application earlier in this chapter. To populate the list of the data-bound ComboBox control, you must set its RowSource property to a Data control, connected to the database and table from which the data will come.

The Data Entry application (in the DEntry folder on the CD) contains a hidden Data control (named Data2) that is connected to the Publishers table of the BIBLIO database. The data-bound ComboBox control's ListField property is the name of the field that will be used to populate the list. In the Data Entry application, this property is set to the Name field of the Publishers table. When the program starts, the data-bound ComboBox control is populated automatically with the names of the publishers in the database, as shown in Figure 17.22.

FIGURE 17.22:

The data-bound ComboBox control on the Form of the Data Entry application contains the names of all publishers in the database.

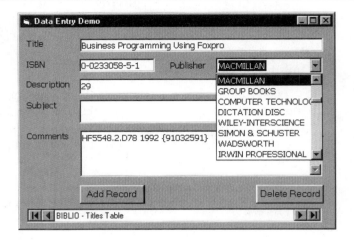

The data-bound ComboBox control has the usual DataSource and DataField properties, just like the other data-bound controls. In the Data Entry application, we want the data-bound ComboBox control to operate as follows:

1. When the program starts, the control is populated with the names of all publishers.

2. When the user navigates through the Titles table, the ComboBox control picks up the publisher's ID from the Titles table, looks up this value in the Publishers table, and displays the Name field of the matching record in the edit box.

3. When appending a new record, the user specifies the book's publisher by selecting a name in the ComboBox control, but the control reports the matching ID to the first Data control.

This sounds like complicated behavior, but it's all built into the data-bound ComboBox control. You've already seen how the first behavior can be implemented with the help of the RowSource and ListField properties. The other two behaviors are typical of a data-bound control. We want to use the edit box of the data-bound ComboBox control as if it were a regular textbox, bound to the PubID field of the Titles table. To achieve this, follow these steps:

1. Select the data-bound ComboBox control, and set its DataSource property to **Data1** (the Data control that sees the Titles table).

2. Set the DataField property to the name of the field you want to update in the database, which is the PubID field.

The PubID field is also the field that should be displayed on the data-bound ComboBox control. But the user now sees IDs in the ComboBox, not their names.

The data-bound ComboBox has one more property, *BoundColumn*, which is the name of the field in its own RowSource that links the field displayed in the list with the actual field to which it is bound. The value of the BoundColumn property must be an index field so that the JET engine can locate it quickly. Set the BoundColumn property to the PubID field and run the application again. This time you'll see the name of the current book's publisher in the ComboBox. If you select another publisher's name in the list, the new publisher's ID will be stored in the current record.

With the help of the DataSource, DataField, and BoundColumn properties, you can use the data-bound ComboBox control as a lookup table in your applications to let the user select meaningful field values, and at the same time, store key values in the database. All this without a single line of code! You will notice that the names of the publishers are not sorted. The data-bound ComboBox control doesn't provide a Sorted property that would sort its entries automatically. You should probably create a new, sorted RecordSet and use it to populate the data-bound ComboBox control.

Using the Data-Bound Grid Control

The data-bound Grid control is one of the most flexible and powerful Visual Basic controls. If you have used Microsoft Access, you'll be familiar with this control. The data-bound Grid control looks a lot like the MSFlexGrid control (discussed in Chapter 9), with two major differences:

- It is populated automatically from a RecordSet.

- It has built-in data-entry mechanisms with which you can edit the Record-Set (if it can be updated).

To fill the control with the data in a RecordSet, all you have to do is to set its Data-Source property to a Data control. The grid is filled with the rows of the RecordSet. Because of the two-dimensional arrangement of the data on the control, you can really see the structure and contents of the entire RecordSet. I used this control to depict RecordSets in some of the figures at the beginning of this chapter. I also used this control to display the results of the SQL statements in the SQLExec application, which we are going to look at next.

VB6 at Work: The SQLExec Project

Earlier in this chapter, we used the SQLExec application to experiment with SQL statements. Now, we are going to build this application. Follow these steps:

1. Start a new Standard EXE project.

2. To add the data-bound Grid control to the Toolbox, right-click the Toolbox, and select Components.

3. In the Components dialog box, check the Microsoft Data Bound Grid Control checkbox. We will also use the Common Dialogs control in this project, so also check the Microsoft Common Dialogs Control 5.0 checkbox, and then click the Close button.

4. Draw the controls you see on the Form shown in Figure 17.23. In addition to the visible controls on the Form, there is a Common Dialogs control (which is invisible at runtime) and a Data control (Data1), whose Visible property is set to False.

FIGURE 17.23:

The SQLExec application lets you query the database with SQL statements and displays the results on a data-bound Grid control.

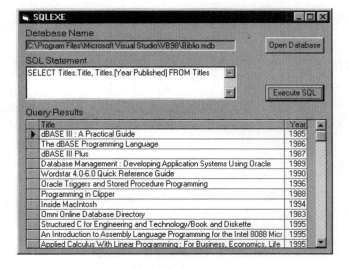

5. The TextBox control on which the SQL statements are typed is called txtSQL. Set its MultiLine property to True, and set its Scrollbars property to 2–Vertical.

6. Now you can program the buttons. The code for the Open Database button opens the File Open dialog box, in which you can select the database with which you want to work. The name of the database is displayed on the Label control next to the Command button.

Code 17.13:   **The Open Database Button**

```
Private Sub DBOpen_Click()
On Error GoTo NoDatabase
CommonDialog1.CancelError = True
CommonDialog1.Filter = "Databases|*.MDB"
CommonDialog1.ShowOpen

    Data1.DatabaseName = CommonDialog1.filename
    Data1.Refresh

    If Err = 0 Then
        Label1.Caption = CommonDialog1.filename
    Else
        MsgBox Err.Description
    End If

NoDatabase:
    On Error GoTo 0
End Sub
```

7. The Execute SQL button retrieves the SQL statement from the txtSQL textbox and assigns it to the Data control's RecordSource property with the following statement:

```
Private Sub ExecuteSQL_Click()
On Error GoTo SQLError

    Data1.RecordSource = txtSQL
    Data1.Refresh
    Exit Sub

SQLError:
    MsgBox Err.Description

End Sub
```

The OnError statement traps any error in the execution of the SQL statement and displays it in a message box. Assigning a new value to the control's Record-Source property doesn't update the contents of the control. You must also call the Refresh method of the Data control to read the new data from the database and to force an update.

Mapping Databases

You design databases using special tools and Visual Data Manager is one of the simplest. These tools let you examine and modify the structure of the database, and in some cases, enter data. You can also access the structure of a database from within an application through a series of objects.

In this section, we will develop a utility that maps the structure of any database, and in the process, you'll see how these objects are used. These objects form a hierarchy, starting with the Database object at the top, and each element in the database is represented by a unique object that can be accessed as a property of the Database object.

The Database Object

In the previous sections, we focused on the contents of a database. Now let's shift our attention to the structure of the database. Even if you know the structure of a database, in some situations you must access its table fields and indices from within your code. For example, you might need to know how many fields a particular table contains or how an index file is defined.

The Database Structure application, shown in Figure 17.24, demonstrates all the objects discussed in this section. First, I'll explain the objects that make up the database, and then we'll look at the implementation of the Database Structure application.

FIGURE 17.24:

The Database Structure application can map any Access database.

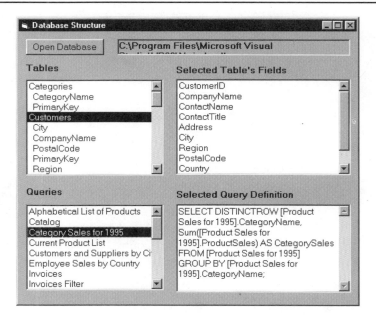

The top-level object is the Database object, which represents the database. To create a Database object and assign a database to it, declare an object variable with a statement like the following:

```
Dim DB As Database
```

The *DB* variable is assigned a Database object with the *OpenDatabase* function, which accepts the path name of an existing database as argument and returns a Database object, as in the following:

```
Set DB = OpenDatabase(dbName)
```

The *dbName* argument is the path name of the database and could be the FileName property of the Common Dialogs control. All the objects we explore in the following sections are properties of the Database object.

Each table in a database is represented by a TableDef object, and a query is represented by a QueryDef object. Each of these objects has its own properties, such as the Name property (which is the table's or query's name) and the Count property (which returns the number of tables in the TableDef object and the number of queries in the QueryDef object).

The TableDef Object: The Tables' Definitions

A *TableDef* object represents the definition of a table in the Database object. All TableDef objects form a collection, the TableDefs collection. The number of tables is given by the property *TableDefs.Count*.

Each table in the database is represented by a TableDef object, whose most important properties are the following:

- **Count** returns the number of rows in the table.

- **Fields** is another collection of Field objects. Each Field object represents a field in the table.

- **Indexes** is another collection of Index objects. Each Index object represents an index of the table.

Assume that you have declared and opened a Database object with the following statements:

```
Dim DB As Database
Set DB = OpenDatabase(dbName)
```

To access the database's table definitions, use the expression DB.TableDefs, which is a collection of objects, one for each table. Through the members of this collection, you can access the properties of the tables in the database. The simplest way to access each table is to first declare a *TableDef* variable, as follows:

```
Dim tbl As TableDef
```

and then scan each element of the DB.TableDefs collection with a For Each…Next structure, like this:

```
For Each tbl In DB.TableDefs
    Debug.Print tbl.Name
Next
```

This loop displays the names of the tables. In addition to the data tables, Access databases contain a few system tables. These tables have names that start with MSYS, and you should skip them. For more information on how to detect and ignore system tables, see the section "VB6 at Work: The DBStructure Project," later in this chapter. You can also access a table's indices, as explained next.

A Table's Indices

Most tables in a database have at least one associated index file, sometimes more. To access the indices of a table, you use the Indexes property of the TableDefs object. Indexes is another collection of objects, one for each index of the table. The simplest way to access each index in a table is to first declare an Index object:

```
Dim idx As Index
```

and then scan each member of the Indexes collection with a For Each…Next structure:

```
For Each idx In tbl.Indexes
    Debug.Print idx.Name
Next
```

The *tbl* entry is a TableDef object, and its declaration was explained in the previous section. The following nested loop displays the names of all tables in the database, and under each table it displays the names of its indices:

```
For Each tbl In DB.TableDefs
    Debug.Print tbl.Name
    For Each idx In tbl.Indexes
        Debug.Print idx.Name
    Next idx
Next tbl
```

You can request the definition of each index with the Fields property, and you use the *Unique* property to determine whether a given index requires unique keys.

A Table's Fields

The most important property of the TableDefs object is the Fields property, which is another collection of objects, one for each field in the table. To access a table's fields, you first specify the table in the database that you want. You specify tables with an index value, which is 0 for the first table, 1 for the second table, up to `DB.TableDefs.Count-1` for the last table. You can access the fields of the first table in the database through the object:

```
DB.TableDefs(0).Fields
```

Alternatively, you can use the table's name in place of the index. The following object represents all the fields in the Titles table of the BIBLIO database:

```
DB.TableDefs("Titles").Fields
```

To access each individual field in the Fields collection, declare a Field object variable, and then scan the collection's members with a For Each...Next structure. The following code segment displays the names and types of each field in the first table of the database:

```
Dim fld As Field

For Each fld In DB.TableDefs(0).Fields
    Debug.Print fld.Name, fld.Type
Next
```

The Type property returns an integer value that represents the type of the field. You must provide a short procedure that converts this number to a string such as "Integer", "String", and so on.

The other properties of the Field object are:

- **OrdinalPosition**   The order of the fields in the table

- **AllowZeroLength**   A Boolean property indicating whether the field can be set to an empty string

- **Size**   The size of the field in bytes

- **Value**   The current value of the field

The QueryDef Object: The Queries' Definitions

In addition to tables, a database can contain query definitions. The queries that are commonly used on a database can be stored in the database and called by name. All the queries stored in a database can be accessed through the QueryDefs object, which is similar to the TableDef object. The *QueryDefs* object is a collection of QueryDef objects, one for each stored query. You can access the following properties of the QueryDefs collection from within your code:

- **Count** returns the number of queries stored in a database.

- **Name** returns the name of the query.

- **SQL** returns the SQL statement of the query.

The number of queries stored in a database is given by the following expression:

```
DB.QueryDefs.Count
```

To access all queries stored in a database, declare a *QueryDef* object variable as follows:

```
Dim qry As QueryDef
```

and then scan the elements of the QueryDefs collection with a For Each…Next loop:

```
For Each qry In DB.QueryDefs
    Debug.Print qry.Name
Next
```

VB6 at Work: The DBStructure Project

The DBStruct application, shown in Figure 17.24 earlier in this chapter, lets you open any database and view the names of its tables, their structure, the queries stored in the database, and their definitions. The tables and queries of the database are displayed in the two lists on the left. Under each table's name you see the names of the indices for the table. Click the name of a table to display its fields, and click the name of a query to display its definition.

Let's start with the code of the Open Database button.

Code 17.14:   **The Open Database Button**

```
Private Sub Command1_Click()
On Error GoTo NoDatabase
    CommonDialog1.CancelError = True
    CommonDialog1.Filter = "Databases|*.mdb"
    CommonDialog1.ShowOpen

' Open the database
    If CommonDialog1.filename <> "" Then
        Set DB = OpenDatabase(CommonDialog1.filename)
        Label1.Caption = CommonDialog1.filename
```

```
        End If
' Clear the ListBox controls
    FldList.Clear
    TblList.Clear

Dim tbl As TableDef
Dim idx As Index
Dim TName As String

Debug.Print "There are " & DB.TableDefs.Count & " tables in the _
        database"
' Process each table
    For Each tbl In DB.TableDefs
        ' EXCLUDE SYSTEM TABLES
        If Left(tbl.Name, 4) <> "MSys" And Left(tbl.Name, 4) _
            "USys" Then
        TblList.AddItem tbl.Name
' For each table, process the table's indices
            For Each idx In tbl.Indexes
                TblList.AddItem "  " & idx.Name
            Next
        End If
    Next

Dim qry As QueryDef
Debug.Print "There are " & DB.QueryDefs.Count & " queries in the database"
' Process each stored query
    For Each qry In DB.QueryDefs
        QryList.AddItem qry.Name
    Next

NoDatabase:
    MsgBoxErr.Description
End Sub
```

Along with the filenames, the program displays the names of the indices for each table below the name of the corresponding table and indents them two spaces.

Let's look at the basic parts of this subroutine. The user-specified database is opened and assigned to the *DB* object variable. It then scans the members of the TableDefs object and appends the name of each table to the Tables list. Notice the following If structure:

```
If Left(tbl.Name, 4) <> "MSys" And Left(tbl.Name, 4) <> "USys"
```

Along with the tables you specify when you design a database, Microsoft Access databases contain a few system tables. The JET engine uses these, and you need not manipulate them from within your code. Actually, you shouldn't. System table names begin with the prefixes *MSys* and *USys*. The program ignores these tables with the previous If statement.

After displaying the name of the current table, the program scans the indices of the table with the help of the current table's Indexes object. After all table and index names are displayed, the program displays the names of all queries stored in the database.

When a table name is clicked in the Tables list, its fields are displayed in the Selected Table's Fields list. Likewise, when a query name is clicked, its definition (a SQL statement) appears in the Selected Query Definition textbox.

Code 17.15:   The Tables List Click Event Handler

```
Private Sub TblList_Click()
Dim fld As Field
Dim idx As Index

    If Left(TblList.Text, 2) = "  " Then Exit Sub
    FldList.Clear
    For Each fld In DB.TableDefs(TblList.Text).Fields
        FldList.AddItem fld.Name
    Next

End Sub
```

If the item that is clicked begins with two spaces, it's an index name, and the program doesn't react. If the item does not begin with two spaces, the program clears the ListBox control where the field names will be displayed and starts filling the list with each field's name. To access the names of the fields, the program scans the elements of the `DB.TableDefs(TblList.Text).Fields` collection. With each iteration, it appends the name of another field (`fld.Name`) to the list. You can also display the field's type with the Type property and the field's size (in bytes) with the Size property.

When a query name is clicked, its definition appears in the multiline textbox.

Code 17.16: **The Queries List Box Click Event Handler**

```
Private Sub QryList_Click()
Dim qry As QueryDef

    txtSQL.Text = DB.QueryDefs(QryList.ListIndex).SQL

End Sub
```

Notice that the objects of the TableDefs are accessed by the name of the table and QueryDefs objects are accessed by the name of the stored query. The alternative is to access them with an index. Since the system tables were omitted, the order of the tables in the Tables list is not the same as the order of the tables in the database; therefore, this method wouldn't work for this application.

The Active Data Objects

- Creating a Data project

- Designing with the DataEnvironment ActiveX Designer

- Using the ADO Data Control

Today's programming languages completely separate the components for accessing databases from the rest of the language. Incorporating data-access technologies into the language makes it inflexible and limited (since you can access only the database management systems supported by the language) and is a sure way to keep the language out of corporate environments. Visual Basic supports several data access tools, with the Active Data objects (ADO) being the most recent addition. Whereas the first Visual Basic data access tools (the Data Access objects, discussed in the previous chapter) allowed programmers to access Access databases only, ADO can access all major databases and is Microsoft's foundation for a universal technology for accessing all types of data in all environments.

With ADO, your Visual Basic application sees three objects:

- A *Connection object*, which establishes a connection to the database, be it a local file or a remote SQL Server

- A *Command object*, which executes commands against the database

- A *RecordSet object*, which holds the records retrieved from the database or the records to be updated on the database

The peculiarities of each database management system are completely transparent to the programmer, which means you don't have to learn the native tools of the database in order to use it.

The components I discuss in this chapter are based on the Active Data objects (ADO), which are different from the Data Access objects I discussed in the last chapter. ADO is the latest data access technology from Microsoft and is meant to gradually replace other technologies, including the DAO. Visual Basic programmers have used the DAO component for many years, and many applications rely on this component. That's why I discussed it at length in Chapter 17. DAO is still the simplest way to break into database programming. As you will see, much of the information you acquired in Chapter 17 applies to programming the Active Data objects as well. ADO, however, supports more sources than DAO does. Whereas DAO was optimized for Access databases, the ADO component can access any database, including SQL Servers.

It is impossible to cover the topic of ADO in a single chapter. There are other books devoted to ADO, and if you plan to develop large-scale database applications, you should get more information on this topic. In this chapter, I mainly want to demonstrate the new visual database tools that come with Visual Basic. As you will see, the visual database tools can simplify some of the most difficult aspects of setting up a database application (reports being one of them). In addition, the ADO model is used on the Web, and in the last chapter of this book, you'll see how to use the ADO objects to access databases from a Web page.

So, is ADO a complicated technology? Even though it exposes fewer objects than DAO, it is more complicated. Its objects support more properties and methods, and ADO was designed to handle complicated database issues. For example, ADO supports batch updates (it lets you download records from a database, process them on the client computer, and update the database after you're done editing). In general, ADO can get quite complicated. It's a much more general tool that addresses the needs of many different databases, not just Access databases. However, some of the tasks you can perform with ADO are quite simple, especially if you use the visual database tools.

In the first part of this chapter, I'm going to concentrate on the visual database tools and show you how to create elaborate Forms for retrieving and displaying records, without any programming—well, perhaps a few lines of code. The examples will focus on data retrieval techniques. They are simple, and you need not design databases, data entry, and validation code. After you are familiar with the basics of ADO, you can consult the documentation or more specific titles to move into more advanced database operations. In the second half of the chapter, I'll present a few simple examples of programming the ADO. As you'll see, some of the names are different, but the principles are the same as with DAO.

Creating a Data Project

To see the new visual database tools in action, start a new project, and in the Project Type dialog box, select Data Project. A Data project is not a special project type. It's basically a Standard EXE project, but Visual Basic loads all the database tools into the project's Toolbox.

In the Project Explorer window, Visual Basic displays a new Form, as usual, and two ActiveX Designers. A *Designer* is a special add-in that simplifies the design of components. Database applications rely on two basic components:

- One or more DataEnvironment component(s)
- One or more DataReport component(s)

The *DataEnvironment* component lets you design a connection to a database and retrieve the desired records. The *DataReport* component lets you design reports and use them from within your applications. Both components are based on visual database tools, and they don't require programming. Of course, you can't go far without programming, but the programming model is similar to the one I discussed in the previous chapter.

The Data project's Toolbox also contains a number of ActiveX controls:

- The ADODC (ADO Data control), which is equivalent to the Data control.

- The DataList and DataCombo controls, which are data-bound versions of the ListBox and ComboBox controls; they work with the ADO Data control (but not with the Data control).

- The MSHFlexGrid control, which is a hierarchical Grid control that also works with the ADO Data control. The MSHFlexGrid is very similar to the MSFlexGrid control (we explored this control in Chapter 9), but it's meant to be populated automatically by the DataEnvironment Designer.

In the following sections, I'm going to discuss the DataEnvironment and DataReport ActiveX Designers. To understand what the ActiveX Designers do and how they can simplify your database projects, we'll take a quick look at the basic requirements of every database application.

To access a database with ADO (or any other data tool), you need two types of objects:

- One or more Connection objects

- One or more Command objects

The *Connection object* connects your application to a database, and the *Command object* retrieves records from the database. The Command object can also update the database, but I won't discuss this topic in much detail here. As you will see, the Command object accepts a SQL statement and executes it against the database. If it's a query statement, the Command object returns a RecordSet with the matching records. If it's an action query, the Command object executes it against the database, where one or more records will be updated (optionally, the Command object can return the records that were affected by the query).

Another just as common and just as important operation in database application design is the generation of reports. Retrieving the required data from the database is not difficult, but printing the report over multiple pages with running totals is quite a task. Most developers use third-party tools to generate reports, especially since printing them on different printers is a real challenge. The DataReport Designer allows you to create the outline of a report with point-and-click operations. You first specify the data to be included in the report with the DataEnvironment object, which works in tandem with the DataReport ActiveX Designer to allow you to implement advanced database operations (queries and reports) without any programming.

Designing with the DataEnvironment ActiveX Designer

Let's start by building a simple database application with the DataEnvironment ActiveX Designer. The Denv1 project is a simple Form that lets you navigate the records of the Customers table in the NWIND database. To design the Form shown in Figure 18.1, we must first establish a connection to the NWIND database; then we retrieve the records of the Customers table and display them on data-bound controls.

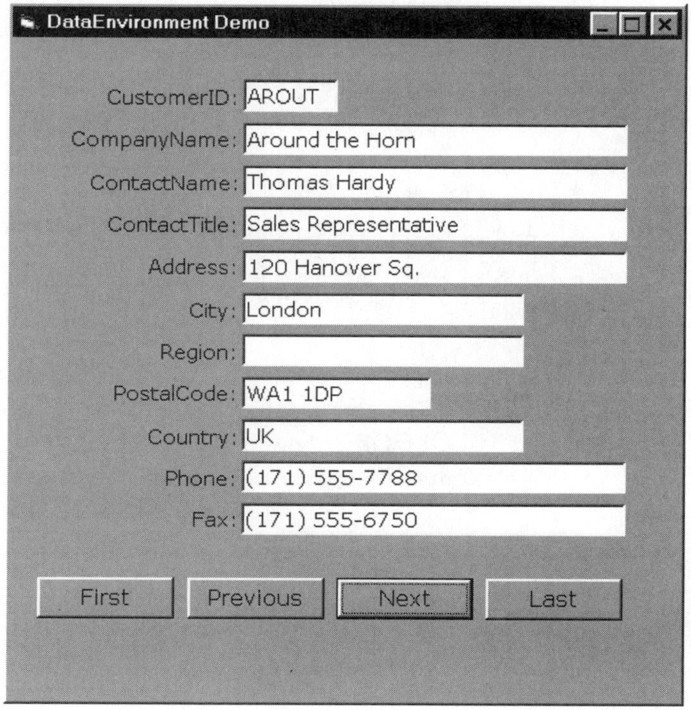

FIGURE 18.1:

The Denv1 project demonstrates the basics of the DataEnvironment ActiveX Designer.

Follow these steps:

1. Start a new project, and in the Project Type dialog box, select Data Project.

2. Double-click the DataEnvironment1 object in the Project Explorer to open the DataEnvironment window:

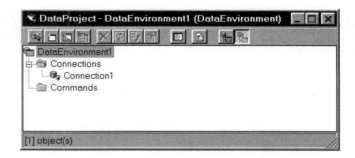

The DataEnvironment of the application consists of a Connection object (the Connection1 object) and one or more Command objects. The Commands folder is empty, but this is where the Command object we'll create later will be stored.

3. Right-click the Connection1 object, and from the shortcut menu, select Properties to open the Data Link Properties window. You use the tabs in this window to specify the database to which you want to connect.

4. In the Provider tab, select the driver between your application and the database.

As you can see, most databases use the OLE DB provider. The OLE DB provider is to databases what OLE is to other applications. Select the Microsoft Jet 3.51 OLE DB Provider. This is the simplest provider that can connect your application directly to a Microsoft Access database.

NOTE   Later in this chapter, you'll see how to use the OLE DB Provider for ODBC drivers.

---

5. Now, select the Connection tab:

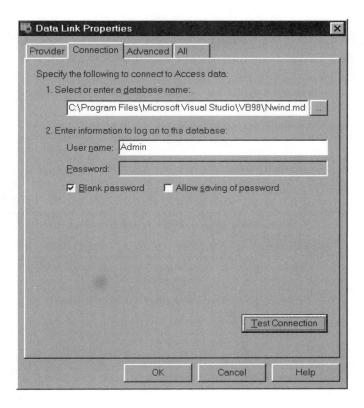

6. Click the button with the ellipsis, and locate the NWIND database (it's in the VB98 folder).

7. Click the Test Connection button to make sure the connection works.

8. If the database requires a user name and password, you'll be prompted to enter them. Supply the same information in the appropriate boxes on the Connection tab.

9. Select the Advanced tab to specify how the database will be opened, as well as other users' rights on the database.

    •   The options Read, Read Write, and Write apply to your application (whether the application will open the database for reading, writing, or both).

    •   The options Share Deny None, Share Deny Read, Share Deny Write, and Share Exclusive determine how other applications can use the database while your application is using it. The Share Deny None option, which is checked by default, means that other applications will be allowed access to the database.

To exclude all other uses of the database while you working with it, check the option Share Exclusive. Normally, you don't want to open a database exclusively and lock out every other user who wants to access it. Your application must use the locking mechanisms to protect the records it needs, but not lock the entire database.

10. Select the All tab to displays all the settings you specified in the previous tabs.

11. Click OK to return to the DataEnvironment window.

We've established a connection to the database and made sure it works. Now, let's create a Command object to request some records. We want to display the records of the Customers table on the Form, so the Command object we'll create must access the Customers table.

To retrieve all the customers from the NWIND database, follow these steps:

1. Right-click the Commands item, and from the shortcut menu, select Add Command. The Command1 object will be added under the Commands folder.

2. Right-click the Command1 object, and select Properties to open the Command1 Properties window:

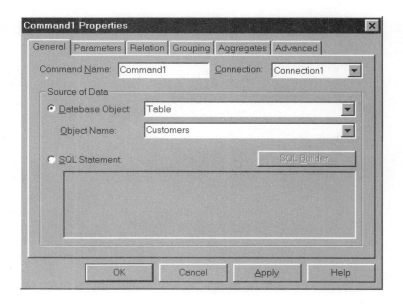

3. In the General tab, set the Command object's name to **Customers** and its Connection to **Connection1** (the Connection object you just created).

> **NOTE**
>
> The data you can request from the database is the Command object's Data Source. It can be a table, a view, or a stored procedure. In this example, we'll use the Customers table.

4. In the Database Object box, select Table, and in the Object Name box, you'll see the names of all the tables in the database.

5. Select the Customers table. If you don't see the names of the tables, click Apply, and then open the Object Name list again. The names of the tables should be there this time. I'll discuss the remaining tabs later in this chapter.

6. Click OK to return to the DataEnvironment1 window, which is organized as a TreeView control.

7. Click the plus sign in front of the Command1 object to display the names of the Customers table's fields.

8. Switch to the project's Form (if you haven't renamed it, it's Form1).

9. With the Form and the DataEnvironment window visible on the screen, drag the Command1 object and drop it on the Form. Visual Basic will create as many pairs of Label and TextBox controls on the Form as needed to display all the fields of the Command object. If you don't want to display all the fields, drag-and-drop the selected fields only.

10. Switch to the Form and arrange the controls on it. This Form lacks the navigation buttons. Place four Command buttons on the Form, as shown earlier in Figure 18.1, and enter the following statements in their Click events.

Code 18.1:   Programming the Navigation Buttons

```
Private Sub Command1_Click()
    DataEnvironment1.rsCommand1.MoveFirst
End Sub

Private Sub Command2_Click()
    If DataEnvironment1.rsCommand1.BOF Then
        Beep
    Else
        DataEnvironment1.rsCommand1.MovePrevious
        If DataEnvironment1.rsCommand1.BOF Then
```

```
            DataEnvironment1.rsCommand1.MoveFirst
        End If
    End If
End Sub

Private Sub Command3_Click()
    If DataEnvironment1.rsCommand1.EOF Then
        Beep
    Else
        DataEnvironment1.rsCommand1.MoveNext
        If DataEnvironment1.rsCommand1.EOF Then
            DataEnvironment1.rsCommand1.MoveLast
        End If
    End If
End Sub

Private Sub Command4_Click()
    DataEnvironment1.rsCommand1.MoveLast
End Sub
```

If you read the previous chapter, this code should be familiar. The Data-Environment1 object exposes the rsCommand1 RecordSet, which contains the records retrieved by the Customers Command object. This record is named automatically according to the name of the Command object (and prefixed with the string "rs"). The DataEnvironment1.rsCustomers object is a RecordSet, which supports most of the properties and methods of the DAO RecordSets.

To navigate through the records use the Move methods (MoveFirst, MoveNext, MovePrevious, and MoveLast). Since the navigation methods can lead to invalid records (the one before the first record and the one after the last record), you must examine the BOF and EOF properties of the rsCustomers RecordSet.

TIP   For a discussion of the EOF and BOF properties and how they are used from within the navigation methods, see Chapter 17.

Using the DataEnvironment ActiveX Designer and a few lines of code, we were able to design a functional Form for navigating through a RecordSet. This example is anything but impressive, though. You can do the same with the Data control, probably faster. In the following section, we are going to build a far more complicated Command object that combines three tables of the same database—all from within the DataEnvironment ActiveX Designer—without a single line of code.

Designing Command Hierarchies

The project we are going to build is called DataRep, and you will find it in this chapter's folder on the CD. In this section, we are going to build a hierarchy of commands. First, we'll retrieve all the company names from the Customers table. For each company (customer), we'll retrieve the invoices issued to it and total their number. Then, for each invoice, we'll retrieve the details and total them. Next, we are going to display this hierarchy of records in a hierarchical Grid control (the MSHFlexGrid control). The MSHFlexGrid control is very similar to the MSFlexGrid control, but MSHFlexGrid one is meant to be used with databases and especially with hierarchical commands.

The first column will contain the names of the companies, the second column, the number of invoices issued to each company, the third column, the total of the invoices issued to the company. The columns that follow display the invoice number, order date, and the invoice's total. Figure 18.2 shows the data displayed on a hierarchical MSFlexGrid control. Notice that the details of some customers are hidden. The plus symbol in front of the customer name means that there are rows with details that can be expanded.

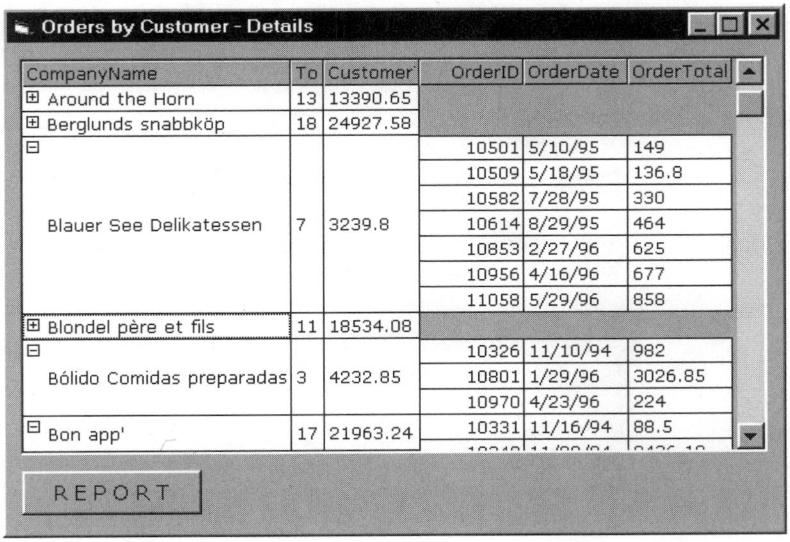

FIGURE 18.2:

A hierarchy of Commands (customers-invoices-totals) displayed on a hierarchical FlexGrid control

CompanyName	To	Customer	OrderID	OrderDate	OrderTotal
⊞ Around the Horn	13	13390.65			
⊞ Berglunds snabbköp	18	24927.58			
⊟			10501	5/10/95	149
			10509	5/18/95	136.8
			10582	7/28/95	330
Blauer See Delikatessen	7	3239.8	10614	8/29/95	464
			10853	2/27/96	625
			10956	4/16/96	677
			11058	5/29/96	858
⊞ Blondel père et fils	11	18534.08			
⊟			10326	11/10/94	982
Bólido Comidas preparadas	3	4232.85	10801	1/29/96	3026.85
			10970	4/23/96	224
⊟ Bon app'	17	21963.24	10331	11/16/94	88.5

REPORT

Follow these steps:

1. Start a new Data project, and create a Connection object to the NWIND database, as explained in the last section.

2. Add a new Command object (Command1), and then open its Properties dialog box (right-click the Command name and select Properties).

3. In the Command1 Properties dialog box, set the Connection to **Connection1**, and then select the Source of Data.

The company names are stored in the Customers table of the NWIND database, so select Table as the Database Object and Customers as the Object Name. As soon as you select Table in the first drop-down list, the names of all tables in the database will appear in the list below.

For each customer, we want to retrieve their invoices. This means we must design another Command object, which will belong to the Command we just designed. The new Command object will be a child of the Command1 object. Every time the Command1 object is repositioned to another customer, the child Command object will contain the new customer's invoices.

4. In the DataEnvironment window, right-click the Command1 object, and from the shortcut menu, select Child Command.

The new Command object will be named Command2. Since Command2 is a child of Command1, it must be executed through the same connection as Command1; therefore, the Connection box is disabled. A child command can't have its own connection. The child command should retrieve the invoices from the Orders table.

5. Specify Table as the Database Object and Orders as the Object Name.

Since Command2 is a child command, we must associate it with the parent Command object.

6. Switch to the Relation tab of the Command2 Properties dialog box, and select Command1 as the parent command (see Figure 18.3).

You must now describe the relationship. The Customers and Orders table share a common field, the CustomerID field. This is the connection between the two commands.

7. Select CustomerID in the ParentFields and Child Fields/Parameters lists, and click Add. The relationship will appear in the lower box as CustomerID TO CustomerID.

Now add another child command under Command2.

FIGURE 18.3:

Use the Relation tab to specify the relationship of a child command to its parent object.

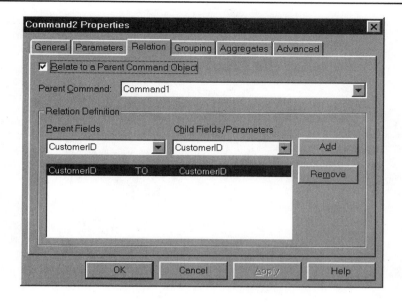

8. Right-click the Command2 entry in the DataEnvironment1 window, select Child Command, and open the Properties dialog box for the new child command.

The new Command object should retrieve the totals for each invoice. The totals are not stored in a table in the NWIND database. Instead, they are calculated with a SQL statement. Because the invoice totals are recalled frequently, they are stored in a View (a *View* is a synonym for a stored procedure). The OrderSubtotals View is a SQL statement that is executed every time the invoice totals are requested and returns a RecordSet (just as if it was a table). Of course, Views can't be updated.

9. Select View as the Database Object, and select Order Subtotals as the Object Name.

The Command3 Properties dialog box should look like the one in Figure 18.4.

Our next task is to add the relation of the Command3 object to its parent object, Command2. Follow these steps:

1. In the Relation tab, specify Command2 as the Parent Command, and select the fields OrderID in the Relation Definition section, as shown in Figure 18.5.

FIGURE 18.4:

The Data Source for the
Command3 object

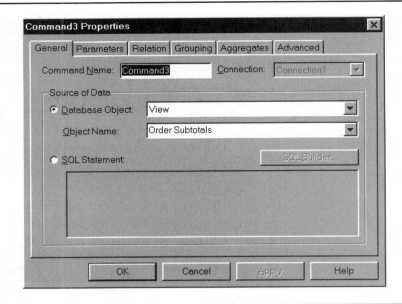

FIGURE 18.5:

The relationship of the
Command3 object to its
parent object

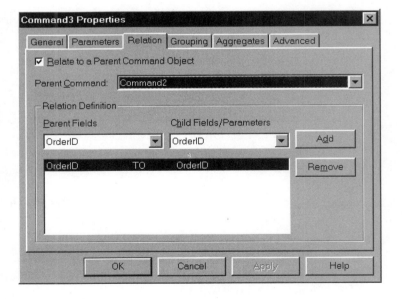

2.   Click the Add button to establish the relationship.

We have now created the hierarchy of commands. We have connected invoice
totals to invoice numbers and invoice numbers to customers. We must now specify

the totals. Totals (or aggregates) are usually specified starting with child commands. Follow these steps:

1. In the Command2 Properties dialog box, select the Aggregates tab.

2. Create a new aggregate and call it **OrderTotal** (click the Add button and specify **OrderTotal** when prompted to enter the name of the new aggregate).

3. The function that will be used in calculating the aggregate is the SUM function, so select Sum in the Function list. We want to add the totals for all invoices in the Command3 object (which contains the details for each invoice).

4. Select Command3 in the Aggregate On list, and select the name of the Subtotal field in the Field list.

OrderTotal is the name of an aggregate with the total for each invoice. This number will reflect the total of the invoice selected in the Command2 object, as shown in Figure 18.6. As far as Command2 is concerned, OrderTotal is just another field of its RecordSet.

FIGURE 18.6:

The Aggregate of the Command2 object

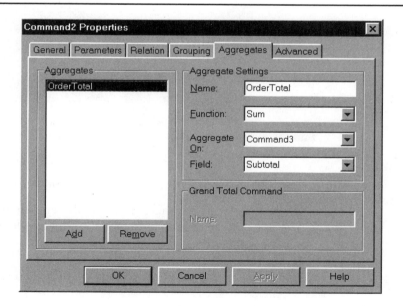

Let's now specify the aggregates of the Command1 object. Follow these steps:

1. Open the Command1 Properties dialog box, and select the Aggregates tab.

2. Add a new aggregate and set its name to TotalOrders. The TotalOrders aggregate will be the number of invoices issued to a customer.

3. Select Count as the Function (we must count invoices, not sum them), select Command2 as the field on which the aggregate will be calculated, and select OrderID as the Field.

The TotalOrders aggregate will count all the invoices in the Command2 object's RecordSet per customer. Figure 18.7 shows the definition of the first aggregate of the Command1 object.

FIGURE 18.7:

The aggregate of the Command1 object

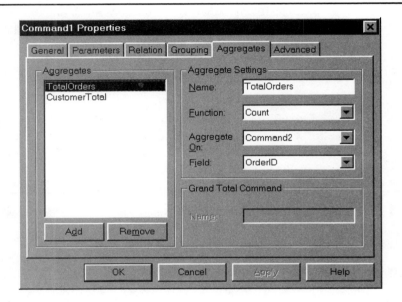

Finally, we must calculate the total of all invoices issued to each customer. Follow these steps:

1. Add a new aggregate, and name it CustomerTotal.

2. This time we want to add the subtotals of all invoices, so select Sum as the Function, select Command2 in the Aggregate On list, and select OrderTotal as the Field value.

OrderTotal is another aggregate, defined in the Command2 object. As far as Object1 is concerned, OrderTotal is just another field. After you enter the definitions of all aggregates, the window of the DataEnvironment1 ActiveX Designer will look like the one shown in Figure 18.8. I have scrolled the contents of this window so that you can see how the aggregates appear under the respective commands.

FIGURE 18.8:

The DataEnvironment window after the aggregates have been defined

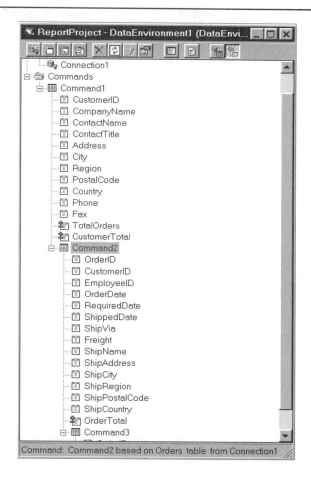

We have designed the Command objects that retrieve the desired records from the database and defined their relationships. How about displaying the data on a Form? There are several options, and we'll explore them in the following sections.

Using the DataEnvironment with the DataGrid Control

The DataEnvironment ActiveX Designer has helped us design a connection and a command hierarchy with point-and-click operations. The records retrieved by the Command object can be dropped on a Form, where they are mapped to data-bound controls. If you drop a few fields from each Command object on a Form, you need only supply the code for navigating the records of the Command1 object. Each time you move to another customer, the child Command fields will be updated to reflect the totals for the selected customer.

In this section, you'll see how the same fields can be inserted in a DataGrid control. The new Form is shown in Figure 18.9. This Form is not part of the project, so I will present the steps you must follow to build the Form.

FIGURE 18.9:

Displaying the fields of a
Command hierarchy on a
DataGrid control

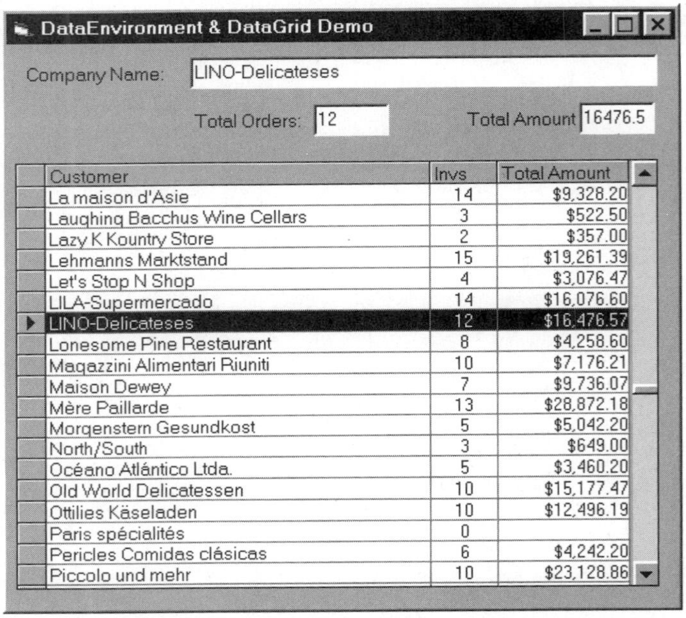

1. Open the project of the last section (it's the Report project on the CD), and from the Project menu, select Add Form to add a new Form to the project. If you have not changed the first Form's name yet, the new Form's name will be Form2.

2. Open the Project menu again, select Project Properties, and make the newly added Form the start-up object of the project.

3. With the DataEnvironment1 window and Form2 visible on the screen, right-click the Command1 object and drag it to the new Form. When you release the mouse, you will see a shortcut menu, which prompts you to select how the fields of the Command1 object will be placed on the Form. Your choices are:

   DataGrid   The selected fields will be placed on a DataGrid control.

   Hierarchical FlexGrid   The selected fields will be placed on an MSHFlex-Grid control.

   Bound Controls   The selected fields will be placed on separate data-bound controls (the type of control is determined by the field type).

4. From the shortcut menu, select Select DataGrid to place a new DataGrid control with two columns on the Form.

5. Right-click the DataGrid control and select Edit to adjust the appearance of the DataGrid control.

6. First, we must add a new column to the grid. Right-click somewhere on the grid's fixed row, and select Insert to add a new column to the DataGrid. You'll now have a total of three columns.

7. Right-click the DataGrid control, outside the fixed row.

8. From the shortcut menu, select Properties to open the Properties Pages dialog box.

9. Switch to the Columns tab (see Figure 18.10), where you can set the caption of each column and the field to be displayed. Set the following captions and field names on this tab:

Column	Caption	DataField
Column 0	Customer	CompanyName
Column 1	Invs	TotalOrders
Column 2	Total Amount	CustomerTotal

FIGURE 18.10:

The Property Pages of the DataGrid control—Columns tab

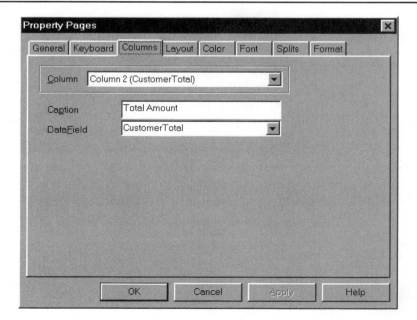

On the Format tab you can specify the format for each column. The default format for each column is General and is determined by the nature of the corresponding field. The last column contains dollar amounts and should be formatted as Custom type.

10. Select the item Column 2 in the Format Item list, and in the Format box, click the Custom item.

11. Enter the following string in the Format String box "$#,###.00" (without the quotes), as shown in the following figure.

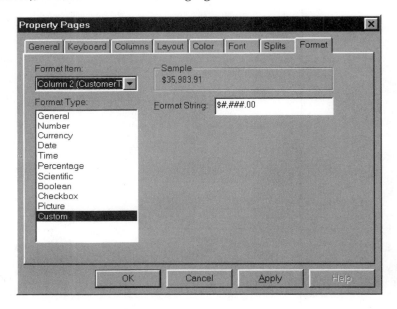

If you run the project now, the invoice data for each customer will appear on the DataGrid control. You will also have to resize the columns manually or insert a few lines of code in the Form's Load event to change the default widths of the columns.

If you place any data-bound controls on the same Form and connect them to the fields of the Command hierarchy (simply drag them from the DataEnvironment window and drop them on the Form), the data-bound controls will be updated to reflect the current selection every time you select another row in the DataGrid.

Using the DataEnvironment with the MSHFlexGrid Control

One of the most interesting new controls in Visual Basic 6 is the hierarchical FlexGrid (or MSHFlexGrid) control. It is very similar to the MSFlexGrid control, which

I discussed in detail in Chapter 9, but it's meant to be used with ADO command hierarchies. Each command is automatically placed in its own band, and you can collapse and expand the rows of the hierarchical FlexGrid control, similar to the nodes of a TreeView control. Figure 18.2, earlier in this chapter, shows the records retrieved by the command hierarchy we designed in the section "Designing Child Commands." Notice the each company name, displayed in the first column, has a + or – sign in front of it. This sign indicates that the corresponding company's details can be expanded or collapsed, respectively.

Let's build the Form shown earlier in Figure 18.2. Follow these steps:

1. Rename the project's Form to DetailsForm, and make it wide enough to hold all the columns shown in the figure.

2. Open the DataEnvironment1 window, and make sure that both windows are visible on the screen.

The hierarchical MSHFlexGrid control isn't added by default to the project's Toolbox. If you have created a Data project, it will be in the Toolbox. If you don't see the MSHFlexGrid's icon in the Toolbox, open the Components dialog box and add the Microsoft Hierarchical FlexGrid Control 6.0 (OLEDB) component. Then place an instance of the control on the Form.

3. Select the MSHFlexGrid control, and locate its DataSource property in the Properties window.

4. Set the DataSource property to DataEnvironment1 (select it from the drop-down list), and set the DataMember property to Command1 (this will map the entire hierarchy of the DataEnvironment1 window to the control). The grid control will be bound to the hierarchical RecordSet returned by Data-Environment1.

5. Right-click the control, and from the shortcut menu, select Retrieve Structure. All the fields listed in the DataEnvironment1 window will be added to the control as headers. Obviously, we don't want to display all the fields, so we must specify which fields will appear in the control's columns and how.

TIP   In the process of setting up the MSHFlexGrid control, you may decide to clear the structure of the control and start all over again. Right-click the control, and select Clear Structure. This action will disconnect (disassociate) the control from the DataEnvironment1 window's fields. Then right-click the control again, and select Copy Structure.

6. From the control's shortcut menu, select Properties to open the MSHFlex-Grid control's property pages:

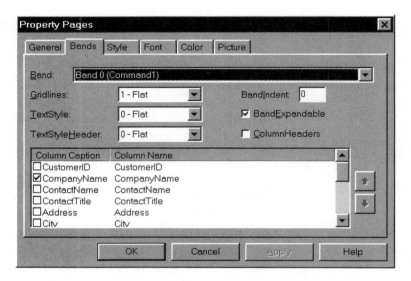

The properties you can set in the General tab are equivalent to the properties of the MSFlexGrid control.

The Bands tab contains information about the control's bands and the fields to appear in each one. A *band* is a section of the control (a collection of adjacent columns) that corresponds to a Command object. The first band corresponds to the Command1 object, and the following bands correspond to the child Command objects. The first band (Band 0) is selected by default. The lower half of the window displays all the fields of the Command1 object. The last two fields are TotalOrders and Customer-Total. These are the aggregates we defined earlier in the DataEnvironment window, but to Command1, they look just like fields.

7. Select the fields you want to display (CompanyName, TotalOrders, and CustomerTotal), and clear the rest.

8. Select Band 1 to displays the fields of the first child command (Command2).

9. Select the fields OrderID, OrderDate, and the aggregate OrderTotal.

10. Select Band 3, and check the field subtotal.

If you run the application now, the hierarchical MSHFlexGrid control will be populated with the selected fields' values. You can collapse/expand each company's invoices by clicking on the minus or plus sign in front of its name.

If you run the project now, the customers and their invoices will appear on the hierarchical grid as previously shown in Figure 18.2. The information on the grid is highly structured, involving two tables and a view of the database, yet you didn't have to enter a single line of code.

We managed to map the structure of a Command hierarchy, which is a fairly complicated structure, to an equally complex control, without any programming. For more demanding applications, you can program the DataEnvironment1 object. I'm sure you noticed the similarities between the DataEnvironment1 object and the Data control. They both act as gateways between your application (specifically, as the data-bound controls of the application) and a database. As you will see later in this chapter, the Active Data object component provides an equivalent Data control, the ADO Data control. It supports many of the same properties and methods as the Data control, and you can program it just as you would program the regular Data control.

Using the DataReport ActiveX Designer

Another equally important operation in database application development is that of generating reports. Generating hierarchical multipage reports with running totals (such as a report for the data retrieved by the Command hierarchy we designed in the previous sections) and printing them properly has been a major headache for developers. We'd rather work with a point-and-click Wizard that generates the report for us and, most important, prints it out correctly. The second ActiveX Designer of Visual Basic 6 is the DataReport Designer, which does exactly that. Let' see how the DataReport Designer can create a report for us based on the (fairly complex) Command hierarchy we generated in the previous section. Follow these steps:

1. Switch to the Report project, and double-click the DataReport Designer in the Project Explorer window to open it. On your screen, you'll see a report template that doesn't correspond to the structure of the Command hierarchy you've created.

2. To connect the DataReport object to the Command1 object, open the DataReport window.

3. In the Properties window, locate the DataSource and DataMember properties, and set them to DataEnvironment1 and Command1.

4. Right-click the DataReport object, and from the shortcut menu, select Retrieve Structure.

The structure of the Command hierarchy will be mapped on the DataReport object, as shown in Figure 18.11.

The DataReport object after retrieving the structure of the Command1 object

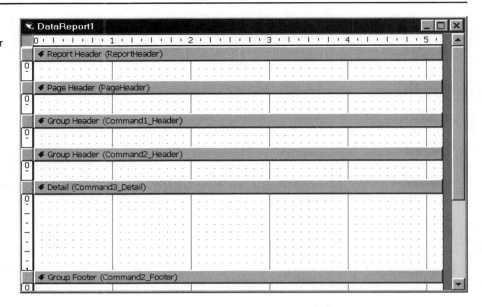

The template now contains a report and a page header. Two more headers follow, the Group headers for Command1 and Command2. As you can see, the report's details are the fields of the Command3 object. After the Details section come the corresponding footers.

Leave the Report header blank (you can place any string you like there later), and follow these steps:

1. To remove the space that's normally allocated to the Report header (even if there's no header), click the gray bar under the Report header (the Page header bar) to select it.

2. Move the pointer near the top of the bar until it assumes the shape of a double (up-down) arrow.

3. Click the mouse, and move the Page header up to close the gap.

> **NOTE**
>
> The Page header should contain a page number (and possibly other items).

4. To display the current page number in this header, right-click the area of the Page header (the white space underneath the bar with the title "Page Header").

5. From the shortcut menu, select Insert Control to open another submenu, as shown in Figure 18.12.

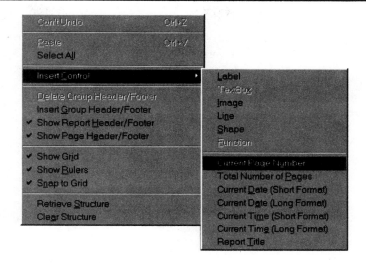

6.   Insert a Label control and a Current Page Number control next to it.

Figure 18.13 shows the Report object at its final design stage. You can use this figure as a guide during the design of your report.

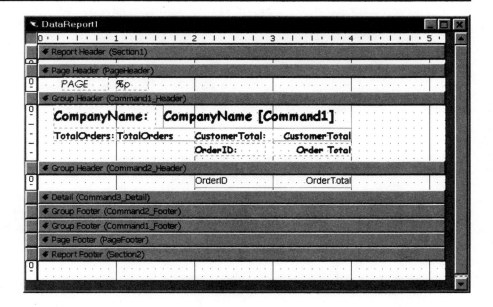

The Label control you just inserted on the report is very similar to the regular Label control. It is called *rptLabel,* and it doesn't provide as many properties as the regular Label control, but it provides enough properties for determining their appearance on the report. You can move it around with the mouse, resize it, and set its basic properties (Font and Caption) through the Properties window. The same is true for the Current Page Number control. It's a Label control, and you can set its Font, ForeColor, and even its Caption property. Its default caption is %p; this is a special value that tells Visual Basic to substitute the current page number.

Then comes the first Group header, which corresponds to the fields of the Command1 object. Obviously, we must place the company name here (you could include a contact name or a telephone number), as well as any field that's unique for each customer. The aggregate fields TotalOrders and CustomerTotal belong here are well. Follow these steps:

1. Place two more Label controls in the first Group Header's area, and set their captions to **Total Orders** and **Customer Total**.

2. Open the DataEnvironment1 Designer, and drop the fields TotalOrders and CustomerTotal under the Command1 object next to the two labels on the Group Header. Set their font appropriately and align them.

The next header corresponds to the Command2 object. This Command object contains the IDs of the invoices (field OrderID) and their totals (field OrderTotal). Place these two fields in the area of the second Group Header. Locate the corresponding fields under the Command2 object in the DataEnvironment1 Designer and drag them to the report.

If you want to print column headers for these two fields, you must place them in the previous Group Header (or else, the column headers will be repeated for each invoice). Place two more Label controls and set their caption to "Order ID" and "Order Total," as shown in Figure 18.13.

Next comes the Detail section of the report. Normally, the fields of the Command3 object should appear here (we used this Command to calculate the aggregates), but we are not interested in any of the fields of the Command3 object. So, our report will not have a Detail section. The second Group header is in essence the report's Details section (this situation is not uncommon in report design). If you want to experiment with the Detail section of the report, place the invoice details there.

Make the Detail section's height 0 by moving the following bars up. For this example, I'm not going to use any footers, but you can design footers in the same way you design the report's headers. You can place any of the controls in the Insert menu and manipulate their properties through the Properties window.

To display a report, call the DataReport1 object's Show method. Place a Command button on the project's Form, name it **Report**, and enter the following statement in its Click event handler:

```
Private Sub Command1_Click()
    DataReport1.Show
End Sub
```

Run the project again, click the Report button, and you will see the report you designed in a separate window on your screen (see Figure 18.14). The two buttons at the top of the DataReport window allow you to print the report on any printer or export the report in text or HTML format. Considering that we didn't have to enter a single line of code, the DataReport Designer did a superb job. The most important aspect of this process is that you don't have to create the printout from within your code. The grid in Figure 18.2 counts as a report, but printing it with straight Visual Basic code would be quite a task.

FIGURE 18.14:

This report was generated by the DataReport ActiveX Designer.

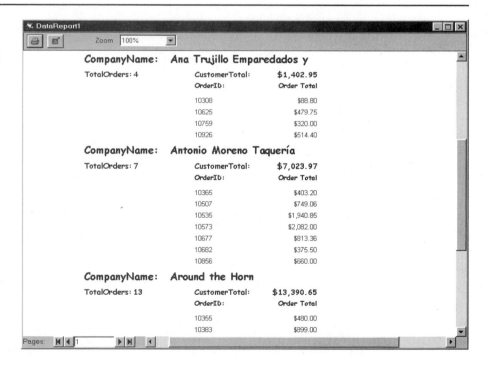

The ADO Data Control

The visual database tools are not the only possibility for developing database applications with Active Data objects. One of the new controls added to the toolbox by the Data project type is the ADO Data control, which is equivalent to the Data control. With the ADO Data control, you can connect to more databases of different types. Yet, as far as your application and your code are concerned, you can access them all with the same interface.

The simplest way to use the ADO in your projects is to add the ADO Data control to your Form and use similar to the way you've been using the Data control. To use the ADO Data control with a standard EXE project, you must add this control to the Toolbox.

Open the Project menu, and select Components to open the Components dialog box. Check the Microsoft ADO Control 6.0 (OLEDB) option. If you want to use any of the advanced data-bound controls, such as the data-bound List and ComboBox controls, you must also check the Microsoft Data List Controls 6.0 (OLEDB) option. Click OK to return to the Visual Basic IDE.

The Toolbox now contains the ADO Data Control and the DataList and Data-Combo controls. The DataList and DataCombo controls are equivalent to the DBList and DBCombo controls, only they can be bound to ADO Data controls and not to Data controls.

Let's start with a trivial example of using the ADO Data control. We'll design a very simple Form that allows you to scan the customers of the NWIND database. The ADODC project, shown in Figure 18.15, consists of a Form, on which several data-bound textboxes display the fields of the Customers table of the NWIND database. The textboxes are bound to an ADO Data control that connects them to the current record in the table. This project doesn't require a single line of code.

FIGURE 18.15:

The ADODC project demonstrates the basic data properties of the ADO Data Control, which are identical to the properties of the Data Control.

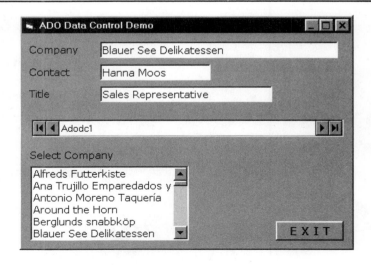

To create the ADODC project, follow these steps:

1. Start a new project, and add the ADO Data control component to the project's Toolbox.

2. Place an instance of the ADO Data control on the Form.

3. Right-click the control, and from the shortcut menu, select Properties to open the property pages of the ADO Data control.

4. Select the General tab, and check the Use ODBC Data Source Name option.

NOTE   ODBC stands for Open Database Connectivity, and it's a standard for accessing different databases uniformly (through a consistent user interface).

You must now specify a Data Source (a database that the ADO Data control will contact). As you will see, you can specify many types of databases, but the application will see them in the same way. It will access the tables and their records with the same statements, regardless of the actual database that provides them.

The Data Source Name is basically a name by which the database is known to the system. Data Source Names must be created once, and after that, any application can use them. If no Data Source name exists on your system, create a new one by following these steps:

1. Click the New button to open the Create New Data Source window. In this window, you can select the type of the Data Source, which can be one of the following:

    File Data Source   A database file that all users on the machine can access.

    User Data Source   A database file that only you can access.

    System Data Source   A database file that any user that can log on the machine can use.

2. Select System Data Source so that you can test the locking mechanisms by logging on to the machine from the network (if you are in a networked environment).

3. Click Next to display the Create New Data Source window in which you must specify the driver to be used to access the database. The driver must obviously match the database.

NOTE   As you can see, the Data Source can be any major database, including Access, Oracle, and SQL Server. In this chapter, we'll deal with Access databases.

4. Select Microsoft Access Driver, and click Next.

The next window informs you that you've selected a System Data Source and you'll be using the Access driver to access it.

5. Click Finish to create the Data Source.

At this point, you're ready to specify which Access database you want to assign to the newly created Data Source. The ODBC Microsoft Access 97 Setup window will appear. Follow these steps:

1. Specify the Data Source's name (**NWIND**) in the first box, and enter a short description (**NorthWind Sample Database**) in the Description box.

2. Click the Select button, and you'll be asked to select the database through a File Open window. Locate the NWINDDB database (it's in the VB98 folder).

When you will return to the ADO Data control's property pages, the new Data Source will appear in the Use ODBC Data Source Name drop-down list (as shown in Figure 18.16).

FIGURE 18.16:

The General tab of the ADO Data control Property Pages

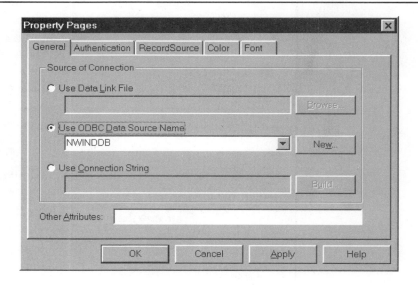

3. Expand the drop-down list, and select NWINDDB.

In essence, you've specified the database you want to use (this is similar to setting the DatabaseName property of the Data Control).The next task is to select the records that the ADO Data control will see in the database (a table or the Record-Set returned by an SQL statement).

4. Switch to the RecordSource tab.

5. In the Command Type drop-down list, select the adCmdTable entry. This is the type of the RecordSource.

6. The list below will be populated with the names of all the tables in the database. Select the Customers table.

The ADO Data Control, which is called Adodc1, sees the records of the Customers table in the NWIND database. We must now bind a few controls to the Adodc1 control, which will accept the fields of the current record.

7. Place three TextBox controls and three Label controls on the Form.

8. Set the Captions of the Label controls as shown in Figure 18.15, and then set the data-binding properties of the TextBoxes as follows:

Control Name	DataSource Property	DataField Property
Text1	Adodc1	CompanyName
Text2	Adodc2	ContactName
Text3	Adodc3	ContactTitle

You can run the project now and scan the records of the Customers table of the NWIND database through the ADO Data control. The ADO Data control behaves just like the regular Data control (or DAO Data control, to make clear which control we're talking about). Setting up the ADO Data control requires a few more steps, but only the first time you create a Data Source. The NWINDDB Data Source has been registered with the system, and you need not create it again. It will appear automatically in the list of ODBC Data Sources on the property pages of the ADO control.

Let's add an advanced data-bound control to our application. We'll add a data-bound List control. The DBList control, which we explored in the previous chapter, doesn't work with the ADO Data control. If you place an instance of the DBList control on a Form and then attempt to set its DataSource or RowSource properties through the Properties window, you'll see that it doesn't recognize the ADO Data control (the names of the ADO Data controls will not appear as choices).

The ADO Data control works with its own advanced data-bound controls, which are the DataList and DataCombo controls. To use them in the project, you must first add them to the Toolbox. Follow these steps:

1. Open the Components dialog box again, and this time check the Microsoft Data List Controls 6.0 (OLEDB) option.

2. Place an instance of the DataList control on the Form.

In this control, we are going to display the names of the companies. Then, we'll connect the DataList control to the ADO Data control so that each time the user selects a new company in the list, the corresponding fields will appear in the data-bound textboxes in the upper half of the Form.

3. To populate the DataList control with the company names from the Customers table, set the following properties:

Property	Value
RowSource	Adodc1
ListField	CompanyName
BoundColumn	CustomerID

If you run the application now, the DataList control will be populated automatically, but selecting a company name in the list will have no effect on the data-bound controls. We must add some code that will reposition the ADO Data control each time the user selects another item in the list. You saw how to do this in the last chapter. Here's the single line of code that will connect the two controls:

```
Private Sub DataList1_Click()
    Adodc1.Recordset.Bookmark = DataList1.SelectedItem
End Sub
```

Each time a new item is clicked in the list, this item becomes a bookmark for the ADO Data control. The ADO Data control retrieves the corresponding record instantly, because the DataList's BoundColumn is the CustomerID field (which happens to be an index field in the Customers table).

The ADODC project has a catch: the list of companies is already sorted, so it's easy to locate the desired company name in the DataList control. If it weren't, though, you wouldn't be able to sort the items of the control. The DataList control doesn't provide a Sorted property or a Sort method, for that matter. In most cases, the data used to populate a DataList control automatically will not be sorted. Figure 18.17 shows a variation of the ADODOC application, which displays a few fields of the Products table in the NWIND database.

If you follow similar steps to build a Form that displays the products, you'll realize that the product names are not sorted in the DataList control. If you can't easily locate an item in a list, what's the point of displaying the items there anyway?

FIGURE 18.17:

The DataList control can't be used as a navigation aid unless its items are sorted.

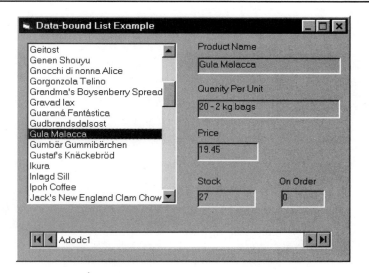

The items that populate the List come from the RecordSet specified by the control's RowSource property, which is Adodc1. In other words, we must make sure that the records of the Products table are read from the Products table in the desired order. To do so, you must change the definition of the ADO Data control's RecordSource property. Follow these steps:

1. Design a Form like the one shown in Figure 18.17.

2. Right-click the Adodc1 control, and in the property pages, set the ODBC Data Source Name to **NWINDB**.

3. Switch to the RecordSource tab, and instead of a table, specify a SQL statement: set the Command Type to **adCmdUnknown**, and enter the following SQL statement in the Command textbox:

       SELECT * FROM Products ORDER BY ProductName

This SQL statement retrieves the same RecordSet as the Products table, only the records are presented in the desired order. The DataList control will be populated with the alphabetic list of product names, and you'll be able to locate the desired item instantly. Below are the settings of the data-binding properties of the ADO Data control and the DataList control of the Form shown in Figure 18.17.

Property	Setting
Adodc1.ConnectionString	"DSN=NWINDDB"
Adodc1.RecordSource	"SELECT * FROM Products ORDER BY ProductName"

Continued on next page

Property	Setting
DataList1.RowSource	Adodc1
DataList1.ListField	ProductName

NOTE   You don't have to manually assign the settings of the properties of the Adodc1 control; use the property pages instead.

Programming the Active Data Objects

As you can see, the code-free approach to database application development, even with the ADO control, isn't the most flexible and powerful, just as with the Data control. To exploit the Active Data objects, you must be able to manipulate them programmatically from within your code. In this section, I'll discuss the ADO object model and show you how to program the basic objects of this model. In the limited space remaining in this chapter, I'm going to discuss the basics of the Active Data objects and give you a few examples that demonstrate the similarities between the ADO and DAO.

The ADO Object Model

The ADO object model is considerably simpler than the DAO model, even though it can handle more databases and supports more features. The ADO model consists of three objects.

Connection   This is the top-level object, and it represents a connection to the Data source. Normally, you establish a connection to a Data Source and then issue commands against the Connection object to retrieve the desired records from the database or to update the database. However, it is possible to establish a connection while you request a RecordSet object. The ADO Connection object is the programmatic equivalent of the Connection object of the DataEnvironment ActiveX Designer.

Command   This object represents a SQL statement or stored procedure that can be processed by the Data Source. The Command object may not return any results (if it updates the database) or return a RecordSet with the requested records. To set up a Command object, you specify the SQL statement or stored procedure and its parameters (if required). The parameters are appended to the Parameters Collection of the Command object. You can then call the Execute method to execute the SQL statement or stored procedure against the Data Source. Another approach is to create a RecordSet object, associate a Command object with it, and retrieve the RecordSet of the qualified records. The ADO Command object is the programmatic equivalent of the Command object of the DataEnvironment ActiveX Designer.

RecordSet   This object holds the results of the execution of a Command object on a database (provided it returns some records). RecordSets can be created without an explicit connection (simply pass the connection string for the Data Source to the RecordSet object's Open method). To access the fields of a RecordSet object, you can use the Fields collection. The ADO RecordSet object represents the records returned by the DataEnvironment ActiveX Designer, only you can access them from within your code, instead of dropping them on a Form.

Using the Active Data Objects

To use the Active Data objects in an application, you must add a reference to the ADO Object library in the References dialog box. Follow these steps:

1. Open the Project menu.

2. Select Project ➤ References to open the References dialog box.

3. Check the Microsoft ActiveX Data Objects 2.0 Library option.

After the ADO Library is added to a project, you can examine the objects it exposes and their members with the Object Browser. If you have used the Remote Data objects with Visual Basic 5, you'll find that the main objects exposed by the ADO object model are similar to the RDO objects and that the process of accessing a database with the ADO is also similar. First, you must create a connection, and then you execute SQL statements or stored procedures against the database and process the results of the query, which are returned in a RecordSet object. In the following sections, we are going to examine these steps and the objects involved in detail.

Establishing a Connection

To establish an explicit connection to a Data Source, declare a *Connection* variable with this statement:

```
Dim ADOConn As New ADODB.Connection
```

(The prefix ADODB is not necessary, unless you are also using DAO objects in the same project, because they will take precedence.) Now, call the ADOConn object's Open method by passing the connection string as an argument:

```
ADOConn.Open "DSN=AdvWorks;UID=xxx;PWD=xxx"
```

(Here, xxx is the appropriate UserID and Password.) The DSN named argument is the name of a Data Source.

Once the Connection object is created, you can assign it to the ActiveConnection property of the RecordSet or Command object.

Executing SQL Statements

ADO is very flexible when it comes to executing SQL statements. You can execute a SQL statement with any of the three objects exposed (Connection, Command, and RecordSet). There are advantages and disadvantages to each, but let's review them first and then evaluate them.

Querying through the Connection Object

The first way to execute SQL statements is to use the Execute method of the Connection object:

```
ADOConn.Execute "SELECT * FROM Products", numRecords, adCmdText
```

The second (optional) argument returns the number of records affected by an action query or the number of records returned by a select query. The last argument, which is also optional, determines whether the first argument is a SQL statement (aCmd-Text) or a stored procedure (aCmdStoredProc).

Querying through the Command Object

The second way is to create a Command object and call its Execute method. The Command object supports a number of properties, but you must at least provide the ActiveConnection and CommandText properties, as shown in the following example:

```
With ADOConn
    .ActiveConnection = connectString
    .CommandText = "SELECT * FROM Products", _
                    numRecords, adCmdText
    .Execute
End With
```

Querying through the RecordSet Object

Finally, you can use the RecordSet object's Open method, whose syntax is:

```
ADORSet.Open SQLstatement, connectString, RecordsetType, _
            LockType, CommandType
```

The *RecordsetType* argument determines the type of the RecordSet and can have one of the following values:

- adOpenDynamic
- adOpenForwardOnly
- adOpenKeyset
- adOpenStatic

NOTE   For an explanation of the four types of RecordSets, see the next section.

The *LockType* argument determines the concurrency control and can have one of the following values:

- adLockBatchOptimistic
- adLockOptimistic
- adLockPessimistic
- adLockReadOnly

NOTE   For an explanation of the four types of locking control, see the next section.

The following statement creates a RecordSet with a simple SQL statement, executed against the RecordSet object itself:

```
Set ADORSet = "SELECT * FROM Products", connectString, _
               adOpenForwardOnly, adLockReadOnly, adCmdText
```

If you are executing SQL statements that affect a lot of records or stored procedures, you should use the Command object. It doesn't create a cursor, and it's the only mechanism that allows you to specify parameters. Avoid executing SQL statements using the RecordSet object, because this object was designed to accept RecordSets, not to create them. Of all objects, only the Command object supports transactions; so if you are executing action queries (which are usually implemented as transactions), you must use the Command object.

Cursor Types and Locking Mechanisms

A *cursor* is the information underlying the RecordSet. A RecordSet is a representation of the selected records, which simplifies the manipulation of the records. As a programmer, you see a table of records, each row made up of fields. ADO, however, doesn't see a table. It sees a cursor, which usually contains information that allows it to present the records to your application as rows of fields. There are four types of cursors: Dynamic, Keyset, Static, and Forward-Only.

To specify the type of cursor that best suits the needs of your application, use the *CursorType* property, which can take one of the values in Table 18.1.

The CursorType property must be set before the RecordSet is opened. If you don't specify a cursor type, ADO opens a forward-only cursor by default.

TABLE 18.1: The Values of the CursorType Property

Cursor Type	Constant	Description
Dynamic	adOpenDynamic	The RecordSet is always synchronized with the records in the database. Allows you to view additions, changes, and deletions made by other users, and supports all Move methods.
Keyset	adOpenKeySet	Behaves like a dynamic cursor, except that it prevents you from seeing records that other users add or delete. Changes made to the selected records by other users will still be visible. It supports all Move methods.
Static	adOpenStatic	Provides a static copy of the qualifying records. It supports all Move methods, but any changes made by other users will not be visible.
Forward-only	adOpenForwardOnly	Identical to the dynamic cursor except that it allows you to only scroll forward through records. This improves performance if you need to make only a single pass through a RecordSet.

The CursorLocation Property   In addition to the type of RecordSet, you can also define the cursor's location with the CursorLocation property. The cursor is usually opened on the server, but you can also open the cursor on the client. Client cursors can speed up the application, provided that you don't have to update the database instantly. Client cursors can be static only, and they can update the database through batch updates (the application modifies the RecordSet and then submits the changes to the server).

> **NOTE**   Batch updates is a fairly complicated topic, which I'm not going to discuss further in this book. One of the implications is what happens when other users have already changed some of the records after your application has read them and before it had a chance to update them. For more information on batch updates, see the documentation of the UpdateBatch method of the RecordSet object.

The LockType Property   Another important property of the RecordSet object is the LockType property, which indicates the type of locks placed on records during editing. Set the LockType property before opening a RecordSet to specify what type of locking the provider should use when opening it. The LockType property can take one of the values in Table 18.2.

> **NOTE**   With the client-side RecordSet object, the LockType property can be set only to ad-LockOptimisticBatch.

TABLE 18.2: The Values of the LockType Property

Value	Constant	Description
Read-only	*adLockReadOnly*	The Recordset is opened for reading only. Use this type of locking to prevent changes of the data.
Pessimistic locking	*adLockPessimistic*	The provider does what is necessary to ensure successful editing of the records, usually by locking records at the Data Source immediately upon editing.
Optimistic locking	*adLockOptimistic*	The provider uses optimistic locking, locking records only when you call the Update method.
Optimistic batch updates	*adLockBatchOptimistic*	Required for batch update mode as opposed to immediate update mode.

Another important aspect of ADO is the so-called *concurrency control*. When your code accesses a record in a database for editing, other users may modify the same record before your code has a chance to write back the edited record. Will your code overwrite the modified record? Will you detect the condition from within your code and notify the user? There's no simple and unique answer to this question—it depends on the application. To deal with similar situations, you must understand how pessimistic and optimistic locking works.

Pessimistic Locking   Pessimistic locking is a sure, but very restrictive method. With pessimistic locking, all the pages that contain the records you've requested are locked. No one else can modify them (but they can read them). The good news about pessimistic locking is that it simplifies your code. However, if the user opens a RecordSet and then walks off, the corresponding page(s) may remain locked for a very long time. If you choose to use pessimistic locking in your code, make sure you use small RecordSets, that can fit in a single page (this number differs among different databases).

Optimistic Locking   With optimistic locking, only the page that contains the record being edited is locked, and only while the record is being updated (which lasts an instance). It sounds more reasonable to lock a page only while you're updating it, but this method doesn't solve the concurrency problem. Two users open the same record for editing; one of them commits the changes to the database. After this event, the second user has an outdated version of the record on his or her screen. ADO doesn't notify the application that a record has changed. Even worse, what will your application do? Overwrite the changes, notify the user, or what?

The answer to this question will be dictated by the needs of the application. You must provide the code to figure out whether the record you're about to update has changed since it was read (you can use a special field for this purpose or re-read the original record from the database), lock it, compare it with the record you read initially, and update the record only if it hasn't changed in the database. If it did, you should probably notify the user and present a list of options (overwrite, abort, start editing the new one) for them to choose.

Manipulating the RecordSet Object

Once you create a RecordSet, you can access its records and their fields with a few methods and properties that are identical to the properties and methods of the DAO RecordSet object. The number of records retrieved is returned by the *RecordCount* property, which has a meaningful value only if you visit the last record. For forward-only RecordSets, you simply can't find out the number of records; you must scan them all and process them as you go along. Or, you can jump to the last record with the MoveLast method and then back to the first record with the MoveFirst method. Then, you can call the RecordCount property to retrieve the number of rows in the RecordSet. Of course, this method will not work with Forward-Only RecordSets.

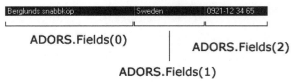

Individual field values in a row (record) can be accessed by the Fields collection. The number of columns in the RecordSet is given by the property *Fields.Count*. Each field in the current row can be accessed by an index (which is the field's ordinal value in the SQL statement) or by its name. If the SQL statement on which the RecSet RecordSet was based is:

```
SELECT ProductName, ProductID FROM Products
```

you can access the product's name in the current record with this expression:

```
RecSet.Fields(0).Value
```

or with this expression:

```
RecSet.Fields("ProductName").Value
```

(You can omit Value because it's the default property of the Fields collection.)

To scan the RecordSet, use the Move methods (MoveFirst, MoveLast, Move-Previous, and MoveNext). In addition to these navigation methods, the RecordSet object provides the *AbsolutePosition* method, which indicates the current record's position in the RecordSet.

To scan a RecordSet, you can use a loop like the following:

```
For Each rec In RecSet
    {process current record}
Next
```

or you can set up a For ... Next loop like this one:

```
RecSet.MoveLast
AllRecs = RecSet.RecordCount
RecSet.MoveFirst
For  i = 1 To AllRecs
    {process current record}
    RecSet.MoveNext
Next
```

You can also set up a similar loop to scan the columns of the RecordSet. The names of the fields are given by the *Fields(i).Name* property. The following loop prints the names of the columns in the RecSet Recordset:

```
For Each fld In RecSet.Fields
    Debug.Print fld.Name
Next
```

You can also sort the RecordSet according to a field's value, or you can filter it to isolate selected records. It's usually best to retrieve only the records you need and in the order you wish. When this is not possible or when you create a client-side RecordSet and you want to process different records in different ways, you can use the Sort and Filter properties of the RecordSet.

The *Sort* property accepts as an argument the name of the field according to which you want to sort the RecordSet. Let's say you have created a RecordSet with the customers of the NWIND database, and you want to sort it according to the Country field. Call the Sort property as follows:

```
RSCustomers.Sort = "Country ASCENDING"
```

To isolate selected records in a RecordSet, use the following statement:

```
RSCustomers.Filter = "Country = 'Germany'"
```

RSCustomers.Filter is not a method and doesn't return a new RecordSet. The Move methods, however, will ignore the records whose Country field is not Germany.

Simple Record Editing and Updating

A major difference between the ADO RecordSet object and DAO RecordSets or RDO ResultSets is that there is no Edit method. You don't have to prepare a record for editing; instead, you can assign a new value to a field. Neither do you have to call the Update method for the changes to be written to the database. When you move off the current record, any changes are automatically saved to the database.

Another interesting feature of the ADO RecordSet object is that it allows you to create arrays of field names and values and use them to add new records. To add a new record, use the *AddNew* method. Here's the code for adding a new record to the current RecordSet (RecSet) using an array:

```
RecSet.AddNew Array("ProductName", "CategoryID", "UnitPrice"),
Array("Ma's Marmelade", 34, 3.45)
```

The new record will be saved to the database when you move to another record or when you call the RecSet.Update method.

Editing the current record is even simpler. You just assign new values to the fields:

```
RecSet.Fields("ProductName") = "Ma's Marmelade"
```

To update many fields in the record, use the Array syntax instead:

```
RecSet.Update Array("ProductName", "CategoryID", "UnitPrice"),
Array("Ma's Marmelade", 34, 3.45)
```

The AddNew and Update methods accept two arrays as arguments. The first one contains the names of the fields, and the second one, their new values.

In the last section of this chapter, we'll look at two simple examples of programming the Active Data objects.

VB6 at Work: The ADO1 and ADO2 Project

On the CD, you will find two simple projects that demonstrate some of the methods and properties of the ADO component. Open the ADO1 and ADO2 projects in the Visual Basic IDE and examine their code. The ADO1 project demonstrates basic record retrieval and manipulation operations. Its main Form contains two lists, which are populated with the names of the various categories (table Categories in the NWIND database) and the names of the products in the selected category, respectively. When the user selects a category in the first list, the other one is populated with the products of the selected category.

The ADO2 project demonstrates the two methods for executing SQL statements against the database:

- The Connection.Execute button retrieves all the category names from the Categories table by passing a SQL statement to the Connection object. It then populates a plain List control with the records.

- The Command.Execute button retrieves all the invoices by invoking the Invoices stored procedure (a SQL statement that has been attached to the database). It then populates a plain Grid control. The program also calculates the totals per customer and displays them on the same grid following each customer's list of invoices.

The invoices are retrieved sorted by date, so the totals per customer are for a specific date only, and the same customer may appear many times. To retrieve all invoices for each customer, you must modify the stored procedure by adding the following clause to the SQL statement:

```
ORDER BY Orders.OrderDate
```

PART VI

Visual Basic and the Web

Introduction to the Web

- Understanding Internet and Web protocols

- Introducing HTML

- Activating the client with VBScript

- Working with Dynamic HTML

If there is one technology that caught up literally overnight and has affected more users than any other, it is the Web. The World Wide Web is the set of all Web sites and the documents they can provide to clients. The computers that host Web sites are called *servers*; their service is to provide the documents that clients request. *Clients* are the millions of personal computers connected to the Internet. To exploit the Web, all you need is a browser, such as Internet Explorer, that can request documents and render them on the client computer.

I assume that most of you are familiar with the Web. This chapter is a compendium of information on how to apply the knowledge you acquired in previous chapters to the Web. Or, to use a popular term, *leverage* your knowledge of Visual Basic by applying it to the Web. To do so, you need a basic understanding of HTML (HyperText Markup Language), the language used to build Web documents, and VBScript, the language for programming the Web client and the Web server.

The first section of this chapter describes the protocols used on the Web and on the Internet, and then I briefly discuss HTML tags and show you how to use HTML to build simple hyperlinked documents (static Web pages). Next, we look at how to activate Web pages by scripting them with VBScript and adding ActiveX controls to them. In short, you will learn how to turn a static Web page into an interactive application that can be executed over the Internet, in the browser's window. We will also build Web pages that use the custom ActiveX controls we developed in the last chapter.

I will also discuss the basics of developing Dynamic HTML pages. DHTML is the latest trend in Web page design, which takes HTML to a new level, allowing Web authors to develop HTML applications that behave like desktop applications, with rich multimedia elements. DHTML is a huge topic to discuss in detail, so I will just demonstrate the principles of DHTML. Since I can't cover everything you need to know about the Web, I'll focus on a few topics that will help you understand how the Web works and how to develop Web pages that behave like applications, and then I'll discuss the role of VBScript in programming Web pages. In the following chapters, you'll find more specific information on how to combine Visual Basic and Web authoring techniques, both on the Web and in your Visual Basic applications. As you will see, it's possible to display HTML pages on VB Forms and exploit the hyperlinked model of the Web from within your applications.

The Web Also Means Intranets

The information in this chapter isn't addressed only to those of you who are going to publish documents on the Internet. You will also find it useful in building *intranet* applications.

The Web caught on so rapidly because it's really simple to use. It has even become an integral part of the operating system itself, and the Windows 98 Desktop is based on the hypertext model.

If Web technology simplified a chaotic structure such as the Internet, why not also use it on local networks? Indeed, many local area networks are designed as miniature Internets. An intranet, or corporate internet, is a local area network that uses Internet technology. On an intranet, you can exploit the Web model to simplify operations, without the security issues you face on the Internet or the limitations imposed by connecting computers with modems.

An intranet is also a network of computers operating on the TCP/IP protocol, but it is not global. Intranets are restricted to the users of a corporation, a university, or some other organization, and they are not accessible by the outside world. Unlike the World Wide Web, intranets don't have more than one server. This machine supplies all the documents requested by the clients.

Many corporations use intranets to provide information to their employees, and they run another Web site for external users. The reason for building corporate intranets is to exploit the technology that made the Web so popular. So, the main characteristic of a corporate intranet is not that it uses TCP/IP, as much as HTTP (HyperText Transfer Protocol).

Internet and Web Protocols

The Internet is a global, distributed network of computers that use a common protocol to communicate—*TCP/IP (Transmission Control Protocol/Internet Protocol)*. TCP/IP is a simple protocol because it had to be implemented consistently on all computers and operating systems. Indeed, TCP/IP is a truly universal protocol, but you needn't know much about it. It's there when you need it and allows your computer to connect to any other computer on the Internet.

Each computer on the Internet has a unique address, for example, 193.25.84.100. Every number is a value in the range 0 through 255, which means the Internet can't have more than 256*256*256*256, or approximately 4,000,000,000 computers. This number isn't as large as it may seem, because many of the possible values are reserved. Others are assigned to organizations that may or may not be using all of them. To accommodate a large number of users, Internet service providers use a pool of addresses (since not all users connect at once, 256 addresses may accommodate 1,000 users or more). It would be nice if we all had a unique IP address, like an e-mail address, but this is not possible. If we did, we could build wide area networks that span the globe easily. However, every time you connect to your Internet service provider you get a different IP address.

If TCP/IP enables any two computers on the Internet to talk to each other, why do we need another protocol? HTTP is the protocol of the Web. Whereas TCP/IP allows two computers to connect on the hardware level, HTTP is the language servers and clients use to exchange information. HTTP is optimized for requesting and supplying HTML documents. The Internet is more than the Web (although it seems the Web is taking over). To exchange files through the Internet, for example, computers use the File Transfer Protocol (FTP). The protocol that is used depends on the type of information to be exchanged. All other protocols, however, run on top of the TCP/IP protocol.

In the following section, I'm going to discuss briefly the components of the Web and the evolution of Web documents.

HTML Pages

The simplest component of the Web is HTML (HyperText Markup Language). HTML is a simple language for formatting documents that are displayed in a Web browser. The primary task of the browser is to render documents according to the HTML tags they contain and display them on the monitor.

Using HTML editors and WYSISYG (What You See Is What You Get) tools, you can publish information in a form suitable for viewing with a browser, on or off the Internet. There's no reason that a company couldn't publish its internal documents in HTML format and make them available on the local area network. The benefits of this approach are many, and Office 97 supports HTML publishing. Any document you can create with an Office 97 application can be converted to HTML format and published on a Web server, either on the Internet or on a corporate intranet. People can locate the information they seek by following hyperlinks, a process they are already accustomed to. Information is up-to-date, at least as much so as the person(s) in charge can make it.

HTML is made up of text-formatting tags that are placed in a pair of angle brackets; they usually appear in pairs. The first tag turns on a formatting feature, and the matching tag turns it off. To format a few words in bold, for example, enclose them with the <B> and </B> tags, as shown here:

```
Some <B>words</B> in the sentence are formatted in <B>bold</B>.
```

Of course, not all tags are as simple. The <TABLE> tag, for example, which is used to format tables, requires additional tags, like the <TR> tag, which delimits a new row in the table, and the <TD> tag, which delimits a new cell in a row. Tags are also assisted by attributes, which are keywords with special meanings within a specific tag. The <A> tag, which is used to insert a hyperlink in the document, recognizes the HREF attribute. The syntax of a hyperlink to Microsoft's home page on the Web would be something like:

```
This <A HREF="http://www.microsoft.com">link</A> will take you to
Microsoft's home page.
```

The text between the <A> and </A> tags is marked as a hyperlink (displayed in a different color and underlined). The HREF attribute in the <A> tag tells the browser which URL, or address, to jump to when a user clicks this hyperlink.

As a VB programmer, you'll have no problem picking up the syntax of HTML. If you are not familiar with HTML, you'll want to peruse the quick introduction in the section "An HTML Primer," later in this chapter. It covers the elements of the language we are going to use in the examples in the following chapters and is addressed to VB programmers—just the essentials. For a complete HTML reference, including all the tags recognized by Internet Explorer and their attributes, visit http://www .microsoft.com/workshop/author/newhtml.

Server-Client Interaction

A Web site consisting of HTML pages is interactive only in the sense that it allows the user to jump from page to page through hyperlinks. The client requests documents from the server, and the server supplies them. In this simple interaction model, which dominates the Web today, Web pages reside on the disks of the servers waiting to be requested by a client. Obviously, updating the information entails editing the HTML documents; no wonder most sites can't provide up-to-date information.

The disadvantage of this model is that the client can't engage in a conversation with the server so that information can flow in both directions. The development of gateway interfaces such as the *Common Gateway Interface* (CGI) has enabled Web authors to add dynamic content to the Web. The client can send specific requests to the server (e.g., "show me the invoices issued last month" or "show me the customers in North America"). The server doesn't return a static page (a page that exists on the disk and can be called by its name). Instead, it executes a script, or application, that extracts "live" data from a database, formats the data as an HTML document, and sends the document to the client. The client sees up-to-date, accurate information.

The disadvantage of gateway programs is that they are difficult to implement and maintain. To simplify CGI programming, Microsoft introduced several technologies, the most recent and popular being Active Server Pages (a topic we'll discuss in the last chapter of this book). Developing Active Server Pages is as simple as developing Visual Basic applications.

Scripting

Initially, the role of the browser was to render Web pages on the client computer. Web pages are simple text files with the text and information as to how the text should appear in the browser's window. HTML is a document-formatting language, as is RTF (Rich Text Format); it's not a programming language. Displaying a Web page in the browser is similar to rendering an RTF file on the RichTextBox control, and you can't use HTML to carry out even simple calculations such as additions or to display the day's name in the browser's window.

Most clients, however, are powerful computers that can do much more than display documents. To exploit the processing power of the clients, scripting languages have been introduced, the simplest being VBScript. Scripting enables Web authors to create dynamic content by embedding executable scripts directly in an HTML page. You can use VBScript to program the elements of a Web page, as well as server applications (through Active Server Pages). You'll see shortly how a Web page can interact (to a limited extent, of course) with the viewer through scripts and how some of the processing that would normally take place on the server can be carried out by the client.

Dynamic HTML (DHTML)

Dynamic HTML (DHTML) is a departure from HTML. It doesn't introduce any new tags, but makes the existing tags programmable. It lets you mix HTML tags with VBScript statements to manipulate the appearance of the document dynamically. For example, it supports layering, which allows you to rearrange elements on a page in response to the user's actions. You can overlap images and specify that the image under the pointer be brought in front of the others. When the pointer is moved over another image, that image is brought on top. Or you can change the color of text elements (such as headings, table cells, and so on) when the pointer moves over them.

DHTML can add rich multimedia effects to a page, such as moving sprites (irregularly shaped images that can be moved around or behind and in front of one another), color gradients across text, dynamic audio mixing, transition effects, and more, without the involvement of the server. DHTML includes animation and multimedia controls that can be used to apply visual effects to selected elements on a page or to the entire page. These controls support filters, animation, and transitions, features that will allow you to build pages with some of the effects used on television today. Multimedia capabilities are no longer added features, but capabilities built into this new flavor of HTML. The multimedia controls you can use in your HTML pages are not discussed in this chapter, but you can find additional information at the following URL:

```
http://www.microsoft.com/workshop/c-frame.htm#/workshop/author/
default.asp
```

Another feature of DHTML, which makes it suitable for business applications, is data awareness. Each data-aware page contains an invisible ActiveX control that communicates with a data source, similar to the Data control of Visual Basic. With this control, you can create Forms with intrinsic, ActiveX controls that are bound to fields in a record. Data entered by the user in the control is saved to the Data Source control, which can transmit the data to the server under program control.

An HTML Primer

HTML is the language you use to prepare documents for online publication. HTML documents are also called *Web documents*. A page is what you see in your browser at any time. Each *Web site*, whether on the Internet or on an intranet, is composed of multiple pages, and you can switch among the pages by following *hyperlinks*. The collection of HTML pages out there makes up the *World Wide Web*.

A Web page is basically a text file that contains the text to be displayed and references to elements such as images, sounds, and of course, hyperlinks to other documents. You can create HTML pages with a text editor such as Notepad or with a WYSIWYG application such as Microsoft FrontPage. In either case, the result is a plain text file that computers can easily exchange. The browser displays this text file on the client computer.

Web pages are stored on computers that act as *servers*: they provide a page to any computer that requests it. Each server computer has an address, or URL, that is something like the following:

```
http://www.mycomputer.com
```

The first portion, `http`, is the protocol used in accessing the server, and `www` `.mycomputer.com` is the name of the server on the Internet. As I mentioned earlier, all computers on the Internet have a unique numeric address, such as 193.22.103.18. This numeric address is known as the IP (Internet Protocol) address, which is more difficult for us humans to remember than names. The server looks up the mnemonic names in tables and translates them into IP addresses.

To post an HTML document on a computer so that viewers can access and display it with their browsers, the computer that hosts the document must run a special application called the Web server. The *Web server* acknowledges requests made by other computers, the client computers, and supplies the requested document. The browser, which is the application running on the client computer, gets the document and displays it on the screen.

URLs and Hyperlinks

The key element in a Web page is the hyperlink, a special instruction embedded in the text that causes the browser to load another page. To connect to another computer and request a document, the hyperlink must contain the name of the computer that hosts the document and the name of the document. Just as each computer on the Internet has a unique name, each document on a computer has a unique name. Thus, each document on the World Wide Web has a unique address, which is called a *URL* (Uniform Resource Locator). The URL for a Web document is something like the following:

```
http://www.someserver.com/docName.htm
```

> **NOTE**   You will notice that some URLs end in **htm** and some end in **html**. They are identical, with the exception that the operating system on which the pages with the extension **htm** were developed doesn't support long file names or the author chose to follow the DOS file-naming conventions. The sample pages you'll find on the CD have the extension **htm**, which is a limitation imposed by the CD production process and has nothing to do with the system on which they were developed.

Every piece of information on the World Wide Web has a unique address and can be accessed via its URL. What the browser does depends on the nature of the item. If it's a Web page or an image, the browser displays it. If it's a sound file, the browser plays it back. Today's browsers (such as Internet Explorer) can process many types of documents. Others can't. When a browser runs into a document it can't handle, it asks whether the user wants to download and save the file on disk or open it with an application that the user specifies.

The Structure of HTML Documents

HTML files are text files that contain text and formatting commands. The commands are strings with a consistent syntax, so that the browser can distinguish them from the text. Every HTML tag appears in a pair of angle brackets (<>). The tag <I> turns on the italic attribute and the following text is displayed in italics, until the </I> tag is found. The statement:

```
HTML is <I>the</I> language of the Web.
```

will render the following sentence on the browser, without the tags and with the word *the* in italics:

```
HTML is the language of the Web.
```

Most tags act upon a portion of the text and appear in pairs. One tag turns on a specific feature, and the other turns it off. The <I> tag is an example, and so are the <B> and <U> tags, which turn on the bold and underline attributes. The tag that turns off an attribute is always preceded by a slash character. To display a segment of text in bold, enclose it with the tags <B> and </B>.

Tags are not case-sensitive; for example, you could also enter the italic tags as <i> and </i>. In this book and on the companion CD-ROM, I use uppercase for HTML commands so that they'll stand out. Most WYSIWYG HTML editors insert HTML tags in lowercase.

NOTE   The matching closing tag is not always required. For example, you don't need to use the pair <P></P> to insert a paragraph; the single <P> tag will insert a line break.

The structure of an HTML document is shown next. If you store the following lines in a text file with the extension HTM and then open it with Internet Explorer, you will see the traditional greeting. Here's the HTML document:

```
<HTML>
<HEAD>
<TITLE>Your Title Goes Here</TITLE>
</HEAD>
<BODY>
Hello, World!
</BODY>
</HTML>
```

To create the most fundamental HTML document, you must start with the <HTML> tag and end with the </HTML> tag. The document's HEAD section, marked with the <HEAD> and </HEAD> tags, is where you normally place the following elements:

- The document's title
- The META and BASE tags
- Scripts

The title is the text that appears in the title bar of the browser's window and is specified with the <TITLE> and </TITLE> tags. META tags don't display anywhere on the screen, but contain useful information regarding the content of the document, such as a description and keywords used by search engines. For example:

```
<HTML>
<HEAD>
<TITLE>Your Title Goes Here</TITLE>
<META NAME="Keywords" CONTENT= _
        "health, nutrition, weight control, _
          chronic illness">
</HEAD>
</HTML>
```

Attributes

Many HTML tags understand special keywords, which are called *attributes*. The <BODY> tag, which marks the beginning of the document's body, for instance, recognizes the BGCOLOR and BACKGROUND attributes, which let you specify the color of the background or an image to appear in the document's background. You can also specify the document's background color (if there's no background image) and the color of the text with the TEXT and BGCOLOR attributes:

```
<HTML>
<HEAD>
<TITLE>Your Title Goes Here</TITLE>
</HEAD>
<BODY BACKGROUND="paper.jpg">
<H1>Tiled Background</H1>
<P>The background of this page was created with a small image, which is
tiled vertically and horizontally by the browser.
<BR>
The image was designed so that its left edge matches with its right
edge and its top edge matches with the bottom edge. Notice that you
can't detect where one instance ends and the next one begins.
</BODY>
</HTML>
```

Background images start tiling at the upper-left corner and work their way across and then down the screen. Figure 19.1 (the top image) shows an example. You can build nicely textured backgrounds by using the successive nature of the tiles, and small image files can tile just as well as large ones. Be careful to merge the edges of the image files though, or you'll end up with a "tiled" look, unless perhaps that's what you're aiming for (see the bottom image in Figure 19.1). Of course, in this particular instance, any color of text would hardly be readable, unless it was large and had good contrast.

FIGURE 19.1:

A background image tiled across the screen

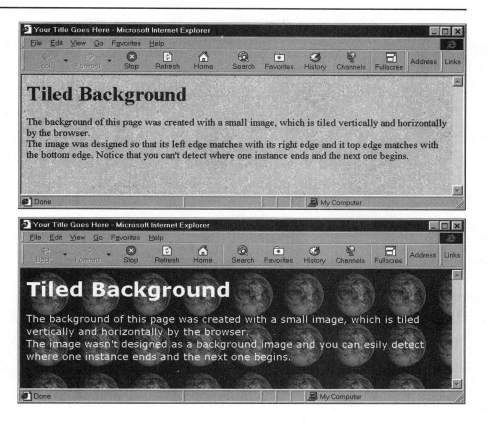

The Basic HTML Tags

No matter what you are going to do on the Web, some basic understanding of HTML is required. HTML is certainly easy for a Visual Basic programmer to learn and use. The small part of HTML presented here is all you need to build functional Web pages. The following are the really necessary tags for creating no-frills HTML documents, grouped by category.

Headers

Headers separate sections of a document. Like documents prepared with a word processor, HTML documents can have headers, which are inserted with the <H*n*> tag. There are six levels of headers, starting with <H1> (the largest) and ending with <H6> (the smallest). To place a level 1 header at the top of the document use the tag <H1>:

```
<H1>Welcome to Our Fabulous Site</H1>
```

A related tag is the <HR> tag, which displays a horizontal rule and is frequently used to separate sections of a document. The document in Figure 19.2, which demonstrates the HTML tags discussed so far, was produced with the following HTML file:

```
<HTML>
    <HEAD>
        <TITLE>
            Document title
        </TITLE>
    </HEAD>
    <BODY>
<H1>Sample HTML Document</H1>
<HR>
<H3>The document's body may contain:</H4>
<H4>Text, images, sounds and HTML commands</H4>
    </BODY>
</HTML>
```

FIGURE 19.2:

A simple HTML document with headers and a rule

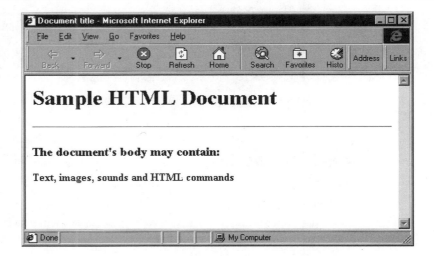

Paragraph Formatting

HTML won't break lines into paragraphs whenever you insert a carriage return in the text file. The formatting of the paragraphs is determined by the font(s) used in the document and the size of the browser's window. To force a new paragraph, you must explicitly tell the browser to insert a carriage return with the <P> tag. The <P> tag also causes the browser to insert additional vertical space. To format paragraphs without the additional vertical space, use the <BR> tag.

How to Test HTML Tags

Although there are WYSIWYG tools for creating HTML documents, a simple editor such as Notepad is all you need to experiment with the few tags discussed in this chapter. Create a simple text file with the basic HTML document structure listed above. Save the file as TEST.HTM (use any name, but the extension must be HTM). When you save this file for the first time, be sure to select All Files in the Save As Type field of the Save As dialog box. If you don't change the default extension, the TXT extension is appended, and you'll end up with a file named TEST.HTM.TXT.

After saving the document, switch to Internet Explorer, and open the document by choosing File ➢ Open. From this point on, you can move back and forth between the text editor and the browser. You can edit the HTML file, save it, switch to the Internet Explorer window, and press F5 to load the updated version of the file.

Character Formatting

HTML provides a number of tags for formatting words and characters. Table 19.1 shows the basic character-formatting tags, and following the table is a description of the FONT tag and its arguments.

TABLE 19.1:   The Basic HTML Character-Formatting Tags

TAG	WHAT IT DOES
<B>	Turns on the bold attribute
<I>	Turns on the italic attribute
<TT>	Turns on the typewriter attribute and is used frequently to display computer listings
<EM>	Emphasizes text and is identical to the <I> tag
<CODE>	Displays text in a monospaced font and is used for computer listings

The <FONT> Tag   Specifies the name, size, and color of the font to be used. The <FONT> tag takes one or more of the following arguments:

- **SIZE**   Specifies the size of the text in a relative manner. The value of the SIZE argument is not expressed in points, pixels, or any other absolute unit. Instead, it's a number in the range 1 (the smallest) through 7 (the largest). The following tag displays the text in the smallest possible size:

  ```
  <FONT SIZE=1>tiny type</FONT>
  ```

The following tag displays text in the largest possible size:

```
<FONT SIZE=7>HUGE TYPE</FONT>
```

- **FACE** Specifies the font that will be used to display the text. If the specified font does not exist on the client computer, the browser substitutes a similar font. The following tag displays the text between FONT and its matching tag in the Comic Sans MS typeface:

```
<FONT FACE = "Comic Sans MS"> Some text </FONT>
```

You can also specify multiple typefaces. The browser uses the one specified first. If it's not available, it tries the next one, and so on, as shown in the following:

```
<FONT FACE = "Comic Sans MS, Arial"> Some text </FONT>
```

If the Comic Sans MS typeface is missing on the client computer, the browser displays the text in Arial (which should not be missing on any Windows machine). Some interesting typefaces designed for Web pages (such as Verdana, Comic Sans MS, and Tahoma) are installed along with Internet Explorer.

- **COLOR** Specifies the color of the text. You specify colors as hexadecimal numbers (#FF00FF) or by name. Internet Explorer recognizes the following color names:

Aqua	Gray	Navy	Silver
Black	Green	Olive	Teal
Blue	Lime	Purple	White
Fuchsia	Maroon	Red	Yellow

The following lines display the text in red:

```
<FONT COLOR=Red>This is red text</FONT>
<FONT COLOR=#FF0000> This is red text</FONT>
```

You can also combine multiple attributes in a single <FONT> tag, as follows:

```
<FONT FACE="Arial, Sans" SIZE=5 COLOR=Red>
```

Hyperlinks

The tag that makes HTML documents come alive is the <A> tag, which inserts hyperlinks in a document. A hyperlink is a string that appears in a different color from the rest of the text; when the mouse pointer is over a hyperlink, the pointer turns into a finger (some browsers may display a different pointer, but it will be clear that the text under the pointer is a hyperlink). When you click the mouse button over a hyperlink, the browser requests and displays another document (which could be on the same or another server).

The <A> and </A> tags enclose one or more words that will be highlighted as hyperlinks. In addition, you must specify the URL of the hyperlink's destination. For example, the URL of the Sybex home page is:

```
http://www.sybex.com
```

The URL to jump to is indicated with the HREF attribute of the <A> tag. To display the string "Visit the SYBEX home page" and to use the word *SYBEX* as the hyperlink, you enter the following in your document:

```
Visit the <A HREF="http://www.sybex.com">SYBEX</A> home page
```

This inserts a hyperlink in the document, and each time the user clicks on the SYBEX hyperlink, the browser displays the main page at the specified URL.

NOTE   You need not specify a document name in the hyperlink. The server supplies the default page, which is known as the *home page*. The home page is usually the entry to a specific site and contains hyperlinks to other pages making up the site.

To jump directly to a specific page on a Web site, use a hyperlink such as the following:

```
View a document on<A HREF = "http://www.sybex.com/HTMLTutorial.htm">
HTML programming</A> on the Sybex site.
```

Most hyperlinks on a typical page jump to other documents that reside on the same server. These hyperlinks usually contain a relative reference to another document on the same server. For example, to specify a hyperlink to the document Images.htm that resides in the same folder as the current page, use the following tag:

```
Click <A HREF=".\Images.htm">here</A> to view the images.
```

If the Images.htm file resides in the Bitmaps folder under the current folder, you use the following statement:

```
Click <A HREF="..\Bitmaps\Images.htm">here</A> to view the images.
```

Inserting Graphics

Graphics play an important role in Web page design. There are hardly any pages on the World Wide Web that don't use graphics, and some pages contain hardly any text. Graphics are not inserted in the HTML document directly. The document itself contains special tags, which reference the image to be inserted by the browser when the page is opened. Because of this, graphics files are downloaded separately and placed on the page by the browser.

On the Web, where every byte counts and downloads must be fast, images must contain as much information in as few bytes as possible. Despite the number of graphics formats available today, two formats have dominated the Web:

- JPEG (Joint Photographic Experts Group)
- GIF (Graphics Interchange Format)

These formats are used because they compress graphics files to a manageable size. JPEG files can be compressed a good deal (albeit with some loss of detail), but they maintain a good image quality overall. The problems become evident when the compressed image is enlarged, but the graphics on Web pages are meant to be viewed in the context of the Web page to which they belong. The GIF file format is an old one, and it supports only 256-color images, but it has a few really handy features. It's the only format that supports transparency, and its compression ratio is quite good.

To insert an image at the current location in the document, use the <IMG> tag with the SRC attribute, which specifies the image to be displayed. Figure 19.3 shows a page with a simple graphic, centered across the page.

FIGURE 19.3:

Inserting a simple graphic file

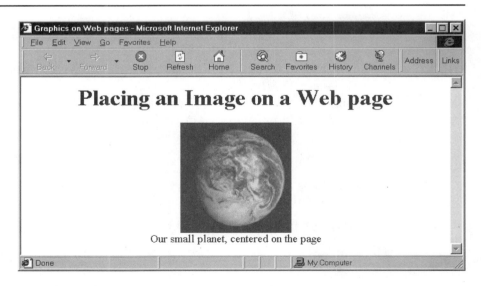

Here is the HTML source code that produced the page in Figure 19.3:

```
<HTML>
<HEAD>
<TITLE>Graphics on Web pages</TITLE>
```

```
</HEAD>
<BODY>
<CENTER>
<H1>Placing an Image on a Web page</H1>
<IMG SRC="earth1.jpg"><BR>
Our small planet, centered on the page
</CENTER>
</BODY>
</HTML>
```

The <IMG> tag has the following syntax:

```
<IMG SRC="picture.jpg">
```

The <IMG> tag recognizes additional attributes, but you must include the *SRC* attribute, which is the location of an image file on the server or any URL on the Web. Most designers use graphics in the same directory as the rest of the Web site files or those in a separate folder used for storing images only. If the image resides on the same server as the document, you should use a relative path name so that the entire project can be moved to another folder or server without having to edit the HTML file.

When you use the following attributes with the <IMG> tag, the browser can manipulate the image in several ways:

- ALIGN aligns the image to the left, right, center, top, bottom, or middle of the screen.

- WIDTH and HEIGHT specify the width and height of the image.

- BORDER adds a border to the image, which is visible only if the image is a hyperlink.

- VSPACE and HSPACE clear space vertically or horizontally. The empty space is specified in pixels.

- ALT includes a text message to be displayed if the user has turned off graphics.

- USEMAP inserts an image map.

The browser can figure out the image's dimensions, but only after it has been downloaded. Specifying the width and the height of an image speeds up the rendering, as the browser doesn't have to rearrange the elements already placed on the page. Although this was the original purpose of the WIDTH and HEIGHT attributes, you can use these values to perform a neat trick.

If you want to change the size of an image, you can specify the size with the WIDTH and HEIGHT attributes, and the browser will size the existing file to the new values. For instance, to create a straight vertical line two pixels wide, simply use a square image two pixels on each side, and set the values to <IMG WIDTH=2 and HEIGHT=200 SRC="picture.jpg">. Your image will stretch 200 pixels high. You can also distort bitmaps with the WIDTH and HEIGHT attributes.

The BORDER attribute specifies the width of the border to appear around an image. Borders two pixels wide automatically surround any image used as a hyperlink. You may want to eliminate this automatic border with the BORDER=none attribute. You can also specify a different size border for an image by including the BORDER attribute with the width value in pixels. Keep in mind, however, that the border won't be displayed unless the image is a hyperlink.

One aspect affecting the appearance of images, especially when they are surrounded by text, is the amount of space between the image and surrounding text. Space can be cleared horizontally and vertically with the HSPACE and VSPACE attributes. Simply specify the amount of space in pixels, for example, HSPACE=10 or VSPACE =20.

The ALT attribute displays alternative text for viewers whose browsers have images turned off (many people turn off the display of images to speed up the loading of the page). The attribute ALT="Company Logo" tells the user that the image is not displayed in the browser. In addition, if the image takes a long time to download, the message "Company Logo" is displayed in the image's space on the page. If for some reason your images are not transmitted or don't show up, the user can still navigate your Web site and get the picture, so to speak.

Tables

Tables are invaluable tools for organizing and presenting data in a grid or matrix. Tables are used in an HTML document for the same reasons they are used in any other document. There is, however, one more reason for using tables with an HTML document: to align the elements on a page. A table's cell may contain text, hyperlinks, or images, and you can use the cell to align these elements on the page in ways that are simply impossible with straight HTML or even other tables. You can even use tables without borders, so your audience doesn't see how you accomplished your amazing (for HTML) feats of graphic design.

The Basic Table Tags

Every table begins with the <TABLE> tag and ends with the </TABLE> tag. The attributes of the <TABLE> tag allow you to specify whether the table has borders, the width of borders, the distance between cells, and the proximity of cell contents to the edge of the cell. You can specify the width and height of the table in either pixels or as a percentage of total screen size.

Within the <TABLE> tags, each table row is marked by the <TR> tag. The closing </TR> tag is optional. Each row's cells are marked by the <TD> tag, whose closing </TD> tag is also optional. Here's the structure of a simple table. If you create an HTML file with the following lines and open it with your browser, you will see the items arranged as a table without any lines around them.

```
<HTML>
<TABLE>
<TR>
     <TD> Row 1, Column 1 </TD>
     <TD> Row 1, Column 2 </TD>
     <TD> Row 1, Column 3 </TD>
</TR>
<TR>
     <TD> Row 2, Column 1 </TD>
     <TD> Row 2, Column 2 </TD>
     <TD> Row 2, Column 3 </TD>
</TR>
<TR>
     <TD> Row 3, Column 1 </TD>
     <TD> Row 3, Column 2 </TD>
     <TD> Row 3, Column 3 </TD>
</TR>
</TABLE>
</HTML>
```

Header and Data Rows

You can use the <TH> tag in place of the <TR> tag to indicate that the row is a header row. The following HTML code produces a simple table with two rows, one of them formatted as header:

```
<TABLE BORDER=1 CELLSPACING=1 CELLPADDING=1>
<TR>
<TH>
</TH>Heading 1
<TH>
</TH>Heading 2
</TR>
<TR>
<TD>Cell 1
</TD>
<TD>Cell 2
</TD>
</TR>
</TABLE>
```

The CELLSPACING and CELLPADDING attributes of the <TABLE> tag determine the spacing between successive cells and the padding around each cell's contents. By default, each cell is made large enough to fit its contents. Use the CELLPADDING attribute to specify additional padding around a cell's contents.

Aligning Cell Contents

The ALIGN and VALIGN attributes specify the alignment of the cell's contents. The ALIGN attribute is used for horizontal alignment and it can have the value LEFT, CENTER, or RIGHT. The VALIGN attribute specifies the vertical alignment of the text, and it can have the value TOP, MIDDLE, or BOTTOM. The default alignment is LEFT (horizontal alignment) and MIDDLE (vertical alignment).

A great deal of control over the alignment, spacing, and placement of cell contents within tables translates directly into excellent formatting capability for documents that would not ordinarily be built as tables. In fact, in HTML there are some effects you just can't get (in a practical way) without the effective use of tables.

Table Width

All the examples we have looked at so far use the default table width, which is determined by the entries of the individual cells. If a column contains a very long entry, the browser will wrap its contents to make sure that all columns are visible. However, it is possible to specify the width of the entire table with the WIDTH attribute of the <TABLE> tag.

The WIDTH attribute can be a value that specifies the table's width in pixels or as a percentage of the window's width. The table defined as:

```
<TABLE WIDTH=50%>
```

occupies one-half of the window's width. Unless you center the table with the CENTER attribute, it will be left-aligned in the browser's window.

The table defined as:

```
<TABLE WIDTH=200>
```

will be 200 pixels wide, regardless of its contents and/or the window's size. If the window is less than 200 pixels wide, part of the table will be invisible. To display the part of the table that's outside the window, you'll have to use the horizontal scroll bar.

Multiple Row and Multiple Column Cells

Quite often, tables don't contain identically sized rows and columns. Some rows may contain fewer and wider cells than the others, and some columns may span multiple rows. The figures in this section contain tables with peculiar formatting.

Figure 19.4 shows a table with cells that span multiple columns and rows. These cells use the ROWSPAN and COLSPAN attributes, which let you create really elaborate tables. Both COLSPAN and ROWSPAN appear in between the <TD> and </TD> tags, and they merge the current cell with one or more of its adjacent cells on the same row (in the case of the COLSPAN attribute) or column (in the case of the ROWSPAN attribute). The number of adjacent cells to be merged with the current one is the value of the COLSPAN and ROWSPAN attributes.

FIGURE 19.4:

This table contains cells that span multiple rows and columns.

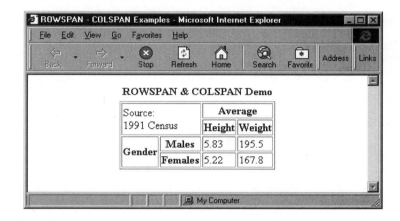

The table in Figure 19.4 was created with the following HTML lines. The only thing I've done differently here is add the COLSPAN attribute in the appropriate <TD> tags to force some cells of the first row to span two columns, and I've added the ROWSPAN attribute to force some cells in the first column to span multiple rows. Other than that, the new table is as simple as those in the previous examples.

```
<HTML>

<HEAD>
<TITLE>ROWSPAN - COLSPAN Examples</TITLE>
</HEAD>

<BODY>

<CENTER>
<TABLE BORDER>
<CAPTION><B>ROWSPAN & COLSPAN Demo</B></CAPTION>

<TR>
    <TD COLSPAN=2 ROWSPAN=2 >Source:<BR>1991 Census</TD>
    <TH COLSPAN=2>Average</TH>
</TR>
```

```
<TR>
     <TH>Height</TH>
     <TH>Weight</TH>
</TR>
<TR>
     <TH ROWSPAN=2>Gender</TH>
     <TH>Males</TH>
     <TD>5.83</TD>
     <TD>195.5</TD>
</TR>
<TR>
     <TH>Females</TH>
     <TD>5.22</TD>
     <TD>167.8</TD>
</TR>
</TABLE>
</CENTER>
</BODY>

</HTML>
```

Frames

The pages you've seen thus far occupy the entire browser window. You can, however, display multiple documents on a page by using frames. You usually create frames with the <FRAMESET> tag. This approach requires some overhead, so I'll describe how to create floating frames using the <IFRAME> tag. You can place a floating frame, such as an image anywhere on the page, and a page can have multiple floating frames. The user can't resize floating frames, but they are quite adequate for the purposes of this chapter and are easier to implement than frames created with the <FRAMESET> tag.

To insert a floating frame on a page, use the following tag:

```
<IFRAME SRC=url WIDTH=xxx HEIGHT=yyy>
```

The *url* variable is the URL of the document to be displayed on the frame, and *xxx* and *yyy* are the frame's dimensions. To place a floating frame in the middle of a document and display the Sybex home page on it, enter the following lines in an HTML file and then open the file with Internet Explorer:

```
<CENTER>
<H1>Floating Frame Example</H1><BR>
<IFRAME SRC="http://www.sybex.com" WIDTH=500 HEIGHT=300>
</CENTER>
```

The output of this document is shown in Figure 19.5. (Everything on the page between the <CENTER> and matching </CENTER> tags is centered.)

FIGURE 19.5:

A floating frame displaying the Sybex home page

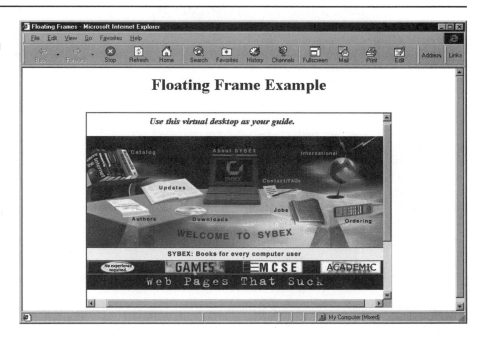

The page in Figure 19.6 was created with a single HTML document that contains two <IFRAME> tags. I specified the contents of each frame with the SRC attribute and used the <CENTER> tag for their placement on the page.

FIGURE 19.6:

This time the floating frames of the page FFRAMES.HTM are nested in another floating frame. The arrangement of the frames on this page doesn't depend on the browser's window size.

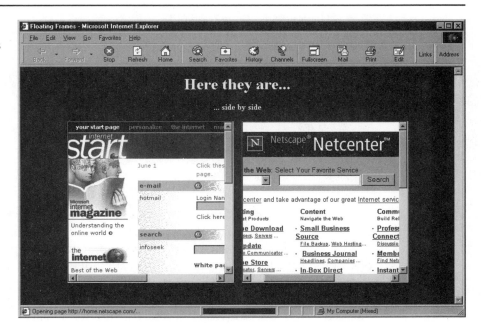

Here's the document FFRAMES.HTM (you will find it in this chapter's folder on the CD):

```
<HTML>
<HEAD>
<TITLE>Floating Frames</TITLE>
</HEAD>

<BODY BGCOLOR=black>
<FONT NAME="Verdana" COLOR=lightyellow>
<CENTER>
<H1>Here they are...</H1>
<H4>... side by side</H4>
<P>
<IFRAME
      SRC="http://home.microsoft.com/"
      NAME="MS"
         WIDTH=325
      HEIGHT=325
         SCROLLING=YES
      MARGINWIDTH=0
      MARGINHEIGHT=0
      HSPACE=8>

</IFRAME>

<IFRAME
      SRC="http://home.netscape.com/"
      NAME="NS"
      WIDTH=325
      HEIGHT=325
      SCROLLING=YES
      MARGINWIDTH=0
      MARGINHEIGHT=0
      HSPACE=8>
</IFRAME>
</FONT>
</CENTER>
</BODY>
</HTML>
```

The page in Figure 19.6 may not look as nice on your computer. If the browser's window isn't at least 700 pixels wide, there will be no room for the two frames to be displayed next to each other, and the second frame will appear below the first one. You'd have the same problem if you attempt to display two images next to each other on a narrow window. The solution in this case is to place the images in adjacent cells of a table without borders. You can do the same with floating frames. Floating frames can be inserted in table cells just like images or text paragraphs.

Activating the Client with VBScript

The Web is by nature a client/server environment. The load is balanced between the server, where the information is stored, and the client, which does the processing. Until recently, processing consisted of rendering a Web page (including its graphics) on the client. With VBScript, you can add small programs to your pages that are executed on the server. With the introduction of DHTML, scripting languages such as VBScript and JavaScript, and ActiveX controls for the Web, an increasing amount of processing will move from the server to the client.

Web pages are by definition interactive: each time visitors click a hyperlink, they are taken to another page. But this isn't the type of interaction with which Windows users are familiar. In addition, this type of interaction requires a trip to the server, at each step. The Web page can't respond to events, such as the click of a button, because HTML isn't a programming language. It can't display the date, or do a simple calculation.

The latest trend in Web design is to make pages active. An *active page* is one that behaves like an application. It has its own user interface, composed of the common Windows elements (Command buttons, textboxes, and all the new ActiveX controls released for the Web), and interacts with the visitor in a manner similar to a Windows application. An active page doesn't require a trip to the server to display the date or do some calculations.

The embedded application is called a *script*. Scripts are simple programs, embedded in the HTML page as ASCII text. When the page is downloaded, the script is downloaded with it and is executed by the browser on the client computer. The idea behind active pages is to exploit the computing power of the client computer. With straight HTML, the client computer's task is to render the HTML documents on the screen. But most clients out there are powerful PCs, and they could do much more than simply display Web pages. Active pages can exploit the available computing power by passing much of the processing that would otherwise take place on the server to the client.

In the following sections, we are going to look the differences between Visual Basic and VBScript. VBScript is a lightweight version of Visual Basic, but before you start developing scripts, you must understand the design philosophy of VBScript. The design environment is also quite different. VBScript doesn't come with an integrated editor. To insert a script on a page, you must edit the HTML file and insert the appropriate code. Once you learn the structure of a script and how it interacts with the rest of the document, you'll be ready to script your Web pages. You'll also be ready to design documents with DHTML, which relies on VBScript for the manipulation of its elements in real time.

Historically (if three years of VBScript evolution can be considered history), VBScript's first use was to program the elements of a Web page that collect user input.

Many pages on the World Wide Web collect input at the client with the help of some basic controls, such as textboxes, radio buttons, and so on. They are primitive compared with the elegant controls used by Windows, but they serve their purpose. To help you understand how VBScript is used on a Web page, I will discuss these controls from a VB programmer's point of view and how they are programmed with VBScript.

Forms and Controls

As you know already, HTML pages contain controls that let the user enter information, similar to the usual Windows controls: textboxes, Option buttons, and so on. The areas on the HTML page where these controls appear are called Forms, and the controls themselves are called *intrinsic controls*. HTML provides special tags for placing intrinsic controls on a Form.

> **NOTE**
>
> In addition to intrinsic controls, you can place ActiveX controls on your Forms. Because ActiveX controls must be downloaded to the client and many visitors don't allow the installation of ActiveX controls on their systems, I am not going to discuss them.

Before placing a control on the page, you must create a Form with the <FORM> tag. Its syntax is:

```
<FORM NAME=name ACTION=action METHOD=method>
</FORM>
```

All the controls must appear between these two tags. The NAME attribute (it's optional) is the name of the Form and is used when a page contains multiple Forms. The ACTION attribute is the name of an application on the server that will be called to process the information. The METHOD attribute specifies how the controls' values will be transmitted to the server. All the information needed by the browser to contact an application in the server is contained in the <FORM> tag. But more on this later, in the section "Passing Parameters to the Server."

HTML provides support for the following intrinsic controls. Figure 19.7 shows a Web page with a Form that contains most of HTML's intrinsic controls. You are going to see the HTML code that produced the page of Figure 19.7 in the section "The FORM.HTM Web Page," later in this chapter.

The Text Control

The Text control is a box in which visitors can enter a single line of text (such as name, address, and so on). To insert a Text control on a Form, use the following tag:

```
<INPUT TYPE = TEXT NAME = "Publisher" VALUE = "Sybex">
```

The VALUE attribute specifies the initial value. After the visitor changes this entry, VALUE holds the new string. To edit the contents of a Text control, the visitor can use the common editing keys (Home, Del, Insert, and so on), but the text can't be formatted.

To control the size and contents of the control use the SIZE and MAXLENGTH attributes. The SIZE attribute specifies the size of the control on the Form, in number of characters, and the MAXLENGTH attribute specifies the maximum number of characters the user can type in the control. A variation of the Text control is the *Password* control, which is identical, but doesn't display the characters as they are typed. Instead, it displays asterisks, and it is used to enter passwords.

The TextArea Control

The TextArea control is similar to the Text control, but it allows the entry of multiple lines of text. All the usual navigation and editing keys work with the TextArea control. To place a TextArea control on a Form, use the <TEXTAREA> tag:

```
<TEXTAREA NAME = "Comments" ROWS = 10 COLS = 30>
The best editor I've ever used!
</TEXTAREA>
```

Because the TextArea control allows you to specify multiple lines of initial text, it's not inserted with the usual <INPUT> tag, but with a pair of <TEXTAREA> tags. The ROWS and COLS attributes specify the dimensions of the control on the page, in number of characters. Notice that the line breaks you insert between the two <TEXTAREA> tags are preserved when the text is displayed on the control. Even if you include HTML tags in the initial text, they will appear as text on the control.

The CheckBox Control

The CheckBox control is a little square with an optional checkmark, which acts as a toggle. Every time the visitor clicks it, it changes state. It is used to present a list of options, from which the user can select one or more. To insert a CheckBox control on a Form, use the <INPUT> tag:

```
<INPUT TYPE = CHECKBOX NAME = "Check1">
```

To initially check a CheckBox control, specify the CHECKED attribute in the corresponding <INPUT> tag. The control's value can be 0 or 1, indicating whether it's checked (1) or cleared (0).

The RadioButton Control

The RadioButton control is round and contains a dot in the center. RadioButton controls are used to present lists of options, similar to the CheckBox controls, but only one of them can be selected at a time. Each time a new option is checked by the visitor, the previously selected one is cleared. To insert a RadioButton control on a Form use the following:

```
<INPUT TYPE = RADIO NAME = "Radio1">
```

Whereas each CheckBox control has a different name, a group of RadioButtons have the same name. This is how the browser knows that a number of RadioButton controls belong to the same group and that only one of them can be checked at a time. To specify the control that will be initially checked in the group, use the CHECKED attribute. The following lines insert a group of four RadioButton controls on a Form:

```
<INPUT TYPE = RADIO NAME = "Level">Beginner <BR>
<INPUT TYPE = RADIO NAME = "Level">Intermediate <BR>
<INPUT TYPE = RADIO NAME = "Level" CHECKED>Advanced<BR>
<INPUT TYPE = RADIO NAME = "Level">Expert <BR>
```

The Multiple Selection Control

The Multiple Selection control is basically a list that can contain a number of options. The visitor can select none, one, or multiple items in the list. The list is delimited with a pair of <SELECT> tags. Each item in the list is inserted with a separate <OPTION> tag. To place a Multiple Selection List on the Form, add the following lines:

```
<SELECT  NAME = "MemoryOptions" SIZE = 3 MULTIPLE = multiple>
<OPTION VALUE=16> 16 MB</OPTION>
<OPTION VALUE=32> 32 MB</OPTION>
<OPTION VALUE=64> 64 MB</OPTION>
<OPTION VALUE=128> 128 MB</OPTION>
<OPTION VALUE=256> 256 MB</OPTION>
</SELECT>
```

The SIZE attribute specifies how many lines will be visible. If you omit it, the list will be reduced to a single line, and the visitor must use the up-down arrow keys to scroll through the available options. If the list contains more lines, a vertical scroll bar is automatically attached to help the visitor locate the desired item. The MULTIPLE attribute specifies that the visitor can select multiple items in the list by clicking their names while holding down the Shift or Ctrl key. If you omit the MULTIPLE attribute, each time an item is selected, the previously selected one is cleared.

The <OPTION> tag has a VALUE attribute that represents the value of the selected item. If the viewer selects the 64MB option in the earlier list, the value 64 is transmitted to the server. Finally, to initially select one or more options, specify the SELECTED attribute:

```
<OPTION SELECTED VALUE=128> 128 MB</OPTION>
```

The Command Button Control

Clicking a Command button triggers certain actions. Without VBScript, Command buttons can trigger only two actions:

- Submit the data entered on the controls to the server.

- Reset all control values on the Form to their original values.

With VBScript, Command buttons can trigger any actions you can program in your pages. You can place three types of buttons on a Form: Submit, Reset, and General.

The most important button is *Submit*. It transmits the contents of all the controls on the Form to the server (the values will be processed by an application, whose URL is specified in the ACTION attribute of the <FORM> tag). The *Reset* button resets the values of the other controls on the Form to their initial values. The Reset button doesn't submit any values to the server. Most Forms contain Submit and Reset buttons, which are inserted like this:

```
<INPUT TYPE = SUBMIT VALUE = "Send data">
<INPUT TYPE = RESET VALUE = "Reset Values">
```

The VALUE attribute specifies the string that will appear on the Command button. The Submit button reads the name of the application that must be contacted on the server (the <FORM> tag's ACTION attribute), appends the values of the controls to this URL, and transmits it to the server.

The third, generic type button has as its TYPE simply BUTTON and functions similar to the other buttons in the Windows interface. Clicking it triggers an event, which you can use to execute some VBScript code. To insert a generic Button control on your Form, use the <INPUT> tag:

```
<INPUT TYPE = BUTTON NAME = "ShowDate">
```

Every time this button is clicked, it triggers the ShowDate_onClick event. Obviously, you must place the code that you want to execute every time this button is clicked in this event's handler:

```
Sub ShowDate_onClick()
    MsgBox "The date is " & Date()
End Sub
```

TIP
If you're going to validate the data on the client's side, you shouldn't use the Submit button because it will transmit the data to the server as soon as the button is clicked. Instead, use the Button control to trigger your data validation routine. After you validate the data, you can submit it with the Submit method.

Here's a typical Command button script that validates the data entered by the user and then submits the Form's contents to an ASP (Active Server Page) application on the server. The Command button is generic and is placed on the Form as follows:

```
<INPUT TYPE = BUTTON NAME = SendData VALUE = "Register Now">
```

Code 19.1: **The Event Handler for the SendData Button's Click Event**

```
<SCRIPT LANGUAGE = VBScript>
Sub SendData_onClick()
    If Instr("@", EMail.Value) = 0 Then
        MsgBox "Invalid e-mail address." & chr(13) & _
                "Please enter a string like _
                yourname@yourserver.com"
    Else If RealName.Value = "" Then
        MsgBox "You can't register without a name"
    Else
        RegistrationForm.Submit
    End If
End Sub
</SCRIPT>
```

This script is invoked when the SendData button is clicked. First, it checks the contents of the *EMail* Text control. If the specified address isn't in the form name@ server.com, it prompts the user to enter a valid e-mail address. It then checks the value of the *RealName* Text control. If the user hasn't specified a name, he or she is prompted accordingly. If both tests fail, the script submits the data on the Form (the Form may contain other controls too) with the Submit method. The Form's Submit method is equivalent to the Submit button. They both cause the browser to contact the application specified by the ACTION attribute of the <FORM> tag and pass to it the values of the controls as parameters. For example, the browser might submit a string such as the following:

```
http://www.servername.com/Register.asp?EMail=EP@SYBEX.COM&Name=Evangelos+P
```

EMail and Name are the names of the parameters expected by the *Register.asp* application on the server (you'll see how to write applications to extract the values passed by the client and process them on the server). The values shown could be anything. Notice that strings are not enclosed in quotes, and spaces are replaced with plus signs.

The FORM.HTM Web Page

The FORM.HTM page, previously shown in Figure 19.7, contains all the controls you can place on a Web page to request information from the viewer. The FORM section of the page is defined with the following tag:

```
<FORM ACTION="ASPages/Register.asp" method="GET">
```

The data collected on this page will be transmitted to the application REGISTER.ASP on the same server, and they will be processed there. You'll learn how to write ASP files (they are text files with VBScript commands) to process the data submitted by the client in the last chapter of the book. What you must keep in mind for now is that the browser will automatically submit the controls' values to the server. All you have to do is specify the URL of the program to intercept them on the server. The URL used in this example contains the path to ASPages folder (under the Web's root folder). The first part of the URL is known to the browser from the address of the current document. The data will be transmitted to the server when the Submit button (Register Now) at the bottom of the Form is clicked.

The rest of the code is trivial. It uses the <INPUT> tag to display the various controls. Most of the controls are grouped into tables for alignment purposes. You can open the FORM.HTM file on the CD to see the statements for creating the page shown in Figure 19.7. I will list the tags for the intrinsic controls only, omitting the table tags in the interest of conserving space:

```
<FORM ACTION="ASPages/Register.asp" method="GET">
<FONT SIZE=4>
```

```
Last Name
<INPUT TYPE=Text SIZE=20 MAXLENGTH=20 NAME="LName">
First Name
<INPUT TYPE=text SIZE=20 MAXLENGTH=20 NAME="FName">
E-Mail Address
<INPUT TYPE=Text SIZE=46 MAXLENGTH=256 NAME="EMail">
My computer is:
My browser is:
<INPUT TYPE=Radio CHECKED NAME="hardware" VALUE="PC"> PC
<INPUT TYPE=Radio CHECKED NAME="browser" VALUE="IE">Internet Explorer
<INPUT TYPE=radio NAME="hardware" VALUE="MAC"> Macintosh
<INPUT TYPE=radio NAME="browser" VALUE="NETSCAPE"> Netscape
<INPUT TYPE=radio NAME="hardware" VALUE="OTHER">Other
<INPUT TYPE=radio NAME="browser" VALUE="OTHER">Other
When I connect I want to see:
<INPUT TYPE=checkbox name="Sports" value="ON"> <STRONG>Sports
<INPUT TYPE=Checkbox NAME="News" VALUE="ON"> News
<INPUT TYPE=Checkbox NAME="Stock" VALUE="ON"> Stock Prices
<INPUT TYPE=checkbox NAME="weather" value="ON"> Weather
<INPUT TYPE=checkbox name="bargains" value="ON">Our Bargains
Do you want to receive e-mail messages?
<INPUT TYPE=Radio CHECKED NAME="mail" VALUE="YES">Yes
<INPUT TYPE=Radio NAME="MAIL" VALUE="NO">No
Click here to submit your registration
<INPUT TYPE=submit NAME="Register" VALUE="Register Now!">
</FORM>
```

If you click on the Register Now button, the browser displays a warning, indicating that it couldn't find the REGISTER.ASP application. This page can't be tested without a Web server. You can view its contents like any other page, but it can't contact the server unless it's opened on a Web server. You'll see how to handle client requests through the Web server in the last chapter of this book. Since the REGISTER.ASP application on the server will be written in VBScript, it's time to explore VBScript.

Embedding a Script

The script is contained in the event handlers of the various controls, as well as procedures, just like regular Visual Basic applications. You place scripts in the HTML file's SCRIPT section, which is delimited with a pair of <SCRIPT> tags. Because there is more than one scripting language, you must also specify the script's language in the <SCRIPT> tag. Here's a typical SCRIPT section:

```
<SCRIPT LANGUAGE = VBScript>
    {your scripting code}
</SCRIPT>
```

When the browser hits the <SCRIPT> tag, it calls the VBScript interpreter to compile and execute the following code. The code is usually placed in event handlers, but you can insert procedures that will be called from within event handlers. If some code appears outside any handler, as shown in the next listing, it is executed as soon as the page is downloaded and before the browser renders the document on the screen. The following script displays the current date as soon as the page that contains it is loaded:

```
<SCRIPT LANGUAGE="VBScript">
    MsgBox "The date is " & Date
</SCRIPT>
```

All intrinsic controls have a Name property (or attribute) that can be used to identify them in the script. Since the intrinsic controls are always placed on a Form, their complete name is the name of the Form, followed by a period and then the name of the control. The Button control, placed on a Form called RegisterForm with the following line:

```
<INPUT TYPE=BUTTON NAME="DateBttn" VALUE="Show Date">
```

can be accessed from within a script with this expression:

```
AppForm.DateBttn
```

For example, you can change the caption of the DateBttn with a statement such as the following:

```
AppForm.DateBttn.Value = "DATE"
```

All intrinsic controls, with the exception of the Select control, have a VALUE attribute too. A button's value is its caption, and a Text control's value is the text displayed on the control. The equivalent property of the Select control is the SelectedIndex property, which is the index of the item currently selected. You can manipulate the Value and SelectedIndex properties of the various controls from within your script.

Finally, the most common event in scripting Web pages is the onClick event, which is generated when the user clicks a control. The Text, TextArea, and Select controls don't recognize this event. The most common event for these controls is the onChange event, which takes place when the text in a Text or TextArea control is changed or when the user makes a new selection in the Select control.

This is all the information you need to start scripting your Web pages. VBScript is similar to Visual Basic, and we can look at an example right away.

Scripting an HTML Page

Scripting allows you to take control of the contents of a page and manipulate them with your program. The first two scripting languages were JavaScript and VBScript.

JavaScript is based on SUN's Java, and VBScript is based on Microsoft's Visual Basic. As you can guess, we are going to explore VBScript in this book.

A script is a short program that manipulates the elements of a page and is inserted in an HTML document with the <SCRIPT> and </SCRIPT> tags. Typically, you place the SCRIPT portion of a document in the HEAD section. Here's a simple script that sets the page's background color and displays a welcome message:

```
<HTML>
<HEAD>
<TITLE>VBScript Demo</TITLE>
<SCRIPT Language = VBS>
Document.fgColor="hFF0000"
Document.bgColor="h00FFFF"
MsgBox "Welcome to the VBScript Demo Page"
</SCRIPT>
</HEAD>
<BODY>
<H1>VBScript Demo</H1>
</BODY>
</HTML>
```

The *Document* entry is an object that represents the document displayed in the browser's window, and you can access the various properties of the document through the Document object. The properties *fgColor* and *bgColor* set (or read) the values of the document's foreground and background colors. The MsgBox() function isn't new to you. There are many similarities between Visual Basic and VBScript, and we need not look at the features of VBScript in detail.

WARNING There is, however, a basic difference: VBScript is a typeless language. You can declare variables of specific types; they are all variants. This has serious implications when you attempt to call Visual Basic functions (such as object methods) from within VBScript. You must either use the proper data conversion functions (discussed in Chapter 2) or enclose the arguments in parentheses to let VBScript and Visual Basic handle the conversion for you.

A scripting language such as VBScript made it possible for Web authors to develop dynamic content for their Web pages. But that isn't all. In less than a year after the introduction of VBScript, Microsoft decided to "activate" Web pages; hence, the term *ActiveX*. Since you have the means to program a Web page, why not add programmable objects to it at will? The programmable objects are nothing less than ActiveX controls. If there was a way to place ActiveX controls on a page, you could access their methods and properties from within VBScript and thereby create an active page. An active page is similar to a small application that runs within Internet Explorer.

The next step was to develop ActiveX controls that could be used on Web pages. And Microsoft released a number of those. Now, with Visual Basic 6, you can create your own ActiveX controls for use on Web pages. In the next section, we'll test the controls we developed in Chapter 16. In the last section of this chapter, we'll look at DHTML, which is nothing more than HTML enhanced with VBScript code segments.

Using Custom ActiveX Controls on Web Pages

You can use ActiveX controls both on Forms and Web pages. This statement is rather brave though, because the Desktop and the Web have different requirements, and it's not always easy to develop controls for both environments. The basic difference in the requirements is in how the two types of applications are used. Desktop applications can safely assume that all the resources are on the local machine where they are executing. Web applications, on the other hand, are executed on a remote computer, and any additional resources, such as images and sounds, must be downloaded as needed. Fortunately, most controls you design for the Desktop will also work on Web pages, but don't expect any control you design to work equally well in both environments.

Microsoft has released a number of ActiveX controls for use on Web pages. Some of these controls come with Internet Explorer, including the Structured Graphics control, the Filter control, and the Sequencer control. You can find information on these controls and examples at `http://www.microsoft.com/workshop` . Practically, every ActiveX control you can place on a Visual Basic Form can also be used on a Web page (of course, it must first be downloaded and installed on the client computer). In the next few sections, we are going to see how the custom ActiveX controls we built in the previous chapters can be used on Web pages.

The ALARM.HTM Page

In this section, you'll build a Web page that uses the Alarm ActiveX control of Chapter 16. Why bother to place an alarm on a Web page (besides demonstrating how to program a custom control with VBScript, that is)? Figure 19.8 shows one reason. This page contains a timer that lets the viewer read a page for 60 seconds. The user can always leave the page by entering another URL in the browser's Address box or by clicking the Back button. If the user keeps this page open for 60 seconds, however, the script takes him or her automatically to another page.

An alarm is handy in several situations. For example, you can use an alarm to update a page with "live" data, or to keep track of time in a game.

FIGURE 19.8:

The Alarm custom control
on a Web page

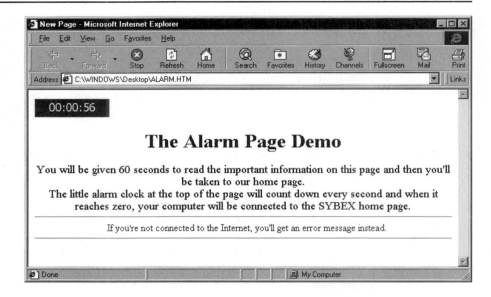

FIGURE 19.8:

The Alarm custom control on a Web page

If you are familiar with ActiveX controls for Web development, you know that there is a Timer control you can use on a Web page, but it's not as simple as the Alarm control. For one thing, when you use a Timer control, you must count time from within your program. You must specify the alarm's time-out period in milli-seconds, and your script must process timer events many times before it actually decides to do something. Like Visual Basic's Timer control, the ActiveX Timer control has no visible components, and if you want your viewers to know what's happening, you must provide visual feedback from within your script.

Let's start with the HTML tags for placing an instance of the Alarm control on a Web page:

```
<OBJECT ID="AlarmCtl" NAME="AlarmCtl"
classid="clsid:7282EB2E-B8A9-11CF-B2FB-005348C101FC"
border="0"
width="120" height="33">
<PARAM NAME="CountDown" value="True">
</OBJECT>
```

The <OBJECT> tag inserts an ActiveX control on the page, but its syntax is peculiar, to say the least. However, you don't have to enter it manually. Each ActiveX control has a Name and an ID property, just like the intrinsic controls. The CLASSID property is a long string, which identifies the control in the Registry. To create the object definition on a page, use a WYSIWYG HTML editor such as FrontPage Express (this one comes with Internet Explorer). Start a new HTML page and insert the desired ActiveX control as follows:

1. Choose Insert ➢ Other Component ➢ ActiveX Control to open the ActiveX Control Properties dialog box:

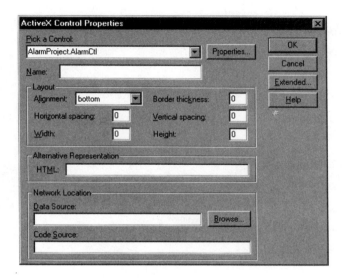

2. Expand the Pick a Control drop-down list and locate the AlarmProject. Alarm-Ctl entry. This is how the Alarm ActiveX control is listed in the Registry. (If the entry doesn't appear in the list, follow the instructions in the sidebar "Registering Custom ActiveX Controls.")

3. Set the control's name to **AlarmCtl**.

4. Click the Properties button to set additional properties for the custom control. For the Alarm control, set its CountDown property to True.

5. Click the OK button to close the dialog box.

6. Choose View ➢ HTML to open a text editor displaying the page's source code. Select the definition of the <OBJECT> tag and copy it to the Clipboard.

7. Switch to the text editor with the HTML document, and paste the definition of the <OBJECT> tag.

Inserting the <OBJECT> tag for a custom control on a Web page isn't complicated, after all. This definition doesn't change, even when it's installed on another computer, so you can copy the same definition from any Web page that contains it.

Registering Custom ActiveX Controls

While you develop custom ActiveX controls, you don't have to register them in order to use them in the test project. If you want to use a custom ActiveX control with a different project, however, you must first register it. The process of registering a custom ActiveX control is explained in Chapter 16, and I repeat it here:

1. Choose File ➢ Make control.ocx (*control* is the name of the custom control) to create the control's OCX file.

2. Open a DOS Prompt window, switch to the folder where the OCX file was saved, and issue the command:

   ```
   C:\windows\system\regsvr32 control.ocx
   ```

   Replace *control.ocx* with the name of the OCX file you want to register.

3. Close the DOS Prompt window.

You're ready to use the new control in any project, even Web pages. In the Visual Basic IDE, the name of the custom control will appear in the Components dialog box (choose Project ➢ Components to open this dialog box). The same name will also appear in Front-Page's ActiveX Control Properties dialog box.

The control's CLASSID value will be different on your system. Therefore, you can't use the ALARM.HTM file on the CD as is. You must change the CLASSID attribute with the value that will be generated on your system.

---

8. Enter the appropriate text and HTML tags on the page, save it as ALARM.HTM, and open it with Internet Explorer.

You should be able to see the Alarm control counting down on the page. Of course, nothing will happen when the alarm times out, because you haven't added any code to the page yet. The script should start the timer as soon as the page is downloaded, and when the alarm times out, it must take the viewer to another page (the Sybex home page, to be exact).

Open the page with a text editor and insert the following script:

```
<SCRIPT LANGUAGE="VBScript">
Sub window_onLoad()
    AlarmCtl.AlarmTime = Time + #00:01.00#
    Call AlarmCtl.StartTimer()
End Sub
```

```
Sub AlarmCtl_TimeOut()
    Call window.navigate("http://www.sybex.com")
End Sub
</SCRIPT>
```

The window_onLoad event is triggered when the page is loaded. In this event, you must initialize the control's properties. Set the AlarmTime property to a minute ahead of the current time and start the timer. You have already set the CountDown property in the definition of the <OBJECT> tag. You could have inserted the statement:

```
AlarmCtl.CountDown = True
```

in the onLoad event's handler. The AlarmTime property can't be set at design time, so it must be set from within the page's script.

When the Alarm control times out, the Alarm_TimeOut event is triggered. In this event's handler, we must program the browser to jump to another page, with the *Window.Navigate* method.

Code 19.2: **The Alarm.htm Page**

```
<HTML>
<HEAD>
<SCRIPT LANGUAGE="VBScript">
Sub window_onLoad()
    AlarmCtl.AlarmTime = Time + #00:01.00#
    Call AlarmCtl.StartTimer()
End Sub

Sub AlarmCtl_TimeOut()
    Call window.navigate("http://www.sybex.com")
End Sub
</SCRIPT>
<TITLE>Alarm Demo Page</TITLE>
</HEAD>
<BODY>

<OBJECT id="AlarmCtl " NAME="AlarmCtl"
classid="clsid:7282EB2E-B8A9-11CF-B2FB-005348C101FC"
border="0"
width="120" height="33">
<PARAM NAME="CountDown" value="True">
</OBJECT>
<CENTER>
<H1>The Alarm Page Demo</H1>
```

```
<FONT SIZE=4>
You will be given 60 seconds to read the important information
on this page and then you'll be taken to our home page.
<BR>
The little alarm clock at the top of the page will count down every
second and when it reaches zero, your computer will be connected to the
SYBEX home page.
<FONT SIZE = 3>
<HR>
If you are not connected to the Internet, you'll get an error message
instead.
<HR>
</BODY>
</HTML>
```

This is the HTML code that produced the page previously shown in Figure 19.8. The HTML tags are simple, and even if you are not familiar with HTML, you can understand the code. To see this control in action, follow these steps:

1. Start Internet Explorer.

2. Choose File ➤ Open, and in the dialog box, locate and open the file Alarm.htm.

3. Wait for 60 seconds, and the script will load the Sybex home page.

The Alarm control works nicely in Internet Explorer, and we don't have to adjust it in any way. It behaves just as it does from within Visual Basic. It even exposes its properties and methods, and you can program its events.

The UINPUT.HTM Page

The UINPUT.HTM page (shown in Figure 19.9) demonstrates how to use the CTextBox custom ActiveX control on a Web page. Use the process outlined in the last section to create the definition of the appropriate <OBJECT> tag with Front-Page and then add the text and HTML tags. The <OBJECT> tag for inserting the CTextBox control is:

```
<OBJECT id="CTextBox"
NAME="CTextBox1"
classid="clsid:7282EB5A-B8A9-11CF-B2FB-005348C101FC"
border="0"
WIDTH="150" HEIGHT="19">
</OBJECT>
```

FIGURE 19.9:

The UINPUT.HTM page uses the CTextBox control to prompt the user for required and optional data.

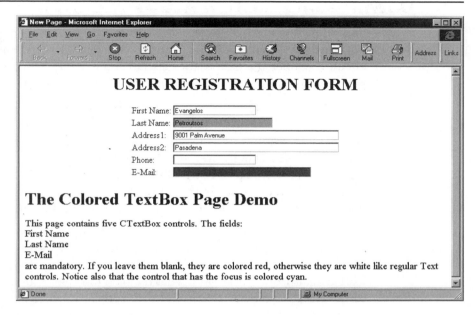

This page's script is simple. It initializes the controls by setting their Mandatory and Text properties:

```
Sub window_onLoad()
    CTextBox1.Mandatory=1
    CTextBox2.Mandatory=1
    CTextBox6.Mandatory=1
    CTextBox1.Text=""
    CTextBox2.Text=""
    CTextBox3.Text=""
    CTextBox4.Text=""
    CTextBox5.Text=""
    CTextBox6.Text=""
End Sub
```

If these controls are used on a page to collect data from viewers, there will also be a Submit button on the Form. Use the button's onClick event to make sure the required fields have values before submitting the data to the server. On the CD, you'll also find the LABEL3D.HTM page, which uses the FLXLabel custom control of Chapter 16 to display carved and raised text on the browser's window. To test the LABEL3D control on a Web page, you must first register the control with your system and then replace the control's CLASSID attribute in the page with the value that Visual Basic will generate on your system.

Downloading Custom ActiveX Controls

Testing custom ActiveX controls on your own computer is simple, and the test pages will always work. If you post the page on a Web server and someone else attempts to open it remotely, they are not going to see the ActiveX control on the page because the control isn't registered on the host system.

If you want to use a custom control on your Web site, you must create a CAB file with the control's OCX file (and any other support files) and post it as well. When Internet Explorer runs into a Web page with a custom control, it looks up for the control's CLASSID in the Registry. If it's found there, Internet Explorer displays the control on the page. If not, it attempts to download the control from the server and install it on the host computer in order to use it. Of course, it will first notify the user that the page contains a control that may not be safe.

Over the Internet, few people will agree to download a control from just any site. Web pages with custom ActiveX controls can be easily used on intranets (after the controls have been installed on the network's computers, they need not be down-loaded again), but you should avoid them on the Web. You can use authentication certificates to convince viewers that your control is safe to download and use. The process is complicated and expensive, and I won't discuss it here.

To download the CAB file for a custom control, Internet Explorer expects to find the CODEBASE attribute in the <OBJECT> tag. The *CODEBASE* attribute is the URL of the CAB file on the Web server. And how about the CAB file? Visual Basic will create it for you with the Package and Deployment Wizard. This is a separate application that is installed along with Visual Basic, and its purpose is to create distribution files for your applications.

NOTE   I don't discuss the Package and Deployment Wizard in this book. It's a straight-forward utility that collects all the information it needs from you and creates an EXE file you can distribute to your clients or a CAB file you can post on a Web site. Users download this file to their computers, and it is installed there automatically by Internet Explorer.

Dynamic HTML

You've seen how to use VBScript to program the intrinsic and custom ActiveX controls on a Web page. Another use of VBScript on the Web (and probably more popular) is to create DHTML pages. As I mentioned, DHTML documents are static HTML pages with programmable elements. For example, you can program a header to change color when the pointer is over it, hide and display text depending on viewer actions, and so on. To make the elements of HTML programmable, though, a few new features had to be introduced. I'll discuss these elements in the next section, and then we'll take a look at how they can be programmed with VBScript.

Extending HTML with Styles and Classes

The origins of DHTML are the so-called *styles*. As I've discussed, many HTML tags recognize attributes, which allow the Web author to modify certain properties of the various elements. The actual look produced by HTML tags, however, can't be modified. The <H1> tag, for instance, displays a level one heading, but you can't change the appearance of the heading.

With DHTML it is possible to redefine just about every HTML tag. For example, the following code is a style definition that will make all level one headers in the page blue and all level two headers red:

```
<STYLE>
    H1 {color:red}
    H2 {color:blue}
</STYLE}
```

If this statement is inserted at the beginning of an HTML document, usually in the HEAD section, it applies to all the <H1> and <H2> tags that follow.

In addition to the modified <H1> and<H2> headers, you might also want to use the original, plain <H1> and <H2> tags. Or, you might want two types of <H1> headers, a red one and a black one. It is possible to define *classes* to differentiate custom tags. A class is a new category of tag, defined by the author. Let's say you want to define two <H1> tags, one for titles and another for summaries. Here are two definitions of custom <H1> tags:

```
H1.title {font-weight: bold; background: white; color: black}
H1.summary {font-weight: bold; color: blue}
```

To use the second <H1> header in a title, you insert the following tag:

```
<H1 CLASS=summary>This is a summary section</H1>
```

A class is practically a new tag, but because it is derived from an existing class, instead of defining an entirely new tag, we define attributes of existing tags. The tag <H1 class=title> has all the attributes of the <H1> tag, except for those specified in the definition of the class: the font's weight, the background color, and the foreground color.

You use classes to customize existing HTML tags as needed in a document. Nonetheless, when you insert a tag in a document, it can't be changed later. The page is still static. As you will see, DHTML lets you redefine the styles after the page has been rendered in the browser's window. For example, you can specify that the color property of an <H1> tag changes when the pointer is hovering over it or when the user takes another action. As you can guess, the browser detects various user actions and generates events for each one of them. If you supply the appropriate event handler, the document will react to these events.

The <DIV> Tag

Internet Explorer renders HTML documents in one pass, working from the beginning of the document to the end. As a result, there is no way for the browser to move back and place one element on top of another. For example, with plain HTML you can't place a caption over an image. Once the image is rendered on the browser's window, you can't step back and place some text over it.

This limitation can be overcome with the help of the <DIV> tag, which lets you break a document into separate entities that can be placed on the page with respect to one another. The <DIV> tag is the heart of DHTML; it let's you break the document into elements (or objects) and manipulate each one independently. Let's look at a deceptively simple example. The STYLES.HTM page, shown in Figure 19.10, looks as if the text appears on top of the background image.

FIGURE 19.10:

The STYLES.HTM page

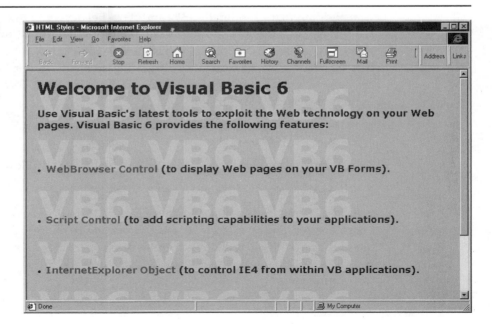

If you open this document with a text editor, you'll see that it contains two sections, each delimited with the <DIV> tag. The first <DIV> tag contains a string that is tiled repeatedly in the document's background. The second <DIV> tag contains the text that's displayed on top of the background. The two sections of the document overlap, because the <DIV> tag allows us to specify its absolute position.

The document contains the following STYLE definition:

```
<STYLE>

    H1.LargeText {color: '#D0D0D0'; font-family: "Verdana"; font-size:
500%}

</STYLE>
```

This Style is a variation of the <H1> header. It uses a very large font and a light gray color (slightly lighter than the silver color of the background). The background pattern may not be noticeable on the printed page; open the STYLES.HTM page to view it. In general, the background shouldn't be busy; if it is, the text on top of it will be hard to read.

The definition of the first <DIV> tag, which creates the background, is:

```
<DIV STYLE="position:absolute; left: 20">
    <H1 CLASS=LargeText>VB6 VB6 VB6 VB6 VB6 VB6
</DIV>
```

The position of this section of the document is defined as absolute and is displaced 20 pixels from the left edge of Internet Explorer's window. To place the text on top of the first section, another <DIV> tag is used, with the same origin. Here's the definition of the section with the text:

```
<DIV STYLE="position:absolute; left=20">
</DIV>
```

Here, I've omitted the actual contents of the section. Whatever appears between the <DIV> tags will be rendered on top of the current contents of Internet Explorer's window. You can open the STYLES.HTM document and examine its code.

The <STYLE> and <CLASS> tags are extensions to HTML, and they allow a Web author to control the properties of the HTML elements and to position them on the page. These two tags were the first significant departure from the straight (and static) HTML model. DHTML gives you the option to manipulate the styles programmatically. Whereas the <CLASS> tag lets you redefine an existing tag, the <DIV> tag lets you apply attributes to an entire section. DHTML takes this capability one step further. It lets you manipulate the background color from within a script, even after the document has been rendered on the browser.

Manipulating the Styles

You have seen how to customize HTML tags with the <STYLE> tag. In this section, we are going to manipulate the styles from within scripts and produce DHTML documents (documents that change their appearance on the browser). Because VBScript is executed on the client, it is possible to include the logic for dynamic content in HTML documents and activate them on the client.

Figure 19.11 shows a simple page with information about Sybex titles. The titles are grouped under the name of the series to which they belong, and they form nested lists. This linear document displays all the information at once, in a lengthy list of series and titles.

FIGURE 19.11:

A simple HTML list

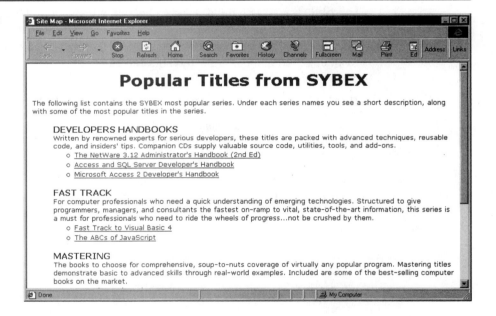

If you were viewing the same information with a Visual Basic application, you'd expect a different organization—most likely a tree structure—where you could expand and collapse the series and view only the titles you're interested in. You can do something similar with HTML, namely, use the series names as hyperlinks to separate documents, each containing the titles in the series. This is how titles are organized at Sybex's Web site on the World Wide Web.

With DHTML, you can organize the series and their titles in an expandable list, without having to make additional trips to the Web server. Each series title can act as a hotspot that, when clicked, expands the following list. Open the document SBXHTML.HTM (in this chapter's folder on the CD) with Internet Explorer and experiment with it. Click the document's title to expand the first-level list (the names of the series), and then click the name of a series to see its titles. If you click again, the list will collapse and make room for other lists. Figures 19.12 and 19.13 show this document in action.

FIGURE 19.12:

DHTML allows you write Web pages that change their look and content based on viewer actions. The Developers Handbooks entry turns red when the pointer hovers over it.

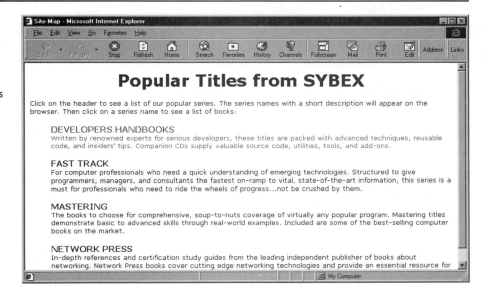

FIGURE 19.13:

This page displays a few titles of the Developer's Handbook series. If the user clicks the Developers Handbook entry again, the title list will collapse, as in Figure 19.12.

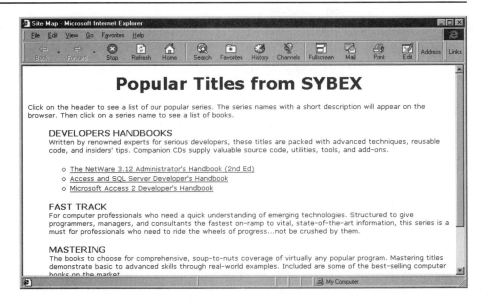

Even the title of the document on the SBXDHTML.HTM page is a hotspot. The first time you open the document, you will see the title only. Click the title to see the names of the series. Then click the title again to collapse the list.

A Dynamic List

To build the SBXDHTML.HTM list, we'll start with a plain HTML document that displays the same document. Here's the HTML for the list with the selected Sybex titles (it's the SBXHTML.HTM document).

Code 19.3: **A Simple HTML List**

```
<HTML>
<HEAD>
<TITLE>Site Map</TITLE>
</HEAD>
<BODY>
<FONT FACE="Verdana" SIZE=2>
<CENTER>
<H1>
Popular Titles from SYBEX
</H1>
</CENTER>
<FONT SIZE=3>
<B>DEVELOPERS HANDBOOKS</B><BR>
<FONT SIZE=2>
<UL>
<LI>The NetWare 3.12 Administrator's Handbook (2nd Ed)
<LI>Access and SQL Server Developer's Handbook
<LI>Microsoft Access 2 Developer's Handbook
</UL>
</FONT>
<P>
<FONT SIZE=3>
<B>FAST TRACK</B><BR>
<UL>
<LI>Fast Track to Visual Basic 4
<LI>The ABCs of JavaScript
</UL>
</FONT>
<P>
<FONT SIZE=3>
<B>MASTERING</B><BR>
<UL>
<LI>Mastering Web Design
<LI>Mastering the Internet (2nd Ed)
<LI>Mastering Windows NT Server 4
```

```
<LI>Mastering Java
<LI>Mastering Windows 95
</UL>
</FONT>
<P>
<FONT SIZE=3>
<B>NETWORK PRESS</B><BR>
<UL>
<LI>The Encyclopedia of Networking (2nd Ed)
<LI>Introduction to Local Area Networks
<LI>Networking The Small Office
</UL>
<FONT>
</BODY>
</HTML>
```

This listing doesn't contain all the text you'll see in the browser's window, just the structure of the list. I also removed the <A> tags that turn each title into a hyperlink, pointing to the corresponding book on the Sybex Web server. You can open the SBXHTML.HTM document with a text editor to see the complete listing. Here's the tag that corresponds to the item *Mastering Web Design* (the first title in the Mastering series):

```
<LI TYPE=DISC><A HREF="http://www.sybex.com/cgi-bin/
category.pl?1911back.html" >Mastering Web Design</A>
```

As you can see in the listing, each series contains a list of items. To display a list with HTML, you enclose the entire list in a pair of <UL> tags (UL stands for Unordered List), and prefix each new item in the list with an <LI> tag. The TYPE=DISC attribute causes a little circle to appear in front of each item, and you can omit it if you don't like the look of the list.

The dynamic version of this list (the SBXDHTML.HTM document on the CD) is a bit more complicated, but it uses the same structure. Each list item that acts as a hotspot must be named so that we can reference it from within our code. Here's the definition of the Mastering series:

```
<DIV ID='Head3'>
<FONT SIZE=3>
<B>MASTERING</B>
<BR>
<FONT SIZE=2>
The books to choose for comprehensive, soup-to-nuts coverage of virtu-
ally any popular program. Mastering titles demonstrate basic to advanced
skills through real-world examples. Included are some of the best-sell-
ing computer books on the market.
</DIV>
```

The <DIV> tags mark the beginning and end of an element. The header "Mastering" and the following description form a distinct element, because they are enclosed in a pair of <DIV> tags. The ID attribute of the <DIV> tag is the name of the element.

Following the "Mastering" header (which we'll turn into a hotspot) is the list of the Mastering titles. The entire list is another element, because we must be able to expand and collapse it. The definition of the Mastering list is based on the straight HTML code presented earlier, but it's enclosed in a pair of <DIV> tags. Here's the "Mastering" list:

```
<DIV ID="TOC3" STYLE="display:none">
    <FONT SIZE=2>
    <UL>
    <LI>Mastering Web Design
    <LI>Mastering the Internet (2ns Ed)
    <LI>Mastering Windows NT 4
    <LI>Mastering Windows 95
     </UL>
    </FONT>
</DIV>
```

Again, I've omitted the definitions of the hyperlinks to make the code easier to read. Notice that this element is called TOC3, and it has a style too. The attribute:

```
STYLE="display:none"
```

tells Internet Explorer not to display the element. The entire document will be downloaded to the client computer, but it won't be displayed because of the STYLE attribute.

As you probably guessed, we must supply the code to hide and display the list each time the visitor clicks the Mastering hotspot. The Mastering section is called Head3. Therefore, we must supply an event handler that will react to the onClick event of the Head3 object:

```
Sub Head3_onClick()
    If TOC3.style.display = "" Then
       TOC3.style.display = "none"
    Else
       TOC3.style.display = ""
    End If
End Sub
```

This event handler is invoked when the visitor clicks the Mastering hotspot. It examines the value of the display attribute of the TOC3 element. If the TOC3 element is visible (its display attribute's value is empty), the code hides it by setting it to *none*. If not, it displays the element by setting its DISPLAY attribute to an empty string.

Notice that in addition to reacting to the mouse click event, the various hotspots react to the movement of the mouse. Every time you move the pointer over a series name, the name of the series and its description turn red. When the pointer is moved over another series, the previously highlighted one is reset to black. Each series is a separate object, so all we have to do is change the color of the object.

The two subroutines that detect when the pointer moves in or out the area of the Head3 element are the Head3_onMouseOver() and Head3_onMouseOut() functions. We must use these subroutines to change the color of the Head3 element so that when the pointer hovers over it, the text color is red, and when it leaves the area, the text color is reset to black. Here are the definitions of the corresponding event handlers:

```
Sub Head3_noMouseOver()
    Head3.style.color = "#FF3300"
End Sub

Sub Head3_onMouseOut()
    Head3.style.color="#000000"
End Sub
```

DHTML is nothing more than programmable HTML. When building a Web page with DHTML, you're basically building an HTML document, and you must make sure that each section of the document that reacts to viewer actions is delimited with a pair of <DIV> tags. Everything that appears between them is a separate element, and its attributes can be manipulated with VBScript statements.

To manipulate the element programmatically, you supply an event handler for each external action to which your document must react. The name of the event handler is made up of the name of the element you want to program (which is the value of the ID attribute of the corresponding <DIV> tag) and the event to which it must react.

The short introduction to the Web and VBScript ends here. By now you should have a good idea of how HTML and VBScript work and understand their role in Web development. As you know, Visual Basic supports a new type of project, the DHTML project, but it doesn't come with all the visual tools you need to develop DHTML documents without a good understanding of the <DIV> tag and how to use VBScript to program the elements of a page. You can experiment with DHTML projects, but unless you understand how HTML works and how to script it, you won't be able to develop DHTML projects with Visual Basic's tools.

You may have found this chapter too general, without many practical applications. That's because you haven't seen the best of VBScript yet. You've learned the prerequisites, and you're ready to apply this knowledge. In the next chapter, you'll learn how to use VBScript to script your own applications and even develop batch files for Windows 98 (yes, VBScript is also the scripting language of the operating system). In the last chapter, you'll see how VBScript is used for developing applications on the server that interact with the client.

CHAPTER

TWENTY

Scripting Objects

- The FileSystemObject object

- Accessing folders and files

- The Script control

- The Windows scripting host

- The Shell object

As you saw in the last chapter, VBScript was introduced to script Web pages and harness the computing power of the client. Scripts are simple programs that are downloaded in text format and executed on the client computer. VBScript itself is the core of a programming language. On its own, VBScript can do very little. The real power in scripting comes from the way that VBScript can access the objects exposed by the browser. If you ignore the objects that can be manipulated through VBScript (such as the <DIV> tags or the intrinsic and ActiveX controls), what's left? A language that can create variables and assign values to them, perform basic operations on these variables, evaluate logical expressions, and repeat several loop structures. If you had a mechanism to perform these operations, you'd be able to build a custom programming language, wouldn't you?

In principle, you can create a custom language and embed it in your applications. All you need is the engine that interprets and executes VBScript code. Add a few objects that expose properties and methods, and you have your own, custom language. DHTML and Internet Explorer expose a number of objects that can be manipulated with VBScript. Later in this chapter, you'll learn how to embed VBScript in your applications and allow users to program your application.

But what about Visual Basic for Applications? VBA is a powerful language for programming Office (and other) applications, but it's not a scripting language. It's considered a programming language, and embedding VBA into an application is not a task for the average VB programmer. Beyond the programming difficulties, VBA is an expensive product. Only large software companies have licensed it so far, and a relatively small number of non-Microsoft applications include VBA (for example, Autodesk's AutoCAD). Embedding VBScript in your applications, on the other hand, is not nearly as complicated, and VBScript is free.

The same technology can also be embedded in other products, including Windows itself. As you probably know, you can automate Windows 98 operations with scripts, which are the equivalent of the old DOS batch files. Windows 98 includes the *Windows Scripting Host (WSH)*, an engine that interprets and executes VBScript code and exposes a few objects needed to script the operating system. One of the objects exposed by the WSH is the Environment object, which gives you access to the environment variables. Another WSH object is the Network object, which gives you access to the network's resources. I'll discuss these objects later in this chapter. For now, keep in mind that the language for scripting the Windows 98 operating system is VBScript, and you can easily apply your programming skills to another scripting area.

In the following section, we are going to look at a very useful object introduced with VBScript, the FileSystemObject object. It gives you access to the host computer's file system and was lacking in Visual Basic. We'll then explore the Script control, which lets you add scripting capabilities to your VB applications. Yes, it is possible to script your own applications with VBScript and make them much more flexible. In the last section of this chapter, you'll see how you can use VBScript to script Windows itself.

The FileSystemObject Object

VBScript introduced several new objects that are also available from within Visual Basic. The most important (from a VB programmer's point of view, at least) is the FileSystemObject object, which gives you access to the host computer's file system. Visual Basic provides a small number of functions and statements for accessing and manipulating the file system, but the *FileSystemObject* object is a very flexible object that provides methods and properties for accessing every folder and file on the host computer's disks.

To gain access to your computer's file system, you create a FileSystemObject variable with the CreateObject() function:

```
Set FSys = CreateObject("Scripting.FileSystemObject")
```

The variable *FSys* represents the file system, and it must be declared as Object:

```
Dim FSys As Object
```

To access text files on the computer's disk, you use the FileSystemObject object's methods, which I'll describe next.

This is how you can access the host computer's file system from within a Windows script. With Visual Basic there's a better method, which exploits early binding to speed up your application. You can add a reference to the Microsoft Scripting Runtime object by choosing Project ➤ References to open the References dialog box. Select the Microsoft Scripting Runtime item, and click OK. Once the reference is added to the project, you can declare the *FSys* variable as follows:

```
Dim FSys As New Scripting.FileSystemObject
```

or simply:

```
Dim FSys As New FileSystemObject
```

In the Code window, as soon as you type the name of the *FSys* variable and the following period, the components of the Scripting object appear in a list, and you can select the desired object. You can then use the *FSys* variable in your code without the CreateObject() function.

Let's exercise the FileSystemObject object. Start a new project and place a Command button on it. In the Form's Code window, enter the following declaration:

```
Dim FSys As New Scripting.FileSystemObject
```

Then enter the following statement in the Command button's Click event handler:

```
Debug.Print FSys.FileExists("C:\AUTOEXEC.BAT")
```

If the file C:\AUTOEXEC.BAT exists, the string "True" will appear in the Immediate window. The FileExists member of the *FSys* variable is a method, which returns True if the specified file exists; otherwise, it returns False.

The FileSystemObject object provides a number of properties and methods for manipulating the file system, as well as for creating new text files (and opening existing ones), to read from or write to. Visual Basic provides its own statements for accessing text files (as well as binary files), so this subset of the FileSystemObject object is not particularly useful to VB programmers. The members of the FileSystemObject object that allow you to open and read from or write to text files are very useful for developing Windows scripts, so I will present them here. This book is addressed to programmers, so I won't discuss them in much detail. Later, I will discuss the members of the FileSystemObject object that are just as useful for developing VB applications as they are for developing Windows scripts.

Being able to write information to text files and read from them is a basic operation in scripting. Many scripts save their results to text files or read their arguments from text files (scripts that process a large number of files, for instance). The methods of the FileSystemObject object for manipulating text files can also be used from within scripts in Visual Basic applications (see the StatClss example later in this chapter).

The CreateTextFile Method

This method creates a new text file and returns a *TextStream* object that can be used to read from or write to the file. The syntax of the CreateTextFile method is:

```
Set TStream = FSys.CreateTextFile(filename, overwrite, unicode)
```

The *filename* argument specifies the name of the file to be created and is the only required argument. *Overwrite* is a Boolean value that indicates whether you can overwrite an existing file (if True) or not (if False). If you omit the *overwrite* argument, existing files are not overwritten. The last argument, *unicode*, indicates whether the file is created as a Unicode or an ASCII file. If the *unicode* argument is True, the new file is created as a Unicode file; otherwise, it is created as an ASCII file. If you omit the *unicode* argument, an ASCII file is assumed.

To create a new text file, create a *FileSystemObject* object variable and then call its CreateTextFile method as follows:

```
Set TStream = FSys.CreateTextFile("c:\testfile.txt")
```

The *TStream* variable represents a TextStream object, whose methods allow you to write to or read from the specified file. (I'll discuss these methods in "The Text-Stream Object" section, later in this chapter.)

The OpenTextFile Method

In addition to creating new text files, you can open existing files with the Open-TextFile method, whose syntax is:

```
FSys.OpenTextFile(filename, iomode, create, format)
```

The OpenTextFile method opens the specified file and returns a TextStream object that can be used to read from or write to the file. The *filename* argument is the only required one. The value of the *iomode* argument is one of the constants shown in Table 20.1.

TABLE 20.1: The Values of the OpenTextFile Method's *iomode* Argument

Constant	Value	Description
ForReading	1	The file is opened for reading existing data.
ForAppending	2	The file is opened for appending new data.

The optional *create* argument is a Boolean value that indicates whether a new file can be created if the specified filename doesn't exist. If it's True, a new file is created. The last argument, *format*, is also optional and can be True (the file is opened in Unicode mode) or False (the file is opened in ASCII mode). If you omit the *format* argument, the file is opened using the system default (ASCII).

To open a TextStream object for reading, use the following statements:

```
Set TStream = FSys.OpenTextFile("c:\testfile.txt", ForReading)
```

Like the CreateTextFile method, the OpenTextFile method returns a TextStream object, whose methods allow you to write to or read from the specified file.

Now that you have seen how the FileSystemObject is used to open and create files, we are ready to look at the TextStream object, which lets you read from and write to files. The FileSystemObject object has more methods, which allow you to access the various drives, copy and delete files or entire folders, and more. I'll come back to the methods of the FileSystemObject object, but first let's see how you can manipulate text files through the TextStream object.

The TextStream Object's Methods

After you create a TextStream object with the CreateTextFile or the OpenTextFile method of the FileSystemObject object, you can use the following methods to read from and write to the file.

NOTE   As its name implies, the TextStream object applies only to text files.

Read   This method reads a specified number of characters from a TextStream object. Its syntax is:

```
TStream.Read(characters)
```

in which *characters* is the number of characters to be read from and *TStream* is a TextStream variable.

ReadAll   This method reads the entire TextStream (text file) and returns the text as a string variable. Its syntax is:

```
fileText = TStream.ReadAll
```

in which *fileText* is a string (or variant) variable.

ReadLine   This method reads one line of text at a time (up to, but not including, the newline character) from a text file and returns the resulting string. Its syntax is:

```
fileText = TStream.ReadLine
```

Skip   This method skips a specified number of characters when reading a text file. Its syntax is:

```
TStream.Skip(characters)
```

in which *characters* is the number of characters to be skipped.

SkipLine   This method skips the next line of the text file, and its syntax is:

```
TStream.SkipLine
```

The characters of the skipped line are discarded, up to and including the next newline character.

Write   This method writes the specified string to a TextStream file. Its syntax is:

```
TStream.Write(string)
```

in which *string* is the string (literal or variable) to be written to the file. Strings are written to the file with no intervening spaces or characters between each string. Use the WriteLine method to write a newline character or a string that ends with a newline character.

WriteLine   This method writes the specified string followed by a newline character to the file. Its syntax is:

```
TStream.WriteLine(string)
```

in which *string* is the text you want to write to the file. If you call the WriteLine method without an argument, a newline character is written to the file.

WriteBlankLines   This method writes a specified number of blank lines (newline characters) to the file. Its syntax is:

```
TStream.WriteBlankLines(lines)
```

in which *lines* is the number of blank lines to be inserted in the file.

The TextStream Object's Properties

Besides its methods, the TextStream object provides a number of properties, which allow your code to know where the pointer is in the current TextStream.

AtEndOfLine   This is a read-only property that returns True if the file pointer is at the end of a line in the TextStream object; otherwise, it returns False. The AtEndOfLine property applies to files that are open for reading. You can use this property to read a line of characters, one at a time, with a loop similar to the following:

```
Do While TSream.AtEndOfLine = False
    newChar = TStream.Read(1)
    {process character newChar}
Loop
```

This loop scans the file represented by the TStream object, and until it reaches the end of the current line, it reads and processes another character.

AtEndOfStream   This is another read-only property that returns True if the file pointer is at the end of the TextStream object. The AtEndOfStream property applies only to TextStream files that are open for reading. You can use this property to read an entire file, one line at a time, with a loop such as the following:

```
Do While TStream.AtEndOfStream = False
    newLine = TStream.ReadLine
    {process line}
Loop
```

Column   This is another read-only property that returns the column number of the current character in a TextStream line. The first character in a line is in column 1. Use this property to read data arranged in columns, without tabs or other delimiters.

Line   This property is another read-only property that returns the current line number in the TextStream. The Line property of the first line in a TextStream object is 1.

VB6 at Work: The MakeFile Project

The MakeFile project (see Figure 20.1) demonstrates several of the TextStream object's methods. This application creates a text file and saves the contents of a TextBox control in it. It then opens the file, reads the text lines, and displays them on the same TextBox control.

FIGURE 20.1:

The MakeFile project demonstrates how to use the TextStreamObject to access a text file.

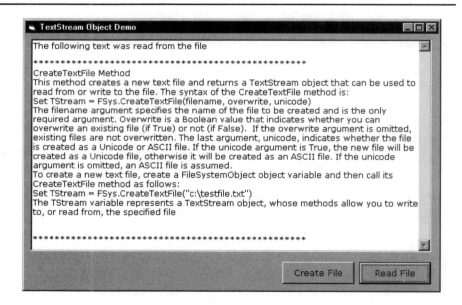

To design the application, follow these steps:

1. Start a new Standard EXE project.

2. Add a reference to the FileSystemObject component.

3. Open the References dialog box, and select the Microsoft Scripting Runtime component.

4. Now, insert the following declaration in the Form's Code window:

```
Dim FSys As New FileSystemObject
```

The *FSys* variable is declared on the Form level so that all procedures can access it.

5. Place the controls shown in Figure 20.1 on the Form, and insert the code shown in Code 20.1 in the two Command buttons' Click events.

The Create File button reads the text on the TextBox control and saves it to the C:\TEXTFILE.TXT file in the application's folder. The code creates a TextStream object and uses it to write the text to the file.

Code 20.1:   **The Create File Button**

```
Private Sub bttnCreateFile_Click()
Dim OutStream As TextStream

    TestFile = App.Path & "\textfile.txt"
    Set OutStream = FSys.CreateTextFile(TestFile, True, False)
    OutStream.WriteLine Text1.Text
    Set OutStream = Nothing
End Sub
```

The second button reads the contents of the same file through another TextStream object. In addition to the text read from the file, it displays a few additional lines to delimit the text read from the file.

Code 20.2:   **The Read File Button**

```
Private Sub bttnReadFile_Click()
Dim InStream As TextStream

    TestFile = App.Path & "\textfile.txt"
    Set InStream = FSys.OpenTextFile(TestFile, 1, False, False)
    While InStream.AtEndOfStream = False
        TLine = InStream.ReadLine
        txt = txt & TLine & vbCrLf
    Wend
    Text1.Text = "The following text was read from the file" & vbCrLf
    Text1.Text = Text1.Text & vbCrLf & String(50, "*")
    Text1.Text = Text1.Text & vbCrLf & txt
    Text1.Text = Text1.Text & vbCrLf & String(50, "*")
    Set InStream = Nothing
End Sub
```

The *FSys* variable represents the file system. *InStream* and *OutStream* are two Text-Stream objects whose WriteLine and ReadLine methods are used to write and read individual lines to the file. After the desired lines have been written to the file, we set both object variables to Nothing to release the resources allocated to it (in effect this statement closes the file).

The file's lines are read with a While…Wend loop, which examines the value of the TextStream object's AtEndOfStream property to find out how many lines to read from the file:

```
While InStream.AtEndOfStream = False
    TLine = Instream.ReadLine
    {process Tline variable}
Wend
```

At each iteration of the loop, the *TLine* variable holds the next line of text in the file.

Accessing Folders and Files

In the previous sections, we looked at the methods of the FileSystemObject object, which allow you to access files on the local disk(s). The FileSystemObject object supports many more methods that apply to files and folders—methods that allow you to copy and delete files or folders, which are much more useful to a VB programmer than the methods for accessing text files. Although there are Visual Basic statements and functions to access the file system, the FileSystemObject object gives you a consistent, hierarchical view of the file system, and you should use it instead.

> **NOTE**   In order to access the file system from within scripts, you can only use the File-SystemObject object.

CopyFile   This method copies one or more files from one folder to another, and its syntax is:

```
FSys.CopyFile source, destination, overwrite
```

The *source* argument is the path of the file to be moved and can contain wildcard characters (for copying multiple files). The *destination* argument is the path of the destination folder to which the file(s) will be copied. The *destination* argument may not contain wildcard characters. The last argument, *overwrite*, is optional, and it's a Boolean value (True/False) that indicates whether existing files are to be overwritten. The CopyFile method produces a runtime error if the destination file has its read-only attribute set, regardless of the value of the *overwrite* argument. See the discussion of the Attributes property for an example of how to overwrite read-only files.

CopyFolder   This method copies a folder from one location to another, including the subfolders (this is called *recursive* copying). The syntax of the CopyFolder method is:

```
FSys.CopyFolder source, destination, overwrite
```

in which *source* is the path of the source folder (where files will be copied from) and may include wildcard characters, in case you want to copy selected files. The *destination* argument is the path of the destination folder (where the files will be copied to), and it may not contain wildcard characters. The last argument, *overwrite*, is optional, and it's a Boolean value that indicates whether existing folders can be overwritten. If it's True, the destination files can be overwritten, if they exist. To protect existing files in the destination folder, set it to False.

To copy all the DOC files from the folder MyDocuments to the folder Work-Docs\February, use the following statement:

```
FSys.CopyFolder "c:\MyDocuments\*.DOC", "c:\WorkDocs\February"
```

in which *FSys* is a properly declared FileSystemObject object variable.

WARNING   The CopyFolder method stops when it encounters the first error. This means that some files have been copied and some have not. The CopyFolder method won't move the copied files back to their source folder, nor will it continue with the remaining files.

DeleteFile   This method deletes one or more files, and its syntax is:

```
FSys.DeleteFile filespec, force
```

in which *filespec* is the name of the file(s) to delete and may contain wildcard characters. The *force* argument is optional, and it's a Boolean value that indicates whether read-only files will be deleted (if True) or not (if False). Like the CopyFile method, the DeleteFile method stops on the first error it encounters.

DeleteFolder   This method deletes a specific folder and its contents, including its subfolders and their files. Its syntax is identical to the syntax of the DeleteFile method:

```
FSys.DeleteFolder folderspec, force
```

Here, *folderspec* is the name of the folder to delete. The specified folder is deleted, regardless of whether it contains files (unlike the RMDIR DOS command). The *force* argument has the same meaning as it has with the DeleteFile method.

MoveFile   This method moves one or more files from one folder to another, and its syntax is:

```
FSys.MoveFile source, destination
```

in which *source* is the path of the file(s) to be moved and *destination* is the path to which the file(s) will be moved. The MoveFile method works identically to the Copy method, but the original files are deleted after they are copied. The *source* argument string can contain wildcard characters to move multiple files, but the *destination* argument can't contain wildcard characters. If you're copying a single file, the *destination* argument can be either a filename or a folder name (in which case, the file is moved to the specified folder). If you're copying multiple files, the destination must be a folder's path, to which the files will be moved. If the *destination* is an existing file's name or an existing folder's name, an error occurs.

MoveFolder   This method moves a folder to another location. Its syntax is:

```
FSys.MoveFolder source, destination
```

in which *source* and *destination* are the specifications of the source and destination folders.

FileExists, FolderExists   These two methods return True if the specified file or folder exists. Use them to make sure a file or folder exists before attempting to use it from within your script. Their syntax is:

```
FSys.FileExists(fileSpec)
```

and:

```
FSys.FolderExists(folderSpec)
```

GetFile, GetFolder   These methods return a File and Folder object, which represent a specific file or folder.

NOTE   The GetFile method doesn't return the entire file, nor does it return the name of the file. It's a reference to a file through which you can access the file's properties. I'll discuss the File and Folder objects later in this chapter.

To create a *File* object variable with the GetFile method, you first create a *FileSystemObject* object variable and then call its GetFile method:

```
Set thisFile = FSys.GetFile("c:\autoexec.bat")
```

The variable *thisFile* represents the file AUTOEXEC.BAT, and you can use its properties and methods to manipulate the file. For example, you can use its Size property to find out the file's size, its DateCreated property to find out when the file was created, and so on. I'll discuss the properties and methods of the File object in the "The File Object" section, later in this chapter.

The GetFolder method is quite similar to the GetFile method, only it returns a Folder object. The argument of the GetFolder method must be an absolute or relative path name:

```
Set thisFolder = FSys.GetFolder("c:\windows\desktop")
```

The variable *thisFolder* represents the Desktop, and you can use its properties and methods to manipulate the Desktop folder. For example, you can use its Size property to find out the size of a folder (including its subfolders), its DateCreated property to find out when the folder was created, and so on. I'll describe the properties and methods of the Folder object in "The Folder Object" section, later in this chapter.

GetFileName   This method returns the last component of specified path, which is a filename with its extension. The GetFileName method is usually called with a File object as an argument, to retrieve the filename. Without the GetFileName method, you'd have to provide your own routine for parsing the path name.

NOTE   The GetFileName method works on its argument, regardless of whether such a path exists.

The Files Collection

The Files Collection contains a File object for each file in a folder. The following script iterates through the files of a specific folder using the For Each...Next statement:

```
Set ThisFolder = FSys.GetFolder(folderName)
Set AllFiles = ThisFolder.Files
For Each file in AllFiles
    {process current file}
Next
```

In the loop's body, you can access the properties of the current file. Its name is file.Name, its creation date is file.DateCreated, and so on. In the following sections, we'll look at the properties and methods of the File object.

The File Object

The File object represents a file and provides properties, which represent the properties of the actual file, and methods, which let you copy, move, and delete files.

To obtain a File object and examine its properties, follow these steps:

1. Create a *FileSystemObject* variable either by declaring it :

   ```
   Dim FSys As New FileSystemObject
   ```

   or by calling the CreateObject() function:

   ```
   Set FSys = CreateObject("Scripting.FileSystemObject")
   ```

2. Use the *FSys* variable to obtain an object that represents a specific file:

   ```
   Set file = FSys.GetFile(fileName)
   ```

   in which *fileName* is the file's path name (c:\Images\Sky.bmp, for example).

3. Now, access the file's properties through the *file* object variable:

   ```
   FName = file.Name
   FDate = file.DateCreated
   FSize = file.Size
   ```

Next, we are going to look at the properties of the File object.

The File Object's Properties

The File object provides the following properties. Many of these properties apply to the Folder object as well, which is discussed in "The Folder Object" section, later in this chapter.

Attributes   You use this property to read or set a file's attributes. To read the attributes of a file, use the syntax:

```
thisFile.Attributes
```

You can also set selected attributes using the syntax

```
thisFile.Attributes = thisFile.Attributes Or new_attribute
```

The *new_attribute* variable can have any of the values shown in Table 20.2. To change multiple attributes, combine the corresponding values with the logical OR operator. The statement:

```
thisFile.Attributes = new_attribute
```

will turn on a specific attribute, but it will clear all other attributes. If a file is read-only and hidden, its Attributes property is 3 (1+2 according to Table 20.2). If you attempt to turn on the Archive attribute by setting its Attributes property to 32, the other two attributes will be cleared. By combining the new attribute (32) and the existing attributes with the OR operator, the file will be Read-only, Hidden, and Archive.

TABLE 20.2: The Values of the *new_attribute* Variable

Constant	Value	Description
Normal	0	Normal file
ReadOnly	1	Read-only file
Hidden	2	Hidden file
System	4	System file
Volume	8	Disk drive volume label
Directory	16	Folder or directory
Archive	32	File has changed since last backup
Alias	64	Link or shortcut
Compressed	128	Compressed file

To find out whether a file is read-only, use this statement:

```
If thisFile.Attributes and 32 Then
     MsgBox "Read-only file"
End If
```

You can also use the MsgBox() function to prompt the user to change the read-only attribute:

```
If thisFile.Attributes And 32 Then
    reply = MsgBox("This is a read-only file. _
          Delete it anyway?", vbYesNo)
      If reply = vbYes Then
          thisFile.Attributes = thisFile.Attributes + 32
Else
    thisFile.Delete
End If
```

Delete is a method of the File object, which deletes the specific file. See the "Delete" section later in this chapter for its syntax.

Normally, when you set a file's attributes, you don't reset its existing attributes. For example, you can choose to add the Hidden attribute from a file that has its ReadOnly attribute set. To turn on the Hidden attribute without affecting the other attributes, use a statement such as:

```
thisFile.Attributes = aFile.Attributes + 2
```

or

```
thisFile.Attributes = aFile.Attributes Or 2
```

To remove a specific attribute, first find out whether this attribute is already set, and then subtract its value for the Attributes property's value. To remove the Hidden attribute, use a structure like the following:

```
If thisFile.Attributes And 2 Then
    thisFile.Attributes = thisFile.Attributes - 2
End If
```

DateCreated   This property returns the date and time that the specified file or folder was created, and it's read-only. To retrieve the date a specific file was created, use the syntax

```
thisFile.DateCreated
```

The following code segment calculates the age of a file in days. You can calculate the file's age in any other time interval by multiplying or dividing the file's age in days by the appropriate constant.

```
Set thisFile = FSys.GetFile("c:\windows\Explorer.exe")
DateCreated = thisFile.DateCreated
MsgBox Int(Now() - DateCreated)
```

To express this difference in hours, divide the difference by 24.

DateLastAccessed   This property returns the date and time that the specified file or folder was last accessed. The DateLastAccessed property is identical in its use to the DateCreated property.

DateLastModified   This property returns the date and time that the specified file or folder was last modified. The DateLastModified property is identical in its use to the DateCreated property.

NOTE   The DateCreated, DateLastAccessed, and DateLastModified properties are read-only. Sometimes, we need to "touch" the files in a folder (change the DateLastAccessed property). If you are using scripts or another automated mechanism for deleting or moving old files, touching them will enable you to exclude certain files from an automatic deletion operation. It would be convenient to touch a file by changing the value of its DateLastAccessed property, but this is impossible. To change the DateLastAccessed property, you should copy the file, delete the original, and then rename the copied file back to the name of the original file.

Drive   This property returns the drive letter of the drive on which the specified file or folder resides. It's read-only, and its syntax is:

```
object.Drive
```

in which *object* is always a File or Folder object.

Name   This property returns or sets the name of a file or folder (the last part of the path). To find out the name of a file, use the statement:

```
FileObject.Name
```

To rename an existing file (or folder), use the following syntax:

```
FileObject.Name = new_name
```

in which *newname* is the new name of the file represented by the *FileObject* variable (or the corresponding *Folder* object variable).

ParentFolder   This property returns a Folder object, which represents the parent folder of the specified file or folder. The ParentFolder property is read-only.

Path   This property returns the path for a specified file or folder. If the file resides in the root folder, the backslash character (\)is not included. In other words, the path for the file C:\Autoexec.bat is "C:" and not "C:\".

If the *FileObject* object variable represents the file c:\windows\desktop\TOC.doc, the expression `FileObject.Path` returns the string "c:\windows\desktop", and the expression `FileObject.Name` returns the string "TOC.doc".

ShortName   This property is similar to the Name property, but it returns the short name (8.3 convention) of the specified file or folder.

Size   When applied to File objects, this property returns the size, in bytes, of the specified file. For folders, it returns the size, in bytes, of all files and subfolders contained in the folder.

Type   This property returns information about the type of a file or folder. For example, for files ending in .TXT, the string "Text Document" is returned.

The File Object's Methods

The File object provides a number of methods for moving files around, and they are similar to the methods of the FileSystemObject object. The difference between the methods of the FileSystemObject object and those of the File object is that you can't operate on multiple files at once with the File object's methods. Each method applies to a specific file only.

Copy   This method copies a file (or folder) from one location to another. Its syntax is:

```
FileObject.Copy destination, overwrite
```

in which *destination* is the new name or folder of the file and may not contain wild-card characters. The second argument, *overwrite*, is optional, and it's a Boolean value that indicates whether existing files or folders are to be overwritten (if True) or not (if False).

Delete   This method deletes a file (or folder). Its syntax is:

```
FileObject.Delete force
```

The *force* argument is optional and indicates whether files with their read-only attributes should be deleted anyway (if True) or not (if False). Unlike the DOS RMDIR command, the Delete method removes a folder regardless of whether it contains files or subfolders.

Move   This method moves a file to a new location (it's equivalent to copying the file to a new location and then deleting the original file). Its syntax is:

```
FileObject.Move destination
```

in which *destination* is the path to which the file is moved. If the *destination* argument is a folder name, the file is moved to the specified folder with the same name. If the *destination* argument also contains a filename, the file is moved and renamed. You can call the Move method with a different filename to simply rename the original file.

OpenAsTextStream   This method opens a specified file and returns a TextStream object that can be used to read from or write to the file. Its syntax is:

```
FileObject.OpenAsTextStream(iomode, format)
```

Both arguments are optional. The *iomode* argument specifies whether the file will be opened as input, output, or appending, and it can have one of the values shown in Table 20.3.

TABLE 20.3:   The Settings of the *iomode* Argument of the OpenAsTextStream Method

Constant	Value	Description
ForReading	1	Opens a file for reading only; you can't write to this file
ForWriting	2	Opens a file for writing; if a file with the same name exists, its previous contents are overwritten
ForAppending	8	Opens a file and writes to the end of the file

The second argument, *format*, indicates whether the file should be opened as Unicode or ASCII, and it can have one of the values shown in Table 20.4.

The OpenAsTextStream method does the same thing as the OpenTextFile method of the FileSystemObject object. They both prepare a file for input or output. Use the OpenAsTextStream method when you have an object variable that represents the file you want to open. If you know the name of the file, use the OpenTextFile method of the FileSystemObject object.

TABLE 20.4: The Settings of the *format* Argument of the OpenAsTextStream Method

Value	Description
−2	Opens the file using the system default
−1	Opens the file as Unicode
0	Opens the file as ASCII

VB6 at Work: The FileMover Project

The FileMover project (you'll find it in the FMover folder in this chapter's folder on the CD) demonstrates how to manipulate multiple files using the FileSystem-Object object's methods. The FMover project is based on the ListDrop project we looked at in Chapter 4. On the Form in Figure 20.2, the user can select any folder on any disk and see its files in the FileListBox control. Any file can be dragged to the ListBox at the bottom of the Form. This list can be populated with filenames from multiple folders, since it stores the full path names of the files. After selecting the files in the ListBox control, the user can copy them with the Copy Selected Files button.

FIGURE 20.2:

The FileMover project uses the FileSystemObject object to move the selected files to the same folder.

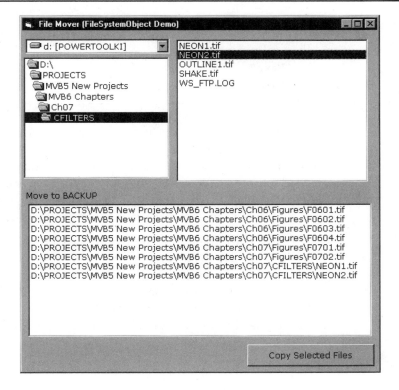

The code for manipulating the drag-and-drop operations is identical to the code in the ListDrop project. As a reminder, each time the user drags an item from the FileListBox control, the program drags the outline of a small TextBox control that matches the size of a single item in the list. At all other times, the TextBox control remains hidden. You can open the project in the Visual Basic IDE and examine the application's code. This is another situation where you can't use the Common Dialogs control; you must build your own Form with the FileSystem controls.

The Command button copies the files stored in the ListBox control to the folder D:\BACKUP. The name of the destination folder is hard-coded in the project, so you must edit this subroutine before testing the application.

Code 20.3:   **Moving the Selected Files**

```
Private Sub Command1_Click()
Dim FSys As New FileSystemObject
Dim thisFile As File
Dim i As Integer

    For i = 0 To TEMPList.ListCount - 1
        Set thisFile = FSys.GetFile(TEMPList.List(i))
' NOTICE: THE FOLDER D:\backup MUST EXIST!
        If Not (thisFile Is Nothing) Then
            thisFile.Copy "D:\BACKUP\" & thisFile.Name
        End If
    Next
End Sub
```

The code scans all the files in the list and uses the GetFile method to create the *thisFile* object variable that references the current file. The GetFileMethod accepts the path name of a file and returns a reference to this file. Notice that the GetFile method returns a reference to a file, not the file's name or its contents. Through the *thisFile* variable, we can manipulate the file. The FMover project copies the selected files, since this is the least dangerous operation for testing purposes.

You can move or delete the file, by calling a different method of the variable *thisFolder*. Or, you can further process the file based on its type, date stamp, and other attributes. For example, you can create a new folder for each ZIP file and call the PKUNZIP application to extract the contents of the ZIP file to the folder by the same name. (To start another application from within you VB code, call the Shell() function, which is described in Appendix A on the CD.)

The Folders Collection

The Folders collection contains a Folder object for each subfolder in a folder. The following script iterates through the subfolders of a specific folder using the For Each...Next statement:

```
Set FSys = CreateObject("Scripting.FileSystemObject")
Set ThisFolder = FSys.GetFolder(folderName)
Set AllFolders = ThisFolder.SubFolders
For Each folder in AllFolders
    {process current folder}
Next
```

In the loop's body you can access the properties of the current folder. Its name is folder.Name, its creation date is folder.DateCreated, and so on.

The various properties of the Folder object are described next. But first, let's look at the AddFolder method, the Folder object's single method.

AddFolder   This method adds a new Folder object to a Folders collection, and its syntax is

```
FolderObject.AddFolders folderName
```

in which *folderName* is the name of the new folder to be added.

The Folder Object

This object represents a folder on a disk; it allows you to manipulate the actual folders on your disk through its properties and methods. To create a Folder object, you first create a *FileSystemObject* object variable, and then you call its GetFolder method, using the folder's path as an argument:

```
Set FSys = CreateObject("Scripting.FileSystemObject")
Set thisFolder = FSys.GetFolder("c:\windows\desktop")
```

After these lines execute, the variable *thisFolder* represents the folder c:\windows\ desktop, and you can manipulate the folder through the variable's properties and objects.

I'll discuss the Folder object's properties next. Since many of these properties are quite similar to corresponding properties of the File object, I'll just mention them briefly and focus on the unique properties of the Folder object.

Attributes   This property returns or sets the attributes of files or folders. See the discussion of the Attributes property of the File object for more information on using this property.

DateCreated   This property returns the date and time that the specified file or folder was created, and it's read-only.

DateLastAccessed, DateLastModified   These properties return the date and time that the specified file or folder was last accessed or modified, and they are read-only.

Drive   This property returns the letter of the drive on which the specified file or folder resides, and it's read-only.

ParentFolder   This property returns the parent folder of a Folder object. See the discussion of the IsRootFolder property for an example.

IsRootFolder   This property returns True if the specified folder is the root folder; otherwise, it returns False. There is no equivalent property for the File object. You can use the RootFolder property to calculate the depth of a folder, with a subroutine such as the following:

```
Sub GetDepth(FolderObject)
If FolderObject.IsRootFolder Then
        MsgBox "The specified folder is the root folder."
Else
    Do Until FolderObject.IsRootFolder
        Set FolderObject = FolderObject.ParentFolder
        fdepth = fdepth + 1
    Loop
    MsgBox "The specified folder is " & fdepth & " levels deep."
End If
End Sub
```

Name   This property returns the name of a specified file or folder (the last part of the folder's path name). See the Name property of the File object for details on using this property.

Path   This property returns the path of a specified file or folder (the folder's path name without the last part). See the Path property of the File object for details on using this property.

ShortName   This property returns the short folder name (8.3 convention) of a Folder or File object.

ShortPath   This property returns the short path name (8.3 convention) of a Folder or File object.

Size   Size is a property of both files and folders, and it returns the size (in bytes) of a file, or it returns the total size of all the files in a folder and its subfolders. To find out the size of a file or a folder, you first create the appropriate File or Folder object variable and then read the variable's Size property:

```
Set FSys = CreateObject("Scripting.FileSystemObject")
Set thisFile = FSys.GetFile("c:\windows\desktop\Message.doc")
```

```
MsgBox "The MESSAGE.DOC file is " & _
       thisFile.Size & " bytes long."
Set thisFolder = FSys.GetFolder("c:\windows\")
MsgBox "The WINDOWS folder's size is " & _
       thisFolder.Size \ (1024*1024) & " MB."
```

The Subfolders Collection

The Subfolders property returns a Subfolders collection, which contains all the subfolders of a specific folder. To obtain the collection of subfolders in the folder C:\WINDOWS, create a *FileSystemObject* variable, use its GetFolder method to obtain a reference to the specific folder, and then create a Collection with its subfolders, using the SubFolders property, as shown in the following statements:

```
Set FSys = CreateObject("Scripting.FileSystemObject")
Set thisFolder = FSys.GetFolder("c:\windows")
Set allFolders = aFolder.SubFolders
For Each subFolder in allFolders
    {process folder subFolder}
Next
```

To scan the subfolder under the specified folder, use a For Each … Next statement, as shown in the above listing. The current folder's name in the loop's body is subFolder.Name. The processing of the current folder could be to examine its files, and this is exactly what we are going to do next.

Scanning a Folder Recursively

Scanning a folder recursively (that is, scanning the folder's files and its subfolders' files to any depth) is a common operation in programming the file system. You have seen how to scan a folder recursively in Chapter 11, using the standard File System controls (the DriveListBox, DirectoryListBox, and FileListBox controls). In Chapter 8, you saw an application that populates a TreeView control with the contents of a drive or a folder. The tree structure is ideal for representing a folder, because the folder itself has a tree structure. In the Explorer project, I used the FileSystemObject object without having discussed it, and I promised I would return to this project to explain how it works. With the information presented so far in this chapter and the discussion of recursive programming techniques in Chapter 11, you're ready to understand the code of the Explorer project.

In this section, I'm going to discuss the FSystem application, which populates a TreeView control with the folders of the C: drive. Change the name of the root directory in the code to map any drive or folder. The Form of the FSystem application is shown in Figure 20.3. Run the application, and click the Populate Tree button to map the folder structure of drive C: on the TreeView control. How long the application takes to map the entire drive depends on how many folders exist in your root drive. So, be patient, or change the code to map a smaller section of the drive.

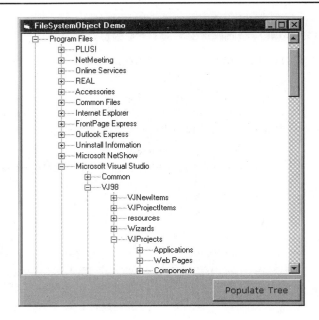

To help you follow the code and experiment with it, I will start with a simpler version of the application, which prints the folder names in the Immediate window. We'll then replace the Debug.Print statements with the appropriate statements to add the folder names to the TreeView control.

Code 20.4:   **Scanning a Drive with the FileSystemObject Object**

```
Dim FSys As New Scripting.FileSystemObject

Private Sub Command1_Click()
Dim folderSpec As String

    Set FSys = CreateObject("Scripting.FileSystemObject")
    ' Specify the folder you wish to map in the following line
    folderSpec = "C:\"
    ScanFolder (folderSpec)
    Debug.Print "*** END OF DIRECTORY LISTING ***"
End Sub
```

```
Sub ScanFolder(folderSpec As String)
Dim thisFolder As Folder
Dim sFolders As Folders
Dim fileItem As File, folderItem As Folder
Dim AllFiles As Files

    Set thisFolder = FSys.GetFolder(folderSpec)
    Set sFolders = thisFolder.SubFolders
    Set AllFiles = thisFolder.Files
    For Each folderItem In sFolders
        Debug.Print
        Debug.Print "*** FOLDER  " & folderItem.Path & "***"
        ScanFolder (folderItem.Path)
    Next
    For Each fileItem In AllFiles
        Debug.Print fileItem.Path
    Next
End Sub
```

The Command button's Click event calls the ScanFolder() subroutine to scan the folder that's specified as an argument to the subroutine. ScanFolder() creates an object variable, *thisFolder*, which represents the current folder. The program then creates a collection of the subfolders in the folder being scanned. This collection, *sFolders*, is scanned, and the names of the subfolders are displayed in the Immediate window. After displaying each folder's name, the ScanFolder() subroutine calls itself to scan the subfolders of the current folder. After the current folder, including its subfolders, has been scanned, the program goes ahead and displays the files in the current folder by iterating through the *AllFiles* collection.

In the version of the FSystem application you'll find on the CD, I've commented out the statements that display in the Immediate window and added the statements to add the names of the folders and files to the TreeView control.

Code 20.5:   **Populating the TreeView Control**

```
Dim FSys As New Scripting.FileSystemObject

Private Sub Command1_Click()
Dim folderSpec As String

    Set FSys = CreateObject("Scripting.FileSystemObject")
    ' Specify the folder you wish to map in the following line
    folderSpec = "C:\wind"
```

```
        folderSpec = UCase(folderSpec)
        TreeView1.Nodes.Add , , folderSpec, folderSpec
        Screen.MousePointer = vbHourglass
        ScanFolder (folderSpec)
        Screen.MousePointer = vbDefault
        TreeView1.Nodes(1).Expanded = True
        MsgBox "File List created"
End Sub

Sub ScanFolder(folderSpec As String)
Dim thisFolder As Folder
Dim sFolders As Folders
Dim fileItem As File, folderItem As Folder
Dim AllFiles As Files

        Set thisFolder = FSys.GetFolder(folderSpec)
        Set sFolders = thisFolder.SubFolders
        Set AllFiles = thisFolder.Files
        For Each folderItem In sFolders
            TreeView1.Nodes.Add folderItem.ParentFolder.Path, _
                    tvwChild, folderItem.Path, folderItem.Name
            ScanFolder (folderItem.Path)
        Next
        For Each fileItem In AllFiles
            TreeView1.Nodes.Add fileItem.ParentFolder.Path, _
                    tvwChild, fileItem.Path, fileItem.Name
        Next

End Sub
```

Notice how the Add method of the TreeView control adds the folder and filenames to the proper location in the tree. Each folder node is a child of the parent folder's node. The expression `folderItem.ParentFolder.Path` is the path name of the folder-Item node's parent node. Likewise, the expression `fileItem.Path` is the current file's path name and it's used as the node's key. In other words, each item's key is its path name, so the keys of identically named files in different folders will end up in the proper place in the tree.

You can easily modify the code of the FSystem project to populate the TreeView control not with all filenames, but with only the names of selected files. The selection can be based on the attributes of the files, such as their size, type, date stamp, and so on. For example, you can select only image files whose size exceeds 100Kb. Or you can select text files that haven't been accessed in a month, and so on.

The Script Control

In addition to scripting Web pages, you can use VBScript to script Visual Basic applications. You can embed the functionality of VBScript in your applications with the help of the Script control, which was released several months before Visual Basic 6. For the purposes of this book, I downloaded the Script control from Microsoft's Web site, at http://www.microsoft.com/scripting. At the same URL, you will find additional documentation on the control and samples. As of this writing, the documentation is sketchy, and the control itself has a few quirks, but scripting Visual Basic applications is an exciting new development, which I couldn't ignore.

So, what can the Script control do for your applications? To begin with, it can evaluate expressions at runtime. Since the Script control can be manipulated from within your application's code, these expressions can be created at runtime (something you can't do with your application's code).

Let's say you want to develop a math calculator that evaluates math expressions. Visual Basic can evaluate any math expression, as long as the expression is entered at design time. Let's say the user of your application needs to evaluate a math expression such as 99.9/log(2.5) at runtime or plot an expression such as 9*sin(x)/cos(x). How would you handle this situation with Visual Basic? Unless you're willing to duplicate the expression evaluation capabilities of Visual Basic (in other words implement your own component that evaluates expressions), not much. In Chapter 6 there is an application that plots functions, but you must hardcode the function definitions into the application. Not the most practical approach, and I'm sure you noticed the limited usefulness of the Graph application in Chapter 6.

Later in this chapter, we'll revise the Graph application so that it can plot any function supplied by the user at runtime. This is the type of functionality the Script control can bring to your application. It allows you to furnish a math expression and ask it to evaluate the expression and return the result. The Script control can evaluate more than math expressions. It can evaluate logical expressions, adjust its course of action based on the result, and execute statements repeatedly. You can use the entire repertoire of VBScript statements and functions with the Script control. For example, you might want to plot the envelope of two functions (evaluate both functions and plot the maximum value at each point). Here's the VBScript code that evaluates the maximum of two functions:

```
Val1= sin(x)/cos(x)
Val2 = cos(x)/atn(1/x)
If Val1 > Val2 Then
    Envelope = Val1
Else
    Envelope = Val2
End If
```

The program will use the value *Envelope* to generate the plot. The user can enter the above code at runtime, and it need not be embedded in the application's source code.

If your application exposes an object model (something like Word's or Excel's objects, which let you manipulate the application behind the scenes), users can script the application by supplying the appropriate VBScript statements. Office applications are programmed with VBA, but as I mentioned, VBA is a full-blown language, can't be easily incorporated in an application, and is very costly. Although very few applications incorporate VBA, a host of applications come with their own scripting languages, which users can deploy to automate operations. The problem with these applications is the multitude of scripting languages. With VBA and VBScript or JavaScript, manufacturers will probably standardize the scripting capabilities of their products and even small applications will be scriptable.

According to the documentation, VBScript is recommended for moderately sized applications (1 to 2MB) and only if you are willing to trade some performance for simplicity. VBScript is an interpreted language and can't match the speed of compiled VB applications. Even worse, VBScript is a typeless language, which means that all its variables are stored internally as variants. This entails a considerable performance penalty, as all variables must be converted to the proper type before they can be used in calculations. Another ramification of a typeless language is that objects can't be early-bound. So, VBScript is not for performance; it's for your convenience only. As you'll see, deploying VBScript with the Script control is straightforward and far simpler than VBA.

Using the Script Control

The Script control has a very simple design philosophy: it stores procedures and can execute any of them at any time. In addition, it can evaluate isolated expressions and return the result. Let's exercise the Script control with a few simple examples.

To use the Script control in a project, you must first add it to the Toolbox. Follow these steps:

1. Start a new project.

2. Right-click the Toolbox, and from the shortcut menu, select Components to open the Components dialog box.

3. Check the Microsoft Script Control 1.0 option (or a newer version, should one become available by the time VB6 is released) and click OK.

4. Once the control is added to the Toolbox, place an instance of the control on the Form.

Let's start by listing the most important members of the Script control, which we'll use momentarily in the examples.

The ExecuteStatement Method

This method executes a single statement and returns the result. It accepts a single argument, which is the statement to be executed. Here's a valid VBScript statement:

```
MsgBox "Programmers of the world unite!"
```

To execute it (and display the string in a message box), you pass the entire statement to the ExecuteStatement method:

```
statement = "MsgBox " & Chr(34) & _
            "Programmers of the world unite!" & Chr(34)
ScriptControl1.ExecuteStatement statement
```

The expression Chr(34) inserts a double quote into a string variable. Another technique is to use two consecutive double quote characters and combine the two statements into one:

```
ScriptControl1.ExecuteStatement _
            "MsgBox ""Welcome to VBScript!"""
```

ExecuteStatement isn't limited to a single function call. Similar to Visual Basic, VBScript lets you place multiple statements in a single line, as long as you separate them with colons. Here's a short VBScript code segment (which is also a VB code segment):

```
X=InputBox("Enter a value from 0 to 5")
If X=3 Then
    X=X+1
Else
    X=X-1
End If
MsgBox "The value of X is: " & X
```

If you execute this VBScript code, you'll be prompted to enter a numeric value. The code will display a new value that is 1 smaller than the value you enter, unless the original value is 3, in which case the value 4 will be displayed. To insert all the statements and execute them with the ExecuteStatement method, place a new Command button on the Form and enter the following code in its Click event handler:

```
Private Sub Command2_Click()
    ScriptControl1.ExecuteStatement "X=InputBox(""Enter a _
        value from 0 to 5""):If X=3 Then X=X+1: Else _
        X=X-1: End If: MsgBox ""The value of X is: "" & X "
End Sub
```

The ExecuteStatement method's argument is created by appending consecutive statements and separating them with a colon. You must enclose the entire argument in double quotes, and you must replace the double quotes in the code with two consecutive double quote characters.

Obviously, this is not the best method for passing long statements to be executed to the Script control. It's best to create a string variable with the statement to be executed and then pass a string variable to the ExecuteStatement method. Here's a clearer coding of the last example:

```
Private Sub Command2_Click()
    script = ""
    script = script & "X=InputBox(""Enter a value _
            from 0 to 5""):"
    script = script & "  If X=3 Then X=X+1:"
    script = script & " Else X=X-1:"
    script = script & "End If: "
    script = script & "MsgBox ""The value of X _
            is: "" & X "
    ScriptControl1.ExecuteStatement script
End Sub
```

The AddCode and Run Methods

Executing simple statements with the Script control is an interesting exercise, but in a practical situation you need to execute more than a simple statement. The Script control can store large segments of code, similar to a Code Module of a Visual Basic project, and execute them at will.

To add one or more procedures to the Script control, use the AddCode method, which accepts a string argument with the code. The code you add to the control may contain Modules (subroutines and functions), and you can later call one of them by name, with the Run method. Here's a simple script that contains a subroutine, which in turn calls a function:

```
Sub Main()
    MsgBox "28908 in hexadecimal notation is " & IntToHex(28908)
End Sub

Function IntToHex(Decimal)
    IntToHex=Hex(Decimal)
End Function
```

The Main() subroutine calls the IntToHex() function to convert a decimal value to hexadecimal notation and display the results in a message box.

There's no need to write a separate function to convert decimal values to hexadecimal notation because this is a simple example meant to demonstrate the

Script control's methods. You can provide your own routines to convert temperatures, if you haven't developed an allergy to the temperature conversion example yet. Place a third Command button on the Form and enter the following code in its Click event's handler:

```
Private Sub Command3_Click()
script = "Sub Main()" & vbCrLf & _
        "    MsgBox ""28908 in hexadecimal notation is "" & _
        IntToHex(28908)" & vbCrLf & _
        "End Sub" & vbCrLf & _
        "Function IntToHex(Decimal)" & vbCrLf & _
        "    IntToHex=Hex(Decimal)" & vbCrLf & _
        "End Function" & vbCrLf
ScriptControl1.AddCode script
ScriptControl1.Run "Main"
End Sub
```

Run the project, click the third Command button, and you'll see the value 70EC in a message box. The statement `ScriptControl1.AddCode` adds the code segment to the control (it's stored internally in a format that you don't have to know). Then, the Run method calls the Main() subroutine by name. The syntax of the Run method is:

```
ScriptControl1.Run procedure_name, param_array()
```

in which *procedure_name* is the name of the procedure you want to invoke, and *param_array* is an array that holds the parameters to be passed to the procedure. The second argument is optional, as in the case of the above example.

You can also invoke the IntToHex() function directly with the Run method. Comment out the line that invokes the Run method in the last example, and enter the following one:

```
ScriptControl1.ExecuteStatement "MsgBox IntToHex(3432)"
```

The value D68 will appear in a message box (the hexadecimal equivalent of the integer 3432).

As you may have guessed, the best way to add procedures to a Script control is to enter the statements in a TextBox control and then add the TextBox control's Text property to the Script control. Later in this chapter, we are going to build an application that lets the user enter scripts with the help of a TextBox control and execute them. But first, let's see some of the Script control's simpler, yet extremely valuable applications.

VB6 at Work: The Revised Graph Project

To demonstrate the Script control, we'll revise the Graph application that we developed in Chapter 6. The Graph application, shown in Figure 20.4, draws one or both of the two functions whose definitions appear at the top of the Form. The original Graph application always plots the same two functions, whose definitions are hard-coded into the application. The revised Graph application, which you'll find in this chapter's folder on the CD, allows the user to specify the functions to be plotted.

FIGURE 20.4:

The revised Graph application lets the user specify the functions to be plotted at runtime.

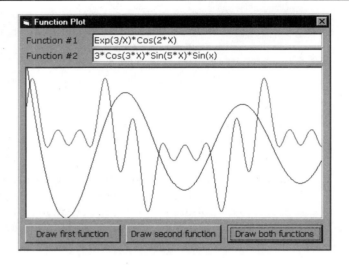

Open the Graph application from Chapter 6, and save its Form and the project itself to a new folder. After the Script control is added to the project, place an instance of the control on the Form. It doesn't make any difference where you place the control on the Form or its size, because the Script control remains invisible at runtime.

The code behind the buttons plots the corresponding functions by calling the functions FunctionEval1() and FunctionEval2(). These functions return the value of the two functions shown at the top of the Form for a specific value of X. If you replace the definitions of these function with the following code, you can plot any user-supplied function.

Code 20.6:   Evaluating Math Expressions at Runtime

```
Function FunctionEval1(ByVal X As Double) As Double
    ScriptControl1.ExecuteStatement "X=" & X
    FunctionEval1 = ScriptControl1.Eval(Trim(Text1.Text))
End Function

Function FunctionEval2(ByVal X As Double) As Double
    ScriptControl1.AddCode "X=" & X
    FunctionEval2 = ScriptControl1.Eval(Trim(Text2.Text))
End Function
```

The revised functions can evaluate any expression entered by the user in the Text-Box controls at the top of the Form. The remaining code, which I will not repeat here, plots these expressions.

Notice that the FunctionEval1() and FunctionEval2() functions do not contain error handlers. Even if you caught an error in these functions, what could you do? The rest of the code would keep calling them anyway (the code that plots the first expression calls the FunctionEval1() function once for each point along the x axis). The error trap is in the code that actually plots the functions. Errors don't need to be caught as soon as they occur. If the procedure in which an error occurs doesn't trap the error, the procedure that called it may trap it with its own error handler.

If you open the Graph project and examine its code, you'll see that I've inserted an error trap in the Cick event handlers of the Command buttons with the statement:

```
On Error GoTo FncError
```

The FncError error handler displays a message indicating that an error occurred and exits:

```
FncError:
    MsgBox "There was an error in evaluating the function"
    Screen.MousePointer = vbDefault
```

This error handler allows us to break the loop that plots the function. Had I caught the error in the FunctionEval1() function, for example, I wouldn't be able to stop the plotting, and the same error would probably come up for all consecutive points.

VB6 at Work: The Script Editor Project

The Script Editor project (you'll find it in the SEdit folder on the CD) consists of single Form with two TextBox controls on it (see Figure 20.5). In the upper box, the user can enter VBScript code and execute it by clicking the Execute Script button. The script must contain a Main() subroutine, which is invoked with the Script control's Run method. The Main() subroutine may call any other procedure.

The script can communicate with the user through the usual message boxes or through the lower textbox. To display something on this textbox, use the Show method, whose syntax is:

```
Show "The file's size is " & Fsize & " bytes"
```

You'll see shortly how the Show method is implemented. In the meantime, you can simply use it to place information in the lower textbox, just like Visual Basic's Debug.Print method.

The code behind the Execute Script button adds the code in the upper textbox to the Script control with the AddCode method and then executes the script by calling the Main procedure.

FIGURE 20.5:

The SEditor application demonstrates how to use the Script control to add scripting capabilities to your applications.

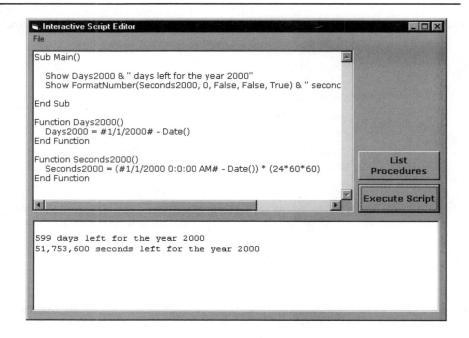

Code 20.7:   **The Execute Script Button**

```
Private Sub bttnExecute_Click()
On Error GoTo CodeError
    ScriptControl1.AddCode Text1.Text
    ScriptControl1.Run "Main"
    Exit Sub
CodeError:
    If ScriptControl1.Error.Number <> 0 Then
        msg = ScriptControl1.Error.Description & bvcrlf
        msg = msg & "In line " & ScriptControl1.Error.Line _
              & ", column " & ScriptControl1.Error.Column
        MsgBox msg, , "Error in script"
    Else
        MsgBox "ERROR # " & Err.Number & vbCrLf & Err.Description
    End If
End Sub
```

The code that executes the script consists of two simple statements. The error-handling code is longer, but I'll cover the topic of error handling during script execution later in this chapter (see the section "Handling Errors"). Error handling is the Script control's weakest point. Only a few syntax errors will be identified correctly. For example, if you enter a statement such as:

```
Limit == 99
```

you'll get a descriptive error message:

```
Syntax errror in Line 2, column 7
```

Most errors, however, generate a general automation error message, and there is no way to extract more information about the line where the error occurred. If you call a nonexistent function, such as Dates() instead of Date(), or if you call a function with the wrong number of arguments, you will see the message "Automation error", because this is all the information the Script control provides.

Run the SEdit application, and execute a few simple scripts by inserting the proper code between the Sub Main() and End Sub statements.

WARNING   When it comes to debugging, you're literally on your own.

To experiment with the Script control, I've included a few scripts in the same folder as the SEditor application, and you can load them by choosing File ➤ Load. You can also save your scripts to disk by choosing File ➤ Save. The Excel script, for example, contacts Excel to perform a calculation and demonstrates how to contact other applications from within VBScript and automate them. Here's the Excel script's code (the same code we used to contact Excel from within VB applications in Chapter 14). To contact an OLE server, you must first create an object variable with the CreateObject() function, and then you call the variable's methods and properties to contact the server.

Code 20.8:   **Contacting Excel from a Script**

```
Sub Main()

    Set EXL = CreateObject("Excel.Application")
    Show EXL.Evaluate("Log(99)")
    Set EXL = Nothing

End Sub
```

Scripting ActiveX Objects

The most powerful feature of the Script control, which makes it possible to use this control to add scripting capabilities to an application, is its ability to manipulate

ActiveX components. In the example in the last section, you saw how to create object variables to access OLE servers such as Excel. If your application uses Classes, it is possible to access them with a VBScript control. All you have to do is create an instance of the Class (or multiple Classes) and store them in the Script control. Then, the properties and methods of the Class can be accessed through an object variable, as if they were VBScript commands.

To add an object to the Script control, use the *AddObject* method, whose syntax is shown here:

```
ScriptControl1.AddObject Name, Object, members
```

The first argument, *Name*, is the name by which the Class can be accessed from within the script, and it's a string variable. The second argument, *Object*, is the actual name of the Class. Let's say your application exposes the DisplayClass Class. To add this Class to a Script control, create an object variable such as the following:

```
Private Display As New DisplayClass
```

and then use a statement like this:

```
ScriptControl1.AddObject "Output", Display
```

After the execution of this statement (which usually appears in a Form's Load event), the script can access the members of the DisplayClass Class through the *Output* object variable. If the Display Class exposes a Show method, any script can access this method as:

```
Output.Show "some message"
```

(The Show method displays a message in the Form's lower textbox.)

The last (optional) argument, *members*, is a Boolean value that indicates whether the members of the Class should be accessed through an object variable. Class members are always accessed through an object variable. If you set the *members* argument to True, the members of the Class can be accessed by name, as if they were VBScript functions. If you add the Display Class to a Script control with the following statement:

```
ScriptControl1.AddObject "Output", Display, True
```

you can access the Show method of the Class from within the script without the object variable's name:

```
Show "some message"
```

VB6 at Work: The Display Class

One of the limitations of VBScript is that it doesn't support input/output functions. This isn't really a limitation, since VBScript is a scripting language, and scripting languages by definition, lack a user interface. If you want to develop applications with visual interfaces, use Visual Basic. In programming, however, especially in the design and testing phase, we need a mechanism to display intermediate results.

The SEditor project's Form has a window in which the script can place its output (similar to the Immediate window). This feature is implemented with the help of the DisplayClass. The DisplayClass exposes two methods:

- The Show method, which prints a string in the lower TextBox control at the bottom of the Form

- The Clear method, which clears the contents of the lower TextBox control

The DisplayClass Class Module is implemented with a few lines of code.

Code 20.9:   **The Display Class**

```
Public Sub Show(message)
    ScriptForm.Text2.Text = ScriptForm.Text2.Text _
                & vbCrLf & message
End Sub

Public Sub Clear()
    ScriptForm.Text2.Text = ""
End Sub
```

To use the DisplayClass's members from within a script without having to register the Display DLL and create an object variable with the CreateObject() function, you add the Display object to the Script control. Insert the following statement in the ScriptForm's Load event:

```
Private Sub Form_Load()
    ScriptControl1.AddObject "Output", display, True
End Sub
```

Notice that the last argument of the AddObject method is True, so the Show and Clear methods can be accessed by name, as if they were VBScript commands.

The SEditor project is a simple application that lets you experiment with VBScript. You can develop really complicated applications, as long as they don't require extensive I/O capabilities (besides the MsgBox() function and the Show method), and you can live with a simple editor. You can't count on this editor to display the members of an object variable or do syntax checking as you type.

Handling Errors

The Script control provides the Error event, which is triggered every time an error occurs. The error may be due to the control (calling a method with the wrong arguments or attempting to set a nonexisting property) or to the script itself. A trappable error is also triggered in the host application, but not before the user is prompted to use the Script Debugger. While you're developing and testing your scripts, let Visual Basic start the debugger and help you debug the script. When you distribute the application, however, you may not want users of your application to see this prompt.

It seems there is no way to suppress this dialog box in the current version of the control, and this makes it difficult to distribute the application. Users may not have the Script Debugger installed, and this prompt will confuse them. The Script control is still rough around the edges, but I hope the next version will be more flexible, and it may even come with a programmer's editor.

In the meantime, you'll have to live with the limitations and the quirks of the Script control. To handle the error, use the *Error* object, which is a property of the Script control, and it's a different object from Visual Basic's Err object. The Error object provides two properties, which identify the location of the error in the script:

- *Line*, which is the number of the line where the error occurred

- *Column*, which is the location of the first character of the offending statement in the error line

You can use these two properties to place the pointer at the location of the error. When you use a TextBox control as an editor, moving to a specific character of a specific line in the control's text isn't simple; there are no methods or properties to take you directly to the specified location in the text.

The Script control's Error object provides additional properties, which are listed in Table 20.5.

TABLE 20.5: Additional Properties of the Script Control's Error Object

Property	Description
Number	The error's number
Description	The error's description
Text	A string with the offending statement
Source	The procedure or Class name where the error took place

Finally, after processing an error, you must call the Error object's Clear method to reset the error.

Let's look at the error handler of the Execute Script button. If the ScriptControl generates a runtime error and the property ScriptControl1.Error.Number is non-zero, we can use the Script control's Error property to extract information regarding the offending statement. In most cases, however, the Script control produces an automation error and doesn't set its Error object. The error handler simply displays the error in a message box.

```
CodeError:
    If ScriptControl1.Error.Number <> 0 Then
        msg = ScriptControl1.Error.Description & bvcrlf
        msg = msg & " In line " & ScriptControl1.Error.Line _
            & ", column " & ScriptControl1.Error.Column
        MsgBox msg, , "Error in script"
    Else
        MsgBox "ERROR # " & Err.Number & vbCrLf & Err.Description
    End If
```

The most common source for errors is the call of invalid methods or object variables. The following statements, for example, invoke Excel and call its Evaluate method:

```
Set EXL = CreateObject("Excel.Application")
MsgBox "The logarithm of 99 is " & EXL.Evaluate("Log(99)")
```

If you misspell the name of the *EXL* variable or if Excel doesn't exist on the host computer, you'll get the same error message, which is an automation error. This simply means that the script couldn't contact the object. If you call the InStr() function with an invalid argument (or the incorrect number of arguments), you'll get the same error message. In fact, only simple syntax errors in your script set the Script control's Error object and can be spotted easily. When working with objects, the Script control can't provide any substantial help.

Retrieving the Procedure Names

The *AddCode* method of the Script control allows you to add many procedures to the control. At some point, you may want to list the names of the procedures in the control. The *Procedures* property is a collection that contains all the procedures you have added to the Script control. As a collection, it has a *Count* property, which returns the number of procedures, and an *Item* property, which returns a specific procedure. The following loop scans all the procedures stored in the Procedures collection:

```
For i = 1 To ScriptControl1.Procedures.Count
    {process element ScriptControl1.Procedures(1)}
Next
```

Each item in the Procedures collection has a *Name* property, which is the corresponding procedure's name, and a *HasReturnValue* property, which returns True if the procedure returns a result (in other words, HasReturnValue returns True if the procedure is a function). The List Procedures button on the ScriptForm of the SEdit project lists the names and types of all procedures in the lower textbox.

Code 20.10:   **Listing the Script Control's Procedures**

```
Private Sub Command2_Click()
On Error GoTo CodeError
    ScriptControl1.AddCode Text1.Text
    For i = 1 To ScriptControl1.Procedures.Count
        If ScriptControl1.Procedures(i).HasReturnValue Then
            Text2.Text = Text2.Text & vbCrLf & "Function    " _
                    & ScriptControl1.Procedures(1).Name
        Else
            Text2.Text = Text2.Text & vbCrLf & "Subroutine " _
                    & ScriptControl1.Procedures(1).Name
        End If
    Next
    Exit Sub
CodeError:
    MsgBox Err.Description
End Sub
```

Notice how the code classifies a procedure as a function or a subroutine based on the value of the HasReturnValue property.

TIP

You'd expect the Procedures collection to have a Code or similarly named property that would return the procedure's listing. Unfortunately, such a property doesn't exist. You simply can't extract the listing of an individual procedure. Moreover, the Script control lacks a method to remove an individual procedure. You can use the control's Reset method to remove all the procedures and then add all but the ones you want to exclude, provided you keep the listings of the control in another control (such as a TextBox control). Even so, the process of removing individual procedures isn't simple. In the SEdit project, for example, you'd have to parse the contents of the top TextBox and extract each individual procedure.

Scripting an Application

If your application exposes Classes, you can add a Script control on a separate Form, such as the ScriptForm, and allow the users of the application to script it.

Let's say you have an application that allows the user to open image files and save them in different formats (TIF, JPEG, NPG, and so on). Users that want to convert numerous image files need not open and save each file individually. They would rather write a script that opens a file at a time, converts it, and then saves it to disk with a different filename.

This Class should expose a small number of methods, such as an *Open(filename)* method to open the image file, a *Convert(format1, format2)* method that converts between two formats, and a *SaveAs(filename)* method that saves the image in the new format. The code for converting image file formats is quite complicated, but it has been published in several books, and you should be able to convert the procedures into methods and attach them to a Class.

VB6 at Work: The StatsClss Project

To demonstrate the scripting of an application, I will use a simple Class that provides a few simple methods to calculate the basic statistics of a data set (see Figure 20.6). In essence, we are going to implement the AXStat Class we developed in Chapter 15 as an ActiveX DLL component and use it to demonstrate how to add scripting capabilities to an application. A Class that exposes an entire object model is beyond the scope of this book, but this simple Class will serve the purposes of this chapter, which is to demonstrate how to add scripting capabilities to your application and enhance it with the members of a Class.

FIGURE 20.6:

The StatClss project lets you write a script to calculate the basic statistics of any data set.

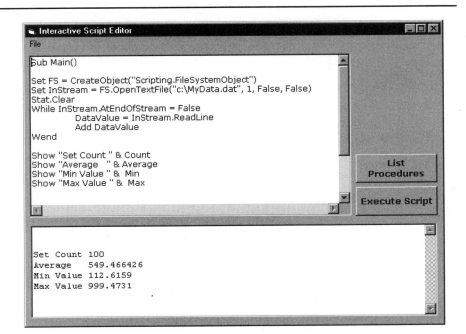

To use StatClss Class with the SEditor project, follow these steps:

1. Open the SEditor project and add a new Class Module.

2. Start a new instance of Visual Basic, open the AXStats project (you will find it in the Chapter 15 folder on the CD), and copy the code of the AXStats Class Module.

3. Switch to the SEditor project, and open the newly added Class Module's Code window.

4. Paste the code you copied from the AXStats Class Module.

At this point, you have a project that consists of the ScriptForm, on which the user can enter and execute scripts, the DisplayClass object, and the AXStats Class that exposes the properties and methods for calculating the basic statistics of a data set. This is a good point to save the components of the new project to its own folder.

> **NOTE**
>
> The methods of the AXStats Class return Double values; however, VBScript, is a typeless language. So how is the script going to contact the AXStats Class and retrieve the values returned by its methods? You can always use the type conversion functions, but you can't expect the user of the application (who's the person that enters the script) to perform all the necessary type conversions. It's much simpler to revise the code of the Class and remove the types. Open the AXStats Class's Code window, and remove all type declarations (the As... part of the declaration of the methods and their arguments). Open the project in the VB IDE to see the code of the AXStats Class after the conversion.

To allow the user to access the members of the AXStat Class and develop scripts to process data sets, you must add a reference to the Class. At the beginning of the ScriptForm's Code window, insert the following declaration:

```
Private Statistics As New AXStats
```

Then, in the Form's Load event, add the Stat object to the Script control with the statement:

```
ScriptControl1.AddObject "Stat", Statistics, True
```

The user of the application can access the members of the AXStat Class either through the members of the *Stat* object variable or by name. Here's a simple script that calculates the average of four data values. Enter the following code in the script editor, and then click the Execute Script button.

Code 20.11:   Scripting the StatClss Application

```
Add 301
Add 44.50
Add 529
Add 124.5
Show "Min Value " & Min
Show "Max Value " & Max
Show "Average   " & Average
```

If you add a few more methods for calculating advanced statistics (standard deviation, correlation, and so on), the users of your application will be able to script it and process data sets in batch mode. If they add a reference to the FileSystemObject object, they'll be able to open files on the local disk for reading data and saving the results.

In the same folder as the StatClss project, you'll find the MakeData and Process scripts. The MakeData script creates a text file on the root folder of the C: drive and stores 100 random values in it. The Process script opens the same file, adds the data values to the data collection of the StatClss, and then calculates and displays the number of data values, their average, and the minimum and maximum data value. Choose File ➤ Load to open the MakeData script, execute it by clicking the Execute Script button, and then load the Process script and execute it.

TIP
You may have noticed a problem with this project. Both Classes expose a Clear method (one for clearing the data set on the AXStat Class and the other one for clearing the lower textbox on the Form). The `Clear` statement will actually clear the textbox. If there are conflicts with the names of the objects you've added to the control, the members of the Class that was added first takes precedence. However, you can still invoke a specific method by prefixing it with the name of the Class to which it belongs. To clear the textbox, use the statement `Output.Clear`, and to clear the data set on the AXStat Class use the statement `Stat.Clear`.

While testing the StatClss project, you must change the Error Trapping settings of the AXStat Class. Follow these steps:

1. Choose Tools ➤ Options to open the Options window.

2. Select the General tab.

3. In the Error Trapping section, check the Break on Unhandled Errors Only option.

If you do not select this option, the application will break in the Class's code every time an error occurs (such as calling the Item method of the AXStat Class with an invalid index value). By turning on the option Break on Unhandled Errors Only, the Class will trigger a runtime error, which you can trap from within the application's code.

The Script control is a convenient way to add scripting capabilities to your applications, but its error-handling capabilities leave a lot to be desired. The control is in its first edition, and by the time this book hits the market, there may be a more stable and more flexible version of the control. If you are really interested in adding scripting capabilities to your applications, you should check the site `http://www.microsoft.com/scripting` for a newer version of the control.

In the last part of this chapter, we'll look at the role of VBScript in scripting the operating system itself. Windows Scripting Host is another area where you can apply your VB knowledge, as long as you familiarize yourself with a few special objects exposed by the Windows Scripting Host.

The Windows Scripting Host

You can also use VBScript, including its FileSystemObject object, to script Windows itself. In this section, you'll learn how to create scripts that run under Windows 98 and automate many common tasks, such as connecting to printers and network drives, cleaning up your folders, and even processing a large number of files in batch mode.

For those of you who are totally unfamiliar with DOS batch files, here's a simple example. Let's say you use two folders (directories in the DOS terminology), the C:\TMP and C:\DOCS\TEMP, where you store temporary files, which should be deleted at the end of the day or every so often. To delete these files, you would execute the following commands:

```
CD C:\TMP
DEL *.*
CD C:\DOCS\TEMP
DEL *.*
```

The CD command (Change Directory) switches to another directory, and the DEL *.* command deletes all the files in the current directory. If the two directories contain subdirectories, the DEL *.* command will not remove them. You must use the DELTREE command instead.

The syntax of DOS batch files is peculiar too. For example, there are no commands to write data to files (or read data from existing files). To send the output of a batch file to a text file, you have to use the redirection symbol (>). To save the (possible) error messages generated by the previous batch file to a text file, you would use the following syntax (assuming that the name of the batch file is DELTEMP.BAT):

```
DELTEMP > ERRMSG.TXT
```

You would then open the ERRMSG.TXT file with a text editor to read the error messages.

If you are familiar with DOS, you probably know the type of operations you can automate with batch files. You can initialize printers, establish network connections, process files en masse, and so on. Any operation that can be carried out with DOS commands from the prompt line can be coded as a batch file.

You can do the same and more with Windows 98. Earlier versions of the Windows operating system didn't support a batch, or scripting, language, and many people wished for a way to automate batch operations. The scripting language of Windows 98 is VBScript, which means you can take advantage of this aspect of the operating system without any additional effort. As a VB programmer, you're ready to develop Windows scripts.

In this chapter, you will learn how to use VBScript to write useful scripts to automate your daily tasks. You will find a number of examples that demonstrate the operations you can automate with scripts and that can become starting points for your own, custom scripts. First, you'll learn how to write simple scripts and execute them. Then, you'll learn about the objects exposed by Windows Scripting Host, and this is all the information you really need.

Writing and Executing a Script

Let's start by building a script that does something and run it. A script is a text file with VBScript commands, which accomplishes a specific task. We'll write a script that displays the number of days left to the end of the century. Start Notepad and enter the lines in Code 20.12.

Code 20.12:   **The YEAR2000.VBS Script**

```
DaysLeft = #1/1/2000# - Date()
Message = DaysLeft & " days left for the year 2000"
MsgBox(Message)
```

Then save the file with the name YEAR2000.VBS on your disk. When saving the file with Notepad, don't forget to select All Files in the Save As Type drop-down list in the File Save dialog box. If you don't select this option, the file will be saved as 2000.VBS.TXT.

The expression #1/1/2000# is a date. In VBScript, dates are enclosed with pound signs. Text is enclosed in double quotes. Date() is another VBScript function that returns the current date. The value returned by the Date() function (a value such as 10/04/1998) is subtracted from the first day of the year 2000, and the result is assigned to the variable *DaysLeft*.

To run this script, locate the file YEAR2000.VBS on the Desktop (or whatever folder you stored it in), and double-click its icon. You will see this dialog box:

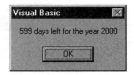

Click OK to close the dialog box.

In the following sections, I'm going to discuss the basics of VBScript: variables, functions, and control flow statements. These sections don't contain any practical examples. Unfortunately, you'll have to learn the basic mechanisms of the language before you'll be able to write any practical scripts.

Running Scripts with WSCRIPT.EXE

Double-clicking the icons of a script is the quickest way to run a script, but this method precludes the use of arguments. Since scripts don't have a visible interface, the only way to alter their behavior is by passing one or more initial arguments to them. To run a script and pass arguments to it, you must invoke the WSCRIPT.EXE application.

Choose Start ➢ Run to open the Run dialog box. Enter the name of the WSCRIPT.EXE application, followed by the name of the script you want to execute. For example, if you have saved the FILEDTR.VBS script in the SCRIPTS folder on the Desktop, enter this line:

```
WSCRIPT C:\WINDOWS\DESKTOP\SCRIPTS\FILEDTR.VBS
```

This command starts the WSCRIPT.EXE program, which executes the script FILEDTR.VBS. If the path contains spaces, enclose the script's path name with double quotes, as shown here:

```
WSCRIPT "C:\WINDOWS\DESKTOP\SAMPLE SCRIPTS\FILEDTR.VBS"
```

You can also pass arguments to a script that's executed with the WSCRIPT.EXE program from the command line, by separating them from the name of the script with spaces:

```
WSCRIPT C:\WINDOWS\DESKTOP\SCRIPTS\FILEDTR.VBS arg1 arg2
```

The two arguments are *arg1* and *arg2*. (You can't test the argument-passing mechanisms right now. You must first learn how to process them from within your script.)

> **NOTE**
> Multiple arguments are separated by a space (or multiple spaces). If you use commas, they will be treated as part of the arguments.

Besides providing an environment for executing the scripts, WSCRIPT.EXE provides a few objects, which let you access special features of the Windows shell that you can't access through VBScript. Practically speaking, you can think of the objects of Wscript as an extension to VBScript. I will start the presentation of the Wscript object with the Arguments collection, which contains the arguments passed to the script. In the following section, you'll learn how to access the arguments to a script and modify the script's behavior based on the values of the arguments.

> **NOTE**
> If you want to pass a large number of arguments to a script (which is a rather common situation), implement the script so that it reads its arguments from a text file, as discussed earlier in this chapter. Users will find it easy to enter the names of a dozen files to a text file and edit it, before using it with a script. Don't expect the users of your scripts to type long path names and get them right the first time.

Using Arguments

So far, you've seen how to build and execute scripts and how to pass arguments to them, but not how to process them from within the script's code. VBScript on its own can't handle arguments. The Arguments property of the Wscript object lets your script read the arguments passed to it. To access the actual arguments, you must create an object variable with the statement:

```
Set Args = Wscript.Arguments
```

The *Args* variable is a collection that provides the Item and Count properties. To iterate through the collection's items, you can use a For...Next loop, such as the following one:

```
For i = 0 to Args.Count - 1
    {process each argument}
Next
```

or a For Each...Next loop, such as this:

```
For Each arg In Args
    {process each argument}
Next
```

In the case of the For...Next loop, you can access each argument with the expression Args(i), and in the case of the For Each...Next loop, you can access them through the variable *arg*. The ARGS1.VBS and ARGS2.VBS scripts demonstrate how to access the script's argument with both methods.

Code 20.13:   **The ARGS1.VBS Script**

```
Set Args = Wscript.Arguments
For i=0 to Args.Count - 1
    txt = txt & Args(i) & vbCrLf
Next
MsgBox txt
```

Each argument is a member of the collection *Args*, and the elements appear in the order in which they were passed to the script.

Code 20.14:   **The GS2.VBS Script**

```
Set Args = Wscript.Arguments
For Each arg In Args
    txt = txt & arg & vbCrLf
Next
MsgBox txt
```

To pass one or more arguments to a script, you execute it with the Run command of the Start menu. Open the Start menu (press Ctrl+Escape), and from the menu, select Run. In the Run dialog box enter this string:

```
WSCRIPT "C:\SCRIPTS\ARGS1.VBS" John Doe 33.5
```

You must modify the path to the script ARGS1.VBS according to your hard disk's structure. The name of the script is enclosed in double quotes because long path names in Windows 98 can contain spaces. After the script's name, supply the arguments using the space as separator. If you call either script with these arguments, the arguments will appear in a message box, as shown in Figure 20.7.

FIGURE 20.7:

The ARGS1.VBA and ARGS2.VBA scripts display their arguments in a message box.

Do not use the comma to separate the arguments of your script. The comma will be attached to the argument that precedes it. If you supply the arguments:

```
WSCRIPT "C:\SCRIPTS\ARGS1.VBS" 1, 2, string
```

the script will display its arguments, as shown in Figure 20.8. The comma is treated like any other character; only the space character is treated differently.

FIGURE 20.8:

Script arguments should not be delimited with the comma character.

If any of the arguments include spaces, you must enclose them in double quotes. For example, if the last argument in our example was a string with a space in it, like the one shown here without the double quotes:

```
WSCRIPT "C:\SCRIPTS\ARGS1.VBS" 1, 2, "string variable"
```

the Arguments collection would contain four arguments: 1, 2, "string", and "variable" (the double quotes themselves are not included in the argument).

The Wscript Object's Properties

The Wscript object provides other properties in addition to the Arguments property. They relate to the Scripting Host (the WSCRIPT.EXE executable) and the script being executed.

Application   This property returns the friendly name of the Wscript object, which is the string "Windows Scripting Host" (the same value is also returned by the property Name).

FullName   This property returns the path and file name of the executable file of the Windows Scripting Host (WSCRIPT.EXE).

Name   This property returns the friendly name of the Wscript object, which is the string "Windows Scripting Host."

Path   This property returns the name of the folder where WSCRIPT.EXE or CSCRIPT.EXE resides (usually c:\windows).

ScriptFullName   This property returns the path and filename of the script being executed by the Windows Scripting Host.

Version   This property returns the version of the Windows Scripting Host (WSCRIPT.EXE). The version that ships with Windows 98 is 5.0.

ScriptName   This property provides the filename of the script being executed by the Windows Scripting Host. The script WSCRIPT.VBS demonstrates several of the properties of the WScript object. Figure 20.9 shows the output.

Code 20.15:   **The WSCRIPT.VBS Script**

```
msg ="Script File Name      " & _
      Wscript.ScriptName & vbCrLf
msg = msg & "Script Path Name      " & _
      Wscript.ScriptFullName & vbCrLf
msg = msg & "Executed by           " & _
      Wscript.Application & " (version " & _
      Wscript.Version & ")" & vbCrLf
MsgBox msg
```

FIGURE 20.9:

The output of the
WSCRIPT.VBS script

The Wscript Object's Methods

The Wscript object provides a number of methods, most of which have an equivalent VBScript function. The most important methods are the CreateObject and GetObject methods, which are identical to the VBScript functions by the same name. Let's start with the simpler methods of the Wscript object.

Echo   This method displays one or more values in a message box. You can display the friendly name of the Windows Scripting Host with the Echo method on a message box, which is identical to the box displayed by the MsgBox() function:

```
Wscript.Echo Wscript.Name
```

You can display multiple values, as long as they are delimited by a comma character. Multiple values are displayed next to each other with a space between them. The following statement will display the message box shown in Figure 20.10:

```
Wscript.Echo "string argument", Wscript.Name, 98.9+1
```

Notice that the Name property is replaced by its value, and the expression 98.9+1 is calculated and substituted by its result.

The Echo method can
display multiple values next
to each other.

Echo is a simple method and is provided as a primitive debugging tool. The
MsgBox() function and the Pop-up method (described next) provide many more
options and should be preferred.

Quit   This method quits the execution of the script and, optionally, returns an
error code. Its syntax is:

```
Wsript.Quit errorCode
```

The optional argument *errorCode* is the error code to be returned. If omitted, the
Quit method returns the error code zero. You can use the error code to specify
whether the script ended its execution normally or to specify the error that pre-
vented the script from completing its execution.

The Shell Object

The Shell object is a property of the Wscript object, which gives your script access to
special items such as the environment variables and the special folders, as well as a
number of methods for manipulating the Registry. Let's start with the Shell object's
properties. Before you can access the Shell object's properties, you must create a
Shell object variable, with this statement:

```
Set wShell = Wscript.CreateObject("Wscript.Shell")
```

The Environment Collection

The Environment property returns a collection with the environment variables.
To iterate through the environment variables, create a Shell object and then request
its Environment collection:

```
Set WShell = Wscript.CreateObject("Wscript.Shell")
Set AllVars = WShell.Environment
For Each evar In AllVars
    txt = txt & evar & vbcrlf
Next
Msgbox txt
```

The *evar* variable represents an environment variable in this form:

```
Variable = setting
```

The output of the ENVVARS.VBS script is shown in Figure 20.11. To access the values of specific environment variables, you can use the Environment object, which is described later in this chapter.

FIGURE 20.11:

The ENVVARS.VBS script displays the names and values of the environment variables.

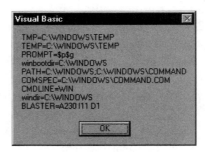

The variables that the Environment method returns by default are the PROCESS environment variables. These are built-in variables, such asWinDir and WinBootDir, as well as variables created with the SET command (this is a DOS command that appears several times in the AUTOEXEC.BAT file). These variables are shown in Table 20.6 (not all of these variables need to exist on every system).

Optionally, you can pass an argument to the Environment method, which causes it to return a different set of environment variables. Windows NT supports several sets of environment variables. Windows 98 supports only the PROCESS and the VOLATILE sets. The VOLATILE environment variables are the ones you set through your scripts, as you will see shortly. Your scripts can use VOLATILE environment variables to communicate with each other. You can dynamically declare and delete VOLATILE environment variables.

TABLE 20.6: The Names of the Environment Variables

Name	Description
NUMBER_OF_PROCESSORS	Number of processors running on the machine
PROCESSOR_ARCHITECTURE	Processor type of the user's workstation
PROCESSOR_IDENTIFIER	Processor ID of the user's workstation
PROCESSOR_LEVEL	Processor level of the user's workstation
PROCESSOR_REVISION	Processor version of the user's workstation
OS	Operating system on the user's workstation

Continued on next page

TABLE 20.6 CONTINUED: The Names of the Environment Variables

Name	Description
COMSPEC	Executable for command Command Prompt (typically CMD.EXE)
HOMEDRIVE	Primary local drive (typically the C: drive)
HOMEPATH	Default directory for users (on Windows NT this is typically \users\default)
PATH	PATH environment variable
PATHEXT	Extensions for executable files (typically .COM, .EXE, .BAT, or .CMD)
PROMPT	Command prompt (typically PG)
SYSTEMDRIVE	Local drive on which the system directory resides
SYSTEMROOT	System directory (for example, c:\winnt); this is the same as WINDIR
WINDIR	System directory (for example, c:\winnt); this is the same as SYSTEMROOT
TEMP	Directory for storing temporary files (for example, c:\temp)
TMP	Directory for storing temporary files (for example, c:\temp)

The SpecialFolders Collection

The SpecialFolders property gives your script access to the special folders on your system. The special folders include the Desktop folder, the Start menu folder, and the personal document folder.

NOTE   The SpecialFolders property returns the path name of the Desktop folder (for example, c:\windows\desktop) and not a Folder object. To access the files and sub-folders of the Desktop folder, you must first create a *Folder* object variable with the GetFolder method of the FileSystemObject object, as shown in the example that follows.

Use the SpecialFolders collection to create new shortcuts on the Desktop or to place new applications in the Start menu folder. The following script displays the names of the files on the Desktop, along with their type. This script (it's called DTOP.VBS, and you'll find it on the CD) uses the FileSystemObject object to iterate through the files of the Desktop folder.

Code 20.16:   **The DTOP.VBS Script**

```
' This script displays all files on the desktop,
' along with their types
Set FSys = CreateObject("Scripting.FileSystemObject")
```

```
Set WShell = Wscript.CreateObject("Wscript.Shell")
DTOPfolder = WShell.SpecialFolders("Desktop")

Set Desktop = FSys.GetFolder(DTOPfolder)
Set DesktopFiles = Desktop.Files
For Each file in DesktopFiles
    txt = txt & file.Name & "  (" & file.Type & ")" & vbCrLf
Next
MsgBox txt
```

This script creates an object variable that references the Desktop folder, by calling the SpecialFolders method of the Shell object. It then retrieves all files on the desktop and stores them to a collection, the DesktopFiles collection, and scans all the items in this collection with a For Each … Next loop. At each iteration of the loop, it can access the current file's properties through the *file* object variable.

You can also access all the special folders on the computer using the Special-Folders Collection. The following script iterates through the computer's special folders and displays their names. The script is called SPFOLDER.VBS, and you will find it in this chapter's folder on the CD.

Code 20.17: **The SPFOLDER.VBS Script**

```
' List all special folders on the host computer
Set WShell = Wscript.CreateObject("Wscript.Shell")
For Each Folder In WShell.SpecialFolders
    msg = msg & Folder & vbCrLf
Next
MsgBox msg
```

If you execute this script, it will display the path names of the following folders:

Application Data	MyDocuments	Recent	Startup
Desktop	NetHood	SendTo	Templates
Favorites	PrintHood	ShellNew	
Fonts	Programs	StartMenu	

The Pop-up Method

This method displays a message box, similar to VBScript's MsgBox function. It has the same syntax, and the only advantage to using this method is that it allows you to specify how many seconds it will remain active on the screen before it shuts itself down. The syntax of the method is:

```
Popup(msg, seconds, title, type)
```

in which *msg* is the message to be displayed; this is the only mandatory argument. If the second argument, *seconds*, is supplied, the message box automatically closes after so many seconds. The argument *title* is the message box's title, and the last argument, *type*, is the same as in the MsgBox() function. It determines which buttons and icons appear in the message box. Its possible values are shown in Tables 20.7 and 20.8.

TABLE 20.7: The Button Combinations You Can Display in a Pop-Up Window

Value	Button(s)
0	OK
1	OK and Cancel
2	Abort, Retry, and Ignore
3	Yes, No, and Cancel
4	Yes and No
5	Retry and Cancel

The icon is specified by one of the values in Table 20.8, which must be added to the value specifying the button to appear in the message box.

TABLE 20.8: The Icons You Can Display in a Pop-Up Window

Value	Icon
16	Stop mark
32	Question mark
48	Exclamation mark
64	Information mark

Depending on which button on the message box was clicked, the Pop-up method returns a value, which is one of those shown in Table 20.9.

TABLE 20.9:   The Values Returned by the Pop-Up Method

Value	Description
1	OK button
2	Cancel button
3	Abort button
4	Retry button
5	Ignore button
6	Yes button
7	No button

The following script displays a pop-up dialog box and waits for 10 seconds. If the user doesn't click on a button during this interval, the dialog box closes, and the program resumes.

Code 20.18:   **The POPUP.VBS Script**

```
Set WShell = Wscript.CreateObject("Wscript.Shell")
Reply = WShell.Popup("Display long file names?", 10, _
        "Timed Dialog Box", 4+64)
If Reply = 6 Then
    Wscript.Echo "OK, here are a few long file names..."
Else
    If Reply = 7 Then
        Wscript.Echo "OK, here are a few short file names..."
    Else
        Wscript.Echo "I selected long file names for you"
    End If
End If
```

The dialog box expires after 10 seconds. In this case, the Pop-up method returns the value –1, and the script makes the default selection (as though the Yes button was clicked). After a Pop-up dialog box expires, there is no reason to display a message box as I have done (for demonstration purposes) in the example.

The CreateShortcut Method

The CreateShortcut method of the WshShell object creates a Shortcut or a URLShortcut object. A *URLShortcut* object is a link to a URL instead of a file on the local disk. When you click URLShortcut, the corresponding page is opened with Internet Explorer.

Creating an actual shortcut on the Desktop is a bit more complicated than using the CreateShortCut method, since you must specify the properties of the shortcut (its name, icon, target, and so on) and then save it. The first step in creating a shortcut, however, is to create a Shortcut object and then use it to set its properties. The process of creating shortcuts is described later in this chapter, but here is a short script that creates a shortcut:

```
Set WShell = Wscript.CreateObject("Wscript.Shell")
Set ShellLink = WShell.CreateShortcut("Run Any Script.lnk")
ShellLink.TargetPath = "WSCRIPT.EXE"
ShellLink.Save
```

Placing these lines in a VBS file and executing them creates a shortcut on the Desktop. The shortcut's icon will be the icon of the WSCRIPT application. This shortcut starts the WSCRIPT.EXE application. Not a very useful shortcut, unless you drop a script on it, in which case it executes the script, as though you'd double-clicked the script's icon.

The *ShellLink* variable is a Shortcut object, which has its own properties and methods (like the TargetPath property and Save method we used in the last example). The Shortcut object's properties are described in the following section.

The WshShortcut Object

The WshShortcut object represents a shortcut and lets you manipulate the properties of an existing shortcut or create a new shortcut. To create a WshShortcut, use these statements:

```
Set WShell = Wscript.CreateObject("Wscript.Shell")
strDesktop = WShell.SpecialFolders("Desktop")
Set aShortcut = WShell.CreateShortcut(strDesktop & _
        "\Encrypt.lnk")
```

If the Encrypt.lnk file exists, the *aShortcut* variable represents the shortcut on the Desktop. If no such shortcut exists, a new one is created.

NOTE   The new shortcut will not appear on the Desktop until you you save it with the Save method.

The properties of the WshShortcut object and its Save method are explained in the following sections. In effect, they are the parameters you can set in the Shortcut tab of the shortcut's Properties window, which is shown in Figure 20.12.

FIGURE 20.12:

A shortcut's Properties
window displays the
properties of a shortcut.

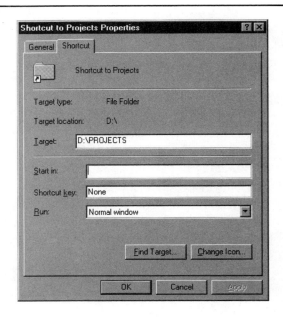

Arguments   This property specifies the arguments to be passed to the shortcut represented by the variable.

Description   This property specifies the description of a shortcut.

FullName   This property specifies the full path name of the shortcut.

Hotkey   This property provides the *hotkey* of a shortcut, which is a keyboard shortcut to start or switch to a program. The hotkey consists of a modifier and a key and has the form Alt+E or Ctrl+Shift+A. The available modifiers are:

ALT+	CTRL+	SHIFT+	EXT+

You can use the following keys in hotkey combinations:

- The characters A–Z
- The digits 0–9
- The special keys:

Back	Tab	Clear	Return
Escape	Space	PgUp	PgDn
Home	End	F1 through F12	

To assign a hotkey combination to the shortcut represented by the variable *myShortCut*, use this statement:

```
myShortCut.Hotkey = "ALT+SHIFT+F"
```

IconLocation This property specifies the location of the icon to be used for a shortcut. Usually, multiple icons are stored in the same file, and the format of the IconLocation property is *Path,index*. If you look for the key Icon in the Registry, you will find values such as the following:

```
C:\Program Files\NetMeeting\conf.exe, 1
```

Here, the icon to be used with NetMeeting is the first one in the CONF.EXE file.

TargetPath This property specifies the target path of a shortcut object (the object it refers to).

WindowStyle This property specifies the window style of a shortcut object. This is the style of the window when the referenced application starts, and it can have one of the values shown in Table 20.10.

TABLE 20.10: Possible Values for the WindowStyle Property

Value	Description
0	Normal
1	Minimized
2	Maximized

WorkingDirectory This property specifies the working directory of a shortcut object.

Save This method saves the shortcut object to the location specified by the Full-Name property.

The WshNetwork Object

The WshNetwork object provides the properties and methods you need to manipulate the shared devices (drives and printers) on the network, as well as the properties of the local computer on the network (its name, domain name, and so on). For information on using the WshNetwork object and the objects it exposes, visit the Web site http://www.microsoft.com.scripting.

CHAPTER
TWENTY-ONE

Visual Basic and the Web

- Web Browsing objects

- The WebBrowser control and InternetExplorer object

- Using hyperlinks in Visual Basic applications

- The Internet Explorer scripting model

- Building Internet-enabled controls

So far, you have seen how to apply Visual Basic to the Web by means of scripting Web pages with VBScript. This chapter demonstrates the merging of the desktop and the Web and includes the related objects and examples. The first topic I'll discuss is the WebBrowser control, which lets you display HTML documents in your VB applications. With this control, you can design a Form that connects the user to your Web site (or a specific page depending on what he or she is doing at the moment) and displays your home page, as if it were viewed with Internet Explorer. Because the WebBrowser control doesn't provide any navigational tools, you can limit the user to your own Web site (unless the site contains hyperlinks to other sites).

In a corporate environment, you can design Forms that display announcements, special instructions, and all types of information that change frequently. The user doesn't have to start the browser to view this information. The WebBrowser control enables you to push information to your users from within applications they use daily.

The WebBrowser control, just like Internet Explorer, can display HTML pages, which must be authored ahead of time and reside on a server (or even on your hard disk). It is also possible to manipulate the document in the control directly, through the IE Scripting Object Model. Through the objects of the IE Scripting Object Model, you can write VB applications that generate HTML code and place it on the WebBrowser control. In other words, it is possible to develop VB applications that generate HTML documents on the fly and display them in the WebBrowser control. It's an exciting capability, especially for authoring interactive tutorials.

The last topic I will discuss in this chapter relates to custom ActiveX controls. One feature of custom ActiveX controls that I didn't discuss in Chapter 16 is how to write controls that can download information from the Internet. It is possible to develop ActiveX controls that can take advantage of the host computer's connection to the Internet and download information from the network, and you'll see how this can be done in this chapter. These controls are called *Internet-enabled*, and I expect that many of you will develop custom controls whose primary function is to connect to servers and download information on demand.

NOTE   Another topic you'd expect to see in this chapter is ActiveX Documents. ActiveX Documents were introduced with VB5, and they are applications that can be executed in Internet Explorer's window. In essence, ActiveX Documents can be executed remotely, through the browser. ActiveX Documents are not among the most popular applications you can build with Visual Basic, so I've decided to omit this topic.

Web Browsing Objects

The two objects you need in order to add Web techniques and hyperlinked documents to your Visual Basic applications are:

- The WebBrowser control
- The InternetExplorer object

The WebBrowser is an ActiveX control that can display HTML documents on Visual Basic Forms. InternetExplorer is an OLE Automation object that you can use to control Microsoft Internet Explorer (and the WebBrowser control) from within your code. The two objects have many common members, and I will discuss them together. The emphasis will be on the WebBrowser control, which VB programmers will find more useful.

The WebBrowser Control

Simply put, the WebBrowser control is Internet Explorer's window. Any HTML document that can be displayed in Internet Explorer can also be displayed in the WebBrowser control. In other words, the WebBrowser control adds browsing capabilities to your Visual Basic applications. It allows the user to browse sites on the World Wide Web, local files, or ActiveX documents, such as Word or Excel documents—all from within a Visual Basic application.

Because the WebBrowser is an ActiveX control, you can place it on any Visual Basic Form. Before you can use it, however, you must add it to the Toolbox. Follow these steps:

1. Right-click the Toolbox, and from the shortcut menu, select Components to open the Components dialog box.

2. Select Microsoft Internet Controls, and then click OK. Two new icons will appear on the Toolbox—the WebBrowser control's icon and the ShelFolderViewOC control's icon.

3. Select the WebBrowser control's icon and draw an instance of the control on the Form.

When you place a WebBrowser control on a Form, it's a borderless rectangle that you can size in any way you like. Because the control can't be resized by the user at runtime, you should try to adjust its size according to the size of its container, which is a Visual Basic Form. When the user resizes the Form, the WebBrowser control should be resized also so that it covers most of the Form.

To display a Web page in the WebBrowser control, use the Navigate method. You can also move through the list of URLs that have been displayed already with the GoBack and GoForward methods. The WebBrowser control automatically maintains the list of visited URLs. We'll look at the control's properties, methods, and events later. Let's start by developing a simple application that demonstrates the basic features of the control.

VB6 at Work: The Browser Project

In this section, we'll develop an application based on the WebBrowser control that demonstrates how to add Web-browsing capabilities to your Visual Basic applications. The project is called Browser, and you will find it on the book's CD. Figure 21.1 shows the Browser application displaying the Sybex Web site. The user can select a URL from the ComboBox control or select a local HTML file by clicking the Open HTML File button.

FIGURE 21.1:

The Browser application shows how to add Web-browsing capabilities to a Visual Basic application.

To build the application, follow these steps:

1.   Start a new Standard EXE project, and add the WebBrowser control to the Toolbox, as shown earlier in this chapter.

2.   Widen the Form and then place an instance of the WebBrowser control on it. Make the control large enough to cover most of the Form's area.

3. Now, place the other controls you see in Figure 21.1 on the Form. In addition to the visible controls (the Command buttons and the ComboBox), there is a Common Dialog control, which will be used to display the Open dialog box and in which the user can select local HTML files to display on the WebBrowser control.

4. Enter the following lines to initialize the ComboBox control when the Form is loaded:

```
Private Sub Form_Load()
    Combo1.AddItem "Microsoft"
    Combo1.AddItem "SYBEX"
    Combo1.AddItem "Infoseek"
    Combo1.AddItem "Excite"
    Combo1.AddItem "RealAudio"
    Combo1.ListIndex = 0
End Sub
```

You can add your favorite URLs here, as long as the name displayed in the box is the name of a commercial Web server. When the user selects the *ServerName* entry in the ComboBox, the program connects to the following URL:

```
http://www.ServerName.com
```

5. The Show URL button creates a complete URL from the computer's name and uses it with the Navigate method to display the specified URL on the WebBrowser control.

Code 21.1: **The Show URL Button**

```
Private Sub Command1_Click()
    WebBrowser1.Navigate "http://www." & Combo1.Text & ".com"
End Sub
```

The Open HTML File button is quite similar, but instead of displaying a remote URL, it prompts the user to select a local HTML file with the File Open dialog box and then renders it on the WebBrowser control.

Code 21.2: **The Open HTML File Button**

```
Private Sub Command2_Click()
    CommonDialog1.CancelError = True
    On Error GoTo CancelOpen
    CommonDialog1.Filter = "HTML Files|*.HTM|Text Files| _
                    *.TXT|All Files|*.*"
```

```
        CommonDialog1.ShowOpen
        If CommonDialog1.filename <> "" Then
            WebBrowser1.Navigate CommonDialog1.filename
        End If
        Exit Sub

    CancelOpen:
        Exit Sub
    End Sub
```

Run the Browser application and check it out. Visit various pages on the World Wide Web, and open HTML files on your local disk (try loading the Web pages developed in the previous chapter). Figure 21.2 shows the Calendar.htm document (which we'll develop later in this chapter) opened with the Browser application. You can also open other types of documents (images, Word documents, Excel spreadsheets, and so on), as long as the browser can handle them.

FIGURE 21.2:

The Calendar.htm page viewed with the Browser application

WARNING If you open a Word document, you will see it as it appears in Word, but you won't see Word's menu and toolbar—which makes it impossible to edit from within the WebBrowser control.

The InternetExplorer Object

The InternetExplorer object allows you to start an instance of Internet Explorer from within your application and manipulate it through OLE Automation. The Internet-Explorer object supports the same properties and methods as the WebBrowser control, plus a few more. We will look at the object's properties and methods shortly, but first let's build an application that controls Internet Explorer. It's called IExplore, and you will find it on the CD.

VB6 at Work: The IExplore Project

To reference Internet Explorer from within your project, you must first add a reference to the InternetExplorer object. Follow these steps:

1. Start a new project and select Standard EXE as the project type.

2. Choose Project ➤ References to open the References dialog box:

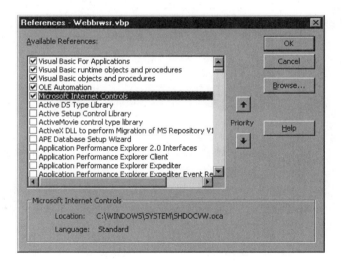

3. Check the Microsoft Internet Controls checkbox.

This time, you won't see a new icon in the Toolbox. But if you open the Object Browser window, you will see that the InternetExplorer Class has been added to the project. In the Members window, you will see the properties and methods exposed by the InternetExplorer Class, and through these members you can OLE automate the Internet Explorer application.

Let's build an application that will control one or more instances of Internet Explorer. The application is shown in Figure 21.3. The user can select a destination in the ComboBox control in the Visual Basic window and click the Show URL button to start an instance of Internet Explorer, in which the selected URL is displayed.

FIGURE 21.3:

Use the IExplore applica-
tion to OLE automate
Internet Explorer.

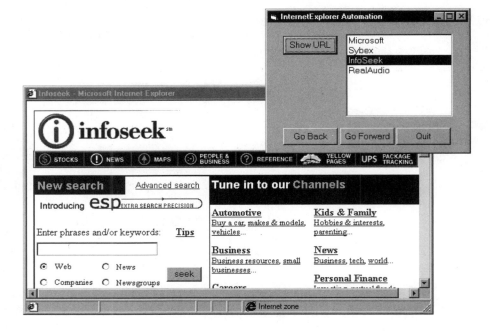

To continue building the application, follow these steps:

4. Design a Form like the one shown in Figure 21.3.

5. Declare a Form-wide object variable, though which you'll be accessing the members of the InternetExplorer Class:

   ```
   Dim IE As New InternetExplorer
   ```

6. Now, add the following initialization code in the Form's Load event:

   ```
   Private Sub Form_Load()
       List1.AddItem "microsoft"
       List1.AddItem "sybex"
       List1.AddItem "infoseek"
       List1.AddItem "realaudio"
   End Sub
   ```

The most interesting part of this application is the code behind the Show URL Command button, which loads an instance of Internet Explorer and opens the selected URL in its window.

Code 21.3:   The Show URL Button

```
Private Sub Command1_Click()
    IE.ToolBar = False
    IE.MenuBar = False
    IE.Visible = True
    IE.Navigate "http://www." & List1.Text & ".com"
End Sub
```

The ToolBar and MenuBar properties determine whether the toolbar and menu bar of Internet Explorer will be visible. Notice that the Internet Explorer window shown in Figure 21.3, earlier in this chapter, has neither a toolbar nor a menu bar. The Navigate method opens the specified document and displays it in the browser's window. (I'll discuss the properties and the methods of the InternetExplorer object and the WebBrowser control in the next section.)

The Back and Forward buttons are implemented with two methods of the Internet-Explorer object, GoBack and GoForward.

Code 21.4:   The GoBack and GoForward Methods

```
Private Sub BackBttn_Click()
On Error GoTo NoBack
    IE.GoBack
    Exit Sub

NoBack:
    MsgBox "There are no URL in the History List"
End Sub

Private Sub ForwardBttn_Click()
On Error GoTo NoForward
    IE.GoForward
    Exit Sub

NoForward:
    MsgBox "There are no URLs in the History List"
End Sub
```

NOTE   We use error-trapping code to prevent runtime errors that will be generated if the user attempts to move in front of or past the history list.

The Properties of the WebBrowser Control and the InternetExplorer Object

In this and the following two sections, we will look at the most common properties, methods, and events of the WebBrowser control and the InternetExplorer object. Most members apply to both, but the following sections focus on the members of the WebBrowser control.

TIP   The InternetExplorer object has a few additional members, which I won't discuss here. For complete documentation, visit the following site: `http://www` `.microsoft.com/intdev/sdk/docs/scriptom`.

Application   This property returns the automation object where HTML documents are displayed (the WebBrowser control or the InternetExplorer object).

Busy   This property returns a True/False value specifying whether the control is navigating to a new URL or is downloading a Web page. If the control's Busy property is True for an unusually long time, call the Stop method to cancel the navigation or the download of a document.

Container   This property returns an object that evaluates to the container of the WebBrowser control, if any. To find out the name of the container, use a statement such as the following:

```
WebBrowser1.Container.Name
```

This expression will return the name of the Form that contains the control.

Document   This property returns the automation object of the active document, if any. This is not the Document object of the Scripting Model (which is covered later in this chapter). To access the document displayed on the control, you use the following expression:

```
WebBrowser1.Document.Script.Document
```

This expression accesses the active document through the script property of the automation object. Later in this chapter, in the section "The IE Scripting Object Model," you'll learn how to manipulate the document from within your code (access its hyperlinks, for example, or even create a new document on the fly and display it on the WebBrowser control).

Height, Width   These two properties return the dimensions, in pixels, of the control that contains the WebBrowser control.

Top, Left   These two properties return the location, in pixels, of the control's upper-left corner on the Desktop.

LocationName   This property returns the title of the Web page displayed on the WebBrowser control.

LocationURL   This control returns the URL of the page displayed on the WebBrowser control. The LocationName and LocationURL properties retrieve information about the location of the displayed document. If the location is an HTML page on the World Wide Web, LocationName retrieves the page's title, and LocationURL retrieves the URL of that page. If the document displayed is a local file, both LocationName and LocationURL retrieve the full path of the file (or its UNC, if it's located on a network).

Type   This property returns a string that determines the type of the contained document object. The type for HTML documents is Windows HTML Viewer.

The Methods of the WebBrowser Control and the InternetExplorer Object

The methods of the WebBrowser control and the InternetExplorer object let you navigate to new URLs or to URLs already visited.

GoBack, GoForward   These two methods navigate backward or forward one item in the history list, which is maintained automatically by the WebBrowser control or the InternetExplorer object. Attempting to move after the most recent URL or before the first URL in the list generates a runtime error. To prevent this, you must include some error-trapping code, similar to the code you saw in the IExplore application, earlier in this chapter.

GoHome, GoSearch   The GoHome method navigates to the current home page; the GoSearch method navigates to the search page, as specified in the Internet Explorer Options dialog box.

Navigate   This method navigates to a URL or opens an HTML file, as specified in the method's first argument. This method has the following syntax:

```
Navigate URL [Flags,] [TargetFrameName,] [PostData,] [Headers]
```

All the arguments except the first are optional. The *URL* argument is the URL of the resource to be displayed on the control. The *Flags* argument is a constant or a value that specifies whether to add the resource to the history list, whether to read from or write to the cache, and whether to display the resource in a new window. It can be a combination of the values shown in Table 21.1.

TABLE 21.1: The Values of the *Flags* Argument

CONSTANT	VALUE	DESCRIPTION
NavOpenInNewWindow	1	Opens the resource or file in a new window
NavNoHistory	2	Does not add the resource or filename to the history list
NavNoReadFromCache	4	Does not read from the disk cache for this navigation
NavNoWriteToCache	8	Does not write the results of this navigation to the disk cache

The *TargetFrameName* argument is the name of a frame in which the document will be displayed. If the document displayed on the WebBrowser control contains frames, you can display the new document in one of the existing frames.

The *PostData* argument is a string to be sent to the server during the HTTP POST transaction. The POST transaction is used to send data gathered on an HTML Form. If this parameter does not specify any post data, the Navigate method issues an HTTP GET transaction (it simply retrieves a document). This parameter is ignored if *URL* is not an HTTP URL (one whose protocol is http).

The *Headers* argument is a value that specifies additional HTTP headers to be sent to the server. These headers are added to the default Internet Explorer headers, and they can specify such things as the action required of the server, the type of data being passed to the server, or a status code. This parameter is ignored if *URL* is not an HTTP URL.

Refresh   This method reloads the page currently displayed on the WebBrowser control.

Refresh2   This method is similar to Refresh, but it lets you specify the refresh level. It has the following syntax:

```
WebBrowser1.Refresh2 level
```

The *level* argument can have one of the values shown in Table 21.2.

TABLE 21.2: The Values of the *level* Argument

CONSTANT	VALUE	DESCRIPTION
REFRESH_NORMAL	0	Performs a quick refresh that does not include sending the HTTP "pragma:nocache" header to the server
REFRESH_IFEXPIRED	1	Performs a quick refresh if the page has expired
REFRESH_COMPLETELY	3	Performs a full refresh by downloading the entire page from the server

In addition, you can prevent the control from using the cache by specifying the *navNoReadFromCache* and *navNoWriteToCache* flags when calling the Navigate method.

Stop   This method cancels any pending navigation or download operation and stops playback of multimedia elements such as background sounds and animations.

The Events of the WebBrowser Control and the InternetExplorer Object

The events of the WebBrowser control and the InternetExplorer object are triggered each time the user moves to another URL with Internet Explorer's navigation buttons or the WebBrowser control's navigation methods. They also monitor the progress of each download and let your application know when the download of a page is finished.

BeforeNavigate2   This event occurs when the WebBrowser control is about to navigate to a different URL. It can be caused by external automation (by calling its Navigate method) or by internal automation from within a script or when the user clicks a hyperlink in the current document. Your application has an opportunity to cancel the navigation by setting the method's Cancel argument to True.

TIP   The BeforeNavigate2 event isn't issued unless the hyperlink is valid. In other words, the control first contacts the Web server and then navigates to the specified document.

The BeforeNavigate2 method has the following declaration:

```
Private Sub WebBrowser1_BeforeNavigate2(ByVal pDisp As Object, _
         URL As Variant, Flags As Variant, _
         TargetFrameName As Variant, PostData As Variant, _
         Headers As Variant, Cancel As Boolean)
```

The first argument, *pDisp*, represents the object on which the document is displayed. Since this object is usually the WebBrowser control, you can use this argument to access the properties of the control. *pDisp.Name* is its name, *pDisp.Width* and *pDisp.Height* are the control's dimensions, and so on.

The *URL* argument is the destination URL (specified by the Navigate method or in the hyperlink that was clicked), and *Flags* is a reserved argument. The *TargetFrameName* argument is the name of the frame in which to display the specified document, or it is NULL if the document is to appear on the control, outside any frames. The *PostData* and *Header* arguments are the same as for the Navigate method.

The application can set the *Cancel* argument (notice that it's passed by reference) to cancel the navigation process. If you set this argument to True, the navigation won't even start. To stop a navigation process in progress, use the Stop method.

NavigateComplete   This event occurs after the control has successfully navigated to the new location. Some of the document's resources may still be downloading (a large image, for instance, may take quite a while), but at least part of the document has been received from the server, and progressive rendering has started already. To interrupt this process, you must call the Stop method.

The NavigateComplete event has the following declaration:

```
Sub WebBrowser1_NavigateComplete(ByVal URL As String)
```

The *URL* variable is the URL of the document being downloaded.

DownloadBegin   This event occurs when a navigation operation is beginning. It's triggered shortly after the BeforeNavigate event (unless the navigation was canceled), and it signals your application to display a busy message or change the pointer's shape. The DownloadBegin event has the following declaration:

```
Sub WebBrowser1_DownloadBegin ()
```

DownloadComplete   This event occurs when a navigation operation is finished, halted, or failed. Unlike NavigateComplete, which may not be triggered if the navigation doesn't complete successfully, this event is always triggered after a navigation starts. Any busy indication by your application must end from within this event. The DownloadComplete event has the following declaration:

```
Sub WebBrowser1_DownloadComplete ()
```

ProgressChange   The WebBrowser control tracks the progress of a download operation and periodically issues the ProgressChange event to inform your application of the progress. The ProgressChange event has the following declaration:

```
Sub WebBrowser1_ProgressChange(ByVal Progress As Long, _
                    ByVal ProgressMax As Long)
```

Both arguments are long integers. The *Progress* argument is the amount of data downloaded so far, and *ProgressMax* is the total amount of data to be downloaded.

TIP   The percentage of data downloaded is *Progress/ProgressMax*, but you must always check the value of *ProgressMax*, because it can be zero (when the control doesn't know the total amount of data to be downloaded). Moreover, the ProgressChange event is triggered for each of the document's resources, and there is no way to know in advance the total size of the components you're downloading. As you have noticed, Internet Explorer displays the progress of each component's download, and not the progress of the entire document.

TitleChange   This event occurs when the title of the current document changes. The title of an HTML document can change; while the document is being downloaded, the URL of the document is also its title. After the real title (if one was specified with the TITLE tag) is parsed, the TitleChange event is triggered, and you can use it to update the Caption property on your Visual Basic Form. The TitleChange event has the following declaration:

```
Sub WebBrowser1_TitleChange(ByVal Text As String)
```

The *Text* argument is the string that appears in Internet Explorer's caption bar.

NewWindow   Although most hyperlinks result in updating the same window in which the document with the hyperlink is displayed, some hyperlinks specify that a new window be opened to display the destination document. When a new window is about to be created for displaying a new document, the NewWindow event is triggered.

This event can be also be triggered if the user holds down the Shift key and clicks the mouse while the cursor is over a hyperlink or if the user chooses New Window ➤ Open in the hyperlink's shortcut menu. The NewWindow event gives your application the opportunity to halt the creation of the new window. When this event is used with Internet Explorer, the new window is another instance of Internet Explorer.

When the NewWindow event is used with the WebBrowser control, however, your application must either create a new WebBrowser control and display the document there or request that the new document be displayed in the same window. If your application creates a new WebBrowser control, it must pass all the parameters from the NewWindow event directly to the Navigate method on the newly created WebBrowser control. If you decide to display the new document on the same control, you must again pass the parameters from this event to the Navigate method in the existing window.

The NewWindow event has the following declaration:

```
Sub WebBrowser_NewWindow (ByVal url As String, _
        ByVal Flags As Long, ByVal TargetFrameName As String, _
        PostData As Variant, ByVal Headers As String, _
        Processed As Boolean)
```

The arguments of the NewWindow event are identical to the arguments of the Navigate method, except for the last argument which is a True/False value indicating whether your application will create the new window (set it to True) or not (set it to False).

FrameBeforeNavigate, FrameNavigateComplete, FrameNewWindow
These three events are identical to the BeforeNavigate, NavigateComplete, and NewWindow events, except that they are triggered from within frames.

Using the WebBrowser Control

You can use the WebBrowser control to build customized Web browsers, because it supports all the browsing functionality of Internet Explorer. You can implement the Back and Forward buttons of Internet Explorer with the GoBack and GoForward methods, capture the jumps to hyperlinks, control which sites the user of the application can visit, and so on.

Of course, the WebBrowser doesn't have all the features of Internet Explorer. The most important limitation is that it can't access the displayed document, and you can't save the current HTML document from within your code. The user, however, can invoke the document's shortcut menu and select View Source.

In the following two sections, we are going to look at two applications that demonstrate how to use the WebBrowser control from within Visual Basic. The first application is a custom Web browser. The second application demonstrates how to exploit the hypertext model of an HTML document from within Visual Basic applications and how to add hyperlink features to a user interface.

VB6 at Work: A Customized Web Browser

Figure 21.4 shows an interesting approach to customized browsers. The Form shown in this figure contains a TabStrip control, with several pages, each displaying a different URL. The URLs can be local files or pages on remote servers. You can use local help files for an application (step-by-step instructions), or you can connect your application's users to a Web server that has up-to-the-minute information.

FIGURE 21.4:

SuperBrowser is a customized Web browser you can insert in any Visual Basic application.

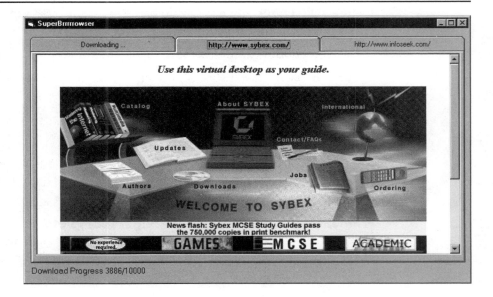

To create the SuperBrowser application, follow these steps:

1. Start a new Standard EXE project, and add a TabStrip control to the Form. Make the Form larger than its default size, and stretch the TabStrip control to fill as much of the Form as possible. You may want to leave some space for a few command buttons, such as Back and Forward (which aren't implemented in this example).

2. If the Toolbox doesn't contain the WebBrowser icon, add it using the Components dialog box (select Internet Controls from the list of available components). You may have to add the TabStrip control to the Toolbox using the Components dialog box also.

3. In the Toolbox, select the WebBrowser control, and place an instance of the control on each of the TabStrip's tabs. The WebBrowser control should cover nearly all the tab's area. The three WebBrowser controls are members of the control array WebBrowser1, and their Index values are 0, 1, and 2.

4. Double-click the Form to open its Code window.

5. In the Form's Load event, enter the following lines, which cause the three WebBrowser controls to navigate to three different Web sites:

```
Private Sub Form_Load()
    WebBrowser1(0).Navigate "http://home.microsoft.com"
    WebBrowser1(1).Navigate "http://www.sybex.com"
    WebBrowser1(2).Navigate "http://www.infoseek.com"
End Sub
```

As soon as the Form is loaded, the corresponding WebBrowser controls download the three pages and display them progressively. You can select the page to view by switching to the appropriate tab of the TabStrip control. All three pages continue downloading, as if you had opened three instances of Internet Explorer, each displaying a different document.

Let's add a few lines of code to display the URL of each page on the corresponding tab. Switch back to the Code window, and enter the following line in the Web-Browser control's BeforeNavigate2 event:

```
Private Sub WebBrowser1_BeforeNavigate2(Index As Integer, _
        ByVal URL As String, ByVal Flags As Long, _
        ByVal TargetFrameName As String, PostData As Variant, _
        ByVal Headers As String, Cancel As Boolean)
    SSTab1.TabCaption(Index) = URL
End Sub
```

This line displays the URL of the page that started downloading to the corresponding tab's caption area.

Once the page is downloaded, the WebBrowser control knows its title. At this point, you replace the URL with the actual title. Enter the code to do so in the NavigateComplete event:

```
Private Sub WebBrowser1_NavigateComplete(Index As Integer, _
        ByVal URL As String)
    SSTab1.TabCaption(Index) = WebBrowser1(Index).LocationName
End Sub
```

Now run the application and watch how the captions on the TabStrip control reflect the contents of each page.

Monitoring the Download Progress

This application provides a good opportunity to experiment with the download events. Switch back to the Code window, and enter the following code in the DownloadBegin and DownloadComplete events:

```
Private Sub WebBrowser1_DownloadBegin(Index As Integer)
    Debug.Print "Started Download for tab #" & Index
End Sub

Private Sub WebBrowser1_DownloadComplete(Index As Integer)
    Debug.Print "Completed download for tab #" & Index
End Sub
```

If you run the application now, you will see the following messages in the Immediate execution window (the order will be different on your computer):

```
Started Download for tab #0
Started Download for tab #1
Started Download for tab #2
Completed download for tab #1
Completed download for tab #2
Started Download for tab #1
Started Download for tab #2
Completed download for tab #1
Completed download for tab #0
Started Download for tab #0
Completed download for tab #0
Completed download for tab #2
```

The WebBrowser control starts and completes several downloads for each page. These messages correspond to the downloads of the various elements of each page. If you want to display the progress as well, you must program the Progress-Change event.

To do so, place a Label control on the first tab of the TabStrip control, and enter the following lines in the WebBrowser control's ProgressChange event:

```
Private Sub WebBrowser1_ProgressChange(Index As Integer, _
        ByVal Progress As Long, ByVal ProgressMax As Long)
    If SSTab1.Tab = Index Then
        If Progress >= 0 Then
            Label1.Caption = "Download Progress " & _
                    Progress & "/" & ProgressMax
        Else
            Label1.Caption = "Page downloaded"
        End If
    End If
End Sub
```

The outer If structure makes sure that only the progress of the selected tab is displayed. If the ProgressChange event reports the progress of a WebBrowser control other than the one on the currently active tab, the event is not processed.

NOTE   If you have a fast connection to the server on which the documents reside, the messages are displayed for only an instant.

Adding Other Features to Your Custom Browser

Another interesting feature you can add to your custom browser is URL monitoring. For example, you can keep a list of URLs visited frequently by the user. When the user selects one of them, you ask whether the user wants to open the pages from the cache or download them again.

Or you can prevent the user from following links outside a given Web. This isn't as outrageous as it may sound in an intranet environment. In this case, you might want to limit certain users to the company's Web and not let them take the trip of the thousand clicks during business hours.

Using Hyperlinks in Visual Basic Applications

What makes Web pages tick is the hypertext model they use to connect to other pages, anywhere on the World Wide Web. Although you can access the functionality of Web technology from within your Visual Basic applications with objects such as the WebBrowser and InternetExplorer, you still can't exploit this technology by making it an integral part of your Visual Basic application.

The WebBrowser controls make it possible to exploit the hyperlink model in your applications, and we'll present an example that uses hyperlinks as part of the user interface of a Visual Basic application.

VB6 at Work: The DemoPage Project

The DemoPage application is shown in Figure 21.5, and you will find it on this book's CD. The DemoPage application consists of two Forms:

- VBForm

- WEBForm

The main Form is VBForm and is used for drawing simple shapes with Visual Basic methods. The WebForm displays an HTML document that contains instructions on the Visual Basic drawing methods. The HTML document contains the instructions and a few hyperlinks. When either hyperlink is activated, it doesn't display another document. Instead, it draws a shape on the first Visual Basic Form.

Design the two Forms as shown in Figure 21.5. The main Form contains a Label control at the top, on which a command is displayed. The second Form (Web-Form) contains a WebBrowser control, on which the Demo.htm page is displayed.

When the first Form is loaded, it loads the second Form and displays the HTML document on the WebBrowser control. All the code in the VBForm Form is located in the Load event.

Code 21.5: **The Load Event**

```
Private Sub Form_Load()
Dim target

    target = App.Path & "\Demo.htm"
    WEBForm.WebBrowser1.Navigate target
    WEBForm.Show

End Sub
```

FIGURE 21.5:

The two Forms of the
DemoPage application

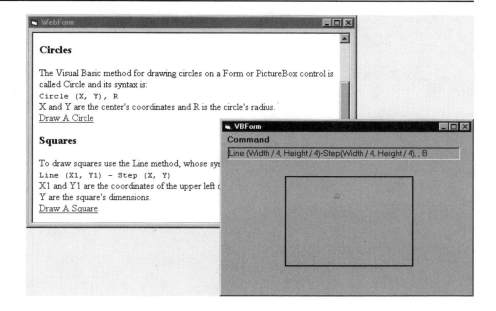

To avoid an absolute reference, the code assumes that the HTML document (the file Demo.htm) is stored in the same folder as the project. The complete Demo.htm page is shown in Figure 21.6.

FIGURE 21.6:

The entire Demo.htm as
displayed by Internet
Explorer

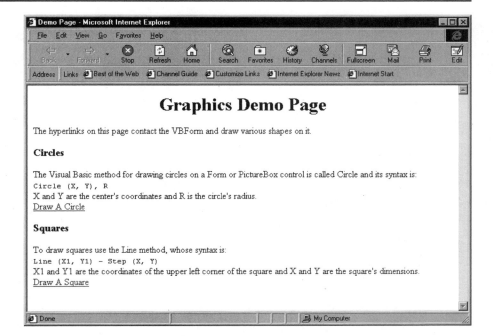

Code 21.6:   **The DemoPage Application**

```
<HTML>
<TITLE>Demo Page</TITLE>

<BODY>
<CENTER>
<H1>Graphics Demo Page</H1>
</CENTER>

The hyperlinks on this page contact the VBForm and draw various
    shapes on it.
<P>
<H3>Circles</H3>

The Visual Basic method for drawing circles on a Form or
    PictureBox control is called Circle and its syntax is:
<BR>
<CODE>Circle (X, Y), R</CODE>
<BR>
X and Y are the center's coordinates and R is the circle's
    radius.
<BR>
<A HREF="http://127.0.0.1/demo.htm#circle">Draw A Circle</A>
<BR>
<BR>
<H3>Squares</H3>
To draw squares use the Line method, whose syntax is:
<BR>
<CODE>Line (X1, Y1) - Step (X, Y)</CODE>
<BR>
X1 and Y1 are the coordinates of the upper left corner of the
    square and X and Y are the square's dimensions.
<BR>
<A HREF="http://127.0.0.1/demo.htm#box">Draw A Square</A>
</BODY>
</HTML>
```

As you may have guessed, the application exploits the BeforeNavigate2 event to find out which hyperlink was activated and then cancels the jump to this hyperlink and does something on the first Form (displays the command in the Label control and draws a shape). The hyperlinks could be fake; all we need is to know which one was clicked. However, the BeforeNavigate2 event isn't triggered unless the destination of the hyperlink is a valid URL.

The definitions of the two hyperlinks are shown next. As you can see, the destinations of the hyperlinks include some information about the kind of shape to be drawn on the first Form.

```
<A HREF="http://127.0.0.1/demo.htm#circle">Draw A Circle</A>
<A HREF="http://127.0.0.1/demo.htm#box">Draw A Square</A>
```

The HTML document doesn't contain any anchors named "circle" and "box", and you don't really need them. The WebBrowser control generates an error message, but all you really need is the name of the anchor. The server address is the IP address of the local machine (127.0.0.1), which is always a valid server name. Let's see how the code of the BeforeNavigate2 event causes some action to take place on the other Form.

Code 21.7:　　　**The BeforeNavigate2 Event**

```
Private Sub WebBrowser1_BeforeNavigate2(ByVal pDisp As Object,_
            URL As Variant, Flags As Variant, _
            TargetFrameName As Variant, PostData As Variant, _
            Headers As Variant, Cancel As Boolean)
Dim Position As Integer, Shape As String
On Error Resume Next

    If UCase(Right$(URL, 8)) <> "DEMO.HTM" Then Cancel = True
    Position = InStr(URL, "#")
    Shape = Mid$(URL, Position + 1)
    If Shape = "circle" Then
        VBForm.Cls
        VBForm.Circle (VBForm.Width / 2, VBForm.Height / 2), _
                    VBForm.Height / 3
        VBForm.Label1.Caption = "Circle (Width / 2, Height / 2), _
                    Height / 3"
    End If
    If Shape = "box" Then
        VBForm.Cls
        VBForm.Line (VBForm.Width / 4, VBForm.Height / 4) _
                -Step(VBForm.Width / 2, VBForm.Height / 2), , B
        VBForm.Label1.Caption = "Line (Width / 4, Height / 4) _
                -Step(Width / 4, Height / 4), , B"
    End If
End Sub
```

The first statement is an error-trapping statement; it tells Visual Basic to ignore errors and continue with the next statement. We know that an error will occur because the destinations of the two hyperlinks are invalid. We then cancel the navigation by setting the Cancel argument to True. The If statement makes sure that other (possibly valid) hyperlinks aren't canceled. The program then examines the last part of the hyperlink's destination URL (everything to the right of the pound sign). If this string is "circle", the program draws a circle on the VBForm Form and displays the command used to draw the circle in the Label control. If the string is "box", it draws a square on the Form and displays the corresponding command on the Label.

You can easily modify this application to accommodate more actions, place detailed instructions in the HTML document, and even create demos for your applications. The approach is rather clumsy, but hyperlinks are not yet part of the Visual Basic interface model. The application does, however, demonstrate how to incorporate the functionality of hyperlinks in your Visual Basic applications.

The IE Scripting Object Model

The Scripting Model is a hierarchy of objects through which you can access the properties of HTML documents displayed in the browser and the properties of the browser itself. The model's organization is similar to the organization of the Database Access objects, which were covered in Chapter 17, *Database Programming with Visual Basic*. If you read Chapter 17, you have already seen a hierarchical organization of objects, starting with the Database object at the top. In the Scripting Model, each object has properties, which are themselves objects. As such, they have their own properties (some of them also being objects), methods, and events.

The top-level object in the Scripting Model is the Window object. The document is rendered within this object. Some basic properties of the Window object are its name (property Name) and the location of the document displayed (property URL). Before we look at these and other properties, though, let's look at the objects of the Scripting Model at large and see what they can do for your Web pages.

The most important property of the Window object is another object, the Document object. The Document object represents the HTML document displayed in the window, which in turn has its own properties, such as background color, title, and so on. A window can also contain frames, which in turn can contain documents. To access the document in a frame, you first access the appropriate frame object and then the document object of the specific frame.

The Properties of the Scripting Objects

The Window is the top-level object and is the container for all other objects. The Window object represents the browser's window, in which HTML documents are displayed. Its properties include the name of the Window and the message displayed in its status bar. To access the Name property of the Window object, use a statement such as the following:

```
win_new = Window.Name
```

You can use the variable *win_new* from within your code to address the window. For example, you can request that another document be displayed in the *win_new* window.

To display a welcome message in the browser's status bar, use a statement such as the following:

```
Window.Status = "Welcome to our Fabulous Site"
```

You can also include VBScript functions in the definition of the status string, such as the date and time functions:

```
Window.Status = "Welcome to our Fabulous Site" & "It is " & _
                date & " and the time is " & time
```

The most important property of the Window object is another object, the Document object. Through the Document object, you can access the properties and methods of the document displayed in the browser's window. Two common properties of the Document object are its background color (property bgColor) and its foreground color (fgColor). To change the document's background color to white, for example, you use the following statement:

```
Window.Document.bgColor = white
```

Just as some of the Window object's properties are objects, the Document object has properties that are themselves objects. One of these objects is the Location object, with which you access the properties of the location of the document. The URL of the document in the browser's window is given by the hRef property of the Location object. You can find out the current document's URL or set this property to the URL of another document. The hHef property is a property of the Location object, and you access it with the following expression:

```
Location.href
```

The Location object is a property of the Document object, and it must be accessed as follows:

```
Document.Location.href
```

Finally, because the Document object is a property of the Window object, the complete expression for accessing the document's URL is the following:

```
Window.Document.Location.href
```

This expression is long, but it's easy to understand. The first-level object is the Window object. The following objects are more specific, and you can step down this hierarchy to reach the desired property. The organization of the scripting objects in a hierarchy simplifies the syntax of its methods and properties.

A window can also contain frames. Frames are accessed though the Frames object, which is an array of objects. The first frame is Frames(0), the second one Frames(1), and so on. To access the document in a specific frame, you start with the Window object and specify the frame whose document you want to access. For example, if you want to access the second frame, you specify the following:

```
Window.Frames(1)
```

Each frame displays a different document and therefore has its own Document property. To access the properties of the document on the second frame, use the following expression:

```
Window.Frames(1).Document
```

What would the background color of this document be? Simply tack on the bgColor property name at the end of the previous expression, and you have it:

```
Window.Frames(1).Document.bgColor
```

As you can see, the same property can be attached to multiple objects. The window has its own Document object, and the document has a Location property. But, if the window contains frames, each frame in the window has its own Location property. You may find this behavior confusing at first, but you'll soon get the hang of it.

The Methods of the Scripting Objects

The scripting objects also have methods. The Document object, for example, provides the Write method, which lets your script place text directly on the Web page. In other words, with the Write method you can create Web pages on the fly.

The Write method displays a string on the current page. The following statement:

```
Document.Write Date()
```

displays the current date on the page. If you use HTML instead, you must hard-code the date and consequently update the document daily. The VBScript Date() function returns the current date, but VBScript doesn't provide any methods for actually displaying the date on the page. To display something on a page from within its script, you use the objects of the Scripting Model.

Let's look at an example. Here's a simple HTML document:

```
<HTML>
<BODY BGCOLOR="#H00FF00">
<H1>Welcome to Visual Basic and the Web</H1>
</BODY>
</HTML>
```

This document displays a page with a green background and a level 1 heading. You can create the same page with the following VBScript code:

```
<HTML>
<SCRIPT LANGUAGE="VBScript">
Document.bgColor = "#H00FF00"
Document.Write "<H1> Welcome to Visual Basic and the Web</H1>"
</SCRIPT>
</HTML>
```

What's the benefit of using the Write method to generate the page? Flexibility. This page is actually generated on the client computer. If you want to display the date and the time this page was opened, you can add the following line of VBScript code:

```
Document.Write "This page was opened on " & date() & _
               ", at " & time()
```

The Write method provides even more flexibility. You can write complicated VBScript code to produce elaborate pages on the fly. For example, you can prompt the user for his or her name and personalize a Web page as follows:

```
UserName = InputBox("Please enter your name")
Document.Write "<H1>Welcome to our Active Pages, " &
UserName & "</H1>"
```

The actual heading will be different on each client computer, depending on the user's response to the prompt. Figure 21.7 shows a typical page generated on the fly with VBScript code that manipulates the IE Scripting Objects.

FIGURE 21.7:

Use the Document object's Write method to create HTML documents on the fly.

Here is the HTML file that produced the page shown in Figure 21.7:

```
<HTML>
<HEAD>
<TITLE>Demo Page</TITLE>
<SCRIPT LANGUAGE="VBSCRIPT">
UserName = InputBox("Please enter your name")
Document.Write "<H1>Welcome to our Active Pages, " _
               & UserName & "</H1>"
Document.Write "<BR>"
Document.Write "This page was opened on " & date() & _
               ", at " & time()
</SCRIPT>
</HEAD>
<BODY>

</BODY>
</HTML>
```

Notice that this document doesn't contain any HTML tags in its BODY section. The entire document was generated from within the page's script section with VBScript commands.

In the following sections, we are going to explore the Document object of the Scripting Model, since this is the most important one from a VB programmer's point of view.

The Document Object

From a programming point of view, the Document object is probably the most important object in the scripting hierarchy. The Document object represents the HTML document displayed in the browser's window or in one of its frames. Through the Document object's properties and methods, you can manipulate the appearance and even the contents of the document. You can use the bgColor property, for example, to read or set the document's background color, and you can use the Title property to read the document's title. You use its Write method to specify the document's contents from within the script and, in effect, create documents on the fly. The following section explains the properties of the Document object and provides short examples that demonstrate the syntax of the properties.

The Properties of the Document Object

The Document object provides a few simple properties that let you set the document's background color, the color of the links, and so on. It also provides a few of the most advanced properties, such as the Cookie property, which lets your script store information on the client computer and read it the next time the document with the script is loaded.

linkColor, aLinkColor, vLinkColor   These properties return or set the color of the links in the document. The linkColor property is the default color of the hyperlinks in the document, aLinkColor is the color of the active hyperlink, and vLinkColor is the color of the hyperlinks already visited. These properties accept color values that can be expressed as hexadecimal numbers or as color names:

```
Window.Document.vLinkColor = #00FFFF
Window.Document.linkColor = blue
```

bgColor, fgColor   These properties return or set the document's background color and foreground color. The foreground color is the color used for rendering text if the HTML code doesn't overwrite this setting. Likewise, the background property can be overwritten by the document if it uses a background image. These properties accept color values.

Title   This property returns the current document's title. This is a read-only property and can't be used to change the document's title at runtime.

Cookie   As you know, scripts written in VBScript are executed on the client computer. VBScript, therefore, had to be a safe language. There is no way for VBScript to access the file system of the client computer and tamper with it. That's why VBScript lacks the file I/O commands of Visual Basic. A language that can't store information locally is rather limited. Scripts can't even open or save a few bytes of data on a local file, and for many applications, this is a serious limitation.

TIP	In the last chapter we discussed the FileSystemObject object, which gives VBScript access to the computer's file system. If you attempt to access the host computer's file system, however, Internet Explorer will not execute the script. Statements that can harm the host computer's system are not considered safe, and Internet Explorer is smart enough to ignore these scripts. If you're using VBScript to script applications or Windows itself, you can access the computer's file system, just as you would access it with Visual Basic statements.

The solution to this problem is to use cookies. A cookie is a property of the Document object and is a string that can be stored on the client computer. Cookies are quite safe, though, because they are text files written and read to and from the disk by the browser, and they live in a specific folder. They are not executable files (they present no threat to the rest of the file system), and they can be accessed only by the browser. Cookies can't be considered a substitute for file I/O, but they can save a piece of information on the client computer so that the next time the script is executed, it will find the information there.

The information stored on the client computer by means of cookies is limited. You can't store large files with text or numbers. But you can store customization information such as the user's name and preferences so that the next time the user requests the same page, the script can find the values it stored on the client computer the last time and customize itself for the user.

NOTE   The most common use for cookies is for storing customization data.

Another practical reason for using cookies is to share information among pages. The shopping basket is a typical example. As you know, a script is limited to a single page. If the page with the script loads another page, the original script ceases to exist. The script (if any) on the newly loaded page takes over. Some sites let viewers select items to purchase on various pages, and they keep track of the items in the user's shopping basket. If each page is a separate entity and the pages can't share information, how is this done?

The answer is the Cookie property of the Document object. When a page wants to pass some information to other pages, it can leave a cookie on the client computer. The page that needs the information can read it. To the viewer, it appears that the various pages are communicating as if they were Forms of an application, to use a Visual Basic analogy.

VB6 at Work: The Cookie Page

To store a string on the client computer's system and access it from another page or to access it the next time the page is opened, use the Cookie property, as outlined in the Cookie page. The Cookie page, shown in Figure 21.8, is a revision of the Page1 page. This time we prompt the user for his or her name, and then we store it in the Document object's Cookie property. The next time you open this page, the user's name appears automatically.

To test the Cookie page, you must have a Web server installed. Opening the Cookie page with Internet Explorer won't do the trick. Cookies are saved on the client computer by the browser and only if they are furnished by a server. You can use any Web server, including the FrontPage Web server or the Personal Web Server.

FIGURE 21.8:

Use the Document object's Cookie property to customize your pages.

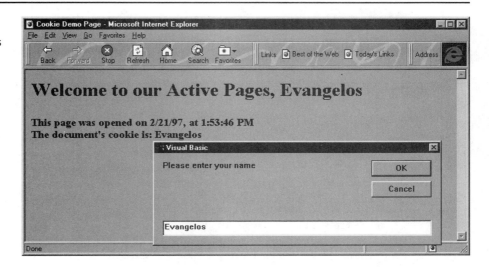

TIP

The Personal Web Server is part of FrontPage and Internet Explorer 4. It is also available from Microsoft's Web site (`http://www.microsoft.com/sitebuilder`).

I used the FrontPage Web server to test this example (which works just like the Personal Web Server). Here are the steps to follow to experiment with the Cookie property:

1. Copy the Cookies.htm file from the CD to the Cookie folder under the Web server's root folder.

2. Rename it to Index.htm.

3. Start the FrontPage Web server or any other server you have installed on your system (if it's not already running).

4. Start Internet Explorer and connect to the following URL:

   `http://127.0.0.1/Cookie`

   The numerals 127.0.0.1 constitute the IP address of the local server, and Cookie is the name of the folder to which the site has been copied (this site contains a single page).

5. When prompted, enter your name. The script displays it on the page and saves it in the Document object's Cookie property.

6. Connect to another URL by entering it in the browser's Address box.

7. Click Back to return to the Cookie page. This time you won't be prompted for your name. It's already stored in the Cookie property.

Now, let's look at the script of the Cookies.htm page.

Code 21.8: **The Cookies.htm Document**

```
<HTML>
<HEAD>
<TITLE>Cookie Demo Page</TITLE>
<SCRIPT LANGUAGE="VBSCRIPT">
If Document.Cookie = "" Then
    UserName = InputBox("Please enter your name")
    document.cookie=UserName
Else
    UserName = Document.Cookie
End If
Document.write "<H1>Welcome to our Active Pages, " &
    UserName & "</H1>"
Document.write "<BR>"
Document.write "This page was opened on " & date() & ",
    at " & time()
Document.write "<BR>"
Document.write "The document's cookie is: " & Document.cookie
</SCRIPT>
</HEAD>
<BODY>

</BODY>
</HTML>
```

The If structure of the script examines the value of the Cookie property. If this property has no value, it prompts the user to enter a name. It then stores the name entered by the user in the Cookie property.

The second time you connect to this page, the Cookie property has a value, and the Else clause executes, which assigns the cookie's value to the *UserName* variable. The rest of the code is the same as that for the Page1 page, with the exception of the last Write method, which displays the current value of the cookie on the page.

Using cookies in this way is slightly unorthodox. Cookies are usually stored as pairs of names and values, separated with a semicolon. A more reasonable cookie value is the following:

```
"UserName = Cibil; Age = 24; Browser=IE3.02"
```

As you can see, you can store many variable values in the cookie, but there are no methods for retrieving the value of a single variable. You must read the entire cookie and then use the string manipulation functions (the InStr(), Mid(), and other string manipulation functions) to isolate each pair and extract the name of the variable and its value.

Cookies Expire

Cookies have an expiration date. If you don't specify an expiration date (I didn't use an expiration date in the Cookie example), the cookie expires after the current session. To create a new session, shut down the Web server and start it again. Shutting down and restarting Internet Explorer won't start a new session.

To specify an expiration date, append a string like this one to the cookie:

```
expires = Thu, 01 Jan 1998 12:00:00 GMT
```

This string must be appended to the cookie as follows:

```
Document.cookie = UserName & " expires = Thu, 01 Jan 1998
12:00:00 GMT"
```

Cookies with expiration dates are actually stored on disk as text files, and you can view them with a text editor. Each Web site's cookies are stored in the Cookies folder under the Windows folder.

Anchor   Anchor is a property of the Document object, and like some other properties, it is also an object. The Length property of the Anchor object returns the number of anchors in the document. The individual anchors are stored in the *Anchors* array, whose elements can be accessed with an index. The name of the first anchor in the document is Anchors(0) (its value is the NAME attribute of the <A> tag that inserted the anchor in the document), Anchors(1) is the second anchor, and so on. The following statements display the number of anchors in the current document in a message box:

```
TotalAnchors = Document.Anchors.Length
MsgBox "The document contains "& TotalAnchors & "anchors"
```

You can also scan all the anchors in a document with a loop such as the following:

```
For i=0 to TotalAnchors-1
    ThisAnchor=Document.Anchors(i)
    {do something with this anchor}
Next
```

Scanning the anchors of the current document from within the same document's script section isn't practical. But you can open another document in a frame and access the anchors of the frame with the *Frame(1).Document.Anchors* array. For another example, see the DocumentLinks example, later in this chapter.

Link   This property is similar to the Anchor property, but instead of representing the anchors, it represents the hyperlinks in the current document. Like the anchors array, the links array is a property of the Document object, which is the only object that can contain links. The basic property of the Link object is the Length property, which returns the number of links in the document.

Each link is a member of the *Links* array. The first link is Links(0), the second one is Links(1), and so on. Because the hyperlinks in a document are destinations, the Link object's properties are identical to the properties of the Location object, but they are read-only.

To obtain the number of links in the document displayed in the browser's window, use the following statement:

```
Window.Document.Links.Length
```

To scan the hyperlinks in the document and examine their destinations, use a loop such as the following:

```
For i=0 to Window.Document.Links.Length-1
    {process the hyperlink}
Next
```

At each iteration of the loop, the current hyperlink is given by the following expression:

```
Window.Dcument.Links(i).href.
```

lastModified   This property returns the date the current document was last modified. You can use the lastModified property of the Document object to display the date and time it was last modified, without having to hardcode this information in the document itself.

Referrer   This property returns the URL of the referring document.

The Methods of the Document Object

The Document object supports a few methods as well, which let you manipulate its contents. The Document object's methods manipulate the contents of the current document.

Open   This method opens the document for output. The current document is cleared, and new strings can be placed on the document with the Write and WriteLn methods.

The Open method of the Document object opens the current document for output and has nothing to do with the Open method of the Window object, which opens a new instance of Internet Explorer and displays a document in it.

Write string   This method writes the *string* variable to the document. The argument is inserted in the current document at the current position, but it doesn't appear until the document is closed with the Close method.

WriteLn string   This method writes the *string* variable into the current document with a newline character appended to the end. The newline character is ignored by the browser anyway, so the WriteLn string method is practically the same as the Write string method.

Close   This method closes the document and causes all the information written to it with the Write and WriteLn methods to be displayed, as if it were placed in an HTML document that is loaded in the browser's window.

Clear   This method clears the contents of the document.

Using the Document Object's Methods

In effect, these methods allow the programmer (or Web author) to create an HTML document from within the script, as the Page1.htm example of the next section demonstrates. The Document object's methods are usually called in the following order:

```
Document.open
Document.write string
. . .
Document.write string
Document.close
```

The *string* variable, or literal, could be anything that normally appears in an HTML document (text, HTML tags, hyperlinks, and so on). Because the Write method's argument can contain HTML tags, you have the flexibility to create Web pages on the fly. The following statements display a level 1 header, centered on the page:

```
Document.write "<CENTER>"
Document.write "<H1>Welcome to our Active Pages</H1>"
Document.write "</CENTER>"
```

If you take the arguments of the Write methods and strip the quotes, you'll get the HTML document that would produce the same page.

The most common use of these methods is to create documents on the fly. The Write method is extremely flexible, and we are going to look at a couple of examples.

VB6 at Work: The Navigate Page

The Navigate.htm document, shown in Figure 21.9, contains a floating frame and two buttons. The first button displays a user-specified URL in the frame by calling the Window object's Navigate method. The second button also displays the user-specified URL in the frame, only this one uses the hRef property of the Location object.

FIGURE 21.9:

The Navigate.htm example demonstrates two methods for navigating to any URL.

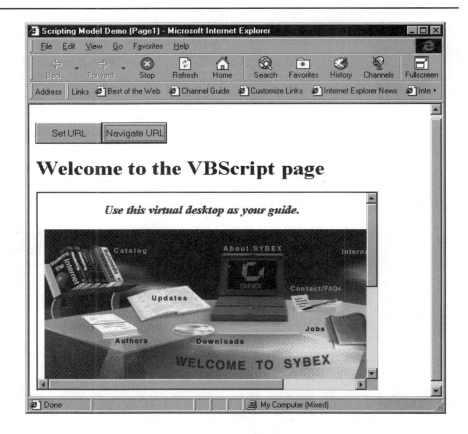

The floating frame was inserted with the following statement:

```
<IFRAME SRC="http://www.sybex.com" WIDTH=600 HEIGHT=300">
```

When the page is first loaded, it displays the Sybex home page in the floating frame. To display another page, click one of the two command buttons. The document's body consists of the following lines:

```
<BODY>
<BR>
<CENTER>
    <INPUT TYPE=Button NAME='Button1' VALUE="Navigate URL">
```

```
            <INPUT TYPE=Button NAME='Button2' VALUE="   Set URL   ">
            <BR>
            <H1>Welcome to the NAVIGATE page</H1>
            <IFRAME SRC="http://www.sybex.com" WIDTH=600 HEIGHT=300>
            </IFRAME>
            </CENTER>
        </BODY>
```

The Command buttons were placed on the page with two <INPUT> tags, and their names are Button1 and Button2. The two buttons react to the onClick event with the following handlers. The first button's code sets the frame's destination to a user-specified URL and is as follows:

```
Sub Button1_onClick()
    newURL=InputBox("Please enter the URL you want to view")
    Call window.frames(0).navigate(newURL)
End Sub
```

The second button does the same, only this time by setting the Href property, which is equivalent to the Navigate method:

```
Sub Button2_onClick()
    newURL=InputBox("Please enter the URL you want to view")
    window.frames(0).location.href=newURL
End Sub
```

The URLs must be complete, including their protocol part. To navigate to Microsoft's home page, enter the URL http://home.microsoft.com, and not just home.microsoft.com.

VB6 at Work: The Calendar.htm Page

The page shown in Figure 21.10 was created entirely from within a script. The calendar is generated by VBScript code on the client's side and displays the days of the current month. By specifying a different date you can create any month's calendar.

The actual calendar doesn't react to mouse clicks, but you can easily turn the dates into hyperlinks that point to documents with information specific to each date.

To understand the code of this application, you need a basic knowledge of building tables with HTML tags. If you are familiar with these tags, you'll find the Calendar page's script straightforward.

FIGURE 21.10:

This calendar was generated with VBScript code.

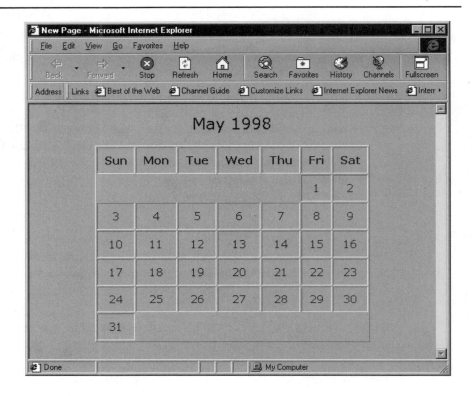

Code 21.9:   The Script for the Calendar Page

```
<HTML>
<HEAD>
<TITLE>New Page</TITLE>
<SCRIPT LANGUAGE="VBSCRIPT">
Dim imonth, thisdate, nextday, cday
imonth=month(date)

    document.bgcolor="#C0C0C0"
    document.write "<CENTER>"
    document.write "<FONT FACE='Verdana' SIZE=5>"
    document.write MonthName(Month(date)) & " " & Year(date)
    document.write "<P>"
    document.write "<TABLE CELLPADDING=10 BORDER><TR>"
    document.write
"<TD><B>Sun<TD><B>Mon<TD><B>Tue<TD><B>Wed<TD><B>Thu<TD><B>Fri<TD><B>Sat"
    document.write "<TR>"
```

```
    thisdate=DateSerial(year(date), month(date), 1)
    nextday=1
    For cday=1 to 7
      If WeekDay(thisdate)>cday Then
        document.write "<TD></TD>"
      else
        document.write "<TD ALIGN=CENTER><FONT SIZE=3>" & nextday & "</TD>"
        nextday=nextday+1
        thisdate=DateSerial(year(date), imonth, nextday)
      End If
    Next
    document.write "<TR>"
    weekDays=1
    while month(thisdate)=imonth
      document.write "<TD ALIGN=CENTER><FONT SIZE=3>" & nextday & "</TD>"
      nextday=nextday+1
      weekDays=weekDays+1
      If weekDays>7 then
        WeekDays=1
        document.write "<TR>"
      End If
      thisdate=DateSerial(year(date), imonth, nextday)
    wend
    document.write "</TABLE>"
    document.write "</CENTER>"

</SCRIPT>
</HEAD>
<BODY>

</BODY>
</HTML>
```

First, the script displays the week's days as headers of the table:

```
document.write _
"<TD><B>Sun<TD><B>Mon<TD><B>Tue<TD><B>Wed<TD><B>Thu<TD><B>Fri
<TD><B>Sat"
```

Next, the program displays the days of the first week with a For…Next loop. The first week of the month is frequently incomplete, and the first few cells in the table are likely to be blank. This loop goes through the seven days in the week until it hits the first day in the month.

After the first day in the month is found, the program creates cells in which it places the value of the variable *nextday*, which is increased with every iteration (it goes from 1 to 31). The following string produces a cell with a number:

```
"<TD ALIGN=CENTER><FONT SIZE=3>" & nextday & "</TD>"
```

This is HTML code, and any references to variables are replaced with the actual value of the *nextday* variable. For example, if the value of the *nextday* variable is 24, the following line is actually written to the document:

```
<TD ALIGN=CENTER><FONT SIZE=3>24</TD>
```

After the first week of the calendar is displayed, the program continues with the following weeks. These weeks are complete, except for the last one, of course.

A While...Wend loop handles the remaining days of the month. At each iteration, the *nextday* variable is increased by one day, and the loop continues to the end of the month.

You can easily turn each day of the month into a hyperlink that points to a file on the server. If you maintain a separate document on the server for each day of the month, you can modify the application so that each day is a hyperlink to this date's file. Instead of writing the number of the day to the output, you can insert the appropriate <A> tags to turn the day number into a hyperlink. For example, if the current value of the *nextday* variable is 24, the following VBScript line:

```
"<A HREF=" & imonth & "-" & nextday & ".htm>" & nextday & "</A>"
```

writes this string, which is indeed a hyperlink, to the document:

```
<A HREF=1-24.htm>24</A>
```

The names of the files specified in the hyperlinks must also exist on the server or in the same folder as the document that opened them.

VB6 at Work: The HTMLEditor Project

The HTMLEditor project is the simplest HTML editor you can imagine. It consists of two panes, which can be resized at runtime with the mouse (see Figure 21.11). The upper pane is a RichTextBox control, where you can enter HTML code. The lower pane is a WebBrowser control, where the HTML code is rendered. The HTMLEditor project (you'll find it in the HTMLEdit folder on the CD) is ideal for experimenting with HTML. There are many WYSIWYG HTML editors around, but in order to get exactly what you want, you must tweak the source HTML code. HTMLEditor combines the operations of HTML editing and rendering in the same window.

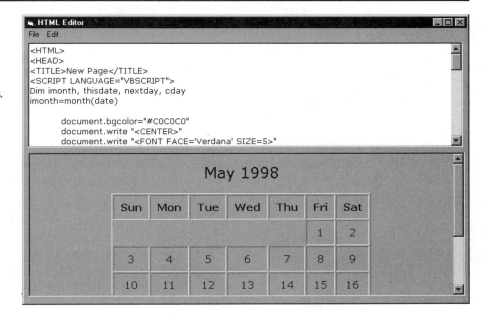

FIGURE 21.11:

HTMLEditor may not be WYSIWYG, but it's quite convenient, and you can customize it according to your needs and preferences.

I could have used a simple TextBox control for editing the HTML source code, but instead I used the RichTextBox control because its built-in features simplify the implementation of many custom editing features. It even allows the use of different colors for HTML tags or lets you convert them to uppercase.

The HTMLEditor can handle every document you could normally display in Internet Explorer, thanks to the WebBrowser control. The upper half of the Form is a simple editor. No HTML specific features were added to this editor, just the built-in editing features of the RichTextBox control. The Edit menu, which is also implemented as a context menu, contains the usual editing commands (Copy, Cut, Clear, Paste, and Select All) plus the Render Document command, which renders the current document on the WebBrowser control.

To access the document displayed in the WebBrowser control, you must first access the Script object of the WebBrowser control's Document property. If you wanted to clear the current document from within a script, you should have used the expression `Window.Document.Clear`. To clear the contents of the WebBrowser control from within your VB application, you use the following expression:

```
WebBrowser1.Document.script.Document.Clear
```

The Script object of the WebBrowser's Document property lets you access the document displayed on the control and manipulate it from within your VB code. But there's a catch here. This expression will work only if, the moment it's called, a document is already displayed. When the HTMLPad application starts, it loads the document Empty.htm, which it expects to find in the current folder. The code of the Render Document command is shown next:

```
Sub RenderDocument()
    HTMLEdit.WebBrowser1.Document.Script.Document.Clear
    HTMLEdit.WebBrowser1.Document.Script.Document.Write _
            HTMLPad.RichTextBox1.Text
    HTMLEdit.WebBrowser1.Document.Script.Document.Close
End Sub
```

The RenderDocument() subroutine is a short procedure that clears the contents of the WebBrowser control, opens the document, and then writes to it the HTML code of the RichTextBox control with the Document object's Write method.

Now that you know how to manipulate the document displayed on the Web-Browser control, you can access any page displayed on the control through your VB code. For example, you can use the *Links* array of the Scripting Model to access the hyperlinks in the document, examine which ones are images, and start another process to download them in the background. Or you can write an application that downloads a Web page and all the documents on the same Web that are referenced on the home page via hyperlinks.

Resizing the HTMLEditor Window

The HTMLEditor application wouldn't be nearly as functional if you couldn't resize its panes. When you're working with the HTML code, you need a large editor window. When you view the rendered document, you want to view as much of the document as possible. The code for resizing the application's window and its panes has nothing to do with the topics covered in this chapter, but because this is such an important feature of the application, I will discuss the code briefly.

First, you must provide the code that resizes and arranges the two controls on the Form. The HTMLEditor Form's Resize event is shown next:

```
Private Sub Form_Resize()
    RichTextBox1.Width = HTMLVal.Width - RichTextBox1.Left - 200
    WebBrowser1.Width = RichTextBox1.Width
    RichTextBox1.Height = 0.3 * HTMLVal.Height
    WebBrowser1.Move WebBrowser1.Left, RichTextBox1.Top + _
            RichTextBox1.Height + 120, WebBrowser1.Width, _
            HTMLVal.Height - RichTextBox1.Top - _
            RichTextBox1.Height - 940
    WebBrowser1.Navigate App.Path & "\empty.htm"
End Sub
```

Another feature of the HTMLEditor application is that the stripe between the two controls acts as a movable bar that lets you change the heights of the editor's and browser's areas. This allows you to give more space to one of them, depending on in which one you're working. To move the bar up or down, place the pointer over the stripe and press the left button. When the pointer turns into a double arrow, move the bar to the desired position, and then release the button.

To implement this feature, you must program the Form's mouse events. When the mouse is first pressed, the code changes the mouse pointer and saves the Y coordinate of the mouse to a Form variable, *DragStartY*. The *ResizeWindows* variable is also set to True to indicate that the two sections of the Form can be resized from within the MouseMove event. Here is the handler of the Form's Mouse-Down event:

```
Private Sub Form_MouseDown(Button As Integer, Shift As Integer, _
        X As Single, Y As Single)
    If Button = 1 And (Y > RichTextBox1.Top + _
            RichTextBox1.Height) And (Y < WebBrowser1.Top) Then
        Screen.MousePointer = vbSizeNS
        ResizeWindows = True
        DragStartY = Y
        WebHeight = WebBrowser1.Height
        HTMLHeight = RichTextBox1.Height
    End If
End Sub
```

In the MouseMove event, you must resize the two controls on the Form by changing their height, as well as the top coordinate of the WebBrowser control:

```
Private Sub Form_MouseMove(Button As Integer, _
        Shift As Integer, X As Single, Y As Single)
On Error Resume Next
    If ResizeWindows Then
        RichTextBox1.Height = HTMLHeight + (Y - DragStartY)
        WebBrowser1.Move WebBrowser1.Left, RichTextBox1.Top + _
                RichTextBox1.Height + 120, WebBrowser1.Width, _
                WebHeight - (Y - DragStartY)
        Form1.Refresh
    End If

End Sub
```

Finally, in the MouseUp event, you must reset the mouse pointer and the *ResizeWindows* variable:

```
Private Sub Form_MouseUp(Button As Integer, Shift As Integer, _
        X As Single, Y As Single)
    ResizeWindows = False
    Screen.MousePointer = vbDefault
End Sub
```

Loading and Rendering Files

The code of the HTMLEditor application has two more interesting procedures. The Save command on the File menu stores the contents of the RichTextBox control (the HTML source code) to a disk file with the SaveFile method of the RichTextBox control. The HTML source code is saved as ASCII text with the following procedure:

```
Private Sub FileSaveAs_Click()
    CommonDialog1.DefaultExt = "htm"
    CommonDialog1.Filter = "HTML Documents|*.htm|All Files|*.*"
    CommonDialog1.ShowSave
    If CommonDialog1.filename = "" Then Exit Sub
    RichTextBox1.SaveFile CommonDialog1.filename, 1
    OpenFile = CommonDialog1.filename
End Sub
```

The Open command is a bit more involved, as it must handle various types of files other than HTML files. When an HTML file is opened, its source code must appear in the editor's box, and the document must be rendered on the WebBrowser control. If the document is an image (a JPG or GIF file), it must be rendered in the WebBrowser control, but the file's contents must not appear in the editor. If it's a sound, it must be played back, but the file's contents must not be displayed. The code of the Open command is:

```
Private Sub FileOpen_Click()
On Error Resume Next

    CommonDialog1.Filter = "HTML Documents|*.htm;*.html|ActiveX _
        Documents|*.vbd|All Files|*.*"
    CommonDialog1.ShowOpen
    If Trim(CommonDialog1.filename) = "" Then Exit Sub
    dPos = InStr(CommonDialog1.filename, ".")
    If dPos > 0 Then ext = Mid$(CommonDialog1.filename, dPos + 1)
    If UCase$(ext) = "HTM" Or UCase$(ext) = "HTML" _
        Or UCase$(ext) = "TXT" Then
        RichTextBox1.LoadFile CommonDialog1.filename, 1
        WebBrowser1.Navigate CommonDialog1.filename
        OpenFileName = CommonDialog1.filename
    End If
' The following lines handle non-HTML file types
' like sounds and images
    WebBrowser1.Navigate CommonDialog1.filename
End Sub
```

If the user selects an HTML or text file in the File Open dialog box, it's displayed in the editor, and the program attempts to render it on the WebBrowser control. If not, the WebBrowser control is navigated to this file. If it's a file that the browser can handle, it does so. If not, no error message is generated. This is a feature of browsers: when they run into information they can't handle, they process as much information as they can or ignore it altogether. But they won't generate any error messages. The error handler was included in case something goes wrong with the VB code.

The History Object

The History object provides methods for navigating through the browser's history. In other words, it lets you access the functionality of the browser's navigation buttons from within your code.

The Methods of the History Object

The History object of the Scripting Model maintains the list of sites already visited, and you can access them through the History object's methods, which are described next. The History object doesn't have its own properties or events.

Back *n*   This method moves back in the history list by *n* steps, as if the user has clicked the browser's Back button *n* times. To move to the most recently visited URL, use the following statement:

```
call Window.History.back(0)
```

Or simply use this statement:

```
call Window.History.back
```

Forward *n*   This method moves forward in the history list by *n* steps, as if the user has clicked the browser's Forward button *n* times.

Go *n*   This method moves to the *nth* item in the history list. The following statement takes you to the first URL in the list:

```
Window.History.go 1
```

The Navigator Object

The Navigator object returns information about the browser. One of the major problems you will face as a Web author is that the two major browsers (Netscape Navigator and Microsoft Internet Explorer) are not totally compatible. Each supports a few unique features that the other doesn't. The truth is, both Netscape and Microsoft try to catch up with each other instead of attempting to establish new standards.

Developing pages that will work on both browsers is not a trivial task, especially for those who design active pages. Even if you can't design a page that can be rendered on both browsers, you can at least have two sets of pages, one for each browser, and display the appropriate pages. Even for this crude technique to work, you must figure out from within a script which browser is opening the page.

The properties of the Navigator object are read-only, and they return information about the browser in which the document is viewed.

AppCodeName   This property returns the code name of the application. Internet Explorer returns "Mozilla."

AppName   This property returns the name of the application. Internet Explorer returns "Microsoft Internet Explorer."

AppVersion   This method returns the version of the application. Internet Explorer 4 under Windows 95 returns "4.0 (compatible; MSIE 4.01; Windows 95." Future versions of Internet Explorer and Windows 98 may return a slightly different string.

UserAgent   This method returns the user agent of the application. Internet Explorer 4 returns "Mozilla/4.0 (compatible; MSIE 4.01; Windows 95)."

Suppose you have prepared an HTML page that can be viewed with any browser (in other words, a generic page), and you have prepared a more advanced version of the same page that includes features supported only by Internet Explorer 4. You can easily detect which browser is running at the client's side, and you can display the advanced page if the browser happens to be Internet Explorer 4 and display the generic HTML page for all other browsers.

To find out the values of the various properties of the Navigator object, run the HTMLEditor application (discussed earlier in this chapter), and create a small script like the following one:

```
<SCRIPT LANGUAGE=VBScript>
    Document.Write Window.Navigator.propName
</SCRIPT>
```

in which *propName* is the actual name of a property of the Navigator object. Then render the document, and the property's value will appear in the lower pane of the HTMLEditor window.

The Location Object

The Location object applies to the Window and Frames objects and provides information about the window's (or frame's) current URL. You've already seen examples of the Location object, but we haven't looked at all its properties yet. Here are all the properties of the Location object. The Location object's properties return information about the URL of the current document. By setting this object's properties, you can navigate to another document.

href   This property returns or sets the complete URL for the location to be loaded into the browser's window. Use this property to connect to another location through your VBScript code. To display the current document's URL, use a statement such as the following:

```
MsgBox "You are currently viewing " & document.location.href
```

You can also display another document in the window or frame with the following statement:

```
document.location.href="http://www.microsoft.com"
```

As you may recall from the discussion of URLs in the previous chapter, URLs have several parts. The properties shown in Table 21.3 return (or set) these parts.

TABLE 21.3:   The Properties That Return or Set URL Parts

PROPERTY	WHAT IT DOES
Protocol	Returns or sets the protocol of the URL (usually http)
Host	Returns or sets the host and port of the URL. The host and port are separated with a colon, as in host:port. The port is optional and rarely used.
Hostname	Reads or sets the host of a URL, which can be either a name or an IP address
Port	Returns or sets the port of the URL (you rarely have to specify the port number in a WWW URL)
Pathname	Returns or sets the pathname of the URL. Use this property when you want to display a document other than the Web's root document.

The Links Object

Another invisible object is the Links object, which represents a link in an HTML document and exposes properties through which you can find out the destination of the link. The number of hyperlinks in the current document is given by the property Links.Length, and each hyperlink in the document is given by the *Links* array. The URL of the first hyperlink is links(0), links(1) is the URL of the second hyperlink, and so on up to links(Links.Length-1).

The *Links* array returns a Links object, which in turn provides information about a hyperlink's attributes. The Links object has the properties shown in Table 21.4.

TABLE 21.4: The Properties of the Links Object

PROPERTY	WHAT IT DOES
Href	Returns or sets the complete URL for the location to be loaded into the frame
Protocol	Returns or sets the protocol of the URL (usually **http**)
Host	Returns or sets the host and port of the URL
Hostname	Reads or sets the host of a URL, which can be either a name or an IP address
Port	Returns or sets the port of the URL
Pathname	Returns or sets the pathname of the URL
Search	Returns or sets the search portion of the URL, if it exists
Hash	Returns or sets the hash portion of the URL
Target	The last property of the Frames object is the target that may have been specified in the <A> frame. The target of the link is the window or frame in which the destination object will be displayed.

Building Internet-Enabled Controls

With the domination of the Internet and the merging of the desktop and the Web—demonstrated by the Active Desktop and the latest release of Internet Explorer—ActiveX controls should be able to connect to the Internet and download information from HTTP servers. No matter how much information you provide along with your control, there will always be more, up-to-date information on a server. An interesting, and in many cases necessary, feature you may want to add to your controls is the ability to connect to HTTP servers and download information on request.

The ActiveX controls you design with Visual Basic support asynchronous down-loading of property values. This means that a property's value may be a file on your company's Web server, and the custom control can contact the server and download information at will. To download a file from a URL, use the AsyncRead method, whose syntax is:

```
UserControl_AsyncRead Target, AsyncType [, PropertyName]
```

The *target* string specifies the location of the data, and it can be a URL to a remote HTTP server or the path to a file on a local or network disk. A URL would be something like `http://www.servername.com/Updates/Latest.txt`, and a path to a local file would be something like: `file://m:\Software\Updates\Latest.txt`.

The type of the file to be downloaded is specified with the *AsyncType* argument, which can be one of the constants shown in Table 21.5.

TABLE 21.5: The Possible Settings of the *AsyncType* Argument of the AsyncRead Method

Constant	Description
vbAsyncTypeFile	The data is provided in a file that can be opened later by Visual Basic.
vbAsyncTypeByteArray	The data is provided as a byte array. The application must handle the elements of the array.
vbAsyncTypePicture	The data is provided in a Picture object.

The last, optional, argument is the name of the property to be downloaded. This name is simply an identifier that you can use later to retrieve the value of the property downloaded or to cancel the downloading of the data. In the examples, I am going to use the *PropertyName* argument to distinguish between multiple properties that are downloaded simultaneously. The *PropertyName* parameter can be any arbitrary name, since its only function is to act as an identifier for this particular data request.

Once the data is requested with the AsyncRead method, the program control returns to the application, which can continue with other tasks. The download may take a while, so the AsyncRead method performs an asynchronous operation. When the download is complete, the AsyncReadComplete event will be raised. The code for handling the downloaded data goes into the AsyncReadComplete event's handler, whose definition is:

```
Sub UserControl_AsyncReadComplete(PropertyValue As AsyncProperty)
```

The *PropertyValue* argument is an object, with the properties listed in Table 21.6.

TABLE 21.6: The Properties of the AsyncProperty Object

Constant	Description
Value	A variant containing the results of the asynchronous download
PropertyName	The property name, as specified with the last argument in the AsyncRead method
AsyncType	An integer specifying the type of the data in the Value property. It takes the same values as the *AsyncType* argument of the AsyncRead method, described earlier.

The AsyncReadComplete event will be raised even if an error occurred during the transmission. If the download didn't complete successfully, a runtime error will occur when you access the Value property of the AsyncProperty object. You should always include an On Error statement in the AsyncReadComplete event handler to trap download errors.

The Value property is the actual value of the property you're downloading. If the type of the requested information was vbAsyncTypeFile, the Value property is the name of a temporary file, which Visual Basic will create for you in the Temp folder on your disk. You can use the standard file I/O functions and statements to process it. If the type of the requested information was vbAsyncTypePicture, the Value property is a Picture object that holds the bitmap. You can assign the Value property to the Picture property of a control (or the UserControl object), or you can transfer the bitmap with the PaintPicture method. Finally, if the type of the requested information was vbAsyncTypeByteArray, *Value* is the array where the bytes are stored.

It is possible to cancel the asynchronous download by calling the CancelAsyncRead method. The syntax of the CancelAsyncRead method is:

```
UserControl.CancelAsyncRead PropertyName
```

PropertyName is the name of the property being downloaded (the last argument of the AsyncRead method). If *PropertyName* is not supplied (because no such property was specified in the AsyncRead method), the last AsyncRead method invocation that was called without a *PropertyName* argument will be canceled.

VB6 at Work: Rates Custom Control

The asynchronous downloading of property values over the Internet is demonstrated in the Rates project, which is shown in Figure 21.12. The Rates Control Demo has a visible interface that consists of a ListBox control, where the most up-to-date currency rates are displayed. The Rates Control Demo also provides methods for retrieving the rates for various currencies so that the control can remain hidden.

FIGURE 21.12:

The Rates Control Demo downloads and displays data over the Internet from an HTTP server.

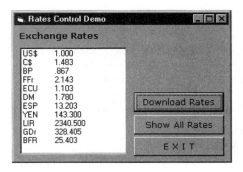

The Rates Control's Members

The Rates control exposes many standard members:

BackColor	ForeColor	MouseMove
Click	KeyDown	MouseUp
DblClick	KeyPress	Refresh
Enabled	KeyUp	
Font	MouseDown	

These members were added to the control with the help of the Wizard, and they are all mapped to the equivalent members of the ListBox control:

In addition to the standard members, the Rates control provides the following custom members.

DownloadRates Method   The DownloadRates method connects to the server and downloads the document with the currency rates. Its syntax is:

```
DownloadRates (RatesURL As String)
```

RatesURL is the URL of a text file with the following structure:

```
<date>
<currency>, <rate>
<currency>, <rate>
 . . .
<currency>, <rate>
```

The first line contains the date of the file's last update so that the client knows how recently the rates have been updated. The following lines contain currency symbols and rates, separated with commas. Here are the lines of the text file that populated the list in Figure 21.12:

```
"5:31 PM 5/18/96"
US$, 1.00
C$, 1.483
BP, 0.867
FFr, 2.143
ECU, 1.103
DM, 1.780
ESP, 13.203
YEN, 143.300
LIR, 2340.500
GDr, 328.405
BFR, 25.403
```

Since the code uses the comma to separate the two items on each line, you can't use the same character to format numbers. The value 2340.500 can't be listed in the Rates.txt file as 2,340.500. This will throw off the code that parses the file and populates the ListBox control.

RatesRead Event   This event is triggered as soon as the data is downloaded.

LastUpdate Property   This property is a date value that returns the date and time the rates were last updated. The value of this property is read from the server, along with the currency rates.

Count Property   This property returns the number of currencies downloaded from the server.

GetCurrencyValue(currency As String)   This method returns the exchange rate for the specified currency. To find out the exchange rate for the German mark, for example, call the GetCurrencyValue as follows:

```
DMRate = GetCurrencyValue("DM")
```

GetCurrencyName Method   This method returns the name of the currency in the location *index* of the ListBox control.

DloadError(ErrNumber As Long, ErrDescription As String)   The DLoad-Error event is triggered from within the AsyncReadComplete event, to notify the application that an error has occurred. The host application can read the error's number and description and act accordingly.

Using the Rates Control

Before examining the actual code of the control, let's see how it's used in the test project. The test project consists of a single Form that contains an instance of the Rates control and a Command button. When the button is clicked, the control contacts a Web server and requests the exchange rates of various currencies. The code behind the Get Rates button calls the DownLoadRates method, passing as argument the URL of a text file.

```
Private Sub bttnGetRates_Click()
    RateControl1.DownloadRates ("http://127.0.0.1/rates.txt")
End Sub
```

The Rates.txt file in this example is in the root folder of the Web server I have installed on my computer. If you have the Internet Information Server or the Personal Web Server installed on your computer or on another computer on a local area network, place the Rates.txt file there, and connect to the server machine to download it. The address is 127.0.0.1, which is the address of the local machine. If you don't have a Web server, see the instructions in the section "Testing the Rates

Control" for information about how to post the file on your Internet service provider's server.

The Rates Control's Code

The standard properties of the control were added with the ActiveX Interface Wizard. We are going to focus on the procedures that download the text file and populate the List-Box control.

Code 21.10:   **The DownloadRates Method**

```
Public Function DownloadRates(RatesURL As String)
On Error GoTo DLoadError

    AsyncRead RatesURL, vbAsyncTypeFile, "Rates"
    Exit Function

DLoadError:
    RaiseEvent DLoadError(1024, "Could not download currency rates.")

End Function
```

The method calls the AsyncRead function, passing the URL of the Web server as an argument. The downloaded information will be stored in a file, and the property name is Rates.

The interesting action takes place in the AsyncReadComplete event of the UserControl object:

```
Private Sub UserControl_AsyncReadComplete(AsyncProp As AsyncProperty)
Dim FileName As String

On Error GoTo DLoadError
    If AsyncProp.PropertyName = "Rates" Then
        FileName = AsyncProp.Value
```

```
            ReadRates FileName
        End If
        Exit Sub


    DLoadError:
        RaiseEvent DLoadError(1025, "Error in Downloading rates ")

    End Sub
```

The code starts by examining the value of the AsyncProp object's PropertyName property. In the Rates control, this property can only be Rates. If the control is downloading multiple files at once, this property tells you which file completed downloading so that you can process it from within your code. When the AsyncRead methods downloads a file, the AsyncProp object's Value property is the name of the file where the file was stored on the local disk. It has nothing to do with the actual filename on the server. It's a unique filename created by the system in the Temporary Internet Files folder. The name of the file is used by the ReadRates() subroutine to display the rates in the ListBox control.

Code 21.11:   **The ReadRates() Subroutine**

```
    Private Sub ReadRates(FileName As String)
    Dim FNum As Integer
    Dim currencyName As String, currencyValue As Currency

        FNum = FreeFile
        CurrencyList.Clear
    On Error GoTo ReadError
        Open FileName For Input As FNum
        Input #FNum, m_LastUpdate
        i = 1
        While Not EOF(FNum)
            Input #FNum, currencyName, currencyValue
            CurrencyList.AddItem currencyName & Chr(9) & _
                        Format(currencyValue, "#.000")
            CurrencyNames(i) = currencyName
            AllRates.Add Str(currencyValue), currencyName
            i = i + 1
        Wend
        RaiseEvent RatesRead
        Exit Sub

    ReadError:
        RaiseEvent DLoadError(1025, "Unkown data format")

    End Sub
```

This is straightforward VB code that opens a text file and appends its lines to the CurrencyList ListBox control. In addition, it stores the currency rates to the AllRates collection, using the currency name as key. This technique will simplify the retrieval of a currency's exchange rate. The ReadRates() subroutine is private to the UserControl object, and it can't be called from the host application.

Notice the error trapping code in all subroutines. When downloading information from the Internet, any number of things can go wrong. The HTTP server may be down, files may be rearranged on the server, transmission errors can occur, and so on. These errors must be trapped and dealt with in a robust manner.

One feature you might want to add to this project is to keep track of the property being downloaded and prevent the host application from initiating another download of the same property while it's being downloaded. Our code will give a generic error message ("Error in downloading rates"). The AsyncRead method can be called to download a file while another one is being downloaded, but it can't download the same file twice simultaneously.

Testing the Rates Control

Testing a control that downloads property values from an HTTP server requires that you connect to the server and the document to be used for testing the control be posted to the server. If you have your own Web server (Internet Information Server or the Personal Web Server), you can just copy the Rates.txt file to one of the Web server's virtual directories. You can just copy it to the root directory and then connect to your own server using the following URL:

```
http://127.0.0.1/RatesPage.htm
```

The address 127.0.0.1 is the address of your own computer on the network. Actually, you don't even need a network. As long as you have a Web server installed on your computer, you can use this URL to connect to it. If the Web server is on another computer on the same network, substitute the actual computer name for the string "127.0.0.1".

Most of you, however, don't have you own Web server. You can still use your Internet service provider's server, as long as you have permission to post files on it (most ISPs offer a few megabytes to their subscribers, where they can post user pages). To test the Rates control with your ISP's server, you must post the Rates.txt file to your directory on the server. To do so, follow these steps:

1. Create a new folder on your hard disk, and place the Rates.txt file in it (if you have any HTML files you would like to post, place them there as well).

2. Start the Web Publishing Wizard (a utility that comes with Windows and FrontPage).

3. The first page of the Web Publishing Wizard is a welcome screen. Click the Next button to display the Select a File or Folder window:

4. In the File or Folder Name box, enter the name of the folder you just created. Click Next.

5. In the next window, specify a friendly name for the Web server and click the Advanced button. You will see another window, where you must select the protocol to be used for transferring the file.

6. Select FTP and click Next.

In the next window, you must specify the URL of your Internet service provider. You must provide the name of the server where the ISP places user pages (don't change the name of the local directory). For most ISPs, this URL is something like:

```
users.ISPname.com/yourname
```

The *yourname* portion is your log-in name. If your address is jdoe@usa1.com, your login name is jdoe, and the URL of your directory on the ISP's server would be:

```
users.usa1.com/jdoe
```

Many ISPs use the tilde character in front of the user name (users.usa1.com/~jdoe). If you search for "user pages" in your ISP's Web site, you'll find all the information you need.

Click Next again to see the last window of the Wizard, where you must click Finish to publish your files.

To test your directory on the server, start Internet Explorer and enter the URL of the Rates.txt file on the server:

```
http://users.usa1.com/jdoe/rates.txt
```

You should see the contents of the Rates.txt file in the browser's window. This means that you have successfully posted the file and that your Rates control will also be able to see it on the server and download it. Copy the URL from the browser's Address box and paste it in your code (pass it as an argument to the DownloadRates method of the Rates control).

The process I describe here will work with many ISPs, but the exact same steps may not apply to all ISPs. If you have problems posting your files to the server, find out from your ISP what it takes to publish your own user, or personal, Web site. Instead of an entire Web site, just place the Rates.txt there. Or, if you already have a Web site, place the Rates.txt file in the same directory. It's not going to affect your Web, since none of the pages contain hyperlinks to this file.

If you download the rates and a few minutes or a few hours later you click the Download Rates button again, chances are that the same values will appear on the control. You may have posted new files on the server several times, but the rates won't change. Experienced Web surfers have already guessed what's happening. The AsyncRead method doesn't contact the server to download the Rates.txt file again. It retrieves it from the cache, stores the information in another temporary file, and the control's code reads it as usual. In effect, the AsyncRead method goes through the InternetExplorer Class and uses the same cache as Internet Explorer.

Where Internet Explorer 4 allows you to refresh a page, the AsyncRead method doesn't provide an argument that will force the data to be read from the server instead of the cache. To bypass this problem, you must change the Cache settings of Internet Explorer. Follow these steps:

1. Start Internet Explorer and choose View ➤ Internet Options.

2. Click the Settings button to open the Settings dialog box:

3. To force Internet Explorer to reload a page from the server (instead of reading from the cache), click the Every Visit to the Page option.

This action will also affect Internet Explorer's operation. Internet Explorer will not use its cache, and every time you move back to a page, even within a few seconds, the page will be reloaded from the server. As this book was ready to go to the press, Microsoft announced the first public beta of Internet Explorer 5. It's also possible that a new AsyncRead method may become available that allows you to specify whether a single page is downloaded or simply refreshed from the cache.

Another interesting approach is to include the InternetExplorer Class to the custom control and call its Refresh2 method to force the download of the file. When the AsyncRead method is called again, it will find the data in the cache, but the cache will contain the most recent data.

Downloading Image Properties

The AsyncRead method can also download picture properties. Pictures can be downloaded as binary files and displayed with the LoadPicture method. Visual Basic can also create a device context and store the downloaded bitmap there. To download an image, call the AsyncRead function with the following arguments:

```
AsyncRead URL, vbAsyncTypePicture, "Image"
```

The constant *vbAsyncTypePicture* tells Visual Basic to download a picture object. No file is created on the host computer, and you can't read the bitmap's pixels. To use the image, you must monitor the progress of the download from within the AsyncReadComplete function. When the download of the property Image (or whatever name you have assigned to the property in the AsyncRead method) completes, you must retrieve the property's value and store it in a Picture object with a statement such as the following:

```
Set Bitmap = AsyncProp.Value
```

If you're downloading multiple images, use different property names to differentiate them. You can then use the Bitmap object's properties, such as Width and Height. The following code segment creates a Picture object with the downloaded bitmap and then calls the ShowImage() subroutine to display the image on a PictureBox control:

```
Private Sub UserControl_AsyncReadComplete(AsyncProp As AsyncProperty)

On Error GoTo DLoadError
    If AsyncProp.PropertyName = "Image" Then
        Set Bitmap = AsyncProp.Value
        ShowImage Bitmap
```

```
          ' Bitmap.Width is the bitmap's width in HiMetric units
          ' to convert it to pixels, use the statement:
          ' Int(ScaleX(Bitmap.Width, vbHimetric, vbPixels))
       End If
       Exit Sub

   DLoadError:
       ' Raise an error event
   End Sub
```

The ShowImage() subroutine uses the PaintPicture method to copy the bitmap from the Bitmap variable onto a PictureBox control:

```
Picture1.PaintPicture Image, 0, 0, _
        Picture1.ScaleWidth, Picture1.ScaleHeight, _
        0, 0, Picture1.ScaleWidth, Picture1.ScaleHeight
```

In summary, downloading image properties from an HTTP server is quite analogous to downloading text files. You must specify the type of data to be downloaded in the AsyncRead function (*vbAsyncTypePicture* constant instead of vbAsyncTypeFile). When the image is downloaded, a Picture object will be automatically created, where the image's bitmap will be stored (just like the text file is generated automatically for you). You can then use the PaintPicture method to transfer the bitmap from the Picture object to a PictureBox control or the User-Control object itself.

Finally, you can download data in array format, by specifying the constant *vbAsyncTypeArray* in the AsyncRead function. This time Visual Basic will create a byte array, and you must process it from within your code.

CHAPTER
TWENTY-TWO

Active Server Pages

- Understanding client-server interaction

- Working with Active Server Pages

- Submitting data to the server

- Processing client data

- Using Server objects

- Building Web applications

In Chapter 19, you saw how a Web server sends information to the client in the form of HTML documents and how the client interacts with the server by means of hyperlinks. You also saw how to design Web pages that collect information from visitors on the client and submit it to the server along with the URL. When the server receives data (or *parameter values*, as they are called) from a client, it must process the data and return the results to the client in HTML format. In this chapter, I am going to discuss how parameters are retrieved by the server and how they are processed. This is the most important part of client-server interaction and (until the release of the Active Server Pages) the most difficult to implement.

The parameters submitted by a client can be anything—registration data, search arguments, customization data, anything. Businesses are interested in the information that is stored in databases and that must be retrieved as needed. To retrieve up-to-the-minute information from a Web server, the client must send back more information than simply the name of a hyperlink. Think about a user on client who requests the sales of a specific product in North Carolina or a list of the most active customers in Texas. This information must be retrieved from a database the moment it's requested; it can't be a document that has been prepared ahead of time, waiting on the server's disk to be retrieved. The requested information must be extracted from the database when it's requested, encoded in HTML format on the fly, and transmitted to the client.

Many companies (of all sizes) are already doing business on the Web. A commercial Web site should be able to present information about the products to a visitor and collect order information (items, quantities, shipping address, and so on). I'll also discuss the requirements of commercial Web sites in this chapter.

NOTE   You won't find information on secure transactions in this chapter, and you'll need that information if you want viewers to transmit sensitive information, such as credit card numbers, or if you want to send back sensitive information that can be viewed by registered users only. You can find all this in the documentation that comes with individual Microsoft products, such as the Commerce Server.

Client-Server Interaction

Figure 22.1 shows a typical Web page that prompts the user to enter information, which will be used later to extract information from a database on the server. The site shown in Figure 22.1 is Infoseek, a widely used search engine on the Web. The search argument is "VB + books" (search for documents about "VB" that also contain the word "*books*").

FIGURE 22.1:

The Infoseek site searches the Web for documents that contain user-supplied keywords.

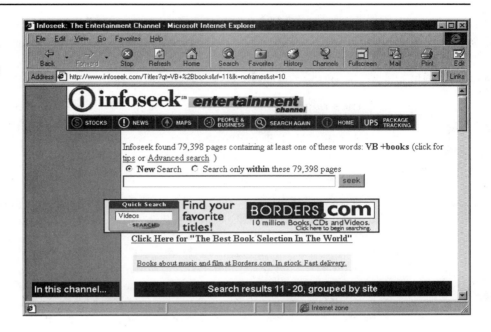

When the Search button is clicked, the client sends the following URL to the server:

```
http://www.infoseek.com/Titles?qt=VB+%2Bbooks&rf=11&lk=noframes&st=10
```

Titles is the name of an application on the server that will search the database and supply the results. It's not an ASP application, but it doesn't make any difference. The same arguments would be supplied if it were an ASP application, and the same document would be returned to the client. The client must transmit the name of the application that will process the parameter values on the server; that's all the client needs to know. This piece of information is supplied in the <FORM> tag of the document (see Chapter 20 for more information on placing controls on a Web page).

Start Internet Explorer, connect to the Infoseek site, and submit some search arguments. When the server returns the requested information, you'll see the name of the application that retrieved the data on the server along with the arguments (a string similar to the one shown above) in the Address Box of the browser.

The information entered by the viewer on the Form is transmitted to the server in the form of parameter values, following the URL of the application that will process them. Parameters have a name and a value and they appear as:

```
parameter=value
```

When you're using a Form to collect data from the visitor, the name of the parameter is the name of a control on the Form, and the value is the control's value. Multiple pairs of parameters are separated by an ampersand character (&), as shown here:

```
LastName=Petroutsos&FirstName=Evangelos
```

The string with the parameters is appended to the URL by placing a question mark (?) after the name of the application that will process it on the server (the name of the ASP file). If the value of a control contains spaces, each space is replaced by a plus sign (+), as in the following example:

```
Title=Mastering+VB6
```

The parameters follow the question mark, which appears at the end of the URL. In the example of the Infoseek site, the first parameter is *qt* (which, most likely, stands for query text), and its value is the string "VB+%2Bbooks". The space was replaced by a plus sign, and the plus sign in the original search argument was substituted with %2B (2B is the hexadecimal representation of the plus sign's ASCII value). The parameter *lk=noframes* tells the application on the server to generate an HTML document without frames, and the parameter *st=10* specifies that it should display the second batch of 10 matching titles. As you can see in Figure 22.1, the search recalled nearly 80,000 documents, but they can be displayed on the client 10 at a time. Each time you click the Next 10 hyperlink, the value of *st* is increased by 10 (and each time you click the Previous 10 hyperlink, the value of the parameter *st* is decreased by 10). This is all the information needed by the Titles application on the server to display the appropriate page with the results of the search.

> **NOTE**
>
> There are many more characters that have special meaning in the HTTP protocol, and they can't appear in the parameter string. For example, the double quote character (") can't appear in the string following the server script's name. Other illegal characters are the forward slash (/) and the ampersand character itself. Any special character (that is, any character that is not a letter or a numeric digit) is replaced with the hexadecimal representation of its ASCII value, prefixed with the % symbol. The & symbol is encoded as &26, and the % symbol is encoded as %25.

The Web server can't decipher the requested URL, but it does have the intelligence to invoke the program whose name appears in the URL string and pass to it the parameters following the program's name. Traditionally, the programs that process client requests in real time on the server are called *scripts*, and most of them were written in Perl.

NOTE

> Perl is an acronym for Practical Extraction and Report Language and is a scripting language for Unix systems with which you can write powerful data and text manipulation routines. However, compared with Visual Basic and VBScript, Perl is a cryptic language, and it's not a language with which Windows programmers are familiar.

Building Parameter Strings

You can use two methods to build URLs that call special applications on the server and supply additional information to them:

- The simple method is to supply all the required information in the <FORM> tag and let the browser contact the server and submit the values of all the controls on the Form.

- The second method is to build the parameter string with VBScript commands and submit it to the server with the Navigate method of the Window object.

Starting with the simple method, let's review the FORM.HTM page we looked at in Chapter 19. The Form section on the page, which is shown in Figure 22.2, was inserted with the following tag:

```
<FORM ACTION="ASPages/Register.asp" METHOD="GET">
```

The ACTION attribute specifies the URL of the application to be invoked. The application is an ASP file that resides in the ASPages virtual folder of the same Web site, which uploaded the current page. The METHOD attribute specifies one of the two methods for submitting data from the client to the server. For the examples in this chapter, we are going to use the GET method. (The alternative is the POST method, but this has a limitation as to the maximum length of the string that can be submitted to the server.)

The Form section of the FORM.HTM page shown in Figure 22.2 contains the controls and values listed in Table 22.1.

When the Submit button at the bottom of the Form is clicked, the client transmits the following string to the server. The browser automatically builds this string (no script is needed in this page).

```
http://127.0.0.1/Register.asp?LName=Brannon&FName=Andrea&EMail=ABrannon@
USA.net&hardware=PC&browser=IE&Sports=ON&Stock=ON&Bargains=ON&mail=YES&
Register=Register+Now%21
```

FIGURE 22.2:

The FORM.HTM page invokes an application on the server and passes the data in the controls as parameters.

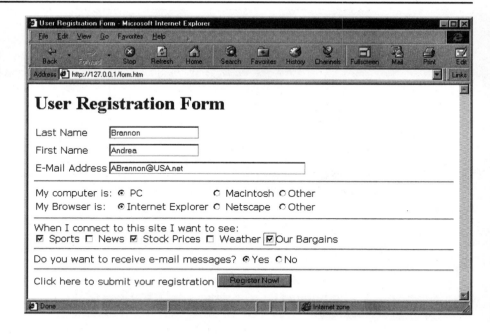

TABLE 22.1: The Controls and Values of the Form Section

Control	Value
Lname	Brannon
Fname	Andrea
Email	ABrannon@USA.net
Hardware	PC
Browser	IE
Sports	ON
News	OFF
Stock	ON
Weather	OFF
Bargains	ON
Mail	YES

The second way to submit the parameter to the server is to build the parameter string with VBScript commands and submit it to the server with the Navigate method of the Window object. Here's how you can contact an application on the server from within a script (when the user clicks a regular Command button, for example):

```
Sub button1_onClick()
    URLsrting =
"http://www.servername.com/Register.asp?Lname=
        Brannon&Fname=Andrea&Email=Abrannon@USA.net"
    Window.Navigate URLString
End Sub
```

The *URLString* variable is a single long line, but it had to be broken somewhere to fit on the printed page. You would normally build this string in pieces, using the concatenation operator. You should use the first method, which is much simpler, except for unusual situations in which the information to be transmitted can't be entered in controls.

Contacting a Server Application

At this point, you probably want to test the information presented so far and see for yourself how the client interacts with the server. This process requires that your pages are processed by a server. You can open the FORM.HTM page by double-clicking its icon, but unless you have a Web server running on your network, you won't be able to see what happens on the server's side. The page won't submit any information to the server, because the page wasn't downloaded from a server.

If you are using the Internet Information Server, you're probably on a local area network, and you can get some help from your network administrator. For the benefit of those who want to experiment with a Web server on a stand-alone computer, I will show you how to configure the Personal Web Server and use it to test the examples in this chapter. The Personal Web Server is a light version of the Internet Information Server, which runs under Windows 95/98 and can be used to service as many as 10 clients simultaneously. For the purposes of this book, the Personal Web Server is quite adequate, and you can use it to build functional Web sites that interact with clients through server-side scripts. When the site has been developed and tested, you can post it on a machine running Internet Information Server.

The Personal Web Server comes with Visual Studio 6 and Visual Basic. To install it, you must install the optional package Windows NT Option Pack. Installing the PWS is a totally automatic process. After its installation, the PWS starts automatically whenever you turn on the computer.

To test the server, copy any of the HTML files you built in previous chapters to the C:\INETPUB\WWWROOT folder. This is the Web server's root folder (unless you specified a different folder during the installation). Visitors that connect to your computer with the HTTP protocol (either via a local network or a modem) will be automatically taken to this folder. One of the files that will be copied there by the installation program is called DEFAULT.HTM, and this file opens by default every time a client connects to the server and doesn't specify a document name.

Before you start experimenting with the examples in this chapter, it's a good idea to create a virtual folder and store your files there. A virtual folder is simply a folder name, such as ASPages, that is mapped by the Web server to any folder on your hard disk (which means ASPages stands for a long folder name such as c:\MasteringVB6\HTML\Active Pages\Samples). To create a virtual folder, follow these steps:

1. Choose Start ➤ Programs ➤ Microsoft Personal Web Server ➤ Personal Web Manager to open the Main window:

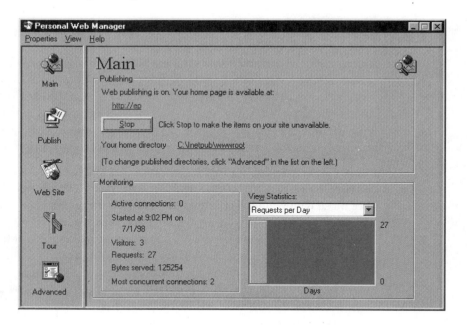

From this window you can start and stop the Web server.

2. Click the Advanced icon in the left pane to display the virtual folders already installed on your system by the installation program.

3. To add a new virtual folder, click Add. The Personal Web Manager will prompt you to select a folder on your hard disk and enter its virtual name.

Notice that the new virtual folder has its Script option checked. This means you can store scripts in it. The folder where the server scripts are stored must have its Scripts option checked; if this option is not checked, the Web server will refuse to execute the scripts in this folder. (If a virtual folder isn't supposed to contain scripts, clear the Scripts option for this folder as a security measure.)

Connecting to Your Web Server

To connect to your own server, start Internet Explorer and enter the following address in the browser's Address box:

```
http://127.0.0.1
```

This is the address of the local computer and is the same on every machine. It's a reserved IP address that connects you to the server running on the same machine from which the request is made. Entering this address (or simply 127.0.0.1) in the browser's Address box displays the Web server's default document. You can copy in the server's root folder any HTML document and open it by specifying its name along with your server's address. Even better, create a virtual folder under the C:\INETPUB\WWWRoot folder (name it MVB6), and place the HTML files you want to test there. The following address will open the Calendar.htm file in the browser's window:

```
http://127.0.0.1/MVB6/Calendar.htm
```

In the following section, you'll see how to develop applications that run on the server and can be invoked from the client. These applications are quite simple to develop (probably simpler than you think). They are scripts, just like the scripts you can embed in HTML pages, only they run on the server. They are called Active Server Pages, and as a VB programmer, you can start writing server-side scripts immediately.

Visual Basic 6 provides a special type of project, the IIS Application type, that automates the process of building Active Server Pages to run on Internet Information Server. Even with the automated tools provided by this application type, you can't go far without a basic understanding of server-side scripts and the objects provided by ASP for interacting with the client.

What Are Active Server Pages?

Microsoft introduced several methods for developing scripts on the server—some of them quite simple (such as the Internet Database Connector and the SQL Web Assistant), and others not as simple. There was a confusing time when companies did their best to simplify the development and deployment of server-side scripts, but none of these methods were particularly easy for Visual Basic developers or even for Web authors.

The situation changed drastically in 1996 with the introduction of Active Server Pages (ASP), an elegant solution to the problem of scripting. Active Server Pages are basically HTML pages that contain VBScript code, which is executed on the server. That's why they are also called server-side scripts or simply server scripts. The results of the VBScript statements (if any) are transmitted to the client. The HTML code is transmitted as is. As a consequence, every HTML page you have authored can be turned into an Active Server Page by changing its extension from HTM to ASP. Not that you'll see any benefits in renaming your HTML documents, but you're ready to activate them with the inclusion of scripts.

The server scripts produce text and HTML tags that are sent to the client, where they are rendered on the screen. A server script can produce any output, but only HTML documents can be rendered on the client. Since VBScript can contact the objects installed on the server, you are not limited to VBScript's native commands. You can contact any ActiveX components installed on the server computer to carry out complicated data processing, to access databases, and so on. A server that supports Active Server Pages is called Active Server, and currently two Web servers support ASP: the Internet Information Server and the Personal Web Server.

The Active Server provides a few built-in objects, which are discussed in the section "The Active Server's Objects," later in this chapter. These objects simplify the development of scripts by taking care of tasks such as reading the parameters passed by the client, querying databases, saving and recalling cookies on the client computer, and so on. In addition to the built-in objects, you can contact any object on the server from within your script with the CreateObject() function. Let's start by building a few Active Server Pages, and then we'll look at the objects of the Active Server.

Creating an Active Server Page

The simplest way to create an ASP page is to change the extension of an existing HTML document, from HTM (or HTML) to ASP. Then place the file in a new folder under your Web server's root folder. In this chapter, all examples will reference ASP pages in the ASPages folder, and you'll find these examples in the ASPages folder on the CD that comes with this book.

ASP Files and Execute Rights

ASP files are text files by content, but they are also programs. When called, their scripts are compiled on demand, and the executable parts are loaded in the cache. Therefore, they must be placed in a folder with Scripts rights.

Through the Web server's administration utility, create a virtual directory, name it Active-Pages, and map it to the ASPages folder under the Web's root folder. (You can create the ASPages directory anywhere on your hard disk, but it's commonly placed under the root folder.) Then set the folder's Scripts permission. You need not set the Execution rights for the folder, because ASP files are not executable files per se.

Let's start with a trivial example from Chapter 20. Here's a simple HTML file that displays the time on the client, as shown in Figure 22.3.

FIGURE 22.3:

The DATETIME.HTM page

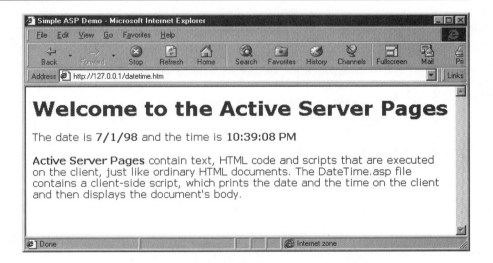

Code 22.1:   **The DATETIME.HTM File**

```
<HTML>
<HEAD>
<TITLE>Simple ASP Demo</TITLE>
<SCRIPT LANGUAGE=VBScript>
Document.Write "<FONT SIZE=3 FACE='Verdana'>"
Document.Write "<H1>Welcome to the Active Server Pages</H1>"
```

```
Document.Write "The date is <B>" & Date() & "</B> and the time is <B>"
& Time() & "</B>"
Document.Write "<P>"
</SCRIPT>
</HEAD>
<BODY>
<B>Active Server Pages</B> contain text, HTML code and scripts that are
executed on the client, just like ordinary HTML documents. The DateTime
.asp  file contains a client-side script, which prints the date and the
time on the client and then displays the document's body.
</BODY>
</HTML>
```

The date and time are displayed from within a client-side script, which calls the functions Date() and Time(). This script is executed on the client, and as a consequence, the date and time are read from the local computer's clock.

We'll revise this page to display the time on the server. To do so, we'll add statements that are executed on the server. Copy the DATETIME.HTM file to the SRVRTIME.ASP file and replace the script with the following:

```
<SCRIPT LANGUAGE = VBScript RUNAT = Server>
Response.Write "<FONT SIZE=3 FACE='Verdana'>"
Response.Write "<H1>Welcome to the Active Server Pages</H1>"
Response.Write "The date is <B>" & Date() & "</B> and the time is <B>"
& Time() & "</B>"
Response.Write "<P>"
</SCRIPT>
```

The Response object is equivalent to the Document object, but the server can't access the Document object, which is available only on the client. Instead, it must use the Response object's Write method to send output to the client. Everything you "write" to the Response object is placed in the output stream and sent to the client as if it were an existing HTML document. The new page will produce the same output, but the date and time displayed will be the date and time on the server. The modifier RUNAT in the <SCRIPT> tag tells the Active Server Pages to execute this script on the server, not on the client.

Server-side scripts can also be enclosed in a pair of <% and %> tags. These tags enclose all the statements that must be executed on the server. Everything between these two tags is considered a server-side script, which is replaced by its output and never seen by the client.

NOTE   If you double-click the name of an ASP file, you will see the HTML code, but none of the server-side statements will be executed. The browser skips the server-side script tags (<% and %>), because it doesn't know how to render them. These statements must be executed on the server, which will happen only if the document is supplied by a Web server.

Here's a more useful ASP page along the same lines. This page, GREET.ASP, displays a different greeting depending on the time of the day.

Code 22.2:   **The GREET.ASP Page**

```
<HTML>
<BODY>
<%
If Time() >=#12:00:00 AM# And Time() < #12:00:00 PM#   Then
  greeting = "Good Morning!"
Else
  greeting = "Good Afternoon!"
End If
%>
<H1> <% =greeting %> </H1>
<BR>
<H2>and welcome to the Active Server Pages.</H2>
<BR>
More HTML lines follow
</BODY>
</HTML>
```

The statements between the first pair of server-side tags (<% and %>) do not produce any output for the client. They simply assign the proper value to the *greetings* variable. The value of this variable is then sent to the client by the line <% =greeting %>. The expression "=variable" (without the quotes, of course) is replaced by the value of the specified variable when the script is executed on the server. The rest is straight HTML, which is rendered on the client as usual.

HTML and server-side statements can coexist on the same line too. The last example could have been implemented as follows:

```
<HTML>
<BODY>
<% If Time()  > = #12:00:00 AM# And Time() < #12:00:00 PM#   Then %
<H1>Good Morning!</H1>
```

```
<% Else %>
<H1>Good Afternoon!</H1>
<% End If %>
<BR>
<H2>and welcome to the Active Server Pages.</H2>
<BR>
More HTML lines follow
</BODY>
</HTML>
```

Your server-side script can also call procedures you supply in addition to built-in procedures such as the Date() and Time() functions. You can write a function that accepts a numeric value and returns it as a string (the value 96, for example, as "ninety-six"). To call this function from within your script, enclose its name in the server-side script tags:

```
<% =NumToString(96) %>
```

The actual definition of the function must appear somewhere in the same file. Since the entire procedure will be executed on the server and since it doesn't contain any HTML code to be sent to the client, you can place it in a pair of <SCRIPT> tags, similar to the client-side scripts, with an added qualifier:

```
<SCRIPT RUNAT=SERVER LANGUAGE=VBScript>
  function  NumToString (Number)
  {
      function's statements
  }
</SCRIPT>
```

The procedure will be executed and return a string, which can be used in the script.

Included Files

Multiple scripts can call common procedures such as the NumToString() function. To avoid repeating code or to maintain identical code in multiple files, you can include a file with one or more procedure definitions in an ASP file. The included file can also contain HTML code; it doesn't really matter. It is inserted as is in the current ASP file and processed along with the rest of the file.

HTML provides the #INCLUDE directive, which inserts the contents of another text file into an ASP file before processing it. The #INCLUDE statement is called a directive, because it's not an executable statement; it simply instructs ASP to perform a simple insertion.

The syntax of the #INCLUDE directive is:

```
<!- #INCLUDE VIRTUAL|FILE="filename" ->
```

The comment tags ensure that this line will not be sent to the client by mistake. If the file resides in a virtual folder (or a subfolder under a virtual folder), use the VIRTUAL keyword. If you'd rather specify an absolute path name, use the FILE keyword. Either keyword must be followed by the path name to the file to be included. Included files do not require a special extension, but the extension INC is commonly used.

To include the NumStrings.inc file in the Support folder under ASPages, use the following line:

```
<!-#INCLUDE VIRTUAL="/ASPages/Support/NumStrings.inc"->
```

If the NumStrings.inc file resides in the same folder as the ASP file in which it will be included, you can use the #INCLUDE directive with the FILE keyword:

```
<!-#INCLUDE FILE="NumString.inc"->
```

If the included file resides in the Support subfolder under the folder of the ASP file, the following line will insert it in the current ASP file:

```
<!-#INCLUDE FILE="Support/NumString.inc"->
```

Relative paths use the ASP file's folder as the starting point. You can also use the ../ qualifier to specify parent folders:

```
<!-#INCLUDE FILE="../Support/NumStrings.inc"->
```

Mixing Server-Side and Client-Side Scripts

An ASP file can contain both server-side and client-side scripts. If you want to include a script section in your Web page, simply insert the scripting commands between the <SCRIPT> tags in the file. Figure 22.4 shows the output of another ASP file that is a variation on the script that displays the server's date on the client. The TIMESRVR.ASP page displays the time on the client through a client-side script, and it displays the time on the server through a server-side script. If the client and server computers are in different time zones, the difference in the time is an integer number of hours, plus a few seconds that it may take for the HTML code to arrive at the client.

Here is the listing of the TIMESRVR.ASP file. Notice that the client-side script is inserted with the <SCRIPT> tag, as if it were included on a regular HTML page. The server-side script isn't really a script, just a call to the Time() function. You could have inserted as many statements as necessary, as long as they were included in a pair of <% and %> tags.

FIGURE 22.4:

The TIMESRVR.ASP page
combines client-side and
server-side scripts to display the time on the client
and the server.

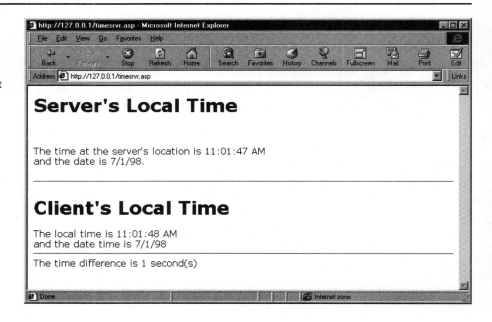

Code 22.3: **The TIMESRVR.ASP Page**

```
<HTML>
<BODY>
<% theTime = Time %>
<% theDate = Date %>
<FONT FACE=VERDANA SIZE=3>
<H1>Server's Local Time</H1>
<BR><BR>
The time at the server's location is <% = theTime %>
<BR>
and the date is <% = theDate %>.
<P>
<HR>
<H1>Client's Local Time</H1>
<SCRIPT LANGUAGE = VBScript>
Document.write "The local time is " & Time
Document.write "<BR>"
Document.write "and the date time is " & Date
Document.write "<HR>"
Document.write "The time difference is " & DateDiff("s",  "<% = theTime
%>", Time) & " second(s)"
Document.close
```

```
</SCRIPT>
</BODY>
</HTML>
```

After this introduction to the basic structure of ASP files, we can turn our attention to the objects of the Active Server and see how they can help you develop interactive Web pages. In developing ASP applications, we are primarily interested in interacting with the server, rather than writing elaborate HTML code or even client-side scripts.

The emphasis is in writing server-side code that reads data submitted by the client, processes them on the server (in most cases, with ActiveX components that reside on the server), and produces Web pages on the fly, which are transmitted back to the client. With any other server, this process requires CGI scripts and, in general, programming in C-like languages. With Active Server Pages and the built-in objects, the tasks that would normally require Perl or C++ programming can be taken care of with VBScript.

In the rest of the chapter, we are going to examine these objects and see how they simplify scripting on the server. At the end of the chapter, we'll look at some of the basic components, especially the Database component, which lets your script access databases on the server.

The Active Server's Objects

HTML is a great language for displaying information on the client. HTML extensions made Web pages colorful, then interactive. But HTML is a simple language. It wasn't designed to be a programming language, and no matter how many extensions are introduced, HTML will never become a proper programming language.

To design interactive Web pages, we need a programming tool. VBScript could be the missing link, but VBScript (and any other scripting language) is also seriously limited because of security considerations. A scripting language that runs on the client must be safe, and, practically speaking, making a language safe for scripting is tantamount to crippling it. So the answer is to do more on the server. The programming tool is still VBScript. However, when it's executed on the server, VBScript can access any object on the server computer (built-in or custom). This means that VBScript on the server behaves more like Visual Basic, and your server-side scripts look more like VB code.

Most of you will be interested in learning how to access databases on the server from the client. The simplest way to access databases through an Active Server

Page is via the Database component, which is based on the Active Data Objects (ADO). As you learned in Chapter 18, ADO is a component that's installed along with ASP, and you can call it from within your ASP pages to access databases. The ADO component provides high-performance connectivity to any ODBC-compliant database or OLE DB data source. As such, it can be used from within a Web page's script to directly access remote databases. In other words, you can use the ADO component on the client script (provided that the component is already installed on the client computer) to build a Web front end for accessing corporate data, without developing additional scripts on the server.

Active Server Pages follow the component-based development paradigm. All the standard functionality you need to build a Web site comes in the form of objects, which can be classified in two major categories:

- Intrinsic
- Basic

Intrinsic objects provide methods and properties that you need to access details of the incoming requests (such as the parameters of the request), handle cookies, and create the response to send back to the client. *Basic objects* provide functionality that is not absolutely necessary, but commonly used in Web development, such as the ADO component for accessing databases, the file system component for writing to and reading from local files on the server, and more. In the following two sections, I'll discuss these objects and give you some examples of how they are used in Web development. It goes without saying that you can build your own objects to address specific requirements.

Intrinsic Objects

ASP includes a number of built-in objects that free the developer from much of the grunt work of writing code to access details such as extracting the parameters submitted along with the URL, storing and retrieving cookies on the client computer, and directing the output to the client.

Request   This object gives you access to the parameters passed to the server by the client along with the URL. These parameters are usually the values of the controls on the Form, but can be any string constructed on the client by a local script. Through the Request object, you can also recall the values of existing cookies on the client or create new ones.

Response   This object provides the methods you need to build the response, which is another HTML document. The output of the Response object is the output stream, which is directed by the Web server to the client, as if it were another HTML document.

Application   This object maintains information that's common to all users of an ASP-based application. The Application object provides events that let you set up variables that will be used by all users of the application.

Session   This object maintains information for single users, while they are interacting with the application. A separate Session object is associated with each user, and its basic function is to maintain a state between pages for that user. You can define variables in the Session object, and they will maintain their value even when the user jumps between pages in the application. The Session object's variables are released when the user terminates the session.

Server   This object allows your server-side script to create instances of ActiveX components that reside on the server. The Server object's CreateObject method is almost identical to the Visual Basic function by the same name, and it lets you incorporate the functionality of ActiveX components into your applications. Similarly, you can create object variables with the Server object and extend your Web pages with capabilities that are way beyond HTML.

Basic Objects

To help you create Web applications, the Active Server provides the following objects that supply the functionality that is not necessary (as is the functionality of the built-in objects), but that is commonly used in building applications for the Web.

Database   This object provides connectivity to any ODBC-compliant database or OLE DB data source. It is based on the Active Data Objects and allows Web developers to easily link a database to an active Web page to access and manipulate data.

File Access   This is another useful object that lets you access text files stored on the server. As with client-side scripts, server-side scripts must be safe for the host system. The File Access object is fairly safe, because it allows developers to write and read text files only in specific folders on the server.

Content Linking   This object manages a list of URLs so that you can treat the pages in your Web site like the pages in a book. You author the pages, and the Content Linking object automatically generates and maintains tables of contents and navigation links to previous and following Web pages. With the methods and properties exposed by the Content Linking object, you can add, delete, and rearrange pages without editing the individual HTML files.

Browser Capabilities   With this object, ASP files can recognize the capabilities of the requesting browser and dynamically optimize the site's content for specific browser features. If you weren't able to write code that automatically recognizes the type of browser for a session, you'd have to create (and maintain) a series of duplicate pages for each browser, or you'd have to notify users that special features on your site can be viewed only with a specific browser.

Advertisement Rotator   As people realize the potential of the Web as a business medium and more and more sites become commercial, the need to manage ads on a Web increases. Web managers can't afford to manually place ads in their designs. Ads must not only be rotated, but selected according to user preferences. If your Web site has a search engine, it wouldn't make sense to advertise cars to a visitor who's looking for books or advertise magazines to people who are searching for programming tools. To simplify the handling of ads on a Web site, Active Server Pages comes with the Advertisement Rotator object. You can use this object to display ads based on preset criteria every time an ASP file is requested.

In this chapter, we'll cover only a few of the basic components of Active Server Pages. We'll discuss the built-in objects and a few of the basic objects, which will help you leverage your VB knowledge to the Web. We won't get into every ASP-related topic.

The Response Object

Use the Response object to send information to the client. ASP files can contain straight HTML code that's sent directly to the client. However, if you want to control the output programmatically from within the script, you must write it to the Response object. The Response object supports the following methods and properties.

The Write Method

Everything you write to the Response object with the Write method is sent to the client. Normally, the information written with the Write method must be an HTML document, just like the Write method of the Document object. Here's a simple, but working example of the Response object's Write method.

Code 22.4:   **Using the Response.Write Method**

```
<HTML>
<SCRIPT LANGUAGE=VBScript RUNAT=Server>
  Response.Write "<HTML>"
  Response.Write "<HEAD>"
  Response.Write "<TITLE>Response.Write Demo</TITLE>"
  Response.Write "</HEAD>"
```

```
    Response.Write "<H1>"
    Response.Write "Response Object:Write Method"
    Response.Write "</H1>"
    Response.Write "This document was created on the fly by an ASP file
on the server"
    Response.Write "</HTML>"
</SCRIPT>
</HTML>
```

The outer pair of HTML tags delimits the ASP file (they are not really required), and the pair of HTML tags written to the Response object delimit the HTML file seen by the client. If there's one method used in nearly every ASP file, it is the Response .Write method, and you will see many more examples of it in this chapter.

The Write method of the Response object is the primary way to send data to the client. The example in Code 22.4 is quite trivial. You could use straight test and HTML tags to produce the same output, or you could place the same arguments in the Document.Write method. All three methods would produce the same output.

The Redirect Method

This method redirects the client to another URL. If you move your site to another URL, write a short ASP application such as the following to redirect the visitor automatically to the new URL.

```
<HTML>
<%
Response.Write "Our site was moved at a new URL."
Response.Write "Your browser will be redirected to the new URL
automatically."
Response.Redirect newURL
%>
</HTML>
```

The *newURL* variable is the Web site's new URL.

The Clear Method

This method clears the data written to the Response object and is used only when the Buffer property is set to True. Normally, the output is buffered until the entire page has been processed, and only then is it sent to the client. To force the information collected so far in the output stream to be transmitted to the client, call the Response object's Clear method.

The ContentType Property

This property determines the type of document you will send to the client. The ContentType property applies to the entire page and must be set before you write any information to the output stream with the Write method.

NOTE   You'll find the various content types in the File Types tab of Windows Explorer's Options dialog box. (In any Explorer window, choose View ➤ Options and select the File Types tab.)

For example, if you want to send source code of an ASP page, set ContentType to `"text/plain"`, rather than to `"text/html"`, which is the default content type:

```
<% Response.ContentType = "text/plain" %>
```

The browser displays the page as text, instead of rendering it as an HTML page (it's like opening a TXT file with the browser).

The Cookies Property

Use this method to send cookies to the client. Cookies are special strings that are stored on the local computer with the Response property, and your ASP application can read them back with the Request method.

In effect, cookies are a way to pass values between the pages of your Web. The HTTP protocol used on the Web is stateless. Each document is requested by the client and transmitted by the server, and the transaction completes at this point. If the same client requests another document from the same server, neither the client nor the server have any recollection of the previous transaction.

Maintaining variables between different pages is a problem with a stateless protocol, which is solved with the help of cookies. If your Web pages use a consistent, but user-defined background color, you can store this value to a cookie, let's call it *BColor*, and then read it before constructing and transmitting a new page. *BColor* is the name of a variable that is stored on the client computer with the Cookies method of the Response object. To read its value, you access the Cookies property of the Request object.

NOTE   For more information on using cookies, see the section "Storing and Recalling Cookies," later in this chapter.

The Buffer Property

By default, the Response object sends its output to the client as soon as it can, and it doesn't wait for the entire page to complete. If you want to process the entire page before sending any output to the client, set the Buffer property of the Response object to True. Let's say that as you process the page (with an ActiveX component or by reading data from a database), you discover that you need not send the previous data to the client or that you must redirect the client to another URL. If the Buffer property was set to True, you can cancel the processing and clear the Response object with the Clear method of the Response object. Here's a typical scenario:

```
<%
Reponse.Buffer = True
{script statements}
If SupplierName = UserName Then
    Response.Clear
    Response.Redirect "/Suppliers/AllSuppliers.html"
    Response.End
End If
%>
```

This script builds a page by reading data from a database, until it discovers that the visitor is actually one of the suppliers and then it clears the output created so far, ends the Response object, and redirects the visitor to another page. If your script takes too long to process, however, nothing will appear on the client's monitor, and visitors may think they are not getting a response. Normal HTML pages are not buffered, so you should not buffer your ASP pages by default.

The Request Object

To interact with the visitor, your script should be able to request information that the visitor enters on a Form and read the values of cookies. Reading data back from the client has been a sore point in server scripting. ASP has simplified the process of reading the data submitted by the client by encapsulating all the complexity of the operation into a few properties of the Request object. This single feature of ASP would be adequate to make it a major server-scripting tool.

The Request object has five properties, all of which are collections:

> **QueryString** contains the values passed to the server with the GET method.
>
> **Form** contains all the Forms on the page.
>
> **Cookies** contains all cookies that have been written to the client by the Web site.

ServerVariables contains all the HTTP variables, which are determined by the server.

ClientCertificate contains all the client certificates installed on the client.

The QueryString Collection

The collection you'll be using most often in developing ASP applications is the QueryString collection. This property gives you access to all the parameters passed along with the URL by the client. If the names of the parameters are known at the time you develop the ASP file, you can request their values by name, with expressions such as the following:

```
reqProdName = Request.QueryString("ProductName")
```

If the names of the parameters are not known when you develop the ASP file or if you want to process them all serially, you can use a loop such as the following:

```
Set Params = Request.QueryString
    For Each param in Params
    {process parameter param}
Next
```

Figure 22.5 shows a simple HTML page with a Form (the SRVRFORM.HTM page on the CD); the user can enter information by selecting options in list boxes. When done, they can click the Recalculate button to submit the information to the server, where the cost of the selected configuration will be calculated and sent back to the client as a new HTML page.

FIGURE 22.5:

A typical Form on an HTML page

The names of the ListBox controls on the SRVRFRM page are: HardDisk, Memory, CD, Speaker, and Software. The possible values for each setting are listed in the <OPTION> tags of each <SELECT> tag. The options of the Select Memory list box have the values 32, 64, 128, and 256. The Memory query parameter will have one of these values, depending on which option was selected on the Form.

Code 22.5:   The SRVRFORM.HTM File

```
<H1>Build Your Own System</H1>
<FORM name=ORDER method="GET" action="aspages/param.asp">
<TABLE>
<TR>
<TD><B>Select Hard Disk</B></TD>
<TD></TD>
<TD><B>Select Memory</B></TD>
<TD></TD>
<TD><B>Select CD</B></TD>
</TR>
<TR>
<TD><SELECT name="HardDisk" size="1">
<OPTION selected value="3.2G">3.2GB Ultra EIDE Hard Drive </OPTION>
<OPTION  value="4.3G">4.3GB Ultra EIDE Hard Drive </OPTION>
</SELECT>
</TD>
<TD>
      
</TD>
<TD>
<SELECT name="Memory" size="1">
<OPTION  value="32">32 MB EDO RAM</OPTION>
<OPTION selected value="64 MB">64MB EDO RAM</OPTION>
<OPTION  value="128">128 MB EDO RAM</OPTION>
<OPTION  value="256">256 MB EDO RAM</OPTION>
</SELECT>
</TD>
<TD>
      
</TD>
<TD>
<select name="CD" size="1">
<option  value="">None</option>
<option selected value="CD12">12 EIDE CD-ROM</option>
<option selected value="CD24">24 EIDE CD-ROM</option>
</select>
</TD>
```

```
</TR>
<TR>
<TD><B>Select Speakers</B></TD>
<TD></TD>
<TD><B>Select Software</B></TD>
<TD></TD>
</TR>
<TR>
<TD>
<select name="Speaker" size="1">
<option selected value="">None</option>
<option value="S90">Altec ACS90 Speakers</option>
<option value="S290">Altec ACS290 Speakers</option>
</select>
</TD>
<TD></TD>
<TD>
<select name="Software" size="1">
<option selected value="WIN95">MS Windows 95</option>
<option value="WIN98">Microsoft Windows 98</option>
<option value="WINNT">Microsoft Windows NT Workstation 4.0 </option>
</select>
</TD>
</TABLE>
<BR><BR>
Select the desired options and click the Recalculate button to see your
system's price
<INPUT TYPE=SUBMIT VALUE="Recalculate">
</FORM>
</HTML>
```

The ASP page that processes this Form is called PARAM.ASP, and it resides in the ASPages virtual folder on the server (its URL appears in the FORM tag). This page doesn't do much. (It doesn't actually recalculate the price of the configuration, but once you know the options specified by the visitor, it's relatively easy to calculate the price of the selected configuration.) The PARAM.ASP script generates another HTML page on the fly with the names and values of the parameters and sends it back to the client. The server's response is shown in Figure 22.6.

The PARAM.ASP page that processes the data on the server uses a For...Each loop to scan all the items of the QueryString collection and display their names and values in a new table. Each parameter is stored in the variable *PValue*. The default property of this variable is the name of the parameter. To access the value of the parameters, use the expression *Params(PValue)*.

FIGURE 22.6:

The names and values of the query parameters submitted to the server by the Form in Figure 22.5

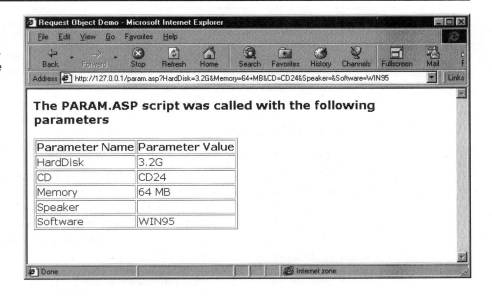

Code 21.6:   **The PARAM.ASP File**

```
<HTML>
<%
  Response.Write "<HTML>"
  Response.Write "<BODY>"
  Response.Write "<TABLE BORDER RULES=ALL>"
  Response.Write "<TR><TD><B>Parameter Name</B></TD><TD><B>Parameter
Value</B></TD></TR>"
  Set Params = Request.QueryString
  For Each PValue in Params
  Response.Write "<TR><TD>" & PValue & "</TD><TD>" & Params(PValue) &
"</TD></TR>"
  Next
  Response.Write "</TABLE>"
  Response.Write "</HTML>"
%>
</HTML>
```

To access individual parameters, you can use the collection Request.QueryString, followed by the name of the parameter whose value you want. The following lines will return the specifications of the memory and the hard disk, as entered by the visitor on the Form in the page SRVRFRM.HTM:

```
MemorySpec = Request.QueryString("Memory")
HDiskSpec = Request.QueryString("HardDisk")
```

TIP It is possible for multiple controls on a Form to have identical names. In this case, the QueryString collection contains an array of values. For example, if the Form contains three TextBoxes named "Name", you can access them as `Request.QueryString("Name")(1)`, `Request.QueryString("Name")(2)`, and `Request.QueryString("Name")(3)`.

The Form Collection

This collection is similar to the QueryString collection in that it contains data that the visitor entered on a Form. Whereas the QueryString collection contains all the parameters submitted to the server, regardless of whether they belong to a Form, the Form collection contains the values of the parameters that come from controls. It is possible to build a URL followed by a number of parameters on the fly, from within a client script. These parameters will be reported by the QueryString collection, but not by the Form collection.

To access the value of a specific parameter in the Form collection, use a statement such as the following:

```
FullName = Request.Form("LastName") & ", " % Request.Form("FirstName")
```

The ServerVariables Collection

This collection contains a number of standard environment variables, which you can access from within your script. Basically, the ServerVariables collection contains all the information available about the client and the server. Here are some of the most commonly used server variables:

SERVER_NAME: The server's DNS or IP address.

SERVER_PROTOCOL: The name and revision number of the protocol used for the request. It's usually HTTP/1.0.

SERVER_PORT: The TCP/IP port number on which the server accepts requests. It's usually 80.

SERVER_SOFTWARE: The name and version of the HTTP server software on the server machine.

SCRIPT_NAME: The path to the script being executed.

QUERY_STRING: The information that follows the question mark (?) in a URL. The GET method uses this variable, and you can retrieve it with the QueryString collection. This string is encoded according to the following two rules:

- Spaces are converted to plus signs.

- Any character may be represented as a hexadecimal number (representing the character's ASCII value) prefixed with the percent sign. The plus sign is encoded as %2B.

REQUEST_METHOD: The HTTP method being used to send client data to the server. The possible values are GET and POST.

CONTENT_TYPE: The type of data sent to the server. This variable is always application/x-www-form-urlencoded.

CONTENT_LENGTH: The length of the string holding the data. This variable is used with the POST method.

REMOTE_HOST: The full domain name of the client that made the request.

REMOTE_ADDR: The IP (Internet Protocol) address of the requesting client.

The file SRVRPARAM.ASP contains a short script that displays all the server variables, as shown in Figure 22.7.

FIGURE 22.7:

The SRVRPARAM.ASP file displays the names of all server variables and their values on a Web page.

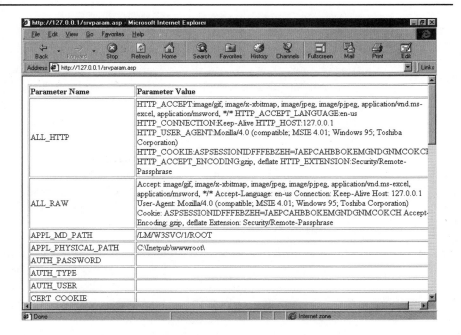

Code 22.7:   **The SRVRPARAM.ASP File**

```
<HTML>
<%
  Response.Write "<HTML>"
  Response.Write "<BODY>"
  Response.Write "<TABLE BORDER RULES=ALL>"
```

```
    Response.Write "<TR><TD><B>Parameter Name</B></TD><TD><B>Parameter
Value</B></TD></TR>"
    Set Params = Request.ServerVariables
    For Each Pvalue in Params
    Response.Write "<TR><TD>" & Pvalue & "</TD><TD>" & Params(pValue) &
"</TD></TR>"
    Next
    Response.Write "</TABLE>"
    Response.Write "</HTML>"
%>
</HTML>
```

The Cookies Collection

This collection is discussed in detail in the section "Storing and Recalling Cookies", later in this chapter. Cookies are basically variables stored by the server on the client computer that can be accessed by name, similar to parameters.

The ClientCertificates Collection

This collection contains all the certificates installed on the client computer and is needed only when your ASP applications install ActiveX components on the client. This property is supported only by Internet Explorer clients.

The Server Object

The Server object controls the environment in which the server-side scripts are executed. The single most important member of the Server object is its CreateObject method, which can create a new instance of an object from a registered class.

The CreateObject Method

This method is identical to the Visual Basic CreateObject() function. It accepts as an argument the programmatic ID (Class ID) of an object and returns an instance of the object. The syntax of the CreateObject method is:

```
Server.CreateObject("progID")
```

To access a database through the ADO component, for instance, you first create a Connection object and a Recordset object with the following statements (see the section "Using ActiveX Data Objects," later in this chapter, for more details on accessing databases through ASP):

```
Set ADOConnection = Server.CreateObject("ADODB.Connection")
Set ADORS = Server.CreateObject("ADODB.Recordset")
```

Similarly, you must create object variables to access the other basic components of ASP, such as the File Access component and the Advertisement Rotator component. You can also use the Server's CreateObject method to create object variables for accessing your own custom ActiveX components. See the section "Using the Active Data Objects" for information on how to contact databases through object variables. In the section "Contacting ActiveX Components," at the end of the chapter, you'll see how to create object variables that contact custom ActiveX components running on the server.

The MapPath Method

Another commonly used method of the Server object is the MapPath method, which maps virtual folders to actual path names. This method is useful in developing server-side scripts for a very simple reason: all the files you access are stored in virtual folders. You can rearrange the entire folder structure of a Web site and then rename a few virtual folders, and your scripts will never know. In some situations, however, you need to know the actual path to a file, and the MapPath method will return this value.

The Session and Application Objects

The Session object maintains variables that apply to a specific session. Before we examine the members of this object and how it's used in developing an ASP application, let's look at how the ASP component maintains sessions with a stateless protocol.

As I mentioned, HTTP is a stateless protocol. Each time the client requests a new document, a new transaction is initiated. Then how does the ASP know that a new request from a client belongs to an existing session? The answer is that ASP uses cookies.

When the client connects for the first time, the server sends the ASPSESSIONID cookie, which is stored on the client computer. Then, every time the client contacts the server, the ASPSESSIONID cookie is transmitted along with the request's header.

NOTE   The header contains information that both computers use to communicate, but you don't have to know what type of information is transmitted or change the default headers.

ASP processes this cookie and uses it to restore the variable values saved previously in the Session object. The ASPSESSIONID cookie doesn't have an expiration value and expires automatically when the client disconnects. The next time the same client connects, a new cookie is sent, and a new session is created. To maintain information between sessions, you must store a cookie with an expiration date on the client, read it as soon as the client connects to the Web server, and use it as a key to a database with relevant data (such as user preferences, access rights, and so on).

> **NOTE**   Some browsers don't support cookies (a rather rare situation today). These browsers don't support Sessions either. Basically the only limitation that ASP imposes on the client (if it can be considered a limitation) is that it support cookies.

The Application object plays a similar role. It maintains a set of variables, not for each session, but for the application. Simple examples are a welcome message that's displayed on each client's window and a visitor counter. To implement a visitor counter with ASP, all you have to do is create an application-wide variable and increment it every time a client hits your home page (which must be an ASP document).

To create a new Session or Application variable, you need only reference it in your code (this is VBScript; you are not required to declare variables). The statement:

```
<% Session("UName") = Request.QueryString("UserName") %>
```

assigns the value of the cookie UserName (which presumably has been set by the client) to the Session variable *UName*. You can also assign function values to the Session variables, as the following statement does:

```
<% Session("Connected") = Now() %>
```

The name of the variable is on the left side of the above expressions. You can use Session variables to build all types of expressions and statements with VBScript. The following statement terminates a client connection if it's been active for more than 12 hours:

```
<% If Hour(Now() - Session("Connected")) > 12 Then
    Session.Abandon
End If
%>
```

The Abandon method terminates the current session. Application variables are declared and used in the same manner, but since multiple scripts can access Application variables, there is always a chance that more than one script will attempt to change the value of an Application variable. The Application object provides the Lock and Unlock methods, which must be called before and after setting the variable:

```
Application.Lock
Application("VisitorCounter") = Application("VisitorCounter") + 1
Application.Unlock
```

The Session and Application objects support object variables too, created with the CreateObject method of the Server object. The difference is that object variables stored in the Session object can't be accessed by other sessions. If you have many clients accessing the same object (the same component on the server), you will be creating many instances of the same component, which may affect performance. This isn't as simple as it sounds. An object can be accessed by multiple sessions only if it has been designed to support multiple threads of execution.

The Start and End Events

Both the Session and the Application objects support Start and End events, which signal when a Session or an Application starts and when it ends. The Start events are:

- Session_OnStart

- Application_OnStart

The End events are:

- Session_OnEnd

- Application_OnEnd

These event handlers include code you should run whenever an application or a session starts or ends. If an application and a session start at the same time, the Application_OnStart event is executed first. These events are important in developing ASP applications, but they are not available from within the script. You must enter them in the GLOBAL.ASA file, which lives in the root folder of the application (the folder where the first ASP file to be requested by the client is stored). Typically, the GLOBAL.ASA file contains the Start and End events of the Session and Application objects, as well as variable definitions.

For example, if you want to implement a variable that stores the number of visitors hitting the site, initialize it in the Application_OnStart event. Enter the following code in the GLOBAL.ASA file:

```
<SCRIPT LANGUAGE=VBScript RUNAT=Server>
Sub Application_OnStart
    Application("Visitors") = 0
End Sub
</SCRIPT>
```

This event takes place every time the Web server software starts. Since you don't want to reset this counter every time you stop and restart the server, you can save the value of the variable *Visitors* to a text file on the server's disk, as explained in

Chapter 20. In the Application_OnStart event, you read the value of the variable from the text file, and in the Session_OnStart event, you increase it by one:

```
<SCRIPT LANGUAGE=VBScript RUNAT=Server>
Sub Session_OnStart
    Application.Lock
    Application("Visitors") = Application("Visitors") + 1
    Application.Unlock
End Sub
</SCRIPT>
```

You must also enter this procedure in the GLOBAL.ASA file. This technique works well. The number will not increase each time a visitor hits the home page during the same session, because the Session_OnStart event is only triggered the first time.

Displaying a fancy counter on your pages is a different story. You can simply display this number in a large font on your home page, or you can generate a GIF file on the fly and display it on the home page. The Structured Graphics control that comes with Internet Explorer 4 lets you create elaborate graphics with simple text commands. This control is probably the simplest way to display a graphic that shows the number of visitors.

If your pages call a specific component frequently during a session, you can declare an object variable in the Session's Start event. This variable will be available from within any page during the current session. Here's a simple example that creates an object variable referencing the MyObject component:

```
<SCRIPT LANGUAGE=VBScript RUNAT=Server>
Sub Session_OnStart
    Set Session("MyObj")=Server.CreateObject("MyObject")
End Sub
</SCRIPT>
```

Any page in the current session can use the *MyObj* object variable, and each session's *MyObj* variable is independent of the other sessions' *MyObj* variable.

Storing and Recalling Cookies

You have certainly noticed that some of the sites you've visited (Microsoft's home page is one of them) can be customized according to the visitor's preferences. How is this done? How does the server know each visitor's preferences between sessions? If each user had a fixed IP address, it would be possible (although not very practical) for the server to maintain a database with IP addresses and the preferences for each user. The IP address of the client computer is given by the Server-Variables collection of the Server object. But clients have different IP addresses each time they connect, so this approach is out of the question.

If you think about it, you will see that the only way for the server to maintain information about specific clients is to store this information on the client computer itself and recall it each time the client connects to the server. The information is stored on the client computer by the browser, in a special folder, in the form of variables and values. But instead of variables, they are called cookies.

You could force your site's visitors to register before they are allowed to connect and store customization information in a database on the server. This approach, however, can only be used by sites of specific interest. A general Web site shouldn't have to maintain an enormous database, when cookies work just as well.

Cookies are also used to pass information between pages of the same site. Let's say you're building a Web site for online orders. The site is made up of many pages, and visitors can order items from each page. How do you keep track of the visitors' orders? Each page can have its own script, and each page can have its own variables, but their scope is limited to the page on which they were declared. There is no way for two or more pages to share common variables. This is direct consequence of HTTP being a stateless protocol. Each time a new page arrives at the client, the browser forgets everything about the current page (except for its URL so that it can jump back to it). Orders made on one page can be stored on the client computer in the form of cookies and read by any other page of the same site.

Since cookies are managed by the browser, Web pages can't access your computer's hard disk directly (that's why cookies are safe). Moreover, when a page requests the values of the cookies, the browser supplies only those cookies that were stored by pages of the same site. In other words, cookies left on your computer by Microsoft's Web site can't be read by pages of other sites. The browser supplies each page with the cookies left by other pages of the same site.

Cookies have expiration dates too. If a cookie is stored without an expiration date, it ceases to exist after the current session. A cookie with an expiration date remains on the client computer until it expires.

To store a cookie on the client computer, use the Cookies property of the Response object. The Cookies property is a collection, and you can create and access individual cookies by name. To create a new cookie, use a statement such as the following:

```
<% Response.Cookies("FavoriteSport")="Hockey" %>
```

If the cookie FavoriteSport exists on the client computer, its value will be overwritten. If it does not exist, a new cookie is created. This cookie is released as soon as the current session ends.

You can specify the expiration date and time with the Expires property of the cookie, as follows:

```
<% Response.Cookies("FavoriteSport").Expires = "December 31, 1998
12:00:00 GTM" %>
```

Cookies have other properties too:

> **Domain**: If specified, the cookie value is sent only to requests from this domain. This property is used along with the Path property.

> **Path**: If specified, the cookie is sent only to requests made from this path on the server, and not to every page on the same site.

> **HasKeys**: Specifies whether the cookie contains multiple keys (in which case it's a dictionary). This property is read-only.

To create cookies with keys, use the same cookie name with multiple attributes, as in the following statements:

```
<%
Response.Cookies("Preferences")("Books") = "Mystery"
Response.Cookies("Preferences")("News") = "Sports"
%>
```

To request the value of a specific cookie from the client, use the Cookies collection of the Request object. The number of cookies in the Cookies collection is given by the Request.Cookies.Count property.

You can write a For…Next loop that scans the collection, or you can write a For Each…Next loop such as the following:

```
<%
For Each cookie In Request.Cokies
    {process current cookie, which is Request.Cookies(cookie)}
Next cookie
%>
```

Normally, the script on the server knows the names of the cookies and can request them by their names:

```
BookType = Request.Cookies("FavoriteSport")
```

If you need to find out the names of the cookies, use the For Each…Next structure. At each iteration, the value of the *cookie* variable is the name of the cookie and *Request.Cookies(cookie)* is its value.

If a cookie has keys, you must access them as elements of a collection. Let's assume you've sent a cookie with keys to the client with the following statements:

```
<%
Response.Cookies("Background") = "Planets.bmp"
```

```
Response.Cookies("Preferences")("Books") = "Mystery"
Response.Cookies("Preferences")("News") = "Sports"
%>
```

The first cookie determines the user's favorite background patterns. The next two values are used to create a custom home page. The following loop reads all the cookie values, including the key values:

```
<%
For Each cookie In Request.Cookies
    If Request.Cookies(cookie).HasKeys Then
        For Each scookie In Request.Cookies(cookie)
            { Process current cookie. Its value is
              Request.Cookies(cookie)(scookie) }
        Next
    Else
        { Process current cookie. Its value is Request.Cookies(cookie)
    End If
Next

%>
```

Cookies are used for many purposes other than to exchange information among different pages of the same site. Every site that provides customized start pages uses cookies to store user information. Some Web sites may store information regarding the topics you search most often and adjust the ads they present to you.

Using ActiveX Data Objects

The most important component of ASP is the Database component, which is nothing less than the ADO. I left this topic for last so that we can use the objects discussed earlier in this chapter to build more elaborate and practical examples. Although you can use other components to access databases on the server, most Web developers use the ADO component.

As you recall from our discussion in Chapter 18, the ADO is the simplest object for accessing databases. Its object model is much simpler than that of DAO (Data Access Objects) or even RDO (Remote Data Objects). Yet, the ADO is the most powerful component and used on most sites that deploy Active Server Pages. You can also use the DAO component and even develop your own Active X components to access databases on the server. This approach will work, but if you are setting up a new Web site, you should seriously consider ADO. It's faster, consumes fewer resources on the server (an important consideration for servers with a heavy load), and will eventually replace the DAO.

Setting Up an ODBC Data Source

To access a database on the server through the Database Component, you first define a System ODBC data source for the database, using the ODBC Administrator. Follow these steps:

1. Choose Start ➤ Settings ➤ Control Panel.

2. Double-click 32bit ODBC (the ODBC Administrator) to open the ODBC Data Source Administrator dialog box:

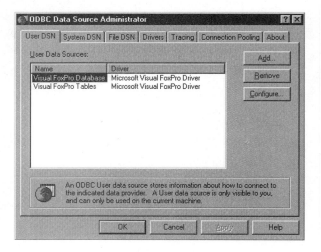

3. Select the System DSN tab to display the installed Data Sources. For the examples in this chapter, we are going to use the NWIND sample database, so let's create a data source for the NWIND database.

4. Click the Add button to open the Create New Data Source Wizard. In this window, you will see the names of all ODBC drivers. Select the Microsoft Access driver and click Finish to open the ODBC Microsoft Access 97 Setup dialog box.

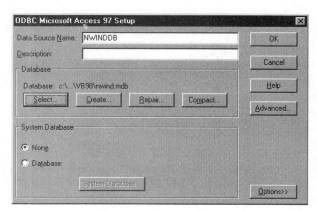

5. In the Data Source Name text box, enter **NWINDDB** (you'll use this name to access the database). Enter a description in the Description text box, and then click Select to select the NWIND.MDB database in your VB folder.

6. Click OK to return to the ODBC Data Source Administrator dialog box. The new data source will now appear.

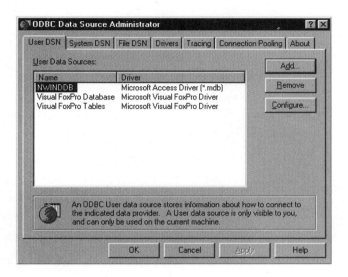

Opening the Database

To access the NWIND database from within an Active Server Page, you must create a Connection object with the Server.CreateObject method, as shown here:

```
Set DBConnection = Server.CreateObject("ADODB.Connection")
```

This variable will be used to establish a connection to the database when you call its Open method, whose syntax is:

```
DBConnection.Open "NWINDDB"
```

The first argument following the Open method's name must be the name of the data source that corresponds to the database you want to access. After you access the database and retrieve the desired records, you must release the Connection object by closing the connection with the Close method:

```
DBConnection.Close
```

> **TIP**
>
> This is the preferred method for accessing Microsoft Access databases. If you use the SQL Server instead, you can set up the *DBConnection* variable in the Application_OnStart event. This way it will be available to all clients that need to access the NWIND database. SQL Server supports multiple threads, and this technique will work. The Microsoft Access ODBC driver does not. Instead, there's a pool of connections, and the first available one is used. That's why you must release each connection object when you no longer need it.

Building a Recordset

After you establish a connection to the database, you can access it with SQL statements. To issue a SQL statement, use the Execute method of the Connection object, and pass the SQL statement as an argument. The syntax of the Execute method is:

```
DBConnection.Execute SQLStatement
```

The *SQLStatement* argument can be a string with the SQL statement or the name of a stored procedure. If the SQL statement returns records (as does the SELECT ·statement), the Execute method returns a Recordset and should be called as follows:

```
Set SelRecords = DBConnection.Execute(SQLStatement)
```

The Execute method accepts two optional arguments:

- The number of records affected by the operation (this parameter is set by the driver)
- Whether the *SQLstatement* is SQL text or the name of a stored procedure

The method's complete syntax is:

```
DBConnection.Execute SQLStatement, numRecords, SQLText
```

The *SQLText* argument can have the value *adCmdText* (for SQL statements) or *adCmdStoredProc* (for stored procedures).

A second way to execute SQL statements against the database is to create a Command object with the statement:

```
Set SQLCommand = Server.CreateObject("ADODB.Command")
```

You can then execute SQL statements with the SQLCommand object's Execute method. The Command object exposes several properties that let you specify the statement and how it will be executed.

For example, you can specify the Connection object to which the Command object applies (should you have multiple connections open), specify parameter values for stored procedures, and so on.

Here's how the Command object is typically used:

```
Set DBConnection = Server.CreateObject("ADODB.Connection")
Set SQLCommand = Server.CreateObject("ADODB.Command")
Set ParamItem = Server.CreateObject("ADODB.Parameter")

SQLCommand.ActiveConnection = DBConnection
SQLCommand.CommandText = "ProductsByCategory"
SQLCommand.CommandType = adCmdStoredProc
ParamItem.Name = "@ProductCategory"
ParamItem.Value = 31
SQLCommand.Parameters.Append ParamItem
SQLCommand.Execute
```

ProductCategory is the name of the parameter that is specified at the same time as the stored procedure. At runtime you supply the value of this variable (31 in the previous example). These statements set up the SQLCommand Command object to execute a stored procedure with parameters. The same code can be simplified using a With structure:

```
Set DBConnection = Server.CreateObject("ADODB.Connection")
Set SQLCommand = Server.CreateObject("ADODB.Command")
Set ParamItem = Server.CreateObject("ADODB.Parameter")

With SQLCommand
    .ActiveConnection = DBConnection
    .CommandText = "ProductsByCategory"
    .CommandType = adCmdStoredProc
    With ParamItem
        .Name = "@ProductCategory"
        .ParamItem.Value = 31
        .Parameters.Append ParamItem
    EndWith
    .Execute
End With
```

Using the Recordset

Most ASP applications that access databases use Recordsets to retrieve and display records, rather than edit them remotely. Recordsets have two important properties:

CursorType indicates the type of cursor used with the Recordset object.

LockType indicates the type of lock to be placed on a record during editing.

For a discussion of the various cursors and locking mechanisms, see Chapter 18.

To navigate through the Recordset, use the MoveNext, MovePrevious, Move-First, and MoveLast methods. You can also bookmark certain pages so that you can return to them instantly. To display all the records in the Recordset, set up a loop like the following:

```
<%
Do While Not SelRecords.EOF
    {process fields}
    SelRecords.MoveNext
Loop
%>
```

To access the fields of the Recordset, use the name of the Recordset and the name of the field or its order in the Recordset. For example, to access the field ProductName in the current record of the SelRecords Recordset, use the expression:

```
SelRecords("ProductName")
```

Or, if the ProductName field is the first one (this is determined by the SQL SELECT statement), use the expression:

```
SelRecords(1)
```

The overview presented in this chapter should be adequate for building interactive ASP Web applications that access databases on the server and display selected records. In the examples that follow, you will see how these objects are used in building Active Server Pages. The following examples are all based on the NWIND sample application, and I am assuming that you have set up a data source for this database.

The ALLPRODS.ASP Page

The ALLPRODS.ASP page displays a list of all the product categories in the NWIND database, as shown in Figure 22.8.

The ASP page retrieves the category names and formats them as hyperlinks. When the visitor clicks a category name, the hyperlink takes him or her to another ASP page, the PRODCAT.ASP page, which displays all the products in the selected category, along with their prices and the number of units in stock The output of the PRODCAT.ASP page is shown in Figure 22.9.

Let's examine the code of the ALLPRODS.ASP page. There's very little HTML code on this page; it's a server-side script that opens the NWINDDB database, creates a Recordset with all the category names, and displays them as hyperlinks.

The line that inserts the hyperlinks is the most interesting code in this listing. If you ignore the expression surrounded by the server-side script tags, it's a simple HTML tag for inserting a hyperlink. Because the hyperlink's name and destination are not known at the time of this file's design, we insert them as expressions, which are substituted by the Active Server Pages when the file is processed.

FIGURE 22.8:

The ALLPRODS.ASP page displays the product categories in the NWIND database as hyperlinks.

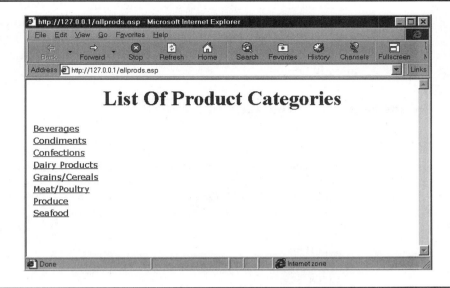

FIGURE 22.9:

The PRODCAT.ASP file displays the products in the category selected in Figure 22.8.

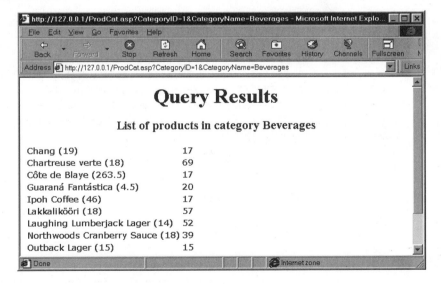

Notice that all hyperlinks call the same URL on the server (the file PRODCAT.ASP), but each hyperlink passes a different parameter to it. The parameter is the ID of the category since this is the field stored in the Products table of the NWIND database, along with each product. The PRODCAT.ASP page uses these parameters to retrieve the products that correspond to the selected category. In addition, it passes the name of the category as the second parameter. This value is not needed in extracting the requested products from the database, but the script uses it to display the name of the selected category. Had we omitted this parameter, the PRODCAT.ASP page would have to open the Categories table to find out the name of the selected category, display it in the page's header, and then open the Products table to retrieve the product names. By passing the name of the category as a parameter, we save the script from establishing a new connection to the database and reading a value that's already known.

Code 22.8: **The ALLPRODS.ASP File**

```
<HTML>
<%
Set DBObj = Server.CreateObject("ADODB.Connection")
DBObj.Open "NWindDB"
SQLQuery = "SELECT CategoryID, CategoryName FROM Categories"
Set RSCategories = DBObj.Execute(SQLQuery)
%>

<CENTER>
<H1>List Of Product Categories</H1>
</CENTER>

<TABLE>
<% Do While Not RSCategories.EOF %>
  <TR>
  <TD> <FONT FACE="Verdana" SIZE=2>
    <% CategoryName = RSCategories("CategoryName") %>
    <A HREF="/ASPages/ProdCat.asp?CategoryID=_
        <% =RSCategories("CategoryID") %>&CategoryName=_
        <% =CategoryName  %> "> <% = CategoryName %> </A>
    </FONT>
  </TD>
  </TR>
<%
RSCategories.MoveNext
Loop
DBObj.Close
%>
</HTML>
```

The PRODCAT.ASP file, which processes requests made by the ALLPRODS.ASP page, is a bit more complicated. First, it must extract the values of the parameters passed by the client. The statements

```
ReqCategory=Request.QueryString("CategoryID")
ReqName=Request.QueryString("CategoryName")
```

store these values to the variables *ReqCategory* and *ReqName*. The QueryString collection contains these values for you, and you don't have to do anything special to read them. Simply access them by name. The value of *ReqCategory* is then used to build the SQL statement that will retrieve the records from the Products table:

```
SQLQuery = "SELECT ProductName, UnitPrice, UnitsInStock _
      FROM Products WHERE CategoryID = " & ReqCategory & " _
      ORDER BY ProductName"
```

This SQL statement returns a Recordset with the products in the selected category. The script scans the records, one at a time, and displays each record on a new row of a table. The code that builds the table looks quite complicated because it combines HTML code and script statements. Replace every expression that appears between the <% and %> tags with a likely value (a product name for the expression <% = RSProducts("ProductName") %> and so on) to see how these lines gradually build the table in Figure 22.9.

Code 22.9:   **The PRODCAT.ASP File**

```
<HTML>
<%
ReqCategory=Request.QueryString("CategoryID")
ReqName=Request.QueryString("CategoryName")
Set DBObj = Server.CreateObject("ADODB.Connection")
DBObj.Open "NWindDB"
SQLQuery = "SELECT ProductName, UnitPrice, UnitsInStock FROM Products
WHERE CategoryID = " & ReqCategory & " ORDER BY ProductName"
Set RSProducts = DBObj.Execute(SQLQuery)
%>

<CENTER>
<H1>Query Results</H1>
<H3>List of products in category <% = ReqName %></H3>
</CENTER>

<TABLE>
<% Do While Not RSProducts.EOF %>
  <TR>
  <TD> <FONT FACE="Verdana" SIZE=2>
      <% = RSProducts("ProductName") & " (" & _
      RSProducts("UnitPrice") & ")"  %>
    </FONT></TD>
  <TD><FONT FACE="Verdana" SIZE=2>
      <% = RSProducts("UnitsInStock") %>
    </FONT></TD>
  </TR>

<%
RSProducts.MoveNext
Loop
```

```
%>
</TABLE>
</HTML>
```

This example was fairly simple. Some of the code may look complicated, but try to separate the expressions that will be evaluated on the server from the pure HTML code. You can use symbolic names—*ProductName* and *UnitPrice* in your code—and after you make sure it works, replace these symbolic expressions with the actual server-side script variables.

A Web Application

So far, we have examined how to build Web pages that interact with the Web server. A collection of Web pages forms a Web site. But how about Web applications? Are they special applications that run over the Internet? The answer is yes and no. They are client-server applications that run over the Internet, but they are not special applications, and there are no new topics to learn. A Web application is a Web site that uses ASP files on the server. The windows of a regular application correspond to the pages of a Web application. The pages exchange information with one another through cookies (as explained earlier in this chapter) or through the Application and Session objects.

To use the Application and Session objects efficiently, you must learn about the ASA files. Every Web application has a GLOBAL.ASA file, which must reside in the server's root folder. This file contains the event handlers of the Application and Session objects and is looked up by the Web server when a Web application or a session starts. A Web application starts when the first connection to the server is made. When the first visitor is connected to the Web server, the server looks up the GLOBAL.ASA file for an Application_onStart event handler. If one is found, it's executed.

At the same time, a new session is established. The server also looks up the GLOBAL.ASA file for a Session_onStart event handler. If one is found, it's executed. At the same time, a new Session object is created, which is associated with the client that established the session. This object remains alive for as long as the client remains connected. When the session is terminated, the server executes the Session_onEnd event handler (which must also reside in the GLOBAL .ASA file).

Let's look at a typical GLOBAL.ASA file. The file shown next contains the code for keeping track of the total number of visitors that have hit the site (variable *Visitors*), as well as the number of users currently connected (variable *Viewers*).

Code 22.10:   A Typical GLOBAL.ASA File

```vbscript
<SCRIPT LANGUAGE=VBScript RUNAT=Server>
Sub Application_onStart
    Application("Viewers")=0
End Sub

Sub Session_onStart
    Application.Lock
    Application("Viewers")=Application("Viewers")+1
    Application("Visitors")=Application("Visitors")+1
    Application.Unlock
    Session("User")=Request.ServerVariables("REMOTE_ADDR")
End Sub

Sub Session_onEnd
    Application.Lock
    Application("Viewers")=Application("Viewers")-1
    Application.Unlock
End Sub
</SCRIPT>
```

When the Web server starts, it creates a new variable, *Viewers*. This variable is initialized to zero when the application starts, and it increases by 1 every time a new session is established. When a session terminates, the *Viewers* variable is decreased by 1. As a result, it reflects the number of users currently connected.

The variable *Visitors* is increased each time a new session is established. This variable reflects the total number of visitors that have hit the site. Of course, this variable is reset to zero every time the Web server is shut down, so you must store its value in a local file and read it from the file when the application starts.

In each session's onStart event handler, we store the IP address of the client to the Session variable *User*. This variable is unique within the scope of the Session object and can be used to identify the client. Each Session object has its own *User* variable, and no other Session object can see it. In fact, you can't even enumerate the *User* variables of all sessions.

Notice that you must lock the Application object when you update the values of its variables, but this is not necessary for the Session object. When a new Session object is initiated, it has its own set of local variables.

To test the GLOBAL.ASA file shown here, you can write an ASP file that accesses the Application and Session variables declared in the GLOBAL.ASA file. The VIEWERS.ASP file, shown next, produces a page like the one shown in Figure 22.10. To test this file, run the WINIPCFG utility (choose Start ➤ Run and type

WINIPCFG), which will display your IP address on the Internet. Share this address with a few friends, and ask them to connect to your server. Each time they establish a new connection, both the *Viewers* and *Visitors* variables will increase. When a user disconnects (by jumping to another URL), the *Viewers* variable is decreased.

Here's the code of the VIEWERS.HTM page that produced the output shown in Figure 22.10 in conjunction with the GLOBAL.ASA file. The VIEWERS.HTM page can reside in any virtual folder on your server, but the GLOBAL.ASA file must reside in the root folder (usually C:\INETPUB\WWWROOT). The page displays how many users are currently connected to the server, the IP address of the session, and the basic properties of the client's browser.

FIGURE 22.10:

The output of the VIEWERS
.ASP Active Server Page

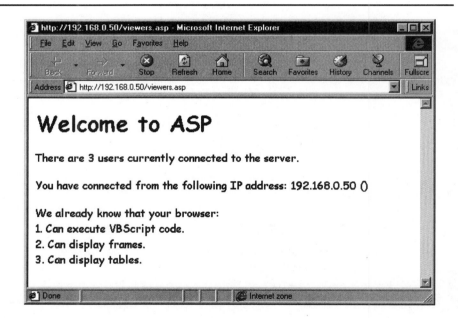

Code 22.11:   **The VIEWERS.ASP Page**

```
<HTML>
<FONT FACE="Comic Sans MS" SIZE=3>
<H1>Welcome to ASP</H1>
There are <% =Application("Viewers") %> users currently connected to
the server.
<P>
You have connected from the following IP address: <% =Session("User")
%> (<% =Session("HName") %>)
<P>
We already know that your browser:
<BR>
```

```
1.
<% Set Browser = Server.CreateObject("MSWC.BrowserType") %>
<% If Browser.VBscript Then
    Response.Write "Can "
Else
    Response.Write "Can't "
End If
%> execute VBScript code.
<BR>
2.
<% If Browser.Frames Then
    Response.Write "Can "
Else
    Response.Write "Can't "
End If
%> display frames.
<BR>
3.
<% If Browser.Tables Then
    Response.Write "Can "
Else
    Response.Write "Can't "
End If
%> display tables.

</FONT>
</HTML>
```

The VIEWERS.ASP page reads the values of the *Visitors, Viewers, User,* and *HName* variables and displays their values on the page it produces. It also demonstrates the BrowserType component, which returns information about the client's browsing capabilities. Active Server Pages produce straight HTML code that can be viewed on any browser, so it's a good idea to consider the basic capabilities of the client before dumping to it a document it can't display properly. Nearly every browser supports tables and frames, but you can't assume that all browsers can also execute VBScript code.

Contacting ActiveX Components

Your Active Server Pages are not limited to the functionality provided by VBScript and the built-in objects discussed in this chapter. The CreateObject method of the Server object can do for your Active Server Pages what the CreateObject() function can do for your VB applications. It opens a door to the services of any existing OLE

Server application, as well as custom ActiveX components (ActiveX DLLs). Actually, it is possible to contact ActiveX EXE components too, but things can get messy. ActiveX DLLs are in-process components: they are loaded and become part of the application that calls them. ActiveX EXEs are out-of-process components. No matter how many applications call an ActiveX EXE component, only one instance of the component is running in the memory. This can lead to hard-to-tackle problems. For example, what if an application sets a global variable and another application changes it? Writing ActiveX EXEs that function properly at all times is not a simple task, and by default, neither the PWS nor the IIS supports ActiveX EXEs.

In Chapter 15, we developed the StringClass component (project NumStr on the CD). As a reminder, Table 22.2 shows the three methods for manipulating numbers and strings that the StringClass provides.

TABLE 22.2: The Methods of the StringClass Component

Method	What It Does
Number2String(number)	Accepts a number as an argument and returns its value as a string. If you call the NumberToString method with the argument 3462, it returns the string "three thousand four hundred sixty-two."
LowerCaps(string)	Accepts a string as an argument and returns the same string in lower caps. If you call the LowerCaps method with the string "MASTERING visual basic" it will return the string "Mastering Visual Basic".
Integer2Binary(number)	Accepts a number (which must be an integer) as an argument and returns its binary representation. If you call the Integer2Binary method passing the number 312 as an argument, it returns the string "000100111000" (without quotes).

To contact the StringClass component from within an ASP file, you must first create the DLL file and then register it with the system. If you haven't done so already, open the NumStr project and make the NumStrings.dll file. Then register it with the REGSVR32 utility (the process is explained in detail in Chapter 15).

To access the methods of the StringClass, you must create an object variable with the following statement:

```
<%
Set STR=Server.CreateObject("NumStrings.StringClass")
%>
```

The STR variable is your gateway to the methods exposed by the StringClass class. To convert a numeric value to a string, use the following line:

```
<% STR.Number2String(4325)) %>
```

Figure 22.11 shows the NUMSTR.ASP page, which uses the Number2String method of the StringClass component to display integers as strings. Notice that the Number2String method returns a lowercase string. To convert it to lower caps, you must call the LowerCaps method. You can combine the two calls into one with the following statement:

```
<% =STR.LowerCaps(STR.Number2String(4325)) %>
```

FIGURE 22.11:

The NUMSTR.ASP page contacts the StringClass component on the server to format numeric values as strings.

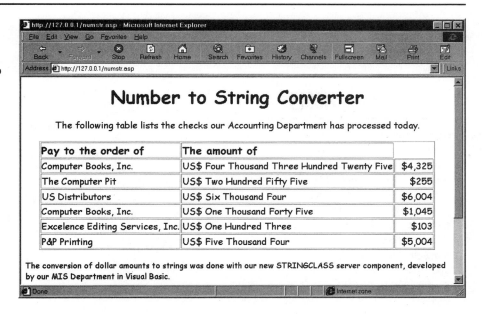

To view the complete listing of the ASP file that produced the output shown in Figure 22.11, open the NUMSTR.ASP file on the CD with a text editor.

To test this ASP file, copy it from the CD to your Web server's root folder, and open it with Internet Explorer by entering its URL in the browser's Address box (127.0.0.1/numstr.asp). You must also make sure that the StringClass component has been registered. To register a Class, you must first create a DLL and then register it with the REGSVR32 utility. Open the NumStr project in the Visual Basic IDE, and choose File ➤ Build StringClass.dll. Once the DLL file is created, close Visual Basic, open a DOS window, and switch to the folder where the DLL resides. Then issue the following command:

```
C:\WINDOWS\SYSTEM\REGSVR32 STRINGCLASS.DLL
```

REGSVR32.EXE is a utility for registering ActiveX components on the host system. For more information on registering ActiveX components, see the section "Registering an ActiveX Component" in Chapter 15.

Once the component is registered, any script running on your server can contact it and call its methods, just like any other system component. You can register all the components you created in Chapter 15 and contact them from your server-side scripts. Notice that these components need not be downloaded.

INDEX

Note to the Reader: Throughout this index **boldfaced** page numbers indicate primary discussions of a topic. *Italicized* page numbers indicate illustrations.

A

B

D

E

G

I

J

K

P

S

T

V

X

Y

Z

Mastering Visual Basic 6 Companion CD

This book's companion CD is an autorun CD that includes the convenient Sybex interface. Just insert the CD into the CD-ROM drive, wait a few seconds, and afterward you will be able to:

- Copy project files and examples created by the author to your hard disk.
- Work through bonus tutorials that teach you interesting projects and basic VB6 features (such as file manipulation commands).
- Install and try out new, powerful software from Installshield, Blue Sky, NuMega, LEADTools, and more.
- Refer to handy VB6 reference information in Adobe Acrobat format.
- Enhance your VB6 applications with multimedia elements.

Custom VB6 Demos by the Author

This book contains numerous applications developed by the author to demonstrate features of the language, ActiveX controls, and general programming topics. You can use any of them in your projects, royalty free. Here are some of the projects you will find in the book.

CDBox This utility allows you to experiment with numerous parameters of the Common Dialog Boxes interactively. Use this tool to find out how to set up a Font or a File Open dialog box and get their parameters right without writing a single line of code.

DirMap Use this application to format and print the contents of any folder on your hard disk, including its subfolders, on a RichTextBox control.

Image Use this image-processing application as your starting point to experiment with custom image-processing techniques. You'll also find an optimized version of this application, which makes extensive use of the Windows API and runs circles around the equivalent VB application.

MDIEdit The fastest way to get up to speed with Multiple Document Interface (MDI) applications is to use this multi-window version of NotePad.

RTFPad An application similar to MDIEdit, only this one allows you to format text, mix fonts, and even print the formatted text.

Globe and **TreeViewScan** Learn how to populate a TreeView control at runtime and save its contents to a disk file. Use the source code of these applications to scan the nodes of any TreeView control from within your application's code.

VBA Sample Code See how you can write VB applications that access Excel's math functions and Word's spell-checking engine. Learn how to make your VB applications mail-aware through Outlook 98.

ScriptEdit Use this sample application's code to add scripting capabilities to your VB applications.

Wipes This application shows you how to set up a slide show with various effects and time the transitions perfectly.

MCIDemo This application lets you prototype multimedia applications with MCI commands (record and play back sounds, animation files, video, and more).

Third Party Software

This CD includes the most valuable software available for Visual Basic programmers. Use this software to speed development work, simplify debugging, create Help files, and more.

Installshield Express Professional 2.1 is a 30 day evaluation copy of the full custom installation product for Visual Basic developers.

RoboHelp HTML 6 enables you to create Microsoft's new HTML Help for Visual Basic applications running in Windows 98.

NuMega's Smartcheck Does more than detect errors—it explains why the errors occurred. This is the smart debugging program that is winning rave reviews.

LEADTools 10 ActiveX controls for a wide range of imaging needs. Scanning, graphics editing, and conversion with more than 500 functions are available for you to try.

Adobe Acrobat Required software for any Web surfer. Use this program to read the tutorials and reference appendices on this CD.

Winzip The number one compression software program. Don't surf the Web without it!